The Restored New Testament

Also by Willis Barnstone

THE
RESTORED
NEW
TESTAMENT

A New Translation with Commentary,
Including the Gnostic Gospels
Thomas, Mary, and Judas

WILLIS BARNSTONE

W · W · Norton & Company   New York London

For information about permission to reproduce selections from this book, write to Permissions, W. W. Norton & Company, Inc., 500 Fifth Avenue, New York, NY 10110

For information about special discounts for bulk purchases, please contact W. W. Norton Special Sales at specialsales@wwnorton.com or 800-233-4830

Manufacturing by RR Donnelley, Crawfordsville, IN
Book design by Margaret M. Wagner
Production manager: Anna Oler

Library of Congress Cataloging-in-Publication Data

Bible. N.T. English. Barnstone. 2009.
The restored New Testament / a new translation with
commentary, including the Gnostic Gospels :
Thomas, Mary, and Judas; Willis Barnstone. — [Rev. ed.].
p. cm.
Rev. ed. of: The New Covenant, commonly called the New Testament.
Includes bibliographical references and index.
ISBN 978-0-393-06493-3 (hardcover)
I. Barnstone, Willis, 1927– II. Title.
BS2095.B37 2009
225.5'209—dc22

2009026133

W. W. Norton & Company, Inc.
500 Fifth Avenue, New York, N.Y. 10110
www.wwnorton.com

W. W. Norton & Company Ltd.
Castle House, 75/76 Wells Street, London W1T 3QT

1 2 3 4 5 6 7 8 9 0

for William Tyndale, Richmond Lattimore, Robert Alter
for pioneer models of biblical translation

Helle Tzalopoulou Barnstone
who led me to Greece and Greek

Sarah Handler
who saw the Restored through its making

Acknowledgments

IN BIBLICAL WORK, mortals begin with error. Many have saved me from mishaps. I want to express warmth to friends who have heartened and helped me immensely in this venture. My deep thanks go to Marvin Meyer, with whom I collaborated in rendering the three Gnostic gospels of Thomas, Mary, and Judas. A Gnostic and Coptic scholar, he brings marvelous authority to *The Restored New Testament*. An unrepentant polymath of ancient cultures and tongues and a close friend, he has collaborated with me on many projects. How lucky I am. I thank Helle Tzalopoulou Barnstone, who led me to all things Greek: demotic, Byzantine, classical, and Koine, in that order. Aliki Barnstone, translator of *The Collected Poems of C. P. Cavafy* from the Greek, has generously coached me through the caverns and peaks of New Testament diction. Tony Barnstone went through the introduction and afterword with tenacious brilliance and nudged me through a narrow gate of clarity. I owe Sarah Handler a bag of denarii for lending her friendly, sharp eye and ear to each page of the volume. For checking all words in Greek, I am once again hugely indebted to William McCulloh, professor of classics at Kenyon College; and for checking all words in Hebrew, I am equally grateful to Joel Segal, my earlier grand editor for *The Gnostic Bible*. I thank Professors James Ackerman and Steven Katz at Indiana University and Robert Alter and Ruth Adler at the University of California, Berkeley, for their crucial scrutiny of the texts for consistency in transcribing proper nouns from Hebrew into English. Professor George Nickelsburg of the University of Iowa, whose abundant work in first-century Judaism and Christianity has for years instructed me, advised and carefully went over the introduction and afterword. David Trobisch, professor of New Testament language and literature at Bangor

Theological Seminary in Maine, has given us *The First Edition of the New Testament* (2000), which convincingly alters traditional notions of the redaction and dating of the first canonical New Testament.

I think constantly of Brother Timothy Meir, the meticulous, charming, and worldly editor at Riverhead of the four gospels and Apocalypse whose sudden early death sorrows us all. I think of good times with Cindy Spiegel and her multiple contributions. And now at Norton, I have had the joy of working with Paul Whitlatch, Adrienne Davich, and Jill Bialosky, who made it all happen. Robert Barnstone cheered our spirits with his design for the Library for Unpublished Writers. I always think of Ruth Stone, Gerald Stern, Yusef Komunyakaa, and Stanley Moss because, like the authors of the New Testament, they are poets. I also greet the indifferent ghost of whimsical time, who has let me enjoy fifteen years of reading and plotting, and held me to the ways of composition and spiritual loneliness.

Order and Names
of the Books

CANONICAL GOSPELS

Creation Prologue to Yohanan	Creation Prologue to John
Markos	Mark
Mattityahu	Matthew
Loukas	Luke
Yohanan	John

GNOSTIC GOSPELS
(Translated by Willis Barnstone and Marvin Meyer)

Toma	Thomas
Miryam of Magdala	Mary of Magdala
Yehuda	Judas

LETTERS OF SHAUL/SAUL/PAUL

Romans	Romans
Korinthians alpha	1 Corinthians
Korinthians beta	2 Corinthians
Galatians	Galatians
Thessalonikians alpha	1 Thessalonians
Filemon	Philemon
Filippians	Philippians

LETTERS ATTRIBUTED TO SHAUL/SAUL/PAUL

Efesians	Ephesians
Kolossians	Colossians
Thessalonikians beta	2 Thessalonians

THREE LATE PASTORAL LETTERS
ATTRIBUTED TO SHAUL/SAUL/PAUL

Timotheos alpha	1 Timothy
Timotheos beta	2 Timothy
Titos	Titus

GENERAL LETTERS

Yaakov	James

The Shimonian Letters

Shimon Kefa alpha	1 Simon Peter
Shimon Kefa beta	2 Simon Peter

The Johannine Letters

Yohanan alpha	1 John
Yohanan beta	2 John
Yohanan gamma	3 John

An Apocalyptic Letter

Yehuda or Judas	Jude

ANONYMOUS

Yehudim or Jews	Hebrews

ACTS

Activities of the Messengers	Acts of the Apostles

APOCALYPSE

Apocalypse or Revelation by Yohanan of Patmos or Efesos	Apocalypse or Revelation by John of Patmos or Ephesos

Contents

Scriptures

CONTENTS

Appendices

Meditations on the Restored New Testament

Yeshua and the Poor

In those days again there was a great crowd who had nothing to eat, and
Calling his students together he said to them,
  I have pity for the crowd,
  And they have already been with me three days
  And have nothing to eat.
  If I send them hungry to their homes,
  They will collapse on the road
  And some have come from far away.

MARK 8.1–3

T HE BOOK of the canonical gospels, which treats the life and death of a rabbi named Yeshua,[1] speaks many notes. It sounds danger, hope, amazement, suffering, a bit of joy, all elaborated with occasional irony and no trace of humor. It is at once riveting and repetitious, since it retells four versions of the same events. It is grave and tragic, since it ends in the terrible torture-death of the crucifixion, which the Romans devised for seditionists and criminals. In the crucifixion, the human body is spiked through and left hanging in torment until death gives it over to the vultures and dogs. There is an epilogue to the Gospel of Mark (a late "orphan" emendation) with a glad resurrection that provides public hope to the rich in faith. But persisting is the personal human agony of a few days earlier when a rabbi nailed to a T-cross calls

---

1. Yeshua is Jesus. The name "Jesus" is from the Greek Ἰησοῦς (Iesous), from the Aramaic יֵשׁוּעַ (Yeshua), a later form of the Hebrew יְהוֹשֻׁעַ (Yehoshua). *Yeshua* was probably Jesus's name in his lifetime.

out in forsaken despair as he gives up the ghost on a Friday afternoon. In response, the earth quakes and the sky blackens and cracks.[2]

Beyond the public event of the crucifixion, the doctrine and the metaphysic, beyond the gathering of followers who will become legion and inform the world-dominating religious movement of Christianity,[3] the gospels speak to the human condition of peasants in an occupied country in times of mean opportunity.

At the heart of the gospels is the wandering and compassionate rabbi Yeshua. We know of his birth-to-death existence through the gospels and Acts.[4] He teaches and feeds the poor. He cures the leper and demoniac, the bleeding woman and a paralyzed on the floor. He restores life to a dead boy and a dead man. He is with Jew and foreigner, children of the carpenter and rich man, official or soldier—all who come to him for medical miracles and spiritual food. He is also a leader who can threaten the bad with eternal pain in hell and promise salvation for the good.[5] There are terrified students[6] who fear for their lives on a boat in a windstorm on the Sea of Galilee[7] until Yeshua tells the winds to fall; and there are the masses whom the wandering rabbi feeds with a few loaves and fishes to satisfy them. The primal physical needs of people

2. When Jesus shouts from the cross, *"Eli, Eli, lama sabachthani?"*—My God, my God, why have you forsaken me? (Matt. 27.46)—he is quoting the first line of Psalm 22 in Hebrew. In Mark, citing the same first line in Psalm 22, he cries his despair to God in Aramaic, *"Eloi, Eloi, lama sabachthani?"* (Mark 15.34), his spoken tongue.

3. "Christianity" or "Messianism" means "those who follow the Christ" or "the anointed." "Christ" is a translation of the Hebrew word for messiah that also means "the anointed." "Christ" comes from the Greek Χριστος (Hristos), from the Hebrew מָשִׁיחַ (mashiah).

4. Paul of the letters knew Jesus as the foretold crucified messiah, but on the basis of the letters he apparently had no knowledge of the messiah's birth, family, disciples, or deeds and cites none of his words or sayings.

5. By the period of Jesus's life, the notion of heaven and hell was common among diverse religious sects in the Near East. In the earlier Hebrew Bible, a time concept of heaven or hell is essentially absent.

6. Disciple from Greek μαθητής (mathetes). The plain meaning of Greek *mathetes* is "pupil" or "student," which is lost in the ecclesiastical inflation to "disciple."

7. Lake of the Galil. Also Lake Tiberius (after the Roman emperor). In modern Hebrew it is Lake Kinnerert, Lake Chinnereth (Num. 34.1). The land around the lake is called Gennesaret (Matt. 14.34).

living close to the edge of life and death show on virtually every page. The book of the gospels is a brief epic of hunger and humility and sicknesses. As such it stands in black-and-white contrast to Homer's prosperous gods and soldiers and islanders, whose sensuality, fun, and adventure, rather than an impoverished human condition, excite us. The gospel figures, described in rudimentary Near Eastern Greek,[8] incite the reader's deep compassion.

That Yeshua comes as an earthly savior to the poor is poignant for us to observe. A woman falls to her knees begging the savior to touch her or her child and enact a cure; the man living in the tombs, possessed by demons, asks Yeshua whether he, too, has come to torment him, and then, cured by Yeshua, begs, unsuccessfully, to accompany him on his wanderings. The unclean are cleansed, the leper is washed, the hungry receive bread, the prostitute is not scorned, the woman (one of the Miryams,[9] wandering in the garden) discovers a resurrected crucified who touches her with hope—all these are the figures of the human landscape that the New Covenant[10] delivers without makeup or guise.

No authority other than Yeshua appeals to us in these pages. But there is a price that the poor must pay for Yeshua's powers, which is a heart-rending fear and degradation. Some call it humility and modesty. There is the shepherd and the sheep, and the sheep, apart from allegory, are beasts of the field who bend their heads to graze. In that surrender and humiliation is the pathos, which makes this picaresque, episodic

8. We lack the original Aramaic or late Hebrew source text or Aramaic oral witness accounts from which derive the existing texts in Greek. Aramaic, not Greek, was the spoken language of the Galilean Yeshua of Nazareth and his followers in Israel.

9. Marys. "Mary" is from the Greek Μαρία (Maria), from Hebrew מִרְיָם (miryam), often Anglicized in English as "Miriam."

10. "New Covenant" is the proper English title for "New Testament," based on the Greek Καινὴ Διαθήκη (Kaine Diatheke), which Paul took from the Hebrew בְּרִית (berit or brit), meaning a "new covenant." In 2 Corinthians 3.6 Paul speaks of a *new covenant* or *pact* with the deity, not a *new testament*, as Saint Jerome erroneously renders the phrase in his Latin Vulgate. In the sixteen hundred years since the Vulgate. Western Europe and much of the world have followed the great translator's early conversion of Καινὴ Διαθήκη (Kaine Diatheke) into "Novum Testamentum," from which "New Testament" derives. New translations of the Greek scriptures sometimes use the formula for its title: "The New Covenant (written in small font), commonly called The New Testament (written in large font)."

book perhaps the most evenly powerful work about the poor in body, soul, and hope. All politic, doctrine, beautiful poetry, parables, aphorisms, and even an ultimate drama and agony of crucifixion pale before the constancy of the common person, who is the human everywhere and in all time. Therein lies the ordinary art and the plain universal passion of the people in the gospels. The picture of primal nakedness covered by a colorless mean cloth, of hurting bodies that speak with needs of the weak and poor, ensures that the gospel tale, independent of faith, doctrine, commandment, fearful warnings, and metaphysic, will always reach those with eyes to hear and feel the human condition of the spirited body waiting on the earth.

A Restoration of Openness

REFORMATIONS in religion and politics bring change and historically have been resisted by or imposed by a sword. We are smart enough to pace the moon but not the earth. The moon has an open transparent society for her rare visitors. Her vast sun-mirror casts light freely and aimlessly on seas and lovers. But on earth where religions everywhere evolve, evolutions still dye streets and paths of all the continents with blood, and eternally in the divisive names of sect, ethnicity, and politic. More than ever we need to tear up all lists of new and old infidels to be slaughtered. It is time to restore or invent a guiltless Eden to a noisy planet.

The reformation in this bible is a return to the old word and idea. Through restoration we can test new truths without fear. Truth is never fixed and has a small "t." Its companion is Heart, with a big "H" so no truth will ever kill. A reformation of openness uses peace to mediate the stranger. Openness roams us into love, stronger than hate. But be careful even of the good. There is no absolute good or truth, no Platonic unchanging idea we can tame down on earth. We are imperfect beings, which opens us to ramble, to lose and find new ways. Such is the wondrous nature of openness. Imperfection in our one long day keeps us looking. But patrons of perfection and the incorruptible kill like Maximilien Robespierre, who beheaded the straggling doubters of the cause, or Oliver Cromwell's "Ironsides," who slaughtered the Irish for being papal Irish, as Jonathan Swift informs in his "Modest Proposal."

Hurray for imperfect stumbling stragglers like Walt Whitman who invent and cheer. Illumination may be anywhere. The blind see. Blind Jorge Luis Borges taught his century dissent and fresh restorations of a multitude of pasts. Picasso made the new by remembering the old.

The artist sees many worlds. The biblical artist sees the outside world as a puzzle and narrates or chants ways and salvations, and sees the inner world of spirit as a blur waiting to be filled with changing light. Scriptures often fill that blur. Good open-minded reader—who may already have closed the book after a few of these random banalities—here is one translator's way to find the past of a book that may bring you light.

INTRODUCTION

WHY A NEW
TRANSLATION?

Why a New Translation?

WHY A NEW TRANSLATION of a biblical text? Why the King James Version in 1611, only eighty-some years after the masterful Tyndale translation, which is as austerely plain and beautiful as a field of wheat? The most obvious answer is that language changes and so too do literary conventions for making speech contemporary and natural. There may also be the call for a new approach, since translation is not only style and period but also way and purpose. The earliest versions in English by John Wyclif in 1380 and William Tyndale in 1525 were created to bring Greek and Latin scripture into the forbidden English vernacular. Wyclif translated from Jerome's Latin Vulgate, whereas Tyndale worked directly from the Greek texts. For their daring acts of replacing Jerome's fourth-century Latin (the authorized Christian Bible in the West) with their English *vulgata*, Wyclif's bones were dug up and burned and Tyndale was strangled and burned at the stake. Wyclif's and Tyndale's purpose had been to bring scriptures to the people. Tyndale, citing the aims of his model the Dutch humanist Erasmus, wrote that the word of the gospels should reach the eyes of all women, Scots and Irishmen, even Turks and Saracens, and especially the farm worker at the plow and the weaver at the loom.[11] Then in the early seventeenth century, the Tyndale and later versions were revised into the monumental King James Version, whose stated purpose by King James I's forty and seven translator-scholars was to bring forth an authorized version for the Protestant peoples of the Church of England. The King James also had a literary and didactic

11. Tyndale also echoes Nehemiah in the Hebrew Bible when he instructs the reading of the Torah "out loud, translating and giving it sense so that people understood what was read" (Neh. 8.7).

aim, which appears in the first line of the prefatory "Translators to the Reader": "Translation it is that openeth the window, to let in the light."

I undertook a new translation of the New Testament to give a chastely modern, literary version of a major world text. In the introduction, annotation, and text itself, I have followed some specific aims. First, I wish to restore the probable Hebrew and Aramaic names and so frame the Jewish identity of the main figures of the covenant, including that of Yeshua (Jesus), his family, and followers; and also the Greek names so that we will not watch Andrew and Mark pausing in London or Chicago but Andreas and Markos walking a Greek city. Second, I would like to clarify the origin of Christianity as one of the Jewish messianic sects of the day vying for dominion. And third, I wish to translate as verse what is verse in the New Testament, as in Yeshua's speech and the epic poem of Apocalypse, following a practice that, since the nineteenth-century Cambridge Paragraph Bible (1873), has prevailed in rendering Hebrew verse as in the Song of Songs, the Psalms, and Job. To the extent that this version rediscovers and restores the Greek and Semitic name and the imprisoned poem behind the text, the Restored New Testament (RNT) may also be thought of as the Rediscovery of the New Testament (RNT). The acronym and its meanings coincide.

Finally, I have made some chronological and thematic reordering of the books, putting Mark historically before Matthew, Letters before Acts, and adding three Gnostic gospels after the canonical gospels.

On all questions of faith versus fact, I take a neutral stance and address them in the annotations. As far as possible, I limit these matters to indicating a historical context of biblical happenings, always with the awareness that more is unknown than known.[12] In her brilliant *Jesus of*

---

12. Events recounted in the gospels are essentially theologically framed accounts confined to the gospels themselves. External references to Yeshua tell us little and are problematic with respect to source: Suetonius (Nero 16.2) mentions the existence of *Christiani* and of Jesus; Tacitus (*Annales* 15.44) mentions Christians and Jesus, who was sentenced to death by Pontius Pilate; Pliny the Younger has a brief reference to Jesus. The main reference to Jesus and his crucifixion is from the Jewish historian Josephus, who wrote in Greek and lived later in Rome, where he composed his histories. His critical paragraph on Jesus is said by Israeli archeologists to be a late forgery, whereas other scholars argue that the reference is authentic and not seventh-century emendation. This passage is not integrated into the text, being unrelated to what precedes and follows it, a characteristic of unskillful emendation.

Nazareth, King of the Jews, Paula Fredriksen presents her first fact, from which all historical speculation must radiate: "The single most solid fact about Jesus' life is his death: he was executed by the Roman prefect Pilate, on or around Passover, in the manner Rome reserved particularly for political insurrectionists, namely, crucifixion. Constructions of Jesus primarily as a Jewish religious figure, one who challenged the authority of Jerusalem's priests, thus sit uncomfortably on his very political, Imperial death: Pilate would have known little and cared less about Jewish religious beliefs and intra-Jewish religious controversy."[13]

As to denominations—Jewish, Christian, Muslim, the world—while respecting all views, I have no pitch for any camp. There is no more polemic or proselytizing here than were this book a new version of the *Odyssey* or of Sappho's fragments, yet I hope that my love for these extraordinary world scriptures will show through. My wish is also that this new covenant of antique persuasions will be read by all and that the text and annotation will be a source of pleasure and information, while giving some awareness of the background from which Yeshua ben Yosef, Jesus son of Joseph, came. In an open eclectic period of rapid change, I like to go back to Tyndale, first hero of the biblical word, transferring the word from its Greek home into our English guesthouse. In old speech his beautiful and daring opening to the world has for decades been my model.

13. Paula Frederiksen, *Jesus of Nazareth, King of the Jews: A Jewish Life and the Emergence of Christianity* (New York: Knopf, 1999), 8.

Villainous Jews

A NUMBER of new translations have changed the word "Jew" in their versions to diminish the accusations of villainy and guilt against Yeshua's coreligionists for their alleged judgment concerning the charismatic rabbi as the foretold messiah of Isaiah. This protective gesture assumes that to be a Jew is inherently a bad and dangerous epithet and that it is best to divest Jesus and other Jews of their religious faith. So Jew is written as "opponent" or "Judean" or some euphemism to spare the Jew abuse and to change the fact that the foundation of anti-Semitism[14] was and remains in the New Testament. Such changes are inaccurate to the texts as we have them, and actually reinforce a much more significant misconception, which is that Yeshua and family and followers were somehow not Jews, that Jesus was not a rabbi preaching in temples (though in the Greek gospels he is addressed as rabbi frequently). By a tradition of using largely Greek names for the Hebrew and Aramaic names of New Testament figures, those who represent what is sometimes called "primitive Christianity" lose their Jewish identity in a grand

14. "Anti-Judaism" is a religious term based on a theological contempt for Judaism and by extension for Jews. The actual term "anti-Semitism" was coined in 1879 by the German agitator Wilhelm Marr to designate anti-Jewish campaigns then underway in central Europe. Anti-Semitism had its beginnings during the first-century Roman Empire when Jews were often segregated for their refusal to participate in emperor worship and, by emerging Christians, for the Jews' failure to accept Jesus as their messiah. Many scholars argue that "anti-Judaism" is a more accurate term, since Jews are only one among Semitic peoples, and "anti-Judaism" means hostility only to religion, not to people. But faith and people are inevitably synonymous. In Protestant Northern Ireland the anti-Catholicism, while not against Irish ethnicity, was directed against Irish people who hold Catholic beliefs. I have used both "anti-Judaism" and "anti-Semitism," depending on whether the hostility is toward the religion or people or both.

identity theft,[15] thereby making it possible for Christians to hate Jews yet not hate Yeshua as a Jew, nor his mother Miryam and father Yosef, nor all his followers. The demeaning hatred of Jews is selective and occurs without awareness of the anomaly of loving Yeshua and hating his people and the religion he practiced and the Jewish Bible,[16] which

15. "Identity theft" is a modern legal term for the crime of assuming another's identity for personal gain. At other levels of deception, the imposter not only steals the identity for oneself but denies identity to the original owner and the totality of his or her work. In ancient literature and scripture, identity theft was commonplace. Abundant spurious works ascribed to major prophets and sages are called pseudepigrapha, especially those of the intertestamental period (200 B.C.E.–200 C.E.). In the first century we have books attributed to Enoch, Moses, Peter, and Paul. More significant is that, with the exception of seven letters by Paul, all books of the Jewish Bible and the Greek scriptures are pseudepigraphic. Authorial names and titles were fixed later. The canonical books ascribed to fabled Moses in the second millennium and David around 1000 B.C.E. somehow find authors who composed them in the sixth century. Such wondrous reinventions and cloning were not unusual. In Elizabethan London, printers facilely added famous authors' names to title pages to increase book sales. Miguel de Cervantes, William Shakespeare, and even Jack London were victims of identity theft. London was flattered that someone else would pose in his name, attire, and habits to sell his own books and impress women.

In the Old and New Testaments we see the identity heist of the original author's religious and group identity, the author's work, and the characters in the work. This cloning is achieved by a concordance of editors who change and emend scriptures and of undiscerning sectarian readers. The concealment extends to the identity of the author, the work, and the characters in the work. In such ways leading Jews in the New Testament are constantly decrying Jews to willing readers. Jane Austen's "sense" and "sensibility" are severely lacking in the preparation and reception of biblical scripture.

16. The Jewish Bible refers to the Bible of the Jews, and when later adopted by the Christians, it became the Bible for Jews and Christians. It is popularly called the Old Testament, a title imposed on it by Christians to make it contrast with the New Testament. When the Old Testament and New Testament are joined, they revert to their shorter and more inclusive epithet: the Bible. Hebrew Bible is the same book as the Jewish Bible or the Old Testament, but the Jewish Bible bears the name of the people and their religion, while the Hebrew Bible recognizes the language of composition, which is Hebrew. The New Testament is often called the Greek scriptures, contrasting it with the Hebrew Bible. In this translation I sometimes refer to the Old Testament as "the first bible," and the New Testament as "the second bible." Finally, on occasion it is useful to use the Hebrew word *Torah*, which specifically refers to the five books of Moses but which has come also to mean the whole Hebrew Bible, which has its own name, "Tanak," from an acronym derived from the first letter identifying each of five major sections of the Bible. For example, "T," the first letter in "Tanak," signifies "Torah."

was his unique guiding scripture. The disappearance of Yeshua's Jewish identity dumbfounds common sense and history, but, alas, this illusion has remained dominantly at the center of Christian reception of the New Testament. Contemporary scholars and some readers know better, but the anachronistic portrayal of Yeshua and his circle as later Christians among enemy Jews permits an unquestioned hatred of the Jew, and is a logical, understandable, and inevitable reading of the New Testament as we have it. Yet the reader need not be a biblical scholar to notice something awry when Yeshua, a Jew, speaks in the voice of a later gentile admonishing Jews of terrible punishment when Rome (four decades after his death) destroys Jerusalem. Such anomalies lead contemporary theologians to make corrective comments. The Christian theologian Marcus J. Borg corrects at all levels:

> Jesus was deeply Jewish. It is important to emphasize this obvious fact. Not only was he Jewish by birth and socialization, but he remained a Jew all of his life. His Scripture was the Jewish Bible. He did not intend to establish a new religion, but saw himself as having a mission within Judaism. He spoke as Jew to other Jews. His early followers were Jewish. All of the authors of the New Testament (with the possible exception of the author of Luke-Acts) were Jewish.
>
> Though I find it hard to believe, some Christians are apparently unaware of the Jewishness of Jesus, or, if they are aware, do not give it much weight. Moreover, Christians have frequently been guilty of conscious or unconscious anti-Semitism, identifying Jesus with Christianity and his opponents with Judaism, and thereby seeing Jesus and the early Christian movement as anti-Jewish. . . . The separation of Jesus from Judaism has had tragic consequences for Jews throughout the centuries. The separation is also historically incorrect, and any faithful image of Jesus must take with utmost seriousness his rootedness in Judaism.[17]

These are ecumenical days, calming old furies of division. In her book *The Bible: A Biography*, religious historian Karen Armstrong writes, "A thread of hatred runs through the New Testament. It is inaccurate to call

17. Marcus J. Borg, *Meeting Jesus Again for the First Time* (San Francisco: Harper-SanFrancisco, 1994), 22.

the Christian scriptures anti-Semitic, as the authors were themselves Jewish." Well-informed Armstrong knows that the authors and main actors, including Jesus, family, and followers, are Jews, but the texts conceal this essential information from the normal reader, enabling a fearfully deceptive presentation. The scriptures are anti-Semitic just because Jews are falsely slammed in "words" that, as Armstrong notes, "for centuries inspired the pogroms that made anti-Semitism an incurable disease in Europe."[18]

I address this dire and central question of disenfranchising Yeshua of his religious identity in two ways: by restoring the probable Hebrew or Aramaic names to biblical figures and framing savage anti-Semitic passages in a historic context in the introduction and the textual annotation. One should first understand that although the extant gospels are only in Greek, and Yeshua speaks Greek in the gospels, Yeshua did not use Greek, if indeed he had any knowledge of it, as his everyday language; and on the cross when he cried in agony to God, Yeshua cried out his forsaken state in Aramaic,[19] a Semitic language close to Hebrew that had by and large become the spoken language of the Jews after their return to Israel from the Babylonian defeat (586 B.C.E.).[20] Hebrew remained the language of the temple and religion. Yet we have Greek names for Yohanan (John—although the Germans retain the Hebrew in Yohan, as in Johann Sebastian Bach), and somehow Yaakov or Jacob in the Hebrew Bible becomes James in English, and Miryam becomes the Greek Maria. By recovering what are the Hebrew and Aramaic names of Testament personages, I believe that the Semitic origin and climate at last persuade in the gospels, and may ameliorate the confusing and relentless fury of anti-Judaism. In the same way that the Homeric names Zeus, Athena, and Artemis are finally heard in twentieth-century trans-

---

18. Karen Armstrong, *The Bible: A Biography* (New York: Grove Press, 2008), 75–76, 77.

19. *"Eloi, Eloi, lama sabachthani?"* (Mark 15.34; first line of Psalm 22). See note 2 above.

20. From the seventh century B.C.E. until the rise of Islam in the seventh century C.E., when Aramaic yielded to Arabic, Aramaic was the lingua franca of the Fertile Crescent and the greater Mesopotamian region and competed with Greek after the coming of Alexander the Great, who conquered the region. The Syrian Christian Church used their dialect of Aramaic, but as Aramaic became associated with pagans, they spoke of it as Syriac and developed an altered alphabet.

lations, no longer romanized as Jupiter, Minerva, and Diana, so too the Jewish names of Yaakov, Yeshua, Yosef, and Yohanan are used here rather than their irrelevant and misleading Greek or Anglicized forms.

In introducing or restoring names, I balance the urgency of restoration with the need for familiarizing the reader with new referents. Hence in the introduction and annotation, the evangelists are still called Mark, Matthew, Luke, and John for easy reference, while in the texts biblical restorations rather than standard Hellenizations are used for many names and places. In the annotation, where other texts are cited, conventional spelling is normally followed. Any change in standard orthography takes a while to absorb, but, like becoming used to new jargon or currency, it is often quickly assimilated. This restoration does wonders to afford a truthful perception of the identity of New Testament peoples. It will help us recall, as Bishop John Shelby Spong, the biblical authority and popular author, among others has observed, that the New Testament was written by Jews about Jews for Jews. The New Testament—though largely unread by Jews and when known may be perceived with deep fear—is the last major Jewish text of biblical Judaism, the parent religion of Christianity and Islam.

The second way I handle traditional anti-Judaism is by placing these remarks in a historical perspective in the introduction and annotations to the texts. There was, of course, the inevitable inflated rhetoric of interfamily rival sects within Judaism, each seeking dominion during Yeshua's life. However, the gospel texts were not fashioned in Greek until late in the first and early in the second centuries, with many unknown hands copying, redacting, and emending the stories and re-creating conversations, even of secret deliberations that allegedly took place behind the walls of the Sanhedrin.[21] By the time these texts were finally accepted by religious councils in the fourth century, what had been a

---

21. Sanhedrin from the Greek συνέδριον (synedrion). The Synedrion was the supreme council or governing body of Alexander the Great's empire. Synedrion later signified the parliament of a Greek city-state as in the Synedrion of the Epirote League. In Jerusalem the council of sages or elders was called the Sanhedrin (סַנְהֶדְרִין, sanhedrin), a Hebraized version of Greek *synedrion*. It was a governing assembly and not, as normally translated, a judicial court presided over by a high priest. In Acts 22.5, Paul refers to the *presbyterion* (elders) as the authority that gave orders to arrest Yeshua. In Mark 15.1, it is called the *symboulion* (council).

first-century controversy between Jewish groups, between Pharisees and messianics, was now seen ahistorically as a conflict between Jews and later Christians, "Christian" being the word "Messianic" or "Messianist" in Greek translation. By then, in name and thought, Christianity was politically separated from Judaism, though it retained the Jewish Bible (Old Testament) as its own Christianized Bible,[22] to which it added the Jewish scriptures of the New Testament.

There is enormous, sad irony in these separations and conflicts, based on misunderstandings and contentions of power. Jews and Christians share one Hebrew Bible, and Christians read the last great biblical document of the Jews, the New Testament, composed by Jews about and for the emerging sect of messianic (Christian) Jews. With so much vitally in common, and believers sharing the same invisible God, why such division and history of hostility? Yet this initial rivalry between Jew and Christian Jew, and in the next century between Jew and Christian, was to be repeated again and again in the inevitable schisms within Christianity. Rome broke away from Constantinople, with equal consequences of fury and death, and there began nearly two millennia of contending Orthodox and Roman Catholics. After the Reformation, the Protestants broke with Catholics and bloody battles ensued. There were the Western crusades against Catharist France, Byzantium, and Islam.

22. In his review "Who Will Praise the Lord?" of Robert Alter's new version of the Psalms, *The Book of Psalms: A Translation with Commentary* (New York: W. W. Norton, 2007), Harold Bloom does not go gently into a dark night of submission: "Alter, a critic of great sophistication, does not allow himself to express any uneasiness with the Christian appropriation of the Bible. I prefer to be rougher about this two-thousand-year-old theft. The Old Testament is a captive work dragged along in the triumphal wake of Christianity. Tanakh, the Jewish Bible, is the Original Testament; the New Testament actually is the Belated Testament. I wince when my Jewish students speak of the Old Testament." (*New York Review of Books*, November 27, 2007, 21)

Frank Kermode, in *The Genesis of Secrecy: On the Interpretation of Narrative* (Cambridge, MA: Harvard University Press, 1979, 88–89), notes how technically the early Christians "transferred the Old Testament" from rolls to codices "to establish consonance between the end of the book [Jewish Bible] and the beginning [New Testament]. . . . The transfer of the Hebrew scriptures to Greek codices enacts the appropriation of those writings for Christian purposes."

These blood schisms do not end. Each year, under changing names and banners, they ravage parts of the globe.

In the end, all people are people, and no people should ever be classified for whatever reason as less than another. Any marker of sect and theology that distinguishes any people adversely is human and humane error. So the gospels and Apocalypse should not be seen for the momentary and external conflicts they may contain, but rather for their greater universality of spirit in a world desperately poor in coming to terms with human consciousness within the perishable body. Happily, the call to spirit is deep and needs no name, and no divisive emblem. The New Testament is a book of the mind; it is infused with compassion and courage and the great questions of being, death, time, and eternity. For the perceptive reader, spirit eludes name, dogma, and even word to reside in the silence of transcendence.

How Old Versions of Bible
Shaped Secular Literature
and New Versions Have Not

HISTORICALLY, the single book most deeply affecting writers in the English language has been the Bible. Imagine John Donne, George Herbert, John Milton, William Blake, Emily Dickinson, Walt Whitman, Gerard Manley Hopkins, T. S. Eliot, and Dylan Thomas without it. But little of this flame—the fires of poetry—came from the New Testament as they knew it, nor from contemporary versions of the Hebrew Bible. Most of the biblical language and tale that entered English literature was found in early translations, those made in that short period between and including the Tyndale publications in the 1520s and 1530s and the King James Version in 1611. Not only was the language of the English Bible established during that period, but English itself, through word inventions in the Bible, became immensely expanded and enriched. In the nineteenth century, there were major scholarly and literary revisions, and in our time, especially in the last decades, there has been an opening and candor in religious studies as never before, permitting all to be said or speculated, doctrinaire and radical. But while theology and history have experienced liberation, in both studies and permissible translation, literary artistry has not done well. Perhaps because the need for intellectual freedom has been so imperative, art and the quality of the word have suffered by neglect in Bible translation.

Early in the twentieth century, T. S. Eliot pitilessly attacked Gilbert Murray's old-fashioned, wooden, Swinburnian translations of the Greek tragedies and called for a renovation of Greek and Latin classics in English. Robert Fitzgerald, Dudley Fitts, and William Arrowsmith answered his plea with consummate renditions. In our time, ancient and modern texts, from the Chinese to the Italian, Spanish, and Russian, have enjoyed a renaissance of excellent translations and translators. Yet despite a renewed academic interest in using more reliable Greek sources to translate more, no imperious Eliot has shown up to rebuke, in the name of art, contemporary translations of holy scripture. We have not the accomplishment of philosopher-theologian Martin Buber, who gave the modern German Bible a flowing, poetic, etymologically keyed alternative to Luther's famous sixteenth-century version. During the past century, we were given variations of the nineteenth-century English and American Revised Versions (1898–1890), of which the best was the recent New Revised Standard Version (1990). The latter aims for accuracy and softening the male-oriented articulation, yet retains the essential archaizing, proper, and pious tone of biblical language. As is often the case with literature deemed sacred, the Bible has been held to criteria alien to the art of literary translation. Reform has often come under the emblem of objectivity where "information transfer," as in technical translation of history, business, and science, is the measure. There are also, for the sake of reader comprehension, interpretive translations and dumbed-down versions of the Bible, yet not in the manner of Mark's plain Greek, but as chatty or off-key street-talk renderings.

The Bible in English deserves what our foremost writers can bring to it. It is a richly complex document, with many levels of expressive meaning, and translation that fails to bring over the maximum semantic load, that slights poetic language, abuses the hope of true equivalence. It is a volume charged with immense connotative meanings, as are all our religious classics, including *Daodejing*, *Bhagavad-Gita*, and *Odyssey*. A version in our day that scarcely goes beyond a word-for-word transfer between tongues signifies that again our age has failed to provide a classical work in English as Tyndale did and the Authorized did. The latter became for many, right or wrong, "an authorized original."

Today's Bible should inspire the devout and the secular reader as the Bible once did. Yet unseen are inspiring new versions. Hence, outside classrooms and religious institutions, the readers of "the great books" are not interested in contending with the Authorized or prosaic updates. Readers of the Bible, especially those outside congregations, have in large part gone away.

Abandoned by our best-known writer-translators and generations of readers, until the last few years we have lacked even those who dedicated themselves to turning one great book of the Bible into a masterpiece, as Sir Philip Sidney and his sister Lady Herbert from Elizabethan London did to give us a new rendition of the Psalms.[23] We have had no contemporary English or American equal to Poland's Nobel laureate in literature, Czeslaw Milosz (who learned Hebrew specifically to translate the Song of Songs into Polish), who might render distinguished books of the Bible in English. Perhaps it is an unfair burden to ask our leading contemporary religious scholars to become the English Luthers and Dantes for our time and refresh the English language. In days of territorial specialization, literature and art are not their terrain. The consequences are clear.

The old versions are remote, and contemporary ones do not sing. In contrast to the King James, whose scholars helped establish a great literary tradition, in new Bibles, after the corrections and recorrections, the seminarian translators have kept repetition of seminal clichés intact in pedestrian speech sullenly removed from literature. So great literature is captive to neglect. It is imperative to remember that these holy books from the coastal strip of Western Asia, of history, religion, and philosophy, contain the most intense concentration of the arts of narration, drama, and poetry the world has assembled.

Apart from the gloom, there are areas of light. If there are not new resplendent Bibles, there are writers infused with Bible light, with a magnificence of language and spirit whose source remains

---

23. See J. C. A. Rathmell, ed., *The Psalms of Sir Philip Sidney and the Countess of Pembroke* (Garden City, NY: Doubleday, 1963), first published in 1823 under the title *The Psalmes of David translated into divers and sundry kindes of verse*. Since noting the absence of our most lyrical and profound ancient document in exemplary English, Robert Alter has published a magisterial version: *The Book of Psalms: A Translation with Commentary* (New York: W. W. Norton, 2007).

the King James Version. Consider T. S. Eliot's "Ash Wednesday," *Murder in the Cathedral*, and *Four Quartets*. For all his cranky urbane anti-Semitism, Eliot is probably the last major poet in the English language to produce enduring pieces deriving directly from the two covenants. Eliot's competitor might be James Baldwin of *Go Tell It on the Mountain*, who uses the full rhetoric of biblical speech preserved in the African-American church. Martin Luther King spoke the language of the Bible in his dream speeches. Of course, these examples mirror the mighty James and not the more accurate, easier-to-read, and invented speech of the archaizing Revised and New Revised and New Revised Standard Version.

One could wish that in the last twenty years of his life, when his own creative well went dry, Eliot had, in the grand tradition, turned his hand to creating the Bible, or some part of it, in English. The task fell to the American classical scholar Richmond Lattimore. Trained in the fullness of the Greek tongue, Lattimore had spent his life turning Homer, Aeschylus, and Pindar into powerful English poetry. In his last years he turned his gaze to the New Testament and gave us a catholic, impeccably smooth version, with dignity, freshness, and a touch of beautiful earlier rhetoric. And although his 1962 publication went largely unnoticed, it remains by far the finest version we have of the words of the New Testament scriptures in English.[24] In translating the New Testament, Lattimore (the first of the Lattimore-Fitzgerald-Fagles triad of splendid Homer translators) is the exception, but his work proves that it is possible to marry scholarship and art in translating the Bible, as was done by his contemporaries in giving us Homer, Sappho, Virgil, Wang Wei, Dante, and Seigyo. What is to be done? At

---

24. Even Richmond Lattimore follows the earlier sacred tradition of blurring Yeshua's identity as a Jew through selectively false translation. After Yeshua praises Nathanael for being "truly a Jew," Nathanael says to Yeshua, "Rabbi, you are the son of God. You are the king of Israel" (John 1.49). In Greek we have *Rabbi*, but Lattimore, the most just literary scholar-translator of his day, here as elsewhere, still renders *Rabbi* in Greek as "Master" in English. More recent translators, however, reflecting the present mood, uniformly translate *Rabbi* as "Rabbi," including the New King James Version (1979), which corrects the King James Version (1611) "Master" to read "Rabbi."

the very least, one should be aware that the larger, once fertile plain is arid. And then, with a hint from the scriptures, one can hope the day of both the Hebrew and Greek scriptures resurrected in English is near.[25]

25. In 1996 Reynolds Price published *Three Gospels* (New York: Scribner, 1996), which includes Mark, Matthew, and John, a revision of an earlier version of the four canonical gospels. It is of the same literary quality throughout as is Lattimore translation, less lofty and more modern, and is very close to the Greek. It has no extra words and is a literary breakthrough. Price uses "wrong" rather than "sin" as one way of reducing what he calls the "puritan" practice in translating from the Koine. As pure observation and no reproach, I note that he comes closer than others but makes no essential break with a strongly Christianizing bias in converting Greek into English and doesn't move the text from a Hellenization of name, place, and spirit back to its Hebrew Bible base. He does mitigate, where he can without stylistic contortions, the domination of male gender words.

Major changes from the pedestrian Hebrew Bible translations that the twentieth century sponsored include the 1996 Genesis versions by Robert Alter and by Stephen Mitchell, and the 1999 translation of 1 and 2 Samuel in *The David Story* and 1999 version of the five books of Moses by Alter. *The Book of Psalms* appeared in 2007 in which King James Version rhetoric has passed into the pen of a scholar deeply informed by the Hebrew texts, and through this literary alchemy Alter has once again enriched the English language.

Mark, the Vernacular Story Teller

WITH RESPECT to common speech for the English translation of Koine Greek, I have found inspiration in the first English translation of the New Testament made directly from the Greek by William Tyndale in 1525. Tyndale's voice is demotic plain speech, not the high rhetoric of the magnificent 1611 King James Version. Tyndale's pioneer texts were deftly lifted into famous later translations, including the King James, along with words and phrases he invented, which we may incorrectly assume were always there, such as "scapegoat," "Let there be light," "gave up the ghost," and "Passover" for Easter. Where Tyndale writes, "He was a luckie fella," the King James will say, "He was a fortunate gentleman." Tyndale keeps his dress plain.

Like Tyndale I have tended to ignore standard entries in biblical Greek-English dictionaries when they are slanted to evoke an erroneous religious or political meaning or when they are common words inflated with grandeur, piety, or a strong ethical statement not inherent in their Greek signification. It is amazing how so many common words have persisted with the same meaning, if not orthography, from ancient Herodotos, through the Byzantines, to the modern Greek of the Nobel Prize poet George Seferis (1900–1971). To preserve these everyday meanings of words, I use "messenger" not "apostle," and "student" not Latin "disciple." If the peasants and fishermen whom the gospels depict have any resonance with the people of ancient Judea, they deserve not to wear robes of sober grandeur in their epithets. Jesus had students around him, not disciples.

Of the books of the New Testament, Mark is fully demotic in speech and is the most accomplished tale of the volume. The author (or authors) of the earliest canonized gospel relates the story of an itinerant rabbi in ancient Israel who talks, heals miraculously, and walks the hills of Judea and alleys of the holy city of Jerusalem; who mesmerizes his followers with his word, at once wise, evasive, lyrical, and surreal; and who suffers, if the story of the Roman crucifixion is accurate, the most dramatic and meaningful death in history. As a wandering preacher, he speaks wisdom and the good life. He brings the dead back to life. To the dispirited and desperate, he offers reward of a new good life of hope; for those who are wicked, he threatens eternal punishment. He is strikingly independent—from the clergy as from the expected behavior toward his family. When his powers are unrecognized by his mother, Mary, he indignantly goes out to the fields to find his faithful followers and his true family. He is gentle but also claims a sword. Recently, theologians have compared Yeshua to a Greek Cynic philosopher, a late Diogenes looking with a lantern in bright daylight for an honest man.

Yeshua's creator is unique in the gospels and perhaps in the whole Jewish Bible in which he is imbued. He is a candid chronicler of the fantastic. With a few strokes Mark creates scene, character, and pathos as his hero moves episodically to the next encounter. Each new encounter contains a magic-realism resolution that participants are ordered to keep secret. Mark lays out events on land and sea without verbal flourish. Spare, making each word vital in his tales of wonder, he is the invisible author, but at the same the modest master of *le mot juste*.

After Mark's tale becomes known, not only are Jesus's followers about to have a document describing a new, small sect of first-century Jews, a new Judaism—which soon takes on its own identity and name, Christianity[26]—but also the book has a breakthrough ethical and metaphysical latitude. In plain speech for the field worker and town dweller, he details Jewish and Greek thought concerning time and eternity, body and spirit, and the life of a skygod residing on earth who dies on a Roman cross and returns to the sky. Though Mark leaves critical assumptions open to later interpretation, never himself saying that Yeshua is God or resurrected, the events he recounts will in the next two thousand years spread around the globe as Christian theology.

26. For further discussion of the complexity of the emerging development of the Yeshua movement, see George W. E. Nickelsburg, "Revealed Wisdom as a Criterion for Inclusion and Exclusion: From Jewish Sectarianism to Early Christianity," in Jacob Neusner and Ernest S. Frerichs, eds., *To See Ourselves as Others See Us: Christians, Jews, "Others" in Late Antiquity* (Chico, CA: Scholars Press, 1985), and Wayne Meeks, *The First Urban Christians: The Social World of the Apostle Paul* (New Haven: Yale University Press, 1983).

The narrative means employed in all the gospels will also alter the use of language. The Greek resting point at which the New Testament exists found its lexicon and style in both the Hebrew Bible and diverse postbiblical scriptures that make up the noncanonical apocrypha and pseudepigrapha of the period. In demotic Mark there is that perfection of the ordinary, the pure, the rude, and the popular. A raconteur could say or dream it, but Aeschylus or even the great Shakespeare of Lear might not notice it as art. Or if they did, their version, as Shakespeare's shorthand borrowings from Plutarch, would be fleshed out beyond recognition. In his lucid minimalism, Mark prefigured a formal revolution in style that occurred two thousand years later when Hemingway, in gnomic works like *The Old Man and the Sea*, and Steinbeck, in the parabolic *The Pearl*, came upon a speech that made the novelists of America and Europe go plain. In the opening picture in the wilderness are Mark's direct rhythmic words and bright plainness:

> Yohanan the Dipper appeared in the desert and preaching an immersion of repentance for the remission of sin. The whole land of Yehuda and all the people of Yerushalayim came out to him and were being immersed by him in the Yarden river, and confessing their sins. And he was clothed in camel hair, and wore a belt of skins around his loins, and he ate locusts and wild honey.
>
> MARK 1.4–6

The author (or authors) of Mark wrote in Koine, a form of demotic or spoken Greek, and his voice is a spoken tale—not a learned written report in elegantly difficult syntax. It is a teller's story, one repeated by Matthew and Luke, each of whose version varies as a teller's account will. Here the Hebrew Bible and the gospels share the medium of talk. The gospels, like Ecclesiastes, are both plain and poetic speech. And nothing is plainer than the talk narration of Genesis, which can be chanted as song.[27] One must remember that God did not write but "spoke" creation through the word; his feats on those six days of labor

27. Academic categories of high and lowbrow rhetoric are helpful but not without paradox. While Genesis has the high rhetoric of Homer, Shakespeare, and Milton, as it moves into description of early figures it has the fast simplicity of a thriller narration, which it also is.

were dictated into the Torah. Mark's gospel story of the days of Yeshua turned out to be divine talk for later Christians. His tone also reflects the unknown sources of his specific tale, which—whether written, oral, or both—certainly carried the same character of common speech.

Mark's plain talk is relentlessly hammered by classical scholars haughty about these foreign latecomers to the narrative and by uneasy biblical scholars largely without a background in classical Greek who accept *fait accompli* Koine's inferiority. It is embarrassing to list the many, including my favorite modern interpreter and biblical expert, Frank Kermode, who while clearly esteeming Mark as the ultimate teller among the evangelists cannot resist repeating the deadly cliché about biblical Greek when he speaks of Mark's crude Greek. If so, then Michel de Montaigne was also crude for writing his *Essais* in French, that "vulgar" version of medieval Latin. Koine, the demotic child of classical Attic Greek, is no more inferior to the classical Greek of Plato (who wrote with flowing dialogic fluency) than French is to old Latin. Koine is the perfect vehicle for the peasant wisdom verse of Yeshua the Mashiah (Jesus the Christ) in swift narrations of the dramatic gospels, for the magical logic and grace of the authentic letters of Paul, for the poem of John's creation prologue and Paul's meditations. Koine is as boundless as it is very Greek in being precise for every whim of philosophical and logical distinction.

Given the spontaneity and overheard tale-teller tone of the gospels, the concern for finding and keeping the fixed word, the exact "letter of the Bible," seems almost an impertinence. The English reader is always dealing with translation and a text that itself is a translation from an unknown written text or witness report, which is sometimes called "oral gospeling" or a half-dozen other words to explain away the absence of a source. Many layers stand between the reader and exact, documentary speech. Talk may be fixed by a playwright or scribe or digital recorder, but with regard to biblical witnessing, such reports are obscure, and their next expression will be different and contain new revelations. This uncertainty pertains to versions of most ancient texts, especially to religious texts, and has its own virtues. The salient virtue of unfixed scripture is its liveliness, its imitation of convincing speech.

Plato cast his writings in the form of dialogues, philosophical talk, precisely to preserve the spontaneous live speech, which, he argued, holds meanings that the written word cannot capture. Speech comes from live persons, who never tell the same story twice. Writing becomes dry ink. Through Socrates' voice, Plato said that "to write with pen and ink is to write in water, since the words cannot defend themselves. The spoken word—the living word of knowledge, which has a soul—is thus superior to the written word, which is nothing more than its image" (Plato, *Phaedrus*, 278b). So at the heart of the gospels is the living, heard voice of Yeshua, usually in the form of Platonic dialogue. The letters (epistles) too are a form of live speech, the voice of one person speaking to others. By contrast, the thinkers Descartes and Hume are master stylists, but unlike the gospels they reason abstractly, never dialogically, nor through the voice of an author intimately addressing the reader. Their texts are eloquent and convincing, but they don't sing.

Each of the gospels has its own genius of style and preserves its authoritative way through discussion. Unlike the intimate tale of the gospels, Apocalypse (Revelation)[28] takes us elsewhere. Although also composed in Koine, Apocalypse, like the many extant apocalypses of the era—Jewish and Christian Jewish—is one long breath of Hebrew Bible prophecy of the end. Like the primeval tales of creation and destruction in Genesis and the grotesque sky beasts in Daniel, its immediate source, the primal grandeur of Apocalypse carries us in vision all over the heavens and under the earth. The gospels of healing, poetry, parabolic wisdom, and the culminating passion along with the angelic vision of Revelation make the New Testament the ultimate Christian-Jewish book.[29]

28. Apocalypses can be found in James H. Charlesworth, *The Old Testament Pseude-pigrapha* (Garden City, NY: Doubleday, 1983–1985), in Willis Barnstone, *The Other Bible* (San Francisco: Harper and Row, 1984; 2nd rev. ed., HarperSanFrancisco, 2005), and in Willis Barnstone, *The New Covenant* (New York: Riverhead Books, 2002). All the other apocalypses are called "apocalypses," but the Apocalypse in the New Testament in most translations into English is "Revelation." In other languages, especially in those where Greek Orthodoxy is followed, the Greek word *apocalypse* is transliterated as "apocalypse" rather than translated as "revelation."

29. In *Omens of Millennium* (New York: Riverhead Books, 1996), Harold Bloom reminds us that apocalyptic tradition, so widespread in intertestamental times and especially in the diverse noncanonical books of Enoch, has a long tradition from Zoroaster to Islam: "From Zoroaster on, apocalyptic expectations flourished and made their way into Judaism and its heretical child, early Christianity, and then into Islam, which sprang forth from Jewish Christianity" (41).

The "ultimate Christian-Jewish book" refers to the fact that although the gospels are Jewish books composed by Jews about Jews, as is each book in the Hebrew Bible, the gospels are also Christian-Jewish books. The later Christians received the gospels as Christian scripture, where "Christian" carries the meaning of "messianic." Yeshua's followers saw him as the foretold Jewish messiah, there being not yet a separate religion one could call Christianity. The increasingly prevalent understanding holds that the gospels are Jewish books written by Christian Jews, which were ultimately appropriated from the Jews and shaped by later Christians who had lost their Jewish centrality and who saw intra-Jewish rivalry in the New Testament as a struggle between gentile Christians and demonized Jews.

In Liberating the Gospels: Reading the Bible with Jewish Eyes, the Episcopal bishop John Shelby Spong asserts that "[t]he Gospels are Jewish Books" (title of chapter 2). He notes that although Christians have been educated to deny that the New Testament is a Jewish book, "the Gospels are Jewish attempts to interpret the life of a Jewish man" and "in a deep and significant way, we are now able to see that all of the Gospels are Jewish books, profoundly Jewish books." He observes that the gospels were written by four Jews (Mark, Matthew, John, and Luke, a convert) about Jews. The bishop goes on to confess his own worldwide, Christian-prejudiced education with regard to the gospels: "How was it that one whose name was Yeshuah or Joshua of Nazareth, whose mother's name was Miryam, could come to be thought of in history as anything but a Jew? . . . Not only did I not understand that Jesus was Jewish, but it never occurred to me to assume that his disciples were Jewish either. I could not imagine Peter, James, John, and Andrew as Jews, to say nothing of Mary Magdalene and Paul." In his extensive study of the New Testament, he tells us, "We are beginning to recognize the Gospels as Jewish books," but as for their historicity, he notes that the dark Judas, the dark "anti-hero of the Christian tradition," was "a later Christian invention. . . . Judas never existed but was a fictional scapegoat created to shift the blame for Jesus's death from the Romans to the Jews.[30] Even while the earliest church fathers were demonizing

30. John Shelby Spong, *Liberating the Gospels: Reading the Bible with Jewish Eyes* (San Francisco: HarperSanFrancisco, 1996), 20, 36, 24–25, 33, 258.
  In her *Judas: A Biography* (New York: W. W. Norton, 2009), Susan Gubar traces

Judas, there was a sympathetic myth about Judas, the Gospel of Judas, in which Jesus selects Judas alone among his students to save and to meet in heaven.

It is sad and hopeful that one must reiterate what is or should be obvious to scholars and eventually to the general readership, which is the centrality of the New Testament as Jewish scripture. It should be as obvious as believing that Plato's *Republic* is Greek philosophy with a Greek cast and author. But Yeshua's Jewishness is not clear. Moreover, in the extant Greek form, it is not meant to be clear. This version, which at least restores the home geography and Semitic identity of the characters, has the fancy that it may incite a journey of understanding.

In a grand book—problematic, imperfect as grand books of all faiths must be since these are the writings of humans, not of God—there is a page behind the page. On the underpage lies the good news of the teacher, rabbi Yeshua ben Yosef. But on other uncertain pages in the New Testament are words reflecting persuasions of later churchmen that have fashioned Yeshua as an alien Galilean denouncing his coreligionists and sending them to a punishment worse than that found in Sodom and Gomorrah. These outbursts should be recognized and understood as perfectly implausible and unworthy of Yeshua's nature and mission. Then begins understanding and good feelings. Then Matthew of the

---

2,000 years of the myth of Judas in scripture, by church fathers, in politics, and especially in literature, music, and painting. The name "Judas," from "Judaism," links Jews to the story. He is rendered as the ugly, greedy, treacherous Jew and the lone Jew among the disciples. He is filled with worms and sexual perversity as seen in the kiss of Judas when he betrays his master. In her unparalleled biography, Gubar studies the nauseating but changing depictions of Judas in the gospels and Acts. She takes us to the second century, when the church leader Papias writes that Judas's "private parts were shamefully huge and loathsome to behold and, transported through them from all parts of his body, pus and worms flooded out together as he shamefully relieved himself." Dante places Judas at the bottom of the inferno, where he is gnawed by Satan. The Inquisition uses Judas as an inspiration to torture. Luther writes that the Jews ate Judas's excrement after he burst in order to sharpen their eyes for money. Judas is a propaganda gift for the Nazis as they round up demonized Jews for execution. Today in media talk, when a politician changes his presidential endorsement he is labeled "Judas." The sound bite works. No one questions the truth of the label. Such is the staying power of the world's cruelest tale. Susan Gubar's history of this tale is her biography of Judas.

lovely Sermon and the empathetic Beatitudes, "Blessed are the gentle /
for they will inherit the earth" (5.5), reaches us and not Jesus militant,
who says, "I have not come to bring peace but a sword" (10.34). The
battle-sword anger and fearful retribution should not, with a positive
twist, be explained away hermeneutically but rejected outright as alien
noises of sectarian rivalry penned by later anonymous hands. Darkness
must not overcome good. Then, released from stains of anger, Jesus's
voice speaks an innocence of light in the heart, of "light filling the
whole body." It becomes a covenant of the noblest and kindest love,
enveloping us in a firmament of soul. And the Christian believer—or
reader of any faith or joy—is released from negation to read the book of
concordance.

Restored New Testament as Poem

THIS Restored New Testament is a literary-historical venture of restoration. If successful it will reach all readers, devout or secular, and provide insight into the words, the message, and, not the least, the lyrical resonance of masterpieces of world literature. With these thoughts in mind I have set all the utterings of Yeshua in poetic form and many of the epistlers and all of Apocalypse in blank verse (loose iambic pentameters). The revision to restore verse locked in prose matches the 1873 Cambridge Paragraph Bible that similarly lineated the poetry of the Song of Songs, Job, Psalms, Proverbs, and much of Ecclesiastes, Isaiah, and the other prophets. The French Jerusalem Bible and its English counterpart have also lineated a large part of the New Testament as verse. So in meaning and sound I would like to think this version can reach a panorama of readers.

A large part of the two covenants is verse. If one looks at any study or well-annotated Bible, one notices that virtually every page, often every paragraph and single line, cites or has a reference to a like passage in the Tanak (the Hebrew Bible). Most of these references come through the veil of the second-century B.C.E. Alexandrian Septuagint Bible, which is a translation into Greek of the complete Tanak for the large community of Jews of Alexandria who could no longer read Hebrew. While the original Hebrew script was not lineated as verse, in great part because of a tradition of saving space on a parchment page, the prosody of echoing parallelism was well known. Robert Alter has written the definitive book on biblical poetry in which he observes that "poetry is quintessentially the mode of expression in which the surface is the depth."[31]

31. Robert Alter, *The Art of Biblical Poetry* (New York: Basic Books, 1987).

Sappho's poems also were not lineated (as was the poetry of all early Greek poets), and often even the words were run together not to waste space on valuable papyrus. Only three centuries after her death did Hellenistic grammarians copy her some five hundred poems in her intended strophic forms. Sappho's elaborate and often original meters and general prosody were imitated by later Greek, Latin, and European poets as was no other figure in antiquity.[32]

The New Testament authors cited Hebrew poetry through the Septuagint, which like the Hebrew source texts was in prose, including the most lyrical poems of the Song of Songs. Even the monumentally poetic King James Version cast them in prose. After the 1873 Cambridge Paragraph Bible, for which effectively all Hebrew poetry in the earlier covenant was uniformly converted into poetic form, it was not until late in the twentieth century that passages in the New Testament with a precursor in the Jewish Bible poetry began to find a poetic stanza. How pitiful that even the Psalms were condemned to prose!

In the Gnostic Gospel of Thomas, which has no narration and is exclusively Yeshua's sayings, Yeshua's words are also preserved in traditional aphorism that can be read as verse. In this version Yeshua's words, Paul's authentic letters, the entire Revelation, and many passages from the letters, gospels, and Acts are rendered in verse as they are in both the French and English editions of the New Testament in the excellent 1990 Catholic Jerusalem Bible.

To most of us it is a secret that Yeshua's speech takes the form of poems. Even more obscure is the notion that the authentic core of the gospels stands in verse. This translation introduces the Jewish messiah of the Christians as the great oral poet of the first century C.E., who heretofore has been our invisible poet.

---

32. For more information on Sappho's poems and prosody, see Anne Carson, *If Not, Winter: Fragments of Sappho* (New York: Knopf, 2002), and Willis Barnstone, *The Complete Poems of Sappho* (Boston: Shambhala Books, 2009).

Three Invisible Poets: Jesus,
John of the Creation Prologue,
John of Patmos

Whitman or Isaiah

WILLIAM BLAKE AND WALT WHITMAN, whose main source for their renovation of poetry into free verse was the Bible, saw, without reference to the verse typography found in the revised versions, that the Bible was an endless fountain of poetry:

> The carpenter measures with a line and makes an outline with a
>   marker;
> He roughs it out with chisels and marks it with compasses.
> He shapes it in the form of man, of man in all his glory, that it
>   may dwell in a shrine.
> He cut down cedars, or perhaps took a cypress or oak.
> He let it grow among the trees of the forest, or planted a pine,
>   and the rain made it grow.
> It is man's fuel for burning; some of it he takes and warms him-
>   self, he kindles a fire and bakes bread.

No, this is not a passage from Walt Whitman's "Song of the Broad-Axe" or "Song for Occupations" but from the New International Version (1973) of Isaiah 44.13–15. These are words translated from the Hebrew of a Jewish poet who wrote in the mid-sixth century B.C.E. Although at the time Whitman was reading the Bible the versions of translated Bible were not yet lineated in verse, he knew what poetry was locked up in its prose typography. Recently, the Jerusalem Bible and John Dominic Crossan have taken New Testament sayings by Yeshua and put them into verse. And Everett Fox's translation of the Torah is pioneer in highlighting new areas of chanted verse.[33] In that grand gesture, he completed the task begun in the nineteenth century when sections of the diverse "Revised" editions of the Hebrew Bible began to be lineated in verse, including the Song of Songs, Psalms, Job, and large segments of the books of the prophets.

Yeshua the Poet

From Sappho to Cole Porter and Aretha Franklin, there are and always will be many technical[34] ways of preserving and presenting the poem. The poem is read or recited or sung. It is recorded on papyrus, parchment, marble, slate, paper, computer screen. It is acoustically recorded joined with music on CDs and transferred to iPods. However presented, the intrinsic poem contains exactly the same words and spelling, and remains the same poem when heard as song. However, as the poem shifts from one medium to another, it can and usually does lose recognition as a poetic utterance. Most of us are not aware that when we hear a song on an iPod, we are listening to a poem. The poem is disguised acoustically in the music of the song, but *all song is poetry*. By way of an earbud the poem reverberates on through the human body. People often assert that they never read poetry, but they hear poetry night and day on radio and through technical devices. It would be a distinguished breakthrough for poetry if one recognized that large CD music stores specialize in selling disks of poetry and music.

As song often goes unrecognized as poem because the melodic song conceals the original verse, most of the New Testament also goes

33. Everett Fox followed his German model, the translation of the Hebrew Bible into German, *Die Schrift,* by Martin Buber and Franz Rosenzweig, who held that the Bible is oral literature written down and that a good translation should reproduce the Hebraic voice.

34. "Technical" is from Greek *techne,* meaning "art," and the adjective "technical" means "artistic" as well as technical. In Greek, art is a technique.

unrecognized as poem. The poem waits behind the text. But if one
looks inventively behind the text and rescues it with poetic lineation and
line breaks, the poet Yeshua son of Yosef, a world poet, appears and is
heard. In the gospels Yeshua is speaking poetry.

If Yeshua's poetic speeches were part of the Hebrew Bible canon,
they would by now be lineated as are Job and the books of the prophets.
By now we are accustomed to believe that poetry resides in the Hebrew
Bible and that the New Testament is a story and a play, a fabling narration
and a drama. If there is any poetry in the New Testament, one assumes
that it consists of segments from the Hebrew Bible, cited in Greek from
the Septuagint translation of the older covenant. Yet Matthew, the gospel with the most dialogue, anthologizes the diverse wisdom talk and
prayers of Yeshua from the other gospels into the Sermon on the Mount,
a famous string of poems that includes the psalm of the Lord's Prayer.
Matthew is mainly poetry.

The poets Jesus and John of Patmos are invisible, obscured in prose.
Readers have been misled by the shape of typography on the page that
is lineated as prose, not poetry. They are also confused by the authorial
questions. Who is the poet and author? Yeshua or the evangelist? Are
the words spoken by Yeshua his or must their authorship be shared with
their presenter? Questions of the *true* original, of the *authentic* creator,
terrorize the arts and nourish the exegetes. They make ink flow and bite.
But let us be grateful that we have a good name—the best name—to
attach to the poetic text, that we can guard and enjoy it as amateurs of
the word and leave dispute and haggle to the wise and learned. We read
and hear Yeshua's voice. Matthew is his recorder and editor. Matthew is
worthy too in that holy concordance of skill in creating a voice. In the
end, we possess Jesus's poems. They are uniformly sonorous in their
metaphysic and of-the-earth peasant, village, fisherman, and farmland
settings. They are poems of the poor with hope.

The Hebrew Bible prophets and the last prophet Yeshua comprise
a garden paradise for authors. This temptation was not lost to Andrew
Marvell, George Herbert, Gerard Manley Hopkins, and Dylan Thomas,
who were among the multitude of poets nourished by biblical scripture. They saw through the prose setting, which in the sixteenth and
seventeenth centuries turned Yeshua's words into magnificent English
story. Then came the somewhat dusty versions in the eighteenth and

nineteenth centuries, where an Orwellian bible-speak set in. But Jesus was not alone in his prose confines. So were the Psalms and the Song of Songs until their release into verse in 1873 when F. H. A. Scrivener published the Cambridge Paragraph Bible, in which he formatted the prose of the KJV in paragraphs and lineated the poetic passages in the Old Testament as poetry. Once released from prose, however, the tradition of rendering in verse the poetry books of the Hebrew Bible was unstoppable and commanded most twentieth-century versions. The New Testament is coming closer to the Old Testament versions in which at last, despite dissenting sighs, chapter and verse were fashioned to sing.

Today there is a good sound of poetry in the air for the Greek scriptures. The passage has taken a century, but ancient song is heard on the land. After millennia of winter ignorance, now a spring beginning. Chaucer's fourteenth-century prologue to the *Canterbury Tales* begins

Whan that aprill with his shoures soote
The droghte of march hath perced to the roote
(When that April with his showers sweet
The drought of March has pierced to the root).

T. S. Eliot's muddy takeoff on Chaucer's prologue begins his *Waste Land* (1922): "April is the cruelest month." But since the era of cool-hand Eliot, who also reminded us, "Gentlemen, it is time," we have invented springing April as Poetry Month. Surely the big bang of biblical verse is near. Then, by acclamation, the world poets of both covenants will be heard first in April, not only in scripture but also in all print and oral venues of poetry, and in all months of the year and in all tongues. Some may awake at last and remember that Matthew all along had it right: "Let those of us with ears hear."

We are there, almost. Some caveats. The concentration of poetry in the New Testament is usually categorized in Anglo-American academic writing as "Jesus' wisdom sayings," a phrase that fails to recognize the poetry. But a good wind, originally out of France, has been the Catholic Jerusalem Bible in French, and now in English, which renders much of John and most of Yeshua into verse. Curiously, the Jerusalem does not do so with Apocalypse, the single long, indisputable poem of the

New Testament. The noble Jerusalem Bible, abundant with enlightened annotation, daringly chose poetry. However, its poetry is not spectacular. And the choice of the poem as the form and proper genre for
the Greek scripture does not in itself ensure the inherent melody of
the verse. Recall how the sixteenth-century Tyndale and seventeenth-
century King James prose renditions are charged with memorable poetry.
Anomaly, not constancy, rules literary history.

Finally, in the twentieth century, the leading modern versions of the
New Testament remain in prose devoid of lyric. The marked exception is
Richmond Lattimore's version, also in prose, but with a magical brightness of the plain word. No wonder for a master translator of Pindar and
the ancient Greek tragedians.

Let us consider briefly a few fragments of New Testament
poems.

The poems in the gospels are clean and incomplete and their endings
elusively open. Even the most gnomic couplets are concentrated wisdom
poems, which, though proverbial, enjoy unlimited grace. They are not
conclusions but a hint for further meditation. Some longer ones ramble
magnificently in the form of parable narrations. Some aphoristically
take a moment of nature, using only images and shunning abstraction,
to give the metaphysics of life on earth and of eternity:

You are the salt of the earth.
But if the salt has lost its taste, how will it recover its salt?
Its powers are for nothing except to be thrown away
And trampled underfoot by others.

MATT. 5.13

With multiple ambiguities, the question is asked about the salt that has
lost its taste and its powers. The salt can only be picked up and thrown
away, obliterated. Or is the recovery of the salt—humankind's redemption on earth—to be attained precisely through its loss and awareness
of loss? Similarly through image alone, the Greek poet Sappho speaks
of love, loss, and the beginning of knowledge in her fragment about the
hyacinth trampled by others into the earth, yet which blooms:

Like a hyacinth crushed in the mountains by shepherds;
lying trampled on the earth yet blooming purple.

SAPPHO, 168

In the verses that follow, Yeshua goes from salt to light, from the element in the earth to the spiritual light inside the *you*, his listener. And that light is so strong that it expands, by its example, as good news to the world. It appears blatantly as a city on a mountain and then returns to the privacy of the house where there too it glows on everyone near it.

You are the light of the world.
A city cannot be hidden when it is set on a mountain.
Nor do they light a lamp and place it under a basket,
But on a stand,
And it glows on everyone in the house.

MATT. 5.14–15

Continuing the image of light, the poet says,

The lamp of the body is the eye.
If your eye is clear, your whole body is filled with light,
But if your eye is clouded, your whole body
Will inhabit darkness.
And if the light in your whole body is darkness,
How dark it is!

MATT. 6.22–23

The poet in Matthew has many moods and voices, largely but not always spoken by Yeshua, including explosions of invective, admonishing survival:

Do not give the holy to the dogs
Or cast your pearls before the pigs.
They will probably trample them underfoot
And turn and tear you to pieces.

MATT. 7.6

43

And there is an abundance of wisdom poetry, among the finest we have from Asia that has entered the West, and later the globe:

> Go in through the narrow gate,
> Since wide is the gate and spacious the road
> That leads to destruction,
> And there are many who go in through it.
> But how narrow is the gate and cramped is the road
> That leads to life,
> And there are few who find it.
>
> MATT. 7.13–14

Among the passages of wondered poetry are the birds of the sky and lilies of the field verses in Matthew 6.26–30. The temporal splendor of flower, clothing, and grass is what we live by. It is here today, yet tomorrow it is all ominously "cast into the oven" to die by fire, a phrase that cannot help but evoke the terrors of the twentieth century. The poet Yeshua in Matthew, evoking the image of emptiness promised to those of little faith, asks the listener to consider what raiment God will offer when those coverings of field and body have disappeared:

> Consider the birds of the sky.
> They do not sow or reap or collect for their granaries,
> Yet your heavenly father feeds them.
> Are you not more valuable than they?
> Who among you by brooding can add one more hour
> To your life?
>
> And why care about clothing?
>
> Consider the lilies of the field, how they grow.
> They do not labor or spin
> But I tell you not even Shlomoh in all his splendor
> Was clothed like one of these lilies.
> And if the grass of the field is there today
> And tomorrow is cast into the oven
> And in these ways God has dressed the earth,

44

Will he not clothe you in a more stunning raiment,
You who suffer from poor faith?

MATT. 6.26–30

John of the Prologue

In the prologue to John, the invisible poet is another unknown John, and the voice is philosophical, making the word an instrument of creation, miming the Genesis phenomenon. John the Evangelist is the author of the fourth gospel who explores spirit and body, eternity and temporal residence. In the great beginning of the Gospel of John, the unknown John blends voices of sundry currents of a period palpitating with philosophy and new religious divisions, especially those of Gnosticism and early Kabbalah. The beginning is a mirror of the creation command in Genesis: "Let there be light." It argues syllogistically about the word in the fashion of the Greek sophists. And influenced by Gnosticism, John of the Prologue elaborates the light of the soul. His word takes us not only to Greek notions of the *logos* as the mind of the world, but to the Kabbalists' notion of the word and creation. In Kabbalah God must first invent letters to make a word with which he speaks the creation. The scholar Gershom Scholem places the beginnings of the Kabbalist word and letters together with the emergence of Jewish Gnosticism[35] in Palestinian Judaism, stating that "[t]he growth of Merkabah mysticism among the rabbis constitutes an inner Jewish concomitant to Gnosis, and it may be termed 'Jewish and rabbinic Gnosticism.'"[36] Like the Kabbalists' word, John's word precedes creation, and his word is all things: God, beginning, life, and light which the darkness cannot apprehend, nor physically seize, nor spiritually understand:

In the beginning was the word
And the word was with God,

35. In the second and third centuries, the classical Christian Gnostics of Alexandria took the evangelist John's gospel as their principal text for exegesis in proof of their dualistic message.
36. Gershom Scholem, *Origins of the Kabbalah* (Princeton: Princeton University Press, 1987), 13.

And God was the word.
The word was in the beginning with God.
Through it everything came about
And without it not a thing came about.
What came to be in the word was life
And life was the light of people
And light in the darkness shines
And the darkness could not apprehend it.

JOHN 1.1–5

In the prologue of John, the light, the first entity to be created in Genesis, immediately takes on a spiritual opposition to the uncomprehending darkness. Light is the ultimate principle of knowledge, which is confirmed throughout the Nag Hammadi Coptic scriptures and especially in "The Creation of the Earth."

John the Evangelist

The poems in the Gospel of John stand alone, or connect in strings, sometimes in strings of three- and four-line related but separate poems (like strings of Japanese tankas), or they inform a dramatic dialogue. In John 4.21–26, Yeshua tells the Samaritan woman that salvation is from the Jews and the hour is coming. Now we can hear Yeshua and the woman as poets, and so distinguish between the opening authorial voice of John and the recorded voice of Yeshua. Because we know no one's name for certain, we have the absolute problem, an impossible but pleasant problem of distinguishing between the unnamed authorial voice and his created or recorded lines of the poet Yeshua. Where one starts and the other ends is the instant where a drop joins the sea. With an Asian simplicity reminiscent of the Asian poets, Yeshua declares himself the savior:

Yeshua said to her,
    Believe me, woman, the hour is coming
    When not on this mountain
    Nor in Yerushalayim will you worship the father.

You worship what you do not know.
We worship what we know
Since salvation is from the Jews.
But the hour is coming and it is now
When the true worshipers will worship the father
In spirit and truth,
For the father seeks such people to worship him.
God is spirit
And those worshiping must worship him
In spirit and truth.

The woman said to him, "I know a mashiah is coming who is called the anointed. When he comes he will declare all things to us."
Yeshua said to her,
I am he, talking to you.

JOHN 4.21–26

Finally, punning with the double meaning of *pneuma*, which is "breath" or "wind over the earth," and by its metaphorical abstraction and later ecclesiastical and Latin usage, God's "spirit," Yeshua again carries on the metaphysic of the temporal and what exists beyond the temporal:

Unless you are born from water and the wind of God
You cannot enter the kingdom of God.

What is born from the flesh is flesh,
What is born from the wind is wind.

Do not wonder that I told you
You must be born again from above.

The wind blows where it wants to and you hear its sound
But you cannot know where it comes from and where it
        goes.
So it is for everyone born from the wind of God.

JOHN 3.5–8

For those who don't believe or understand his statement, he tells us plainly,

> The breath keeps us alive.
> The flesh is of no help.
> The words I spoke to you are the breath of spirit
> And are life.
>   JOHN 6.63

The voice revealed through translation of his words into the Greek, and now into English, is that of a world poet. To call an unidentified poet Yeshua of the gospels or John the Evangelist or Luke of the ballad of the poignant "Lost Son," or surreal John of the Apocalypse is a shadowy name and distinction, since in each case there is a poet or recorder of the poet behind that voice: the evangelists in the case of Yeshua, and John and a Greek Jew, said to be from Patmos or Ephesos—though his origin is quite dubious—behind the great revelation in the Apocalypse. The voices, of uncertain name and of distinctive mystery of origin, must be perceived so we may hear them as we have heard other ancient wisdom poets of Asia, of a religious and metaphysical cast, from China's Laozi tradition, India's Mahadevi, Sumeria's Enheduanna, and Israel's many-voiced prophets. Isaiah and Laozi are, respectively, the great poets of the Hebrew Bible and the Chinese Daoist *Daodejing*, yet in each case what is held together under each name are several voices. We speak of Isaiah 1, Isaiah 2, Isaiah 3. We speak of Laozi as the author of the *Daodejing* or Confucius (Kong Fuzi) as the author of the Confucian odes. But in each instance we know it is many songs under a single name. In short, under each name is a tradition. In the New Testament, the most distinctive voices are Yeshua and the two Johns (of gospel and Apocalypse). Following the tradition of retelling the gospel story in different voices, in each gospel the poems take distinctive wordings as they are retold.

John of Patmos

The poet of the Apocalypse has given us a single book by the last invisible poet of the New Testament. He is the one of epic breath, whom John Milton seems to have invented as his primary precursor for his paradises lost and found. We speak of John of the white island of Patmos or of the marble city of Ephesos, the author of the apocalyptic narration purportedly done in a cave near the port in Patmos. The monastery and cave are there, and you can see the rock where John, during a two-year retreat, is said to have written Apocalypse. His identity and actual location, as with all figures in the New Testament with the exception of Paul, are similarly clouded. But we see his markings when his lamb opens the seals, the cosmos shudders, and the sun becomes black like sackcloth of hair:

> When the lamb opened the sixth seal I looked
> And there took place a great earthquake
> And the sun became black like sackcloth of hair
> And the full moon became like blood,
> And the stars of the sky fell to the earth
> As the fig tree drops its unripe fruit
> Shaken by a great wind. And the sky
> Vanished like a scroll rolling up
> And every mountain and island of the earth
> Was torn up from its place and moved.
> And the kings of the earth and the great men
> And commanders of thousands and every slave
> And the free hid in caves and mountain rocks,
> And said to the mountains and rocks, "Fall on us
> And hide us from the face of him who is sitting
> On the throne and from the anger of the lamb
> Because the great day of his anger has come,
> And before him who has the force to stand?"
>
> JOHN 6.12–17

We are in an inferno when we see the beasts of the Apocalypse, appropriated from Daniel, and we soon know where Dante, Milton, and Blake found the tradition of their bestial apocalyptic visions:

> Then I saw a beast coming up from the sea,
> With ten horns and seven heads and on his horns
> Ten diadems, and on his heads were the names
> Of blasphemy. The beast I saw was like a leopard,

49

His feet like a bear and his mouth like the mouth
Of a lion. And the dragon gave him his power
And his throne and fierce power of dominion.
One of his heads seemed to be stricken to death
But the wound causing his death was healed
And the whole world marveled after the beast.

JOHN 13.1–3

These poets, Jesus son of Joseph, John of the Creation Prologue, John the Evangelist, and John of Patmos, are the poetic constellations of the New Testament—a book unjustly in shadow to the poetic grandeur of the Hebrew Bible. We have felt them, heard them, but failed to identify their poetic profile, and that very failure of identification, of assigning an identity card, has preserved their nameless solitudes as poets. Yet only from the collaboration of a single poetic solitude and a rich tradition could such poetry have emerged. Homer (one, two, male or female) is also invisible and unknown, but no one has thought of taking the title of poet from him.

The New Testament poets have been concealed in unfriendly typography. They are orphans of uncertain name, of dubious pedigree, even of dubious Greek (a stupidity), and yet these poets from Asia's Mediterranean lands were filled with rabbinic light from a millennium of prophetic verse. On their own, despite the enigma concerning identity, their light has glowed over into Coptic Egypt, down to Ethiopic Africa, east through Armenia of Persia, north crossing the Syriac bridge up to Byzantium, Old Slavonic principalities, on their way to Latin Europe, and then through the entire world.

We also know very little about Shakespeare and Homer, but works carrying their names exist. The texts reveal little if anything solid about the author. By contrast, Jeremiah and Isaiah are tremendous personalities in their prophetic works. We know these figures. If you clamor and remonstrate like Jeremiah you have uttered a "jeremiad." It is loony that the major poetic voices of the Bible are not, along with Sumerian Enheduanna, Greek Sappho, and Latin Catullus, laureled as great poets of antiquity. They don't lack fame—only the proper form to celebrate the genre of poetry.

Why not truly and fully detect New Testament poetry? *It is time.* Then we could include both the prophets and Yeshua and the many Johns in poetry anthologies. The Song of Songs has already entered anthologies, but who is the author? He/she is gloriously anonymous. Anonymous New Testament authors, who have been assigned traditional names, possess a treasure of bright words singing deep in compassionate narrations and one amazing apocalyptic vision.

Restoration of Torah Names
in the New Testament

THE JEWISH BIBLE is at the core of the New Testament Greek scriptures, cited through the Greek Septuagint translation, paraphrased, and imitated on every page. The setting is the same—Israel; the people are the same—Jews, all of them, the actors on stage and the authors who record them, except for the traditional enemies. Here the outside foe is the Roman army. As the tale unfolds, its leader, Pontius Pilatus, alone chooses to end the life of the young itinerant rabbi Yeshua ben Yosef, who has been perceived, or will be, as the messiah foretold in the Jewish Bible.

English versions of Greek scriptures have linguistically muffled the ordinary Greek, Aramaic, and Hebrew names of *Andreas*, *Yaakov*, *Yohanan*, and *Miryam* as "Andrew," "James," "John," and "Mary." There has also been a fudging of identity when the same person in the Hebrew Bible and the New Testament acquires dissimilar names in English. So *Yaakov* in Hebrew is "Jacob" in English as the Jewish Bible patriarch but a suspect James in English as Jesus's brother and all the other James's. A Bible sleuth will uncover deep theological mischief when the same Yehoshua (or Yeshua by his Aramaic nickname) is Joshua in the Old Testament and Jesus in the New Testament.

The effect of name manipulation, as noted, has been an eager over-naturalization of the immigrant Semites into Anglo-Saxon characters, making Jerusalem Jews named Elisheva or Kefa into local friends called Elizabeth or Peter. When the name is changed, the ethnic heritage is clouded. The ambience and original people have vanished with all their regional color. Here the names are restored. Imagine if we abused foreign classics as we do the Bible. Think of Don Quijote Anglicized to Donald Quincy, Lady Murasaki to Mrs. Murray, and Fyodor Dostoyevsky to Fred Dustman. Unknown to the reader, the translators of earlier bibles transformed our biblical ancestors from the Semitic Levant—none of them from Europe—into European folk. A king from England or Scotland carries the noble name "James," derived from Hebrew *Yaakov*, and "James" fits a golden monarch or a faithful butler from *Remains of the Day*, free of any whiff of origins in the Jewish Bible or with anyone in the local ghetto who happens to share the source name *Yaakov*.

In this version, as well as I can, I repair a perplexing tradition of appellation, restoring original names. An evangelist, epistler, patriarch, or lowly student from the ancient kingdom of Yehuda (Judea) keeps his or her noble name as they would have been in Latin, Greek, Aramaic, or Hebrew.

As all the ancient Greeks are Greeks when we read them in English (despite phonetic changes), may all the Jews be Jews as they act out their ordinary, ecstatic, and tragic lives in the New Testament. If this version manages to return us to our true biblical cast, whose single-named actors from both testaments stroll alleys in the kingdom of Yehuda rather than the byways of Cape Cod or the Lake District, the restored scene may evoke a strange earthly miracle that emerged when the heart of the Abrahamic world gave us these astonishing new scriptures.

The Restored New Testament is a new translation based on Greek and Semitic sources in its naming and historical annotation. Ever since the return of perhaps forty thousand Jews from Babylonia in 538–537 B.C.E. after some seventy years of captivity, the spoken language in the post-exilic kingdom of Judea was Babylonian Aramaic while the temple and written language continued to be Hebrew.[37] By Jesus's time the Semitic sources of both Aramaic and Hebrew were found in common

---

37. Aramaic was the tongue of the Babylonians and a lingua franca of the Near East and its Eastern Mediterranean littoral, often called the Levant, extending from the Euphrates to the Nile. Aramaic took its orthography from the Phoenicians, and Hebrew adopted the Aramaic alphabet squares for its own script. Large sections of Daniel and Ezra, late volumes of the Jewish Bible, were in Aramaic, as was the later Talmud (meaning "study"), which contains commentaries on the Bible.

names.[38] So Jesus's full Hebrew name was *Yehoshua* or shortened to *Yeshua*, which had also become a name in Judeo-Aramaic, the language Jesus spoke.

Where does the English "Jesus" come from? We must go back four levels to find his name as it appears in the Jewish Bible. "Jesus" is from medieval and Vulgate Latin *Iesus*, from Greek Ἰησοῦς (Iesous), from Aramaic יֵשׁוּעַ (Yeshua), a later form of Hebrew יְהוֹשֻׁעַ (Yehoshua), meaning "Yahweh is salvation." If translations were consistent about matching root names in the Old and New Testaments, then Jesus should have one name in both testaments: either Jesus, Joshua, Yeshua, or Yehoshua. None of these pairings have prevailed. For blurring or concealing religious identity, we read "Jesus" in the New Testament and "Joshua" in the Old Testament. "Jesus" gives no hint of its Aramaic/Hebrew origin in *Yeshua*.[39]

These linguistic irregularities of the past have not gone unnoticed in scholarly publications. The selective inconsistency of names would especially seem to alert the teams of biblical scholars, of diverse faith backgrounds, who in the twentieth century gave us new versions of the New Testament. But their naming has retained the traditional evasions of earlier versions. Biblical scholars today contend on lines of faith and history, marking traditional interpreters from religious studies historians. While it is not shameful for the ancient people of Israel and the Bible to carry their probable names, traditionalists have prevailed in

38. Proper nouns often carry language history even when the original tongue is no longer used. In Massachusetts and Connecticut, thousands of Native American names persist for villages, rivers, mountains, and states, though few Indian words are used in English. In the American West are thousands of Spanish geographical names— Colorado (red), Montana (mountain), Nevada (snow covered)—but few Spanish words in American English. Centuries after spoken Hebrew gave way to post-exilic Aramaic, old Hebrew words for person and place were in common usage.

39. Many Old Testament names in the Greek scriptures are taken from the Jewish second-century B.C.E. Septuagint translation into Greek of the Old Testament. In the Septuagint, "Yeshua" is *Iasous*, which the New Testament adopts in its two references to Joshua (Acts 7.45 and Heb. 4.8). New Testament Greek for "Jesus" is *Iesous*, one vowel away from *Iasous*. The slight change is consistent with the practice of separating New Testament from Old Testament figures by rendering them with distinct names in Greek, and by distinct names in translation out of the Greek into other tongues.

uniformly and unwaveringly marking them with impermeable English nametags.

By eliminating Semitic appellations, the translators have deracinated New Testament characters. Through the linguistic magus of name conversion, the common reader shares the illusion that Christians and Jews in the first century were distinct peoples and religions, one unrelated to the other. The critical deed of name changing conveys that John the Baptist and Jesus and his family were not Jews but somehow Christians before there were Christians, and before there was a lexicon to name members of the emerging sect.

As for the Jews who remained looking for their messiah, in the Old and in the New Testament, they have two incarnations in the Christian Bible. In the New Testament they are portrayed relentlessly as sinister, shouting and scheming fellows lacking virtue and respectability. The Roman authorities are their obedient pawns and persuade a reluctant Pilatus (Pilate), the Roman military prefect, to kill Jesus. We know their malice because the Jews' secret plot was somehow implausibly hatched and recorded in the Sanhedrin, the Jewish council. Serious scholars ask today, by whom was the alleged plot overheard in the Sanhedrin and who reported it to whom?

The *anger* against the Jews, based on overheard secret deliberations in a council room, lacks credence, but the very invention of the story in order to blame the Jews for extreme perfidy depends on a false separation of Jews into the two gospel categories: good Jews who are no longer identified as Jews but are now Christian, and bad Jews who pass only as Jews. The historical cover-up has endured for two millennia.

Is Rabbi Jesus a Christian?

JESUS ON THE CROSS is not remembered as the circumcised child, the wandering rabbi as Mark depicts him in Greek with his proper title "rabbi," which in English traditionally comes out as "Lord, Master, or Sir,"[40] but as the earthly incarnation of "Lord." In the intentional confusion of epithets, one forgets the clarion fact that all these first Christians are observant Jews, now called by scholars Christian Jews (or Jewish Christians) because of their conviction that Jesus is the Isaiah-predicted Jewish messiah. But Jesus himself is not a Christian, a Christian Jew, or a Jewish Christian as he is almost universally taken to be. And as he is not a Christian, he cannot be the *first* Christian, another post he occupies in the popular mind. Jesus as the Christ cannot share the excellent epithet of Christian, since he is not a faithful follower of himself. He *is* the Christ. "He's the tops," as Fred Astaire sang. He is no less and no more than himself, which is to say a world.

To make this crucial distinction between leader and follower clear, permit an analogy. A Stalinist or a Wagnerite is an admirer and follower of Stalin or Wagner, but Joseph Stalin is not a Stalinist, nor Richard Wagner a Wagnerite. They are themselves alone, Stalin and Wagner, not their disciples and friends. Similarly Jesus is the Christ or Messiah, not the disciples and friends. He is the observant Jew deemed the messiah.

In the linguistic confusion of adjective and noun, "Jesus" is a noun and has no syntactic role of modifying a noun. As the early Christians

---

40. In the recent modernized New King James Version, for the first time (except in *The New Covenant*) Greek "rabbi" as Jesus's epithet is throughout translated as "rabbi."

expand their movement, they take on the epithet "Christian," which is syntactically both a noun and an adjective. As a noun the Christian is simply a follower of the Christ. "Christian" without an article is an adjective and has the syntactic role of modifying the Christ and Christianity. So, by analogy, to call Jesus, as opposed to his followers, a Christian is a semantic blunder, imposing the adjective on the noun, reducing Jesus the Christ from his role of being the messiah to being his own follower. This semantic blunder has prevailed, however preposterous and illogical it is, and has successfully served the program of identity theft and denial. The name change from Semitic *Yeshua* to Latin *Jesus* serves the same program of forgetting. These omnipotent semiotic leaps of camouflage have prevented Jesus, for the majority of the world, from being immediately perceived as the most famous of all Jews after Yahweh-created Adam, Moses, and David. Let Jesus be himself, the illuminated Jew perceived as the messiah savior, not a mere follower from another time and another land.

This muddle of misused words befuddles. Equally baffling is the picture of Pontius Pilatus as the unwilling Roman officer, in part Judaized as he follows the Jewish ritual of washing his hands of all guilt. He comes through as sympathetic to Jesus. Though they have no common language (the Roman has Latin, Jesus Aramaic), Pilatus converses in Greek with Yeshua, exchanging wisdom barbs. But then Pilatus, under pressure from the evil Jews, issues the order of the crucifixion during the Seder when somehow the crowds are not in their houses lighting the candles of Passover hope. For his honorable role in ordering the execution of the Messiah, Pilatus is a saint in some Eastern Orthodox sects.

In the Old Testament, in Christian and Jewish translation of the Tanak, the Jew is also rarely seen as a Jew. The mythical patriarchs, prophets, and kings, along with the common Jews of Judea and Israel, are normatively Israelites (Greek nominative plural of Hebrew *Yisraeli/ Israeli*) or children of Israel. Except for the late books of Esther and a few times in Ezra and Daniel, we rarely read the word "Jew" in the long Jewish Bible in its English translation.

In the short New Testament the wicked Jew appears more than two hundred times and seems unrelated to his fabled coreligionists in the Old Testament. Likewise, the Jew stands apart from his coreligionist primitive Christian Jews in the New Testament. How can the term be used selectively throughout the New Testament, used only when referring to those who are not believers in Jesus as the messiah, but never employed when referring to the Jewish followers of rabbi Yeshua? It is sorrowfully clear why this obscuration of the Jew who can pass for Christian occurs. One should remember, however, that on the Nazi railroad platforms by the death camps, where Jews were separated from Christians, none of the New Testament Christian Jews, not Jesus nor his family, could have passed. All would have been gassed because of their religious and blood identity. In killing Jews, the Nazis were symbolically exterminating the Jewish pioneers and founders of earliest Christianity.

The central conundrum persists: the figures who dominate the New Testament—Jesus, his kin and students, the epistlers and the evangelists, the early saints—are Jews who have discovered the foretold messiah whom as Jews they had awaited. Yet for the common reader they wear no identifying costume. As observed by most readers, these actors on the New Testament stage wear masks concealing who they are, giving them anachronistic and profoundly confusing identities. That deception is a blood tragedy, and the essential historical source of inhumanity for Christian and Jew alike.

The hiding and muddling of true identity has tragically persisted since the beginnings of the worldwide Abrahamic sect of Messianism. It besets the majority of well-minded Christians and Jews. Jews are as confused as Christians. Jews are popularly unfamiliar with the New Testament and are, except in specific academic circles, unaware of the actual wording and making of their portraiture. However, despite scriptural ignorance of the New Testament, Jews sense themselves painted as villains in this major global book. Two millennia of somber treatment in Christendom is, alas, connected directly with pages of these extraordinary chapters of wisdom, social hope for the poor, and faith. The history of Jews convinces them there is no love for them in this book of love.

But the restoration of names and thereby identity may dramatically change world thought with respect to the early family of Jews and Christians.

In keeping with other technical and information intimacies, the restoration of earlier names has become worldwide in scholarship, journalism, and popular speech. This revelatory practice seeks cultural transparency in translation and respect for the actual speech in the foreign tongue. Rather than Anglicizing most foreign names, now we write and say *Beijing*, not "Peking," for China's capital, and *Livorno*, not "Leghorn," for the birthplace of the Italian painter Amedeo Modigliani. Here, in addition to Greek, Aramaic, and Hebrew, some Latin names are given their Latin original. Hence from Latin it is *Pilatus*, not "Pilate,"[41] for the Roman crucifier; from Greek it is *Andreas*, not "Andrew," for Jesus's student; from Aramaic it is *Yeshua*, not "Jesus," for the messiah; and from Hebrew it is the *Galil*, not "Galilee," for the sea in northern Judea.[42]

41. Pontius Pilatus's name in biblical Greek is *Pontios Pilatos*. His origin is unknown. His obscure existence was recently confirmed historically by archeologists after the discovery of a limestone block in the ruins of an amphitheater called Caesarea Maritima that refers to Pilate as "Prefect of Judea" (26–36), reading as follows: [*DIS AUGUSTI*]S TIBERIEUM [*PO*]NTIUS PILATUS [*PRAEF*]ECTUS IUDA[*EA*] E. Bracketed letters are conjectural.

42. "Judea" is the general name of the Jewish kingdoms under the rule of the Herodian kings, of whom the most significant was Herod the Great (74–4 B.C.E.), an Idumaean Jew who was Rome's client king. Herod's greatest achievement was the construction of the Second Temple in Jerusalem. By the time of Jesus, the Kingdom of Judea had absorbed the Kingdom of Israel in the north. The term "Judea" referred to a region in Israel as well as the whole kingdom, including Galilee in the north. The Latin word *Judaea* was adopted from יְהוּדָה (yehuda). In the second century, after the failed Jewish rebellion of Bar Kokhba in 132–135 C.E., most of the Jews in Judea (not in Samaria or Galilee) were sent into exile, and the Roman emperor Hadrian renamed Judea *Syria Palaestina* in order to erase Jewish ties to the land. *Palaestina* derives from "Philistine," from Hebrew פְּלִשְׁתִּים (pelishtim). Hence, the kingdom earlier ruled by David, King of Israel, became Palestine, an epithet used—except by Jews—universally by religious scholars, historians, statesmen, and journalists until shortly after World War II. But in the century before Romans coined the territorial name, neither Jesus, coreligionists, nor early Christians knew the word "*Palaestina*," the future epithet for lands surrounding Jerusalem.

Vagaries of Translation
in Finding a Word
for "Messiah"

⁓

WE CAN WONDER but never be certain why the epistlers and evangelists chose not to return to the original Hebrew text for the multiple references to the Old Testament that appear on almost every page in the New Testament. They could read the Hebrew, probably had access to it, yet they preferred to cite the second-century B.C.E. Greek Septuagint translation of the Jewish Bible. The writers of the letters were closer in years to their fully Jewish background. By the time of the evangelists, whose dispersed geographies and identities remain uncertain, perhaps they, like the diaspora Jews of Alexandria, found it convenient to absorb the Hebrew Bible in the Greek Septuagint, which gave them a ready-made Greek lexicon for their compositions. Always there was the preference to distance themselves from Jews who did not accept Jesus as their messiah and from their Bible in Hebrew, which the early Christian Jews and Christian Greeks claimed as their own Bible. A mountain of passages in the New Testament are quotations from the Hebrew Bible, yet they are not cited directly from the Bible in Hebrew but from their Greek Septuagint translation. The passages are copied and disclose neither that they are citations, nor their specific source, such as Genesis or the Songs or Isaiah. Modern study bibles, through annotation, clarify the biblical source.

Christianity depended on the Jewish Bible for its origin, for the creation story, the Isaian predictions, for the religion of Jesus, the apostles and evangelists. Though the Jewish Bible appears on every page of the New Testament, eventually the New Testament would loom larger than the Jewish Bible in Greek Orthodoxy and Roman Catholicism until the

Protestant Reformation, when the Old Testament was retranslated into vernaculars, and many Hebrew names such as "Elizabeth," "Samuel," and "Isaiah" became popular. The New Testament, approximately as we have it today, was confirmed at the first Council of Nicaea in 325 C.E., convoked by Roman Emperor Constantine. By the Council of Nicaea, doctrinal orthodoxy and the canon of New Testament scriptures, in a state of ceaseless debate, were fixed.

The main lesson of the Jewish Septuagint example is that because the New Testament authors' citations from the Hebrew Bible were taken intact from the Septuagint Greek, bypassing the Hebrew, the Hebrew original became secondary to its Greek translation. Similarly, after the emergence of the Latin Vulgate translation for the papal areas of Europe, the Greek gospels themselves, along with all their citations from the Hebrew original, became secondary to Jerome's Latin version. Such are the authorizing manners of denial and affirmation in translation. In the papal West, the Latin Vulgate was the true Bible, and the Greek original of the New Testament and Old Testament was secondary. By similar disrespect, in Eastern Orthodoxy of Greece, the Balkans, and Russia, the Latin Vulgate and all the beautiful illuminated texts did not exist except as would-be usurpers of their holy Greek scripture.

The practice of skipping the originals continued in Bible translation. The mystical Spanish poet Luis de León (1527–1597), Augustinian monk and professor of Latin, Greek, and Hebrew at the University of Salamanca, was imprisoned for five years in the Inquisitional prison at Valladolid for Judaizing, that is, for translating the biblical Song of Songs into Spanish from Hebrew, the "corrupt original," rather than from the approved Latin Vulgate.[43] Similar sins of translation were being punished in France and England. William Tyndale's direct translation of the New Testament from Greek into English in 1525 was a heresy for which he was strangled and burned at the stake in 1535 by a joint collaboration of Carlos V of Spain and the still-Catholic Henry the VIII. Until the Tyndale version, there had been no translation into English of the Jewish Bible or the Greek scriptures that had not been entirely based on the Latin of Jerome's authorized Vulgate. And in the same tradition

43. While in the sixteenth century Luis de León was punished for taking the original Hebrew as a worthy source for his unparalleled translations, today he is universally esteemed, by the laity and the Spanish Catholic church, as the finest translator in the Spanish language.

of bypassing the original language texts, even the magnificent King James Version took not less than eighty percent of its New Testament directly from the Tyndale translation, albeit elevating its rhetoric to its own splendor. The forty-seven translators bypassed the Greek source for most of their version just as the first-century evangelist authors of the New Testament had bypassed the Hebrew scripture by relying exclusively on the Greek Septuagint translation of the Tanak.

To understand the origin of the cardinal words "messiah" and "messianic" in the history of religion, we examine the Septuagint Greek Bible, the second-century translation of the Hebrew Bible.[44] The normative transliteration of Hebrew מָשִׁיחַ (mashiah) into Greek is Μεσσίας (Messias) and into English is "messiah." However, the Septuagint Bible chose not to *transliterate* but to *translate mashiah* מָשִׁיחַ into Greek *hristos/ christos* (χριστος), meaning "the anointed." When the authors of the letters wrote about the Christian Jews and the Greek converts, and when the authors of the gospels composed the life and death of Yeshua the Mashiah, they all turned to the Septuagint Bible in Greek of the Jews in Alexandria to determine "Christ" (Hristos) as Jesus's epithet. The Greek language worked for a Greek-speaking reader but not for readers of other languages. In other tongues the reader did not read the word "Christ" as χριστος, meaning "the Anointed who is Messiah."

44. The traditional story is that seventy-two Jewish scholars translated the Hebrew Bible into Greek in seventy-two days in the third century B.C.E. in separate chambers on the Alexandrian island of Pharos (Lighthouse). After this period they compared translations and found all to be identical. However, the translation, which began in the second century B.C.E., not the third, actually took some 115 years to complete. See *Aristeas to Philocrates* [*Letter to Aristeas*], ed. and trans. Moses Hadas (New York: Ktav Publishing, 1974). The Septuagint was accomplished under Ptolemy II Philadelphus's rule for the Jews of Alexandria, who could no longer read the Bible in Hebrew. The fourteen books of the canonical Apocrypha, accepted by Jews and Orthodox and Roman Catholics as deuterocanonical, appear in the Septuagint. They were considered "secondarily" canonical because the original Hebrew was not found in the available Hebrew texts. Since the discovery of the Dead Sea Scrolls, fragments of most of the Apocrypha have been found, as have several complete versions of Tobit in Hebrew and Aramaic. The Jews, Greek and Eastern Orthodox, Catholics, and Armenians accept the Apocrypha as deuterocanonical, though the numbers and selection of the fourteen texts vary. The Protestants accept none, and hence the King James Version today contains none. The original King James Version of 1611 included the Apocrypha, but after 1629 they were increasingly omitted. Beginning around 1840 the British and American Bible Societies regularly omitted them.

Messiah and the Anointed

THE MESSIAH in Jewish theology is a redemptive earthly leader who, along with kings, prophets, and patriarchs, is anointed. In Christianity the messiah and the Christ are frequently asserted as synonymous, in theology and everyday meaning. In practice the messiah conveys one reality, and Christ the Anointed conveys another. Christ the Anointed is actually a redundancy, meaning "Anointed the Anointed." We have reached these discrepancies in English once again through the dominion of translation, as ideas and words pass from one book, one language, and one religion to another.

Let us again consider the comparative philology of the names as they hop nation and sect. For the Jew reading Septuagint Greek, as well as for an ancient or modern Greek Christian, Greek *hristos* is, or should be, understood to be a translation of an attribute, the anointed, to represent the *mashiah* just as אָדוֹן (adon), meaning "lord," or "my lord" as in "Adonai," is a code word for the unutterable tetragrammaton YHWH (יהוה—yahweh). The Greek reader understands because he or she reads *hristos* as a translation of the Hebrew *mashiah*, albeit a translation only of his attribute. In English, as in all other languages except Greek, the word "Christ" is not translated but merely transliterated, and is neither a code word for "anointed" nor for "messiah." In their confusing Anglicization from the Greek through Latin, the messiah and the Christ lost their way.

Being the anointed signifies having an attribute of messiah. And therefore the anointed operates as a metonym for messiah, as crown stands for king. But as the crown may evoke the notion of king, a crown is not the king. So too the anointed evokes the notion of the messiah, and to be the anointed is to be only one aspect of the messiah. In this limiting grammatical puzzle, by constant usage the word "Christ" has taken on its own meaning. Indeed, by usage Christ is such a dominant entity— man god, son of man, son of God, God himself—that the many roles of the Christ have altered our understanding of the original meaning of Christ as a Greek synonym for messiah. And the messiah's title becomes Jesus's last name, that is, Jesus's surname in "Jesus Christ."

But Christ is his title as the Messiah and is not a family name. In this regard, there are few people, Christian or other, who are not completely muddled as to meaning and distinctions when they utter the English words "Jesus Christ." The most common question is, *What is the difference between Jesus and Christ?*

Even Paul, the most cognizant of Jesus's spiritual messiahship, normally writes "Jesus Christ" rather than "Jesus the Christ" or, more sensitive to his background, "Jesus the Messiah." Had Jesus been a messiah with a name in Isaiah, the King James Version, according to its Anglicization of Hebrew words, would have named him Joshua the Messiah. We can go a step further by permitting Jesus's Aramaic and Hebrew root names to glow by calling him "Yeshua the Mashiah." Thereby Jesus Christ can be restored to his native Israel and his family speech. We can restore his name with glee, with no fear of stumbling linguistically or theologically. The huge receptive English tongue takes in diverse word immigrants with pride, grace, and generosity. In these texts the reader will find "Yeshua the Mashiah."

If indeed those who chose to prefer the notion of "the Anointed" (the meaning of "Christ") to "the Messiah," they might have chosen the word that cannot be misunderstood as a surname, which in English would be Anointeds or Anointees, which is the practice of other sects of Christianity who call themselves by attributes, such as the Shakers, Holy Rollers, Baptists, and more quietly the exclusionary Select.

I offer the unlikely epithet "Anointed" or "Anointee" largely because the epithet "Christian" has lost both the original meaning of messiah and the attributive meaning of anointed. Perhaps it is better and less exclusionary to have a name, such as Christ, which is imbued with awe but has only titular or surname meaning as a unifying gesture (except in Greek, where it is understood as a translation of anointed, a quality of the messiah). Only the Greeks recognize *hristos* to mean both "Anointed" and "Messiah." In English we understand neither Anointed nor Messiah when we utter the word "Christ." The intention of asserting the revelation of the true Messiah is not enhanced by the name "Christ," which, from Paul to the present, fails to mean or suggest "Messiah."

What are we to do? Perhaps nothing but have a bit more understanding of what we are saying. "Messianics" is the correct word for those who have found the Messiah (Mashiah). Or a possible word could be "Anointeds" if one wishes, like the Quakers, to choose a metanomic word to reveal a bodily attribute for the revelation of divinity (the trembling at seeing the inner light of God). "Anointed" is exactly what the word "Christ" means in Greek. Yet why stick to the Greek translation in the Jewish Septuagint and not reread the Hebrew original and then bring it into English? Then we can bypass the vagaries of translation. The transliteration from Hebrew *mashiah* to English "messiah" is easy and appropriate. Christianity or Messianism? Christ or Messiah? We would turn the Bible to its original truth if we made this gesture of restoration and transparency and went all the way, if Christian and Christianity were called by their correct and evocatively meaningful original titles: "Messianic" and "Messianism." Then Christians' Christianity would be restored, in word and meaning, to its original messianic mission and exultation of enlightenment.

WHERE GOES JOHN'S WORD?

Creation Prologue to John

In the first Bible, the Jewish or Hebrew Bible, Genesis recounts beginnings, and though in its composition Genesis is not the earliest book among the scriptures, the Bible opens with Genesis. It is there at the beginning where it must be in order to narrate the creation and early legendary events: Eden, Babel, the flood, and the wanderings of Abraham and his descendants from Abraham's birthplace in Ur, a city south of present-day Baghdad, down to Egypt and across the desert to Canaan and to lands where a Jerusalem will grow and its histories be recorded in the Old Testament.

In the Greek New Testament the Genesis story of beginnings is found in the prologue to the Gospel of John, last of the canonical gospels in order and date of composition.

In Genesis 1.1 God of the Hebrew Bible creates our planetary system with the words "In the beginning God created the heavens and the earth." In Genesis 1.3 he speaks the whole cosmos into being through the words "Let there be light."[45] In parallel manner, the evangelist John begins his gospel in the New Testament with a prologue in which he makes "the word" the immediate author of creation: "In the beginning was the word," followed by "and the word was with God, and God was the word." Here we find the crucial dictum, which for two millennia has provoked debates over the "true" nature of Christ, of the Messiah, and of God. That discourse, subsumed under the academic category of "Christology," finds its starting point in the revolutionary notion that John initiates by making God or the divinity co-equal with the word.

---

45. Gen. 1.3, יְהִי אוֹר (*yehi or*). With these words came the biblical big bang creation when the cosmos came into being.

However, before using the word to create the world, the word itself must be created. Or so one might presume.[46] But if God is the word already, then he has no need to create his instrument of creation? The answer may be that the metaphor of "God is word" is not a metaphor of difference, not of whole versus attribute, but a metaphor of total identity. In the unending debates and word games concerning the meaning of the word, there will be more who pursue definitions of this enigma, though part of its elusive power is that it will remain unsolved as enigma. What happens when the word reaches our globe?

Since God sends the word, himself who is the word, down to earth, and in human form, the implications are unending. Since God is the word and comes down onto the earth in the form of a human carrier of the creating word, he may be God witnessing his creation, or a filial attribute of himself, the messiah. If the metaphor means the latter, we have the second miracle after the earth's creation: God assuming a human form, who may be the messiah born of a woman.[47] John's passage is a powerful metaphor, and like the best mystery declarations it will not disclose more.

Here is John:

In the beginning was the word
And the word was with God,
And God was the word.[48]

JOHN 1.1

46. The ancient Kabbalists who take us to a time before there was a word declare that in the beginning God created the letters of the alphabet, the letter of fire on a black velvet cloth, in order to create the word. See Gershom Scholem, *Origins of the Kabbalah* (Princeton: Princeton University Press, 1987).

47. We are familiar with gods assuming human forms, of whom the most notorious in the West is Homer's ubiquitous skygod Zeus.

48. John 1.1. Ἐν ἀρχῇ ἦν ὁ λόγος, καὶ ὁ λόγος ἦν πρὸς τὸν θεὸν, καὶ θεὸς ἦν ὁ λόγος (En arhe en o logos, kai o logos en pros ton theon, kai theos en o logos). Verses 1–18, among the most significant and beautiful in the Bible, have textual problems as do many verses in the gospels. Bart D. Ehrman, calling these eighteen lines a prologue, notes, "This highly celebrated poem speaks of the 'Word' of God, who existed with God from the beginning and was himself God, and who 'became flesh' in Jesus Christ. The passage is written in a highly poetic style not found in the rest of the Gospel. . . . Is it possible that this opening passage came from a different

Near the ending of the prologue, he elaborates the meaning, making the word equal to both God and human beings:

> And the word became flesh
> And lived among us.
> And we gazed on his glory,
> The glory of the only son born of the father,
> Who is filled with grace and truth.
>
> JOHN 1.14[49]

If the only son is born of a woman, does he have a mother? If the mother is Mary, is Jesus a demigod or does the virgin birth take care of that? In John, however, unlike the synoptic gospels, there is no virgin scene. We go immediately to Jesus as an adult. By complicating the nature of God, by converting himself into a verbal entity, John insinuates not only the spoken word for creating the world, but also the same powerful word in the art of writing, and in particular the writing of a bible. What could be more appropriate than to begin a new bible with all the verbal means of bringing not only the world, humanity, and a messiah into being, but also the record of these creations through the written word in a bible? And apart from world literature, if there is any doubt of the ancient importance of the word, at the instant of the creation of the word (the *logos*) it already prevailed, being God, God's instrument for creation, his agent on earth embodying the word, and finally the word embodied in us, which we use for thinking, speaking, hearing, writing, and reading. The word is our beginning.

Each of the parallel canonized Bibles contains a sentence speaking of creating the beginning: "In the beginning God created the world" (Gen. 1) and "In the beginning was the word" (John 1). Clearly John sees his prologue as a restatement, with major new nuances, of the cosmic words of Genesis. Each proclaims the birth of the world. With this in mind, a

---

source than the rest of the account, and that it was added as an appropriate beginning by the author after an earlier edition of the book had already been published?" See Bart D. Ehrman, *Misquoting Jesus: The Story Behind Who Changed the Bible and Why* (San Francisco: HarperSanFrancisco, 2005), 61–62.

49. For more, see annotation of this passage in the Gospel of John.

translator-editor confronts a radical temptation. Since John alone among the gospels speaks of the world's beginning, why not begin the Greek scriptures with John rather than Mark? Moreover, apart from giving us the only creation passages in the New Testament, John's prologue contains the most provocatively philosophical and theological passages in the gospels in splendid gnomic wisdom verse.

Given John's luminous beginning, there are major reasons why one might begin the New Testament genesis with John, though chronologically John was composed after the synoptics. Since the prologue poem (which could have been composed before or after John) is almost certainly not by John but an emendation inserted later into the text by an unknown author, why not move at least the prologue for thematic purpose to the beginning of the gospels? Thereby, following the intention of its author, the prologue would assume its role as a parallel Genesis to begin the tale of Jesus? That would make it unnecessary to move the whole of John, last in composition, while moving the pertinent cosmic beginning where it makes its keenest impression.

It is wondrous and sensible for the New Testament to begin with its creation poem, and I confess I have gone back and forth on the implications of the change. As Mark is here the first gospel, as he is among scholars and in recent translations, I have reasoned it best to find some solution that can serve multiple purposes. By beginning the canonical gospels with the John prologue, but also including the same prologue as page one of the full gospel of John, we have a solution that may please and displease. Any change from tradition costs. Here the change is crucially limited to repeating perhaps the most memorable lines in the fugue that is already the gospels, which already have the habit of saying each of their stories four times as the Jewish Bible repeats "The Ten Commandments" twice.[50]

Finally, apart from the weight of tradition, there are obvious benefits for repeating this poem of beginning, letting it also stand where it is traditionally intrinsic to the John gospel. John provides the most intriguing and distinct meditation of the gospels, and the disparate prologue preceding the gospel, albeit by another hand, lives in elliptical harmony with the rest of the scripture. Let us say optimistically that we are immensely richer for the odd conjunction of the prologue poem

50. Exod. 20.2–17; Deut. 5.6–21.

of creation as the genesis of the gospels as well as at its imperative place at the beginning of the last gospel of the life and death of Yeshua, which is the Gospel of John.

John is the favored book of philosophers of Christianity and of the Gnostic claimers of Christianity, whose Alexandrian exegesis of John set a standard imitated by Origen and other early Church fathers, giving them a method of critical analysis to emulate.

Now to the question of moving entire gospels around, or other books in the New Testament. Though the order of the New Testament, with few exceptions, has been constant, the order of the Hebrew Bible, including questions of the Apocrypha, has been in flux, determined by the particular sect, varying from England to Ethiopia, from Armenia to the closed and often underground portals of Beijing. There has emerged a number of initiatives to reconsider the order and actual canon of the New Testament, particularly with respect to the placement of Mark, and the inclusion of the reconstructed precursor Q and the recently uncovered Gospel of Thomas.

In this volume we might have begun the gospels with Gnostic Thomas, which may or may not be the earliest of the many extant gospels, fragmentary and full.[51] Although I argue elsewhere for the earlier assigned dating, what is relevant is that this wisdom dialogue of 114 questions and answers between Jesus and his student is itself a source of or parallel to a development of similar passages in the canonical gospels. Thomas is a wisdom poem but not a narration. We see Jesus only as a speaker. Thomas is also one of the major extant early Christian-Jewish documents, a masterpiece of world literature, first found in Greek and Syriac fragments (Syriac is the name given to early Aramaic-Christian scripture) and uncovered in later Coptic translation in the Nag Hammadi Library trove in Egypt.[52] However, despite the probable early dating of Thomas, it is more appropriate to place Thomas with the other two Gnostic gospels, Mary and Judas, immediately after the canonical gospels.

51. For a nearly complete selection of some seventeen gospels, with commentary, found among the intertestamental scriptures, see Willis Barnstone, *The Other Bible* (San Francisco: Harper and Row, 1984; 2nd rev. ed., HarperSanFrancisco, 2005).
52. Thomas appears in translation by Marvin Meyer in *The Gospel of Thomas* (San Francisco: HarperSanFrancisco, 1992).

Canon of the Restored New Testament: A Movable Feast

A Movable Feast

THE STANDARD New Testament contains twenty-seven books:
four gospels, a book of acts, twenty-one letters, and an apocalypse.
In 2003 I published *The New Covenant*, containing the four gospels
and Apocalypse (Revelation). The present volume completes the New
Testament by adding Acts and Letters, and three Gnostic gospels:
Thomas, Mary, and Judas. Here below is a comparative list and order
of books found in other New Testaments and in the Restored New
Testament (RNT) and the main areas of restoration, including number
and order:

STANDARD NEW TESTAMENT	RESTORED NEW TESTAMENT
27 *books:*	30 *books*:
4 gospels	4 canonical + 3 Gnostic gospels
1 book of acts	21 letters
21 letters	1 book of acts
1 apocalypse	1 apocalypse

Gnostic Gospels

IN CONTEMPORARY PUBLICATIONS of the whole Bible, there is an increasing tendency to include the Apocrypha, even for an audience predominantly Protestant, though there are no Apocrypha in today's King James Version. Some scholars argue for the inclusion of the hypothetical Q document, invented by New Testament scholars to replace a presumed lost text that contained material shared in Matthew and Luke but not found in their common Markan source. Members of the Jesus Seminar, including James M. Robinson, and Helmet Koester have maintained that both Q and Thomas represented the earliest Christian logia that ultimately led to the canonical gospels.

The Gospel of Thomas contains 114 sayings of Jesus in a Platonic discourse, but no story of the life and death of Jesus.[53] There is sharp debate concerning the dating of Thomas, dividing scholars into an "early camp" and a "late camp." The early camp sees Thomas composed in the 50s, the late camp in the 100s. In *Beyond Belief*, Elaine Pagels sees textual conflict between the Gospel of John and the Gospel of Thomas concerning the nature of Jesus. In Thomas she sees the Gnostic notion of Jesus as teacher, who is not the light of the world but one who proclaims a divinity of light in each of us.[54]

I see Thomas as an early direct or indirect source coming two decades before the canonical gospels. But whether it was written before or after

---

53. See Robert W. Funk, Roy W. Hoover, and the Jesus Seminar, eds., *The Five Gospels: The Search for the Authentic Words of Jesus: New Translation and Commentary* (New York: Macmillan, 1993).

54. Elaine Pagels, *Beyond Belief* (New York: Vintage Books, 2004).

the gospels, it is a key gospel work of Jesus's words, thoughts, and wisdom, and as authentic as a mirror of Jesus as any canonical document. That fact alone invites its inclusion.

Elaine Pagels and Karen King, the authors of one of the new translations of the Gnostic Gospel of Judas, state that the canon as we have it now, varying with each major Christian sect, represents the winners, not the losers, in the struggles over canonicity.[55] The three gospels added here to the Restored New Testament may be thought of as having a parallel relation to the immigrant status of the Apocrypha of the Hebrew Bible: not fully canonical but essential to be included and read as part of the tradition.

The Gospel of Judas, which has caused a worldwide religious earthquake, is similarly essential. None of these works is entirely new to us, some even preceding the great discovery in 1945 in Egypt of the Nag Hammadi Library and its fifty-one mainly Gnostic scrolls in Coptic translation from second-century Greek scripture. Some of it comes from earlier Greek and Syriac sources if Thomas is indeed a first-century creation.

In the work of the early fathers "against the Gnostics," we have a clear picture of the critical theology of each major Gnostic sect. In the second century, Irenaeus, bishop of Lugdunum (present-day Lyon, France), wrote in his *Against Heresies* (1.31.1) that a "Gnostic gospel portrayed Judas in a positive light, as having acted in accordance with Jesus's instructions." Jorge Luis Borges, in the published story-essay "Three Versions of Judas" in his book *Labyrinths* (1944), tells the same tale of Judas as suggested by Irenaeus and now fleshed out in the Gospel of Judas. In a second story, half-pretend scholarship, half-Borgesean imagination, he re-creates the same notion of Judas as one of the worshiped figures among those at the cross. It is called *The Sect of the Thirty*, based on a dissident group named the "Thirty Pieces of Silver." Borges writes, "Of knowing actors, there were but two: Judas and the Redeemer. Judas cast away the thirty coins that were the price of our souls' salvation and immediately hanged himself. At that

55. Elaine Pagels and Karen L. King, *Reading Judas: The Gospel of Judas and the Shaping of Christianity* (New York: Viking, 2007).

moment he was thirty-three years old, the age of the Son of Man. The sect venerates the two equally, and absolves the others."[56]

The Argentine maestro Jorge Luis Borges understood the ancient debate over Judas, found in the work by Irenaeus and elsewhere, sixty years before the world was at last given a bestseller version in translation from the Coptic of the Gospel of Judas.

56. From *The Sect of the Thirty* in Jorges Luis Borges, *Collected Fictions*, trans. Andrew Hurley (New York: Viking, 1998), 445.

Where Goes Mark?

Until recently the New Testament began with Matthew's genealogy of Jesus. However, Mark is the earliest of the canonical gospels in composition and Mark is the main source of Matthew and Luke. Here, Mark, among the "synoptic gospels" (a term for Mark, Matthew, and Luke), comes first. But Mark's place at the beginning is not traditional. Until the posthumous publication of the lucid and formidable translation of the complete New Testament by Richmond Lattimore,[57] who made Mark the first gospel, no one had dared to tamper with the traditional Catholic Augustinian hypothesis (Matthew → Mark → Luke) or the later Protestant Griesbach hypothesis (Matthew → Luke → Mark) for the ordering of the synoptics. Moving or excluding the Apocrypha is another matter and is distinctive in almost all major denominations.

From earliest Greek and Latin versions, Matthew was first, except for the first canonist, Marcion, who did not even include Matthew among the books he selected for a primitive New Testament. Matthew begins with the genealogy of "Jesus the Messiah," which traces the infant child from Abraham through King David to "Joseph the husband of Mary, of whom Jesus was born." More significant, Matthew contains the birth of Jesus in Beit Lehem (Bethlehem, meaning "the house of bread"). But tradition rather than content has surely determined the unchallenged universal trinity of Matthew, Mark, and Luke. Today, the "two-source theory" finds earlier Mark, along with the hypothetical Q document, the source and model of Matthew and Mark, a notion accepted in one form or other by most biblical scholars. Now with the

---

57. Richmond Lattimore, *The New Testament* (New York: North Point Press, 1997).

discovery of the Gospel of Thomas, we have a third possible source for the canonical gospels. One wonders why the chronological order of composition remains ignored. In analyzing the gospels, virtually every scholar begins with Mark and then notes how a parallel (or lack of a parallel) event is handled in later Matthew and Luke. We should let the reader know and experience the order that scholars know and use in their studies.

An advantage to beginning with Mark is found not only in seeing how he presents the information but also in noting what information is omitted. There are many charts and even editions showing the parallel presentation of passages. We learn as much from the absence of a parallel passage as from its presence. Mark does not contain a scene of Mary and Joseph and the birth of the infant messiah. Matthew and Luke do. The absence of this crucial tenet of Christianity in Mark means that the miraculous birth of Jesus, with Mary seeded by a messenger of God, came to the evangelists from another source or was composed by the authors of Matthew and Luke, but was almost certainly unknown to Mark. Most passages in Mark do have a parallel in the other synoptics. The progressive changes and additions in word and setting are only clear when Mark precedes Matthew.

Of huge interest is the abrupt ending of Mark. Here is the major absence. There is no resurrection scene in Mark. In contrast to the other three gospels, where the resurrection is a major element, as it will be to Christianity, Mark offers some enigmatic words about a possible after-death appearance. But Jesus does not appear alive to his students (disciples). Three verses in the last chapter of Mark (16.5–7) reveal a young man in a white robe who has been sitting in the empty tomb (identified by Matthew as an angel, Matt. 28.2) and who says, "He was raised" and he tells them to go to the Galil (Galilee) to see him. To compensate for ending the gospel not on hope but with the women's fear and, crucially, without a true witnessed resurrection episode, two "orphan" endings have been clumsily added to Mark. They are called "orphan" endings, not because they stand alone, though some may interpret the term in that innocent manner, but because here "orphan" is a euphemism for spurious. One orphan ending is barely two lines. It is a scribal addition, written as a declamation and prayer in tone and Greek alien to Mark:

All that had been commanded they reported briefly to those around Shimon Kefa [Peter]. After that, Yeshua himself, from east to west, sent through them the holy and deathless proclamation of eternal salvation. Amen.

The longer ending is fleshed out, and in almost a full page Jesus appears to Mary of Magdala and then to the disciples. But the orphan passage has neither the grace nor the mysterious beauty of the resurrection scenes in the other gospels. Its clear purpose is to *create* a resurrection scene that the authentic Mark lacks. To do so it imitates the words of the other gospels. The orphan ending concludes with words by a later cleric scribe asserting the role of the apostles and the place of Jesus in the hierarchy of divinity, crucially not as God himself but as lord Jesus sitting at God's right-hand side:

> After speaking to them, lord Yeshua was taken up into the sky, and he sat down at the right hand of God. And they went out and preached everywhere. The lord was working with them and confirmed the word through accompanying signs.
>
> MARK SUPPLEMENT 20

The absence of a resurrection scene and the need to forge another ending allow us to understand the elaboration of the concept of Jesus as a resurrected messiah. But we should hear Mark alone, for his haunting ending, a high moment in religious literature. His own austerely moving and dramatic narrative ends with the desperate passage in the cave when two of the women—Miryam of Magdala and Miryam of Yaakov and Shelomit—flee the tomb after they discover that Jesus's body is gone:

> So they went out and fled from the tomb, seized by trembling and ecstasy. And they said nothing to anyone. They were afraid.
>
> MARK 16.8

It is a fitting ending for one of the singular literary documents in the world.

What Are the Letters?

OF THE twenty-seven books in the New Testament, twenty-one are letters. Or twenty are letters if one thinks of the anonymous letter, Jews, as a meditative sermon. These letters were dictated and recorded decades before the composition of the gospels and yield the first statements and knowledge we have concerning a religious movement that was to be called Christianity. Chronologically they come first in moral thesis and edicts of a young community centering its faith on the significance of the crucifixion of the young rabbi, who is perceived as the true messiah. For mapping the new messianic movement, the letters are our base.

What are they?

The letters or directives are ancient missives by apostolic leaders to congregations, leaders, and specific persons. They were normally dictated to a scribe or amanuensis. They comprise the oldest documents we have in what came to be known as the New Testament. Before elaborating the circumstance, meaning, and placement of the letters, I wish to spend a few words on the title "New Testament" that provides framing information for our second bible out of the New East. In the letters we find the Pauline words of a new agreement, a new covenant, which later will lead others to give name to the collection as the New Testament.

While Paul gave us the words for a new covenant, he had no body of scripture in mind, and of course his own letters were letters, not holy words of a sacred bible. For him the covenant was not a book or anthology of books but a personal pact with the deity. Here he was with Noah, Abraham, the prophets, and the many Bible figures who spoke their new covenants, their new vows, as well as their longing for the earthly messiah who would bring them into a realm of peace, happiness, and intimacy with a benevolent and loving God.

How did Paul's new covenant attain its present name of New Testament in Western Europe? "New Testament" is derived from a Latin title devised by Saint Jerome (Eusebius Sophronius Hieronymus) (347–420). Under orders from Pope Damasus I in 382 to revise the four gospels of the existing Old Latin version (*Vetus Latina*) from the best Greek texts, Jerome finished this initial venture. Then, exiled from Rome, he learned Hebrew in Jerusalem and in 390 began to translate directly from Hebrew and Greek, becoming the principal translator of the Vulgate (from the Latin *Vulgata*) and finishing it in 405. Though the Septuagint translation into Greek of the Tanak[58] (the Jewish Bible) continued to be the Old Testament for Greek-speaking Christians and the source of translations for Eastern Europe, the Vulgate to this day remains the Bible of Roman Catholicism.

The title of Jerome's version of the Greek scriptures, "Novum Testamentum," from which the English "New Testament" is derived, is a mistaken conversion of its Greek title Καινὴ Διαθήκη (Kaine Diatheke, meaning "New Covenant"). Titles are always the least reliable word or words of an ancient document, and it is unknown whether Jerome, another translator, or a scribal tradition gave us the Latin title. After the Jerome Vulgate[59] appeared, it soon became the prescribed Latin version, and such was its power and the church of Rome's authority behind its usage that later a death penalty was enacted for translation of the Vulgate into a vernacular, that is, a vulgar tongue. That prohibition reeks with irony, since the word "Vulgate" means "vernacular" or "for the populace," from the Latin *vulgar, vulgaris*. Once the official death penalty was lifted, there were many translations. Too often they led to the execution or long imprisonment of those who translated scripture into the Western tongues of Italian, French, and English.

58. Tanak (or Tanakh; Tenak) is an acronym for the three main divisions of the Hebrew Bible: Torah—תּוֹרָה, meaning "Instruction" (five books of Moses); Neviim—נְבִיאִים, meaning "Prophets"; and Ketuvim—כְּתוּבִים, meaning "Writings."
59. Vulgate from Latin *Vulgata* or *Nova Vulgata*, "New Vulgate." Latin *Vulgata* is often used in English as a synonym of "Vulgate."

As for Jerome's title for the new covenant, his New Testament persists in all but a few new versions.[60]

If we go back to Paul, the early epistler gave us the notion of a new "covenant." His word διαθήκη (diatheke) comes from Hebrew בְּרִית (berit, "a cutting"), meaning "circumcision" as well as "covenant" or "pact," going back to Abraham's covenant with God, who tells Abram to be circumcised. The rite of the בְּרִית, the circumcision, became metonymically the abstract word for "covenant." If Abram keeps the covenant of being circumcised, he will become Abraham, king and leader of nations. Paul in turn, by altering the conditions of that Old Testament covenant, proclaims a new covenant (Rom. 2.27) and, evoking the etymological root meaning of בְּרִית, sharply declares that our new "circumcision"—περιτομή (peritome)—must be a spiritual one of the heart, not of the flesh. He cites as his authority Deuteronomy 30.6, where Torah calls for a circumcision—וּמָל (umal, an alternate form of the Hebrew word for circumcision)—of the heart, not of the flesh.[61]

> Someone is not a Jew by what is seen.
> Rather, one is a Jew by what is hidden.
> Circumcision is of the heart, the spirit,

60. The reader may ask why, given the discussion of Jerome's mistake in his Latin naming of the Καινὴ Διαθήκη (new covenant), his error is perpetuated here by not uniformly speaking of New Covenant rather than New Testament. The same holds true for my references to Jesus, Paul, and James rather than to Yeshua, Paulus or Shaul, and Yaakov. Paul's Hebrew name was Shaul, but since he wrote in Greek, I preserve the Greek name. In contemporary Greek the upsilon is usually the English "v" and he would be Pavlos. In the scripture the restored names are used throughout, where the main concern is. In the introduction, the usage is not consistent because it is important to introduce the reader gradually to a restored lexicon. In the thematic essays in the afterword, the restored terminology is used predominantly. Here as elsewhere it is good for a reader to rock back and forth between usages in order to become accustomed to the restoration while remembering the traditional patterns. To have an awareness of the history of names, whether it be Asian or African nations whose titles change with the historic and political winds, or the names of peoples and people and even institutions is not only helpful but also crucial if one wishes to see the many faces of the past.

61. See notes on Romans 2.25–29 for more on circumcision.

> Not from the literal law. So one finds praise
> Not from the ranks of men. It comes from God.
>
> ROM. 2.28–29

By changing the nature of circumcision to avoid the cutting of the flesh, Paul opens the way for the uncircumcised "ethnics," as he calls the pagan Greeks, to enter the emerging congregations of Christian Jews.

While Paul speaks of a new covenant with God, only late in the second century do the Christian fathers speak of a new covenant as a title for the books in the Greek Bible. Paul, who uttered the names that ultimately were to frame the Greek scriptures, died before the gospels were composed. And he did not dictate his letters as holy scripture but rather as information and admonitions to the emerging congregations. He had no canonical aspirations for these unparalleled documents. The decades-later gospels, acts, and apocalypse of a second bible were not yet conceived or composed.

The common ancient Greek word for letter is ἐπιστολή (epistole) from which the English word "epistle" comes. The canonical letters were earlier called epistles, elevating them back to their Greek root, but today they are simply called the letters, which is faithful to the original demotic tenor of biblical Koine (common) Greek. An awkward compromise to please all, or no one, is "letters/epistles." We also speak of them interchangeably as "books" when referring to the entire Greek scriptures, which includes letters, gospels, acts, and an indefinable apocalypse or revelation, which is the epic poem of the New Testament.

Since twenty-one books of the New Testament are letters, they are the predominant literary form in the Greek Bible. Of these, fourteen, if we include Jews, are traditionally attributed to Paul; and at least seven, if Philemon is included, are by Paul himself, in whole or in part. Paul, the essential shaper of Christianity, dictated them to his scribe. In the resonant "To the Romans" his scribe inserts at the end, "And I Tertios, who wrote down this letter, send you greetings in the lord" (Rom. 16.22). Paul dispatched his letters to synagogues and the newly forming churches. They carry the titles of their recipients: To the Romans, To the Thessalonikians,[62] To Philemon. The titles are arbitrary, added by later scribes and editors in the process of establishing the canon of the Greek scriptures.

The act of dictation gives these first documents a lively immediacy, perfect for their proselytizing and admonishing purpose. Not only were they spoken to the scribe but upon reception they were to be read aloud to specific congregations or persons. The letters vary from philosophical meditation and idealist spiritual love expressed in supreme poetry to legalist instructions, such as the troubling early missive To Philemon. Here Paul sends the escaped slave Onesimos, whom Paul has converted to Christianity, back to his master Philemon, noting that while Onesimos the slave is free now in Christ, in this world according to Roman law he belongs to Philemon and must serve him. More, the penalty for lost workdays due to his absence must be paid up. Throughout the letters, as in the gospels, flows a mixture of eschatological theology coupled with detailed instruction about everyday behavior at home and in the market.

---

62. The Greek title of the letter Πρὸς Θεσσαλονικεῖς—To the Thessalonikians— means "to people of Thessaloniki (Salonica)," the northern port city of Greece in whose extant synagogue, now an excavation in the main square, Paul once preached. Thessalonians, the common name for Paul's letters carrying this title, were people from the capital city of Thessaloniki. Thessaloniki means "Victory of the Thessalians," referring to the brave horsemen from Thessaly who helped Philip II of Macedon to defeat the Phocians. To commemorate his victory (Greek *nike*), Philip named his newborn daughter Thessaloniki. She was to marry Cassander, king of Macedon, who founded the port city, and gave it his wife's name, Thessaloniki.

Should Letters Go before Acts?

THE LETTERS' PLACE in the canon raises fascinating questions. Despite their depth and frequent rhetorical majesty, the letters were not, as noted, conceived or composed as religious scripture. Yet as purported words of the first saint historians of Christendom, the messages had a core significance and could not be ignored. But some early Church fathers wished to seriously reduce the number. At one extreme we have Marcion of Sinope (ca. 110–160), who was probably the first Christian to attempt to establish a canon. Marcion excluded the entire Hebrew Bible and included only parts of Luke, parts of ten letters by Paul, and a gospel of his own sayings. Though Marcion later received the official designation of heretic, especially for his flirtations with the Gnostics, the fact that he probably initiated the notion of a sacred collection of holy books can never be minimized. Marcion was also the first to identify and choose some of Paul's letters for inclusion in his minimal bible.

After centuries of wrangling over selection, the letters remained in the final canon, a tribute to their intrinsic complexity, beauty, and the compilers' wisdom. Unlike the histories of the Old Testament, however, which are found at the core of the Hebrew Bible, the letters, their chronology ignored, share a dim deutercanonical aftermath placement near the end of the New Testament. The less-than-prominent placement is not unintentional, and reflects less interest in historical accounts than in story. That Acts of the Apostles (Activities of the Messengers) now precedes the messenger Paul's own account of his work and ideas is arguable,[63] but makes little sense. The hero of Paul's letters and Acts is

63. The placement of Acts immediately after the Gospel of Luke is traditionally justified by claiming that both Luke and Acts were authored by Luke (authors' actual

Paul himself. The letters are first-person historical. While Acts with its Jack London adventures compliments the letters, it lacks the plain quirky veracity, the cranky gloom, and the towering passion and philosophical eloquence of Paul. One should not hide or postpone Paul's unparalleled discourse on love in 1 Corinthians 13. If wisdom, theology, history, and love are most welcomed after the gospel story of Jesus, then the reader should first hear Paul, whose letters on the crucified messiah are the initial and significant cause of Christianity's foundation. Paul in Acts is profoundly different from the soul-creating author of the letters. In Acts Paul is not a normal mortal but one endowed with amazing powers to heal the gravely sick and raise the dead. Paul has been re-created as a later messianic Jesus, endowed with the personal powers of miracle. Yet there is no hint of such powers in any chapter or verse of Paul's letters. In Paul's panorama of conflict with congregations and his religio-political obstacles from rival missionaries and civil authorities, it is certain that he would have welcomed any otherworldly help to his mission and they would have been inscribed in detail in his letters.

As a result of the letters' placement in the New Testament right before the concluding Revelation, it is the unusual reader who knows their historical significance at the inception of Christian messianism or who commands them as intimately as the gospels. Unless a preacher looking for sermon material, most readers skip the letters (except perhaps to pause at Paul's definition of love) and go directly to Revelation. Here the letters appear before rather than after Acts.

Acts is not about events that happened before the letters, but is chronologically a continuation of Paul's own narrations, composed long after Paul's letters. In all the arts the authorial composition precedes a re-creational summary by others. Since Acts is in reality a long third-person letter describing the life of the letter-writer, Paul, it should follow Paul's own letters. Such a new ordering solves the question of chronology, since the letters obviously preceded Acts, and we should first know the philosopher-preacher Paul before the later miracle-performing Paul.

---

names are unknown), based on the brief, clearly interpolated prefaces to Luke and Acts by one, or more probably two unknown apologists. In artificial formal Greek speech, fathoms apart from the fluent and dramatic speech of the gospels, the author or authors unconvincingly claim a Lukan authorship for both books.

The first-person Paul of the letters, the wonderful, petulant, meditative, and poetic Paul, is not the semi-mythical Paul in Acts, the magician who can heal and raise the dead. Rather, he is the down-to-earth thinker, the founder and creator of a new version of Judaism infused with Platonic idealism and radically new ideas concerning the traditional messiah. His place as the predominant letter writer, along with the other letter writers, must precede the fantastic Paul in Acts, the last of the epistles.

Finally, it is also better for Acts to directly precede the allegory of the Apocalypse. Acts and Revelation flow together. Thereby, the new ordering of the New Testament gives us a story. Acts gives us a post-gospel story, followed by the resolution of all in Revelation that takes us back to an allegorical Babylonia. It tells us in coded terms of the persecution by a Roman Caesar (not Nero, the obviously wicked Caesar as usually claimed)[64] of early Christian Jews trying to survive Roman brutality in underground caves in Cappadocia in central Anatolia and everywhere they strove to survive and practice their new faith.

The letters serve many purposes. Being the oldest New Testament documents, they inform us of the formative years. Without them Christianity would have sprung from nowhere. They speak of Jesus Christ the Messiah. Without them there would be no corroboration beyond the gospels themselves to speak of the death of the messianic figure of Christianity.[65] Equally significant as documents originating in

64. In Revelation 13.18, the number of the beast 666 has been read as a code name for the emperor Nero. Recent testing at the Stanford Linear Accelerator Center suggests "616" for the beast emperor, which corresponds to the oldest-known record of this verse found in a papyrus fragment at the Oxyrhynchus site in Egypt. There the photographed number clearly appears as 616 (χις). In *The Messiah before Jesus: The Suffering Servant of the Dead Sea Scrolls* (Berkeley: University of California Press, 2002), Israel Knohl convincingly reveals that the beast coded "666" (or 616) is not Nero and corresponds in all ways to Caesar Augustus.

65. Paul tells us of the death of Jesus Christ but nothing about his life, family, or the life of his followers leading to Passion. One corroborating outside source for the life and death of Jesus is from the Jewish historian Josephus. However, the passage in Josephus's *Josephus Antiquities* (18.3.3) regarding Jesus in Testimonium Flavianum 3.3 is out of context and probably a late interpolation, and the brief reference by Tacitus, in book 15, chapter 44, of his *Annales*, is unverified information probably given to Tacitus from an early Christian who was not witness to the noted event. The dating of Tacitus's references is wrong. What stands out is that in a time of abundant

Greek by Greek-speaking Jews who had found the messiah, their claim to historicity has an ostensibly larger base of corroboration than the gospels, whose authors and sources are unknown, and which were composed so many decades after the dates assigned to Jesus's crucifixion.

While there are also no reliable sources for Paul's own life outside the New Testament, his ascetic letters, with their abundance of reference to specific person and place, carry with them an intimate sense of the author. The general letters of the other messengers, Peter (Kefa), John (Yohanan), and James (Yaakov), are equally compelling personal histories, though here, as in half the letters of Paul, the public name of the author is unknown and unknowable.

Besides the double Paul we find in the letters and Acts, there are other figures who share a common name but represent distinctive qualities of that person or of more than one person. The letter-writer names of James, John, and Peter cannot have the multiple identities traditionally assigned to them. The name "Peter" is as arbitrary as "Isaiah" for the three-sectioned book of 1 Isaiah, 2 Isaiah, and 3 Isaiah. The eloquent, angry, conservatively Jewish letter-writer Peter does not speak as the former disciple and companion of Jesus. Peter in the gospels, the fisherman, is ever in trouble and rebuked by his master for his doubts and heavenly ambitions. Jesus states that Peter will deny him three times before the cock crows. When Jesus is seized, Peter three times denies any connection with the arrested rabbi.

That fisherman companion is not the letter writer and founder. And the letters attributed to the epistler Peter appear to be composed years after Paul's death. Nor is John, as orthodoxies of the Greek and Roman churches claim, the single author of the Gospel of John, the very late letters of John, and the even later Apocalypse of John. Can John of the letters and the gospel be John of Patmos or Ephesos, author of Revelation, which was composed no less than seven decades after the crucifixion? Few scholars hold to the traditional assertion of a singular

---

record keeping that provides details of minor and major messianic figures, there is nothing outside the New Testament concerning Jesus in life and death. For information about Galilean messiahs, see Geza Vermes's illuminating book *The Changing Faces of Jesus* (New York: Viking Compass, 2001).

Johannine authorship for the three books that carry the name "John" on the title page.[66]

Another unknown with respect to the letters is the loss of replies that might have found their way into the canon. By even a superficial perusal of the letters, we learn that the letters were answered, many of them being themselves responses to other letters. This should not surprise us. And the absence of respondents' letters should not upset us. Their absence does not add or diminish questions of authorship and authenticity of the canonical letters. Their loss is unquestionably due to the value of the piece and who chose to preserve them and the importance of whatever name, authentic or inauthentic, is attached to it. It must be remembered that virtually all ancient writings, classical or biblical, survive because there has been since their composition an unbroken history of copying and recopying.[67]

66. Given these diverse doubts concerning authorship and sources, with particular reference to the gospels, the questions of origin and other mysteries of the gospels do not lessen their intrinsic value and wonder. At the same time, the contradictions, mistakes, and absence of source material compose a fact that does not help confidence in the gospels' every word and event.

67. The extent of tomb and library texts is limited, though especially in the Egyptian Fayum and in sites in Syria, not to mention Antioch, Athens, Rome, Sinai, Mount Athos, or some library storage area in an old European university, or in a palimpsest that modern technology can now decipher, there is always hope that old work may surface. The ways of survival are the copiest's shop, monk's cell, a Dickinson or a Melville attic. As for the process of copying, there changes abound. As in revised editions of books, the errors or intentional changes depend on the copiest, who often feels free to shape the work according to his or her religious or political mind. What exits from antiquity is what was popular enough to have been copied and recopied, and popular enough to be buried in a tomb. Surviving versions often differ dramatically. With respect to the Hebrew Bible and the Greek scriptures, the textual history is longer than the scripture. Outstanding among chance finds are the Dead Sea Scrolls and the Gnostic Nag Hammadi Library, which are also copies of copies.

The King James Version was based on copies dating back only to the thirteenth century C.E., while recent editions of Greek scripture go back to about the eighth century C.E., as is also true for the Torah (the Jewish Bible we call the Old Testament). Indeed the Septuagint Greek translation of the Old Testament (which includes the canonical Apocrypha), presumably accomplished in the third century B.C.E. but actually in the second century B.C.E., exists today in fourth-century parchments, thus preceding surviving Old Testament parchments by at least four centuries.

FINALLY, one may ask why is Jews by its lonesome between the letters and Acts? One has never known what to do with this secret jewel of the New Testament. It is a letter, and even the most conservative of religious scholars acknowledge that it is not by Paul and has nothing to do with Paul's thought or sonorous philosophy. Nor does anything in it, unlike the pseudo-Pauline letters, display or attempt to display a similarity to Paul. As a unique piece it contains many paradoxes. While it is absolutely anonymous, we know much more of the background of this author than we do of the authors of the general letters, less than convincingly attributed to James, Simon Peter, John, and Jude. The author of Jews is an Alexandrian Christian Jew who in his learned sermon poem fervently defends the emerging Jesus movement. He does so not by denigrating the Jews but by returning to main early Torah tales to enforce his convictions that the salvific messiah has appeared on the globe for us to hear. But the Jesus he extols is more clearly than elsewhere neither a specific nor a vaguely allegorical presentation of God. Jesus is Jesus, the messiah, here presented as very much like the Isaian messiah as virtuous leader, but also distinctive in that he has a divine presence as mediator to salvation. And his description of the messiah is a poetic highlight of the *Restored New Testament*:

Now Mashiah has come as the high priest[68]
By way of a greater and perfect tent

Not made by hands, not hands of this creation,[69]
And not by blood of goats and bulls but through

His unique blood. He entered once into
The holy place to gain for us eternal

Redemption. But if blood of goats and bulls
And sprinkled ashes of a heifer hallow

68. "of good things to come," not in all ancient texts.
69. Or world.

94

Those who have been defiled so that their flesh
Is purified, how greater is the blood

Of the Mashiah. Though eternal spirit
He gave himself blameless to God to purify

Our conscience far away from mere dead works
That serve us when we worship living God.

JEWS, 9.11–14

Of immense erudition, this Alexandrian more than any author of the
New Testament is rich in the discursive dexterity—not the doctrine—
of the Gnostics. So like Valentinos or Basilides, the great original
Alexandrian Gnostic thinkers, authors, and exegetes, he too could be
a source for Origen and the first Church father scholars who applied
Alexandrian learning in a hermeneutic reading of the two covenants.

Arbitrarily Jews has routinely appeared between the letters of and
attributed to Paul and the general letters of James, Peter, John, and Jude.
I place it by itself as the last letter and closest to Acts and Revelation,
both of which are sermon, poetry, and story as is Jews. I hope the world
will recognize this literary and philosophical masterpiece in equal
frames of glory with the best epistles of Paul and John. It follows its own
solitary early way and messianic message out of Hellenistic Alexandria
during a period of intense spiritual ferment. It is surprising that this
anonymous distinctive sermon letter found its way into the canon. One
can thank its early mistaken attribution to Paul.[70] Sir Anonymous made
the canonical cut. Now the recognition of his work as an extended and
defining moment of the New Testament is due this very day.

70. Most of the mountains of pseudepigrapha are by their very name attributed,
often foolishly, to a grand figure, often a clearly first- or second-century piece to
Moses or one of the evangelists or Apocalypse John. Since the names of both covenants are for the most part later attached to the scriptures, these intertestamental would-be members of the party are not to be disparaged. On the contrary, the
infancy gospels, the other acts, gospels, and apocalypses of the Intertestament are
of immense value and usually of deep beauty.

Should Paul's Letters
Precede the Gospels?

WE HAVE LOOKED at the content priority of John's metaphysical creation story and at the chronological priority of Mark, which begins the canonical gospels in all significant ways of style, development, content, and influence. After Mark's austere narration we see modifications of his Jesus tale in Matthew and the other gospels.

If we look at the compositional chronology of the whole New Testament, then the first letters precede the canonical gospel by at least two to three decades. The letters represent pioneer Christianity (early Messianism), and the depiction of Jesus in the letters is fundamentally different from his portrait in the elaborate narration in the gospels. Since the first breath of the Christian Jews occurs in the letters, why not first read how these early activists, proselytizers, and now our early saints saw the Christ and early Christianity develop? It would be a boon to historicity to begin with the letters. And it would add to our information to fuel the unending discussion of the nature of Christ, which takes place in that large playing field of Christology.

Jesus of the letters and Jesus of the gospels are distinct portraits. Jesus of the letters is not a person whose first name happens to be Jesus, but the Christ, the messiah, the awaited one who promises salvation and eternity, who died and who will very soon return to earth. Therein the awaited Second Coming.

As for the placement of gospels and letters, we note the intended parallels between the two testaments in compiling the New Testament. Genesis begins Torah, though its date of composition, as with all pre-exilic books of Torah, is uncertain.[71] It was composed at a later date than many books in the Jewish Bible. We place the gospels at the beginning of the New Testament, before the earlier-written letters, because thematically the gospels tell the original mythic tale of Christianity. Genesis tells the creation of the universe and of earth, and by the end of the sixth day on earth Adam and Eve have come into being in a garden of immortality. It describes Yahweh hurling Adam and Eve, who disobeyed, into mortal time.[72] Obviously, Genesis (meaning "birth," "origin," "beginning") must begin the Tanak.[73] So too the gospels must come first, since they, like the creation myth, tell the ultimate tales of the New Testament on which Christianity is based. Moses's forty years of struggle and reformation in the desert before the return to the lands of Canaan find their parallel in Jesus's forty days of spiritual struggle and learning in the wilderness before his return to the kingdom of Judah. As Genesis must begin Tanak (though it is not the earliest Hebrew Bible composition), the gospels must begin the New Testament. In like manner, we follow the thematic rather than the compositional chronology in the ordering of New Testament books.

The informed reader and the scholar should keep a perspective of Christianity's development in scripture, however, by examining the letters, which predate the gospels. We can speculate but do not know how the gospel stories arose. We do know that not only the gospels but also

71. Dating of the early books of the Hebrew Bible varies from traditional dating, going back to 1500 B.C.E., to dating by textual scholars who argue for between the tenth and sixth centuries. The Torah was fixed as it is in the canons by perhaps the early Hasmonean period of the early second century B.C.E., but there is little consensus. We have no more hard evidence outside the Hebrew Bible itself of legendary Moses and equally mythic King David in the period of the United Monarchy (kingdoms of Israel and Judah), 1050–930 B.C.E., than we do of Jesus and his students. We do have reasonable dating for Nevi'im (Prophets) based on historical events, from 561 to 538, the latter being the year Cyrus decreed the Jews in Babylonia free, and free to return to Judah.

72. Eve chose to pick fruit from the tree of the knowledge of good and evil, which she was commanded not to. Because she chose knowledge, *gnosis*, in the major Gnostic sects she is the first heroine who gave up immortality for gnosis. See Elaine Pagels, *The Gnostic Gospels* (New York: Random House, 1979).

73. Old Testament.

the basic tales of the gospels in any form were unknown to the apostles who were championing the coming, life, death, and future return of their Christ the Messiah. Given the revolutionary importance of the gospel story, the absence of significant reference to them in the letters is overwhelming evidence that the apostles had no knowledge of Jesus's life, no thought concerning his family, disciples, or the Romans. There are no words about the narrative of Mary and the virgin birth of Jesus, about his teachings and the parables; no word about Judas's betrayal (or noble loyalty as in the Gnostic Gospel of Judas), no Sermon on the Mount. In short, the epistlers had knowledge of no key figure or event in the gospels other than the fact of a crucifixion. (The exception is the very late epistler Peter, who in 2 Peter 1.17 actually quotes Matthew 17.5, in which God on a mountain says of Jesus, "This is my son / Whom I love, / In whom I am happy.") And of the crucifixion they had no details, not of Roman Pilatus nor of his conversations with Jesus or the disciples. We can guess but perhaps never know why the gospel story, accounting for half the New Testament, has no presence in the letters. This enigma is unknowable. After all, Paul's letters were composed not long after the purported life span of Jesus, and if anyone was deeply informed about the messiah, it was Paul, who had lived in Jerusalem before and after the crucifixion. The letters contain the heavenly sky of Christ the crucified but only a shade of a living Jesus. Paul's good news is not that of the gospels. What then can be the main source of the gospel story? Its apparent absence invites speculation as to what degree the gospels were source-inspired and to what degree they were created by the evangelists.

The crucifixion, resurrection, and predicted return of the Christ the Messiah is the predominant theme of the epistlers. The letters reveal the messiah as Jesus Christ who gave his life for our human sins in order to save us. More, he will return a second time and deliver to us our reward, and very soon, presumably within the apostles' lifetime. The sole references to a gospel-described Jesus in the letters are a reference to the Last Supper (the Seder) in 1 Corinthians 11.23 and one or two others. Apart from these isolated quick shots, whether or not they are authentic or among the many later patches to the letters and pseudo-letters, the scene is empty. In the end no piece of scripture is absolutely verifiable, but much of Paul is more than reasonably verifiable. By verifiable I refer to the texts being his own, patched together to be sure, not written by him but dictated by him. By verifiable I refer solely to his authorship, not his beliefs.

The apostles were the most eloquent and knowledgeable proselytizers of their day, avid for information in order to spread the word about the Messiah. How did the apostles come on the notion of a messiah deity who after his death would return to earth to save the faithful? Indeed, what Jewish sects of that time believed in resurrection?

Flavius Josephus and others describe the Pharisees as the main Jewish sect believing in the resurrection of the dead. The Sadducees were not similarly creedal, denying afterlife (Josephus, *Antiquities*, 2.164–165). Consider Paul's background and theological training. Paul, fountainhead of the epistlers, was a Pharisee rabbinically trained by Gamaliel, grandson of the famous rabbi Hillel.[74] As once a Pharisee, rabbi Paul was with those who believed in the coming of a divine messianic age. He absorbed the Platonic notion of the immortality of the soul that the Pharisee espoused.

Unlike the letter-of-the-law Sadducee priest caste, the Pharisees

74. Although Rabban (our great master) Gamaliel was rabbinical head of the Sanhedrin at the time of its alleged plot to have Jesus killed, he is spoken of with deep respect by Luke in Acts (5.34–40; 22.3) as Paul's teacher, "a Pharisee and celebrated scholar of the Mosaic Law," and according to Christian tradition he was singled out by Clement as a Jew especially kind to early Christians. Later he was to have converted to Christianity, and his body has been revered in Pisa, Italy, where as a Christian he died. Until 1956 Rabbi Gamaliel was among the first millennium of saints, "by public acclaim," in the Roman martyrology. However, since 1956, while still in highest esteem, his saintly status has been on hold for lack of verification. Whether there is truth or wishful thinking that Gamaliel was among the early saints (most of the early Christian saints were Jews), what is most significant is that the gospels and Acts do not have their act together about the Sanhedrin with respect to its leader Gamaliel. On the one hand, the gospels vilify the Sanhedrin for deicide, while on the other, Luke, who is popularly (and falsely) held to be the author of both the Gospel of Luke, which accuses the Sanhedrin of the Jesus plot, and the Acts, praises Gamaliel, the Sanhedrin's leader, as the most learned Jew of his time. In short, Gamaliel was guilty of deicide and a Christian martyr and saint. In this, Gamaliel surpassed Paul, himself in paradox, who writes that before his conversion he joined in the martyrdom of Stephen, yet we also know through chapter 13 of 1 Corinthians that Paul invented the most generous, profound, and pervasive notion of love in the Western world.

followed the oral tradition of freely interpreting Torah. Like the Pharisees and Jesus of the gospels, Paul freely threw away rules of Sabbath, diet, and circumcision for the gentile converts. As the poor's final reward, Paul of love promised after-death resurrection. The Pharisees, themselves poor, were scribes and sages of the poor, as opposed to the Sadducees, who were the rich aristocratic clan of Hasmonean Temple priests favoring King Herod appointed by Rome. Pharisee in Hebrew is פָּרוּשׁ (Parush), meaning "separatist" and "deviant." The Pharisees opposed the dominating alien Temple and set up their own small synagogues in opposition.

I suggest that Paul of the letters would have rejected any later portrait that has Jesus demonizing Pharisee brethren as arrogant "offspring of vipers" who place the letter of law over the human spirit, as rich Temple hypocrites in league with the devil and collaborating with enemy Rome. Paul knew, as would any informed figure of his day, that the Sadducees, not the Pharisees, were backed by Rome and controlled the Temple with Herod's blessing. Indeed, the Pharisees, the *Prushim*, as their name indicates, were outsiders bearing no resemblance to their wicked caricature in the gospels that reverse the role of Pharisee and Sadducee.

The cartoon version of Pharisee as "hypocrite" persists in the dictionary.

Yeshua in Letters and Gospels

SINCE THE EARLY letter-writing apostles, who were much closer to the Jesus drama in time, lacked the elaborate "good news" that impelled the later evangelists, one might ask, who gave the story to the evangelists? The gospel authors found their life and death of Jesus three to five decades after the purported date of Jesus's death. Did they find their information in an oral gospel tradition as some contend, or in a lost document? Could the evangelists be inventors? It is a safe assumption that they composed the majority of changes in the parallel texts as they moved from Mark to Matthew to Luke. We cannot know the author or authors of any source beyond the gospels themselves. The authors' names were accorded to them, it is believed, in the early second century. As for the story itself, one does not ask for mathematical concordance of statement, since scripture, like all literature, is connotative rather than denotative, and without human contradictions, be it in Whitman or the evangelists, we have no oeuvre. The veracity of the gospels and of their origin does not stand or fall on contradictions, mistakes, allegorical exaggerations, or any literary device that has made these books extravagantly significant. Many books have gained bestseller prominence by informing us of error. But whether they be skepticism concerning detail voiced by Presidents Jefferson and Lincoln, or Bart D. Ehrman's observations on misquotations in emendations to the gospels, what counts most is credulity in the major passages and situations.[75]

In citing some cruel passages that are *invraisemblable*, I return to and repeat what scores of Christian theologians have earlier noted: The Sanhedrin could not have been in session on the night of the Seder

75. Bart D. Ehrman, *Misquoting the Bible* (San Francisco: HarperOne, 2007).

(Passover), and night trials were forbidden. But on the Seder night in Matthew 26.57–67, the tribunal council is in session and a choir of voices plot the crucifixion of Jesus. There follows, in Matthew 27.23, masses of Jews in the streets, again on the Seder when none would be in the street, shouting, "Crucify him!" When Pilatus, who is in Rome, washes his hands and says, "I am innocent of the blood of this man," we read, "all the people answered, 'Let his blood be upon us and upon our children!'" (Matt. 27.24). Can it be that Jews call on God to bring his eternal curse upon themselves and on their blood descendants at the death of the "King of the Jews." Such collective masochism cannot hold. As holy scripture and creed, the Jew is demonized here at the peak of the passion tale. And so was launched two millennia of retribution.[76]

The history of religion is one of internal conflict, of demonizing the other, especially the one competitively close, and so the internecine wars or massacres of Christians and Gnostics, Orthodox and Arians, Protestants and Catholics, Shias and Sunnis, Sri Lankan Hindus and Buddhists. Rare is the religious sect from any century or land that has not seen torture and execution in the name of the true faith.

Here the unfriendly transmission of information may originate in the duel between Messianic Jews who believed and those who did not believe that Yeshua was the messiah announced in Isaiah. Paul was not part of that cruel duel of the good and wicked. On the contrary, in Romans he speaks with profound grace about the Jews who believe in the newfound messiah and those who don't. He suggests a temporal relativism concerning belief in God's diverse manifestations. Belief or lack of it does not threaten the ultimate truth, which in the end, Paul writes, is the truth of God:

What then is the advantage to the Jew,
What is the value of circumcision?

76. Frank Kermode writes in *The Genesis of Secrecy: On the Interpretation of Narrative* (Cambridge, MA: Harvard University Press, 1979, 20), "I know of no better example of the way in which privileged interpretation, propounded by an elite believing that it alone has access to the true spiritual sense of a text, may determine matters of life and death—unless it is the horrible success of Matthew's that the Jews, after Pilate washed his hands, voluntarily took upon themselves and their children the blood-guilt of the Crucifixion."

Great in all ways. In the first place, the words
Of God were entrusted to them. What then?
What if some of them did not find belief
In words of God? If some did not believe,
It did not void belief in God. Never!
Let God alone be true.

ROM. 3.1–4, Ps. 51.4

Many messiahs were popping up in the provinces, especially in the
Galil highlands and the Essene deserts south of Jerusalem. The very
intensity of rivalries may account for the cruelties in the elaboration
of the later Passion scenes. Given that the earlier apostles were in the
dark with respect to the life of Jesus, the conspiracy story behind the
crucifixion is a confounding factual mystery whose elaboration rests in
the faith evidence of the gospels themselves.[77]

As for all these enigmas, especially the confusing identity of its
major figures, such mysteries are alive and constant in all major ancient
religious scriptures. In contrast to the highly documented Greeks and
Romans, while we have abundant and beautiful scriptures of the Buddha
and Laozi (who were Plato's contemporaries) we lack historical sources.
The chronicle events of the Asian masters dwell in a cloud of fable and
contradiction, which in no way lessens their spiritual message, nor their
eloquent speech. Such emptiness, to use a favored Buddhist word, may
be there to stimulate thought and investigation.

77. As to how the gospel evangelists could be in the dark about the epistlers, one
can say that the gospels dealt with the life of Jesus, and therefore why bring in the
epistlers? This may seem to be a valid point, yet surely something of the theology of
the letters would have found its way into the gospels. Paul was not an insignificant
thinker and religious philosopher, as proved by how in Acts, erroneously attributed
to Luke, Paul is the central apostle philosopher and letter writer. And if one were
to take the conservative view that evangelist Luke was the author of Acts, it would
seem inexplicable that one who knew Paul so intimately would not have introduced
Pauline theology into Luke's own gospel and similarly why Paul himself was not
informed of the life of Jesus as revealed in the gospels.

From Christ to Jesus
and Back to Christ,
and Who Is God?

JESUS CHRIST has many presences and transformations. In the letters, as noted, there is not a life-on-earth Jesus depicted. Rather, the figure of divinity is divine throughout. He is Christ the Messiah, Yeshua ha-Mashiah of the faithful. But Yeshua's birth, circumcision on the eighth day, youth, family, his itinerant life of teaching wisdom to followers, nothing of that rich life and death as a visionary rabbi comes into prominence in the letters. There is a void with respect to a seeable and hearable person of Jesus on earth. Christ is the crucified Messiah. That void of a personal Jesus in the Pauline letters also pertains to the other epistlers.

This void is not in the gospels, where Jesus is fleshed out completely, from birth in the lowdown stable to the cruel apogee on cross. The evangelists beheld a human miraculously born on earth, apparently not of human sperm. They witnessed the many aspects of his life, death, and resurrection. How astonishing that the epistlers and the evangelists, the authors of the two major sequences of New Testament scripture, knew next to nothing of each other. Or if somehow each group was aware of each other and their writings, nothing in the writings of the letters or the gospels reveals acquaintance.

In the ancient world, despite the absence of electronic mail or any form of invisible particle waves to speed words and ideas through the ether, precious information dropped like lightning from heaven. Plato and Platonism went everywhere at cable speed across continents, as did later Christianity and Gnosticism. With such seemingly universal intimacy of ideas, it is hard to account for the lack of contact and mutual influence amid this relatively small group of proto-Christians of the letters and of the gospels. Though these authors were equally devoted to the messianic leader, they existed as two solitudes whose circles did not coincide.

The letters are theological and moral documents. They express deepest faith in Christ the messianic savior, and tell how to lead a spiritual life in the community, congregation, and in one's own soul. In addition to personal and societal advice and prescriptions, the letters also address the grand ethical issues of the Hebrew Bible, namely, how to live on earth; the three do's or do not's of circumcision, diet, and the Sabbath; and how to live with a personal God.

In the epistles Christ is already there. He is confirmed, reigns, and is present as the director and judge on earth and for a promised realm of eternity.

In the gospels Jesus a child is born.

In the traditional Matthew, Mark, Luke, and John, we begin with Jesus's ancient genealogy in Matthew, which in Luke is again recorded but in reverse order. In Luke we have the nativity passages, the life events, teaching, parables, death, and statements after resurrection to amazed students. If we include the orphan ending of Mark, which turns Jesus into the Christ, the portrait of a roving rabbi becoming the martyred Christ appears in four visions, which are the four gospels. And for more information on Jesus and the Christ, we can go to the later intertestamental scripture and pseudepigrapha. They provide us with the infancy gospels of Jesus's childhood, the boy's maternal grandparents, and many anecdotal events that have found their way into ecclesiastic writing and the iconography of church wall mosaics, paintings, and the hand-copied books of the time.

The culminating event of the gospels is the crucifixion. It is also the culminating event that gives later Christianity a logos. The logos of the cross is an identity symbol as are the six-pointed star of the Jews and the five-pointed star and crescent of the Muslims. Though presented in unrelated fashion, the resurrection is the constant for the epistlers and the evangelists. In the letters the Christ is crucified. In the gospels Jesus, whom the Roman soldiers taunt as "King of the Jews," is crucified. The differences in presentation prescribe the movements from a Christ to a Jesus and back to a Christ.

This changing nature of the deity persists in a cycle of godheads competing for dominion in the eyes of church leaders and the faithful who perceive and re-create the nature of both the Christ and Jesus. The lord of lords, the immediate master to whom one prays for comfort and action, rises and falls in authority according to sect and century. The competition sways back and forth between "Christ is lord" of the letters and "Jesus is lord" of the gospels. In these Christological debates on the nature of Christ, the place of God is less conspicuous. God subsists in the Holy Trinity. The immediate work on earth falls to God's son Jesus the Christ, who is God's son at his side or God's equal by another name. Such a formulation bothered some, since for God to exist "under" or "within" the Trinity seemed to threaten God's preeminence. The Protestant Reformation emphasizes the Hebrew Bible and abolishes idolatry and the iconic representation of Jesus, angels, and saints in the churches. While it accepts the Trinitarian doctrine, God the father, for at least the main early Protestants, regains everyday dominion over the earthly world, though in the New Testament God himself doesn't speak.

One can see the fluctuating roles of God versus Christ, his messiah, in the iconic appearance of the Pantokrator (ruler or strength of the world) in the early Eastern Orthodox Church. In Byzantine churches the Pantokrator is the omnipotent Jesus. His face is the stern, implacable judge and commander, distinct from the features of the sensitized suffering Jesus on the cross. He usually occupies the central dome of the church, in mosaic, gesso, or paint, and looks down from the heaven of the ceiling, as he does in Greece in splendid mosaic at Ossios Lukas and in paint on gesso at Daphne. His equivalent in the West is Christ in Majesty. When the Pantokrator is seen in half-length image, he is teaching or blessing with his right hand while in his left he carries a copy of the New Testament, showing his source and identity. But in the ten references to the Pantokrator in the New Testament, they are to God, not Jesus. In 2 Corinthians 6.18, Paul cites verses from the Hebrew Bible through the Septuagint Greek:

And I will be your father and you will be my sons
And daughters, says the lord of the mountains.

The NRSV translates Greek *pantokrator* (Παντοκράτωρ) as "Lord Almighty." In the New Testament the Pantokrator is God. In the Old Testament in Greek translation (the Septuagint), "Pantokrator" appears as a synonym for God. The other nine references occur in Revelation and are also to God, not the Christ.

We might add that the Greek word *pantokrator* is the Septuagint Greek translation of one of the most mysterious Hebrew names for God in the Old Testament, *El Shaddai* (אֵל שַׁדַּי), meaning "almighty God," or more properly "God of the Mountain." By the time the Pantokrator finds a rare place in Protestantism, he has gone back to being God, not Jesus. And the grave resplendent images of God Pantokrator—God Almighty—have also disappeared because in the Protestant churches God is invisible.

So the voyage of the Pantokrator goes from 1) *God* in the Septuagint and New Testament, to 2) *Christ* in the iconography and liturgy in Eastern Orthodoxy and Catholicism, and back to 3) *God* in Protestantism, where he also sheds his visual representation. The larger metaphor of the Pantokrator is a grand movement in all aspects of church life, ritual and everyday creedal emphasis, from God in New Testament Paul, to Jesus in Orthodoxy and Catholicism, and God in Protestantism.

The balancing roles of God and his son Jesus point to underlying theological doctrines in flux, concerning the nature of not only Christ but also God himself or herself. The larger question in the monotheistic Abrahamic religions of Judaism, Christianity, and Islam concerns the nature of, or competition between, God and his messiah.

In Judaism there is no competition. The messiah (the anointed one) is an earthly mortal descended from the house of David who will deliver his people to peace and freedom in Israel. The Torah messiah is not God nor is he his son, and all who claim so spell a return to polytheism idolatry. The notion of a messiah as lord, son of God, or God himself opposes the underlying imperative of the *shema* (hear). "Hear, O Israel, the lord our God, the lord is one" (שְׁמַע יִשְׂרָאֵל יְהוָה אֱלֹהֵינוּ יְהוָה אֶחָד)—shema yisrael adonai eloheinu adonai echad) (Deut. 6.4–9).

In Christianity the gospels, not the letters, give us the Trinitarian doctrine, which is heard in countless prayers, liturgies, and rites and originates with the command to baptize nations in the name of the father, son, and holy ghost[78] (Matt. 28.19): "in the name of the father and the son and the holy spirit" (εἰς τὸ ὄνομα τοῦ πατρὸς καὶ τοῦ υἱοῦ καὶ τοῦ ἁγίου πνεύματος—eis to onoma tou patros kai tou uiou kai tou hagiou pneumatos, and in the Latin Vulgate, in nomine Patris et Filii et Spiritus Sancti). The notion of the Orthodox fourth-century Nicene Trinitarian doctrine has dominated Christianity despite expected sectarian spats over interpretation of the formula.[79]

In Islam, Muhammad (in Arabic محمد) is the last great prophet and a messiah only in the Jewish sense of prophet, leader, and God's foremost messenger. Muhammad (ca. 570–632) restored religion against "earlier corruption," bringing Islam back to its monotheistic world of Adam, Abraham, and the unique worship of Allah (الله), Arabic for "God." His scriptural source was given to him by the angel Gabriel, who commanded him to recite and record verses sent by God. The prophet Muhammad's writings are the bible of Islam, known as the Qur'an (in Arabic القرآن, al-ḳur'an). A singular principle rejected in Qur'an is the Trinitarian doctrine, which to Islam created a messiah who was not simply an angel or messenger of God but another deity equal to or competing with God. Returning to the biblical proscription against graven images, the mosque, like the synagogue, permits abstract decoration but no depiction of God, angels, and God's creations on earth.

78. In reference to baptism, the Trinitarian Formula is called "Great Commission," exhorting the apostles to go to all nations and baptize their people in the name of the son, the father, and the holy ghost.

79. In modern times the liberal Jesus Seminar has "voted" that this crucial passage in Matthew is a later scribal emendation and not voiced by Jesus. Whether by Jesus or not, the Seminar acknowledges that despite questions such as those about unity and equality with respect to the father, son, and holy ghost, the Trinity Formula guided Christianity from its formative years to the present.

Jesus, a Semite Who May Have Been Called Yeshua ben Yosef

WHO IS JESUS of the gospels? The New Testament begins with four stories of the life and death of a young rabbi who preached in the synagogues, and who in his lifetime would have been called "Yeshua ben Yosef" or "Yeshua bar Yosef" (using Aramaic *bar* for "son"). If we followed usual Anglicization of his name, in English he would be "Jesus son of Joseph." After he died, the followers who accepted him as the messiah of the Jews may have called him "Yeshua ha-Mashiah," in standard English, "Jesus the Messiah." I note the probable original name because in later diverse translations the names have been changed by which the world knows him. In their changes is a story that I hope will permit Jesus, a Semite from the Levant where the sun rises, to return and be seen in the full light of his homeland.

Jesus the Messiah should not appear as an alien with strange names in a distant culture and certainly not as a non-Jew Galilean Aryan, as the nineteenth-century French author Ernest Renan (1823–1892) depicted him in his *Vie de Jésus* (1863).[80] Renan's invention of a "historical" Jesus as a non-Jewish Caucasian from an Aryan people who happened to be living in Galilee served the Nazi historians well. Renan was popularly the first to deal with the historical Jesus before Albert Schweitzer's significant *Quest of the Historical Jesus* (1906).[81] Although we lack modern

80. Ernest Renan, *Life of Jesus*, trans. William J. Hutchison (Whitefish, MT: Kessinger Books, 2003).
81. Albert Schweitzer, *The Quest of the Historical Jesus*, trans. W. Montgomery (New York: Macmillan, 1968).

evidence outside the gospels on Jesus's existence, this has no bearing on the name identity of Jesus, the letter writers, and the evangelists. Jesus was a Jew. Socrates was a Greek, in life and death, and was so perceived without ambiguity. It is not too much to ask that Socrates, though he was historically put to death by the Greek governing body, not by a foreign official, be perceived without equivocation as a Greek. Identically, for truth and history it is imperative to know at all moments that Jesus and his kin and friends were Jews and that he was put to death by the Romans.[82] His followers were Jews, as were the authors of the authentic letters, Paul, Peter, John, James, Jude (Judas), and the evangelists, though the actual names of the authors, with the exception of Paul, of seven letters are unknown.

In the second century the term "Christian" (meaning "anointed ones") was used rather than "Messianic," an accurate translation for the followers of the messiah. As the new sect developed, the letter authors wrote to each other, often in fierce debate, such as the one between Paul and Peter over circumcision, Sabbath, diet, and what non-Jews, the ethnics, meaning Greeks, must do to be qualified to join these dissenters for whom the messiah had at last come.

---

82. Traditionally, Pontius Pilate crucified Jesus; however, apart from forged evidence by Josephus and a suspect secondhand report by Tacitus, whose dating is wrong, there is no existing evidence of the crucifixion of Jesus outside the gospels.

Rabbi Paul

PAUL WAS EDUCATED as a Pharisee in Jerusalem in the school of Hillel when Jesus was presumably teaching in the same city. Until the road-to-Damascus revelation, as recounted in 1 Corinthians 15.1–11, Paul had not heard of Jesus or his crucifixion. One considers how the earliest apostolic historian in the New Testament, almost a contemporary in age in Jerusalem, was unaware of the messiah on whom his faith was based. As depicted in the gospels, the crucifixion was a huge event, filling the central square and presided over by Pilate the governor. But on reading Paul, one realizes that his notion of the religious movement, which he set in motion, did not require knowledge of the messiah's life. As for when, where, and under what circumstances a crucifixion occurred, these thoughts have no place in his letters. There were many messiahs recounted in reliable sources, but for Paul what counts and on which he establishes faith is that the true Jewish messiah, the Christ forecast in Tanak, has come. He has seen him only in vision. He will come again to save us. He tells his parishioners that we will be in heaven with God. In incomparable lines Paul speaks about the resurrection of the dead, telling us, "If there is a natural body, there is also a spiritual one" (1 Cor. 15.44), and,

> The ram's horn will blow and the dead will wake
> Uncorrupted, and we shall all be changed.
> Then the perishable body will put on
> Imperishability, and the mortal body
> Immortality. When the perishable
> Puts on immortality, then the word
> Will be fulfilled as written in Yeshayahu

And Hoshea:
> Death is swallowed up in victory.
> Where, death, is your victory?
> Where, death, is your sting?

1 COR. 15.52–55

Here, Paul, as a former Pharisee deeply dependent on the Platonist idea of the immortality of the soul, adds a new Pharisaic element as he asserts that we will be resurrected in both body and soul, with body transformed into spiritual body.

In parallel manner, as there is an absence of a living Jesus in the letters, in the gospels, the evangelists, as observed, don't know the letters or their writers. It is true that the letters were competing with mountains of intertestamental documents, all written under assumed names for the privilege and hope of being accepted as canonical scripture.[83] One wonders how, amid the plenitude, even the letters of the New Testament found their final inclusion.[84] But among the documents passed around, one would have supposed that the letters that survived for two millennia might also have reached the eyes of the evangelists.

When Paul speaks of the messiah, he is the awaited Jewish messiah who will bring peace on earth and save the Jews from the horrors of Roman occupation. The messiah will bring not only peace and safety on earth but also deliverance and eternal salvation. It would seem, then, as a Jew believing ardently in the truth of Tanak, he would not address the followers of Jesus Christ as "Christians" but as "Messianics." Neither term is used. In reality he avoids the question altogether because in the Greek letters of Paul there is no designation of the faithful as "Christians." We find the sectarian name of Χριστιανός (Christian) used for the first time in 1 Peter 4.16 and then not until Acts 11.26, which

---

83. See Willis Barnstone, *The Other Bible* (San Francisco: Harper and Row, 1984; 2nd rev. ed., HarperSanFrancisco, 2005).

84. For the earliest attempt at canon for books to be included in the New Testament, see David Trobisch, *The First Edition of the New Testament* (New York: Oxford University Press, 2000). For the most authoritative and concise history of the transmission, corruption, and restoration of New Testament scripture, see Bruce M. Metzger, *The Text of the New Testament: Its Transmission, Corruption, and Restoration*, 3rd ed. (New York: Oxford University Press, 1992).

reads, "and it was in Antioch that the students [disciples] were first called Messianics [Christians]," and "Christians" is read again in Acts 26.28: "In a little while you will persuade me to become a Christian."

Since the words "Messiah" and "Messianics" would be the proper names for the salvific messiah and his followers, where did the epithets "Christ" and "Christian" come from?

Here we encounter tricky but essential problems of translation, from at least three languages before reaching English—Hebrew, Greek, Latin—and to use the banal phrase, much is lost in translation, by error or intention.

Order of Paul's Letters
Singing to the World

I WILL TRY TO MAKE the chronology as clear as possible, going back to source tongues, without skipping the complications. We do not know the true chronology of the letters, but we can make informed guesses. We have a plausible dating for the Pauline letters that has been around for a long time.[85] The normal order of the letters has little or nothing to do with chronology or even theme, mixing the authentic with the dubious letters for no apparent reason. I group the probably authentic Pauline letters together, followed by the pseudo-Pauline letters, and end with the least likely Pauline letter, Jews (Hebrews), which is for many reasons one of the most fascinating of these missives. The letter to the Jews is revealing because of the large role the "dangerous and deceitful Gnostics" play as potential corrupters of the congregation.

The uncontested Pauline letters are not in their probable chronology of composition but follow a strategy of importance. So Romans here, as elsewhere, is number one, followed by Corinthians 1 and 2, the order in Orthodox, Catholic, and Protestant Bibles. All sects have traditionally held to one ordering of the letters. In Paul this means lumping the authentic with the apparently false. Here, except for the grouping in Paul, I follow the traditional format, starting with long Romans and ending with short Jude.

The letters to the Romans (probably his last letter) and the Corin-

---

85. Some scholars are working on the larger question of dating all of the letters, notably Patricia Allen at Oxford University, who joins science, technology, and textual expertise to gain answers to the chronology.

thians show Paul at the peak of thought and rhetorical magic. He achieves language magic in a demotic Greek (Koine), with a flare of the classical period while keeping to the simplified syntax and virtues of the vernacular. He has the high flow of Plato, who wrote in Attic Greek, in his own less inflected tongue. To repeat my argument about the glory of Mark's Greek, Paul's work is not less effective for being composed in a vernacular development of Attic Greek any more than Michel de Montaigne is less for writing in French, the regional vernacular of Cicero's Latin. Indeed, in terms of change, Paul's Greek is closer to Plato than E. M. Forster's English is to Shakespeare. Greek, in spelling, grammar, and usage, was very early established, while in English the dictionary thoroughness of Samuel Johnson, who established norms for English spelling and usage, did not enter the scene until midway between Forster and Shakespeare.

If this volume were predominantly a study Bible, then it would begin with Paul's 1 Thessalonians, which, if not supreme, carries the authority and beauty of all his authentic letters. And despite the above encomia for the apostle's key letters, there are advantages at least for study purposes to keep in mind the probable order of Paul's work. He grows as his movement grows, and his work moves to the climactic pivotal letters. A chronological order, even the thought of one, would provide an unbiased historical frame for secular and sectarian events and reveal the material culture scene of the Jews, Christian Jews, Greeks, and Romans who participate in the drama of each book.

While I separate the authentic Pauline letters from the pseudonymous, from a stylistic point of view, the would-be Paul letters do not jar. Being pseudepigraphic they imitate Paul's style, if not his depth and breadth. The weakest are among the latest, commonly called the Pastorals: Timothy 1 and 2 and Titus. They are said to have been written between 62 and 63 C.E., but they are just as likely to have been composed in the second century, perhaps after Revelation.

But where does one put late Philemon, a short authentic account of a runaway slave, which some think the earliest of the letters? Philemon is considered by some authentic, by others an imitation. As a testy epistle, Philemon is more important sociologically and politically than for its spirit and poetry. If the letter is by Paul, it presents a Paul hobbled by his time in justifying the duties of the slave to return and pay for lost time to the master. Its disturbing message reveals how strong were the ties of many early Christian Jews with the Roman Empire and its vast slave network, which Paul, as a possible Roman citizen, espouses without criticism.

For all these good reasons, because the Bible should sing us into its depths and rapture, Romans and Corinthians begin the letters. A Bible like a novel, play, or opera has a movement leading to the reader's pleasure and enlightenment. As with the classical drama, following Aristotle's dictum, we have a suspension of disbelief in order to become fully involved in the drama and achieve catharsis. All these instructions are applicable to the Bible, and they work for the believer and the skeptic.

The Bible is a work of art. Were it not art, were it simply an instruction manual, it would not satisfy or convince, and very likely would not have survived. So, to be faithful to the original work, which in Greek is normally chanted in the churches, as the Torah is chanted in the temple and the Qu'ran is melismatically chanted in the mosque (and plainsong chant is characteristic of all religions of the world), the Bible here must resonate.

As for the sequence and reasons for making it work, I remember the words of the Argentine author Jorge Luis Borges when asked what his criteria were for reading a book. He answered, "I read the first page, and if I like it I go on to the second. If I do not, I close the book."[86] Here I wish the reader to go on to the second page until the last.

86. See Willis Barnstone, *With Borges on an Ordinary Evening in Buenos Aires: Memoir with Poems* (Champaign/Urbana: University of Illinois Press, 1993).

BON VOYAGE

Bon Voyage

AFTER TWO MILLENNIA a bible is a rainfall of languages. Jesus, or more properly, Yeshua, is bizarrely speaking to us in late-first- and second-century demotic Greek, which has somehow entered this book as English. We receive the story and his words with astonishment and do not question circumstance, which is just as well, for the story is a universe, whatever our background of origin or faith or doubt. All ethno-religious epithets fade as clouds fade before the strong morning sun, and we enter the day and the night of the tale, never to return the same.

Bon Voyage

SCRIPTURES

Canonical Gospels

A Note on
New Testament Scripture

THE NEW TESTAMENT is a collection of gospels, acts (a sequel Luke), and letters, and, like the Hebrew Bible, an anthology of distinct literary genres. Specifically, the New Testament consists of the canonical gospels, Acts of the Apostles, Letters, and Apocalypse (Revelation). A gospel (meaning, a book of "good news") tells the life, teachings, and death by crucifixion of Yeshua the Mashiah (Jesus Christ) and is also an account of the followers of Yeshua (Jesus). The followers included his students (disciples) and the crowds that traveled with this itinerant rabbi and healer around the hills of Upper and Lower Galilee, the fields of Yehuda, and the streets of Yerushalayim.

Yeshua ben Yosef was born in turbulent times of rebellion against the Roman occupiers of Israel in about 7–3 B.C.E. It may seem strange to say that Christ was born before Christ, but it is now generally accepted among scholars that the date set for Yeshua's birth, by Dionysius Exiguus, the creator of the Christian calendar, was off by several years.

The earliest texts of the New Testament we have are written in Greek. Although Paul's letters were written in Greek, the gospels of Matthew, Mark, Luke, and John are later Greek versions of earlier lost accounts, oral or written, from Aramaic and probably Hebrew sources. The scriptures of the Christian New Testament concern the lives of Jews who followed Yeshua and Paul and Peter, who reflected one sect among other revolutionary Jewish sects, which included the Pharisees, Zealots, Essenes, Hasidim, and early Gnostics. The gospels of the New Testament were written by or ascribed to Matthew, Mark, Luke, and John, who are called the evangelists. They are traditionally thought to be three Jews and a convert to Judaism (Luke), though any knowledge of the evangelists outside of the texts ascribed to them does not have a scholarly or historical basis. Like the Hebrew Bible, the Greek scriptures of Christianity underwent countless modifications and radical restructuring as they moved from oral history to a fixed place in the canon. As for the extent to which the narration itself has a historical base, again we have essentially no source outside the gospels themselves. We do not know what scribal hands copied, redacted, and fashioned the gospels into their present narration. In a few documents, from Tacitus, Philo, and Josephus, it is noted that there was a man named Jesus who was crucified by the Romans.

In the first years after the crucifixion, the Christian Jews (those who followed Yeshua) were in contention with other Jews in the synagogues for dominance. Paul wrote letters to the congregations of the synagogues in Rome, Corinth, Thessaloniki, Antioch, and Athens to persuade his coreligionists to follow Christ. By the time of the destruction of Jerusalem by Titus in 70 C.E. and the subsequent diaspora of the inhabitants of the city, the division between Christian Jews and those who did not receive Yeshua as the mashiah became more decisive; by the second century the separation between Jew and Christian was irreversible. But the new Christians had no scripture of their own. The Pauline letters were not then considered holy documents. The Hebrew Bible was the sole Christian Bible, which most of the "primitive Christians" read in its Greek Septuagint translation or in later Christianized versions of the Septuagint. The New Testament gradually was assembled, with an initial edition around 150. Through the next centuries its contents were debated fiercely by the Church fathers until the end of the fourth century, when there was a consensus. Athanasios (293–373) is nominally credited with setting the twenty-seven books in the order we have them today in 367, but in all probability *The First Edition* was published around 150, and it already established the selection, if not the final order or wording. Then, after the councils of Laodicea (363), Hippo (393), and Carthage (397), the Athanasian collection was accepted as canon. With his revision of earlier Latin translations of the Hebrew Bible, and from the Greek New Testament, followed by his own new translation of Hebrew texts, which he studied in Israel and available Greek texts found elsewhere, Saint

Jerome (347–420) produced in about 405 the Latin Bible of the Catholic Church. For the first time, the Christians who depended on Rome at last had a complete Bible in Latin, the famous Vulgate (*editio vulgata*). In 1546, the Council of Trent declared Jerome's version to be the exclusive Latin authority for the Bible.

A Note on
the Greek Source Texts

THE SOURCE TEXT for this translation is *The Greek New Testament*, fourth edition (1993), published by the United Bible Societies, which is a unified edition of the United Bible Societies (the UBS) text, and the twenty-sixth edition of *Novum Testamentum Graece,* edited by Eberhard and Erwin Nestle, based on an earlier edition by Kurt Aland (1979). An earlier but still available Greek text from which translations have been made is the Majority Text, which is based on a consensus of manuscripts that includes some passages generally omitted in the UBS and other available editions, including the Alexandrian Text. The UBS and Alexandrian Text consult manuscripts discovered in the late nineteenth and early twentieth centuries, in particular, the Codex Vaticanus and Codex Sinaiticus, both from the fourth century. In some instances, I have noted the Majority Text reading, where it differs from the prevailing UBS text used in this translation. In one crucial instance, in the Lord's Prayer, in Matthew 6.9–13, I include, in brackets indicating interpolation, the last lines of the model prayer: "For yours is the kingdom and the power and the glory forever and ever. Amain." The UBS and other modern Greek texts and translations such as the New Revised Standard Version exclude this famous ending. It was added by the early church as an appropriate concluding doxology to Yeshua's prayer in keeping with David's prayer in 1 Chronicles 29.11–13. The extraordinary but uncertain ending is, however, found in Tyndale (1534), which used the best Greek texts available at the time and in the King James Version (1611), based on the *Textus Receptus* (1516), which derives from few manuscripts and not the better or older ones that we now have in our possession.

Although more than five thousand manuscripts exist in Greek, and many more in Latin translation from the Greek, it is unlikely that there will be a final correct edition of the Greek text, much less a true Aramaic or Hebrew source text for the gospels. The most engaging possibility of an earlier textual source for the gospels is the Gospel of Thomas, limited to wisdom sayings of Yeshua, found in 1945 at Nag Hammadi, Egypt, along with classical Gnostic scriptures, all translated into Coptic (the language of non-Greek Egyptians). Some, though not most, scholars suggest that Thomas may precede Mark (ca. 70–80 C.E.) by twenty years, and hence presents us with the earliest extant translated words of Yeshua.

IN ITS PRESENTATION, brackets signify that a translation has been made from a Greek word or phrase that appears in the earlier Majority Text, but not in the UBS fourth edition (the source of this translation), and indicates that such a word or phrase does not appear in our earliest extant, full ancient texts.

The brief subtitles before passages throughout, which most translations into English since the Revised include, generally follow their placement in other versions. The titles help locate each distinct segment and show the episodical nature of the short pieces that comprise the narration. The titles reveal but do not scoop the story. They do not interpret, nor say so much as to replace or lessen the reading experience.

Annotation is light and generally explanatory or linguistic. Though not a study Bible, the linguistic resource gives derivations from Greek, Aramaic, and Hebrew so that the interested reader may pursue that course of inquiry. The etymology of changing names provides a historical key to sectarian and ethnic politics of the New Testament.

Creation Prologue to Yohanan (Creation Prologue to John)

In the beginning was the word

    In the beginning was the word[1]
    And the word was with God,
    And God was the word.
  2 The word was in the beginning with God.
  3 Through it[2] everything came about
    And without it not a thing came about.
    What came to be 4 in the word was life
    And the life was the light of people
  5 And the light in the darkness shines
    And the darkness could not apprehend it.

---

1. John informs us in "In the beginning was the word," Ἐν ἀρχῇ ἦν ὁ λόγος (En arhe en ho logos) (John 1.1). God created through the word, ὁ λόγος. With that utterance God translates divine sound into matter and being, thereby bringing the cosmos, the earth, and the earth's inhabitants, great and small, into temporal existence. The creation through the word in John parallels the creation in Genesis 1.1 of the Hebrew Bible: "In the beginning when God created the heavens and the earth": בְּרֵאשִׁית בָּרָא אֱלֹהִים אֵח הַשָּׁמַיִם וְאֵת הָאָרֶץ (bereshit bara elohim et ha-shamayim veet ha-aretz). God in Genesis uses "the word" to speak the world into being through his order, "Let there be light," יְהִי אוֹר (yehi or), while in John "the word" of creation may be spoken or written, but it also is the initial cause of creation. And as in the Hebrew Bible, that word is immediately commingled with light. It has been observed that in this prologue, the use of the logos offers a link between the divine mind and the human mind, which is rational and apprehends the word through reason, reason being another meaning of "logos." This beginning is often presumed to be a separate poem added or adapted to the gospel.

    John is considered the most Gnostic of the gospels, and especially in this prologue. The logical sequence of this poem also suggests the syllogistic reasoning of the Sophists as well as the Cynics to whom leading theologians sometimes compare Yeshua. See John Dominic Crossan, *The Birth of Christianity* (San Francisco: HarperSanFrancisco, 1998), and Burton L. Mack, *Who Wrote the New Testament? The Making of the Christian Myth* (San Francisco: HarperSanFrancisco, 1995). More broadly, "logos" may be given multiple meanings: the word of God, knowledge, science, the Greek principle of reason ordering the universe, and a Kabbalist principle of the primacy of creating words and, before words, an alphabet of letters, so that God has the means of speaking the universe into being.

2. "Through it" is also translated as "Through him."

Yohanan came to proclaim light[3]
> 6There was a man sent from God.
> His name was Yohanan.[4]
> 7He came as a witness in testimony of the light
> So that all might believe through him.
> 8He was not the light,
> But came to testify about the light.[5]
> 9The light was the true light
> Which illuminates every person
> Who comes into the world.

Light was in the world
> 10He was in the world
> And through him the world was born,
> And the world did not know him.[6]
> 11He went to his own
> And his own did not receive him.[7]
> 12To all who received him
> He gave power to become the children of God,

---

3. Yohanan the Dipper (John the Baptist).

4. John from the Greek Ἰωάννης (Ioannes), from the Hebrew יוֹחָנָן (yohanan).

5. Yohanan was not the light, meaning not Yeshua the Mashiah, but the lamp carrying the light, defining the testimony of Yohanan the Dipper (John the Baptist) as prophetic but in a secondary role to Yeshua, who is the messiah, and also suggesting rivalry between early followers of the messiah, some favoring Yohanan, who electrified Judaism with his arrival in ways foretold in Isaiah (Isa. 9.2, 42.6–7, 60.1–3). The majority favor Yeshua, but there is considerable evidence that by the second century of the Common Era the number of those favoring Yohanan over Yeshua as the messiah was increasing alarmingly.

6. Yeshua the Mashiah.

7. The Jews in Isaiah and other prophets spoke of one messiah, whom the majority of Jews did not accept when he came. The Jews, who did recognize Yeshua, the early Messianics, who late in the first century broke off from mainstream Jewry, were the Christian Jews (meaning "Messianics," followers of the messiah). They shared with traditional Jews the Torah as their sole holy scripture, since the New Testament was not to be firmly set and canonized until centuries later.

To those who believed in his name,
13Who were born not from blood
Or from the will of the flesh
Or from the will of a man,
But were born of God.

Word became flesh
14And the word became flesh
And lived among us.[8]
And we gazed on his glory,
The glory of the only son born of the father,
Who is filled with grace and truth.

*Yohanan cries out about him who will come after
and who was before*
15Yohanan testifies about him and cries out, saying,
He is the one of whom I said,
"One who will come after me was before me,
Because before me he was."
16From his bounty we have all received grace upon grace,
17And as the law was given through Moshe,[9]
Grace and truth have come through Yeshua the Galilean.
18No one has ever seen God.
Only the one born of God,[10]
Who is in the heart of his father,
He has made him known.

---

8. God's word became human flesh in the person of Yeshua.

9. Moses from the Greek Μωϋσῆς (Moyses), from the Hebrew מֹשֶׁה (moshe).

10. Other texts have "only begotten son."

Markos
(Mark)

Markos
(Mark)

As in the other gospels, there is no internal evidence of the authorship of the book of Mark. An early church figure, Bishop Papias (ca. 130–140 C.E.), states that Mark was John Mark, a close associate of Peter, and that the Gospel of Mark is essentially an arrangement of Peter's preachings in Rome. The second-century bishop Irenaeus also places Mark in Rome. Another tradition claims Alexandria as the place of origin. Others assume that because the Markan gospel is probably the earliest, it was composed in Israel. Mark was written at least thirty to forty years after Yeshua's death, and the gospel authors' names were appended to the gospels more than a hundred years after Yeshua's death. The traditions that assert authorship of the gospels frequently deny each other, and here, as elsewhere, none has a strong historical probability. Authorship in the New Testament remains an enigma.

Like Luke 1.1, Mark 1.1 begins with the presentation of "the good news" about Yeshua the Mashiah. Mark stresses Yeshua's miracles and his powers of healing, the drama and mystery of his death. The first verses quote the prophet Isaiah to prove that Yeshua is "the voice of one crying out in the desert" and that he is therefore God's messenger. But after this initial declaration, Mark plunges directly into the stories of John the Baptist and of Yeshua tempted for forty days in the desert by Satan (which parallels Moses's forty years in the desert tempted by Baal). It follows his wanderings through the land of Israel, where he takes on disciples and crowds of followers, who accompany him in his ministry. Mark gives us a series of miracles, teachings through parables, and finally the "Passion Week" of Yeshua's arrest, trial, death, burial, and disappearance from the tomb. Here the gospel ends. This so-called abrupt ending has bothered theologians and has caused some to speculate that we have a truncated or unfinished gospel. Most disturbing is that there is no mention of Christ risen, and since Mark is the source of Matthew and Luke, the absence of a resurrected Yeshua is not desirable. As a probable result of this discomfort with the present ending, two later endings were appended to Mark, the "Shorter Ending of Mark" and the "Longer Ending of Mark." The very short one has Yeshua send word of eternal salvation out from east to west. The longer one has Yeshua appear resurrected before Mary Magdalene and the disciples and then describes Yeshua ascending into heaven. The shorter ending may have been added in the fourth century, the longer one as early as the third or second. Both endings are termed "orphans," because they are spurious, and do not exist in the earliest manuscripts, which are the Vaticanus and Sinaiticus codexes.

Mark is most often characterized as an author whose Greek is crude and rudimentary in contrast especially to Luke, who is more classical, and John, who is clearly influenced by Greek philosophical and Gnostic models. But Mark is in many ways the greatest stylist among the evangelists. Mark writes with plain clarity, concision, with dramatic power, minimal and striking diction. The original ending of the Gospel of Mark may be less satisfying as theology, but it is overwhelmingly dramatic and mysterious in its understatement of the sublime terror of Yeshua's disappearance from the tomb. When the two Marys enter the tomb and find that Yeshua is not there, Mark writes, "So they went out and fled from the tomb, seized by trembling and ecstasy. And they said nothing to anyone. They were afraid" (16.8).

Chapter 1

Good news

1The beginning of the gospel[1] of Yeshua the mashiah,[2] son of God.
2As it is written in Yeshayahu[3] the prophet:

> Look, I send my messenger ahead of you,[4]
> And he will prepare your road;
> 3The voice of one crying out in the desert,
> "Prepare the way for Adonai[5] and make his paths straight."[6]

Yohanan the Dipper in the desert

4Yohanan the Dipper[7] appeared in the desert, preaching an immersion of repentance for the remission of sin.[8] 5The whole land of

---

1. Gospel from the Greek εὐαγγέλιον (euangelion), meaning "good news" or "good tidings" as well as "gospel." "The beginning" in Mark is parallel to "In the beginning," the first words in Genesis.

2. Jesus the Messiah. "Jesus" is from the Greek Ἰησοῦς (Iesous), from the Hebrew יֵשׁוּעַ (yeshua), from the Hebrew יְהוֹשֻׁעַ (yehoshua); and "messiah" is a translation of Christ (the Greek word for "the anointed") from the Greek Χριστος (Hristos) translated from the Hebrew מָשִׁיחַ (mashiah). "Messiah" is a free transliteration of the Hebrew *mashiah*.

3. Isaiah from the Greek Ἠσαΐας (Esaias), from the Hebrew יְשַׁעְיָהוּ (yeshayahu).

4. "Before your face" in the Greek.

5. "Lord" or "Adonai" from the Greek κύριος (kyrios or kurios). When referring to the divine lord, the Greek κύριος may be translated as "lord" or "Adonai" (אֲדֹנָי) as here in the Hebrew text cited from Isaiah; when referring to Jesus, *kyrios* may be translated as "sir," "master," "teacher," or "rabbi," when the implicit Hebrew source is רַבִּי (rabbi).

6. Isa. 40.3.

7. John the Baptist, John from the Greek Ἰωάννης (Ioannes), from the Hebrew יוֹחָנָן (yohanan). "The Dipper" is from the Greek ὁ βαπτιστής (ho baptistes), meaning "one who dips, washes, or immerses" as in Jewish ritual washings.

8. Sin from the Greek ἁμαρτία (hamartia), also translated literally as "missing the mark," "wrong," "wrongdoing," or "error."

Yehuda[9] and all the people of Yerushalayim[10] came out to him and were being immersed by him in the Yarden[11] river and confessing their sins. 6And he was clothed in camel hair and wore a belt of skins around his loins, and he ate locusts and wild honey. 7He preached, saying,

> After me will come one more powerful than I am
> Of whom I am not fit to stoop down and untie the strap
> of his sandals.
> 8I immersed you in water,
> But he will immerse you in holy spirit.[12]

Yeshua immersed

9And it happened in those days that Yeshua came from Natzerot[13] in the Galil[14] and was immersed in the Yarden[15] by Yohanan. 10And as soon as he came out of the water, he saw the heavens torn open and the spirit like a dove descending on him. 11And there came a voice out of the skies:

> You are my son whom I love.
> With you I am well pleased.

---

9. Judea from the Greek Ἰουδαία (Ioudaia), from the Hebrew יְהוּדָה (yehuda). Also is the name Yehuda.

10. Jerusalem from the Greek Ἰερουσαλήμ (Ierousalem), from the Hebrew יְרוּשָׁלַיִם (yerushalayim).

11. Jordan from the Greek Ἰορδάνης (Iordanes), from the Hebrew יַרְדֵּן (yarden).

12. Yohanan the Dipper is introduced competitively with Yeshua, for Yohanan baptizes in water while Yeshua baptizes in the spirit. Joseph Campbell's *The Masks of God: Occidental Mythology* (New York: Penguin Arkana, 1991) and David Fideler's *Jesus Christ, Son of God: Ancient Cosmology and Early Christian Symbolism* (Wheaton, IL: Quest Books, 1993) trace Yohanan back to the traditional Sumerian god of water and Yeshua to the god of sun. For more than two centuries there was serious rivalry, in both Orthodox Christian and Gnostic Christian sects, between those who favored Yeshua and those who favored Yohanan as the true foretold messiah.

13. Nazareth from the Greek Ναζαρέτ (Natzaret), from unknown village in Galilee probably spelled Natzeret.

14. Galilee from the Greek Γαλιλαία (Galilaia), from the Hebrew גָּלִיל (galil). "Galil" is a "circle," "district," or "province." It is often used in the phrase גְּלִיל הַגּוֹיִם (gelil hagoyim), meaning "province of the goyim (gentiles)."

15. Jordan.

Temptation in the desert

12And at once the spirit drove him out into the desert. 13He was in the desert forty days, tested by Satan, and he was among the wild beasts, and the angels attended him.

Preaching in the Galil and first students

14After Yohanan was arrested, Yeshua came into the Galil preaching the gospel of God,[16] 15and saying,

The hour is fulfilled and the kingdom[17] of God is near.

---

16. "God" in the New Testament may be more properly translated *El, Eloah, Elohim* (plural or plural of majesty of El) or *Yahweh* or "YHWH" (which is closest to the un-voweled Hebrew consonants), or "Adonai." In Matthew 27.46, where he addresses God in the Aramaic/Hebrew rather than in the Greek, Yeshua cries out in Greek transcription, ἤλι ἤλι λεμα σαβαχθανι; (eli eli lema sabachthani?), "My God, my God, why have you forsaken me?" repeating "My God," the first line of Hebrew Psalm 22, "My God, my God, why have you forsaken me?" So in Matthew 27.46 in recent translations from the Hebrew Bible, as in Everett Fox's *The Five Books of Moses* (New York: Schocken Books, 1995) and now elsewhere, "God" is translated "YHWH." "God" in English is derived from Middle English and Germanic *god*. Please see "Names of God" in the Appendices.

Yeshua in the New Testament is called diversely "rabbi," "teacher," "master," and "lord." "Rabbi," from Hebrew רַבִּי *rabbi*, master + -*i*, my, and "rabboni" appear many times in the gospels (Mark 9.5, 10.51, 11.21; Matt. 23.7, 23.8; John 1.39, 1.49, 3.2, 3.26, 6.25, 20.16). In the synoptic versions of Matthew in Mark and Luke "rabbi" usually becomes in Greek "teacher" (διδάσκαλος), "master" (ἐπιστάτης), or "lord" (κύριος), suggesting that the word "rabbi" in these Greek texts and other instances of address has been changed in order to dissociate Yeshua from the Jews. These changes of "rabbi" to "master," "lord," and "teacher" occur not only in going from one Greek text to another, from Mark to Matthew and Luke, but also when "rabbi" in the Greek text is translated into English. So the King James Version (1611) of Mark 9.5, "Rabbi, it is good for us to be here," becomes "Master, it is good for us to be here." Other early English Bibles— Tyndale (1525), Great (1539), Geneva (1562), Bishops' (1568)—similarly change "rabbi" in Mark 9.5 to "master" or "teacher." Only the Rheims-Douai (1582), a Catholic Bible translated into English by persecuted English exiles in France, renders Greek "rabbi" of Mark 9.5 (as most versions do today) as "rabbi." Please see Afterword.

17. In the Oxford *New Testament and Psalms*, each instance of "kingdom" is replaced by "dominion," since "kingdom," βασιλεία (basileia), contains the word "king," βασιλεύς (basileus). "Kingdom" is not gender free, and "dominion" is a rich alternative, but to use "dominion" would mask the intended meaning, which is "to evoke the dominion of a king."

Repent and believe in the good news.[18]

16And as Yeshua went by the Sea of the Galil, he saw Shimon[19] and his brother Andreas[20] casting nets into the sea, for they were fishermen, 17and Yeshua said to them,

Come follow me,

And I will make you fishers of people.

18And at once they dropped their nets and followed him.

19And going on a little farther he saw Yaakov[21] the son of Zavdai[22] and his brother Yohanan in their boat mending their nets. 20And at once he called them, and leaving their father Zavdai in the boat with the hired hands, they followed him.

An unclean spirit

21They came into Kfar Nahum[23] and on Shabbat[24] he went into the synagogue and taught.

22The people were in wonder at his teaching, for he taught them as one who has authority and not like the scholars.[25] 23Suddenly in their

---

18. See note on Mark 1.1.

19. Simon from the Greek Σίμων (Simon), from the Hebrew שִׁמְעוֹן (shimon).

20. Andrew from the Greek Ἀνδρέας (Andreas). Andreas, like Markos and Lukas, are Greek names used by Jews in Israel.

21. James (Jacob) from the Greek Ἰάκωβος (Iakobos), from the Hebrew יַעֲקֹב (yaakov). When referring to New Testament followers of Yeshua, *Iakobos* is given a Greek ending; when the same Hebrew name refers to the Old Testament patriarch Jacob, it is undeclined in the Greek as Ἰακώβ (Iakob), thereby distinguishing Old Testament from New Testament personages. "James" is an English name derived freely from the Greek, which does not suggest "Jacob." In French it is *Jacques*, in Spanish *Jaime*, *Diego*, or *Santiago* (St. James). In German and other languages, *Iakobos* is usually rendered in a way to suggest "Jacob," thereby referring it back to the Hebrew Bible name.

22. Zebedee from the Greek Ζεβεδαῖος (Zebedaios), from the Hebrew זַבְדִּי (zavdai).

23. Capernaum. Latin *Capernaum* from the Greek Καφαρναούμ (Kafarnaoum), from the Hebrew כְּפַר נָחוּם (kfar nahum), meaning "village of Nahum."

24. Sabbath from the Greek σάββατον (sabbaton), from the Hebrew שַׁבָּת (shabbat).

25. From the Greek γραμματεύς (grammateus), traditionally translated as "scribe" but in more recent translations rendered as "scholar."

synagogue there was a man with an unclean spirit and he screamed, 24"What are you to us, Yeshua the Natzrati?[26] Did you come to destroy us? I know who you are. God's holy one!"

25Yeshua rebuked him, saying,

Be silent and come out of him!

26And convulsing him and crying out in a great voice, the unclean spirit came out of him.

27Everyone was so amazed they started to ask each other, "What is this? A new teaching? What authority does he possess?" And he commanded the unclean spirits and they obeyed him. 28Word of him at once went out everywhere through all the surrounding countryside of the Galil.

Healing at Shimon's house

29As soon as they left the synagogue they went into the house of Shimon and Andreas with Yaakov and Yohanan. 30Shimon's mother-in-law was lying in bed with a fever and right away they told Yeshua about her.

31He came to her, and holding her hand he raised her.

The fever left her and she served them.

32When dusk came and the sun set, they brought him all the sick and those possessed by demons.[27] 33And the whole city gathered together at the door. 34He cured many who were sick with various diseases and expelled many demons, and would not let them speak, because they knew him.

In a desolate place

35Early in the morning while it was still like night, he got up and went to a desolate place, and there he prayed. 36Shimon and those with him

---

26. Nazarene from the Greek Ναζαρηνός (Nazarenos), from Natzeret, that is, a Natzrati.

27. From the Greek δαιμονιζομένους (daimonizomenous), meaning "possessed by demons" or "demonized." The KJV translates "demons" as "devils," suggesting hell's evil and Satan. The ancient Greek word *demon*, as dark and evil as it is, carries no Jewish or later Christian reference to the devil. Contemporary translations render "demon."

searched for him, 37found him, and said to him, "Everyone is looking for you."

38He said to them,

> Let us go elsewhere into the neighboring towns
> So I may preach there also. For this I came.

39And he went all over the Galil, preaching in the synagogues, and cast out demons.

With a leper

40A leper came to him begging on his knees,[28] and said to him, "If you wish to, you can make me clean."

41And filled with pity, he stretched out his hand and touched him and said,

> I wish to. Now be clean.

42At once the leprosy went from him, and he was made clean. 43Then warning him sternly, he sent him away at once. 44And he said to him,

> See that you say nothing to anyone,
> But go and show yourself to a priest and offer
> For your cleansing what Moshe[29] commanded
> As a testimony to others.

45But the man went out and began to proclaim many things and to spread the word, so that Yeshua could no longer go into a city openly, and kept to desolate places.

And they came to him from everywhere.

---

28. "On his knees" or "kneeling" is omitted in more recent Greek texts.

29. Moses from the Greek Μωϋσῆς (Moyses), from the Hebrew מֹשֶׁה (moshe).

Chapter 2

A paralytic

After a few days Yeshua went back to Kfar Nahum[30] and it was heard that he was in a house. 2And many gathered so there was no room, not even at the door, and he spoke the word to them. 3They came, bringing him a paralytic carried by four men. 4But when because of the crowd they could not reach him, they uncovered the roof above Yeshua, and when they had made an opening in it they lowered the bed on which the paralytic lay.

5When Yeshua saw their faith, he said to the paralyzed man,

My child, your wrongs are forgiven.

6But there were some scholars sitting there, debating these things in their hearts. 7"Why is he speaking like this? He blasphemes. Who can forgive sins but God alone?"

8Yeshua immediately knew in his soul what they were saying to each other, and he told them,

Why do you argue these things in your heart?
9What is easier to say to the paralytic,
"Your wrongs are forgiven" or to say,
"Stand, pick up your bed, and walk"?
10But so you know that the earthly son[31]
Has the powers to forgive wrongs on earth,

he said to the paralytic,

11I tell you, "Stand up, pick up your bed,
And go to your house."

---

30. Capernaum.

31. "Son of Man" or "son of man" is the usual translation from the Greek ὁ υἱὸς τοῦ ἀνθρώπου (ho huios tou anthropou), which literally means "son of a person" or "son of people." The Greek ἀνθρώπου is not "man" but without gender, like "person." In the Hebrew Bible, "son of people" was an idiomatic way of saying "human being." In the gospels it may also suggest the son on earth as opposed to the son in heaven. Hence, "earthly son," rather than "son of man," "son of people," or "human being," may work better poetically and theologically.

12And he stood up, and immediately took his bed and went outside in front of everyone so that all were astonished and glorified God, saying, "We have never seen anything like this!"

Calling on Levi the tax collector

13Yeshua went out again by the sea, and the whole crowd came to him and he taught them. 14And passing by he saw Levi[32] the son of Halfai[33] sitting in the tax office, and he said to him,

>Follow me.

And he stood up and followed him.

15As he sat in Levi's house, many tax collectors and sinners lay back with Yeshua and his students.[34] There were many who followed him.

16When the Prushim scholars[35] saw that he was eating with sinners

---

32. Levi from the Greek Λευί (Levi), from the Hebrew לֵוִי (levi), the tax collector in scripture, is usually identified as Matthew, which later, probably in the second century, became the evangelist's apostolic name: מַתִּתְיָהוּ (mattityahu).

33. Alphaeus from the Greek Ἀλφαῖος (Halfaios), from the Hebrew חַלְפִּי (halfi).

34. "Lay back" suggests lying or leaning back on a couch, which was the customary way of sitting in a house, alone or at a table, whether for talk or eating. "Student" is from the Greek μαθητής (mathetes), meaning "student" or "pupil." In Latin, "student" is discipulus, from which "disciple" comes. Through usage the more formal "disciple" has become a standard translation of the New Testament Greek mathetes. Here "student" or "disciple" is used, depending on context.

35. Pharisees from the Greek Φαρισαῖος (Farisaios), from the Hebrew פְּרוּשִׁים (prushim). "Pharisee" (s.) is Parush. Historically, Pharisees, like Yeshua and Paul, reflect an open, oral interpretation of law, messiahship, and afterlife. In this first mention in the gospels of the Pharisees, the group is here and elsewhere depicted as a body of religious hypocrites and legalists who are enemies of Yeshua, plotting his downfall and death. The reader is instructed to hate the Pharisees, who embody the soul of the Jews. Many modern scholars view the historical Yeshua as a rabbi of the Pharisees, placing him, therefore, with those who strongly opposed Roman occupation of Israel. The Pharisees embodied central ideas of Paul and the evangelists: the immortality of the soul and resurrections. (See Geza Vermes, The Resurrection, New York: Doubleday, 2008). In matters of Jewish law the Pharisees favored a personal creed, outside temple and priesthood, not a legalistic but a pragmatic tradition in which the good corresponded to circumstance and need. As such they were more sympathetic than any Jewish sect to the relaxation of the laws of diet, circumcision, and Sabbath, which in Paul was to open his Judaism to Greeks and

and tax collectors, they said to his students, "Does he eat with sinners and tax collectors?"

17When Yeshua heard, he said to them,

> The strong ones have no need of a doctor,
> But the sick do.
> I came not to call on the just but on the wrongdoers.

Fasting

18Then Yohanan's students and the Prushim were fasting, and people came to him and said, "Why are the students of Yohanan and the students of the Prushim fasting, but your students do not fast?"

19And Yeshua said to them,

> Can the attendants of the bridegroom fast
> While the bridegroom is with them?
> As long as they have the bridegroom with them,
> They cannot fast. 20But days will come
> When the bridegroom is taken away from them.
> Then on that day they will fast.
> 21No one sews an unshrunk patch of cloth
> On an old garment
> Since the new pulls the patch away from the old
> And the tear becomes worse.
> 22No one pours new wine in old skins,
> Since the wine splits the skins
> And both wine and skins are lost.
> No, put new wine in new skins.

Hunger on Shabbat[36]

23It happened on Shabbat that he was walking through the grain fields, and as his students made their way they were plucking ears of wheat.

24The Prushim said to him, "Look, why are you doing what is forbidden on Shabbat?"

---

other pagans. Pharisees were also a principal opponent of Rome and the *Herodians*, who supported Rome, as suggested in Mark 3.6.

36. Sabbath.

25He said to them,

> Have you never read what David did when he had need
> And hungered
> He and those with him?

26How in the days of the high priest Evyatar[37]

> He went into the house of God and ate the loaves
> Of consecrated bread,
> Which only priests are allowed to eat,
> And gave it also to those with him?

27And he said to them,

> Shabbat was made for a man and woman,
> Not a man and woman for Shabbat.

28So the earthly son is rabbi even of Shabbat.

Chapter 3

Man with a shriveled hand

Once again he entered the synagogue and there was a man who had a shriveled hand. 2They were watching him to see if he would heal on Shabbat so they might accuse him.

3He said to the man with the shriveled hand,

> Stand here in the middle.

4And he said to them,

> Is it right on Shabbat to do good or do harm,
> To save life or to destroy?

But they were silent.

5He looked around at them with anger, and grieved at the hardness of their heart. He said to the man,

> Stretch out your hand.

He stretched it out and his hand was restored.

6Then the Prushim left and at once began to plot against him with the Herodians as to how to destroy him.

---

37. Evyatar from the Greek Ἀβιαθάρ (Abiathar), from the Hebrew אֶבְיָתָר (evyatar).

At the sea and on the mountain with his twelve students

7Then Yeshua with his students withdrew to the sea. 8On hearing what he did, a great multitude from the Galil followed him, and they came also from Yehuda and from Yerushalayim and from Edom[38] and from beyond the Yarden and the region around Tzor[39] and Tzidon.[40] 9And he told his students to have a boat[41] ready for him, because of the crowd, so they would not crush him. 10He had healed many, and those who were in torment pushed forward that he might touch them. 11When the unclean spirits saw him they fell down before him and cried out, saying, "You are the son of God!"

12He warned them forcefully not to make him known.

13Then he went up on the mountain and called to those whom he wanted, and they came to him. 14He appointed twelve, whom he named messengers,[42] to be with him so he might send them out to preach 15and have the right to cast out demons.[43] 16He gave Shimon[44] the name

---

38. Edom. Idumaea in its Latin version from the Greek Ἰδουμαία (Idoumaia), from the Hebrew אֱדוֹם (edom). Here it refers to an area south of Yehuda.

39. Tyre from the Greek Τύρος (Tyros), from Hebrew צוֹר or צֹר (tzor), meaning "hard quartz" or "a flint knife," from the Aramaic טוּר (tur), meaning "a rock."

40. Sidon from the Greek Σιδών (Sidon), from the Hebrew צִידוֹן (tzidon).

41. From the Greek πλοιάριον (ploiarion), "a small ship" or "boat." "Boat" is often favored, since "ship" implies a larger vessel as in πλοῖον (ploion), which, depending on context, as in Mark 4.1, where the vessel is obviously a small one, may also be translated as "boat."

42. "Whom he named messengers" is omitted in many Greek texts. "Messenger" or "envoy" rather than "apostle" is the common meaning of *apostolos*. *Apostolos* (in most translations "apostle") means "one from Yeshua's inner circle who is sent out on a mission." Another classical Greek word for "messenger" is ἄγγελος (angelos), whose New Testament meaning is "angel" or "God's messenger." So there is an earthly messenger, ἀπόστολος, and a heavenly messenger, ἄγγελος. "Angel" has its lexical source in the earlier Septuagint Bible (the second-century B.C.E. Hebrew Bible in Greek translation for Jews of Alexandria). New Testament Greek words that differ in meaning from their classical Greek source, by having acquired a religious and ethical dimension, usually are taken from the Septuagint.

43. In other texts the phrase "he appointed the twelve" is repeated.

44. Simon.

Kefa.[45] [17]And Yaakov[46] son of Zavdai and Yohanan brother of Yaakov he named Benei Regesh,[47] which means "Sons of Thunder." [18]And Andreas and Filippos[48] and Bartalmai[49] and Mattai and Toma[50] and Yaakov son of Halfai and Taddai and Shimon the Cananean,[51] [19]Yehuda of Keriot,[52] who betrayed him.

If a house is divided

[20]He came into a house, and the crowd gathered again so they could not even eat their bread. [21]On hearing this, his family went out to restrain him, for they said, "He has lost his mind."[53] [22]And the scholars who came

---

45. Peter. The name *Petros* from the Greek Πέτρος means "rock" or "stone" and is a translation of the Aramaic כֵּיפָא (kefa), also meaning "rock" or "stone." However, in John 1.42 and in three letters of Paul, Peter is called by his Aramaic name Kefa, which has been transliterated into the Greek and given a Greek ending to make it Κηφᾶς (Kefas), which is then romanized into English to read as Cephas. *Shimon Kefa* would be a fully Aramaic/Hebrew equivalent to the English "Simon Peter." Peter's Semitic name *Kefa* is far removed from English, being a translation and not a transliteration, and hence cannot, without a glossary, be recognized as "Peter" by the English reader, unlike *Yosef*, which is readily seen to be "Joseph."

46. James from the Greek Ἰάκωβος (Iakobos), from the Hebrew יַעֲקֹב (yaakov).

47. Boanerges from the Greek Βοανηργές, from the Hebrew בְּנֵי רֶגֶשׁ (benei regesh), meaning "sons of anger" or "thunder."

48. Philip from the Greek Φίλιππος (Filippos).

49. Bartholomew from the Greek Βαρθολομαῖος (Bartholomaios), from the Hebrew בַּר תַּלְמַי (bar talmai). "Bartalmai" means "son of Talmai." Talmai may be Ptolemy, an Egyptian king.

50. Thomas from the Greek Θωμᾶς (Thomas), from the Hebrew תְּאוֹם (teom). Thomas elsewhere in the gospels is called Θωμᾶς Δίδυμος (Thomas Didumos), meaning "Thomas the Twin."

51. In Matthew 10.4 in the list of the twelve messengers or apostles it is "Shimon the Zealot."

52. Iscariot from the Greek Ἰσκαριώθ (Iskarioth), from the Hebrew אִישׁ קְרִיּוֹת (ish keriot), meaning "man of Keriot." In English, "Keriot" is also transcribed "Kerioth." Keriot is a village or town some twenty miles south of Jerusalem. Yehuda of Keriot, or more fully, Yehuda ben Shimon ish Keriot, Yehuda son of Shimon, man of Keriot, John 6.71, is normally Anglicized as "Judas son of Simon Iscariot."

53. The family of Yeshua and especially his mother Mary are portrayed negatively

down from Yerushalayim said, "He has Baal Zebul⁵⁴ in him, and it was
through the prince of the demons that he drove out demons."

₂₃Gathering them together, he spoke to them in parables,
> How can Satan cast out Satan?
> ₂₄If a kingdom is divided against itself

---

through the Gospel of Mark, in contrast to Luke's positive portrayal. Here the family
accepts the crowd's view that Yeshua "has lost his mind" and may be demonized, and
seizes him to restrain him. Yeshua resentfully rejects his family for their lack of faith in
his powers, stating that his true mother and brothers are those out in the fields (Mark
3.33–35) and that a prophet is without honor in his own house and in his own family
(Mark 6.4).

54. Beelzebul is a pejorative name for the Philistine deity Baal. Beelzebul is usually translated as "Lord of the Flies," implying "Satan," but its etymological meaning suggests "Lord of Filth," whereas Beelzebub, the original word, is "Lord of the
Flies." Beelzebul is from the Greek Βεελζεβούλ (Beelzeboul), from the Hebrew
בַּעַל זְבוּל (Baal Zebul), and seems to be a corruption of בַּעַל זְבוּב (Baal Zebub)
(2 Kings 1.2, 1.16). As the word "Beelzebub" moved from Hebrew through Greek to
English, it became "Beelzebul." The philology of its usage and meaning is at best
confusing and arbitrary. Whatever their metaphoric image, Lord of Flies and Lord
of Dung, "Baal" implicitly means a Satanic undefined evil.

The unchanging root "Baal" is a Semitic word meaning "lord" or "owner." Baal was
the Canaanite storm and fertility god. In his pantheon, Baal's progenitor and head
god was El or Eli, but Baal was the most significant god in the Hebrew Bible after
Yahweh. He was a thunderstorm deity just like Yahweh as in "rider of clouds" (Ps.
18.10), a title going back to Ugaritic epics where Baal was the "rider of clouds." His
symbolic representation was the bull. In early Judaism Baal was a threat, competing for Moses's loyalty, even while he was slowly crossing the desert from Egypt back
to an Israel he could see from a mountain but not enter. In the Solomonic period
the Jews were acutely apprehensive of the religion and theology of their immediate neighbors, as in the figure of the Philistine deity Beelzebul worshiped at Ekron,
just to the west of Jerusalem (2 Kings 1.2–18). That close was the wind of apostasy
in Baal, whose very name, like that of his father *El* or *Eli*, is the source of the sundry names of God, from *Elohim* ("God" or "Gods"), the third word of the first line of
Genesis, to the last words of Jesus on the cross, as in Matthew 27.45: "*Eli, Eli, lama
sabachthani?*"—"God, God, why have you abandoned me?"

By the time Beelzebul reached John Milton, erudite in Hebrew, the epic poet
portrayed the earlier Beelzebub in *Paradise Lost* as a fallen angel second in station
only to Lucifer, whereas in John Bunyan's *Pilgrim's Progress*, the self-inventing Beelzebub prowls as a nasty character on the road, shooting arrows everywhere.

That kingdom cannot stand.
25If a house is divided against itself
  That house cannot stand.
26And if Satan rises against himself and is divided
  He cannot stand but comes to an end.
27No one can enter the house of the strong man
  To plunder his possessions
  Unless he first ties up the strong man,
  And then he will plunder his house.

28Truly I tell you,

  The children of man and woman will be forgiven
  For everything, their wrongs and blasphemies
  As much as they blaspheme.
29But whoever blasphemes against the holy spirit
  Will be unforgiven everlastingly
  And be guilty of everlasting wrong,
30For they had said "his spirit is unclean."

Yeshua rejects his mother and brothers
  31Then his mother came and his brothers, and standing outside they
sent someone in to call him. 32A crowd sat round him and said to him,
"Look, your mother and your brothers55 are outside looking for you."56
  33He answered them, saying,
    Who is my mother and who are my brothers?
34And looking at those sitting around him in a circle, he said,
    Here are my mother and my brothers!
  35Whoever does the will of God,
    That one is my brother and sister and mother.57

---

55. Other texts add "and your sisters."

56. The reference to Yeshua's brothers indicates Mark's ignorance of the later doctrine of Mary's perpetual virginity. The brothers are mentioned later as James, Joseph,
Judas, and Simon.

57. In Mark and the other gospels there is a thread of resentment against his mother

Chapter 4

Sower parable

Again he began to teach beside the sea, and a great crowd was gathered near him so he got into a boat and sat on the sea, and all the crowd near the lake was on the land. 2He taught them much in parables, and told them in his teaching, 3listen,

> Look, the sower went out to sow
> 4And it happened that as he sowed
> Some seed fell on the road
> And birds came and ate it.
> 5Another fell on stony ground
> Where there was little soil,
> And at once it sprang up
> Because it had no deep soil.
> 6And when the sun rose
> It was burnt, and because
> It had no roots it dried away.
> 7Another fell among the thorns
> And the thorns came up
> And choked the sprouts
> And it bore no fruit.
> 8But some fell into good soil
> And it bore fruit, shooting up
> And increasing and it bore
> Thirty and sixty and one hundredfold.

9And he said,

> Who has ears to hear, hear.

Secret of the kingdom

10When he was alone, those who were around him along with the twelve asked him about the parables. 11He said to them,

---

and brothers (and sisters) who are always elsewhere, outside when he is inside, inside when he is preaching in the meadows. See note 53 on Mark 3.21.

You have been given the mystery of the kingdom of God.
For those outside, everything comes in parables
12So that as Yeshayahu said,

> "Looking they might look and not see,
> Hearing they might hear and not understand,
> Lest they might turn and be forgiven."[58]

13And he said to them,

> Do you not know this parable
> And how will you know all the parables?
> 14The sower sows the word.
> 15And these are the ones by the road
> Where the word is sown.
> When they hear it, at once Satan comes
> And takes the word sown in them.
> 16These are ones sown on stony ground,
> And when they hear the word
> At once they receive it happily
> 17And have no root in themselves
> But are people of the moment.
> When trouble or persecution comes
> Because of the word's sake,
> At once they are shaky and fall.
> 18Others are those sown among thorns.
> These are ones who heard the word,
> 19But worldly cares and lure of wealth
> And desires for other things come in
> And choke the word and it turns barren.
> 20And there are ones sown on good earth,
> Who hear the word, receive it, and bear fruit
> Thirty and sixty and one hundredfold.

Lamp on a stand
21Then he said to them,

> Is a lamp brought inside to be placed

---

58. Isa. 8.16.

Under a basket or under a couch
Rather than set on a lampstand?
22So nothing is hidden except to be disclosed
Or secret except to come into the open.
23If someone has ears to hear, hear.

Measure
24He was saying to them,
Consider what you hear. The measure
By which you measure will measure you,
And more will be added for you.
25Whoever has, more will be given,
And whoever has nothing, even that nothing
Which he has will be taken from him.

Seed on the earth
26And he was saying,
The kingdom of God is as if a man threw seed on the earth,
27And would sleep and rise night and day
And the seed sprouts and grows big
In a way he does not perceive.
28On its own the earth bears fruit,
First grass then a stalk then the full grain in the ear.
29But when the grain is ripe, immediately
He takes out his sickle. The harvest has come.

The mustard seed and the kingdom of God
30And he said,
To what can we compare the kingdom of God
Or in what parable shall we place it?
31Like a mustard seed which is sown on the earth,
Smaller than all the seeds on the earth,
32Yet when it is sown it grows and becomes greater
Than all garden plants,
And makes branches so big that under its shade
The birds of the sky
May find there a place to nest in its shade.

33With many such parables he spoke the word to them insofar as they could understand, as far as they were able to hear. 34He spoke to them only in parable, but to his own students privately he explained all.

Calming the storm and the sea

35And on that day, as dusk took over, he said to them,

> Let us cross over to the other side.

36And leaving the crowd behind, they took him with them into the small ship, just as he was. Other vessels were with him. 37There arose a furious wind storm and the waves were crashing against the boat so that it was beginning to fill. 38He was in the stern, sleeping on a pillow.

They woke him and said to him, "Rabbi, don't you care that we are perishing?"

39He got up and scolded the wind and spoke to the sea,

> Silence, be still.

The wind died down and there was a dead calm.

40And he said to them,

> Why are you cowards? Have you still no faith?

41And they feared with great dread and said to one another, "Who is this that even the wind and the sea obey him?"

Chapter 5

Demoniac and the pigs

They came to the other side of the lake to the region of the Gerasenes.[59] 2When Yeshua stepped out of the ship, at once a man with an unclean spirit came out of the tombs and met him. 3He lived in the tombs, and not even a chain could hold him back. 4He had often been bound with shackles and chains and he tore the chains apart and smashed the shackles. No one was strong enough to subdue him. 5Night and day in the tombs and in the mountains, constantly he was screaming and

---

59. In the KJV, "Gerasenes" is rendered as "Gadarenes." The capital of the Gadarenes, Gadara, is a sizable Greco-Roman city in what is now Jordan.

smashing himself with stones. 6Seeing Yeshua from a distance, he ran and fell to his knees before him 7and screaming in a great voice, he said, "What am I to you, Yeshua son of the highest God? I beg you, don't torment me."

8Yeshua was saying to him,

> Foul[60] spirit, come out of this man!

9He asked him,

> What is your name?

The man said to him, "My name is Legion, for we are many." 10And he implored him again and again not to send them out of the country.

11Now near the mountain was a big herd of pigs feeding. 12The demons begged Yeshua, "Send us to the pigs so we can go into them."

13And he consented.

The foul spirits came out and went into the pigs. And the herd rushed down the steep slope into the sea, about two thousand, and they drowned in the sea.

14Those feeding the pigs fled and reported it in the city and on the farms. And people came to see what happened. 15They came to Yeshua and saw the man who had been possessed by the legion of demons, seated, dressed, and of sound mind. And they were afraid. 16Those who saw what happened to the demoniac and the pigs reported it. 17And they began to plead with Yeshua to leave their district.

18As he was boarding the ship, the demoniac begged Yeshua to take him with him.

19He would not take him, but he said to him,

> Go to your house and to those who are yours
> And say how much Adonai has done for you
> And how much he has pitied you.

20And the man left and spread word in Dekapolis[61] of how much Yeshua did for him.

Everyone wondered.

---

60. Foul from the Greek ἀκάθαρτον (akatharton). Literally, "unclean."
61. Dekapolis from the Greek Δεκάπολις, translated as "Ten Towns."

Girl near death and a woman bleeding

21When Yeshua crossed over again in the ship to the other side, a big crowd gathered around him beside the lake. 22One of the synagogue leaders named Yair[62] came, and seeing him, fell to his knees 23and begged him intensely, saying, "My daughter is at the point of death. Come and put your hand on her so she may be healed and live."

He went with him. 24And a great crowd went with him and pressed against him. 25There was a woman who for twelve years had a flow of blood. 26She suffered much under many doctors, and spent all she had but she was no better. Rather she got worse. 27She had heard about Yeshua, and coming up behind him in the crowd she touched his garment. 28She was saying, "If I can even touch his garments, I will be healed."

29At once the source of her blood dried up and she knew in her body that she had been healed of her terrible disease.

30Immediately aware in himself that power had gone out from him, Yeshua turned around in the crowd and said,

Who touched my clothing?

31His students said to him, "You see the crowd pressing against you, and you say, 'Who touched me?'"

32He looked around to see who had done it.

33Then the woman—in fear and trembling, knowing what had happened to her—came and fell before him and told him the whole truth.

34He said to her,

Daughter, your faith has healed you.

Go in peace and be cured of your affliction.

35While he was speaking, some people came from the house of the leader of the synagogue. "Your daughter died," they said. "Why are you still bothering the rabbi?"

36But overhearing what they said, Yeshua said to the leader of the synagogue,

Do not fear. Only believe.

---

62. Jairus from the Greek Ἰάϊρος (Iairos), from the Hebrew יָאִיר (yair).

37And he let no one follow him except Shimon Kefa[63] and Yaakov and Yohanan, brother of Yaakov.[64]

38They came to the house of the leader of the synagogue and saw a commotion and people weeping and wailing loudly. 39On going inside, he said to them,

Why this commotion and weeping?
The child didn't die. No, she is sleeping.

40But they laughed at him.

Then he put everyone outside, and took the child's father, mother, and those with him, and went inside where the child was. 41He took the child's hand and said to her,

Talitha koum,[65]

which translated from Aramaic means, "Little girl, I say to you, Awake!"

42And at once the girl got up and walked around. She was twelve years old.

They were amazed and in great ecstasy.

43He gave them repeated orders that no one should know this and said to give her something to eat.

Chapter 6

Rejected in his town and by his family

Yeshua left that place and went to his home town,[66] and his students followed him. 2When Shabbat came, he began to teach in the synagogue

---

63. Simon Peter.

64. James and John, brother of James.

65. An Aramaic expression. Aramaic was the lingua franca of the region from Canaan to Phoenicia and was the language Yeshua would have commonly spoken. Hebrew by his time was the language of the book and the synagogue.

66. From the Greek πατρίς, ίδος (patris, idos), meaning "hometown," "native land," "fatherland," or "country." Since Nazareth was surely a small village yet is referred to as a *polis* (πόλις), a "city," it is difficult to find one word that fairly represents *patrida* (πατρίδα, accusative).

and many who heard him were amazed, saying, "Where did he learn all these things, and what is this wisdom given to him, and how is it that such powers[67] have come into his hands? 3Isn't he the carpenter, the son of Miryam[68] and brother of Yaakov and Yosef[69] and Yehuda and Shimon? And are his sisters not here with us?"

They were offended by him.

4Yeshua said to them,

> A prophet is not without honor except in his own country,
> In his own family, and in his own house.

5He could not perform his powers except on a few sick people, laying hands on them, and healing them. 6He was astonished by their disbelief.

Shake the dust off from under your feet

7Then he went around the villages, teaching. And he called the twelve and began to send them out two by two, and he gave them authority over unclean spirits, 8and ordered them to take nothing on the road except a staff, but no bread, bag, no copper coins in their belts. 9To wear sandals and not to wear two tunics. 10He told them,

---

67. From the Greek δύναμις (dynamis). From *dynamis*, "power" or "strength," as in dynamism. *Dynameis* is translated as "miracles" in New International Version, New American Standard Bible, and Annotated Scholars. In New Revised Standard Version, it is "deeds of power." Lattimore gives "powers," Reynolds Price "acts of power." In Tyndale, we have "virtues," in KJV "mighty works," in the New American Bible "mighty deeds." Although New Testament lexicons accommodate "explanatory" ecclesiastical meanings, in the standard Liddell and Scott's *Greek-English Lexicon*, "miracle" is not given as a meaning for the Greek δύναμις (dynamis). The miracle is essential to the figure of the messiah, who with transcendental powers operates in disregard to laws of nature. In other instances I have used "miraculous powers" to suggest the clear intention of miracle, but Tyndale, KJV, and most modern translations of this crucial word have resisted endowing their versions with the heresy of explanation and give us only what the Greek states.

68. Mary from the Greek Μαρία (Maria), from the Hebrew מִרְיָם (miryam), often Anglicized in English as Miriam.

69. Joseph from the Greek Ἰωσήφ (Iosef), from the Hebrew יוֹסֵף (yosef).

Wherever you go into a house,
Stay there until you leave there.
11And when a place will not receive or hear you,
As you leave there, shake the dust off from under your feet
As a testimony against them.[70]

12They went out and preached the message of repentance. 13They cast out many demons, rubbed olive oil[71] on many who were sick, and healed them.

Herod and Yohanan's head

14At that time King Herod[72] heard about Yeshua, for his name had become well known, and people were saying that "Yohanan the Dipper had been raised from the dead which is why those powers are at work through him." 15But others were saying, "It is Eliyahu";[73] and others said, "It is a prophet." 16But when Herod heard, he said, "It is Yohanan whom I beheaded. He has been raised."

---

70. The KJV continues Mark 6.11: "Verily I say unto you, it shall be more tolerable for Sodom and Gomorrah [Sedom and Amorah] in the day of judgment, than for that city." The vindictive response of "shake the dust off from under your feet as a testimony against them" becomes more specifically destruction and intolerable punishment if the apostles' ministry is refused. The Greek text is disputed and not translated in modern versions other than the Amplified Bible (1958), which puts it in italics. The older Rheims Bible (1588) also omits this passage.

71. "Rubbing olive oil" has the religious meaning of "anointing," from the Greek ἀλείφω (aleifo), from the Hebrew מָשִׁיחַ (mashiah), "the anointed one," giving us the word "messiah." Another Greek word, also for anointing, gives us the word "Christ": χρίω (chrio or hrio), from which comes Χριστος (Christos or Hristos). In Greece and the Near East the people anointed with oil (usually olive oil) and spice (often myrrh). Olive oil was used as a medicine to rub on as a balm and also for athletes.

72. The Greek title for Herod Antipas, son of Herod the Great, who was tetrarch of Galilee. Mark calls him "King."

73. Elijah or Elias from the Greek Ἠλίας (Elias), from the Hebrew אֵלִיָּהוּ (eliyahu).

17Herod himself had sent to have Yohanan arrested and bound in prison because of Herodias, the wife of his brother Filippos. Herod had married her. 18Yohanan told Herod, "It is not lawful for you to take the wife of your brother." 19So Herodias bore a grudge against him and wanted to kill him, but she was unable to. 20Herod feared Yohanan, knowing that he was a just and holy man, and he protected him. When he heard him, he was greatly disturbed, yet gladly he listened to him.

21Then came an opportune day when Herod on his birthday had a banquet for the great courtiers and military commanders and foremost people of the Galil. 22When his daughter Herodias came in and danced, she delighted Herod and those reclining at the table. And the king said to the girl, "Ask me whatever you want and I will give it to you." 23He swore to her, "Whatever you ask of me, I will give you up to half my kingdom."

24She went out and said to her mother, "What must I ask?"

And she said, "The head of Yohanan the Dipper."

25At once she rushed back eagerly to the king and made her request: "I want you to give me right now on a platter the head of Yohanan the Dipper."

26The king was despondent because of his oaths and those reclining at the table and he didn't wish to refuse her. 27At once the king sent an executioner and commanded him to bring the head of Yohanan.

The guard left and beheaded him in the prison, 28and brought his head in on a platter, and the girl gave it to her mother. 29Hearing about this, his students came and took his corpse and placed it in a tomb.74

---

74. The story of Herod the Great's son Herod Antipas and his daughter Salome (not Herodias, as in Mark and Matthew) is the legendary subject of gospel, play, and opera. However, the historian Josephus tells us that John was imprisoned and executed by Herod, not in his palace but in his grim fortress of Machaeros, and identifies Herod's daughter as Salome and her mother as Herodias. In this incident, as told in Mark and Matthew, the villain is the wife, and her daughter is obeying her mother's orders. Herod, like Pontius Pilate, respects and admires the prisoner but is unhappily fulfilling a trick promise. In both incidents, the rulers, Herod and Pilate, strong repressive figures loyal to the Romans, are exonerated from the unpleasant act of executing major Christian heroes, which thereby reduces Rome's responsibility for wrongdoing in the drama of emerging Christianity.

Bread for the five thousand on the green grass

30The messengers[75] rejoined Yeshua and reported to him everything they had done and taught. 31He said to them,

> Come yourselves alone to a deserted place
> And rest a while.

For many of them were coming and going and they had no chance even to eat. 32And they went off in a ship to a deserted place by themselves.

33Now many saw them going and had heard of them, and from all the towns they ran there on foot and got there ahead of them.

34On coming ashore, Yeshua saw a great crowd and he pitied them, for they were like sheep without a shepherd, and he began to teach them many things.

35When it was already late the students came to him, saying, "This is a deserted place and it is already late. 36Send them off so they can go into the surrounding farms and villages and buy themselves something to eat."

37But he answered, saying to them,

> You give them something to eat.

They said to him, "Shall we go and buy two hundred denarii[76] worth of loaves and give them that to eat?"

38And he said to them,

> How many loaves do you have?
> Go and see.

When they found out, they said, "Five, and two fish."

39He told them all to sit down in groups on the green grass. 40They sat down in groups of hundreds and fifties.

41He took the five loaves of bread and the two fish, and looking up into the sky he blessed and broke the loaves and gave them to his students to set before the people, and the two fish he divided among them all. 42Everyone ate and they were filled. 43And they picked up twelve full

---

75. See note 42 on Mark 3.14.

76. "Denarii" is a plural of "denarius," a silver Roman coin worth about the day's wages of a laborer.

baskets of crumbs and fish. 44Those who had eaten were five thousand men.[77]

Walking on the sea

45Immediately Yeshua had his students climb into the ship and go ahead to the other side, to Beit Tzaida,[78] while he dismissed the crowd. 46And after saying goodbye to them he went off to the mountain to pray.

47When dusk came the ship was in the middle of the sea and he was alone on the land. 48Seeing the students straining at the oars—the wind was against them—about the fourth watch of the night[79] he came toward them, walking on the sea, and he wanted to pass by them. 49But seeing him walking on the sea they thought he was a phantom, and they cried out. 50They all saw him and they were terrified.

At once he spoke with them and said,

> Take courage. It is I. Don't be afraid.

51Then he climbed into the boat and the wind fell, and deep in themselves they were astonished. 52They had not understood about the loaves and their hearts hardened.

The sick on stretchers at Gennesaret

53When they crossed over to the land, they came to Gennesaret[80] and anchored. 54They got out of the ship, and people immediately recognized him 55and rushed about over the countryside and began to bring the sick on litters to wherever they heard he was. 56Wherever he went, into villages or cities or farms and in the marketplaces, they laid out the sick

---

77. Here the word is specifically "men" rather than "people," from the Greek ἀνήρ (aner), ἀνδρός (andros). Another word for "man" is ἄνθρωπος (anthropos), which may mean "man" or also "a genderless person." It is possible, though unlikely, that the multitude consisted entirely or largely of men. Probably the text followed the habit in most languages of men meaning "people" (male and female).

78. Bethseda from the Greek Βηθσαϊδά (Bethsaida), from the Hebrew בֵּית צָיְדָה (beit tzaida), which is a place north of the Sea of Galilee.

79. About three in the morning.

80. Village on the north side of the Sea of Galilee.

and begged that they might touch even the fringe of his garment. And those who touched him were healed.

Chapter 7

On ways of washing

The Prushim and some scholars who had come from Yerushalayim gathered around him. 2They saw that some of his students were eating bread with impure, that is, unwashed, hands. 3The Prushim and all the Jews will not eat unless they wash, hand against fist, so keeping the tradition of the elders, 4and eat nothing from the markets unless they wash. And they keep many other traditions about washing cups and pots and copper cauldrons. 5The Prushim and the scholars questioned him, "Why do your students not walk according to the tradition of our elders, but eat bread with impure hands?"

6Yeshua said to them,

> Yeshayahu prophesied rightly about you hypocrites,
> As it is written:
>> "This people honors me with their lips
>> But their hearts are far away from me.
>> 7They worship me in vain,
>> Teaching teachings that are commands of men."[81]
> 8You abandon God's commands, you hold to human ways.

9And he said to them,

> You fully reject the commandment of God
> So your own tradition of men can stand.

10Moshe said, "Honor your father and your mother"

And "Whoever reviles[82] a father or mother must die."

11Yet you say if a person tells his father or mother,

---

81. Isa. 29.13. Isaiah says that "these are rules taught by men," suggesting that the commandments do not come from God.

82. From the Greek κακολογέω (kakologeo), "to speak poorly" or "evilly" or "reviling." Literally, it is "badspeaking," which is close in spirit to "bad mouthing."

"What you might have got from me is Korban,[83]
Meaning an offering to God,
12Then you are free to do nothing for your father and mother,"
13And you erase the word of God
By the way you pass on your tradition.
And you do many such things!

Parable of food and defilement
14Then he called the crowd again, and said to them,
Hear me all of you and understand.
15There is nothing outside a person
Which by going in can defile,
But what comes out,
These are the things that defile a person.[84]
17When he entered a house from the crowd, the students asked him about the parable. 18He said to them,
Are you that mindless? Don't you understand,
Anything that goes into a person from the outside
Cannot defile
19Since it doesn't enter the heart but the stomach
And goes into the sewer, purging all foods.
20He said,
What goes out of a person defiles
21Since evil thoughts come out of the heart—
Copulations, thefts, murders, 22adulteries,
Greeds, wickednesses, deceit, lasciviousness,
Evil eye, blasphemy, pride, and folly.

---

83. Corban from the Greek κορβᾶν (corban), from the Hebrew קָרְבָּן (korban), meaning "an offering to God," as in Leviticus 1.2 and Numbers 7.13. Mark uses "corban" in a convoluted way to suggest that one can declare an offering to God and so avoid supporting one's parents. The notion appears to have no earlier meaning as Mark defines it, and the later Mishnah states that one can break vows of payment to the synagogue if one is without means of supporting one's parents.

84. There is no verse 16. In some ancient texts, there is appended the line, as in 4.9, "Who has ears to hear, hear."

23All these wicked things of the earth
  Come out from within and defile.

Greek girl with a demon

24Arising from there he went off to the region of Tzor. He entered into a house and wanted no one to know, but he could not remain hidden.

25For a woman, whose little daughter had an unclean spirit, immediately heard about him. She came and fell down at his feet. 26The woman was a Greek, by birth a Phoenician from Syria, and she asked him to expel the demon from her daughter.

27He said to her,
  Let the children first be fed,
  For it is not good to take the bread of the children
  And throw it to the dogs.
28But she answered and said to him,
"Sir, even the dogs under the table
Eat the children's crumbs."
Then he told her,
  29Because of this word, go.
  The demon has left your daughter.
30She left and went into her house, found the child lying on her bed, and the demon was gone.

Fingers and spittle for a deaf mute

31Once again on leaving the region of Tzor, he came through Tzidon to the Sea of the Galil and into the middle of the region of Dekopolis. 32They brought him a deaf mumbler who could barely speak, and they begged him to lay his hand on him. 33He took him away from the crowd where they were alone, put his fingers into the man's ears, spat, and touched his tongue. 34Then after looking up into the sky, he groaned and said to him, *Effatha!*,[85] which means "Be opened!"

35The man's ears were opened, the bond of his tongue loosened, and he spoke plainly.

----

85. From the Greek ἐφφαθά (effatha), which is derived from the Aramaic.

36Then Yeshua ordered them to tell no one, but the more he ordered, the more they spoke of it everywhere. 37People were overcome with wonder, saying, "He has done everything good, he makes the deaf hear and the dumb speak."

Chapter 8

Bread for the four thousand in the desert

In those days again there was a great crowd who had nothing to eat, and calling his students together he said to them,

2I have pity for the crowd,
 For they have already been with me three days
 And have nothing to eat.
3If I send them hungry to their homes,
 They will collapse on the road
 And some have come from far away.

4His students answered him, "Where will anyone find bread to feed them here in the desert?"

He asked them,

5How many loaves do you have?

"Seven," they said.

6Then he ordered the crowd to lie back on the ground. He took the seven loaves, and after giving thanks he broke them and gave them to his students to serve.

They served the crowd.

7They had a few small fish. After giving thanks for them he gave them to the students and ordered these to be served also.

8They ate and were filled. And there were seven basketfuls of leftover pieces. 9There were about four thousand people and he sent them off.

10At once he got into his ship with his students and came into the region of Dalmanutha.[86]

---

86. Matthew says he went to Gennesaret (Matt. 15.39). They may be different names for the same place or two places near each other. Variant readings are Magadan, Magedan, and Magdala, the latter suggesting it may be Magdala, as in Miryam of Magdala.

A sign from the sky

11Then the Prushim came out and began to argue with him, asking him for a sign from the sky. They were testing him.

12Groaning in his soul, he said to them,

> Why does this generation ask for a sign?
> Amain,[87] I say to you.
> No sign will be given to this generation.

Understanding bread

13He left them, and got into his ship again and left for the other side.

14They forgot to take bread, and except for one loaf they had nothing for themselves on the boat.

15Yeshua gave orders, saying,

> Look, and watch out for the Prushim's leaven
> And the leaven of Herod.

16They argued with one another about not having bread.

17Knowingly, he said to them,

> Why do you argue about not having bread?
> Do you still not see or understand?
> Has your heart hardened?
> 18You have eyes, do you not see?
> You have ears, do you not hear?
> Don't you remember 19when I broke the five loaves
> For the five thousand,
> How many baskets filled with scraps you picked up?

They said to him, "Twelve."

> 20When it was seven for the four thousand,
> How many baskets filled with scraps did you pick up?

They said to him, "Seven."

---

87. Amen from the Greek ἀμήν (amen), from the Hebrew אָמֵן (amein). The Hebrew word *amain* (*amein* would work just as well for free-sounding English) was used by Paul in his Greek, as it is used in Hebrew at the end of a passage as a liturgical "in truth" or "so be it." Both the Greek and Hebrew words were probably pronounced with a long ay, as in "main." It is appropriate to pronounce English "amen," as in Greek and Hebrew; hence here it is given as *amain*.

21And he said to them,

> Do you still not understand?

Saliva on a blindman's eyes

22They came to Beit Tzaida. Some people brought him a blindman and they begged him to touch him.

23He took the blindman's hand and took him outside the village and spat on his eyes, lay his hands on him, and asked him,

> Can you see?

24He looked up and said,

> I see people but they look like trees walking.

25Then Yeshua again put his hands on the blindman's eyes. The man looked hard, his eyes were restored, and saw all things clearly.

26Then he sent him to his house, saying,

> Don't go into the village.

Who do people say I am?

27Then Yeshua and his students went out to the villages of Caesarea Filippi.[88] On the way he questioned his students, saying to them,

> Who do people say I am?

28They answered, saying, "Yohanan the Dipper, and others say, Yeshayahu, but others one of the prophets."

29He asked them,

> But who do you say I am?

Shimon Kefa[89] said to him, "You are the mashiah."

30He warned them not to tell anyone about him.

I will die and be arisen

31He began to teach them that the earthly son[90] must suffer many things and be rejected by the elders and the high priests and the

---

88. Caesarea Philippi.
89. Simon Peter.
90. Son of Man.

scholars, and be killed and after three days rise. 32And he said the word openly.[91]

Shimon Kefa took him aside and began to warn him.

33But Yeshua turned and looked at his students and reproved Kefa, and said,

> Go behind me, Satan!
> Because you are thinking not the things of God
> But of earthly beings.[92]

Follow me

34Then calling the crowd together with his students, he said to them,

> If some of you would follow me,
> Deny yourself and take up your cross
> And follow me.

Losing life to find the soul

> 35Whoever of you would save your life
> Will lose it.
> Whoever of you loses your life for me
> And for the good news
> Will save it.
> 36How does it help a person to gain the whole world
> And forfeit the soul?
> 37What can a person give in exchange for the soul?

Whoever is ashamed of me

> 38Whoever of you is ashamed of me and my words
> In this adulterous and wrongful generation,
> The earthly son will be ashamed of you
> When he comes
> In the glory of his father with the holy angels.

---

91. Others translate "said the thing" or "said all this," and so forth, but "said the word" is literal, mysterious, yet less vague.

92. Peter is frequently mocked or rebuked by Yeshua, here calling him Satan. The reproach is severe.

Chapter 9

Tasting death

And he said to them,
>Amain, I say to you,
>There are some of you standing here
>Who will not taste death
>Until you see that the kingdom of God has come
>With power.

Transfigured, his clothing gleaming white

2After six days Yeshua took Shimon Kefa and Yaakov and Yohanan and led them up a high mountain, alone, by themselves. And he was transfigured[93] before them, 3and his clothing became a white so gleaming that no bleach on the earth could so whiten them. 4And there appeared to them Eliyahu with Moshe talking to Yeshua.

5Then Shimon Kefa said to Yeshua, "Rabbi, it is good for us to be here, and let us make three shelters,[94] one for you and one for Moshe and one for Eliyahu."

6He didn't know what to say, they were so terrified.

7Then a cloud came and cast a shadow over them, and a voice came out of the cloud:
>This is my beloved son. Hear him.

8And suddenly as they looked around, they no longer saw anyone but Yeshua, alone with them.

---

93. Verses 2–8 are commonly called the Transfiguration. Following the tradition of Jewish apocalypticism, Yeshua is supernaturally transformed into a dazzling white vision of the mashiah in heaven.

94. Tabernacle from the Greek σκηνή (skene), "tent," from the Hebrew סֻכָּה (sukkah), "shelter" or "tent." The three tents are associated with the Jewish Sukkah, also called Sukkoth, or the Festival of the Tabernacles or Booths, חַג הַסֻּכּוֹת (hag hasukkot), an eight-day celebration for the autumnal harvest, beginning on the eve of the 15th of Tishri. The sukkah is a small lean-to-like tent in the fields. One dwells in the sukkah in commemoration of God's protection of Israel when its people were wandering in the desert (the wilderness) after their escape from Egypt.

Eliyahu has come

9As they came down the mountain, he ordered them to tell no one what they had seen until the earthly son has risen from the dead.

10And they kept that word to themselves, discussing what is "to rise from the dead." 11They asked him, saying, "Why do the scholars say that first Eliyahu must come?"

12He said to them,

> Eliyahu will come first and restore everything.
> How has Yeshayahu written about the earthly son
> That he must suffer much and be rejected?[95]
>   13But I tell you that Eliyahu has come
> And, as written,
> They did to him whatever they pleased.

A mute child foaming and grinding his teeth

14When their party came to the students, they saw a great crowd around them and the scholars arguing with them. 15The whole crowd when they saw him were at once amazed and ran up to him and greeted him.

16He asked them,

> What are you arguing about with them?

17Someone from the crowd answered him, "Rabbi, I brought my son to you. He has a speechless spirit. 18When it seizes him, it throws him down, he foams and grinds his teeth and becomes stiff.[96] I asked your students to drive it out, but they could not."

19Yeshua responded to them, saying,

> You faithless generation, how much longer must I be among
>   you?
> How much longer must I put up with you?

---

95. Isa. 52.13–53.12, the suffering servant passage. In Isaiah we read of the messianic figure who "grew up before God like a tender shoot" (Isa. 53.2); who was despised and rejected (53.3); who was pierced for our transgressions, whose pain brought us peace and by whose wounds we are healed (53.5); he was led like a lamb to the slaughter (53.7); and after his suffering he will see the light (53.11); he bore the sins of many, and for his suffering will gain God's place with the great (53.12). These passages are standardly interpreted in Christian reading of the Hebrew Bible as prophecy of the suffering, crucifixion, and resurrection of the Christ.

96. The boy has the symptoms of epilepsy.

Bring him to me.

20And they brought him to him. When the spirit saw Yeshua, at once it convulsed the boy, who fell on the ground and rolled about, foaming.

21Then Yeshua asked his father,

How long has this been happening to him?

"Since childhood," he said, 22"and often it threw him into the fire and into the water to destroy him. But if you can do anything, have pity on us."

23Yeshua said to him,

If you are able, all things are possible for the one believing.

24At once the child's father cried out, saying, "I believe! Help my unbelief!"

25Yeshua, seeing that the crowd was growing around him, warned the unclean spirit, saying to it,

Speechless and deaf spirit, I command you,

Come out of him, and enter him no more.

26After it screamed and convulsed, it came out and the boy became like one dead, and many said he had died.

27But Yeshua holding his hand lifted him and he stood up.

28When he went into a house his students asked him privately, "Why were we unable to cast it out?"

29And he said to them,

This kind will come out only through prayer.

I will die and be arisen

30After leaving there they went through the Galil, and he didn't wish anyone to know. 31He was teaching his students and said to them,

The earthly son will be handed over into human hands

And they will kill him,

And three days after being killed he will arise.

32But they didn't understand his word and they were afraid to ask him.

The first will be last but who receives the child receives me

33Then they came into Kfar Nahum[97] and once in the house he questioned them,

On the road what were you arguing about?

---

97. Capernaum.

34They were silent, for they argued on the road about who was the greatest.

35He sat down and called the twelve and said to them,

> Who would be first will be last
> And a slave to all.

36Then he took a child and placed him in their midst and taking him into his arms he said to them,

> 37Whoever welcomes a child like one of these
> In my name
> Welcomes me.
> And whoever welcomes me, not only welcomes me
> But the one who sent me.

Demons and a cup of water

38Yohanan said to him, "Rabbi, we saw someone casting out demons in your name, and we stopped him because he was not one who followed us."

39But Yeshua said,

> Don't stop him,
> For no one can perform a power[98] in my name
> And speak poorly about me.
> 40Whoever is not against us is for us.
> 41Whoever gives you a cup of water to drink in my name
> Because you are of the mashiah,
> I say to you that he won't lose his reward.

A millstone around the neck

> 42Whoever makes one of these little ones who believes stumble,
> It would be better for him to hang a millstone[99]
> Around his neck and be thrown into the sea.

> 43And if your hand makes you stumble, cut it off.
> It is better for you to enter life maimed

---

98. Elsewhere translated as "a deed of power" or "a miracle."

99. Literally, "donkey stone," meaning that a mule turned a great millstone. Verses 42–48 are the first warnings of hell and its pains.

Than to have two hands and go into Gei Hinnom[100]
Into unquenchable fire.[101]
45And if your foot makes you stumble, cut it off.
It is better for you to enter life maimed
Than to have two feet and go into Gei Hinnom.
47And if your eye makes you stumble, tear it out.
It is better for you to enter one-eyed into the kingdom of God
Than to have two eyes and be flung into Gei Hinnom
48where the worm does not die
and the fire is unextinguished[102]

Salted with fire
49Everyone will be salted with fire.
50Salt is good, but if salt loses the taste of salt,
What will you season it with?
Keep the salt in yourselves and be at peace
With one another.

Chapter 10

What God joined together let no one separate
Rising from there he came into the region of Yehuda and beyond the Yarden River, and again crowds gathered around him, and again as was his custom he taught them. 2The Prushim came near and asked him if it was allowable for a man to divorce his wife. They were testing him.
3He answered and said to them,
What did Moshe command you?

---

100. Gehenna from the Greek γέεννα (Geenna), from the Hebrew גֵּיא הִנֹּם (gei hinnom), meaning the "valley of Hinnom." Gei Hinnom is a special pit of darkness of the Hebrew Bible. *Gei Hinnom* and *Sheol* are normally translated into English as "hell."

101. Verses 44 and 46 are not in ancient texts and were added later. They repeat what is in verse 48.

102. Isa. 66.24.

4They said, "Moshe allowed a man to write a notice of separation[103] and to divorce his wife."

5Then Yeshua said to them,

> Because of your hardheartedness he wrote this commandment
> > for you.

6But from the beginning of creation:

> He made them male and female[104]

7Because of that a person will leave the father and mother

8And the two will be one flesh.[105]

> So they are no longer two but one flesh.

9Therefore what God joined together let no one separate.[106]

10The students in the house again questioned him about that.

11And he said to them,

> Whoever divorces his wife and marries another
> Commits adultery with her.

12And if she divorces her husband and marries another,

> She commits adultery.

Let the children come to me

13Then they brought him children for him to touch them, but the students scolded them. 14Seeing this, Yeshua became angry and said,

> Let the children come to me.
> Do not stop them. For the kingdom of God
> Belongs to them.

15I tell you,

> Whoever does not receive the kingdom of God
> Like a child

---

103. The separation stated in the Greek ἀποστάσιον (apostasion) has its root meaning in "standing apart from." In contemporary translation, there is a temptation to use contemporary legal terms. It may be interpreted as "a divorce," "a legal transfer of property," or "the act of releasing or dismissing."

104. Gen. 1.27. "He" is God.

105. Gen. 2.24.

106. The injunction against separation (divorce) is Yeshua's addition to the Hebrew verses in Genesis and remains the source for the Christian sanctity of marriage.

Will never enter therein.

16And he took them in his arms and blessed them and placed his hands on them.

Dilemmas of a rich man

17As he went out on the road, a man ran up and kneeling before him asked him, "Good rabbi, what must I do to inherit eternal life?"

18Yeshua said to him,

> Why do you call me good?
> No one is good but God alone.
> 19The commandments you know:
>> "Do not murder.
>> Do not commit adultery.
>> Do not steal.
>> Do not bear false witness.
>> Do not defraud.
>> Honor your father and mother."[107]

20He said to him, "Rabbi, all those things I have kept since my youth."

21Then Yeshua looked at him and loved him, and said,

> One thing you lack. Go, and sell all you own
> And give to the poor
> And you will have a treasure in heaven.
> Then come follow me.

22But he was downcast by the word and went away grieving. He had many possessions.

Heaven through the eye of a needle

23Then Yeshua looked around him and said to his students,

> How hard it will be for those who have money
> To enter the kingdom of God!

24His students were astonished by his words.

But Yeshua said to them again,

> Children, how hard it is to enter the kingdom of God.

---

107. Exod. 20.12–16; Deut. 5.16–20.

25It is easier for a camel to go through the eye of a needle
    Than for a rich person to enter the kingdom of God.[108]
26They were even more astonished and said to each other, "Then who can be saved?"
27Looking at them, Yeshua said,
    For humans it is impossible, but not for God.
    All things are possible for God.

The last will be first

28Shimon Kefa began to say to him, "Look, we left everything and have followed you."
29Yeshua said,
    Amain, amain, I say to you,
    There is no one who gave up home or brothers or sisters
    Or mother or father or children or farms
    For my sake and for the good news,
    30Who will not receive a hundredfold,
    Now in this age—houses and brothers
    And sisters and mothers
    And children and farms with persecutions—
    And in the age to come life everlasting.

---

108. This famous passage has often been commented on for its hyperbole of a camel passing through the eye of a needle. Because such an event is utterly impossible, it is removed from ordinary reality to an allegorical or surreal level, which makes it acceptable. The reader is informed not to reject the comparison for reasons of exaggeration, but to accept it "symbolically." So this wonderful literary trope works. In all probability we have a happy accident of conversion from the Aramaic or the Hebrew source. The root consonants for "camel" and "coarse thread" are the same in the Semitic original (vowels distinguishing meaning and pronunciation were written under the letters only much later in the Masoretic texts). Were we to have an accurate translation of the probable meaning of the aphorism, "It is easier for a coarse thread to pass through the eye of a needle than for a rich person to enter the kingdom of God," we would have a bland and forgettable bit of wisdom verse. Although it is always astonishing to read Yeshua conversing in Greek with Jewish peasants rather than in Aramaic and quoting Hebrew to them, in this instance, in comparison with the extant Greek translation, the passage probably suffers in the original.

31But many who are first will be last
And the last will be first.

I will die and be arisen[109]

32They were on the road going up to Yerushalayim, and Yeshua was leading them. They were astounded, and those following them were afraid. He took the twelve aside again and began to tell them what was going to happen to him,

33Look. We are going up to Yerushalayim
And the earthly son will be handed over to the high priests
And the scholars,
And they will condemn him to death
And hand him over to the gentiles[110]
34And they will ridicule him and spit on him and flog him
And kill him,
And after three days he will rise again.

Seated in glory

35Yaakov and Yohanan—the sons of Zavdai[111]—came up to him, saying, "Rabbi, we want you to do for us whatever we ask you to."
36He said to them,
What do you want me to do for you?

---

109. This is the third time Yeshua foresees his death and resurrection.

110. Foreigners or non-Jews. Gentile from the late Latin *gens*, meaning "pagan," from the Greek ἔθνος (ethnos), meaning literally a "national" as in "people" or "nation," and in the plural "non-Jews, Christian Jews, Christians, pagans," or "heathens," from the Hebrew גּוֹי (goy), plural גּוֹיִם (goyim), meaning "a people, nation, non-Jew." The diverse meanings given in usage and especially in translation of the Greek depend on the context. Normally, in the gospels and Acts an *ethnos* means a non-Jew who may be converted to Jewish Messianism or, as in later church koine, a "Christian Jew who is a convert from paganism," as in parts of Acts and the letters; and if the word is used disparagingly to mean both a non-Jew and non-Christian, it refers to a pagan. In its fully wicked sense, *ethnikos* (like a gentile) means a "heathen." In modern English the commonest meaning of "gentile" has come to be a Christian as opposed to a Jew.

111. The sons of Zebedee (Zavdai) are the Boanerges (Benei Regesh), known for their fiery zeal.

37And they said to him, "Let one of us sit on your right and one on your left in your glory."

38Yeshua said to them,

> You do not know what you are asking.
> Can you drink the cup I am drinking
> Or be dipped in the waters I am dipped in?[112]

39They said to him, "We can."

Then Yeshua said to them,

> The cup I will drink you will drink
> And the waters I am dipped in
> You will be dipped in.
> 40Yet to sit on my right or my left is not mine to give.
> It is for those for whom it was prepared.

To be first, be a slave

41When the other ten heard about this, they began to be angry with Yaakov and Yohanan, 42and Yeshua called them and said to them,

> Among the gentiles those who are called the rulers
> Lord over the people and their great ones wield power.
> You know that. 43But it's not so with you.
> Whoever would be great among you must become your servant
> 44Whoever would be first must be the slave of all.
> 45The earthly son did not come to be served but to serve
> And give his life as ransom for the many.

A blind beggar in Yeriho

46They came to Yeriho.[113] As he and his students and a large crowd were leaving Yeriho, Bar Timai, son of Timai,[114] a blind beggar, was sitting by the road. 47When he heard that Yeshua the Natzrati was coming, he began to cry out and to say, "Son of David, have pity on me!"

---

112. Presumably "the waters of the spirit."

113. Jericho from the Greek Ἰεριχώ (Ieriho), from the Hebrew יְרִיחוֹ (yeriho).

114. Bartimeus from the Greek Βαρτιμαῖος (Bartimaios), from the Aramaic בַּר טְמַי (bar timai). *Timai* is a Greek word in Aramaic and Hebrew, probably τιμή (time), meaning "value" or "honor," or a shortened form of Τιμόθεος (Timotheos), "Timothy," meaning "valued by God."

48Many warned him to be quiet but he shouted even louder.

49But Yeshua stopped and said,

> Call him.

And they called the blindman, saying to him, "Be happy. Stand up. He's calling you."

50Then throwing off his cloak, he sprang up and came to Yeshua.

51And answering him Yeshua said,

> What do you want me to do?

The blindman said to him, "Rabboni,[115] let me see again."

52And Yeshua said to him,

> Go, your faith has cured you.

At once he saw again and followed him on the road.

Chapter 11

Entering Yerushalayim on a colt

And as they neared Yerushalayim, at Beit Pagey[116] and Beit Aniyah[117] toward the Mountain of Olives, he sent two of his students 2and said to them,

> Go into the village before you
> And once you are inside you will find a tethered colt
> On which no one has sat.
> Untie it and bring it.
> 3If someone tells you, "Why are you doing this?" say,
> "The master needs it and he will send it back at once."

4They went away and found a colt tethered to a door out on the street and they untied it.

5Some of those standing there said to them, "What are you doing untying the colt?"

---

115. *Rabboni*, meaning "my great rabbi."

116. Bethphage from the Greek Βηθφαγή (Bethfage), from the Hebrew בֵּית פַּגֵּא (beit pagey). Bethphage is thought to be a village east of Jerusalem on the Mountain of Olives.

117. Bethany from the Greek Βηθανία (Bethania), from the Hebrew בֵּית אֲנְיָה (beit aniyah). Beit Aniyah is also east of Jerusalem, near Beit Pagey.

6They told them just what Yeshua had said to them.

And they let them alone.

7Then they brought the colt to Yeshua and piled their clothing on the colt, and he sat on it. 8Many people spread their clothing on the road, and others strewed leafy branches they had cut in the fields. 9The ones leading and the ones following cried,

> Hosanna!
> Blessed is the one who comes in the name of the lord.
> 10Blessed is the coming kingdom of our father David.
> Hosanna in the highest.[118]

11Then he entered Yerushalayim, into the Temple, and looking around at everything, since the hour now was late, he went out to Beit Aniyah with the twelve.

Cursing the fig tree

12On the next day as they left from Beit Aniyah, he was hungry. 13And seeing a fig tree in leaf in the distance, he came to see if he might find something on it. When he came to it he found nothing but leaves. It was not the season for figs. 14He spoke out, saying to it,

> Let no one ever eat your fruit again.

His students heard him.

Driving the traders and dove sellers from the Temple

15Then they came to Yerushalayim. And Yeshua entered the Temple and began to drive out those who sold and bought in the Temple. He overturned the tables of the money changers and the chairs of those selling doves. 16He did not allow anyone to carry goods through the Temple.[119] 17He taught and said to them,

> Is it not written in Yeshayahu and Yirmiyahu:[120]

---

118. Ps. 118.25–26.

119. Market merchants would have been outside the restricted Temple, in the adjacent courtyards where the sacrificial animals were taken to be sold in specific areas reserved for commerce and where non-Jews were permitted to buy and sell. Since commerce was restricted to courtyards, it casts doubt on the location of Yeshua's house cleaning as within the Temple itself.

120. Jeremiah from the Greek Ἰερεμίας (Ieremias), from the Hebrew יִרְמְיָהוּ (yirmiyahu).

"My house will be called a house of prayer for all
　　nations"?[121]

But you have made it into "a cave of robbers"?[122]

18The high priests and scholars heard and looked for a way to destroy
him. They feared him, for the crowd was amazed by his teaching.

19When it was late they went out of the city.

The fig tree dried up

20In the morning as they passed by, they saw the fig tree dried up from
the roots.

21Then Kefa remembered and said to him, "Rabbi, look! The fig tree
you cursed has dried up."[123]

Moving mountains

22Yeshua answered, saying to them,

　　Have faith in God. 23Amain, I say to you,

　　If you tell this mountain, "Rise and leap into the sea,"

　　And have no doubt in your heart

　　But believe what is said will happen,

　　It will be yours.

24So I say to you,

　　All you pray for and ask, believe you have received it

　　And it will be yours.

25When you stand praying, if you hold something

　　Against someone, forgive

　　So your father in heaven will also forgive your wrong steps.[124]

---

121. Isa. 56.7.

122. Jer. 7.11.

123. Destructive miracles are uncommon in the New Testament, though not infre-
quent in noncanonical scripture. Here the conventional theological explanation is
that Yeshua's curse on the fig tree is a metaphor for the future punishment of the
faithless Jews for failing to be fruitful in recognizing Yeshua as the mashiah and is a
prophecy of "the destruction of the temple that similarly failed to bear proper religious fruit" (*The HarperCollins Bible Dictionary*, ed. Paul J. Achtemeier, San Francisco: HarperSanFrancisco, 1993, 338).

124. From the Greek παράπτωμα (paraptoma), meaning "wrong or false step,"
"transgression," or "sin." The usually translated "trespasses" and "transgressions" are

Back in Yerushalayim, outwitting priests and scholars

27They came again to Yerushalayim. As he was walking about in the Temple, the high priests and scholars and elders came to him 28and said, "By what authority do you do these things?" or "Who gave you this authority to do these things?"

29Yeshua said to them,

> I will ask you one word, and answer me
> And I will tell you by what authority
> I do these things.
> 30Did Yohanan's immersion come from heaven
> Or from people? Tell me.

31They discussed this among themselves, saying, "If we say 'From heaven,' he will say, 'Why didn't you believe him?' 32But if we say, 'From people.'" . . . They were afraid of the crowd, for everyone held Yohanan to be truly a prophet.

33They answered Yeshua, saying, "We do not know." And Yeshua said to them,

> Then neither will I tell you by what authority
> I do these things.

Chapter 12

The unbridled tenants

> And he began to speak to them in parables,
> A man planted a vineyard and put a fence
> Around it, dug a wine vat, and built a tower.[125]
> He rented it to farmers and left the country.

Latin words that also have the original image in them of losing one's footing, but that through usage have lost their primary image and metaphor and convey a conceptual meaning of "fault" or "sin." Unless the primary image remains, the metaphor is lost, and the two cognitive levels of image and concept do not intensify each. Note that verse 26 does not appear in the earliest texts and was later appended but not accepted in modern editions.

125. Tower from the Greek πύργος (pyrgos). *Pyrgos* is the common word for "tower" and often is translated as "watchtower," as in Jehovah Witnesses' Watchtower.

2At the harvest he sent a slave to the farmers
  To take back some fruits from the vineyard.
3But they seized him, lashed him, and sent him away
  Empty. 4Again he sent another slave to them
  And him they struck on the head and insulted.
5He sent another and that one they killed,
  And many more, lashing some, killing others.
6He still had one beloved son. He sent him
  Finally to them, saying, "They will respect
  My son." 7But those farmers said to one another,
  "This is the heir. Come, let us kill him
  And the inheritance is ours." 8They seized him
  And killed him and threw him outside the vineyard.
9What will the owner of the vineyard do?
  He will come and destroy the farmers and give
  The vineyard to others. 10Have you not read
  In the Psalms: "A stone that the builders rejected
  Became the cornerstone. 11From the lord
  It came to be and is wonderful in our eyes.[126]

12The priests and scholars were seeking a way to arrest him, but feared the crowd. They realized that he had told the parable against them. So they left him and went away.

Paying coins to Caesar

13Then they sent some Prushim and Herodians to him to trap him in a word. 14They came and said to him, "Rabbi, we know that you are truthful, and favor no one. You do not look at a person's face but rather you teach the way of God in accordance with truth. Is it right to pay the tax to Caesar or not? Should we give or not give?"[127]

---

126. Ps. 118.22–23.

127. Historically, this period (preceding all-out rebellion against Roman rule, culminating in 70 C.E. with the destruction of the Temple) was a touchy time of contention between Jew and Roman over religious matters—such as Caligula's attempt in 44–45 C.E. to set up a statue of himself in the Temple. In the gospels, however, the Romans are not perceived as occupiers of a suppressed Israel. Since the scriptural

15But he saw their hypocrisy and said to them,
> Why are you testing me?
> Bring me a denarius to look at it.
16They brought one.
And he said to them,
> Whose image is this and whose name?
They said to him, "Caesar's."
17Yeshua said to them,
> The things of Caesar give to Caesar
> And the things of God give to God.
.And they were amazed at him.

Who is one's wife in heaven?

18Then Tzadokim[128] came to him, who say there is no resurrection, and they questioned him, saying, 19"Rabbi, Moshe wrote for us that if 'a man's brother dies and leaves a wife and no child, the brother should take the wife and raise the seed for his brother.' 20There were seven brothers and the first took a wife and when he died he left no seed. 21The second took her and he died without leaving seed. And the third likewise. 22The seven did not leave seed. Last of all the woman died. 23In the resurrection, whose wife will she be? Seven had her as a wife."

24Yeshua told them,
> Are you not wrong in not knowing the scriptures

---

position sees Roman authority as good and Jewish authority as bad (as represented by the Pharisees, who historically strongly opposed both Hellenization and Roman occupation), it is imperative to prove that tribute to Rome in the form of payment to Caesar does not interfere with tribute to God. So this passage of the coin showing Caesar's head establishes three principles: Yeshua's recognition of the authority of the emperor for things of the emperor, the hypocrisy of Jewish authorities who cast doubt on the authority of the emperor, and that payment to the emperor does not imperil the things that are God's. Reflecting loyalties in the gospels, while deeming it proper to pay coins to Rome, Yeshua disdains the yearly upkeep tax for local Temple tax in Capernaum (Kfar Nahum). To avoid scandal, he orders Peter to pay it with a coin he will find in the mouth of a fish he will hook in the sea (Matt. 17.24–27).

128. Sadducee from the Greek Σαδώκ, from the Hebrew צָדוֹק (tzadok). "Sadducees" (pl.) is *Tzadokim. Tzadok* (Tsadok) was High Priest in the time of King David and means "the just."

Or the power of God?

25When they rise from the dead they do not marry

Nor are they given away in marriage.

They are like angels in the skies.

26As for raising the dead, in the Book of Moshe

Have you not read how at the thornbush

God spoke to Moshe saying,

> "I am the God of Avraham and the God of Yitzhak

> And the God of Yaakov"?[129]

27He is not the God of the dead but of the living.

You are deeply wrong.

Hear O Yisrael[130]

28One of the scholars came near, heard them debating, and seeing that he had answered them well, asked him, "What is the first commandment of all?"

29Yeshua answered,

The first is:

> "Hear O Yisrael, the lord our God, the lord is one.

> 30And you shall love the lord your God with all your heart

> And all your soul and all your mind and all your

> strength.[131]

31The second is:

> "You shall love your neighbor like yourself."

There is no commandment greater than these.

32The scholar said to him, "Well said, rabbi, you are right in saying that he is one and there is no other but he. 33To love him with all your heart and with all your understanding and with all your strength, and to love your neighbor like yourself is greater than all burnt offerings and sacrifices."

34Yeshua seeing that he answered wisely said to him,

---

129. Exod. 3.6 and 3.15.

130. Israel from the Greek Ἰσραήλ, from the Hebrew יִשְׂרָאֵל (yisrael).

131. Deut. 6.4–5.

You are not far from the kingdom of God.
Nobody dared question him further.

Watch out for scholars

35While he was teaching in the Temple, he said,
>How can the scholars say the mashiah is David's son?
36Through the holy spirit David himself declared,
>"The lord said to my lord,
>'Sit at my right
>Until I put your enemies under your feet.'"[132]
37David calls him lord so how can he be his son?
The great crowd heard him with delight.
38And in his teaching he said,
>Beware of the scholars, the ones in long robes
>Who love to stroll about, be greeted in the marketplaces,
39And claim the best seats in the synagogues
>And the foremost couches at dinners,
40Who eat up the widows' houses
>And solely for show say long prayers.
>They will receive the greater condemnation.[133]

The widow's copper coins

41Then he sat down opposite the treasury and observed how the crowd threw copper coins into the treasury. Many rich tossed in many coins. 42A poor widow came and threw in two lepta, worth a penny. 43He called his students and said to them,
>Amain, amain, I say to you,
>That poor widow threw in more than all who cast money into
>>the treasury.
44All have thrown in from their abundance.
>She has thrown in from her poverty,
>She gave all that she had for living on.

---

132. Ps. 110.1.

133. The scholars of Torah were dependent on patrons for their salary. Here they are condemned for their vanity and exploitation of vulnerable widows.

Chapter 13

The great buildings will be thrown down

As he was leaving the Temple, one of his students said to him, "Rabbi, look, what enormous stones, what enormous buildings!"

2Yeshua said to him,

> Do you see these great buildings?
> No stone on stone will be left that will not be thrown
> down.[134]

3When he was sitting on the Mountain of Olives opposite the Temple, Shimon Kefa and Yaakov and Yohanan and Andreas[135] asked him privately, 4"Tell us when these things will be and what will be the sign when they will be fulfilled."

5Yeshua began to say to them,

> Beware that no one leads you astray.
> 6Many will come in my name saying, "I am,"[136]
> And they will lead many astray.
> 7But when you hear of wars and rumors of wars
> Do not be frightened. These things must occur.
> But the end is not yet.

---

134. This famous prophecy of the destruction of the Temple in 70 C.E. suggests a dating of Mark after the year 70 or, if as early as 66 as some venture, a later scribal interpolation. Mark's prophecy is in the tradition of the oracle writing of the Sibyls. The Sibyls were women who proclaimed future events in a state of ecstasy. Usually, their prophecies were placed in a period earlier than that of their authors, so that the catastrophes foretold had already occurred, thereby guaranteeing the Sibyls' accuracy. For a discussion of the Greek, Jewish, Christian-Jewish, and Christian sibyllines, see Willis Barnstone, "The Sibylline Oracles," 501–505, and "Christian Sibyllines," 554–566, in *The Other Bible* (San Francisco: Harper and Row, 1984).

135. Peter and James and John and Andrew.

136. From the Greek ἐγώ εἰμι (ego eimi), "I am." *Ego eimi* suggests "I am he," meaning "the messiah," or colloquially "it's me," as the response to "Who is it?" or "Who's here?" However, the strong literal meaning in Greek of *Ego eimi*, "I am," also conveys an oracular tone of stating his existence, as in the Hebrew Bible "I am that I am," which any of these common English translations loses.

8Nation will rise against nation, kingdom against kingdom,
There will be earthquakes in the lands
And there will be famines.
These things are the beginnings of the last agonies.[137]

Lashed in the synagogues
9Look out for yourselves. They will hand you over
To the Sanhedrin[138] and lash you in the synagogues
And you will stand before governors and kings
Because of me and testify to them. And first
10The good news must be preached to all peoples.
11When they turn you over and bring you to trial,
Don't worry beforehand about what you will say.
Whatever is given to you in that hour, say it,
For it is not you who speak but the holy spirit.
12Then brother will hand over brother to death
And father his child, and children will rise up
Against parents and put them to death.
13And you will be hated by everyone
Because of my name. But whoever survives
To the end, that person will be saved.

---

137. The gospels were written following the destruction of the Temple and the consequent diaspora of both Jews and contending Christian Jews, and the memory and implications of that catastrophe permeate the scriptures. In the Sermon on the Mount, the prediction of rebellion of nation against nation, kingdom against kingdom, and, specifically, Israel against Rome, tells the price paid for revolution: the dispersal of both Jews and Christian Jews from Israel; the destruction of Israel as a religious power base for Jews as well as Peter's and James's Messianic Jews in Jerusalem; and, as a result of the diaspora, an increasing distinction in identity between Jews and Christian Jews, leading in foreign lands to the creation of two interdependent but separate religions, in larger domains outside of Israel, greatly increasing the proselytizing of others to both Judaism and emerging Christianity. The destruction of Israel "is not the end," not the apocalypse, for, as the following lines show, after much suffering, humiliation, and death, "the good news [of the messiah] will be proclaimed to all nations."

138. Councils.

Desolation

14When you see the "abomination of desolation"[139]
Standing where it should not—let the reader
Understand—then let those in Yehuda flee
To the mountains, 15and someone on the rooftop
Not come down or go into the house
To take things away, 16and a man in the fields
Not go back to pick up clothing left behind.
17Grief to women with a child in the womb
And to women nursing babies in those days!
18Pray that it may not happen in the winter.
19In those days there will be an affliction
Which has not happened since the beginning
Of creation, which God created, until now,
And will in no way again take place.
20And if the Lord had not shortened the days,
No flesh would be saved. But for the ones
Whom he chose, he did shorten the days.

The earthly son comes in the clouds

21And then, if someone says to you, "Look,
Here is the mashiah, look, he is there,"
Do not believe. 22False mashiahs and false prophets
Will rise up and perform signs and wonders
To mislead the chosen, if they can.
23But beware! I have forewarned all to you.[140]

---

139. The phrase is from Daniel 9.27, and alludes to the Hellenistic ruler's attempt in the second century B.C.E. to convert the Temple into a shrine for Zeus. In Daniel we have, "And on a wing of the temple he will set up an abomination that causes desolation." This example from the past is also interpreted as a prelude to the apocalyptic destruction by Titus of the Temple and of Israel three and a half decades after Yeshua's death.

140. Those "false messiahs" and "false prophets" are not other traditional Jews but the Gnostics, those who come with knowledge. The Gnostics were the main ideological enemies during the later period of church formation. As such, these warnings

24But in those days after that affliction,
  The sun will be darkened
  And the moon not give its light
25And the stars will fall out of the sky[141]
  And the powers in the skies will quake.
26Then you will see the earthly son coming
  On clouds with great power and glory.
27Then he will send out angels and gather in
  The chosen from the four winds from the end
  Of the earth to the end of the sky.

Stay awake for the coming
28From the fig tree learn the parable.
  When its branch is tender again and shoots out leaves,
  You know that summer is near.
29So when you see these things happening
  You know that the earthly son is near the doors.
30Amain, amain, I say to you,
  This generation will not pass away before
  All these things have come about.
31The sky and the earth will pass away
  But my words will not pass away.
32But of that day or the hour no one knows,
  Neither the angels in heaven nor the son.
  Only the father. 33Be watchful, stay awake.
  You do not know when the time will come.
34It is like when a person goes on a journey
  And puts slaves in charge, to each his task,
  And commands the doorkeeper to be watchful.
35Beware then, you never know when the lord
  Of the house comes, in the evening or midnight
  Or at cockcrow or dawn, 36or coming suddenly

---

are anachronistic, reflecting not specific concerns in Jesus's lifetime but the fierce sectarian rivalries in the period of the later evangelists.

141. Isa. 13.10 and 34.4.

He may find you asleep.
37What I say to you I say to everyone. Beware.

Chapter 14

Plotting

After two days it would be Pesach,[142] the Supper of the Matzot Bread,[143] and the high priests[144] and the scholars were looking for a way to arrest him by treachery and to kill him. 2"Not at the festival," they were saying, "for there would be an outcry from the people."

Anointed in the house of the leper

3While he was in Beit Aniyah[145] in the house of Shimon the leper, reclining, a woman came with an alabaster jar of myrrh, a pure and costly spikenard ointment. Breaking the alabaster jar she poured it on his head. 4Now some grumbled to each other, "Why was there this waste of myrrh?" 5This ointment could have been sold for more than three hundred denarii and the money given to the poor. And they scolded her.

---

142. On the first two evenings of Passover is the Seder, the supper of the Matzot (unleavened bread). *Pesach* is "Passover" from the Greek πάσχα (pasha), from the Hebrew פֶּסַח (pesach), "passed over," referring to the escape from bondage in Egypt. Pesach is celebrated at the Seder by eating the paschal lamb. See Exodus 12.1–13.16.

143. The Greek word ἄζυμος (azymos) means "unleavened bread," which is a translation from the Hebrew מַצּוֹת (matzot), meaning "unleavened bread." The matzot bread is sometimes called a loaf, which suggests round and oblong. It was more likely flat like East Indian bread or a tortilla. It is not indicated in the Torah or Mislanah that, like modern matzos, it was dry, heavily salted, and brittle.

144. High priests are the *cohanim*. A high priest is a *cohen* or *koben*. In Torah (Pentateuch), the priesthood is limited to the Levites, the family of Levi, son of Jacob. Matthew, to whom the Gospel of Matthew is traditionally attributed, is said to be a second-generation Christian Jew whose name, in the gospel of Matthew, is Levi.

145. Bethany.

6But Yeshua said,
> Let her be. Why do you bother her?
> She has done a good thing for me.
> 7You always have the poor with you
> And whenever you want you can do good for them.
> But me you do not always have.
> 8She did what she could.
> She has anointed my body beforehand for its burial.
> 9I say to you,
> Wherever in the whole world the good news is preached,
> What this woman did will speak her memory.

Yehuda and the promise of silver

10Yehuda, man of Keriot,[146] one of the twelve, went to the high priests to betray him to them.[147]

11Hearing of this they were happy and promised to give him silver. He was looking for an easy way of betraying him.

Planning the Seder in an upper room

12On the first day of the Feast of the Matzot, when the Pesach lamb was sacrificed, his students said to him, "Where do you want us to go to arrange for you to eat the Pesach lamb?"

13And he sent two of his students and said to them,
> Go into the city and you will meet
> A man carrying a clay pot of water.
> Follow him 14and wherever he enters tell
> The owner of the house, "The rabbi[148] asks,

---

146. Judas Iscariot.

147. For more on the origin of the betrayer tale of Judas in scripture and post-biblical portrayals in history and the arts, see note 30 on p. 33, in "Mark, the Vernacular Story Teller." For a more complete account of Judas from the Bible to modern times, see Susan Gubar's *Judas: A Biography* (New York: W. W. Norton, 2009).

148. In his instructions, where he wishes to assert his authority for a Jewish ceremonial feast, it is unlikely that Yeshua would not have used the normal epithet "rabbi" rather than *didaskalos* (διδάσκαλος) or *epistates* (ἐπιστάτης) for "teacher."

'Where is my guest room where I may eat
The Pesach supper with my students?'"
15And he will show you a large upper room
Furnished and ready. There prepare for us.
16And the students left and came into the city and found things just as they were told and they prepared the Pesach meal.

One of you will betray me

17When it was evening, he came with the twelve. 18As they were reclining at the table and eating, Yeshua said to them,

Amain, amain, I say to you,
One of you will betray me,
One who is eating with me.
19They became forlorn and said to him, one by one, "Surely not me?"
20He said to them,
One of the twelve who is dipping matzot in the bowl.[149]
21The earthly son will go just as Yeshayahu wrote of him.[150]
But a plague on him who betrayed the earthly son!
It would be good for him had he never been born!

This is my body, this is my blood

22While they were eating he took the matzot, and blessing it he broke it and gave it to them and said,
Take it. This is my body.
23And he took a cup and after giving thanks,[151] he gave it to them, and they all drank from it. 24And he said to them,

---

149. Presumably dipping "bread" in the bowl.

150. The Greek says "just as it is written," meaning, for the informed reader, Isaiah 1–12, in which Isaiah describes the birth, life, and sacrificial death of the coming mashiah. The "earthly son" translates the probable meaning of a human as opposed to a heavenly being, but here, more clearly than elsewhere, Yeshua explains his self-given epithet as being the mashiah, making "mashiah" a reasonable translation of *ho huios tou anthropou* (ὁ υἱὸς τοῦ ἀνθρώπου), but such would be explanation, not translation.

151. The word "Eucharist" is derived from the Greek εὐχαριστία (euharistia), "thanksgiving," which appears in this passage of the Pesach supper (14.23).

This is my blood of the covenant[152]
Which is poured out for many.
25Amain, amain, I say to you,
I will no longer drink the fruit of the wine
Until that day when I drink it new in the kingdom of God.

Before the cock crows twice
26After singing the psalm they left for the Mountain of Olives.
27Then Yeshua said to them,
You will all stumble and fail me as Zeharyahu[153] wrote.
"I will strike down the shepherd
And the sheep will be scattered."
28But after I am raised up I will lead the way
For you into the Galil.
29But Shimon Kefa said to him, "Even if everyone stumbles and fails,
I will not."
30And Yeshua said to him, "Amain, I say to you,"

---

152. From the Greek διαθήκη (diatheke), "the covenant," and in Hellenistic Greek, "testament" or "will." In the KJV, the word "new" is added and so it reads, "This is my blood of the new testament." "New" (καινή) is not in the Greek text. In Greek and East European orthodoxy, the title for the scriptures is "New Covenant." New Testament came into Latin and modern West European languages through Jerome's mistranslation of *diatheke* as *testamentum*, "testament" rather than "covenant." "Covenant" derives from the Hebrew בְּרִית (berit). "New Covenant" in the Greek is Καινὴ Διαθήκη (Kaine Diatheke), and in Torah בְּרִית חֲדָשָׁה (berit hadashah), found in Jeremiah 31.30.

The "blood of the covenant" derives from the covenant between God and Moses at Sinai: "Moses then took the blood, sprinkled it on the people and said, 'This is the blood of the covenant that the Lord has made with you in accordance with all these words'" (Exod. 24.6–8). Moses has set up "twelve stone pillars representing the twelve tribes of Israel." The sacred symbolism of the twelve, representing all the tribes of Israel, is repeated in having Yeshua choose to be followed by twelve students. The major covenants in the Hebrew Bible between God and Israel and the patriarchs are through Noah (Gen. 9.9), Abraham (15.18), Moses (Exod. 19.5, 24.7), and David (2 Sam. 7.14). In the New Testament there are covenants in Matt. 26.28; Mark 14.24; 1 Cor. 11.25; and Heb. 7.22, 8.8–13, 9.15, and 12.24.

153. Zechariah or Zacharias from the Greek Ζαχαρίας (Zaharias), from the Hebrew זְכַרְיָהוּ (Zeharyahu).

Today on this same night before the cock crows twice
You will deny me three times.
But he said forcefully, "If I must die for you, I will not deny
      you."
And all of them said the same.

Terror and prayer at Gat Shmanim

32And they came to a place whose name was Gat Shmanim[154] and he said to his students,

Sit here while I pray.

33And he took Kefa and Yaakov and Yohanan with him and he began to feel terror and anguish 34and he said to them,

My soul is in sorrow to the point of death.
Stay here and keep awake.

35And going a little farther he threw himself on the ground and prayed that, if it were possible, the hour might pass from him. 36And he said,

Abba,[155] my father, for you all things are possible.
Take this cup from me. Yet not what I will
But what you will.

37And he came and found them sleeping, and said to Shimon Kefa,

Shimon,[156] are you sleeping? Did you not have
The strength to keep awake for an hour?

38Stay awake and pray that you are not tested.
Oh, the spirit is ready but the flesh is weak.

39He went away again and prayed, saying the same words.

40And he came again and found them sleeping. Their eyes were very heavy, and they did not know what to say to him.

---

154. Gethsemane from the Greek Γεθσημανί (Gethsemani), from the Hebrew גַּת שְׁמָנִים (gat shmanim), meaning "olive press." It was the name of an olive orchard on the Mountain of Olives.

155. Abba from the Greek Αββα ὁ πατήρ (abba o pater). Abba from Aramaic אַבָּא (abba, father).

156. "Shimon Kefa" is Simon Peter or Simeon Peter. Here Yeshua is addressing Peter by his proper name, *Shimon*, not by his nickname, *Kefa* (the rock), which is translated from Aramaic into Greek as *Petros* and into English as "Peter."

41And he came a third time and said to them,

> Sleep what is left of the night and rest.
> Enough! The hour has come.
> Look, the earthly son is betrayed
> Into the hands of those who do wrong.

42Get up and let us go.

> Look, my betrayer is drawing near.

The rabbi is kissed and arrested

43Immediately, while he was still speaking, Yehuda,[157] one of the twelve, arrived, and with him a crowd with swords and clubs from the high priests and the scholars and the elders. 44His betrayer gave them the signal, saying, "The one I kiss is the one. Hold him and take him away under guard."

45When he came, at once he went up to Yeshua and said, "Rabbi," and kissed him.

46They got their hands on him and held him.

47But someone standing near him drew his sword and struck the slave of the high priest and cut off his ear.

48Then Yeshua spoke out to them,

> As against a thief have you come with swords
> And clubs to arrest me?

49I was with you every day in the Temple, teaching,

> And you did not seize me,
> But only now so that the scriptures may be fulfilled.

50And all left him and fled.

51And one young man followed him, dressed in linen cloth around his naked body, and they seized him. 52But he left the linen cloth behind and fled.

---

157. Judas the Iscariot. Judas from the Greek Ἰούδας (Ioudas), from the Hebrew יְהוּדָה (yehuda). The name for the messenger (apostle) Judas in Hebrew, *Yehuda*, was surely invented because it suggests the Hebrew word for "Jew," which is יְהוּדִי (yehudi); thereby the betrayer of Yeshua among his followers was a Jew, as opposed to the others who escape that identity.

False testimony in the Sanhedrin

53They led Yeshua to the high priest. All the high priests and the elders and the scholars were assembled.[158]

54Shimon Kefa followed him from a distance until he was inside the high priest's courtyard and he sat together with the servants, warming himself near the light of the fire.

55The high priests and the whole Sanhedrin were looking for evidence against him to put him to death, but they didn't find any. 56Many gave false testimony against him, and their testimonies did not agree. 57Some stood up and gave false testimony against him, saying, 58"We heard him say, 'I will tear down this Temple that was made with hands and after three days I will build another not made with hands.'" 59But on this point too their testimony did not agree.

60Then the high priest stood up in their midst and questioned Yeshua, saying, "Won't you answer anything that they have testified against you?"

61But he was silent and gave no answer to anything.

Again the high priest questioned him and said to him, "Are you the mashiah, the son of the blessed one?"

62Yeshua said,

> I am.
>> "And you will see the earthly son seated on the right of
>>> the power"
>> And "coming with the clouds of heaven."[159]

63The high priest tore his own tunic, saying, "What further need do we have of witnesses? 64You heard this blasphemy. How does it seem to you?"

They all judged him as deserving death.

---

158. The night session at the Sanhedrin is problematic, raising many questions. Trials during Passover as well as night trials were forbidden by Jewish law. By Roman law, Jews could not pass death sentences. There is no document or testimony outside the gospels or testimony in the gospels as to how such conversations were recorded and obtained about false testimony.

159. Hebrew scripture cited combine words and ideas in Daniel 7.13, and line 1 from Psalms 110.1.

65And some began to spit on him and to cover his face and beat him. They said to him, "Prophesy!" And the servants took hold of him and pummeled him.

Shimon Kefa and the crowing cock

66While Shimon Kefa was below in the courtyard, one of the serving maids of the high priest came 67and when she saw Shimon Kefa warming himself she stared at him and said, "You were also with the Natzrati,[160] with Yeshua."

68But he denied it, saying, "I don't know or understand what you are saying." Then he went outside into the forecourt. [And the cock crowed.][161]

69And the maid seeing him began again to say to those standing by, "This is one of them."

70Again he denied it.

After a short while those standing by said to Shimon Kefa, "Surely you must be one of them, since you are a Galilean."

71He began to curse and to swear, "I don't know this man you're talking about."

At once the cock crowed a second time.

72And Kefa remembered the words Yeshua said to him,

> Before the cock crows twice
> You will deny me three times.

And he broke down and wept.

Chapter 15

Pilatus[162] asks, Are you the king of the Jews?

As soon as it was morning, the high priests with the elders and scholars held a meeting. And they bound Yeshua, led him away and handed him over to Pilatus.

---

160. Nazarene.

161. "And the cock crowed" is omitted in other texts and bracketed in the Nestle-Aland, as here.

162. Pilate from the Latin *Pilatus*.

2Pilatus asked him, "Are you the King of the Jews?"

Answering him, he said,

> You say it.

3The high priests brought many charges against him.

4Pilatus again questioned him, saying, "Have you no answer? Look how much you are accused of."

5But Yeshua still said nothing.

Pilatus was amazed.

Crucify him!

6Now at that festival he used to release one prisoner to the people, whichever one they asked for. 7There was a man called Bar Abba[163] who was bound along with other revolutionaries, who in the uprising had committed murder.

8So the crowd came and began to ask Pilatus for what he did for them.

9But Pilatus answered them, saying, "Do you want me to release the King of the Jews?" 10He knew that the high priests had handed him over to him out of envy.

11But the high priests incited the crowd to release Bar Abba instead to them.

12Pilatus again answered, saying to them, "What do you want me to do with the King of the Jews?"

13"Crucify him!"[164]

---

163. Barabbas from the Greek Βαραββᾶς, from the Aramaic בַּר אַבָּא (bar abba), meaning "son of Abba" (father). Nothing is known of Barabbas, but from his revolutionary activities it is assumed that he was a Zealot, a member of a Jewish sect that was rebelling against Roman occupation. Insurrectionists were treated by the Romans as seditionists and hence crucified. It is only from the gospels that we have the notion that the Romans had the custom of releasing one prisoner during the Passover. In Matthew, his name is given as "Yeshua Barrabas". "Barrabas" means "son of the father," or "son of God." See Matthew 27.17.

164. This pivotal but unlikely scene that has the crowd shout "Crucify him," which is to say "crucify a dissident rabbi," suggests not the voice of a Jewish mob in the street but the voice of Rome enunciated in highly redacted texts attributed to the evangelist. The voice of Rome comes through more emphatically in Matthew's elaboration of the same scene, in which Pilate declares both his own innocence and

14Pilatus said to them, "What wrong did he do?"

But they cried out louder, "Crucify him!"

15So Pilatus, wanting to satisfy the crowd, released Bar Abba to them, and had Yeshua flogged and handed him over to be crucified.

Soldiers clothe him in purple and a crown of thorns and club him

16The soldiers led him away into the courtyard, which is the prae-torium,[165] and assembled the whole cohort. 17And they clothed him in purple and twisted some thorns into a wreath, and placed it on his head. 18Then they began to salute him, "Hail, King of the Jews." 19They beat him on the head with a reed club and spat on him, and going down on their knees they worshiped him. 20And after mocking him, they stripped off the purple and put his own clothes on him. Then they led him out to be crucified.

Gulgulta, the Place of the Skull

21And a certain Shimon of Cyrene,[166] the father of Alexandros and Rufus, was passing by from the countryside, and they forced him to carry

---

Yeshua's innocence, and blames the crowd: "When Pilatus saw that he could do nothing and that an uproar was starting, he took water and washed his hands before the crowd, saying, 'I am innocent of the blood of this man. You see to it'" (Matt. 27.24). In Mark, to clear himself and, by extension, Rome, of responsibility for the crucifixion, Pilate asks the crowd, "What wrong did he do?" By revealing to the crowd—and to the reader—his conviction that Yeshua did no wrong, he places himself squarely on Yeshua's side at the very moment that he orders the rabbi to be flogged and crucified. Mark paints Pilate as the helpless tool of a murderous mob whom he feels obliged to please. Sects of the Eastern Orthodox Church will later elevate the same Roman governor to sainthood. The historical view of Pilate depicts the procurator of Judea, Idumea, and Samaria, 26–36 C.E., as an unusually brutal ruler of peoples under Roman occupation. He was recalled to Rome for the massacre of the Samaritans in 36 C.E. It should also be noted that crucifixion was a Roman means of execution, one neither practiced by Jews not conceivably ordered by Jews against a Jew. Unless Yeshua were a common thief, such punishment would have been for an opponent of Roman occupation, and it may be assumed that Yeshua was an opponent of Roman rule, which earned him his death.

165. The governor's residence.

166. Cyrene. Modern Libya.

his cross. 22They brought him to the place Gulgulta,[167] which translated is the Place of the Skull. 23And they gave him wine mixed with myrrh,[168] but he didn't take it.

24And they crucified him.

The soldiers divided his clothes, casting lots to see who would take them.[169]

Crucifying him

25It was the third hour, nine in the morning, when they crucified him. 26The inscription of the charge against him was written above:

THE KING OF THE JEWS.

27With him they crucified two thieves, one on the right and one on the left of him.[170]

29And those passing by blasphemed him, shaking their heads, and saying, "Ha! You who would destroy the Temple and rebuild it in three days, 30save yourself by coming down from the cross." 31Likewise the high priests mocked him among themselves and with the scholars said, "He saved others but he can't save himself. 32Let the mashiah, the King of Yisrael, now come down from the cross so we can see and believe." And those who were crucified with him taunted him.

Darkness at noon

33At when it was the sixth hour, at noon, the whole earth became dark until three in the afternoon. 34At three o'clock, Yeshua called out words from the Psalms in a loud voice,

Eloi Eloi, lama sabachtani?

which translated is,

My God, my God, why have you abandoned me?[171]

---

167. Golgotha from the Greek Γολγοθα (Golgotha), from the Aramaic גֻּלְגֻּלְתָּא (gulgulta).

168. In the Talmud, incense is mixed with wine to deaden pain.

169. Ps. 22.18. These passages contain many citations from Psalms.

170. Verse 28 was an ancient emendation, saying, "and the scripture was fulfilled that says, 'he was counted among the lawless.'"

171. Ps. 22.1. Yeshua's words are in Aramaic.

35Some of those standing near heard him and said, "See, he calls to Eliyahu."172 36And someone ran up with a sponge soaked in vinegar,173 placed it on a reed stick, and gave it to him to drink, saying, "Let him alone. Let us see if Yeshayahu comes to take him down."

37But Yeshua let out a great cry and breathed his last breath.

38And the curtain of the Temple tore in two from top to bottom.

39The centurion who was near saw him breathe his last and said, "Truly this man was the son of God."174

His women look on

40There were also women looking on from a distance, among whom were both Miryam of Magdala175 and Miryam mother of Yaakov the younger and of Joses,176 and Shlomit,177 41who were in the Galil following

---

172. The bystanders mistakenly heard "Eliyah" for *Eloi,* "my God."

173. From the Greek *oxous,* meaning "vinegar" or "sour wine."

174. A centurion was a commander of 100 Roman soldiers. In the story of the crucifixion, after Yeshua has been mocked by Jewish bystanders, the high priests, and those crucified with him, and the curtain in the Temple has sympathetically torn in two, foretelling the Temple's imminent doom, the first to recognize that Yeshua was the son of God is the commander of the execution squad. This exoneration of Roman leadership, who now are not only guiltless in Yeshua's execution but the first in Jerusalem to state his divinity, follows the pattern of preparing the move of the authority of Yeshua's messiahship to Rome. See notes 35, Mark 2.16, and 191, Matt. 27.54.

In the pseudo-Pauline letter Hebrews 9.8–10, 9.12, and 10.19–20, the narrator tells us that the tearing of the curtain means that Yeshua has entered heaven for us so that we too now may enter God's presence.

175. Mary Magdalene from the city of Magdala.

176. It is not known who Miryam mother of Yaakov the younger and of Joses is. She may be Yeshua's mother, though there is not a consensus in favor of this view. Since she is called the mother of Yaakov rather than of Yeshua, it is unlikely that Mark intended to identify her as Miryam mother of Yeshua. Elsewhere Yeshua's brothers are identified as James, Joses (Joseph), Judas, and Simon, that is, Yaakov, Yosef, Yehuda, and Shimon. In Mark, Yeshua's mother is not portrayed sympathetically, but by Luke, the last synoptic gospel, Miryam is glorified. The virgin birth is stated in the birth stories of Matthew and Luke, and the nativity in Luke fixes her later image. Please see note 53 on Mark 6.21.

177. Salome from the Greek Σαλώμη (Salome), from the Hebrew שְׁלֹמִית (shlomit or shelomit). Salome may be the wife of Zebedee and so the mother of James and John.

him and serving him, and there were many other women who had gone up with him to Yerushalayim.

The body in linen entombed in rock

42Evening had already come, and since it was Friday (day of Preparations), the Day-Before-Shabbat,[178] 43Yosef of Arimathaia,[179] a prominent member of the Sanhedrin, who was also looking for the kingdom of God, boldly went to Pilatus and asked for the body of Yeshua.

44Pilatus marveled that he was already dead and called the centurion, and asked him if he was already dead. 45Informed by the centurion, he gave the corpse to Yosef.

46Then Yosef bought a linen cloth, took him down, and wrapped him in the linen cloth and placed him in a tomb which had been cut out of the rock, and he rolled a stone against the entrance to the tomb.

47Miryam of Magdala and Miryam of Joses saw where he was laid.

Chapter 16

The women in the empty tomb

When Shabbat was over, Miryam of Magdala and Miryam of Yaakov and Shlomit bought aromatic spices so they might go and anoint him. 2And very early on the first day of the week, they came to the tomb as the sun was rising. 3They said to each other, "Who will roll away the stone for us from the entrance to the tomb?" 4They looked up and saw that the stone had been rolled away. And it was huge. 5Then on going into the

---

178. The Greek word for "preparation," παρασκευή (paraskevi), has come to mean "Friday" in the Greek. Here, it means both Friday and preparation for the Pesach. Another word for "Friday" is *Prosabbaton* (προσάββατον), meaning "the day before Shabbat (the Sabbath)."

179. Yosef of Arimathea was presumably a member of the Sanhedrin, the council that, according to the gospels, asked for Yeshua's death. This apparent contradiction of role may be softened by the description of his piety and vision of the kingdom of God. "Arimathea" is from the Greek Ἀριμαθαία (Arimathaia) and is identified with either Ramathaim or Rentis, fifteen or twenty miles east of Jaffa.

tomb they saw a young man sitting on the right, dressed in a white robe, and they were utterly astonished.[180]

6He said to them, "Don't be alarmed. You are looking for Yeshua of Natzeret, the one who was crucified. He was raised. He is not here. See the place where they laid him. 7But go tell his students and Shimon Kefa, 'He is going ahead of you to the Galil. There you will see him, just as he told you.'"

8So they went out and fled from the tomb, seized by trembling and ecstasy. And they said nothing to anyone. They were afraid.[181]

---

180. Matthew identifies the young man as an angel (28.2).

181. The earliest manuscripts end with the dramatic fear of the women in *ekstasis*, here rendered "ecstasy," which conveys the literal meaning of "being outside themselves" as well as "ecstasy" with its multiple meanings of "amazement" in "being elsewhere" and "beside themselves" with fear.

Two Supplements to Mark

THE ENDING OF MARK has been called abrupt, although not in this translator's opinion or in that of many scholars. The ending is mysterious and dramatic, reflecting the uncertain movement during a period of turmoil. The notion of "abruptness" or "incompletion" has probably been suggested to consider or justify the inclusion of two orphan supplements, the shorter and the longer, that do not appear in the Codex Vaticanus or the Codex Sinaiticus, the two earliest manuscripts of the New Testament. The dating and authorship of the emendations are unknown. While dating and authorship for all books of the New Testament and the Hebrew Bible are in question (with the exception of seven of Paul's letters), these orphans, as they are called, cannot be considered part of original Mark. Therefore, without manuscript evidence for inclusion, these supplements are not found in Lattimore and recent translations. When included in others, they are bracketed to indicate that they are pseudepigraphical.

The shorter supplement is a few lines, the longer about a page, continuing chapter 17 from 9–19. The purpose of the "Shorter Ending" is to mend fences with Peter and Peter's faction in Jerusalem. Peter fares poorly in the last chapters, having been rebuked by Yeshua for his irresolution. There is the briefest suggestion of resurrection in that Yeshua is sending through the Peter circle the message of eternal salvation. It is a dull, bureaucratic anticlimax. The "Longer Ending" is more substantive and may be a second-century addition to make Mark conform to the personal appearances of the resurrected messiah as revealed in the other gospels. Belief in Yeshua's resurrection was crucial to second-century emerging Christianity.[182] The earliest gospel is Mark (it is not known when the theory of order was "first" generally accepted), and to let Mark, either the foundation of the Synoptics or at the very least a core member, not end with a clear resurrection scene, which shows Jesus walking and talking, is a serious inconsistency that could cast doubt on the historical reliability of the other gospel documents. Hence, the compiler or compilers assumed their tasks and composed these suitable didactic summaries, these new orphan endings that abruptly change the tensely fearful tone and dramatic climax to Mark.

182. For an outstanding study of the notion of resurrection in the Hebrew Bible and the New Testament, see Geza Vermes, *The Resurrection* (New York: Doubleday, 2008).

The Shorter Ending of Mark

ALL THAT had been commanded they reported briefly to those around Shimon Kefa. After that, Yeshua himself, from east to west, sent through them the holy and deathless proclamation of eternal salvation. Amain.

The Longer Ending of Mark[183]

⁓

9Now AFTER he rose early on the first day of the week, he appeared first to Miryam,[184] from whom he had cast out seven demons. 10She left and informed those who had been with him, who were mourning and crying. 11But those who had heard that he was alive and was seen by her did not believe her.

12After this he appeared in another form to two of them as they were walking into the countryside. 13And they returned and reported it to the rest, but they did not believe them.

14But later, as the eleven were reclining at the table, he appeared and rebuked them for their disbelief and hardheartedness, for they did not believe those who had seen him risen. 15And he said to them,

> Go into all the world and proclaim the good news to all creation.
> 16Who believes and is immersed will be saved,
> And who is unbelieving will be condemned.
> 17And signs will accompany the believers.

---

183. Some ancient authorities give what is clearly a later addition, inserted between 16.14 and 16.15 of the Longer Ending of Mark: "And they excused themselves, saying 'This age of lawlessness and unbelief is under the sway of Satan, who does not allow the truth and power of God to prevail over the unclean things of the spirits. Therefore reveal your justice now.' In such way they spoke to Christ. And Christ replied to them, 'Satan's term of years has been fulfilled, but other terrible things are coming. Because of those who sinned I was delivered to death so that they may return to the truth and no more sin all in order that they may inherit the spiritual and imperishable glory of justice that lies in heaven.'"

184. Mary Magdalene.

In my name they will cast out demons,
18And speak in new tongues.
They will pick up serpents with their hands,[185]
And if they drink poison, it will not harm them,
19They will lay their hands on the sick who will be well again.
20After speaking to them, lord Yeshua was taken up into the sky, and he sat down at the right hand of God. And they went out and preached everywhere. The lord was working with them and confirmed the word through accompanying signs.

---

185. "With their hands" appears bracketed as doubtful in the UBS fourth corrected edition of the Greek texts.

Mattityahu
(Matthew)

Mattityahu[1]
(Matthew)

THE AUTHORSHIP and place and date of composition of the Gospel of Matthew are matters of speculation. In the gospel itself, the writer is identified as Levi the tax collector. "Matthew" is apparently the apostolic name of Levi, given to him by churchmen in the second century. Biblical scholarship describes Matthew as steeped in rabbinical reference and learning and as a Greek-speaking Christian Jew of the second generation. Though there is no scholarly consensus about the dating of the gospels, Matthew was probably composed a decade after 70 C.E., the year of the destruction of the Temple by Titus, which is alluded to in Matthew and in the other gospels. The allusion to this specific historical event of 70 C.E. is sufficient evidence to place the composition of all the gospels at least after that year.

Traditionally, Matthew is placed first in the order of the gospels, but this placement is not chronological, for Matthew derives from Mark and probably from a lost sayings gospel, the so-called Q source. The Gnostic Gospel of Thomas found at Nag Hammadi, Egypt, in 1945 is a sayings gospel and may have been one of those sayings books of Yeshua's aphorisms and parables that fed into the sources from which Matthew derives. Matthew begins with a genealogy (most certainly appended at a later date) and with the birth of Yeshua. Since Luke also begins with a genealogy followed by the famous nativity scene of Yeshua's birth in

---

1. Matthew's name in English comes from the Greek Ματθαῖος (Maththaios), from the Hebrew מַתִּתְיָהוּ (Mattityahu) or מַתִּתְיָה (Mattityah), meaning "gift of Yahweh." Another candidate for Matthew's name is the Hebrew *Mattai* or the Aramaic *Matai*.

Bethlehem in a feeding trough, the manger, and the story of Yeshua's life, there is as much reason for beginning the New Testament with Luke as with Matthew, though it appears in terms of dating and influence that Matthew precedes Luke. That Mark is the earliest of the gospels and a direct source for Matthew and Luke is widely accepted, and in recent years the traditional presentation of the gospels has been changed, placing Mark at the beginning of the New Testament, as in the Richmond Lattimore and the Jesus Seminar translations.

There are more allusions to the Hebrew Bible in this gospel than in the others. Matthew wrote to persuade Jews that Yeshua was the foretold messiah so they might become Christian Jews. Biblical scholarship suggests that passages of extreme anti-Semitism, such as "Let his blood be upon us and upon our children!" (27.25), in which the Jews in the street shout a curse upon themselves now and on their progeny forever, are later interpolations, thereby creating a polemic external to Matthew and his days.

Matthew may be said to be the most aphoristic and poetic of the gospels and closest to a sayings book. This teaching book does not have the same austere plainness and drama of Mark, which is more uniformly narrative and ends abruptly at a moment of fear and ecstasy in the cave where Yeshua's body has disappeared. But Matthew also has a deep pathos and conveys a sense of Yeshua as a leader of the poor, of the disenfranchised, in an epic of hunger and hope. Matthew covers many aspects of Yeshua's life and mission, including his discourse dealing with death, resurrection, and immortality (24.1–25.46). Many of the critical moments in the New Testament are fully elaborated in Matthew, including the coming of the Magi, the birth of Yeshua, the baptizing mission of John the Baptist, John's arrest and execution, and the Passion Week scene of Yeshua's arrest, crucifixion, and the risen Yeshua. Matthew's most extraordinary literary and philosophical contribution is the Sermon on the Mount (5.1–7.29), including the Beatitudes (5.3–12) and the Lord's Prayer (6.9–13). Much of the material in the Sermon on the Mount also appears dispersed through the other synoptic gospels (Matthew, Mark, and Luke, but not John), and the Lord's Prayer, in a shorter form, also appears in Luke 11.2–4. Apart from Apocalypse (Revelation), which I believe is the epic poem of the New Testament, the poetry in Matthew takes its place among the great bodies of world poetry.

Chapter 1

Yeshua's genealogy[2]

The book of the generation[3] of Yeshua the Mashiah[4] son of David son of Avraham.[5] 2Avraham fathered Yitzhak,[6] and Yitzhak fathered

---

2. The genealogy in Matthew importantly establishes Yeshua's Davidic descent. While Luke's genealogy (3.23–31) traces Yeshua's lineage all the way back to Adam, the son of God, Matthew's begins with Avraham, the father of the Jewish people. It goes forward, ending with "and Yaakov fathered Yosef, the husband of Miryam, from whom was born Yeshua (Yehoshua) who is called the mashiah." Matthew states that Yeshua was born of Miryam. Since the genealogy is patrilineal, it traces Yeshua's origin not through Miryam's ancestors but Yosef's lines, which go back to Avraham. If it is to be understood that Yeshua was born of the virgin Miryam (seeded by the Holy Ghost) and that Yosef was *not* his biological father, then Matthew's patrilineal genealogy fails to establish Yeshua's blood descent from Avraham, David, and the listed ancestors, and pertains to Yeshua only in affirming who was his mother. To explain this genealogical dilemma, scholars have said that Matthew traces the *legal* descent of Yeshua, since Yosef was Yeshua's legal father, if not his blood relative.

The genealogy (Matt. 1.1–16) is prefatory to the gospel and its author uncertain. It may have been added in a later period.

3. "Generation" may also be translated as "birth," "beginning," "history," or "genealogy." The two first words of Matthew are βίβλος γενέσεως (biblos geneseos), "the book of the generation." The beginning parallels Genesis 1.1, "In the beginning"; Genesis 2.4, "These are the generations of the heavens and the earth when they were created"; and exactly Genesis 5.1, "This is the book of the descendants" (זֶה סֵפֶר תּוֹלְדֹת, ze sefer toldot). In *An Introduction to the New Testament* (New York: Doubleday, 1997), Raymond E. Brown notes the competitive meaning of Matthew 1.1: "A polyvalent sense of *genesis* is a possibility: The phrase prefaces the ancestral origin, birth, and beginnings of Jesus; but it also encompasses a view of the whole story of Jesus as a new creation, even greater than the old" (174).

4. Jesus from the Greek Ἰησοῦς (Iesous), from the Hebrew יֵשׁוּעַ (yeshua), from the Hebrew יְהוֹשֻׁעַ (yehoshua), and Christ from the Greek Χριστος (Hristos), translated from the Hebrew מָשִׁיחַ (mashiah). The Greek translation of *Yeshua the Mashiah* is "Jesus the Christ." *Mashiah* is a free transliteration of Hebrew *mashiah*.

5. Abraham.

6. Isaac.

Yaakov,[7] and Yaakov fathered Yehuda[8] and his brothers, 3and Yehuda fathered Peretz[9] and Zerah whose mother was Tamar,[10] Peretz fathered Hetzron,[11] and Hetzron fathered Ram,[12] 4and Ram fathered Amminadav,[13] Amminadav fathered Nahshon, and Nahshon fathered Salmon, 5and Salmon fathered Boaz, whose mother was Rahav,[14] and Boaz fathered Obev,[15] whose mother was Rut,[16] and Obev fathered Jesse, 6and Jesse fathered David the King.

And David fathered Shlomoh,[17] whose mother had been Uriyah's wife, 7and Shlomo fathered Rehavam,[18] and Rehavam fathered Aviyah,[19] and Aviyah fathered Asa,[20] 8and Asa fathered Yehoshafat,[21] and Yehoshafat fathered Yoram,[22] and Yoram fathered Uziyah,[23] 9and Uziyah fathered Yotam,[24] and Yotam fathered Ahaz, and Ahaz fathered Hizikiah,[25] 10and Hizikiah fathered Menasheh,[26] and Menasheh fathered Amon, and

---

7. Jacob.

8. Judas.

9. Perez.

10. Tamar, Thamar.

11. Hezron or Estrom.

12. Aram.

13. Amminadab.

14. Rahab.

15. Obeb.

16. Ruth.

17. Solomon.

18. Rehoboam.

19. Abijah.

20. Asaph. (Matthew gives "Asaph," confusing King Asa, son of the Judean king Aviyah, with a minor figure named Asaph.)

21. Jehoshaphat.

22. Joram.

23. Uzziah.

24. Jotham.

25. Hezekiah.

26. Manasseh.

Amon fathered Yoshiyah,[27] 11and Yoshiyah fathered Yehoniah[28] and his brothers at the time of the exile to Babylon.

12After the exile to Babylon, Yehoniah fathered Shealtiel,[29] and Shealtiel fathered Zerubavel,[30] 13and Zerubavel fathered Avihud,[31] and Avihud fathered Eliakim,[32] and Eliakim fathered Azur,[33] 14and Azur fathered Tzadok,[34] and Tzadok fathered Yahin,[35] and Yahin fathered Eliud,[36] 15and Eliud fathered Elazar,[37] and Elazar fathered Mattan,[38] and Mattan fathered Yaakov, 16and Yaakov fathered Yosef, the husband of Miryam,[39] from whom was born Yeshua (Yehoshua) who is called the mashiah.

17So all the generations from Avraham to David are fourteen, and from David until the exile in Babylon fourteen generations, and from the exile in Babylon until the mashiah fourteen generations.

An angel in Yosef's dream tells of Miryam with child

18The birth of Yeshua the Mashiah happened in this way. Miryam[40] his mother was engaged to Yosef,[41] yet before they came together she discovered a child in her womb, placed there by the holy spirit. 19Yosef her husband, a just man and loath to expose her, resolved to divorce

---

27. Josiah, Josias.
28. Jechoniah.
29. Shealtiel or Salathiel.
30. Zerubbabel.
31. Abiud.
32. Eliakim.
33. Azor.
34. Zadok.
35. Achim.
36. Eliud.
37. Eleazar.
38. Matthan.
39. Mary.
40. Mary from the Greek Μαρία (Maria), from the Hebrew מִרְיָם (miryam).
41. Joseph from the Greek Ἰωσήφ (Iosef), from the Hebrew יוֹסֵף (yosef).

her secretly. 20But as he was making plans, look, an angel of the Lord[42] appeared to him in a dream and said,

>Yosef, son of David, do not fear to take Miryam as your wife.

>The child engendered in her came from the holy spirit,

>21And she will give birth, and you will name him Yeshua,

>For he will save[43] his people from their wrongdoings.

22All this was done to fulfill the word of God uttered through his prophet Yeshayahu,[44] saying,

>23"Listen. A young woman will have a child in her womb

>And give birth to a son, and his name will be Immanuel."[45]

24When Yosef rose from his dream, he did what the angel of the Lord told him, and he accepted her as his wife, 25yet he did not know her until after she gave birth, and he called the child the name Yeshua.

---

42. Angel of the Lord from the Greek ἄγγελος κυρίου (angelos kyriou), from the Hebrew מַלְאַךְ יהוה (malakh yahweh), as in Genesis 48.16. A literal rendering would be *Yahweh's malakh* or "messenger." *Malakh* (מַלְאַךְ) is the Hebrew word for "angel." "Angel" is a Greek word meaning merely "a messenger," associated with Hermes, without the divine powers of Yahweh's *malakh*. In biblical Greek, however, "angel" has taken on meanings of divinity and connotes "great beauty" and "fear."

43. The naming of the infant messiah as Jesus, *Iesous* in the Greek, is followed by the reason for naming him "Jesus," explaining that the name means "he will save." But Jesus in the Greek, *Iesous* (Ἰησοῦς), has no meaning in the Greek other than being a transliteration of the Hebrew Yeshua, from *Yehoshua*, which does mean "Yahweh saves." This passage suggests either an earlier text in the Hebrew or the Aramaic or that the author of the Greek Matthew was a Greek- and Hebrew-speaking Jew who had in mind the Hebrew or Aramaic name *Yeshua* or *Yehoshua* for the salvific lord and expected the readers or listeners to understand the name of the salvific lord in Hebrew embedded in the name *Yeshua* or *Yehoshua*. There seems to be no other explanation for attributing "for he will save" to a Greek name which itself is meaningless.

44. Isaiah from the Greek Ἡσαΐας (Esaias), from the Hebrew יְשַׁעְיָהוּ (yeshayahu). Isaiah is not mentioned in the text, but the passage quoted is by the prophet Isaiah (7.15). Since an ancient reader or listener presumably knew, or was expected to know, which prophet was being cited—and the modern reader would normally not have such knowledge—the name of the prophet here, and in each instance where the text attributes a passage to a prophet or to a book in the Hebrew Bible, is included in the text itself rather than in the margin or in bottom-of-page annotation.

45. Immanuel means "God is with us."

Chapter 2

A star in the east

Now when Yeshua was born in Beit Lehem[46] in Yehuda[47] in the days of King Herod, look, some Magi, astrologer priests from the east, came to Yerushalayim[48] 2and said,

> Where is he who was born King of the Jews?
> We saw his star in the east
> And we came to worship him.

3Hearing this, King Herod was troubled and all Yerushalayim with him, 4and calling together all the high priests and the scholars of the people, he asked them where the mashiah was born.

5And they said to him, "In Beit Lehem in Yehuda, for so it is written by the prophet Malachi":

> 6And you, Beit Lehem, in the land of Yehuda,
> You are in no way least among the leaders of Yehuda,
> For out of you will come a leader
> Who will be a shepherd of my people Yisrael.[49]

7Then Herod secretly called in the Magi astrologers and learned from them the exact time of the star's appearance, 8and he sent them to Beit Lehem, saying, "Go and inquire precisely about the child. When you find him, bring me word so that I too may go to worship him."

9After hearing the king they set out, and look, the star, which they had seen in the east, went before them until it stood above the place where the child lay. 10When they saw the star, they were marvelously glad. 11And they went into the house and saw the child with Miryam his mother, and fell to the ground and worshiped him. Opening their treasure boxes, they offered him gifts of gold and frankincense and myrrh.

---

46. Bethlehem from the Greek Βηθλέεμ (Bethleem), from the Hebrew בֵּית לֶחֶם (beit lehem), meaning "house of bread."

47. Judea from the Greek Ἰουδαία (Ioudaia), from the Hebrew יְהוּדָה (yehuda). Also is the name Yehuda.

48. Jerusalem from the Greek Ἰερουσαλήμ (Ierousalem), from the Hebrew יְרוּשָׁלַיִם (yerushalayim).

49. Israel from the Greek Ἰσραήλ, from the Hebrew יִשְׂרָאֵל (yisrael).

12Then having been warned in a dream not to go back to Herod, they returned by another road to their own country.

An angel warns and a family flees to Egypt

13When they had gone, an angel appeared to Yosef in a dream, saying, "Arise, take this child and his mother, and fly into Egypt, and remain there until I tell you. Herod is looking for the child to destroy him."

14Then he arose and took the child and his mother through the dark of night and went to Egypt, 15and he stayed there until the death of Herod, thereby fulfilling the word uttered through Hoshea[50] his prophet, saying,

> Out of Egypt I have called my son.

Herod enraged and killing

16When Herod saw that he had been outfoxed by the three astrologers, he was in a great rage and sent his men to kill all the male children in Beit Lehem[51] and in all the region who were two years and under, according to the exact time of the star, ascertained from the Magi. 17Thereby was fulfilled the word spoken through the prophet Yirmiyahu,[52] saying,

> 18A voice was heard in Ramah,
> Weeping and grave lamentation,
> Rahel[53] weeping for her children,
> And she would not be comforted,
> Because her children are gone.

Back into the land of Yisrael

19Now when Herod died,[54] look, an angel appeared in a dream to Yosef in Egypt, 20saying,

---

50. Hosea from the Hebrew הוֹשֵׁעַ (hoshea).

51. Bethlehem.

52. Jeremiah from the Greek Ἰερεμίας (Ieremias), from the Hebrew יִרְמְיָהוּ (yirmiyahu).

53. Rachel from the Greek Ῥαχήλ (Rahel), from the Hebrew רָחֵל (rahel).

54. The story of Herod's massacre of the sons at the birth of Yeshua as it is written echoes pharaoh's massacre of the sons at the birth of Moses (Exod. 1.12–22), thereby making a parallel between Moses and Yeshua and Yeshua as leader of their Israel, each having been called by God "out of Egypt."

> Arise, take the child and his mother
> And go to the land of Yisrael.
> Those who sought the child's life are dead.

21Yosef arose, took the child and the mother, and went to the land of Yisrael. 22But when he heard that Archelaos was now King in Yehuda, replacing his father Herod, he was afraid to go there. And being warned in a dream, he withdrew to a place in the Galil,[55] where he went 23and lived in a city called Natzeret.[56] So the prophets' word was fulfilled:

> And he will be called a Natzrati.[57]

Chapter 3

Yohanan the Dipper in the desert

In those days came Yohanan the Dipper[58] preaching in the desert of Yehuda, 2saying,

> Repent, for the kingdom of the skies is near.

3He was the one mentioned by the prophet Yeshayahu,[59] saying,

> A voice of one crying in the desert:
> Prepare the way of the Lord and make his road straight.

4Now Yohanan wore clothing made of camel's hair and a belt of hide around his waist, and his food was locusts and wild honey. 5At that time the people of Yerushalayim came to him and also all of Yehuda and the whole countryside about the Yarden.[60] 6He immersed them in the river

---

55. Galilee from the Greek Γαλιλαία (Galilaia), from the Hebrew גָּלִיל (galil). "Galil" is a "circle," "district," or "province." It is often used in the phrase גְּלִיל הַגּוֹיִם (galil hagoyim), meaning "province of the goyim (gentiles)."

56. Nazareth from Greek Ναζαρέτ (Natzaret), from unknown village in Galilee probably spelled "Natzeret."

57. Nazarene from the Greek Ναζαρηνός (Nazarenos), from the Natzeret, that is, a Natzrati.

58. John the Baptist. "John" is from the Greek Ἰωάννης (Ioannes), from the Hebrew יוֹחָנָן (yohanan). "The Dipper" is from the Greek ὁ βαπτιστής (ho baptistes), meaning "one who dips, washes, or immerses," as in Jewish ritual washings.

59. Isaiah.

60. Jordan from the Greek Ἰορδάνης (Iordanes), from the Hebrew יַרְדֵּן (yarden).

Yarden, and they confessed their sins. 7But when he saw many of the
Prushim and Tzadokim[61] coming to the dipping, he said to them,

> You offspring of vipers, who warned you to flee from
> The coming wrath? 8Prepare fruit worthy of your repentance.
> 9And do not plan to say among yourselves,
> "We have Avraham as our father."
> For I say to you that out of these stones
> God is able to raise up children to Avraham.
> 10Even now the axe lies set against the root of the trees,
> And so every tree that fails to yield good fruit
> Is cut down and cast into the fire.
> 11I immerse you in water for repentance,
> But after me will come one stronger than I,
> And I am not fit to carry his sandals.
> He will dip you in the holy spirit and fire.
> 12His winnowing fork is in his hand,
> And he will clear his threshing floor and
> Put his grain in the storehouse,
> But he will burn the chaff in unquenchable fire.

Yeshua immersed

13Then came Yeshua from the Galil to the Yarden and to Yohanan to
be immersed by him. 14Yohanan tried to stop him, saying, "I need to be
immersed by you, yet you come to me?" 15But Yeshua answered, saying
to him,

> Leave things as they are.
> It is right for us in this way
> To fulfill all that is just.

Then Yohanan consented.

16And when Yeshua was immersed, at once he came out of the water
and look, the skies opened, and he saw the spirit of God coming down like
a dove, coming down upon him. 17And look, a voice from the skies said,

---

61. Pharisees from the Greek Φαρισαῖος (Farisaisos), from the Hebrew פְּרוּשִׁים
(prushim). "Pharisee" (s.) is *Parush*. Sadducee from the Greek Σαδώκ, from the
Hebrew צָדוֹק (tzadok). "Sadducees" (pl.) is *Tzadokim*.

This is my son whom I love,
In whom I am well pleased.

Chapter 4

Temptation in the desert

Then Yeshua was led by the spirit up into the desert to be tempted by the devil. 2 And he fasted forty days and forty nights, and afterward he hungered. 3And coming up to him, the tempter said,

If you are the son of God, speak
And make these stones loaves of bread.

4But Yeshua answered, saying,

It is written in Deuteronomy:
One lives not on bread alone
But on every word coming through the mouth of God.[62]

5Then the devil took him to the holy city, and set him on the parapet of the Temple 6and said to him,

If you are the son of God, cast yourself down,
For in the Psalms it is written:

He will command his angels to care for you,
And with their hands they will hold you up
So you will not smash your foot against a stone.[63]

7Yeshua said to him,

Again in Deuteronomy it is written:

You must not tempt the lord, your God.[64]

8Once more the devil led him to a very high mountain and showed him all the kingdoms of the world and their glory, 9and said to him,

All this I will give you
If you fall down before me and worship me.

10Then Yeshua said to him,

---

62. Deut. 8.3.
63. Ps. 91.11–12.
64. Deut. 6.16.

Go away, Satan, for it is also written:
> You will worship the lord, God, and you will serve him
> alone.[65]

11Then the devil left him, and look, angels came down and cared for him.

Preaching in the Galil

12Now when he heard that Yohanan had been arrested, Yeshua withdrew to the Galil, 13and leaving Natzeret he came to and settled in Kfar Nahum[66] by the great lake, in the districts of Zvulun and Naftali. 14He came to fulfill the words spoken through the prophet Yeshayahu:

15Land of Zvulun and land of Naftali,
The way to the sea beyond the Yarden,
The Galil of the foreigners,
16The people who were sitting in darkness
Saw a great light,
And for those sitting in the land and shadow of death
The light sprang into dawn.[67]

17From that instant Yeshua began to preach his word and said,
Repent, for the kingdom of the skies is near.

Gathering the fishermen

18And as he was walking by the Sea of the Galil, he saw two brothers, one called Shimon Kefa,[68] and his brother Andreas,[69] casting their net into the sea, for they were fishermen. 19He said to them,
Come, and I will make you fishers of people.
20And they immediately dropped their nets and followed him.

---

65. Deut. 6.13.

66. Capernaum. Latin *Capernaum* from the Greek Καφαρναούμ (Kafarnaum), from Hebrew כְּפַר נַחוּם (kfar nahum), meaning "village of Nahum."

67. Isa. 9.1–2.

68. Peter from the Greek Πέτρος (Petros), translated from the Aramaic כֵּיפָא (kefa), meaning "rock" or "stone." Full name is Simon Peter, in Aramaic Shimon Kefa.

69. Andrew.

21Going on from there he saw two more brothers, Yaakov[70] the son of Zavdai[71] and Yohanan his brother, in the boat with Zavdai their father, mending their nets. He called out to them. 22And they left their boat and their father, and followed him.

Healing the possessed

23Yeshua went all over the Galil, teaching in the synagogues, preaching the good message of the kingdom, and healing every sickness and infirmity among the people. 24His fame spread into all of Syria. And they brought him all who suffered diverse diseases and were seized by pain and those who were possessed by demons, epilepsy, and paralysis, and he healed them. 25And huge crowds followed him around from the Galil and Dekapolis and Yerushalayim, Yehuda, and from beyond the Yarden.

Chapter 5

Teaching from the mountain[72]

And seeing the crowds, he went up the mountain. When he was seated, his students came to him. 2And he opened his mouth and from the mountain gave them his teachings:

3Blessed are the poor in spirit
   For theirs is the kingdom of the skies.
4Blessed are they who mourn
   For they will be comforted.
5Blessed are the gentle

---

70. James (Jacob) from the Greek Ἰάκωβος (Iakobos), from the Hebrew יַעֲקֹב (yaakov).

71. Zebedee from the Greek Ζεβεδαῖος (Zebedaios), from the Hebrew זַבְדִּי (zavdai).

72. Chapters 5–7, 10, 13, 18, 24–25 are commonly known as the Sermon on the Mount, a phrase that does not appear in the New Testament. The Sermon is a compilation of wisdom sayings of Yeshua and contains the Beatitudes ("blessings") (5.3–12). Parts of the Sermon are found dispersed in the other gospels and have a counterpart in Luke's Sermon on the Plain (Luke 6.20–49).

For they will inherit the earth.

6Blessed are the hungry and thirsty for justice

For they will be heartily fed.

7Blessed are the merciful

For they will obtain mercy.

8Blessed are the clean in heart

For they will see God.

9Blessed are the peacemakers

For they will be called the children of God.

10Blessed are they who are persecuted for the sake of their
justice

For theirs is the kingdom of the skies.

11Blessed are you when they revile, persecute, and speak

Every cunning evil[73] against you, lying, because of me.

12Rejoice and be glad, for your reward in the heavens is huge,

And in this way did they persecute the prophets before you.

Salt and light

13You are the salt of the earth.

But if the salt has lost its taste, how will it recover its salt?

Its powers are for nothing except to be thrown away

And trampled underfoot by others.

14You are the light of the world.

A city cannot be hidden when it is set on a mountain.

15Nor do they light a lamp and place it under a basket,

But on a stand,

And it glows on everyone in the house.

16So let your light glow before people so they may see

Your good works and glorify your father of the skies.

---

73. The adjective poneros (πονηρός) in classical Greek often has a positive meaning, as in "nimble-witted" or "cunning" Odysseus, and has retained that specific
earthly meaning into modern Greek. Some sense of the shade of cunning or earth-
iness is desired in the New Testament usage, where it is usually rendered "evil" or
"wicked."

Law and prophets

17Do not think that I have come to destroy the law or the
prophets.

I have not come to destroy but to fulfill.

18And yes I say to you, until the sky and the earth are gone,

Not one tiny iota or serif will disappear from the law

Until all has been done.

19Whoever breaks even the lightest of the commandments

And teaches others to do the same

Will be esteemed least in the kingdom of the skies,

But whoever performs and teaches them

Will be called great in the kingdom of the skies.

20I say to you, if you don't exceed the justice

Of the scholars and the Prushim,

You will never enter the kingdom of the skies.

Anger and the fire of Gei Hinnom[74]

21You have heard our people in ancient times commanded in
Exodus,

You must not murder,

And whoever murders will be liable to judgment.

22I say to you, whoever is angry with a companion

Will be judged in court,

And whoever calls a companion a fool will go before the
Sanhedrin, the highest court,

And whoever calls a companion a scoundrel

Will taste the fire of Gei Hinnom.

23If then you bring your gift to the altar,

And there you remember your companion holds something
against you,

24Leave your gift before the altar,

And go first to be reconciled with your companion

---

74. Gehenna from the Greek γέεννα (Geenna), from the Hebrew גֵּיא הִנֹּם (gei hinnom), meaning the "Valley of Hinnom." *Gei Hinnom* and *Sheol* are normally translated as "hell."

And then come back and present your offering.

25When you are with your adversary walking in the street

On the way to the court,

Quickly, be of good will toward him and reconcile

26Or your accuser will hand you over to the judge,

The judge to the bailiff,

And you will be thrown into prison.

I tell you, there will be no way out

Until you have paid back the last penny.

Adultery in the heart

27And you have heard in Exodus the words,

"Do not commit adultery."

28Yet I say, if a man looks at a woman with lust

He has already slept with her in his heart.

29So if your right eye causes you to stumble,

Tear it out and cast it away.

It is better to lose a part of your body

Than for your whole body to be cast into Gei Hinnom.

30And if your right hand causes you to stumble,

Cut it off and cast it away.

It is better to lose a part of your body

Than for your whole body to be cast into Gei Hinnom.

Sending a wife away

31And you have heard in Deuteronomy,

If a man sends his wife away,[75]

Give her a proper bill of divorce,

32But I also tell you that any man divorcing and sending his
wife away,

Except for dirty harlotry,

Makes her the victim of adultery;

And any man who marries a woman divorced and sent away

Is himself an adulterer.

---

75. Deut. 24.1–4.

Do not swear

33You have heard said in ancient times in Exodus,

You must not swear false oaths,

But make good your oaths before God.

34But I tell you not to swear at all:

Not by heaven, for heaven is God's throne,

35Nor by earth, for earth is God's footstool,

Nor by Yerushalayim, for Yerushalayim is the city of the great
king.

36Do not swear by your own head,

Since you cannot make one hair white or black.

37If your word is yes, say yes.

If your word is no, say no.

To say more is to indulge in evil.

Turn your cheek

38And you have heard in Exodus,

"An eye for an eye and a tooth for a tooth."

39But I tell you not to resist the wicked person,

And if someone strikes you on the right cheek,

Turn your other cheek as well.

40If someone wants to sue you for your shirt,

Give him your cloak as well.

41If someone forces you to go a mile with him,

Go a second mile with him.

42Give to who asks you. And do not turn away one

Who wants to borrow from you.

Love your enemies

43You have heard it said in Leviticus,

"You will love your neighbor and hate your enemy."[76]

44I say to you to love your enemies

And pray for those who persecute you

---

76. Lev. 19.18.

45So you may become the children of your father of the skies,
　For he makes the sun rise over the evil and the good,
　And he brings the rains to the just and the unjust among us.
46If you love those who love you, what reward have you?
　Do not even the tax collectors do the same?
47If you greet only those who are your friends,
　How have you done more than others?
48Have you done more than the gentiles?[77]
　Be perfect as your father the heavenly one is perfect.

Chapter 6

Actors in the synagogue
　Take care not to perform your good deeds before other people
　So as to be seen by them,
　For you will have no reward from your father of the skies.
2When you give alms, don't sound a trumpet before you
　Like the actors[78] in the synagogues and in the streets,

---

77. Gentile from the late Latin *gens*, meaning "pagan," from the Greek ἔθνος (eth-nos), meaning literally a "national" as in "people," or "nation," and in the plural "non-Jews, Christian Jews, Christians, pagans," or "heathens," from the Hebrew גּוֹי (goy), plural גּוֹיִם (goyim), meaning "a people, nation, non-Jew." The diverse meanings given in usage and especially in translation of the Greek depend on the context. Normally, in the gospels and Acts an *ethnos* means a non-Jew who may be converted to Jewish Messianism or, as in later church koine, a "Christian Jew who is a convert from paganism," as in parts of Acts and the letters; and if the word is used disparagingly to mean both a non-Jew and non-Christian, it refers to a pagan. In its fully wicked sense, *ethnikos* (like a gentile) means a "heathen." In modern English the commonest meaning of "gentile" has come to be a Christian as opposed to a Jew.

78. Actor from the Greek ὑποκριτής (hypokrates). An "actor" or "player" is the ancient meaning. In New Testament Greek, an actor is a pretender or hypocrite. In this instance of ostentatious acting in the synagogue, for the metaphor for hypocrisy to work it is essential that the primary meaning of "actor," rather than the moral abstraction of "hypocrite," come through first.

Who seek the praise of the onlookers.
I say to you, they have their reward.
3Yet when you give alms, do not let the left hand know
What the right hand is doing
4So the alms may be given in secret,
And your father seeing you in secret will repay you.

5And when you pray, do not do so like the actors.
They love to stand in our synagogues and on the corners
Of the open squares, praying
So they will be seen by others.
I say to you, they have their rewards.

A secret prayer
6When you pray, go into your inner room and close the door
And pray to your father who is in secret,
And your father who sees you in secret will repay you.
7Yet when you pray, do not babble empty words like the
        gentiles,
For the gentiles think by uttering a glut of words
They will be heard.
8Do not be like them,
For your father knows what you need before you ask him.

Prayer to the father in the firmament
9And pray like this:
Our father in heaven, hallowed be your name.
10Your kingdom come, your will be done
On earth as it is in heaven.
11Give us today our daily bread
12And forgive our debts
As we have forgiven our debtors.
13And do not lead us into temptation,
But rescue us from the evil one.[79]

---

79. The figure referred to is probably the devil.

> [For yours is the kingdom,
> And the power and glory forever. Amain.][80]

Forgiving

14If you forgive those who have stumbled and gone astray
  Then your heavenly father will forgive you,
15But if you will not forgive others
  Your father will not forgive your missteps.

Oil on your head when fasting

16When you fast, do not scowl darkly like actors.
  They distort their faces to show others they are fasting.
  Yes, they have their reward.
17But when you fast, anoint your head with oil
  To make it smooth and wash your face
18So your fasting will be unknown to people
  And known only to your father who is not visible.
  Your father who sees you in secret will repay you.

Treasures in heaven

19Do not hoard your treasures on earth
  Where moth and earthworms consume them,
  Where thieves dig through walls and steal them,
20But store your treasures in heaven
  Where neither moth nor earthworm consumes
  And where thieves do not dig through the walls and steal,

---

80. This famous ending of the Lord's Prayer is in brackets, since this doxology, based on David's prayer in 1 Chronicles 29.11, does not appear in the earliest Greek texts. It does appear in the later Majority Greek Text, in Tyndale, and in the Authorized translations. See Introduction for further discussion.

Amen from the Greek ἀμήν (amen), from the Hebrew אָמֵן (amein). The Hebrew word *amain* (*amein* would work just as well for free-sounding English) was used by Paul in his Greek, as it is used in Hebrew, at the end of a passage as a liturgical "in truth" or "so be it." Both the Greek and Hebrew words were probably pronounced with a long ay, as in "main." It is appropriate to pronounce English "amen," as in Greek and Hebrew; hence here it is given as *amain*.

21Since your treasure is also there
Where your heart will be.

Lamp of the body

22The lamp of the body is the eye.
If your eye is clear, your whole body is filled with light,
23But if your eye is clouded, your whole body
Will inhabit darkness.
And if the light in your whole body is darkness,
How dark it is!

Dilemma of two masters

24No one can serve two masters.
You will either hate one and love the other
Or cling to one and despise the other.
You cannot serve God and the mammon of riches.

Life more than food

25So I tell you, do not worry about your life
Or say, "What am I to eat? What am I to drink?"[81]
And about the body, "What am I to wear?"
Isn't life more than its food, and your body more than its
clothing?

Birds of the sky and lilies of the field

26Consider the birds of the sky.
They do not sow or reap or collect for their granaries,
Yet your heavenly father feeds them.
Are you not more valuable than they?
Who among you by brooding can add one more hour
To your life?

27And why care about clothing?

---

81. "What am I to drink?" is missing in many texts.

28Consider the lilies of the field, how they grow.
   They do not labor or spin
29But I tell you not even Shlomoh[82] in all his splendor
   Was clothed like one of these lilies.
30And if the grass of the field is there today
   And tomorrow is cast into the oven
   And in these ways God has dressed the earth,
   Will he not clothe you in a more stunning raiment,
   You who suffer from poor faith?

Brooding about tomorrow

31Do not brood, mumbling, "What is there to eat or drink?"
   Or "What shall we wear?"
32All those things the gentiles set their hearts on.
   Your heavenly father knows you need all these things.
33But seek first his kingdom and his justice
   And all things will be given to you.
34Do not worry about tomorrow,
   For tomorrow will worry about itself.
   Each day has enough troubles of its own.

Chapter 7

Splinter in the eye

Do not judge so you may not be judged,
2For by your judgment you will be judged
   And by your measure you will be measured.
3Why do you gaze at the splinter in your brother's eye
   Yet not recognize the log in your own eye?
4Or why say to your brother,
   "Let me take the splinter out of your eye"

---

82. Solomon from the Greek Σολομών (Solomon), from the Hebrew שְׁלֹמֹה (shlomoh).

When your own eye carries a log of wood?
5You hypocrite, first remove the log from your own vision,
And you will see clearly enough
To pluck the sliver from your brother's eye.

Pearls and pigs

6Do not give the holy to the dogs
Or cast your pearls before the pigs.
They will probably trample them underfoot
And turn and tear you to pieces.

Knock and the door will be opened

7Ask and it will be given to you.
Seek and you will find.
Knock and the door will be opened for you.
8Everyone who asks receives
And the seeker finds,
And the door will be opened to one who knocks.
9And who among you if your son asks for bread
Will give him stone?
10Or if he asks for fish will give him snake?
11If you, who are cunning, know how to give good gifts
To your children,
How much more will your father of the skies
Give good gifts to those who ask him?

Doing for others

12Whatever you wish others to do for you,
So do for them.
Such is the meaning of the law and the prophets.

Narrow gate

13Go in through the narrow gate,
Since wide is the gate and spacious the road
That leads to destruction,
And there are many who go in through it.
14But how narrow is the gate and cramped is the road

That leads to life,
And there are few who find it.

Wolves in sheep's clothing

15Beware of false prophets
Who come to you in sheep's clothing,
But who inwardly are wolves.

Tree and fruit

16From their fruit you will know them.
Can you gather grapes from thorns or pick figs from thistles?
17Every good tree bears delicious fruit,
But the diseased tree bears rotting fruit.
18A good tree cannot yield rotting fruit,
Nor a diseased tree delicious fruits.
19Every tree incapable of delicious fruit is cut down
And tossed in the fire.
20So from their fruit you will know them.

Who enters heaven

21Not everyone who says to me, "Adonai, Adonai,"[83]
Will come into the kingdom of the skies,
But only one who follows the will of my father,
Who is in the heavens.
22On that day of judgment many will say to me,
"Adonai, Adonai, did we not prophesy in your name
And in your name cast out demons
And in your name take on great powers?"
23And then I will say my word clearly to them:

---

83. Kyrie, kyrie (κύριε κύριε), lord. When the scriptures give *theos*, "God," it is uncertain which of the multiple words for "God" would have been used by Yeshua in the Hebrew or the Aramaic. However, when *kyrie* is used to mean "Lord as God," it may be as in *Adonai*, "my Lord," from the Hebrew אָדוֹן (adon) "Lord," or from *Yahweh* יהוה, another word for "God" or "Lord." *Kyrie* can also mean simply "sir," "lord," or "master."

"I never knew you. Go from me,
You who are working against the law."

Wind battering houses
24Everyone who hears my words and follows them
Will be like the prudent man who built his house upon the
rock.
25The rain fell and the rivers formed
And the winds blew and battered that house
And it did not fall down
Because it was founded upon the rock.
26But everyone who hears my words and doesn't follow them
Will be like the foolish man who built his house upon the
sand.
27The rain fell and the rivers formed
And the winds blew and battered that house
And it fell down and it was a great fall.

28And it happened that when Yeshua ended these words, the crowds
were amazed at his teaching, 29for he taught them as one who has authority and not like one of their scholars.

Chapter 8

With a leper
When he came down from the mountain, many multitudes followed
him. 2And look, a leper[84] came near and bent low before him, saying,
Sir, if you want to, you can make me clean.
3Stretching out his hand, Yeshua touched him and said,
Yes, I want to. Be clean.
And at once his leprosy was cleansed away.
4And Yeshua said to him,

---

84. The word "leper" can refer to someone with any of several skin diseases.

Be sure to say nothing, but go to the priest
And offer the gift that Moshe commanded.
Offer it to them as testimony of your cure.

5When he came into Kfar Nahum, a centurion, a Roman officer, came near, 6beseeching him. "Sir, my servant boy is lying paralyzed in my house, and in terrible pain."

7And he said to the centurion,
    I will come to heal him.

8The centurion answered, "Sir, I don't deserve to have you under my roof. Only say a word and my servant will be healed. 9I am also a man under orders, with soldiers under me, and I say to this man, 'Go,' and he goes, and to another, 'Come,' and he comes, and to my slave, 'Do this,' and he does it."

10Hearing him, Yeshua was amazed and said to his followers,
        Yes, I tell you, in Yisrael
        I have found no one with such deep faith,[85]
    11And I tell you, many from the east and west
        Will come and lie down beside the table
        to eat with Avraham and Yitzhak and Yaakov
        in the kingdom of the skies.
    12And sons of the kingdom will be thrown out
        into the far outer darkness.

---

85. Matthew portrays the centurion as humble toward Yeshua, but of a faith greater than anyone in Israel. This astonishing portrait of an officer of the Roman army is repeated when the centurion who commands the execution squad is the first to recognize and announce Yeshua's divinity immediately upon Yeshua's death on the cross (27.54). This benign view of members of an army hostilely occupying Israel, and which executed Yeshua and other Jews and, subsequently, great numbers of Christians, is consistent with the exoneration of Rome in the gospels by an early Christian church whose seat was in Rome and in the new Roman empire in Constantinople. See Afterword. The portrait ends with Matthew's familiar warning that earlier Hebrew Bible patriarchs, Abraham, Isaac, and Jacob, as well as those from east and west (gentiles), will dine in heaven but those other sons of the kingdom (Jews who do not accept Yeshua as the messiah) will be thrown into the darkness and torment of Hell.

There will be weeping and gnashing of teeth.
13Yeshua said to the centurion,

> Go back to your home. Since you have had faith,
> let the event take place for you.

And his son was healed in that hour.

Healing at the house of Kefa

14Then Yeshua went into the house of Shimon Kefa, whose mother-in-law he saw lying in bed with a fever, 15and he touched her hand and the fever left her. She got up and served him.

16That same evening they brought him many who were afflicted with demons. With a word he cast out the spirits and he healed all their sicknesses. 17He was fulfilling the words of the prophet Yeshayahu:

> He attended our sicknesses
> and removed our diseases.[86]

I will follow you

18Now when Yeshua saw the great crowds all about him, he ordered them to cross over the water to the other side. 19A scholar came up to him and said, "Rabbi, I will follow you wherever you go."

20And Yeshua answered,

> Foxes have holes in the earth and birds of the sky
> Have nests,
> But the earthly son[87] has no place to rest his head.

21Another student said to him, "Sir, first let me go and bury my father."
22But Yeshua told him,

> Follow me
> And let the dead bury their own dead.

Dead calm

23When he got into the ship, his students followed him. 24And suddenly a great storm sprang up on the sea, so powerful that the ship was

---

86. Isa. 53.4.
87. See note 31 on Mark 2.10 for "earthly son."

hidden under the waves, but he was sleeping. 25And they came and woke him and said,

> Sir, save us, we are perishing!

And he said to them,

> 26Why are you frightened, you of little faith?

Then he got up and admonished the winds and the sea, and there was a dead calm.

27And the people marveled, and said,

> What kind of a man is he?
> Even the winds and the sea obey him.

Demoniacs and pigs

28When he crossed over into the country of the Gadarenes, two men possessed by demons, coming out of the tombs, accosted him on the road. They were wild and fierce and no one could get through. 29Suddenly they screamed, "What do you want with us, son of God? Are you here before your time simply to torment us?"

30Far off there was a herd of many pigs, feeding.

31And the demons pleaded, "If you cast us out, send us into the herd of pigs!"

32And he said to them,

> Go!

So they came out and entered the pigs and look, the whole herd raced down the slope into the sea and died in the waters. 33Those tending the pigs ran off, and when they came to their city they told the story of those who had been possessed by demons.

34And look, the whole city came out to meet Yeshua. But when they saw him they begged him to leave their region.

Chapter 9

Stand up and walk

Then he stepped back into a ship, crossed over the sea, and came to his own city. 2And look, the people brought him to a paralytic lying on a bed. When he saw their faith, he said to the paralytic,

> Be happy, my child, your wrongs are forgiven.

3And look, some of the scholars said among themselves, "This man is blaspheming."

4When Yeshua noticed what they were thinking, he said,

Why do you harbor bad thoughts in your hearts?

5Which is easier: to say, "Your wrongs are forgiven"

Or to say, "Stand up and walk"?

6So that you will know that the earthly son

Has the power to forgive sins,

Stand up, take your bed with you, and go home.

7And the paralytic stood up and went off to his house.

8When the crowds saw this, they were afraid and glorified God, who gave such powers to people.

Dining with a tax collector

9As Yeshua walked along, he saw a man seated in the toll house. His name was Mattityahu,[88] and he said to him,

Follow me.

And Mattityahu stood up and followed him.

10And it happened that while he was eating in Mattityahu's house, look, many other tax collectors and sinners came to recline at the table to dine with Yeshua and his students. 11When the Prushim saw this, they were saying to the students, "Why does your rabbi eat with tax collectors and sinners?"

12Yeshua heard them and responded,

The strong and healthy do not need a doctor

But the sick do. Go and learn the meaning of

13"I wish mercy and not sacrifice."[89]

I came not to call on the upright but the sinners.

Fasting and the bridegroom

14Then Yohanan's students came and asked him,

Why do we and the Prushim often fast,

---

88. Matthew. Also called Levi, Λευί (לֵוִי), by Mark 2.14 and Luke 5.27. See note 32 in Mark.

89. Hos. 6.6.

But your students do not fast?
15Yeshua answered,
> Surely the members of the wedding party cannot mourn
> While the bridegroom is with them?
> But the days will come when the groom
> Is taken away from them,
> And then they will be fasting.

Unshrunk cloth and new wine

> 16No one sews a patch of unshrunk cloth on an old coat,
> Since the patch pulls away from the coat
> And makes the tear worse.
> 17Nor do they pour new wine into old wineskins.
> If they do, the skins burst, the wine gushes out,
> And the wineskins are ruined.
> No, they pour new wine into fresh wineskins
> And both are preserved.

Dead girl and a bleeding mother

18While he was saying these things, a leader of the synagogue[90] came near, bowed low before him, and said,
> My daughter has just died.
> But come and put your hand on her
> And she will live.

19Yeshua rose and he and his students followed the official. 20And look, a woman, who had been bleeding for twelve years, came from behind him and touched the fringe of his cloak. 21She was saying to herself, If only I might touch his garment I will be healed.

22Yeshua turned and saw her and said,
> Be happy, daughter. Your faith has healed you.

And in that instant the woman was healed.

23When Yeshua entered the official's house and saw the flute players and the noisy crowd, 24he said,

---

90. The Greek lacks "of the synagogue."

Go away. The girl has not died. She is asleep.
They laughed at him.

25But when the crowd was put outside, he went in and took her hand, and the girl woke.

26And the news of this spread throughout the land.

With the blind

27As Yeshua was leaving, two blind men followed him, weeping and saying,

"Pity us, son of David."

28When he had gone indoors, the blind men came to him, and he asked them,

Do you believe that I can do this?
They said to him, "Yes, lord."

29Then he touched their eyes and said,

As you have faith, let your eyes be healed.

30And their eyes were opened.
Then Yeshua warned them sternly,

See that no one knows of this.

31But they left and spread the news throughout the land.

With a mute

32And just as they were going out, look, they brought him a mute and he was possessed by a demon. 33When he cast the demon out, the mute spoke. The crowd stood in wonder and exclaimed,

Never have these things happened in Yisrael!

34However, the Prushim said,

He drives out demons through the prince of demons.

Sheep and a shepherd

35Then Yeshua went through all the cities and villages, teaching in their synagogues, and preaching the good news of the kingdom, and healing every disease and sickness. 36When he saw the crowds, he felt pity for them, because they were harassed and helpless like sheep without a shepherd. 37Then he said to his students,

The harvest is abundant but the field workers are few.

38Ask the harvest owner to send his workers into the fields.

Chapter 10

Missions for the twelve on the road

Then he called his twelve students together, and gave them authority over unclean spirits to cast them out, and to heal every disease and sickness. 2The names of the twelve messengers[91] are: first, Shimon,[92] who is also called Kefa, and his brother Andreas, and Yaakov the son of Zavdai, and his brother Yohanan, 3Filippos and Bartalmai, Toma,[93] and Mattityahu the tax collector, Yaakov the son of Halfi,[94] and Taddai,[95] 4Shimon the Zealot, and Yehuda of Keriot,[96] the one who betrayed him.

5These twelve Yeshua sent out with instructions, saying,

> Don't go on the road where there are gentiles
> And don't enter the city of the Shomronim.[97]

6Go rather to the lost sheep of the house of Yisrael.

7And as you go, preach
> And say that the kingdom of the skies is coming near.

8Heal the sick, raise the dead, cleanse the lepers,

---

91. Apostles. See note 42 on Mark 3.14.

92. Simon from the Greek Σίμων, from the Hebrew שִׁמְעוֹן (shimon).

93. Thomas.

94. Alphaeus from the Greek Ἀλφαῖος (Halfaios), from the Hebrew חַלְפִּי (halfi).

95. Thaddeus from the Greek Θαδδαῖος (Thaddaios), from the Hebrew תַדִּי (taddai).

96. Judas the Iscariot. Judas from the Greek Ἰούδας (Ioudas), from the Hebrew יְהוּדָה (yehuda). The name for the messenger (apostle) Judas in Hebrew, *Yehuda*, was surely invented because it suggests the word in Hebrew for "Jew," which is יְהוּדִי (yehudi), thereby the betrayer of Yeshua among his followers was a Jew, as opposed to the others who escape that identity. For more on the origin of the betrayer tale of Judas in scripture and post-biblical portrayals in history and the arts, see note 30 on p. 33, in "Mark, the Vernacular Story Teller." For a more complete account of Judas from the Bible to modern times, see Susan Gubar's *Judas: A Biography* (New York: W. W. Norton, 2009).

97. Samaria from the Greek Σαμάρεια (Samareia), from the Hebrew שֹׁמְרוֹן (Shomron). Samaritan from the Greek Σαμαρίτης (Samarites), from the Hebrew שֹׁמְרֹנִי (Shomroni). "Samaritans" (pl.) is *Shomronim*.

And cast out the demons.
Freely you have received, freely give.
9Don't take gold and silver and copper in your belts,
10Or a bag for the journey
Or two tunics or sandals or a staff,
For the laborer earns his food.

Shake the dust from your feet
11In whatever city or village you enter,
Find out who in it is worthy
And stay there until you leave.
12As you go into a house, greet it,
13And if the house is worthy
Let your peace be upon it.
But if the house is not worthy,
Let your peace return to you.
14If someone doesn't welcome you
Or listen to your words,
As you go out of that house or city
Shake the dust from your feet.
15Amain, I say to you,
Sedom and Amorah[98] will be more tolerable
On the day of judgment
Than the fate of that city.

Be crafty as snakes, innocent as doves
16Look, I send you out as sheep among wolves,
So be crafty as snakes and innocent as doves.
17Be careful of people who will hand you over to the councils
And flog you in their synagogues.
18You will be dragged before governors and kings,
Because of me, to bear witness before them

---

98. Sodom from the Hebrew סְדֹם (sedom) and Gomorrah from the Hebrew
עֲמֹרָה (amorah).

And before the gentiles.
19But when they hand you over,
  Do not worry about how and what you are to say.
  In that hour what you say will be given to you,
20For you will not be speaking.
  The spirit of your father will be speaking through you.

21Brother will turn in brother over to death,
  And a father will turn in his child,
  And children will rise against their parents
  And have them put to death.
22You will be hated by all because of my name,
  But the one who endures to the end will be saved.
23And when they persecute you in one city,
  Escape to another.
  Amain, I say to you,
  You will not have gone through the cities of Yisrael
  Before the coming of the earthly son.

Student to teacher, slave to master
24A student is not above the teacher,
  Nor a slave above the master.
25It is enough for the student to be like the teacher
  And the slave like the master.
  If they call the master of the house Baal Zebul,99
  Lord of the flies,
  How much worse will they call the members of
  The household!

Uncovering darkness
26So do not fear them.
  There is nothing concealed that will not be revealed
  And nothing hidden that will not be known.
27What I say to you in darkness, speak in the light,

---

99. Beelzebul. See note 54 on Mark 3.22.

And what you hear whispered in your ear,
Proclaim from the housetops.
28And have no fear of those who kill the body
But are unable to kill the soul.
Fear rather the one who destroys both soul and body
in Gei Hinnom.

Two sparrows and a penny

29Are two sparrows not sold for a penny?
Yet not one of them will fall to the earth
Without your father,
30Even the hairs of your head are each counted,
31So have no fear.
You are worth more than many sparrows.

Heralding or denying

32Anyone who heralds me before others,
I will herald before my father of the skies,
33And whoever denies me before others,
I will deny before my father in the skies.

Not peace but a sword

34Do not think I have come to bring peace on the earth.
I have not come to bring peace but a sword.
Mihaihu[100] said,
35I came to set a man against his father
And a daughter against her mother,
And a bride against her mother-in-law
36And one's enemies will be in one's household.[101]

Finding soul

37If you love your father or mother more than me,
You are not worthy of me,

---

100. Micah from the Hebrew מִיכָה (mihah), from מִיכָיְהוּ (mihaihu).
101. Mic. 7.6.

251

If you love your son or daughter more than me,
You are not worthy of me,
38And if you do not take up the cross and come along
Behind me,
You are not worthy of me.
39Whoever finds his soul will lose it,
Whoever loses his soul, because of me, will find it.

Even a cup of cold water
40Whoever accepts you, accepts me.
Whoever accepts me, accepts the one who sent me.
41Whoever accepts a prophet in the name of the prophet
Will have the reward of a prophet,
And whoever receives a just person in the name
Of a just person
Will have the reward of the just.
42And whoever gives even a cup of cold water
To one of these children in the name of a student,
I tell you none will go unrewarded.

Chapter 11

Teaching in the cities
And when Yeshua had finished instructing his twelve students, he left the region to teach and preach in their cities.

Word from Yohanan in jail
2When Yohanan heard in prison what the mashiah was doing, he sent his own students 3to ask him, "Are you the one who is to come[102] or shall we look for another?"
4And Yeshua answered, saying to them,
Go and tell Yohanan what you see and hear.

---

102. "Who is to come" refers to "the mashiah (Christ)."

In the words of our prophet Yeshayahu:
> 5The blind will see again and the lame walk,
> The lepers are made clean and the deaf hear,
> The dead are raised and the poor hear the good news.[103]
> 6Blessed is the one who has not stumbled because of
> me.

Yohanan, who is Eliyahu preparing the way

7As Yohanan's students were leaving, Yeshua began to speak to the crowd about Yohanan,

> What did you go into the desert to see?
> A reed shaken by the wind?
> 8But what did you go out to see?
> A man dressed in soft robes?
> Look, those who wear soft clothing are in the houses of the
> kings.
> 9What did you go out to see?
> A prophet? Yes, I tell you, and he is more than a prophet.
> 10He is the one of whom the prophet Malachi wrote:
> > See, I send my angel messenger before your face,
> > Who will prepare the way before you.[104]
> 11I say to you, no one risen among us born of women
> Is greater than Yohanan the Dipper.
> Yet who is least in the kingdom of the skies
> Is greater than he is.
> 12From the days of Yohanan the Dipper until now
> The kingdom of the skies has been violated
> And violent men seize it.
> 13The prophets and all the law prophesied
> Until Yohanan's coming,
> 14And, if you are willing to accept it,
> Yohanan is the Eliyahu who is about to come.
> 15Whoever has ears to hear, hear.

---

103. Isa. 35.5–6. See also Isa. 26.19, 29.18, 42.7, 42.18, 61.1.
104. Mal. 3.1.

Like children sitting in the market place

16But to what shall I compare our generation?
  We are like children sitting in the market places,
  Calling out to one another, 17saying,
  "We played the flute for you and you didn't dance.
  We sang a dirge and you didn't mourn."
18When Yohanan came he was not eating or drinking,
  And they say, "He has a demon."
19The earthly son came eating and drinking,
  And they say, "Look at that glutton and drunk,
  A friend of tax collectors and sinners,"
  Yet wisdom is justified by her deeds.

Punishment of cities

20Then he began to blame the cities in which his greatest powers[105]
were revealed, because they had not changed their ways,
  21A plague on you, Horazim[106] and Beit Tzaida![107]
  If these powers had been revealed in Tzor[108] and Tzidon[109]
  That were revealed among you,
  Long ago they would have repented in sackcloth and ashes.
  22But I tell you, it will be more tolerable for Tzor and Tzidon
  On the day of judgment than for you.
  23And you, Kfar Nahum,
    Will you be raised into the skies?
    No, you will descend into the pits of hell.[110]

---

105. Powers from the Greek δύναμις (dynamis), meaning "power." *Dynamis* is traditionally translated as "miracle," though not in most new versions, where it is rendered as "power" or "deed of power," its classical as well as koine meaning in the Greek.

106. Chorazin from the Greek Χοραζίν (Horazin). The Hebrew *Horazim* is uncertain.

107. Bethseda from the Greek βηθσαϊδά (Bethsaida), from the Hebrew בֵּית צֵיְדָא (beit tzaida), which is a place north of Lake Gennesaret.

108. Tyre from the Greek Τύρος (Turos), from the Hebrew צוֹר (tzor), צֹר (tzor), or טוּר (tur), meaning "hard quartz" or "a flint knife," from the Aramaic טוּר (tur), meaning "a rock."

109. Sidon from the Greek Σιδών (Sidon), from the Hebrew צִידוֹן (tzidon).

110. Isa. 14.13 and 14.15.

> If these powers had been revealed in Sedom
> That were revealed among you,
> Sedom would be here today.
> 24Yet I tell you, it will be more tolerable for the land
> Of Sedom on the day of judgment than for you.

Revealed to little children

> 25At that time Yeshua said,
> I praise you, lord of the sky and of the earth,
> Because you have hidden these things from the wise
> And the learned,
> And revealed them to little children.

Father and son

> 26Yes, father, in this way it was pleasing to you.
> 27All things were given to me by my father,
> And no one knows the son except the father,
> And no one knows the father except the son
> And any to whom the son wishes to reveal it.

Rest for your souls

> 28Come to me, all who labor and are sorely burdened,
> And I will give you rest.[111]
> 29Take my yoke upon you and learn from me
> Because I am gentle and humble in heart,
> And you will find rest for your souls
> 30For my yoke is easy and my burden is light.

Chapter 12

Shabbat[112] in the grain fields

At that time Yeshua walked on the Shabbat through the sown fields. His students were hungry and they began to pick the ears of grain and

---

111. Jer. 31.25.

112. Sabbath from the Greek σάββατον (sabbaton), from the Hebrew שַׁבָּת (shabbat).

eat them. 2But the Prushim saw it and said to him, "Look, your students are doing what is forbidden to do on Shabbat."

3But he said to them,

> Have you not read what David did
> When he and his companions were hungry?
> 4How he went into the house of God
> And ate the bread for the presentation,[113]
> Which he was not permitted to eat,
> As were not those who were with him,
> For that bread was for the priests alone?
> 5Haven't you read in the law that priests in Temple
> Break the Shabbat by their labors,
> Yet they must be held innocent?
> 6I tell you here is something greater than the Temple,
> 7And if you knew what our prophet Hoshea
> Meant by "I wish mercy and not sacrifice,"[114]
> You would not condemn the innocent.
> 8The lord of the Shabbat is the earthly son.

A sheep in a pit, a withered hand

9And leaving that spot he went inside the synagogue 10and suddenly he saw a man with a withered hand. They asked him, "Is it lawful to heal on Shabbat?" They questioned him, hoping to trap and accuse him. 11But he said to them,

> If you who had only a single sheep
> And it fell on Shabbat into a pit,
> Wouldn't you grab it and pull it out?
> 12A person is worth more than a sheep,
> So on the Shabbat one can do good.

13Then he said to the man,

> Hold out your hand.

And it was restored, sound like the other one.

14But the Prushim went out and plotted against him to destroy him.

---

113. Twelve consecrated loaves of bread, changed weekly, set out in the synagogue as a symbol of communion with God. Also called "the bread of presence."

114. Hos. 6.6. Hosea from the Hebrew הוֹשֵׁעַ (hoshea).

Yeshayahu and hope for foreigners

15Aware of this, Yeshua departed. And many followed him and he healed them all. 16But he warned them not to reveal who he was 17in order that he might fulfill the prophecy of Yeshayahu, saying,

18Look, here is the servant I have chosen,
My love in whom my soul delights.
I will place my spirit in him
And he will announce judgment for the foreigners.[115]
19He will not quarrel or shout;
No one will hear his voice in the main streets.
20He will not break a bruised reed
Or quench a smoking wick of flax
Until he brings in the victory of judgment.
21In his name the foreigners will hope.[116]

With a blind and deaf demoniac

22Then they brought him a blind and deaf demoniac and he healed him, so that the mute was able to speak and to see. 23The crowds were amazed and were saying, "Is he not the son of David?"

Yeshua and demons

24But the Prushim heard this and said, "This man doesn't drive out demons except through Baal Zebul,[117] the prince of the demons."
25Yeshua knew their thoughts and said to them,
Every kingdom divided against itself turns into a desert,
And every city or house divided against itself will not stand.
26And if Satan casts out Satan, he is divided against himself.
How then will his kingdom stand?
27If through Baal Zebul I cast out the demons,
Through whom do your sons cast them out?
Therefore they will be your judges.

---

115. Foreigner or gentile.
116. Isa. 42.1–4.
117. Beelzebul.

28But if through the spirit of God I cast out the demons,
The kingdom of God has come to you.

Plundering a strong man's house

29Or how can one enter the house of a strong man
And carry off his possessions
Without first tying up the strong man?
Then his house can be plundered.

Standing firm

30Who is not with me is against me
And who will not assemble with me scatters my gatherings.
31So I tell you, every sin and blasphemy
By people will be forgiven,
32And whoever speaks against the earthly son will be forgiven,
But whoever speaks against the holy spirit
Will not be forgiven,
Either in this age or in the age to come.

Fruit, vipers, and words

33Either make the tree good and its fruit good
Or make the tree bad and its fruit bad,
Because from the fruit the tree is known.
34Offspring of vipers, how can you speak of the good
When you are evil?
The mouth speaks from an abundance in the heart.
35The good person from a good storehouse draws good,
The evil one from an evil storehouse draws evil.
36But I tell you, that each idle word you utter
You will account for on the day of judgment,
37For by your words you will be justified
And by your words you will be condemned.

The sign of Yonah

38Then some of the scholars and Prushim answered him, saying,
"Rabbi, we wish to see a sign from you."
39He answered and said to them,

A corrupt and adulterous generation asks for a sign
But no sign will be given to it
Except for the sign of Yonah[118] the prophet.
40For as Yonah was in the belly of the sea monster
Three days and three nights, so three days and three nights,
The earthly son will be in the heart of the earth.
41The men of Ninevah will stand up on the day of judgment
Of this generation, and they will condemn it,
Because they repented with the preaching of Yonah,
And look, there is more than Yonah here.
42The Queen of the South[119] will rise on the day of judgment
Of this generation, and they will condemn it,
Because she came from the ends of the earth to listen
To the wisdom of Shlomoh,
And look, there is more than Shlomoh here.

Unclean spirit

43When the unclean goes out of a person,
It wanders through waterless places,
Seeking a place to rest and finds none.
44Then it says, "I will return to the house I came from,"
And finds it empty and swept and put in order.
45Then it goes and picks up seven other spirits,
Each worse than itself.
And they go into the house and live there,
And the end for that man is worse than the beginning.
Such it will also be with this evil generation.

Yeshua rejects Miryam and his brothers

46While he was still talking to the crowds, look, his mother Miryam
and his brothers were standing outside, wanting to speak with him. 47And

---

118. Jonah from the Greek ᾽Ιωνᾶς (Ionas), from the Hebrew יוֹנָה (yonah).
119. The Queen of Sheba (1 Kings 10.1–13; 2 Chron. 9.1–12).

someone said to him, "See, your mother and your brothers are standing outside, wanting to speak with you."[120]

48And Yeshua answered him,

> Who is my mother and who are my brothers?

49And pointing to his students, he said,

> Look at my mother and my brothers.
> 50Whoever does the will of my father of the skies
> Is my brother and my sister and my mother.

Chapter 13

Parables by the sea

On that day Yeshua went out of his house and sat by the sea. 2And a great multitude gathered before him, so that he got into a boat and sat there, and all the crowd stood on the shore. 3And he told them many things in parables.

The sower

He said,

> Look, a sower went out to sow
> 4And as he was scattering the seed,
> Some of the grain fell on the path
> And some birds came and ate it.
> 5Other seed fell on stony ground
> Where there was not much soil
> And the grain sprang up quickly,
> For the soil had no depth.
> 6But when the sun came up
> The seedlings were parched
> And, having no roots, withered.
> 7Some fell among the thorns
> And the thorns grew and choked them.
> 8But some fell on good earth and bore fruit.

---

120. Verse 47 is omitted in some texts.

A hundredfold and sixty and thirty.
9Whoever has ears to hear, hear.

Why parables?

10Then the students came near him and asked, "Why do you talk to them in parables?"

11He answered them and said,

You are given a knowledge of the secrets
Of the kingdom of the skies,
But that knowledge is not given to them.
12When one has, more is granted; when one has not,
That little is taken away.
13So I talk to them in parables,
For while they see, they do not see,
And while they hear, they do not hear or understand.

14And so the prophecy of Yeshayahu is fulfilled, saying,

You hear, yet in hearing, you do not understand
And you see, yet in seeing, you do not see.
15For the heart of this people has become calloused
And with their ears they hear poorly and their eyes are closed,
Otherwise they might see with their eyes,
And hear with their ears
And with their heart understand and turn
And I would heal them.[121]

16But blessed are your eyes because they see
And your ears because they hear.
17I say to you that many prophets and good people
Have longed to see what you see and did not see it.
And to hear what you hear and did not hear it.

Sower parable given light

18Now listen to the parable of the sower.
19When someone hears the word of the kingdom

---

121. Isa. 6.9–10.

And does not understand it,
The evil one comes and seizes what was sown in the heart.
That is what was scattered on the path.
20The one who received seed dropped into the stony ground is
the one
Who hears the word and at once accepts it with joy.
21But since he has no roots within himself,
All is brief and transitory,
And when affliction or persecution comes because of the word,
That sower weakens and falls away.

22Now the seed dropped among the thorns is the one
Who hears the word, but the worries of the age
And the lure of riches choke the word and it gives no fruit.
23But the seed sown in the good earth is the one
Who hears the word and understands
And who bears fruit a hundredfold and sixty and thirty.

Weeds sown among the wheat
24He set another parable before them, saying,
The kingdom of the skies is like someone
Who sowed good seed in his field
25And while the people were asleep
His enemy came and sowed weeds among the wheat
And went away.
26When the plants grew and bore fruit
Then the weeds also appeared.
27The slaves came to the master of the house,
And said to him,
"Sir, did you not sow good seed in the field?
Where do the weeds come from?"
28The master told them, "My enemy did this."
"Do you want us to go and pull them out?"
Said the slaves.
29"No, in pulling the weeds you would uproot the wheat.
30Let both grow together until the harvest.
Then at the harvest I'll tell the reapers,

'First pull the weeds and tie them in bundles to burn,
But store the wheat in my granary.'"

Mustard seed and the birds

31He set another parable before them, saying,
The kingdom of the skies is like a mustard seed
That someone took and planted in the field,
32That is the smallest among all the seeds
But when it grows it is the greatest of the green shrubs
And becomes a tree
So birds of the sky can come and nest in its branches.

Yeast and heaven

33He set another parable before them, saying,
The kingdom of the skies is like yeast
A woman hid in three measures of flour
So that the dough was leavened and rose.

Parables opening the hidden

34All this Yeshua told the crowd in parables, and he talked solely in
parables 35so as to fulfill the words spoken by the prophet in the Psalms,
saying,
I open my mouth in parables,
I will pour out what has been hidden since the creation.[122]

Weed parable given light

36Then he left the crowds and went into the house and his students
came up to him and said, "Clarify the parable of the weeds in the field
for us."
37And he answered,
The one who sows the good seed is the earthly son
38And the field is the cosmos,
The good seeds are the children of the kingdom,
But the weeds are the children of the evil one,

---

122. Ps. 78.2.

39And the enemy who sowed them is the devil.
The harvest is the end of an age,
And the reapers are angels.
40Then as the weeds are pulled up and burned in the fire
So it will be at the end of the age.
41The earthly son will send out his angels
And they will gather from his kingdom
All scandalous things and those practicing lawlessness
42And cast them into the furnace of fire
Where there will be weeping and gnashing of teeth.
43Then the just will shine like the sun in the kingdom of the
father.
Whoever has ears to hear, hear.

Three parables:

Of treasure
44The kingdom of the skies is like treasure
Hidden in a field,
Which someone found and concealed,
And out of his joy
He goes away and sells everything he ever bought
And buys that field.

Of a pearl
45Again, the kingdom of the skies
Is like a merchant seeking fine pearls.
46After finding one valuable pearl he sold everything
He had and bought that pearl.

Of a net
47Again, the kingdom of the skies is like a net
Cast into the sea and catching every kind of fish.
48When it was full and they dragged it up on the shore,
They sat down and put the good fish in baskets,
But the rotted ones they threw out.
49So it will be at the end of the age.
The angels will come and separate the evil from the just

50And will cast them into the furnace of fire,
Where there will be weeping and gnashing of teeth.

51All these things, did you understand them?
52"Yes," they said to him.
And he said to them,
Every scholar who is learned about the kingdom
Of the skies
Is like one who is master of a household,
Who takes the new and the old
From the storeroom of the treasures.

Prophets without honor

53And it happened that when Yeshua finished the parables, he left
the region 54and came to his home country and taught them in their
synagogue. They were astonished and they said, "Where has this man
found his wisdom and powers? 55Isn't he the carpenter's son? Isn't his
mother called Miryam, and his brothers Yaakov and Yosef and Shimon
and Yehuda? 56And aren't all his sisters with us too? Where did this man
get all these powers?" 57And they were offended by him.
But Yeshua said to them,
A prophet is not dishonored
Except in his own country and house.
58And due to their lack of faith, he performed few deeds of power
there.

Chapter 14

Herod and Yohanan's head

At this time Herod the tetrarch[123] heard the reports about Yeshua,
2and he said to his servants, "This is Yohanan the Dipper. He has risen
from the dead, which is why these powers are at work in him."
3Herod had seized Yohanan and bound him and put him in prison,
because of Herodias, the wife of Filippos his brother. 4Yohanan had said to

---

123. Tetrarch. Greek for "ruler." Also referred to as "king."

him, "It is not lawful for you to have her." 5Herod wanted to kill Yohanan, but he feared the crowd, because they held him to be a prophet.

6Now on Herod's birthday celebration, it happened that the daughter of Herodias danced before them and she captivated Herod, 7and he took an oath and agreed to give her anything she asked for. 8The daughter, guided by her mother, said, "Bring me, here on this platter, the head of Yohanan the Dipper."

9The king was distressed, but because of his oath and his dinner guests he ordered that it be given her, 10and sent word and had Yohanan beheaded in prison. 11The head was brought in and given to the girl, and she took it to her mother.

12Yohanan's students came and took the body away and buried it. Then they left and reported it to Yeshua.

Bread for five thousand on the grass

13When Yeshua heard what had happened, he withdrew quietly from there by boat to a desolate place. But when the crowds found out, they followed him on foot from the villages. 14When he came ashore, he saw a great crowd and pitied them and healed the sick among them.

15When it was evening, his students came to him and said, "This is a deserted place and it is already late. Send the crowds away so they can return to the villages and buy food."

16But Yeshua said to them,

> They need not go away.
> You give them something to eat.

17"We have only five loaves of bread and two fishes," they answered. 18But he said,

> Bring them here to me.

19Then he ordered the crowd to sit down on the grass, and took the five loaves and two fishes, gazed into the sky, and gave a blessing, broke the bread and gave the loaves to his students. The students gave them to the crowds. 20And everyone ate and was satisfied. They picked up the broken pieces of the leftovers in twelve baskets full. 21And those who ate were about five thousand men apart from the women and children.

Yeshua walking on the sea at daybreak

22Then he made the students board the ship, and go on ahead of him to the other side while he dispersed the multitude. 23And when the crowds had vanished, he went up on the mountain, by himself, and prayed. When evening came, he was alone there.

24By this time the ship was a great distance from the land and battered by the waves, for the wind was against them. 25In the fourth watch of the night, near dawn, he came toward them, walking on the sea. 26When the students saw him walking on the sea, they were terrified. "It's a phantom!" they said, and cried out in fear.

27Yeshua quickly spoke to them,

Take heart, it is I. Do not be afraid.

28"Sir, if it is you, command me to come to you on the waters," answered Shimon Kefa.

29And he said,

Come.

Kefa climbed down from the boat and walked on the waters and he went toward Yeshua. 30But when he saw the storm he was frightened, and began to sink, and cried out, "Lord, save me!"

31At once Yeshua stretched out his hand, caught him, and said,

You of poor faith, why did you doubt?

32As they climbed into the ship, the wind ceased. 33Those who were on the ship worshiped him and said, "Truly you are the son of God."

Touching the sick in Gennesaret

34Then they crossed over and went to the land of Gennesaret. 35The men in that area recognized him and sent word all over the surrounding country and brought him all who were afflicted with sickness, 36and they begged him just to let them touch the fringe of his cloak. And those who touched it were cured.

Chapter 15

You hypocrites!

At this time, Prushim and scholars came to Yeshua from Yerushalayim, saying, 2"Why do your students break the tradition of the elders? They don't wash their hands before eating bread."

3But he answered them,

Why do you also break the commandment of God
Because of our tradition? 4God said,

Honor your father and your mother,[124]
And whoever curses his mother or father must die.
5You claim whoever tells their mother or father,
"Whatever help you might have had from me
Is a gift to God," need not honor the father.
6So you have made empty the word of God,
Because of our tradition. 7You hypocrites!
Our Yeshayahu was right when he prophesied
About you, saying,
8This people honors me with their lips,
But their heart is remote from me.
9They worship me in a hollow way.
Their teachings are the rules of men.

Parable of food and defilement
10Then calling the crowd together, Yeshua said to them,
Hear and understand,
11Not what goes into the mouth defiles
But what comes out of the mouth.
12Thereupon his students came near him. "Do you know that the Prushim were offended when they heard your words?" they asked.
13He answered, saying,
Every plant that my heavenly father has not planted
Will be uprooted.
14Leave them. They are blind guides of the blind.
When the blind lead the blind,
They both fall into a pit.
15But Shimon Kefa said to him, "Explain this parable to us."
And he said,
16Shimon Kefa, don't you understand yet? Don't you know
17That everything that goes into the mouth
Goes into the stomach and into the sewer?
18But what comes out of the mouth comes from the heart,

---

124. Exod. 20.12.

And that makes a person unclean,
19For from the heart come vile thoughts, murders, adulteries,
Fornications, thefts, false testimonies, and blasphemies.
20These are what make a person unclean.
But eating with unwashed hands does not defile.

Not only the lost sheep of Yisrael

21Then Yeshua left that place and withdrew to the districts of Tzor[125] and Tzidon.[126] 22And look, a Canaanite woman from that region came out crying and saying, "Pity me, lord, son of David. My daughter is tormented by a demon."

23But he didn't say a word to her.

His students came near, and urged him, saying, "Send her away, for she is following us, and keeps crying out."

24He answered her,

I was sent here solely for the lost sheep
Of the house of Yisrael.

25But she came and bowed before him, saying, "Lord, help me."
26He answered her,

It is not good to take the children's bread
And throw it to the dogs.

27But she said,

Yes, sir, but even dogs eat the crumbs
Fallen from the tables of their masters.

28Then he responded, saying to her,

Woman, great is your faith.
Let your wish be carried out.

And her daughter in that hour was healed.

To his mountain came the lame

29Then Yeshua left that place and came to the shores of the Sea of the Galil. He went up the mountain 30and sat there. Great crowds of people

---

125. Tyre.
126. Sidon.

came to him, bringing with them the lame, blind, crippled, deaf, and dumb, and many others, and put them at his feet. And he healed them. 31The crowd was amazed to see mutes talking, cripples healthy, the lame walking around, and the blind seeing.

And they glorified the God of Yisrael.

Bread for four thousand on the shore
32Yeshua summoned his students and told them,

> I pity the crowd. They have stayed with me
> For three days and have nothing to eat.
> I don't wish to send them away hungry
> For fear they will collapse on their way.

33His students asked him, "Here in the desert, where can we find enough loaves to feed such a crowd?"

34He asked them,

> How many loaves of bread do you have?

"Seven loaves and a few fish," they said.

35He told the crowd to sit down on the ground. 36He took the seven loaves and the fish, gave thanks, and he broke them and gave them to his students, and the students to the crowds. 37And everyone ate and was satisfied. And the broken pieces of the leftovers were seven baskets full. 38And those who ate were four thousand men, apart from the women and children.

39Then he sent the people away and got into his ship and came to the region of Magadan.

Chapter 16

A sign from the sky

Then Prushim and Tzadokim came to him, and tested him, asking him to show them a sign in the sky.

2He told them,

> Evening comes and you say it will be good weather,
> For the sky is fire red.
> 3Dawn comes and today will be stormy weather,
> For the sky is fire red and very dark.
> Do you know how to judge the face of the sky

And not make out the signs of the times?
4A corrupt and adulterous generation asks for a sign
But no sign will be given to it
Except for the sign of Yonah the prophet.
Then he left them and went away.

Understanding bread

5When the students crossed to the other side they forgot to take the bread.

Yeshua said to them,

6Be alert and beware of the yeast of the Prushim
And Tzadokim.

7But they were talking it over among themselves, saying, "We didn't bring the bread."

8Yeshua knew their thoughts. He asked them,

Why are you talking it over among yourselves?
You of poor faith, talking about having no bread.
9Don't you see, don't you remember the five loaves
For the five thousand and all the full baskets
You took away? 10Or the seven loaves for the four thousand
And how many baskets you took away?
11Couldn't you see that I wasn't talking about bread?
But guard against the yeast of the Prushim and Tzadokim.

12Then they understood. He did not say to guard against the yeast of the bread but against the teachings of the Prushim and the Tzadokim.

Keys of the kingdom

13When Yeshua came into the region of Caesarea Filippi,[127] he questioned his students,

Who do the people say is the earthly son?

14They said to him, "Some say Yohanan the Dipper, some Eliyahu[128] and others say Yirmiyahu[129] or one of the prophets."

---

127. Caesarea Philippi.

128. Elijah or Elias from Greek Ἠλίας (Elias), from Hebrew אֵלִיָּה (eliyah) or אֵלִיָּהוּ (elyahu).

129. Jeremiah from the Hebrew יִרְמְיָהוּ (yirmiyahu).

He said to them.

15But you, who do you say I am?

16Kefa, called Shimon Kefa, "You are the mashiah, the anointed, the son of the living God."

17Yeshua answered him, saying,

> You are blessed, Shimon bar Yonah.[130]
> It was not the flesh and blood that revealed to you this vision,
> But my father who is in the skies.

18And I tell you that you are Kefa the rock

> And upon this rock I will build my church,[131]
> And the gates of Gei Hinnom will not overpower it.

19I will give you the keys of the kingdom of the skies,

> And whatever you close upon the earth
> Will be closed in the heavens,
> And whatever you open on the earth
> Will be open in the heavens.

20Then he warned his students not to tell anyone that he was the mashiah.

---

130. Barjonah, son of Jonah from the Greek Βαριωνᾶ (Bariona), from the Hebrew בַּר יוֹנָה (bar yonah). Some have suggested a secondary derivation from the Hebrew בַּר יוֹחָנָן (bar yohanan).

131. The Greek words ἐκκλησία (ekklesia) and συναγωγή (synagoge) mean an "assembly," "gathering," or "congregation," and both words can refer to "synagogue." However, *ekklesia* (except in the Septuagint Greek version of the Hebrew Bible) is normally translated as "church" and is the common Greek word designating the later Christian church, while *synagoge* is the common word for "synagogue." Here, in Yeshua's prophecy, the intentional futurity of "I will build my church" is contrasted with the old Jewish tradition represented by *Gei Hinnom*, the Hebrew word for "hell." Yeshua's dramatic message is that he will build on a rock the *new church* that will overcome the *old synagogue*, and that *Christian heaven* will overcome *Jewish hell*. In his lifetime there was no Christian church, and Yeshua preached in the synagogues. For this observant Jew to say that he would "build a church" is an anachronism, revealing not his voice but that of churchmen many decades later when a Christian church as a building and institution did exist. The superimposition of later terminology, theology, and history on the figures of Yeshua and his followers remains the essential dilemma of the New Testament.

I will die and be arisen

21From that time on Yeshua began to explain to his students that he must go to Yerushalayim, and to suffer much from the elders and the high priests and the scholars, and be killed and on the third day after his death be raised.

22But Shimon Kefa took him aside, and began to rebuke him, saying, "God forbid it! Sir, this must never happen!"

23Yeshua turned to Kefa and said,

> Go behind me, Satan!
> To me you are an obstacle,
> For you are thinking not the thoughts of God
> But of earthly beings.

Losing life to find the soul

24Then Yeshua said to his students,

> If anyone wishes to be my follower,
> Deny yourself and take up the cross
> And follow me.

> 25If anyone wishes to save your soul
> You will lose it.

> But if you lose your soul because of me,
> You will find it.

> 26What good will it do you to gain the whole world
> But you forfeit your soul?

> And what will you give
> In exchange for your soul?

> 27The earthly son will come,
> With his angels in the glory of his father,
> And reward you by your deeds.

> 28Some of you who stand here
> Will not even taste death

Until you see the earthly son
Coming in his kingdom.

Chapter 17

Transfigured, his face like the sun

After six days, Yeshua took Shimon Kefa and Yaakov and Yohanan his brother, and led them up a high mountain and they were alone. 2And he was transfigured before them and his face shone like the sun, 3and his clothing became white as light. And look, Moshe and Eliyahu were talking with him.

4Kefa said to Yeshua, "Lord, it is good for us to be here. If you wish I will set up three shelters,[132] one for you and one for Moshe and one for Eliyahu."

5While he was speaking, look, a shining cloud covered them in shadow and a voice from the cloud was speaking,

This is my son
Whom I love,
In whom I am happy.
Listen to him.

6When his students heard this, they fell on their faces and were greatly afraid. 7But Yeshua came and touched them and said,

Arise and do not be afraid.

8When they raised their eyes, they saw no one but Yeshua alone.

9And as they were coming down the mountain, Yeshua instructed them, saying,

Speak to no one of the vision
Until the earthly son is raised from the dead.

Who is coming first?

10Thereupon his students asked him, "Why do the scholars say Eliyahu must come first?"

---

132. Sukkah or Tabernacle, for the Festival of the Tabernacles or Booths. See Mark 9.5, note 94.

He replied,

11Eliyahu is coming and will set all things right.

12But I tell you Eliyahu has already come

And they didn't know him and did with him as they cared to.

So also the earthly son is to suffer at their hands.

13Then his students understood that he was talking about Yohanan the Dipper.

A boy who falls into fire and water

14As they neared the crowd, a man came who kneeled before him and said, 15"Sir, take pity on my son. He is epileptic and suffers deeply. He often falls into the fire and falls into the water. 16I took him to your students and they were not able to heal him."

17Yeshua answered, saying,

You faithless and depraved generation!

How much longer must I be with you?

How much longer must I endure you?

Bring him to me here.

18Yeshua scolded him and the demon went out of him, and from that hour on the child was cured.

19His students came to Yeshua privately, and asked, "Why could we not cast it out?"

20He said to them,

You failed because of your poor faith.

I say to you, even if your faith is no bigger

Than a mustard seed,

When you say to the mountain to move

It will be moved

And nothing will be impossible for you.[133]

The earthly son will die and be arisen

22And when they came back together in the Galil, Yeshua said to them,

The earthly son is about to be handed over

---

133. The earliest manuscripts do not contain line 21 found in later ancient manuscripts: "But this kind does not come out except by prayer and fasting."

To human hands and they will kill him
23And on the third day he will be raised.
And they felt bitter sorrow.

A coin for the Temple

24When they all reached Kfar Nahum, those who collect the half-shekel Temple tax came up to them.[134] "Doesn't your rabbi pay the Temple tax?" they asked Shimon Kefa.

"Yes," he answered.

25And Kefa went into the house. Yeshua anticipated his student's thoughts, and told him,

Kefa, what are you thinking?
From whom do the kings of the earth collect duty
And taxes?
From their children or from strangers?"

26"From strangers," Shimon Kefa said.

27Yeshua responded,

Then the children are free of them.
But so as not to offend them, go to the sea and cast
A fishhook into the waters
And take the first fish coming up, open its mouth.
You'll find a coin. Take it,
And give it to them, for me and you.

Chapter 18

Becoming like children

In that hour the students came to Yeshua and asked, "Who is the greatest in the kingdom of the skies?"

2He called a little child to him and had her stand among them and told them,

---

134. Half-shekel. Greek has *didrachma*, a two-drachma coin. The half-shekel tax was paid each March for the upkeep of the Temple.

3I tell you, unless you change and become like children,
  You will never enter the kingdom of the skies.
4But whoever becomes little like this child
  Will be greatest in the kingdom of the skies,
5And whoever in my name accepts a child
  Like this one also accepts me,
6But whoever leads one of these children to stumble
  Who believes in me, for him it would be better
  To hang a donkey's millstone around his neck
  And be drowned in the depth of the sea.

Better to enter life one-eyed

7A plague be on the world because of stumbling blocks.
  Stumbling occurs
  But a plague on one through whom these falls come.

8And if your hand or foot causes you to stumble,
  Cut it off and throw it away from you.
  It is better for you to enter life maimed or lame
  Than to have two hands or two feet
  And be hurled into eternal fire.

9And if your eye causes you to stumble,
  Rip it out and throw it away.
  It is better for you to enter life one-eyed
  Than to have two eyes
  And be hurled into the Gei Hinnom of fire.

Parable of a little sheep lost

10Take care. Do not despise one of these little ones.
  I tell you that their angels in the air constantly gaze
  At the face of my father who is in the heavens.[135]
12What seems right? If a person has a hundred sheep

---

135. Other ancient authorities add verse 11: "For the earthly son came to save the lost."

And one of them wanders away,
Will she not leave the ninety-nine on the mountain
And go and look for the one who has wandered off?
13And if she happens to find him,
I tell you she is happier than over the ninety-nine
Who never went astray.
14So it is the wish of your father in the heavens
That none of these little ones be lost.

A brother hurting you

15If your brother hurts you, go alone and show him
Your hurt. If you are heard, you have won the brother.
16But if you are unheard take one or two witnesses
So two or three may confirm each word from your mouth.
17But if you are still unheard, take it to the synagogue
And if he will not even listen to the synagogue
Let him be to you like a gentile or a tax collector.

On earth and in heaven

18I tell you, whatever you close on earth
Will be closed in heaven
And whatever you free on earth
Will be free in heaven.
19Again I say, if two agree about everything on earth they ask
for,
It will be done for them by my father in the skies.
20Where two or three come together in my name,
There I am among them.

How many forgivenesses?

21Then Shimon Kefa came to him and said, "Sir, how many times shall
I forgive my brother? As many as seven times?"
22Yeshua said to him,
I do not say to you as many as seven
But as many as seventy times seven.[136]

---

136. Others render the number seventy-seven.

Parable of a king and an unforgiving slave

23So the kingdom of the skies is like a king
  Who wished to settle accounts with his slaves.
24As he was counting, a debtor of ten thousand talents
  Was brought in 25who could not pay,
  And his master ordered him to be sold,
  And also his wife, children, and all they possessed
  In order that his owner be repaid.
26Then the slave fell on his knees before him
  And said to him, "Delay your anger with me
  And I will pay you back everything."
27The lord had compassion for his slave
  And he pardoned him and forgave the debt.
28The slave went out and met a fellow slave,
  Who owed him one hundred denarii,
  And he seized him and choked him.
  "Pay me back what you owe me," he said.
29His fellow slave fell to the ground and begged him,
  "Delay your anger, and I will repay you,"
30But the freed slave was unwilling
  And he left and threw him into prison
  Until his fellow slave could pay the debt.
31When the other slaves saw this they grieved immensely
  And went and reported these things to their master.
32The master called the wicked slave to him
  And said, "I forgave you because you begged me.
33Should you not have pity on your fellow slave
  As I had compassion for you?"
34And his master was angry and handed him
  Over to the torturers in the prison
  Until he paid back everything he owed.
35In this way my father in the skies will handle
  Each one of you unless you forgive
  Your brother or sister from your heart.

Chapter 19

What God joined together let no one separate

Now it happened that when Yeshua finished speaking these words, he left the Galil and came into the regions of Yehuda beyond the Yarden, 2and huge crowds followed him and there he healed them.

3Then the Prushim came near him and to trap him they asked, "Is it lawful for a man to divorce his wife for any reason?"

4He answered,

> Have you not read in Genesis that "in the beginning"
> The creator "made them male and female"?[137]
> 5And it is said, "because of this a man will leave his father
> And his mother,
> And he will be joined to his wife
> And the two will be one flesh.[138]
> 6So they are no longer two but one flesh
> And what God joined together let no one divide.

7Then they asked him, "Why did Moshe decree that one might give a certificate of divorce and divorce her?"

He replied to them,

> 8It is solely because of your hard hearts
> That Moshe let you divorce your wives.
> Yet it was not so from the beginning.
> 9I say that he who divorces his wife,
> Except in the instance of harlotry,
> And marries another is an adulterer.

Eunuchs and the gift of celibacy

> 10His students asked him,
> If this is so between husband and wife,
> Is it not better not to marry?

---

137. Gen. 1.27 and 5.2.
138. Gen. 2.24.

11Yeshua replied,

> Not everyone can understand this word.
> Only those to whom it is given.[139]
> 12There are eunuchs who from their mother's womb
> Were born to be sterile.
> And there are eunuchs who were made into eunuchs by others,
> And there are eunuchs who made eunuchs of themselves
> For the sake of the kingdom of the skies.
> Let anyone who can comprehend, comprehend.

Let the little children come to me

13Then children were brought to him that he might lay his hands on them and pray for them. But his students scolded those who brought them in.

14Yeshua said,

> Let the children be and do not stop them
> From coming to me,
> For of such is the kingdom in the heavens.

15And he laid his hands on them, and went on his way.

Dilemmas of a young rich man

16And look, someone came to him and said,

> Rabbi, what good deed must I do to have eternal life?

17He replied,

> Why do you ask me about the good?
> There is only one who is good. But if you wish
> To enter into life,
> Keep the commandments.

And he said, "Which ones?"

18And Yeshua said,

> You must not murder or commit adultery or steal
> Or bear false witness. 19You must honor your father
> And mother,

---

139. Probably the gift of celibacy, which being a eunuch ensures.

And love your neighbor as yourself.
20The young man replied,
> All these commandments I have observed.
> What am I missing?
21Yeshua said to him,
> If you wish to be perfect, go and sell
> What belongs to you and give it to the poor,
> And you will have a treasure in heaven.
> Then come and follow me.
22The young man was downcast when he heard these words, and went away grieving since he had many possessions.

Heaven through the eye of a needle
23And Yeshua said to his students,
> 24Amain, I say to you,
> > It will be hard for a rich man to enter the kingdom of the skies.
> > I say it is easier for a camel to go through the eye of a needle
> > Than for a rich man to enter the kingdom of God.[140]
25When the students heard this, they were greatly amazed and asked, "Who then can be saved?"
26Yeshua looked at them and said,
> For people this is impossible
> But for God all things are possible.

Life everlasting
27Shimon Keťa answered him, saying, "Look, we have given up everything and followed you. What will there be for us?"
28He responded to them,
> Amain, I say to you,
> In the next life when the earthly son
> Is seated on his throne of glory,
> You who have followed me

---

140. See note 108 on Mark 10.25.

Will also be seated on the twelve thrones
And judge the twelve tribes of Yisrael.
29And anyone who has given up houses or brothers
  Or sisters or father or mother
  Or children or fields in honor of my name,
  Will have them back a hundred times over
  And inherit life everlasting.

30Many who are first will be last, and the last will be first.

Chapter 20

Parable of the laborers in the vineyard
    The kingdom of the skies is like a man,
    The master of a house, who went out at daybreak
    To hire laborers for his vineyard.
  2After agreeing on a silver denarius a day,
    He sent the laborers into the vineyard.
  3About the third hour after dawn he went out
    And saw others standing idle in the marketplace,
  4And said to them, "Go into the vineyard
    And I will give you what is right."
  5And they went to the vines.
    Again about the sixth and the ninth hour
    He went out and did the same.
  6And about the eleventh hour after dawn
    He saw others standing idle
    And he asked them,
    "Why have you been standing here all day, idle?"
  7They told him, "Because no one hired us."
    He said to them, "Go into the vineyard."
  8When evening came the owner of the vineyard
    Told his foreman,
    "Call the laborers and give them their wages,
    Beginning with the last who came
    And then going on to the first."

9And those who had come at the eleventh hour
  Each took away a silver coin.

10And those who had come first thought their pay
  Would be greater
  But each took away a silver coin.
11When they took it they grumbled against the master,
12Saying, "The last ones worked an hour
  And you made them equal to us
  Who bore the weight of the day and the heat."
13But he told them, "Friend, I am not cheating you.
  Didn't you agree with me on one silver coin?
14Take what is yours and go.
  But I wish to give to the last as I gave to you.
15Can't I do what I want with what is mine
  Or is your eye envious that I am kind?"

16So the last will be first and first will be last.

I will die and be arisen

17Then as Yeshua went up to Yerushalayim, he took the twelve with
him aside, and on the road said to them,
  18Look, we are going up to Yerushalayim
  And the earthly son will be given into the hands
  Of the high priests and scholars
  And they will condemn him to death.
  19And they will give him into the hands of the gentiles[141]
  To mock and flog and crucify,
  And on the third day he will be raised.

Seats for my sons

20Then the mother of the sons of Zavdai[142] came to him, along with
her sons, and bowed before him. She had a request.

---

141. Here "gentiles" would be the Roman soldiers.
142. Yeshua's students Yaakov and Yohanan (James and John).

21He said to her,

> What do you want?

She said to him, "Tell me that my two sons will sit on your right hand and on your left in your kingdom."

22And Yeshua answered,

> You don't know what you are asking for.
>
> Can you drink the cup I'm about to drink?

The brothers said to him, "Yes, we can."

23He told them,

> You will drink from my cup,
>
> Yet to be seated on my right and my left I cannot grant.
>
> These places belong to those who have been chosen
>
> By my father.

24Hearing this, the other ten were indignant about the two brothers.
25But Yeshua called them together and said,

> You know that the rulers of the gentiles
>
> Lord it over their people
>
> And the high officials tyrannize them.
>
> 26It will not be so for you,
>
> For whoever among you wishes to be great
>
> Will be your servant,
>
> 27And whoever among you wishes to be first
>
> Will be your slave.
>
> 28So the earthly son did not come to be served
>
> But to serve and to give his own life
>
> For the redemption of the many.

Touching blind eyes in Yeriho

29As they were leaving Yeriho, a great crowd followed him. 30And look, two blind men were sitting beside the road. When they heard that Yeshua was passing by they cried out, saying, "Have pity on us, lord, son of David."

31The crowd scolded them and told them to keep quiet, but again they cried out, saying, "Have pity on us, lord, son of David."

32Yeshua stopped and called to them, saying,

> What do you want me to do for you?

They said, 33"Lord, let our eyes be opened."

Yeshua pitied them and touched their eyes and at once they saw and followed him.

Chapter 21

Entering Yerushalayim on a colt

Then as they came near Yerushalayim and reached Beit Pagey[143] at the Mountain of Olives, Yeshua sent two students ahead, 2saying to them,

> Go on into the village ahead of you
> And soon you will find a donkey tethered
> And her foal beside her.
> 3Untie them and bring them to me.
> And if anyone should say anything to you,
> Say that their master needs them.
> And he will send them at once.

4This was done to fulfill the word spoken
by our prophets Zeharyahu[144] and Yeshayahu, saying,

> 5Tell the daughter of Zion,
> Look, your king is coming to you,
> Modest and riding on a donkey,
> And with a colt, the son of the donkey.[145]

6His students went and did as Yeshua instructed them. 7They brought the donkey and the colt and placed their cloaks upon them, and he sat on them. 8And the enormous crowd spread their cloaks on the road. Others cut branches from the trees and spread them on the road. 9And the crowds who went ahead and those who followed were shouting,

> Hosanna to the son of David!
> Blessed is he who comes in the name of the lord!

---

143. Bethphage from the Greek Βηθφαγή (Bethfage), from the Hebrew בֵּית פַּגֵּא (beit pagey).

144. Zechariah or Zacharias from the Greek Ζαχαρίας (Zaharias), from the Hebrew זְכַרְיָהוּ (zeharyahu).

145. Isa. 62.11; Zech. 9.9.

Hosanna in the highest realm!

10When he entered Yerushalayim, the whole city trembled, saying, "Who is this?"

11And the crowds were saying, "This is the prophet Yeshua of Natzeret in the Galil."

Driving the traders and dove sellers from the Temple

12Then Yeshua entered the Temple and drove out all who bought and sold in the Temple, and he overturned the tables of the coin changers and the chairs of those who sold doves. 13He said to them,

As it is written in Yeshayahu and Yirmiyahu,[146]
"My house will be called a house of prayer,"
But you have made it a den of robbers.

Healing in the Temple and consternation of priests

14And the blind and the lame came to him in the Temple, and he healed them.

15But when the high priests and the scholars saw the wonders[147] he performed and the children crying out in the Temple, "Hosanna to the son of David," they were indignant, 16and said to him, "Do you hear what they are saying?"

And Yeshua answered,

Yes. Have you never read in the Psalms:
"From the mouths of children and infants
You have composed praise for yourself"?[148]

17And he left them and went out of the city to Beit Aniyah[149] where he spent the night.

---

146. Isa. 56.7; Jer. 7.11.

147. From the Greek τὰ θαυμάσια (ta thaumasia), meaning "wonders" or "wonderous things." "Wonder" from the Greek θαυμα (thauma) and "power" from the Greek δύναμις (dynamis) are the words in the gospels for "miracle."

148. Ps. 8.2 (Septuagint).

149. Bethany from the Greek Βηθανία (Bethania), from the Hebrew בֵּית אָנִיָה (beit aniyah).

Cursing and drying up the fig tree

18Early in the morning he came back to the city, and he was hungry.
19And seeing a single fig tree by the road, he went up to it and found
nothing on it but leaves, and said to it,

> Let you bear no fruit forevermore.

And at once the fig tree dried up.[150]

20His students seeing it were astonished, and asked, "How did the fig
tree suddenly dry up?"

21Yeshua answered them, saying,

> Amain, I say to you.
> If you have faith and do not doubt,
> Not only what happened to the fig tree
> Will be in your domain,
> But you can say to the mountain,
> "Rise up and hurl yourself into the sea,"
> And it will be done.
> 22All things you ask for in prayer with faith
> You will receive.

By what authority?

23Now when he had gone into the Temple and was teaching there, the
high priests and the elders of the people came to him, saying, "By what
authority do you do these things?"

24And Yeshua replied to them,

> I too will ask you one thing, and if you tell me
> I will tell you by what authority I do these things.
> Where did Yohanan's baptism come from?
> Was it from heaven or from people on earth?

25They discussed it among themselves, and said, "If we say 'from
heaven,' he will tell us, 'Then why did you not believe him?' 26But if we
tell him 'from people on earth,' we will fear the crowds, for everyone
holds Yohanan to be a prophet."

---

150. Here the incident in Mark is developed to say that, had the fruit tree had faith,
its fruit would not have dried up, but with faith one can move mountains. For more
on the metaphor, see note 123 on the withering of the fig tree, Mark 11.20–21.

27So they told Yeshua, "We do not know."
He said to them,

> Then neither will I tell you by what authority
> I am doing these things.

Parable of the two sons

> 28What do you think?
> A man had two children.
> To the first he said, "Son, go out today and work in the
>   vineyard."
> 29But the son said, "I don't want to."
> Later, he changed his mind and went.
> 30To the second he asked the same.
> He said, "I will go, sir," but didn't go.
> 31Which of the two did the father's will?

They said, "The first."
Yeshua responded, telling them,

> Amain, I tell you,
> The tax collectors and the prostitutes
> Will go before you into the kingdom of God.
> 32Yohanan came to you on the path of justice
> And you did not believe him,
> But the tax collectors and the prostitutes
> Believed in him,
> And even after you saw, you did not later repent
> And believe him.

Parable of the wicked tenants

> 33Listen to another parable.
> There was a man who was a landowner
> Who planted a vineyard and put a fence around it,
> And dug a wine press in it,
> And built a tower and leased it all to farmers
> And left the country.

> 34And when the time of the vintage was near,
> He sent his slaves to the farmers to take the vintage.

35But the farmers seized the slaves
  And one they beat, one they killed, one they stoned.
36Again he sent slaves, more than the first group,
  And they dealt with them the same.

37After this he sent his son, saying,
  "They will respect my son."
38But once the farmers saw his son,
  They said among themselves, "He is the heir.
  Come, let us kill him and take his inheritance."
39And they seized him, threw him out of the vineyard,
  And they killed him.

40Now, when the lord of the vineyard comes,
  What will he do to those farmers?
41They said to him, "Those wicked ones he will destroy and he will lease the vineyard to other farmers who will give him his share of the grapes at vintage time."
And Yeshua replied,
  42Have you never read in the Psalms:
    "The stone that the builders rejected,
    It has become the cornerstone.
    It was made by the lord
  And is a wonder to our eyes"?[151]
43For this reason I tell you,
  The kingdom of God will be taken away from you
  And given to a people producing its harvest.
[44And the one falling on this stone will be broken
  And it will crush anyone on whom it falls.][152]
45And when the high priests and the Prushim heard his parables, they knew that he spoke of them. They were looking for a way to seize him, but they feared the crowds, since they held him to be a prophet.

---

151. Ps. 118.22–23.

152. Other early texts lack verse 44.

Chapter 22

Parable of the wedding guest without a wedding garment
Once more Yeshua spoke to them in parables, saying,
2The kingdom of the skies is like a king
  Who held a wedding banquet for his son.
3And he sent out his slaves to call on those invited to the feast
  But they did not wish to come.
4He sent out more slaves, saying, "Tell the guests,
  Look, I have prepared a dinner. The oxen and fatted calves
  Are slaughtered,
  And all is ready. Come to the wedding."
5But they were unconcerned and went their way,
  One going to lands, one to business,
6While others seized the slaves and outraged them
  And killed them.

7So the king was angry and sent out his armies
  And destroyed those murderers and burned their city.
8He said to his slaves, "The wedding feast is ready,
  But our invited guests were unworthy.
9So go out to the open crossroads and invite everyone
  To the wedding."
10And those slaves went out to the roads
  And gathered everyone they found, good and bad,
  And filled the wedding hall with guests.

11But when the king went in to observe them at dinner,
  He saw a man not wearing a wedding garment.
12He said to him, "Friend, how did you come in
  Without a wedding garment?"
  The man was speechless.
13Then the king said to his servants,
  "Bind his hands and legs and cast him into the outer darkness
  Where there will be weeping and gnashing of teeth."
14Many are called, few are chosen.

Paying coins to Caesar

15Then the Prushim went and conferred on how to trap Yeshua through his words. 16They sent their students, along with supporters of Herod, saying, "Rabbi, we know that you are truthful and you teach the way of God in the truth and show no favor to anyone, for you do not judge people by their face. 17So tell us what seems right. Is it right to pay taxes to Caesar, or not?"

18But aware of their craftiness, Yeshua said,

> Why do you test me, hypocrites?
> 19Show me the tax coin.

And they brought him a denarius.

20And he said to them,

> Whose image is this and whose name?

21"Caesar's," they said to him.

He told them,

> Then give the things of Caesar to Caesar
> And the things of God to God.¹⁵³

22When they heard this, they were left in wonder, and they turned and went away.

A wife in heaven

23On that same day the Tzadokim, who say there is no resurrection, came to him and questioned him, saying, 24"Rabbi, Moshe told us that if someone dies without children, his brother must marry the widow and raise offspring for his brother. 25Now there were seven brothers among us. The first one married, and not having children he left his wife to his brother. 26The second did the same, also the third and all the way until all seven had married her. 27Last of all, the woman died. 28So in the resurrection, whose wife will she be? For they all had her as wife."

29Yeshua responded,

---

153. This episode presents the prevailing view in the gospels to cooperate with Roman rule. For more information, see note 127 on Mark 12.14.

You are wrong not to know the Torah[154] or the power of God.
30In the resurrection they do not marry nor are given in marriage
But are like angels in the air.
31As to the resurrection of the dead,
Haven't you read God's word in Exodus speaking to you:
32"I am the God of Avraham and the God of Yitzhak and the
God of Yaakov"?
God is not God of the dead but of the living.

33And hearing this, the crowds were struck with wonder by his teaching.

Loving God and neighbors

34When the Prushim learned how he had silenced the Tzadokim, they assembled together, 35and one of them, an expert in the law, questioned him in order to test him. 36"Rabbi, which is the great commandment in the Torah?"

37And Yeshua said to them,

"You shall love the lord your God with all your heart
And with all your soul and with all your mind."
38This is the great and first commandment.
39And the second is like it:
"Love your neighbor like yourself." 40All the law
And the prophets hang on these two commandments.

Son and lord of David

41When the Prushim were gathered together, Yeshua questioned them, saying,

42What do you think is right concerning the mashiah?
Whose son is he?
"The son of David," they told him.
He said,

---

154. Torah is specifically the five books of Moses but is normally a synecdoche for the Hebrew Bible.

43How then did David, moved by the spirit,
Call him lord? For it says in the Psalms,
44"The lord says to my lord,
'Sit at my right hand until I make your enemies
A footstool under your feet.'"[155]
45If then David calls him lord, how can he be his son?
46And no one could say a word in reply, and from that day on no one dared to ask him any more questions.

Chapter 23

They speak and do nothing
Then Yeshua spoke to the crowds and to his students, 2saying,
On the seat of Moshe[156] sit the scholars and Prushim.[157]

---

155. Ps. 110.1.

156. Moses represents the covenant of Sinai that is transcended by the New Testament. The Pharisees sit on Moses's seat, identifying these wicked scholars with the Jewish Bible and its old law and commandments now superceded by Matthew's sermons and good news, although elsewhere the Torah is cited as the authenticating source of Yeshua as the promised messiah, who is dignified by his Davidic sonship as in Matthew 1.1. See note 2 on Matthew 1.1 and Raymond E. Brown's analysis of "the story of Jesus as a new creation, even greater than the old," in *An Introduction to the New Testament* (New York: Doubleday, 1997).

157. Matthew 23 "is a litany of angry fulminations against (some of) the Pharisees" (*The New Oxford Annotated Bible, with the Apocryphal/Deuterocanonical Books, New Revised Standard Version*, ed. Bruce M. Metzger and Roland Murphy, New York: Oxford University Press, 1994 417). And literarily it is a compendium of great poetic curses. It represents the views of an already competitive early Christian polemic against the Pharisees, though we have no idea when these denunciations may have been composed or added to a changing text, constantly recopied and freely redacted. Some contemporary scholars conjecture that Yeshua was a Pharisee rabbi, which is why, in the early assembling of a New Testament text, it became necessary to distance Yeshua furiously from his Jewish source, a view elaborated by Burton Mack, in *Who Wrote the New Testament? The Making of the Christian Myth* (San Francisco: HarperSanFrancisco, 1995), and Hyam Maccoby, in *The Mythmaker: Paul and the Invention of Christianity* (San Francisco:

3Do and observe all that they tell you,
  But do not do as they do. They speak and do nothing.
4They tie up heavy bundles
  And lay them on the shoulders of other men,
  But will not lift a finger to move them.
5All they do is for show.
  They spread their tephillin[158] and lengthen their tassels
6And love the foremost couch at the dinners,
  The front seats in the synagogues,
7To be greeted in the market places
  And to be called rabbi by the people.

8But you must not be called rabbi,

HarperSanFrancisco, 1986), among others. (See Afterword for more on Pharisees.) If Yeshua was not a Pharisee, he was at the very least closer to them than to the Essenes, with whom he is often compared, in that the Pharisees took up and emphasized ideas that are essential to New Testament eschatology: a belief in the messiah and his resurrection and in the immortality of the soul, which had been a dominantly Greek Platonic rather than a Jewish notion. The Pharisees also represented an oral Jewish tradition that was constantly changing. Of the some seventeen sects of Jews at the time of Yeshua (as identified by James H. Charlesworth in *The Old Testament Pseudepigrapha*, 2 vols., Garden City, NY: Doubleday, 1983–1985), the Pharisees as a prominent sect distinguished themselves from the Sadducees, who did not believe in the immortality of the soul, resurrection, or angels, but who, in contrast to the Pharisees, did support the Hasmonean priest-kings, who represented Hellenization and who during Yeshua's life were surrogates for Roman rule. The prevailing politics of the gospels is an exoneration of Pilate, depicted as innocent, and of Rome and the Roman occupation of Israel. Since the Sadducees were the natural allies of the Hasmonean-Roman power base, in the gospels they do not receive the sustained polemic reserved for the Pharisees. By contrast, the hated Pharisees, by sharing Yeshua's views, made their rejection imperative if Christianity were to distinguish itself from its early reality as a Jewish sect of Christian (messianic) Jews. Yeshua was, like the Pharisees (as opposed to the cooperative Sadducees), troublesome and probably deemed a revolutionary figure. The Romans saw fit to crucify him as they did thousands of Jewish opponents in the first century. "Innocent" Pilate had a dominantly bloody role in the massacres.

158. Phylacteries.

For you have one teacher and are all brothers.

9On earth call no one father. You have one father in
heaven

10And do not call yourselves instructors.

You have one instructor, the mashiah.

11The greatest among you will be your servant.

12Whoever raises himself high will be brought low

And whoever brings himself low will be raised high.

A plague on you!

13A plague on you, scholars and Prushim, hypocrites!

You lock people out of the kingdom of the skies.

You do not enter, nor let others go in.[159]

15A plague on you, scholars and Prushim, hypocrites!

You sweep the sea and the dry land

To enroll a single convert,

And make your convert into a child of Gei Hinnom

And twice as much of hell as you.

16A plague on you, blind leaders who say, "If you swear

By the Temple, it means nothing,

But if you swear by the gold of the Temple, it is binding."

17Fools and blindmen, which is greater,

The gold or the Temple that hallows the gold?

18And if you swear by the altar, it means nothing,

But if you swear by the gift on the altar, is it binding?

19Blindmen, which is greater, the gift or the altar that hallows
the gift?

20So one who swears by the altar swears by it and by everything
on it

---

159. Verse 14, not found in the most ancient texts, is omitted in the UBS fourth edition used here, but appears in other ancient texts and translations as "A plague on you, scholars and Pharisees, hypocrites! You devour widows' houses and for appearance make long prayers. So you will receive the greater condemnation."

21And one who swears by the Temple swears by it and by the one
   Who dwells in it.
22And the one who swears by heaven swears by the throne of
       God
   And by the one sitting upon it.

23A plague on you, scholars and Prushim, hypocrites,
   Because you pay a tenth on the mint and the anise and the
       cumin
   And pass over what is grave in the law: justice and mercy
       and faith
   You should have done the last and not passed over the first.
24Blind leaders, you strain the gnat but swallow the camel.

25A plague on you, scholars and Prushim, hypocrites,
   Because you clean the outside of the cup and the dish
   But the inside is filled with greed and dissipation.
26Blind Parush, first scour the inside of the cup
   So the outside will also be clean.

27A plague on you, scholars and Prushim, hypocrites,
   Because you are like graves that are whitewashed,
   Which on the outside seem beautiful
   But the inside are filled with the bones of the dead
   And all uncleanness.
28So you too on the outside seem to the people to be just
   But on the inside you are filled with hypocrisy and law-
       lessness.

29A plague on you, scholars and Prushim, hypocrites,
   Because you build the tombs of the prophets
   And decorate the monuments of the just
30And say, "Had we lived in the days of our fathers,
   We would not have been guilty of spilling the blood of the
       prophets."
31So you testify against yourselves that you are the children
   Of those who murdered the prophets

32And you are the full measure of your fathers.

33Snakes, offspring of vipers, how can you escape

From the judgment of Gei Hinnom?[160]

34Therefore, look, I am sending you prophets and sages and
scholars,

Some of them you will kill and crucify,

And some of them you will flog in the synagogues

And chase from city to city

35So that all the righteous blood spilled on the earth

Will descend upon you,

From the blood of Hevel[161] the just to the blood

Of Zeharyahu,[162] son of Berehyahu[163]

Whom you murdered between the Temple and the altar.

36Amain, I say to you,

All this will descend on this generation.[164]

Yerushalayim, Yerushalayim

37Yerushalayim, Yerushalayim, who kills the prophets[165]

---

160. In 31–32, Yeshua accuses the Jews, as represented by Moses and the Pharisees, of being the children of the "murderers" of the prophets and tells them that as offspring of vipers they will be sent to hell. So the guilt of the fathers is transferred to the children, always with the implicit charge of killing the messiah. The legend of killing the prophets and the charge of killing the foretold Righteous One is repeated in Acts 7.52–53: "Which of the prophets did your ancestors not persecute? They killed those who foretold the coming of the Righteous One, and now you have become his betrayers and murderers" (translation from the New Revised Standard Version).

161. Abel from the Greek Ἄβελ (Abel), from the Hebrew הֶבֶל (hevel).

162. Zechariah.

163. Barachiah from the Greek Βαραχίας (Barahias), from the Hebrew בֶּרֶכְיָהוּ (berehyahu).

164. The preceding attacks on the scholars and Pharisees are called the seven woes (plagues) or seven denunciations.

165. "Yerushalayim, Yerushalayim" (Jerusalem, Jerusalem) is an allusion to the famous "If I forget thee, O Jerusalem" in Psalm 137, a scriptural citation to support Yeshua's accusation that Jerusalem has the habit of "kill[ing] its prophets." However, no words in Psalm 137, in the Hebrew Bible, or from external documents confirm this charge. These words, placed in the lips of the mashiah, reflect not the affecting Yeshua in

And stones those who were sent to her,
How many times I wished to gather in your children
As a hen draws her brood under her wings,
But you would not let me.

38Look, your house has been left desolate.
39I say to you that you will not see me until you say,
"Blessed is the one who comes in the name of the lord."

Chapter 24

Prophecy of the Temple stones thrown down
And Yeshua left the Temple and was on his way when his students came to him to show him the buildings of the Temple. 2But he said to them,

Do you not see all this? Amain, I tell you,

---

the fields preaching Beatitudes of love, but a militant Yeshua speaking against Jews. The time frame in Matthew is the travail of the Jews in the period after the Jewish Wars, 66–70 C.E., and the resultant destruction of Jerusalem and exile of Jews and Christian Jews. By alluding to Psalm 137 in "Jerusalem, Jerusalem," the evangelist belies his own message since the psalm is a lament for Zion and Jerusalem as a result of the Babylonian Captivity (587 B.C.E.):

By the rivers of Babylon, there we sat down, yea, we wept when we
    remembered Zion . . .
If I forget thee, O Jerusalem, let my right hand forget *her cunning*.
If I do not remember thee, let my tongue cleave to the roof of my mouth;
    if I prefer not Jerusalem above my chief joy
—Ps. 137.1, 5–6, King James Version

Psalm 137 ends with a tirade against the Edomites who with the Babylonian king Nebuchadnezzar II have destroyed the Temple, razed and plundered Jerusalem, and slaughtered its inhabitants. In Matthew, however, the Jews are not victims of the Babylonians and Edomites, but, by reversing roles in a historical event, the Jews have implausibly become the aggressor.

A few lines later, in verse 39, Yeshua, quoting a second Hebrew psalm, Psalm 118.26, says that the house of the Jews will remain desolate until they say, "Blessed is the one who comes in the name of the lord." There is nothing in the psalm saying or suggesting that "your house has been left desolate."

Nothing here will escape destruction. No stone
Upon a stone will not be thrown down.

Earthquakes, famines, signs of the end and the coming[166]

3While he was sitting on the Mountain of Olives, his students came
to him privately. "Tell us," they said, "when will this happen and what
will be the sign of your coming and the end of the world?"

4And Yeshua answered them,

See to it that no one leads you astray,
5Because many will come in my name, saying,
"I am the mashiah,"
And they will lead many astray.
6You will hear of wars and rumors of wars.
See to it that you are not alarmed.
For this must happen, but it is not yet the end.
7Nation will rise up against nation
And kingdom against kingdom
And there will be famines and earthquakes
In place after place.
8All these are the beginning of birthing pains.

9Then they will hand you over to be tortured
And they will kill you and you will be hated
By all the nations because of my name.
10And many will fall into sin
And they will betray and hate one another
11And many false prophets will rise and lead many astray.
12And through the abundance of lawlessness,
The love of many will grow cold.
13But the one who endures to the end will be saved
14And the good message of the kingdom will be preached
Throughout the world as a testimony,
And then the end will come.

---

166. Parousia. "The coming." The Parousia is the "coming of the messiah."

15So when you see the abomination of desolation
   Standing in the holy place,
   Foretold through Daniel the prophet
   (Let the reader understand),
16Then let those who are in Yehuda flee to the mountains.
17Let no one on the roof come down
   To carry away anything from the house.
18Let no one in the field go back to pick up his cloak.

19A plague on you pregnant women and mothers nursing babies.
20Pray that your flight not come in the winter or on Shabbat,
21For then there will be great affliction
   Unequaled from the beginning of the world till now
   And never equaled again.
22And if those days had not been cut short,
   There would be no living flesh saved,
   But for the sake of the chosen ones those days will be cut
      short.

23If anyone tells you, "Look, here is the mashiah!"
   Or "He's there," don't believe it. 24False mashiahs will arise
   And false prophets and they will give great signs
   And portents to lead astray, if possible, even the chosen.
25Look, I have warned you.
26If they tell you, "Look, he is in the desert,"
   Don't go out to it, or "Look, he's in the inner rooms,"
   Don't believe it.
27For as lightning comes out of the east and flashes as far as
      the west,
   So will be the coming of the earthly son.
28Wherever the corpse may be, the vultures will gather.

Coming of the earthly son
   29And suddenly after the suffering of those days,
      The sun will be darkened
   And the moon not give its light
   And the stars fall out of the skies

And the powers of the heavens be shaken.[167]

30 Then the sign of the earthly son will shine in the sky,
  And all the tribes of the earth will beat themselves mourning
  And they will see
      The earthly son coming on the clouds
      In the high air
      With power and multiple glory,[168]

31 And he will send out his angels with a great ram horn blast
  And they will gather the chosen ones from the four winds,
  From one peak of the skies to the other peak.

Lesson of the fig tree

32 From the fig tree learn the parable,
  When its branch is already tender and issues leaves
  You know that summer is near.

33 So when you too see all these things,
  You know that he is near, at your doors.

34 Amain, I say to you,
  This generation will not fade before all these things are done.

35 The sky and earth will disappear
  But my words will not pass away.

36 As to that day and hour, no one knows.
  Not angels in the air [nor the son].[169]
  None but the father alone.

37 For as the days of Noah came,
  So will be the coming of the earthly son.

38 For as in those days before the flood,
  They were eating and drinking, marrying husbands and wives
  Until the day Noah went into the ark,

---

167. Isa. 13.10, 13.13, and 34.4. The language echoes Isaiah as well as other prophets.

168. Dan. 7.13–14.

169. Lacks Greek in some earlier texts.

39And they knew nothing until the flood came
  And carried everything away,
  So will be the coming of the earthly son.
40Then two men will be in the field:
  One is taken away and one is left.
41Two women will be grinding flour at the mill:
  One is taken away and one is left.
42So be watchful, since you don't know on what day
  Your lord is coming.
43But you know that if the master of the house
  Had known at what hour of the night the thief was coming,
  He would have kept awake
  And not allowed his house to be broken into.
44Therefore, you also must keep awake,
  For in an hour unknown to you comes the earthly son.

Master and slaves
  45Who then is the faithful and wise slave
    Whom the master sets over the household
    To give out the food at the proper time?
  46Blessed is that slave found working away
    When the master barges into the room.
  47I tell you, the master will choose only him
    To be in charge of all his possessions.
  48But if that other wicked slave says in his heart,
    "My master is delayed and will not come soon,"
  49And he begins to flog his fellow slaves
    And he eats and drinks with the drunkards,
  50The master will come on a day of surprise
    And at an hour when he is not expected,
  51And he will cleave him into small pieces
    And deliver the parts to the hypocrites,
    And there will be weeping and gnashing of teeth.

Chapter 25

Ten virgins and their oil lamps

Then the kingdom of the skies can be compared
To ten young virgins who picked up their lamps
And went out to meet the bridegroom.
2Five of them were foolish and five were wise.
3The fools took their lamps but not the oil.
4The clever ones took flasks of oil with their lamps,
5But when the bridegroom was delayed,
The virgins all grew drowsy and fell asleep.

6In the middle of the night there was a shout.
Look, it is the bridegroom. Go out to meet him.
7Then the women woke and trimmed their lamps,
8But the fools said to the wise, "Give us some
Of your oil, because our lamps are going out."
9But the wise ones answered, saying, "No,
There would never be enough for us and you.
Better go out to the merchants and buy some for yourselves."

10And while they were gone to buy the oil,
The groom came and the virgins ready with light
Went with the groom into the wedding,
And the door was shut. 11Soon the others came crying,
"Lord, lord, open the door to us!"
12But the master answered them in turn,
"I tell you, I don't know you." 13Be watchful,
For you do not know the day or the hour.

Landlord and slaves

14Again, it is like a man going on a journey
Who called his slaves together
And handed his possessions over to them.
15And to one he gave five talents, meaning many pounds
Of silver coins,

To another slave two sacks of coins,
And to another one talent, each according to his skills,
And he went off at once on his journey.

16The one who received five talents left at once,
Put his money to work, and gained another five.
17Likewise the one with two gained another two.
18But the one who received one talent went out
And dug a hole in the ground and hid the money
That his master had given him.
19After a long time the master of those slaves came back
And settled accounts with them.

20The slave who got five talents came forward
And showed the other five to him, saying,
"Master, you gave me five talents. See, I have made five talents
more."
21His master said, "Well done, good and faithful slave.
You were faithful in small things. I will put you in charge
of much. Enter into your master's joy."
22And the slave who got two talents came forward
And showed the other two to him, saying,
"Master, you gave me two talents. See, I have made two
talents more."
23His master said, "Well done, good and faithful slave.
You who were faithful over a few things
Now I will put you in charge of much.
Enter into your master's joy."

24And the slave with one talent came forward, saying,
"Master, I knew you were a harsh man,
Harvesting where you didn't sow and gathering
Where you didn't scatter seed.
25And so I was frightened and went away
And hid my one sack of silver coins in the ground.
Here, I return to you what is yours."

26The master of the mansion answered him,
  "Wicked and timid slave, so you knew that I harvest
  Where I don't sow, that I gather where I don't scatter seed?
27You should have placed your money with the bankers
  And I would have received my part with interest.
28So take away the sack of coins from him
  And give it to him who has ten talents."
29To all who have will be given, even in excess,
  And from those who have nothing,
  Even what they do have will be taken from them.
30And cast this worthless slave into outer darkness.
  There will be weeping and gnashing of teeth.

Judgment day for the kingdom
31When the earthly son comes in his glory
  And all the angels with him,
  Then he will sit upon the throne of his glory.
32And all the nations will be assembled before him
  And he will separate them one from the other
  As the shepherd separates the sheep from the goats.
33And he will place the sheep at his right hand
  But the goats he will place at his left.

34Then the king will say to those at his right,
  "Come, you who are the blessed by my father,
  And inherit the kingdom prepared for you
  Since the creation of the world.
35For I was hungry and you gave me to eat,
  I was thirsty and you gave me to drink,
  I was a stranger and you took me in,
36I was naked and you gave me clothing,
  I was sick and you took care of me,
  I was in prison and you came to me."

37Then the just will answer the king, saying,
  "Lord, when did we see you hungry and feed you,
  Or thirsty and give you to drink?

38And when did we see you a stranger and take you in,
  Or naked and give you clothing?
39And when did we see you sick or in prison
  And come to you?"
40And the king will answer them, saying,
  "I tell you that all those things you have done
  For one who was least in my family,
  You have also done for me."

41And he will say to those at his left,
  "Go from me, cursed, into the everlasting fire
  Prepared for the devil and his angels.
42For I was hungry and you didn't feed me,
  I was thirsty and you gave me nothing to drink,
43I was a stranger and you didn't take me in,
  Naked and you didn't give me clothing,
  Sick and in prison and you didn't come to me."
44Then they will also answer him, saying,
  "Sir, when did we see you in hunger or thirst
  Or as a stranger or naked or sick or in prison
  And we did not help you?"

45And the king will answer them,
  "Amain, I say to you, since you did nothing for one
  Who was least of my family, you did nothing for me."
46And these will go into everlasting punishment,
  But the just will enter life everlasting.

Chapter 26

Plotting
  And it happened that when Yeshua finished saying all these words, he
told his students,
    2You know that in two days the Pesach comes,[170]

---

170. Passover, the Feast of Unleavened Bread.

And the earthly son will be given over to be crucified.

3Then the high priests and the elders gathered in the courtyard of the high priest, whose name was Kayfa,[171] 4and they made plans to capture Yeshua by treachery and kill him. 5But they said, "Not during the feast days, or there might be a noisy riot among the people."

Anointed in the house of the leper

6Now while Yeshua was in Beit Aniyah[172] in the house of Shimon the leper, 7a woman came to him with an alabaster flask of precious myrrh and poured it on his head, anointing him, while he was reclining at the dinner table. 8When his students saw this, they were indignant and said, "Why this waste? 9This ointment could have been sold for a great price and the money given to the poor."

10Yeshua heard them and said,

> Why are you troubling this woman
> Who has done a good thing for me?
> 11The poor you always have with you,
> But me you will not always have.
> 12When she poured myrrh on my body,
> She prepared me for my burial.
> 13Amain, I say to you, where in all the world
> The good news is proclaimed,
> What she has done will be told
> In memory of this woman.

Yehuda and the silver

14Then one of the twelve, who was called Yehuda of Keriot, went to the high priests and 15said, "What are you willing to give me if I hand him over to you?"

And they weighed out thirty pieces of silver for him.

16And from that moment, Yehuda looked for a chance to betray him.

---

171. Caiaphas from the Greek Καϊάφας (Kaiafas), from the Aramaic and Hebrew כָּיְפָא (kayfa).

172. Bethany.

Planning the Seder in an upper room

17On the first day of the Feast of the Matzot Bread, the students came to Yeshua, saying, "Where do you wish us to make preparations to eat the Pesach[173] supper?"

18And he said,

> Go into the city to a certain man and tell him,
> "The teacher says: My time is near. With you
> I will celebrate the Pesach with my students."

19And the students did as Yeshua instructed and they prepared the Seder.

One of you will betray me

20When evening came, he took his place reclining at the table with the twelve. 21And as they were eating, he said,

> I tell you that one of you will betray me.

22Bitterly sorrowful, they began to say to each other, "Surely not I, lord?"

23He answered, saying,

> The one who has dipped his hand
> In the bowl with me will betray me.
> 24Yes, the earthly son departs
> As the prophets wrote of him,
> But agony is prepared for him
> Who betrayed the earthly son.
> Better had he not been born!

25Then Yehuda, the one betraying him, said,

> Surely not I, Rabbi?

Yeshua replied,

> You have said it.

---

173. The Pesach supper is the Seder. The Feast of the Matzot is the Festival of Unleavened Bread. The Greek word ἄζυμος (azymos) means "unleavened bread," which is a translation from the Hebrew מַצּוֹת (matzot), "unleavened bread." See note 143 on Mark 14.1. *Pesach* is "Passover" from the Greek πάσχα (pasha), from the Hebrew פֶּסַח (pesach), "to pass over," referring to escape from bondage in Egypt, celebrated at the Seder by eating the paschal lamb. See Exodus 12.1–13.16.

This is my body, this is my blood

26As they were eating, Yeshua took the matzot, and after giving thanks he broke it, gave it to his students, and said,

> Take it and eat.
> This is my body.

27Then he took the cup and after giving thanks, he gave it to them, saying,

> Drink from it, all of you,
> 28For this is my blood of the covenant,[174]
> Poured out for the many for forgiveness of sins.
> 29I tell you, I will no longer drink this fruit of the vine
> Until that day I drink it new with you
> In the kingdom of my father.

30And they sang a psalm and went out to the Mountain of Olives.

Before the cock crows twice

31Then Yeshua said to them,

> You will all desert me this night,
> For it is written in Zeharyahu.
>> I will strike down the shepherd
>> And the sheep of his flock will be scattered.[175]

> 32But after I am raised up,
> I will go ahead of you to the Galil.

33"Though all the others fail you, I will never fail you," Shimon Kefa protested.

34Yeshua said to him,

> Amain, I say to you.

---

174. From the Greek διαθήκη (diatheke), "the covenant," and in Hellenistic Greek "testament or will." In the King James Version, the word "new" is added and so it reads, "This is my blood of the new testament." "New" (καινή) is not in the Greek text. In Greek and East European orthodoxy the title for the scriptures is "New Covenant." "New Testament" came into Latin and modern West European languages through Jerome's mistranslation, or repetition of an earlier mistranslation, of *diatheke* as *testamentum*, "testament" rather than as "covenant." "Covenant" derives from Hebrew בְּרִית (berit). "New Covenant" in Greek is Καινὴ Διαθήκη (Kaine Diatheke), and in Torah בְּרִית חֲדָשָׁה (berit hadashah), found in Jeremiah 31.31.

175. Zech. 13.7.

During this night before the cock crows,

You will deny me three times.

35"Even if I must die with you, I will not deny you," Shimon Kefa answered.

And all the students said the same.

Terror and prayer at Gat Shmanim

36Then Yeshua went with them to a place called Gat Shmanim and he told his students,

Sit down here while I go over there to pray.

37He took with him Shimon Kefa and the two sons of Zavdai and then he fell into pain and sorrow. He told them,

38My soul is in anguish to the point of death.

Stay here and keep awake with me.

39And going a little farther, he threw himself down on his face and prayed,

My father, if it is possible,

Let this cup pass from me,

But not as I wish, but as you wish.

40Then he went back to the students and found them sleeping, and said to Kefa,

Were you not strong enough to stay awake

With me for one hour? 41Stay awake and pray

That you are not brought to the test.

The spirit is eager but the flesh is weak.

42Again he went off and prayed, saying,

My father, if this cup cannot pass from me

Without my drinking it,

Let your will be done.

43And returning once more, he found them sleeping, for their eyes were heavy. 44He went off a third time and prayed and said the same words as before. 45Then he came back to his students and told them,

Are you still asleep and resting?

Look, the hour is near, and the earthly son

Will be betrayed into the hands of sinners.

46Wake up, let us go.

Look, the one betraying me is near.

The rabbi is kissed and arrested

47While he was speaking, look, Yehuda, one of the twelve, came, and with him a great crowd with swords and clubs from the high priests and the elders of the people. 48And the betrayer told them the signal, which was, "The one I kiss is the man. Seize him."

49And at once he came up to Yeshua and said, "Hello, Rabbi." And he kissed him.

50And Yeshua said,

> Friend, do what you are here to do.

Then they came and laid their hands on Yeshua and seized him.

51And look, one of those with Yeshua put out his hand, drew his sword, and struck the high priest's slave, cutting off his ear. 52But Yeshua said to him,

> Put your sword back into its place,
> For all who draw the sword will die by the sword.
> 53Do you suppose I don't have the power to call on my father
> To send me at once twelve legions of angels?
> 54How else would the scriptures be fulfilled
> That say in this way these things must happen.[176]

55At that moment Yeshua said to the crowds,

> Have you come to arrest me with swords and clubs
> As if I were a robber?
> Day after day I sat in the Temple, teaching,
> And you did not take hold of me.
> 56But all this happened so the scriptures of the prophets
> Might be fulfilled.

Then all his students deserted him and fled.

False testimony in the Sanhedrin

57But those who had seized Yeshua led him to Kayfa the high priest, where the scholars and the elders had gathered.[177] 58And Kefa followed

---

176. 2 Kings 6.15–17; Ps. 24.8–10; Rev. 19.14.

177. The night session at the Sanhedrin is problematic, raising many questions. Trials during Passover as well as night trials were forbidden by Jewish law. By Roman law, Jews normally could not pass death sentences, but by the first century "the

him at a distance, as far as the courtyard of the high priest, and went inside and sat down with the servants to see the outcome. 59The high priests and the entire Sanhedrin were looking for false witnesses against Yeshua so they could put him to death. 60But they found none, though many false witnesses came forward.

Later, two came forward 61and declared, "This man said, 'I can tear down the Temple of God and rebuild it within three days.'"

62The high priest stood up and said to the captive, "Do you answer nothing? What is this testimony these men bring against you?"

63But Yeshua was silent.

And the high priest said to him, "I charge you under oath by the living God to tell us if you are the mashiah, the son of God."

Yeshua told him,

> 64You said it. But I say to you,
>
> From now on you will see the earthly son
> Seated at the right hand of the power
> And coming upon the clouds of the sky.[178]

65Then the high priest tore his clothing and said, "He has blasphemed! Why do we still need witnesses? Look, now you have heard the blasphemy. 66What do you think?"

They responded, "He deserves death."

67Then they spat in his face and struck him with their fists. And slapped him, 68and said, "Tell us your prophesy, mashiah. Who hit you?"

Shimon Kefa and the crowing cock

69Now Shimon Kefa was sitting outside in the courtyard, and a servant girl came to him and said, "You were with Yeshua of the Galil."

Roman authorities voluntarily authorized the Sanhedrin and the High Priest to try capital cases," M. Stern writes in "The History of Judea under Roman Rule," in H. H. Ben-Sasson, ed., *A History of the Jewish People* (Cambridge, MA: Harvard University Press, 1976), 250. However, this authority would not have extended to the instance of Yeshua whom, it is generally agreed, was tried as a seditionist, as the "King of the Jews."

178. Daniel 7.13, which he cites, reads, "I saw one like a person / coming upon the clouds of the sky."

70But he denied it before everyone, saying, "I do not know what you are saying."

71When he went to the gate, another girl saw him and said to the people there, "He was with Yeshua of Natzeret."

72And again he denied it, with an oath, saying, "I do not know the man."

73A little later, those who were standing there came up to Kefa and said, "Certainly you are one of them. Your Galilean accent betrays you."

74Then he began to curse, and he swore an oath, "I do not know the man!"

At that moment a cock crowed.

75Kefa remembered what Yeshua had said,

> Before the cock crows you will deny me three times.

And he went outside and wept bitterly.

Chapter 27

Yeshua before Pilatus

When early morning came, all the high priests and the elders of people held a meeting against Yeshua to have him put to death. 2They bound him and led him away and handed him over to Pilatus the governor.

Yehuda with silver and rope

3When Yehuda, who betrayed him, saw that Yeshua was condemned to die, he was seized with remorse, and returned the thirty silver coins to the high priests and the elders.

4"I have sinned in betraying innocent blood," he told them.

But they said, "What is that to us? You live with it."

5He flung the silver coins into the Temple and left. Then he withdrew and hanged himself.

6After the high priests picked up the silver coins, they said, "It's not permitted to put this into the treasury, since it is blood money."

7Then they took counsel again, and used the money to buy the potter's field to bury foreigners in. 8To this day that field has been called the Field of Blood.

9With this, the word spoken through Yirmiyahu the prophet was fulfilled, saying,

> And they took the thirty silver coins,
>
> The price fixed on him by the children of Yisrael,
>
> 10And used them to buy the potter's field
>
> As the lord commanded me.[179]

Pilatus asks, Are you the king of the Jews?

11Later, Yeshua stood before the governor, and the governor asked him, "Are you the king of the Jews?"

And Yeshua said,

> You say so.

12When the high priests and the elders accused him, he answered nothing.

13Then Pilatus said to him, "Do you not hear all the charges against you?"

14But he gave no reply to a single charge, and the governor was greatly amazed.

Crucify him!

15For the holidays of Pesach, the governor had the custom of releasing a prisoner to the crowd, whichever one they wished. 16At that time they had a learned prisoner[180] who was called [Yeshua] Bar Abba.[181] 17So after they assembled, Pilatus said to them, "Which one do you want me to release to you, Yeshua Bar Abba[182] or Yeshua who is called the mashiah?" 18He knew that out of jealousy the latter had been handed over to him.

---

179. The passage is not from Jeremiah, though Jeremiah mentions buying land and visiting a potter. The passage is loosely derived from Zechariah 11.12–13.

180. The prisoner's epithet is from the Greek ἐπίσημον (episemon). In virtually all translations Barrabas is "notorious," with the exception of the KJV, which is neutral to positive, where he is called "a notable prisoner."

181. Barabbas from the Greek Βαραββᾶς, from the Aramaic בַּר אַבָּא (bar abba), meaning "son of Abba" (father).

182. Jesus Barabbas. Barabbas means "son of the father" or "son of God." It is assumed that Jesus Barabbas was a revolutionary of the Zealots, a Jewish sect which opposed payment of taxes to the Roman emperor, use of the Greek language, and Roman occupation of Israel. Their rebellion, referred to in the "uprising" in Mark 15.7, ended with the Roman assault on the fortress at Massada and their mass suicide in the fortress after which the sect largely disappeared.

19While Pilatus was sitting on the judgment seat, his wife sent word to him, saying, "Have nothing to do with that just man, for I have suffered much today because of a dream about him."

20But the high priests and the elders persuaded the crowds to ask for Bar Abba and to destroy Yeshua.

21The governor again said to them, "Which of the two do you want me to release to you?"

"Bar Abba!" they cried.

22"Then what should I do with Yeshua, who is called the mashiah?" he asked.

"Let him be crucified,"[183] they all said.

23"What harm has he done?" he told them.

But they screamed all the more, "Crucify him!"

24When Pilatus saw that he could do nothing and that an uproar was starting, he took water and washed his hands before the crowd, saying, "I am innocent of the blood of this man.[184] You see to it."

25Then all the people answered, "Let his blood be upon us and upon our children!"[185]

26So Pilatus released Bar Abba to them.

He had Yeshua flogged and sent him off to be crucified.

Soldiers clothe him in scarlet and a crown of thorns and club him

27Then the soldiers of the governor took Yeshua to the governor's residence[186] and drew up the whole battalion around him. 28And they

---

183. See note 164 on Mark 15.13 for questions arising from this scene.

184. For more on Pilate's "innocence" and his subsequent sainthood in sects of the Eastern Orthodox Church, see note 164 on Mark 15.13.

185. This line, "Let his blood be upon us and upon our children has given rise to much dispute and skepticism. The Jews in the street are shouting, "Let the guilt of his murder be upon us, the Jews, forever." On Passover evenings the Jews would be in their houses, celebrating the Passover meal. They would not be in the street asking the Romans to crucify a rabbi, and had they been, they would not be shouting for crucifixion and at once declaring their guilt forever by shouting for crucifixion.

186. The praetorium.

stripped him and wrapped a scarlet robe around him, 29and twisted thorns in a wreath and put it on his head and placed a reed staff in his right hand. Then they knelt before him and mocked him, saying, "Hail, king of the Jews!" 30And they spat at him and took his reed staff and struck him on the head with it. 31After mocking him, they took off his scarlet robe and dressed him in his own garments and led him away to be crucified.

Gulgulta, the Place of the Skull

32As they came out they found a man from Cyrene by the name of Shimon. They forced him to carry the cross. 33And they came to a place called Gulgulta, which is called the Place of the Skull.[187] 34They gave him wine mixed with gall to drink. When he tasted it, he didn't wish to drink it.

Crucifying him

35Then they crucified him, divided up his clothing by casting lots, 36and sat there and kept watch over him. 37Above his head they put the charge against him, which read,

THIS IS YESHUA THE KING OF THE JEWS.

38They crucified two thieves with him, one on his right and one on his left. 39And those who passed by cursed him, shaking their heads, 40and said, "You who can tear down the Temple and rebuild it in three days, save yourself if you are the son of God, and come down from the cross." 41So too the high priests along with the scholars and the elders mocked him, saying, 42"He saved others, but cannot save himself. He is the king of Yisrael. Let him come down now from the cross and we will believe in him. 43He trusted in God. Let God rescue him now if he wants him, for he said, 'I am the son of God.'"

44And similarly the thieves who were crucified with Yeshua taunted him.

---

187. Golgotha from the Greek Γολγοθᾶ (Golgotha), from the Aramaic גֻּלְגֻּלְתָּא (gulgulta), meaning "skull."

Darkness at noon

45From noon on, darkness came over all the land until three in the afternoon.[188] 46And about three o'clock, Yeshua cried out in a great voice,

> Eli, Eli, lama sabachthani?

meaning,

> My God, my God, why have you forsaken me?

47Some of those standing there heard and said, "This man is calling for Eliyahu."

48All at once one of them ran and took a sponge, filled it with poor wine,[189] put it on a stick, and gave it to him to drink. 49But the others said, "Leave him alone. Let's see if Eliyahu comes to save him."

50And Yeshua again let out a great cry and breathed his last breath.

51And look, the curtain of the Temple tore in two from top to bottom, and the earth shook and the rocks were split, 52and the tombs opened and many bodies of the saints[190] who had fallen asleep were raised. 53And

---

188. In Greek, noon is the sixth hour, and three in the afternoon is the ninth hour.

189. A popular wine of the poor, also translated "vinegar" or "vinegared wine," from the Greek ὄξος (oxos), which was supposed to be more effective than water in eliminating thirst. The classical Greek definition of *oxos* gives "poor wine," that is, a wine poor in quality and for the poorer classes. The KJV gives "vinegar" and most modern translations "soured wine." The standard annotation explains that the motive of the sponge soaked with sour wine was not to comfort Yeshua but to revive him and prolong his agony, and is taken as a symbol of Jewish malice to their enemy, fulfilling scripture, as in Psalm 69.20–21: "I looked for pity, but there was none, and for comforters, but I found none. They gave me poison (gall) for my food (meat) and vinegar to drink." Line 27.48 in Matthew states only that after Yeshua's plea to God, a bystander who heard got a sponge soaked with poor wine and ran forward and put it to Yeshua's lips to drink. Whether this was the act of a brave sympathizer or a taunting foe cannot be known, since no motive is indicated in verse 27.48, nor is it clarified by turning to verses in Psalm 69 of David, which begins with a Jew saying, "Save me, O God, for the waters have come up to my neck. I sink in deep mud where there is no foothold." However, the next verse does seem to depict the offerer as a comforter rather than a villain since he is derided by another bystander who says, "Leave him alone. Let's see if Eliyahu comes to save him" (27.49).

190. Saints or, literally, the "holy ones." The Greek word (*hagios*, saint) normally refers to a Christian saint, and in this instance is probably an anachronism since

after his resurrection they came out of their tombs and went into the holy city and they appeared to many people there. 54When the centurion and those with him guarding Yeshua saw the earthquake and all that took place, they were terrified, and said, "Surely he was the son of God!"[191]

His women look on

55And there were many women watching from a distance. They had followed Yeshua from the Galil and had provided for him. 56Among them were Miryam of Magdala,[192] and Miryam the mother of Yaakov and Yosef, and the mother of the sons of Zavdai.[193]

The body in linen entombed in rock

57When evening came, a rich man from Arimathaia[194] named Yosef appeared. He was also a student of Yeshua. 58He went to Pilatus and asked for the body of Yeshua. Then Pilatus ordered it to be given to him. 59Yosef took the body, wrapped it in clean linen, 60and laid it in his own new tomb, which he had cut out of the rock. He then rolled a great stone to the door of the tomb and went away.

61Miryam of Magdala and the other Miryam were there, sitting opposite the tomb.

---

there were not yet Christian saints to fall out of their tombs. If they were meant to be pre-Christian Jewish saints, this meaning does not come through.

191. Centurion is a Roman commander of a century, that is, one hundred soldiers. Here the centurion is the head of the execution squad that mocks and crucifies Yeshua, and he and his soldiers are also the first to state that Yeshua is the son of God. This deus ex machina declaration foretells Yeshua's resurrection.

192. Mary Magdalene from the Galilean town of Magdala.

193. Mother of the sons of Zebedee. Her sons were James and John. Of the three Marys at the crucifixion, Mary, mother of Yeshua, is notably absent in Mark, Matthew, and Luke. However, in John, Mary, mother of Yeshua, is there, and there is a moving recognition: "Woman, here is your son." Then Yeshua says to the student he loved, "Here is your mother." The unknown student then takes Mary to his own home (John 19.26–27). In the gospels, it is Mary Magdalene who goes to the tomb and speaks to the risen Yeshua in the garden. See note 191, Matt. 27.54.

194. Arimathea from the Greek Ἀριμαθαία (Arimathaia) and identified with either Ramathaim or Rentis, fifteen or twenty miles east of Jaffa.

Guard at the tomb

62On Shabbat, the next day after Preparation Day,[195] the high priests and the Prushim gathered before Pilatus 63and said, "Sir, we remember what the imposter said while he was alive, 'After three days I will rise again.' 64Therefore, command that the tomb be guarded until the third day so his students will not come and steal his body and say to the people, 'He has been raised from the dead.' And that will be the ultimate deception, worse than the first."

65Pilatus said to them, "You have a guard of soldiers. Go, and make it as secure as you know how."

66And they went to police the tomb and they secured the stone with the guard.

Chapter 28

The women at the empty tomb

After Shabbat, at the first dawnlight of Sunday, Miryam of Magdala and the other Miryam came to look at the tomb. 2And look, there was a great earthquake. An angel of Yahweh came down from the sky and approached the tomb, rolled away the stone, and was sitting on it. 3And his appearance was like lightning and his clothing white as snow. 4And those who were on guard shook with fear, and became like dead men.

5But the angel said to the women,

> Don't be afraid. I know you are looking for Yeshua who was
>   crucified.
> 6He is not here. He has risen just as he said.
> Come see the place where he lay.
> 7Then go quickly and tell his students,
> "He has risen from the dead, and look,
> He goes before you into the Galil.
> There you will see him." Look, I have told you.

---

195. Friday.

Risen

8The women left the tomb with fear and great joy, and ran to tell the news to the students. 9And look, Yeshua met them and said,

>   Hello!

And they came near him and grabbed his feet and worshiped him. 10Yeshua said to them,

>   Do not fear. Go and tell my brothers and sisters
>   To go to the Galil and there they will see me.

Report of the guards

11And while the women were on their way, look, some of the guards went into the city to report to the high priests all that had happened. 12And they met with the elders and took enough silver coins to give to the soldiers 13and told them, "Say that during the night the students came and stole his body while we were sleeping. 14And if the governor hears of this, we will confer with him and keep you out of trouble."

15The soldiers took the money and did as they were instructed. And this story is known among the Jews to this day.

Yeshua in the Galil with his students

16Now the eleven students went to the Galil, to the mountain where Yeshua had commanded them to go. 17And look, when they saw him they worshiped him, but some doubted. 18And Yeshua came up to them and spoke to them, saying,

>   To me was given all authority in heaven and on earth.
>   19Go and make students of all nations,
>   Washing them in the name of the father and the son
>   And the holy spirit,
>   20Teaching them to hold to all I have commanded you.
>   And know I am with you
>   All the days until the end of eternity.[196]

---

196. "Age" in Greek is αἰών (aion). The KJV and Lattimore version have chosen to translate the completion of the aeon as "the end of the world," which is more dramatic and beautiful. The Greek wording also has a mysterious note conveying "until the end of eternity."

Loukas
(Luke)

Loukas
(Luke)

THERE IS GENERAL AGREEMENT among scholars that little is certain about authorship, place, and date with regard to Luke. While this uncertainty exists for all the gospels, Luke remains a special case. Older scholarship has given us the authorial name "Luke" and the places of his gospel composition as Rome or cities in the East such as Achaia, Ephesos, or Caesarea in Israel. The name "Luke" appears to come from Bishop Irenaeus (late second century), who claimed that Luke was Paul's "inseparable collaborator" in Antioch. But the depiction of Paul in the Acts, which is also ascribed to Luke, has little to do with the self-portrait of Paul that emerges in the apostle's own letters. There are also traditions, of no more certainty, that speak of Luke as "the beloved physician," as a "convert" to the Christian Jews, and as the evangelist who wrote for gentile converts. There is no substantial evidence for any of this. It is clear that Luke the author never read or even knew of Paul's letters, and hence all attempts to identify who the author of Luke was, who his associates were, for whom he wrote, and what city or country he wrote in, fall apart. Luke was almost certainly not the companion of Paul. Regardless of unproved speculations about the person of Luke, the Gospel of Luke is a splendid achievement.

Luke is the longest of the gospels, and, according to most commentators, the most skillfully constructed one, composed in an elegant Greek at times approaching classical Hellenistic Greek of the first century. The main example cited by scholars to demonstrate Luke's classical Greek is the brief prologue (1.1–4). This text resembles the prologue to Acts and has been used as proof that Luke is the common author of the Gospel of Luke and the Acts of the Apostles. While it is true that the prologue is a good example of the Hellenistic complexity of rhetoric, its convoluted discourse is polite and also heavy. The prologue, in fact and in spirit, is not by the same author who wrote the rest of the Gospel of Luke. And whether or not the same author wrote Luke and the Acts should not be proved by the similarities of the prologues, which in Acts, again, does not share the spirit of the scripture it prefaces. Once we go beyond the prologue, the Greek of Luke is different, is more inflected, but not decisively removed from that of Mark and Matthew. The Koine (demotic) Greek of the four gospels is a perfect vehicle for the narration and poem of the New Testament.

The Gospel of Luke reads as a fluent late text, greatly enlarging the scope of the New Testament. Its immediate sources in the synoptic chain are the unknown Q source, which is presumed to be a sayings gospel, and both Mark and Matthew. Luke expands on Mark and Matthew, and we cannot explain the sources for this additional material. Perhaps the most original and beautiful passages in Luke (for which there are no counterparts in the other gospels) are the annunciation (1.26–38), Mary's visit to Elizabeth (1.39–56), the nativity scene of the birth of Yeshua in the manger (2.1–7), the parable of the Good Samaritan (10.29–37), and the parable of the Prodigal Son (15.11–32). Only the rich treasure of Luke gives us the birth of John the Baptist (1.5–25, 57–80), the angelic announcement and the visit of the shepherds (2.8–20), as well as the prayers of Simeon and Anna (2.25–38). Among the poetic masterpieces in the New Testament is Mary's song, the "Magnificat" (1.39–55), beginning "My soul magnifies the lord."

Much has been written about Luke as the great narrator, which is true, and Luke's means are often contrasted with Mark's more modest style. The comparison is mistaken. Both Mark and Luke are master narrators of the New Testament, and Luke is closer to Mark than is normally acknowledged. The clichés of Mark as a rude populist and Luke as an elegant Henry James are unfounded. In their best moments, especially in the rush and drama of the passion week, the two authors are cut from the same cloth. Although Mark has no resurrection scene and Luke does, the ending of Luke resembles the narrative genius of Mark. Luke speaks of Yeshua, who has come back to life and is walking the roads of Israel, startling his disciples and friends, and engaging in the most profound and compelling conversation of the gospels.

Prologue[1]

So you may know the truth, excellent Theofilos

Since many have set their hand to composing a narrative of those things which have been fulfilled among us 2 as they were handed on to us from the beginning by eyewitnesses and servants of the word, 3 it seemed also good for me, since I was the first to follow everything closely, to write them down in good order for you, excellent Theofilos, 4 that you may know the truth concerning these words about which you have been instructed.

Chapter 1

Angel with good news for barren Elisheva

5 In the days of Herod, king of Yehuda[2] there was a certain priest named Zeharyahu,[3] from the priestly order of Aviyah,[4] and his wife came from the daughters of Aharon[5] and her name was Elisheva.[6] 6 They were both upright before God, walking blamelessly in all the commandments and regulations of God. 7 But they had no child, because Elisheva was barren, and both of them were advanced in their days.

---

1. In Paul's letter to Philemon, 1.24, Luke is Paul's "fellow worker," and in Colossians 4.14 he is "the beloved physician." Acts begins, "In the first account, O Theofilos, I wrote about everything that Yeshua began to do and teach . . ." This reference to "the first account" has been taken as an allusion to the Gospel of Luke and remains at the center of the Luke-Acts' controversy over authorship. While these late brief prefaces do not prove common authorship for Luke and Acts, their almost identical voice, each addressed to the honorific patron Theophilos, may mean their own single authorship, or one author imitating another. The heart of Luke is composed in graceful popular Greek, and the notion of the elevated classical style is rumor.

2. Judea (and Judas, Juda, Judah, Jude, and feminine of Jew) from the Greek Ἰουδαία (Ioudaia), from the Hebrew יְהוּדָה (yehuda).

3. Zechariah from the Greek Ζαχαρίας (Zaharias), from the Hebrew זְכַרְיָהוּ (zeharyahu).

4. Abijah from the Greek Ἀβιά (Abia), from the Hebrew אֲבִיָּה (aviyah).

5. Aaron from the Greek Ἀαρών (Aaron), from the Hebrew אַהֲרֹן (aharon).

6. Elizabeth from the Greek Ἐλισάβετ (Elisabet), from the Hebrew אֱלִישֶׁבַע (elisheva).

8Now it happened that in his priestly duty when it was the turn of his division to be before God, 9Zeharyahu was chosen by lot, according to the custom of the priesthood, to go into the Temple of the lord and burn incense. 10And a huge gathering of people was praying outside at the hour of the incense offering. 11Then an angel of the Lord appeared to him, standing to the right side of the incense altar. 12He was terrified at what he saw and fear fell upon him.

13But the angel said to him.[7]

> Do not be afraid, Zeharyahu, your prayer
> Was heard and your wife Elisheva will bear
> You a son and you will name him Yohanan[8]
> 14And he will be your joy and exultation,
> And many will rejoice at his birth,
> 15For he will be great before the eye of the lord
> And he will never swallow wine or strong drink
> And he will be filled with the holy spirit
> While still in his mother's womb, and will turn
> 16Many sons of Yisrael[9] toward the lord their God.
> 17And he will advance with Eliyahu's spirit and power
> To turn the hearts of fathers toward their children
> And the disobedient to the wisdom of the just,
> And to prepare a people ready for the lord.

18And Zeharyahu said to the angel,

> How will I know this? I am an old man
> And my wife is weak in the years of her life.

19The angel answered, saying to him,

> I am Gavriel.[10] I stand in the presence of God
> And was sent to speak to you and to announce
> These things to you. 20And look, you will be silent,

---

7. The poem that follows is in the manner of the Hebrew Bible as Luke understood it through the Septuagint (the Greek translation of the Hebrew Bible for the Jews of Alexandria, 250–100 B.C.E.), the first words of the narrative after the prologue are in conscious imitation of the Septuagint phrasing, with words taken from Numbers 6.1–4; Judges 13.4; Jeremiah 1.5; Malachi 4.5–6; and Genesis 17.17.

8. John from the Greek Ἰωάννης (Ioannes), from the Hebrew יוֹחָנָן (yohanan).

9. Israel from the Greek Ἰσραήλ, from the Hebrew יִשְׂרָאֵל (yisrael).

10. Gabriel.

Unable to speak till the day these things happen
Because you did not believe my words,
Which will be fulfilled in their own time.[11]

21Now the people were waiting for Zeharyahu and they wondered at
the time he spent in Temple. 22But when he came out he could not speak
to them, and they knew he had seen a vision in the Temple. He kept
nodding to them and remained speechless. 23And it happened that when
the days of his liturgies[12] were completed, he went to his house.

24After those days his wife Elisheva conceived, and she hid away for
five months, saying,

25This is what the lord has done for me
In the days he looked on me with favor
And took away my disgrace among people.[13]

Angel with troubling news for Miryam[14]

26In the sixth month the angel Gavriel was sent by God to a city in
the Galil[15] called Natzeret,[16] 27to a virgin engaged to a man whose name
was Yosef,[17] from the house of David, and the name of the virgin was
Miryam.[18] 28And he came near her and said,

Hello, favored one, the lord is with you.

---

11. She would become pregnant, and her child would become known as John the
Baptist.

12. From the Greek λειτουργία (leitourgia), "liturgy." Usually translated as "ministries" (King James Version) or "service(s)" in modern versions, but liturgy also means,
as in English, a liturgy, "a ceremonial chant in service of attending a parishioner."
The root meaning of the word is "work for people." Since both the musical notion
of ceremonial liturgy and work are suggested in the Greek, it is important to convey this in English.

13. Elizabeth's disgrace was for having been infertile.

14. In the *Harper NRS Study Bible*, the subtitle is "The Birth of Jesus Foretold"; in
the Jerusalem Bible it is "The Annunciation."

15. Galilee from the Greek Γαλιλαία (Galilaia), from the Hebrew גָּלִיל (galil).
"Galil" is a "circle," "district," or "province" and is usually written in the Hebrew as
גְּלִיל הַגּוֹיִם (galil hagoyim), meaning "province of the goyim (gentiles)."

16. Nazareth from the Greek Ναζαρέτ (Natzaret), from unknown village in Galilee
probably spelled Natzeret.

17. Joseph from the Greek Ἰωσήφ (Iosef), from the Hebrew יוֹסֵף (yosef).

18. Mary from the Greek Μαρία (Maria), from the Hebrew מִרְיָם (miryam).

29But Miryam was deeply troubled by his words and pondered what kind of greeting this might be.

30The angel said to her,

Do not fear, Miryam, for you have found favor with God.

31Look, you will conceive in your womb and bear a son

And you will name him Yeshua.

32He will be great and be called son of the highest,

And the lord God will give him the throne of his father David,

33And he will rule over the house of Yaakov through the ages,

And of his kingdom there will be no end.

34But Miryam said to the angel,

How will this be since I do not know a man?[19]

35The angel answered her,

The holy spirit will come to you

And the power of the highest will overshadow you.

So the one being born will be called the holy son of God.

36And look, Elisheva your kinswoman

Has also conceived a son in her old age

And this is her sixth month, she who had been called barren.

37With God nothing is impossible.[20]

38Miryam said,

---

19. The old versions in English, Tyndale, and the Rheims in the sixteenth century and KJV in the seventeenth century accord the English version of this phrase the accurate dignity of the Greek ἄνδρα οὐ γινώσκω (andra ou ginosko?). Tyndale: "I know not a man?" Rheims: "I know not man?" KJV: "I know not a man?" However, modern versions commit the heresy of explanation. New International Version: "I am a virgin?" New Revised Standard Version: "I am a virgin?" New American Standard: "I am a virgin?" Oxford Inclusive Version: "I am a virgin?" Going further into explanation, the New American Bible reads, "I have no relations with a man?" The Annotated Scholars reads, "I've not had sex with any man." As usual, Lattimore breaks the modern mold and returns to the Greek: "I know no man?" His interpretation differs slightly in that here the negative is connected with the verb, and Lattimore negates the object noun.

20. The texts vary on line 1.37, some putting it in doubt.

Look, here I am, the slave of the lord.
May it happen to me according to your word.
The angel left her.

Miryam visits Elisheva[21]

39And Miryam rose up in these days and went into the hill country
to a city in Yehuda.[22] 40She entered the house of Zeharyahu and greeted
Elisheva.

Elisheva sings

41It happened that when Elisheva heard Miryam's greeting, the child
leapt in her womb. And Elisheva was filled with the holy spirit. 42She
spoke out, with a great cry,

You are blessed among women
And blessed is the fruit of your womb.

43How has it happened to me that the mother
Of my lord comes to me?

44Look, as soon as the sound of your greeting came
To my ears, a child in my womb leapt for joy!

45Blessed is she believing in the fulfillment
Of what was told her by the lord.

Miryam sings

46And Miryam sang,[23]
47My soul magnifies the lord
And my spirit is joyful in God my savior,

---

21. Harper NRSV has "Mary Visits Elizabeth"; the Jerusalem "The Visitation."

22. Judea. See note 2 for Luke 1.5 on Judea.

23. Mary's song, popularly known through the Latin title the "Magnificat," resembles Hannah's song over Samuel's birth (1 Sam. 2.1–10) and the immediately preceding Elisheva's song.

48For he has looked upon his young slave
   In her low station.

Hereafter all generations will call me blessed,
49For through his powers the great one did wondrous

Things for me. His name is holy.
50His mercy goes from generation to generation

To those who fear him.
51He has shown the strength of his arm,

And scattered those who were proud
In the mind of their heart.

52He has toppled monarchs from their thrones
And raised the poor to their feet.

53He filled the hungry with good foods
And sent the rich away empty.

54He has helped Yisrael his servant and child
Through the memory of his mercy,

55Just as he spoke to our fathers,
   To Avraham and to his everlasting seed.
56Miryam stayed with Elisheva about three months and went back to
her own house.

Yohanan born

57Now for Elisheva the time was completed for her to give birth, and
she bore a son. 58Her neighbors and relatives heard that the lord had
made great his mercy to her and they rejoiced with her.

Yohanan circumcised and named

59And it happened on the eighth day they came to circumcise the
child and they were calling him by the name of his father Zeharyahu.
60His mother said, "No, but he will be called Yohanan."

61They told her, "There is no one among your relatives who is called by that name."

62And they made signs to his father to learn what he wanted to call him.

63He asked for a tablet and wrote, "Yohanan is his name."
And all were amazed.

64His mouth was open and his tongue immediately set free, and he spoke praising God.

65Then fear took hold of all those living near them, and in all the hill country of Yehuda those sayings were on everyone's lips. 66All who heard them placed them in their heart, saying, "What will this child be?"
The hand of the lord was with him.

Zeharyahu's prophecy

67His father Zeharyahu was filled with the holy spirit and he prophesied, saying,

68Blessed be the lord God of Yisrael.
　He visited his people and shaped their deliverance
69And raised a horn of salvation for us
　In the house of his servant David 70as he spoke
　Through the mouth of the ancient holy prophets:
71We will be delivered from our enemies
　And from the hand of those who hate us.
72He will show mercy to our fathers
　And remember his holy covenant
73In which he swore to Avraham our father:
74To grant us deliverance without fear
　From the hand of our enemies
　And that we serve him 75in holiness and justice,
　And be before him all of our days.
76You, child, will be called the highest prophet.
　You will go before the lord to make ready his ways,
77To give knowledge of salvation to his people
　Through the forgiveness of their sins.
78Through the tender mercies of our God
　The dawn sun will visit us from its heights
79To illuminate those of us who are sitting
　In darkness and the shadow of death,
　And to guide our feet along the way of peace.

Yohanan in the deserts

80And the child grew and became strong in spirit, and he was in the deserts[24] until the day of his appearance before Yisrael.

Chapter 2

Yeshua born in a stable

It happened in those days that a decree was sent out from Caesar Augustus to enroll the whole world.[25] 2This was the first census, when Quirinius was governor of Syria. 3And all went to their own cities to be registered.

4Now Yosef also went up from the Galil, from the city of Natzeret,[26] to Yehuda, to the city of David which is called Beit Lehem,[27] because he was of the house and family of David. 5He went to be enrolled with Miryam, who was engaged[28] to him and who was pregnant.[29] 6And it happened that while they were there, the days were completed for her to give birth, 7and she bore a son, her first-born, and she wrapped him in strips of cloth and laid him in a feeding trough[30] of a stable because there was no room for them in the inn.

---

24. "In the deserts" from the Greek ἐν ταῖς ἐρήμοις (en tais eremois) is often translated as "in the wilderness."

25. A census presumably in the whole Roman world that could be used for purposes of taxation and military service.

26. Nazareth from the Greek Ναζαρέτ (Nazaret). Since the town is not mentioned by name in the Hebrew Bible or the Talmud, the Hebrew form of the word is uncertain. It could be from Netzeret, meaning "sentinel," or Natzoret, meaning "watchtower."

27. Bethlehem from the Greek Βηθλέεμ (Bethleem), from the Hebrew בֵּית לֶחֶם (beit lehem), meaning "house of bread."

28. To make plausible Mary's virginity, Joseph was engaged, not married, to Mary. There is no reference in the gospels to a later marriage between Joseph and Mary, though Yeshua will later have four brothers, who are named, and probably two sisters, who are unnamed.

29. It was important to establish Yeshua's lineage through Joseph, who was of the family of David, as indicated in Luke's genealogy, 3.23–37, but with the reservation "as it was thought." The virgin birth would, it would seem, deprive Yeshua of the biological paternal link back to David, but through Mary there was a blood line.

30. From the Greek φάτνη (fatne), "feeding trough." "Manger" is a feeding trough

8And there were shepherds in the region, camping in the fields at night and keeping guard over their flock. 9An angel of the lord stood before them and the glory of the lord shone about them, and they were terrified.

10The angel said to them,

> Don't be afraid. Look, I tell you good news,
> A great joy for all people.
> 11Because on this day was born to you in the city of David
> A savior who is the mashiah the lord.
> 12Here is your sign. You will find a child wrapped in cloths
> And lying in a feeding trough of a stable.

13And suddenly with the angel there was a multitude of the heavenly army praising God and saying,

> 14Glory to God in the highest sky
> And on earth peace among people of good will.[31]

15And it happened that after the angels had gone from them into the sky, the shepherds said to one another, "Let us go to Beit Lehem and see what has taken place, which the lord has made known to us."

16And they left, hurrying, and found Miryam and Yosef, and the baby boy lying in the feeding trough. 17When they saw them, they made known what had been said to them about the child. 18And all who heard were amazed at what the shepherds told them.

19But Miryam took all these words in and pondered them in her heart.

20The shepherds returned, glorifying and praising God for all they had heard and seen, as it had been told them.

Yeshua circumcised and named

21Now after eight days had passed it was time for his circumcision, and he was called by the name Yeshua, the name called by the angel before he was conceived in the womb.

22When the days for their purification[32] had passed, according to the

---

for animals. Though a beautiful and evocative word, "manger" has come, incorrectly, to signify the stable itself rather than the feeding box, which conveys a more extraordinary incident.

31. From the Greek εὐδοκία (eudokia), "of goodwill" or "good pleasure," or variously translated as "whom he favors."

32. Forty days after the birth of a male child.

law of Moshe,[33] they brought him up to Yerushalayim[34] to present him before the lord, 23 as it is written in Exodus[35] in the law of the lord:

Every male child who opens the womb
will be called holy to the lord.[36]

24 And a sacrifice was offered according to what is said in the law of the lord,

A pair of turtledoves or two young pigeons.

Song of Shimon[37]

25 And look, there was a man in Yerushalayim whose name was Shimon,[38] and he was just and circumspect and he looked forward to the

---

33. Moses from the Greek Μωϋσῆς (Moyses), from the Hebrew מֹשֶׁה (moshe).

34. Jerusalem from the Greek Ἰερουσαλήμ (Ierousalem), from the Hebrew יְרוּשָׁלַיִם (yerushalayim).

35. Exod. 13.2.

36. This famous passage of the nativity scene, based on Exodus 13.2, is translated accurately from Luke's Greek, without interpretation, in the KJV and in Lattimore. Luke has made a loose reference to Exodus 13.2. Perhaps to complete Luke's free reference to Exodus 13.2, most standard contemporary translations, including NRSV, NIV, Jerusalem, and Oxford Inclusive, have added and subtracted words in their versions of Luke. NRSV has, "Every firstborn shall be designated as holy to the Lord." NRSV's own version of Luke's source (probably by way of the Septuagint) in Exodus 13.2 reads, "Consecrate to me all the firstborn; whatever is the first to open the womb among the Israelites." Luke does not say "firstborn," which most modern translations add. But Luke does repeat the very strong Hebrew metaphor "open the womb," here in the Greek διανοῖγον μήτραν (dianoigon metran), which modern translations omit.

37. "Simeon" is a name not everyone knows for "Simon," much less for "Simeon Peter," but the poet T. S. Eliot knew it well, and becomes one with Simeon in his "Song for Simeon," which begins unforgettably:

Lord, the Roman hyacinths are blooming in bowls and
The winter sun creeps by the snow hills;
The stubborn season has made stand.
My life is light, waiting for the death wind,
Like a feather on the back of my hand.
Dust in sunlight and memory in corners
Wait for the wind that chills towards the dead land.

38. Simon from the Greek Σίμων (Simon), from the Hebrew שִׁמְעוֹן (shimon). Here Luke refers to Simon as Simeon, from the Greek Συμεών (Simeon).

consolation of Yisrael,[39] and the holy spirit was upon him. 26It had been revealed to him by the holy spirit that he would not see death until he saw the mashiah of the lord. 27And through the spirit he came into the Temple. When the parents brought in the child Yeshua, to do for him what was the custom under the law, 28Shimon took him in his arms and praised God and said,

> 29Rabbi, in accordance with your word,
>> Now you release your slave in peace,
> 30For my eyes have seen your salvation,[40]
> 31Which you prepared before the face of all the people,[41]
> 32A light of revelation to the gentiles[42]
>> And a glory to your people Yisrael.

33And his father[43] and mother were in wonder at the things said about their child.

34Then Shimon blessed them and said to Miryam his mother,

> See, the child is appointed for the fall and rise of many in
>> Yisrael,

---

39. The consolation that the coming of the messiah would bring to Israel.

40. Isa. 52.10 and 46.13.

41. Isa. 42.6 and 49.6; John 8.12b.

42. Gentile from the late Latin *gens*, meaning "pagan," from the Greek ἔθνος (ethnos), meaning literally a "national" as in "people" or "nation," and in the plural "non-Jews, Christian Jews, Christians, pagans," or "heathens," from the Hebrew גּוֹי (goy), plural גּוֹיִם (goyim), meaning "a people, nation, non-Jew." The diverse meanings given in usage and especially in translation of the Greek depend on the context. Normally, in the gospels and Acts an *ethnikos* (like a gentile) means a non-Jew who may be converted to Jewish Messianism or, as in later church koine, a "Christian Jew who is a convert from paganism," as in parts of Acts and the letters; and if the word is used disparagingly to mean both a non-Jew and non-Christian, it refers to a pagan. In its fully wicked sense, *ethnos* means a "heathen." In modern English the commonest meaning of "gentile" has come to be a Christian as opposed to a Jew. Here, since Luke, the nominal author of Luke, was traditionally called the non-Jew among the four evangelists, the appearance of "the gentiles" in the Song of Simeon is said by commentators to reflect Luke's careful emphasis on affirming that salvation is offered to gentile as well as Jew.

43. The reference to Joseph as πατήρ (pater), "father" rather than "stepfather," reveals the difficulty of speaking of Yeshua's parents without raising the question of his lineage.

And destined to be a sign that will be opposed,
35And through your own soul a sword will pierce
So that secrets from many hearts may be revealed.

Hannah, Temple prophet

36And there was Hannah, a prophet, daughter of Fanuel,[44] of the tribe of Asher. She was well advanced in her days, having lived with her husband seven years after her virginity,[45] 37and she was a widow until she was eighty-four years. She did not leave the Temple, serving there with fasting and prayers night and day. 38At that hour she came in, standing near, and praised God and spoke of the child to all who looked forward to the deliverance of Yerushalayim.

Yeshua's childhood in Natzeret

39When they completed everything according to the law of the lord, they went back to the Galil to the city of Natzeret. 40And the child grew and became strong, filled with wisdom, and the grace of God was upon him.

After Pesach in Yerushalayim, twelve-year-old Yeshua stays on alone to talk with the rabbis in the Temple

41Now his parents journeyed every year to Yerushalayim for the Seder of the Pesach.[46] 42And when he was twelve years old, they went up as was their custom for the Seder. 43When the feast days were over and they

---

44. Anna from the Greek Ἄννα, from the Hebrew חַנָּה (hannah). Phanuel from Greek Φανουήλ (Fanouel), from Hebrew פְּנוּאֵל (penuel). Hannah's words and Shimon's song are seen as prophecies.

45. Virginity from the Greek παρθενία (parthenia), "virginity," "purity," or "maidenhood." Here the word means "from her marriage" as indicated by the time since maidenhood was lost. It is important not to lose in translation the physical immediacy of the Greek word for "virginity," which may suggest marriage but does not say it, by giving its less rich equivalent or an explanation. As with many expressions, the Greek works from a metaphorical image, which the reader understands at both ends of the metaphor. In his 1525 New Testament, William Tyndale and the 1611 KJV translate "parthenia" as "virginity."

46. Passover feast or Seder, a ceremonial meal on the first or first two evenings of Pesach, a festival commemorating the escape of the Jews from captivity in Egypt.

returned, the boy Yeshua remained in Yerushalayim, but his parents did not know it. 44Thinking he was with a caravan of travelers, they went a day on the road, looking for him among their relatives and acquaintances. 45When they didn't find him, they went back to Yerushalayim and searched for him.

46And it happened that after three days they found him in the Temple, sitting among the rabbis, listening to them and asking them questions. 47And all who listened to him were amazed at his intelligence and his answers.

48And when his parents saw him they were astonished, and his mother said to him, "Son, why did you do this to us? Look, your father and I were in sorrow, searching for you."

49And he said to them,

> Why were you looking for me?
> Didn't you know I must be in my father's things?[47]

50And they didn't understand the words he spoke to them.

Yeshua in Natzeret grows into manhood

51Then he went down with them and they came to Natzeret, and he was under their authority.[48] And his mother kept all his sayings in her heart.

52Yeshua increased in wisdom and in stature and in the favor of God and people.

Chapter 3

Yohanan the Dipper in the desert

In the fifteenth year of the reign of Tiberius Caesar,[49] while Pontius Pilatus[50] was governor of Yehuda, and Herod was tetrarch of the Galil,

---

47. Other translations have rendered "my father's things" as "my Father's house," which is not stated in the Greek, and while it may be implied, the range of meanings of "things" thereby becomes limited by specific interpretation.

48. A polite way of saying he was obedient to them.

49. Literally, "hegemony." The reign of Tiberius Caesar (14–37 C.E.).

50. Pontius Pilate.

and his brother Filippos[51] was tetrarch of the region of Ituraea and Trachonitis, and Lysanias was tetrarch of Abilene, 2during the priesthood of Hannan[52] and Kayfa,[53] the word of God came to Yohanan son of Zeharyahu in the desert. 3And he went into all the surrounding region of the Yarden,[54] preaching ritual washing of repentance for the forgiveness of sins, 4as it is written in the book of words of the prophet Yeshayahu,

> I am the voice of one crying out in the desert:
> "Prepare the way of Adonai, make his paths straight!
> 5Every ravine will be filled
> And every mountain and hill will be leveled low,
> And the crooked will be straight
> And the rough roads smooth
> 6And all flesh will look upon the salvation of God."[55]

Yohanan forewarns the offspring of vipers

7Yohanan said to the crowds that came out to be dipped by him,

> Offspring of vipers!,
> Who warned you to flee from the coming anger?[56]

---

51. Philip from the Greek Φίλιππος (Filippos).

52. Annas. *Hannan* or *Anan* means "high priest" in the Hebrew, from the Greek Ἄννας (Annas), from the Hebrew חָנָן (hannan), "priest" or "gracious one."

53. Caiaphas from the Greek Καϊάφας (Kaiafas), from the Hebrew כֵּיפָא (kayfa), meaning "a depression." The high priests were under Rome and subject to appointment. Kayfa was appointed by Valerius Gratus, governor of Judea.

54. Jordan from the Greek Ἰορδάνης (Iordanes), from the Hebrew יַרְדֵּן (yarden).

55. The prayer, which appears in other gospels, comes from Isaiah 40.5.

56. The furious curse and anger by John at his entrance are taken as a warning of forthcoming punishment to the people who do not recognize the messiah, which is the coming destruction of the Temple in 70 C.E., which has occurred by the time of the gospel's composition. The familiar anger against Jews is historically anachronistic, since John belonged to the same tribe as the "offspring of vipers." The Annotated Scholars edition translates the phrase "offspring of vipers" (Matt. 23.33) as "You spawn of Satan," so interpreting "vipers" to be both "the snake as Satan in the garden" and "the snake as Jew." This early segment of warning and condemnation in Luke, given in John's voice, duplicates the word and sentiment found in the

8Bear fruits that are worthy of repentance,
And do not begin to say among yourselves,
"We have Avraham for our father."[57]
For I say to you that out of these rocks
God can raise up children for Avraham.
9Even now the ax is set against the root of trees
So every tree that does not bear good fruit
Is cut down and cast into the fire.

10And the crowds questioned him, saying, "What should we do then?"
11Yohanan answered them, saying,
One who has two coats should share them
With one who has none.
One who has meat[58] should share it
In the same way.

12Then came tax collectors to be dipped, and they said to him, "Rabbi, what should we do?"
13He said to them,
Collect no more than you are ordered to.

14Then soldiers in service also questioned him, saying, "What should we do?"
And he said to them,
Do not slanderously blackmail, do not extort,
And be satisfied with your wages.

Who is the mashiah?

15And as the people had great expectations and wondered in their hearts about Yohanan, whether he might be the mashiah, 16Yohanan answered them all, saying,

---

other gospels, however, at later moments in the narrative. Here the curse is introduced early in John's voice. Another such example of a curse by a Jew on Jews is the implausible passage in Matthew in which the Jews are out in the street, shouting their own future and eternal punishment, "Let his [Yeshua's] blood be upon us and upon our children!" (Matt. 27.25).

57. 2 Chron. 20.7.

58. Also translated as "food."

I wash you with water,
But one is coming who is stronger than I,
And I am not worthy to untie the strap of his sandals.
He will immerse you in holy spirit and fire.
17His winnowing fork is in hand to clean out the threshing
floor
And to gather the grain into his storehouse,
But the chaff he will burn up in quenchless fire.

18And with many other words of exhortation, Yohanan proclaimed the good news to the people.

Yohanan imprisoned

19But Herod the tetrarch, whom Yohanan had rebuked about Herodias his brother's wife and about all the misdeeds that Herod had done, 20added one more to them all: he locked Yohanan up in prison.[59]

Yeshua baptized

21Now it happened that in washing all the people and also Yeshua while he was praying, the sky opened 22and the holy spirit descended on him in the bodily form of a dove. A voice came out of the sky, saying,

You are my son whom I love.
In you I am pleased.[60]

His ancestry

23And Yeshua was about thirty years old when he began his work, being the son (as it was thought) of Yosef, son of Eli,[61] 24son of Mattat,[62] son of Levi, son of Malki,[63] son of Yannai,[64] son of Yosef, 25son of Mattatias, son

---

59. According to Josephus, John was imprisoned in Machaerus, Herod Antipas's fortress palace overlooking the Dead Sea, later in Yeshua's life (*Antiquities* 18.5.2).

60. Other manuscript readings give, "Today I have begotten you."

61. Heli.

62. Matthat.

63. Melchi.

64. Jannai.

of Amos,[65] son of Nahum, son of Hesli,[66] son of Naggai, 26 son of Mahat,[67] son of Mattathiyah, son of Shimi,[68] son of Yoseh,[69] son of Yodah,[70] 27 son of Yohanan,[71] son of Reisha,[72] son of Zerubavel,[73] son of Shaltiel,[74] son of Neri, 28 son of Malki, son of Addi, son of Kosam,[75] son of Elmadam,[76] son of Er, 29 son of Yeshua, son of Eliezer, son of Yoram,[77] son of Mattat, son of Levi, 30 son of Shimon, son of Yehuda, son of Yosef, son of Yonam, son of Eliakim,[78] 31 son of Malah,[79] son of Manah,[80] son of Mattatah,[81] son of Natan,[82] son of David, 32 son of Yishai,[83] son of Obev,[84] son of Boaz, son of Salmon, son of Nahshon, 33 son of Amminadav,[85] son of Admin,

---

65. Amos, as in the prophet, is not to be confused with Amos, the father of Isaiah.

66. Esli.

67. Maath.

68. Semein.

69. Josech.

70. Joda.

71. Joanan, John. The Hebrew name passing through the Greek comes out as *Joanan*, when referring to a Hebrew Bible figure, and "John," when a New Testament figure, taking it from the Greek Ἰωάννης (Ioannes), from the Hebrew יוֹחָנָן (yohanan). "John" in English is farther removed from its Semitic source than is *Yohanan*.

72. Rhesa.

73. Zerubbabel.

74. Shealtiel.

75. Cosam.

76. Elmadan.

77. Jorim.

78. Eliakim.

79. Melea.

80. Menna.

81. Mattatha.

82. Nathan.

83. Jesse.

84. Obeb.

85. Amminadab.

son of Arni, son of Hetzron,[86] son of Peretz,[87] son of Yehuda, 34 son of Yaakov, son of Yitzhak, son of Avraham, son of Terah, son of Nahor, 35 son of Serug, son of Reu, son of Peleg, son of Ever,[88] son of Shelah, 36 son of Keinan,[89] son of Arpahshad,[90] son of Shem, son of Noah, son of Lemeh,[91] 37 son of Metushelah,[92] son of Hanoh,[93] son of Yered,[94] son of Mahalalel,[95] son of Keinan, 38 son of Enosh,[96] son of Shet,[97] son of Adam, son of God.

Chapter 4

Temptation in the desert

Filled with the holy spirit, Yeshua returned from the Yarden[98] and was led by the spirit into the desert 2for forty days, being tested by the devil. And he ate nothing in those days and when they were ended, he hungered.

3The devil said to him,

> If you are the son of God,
> Tell this stone to become bread.

4And Yeshua responded to him,

> As it is written in the Torah:

---

86. Hezron.
87. Perez.
88. Eber.
89. Cainan.
90. Arphaxad.
91. Lemech.
92. Methuselah.
93. Enoch.
94. Jared.
95. Mahalaleel.
96. Enos.
97. Seth.
98. Jordan.

"One does not live by bread alone."[99]

5Then the devil led him very high and showed him all the kingdoms of the world in a flash of time, 6and said to him,

> I will give you authority over all these places
> Along with the glory of these things,
> Since this has been handed over to me,
> And I give it to whomever I please.
> 7If you worship me it will all be yours.

8And Yeshua answered, saying to him,

> It is written in the Torah:
> "You will worship the lord our God
> And will serve him alone."[100]

Temptation from the Temple rooftop

9The devil led him to Yerushalayim and placed him on the pinnacle of the Temple and said to him,

> If you are the son of God, leap down from here,
> 10For it is written in Psalms:
> > He will command his angels to protect you,
> > 11And on their hands they will hold you up
> > So you won't smash your foot against a stone.[101]

12Yeshua answered, saying to him,

> You will not test the lord your God.[102]

13When the devil had completed every test, he left him for a better time.

Teaching in synagogues in the Galil

14And Yeshua returned in the power of the spirit to the Galil. And

---

99. Deut. 8.3. The Torah is specifically the five books of Moses but is normally used as a synecdoche for the entire Hebrew Bible.

100. Deut. 6.3.

101. Ps. 91.11–12.

102. From the Greek πειρασμός (peirasmos), "test." Also translated as "temptation," which lightly heightens specific "test" to conceptual religious "temptation."

rumor went out about him in the surrounding countryside. 15He taught in their synagogues, honored by all.[103]

Saying Yeshayahu's prophecy in synagogue in Natzeret

16He came to Natzeret where he had been raised, and on Shabbat[104] he entered the synagogue as was the custom, and stood up to read. 17He was given the book of the prophet Yeshayahu. And he unrolled the scroll[105] and found the place where it was written,

> 18The spirit of the lord is upon me,
> Through which he anointed me
> To bring good news to the poor.
> He sent me to preach release of captives
> And vision to the blind,
> To let the downtrodden go free,
> 19To proclaim the year of the lord's favor.[106]

20He rolled up the book, gave it back to the servant, and sat down. And the eyes of all in the synagogue were fixed on him. 21He began to speak to them,

> Today the Torah is fulfilled in your ears.

---

103. From the Greek ἐν ταῖς συναγωγαῖς αὐτῶν (en tais synagogais auton), "in their synagogues." *Auton,* meaning "of them" or "their," is a crucial distancing pronoun; it implies a distinction of identity between Yeshua and the Jews of the synagogue. If Yeshua, a Galilean, is to be fully identified as a Jew, it should be "in *the* synagogues" or "in *his* synagogues," since he was in his homeland of Galilee. One would not say that Augustine taught "in their churches." Augustine would be teaching "in the churches," for he and the congregation were identified as one, whether it was Galilee or Rome.

104. Sabbath from the Greek σάββατον (sabbaton), from the Hebrew שַׁבָּת (shabbat).

105. The Greek uses βιβλίον (biblion), "book." Here a "book" is a "scroll."

106. The basic tenets of Yeshua's ministry and his later title appear in this passage from Isaiah 61.1–2 and 58.6: the spirit of the lord in him; anointment by God; bringing the good news (the evangels); setting free captives; vision to the blind (in physical and metaphorical sense); freeing the poor; a year of the lord's favor (coming of the time of deliverance).

Prophet unwelcome in one's country

22And all spoke well of him and marveled at the grace in the words that came from his mouth, and said, "Isn't this Yosef's son?"

23He said to them,

Surely you will tell me the parable,

"Doctor, heal yourself," and you will say,

"All that we heard that happened in Kfar Nahum,[107]

Accomplish here in my own country."

24But he said, "Amain,[108] I tell you,"

No prophet is welcome in his own country.[109]

25But truly there were many widows in Yisrael in the days of Eliyahu[110]

When the sky was closed for three years and six months

And so there was great famine over all the land

26And Eliyahu was sent to no one except to a widow

At Tzarfat[111] in Tzidon.[112]

27And many lepers were in Yisrael in days of the prophet Elisha,[113]

And none of them was made clean except Naaman the Syrian.

28Then all those in the synagogue were filled with anger when they heard these things 29and rose up and drove him out of the city. They led

---

107. Capernaum.

108. Amen from the Greek ἀμήν (amen), from the Hebrew אָמֵן (amein). The Hebrew word *amain* (*amein* would work just as well for free-sounding English) was used by Paul in his Greek, as it is used in Hebrew at the end of a passage as a liturgical "in truth" or "so be it." Both the Greek and Hebrew words were probably pronounced with a long ay, as in "main." It is appropriate to pronounce English "amen," as in Greek and Hebrew; hence here it is given as *amain*.

109. See note 57 on Mark 3.35.

110. Elijah from the Greek Ἠλίας (Elias), from the Hebrew אֵלִיָּהוּ (eliyahu).

111. Zarephath from the Greek Σάρεττα (Sarepta), from the Hebrew צָרְפַת (tzarfat).

112. Sidon from the Greek Σιδών (Sidon), from the Hebrew צִדוֹן (tzidon).

113. Elisha or Eliseus from the Greek Ἐλισαῖος, from the Hebrew אֱלִישָׁע (elisha).

him up to the edge of the hill, on which the city was built, to fling him over. 30But he passed through their midst and went on his way.

With a demoniac

31And he went down to Kfar Nahum, a city in the Galil, and he taught them on days of Shabbat, 32and they were astonished at his teaching because of the authority of his word.

33And in the synagogue there was a man who had the spirit of an unclean demon[114] and he cried out in a great voice, 34"Ha! What are you to us, Yeshua of Natzeret? Did you come to destroy us? I know who you are, the holy one of God!"

35Yeshua reproved him, saying,

> Be silent and come out of him.

The demon threw the man down in the middle of them and he came out of him without harming him.

36Then wonder came over everyone and they talked to one another, saying, "What is this word that in its authority and power he commands unclean spirits and they come out?"

37And rumor went out about him into every place of the surrounding region.

Shimon's feverish mother-in-law

38Then he rose up from the synagogue and entered the house of Shimon.[115] Shimon's mother-in-law was suffering from a great fever and they asked him about her.

39He stood over her and reproved the fever and it left her.

At once she got up and served them.

Demons cry, "You are God's son"

40As the sun was setting, all who had people sick with various diseases

---

114. Reflecting the pattern of inserting or elevating a religious significance to the lexicon, "demon," from the Greek δαίμων (daimon), is translated as "devil" in Tyndale, KJV, and other early versions. After the Revised, "demon" is translated as "demon." In classical Greek, as in Homer's theogony, *daimon* is a "divinity" or "god."

115. In this brief episode, Shimon or Simeon will be Shimon Kefa (Simon Peter). See note 45 on Mark 3.16 for the derivation of "Simon Peter."

brought them to him, and he laid his hands on each of them and healed them. 41Demons came out of many of them, shouting, "You are the son of God."

But he rebuked them, forbidding them to speak, because they knew he was the mashiah.

From a deserted place Yeshua goes on to preach in Yehuda

42When day came he left and went into a deserted place and the crowds were looking for him and came up to him and held him back so that he could not go away from them. 43But he said to them,

> I must preach the good news of the kingdom of God
> In other cities, since for this I was sent.

44And he preached in the synagogues of Yehuda.[116]

Chapter 5

Calling his first students, who are fishermen

Now it happened that while the crowd pressed in around him to hear the word of God, Yeshua was standing beside the lake of Gennesaret. 2He saw two ships there beside the lake. But the fishermen had got out of them and were washing their nets. 3He climbed into one of the ships, one that was Shimon's, and asked him to take him out a little away from the shore. Then he sat down and from the boat he taught the crowds.

4When he stopped speaking, he said to Shimon,

> Go out into the deep waters
> And drop your nets and fish.

5Shimon answered and said, "Rabbi, all through the night we worked hard and caught nothing. But on your word I will lower the nets."

6And when they did this, they caught such an abundance of fish that their nets were breaking. 7They signaled their partners in the other ship to come help them. They came and they filled both ships so much it was sinking them.

---

116. Other early texts, which the KJV used, say "Galilee" rather than "Judea." The Nestle-Aland gives "Judea."

8Shimon Kefa fell down at Yeshua's knees and said, "Go away from me, lord. I am a sinful man."[117]

9He and all who were with him were amazed at the haul of fish they took in. 10And so were Yaakov[118] and Yohanan, sons of Zavdai,[119] who were partners with Shimon.

Yeshua said to Shimon,

> Do not be afraid. From now on
> You will be catching people.

11And they beached their boats and left everything and followed him.

With lepers

12It happened that while he was in one of the cities, look, there was a man full of leprosy. On seeing Yeshua, he fell on his face and implored him, saying, "Sir, if you want to, you can make me clean."

13Then stretching out his hand, Yeshua touched him, saying,

> I want to. Now be clean.

And at once the leprosy left him.

14He ordered him,

> Tell no one but go,
> And then show yourself to the priest
> And, as Moshe commanded, make an offering
> For your cleansing,
> And do this as a testimony to them.

15But the word about him spread even more, and great crowds came together to hear him and be healed of their sicknesses.

16Yeshua withdrew into the desert and was praying.

---

117. "Sinful" from the Greek ἁμαρτωλός (hamartolos) is the usual New Testament translation. In ancient Greek, the word means one who "misses the mark," who "fails" or "goes astray."

118. James (Jacob) from the Greek Ἰάκωβος (Iakobos), from the Hebrew יַעֲקֹב (yaakov).

119. Zebedee from the Greek Ζεβεδαῖος (Zebedaios), from the Hebrew זַבְדִּי (zavdai).

A paralytic

17It happened that on one of those days while he was teaching, seated there were Prushim[120] and rabbis of the law, who had come from every village of the Galil and Yehuda and from Yerushalayim. The power of the lord was in him to heal. 18And look, men, carrying a man on a stretcher, who was paralyzed, and they tried to carry him in and place him before Yeshua. 19And finding no way to bring him in because of the crowd, they went up on the roof and lowered him on the stretcher through the tiles into the middle, in front of Yeshua. 20When he saw their faith he said,

> Friend, your sins are forgiven.

21Then the scholars and the Prushim began to reason, saying, "Who is this who speaks blasphemies? Who can forgive sins but God alone?" 22Yeshua perceived their reasoning, and answered, saying to them,

> Why do you reason in your hearts?
> 23Which is easier: to say, "Your sins are forgiven,"
> Or to say, "Stand up and walk"?

Then to the paralytic, he said,

> 24But for you to know that the earthly son
> Has authority on earth to forgive sins,
> I tell you, "Stand up and take up your bed
> And go to your house."

25And at once he stood up before them all, and took up what he was lying on, and he left for his house, glorifying God.

26And ecstasy overcame everyone, and they glorified God and they were filled with fear, saying, "Today we saw the extraordinary."

With Levi the tax collector

27After these things he went outside and saw a tax collector named Levi,[121] sitting in the tax booth. And he said to him,

> Follow me.

28Leaving everything behind, he got up and followed him.

---

120. Pharisees from the Greek Φαρισαῖος (Farisaisos) from the Hebrew פְּרוּשִׁים (prushim). "Pharisee" (s.) is *Parush*.

121. Levi from the Greek Λευί (Levi), from the Hebrew לֵוִי (levi), is identified with the evangelist Matthew.

29And Levi arranged a great feast for him in his house, and there was a throng of tax collectors and others who were with him reclining at the table.

30The Prushim and their scholars were grumbling to Yeshua's students, saying, "Why do you eat and drink with sinners?"

31And Yeshua answered and said to them,

> The healthy do not need a physician
> But the sick do.
> 32I did not come to call the just to repent
> But the sinners.

33But they said to him, "The students of Yohanan often fast and say prayers, and so too the students of the Prushim, but your students eat and drink."

34Then Yeshua said to them,

> Can you ask the members of the wedding party to fast
> While the bridegroom is still with them?[122]
> 35The day will come when the bridegroom
> Will be taken away from them,
> And in those days they will fast.

New wine in old wineskins

36He told them a parable,

> No one tears a patch of cloth from a new coat
> To sew on an old coat
> For the new one will tear
> And the piece from the new will not match the old.
> 37No one pours new wine into old wineskins,
> Since the new wine will split the skins
> And the wine be spilled and the skins destroyed.
> 38But new wine must be put in new skins.

And he added,

> 39Yet no one drinking old wine wants the new.
> The old is good.

---

122. Members of the wedding from the Greek υἱοὺς τοῦ νυμφῶνος (uious tou num-fonos), meaning "sons" or "children of the bridal chamber" and may also be understood as "attendants of the bridegroom."

Chapter 6

Shabbat in the grain fields

It happened on Shabbat that he passed through grain fields, and his students picked and ate the ears of grain, rubbing them in their hands.

2And some of the Prushim said, "Why are you doing what is not permitted on Shabbat?"

3Yeshua answered and said to them,

> Have you not read what David did when he
> Was hungry and those with him were hungry,
> 4How he went into the house of God
> And took the show bread and ate it
> And gave bread to those who were with him,
> Which can only be eaten by the priests?

5And he said to them,

> The earthly son is the lord of Shabbat.[123]

Man with a shriveled hand

6And it happened that on another Shabbat he went into the synagogue and taught. There was a man there and his right hand was crippled. 7The scholars and the Prushim were watching Yeshua to see whether he healed on Shabbat so they might accuse him. 8But he knew their thoughts, and said to the man with the crippled hand,

> Rise and stand before everyone.

And he rose and stood there.

9Yeshua said to them,

> I ask you if it is lawful
> To do good or do evil on Shabbat,
> To save or to destroy?

10And after looking around at all of them, he said to him,

> Stretch out your arm.

And he did so and his arm was restored.

---

123. There exists in English the beautiful phrase "Lord of the Sabbath," which comes from Luke 6.5. The Internet search engine Google lists 165,000 entries for "Lord of the Sabbath," carrying us from Tyndale to Dylan Thomas.

11But they were filled with fury and talked with each other about what they could do to Yeshua.

Choosing his twelve messengers

12And it happened in those days that he went out to the mountains to pray, and he spent the whole night in prayer to God. 13And when it was day he summoned his students and chose twelve of them, whom he named messengers.[124] 14Shimon whom he named Kefa,[125] and Andreas[126] his brother, and Yaakov, and Yohanan and Filippos and Bartalmai,[127] 15and Mattityahu[128] and Toma[129] and Yaakov son of Halfi,[130] and Shimon who was called the Zealot, 16and Yehuda[131] son of Yaakov, and Yehuda, man of Keriot,[132] who became a traitor.

Sermon on the Plain[133]

17He went down with them and stood on the plain,[134] and there was a huge crowd of students and a great multitude of people from all Yehuda and Yerushalayim and the coastal region of Tzor[135] and Tzidon.

---

124. Apostles. See note 42 on Mark 3.14.

125. Peter called him "Cephas" (Greek transliteration of *Kefa*), meaning "stone" or "rock" in Aramaic.

126. Andrew from the Greek Ἀνδρέας (Andreas). Andreas, like Markos and Loukas, are Greek names used by Jews in Israel.

127. Bartholomew from the Greek Βαρθολομαῖος (Bartholomaios), from the Hebrew בַּר תַּלְמַי (bar talmai).

128. Matthew from the Greek Μαθθαῖος (Maththaios), from the Hebrew מַתִּתְיָהוּ (mattityahu).

129. Thomas from the Greek Θωμᾶς (Thomas), from the Aramaic תְּאוֹם (teom).

130. Alphaeus from the Greek Ἀλφαῖος (Halfaios), from the Hebrew חַלְפִּי (halfi).

131. Judas from the Greek Ἰούδας (Ioudas), from the Hebrew יְהוּדָה (yehuda).

132. Iscariot from the Greek Ἰσκαριώθ (Iskarioth), from the Hebrew אִישׁ קְרִיּוֹת (ish keriot), meaning "man of Keriot." In English, "Keriot" is also written "Kerioth."

133. The Sermon on the Plain (the title does not appear in the New Testaant), 6.20–49, is often compared to the larger Sermon on the Mount in Matthew in chapters 5–7, 10, 13, 18, 24–25.

134. Literally, a level place.

135. Tyre from the Greek Τύρος (Tyros), from the Aramaic טוּר (tur), from the Hebrew צוּר (tzor), meaning "hard quartz" or "a flint knife."

18Those who came to hear him and be healed of their diseases, and those troubled with unclean spirits were cured. 19And all in the crowd tried to touch him.

Blessings
20He raised his eyes to the students and said,[136]
> Blessed are the poor
> For yours is the kingdom of God.

> 21Blessed are you who are hungry now
> For you will be fed.

> Blessed are you who weep now
> For you will laugh.

> 22Blessed are you when people hate you,
> When they ostracize you and blame you

> And cast your name about as evil because of the earthly son.
> 23Be happy on that day and spring and leap,

> For look, your reward is great in the sky.
> For in the same way their fathers treated the prophets.

Plagues
> 24But a plague on you the rich,[137]
> For you have received your consolation.

> 25A plague on you who are filled now,
> For you will hunger.

---

136. 20–23. These four passages are commonly called the "Beatitudes" or "blessings," as in Matthew's eight Beatitudes, 5.3–10.

137. 24–26. These are commonly called the "woes" or "curses." The word "woe" is archaic in English. The cliché "a plague on" comes closer to the Greek *woe* than does "woe" or "curse."

A plague on you who laugh now,
For you will mourn and weep.

26A plague on you when all people speak well of you,
For so did their fathers treat the false prophets.

27But I say to you who listen,
Love your enemies, do good to those who hate you,
28And praise those who curse you.

Sayings of love and enemies
Praise those who curse you.
Pray for those who abuse you.

29When one slaps you on the cheek,
Offer the other cheek as well.

From one who takes your coat,
Do not withhold your shirt.

30To all who ask you,
Give what you have.

From one who takes what is yours,
Ask nothing back.

31As you wish people to do for you,
Do for them.

32If you love those who love you, what grace is yours?
Even sinners love those who love them.

33And if you do good to those who do good,
What grace is yours? Sinners do the same.

34If you lend to those from whom you hope return,
    what grace is yours?
Even sinners lend to sinners for a like return.

35But love your enemies and do good,
And when you loan, ask nothing in return.

Your reward will be great.
You will be the children of the highest.

He is kind to the ungrateful as he is to the cunning.[138]
36Be compassionate as your father is compassionate.

Sayings of judgment

37Do not judge and you will not be judged.
Do not condemn and you will not be condemned.

Forgive and you will be forgiven.
38Give and you will be given.

A good measure of wheat[139] shaken, packed down
And overflowing will be placed in your lap,

Since the measure of your measure
Will be the measure of your return.

Sayings and parables

39Then he told a parable,
Surely the blind cannot guide the blind?
Will they not both fall into a pit?

40A student is not above the teacher,
But fully trained, everyone is like the teacher.

41Why do you see the splinter in the eye of your brother
When the log in your own eye you cannot perceive?

---

138. Also has the New Testament meaning of "wicked."

139. "Wheat" is not in the Greek. The implication is probably that a measure of wheat will be pressed into the fold of the garment and overflow.

42How can you say to your brother, "Let me take out
  The splinter in your eye"
  When the log in your eye you do not see?

  Hypocrite! First take the log out of your eye
  And then you will see clearly to take the splinter
    out of the eye of your brother.

Tree and its fruit

43No good tree bears rotten fruit,
  And so no rotten tree bears good fruit.
44Each tree is known by its own fruit.

  Not from thorns are figs gathered
  Nor from brambles are grapes picked.

45The good person from the good treasure house of the heart
  Brings forth good,
  And the cunning person out of cunning brings forth cunning.

  Out of the fullness of the heart, the mouth speaks.

Parable of house and foundation

46Why do you call me "lord, lord,"140
  And do not do what I say?
47When anyone comes to me and hears my words
  And does them,
  I will show you who that person is like.

---

140. "Lord" from the Greek κύριος (kyrios) is always ambivalent, since it means
"Lord," "lord," "master," and "Mr." and "Sir." Here it appears to mean primarily
"Adonai," that is, "Lord," which in the Aramaic and Hebrew of Yeshua's day would
be אָדוֹן (adon) "lord," or "Adonai, my lord." "Lord" could also have been "YHVH,"
from the Hebrew יְהֹוָה (with the Masoretic vowels added), the Hebrew tetragrammaton representing the name of God. "Adonai, my lord," is one of the alternate ways
of expressing the presumably unsayable "YHWH" (or "YHVH"), made up of the letters *yodh he vav he.* However, the vowels under the letters do make "YHWH" pro-
nounceable as *Yahweh* or *Yahveh.* See glossary for *Yahweh* and "YHWH."

48That person is like the man building a house
Who dug and went down deep and laid a foundation on rock.

The flood came and the river burst against that house
And it was not strong enough to shake it,
Because the house was well built.
49But one who hears and does not do
Is like the man who built a house on the earth
Without any foundation,
Against which the river burst
And at once the house collapsed under the river
And the ruin of that house was great.

Chapter 7

With a Roman officer's slave boy

After he had completed all his sayings for the people to hear, he entered Kfar Nahum. 2A centurion[141] had a certain slave, whom he highly prized, who was sick and near death. 3Hearing about Yeshua, the Roman sent some Jewish elders to go to Yeshua, asking him to cure his slave. 4When they came to him, they pleaded with him urgently, saying, "He is worthy of your doing this, 5for he loves our people and he built our synagogue.[142]

---

141. A Roman officer usually commanding one hundred men.

142. The role of Roman officers is presented as benevolent. In these years of common Roman crucifixion, Rome is portrayed in the gospels as benign, and her destruction of the Temple in 70 C.E. is prophesied as a fit punishment of the Jews, both for their wickedness in opposing Rome and for their failure to recognize Yeshua as messiah. The centurion commanding the execution squad and the squad itself are the first to affirm the crucified Yeshua as God's son. In the above passage, implausibly, the Jewish elders claim that the Roman officer loves the nation and has built their synagogue. And in Luke 7.9, Yeshua tells us that the Roman officer's faith goes beyond that of anyone in Israel, and so beyond that of his own followers and students. Passages such as Yeshua's heaping praise on the officer's faith reflect layers of scribal emendation that make the gospels an apology for Rome and the later Christian church in Constantinople and Rome. As such, the gospels stand in contrast to Apocalypse, which is violently anti-Roman, revealing the plight of early Christian Jews and Christian gentiles, who, as in Cappadocia, built churches in underground caves and lived in terror of Roman purpose and acts.

6And Yeshua went with them.

But when he was not far from the house, the centurion sent friends to tell him, "Sir, do not trouble yourself, for I am not fit to have you come under my roof. 7Therefore I didn't think myself worthy to come to you. But say the word, and let my boy be healed. 8I am also a man placed under orders, with soldiers under me. I say to this one, 'Go,' and he goes, and to another, 'Come,' and he comes, and to my slave, 'Do this,' and he does it."

9Yeshua hearing this was amazed by him, and he turned to the crowd following him and said,

> I tell you,
> I have not found such faith in Yisrael.

10When those who had been sent returned to the house they found the slave in good health.

Touching a coffin in Nain

11And it happened on the next day that he went to a city called Naïn,[143] and his students and a large crowd went along with him. 12As he came near the gate of the city, look, there was a dead man being carried out, the only son of his mother, and she was a widow. A sizable crowd from the city was with her.

13When he saw her, the lord pitied her and said to her,

> Don't weep.

14And coming near he touched the coffin, and those carrying it stopped, and he said,

> Young man, I tell you, stand up.

15And the dead man sat up and began to speak, and Yeshua gave him to his mother.

16Fear seized all of them and they glorified God saying,

> A great prophet has risen among us!
> God has looked on his people!

17The word about him went out through Yehuda and in all the surrounding countryside.

---

143. Nain. Probably *Naim* in the Hebrew.

Who is mashiah? Who is prophet?

18Yohanan's students brought him news of all these things. And Yohanan summoned two of his students 19and sent them to Yeshua to say,

> Are you one who is to come
> Or should we look for another?

20And when the men came to him they said, "Yohanan the Dipper sent us to ask you, 'Are you the one who is to come or should we look for another?'"

21In that time he healed many with diseases and afflictions and evil spirits and many blind he graced with sight. 22He answered, saying to them,

> Go and tell Yohanan what you have seen and heard.
> "The blind see again, the lame walk, lepers are cleansed,
> The deaf hear, the dead arise,
> The poor are told good news."

23And blessed is one who does not stumble
> And fall into wrong because of me.

Yeshua commending Yohanan

24When the messengers of Yohanan left, Yeshua began to talk about Yohanan to the crowds,

> What did you come into the desert to see?
> A reed shaken by the wind?

25But what did you come out to look at?

> A man dressed in soft clothing?
> Look, those who are in splendid clothing
> And luxury are in the palaces of the kings.

26But what did you go out to see? A prophet?

> Yes, I tell you. And more than a prophet

27This is he about whom Malachi writes.[144]

> "Look, I send my messenger before your face

---

144. Mal. 3.1. The words are directly from Malachi, but they also appear earlier in Exodus 23.20. "Malachi" comes from the Hebrew מַלְאָכִי (malahi), meaning "my" or "like a messenger" or "angel."

Who will prepare the way before you."
28I tell you, among those born of women
There is no one greater than Yohanan.
But there is one who is the very least,
Yet in the kingdom of God greater than he.
29And all the people who heard this, including the tax collectors, found justice in God, since they had been cleansed with Yohanan's immersion. 30But the Prushim and the lawyers rejected God's will, since they had not been immersed by him.

They call me a glutton and a drunk
    Yeshua said,
        31What are the people of this generation like
        And to whom shall I compare them?
        32They are like children in the marketplace,
        Sitting and calling out to each other, who say,
                We played the flute for you
                And you did not dance.
                We sang a dirge
                But you did not weep.
        33Yohanan the Dipper came and ate no bread
        And drank no wine, and you say, "He has a demon."
        34The earthly son comes and eats and drinks
        And you say, "Look, this man is a glutton and a drunk,
        A friend of tax collectors and sinners."
        35But wisdom is proved right by all her children.

A woman washes Yeshua's feet with her tears and
dries them with her hair
    36One of the Prushim asked Yeshua to eat with him, and he went into the house of the Parush and reclined at the table. 37And look, there was a woman of the city who was a sinner.[145] When she learned that he was reclining in the house of the Parush, she brought in an alabaster jar of

---

145. A prostitute.

myrrh. 38Standing behind his feet and weeping, she began to wash his feet with her tears. She dried them with her hair and kissed his feet and anointed them with myrrh.

39When the Parush who had invited him saw this, he said to himself, "If this one were a prophet, he would have known who and what kind of woman is touching him, since she is a sinner."

40Yeshua answered and said to him,

> Shimon, I have something to say to you.

"Rabbi," he said, "Speak."

> 41A money lender had two people in his debt.
> One owed five hundred denarii, another fifty.
> 42When they couldn't pay, he forgave them both.
> Now which of them will love him more?

43Shimon answered, saying, "I suppose the one whom he forgave more."

He said to Shimon,

> You judged right.

44And turning to the woman, he said to Shimon,

> Do you see this woman?
> I came into your house.
> You did not give me water for my feet,
>
> But she washed my feet with her tears.
> 45You gave me no kiss,
> But from the time I came in
>
> She has not stopped kissing my feet.
> 46You did not anoint my head with olive oil,
> But she anointed my feet with myrrh.
>
> 47Therefore, I tell you, her many sins
> Are forgiven, for she loved much.
> But one who is forgiven little, loves little.

48And he said to her,

> Your sins are forgiven.

49And those who were reclining at the table began to say to each other, "Who is this who even forgives sins?"

50And he said to the woman,

> Your faith has saved you. Go in peace.[146]

Chapter 8

Women with Yeshua

And it happened after this that he went through every city and village preaching and bringing good news of the kingdom of God, and the twelve were with him. 2And some women were cured of crafty spirits and sicknesses: Miryam who was called Miryam of Magdala[147] from whom seven demons had gone out, 3Yohannah[148] wife of Herod's steward Kuza,[149] and Shoshannah,[150] and many others.

These women provided for Yeshua and the twelve from their own possessions.

Parable of the sower

4When a large crowd assembled and people from every city made their way to him, he said through a parable,

> 5The sower went out to sow his seed
>
> And as he sowed some seed fell by the road
>
> And it was trampled down and birds of the sky ate it.
>
> 6And some fell on the rock
>
> And after growing it dried up because it had no moisture.
>
> 7And some fell in the midst of thorns,
>
> And when the thorns grew they choked it.
>
> 8And some fell into good earth

---

146. "Go in peace" in the Hebrew is שָׁלוֹם (shalom).

147. Mary Magdalene from the Galilean town of Magdala.

148. Joanna from the Greek Ἰωάννα or Ἰωάνα (Ioanna or Ioana), probably a feminine form of John, from the Greek Ἰωάννης (Ioannes), from the Hebrew יוֹחָנָן (yohanan), from which *Yohannah* is derived.

149. Chuza.

150. Susanna from the Greek Σουσάννα (Sousanna), from the Hebrew שׁוּשַׁן (shushan), "lily," from which the name *Shoshannah*, שׁוֹשַׁנָּה (shoshannah), is derived.

And after growing it made a hundredfold of fruit.
As he said these things, he called out,
    Whoever has ears to hear, hear.
9Then his students asked him what the parable meant.
10And he said,
    You are given knowledge of the mysteries of the kingdom of
        God
    But to others I speak in parables
    So that, as Yeshayahu says,
        Looking they may not see,
        And hearing they may not understand.[151]

Telling the mysteries

11Now this is the parable:
    The seed is the word of God.
    12The ones on the side of the road are those who heard.
    Then comes the devil, who takes away the word from their
        heart
    So they will not believe and be saved.
    13Those on the rock are those who when hearing
    The word receive it joyfully. But they have
    No root. They believe for a while and in time
    Of trial fall away. 14As for what fell among
    The thorns, they are the ones who hear
    But are choked with worries and riches
    And pleasures, and nothing they do bears fruit.
    15What is in the good soil are those who hear
    The word with a good and generous heart
    And hold to it and bear fruit with patience.

Lamp and light

16No one lights a lamp and puts it in a jar
    Or under the bed.
    One puts it on a lampstand

---

151. Isa. 6.9.

So that those who come in may see the light.

17For nothing is hidden that will not become visible,
And nothing is obscure[152] that will not be known
And come into the light.

Who has and has not

18See how you listen, for to anyone who has,
More will be given,
And whoever has not, even what one thinks one has
Will be taken away.

Yeshua rejects his mother and brothers

19Then his mother and his brothers came to him, but could not reach him because of the crowd. 20Word came to him, "Your mother and brothers are standing outside, and wish to see you."

21But he answered, saying to them,
My mother and my brothers are those
Who hear the word of God and do it.[153]

Calming the storm and the sea

22Now it happened on one of those days, he got into a ship, he and his students, and he said to them,
Let us cross to the other side of the lake.
And they set out.

23While they sailed he fell asleep, and a wind storm fell down on the lake and they were filling with water and were in danger.

---

152. Obscure from the Greek ἀπόκρυφον (apokryfon), here translated as "obscure" but may also be rendered "secret" or "hidden." This lamp parable appears again, with variations, in 11.33–36.

153. This instance of Yeshua's rejection of his mother Mary and his brothers (and sisters) for their apparent lack of faith in his messiahship occurs in the other gospels in various forms. Here, as in Mark 3.21 and 31–35 and in John 7.5, Yeshua states that his true mother and brothers are those in the fields listening to him. When Yeshua avoids his mother and brothers who unsuccessfully seek him out in the fields, the poignancy of familiar conflict is heightened. The scene corresponds to his earlier complaint: "No prophet is welcome in his own country" (Luke 4.24).

24They went to him and woke him and said, "Rabbi, rabbi, we are lost!"
But he woke and rebuked the wind and the rough water and they
stopped and it was calm. 25And he said to them,

> Where is your faith?

And they were afraid and wondered, saying to one another, "Who is
this who commands even the winds and the water and they obey him?"

Demoniac and the pigs

26Then they sailed down to the country of the Gerasenes, which is
across from the Galil. 27And as he came upon the land, a man from the
city met him, a man who had demons[154] and for some time had worn no
clothing and did not live in a house but in the tombs. 28When he saw
Yeshua, he cried out and fell down before him and in a great voice said,
"What am I to you, Yeshua son of the highest God? I beg you, don't
torment me."

29For Yeshua had ordered the unclean spirit to come out of the man.
Often it had seized him and he had been bound with chains and
shackles and was guarded, but he would break his bonds and go, driven
by the demon into the desert.

30But Yeshua asked him,

> What is your name?

"Legion," he said, because many demons had entered him.

31Now the demons implored him not to command them to drop back
into the abyss.

32There was a herd of pigs feeding on the mountain. The demons
begged him to let them enter them.

---

154. Demons from the Greek δαιμόνια (daimonia), "demons." In Tyndale, "demon"
(δαίμων) is translated as "devil" or "fiend." In KJV and even the Jerusalem Catholic version, the Greek δαίμων is also "devil." In the Revised and most contemporary
versions, δαίμων is translated as "demon." The older translation practice of making
"demons" into "devils" is a *devilizing* (not *demonizing*) of the many demon-possessed
figures in the gospels. Contrary to common perception, here Luke's treatment of
the episode gives us a richer and more psychologically complex picture of the wild
man. He has not fully demonized him. The wild man is initially described as being
possessed by "unclean spirits," not "demons." Once cured, however, he is referred
to as "the man who had been demonized."

And he let them.

33When the demons came out of the man, they entered the pigs, and the herd rushed down the slope into the lake and drowned.

34When those feeding them saw what happened, they fled and reported it in the city and in the farmlands. 35Then people came out to see what happened and came to Yeshua and they also found the man, from whom the demons left, seated at the feet of Yeshua, clothed and in his right mind. And they were afraid. 36Those who had seen it told them how the demon-possessed was saved.

37The whole population of the region asked him to leave them, because they were seized by great fear. So he got into his ship and returned.

38The man from whom the demons had gone out pleaded to go with him, but he sent him away, saying,

> 39Return to your house and declare how much
> God did for you.

And he went away, proclaiming throughout the city how much Yeshua did for him.

Girl near death and a woman bleeding

40When Yeshua returned, the crowd welcomed him, for they were all expecting him. 41And look, a man came to him whose name was Yair,[155] who was a leader in the synagogue, and he fell at Yeshua's feet. He pleaded with him to enter his house 42because his only daughter, who was twelve, was dying.

42As he went the people were crowding around him. 43There was a woman who had been bleeding for twelve years, and [though she had spent all she had on physicians,] no one could heal her.[156] 44Coming from behind she touched the hem of his cloak and immediately her flow of blood stopped.

45Then Yeshua said,

> Who touched me?

When everyone denied it, Shimon Kefa said, "Rabbi, the crowds are pressing in and squeezing you."

---

155. Jairus from the Greek Ἰάϊρος (Iairos), from the Hebrew יָאִיר (yair).
156. Other editions lack the passage enclosed in brackets.

46But Yeshua said,

> Someone touched me. I felt the power
>
> Go out from me.

47When the woman saw that she had not gone unnoticed, she came trembling and fell down before him. And in the presence of all the people, she declared why she had touched him and how she had been healed at once.

48He said to her,

> Daughter, your faith has saved you.
>
> Go in peace.

49While he was speaking, someone came from the house of the leader of the synagogue, saying to him, "Your daughter is dead. Do not trouble the rabbi any longer."

50But Yeshua heard and answered him,

> Do not be afraid. Only believe
>
> And she will be saved.

51And he went into the house and did not let anyone enter with him except Shimon Kefa and Yohanan and Yaakov and the father of the child and the mother. 52All were weeping and mourning her, but he said,

> Do not weep. She did not die
>
> But is sleeping.

53And they laughed at him, knowing that she was dead.

54He took her hand, and called out, saying,

> Child, get up!

55The spirit came back to her and at once she stood up and he ordered them to give her something to eat.

56Her parents were amazed, but he instructed them to tell no one what happened.

Chapter 9

Missions for the twelve on the road

And he called together the twelve and gave them power and authority over all demons and to heal sicknesses. 2He sent them out to preach the kingdom of God and to heal. 3And he said to them,

> Take nothing for the road,

No staff, no bag, no bread, no silver,
Not even two tunics.
4Whatever house you go into, stay there,
And leave from there.
5And whoever does not receive you,
As you go out of that city shake the dust
From your feet
In testimony against them.

6And they went out going around through each village, preaching the good news and healing everywhere.

Herod and Yohanan's head

7Now Herod the tetrarch heard about these things happening everywhere, and he was perplexed because it was said by some that Yohanan had been raised from the dead, 8by some that Eliyahu had appeared, but by others that one of the ancient prophets had arisen. 9And Herod said, "Yohanan I beheaded, but who is this about whom I hear such things?" And he sought to see him.

The twelve withdraw with Yeshua to Beit Tzaida

10The messengers returned and told him what they had done. And taking them with him, he withdrew privately to a city called Beit Tzaida.[157] 11When the crowds learned of it, they followed him. After welcoming them, he spoke to them about the kingdom of God, and those in need of treatment he healed.

Bread for five thousand on the grass

12The day began to fade, and the twelve came to him, and said to him, "Send the crowd away so that they may go into the surrounding villages and farms to find places to sleep and food to eat. Here we are in a desolate place."

13And he said to them,
You give them something to eat.

---

157. Bethseda from the Greek Βηθσαϊδά (Bethsaida), from the Hebrew בֵּית צַיְדָא (beit tzaida), which is a place north of the Sea of Galilee.

But they said, "We have only five loaves and two fish unless we go to buy food for all these people."

14There were about five thousand men.

He said to his students,

Have them sit down in groups of fifty.

15And they did so and they made everyone sit down.

16Then he took the five loaves and the two fish and looked up to the sky, and blessed them and broke them and gave them to the students to set before the crowd.

17And they ate and all were fed. What was left over by them was picked up and filled twelve baskets with broken pieces.

Who do you say I am?

18Once when Yeshua was praying alone, the students were with him, and he asked them, saying,

Who do the crowds say I am?

19They answered, saying,

Yohanan the Dipper, but others say Eliyahu,

And some say an ancient prophet has risen.

20And he said to them,

You, who do you say I am?

Shimon Kefa answered,

The mashiah of God.

21He warned them and ordered them to tell no one of this.

I will die and be arisen

22And he said,

The earthly son must suffer much

And be rejected by the elders and high priests and scholars

And be killed and on the third day be raised up.

Deny and follow me

23Then he said to everyone,

Whoever wants to come after me,

Deny yourself

And raise your cross each day

And follow me.

Losing life to find the soul

24Whoever wants to save the soul
  Will lose it,
  But whoever loses the soul because of me
  Will save it.

25What benefit is there to gain the whole world
  And lose or punish yourself?

Earthly son in his kingdom

26Those who are ashamed of me and my words
  Will be ashamed of the earthly son
  When he comes in his glory
  And the glory of his father and the holy angels.
27But I tell you truth:
  There are some standing here who will not taste death
  Until they see the kingdom of God.

Transfigured, his clothing lightning white

28And it happened about eight days after these sayings, Yeshua took Shimon Kefa and Yohanan and Yaakov with him and they went up to the mountain to pray. 29While he was praying, the appearance of his face changed and his clothing was lightning white. 30And look, two men were talking with him, Moshe and Eliyahu 31who shone in glory, spoke about his departure, which he was to fulfill in Yerushalayim.

32Shimon Kefa and those with him were heavy with sleep. But they woke and saw his glory and the two men who were standing with him. 33And it happened that as they left him, Shimon Kefa said to Yeshua, "Rabbi, it is good for us to be here. Let us make three shelters,[158] one for

---

158. Tabernacle from the Greek σκηνή (skene), "tent," from the Hebrew סֻכָּה (sukkah), "shelter" or "tent." The three shelters are associated with the Jewish Sukkoth, the Festival of the Tabernacles or Booths, חַג הַסֻּכּוֹת (hag hasukkot), an eight-day celebration for autumnal harvest, beginning on the eve of the 15th of Tishri. The sukkah is a small lean-to-like shelter in the fields. One dwells in the sukkah in commemoration of God's protection of Israel when the people were wandering in the desert after their escape from Egypt.

you and one for Moshe and one for Eliyahu." He didn't know what he was saying.

34While he spoke, a cloud came and overshadowed them. They were frightened as they went into the cloud. 35And a voice came out of the cloud saying,

> This is my son, the chosen,[159] hear him!

36And as the voice vanished, Yeshua was found alone. They were silent and no one in those days reported anything they had seen.

Down the mountain to a boy foaming at the mouth

37On the next day when they came down from the mountain a large crowd met him. 38And look, a man from the crowd cried out, saying, "Rabbi, I beg you to look at my son, for he is my only son. 39And look, a spirit takes hold of him and suddenly he screams and it convulses him and he foams at the mouth, it bruises him, and barely leaves him.[160] 40I begged your students to cast it out, and they could not."

41And Yeshua answered, saying,

> O unbelieving and crooked generation,
> How long will I be with you and endure you?
> Bring your son to me.

42While he came near him, the demon threw the boy to the ground and convulsed him, but Yeshua rebuked the unclean spirit and healed the child and returned him to his father.

43And all were astounded at the greatness of God.[161]

I will die

And while all were in wonder at all he was doing, he said to his students,

> 44Store these words in your ears,

---

159. Other ancient Greek texts have "my beloved."

160. Symptoms of epilepsy.

161. Only in Luke is there a frequent equation of Yeshua and God before the resurrection. As the latest of the synoptic gospels, there is a formalization of ideas in which the notion of a messiah, born of humans, "the earthly son," and divine God are one.

For the earthly son is to be turned over
Into human hands.

45But they did not understand this saying. It was hidden from them so they might not perceive it, and they were afraid to ask him about it.

Greatness and the child

46Then there arose a dispute among them as to who might be the greatest of them.

47Yeshua, seeing the thought in their heart, took a child standing near him, 48and he said to them,

Whoever receives this child in my name
Receives me,
And whoever receives me receives the one
Who sent me.
For whoever is smallest among you all,
That one is great.

Of one not our follower

49And Yohanan said, "Rabbi, we saw someone in your name casting out demons and we tried to stop him, because he is not one of our followers."

50But Yeshua said,

Do not stop him.
Whoever is not against you is for you.

Shall we burn the Shomronim village with heaven's fire?

51And it happened that as the day of his ascension came near, he set his face to go to Yerushalayim. 52And he sent messengers ahead of him. They went into a village of Shomronim[162] to make things ready for him, 53 but they did not receive him because his face was set for going to Yerushalayim. 54When his students Yaakov and Yohanan saw this, they said,

Lord, do you want us to summon fire
Down from heaven to consume them?

---

162. Samaritans from the Greek Σαμαρίτης (Samarites), from the Hebrew שִׁמְרֹנִי (Shomroni). *Shomronim* is "Samaritans." *Shomron* is "Samaria."

55But Yeshua turned and reproved them.[163] 56And they went to another village.

Rest nowhere

57As they went along the road, someone said to him, "I will follow you wherever you go."

58And Yeshua said to him,

> Foxes have holes and birds of the sky have nests,
> But the earthly son has no place to lay his head.

Let the dead bury the dead

59And he said to another,

> Follow me.

But the man said, "Let me go first to bury my father."

60But Yeshua said to him,

> Let the dead bury their own dead,
> And as for you,
> Go and proclaim the kingdom of God.

Do not look back

61And another said, "I will follow you, lord, but first let me say goodbye to my people in my house."

62But Yeshua said,

> No one who puts a hand on the plow and looks back
> Is fit for the kingdom of God.

Chapter 10

Seventy lambs on the road

After these things, the lord appointed seventy[164] others and sent them

---

163. Having just been given powers of healing and over demons, the messengers (apostles) test Yeshua, asking whether they should use holocaust fire to consume the village and the lives of these inhospitable Samaritans, but Yeshua quickly scolds them and they go on to the next village.

164. Other texts have seventy-two.

two by two ahead of him into every city and place where he was going
to go. 2And he said to them,

> The harvest is abundant, but the workers few.
> So ask the master of the harvest
> To send out workers into his harvest.
> 3Go forth. Look, I send you as lambs
> Into the midst of wolves.
> 4Carry no purse or a bag or sandals,
> And greet no one along the road.

Shake the dust from your feet

> 5Whatever house you enter, first say, "Peace to this house."
> 6And if a child of peace is there,
> Your peace will stay with that one.
> And if not, it will return to you.
> 7Remain in the same house, eating and drinking with them,
> For the worker deserves his wages.
> Don't wander from house to house.
> 8And when you go into any city and they receive you,
> Eat what they set before you
> 9And heal those who are sick and say to them,
> "The kingdom of God is near."

> 10But when you go into any city
> Where they do not receive you,
> Go out into its open places and say,
> 11"Even the dust from this city clinging to our feet
> We wipe off against you.
> But know this. The kingdom of God is near."
> 12I tell you on that day it will be more bearable
> For Sedom[165] than for that city.

---

165. Sodom from the Greek Σόδομα (Sodoma), from the Hebrew סְדֹם (sedom or sdom).

What awaits unrepentant cities

13A plague on you, Horazim,[166] a plague on you, Beit Tzaida.

If the miraculous powers[167] shown among you

Had been shown in Tzor and Tzidon,

They would have repented long ago,

And sat in sackcloth and ashes.

14But for Tzor and Tzidon at the day of judgment

It will be more tolerable than it will be for you.

15And you Kfar Nahum, as said in Yeshayahu:

"Will you be exalted to the sky?

No. You will be thrown into Sheol."[168]

16Whoever hears you hears me

And whoever rejects you rejects me

And whoever rejects me rejects the one who sent me.

---

166. See note 106 on Matthew 11.21.

167. Powers from the Greek δύναμις (dynamis), "power." The translation of *dynameis* splits between "powers" in the Revised Standard Version and Lattimore, which is the immediate classical meaning, and "miracles" in NIV and older versions, which is certainly the intended meaning. If the reader knows that "powers" has taken on the meaning of a "miracle," then to give the vital "powers" would be preferable. However, most readers do not know the ambiguity of the word. Therefore, here, "miracles" seems the appropriate choice, since Luke is, in its majority, a book of miracles. The reader is asked, however, to sense the original meaning of "powers" operating behind the event, which is interpreted as the miracle.

168. Sheol from the Greek ἄδης (Hades), from the Hebrew שְׁאוֹל (sheol). These two lines of exaltation and damnation are a translation from Isaiah 14.13–15, taken directly from the Septuagint version of the Torah. In the Hebrew text of Isaiah 14.15, *Sheol* means "pit" or "underworld of the dead," which may be thought of as a relatively benign Greek Hades as opposed to fiery Gei Hinnom (Gehenna), which, as a *fiery* pit outside Jerusalem, suggests the more fierce notion of Old Norse hell. Both the Septuagint Greek Bible and the Greek gospels erroneously translate Isaiah's *Sheol* into English as "Hades." In doing so they follow the New Testament pattern of Hellenizing the Hebrew Bible, here taking an essential Jewish figure and replacing it with a figure from Greek myth and religion. *Sheol*, an accurate transliteration of the Hebrew, is a strong word to represent "the underground place of the dead" and to return its geography from Greece to Israel.

Return of the seventy

17And the seventy returned with joy, saying, "Sir, even the demons submit to us in your name."

He said to them,

18I saw Satan falling from the sky like a flash of lightning.

19Look, I have given you authority to walk on snakes

And scorpions,

And over all the power[169] of the enemy,

And nothing will ever harm you.

20But do not rejoice that the spirits submit to you.

Rejoice that your names are written in the skies.

Revealing only to the children

21In that same hour Yeshua rejoiced in the holy spirit, and said,

I thank you, holy father, lord of sky and earth,

For you have hidden these things from the wise and the learned

And revealed them to little children.

Yes, father, for so it pleased you.

22All was given to me by my father,

And no one knows who the son is except the father

And who the father is except the son

And anyone whom the son wishes to reveal it to.

What his students have seen

23And turning to his students privately, he said,

Blessed are the eyes that see what you have seen.

24I tell you that many prophets and kings

Wanted to see what you see and have not seen,

And to hear what you hear and have not heard.

---

169. The same tradition that makes Yeshua's "powers" be rendered as "miracles" can also make the powers of the enemies understood to be "miracles."

How to find eternal life?

25And look, a lawyer stood up to test him, saying, "Rabbi, what must I do to inherit eternal life?"

26And he said to him,

> What is written in the law of the Torah?[170]
> How do you read it?

27The man answered and said,

> "You will love the lord your God with all your heart,
> With all your soul, with all your strength
> And with all your mind,
> And you will love your neighbor as yourself."

28And Yeshua said to him,

> You answered right. Do this and you will live.

Parable of the Good Shomroni[171]

29But wishing to justify himself he said to Yeshua,

> And who is my neighbor?

30Yeshua answered and said,

> A man was going down from Yerushalayim
> To Yeriho[172] and fell into the hands
> Of robbers. They stripped him and beat him
> And went away leaving him half dead.
> 31By chance a priest went down the same road
> And when he saw him he passed by on the other side.
> 32And a Levite also came by and saw him
> And passed by on the other side.
> 33But a Shomroni on his journey came near
> And when he saw him he pitied him.
> 34He went to him and bound his wounds

---

170. Here these basic commandments come from Deuteronomy 6.5 and Leviticus 19.18.

171. Samaritan. See note 161 on Luke 9.52.

172. Jericho from the Greek Ἰεριχώ (Iericho), from the Hebrew יְרִיחוֹ (yeriho).

And poured olive oil and wine over him,
And set him on his own beast, and took him
To an inn where he cared for him.
35And on the next day he took out and gave
Two denarii to the innkeeper and said,
"Take care of him and what costs you still may have,
I will repay when I return."
36Which of the three seems to you the neighbor
Of the man who fell before the robbers?
37And the lawyer said,
The one who treated him with mercy.
Yeshua told him,
Go and you too do the same.

With Marta and Miryam

38And on their journey he went into a certain village. A woman named Marta[173] took him in. 39And she had a sister named Miryam, who sat at the feet of the lord and listened to his word. 40But Marta was distracted by her many house duties and stood near him and said, "Sir, do you not care that my sister has left me to serve by myself? Tell her to help me."
41And he answered, saying to her,

Marta, Marta, you worry and fret
About many things, 42yet few are needed.
Miryam chose the good portion,
And it will not be taken from her.

Chapter 11

How to pray

And it happened that while he was praying in a certain place, when he stopped, one of his students said to him, "Sir, teach us to pray, as Yohanan taught his students."

---

173. Martha from the Greek Μάρθα (Martha), from the Aramaic מָרְתָא (marta).

2And he said to them that when you pray, say,
    [Father,]174 hallowed be your name.
    Your kingdom come.
    Give us each day our daily bread
    And forgive our sins
    As we have forgiven the debts of others
    And do not lead us into temptation.175

Midnight friend and bread
  5And he said to them,
      Who among you has a friend and will go
      To him at midnight and say to him,
      "Friend, lend me three loaves, 6because my friend
      Has come in from the road to my house
      And I have nothing to set before him."
    7And the one inside answers and says,
      "Don't bring me troubles. I've already locked
      The door and my children are in bed.
      I cannot get up to give you anything."
    8I tell you, even if he will not get up
      And give it to him because he is a friend,
      Yet he will wake up and give him
      What he needs because of his persistence.

Knock and the door opens
    9I tell you, ask and it will be given you,
      Seek and you will find,
      Knock and the door will be opened for you.
    10For all who ask receive
      And the seeker finds,
      And for who knocks the door will be opened.

---

174. "Father" is not in the earliest texts.

175. The KJV uses other texts that add "And deliver us from evil (cunning)," but modern texts do not include this sentence, which does appear in Matthew's Lord's Prayer.

Son asking for a fish

11Who among you has a son who would ask his father for a
  fish
And instead of a fish he will give him a snake?
12Or even if he asked for an egg,
  Will he give him a scorpion?
13If then you who are cunning know how to give
  Good gifts to your children,
  By how much more will the father from the sky
  Give holy spirit to those who ask him?

Division and desolation

14He was casting out a deaf man's demons. And it happened that as
the demons came out, the deaf man spoke and the crowds marveled.

15Yet some of them said, "It is through Baal Zebul[176] ruler of the demons
that he cast out the demons." 16Others tested him, asking him to bring a
sign down from the sky. 17But he knew their thoughts, and said to them,
  Every kingdom divided against itself becomes desolate
  And a house against its own house falls.
18And if Satan is also divided against himself,
  How will his kingdom stand?

How I cast out demons

  You say I cast out demons through Baal Zebul.
19But if through Baal Zebul I cast out demons,
  By whom do your sons cast them out?
  So they will be your judges.
20Yet if through the finger of God I cast out demons,
  Then the kingdom of God has come to you.

Strong man and peace

21When a strong man, fully armed, guards his own castle,
  His possessions are in peace.
22But when one stronger than he attacks and overpowers him,

---

176. Beelzebul. See note 54 on Mark 5.22.

He takes off his armor in which he trusted
And gives away his plunder.

Who is not with me

23One who is not with me is against me
And who does not gather with me scatters.

Wanderings of unclean spirit

24When an unclean spirit goes out of a person,
It goes through waterless places seeking a place to rest,
And finding none, it says,
"I shall return to my house from which I came out of."
25And when an unclean spirit goes back,
It finds the house swept and in order.
26Then it goes and picks up other spirits slyer than itself,
Seven of them who all go in and live there,
And the last condition for that person
Is even worse than the beginning.

The blessed

27And while he was saying this, a woman in the crowd raised her voice and said to him, "Blessed is the womb that carried you and the breasts that you suckled."
28But he said,

Blessed rather are those who hear the word
Of God and obey it.

Sign of Yonah

29As the crowds increased he began to say,

This generation is a malicious generation.
It seeks a sign and it will be given no sign
Except for the sign of Yonah.[177]

---

177. Jonah from the Greek Ἰωνᾶς (Ionas), from the Hebrew יוֹנָה (yonah). Jonah was three days in the huge fish as Yeshua was buried for three days before his resurrection.

30Just as Yonah became a sign to the people of Nineveh,
  So is the earthly son for this generation.
31The Queen of the South[178] will rise up
  On the day of judgment with the men of this generation
  And she will condemn them, for she came
  From the ends of the earth[179] to hear the wisdom of Shlomoh,[180]
  And look, one greater than Shlomoh is here.
32The men of Nineveh will rise up
  On the day of judgment with this generation
  And condemn it because they repented
  On hearing the preaching of Yonah,
  And look, one greater than Yonah is here.

Lamp on a stand

33No one lights a lamp and puts it in a hidden place,
  But on the lampstand[181]
  So that those who come in may see the light.
34The lamp of the body is your eye.
  When your eye is clear, then your whole body
  Is filled with light.
35But when it is clouded, then your body is darkness.
36So if your whole body is filled with light,
  With no part dark,
  You will be all light as when the lamp illumines you
  With its beams.

Insulting Prushim

37While he was speaking, a Parush asked him to dine with him. So he went inside and reclined at the table. 38The Parush saw this and was astonished that he did not first wash before the meal.

---

178. The Queen of Sheba.

179. Ethiopia.

180. Solomon from the Greek Σολομών (Solomon), from the Hebrew שְׁלֹמֹה (shlomoh).

181. Other texts add "nor under a measuring bucket."

39But the lord said to him,
> You Prushim clean the outside of the cup
> And dish, but inside you, you are full of greed
> And cunning. 40You fools! Did not the one
> Who made the outside make the inside too?
> 41But give away what is inside as charity,
> And look, everything will be clean for you.
> 42But a plague on you Prushim![182]
> Though you tithe mint and rue and every herb
> You neglect justice and the love of God.
> You should have practiced tithing
> Without neglecting to do the others.
> 43A plague on you Prushim! Because
> You love the place of honor in the temples
> And the greetings in the marketplaces.
> 44A plague on you! You are like invisible graves;
> People walk over you and don't know it.

Insulting lawyers

45One of the lawyers answered, saying to him, "Rabbi, in saying these things you insult us too."

46But Yeshua said,
> And a plague on you too, lawyers!
> You burden people with loads hard to carry,
> Yet you don't touch the loads with one
> Of your fingers. 47A plague on you
> Because you build the tombs of the prophets,
> But your fathers killed them. 48And you are witnesses
> And you approve of the deeds of your fathers,
> Since they killed them and you build their tombs.
> 49That is why the wisdom of God has said,
> "I will send them prophets and messengers,
> Some of whom they will kill and persecute."

---

182. These are the six tribulations.

50So this generation will be charged
With the blood spilled of all the prophets
From the creation of the world, 51from the blood
Of Abel to the blood of Zeharyahu,
Who was killed between the altar and the Temple.
Yes, I tell you, this generation will be charged.[183]
52A plague on you lawyers, because
You took away the key of knowledge.
You did not go in yourselves, and blocked
The way of those who tried to go in.
53When he went outside, the scholars and the Prushim were fiercely

---

183. Through the voice of Yeshua, Luke reminds the reader that the Jews are murderers of their own prophets, and that this generation approves the killing deeds of their fathers and hence is guilty of all the blood spilt from the blood of Abel to the blood of Zechariah, and hence charged "from the creation of the world to this generation." The figures of Abel and Zechariah are cited as examples of prophets whom the Jews killed, Abel by his brother Cain (Gen. 4.8–10), and Zechariah a priest murdered in the Temple (2 Chron. 24.20–22). In the Hebrew Bible they are not identified as prophets. The role of the prophet was firmly established in the pre-exilic monarchic society of Israel, and there are no references in Hebrew scripture to killing prophets. This particularly strong vitriol against the Jews of the Hebrew Bible reflects the imagination of later churchmen rather than the utterance of a first-century itinerant rabbi.

At the time of the composition of the gospels, the early Christian Jews and gentile converts had only the Hebrew Bible (Tanak) as scripture, which was seen with disturbed ambivalence not only as their own book but also as the book of Jews from whom they urgently wished to distinguish themselves. While the Hebrew Bible is quoted abundantly and in a positive light on virtually every page of the gospels, it is also fiercely condemned as the Old Testament, as opposed to the New Testament. Troubling to resolve was that the people of the Hebrew Bible—the patriarch Abraham, king Solomon, and the prophet Isaiah—were Jews as were Yeshua and all his lifetime followers. The problem of identity was imperfectly resolved by having Yeshua condemn his contemporary Jews as inheritors of the guilt of being murderers of their Jewish prophets, while he, his followers, and his family are presented less distinctly as Jews and exempt from the wicked inheritance of the Jews and the consequent punishments. In this instance, now even the vaguely unscathed "Israelites," who inhabit the translations of the Hebrew Bible, have become Jews and are associated with Jews of the New Testament, who bear the guilt of their ancestors for having killed their prophets.

hostile to him and questioned him closely about many things, 54plotting
to trap him on something out of his mouth.[184]

Chapter 12

Be on guard against the Prushim
    Meanwhile, as a crowd of thousands gathered and trampled one
another, he began to speak first to his students,
        Be on guard against the yeast of the Prushim,
        Which is their hypocrisy.

Hidden into light
        2There is nothing hidden that will not be revealed,
        And nothing secret that will not be known.
        3What you have said in darkness will be heard in the light,
        And what you said to the ear in inner rooms
        Will be proclaimed on the housetops.

Fear and killing the body
        4I tell you my friends, do not be fearful of those who kill the
            body
        But after that can do nothing more.
        5I will show you one to fear.
        Fear the one who after killing you has the power
        To throw you into Gei Hinnom.[185]
        Yes, I tell you, that one you should fear.

---

184. Out of his mouth from the Greek ἐκ τοῦ στόματος αὐτοῦ (ek tou stomatos
autou). Contemporary translations do not render the powerful, literal metaphor "out
of his mouth," but the Tyndale and the KJV follow the Greek to the word. The Revised
and later versions explain the metaphor as "something he might say" or "something
he might let fall" (Lattimore) or "with his own words" (Annotated Scholars).

185. Gei Hinnom from the Greek γέεννα (Geenna), "hell," from the Hebrew
גֵּיא הִנֹּם (gei hinnom), meaning the "Valley of Hinnom." Gei Hinnom is a "special
pit of darkness" of the Hebrew Bible. *Gei Hinnom* and *Sheol* are normally translated into English as "hell."

God's memory of sparrows and pennies

6Are five sparrows not sold for two pennies?[186]
And not one of them is forgotten before God.
7But even the hairs of your head are all counted.
Do not fear.
You are worth more than many sparrows.

Accepted or denied by angels of God

8I tell you, whoever accepts me before people,
The earthly son will accept before the angels of God.
9But whoever denies me before people
Will be denied before the angels of God.
10And whoever speaks a word against the earthly son
Will be forgiven,
But one who blasphemes against the holy spirit
Will not be forgiven.
11And when they bring you before the synagogues
And its rulers and authorities,
Do not worry how or what you should speak in your defense
Or what you should say.
12For in that very hour the holy spirit will teach you
What you must say.

Rich man and death

13Someone in the crowd said to him, "Rabbi, tell my brother to share his inheritance with me."
14But he said to him,
Sir, who appointed me to be the judge
Or arbiter between both of you?
15He said to them,

---

186. Pennies or assars from the Greek ἀσσάριον (assarion), a Roman copper coin, worth about one-sixteenth of a denarius. Three words are used for Roman coins: denarius or denar (δηνάριον) or denarion, assarion (diminutive of Latin *as*), and kodrantes (κοδράντης), a loan word from the Latin *quadrans*, and worth about a quarter of a cent. "Assarion" is translated as "penny," "nickel," "copper," or "farthing."

Look and guard against every kind of greed.
Life is not in the possessions one piles up.
16Then he told them a parable, saying,
The farm of a rich man bore excellent crops
17Yet he asked himself, "What should I do
Since I have no place to store my crops?"
18And said, "I'll tear down my barns and build bigger ones.
I'll gather all my grain and goods there
19And say to my soul, 'You have many goods
Stored away for many years. Rest, eat, drink, and be happy.'"
20But God said to him, "You fool. This night
They demand your soul.
To whom will go all you have prepared?"
21So it goes for one who stores up treasures
For himself but is not rich before God.

Consider the ravens of the sky

22And Yeshua said to the students,
So I tell you this. Do not worry about your life,
What you eat, about your body, or how you clothe yourself.
23The soul is more than food and the body more than clothing.
24Consider the ravens who do not sow or reap,
Who have no storehouse or barn,
And God feeds them.
How much more are you worth than the birds!
25Who among you by brooding can add one more hour to your
life?
26If you cannot do a little thing, why worry about the rest?

Consider the lilies

27Consider the lilies, how they grow.
They do not labor or spin,
But I tell you, not even Shlomoh in all his glory
Was clothed like one of these lilies.
28But if God so dresses the grass of the field
Which is here today
And tomorrow is cast into the oven,

How much better he will clothe you,
O you of little faith!

Setting hearts on the kingdom

29And look not for what you can eat and drink,
   And do not worry.
30All the nations of the world seek them,
   But your father knows you are in need.
31Seek only his kingdom
   And these things will be added for you.
32Little flock, do not fear, for your father
   Is happy to give you the kingdom.

Give and no moth or thief destroys

33Sell your possessions and give charities.
   Make yourselves purses that never wear out,
   Be an inexhaustible treasure in the skies
   Where no thief comes near or moth destroys.
34Where your treasure is,
   There also will be your heart.

Master may come at any hour

35Let your loins be girded about and the lamps burning
36And be like people waiting for their master
   When he comes back from the wedding,
   So that when he comes and knocks
   They will open for him at once.
37Blessed are the slaves whom the lord
   On his return finds wide awake.
   Amain, I tell you, he will gird himself up
   And have them recline to eat and he will come near
   And he will serve them.
38And if he comes in the second watch[187] or third watch[188]

---

187. Midnight.
188. Three in the morning.

And finds them alert, they will be blessed.
39But know this. If the master of the house
    Knew what time the thief was coming,
    He would not have let his house be broken into.
40Be ready, for the earthly son comes
    In the hour when you least expect him.

Lashes and death for slaves unprepared
for the master's return

41And Shimon Kefa said, "Lord, is your parable for us or do you speak
to everyone?" 42And the lord said,
        Who is the faithful steward, the prudent one,
        Whom his master will set over his servants
        To give them their measure of bread
        At the right time? 43Blessed is that slave
        Whom the lord when he comes will find
        At work. 44I tell you truth, he will put him
        In charge of all the possessions.
45But if that slave says in his heart, "My master
    Is long in coming," and he begins to beat
    The men servants and women servants,
    And to eat and to drink and to get drunk,
46The lord of that slave will come on a day
    When he does not expect him and in an hour
    Which he does not know, and cut him to pieces
    And cast him out with the unfaithful.[189]
47That slave who knows the master's will
    But who is not prepared or flaunts his own will
    Will be flogged with many blows.
48But the one who knows nothing and does
    What merits a whipping will be flogged lightly.
    Everyone to whom much is given will have

---

189. The fate of the unfaithful, of not accepting the messiah, is death and everlasting punishment.

Much to return. To whom much was entrusted,
Even more they will ask from him.

I came with fire

49I came to cast fire over the earth
And how I wish it were already ablaze!

His need to be washed

50There is a dipping I must undergo,
And how I am afflicted until it is done!

I do not bring peace but division

51Do you think I came to bring peace on earth?
No, I tell you, I came to bring division.
52From now on there will be five in one house
Dissenting against two and two against three.[190]
53Father will be divided against son and son against father,
Mother against daughter and daughter against mother,
Mother-in-law against daughter-in-law
And daughter-in-law against mother-in-law.

---

190. This passage here and in Matthew 10.34 have traditionally been interpreted to mean that there will be conflict between the competing religious sects. The contemporary *NIV Study Bible: New International Version* (gen. ed. Kenneth Barker, Grand Rapids, MI: Zondervan Publishing House, 1995), alluding to John 8.44, where the Jews are declared the children of the devil ("You are from your father the devil"), interprets: "Yet the inevitable result of Christ's coming is conflict—between Christ and the antichrist, between light and darkness, between Christ's children and the devil's children." *The HarperCollins Study Bible: New Revised Standard Version* (gen. ed. Wayne Meeks, New York: HarperCollins, 1993), comments mildly, "The promise of peace . . . becomes a threat of *division* if the messiah is rejected." The passage is a threat of division and fire on the day of judgment. One can also read the passage as a commentary on an already divisive Israel, within families, including Yeshua's family, between sects, which may coincide with the meaning of the affirming passage then quoted from Micah 7.6, which reads, "For the son dishonoureth the father, the daughter riseth up against her mother, the daughter in law against her mother in law; a man's enemies *are* the men of his own house" (KJV).

Reading rain clouds and paying debts
    54And he said to the crowds,
> When you see a cloud rising in the west,
> At once you say a rain storm is coming.
> 55And so it comes. When a south wind blows
> You say it will be hot. 56You hypocrites!
> The face of the earth and the sky you know
> How to read. Why don't you know how to read
> These times? 57Why don't you judge on your own
> What is right? 58As you go with your opponent
> To the magistrate, try on the way there
> To reconcile with him, or you may be dragged
> Before the judge, and the judge will hand you
> Over to the bailiff and the bailiff throw you
> In jail. 59I tell you, you will never get out
> Of there until you pay back the last penny.

Chapter 13

Repent or perish
    At that time some who were there told him about the Galileans whose blood Pilatus had mingled with their sacrifices.[191] 2And he answered and said to them,
> Do you think these Galileans, because
> They suffered in this way, were the worst sinners
> Of all the Galileans? 3No, I tell you,

---

191. This is the only information we have about a slaughter of Galileans in the midst of religious ceremonies. It seems to say that Pilate's soldiers killed some Galilean Jews in the act of their sacrifices and mixed their blood with their offerings. Pilate's brutal reprisals and disdain of religious practice are elaborated in Josephus's *Antiquities* 18.85–89. Other commentators conjecture that Pilate may have been concerned with an insurrection of the Jews (which came much later). Yeshua's anger against Pilate's killing of Galileans conflicts with the benign picture of Pilate, who washes his hands in a symbol of his innocence in ordering the crucifixion of Yeshua.

But unless you repent you will all perish
Like them, ₄or like those eighteen when the tower
Of Shiloach fell on them and killed them.[192]
Do you think they were more guilty
Than the people living in Yerushalayim?
₅No, I tell you, but unless you repent
You will perish too just as they all did.

Parable of the barren fig tree

₆Then Yeshua told this parable,

A man had a fig tree planted in his vineyard
And he went looking for fruit on it
And found none. ₇He said to the gardener,[193]
"Look, for three years I have come looking
For fruit on this tree and have found none.
Cut it down. Why should it be wasting the soil?"
₈But he answered and said to him, "Sir, let it go
For another year while I dig around it
And throw manure on it. ₉Then it may bear fruit
In the future. And if not, cut it down."

Working good on Shabbat

₁₀He was teaching in one of the synagogues on Shabbat. ₁₁And look, a woman who had a spirit of sickness for eighteen years and she was bent over and unable to stand up straight at all. ₁₂When he saw her, Yeshua called her over and said to her,

Woman, you are released from your weakness.

₁₃And he placed his hands on her and at once she stood straightened out and was glorifying God.

₁₄But the leader of the synagogue, angered because Yeshua had healed on Shabbat, said to the crowd, "There are six days on which one must work. So come and be healed on these days and not on the day of Shabbat."

---

192. Siloam. The tower of Siloam was built inside the southeast section of Jerusalem's walls.

193. Literally, "vinekeeper" or "vinedresser."

15The lord answered him and said,
>Hypocrites.[194] Each of you on the Shabbat,
>Do you not untie your ox or your donkey
>From the feeding trough and lead it away
>To give it water? 16And this daughter of Avraham
>Whom Satan, look, bound for eighteen years,
>Should she not be loosened from this bondage
>Even if it is the day of the Shabbat?

17And when he said this, all who opposed him were put to shame, and the entire congregation rejoiced over all the glorious things that came through him.

Mustard seed and kingdom of God

18Then he said,
>What is the kingdom of God like
>And to what shall I compare it?
>19It is like a mustard seed that a man threw
>Into his garden and it grew into a tree,
>And the birds of the sky nested in its branches.

Yeast and kingdom of God

20And again he said,
>What is the kingdom of God like?

---

194. After the first statement, the debate concerning the meaning of the Sabbath (Shabbat) turns to severe insult. The inflammatory language by Yeshua was also found commonly in the Hebrew Bible, voiced by prophets and Yahweh himself. There it was perceived as conflict and condemnation within the tribe. In the New Testament, although the conflict of ideas is still between Jews (Christianity did not exist), it is presented and, more significant, has been virtually universally perceived anachronistically, as a conflict between Christian and Jew, and hence this pattern of vilification has been a primary source of traditional anti-Semitism. It is not known when the invective found its place in scripture, whether it was in the original assemblage or added to it in the course of scribal copying. If the hate word "hypocrites!" did not initiate Yeshua's response, the argument would be perfectly ordinary, and the hearts of the congregation, who are won over to Yeshua's humane interpretation of the Sabbath, would have been no less likely to be won over joyfully. But being there, the invective entirely alters the tone, level, and consequence of the discourse.

21It is like yeast that a woman took and concealed
    In three measures of wheat until it was all leavened.

Narrow gate[195]

22And he walked through cities and villages, teaching and making his way
to Yerushalayim. 23Someone said to him, "Sir, will only a few be saved?"
    And he said to them,

    24Struggle to go in through the narrow door,
      Because many, I tell you, will try to get in
      And will not succeed, 25for once the master
      Of the house wakens and shuts the door,
      You will begin to stand outside and knock,
      Saying, "Lord, open for us." And he will answer,
      Saying to you, "I do not know you or where
      You come from." 26Then you will begin to say,
      "We ate and drank with you, and you taught
      In our broad streets." 27Then he will tell you,
      "I do not know where you come from.
      Go away from me, all you workers of iniquity!"
    28There will be the weeping and gnashing of teeth
      When you see Avraham and Yitzhak and Yaakov
      And all the prophets in the kingdom of God,
      But you will be cast alone outside.

    29And they will come from east and west
      And from north and south and they will recline
      At a table in the kingdom of God. 30And look,
      The last will be first and the first will be last.

A prophet must die in Yerushalayim

31In the same hour some Prushim came near him and said, "Go and
make your way out of here, because Herod wants to kill you."

---

195. In Matthew 7.13–14 the narrow gate leads to life; here the narrow gate leads
to salvation.

32And he said to them,

> Go and tell that fox, look, I cast out demons
> And I perform cures today and tomorrow
> And on the third day I am done. 33Yet today
> And tomorrow and the next day I must go
> On my way, for it is not possible for a prophet
> To die outside Yerushalayim. 34Yerushalayim,
> Yerushalayim, who kills the prophets
> And stones those who are sent to her! How often
> I wanted to gather your children together
> Just as a bird her brood under her wings
> And you were unwilling! 35Look, your house
> Abandons you. But I tell you, you will not
> See me until the time you can say: "Blessed
> Is one who comes in the name of the lord."196

Chapter 14

Healing a man with dropsy on Shabbat

It happened that when he went into the house of a leading Parush on Shabbat and ate bread, they were watching him closely. 2And look, there was a man before him suffering from dropsy. 3And Yeshua spoke to the lawyers and Prushim, saying,

> Is it lawful or not to heal on Shabbat?

4But they were silent.

5And he said to them,

> Who among you who has a son or an ox
> Fallen into a well
> Will not lift it out immediately
> On the day of Shabbat?

6And they were unable to answer.

---

196. Ps. 118.26.

Choosing a place at the table

7And observing how places of honor at a meal are selected, he told them a parable,

8When you are invited by someone to
A wedding, do not recline at the table
In the place of honor, for possibly one
With more honors than you has been invited
By him. 9Then he who invited you will say
To you, "Give up your place," and you will slip
With shame into the very last place.
10But when you are invited, go and take
The lowest place, so when your host comes
He will say to you, "Friend, move up higher."
Then glory will come to you before all
Who are reclining at the table with you,
11Because all who exalt themselves high
Will be humbled low, and those who choose
To humble themselves will be exalted.

Choosing guests

12He also said to the one who was his host,
When you prepare a lunch or supper,
Do not invite your friends or your brothers
Or your relations or rich neighbors,
For possibly they will invite you in return
And it will be a repayment to you.
13When you prepare a banquet invite
The poor, the crippled, the lame, the blind.
14Then you will be blessed, for they have no means
To repay you, but you will be repaid
At the resurrection of the good.

Fate of guests who do not come

15Hearing this, one of the guests at the table said to him, "Blessed is one who eats bread in the kingdom of God."

16Yeshua said to him,
There was a man preparing a great banquet
And he invited many, 17and at the dinner hour

He sent his slave to say to those who were
Invited, "Come, because now it is ready."
18Then one and all asked to be excused.
The first said to him, "I bought a field
And I must go out and look at it. I ask
You to excuse me." 19Another said, "I bought
Five yokes of oxen and I'm going out
To try them out. I ask you to excuse me."
20Another said, "I took a wife and so
I cannot come." 21When the slave returned
And reported these things to his lord,
Then the master of the house got angry
And told his slave, "Go quickly into the squares
And alleys of the city and bring in the poor
And the crippled and the blind and the lame."
22The slave said, "Master, what you ordered
Has been done and there is still room." 23The master
Said to the slave, "Go out to roads and hedge roads
And compel the people to come in to fill
My house. 24I tell you not one of those men
Who were invited will taste my dinner."

*Hate your father and mother, renounce everything
and follow me*
25And there was a large crowd accompanying him and he turned and
said to them,
26If someone comes to me and does not hate
His father and mother and wife and children
And brothers and sisters and even life itself,
He cannot be my student. 27Whoever does not
Carry the cross and follow me cannot be
My student. 28Who among you who wants to build
A tower will not first sit down and calculate
The cost to see if you have enough to finish it?
29For if you have put the foundation in place
And cannot finish it, everyone who sees it
Will begin to make fun of you 30and say,
"This one began to build and was not able

To complete it." 31Or what king going to war
With another king would not first consider
If with ten thousand he is strong enough
To combat one who comes against him
With twenty thousand? 32If he lacks the force,
While the enemy is still far away, he sends
An envoy to ask for terms of peace.
33So those of you who do not surrender
All possessions cannot be my students.

Taste of salt

34Salt is good. But if salt has lost its taste
How can it be seasoned?
35It is not fit for the land or a dunghill.
They throw it out.
Whoever has ears to hear, hear.

Chapter 15

Three parables

Now all the tax collectors and wrongdoers were coming near him to
listen to him. 2And the Prushim and the scholars were grumbling and
saying, "This man welcomes wrongdoers and eats with them."

3But Yeshua told them this parable:

Parable of the lost sheep

4Who among you who has a hundred sheep
And has lost one of them will not leave
The ninety-nine in the wilderness
And go after the one lost until it is found?
5Once he finds it he sets it on his shoulders
And is happy. 6And when he comes home
He calls his friends and neighbors together
And tells them, "Celebrate with me,
For I have found my sheep that was lost."
7I say to you there will be more joy

In heaven over one sinner who repents
Than over ninety-nine of the just
Who have no need of repentance.

Parable of the lost drachma

8Or what woman who has ten drachmas[197]
If she loses one will not light a lamp
And sweep the house and search carefully
Until she finds it? 9And finding it, she calls
Together friends and neighbors, saying,
"Celebrate with me, for I have found the coin
I lost." 10So I tell you, there is joy
Among the angels over one sinner who repents.

Parable of the lost son[198]

11And he said,
There was a man who had two sons.
12The younger said to his father, "Father,
Give me the share of the property
That will belong to me." So he divided
His resources between them. 13And not
Many days later the younger son
Got all his things together and went off
To a far country and there he squandered
His substance by riotous living.

14When he had spent everything he had,
There came a severe famine throughout
That country, and he began to be in need.
15And he went and hired out to a citizen
Of that land, who sent him to his fields
To feed the pigs. 16He longed to be fed
On the pods the pigs were eating, but no one

---

197. The drachma was a Greek silver coin. A drachma was worth about a day's wage.
198. Commonly called "The Prodigal Son."

Gave him anything. 17He came to himself[199]
And said, "How many of the day laborers
Of my father have bread left over and here
I'm starving and dying. 18I will rise up
And go to my father and I will say to him,
'Father, I have sinned against heaven
And before you. 19I am no longer worthy
To be called your son. Make me
Like one of your hired hands.'" 20And he rose up
And went to his father. While he was still
Far off, his father saw him and was filled
With compassion and tears fell on his neck
And he kissed him. 21And the son said to him,
"Father, I have sinned against heaven
And before you. I am no longer worthy
To be called your son." 22But his father said
To his slaves, "Quick, bring out the finest robe
And put it on him, and give him a ring
For his hand and sandals for his feet.
23And bring the fatted calf, slaughter it,
And let us eat and celebrate, 24for my son
Was dead and he came back to life,
He was lost and he has been found."
And they began to celebrate.

25Now the older son was in the fields
And as he drew near the house he heard
Music and dancing. 26And he called over
One of his slaves and asked what was going on.
27He told him, "Your brother is here,
And your father has slaughtered the fatted calf
Because he took him back in good health."
28He was angry and did not want to go in,
But his father came out and pleaded with him.
29Yet he answered and said to his father,

---

199. Meaning "he came to his senses."

"Look, so many years I have served you
And never disobeyed an order of yours,
And for me you never gave a young goat
So I could celebrate with my friends.
30But when this son of yours came, who ate up
Your property with prostitutes, for him
You slaughtered the fatted calf." 31And he said
To him, "Child, you are always with me,
And everything that is mine is yours,
32But we must be happy and celebrate.
Your brother was a dead man and he lived
And he was lost and has been found."

Chapter 16

Crafty steward

Then Yeshua said to his students,
There was a rich man who had a steward[200]
And this steward was accused of squandering
His possessions. 2So he summoned him
And said, "What is this I hear about you?
Give me a statement of your stewardship,
Since you can no longer be my steward."
3Then the steward said to himself,
"What will I do now that my master
has taken my stewardship from me?
I am not strong enough to dig. I am
Ashamed to beg. 4Now I know what to do
When I am removed from my stewardship
So people will welcome me in their houses."
5And he summoned all the debtors
Of his master, one by one. He told the first,
"How much do you owe my master?"
He said, "A hundred measures of olive oil."

---

200. Also translated as "manager."

6"Take your bills, sit down, and quickly write in
Fifty." 7Then to another he said, "How much
Do you owe?" "A hundred bushels of wheat,"
He said to him. "Take your bills and write in
Eighty." 8And his master praised the steward
For his dishonesty since he had acted shrewdly.
The people of this age are wiser than
The children of light of their generation.
9I say to you: Make friends for yourselves
By way of the mammon of dishonesty,
So when that wealth is gone, you will
Be welcomed into the eternal tents.

Faithful in money

10One who is faithful in the little thing
Is faithful in the bigger, and one who is
Dishonest in the little is also dishonest
In the bigger. 11So then if you have not
Been faithful with dishonest wealth,
Who will believe in you for true riches?
12And if you have not been faithful
With what belongs to another,
Who will give you what is your own?

Dilemma of two masters

13No house slave can serve two masters.
Either he will hate one and love the other
Or be devoted to one and despise the other.
You cannot serve God and mammon.[201]

Against Prushim who love silver

14When the Prushim, who loved silver,[202] heard all these things, they
derided him.

15Yeshua said to them,

---

201. Riches or money.
202. Also means by extension "fond of money."

You are the ones who justify yourselves
In the eyes of the people, but God knows
Your hearts. For what among people is exalted
Is in the eyes of God an abomination.

Law and prophets, then the kingdom

16Until Yohanan came it was the law
And the prophets. Since then the kingdom of God
Is preached, and all try to force their way in.
17But it is easier for the sky and the earth
To disappear than for one hook of the letter
Of the law in the Torah to fall away.

Divorce and adultery

18Anyone who divorces his wife and marries another commits
adultery.
Anyone who marries a woman divorced from her husband
commits adultery.

Rich man in burning Sheol, begging help from Avraham in heaven

19There was a rich man dressed in purple
And fine linen, and he feasted every day
In splendor. 20And at the gate lay a poor man
Named Elazar,[203] covered with sores,
21And longing to be fed with the crumbs
That fell from the rich man's table.
Even the dogs came to lick his sores.
22And it happened that the poor man died
And was carried away by angels to Avraham's side.

The rich man also died and was buried.
23And in Sheol[204] where he was in torment,

---

203. Lazarus from the Greek Λάζαρος (Lazaros), from the Hebrew אֶלְעָזָר (elazar).
204. The underworld.

He raised his eyes and saw Avraham far away
And Elazar lying on his chest. 24And he called
And said, "Father Avraham, have mercy on me
And send Elazar to dip his fingertip into water
And cool my tongue, for I am in agony
In this flame." 25But Avraham said, "Child,
Remember that you received the good things
In your life, and Elazar got the bad.
But now he is comforted here and you suffer.
26And more than that, between us and you
   A great chasm has been fixed so that those
   Who want to cross over from here to you
   Cannot, nor can they cross from there to us."

27And he said, "Then I ask you, father, to send
   Him to my father's house. 28I have five brothers.
   He may warn them so they will not also come
   To this place of torment." 29But Avraham said,
   "They have Moshe and the prophets. Let them
   Listen to them." 30Yet he said, "No, father Avraham,
   If someone goes to them from the dead
   They will repent." 31But Avraham said to him,
   "If they do not listen to Moshe and the prophets,
   Nothing will persuade them to repent
   Even if someone rises from the dead."

Chapter 17

Millstone to drown one who leads others astray
  Yeshua said to his students,
     It is impossible that traps will not be set
     For stumbling into, but a plague on
     Anyone who falls in! 2It would be better
     If a millstone were hung around his neck
     And he were cast into the sea
     Than to cause these little ones to go astray.

When your brother does wrong

3Watch yourselves. If your brother does wrong
And repents, forgive him. 4And if he does wrong
Seven times a day against you and seven times
Turns around to say, "I repent," forgive him.

Faith uprooting a black mulberry tree

5The messengers said to the lord, "Give us more faith."
6But the lord said,

If you have faith like a grain of mustard seed
You could say to this black mulberry tree,
"Pluck yourself up by the roots and plant yourself
In the sea," and it would still obey you.

Duty of a slave plowing

7But who among you with a slave plowing
Or tending sheep, who comes in from the fields,
Will say to him, "Come here at once and eat
With me at the table"? 8Will he not say,
"Prepare something for supper, wrap an apron
Around you, serve me while I eat and drink,
And after all this, you may eat and drink"?
9Does he thank the slave for doing as he
Was commanded? 10So when you too do all
You were told to do, say, "We're worthless slaves
And what we did was our duty to do."

With ten lepers

11And it happened on his journey to Yerushalayim, Yeshua passed
through the middle of Shomron[205] and the Galil. 12As he went into a
certain village ten men who were lepers met him, keeping their distance,
13and raised their voices, saying, "Yeshua, master, have mercy on us!"

14When he saw them, he said to them,

Go and show yourselves to the priests.

---

205. Samaria.

And it came about that as they went away they were made clean.

15And one of them, seeing that he was healed, turned, glorifying God in a great voice. 16He fell on his face at his feet, thanking him. And this man was a Shomroni.206

17Yeshua answered him and said,

> Were not ten made clean? Where now are the nine?
> 18Has no one come back to glorify God
> Except this stranger?

19And he said to him,

> Rise and go. Your faith has saved you.

Coming of the kingdom of God mysteriously inside

20When he was asked by the Prushim when the kingdom of God was to come, he answered them and said,

> The kingdom of God is not coming
> In an observable way,
> 21Nor will people say, "Look, it is here!"
> Or, "It is there!"
> For look, the kingdom of God is inside you.

Coming of the earthly son

22Then he said to the students,

> The days are coming when you will long to see
> One of the days of the earthly son,
> And you will not see it.
> 23And they will say to you, "Look, there!" or "Look, here!"
> Do not go after them! Do not follow them!
> 24For as lightning burns at one end of the sky
> And then at the other end of the sky glistens,
> So will be the coming of the earthly son.
> 25But first he must suffer multiple wrongs
> And be rejected by this generation.
> 26And as it happened in the days of Noah,
> So it will be in the days of the earthly son.
> 27The people were eating, drinking, marrying,

---

206. Samaritan.

And given away in marriage until the day
Noah went into the ark and the flood came
And destroyed all of them.[207] 28It was the same
As in the days of Lot. They were eating,
Drinking, buying, selling, planting, building.
29But on the day Lot went out of Sedom[208]
It rained fire and sulfur from the sky
And destroyed everything. 30So it will be
On the day the earthly son is revealed.

31On that day if a man is on the roof and his goods
Are in the house, let him not come down
To carry them away. And one in the field
Likewise let him not turn back for anything
Left behind. 32Remember the wife of Lot.
33Whoever tries to preserve her life will lose it,
But whoever loses it will bring it to life.
34I tell you, on that night there will be two men
In one bed. One will be taken, the other left.
35There will be two women grinding meal
At the same place. One will be taken, the other left.[209]

37And they asked him, "Where, lord?"
He said to them,
Where the body is, the vultures will assemble.[210]

---

207. This passage contains a warning of impending apocalypse when Yeshua is revealed. There is established a vital parallel between the suffering of Yeshua and his rejection by "this generation" in Israel, and an equivalent rejection by the world's population of God's word in the days of the Hebrew Bible. For this impiety comes a flood, an absolute holocaust, which destroys all living people on earth except for the single family of Noah. The parallel of apocalyptic judgment is then extended to the iniquitous inhabitants of Sodom and the lone-surviving family of Lot.

208. Sodom.

209. Other ancient authorities have added verse 36: "Two will be in the field; one will be taken and the other left."

210. This aphorism may be reworded as "where the corpse is, the vultures or eagles will assemble."

Chapter 18

Parable of the unjust judge and widow

Then he told them a parable about the need always to pray and not weaken, saying,

2In a certain city there was a judge
   Who did not fear God or respect people.
3And in that city there was a widow
   Who was coming to him and saying,
   "Grant me justice against my adversary."
4And for a time he would not, but later
   He said to himself, "Though I do not fear God
   Or respect people, 5since this woman gives
   Me trouble, I will grant her justice for fear
   She will keep coming and at last wear me down."

6And the lord said,
   Listen to what the unjust judge says.
   7Will God not do justice to his chosen ones
   Who cry out to him day and night?
   Will he set them at a distance from him?
   8I tell you he will quickly give them justice.
   But when the earthly son comes,
   Will he then find faith on the earth?

Parable of the Parush and tax collector

9And to some who confidently saw themselves as just and looked upon others with contempt, he told this parable,

10Two men went up to the Temple to pray,
   One a Parush and the other a tax collector.
11The Parush stood alone and prayed
   In this way, "God, I thank you that I am
   Not like the other people—grasping, unjust,
   Adulterous—or even like this tax collector.
12I fast twice a week, I give a tithe on all
   I have." 13Now the tax collector stood far off

And did not wish to raise his eyes to the sky
And he beat his chest, saying, "God, have mercy
On me a sinner." 14I tell you this man went back
To his house justified while the other,
Because he exalted himself, will be humbled,
And he who humbles himself will be exalted.[211]

Let the children come to me

15They even brought him babies for him to touch, and seeing this the students scolded them. 16But Yeshua called for them and said,

---

211. Officials of the Roman occupation of Palestine (in which Judea, its Roman name, was a Roman province ruled by Roman governors) are seen positively by the evangelists, while the Pharisees, with their opposition to Roman occupation during Yeshua's life and during the failed rebellion, their emphasis on the oral (*Halakhah*) rather than the written word (the domain of the Sadducees), and their belief that the soul survives death, would seem to fall in Yeshua's camp. While the Sadducees represented the rich and the ruling class, the Pharisees in the first century were typically the liberal theologians who spoke for the poor and reflected the larger people of Israel, who saw Judaism as a living and changing religion, which was the *Halakic* oral tradition of discourse exemplified in Yeshua's speech of using and at the same time altering the written law. In the gospels, however, the Pharisee is the sinister scapegoat Jew. Although there is disagreement with regard to Pharisee opposition to Herodean (Hasmonean) and Roman authority, Josephus was disturbed by the Pharisees as a dissident group opposing Rome, and Paul, an ultimate dissident who may have been executed by Rome, who wrote and died before the gospels were composed, was proud of his dissident Pharisee background (Philippians 3.5). The early Christian polemic against the Pharisees as hypocrites and legalistic conspirators is largely discredited as self-justifying rant. But in the gospels the division between supporters of state authority by way of Pilate, centurions, and even a lowly tax collector (Matthew's profession) and opponents by way of the Pharisees is constant, and hence it is natural that in this parable the Pharisee is depicted as a self-exalting hypocrite and the tax collector as a modest repentant who will find salvation. The gospels, through Yeshua's voice, have made Yeshua, who many scholars assert was a Pharisee (as Paul claimed to be), militantly opposed to the Pharisees and an apologist for Rome and some of those in its employ. In this parable, the gospel's prophecy is that Israel will be humbled, Rome exalted, the Rome that will crucify Yeshua. In contrast to the gospels, Acts and Revelation narrate Rome's massacre and martyrdom of early Christians, and there is no love affair with Rome.

Let the children come to me
And do not stop them, for the kingdom of God
Belongs to them.
17Amain, I tell you,
Whoever does not receive the kingdom of God
Like a child
Will never enter therein.

Rich ruler

18And a certain official asked him, "Good rabbi, what do I do to inherit eternal life?"

19And Yeshua said to him,
Why do you call me good? No one is good
Except God alone. 20The commandments you know.
Do not commit adultery, do not murder,
Do not steal, do not bear false witness,
Honor your father and your mother.
21And he said, "All those I kept since my youth."
22Hearing this Yeshua said to him,
You still have one thing missing.
Sell all you own and give it to the poor
And you will have a treasure in heaven,
And then come and follow me.
23But when he heard this, he grieved, for he was rich.
24Yeshua looked at him and said,
How hard it is for the wealthy to enter the kingdom of God!
25It is easier for a camel to enter through the eye of a needle
Than for a rich man to enter the kingdom of God.[212]

Who can be saved?

26Those hearing him said, "And who can be saved?"
27He said,
What is impossible for people
Is possible for God.

212. See note 108 on Mark 10.25.

Rewards for abandoning family for the kingdom

28Then Shimon Kefa said, "See, we have given up what we had and followed you."

29And Yeshua said to them,

> Amain, amain, I say to you.
> There is no one who has left house or wife
> Or parents or children for the kingdom of God
> 30Who will not receive back many times more
> In this age,
> And in the age to come of life everlasting.

I will die and be risen

31Then taking the twelve aside, he said to them,

> Look, we are going up to Yerushalayim
> And all that has been written by the prophets
> About the earthly son will be fulfilled.
> 32He will be handed over to the foreigners,[213]
> And they will mock and insult and spit on him,
> 33And after scourging him they will kill him
> And on the third day he will rise again.

34But they understood nothing of this, and this word was concealed from them and they did not know what was being said.

Blind beggar in Yeriho

35And it happened as he drew near Yeriho there was a blind man sitting by the road, begging. 36And when he heard the crowd going by, he asked what was going on. 37They informed him that Yeshua the Natzrati[214] was going by. 38And he cried out, saying, "Yeshua, son of David, have pity on me!"

39Those who were in front of him rebuked him and told him to be quiet, but he cried out much louder, "Son of David, have pity on me!"

40Yeshua stood still and ordered him to be brought to him. Drawing near him, he questioned him,

---

213. See note 42 on Luke 2.32: gentiles, foreigners, pagans, heathens.
214. Nazarene.

41What do you want me to do?

And he said, "Lord, let me see again."

42Then Yeshua said to him,

See again. Your faith has healed you.

43And at once he saw again and followed him and glorified God. And all the people, seeing this, gave praise to God.

Chapter 19

Zakai, rich tax collector who will be saved

And he entered Yeriho and was passing through it. 2And look, a man named Zakai[215] was a chief tax collector, and he was rich. 3He was trying to see who Yeshua was, but was unable to because of the crowd, since he was short. 4So he ran ahead to the front and climbed a sycamore tree to see him. He was about to pass by. 5As Yeshua came to the place, he looked up and said to him,

Zakai, hurry and come down,

For today I must stay at your house.

6And he quickly climbed down and welcomed him with joy.

7When they saw this, everyone muttered, saying, "He has gone in to stay with a sinful man." 8Zakai stood there and said, "Lord, I am giving half my possessions to the poor, and if I have cheated anyone I am paying it back four times over."

9And Yeshua said to him,

Salvation has come to this house today,

Because he too is a son of Avraham.[216]

10The earthly son came to seek out and save the lost.

---

215. Zacchaeus from the Greek Ζακχαῖος (Zakhaios), from the Hebrew זַכָּי (zakai). The Hebrew name in Luke is given in Greek form and is ordinarily Romanized in English. See note 211 on Luke 18.14 for information on the "lowly" Roman tax collector. *Zakai* is found in Ezra 2.9 and Nehemiah 7.14.

216. "Son of Abraham" meant a true Jew and not one to be excluded from society because, as a tax collector, he was working for the Roman occupiers.

Parable of the king and his slaves

11As they were listening to this, he went on to tell a parable, because he was near Yerushalayim and they supposed the kingdom of God would appear immediately. 12Then he said,

> A man of high birth journeyed to a far land
> To acquire a kingdom for himself and then
> Return. 13He summoned ten of his slaves
> And gave them ten minas²¹⁷ and told them,
> "Carry on the business with this silver
> Until I return." 14But his citizens hated him
> And they sent a delegation after him, saying,
> "We do not want this man to rule
> Over us." 15Now it happened on his return,
> After he obtained his appointment as king,
> He summoned his slaves to whom he had given silver
> So he could find out what profit they made.
> 16The first one came and said, "Master, your mina
> Has made you ten minas." 17And he said to him,
> "Well done, good slave. Since in every detail
> You were faithful, take charge of ten cities."
> 18And the second came saying, "Master, your mina
> Made five minas." 19And he also said to him,
> "Rule over five cities." 20And the other came
> Saying, "Master, see the mina you gave me,
> Which I hid away in a napkin. 21I was afraid
> Because you are a severe man. You take
> What you did not lay down, and you harvest
> What you did not sow." 22He said to him,
> "Out of your own mouth I judge you, crafty slave!
> Didn't you know I am a severe man
> And take what I did not lay down and harvest
> What I did not sow? 23Why did you not put
> My money into the bank? Then when I came

217. One talent is 60 minas, and a mina is 100 drachmas. A drachma is about a day's wage.

I could have taken it out with interest."
24And to those who were standing near he said,
"Take this mina from him and give it to the one
With ten minas." 25And they said to him,
26"Master, he has ten minas." "I tell you, everyone
Who has will be given. But from one with nothing,
Even that nothing will be taken away. As for
27My enemies who have not wanted me to rule,
Bring them here and slaughter them before me."[218]

Entering Yerushalayim on a colt

28And after Yeshua said this, he went on ahead, going up to Yerusha-layim. 29And it happened as he came near Beit Pagey[219] and Beit Aniyah,[220] near the place called Mountain of Olives, he sent two of his students ahead, 30saying to them:

Go into the village just ahead
And as you enter you will find a tethered colt
On which no one has ever sat.
Untie it and bring it here.
If someone asks you, "Why are you untying it?"
31You will say, "His master needs it."

32So those whom he had sent left and found what he told them. 33While untying the colt, its owners said to them, "Why are you untying the colt?"

34They said, "His master needs it."

35And they led it to Yeshua.

Then after spreading their clothing on the colt, they mounted Yeshua on it. 36And as he rode on they strewed their clothing on the road.

---

218. Virtue in this parable is to reward good financial performance and to punish caution and timidity. In the last lines, the slaughter of those who oppose and lack faith in their master as king is ominous. Common interpretation has the overlord's departure to be appointed king an allegory for Yeshua's own departure and exaltation.

219. Bethphage from the Greek Βηθφαγή (Bethfage), from the Hebrew בֵּית פַּגֵּא (beit pagey).

220. Bethany from the Greek Βηθανία (Bethania), from the Hebrew בֵּית אָנְיָה (beit aniyah).

37As he came near the descent from the Mountain of Olives, the whole multitude of his students began joyfully to praise God in a great voice for all the miracles they had seen, 38and said from the Psalms,

> Blessed is the king who comes in the name of the lord!
> Peace in heaven and glory in the highest.[221]

If his students are silent the stones will cry out

39Some of the Prushim in the crowd said to him, "Rabbi, reprove your students."

40And he answered them and said,

> I tell you, if these are silent,
> The stones will cry out.

Weeping for Yerushalayim, which will be punished, its children crushed

41As he came near and saw the city, he wept over it, 42saying,

> If you only knew on this day those things
> Creating peace! Yet now they are hidden
> From your eyes. 43But days will come upon you
> And your enemies will set up ramparts
> Against you and encircle you and hem you in
> From all sides. 44They will crush you and your children
> And not leave a stone on a stone intact in you[222]
> Since you did not know the time of your visitation.

Driving the vendors from the Temple

45And he went into the Temple and began to throw out the vendors, 46saying to them as written in Yeshayahu and Yirmiyahu,

> My house shall be a house of prayer
> But you have made it into a cave of robbers.[223]

---

221. Ps. 118.26.

222. In this passage Yeshua foresees the destruction of Jerusalem in 70 C.E. by the Roman general Titus, son of the emperor and future emperor himself. The city will fall because of her disobedience to Rome and her impiety toward Yeshua. For more information, please see Afterword.

223. Isaiah 56.7 writes, "My house shall be a house of prayer." Jeremiah 7.11 writes, "Has this house, which bears my Name, become a den of robbers to you?"

Teaching in the Temple

47And he was teaching every day in the Temple. The high priests and the scholars sought to kill him, and also did the leaders of the people, 48but they could not find what to do, for the people were all hanging on his words.

Chapter 20

Sparring with authorities in the Temple[224]

And it happened on one day when he was teaching in the Temple[225] and preaching the gospel, the high priests and the scholars came by, and also the elders, 2and they said to him, "Tell us by what authority you do these things? Who gave you this authority?"

3He answered and said to them,

> I too will ask you a word and you tell me.
> 4Was the immersion of Yohanan come from heaven
> Or from humans?

5They discussed this among themselves, saying, "If we say from heaven, he will say, 'Why do you not believe him?' 6But if we say from humans,

---

224. The subtitles given in modern translations to conspiracy passages reveal positions of the translator editors. Such unconfirmed private conversations in the New Testament are, for a historian, true, speculative, or fictional, depending on witness accounts of which there are none outside the gospels. Given the uncertainty and crucial importance of conspiracy passages in the religious politics of the scriptures, the translators may choose neutral or inflammatory speech in their own additions to the texts, which are the subtitles. Reflecting four Bible versions, the 1993 *HarperCollins Study Bible*'s subtitle has "The Authority of Jesus Questioned," the 1986 Zondervan *NIV Study Bible* also has "The Authority of Jesus Questioned" (normally subtitles in these major translations differ), and the 1995 Oxford *New Testament and Psalms* has "Jesus Authority Is Questioned." However, the 1990 revised edition of the *New Jerusalem Bible* has "The Jews question the authority of Jesus." Here the Jerusalem subtitle is inflammatory, pitting Jews against Yeshua, giving credence to an underlying notion that Yeshua is not of the Jews. "Jew" in their subtitle enforces "Jew" as a loaded hate word, based on the New Testament fiction that Yeshua and the ordinary inhabitants of Jerusalem and Israel who were Yeshua's followers ceased to be Jews insofar as they became his followers. The anti-Semitism whose voice begins in the Jewish scripture of the New Testament intensified in the *New Jerusalem Bible* by its invention of a subtitle that logically makes Yeshua seen as the non-Jew.

225. Yeshua was probably teaching in the Temple courts.

all the people will stone us, for they are convinced that Yohanan is a prophet." 7So they answered that they didn't know where he came from.

8And Yeshua said to them,

> Neither will I tell you by what authority
> I do these things.

Parable of wicked tenants

9He began to tell the people this parable,

> A man planted a vineyard and leased it
> To farmers and left the country for some time.
> 10And when the time came he sent a slave
> To the farmers so they would give him
> Some of the fruit of the vineyard.
> But the farmers beat him and he came back
> Empty-handed. 11Then he sent another slave,
> But they also beat him and humiliated him
> And sent him back with nothing. 12And he sent
> A third. They wounded him and threw him out.

> 13The owner of the vineyard said, "What can I do?
> I'll send my beloved son. This one maybe
> They will respect." 14But when the farmers saw him,
> They talked it over and said, "He is the heir.
> Let us kill him so the inheritance
> Will become ours." 15And they drove him out of
> The vineyard and killed him. What will
> The owner of the vineyard do to them now?
> 16He will come and destroy these farmers
> And give the vineyards over to others.

And when they heard it they said, "May it never happen!" 17But he looked at them and said,

> What is the meaning of this phrase in Psalms:
>> "This stone which was rejected by the builders
>> Has become the cornerstone"?[226]

---

226. Ps. 118.22.

18Anyone who falls on that stone will be broken to pieces
And anyone it falls on will be crushed.[227]

19The scholars and the high priests were looking for a way to lay their hands on him at that very time but they were afraid of the people, for they knew he had spoken that parable against them. 20And they watched for an opportunity and sent spies who pretended to be just so they might trap him through his word and turn him over to the rulers and authority of the governor.

Paying coins to Caesar

21And they questioned him, saying, "Rabbi, we know that you speak and teach straight, and do not favor any person but truthfully teach the way of God. 22Is it right for us to pay the tax to Caesar?"
23But he knew their craftiness and said to them,
24Show me a denarius silver coin.
Whose image and name are on it?
"Caesar's," they said.
25And he said to them,
Then give the things of Caesar to Caesar
And the things of God to God.[228]
26And they were not able to catch him on his saying before the people, and they were confounded at his answer and were silent.

A wife in heaven

27Some of the Tzadokim[229] came near him, those who say there is no resurrection. 28They questioned him: "Rabbi, Moshe wrote for us that if one's brother dies, and he is childless, then his brother should marry

---

227. The stone is "the new rock of Christianity." Whoever rejects Yeshua will be crushed. When this brief parabolic phrase from the Psalms was added and explained in the New Testament cannot be known. It is routine in the gospels to draw from the Hebrew Bible to prove the truth of Yeshua as the foretold messiah.

228. This episode of the coin presents the synoptic gospels' view of cooperation with Roman officials. For more information, see note 127 on Mark 12.14.

229. Sadducee from the Greek Σαδώκ, from the Hebrew צָדוֹק (tzadok). "Sadducees" (pl.) is *Tzadokim*. *Tzadok* (Tsadok) was High Priest at the time of David and means "the just."

the widow and raise children for his brother. 29Now there were seven brothers. And the first who married the widow died childless, 30and the second took her and the third, 31and in the same way all seven died childless. 32Finally, the woman died too. 33In the resurrection whose woman will she be? For all seven had her as wife."

34Yeshua said to them,

> The sons in this age marry, are given in marriage,
> 35But those who are thought worthy
> In this age to attain life in the resurrection
> From the dead do not marry or are given
> In marriage. 36But they can no longer die
> For they are like angels, they are children
> Of God, being children of the resurrection.
> 37That the dead are raised Moshe revealed
> In the burning bush,[230] where he calls the lord
> The God of Avraham and Yitzhak and Yaakov.
> 38But God is not of the dead but of the living,
> Because to him everyone is alive.

39Some of the scholars answered and said, "Rabbi, you have spoken well." 40They no longer dared to question him on anything.

The mashiah is son and lord of David

41And Yeshua said to the people,

> How can they say that the mashiah is the descendant
>   Of David?
> 42For David himself says in the book of Psalms:
>   "The lord said to my lord,
>   'Sit at my right side
>   43While I make your enemies your footstool.'"[231]
> 44Since David calls him lord, how can he be his son?

Condemning scholars

45And in the hearing of all the people, he said to his students,

---

230. Exod. 3.2.
231. Ps. 110.1.

46Beware of the scholars, who like to walk around
In long robes, who love to be greeted
In market places, in their high seats in the synagogues
And at the places of honor at the dinners,
47Who eat up the houses of the widows,
And, for mere appearance, say lengthy prayers.
They will receive the harshest judgment.

Chapter 21

The widow's copper coin
Then he looked up and saw the rich casting their gifts into the treasury.
2And he saw a poor widow casting in two copper leptas.232 3And he said,
Truly I tell you,
This widow who is poor
Has cast in more than anyone else.
4All of them put in gifts from their abundance
While she in her poverty cast in
All the pennies she had to live on.

Destruction of the Temple foretold
5And when some were saying that the Temple was adorned with beautiful stones and sacred gifts, Yeshua said,
6As for what you see,
The days will come
When there will be
Not one stone on a stone
Not thrown down.233

False mashiahs and terrifying signs
7And they questioned him, saying, "Rabbi, when will this be and what sign when it will take place?"

---

232. A small copper coin of which 100 make a drachma.

233. The reference is again to the Romans' taking of Jerusalem and the burning of the Temple.

8And he said,

>Beware that you are not fooled.
>Many will come in my name, saying, "I am he."
>The time is near. Do not follow them.

9When you hear about wars and uprisings,

>Do not be alarmed, for these must happen first,
>But the end will not come soon.

10Then he said to them,

>Nation will rise up against nation
>And kingdom against kingdom.

11There will be great earthquakes,

>And in many places there will be famines and plagues, and
>   horrors,
>And there will be great signs from the sky.

Betrayal and persecutions because of my name

12But before all these things, they will lay their hands on you

>And persecute you
>And turn you over to the synagogues and jails,
>And you will be brought before kings and governors,
>Because of my name.

13This will be your time to testify.

14So keep in your hearts that you must not prepare

>To defend yourselves,

15For I will give you such a tongue and wisdom

>That all those opposed to you
>Will not resist or stand against you.

Though parents and friends betray and kill you, you gain your souls

16You will be betrayed even by parents

>And brothers and relatives and friends,[234]

---

234. The betrayal by parents and brothers reflects Yeshua's by-now frequent indignation not only in the broader sense against those who are not followers but also against his own family and the failure of his mother and brothers and sisters to have faith in him as the messiah. See Mark 3.32 and Luke 8.19.

And they will put some of you to death,[235]
17And you will be hated by all because of my name.
18Yet not a hair of your head will perish.
19In your endurance you will gain your souls.

Desolation of the siege of Yerushalayim

20When you see Yerushalayim encircled
By armies, then know that its devastation is near.
21Then those in Yehuda must flee to the mountains
And those in the city must escape
And those in the fields not go into her,
22For these are days of vengeance to fulfill
All that has been written by the prophets:
23A plague on those women who have a child
In their womb and women who are nursing
In those days. There will be great distress
On the earth and anger against the people.
24And they will fall to the edge of the sword
And they will be taken away as captives
Into all nations, and Yerushalayim
Will be trampled by foreigners until the time
Of the foreigners has run its course.[236]

Cosmic disasters and coming of the earthly son

25There will be signs in sun and moon and stars,
And on the earth the dismay of foreign nations
In bewilderment at the sound of the sea

---

235. Reference of this prophecy is to Stephen in Acts 7.54–60 and James in Acts 12.2. Yeshua's prophecies, here and throughout the scriptures, indicate that the author of Luke created these words for Yeshua since Stephen's death took place after his crucifixion. All knowledge by Yeshua, including the destruction of Jerusalem elaborated in Luke 19.41–44 and 21.20–24, suggests either that Yeshua had knowledge of the future or that in the future the assemblers of the scriptures put knowledge of the future into Yeshua's speech.

236. These prophecies of disaster are from Isaiah 63.4–5 and 63.18 and Daniel 8.13 and 9.24–27.

And surf. 26People will faint from fear
And foreboding of what is coming upon the world,
For the powers of the skies will be shaken.
27And then they will see the earthly son coming
On a cloud with power and enormous glory.[237]
28When these things happen, stand up straight
And raise your heads, for your redemption is near.

Parable of the budding fig tree
29And he told them a parable,
Look at the fig tree and all the trees.
30When they sprout leaves, you look at them
And know that summer is already near.
31So too when you see these things happening
You know the kingdom of God is near.
32I tell you truth. This generation will not
Pass by until all these things take place.
33The sky[238] and the earth will pass away
But my words will not pass away.

Don't burn up before the day rushing in on all of us on the face of the earth
34Be careful that you don't weigh down your hearts
With dissipation and drunkenness and worries of life
Test that day suddenly come upon you 35as a trap,

---

237. Dan. 7.13–14.

238. Sky from the Greek οὐρανός (ouranos), translated as "sky" or "heaven." In Greek, as in many languages, the word for heaven and sky is the same. Normally, translations raise the possible religious or moral meaning of words, and hence *ouranos* is regularly translated as "heaven" regardless of context, as it is in this instance by NRSV and NIV, with the notable exception of Richmond Lattimore and the Annotated Scholars' translation. In this version, the intention is not to blur the distinction between heaven and the physical sky above the earth, for then the image of paradise, God's abode and the abode of the saved, would also be blurred. So either "heaven" or "sky" is used to translate *ouranos*, depending on its usage, and in very many cases the choice is difficult, because either or both meanings are possible.

For it will rush in on all
Who are sitting on the face of the whole earth.
36Be alert and pray at all times for strength
To escape the many things that are to happen,
And to stand before the earthly son.

Days in the Temple, nights on the Mountain of Olives

37Now during those days he was in the Temple, teaching, and in the nights he went out and stayed on the mountain, the one called "Of the Olives."239 38And all the people rose at dawn to go to the Temple to hear him.

Chapter 22

Plotting before Pesach

The Feast of the Matzot Bread240 was approaching, which is called Pesach.241 2The high priests and the scholars were looking for ways to destroy him, because they were afraid of the people. 3Then Satan entered Yehuda, who is called the one from Keriot, who was one of the number twelve.242 4And he went to speak with the high priests and

---

239. The Mountain of Olives.

240. Matzot Bread from the Greek ἄζυμος (azymos), "unleavened bread," from the Hebrew מַצּוֹת (matzoh).

241. Festival of the Matzot Bread is the Festival of Unleavened Bread. *Pesach* is "Passover" from the Greek πάσχα (pasha), from the Hebrew פֶּסַח (pesach), "passed over," referring to escape from bondage in Egypt, celebrated at the Seder by eating the paschal lamb. See Exodus 12.1–13.16. In other instances I have transliterated the Hebrew *heth*, ח as "h," so it is *Yohanan*, not *Yochanan*, which would also be acceptable and emphasize the guttural "ch." However, "ch" may also be understood in English as "ch" in "child." Hence ח is always "h" except in *Pesach* (chosen rather than *Pesah*), since *Pesach* is already a Hebrew word used in English and found in English dictionaries.

242. The demonization of the Jew is epitomized by introducing an earlier story of the betrayer into the gospels and giving the figure the name "Judas" (Yehuda), meaning "the Jew." For more on the origin of the betrayer tale of Judas in scripture and post-

generals[243] about a way to hand him over to them. 5They were very happy and agreed to pay him money. 6And he consented and looked for an opportunity to betray him when the crowd was not there.

Preparation for the Seder

7The day of the Matzot Bread came when it was necessary to sacrifice the Pesach lamb. 8And he sent Shimon Kefa and Yohanan, saying,

> Go and prepare the Pesach meal for us
> So we can eat.

9And they said to him, "Where do you want us to prepare it?"
10And he said to them,

> Look, as you go into the city,
> A man carrying a jar of water will meet you.
> Follow him into the house he enters
> 11And say to the owner of the house,
> "The rabbi says to you, 'Where is the guest room
> Where I am to eat the Pesach meal
> With my students?'" 12And he will show you
> A large upstairs room, already furnished.
> Prepare it there.

13So they left and found things just as he had told them and they prepared the Pesach supper.

The Seder

14When the hour came, he reclined at the table, and the messengers with him. 15And he said to them,

> I greatly desired to eat this Pesach with you
> Before I suffer.

16I tell you truth,

> I will not eat it again until it is fulfilled
> In the kingdom of God.

---

biblical portrayals in history and the arts, see note 30 on p. 33, in "Mark, the Vernacular Story Teller." For a more complete account of Judas from the Bible to modern times, see Susan Gubar's *Judas: A Biography* (New York: W. W. Norton, 2009).
243. Temple officers.

17And taking the cup he gave thanks and said,

> Take this cup from me and share it among you.

18I say to you,

> As of now I will not drink of the fruit
> Of the vine
> Until the kingdom of God comes.

19And taking the matzot he gave thanks, broke it, and gave it to them, saying,

> This is my body [which is given for you.
> Do this as a memory of me.²⁴⁴

20And he did the same with the cup, after supper, saying,

> This cup is the new covenant²⁴⁵ in my blood,
> Which is poured out for your sake.]²⁴⁶

Foretelling the hand of the betrayer

21But look, the hand of the betrayer is with me

> On the table.

22Because the earthly son is going away

> As has been determined,
> But a plague on that man who betrayed him.

23And they began to ask each other who of them would do this.

Who is the greatest?

24Then a quarrel took place among them as to who was thought to be the greatest.

25And he said to them,

> The kings of nations lord it over them
> And those in power are called benefactors,

26But with you it is not so.

---

244. The ceremony of the thanksgiving, known as the Eucharist, from the Greek εὐχαριστία (eucharistia), "giving thanks (to God)."

245. From this Greek phrase, καινὴ διαθήκη (kaine diatheke), we have "New Covenant," the Greek name for the Christian scriptures.

246. In many translations, the bracketed section is omitted or included with brackets, indicating uncertainty about its ancient authenticity.

Let the greatest among you be the youngest
And the leader the one who serves.
27 Who is greater?
The one who reclines at the table
Or the one serving?
I am among you as one who serves.

You will eat and drink at my table in my kingdom
28 You are the ones who have stood by me
In my trials. 29 And just as my father
Has conferred a kingdom on me, I confer on you
30 That you may eat and drink at my table
In my kingdom, and you will sit on thrones
And judge the twelve tribes of Yisrael.

Shimon Kefa, you will deny me
31 Shimon, Shimon, look, Satan asked for you
To sift you like wheat,
32 But I have prayed that your faith not fail you,
And you, when you return, strengthen your brothers.
33 And he said to him, "Lord, with you I am ready to go to prison and
to death."
34 He said to him,
I tell you, Shimon Kefa, the cock will not crow today
Until you have three times denied knowing me.

Now go out with a purse, bag, and sandals and buy a sword
35 And Yeshua said to them,
When I sent you without a purse and bag
And sandals, were you in need of anything?
They answered, "Nothing."
36 And he said to them,
But now let the one who has a purse
Let him take it, and also the bag,
And the one who has no sword,
Let him sell his coat and buy one.
37 For I tell you, what Yeshayahu wrote

Must be fulfilled in me.[247]

"Even he was counted among the lawless."

And what is said about me will find its resolution.

38And they said to him, "Lord, look, here are two swords."

He said to them,

It is enough.

An angel comes to him while he is praying on the Mountain of Olives

39He came outside, and then, as was his custom, he went to the Mountain of Olives. And the students followed him. 40When he came to the place he said to them,

Pray that you do not come to the time of trial.

41And he withdrew from them about a stone's throw, went to his knees, and prayed, saying,

42Father, if you choose, take this cup from me,

And let not my will but yours be done.

[43Then an angel from the sky appeared, giving him strength. 44And being in agony he prayed more intensely. His sweat became drops of blood falling on the ground.][248]

Why are you sleeping?

45He stood up from prayer and went to his students and found them sleeping after their grief. 46And he said to them,

Why are you sleeping? Get up and pray

That you may not enter the time of trial.

The rabbi is kissed and arrested

47Yet while he was speaking, look, a crowd came, and the one called Yehuda, one of the twelve, was leading them, and he came up to Yeshua to kiss him.

48And Yeshua said to him,

---

247. Isa. 5.12.

248. Verses 22.43–44 appear in some texts and not in others. They are not found in the earliest manuscripts.

Yehuda, are you betraying the earthly son
　　With a kiss?
49When his companions saw what was to happen, they said, "Sir, shall we strike with a sword?"

50And one of them struck a slave of the high priest and cut off his right ear.

51But Yeshua answered and said,
　　No more of this!
And he took hold of the man's ear and he healed him.

52Yeshua said to the ones coming against him, high priests and generals of the Temple and elders,
　　Did you come out with swords and clubs
　　As if I were a robber?
53Each day I was with you in the Temple,
　　You did not lay your hands on me.
　　But this is your hour and the power of darkness.

Shimon Kefa and the crowing cock

54They seized him and led him away and took him to the house of the high priest. Shimon Kefa was following at a distance. 55And when they lit a fire in the middle of the courtyard and sat down together, Shimon Kefa was among them. 56When a serving girl saw him sitting near the light, she stared at him and said, "This man was also with him."

57But he denied it, saying, "Woman, I do not know him."

58And after a short while someone else saw him and said, "You are also one of them."

But Shimon Kefa said, "Sir, I am not."

59And after an hour passed, another insisted, saying, "Truthfully, this man also was with him. He is even a Galilean."

60But Shimon Kefa said, "Sir, I do not know what you are saying."

And suddenly while he was speaking the cock crowed.

61The Lord turned and looked at Kefa, and Shimon Kefa remembered the words of the Lord, how he had told him,
　　"Before the cock crows today
　　You will deny me three times."
62And he went outside and wept bitterly.

Men holding Yeshua mock and beat him

63And the men who had hold of Yeshua ridiculed him, beat him, 64and blindfolding him questioned him, saying, "Prophesy! Who is it who hit you?"

65And they uttered many other blasphemies against him.

Before the Sanhedrin

66And when it was dawn, the elders of the people assembled, high priests and scholars, and they led him away to the Sanhedrin.[249] They said, 67"If you are the mashiah, tell us."

But he said to them,

> If I tell you, you will not believe me,
> 68And if I question you, you will not answer.
> 69But from now on the earthly son
> Will be sitting on the right of the power of God.[250]

70And they all said, "Then you are the son of God?"

But he said to them,

> You say that I am.

71Then they said, "Why do we still need a witness? For we ourselves have heard it from his mouth."

Chapter 23

Yeshua before Pilatus

Then the whole assembly rose as a multitude and led him before Pilatus.[251] 2And they began to accuse him, saying, "We found him misleading our nation, forbidding taxes to be paid to Caesar[252] and saying that he is the mashiah and king."

3Pilatus questioned him, "Are you the king of the Jews?"

He answered him and said,

> You say it.

---

249. The council.

250. Ps. 110.1.

251. Pilate.

252. For more information on this passage, please see Afterword.

4And Pilatus said to the high priests and the crowds, "I find no guilt in this man.²⁵³

5But they insisted, saying, "He inflames the people with his teaching throughout all Yehuda, from the Galil where he began and up to here."

6When Pilatus heard this, he asked whether the man was a Galilean, 7and learning that he was under the authority of Herod, who in these days was also in Yerushalayim, he sent him off to Herod.

Yeshua before Herod

8Herod was exceedingly pleased to see Yeshua, for he had heard about him and hoped to see him perform a miracle.²⁵⁴ 9And he questioned him at some length, but Yeshua gave him no answer.

10The high priests and scholars stood there, vehemently accusing him. 11Herod and his soldiers despised and mocked him, putting shining clothing on him, and sent him back to Pilatus. 12Herod and Pilatus became friends on that same day, though earlier they had been enemies.

Yeshua again before Pilatus

13Pilatus assembled the high priests and the leaders and the people 14and said to them, "You brought this man before me as one who was inciting the people to rebellion, and look, I have judged him in your presence and found him not guilty of any charges you bring against him. 15Nor did Herod, for he sent him back to us. And look, he has done nothing to deserve death. 16So I will have him flogged and release him.²⁵⁵

18But they all screamed together, "Take him away and release Bar Abba to us!"²⁵⁶

19Because of some uprising in the city, and a murder, he was there in prison.

20And again Pilatus spoke to them, wanting to let Yeshua go.

---

253. In this passage begins Pilate's exoneration.

254. In this context, the Greek σημεῖον (semcion), "sign," may be translated as "miracle."

255. Other ancient authorities add verse 17: "Now he was obliged to release someone for them for the festival."

256. Barabbas from the Greek Βαραββᾶς, from the Aramaic בַּר אַבָּא (bar abba), meaning "son of abba" (father).

21But they cried out saying, "Crucify! Crucify him!"

22A third time, he said to them, "What harm has this man done? I found nothing in him to deserve death. I will have him flogged[257] and let him go."

23But in loud voices they insistently demanded that he be crucified.

24And Pilatus decided to grant their demand. 25And he released the one they asked for, who had been thrown into prison for insurrection and murder. But Yeshua he delivered to their will.

Shimon a Cyrenian forced to carry the cross

26As they led him away, they seized a man named Shimon, a Cyrenian,[258] who was on his way in from the country, and they loaded the cross on him to carry it behind Yeshua. 27A huge crowd of people followed him and women who mourned and lamented him.

28And Yeshua turned to them and said,

> Daughters of Yerushalayim,[259] don't cry for me,
> But cry for yourselves and for your children,
> 29For look, the days are coming when they'll say,
> > Blessed are the barren and the wombs
> > That do not bear and breasts that do not nurse.
> 30Then they will say to the mountains,
> > "Fall upon us,"
> And say to the hills,
> > "Cover us."[260]
> 31If they do this when a tree is wet and green
> What may happen when it is dry?[261]

---

257. Flogged from the Greek παιδεύω (paideuo), meaning "to discipline as in whipping, flogging, or scourging."

258. From Cyrene, a city in Libya, where there was a large Jewish community.

259. The epithet "Daughters of Yerushalayim" from the Greek θυγατέρες Ἰερουσαλήμ (thygateres Ierousalem), from the Hebrew בְּנוֹת יְרוּשָׁלַיִם (benot yerushalayim) is from the Song of Songs.

260. Hos. 10.14. Can be read, by extension, as "bury us."

261. Ezek. 20.47. In his last speech prior to his resignation, as always Yeshua speaks in aphoristic verse, citing the prophets, here enigmatically, probably to suggest that if the messiah is here now to help them, what will happen when he is gone.

Crucifying him

32Two other men, both criminals, were led away to be executed. 33When they came upon a place called Skull,[262] there they crucified him and the criminals, one on the right, one on the left. 34[And Yeshua said,

> Father, forgive them.
> They do not know what they are doing.][263]

The soldiers divided up his clothing and cast lots for it. 35The people stood around watching.

But the leaders ridiculed him, saying, "He saved others, let him save himself if he is God's mashiah, the chosen one."

36The soldiers also came up to him, ridiculed him, offering him sour wine,[264] and they said, 37"If you are king of the Jews, save yourself!"

38And there was a sign over him:

THIS ONE THE KING OF THE JEWS.

With me in paradise

39One of the criminals hanging there insulted him and said, "Are you not the mashiah? Save yourself and us!"

40But the other one reproved the first criminal and said, "Do you not fear God, since you shared the same sentence? 41And we were justly punished, and are getting what we deserve, but he did nothing wrong." 42Then he said, "Yeshua, remember me [when you enter your kingdom]."[265]

43And Yeshua replied,

> Amain, I say to you, today you will be with me
> In paradise.

---

262. In the other gospels, the Place of the Skull is identified as Golgotha. "Golgotha" is from the Greek Γολγοθα (Golgotha), from the Aramaic גָּלְגָּלְתָּא (gulgulta).

263. The passage in brackets is not included in many ancient texts and is often omitted or placed in notes.

264. Also translated as "poor wine" or "vinegar." See note 189 on Matthew 27.48 where a sympathetic bystander, not a soldier, offers the wine.

265. These words are not found in very early manuscripts.

Darkness at noon

44And it was noon and darkness came over the whole land until three in the afternoon,[266] 45the sun was eclipsed, and the curtain of the Temple was torn down the middle.

46Yeshua cried out in a great voice,

> Father, into your hands I commend my spirit.[267]

As he said this he breathed his last.

47When the centurion, commander of the company of soldiers, saw what had happened, he glorified God, saying, "Surely this was a just man.[268]

48And when all the crowds gathered for this spectacle saw what had happened, they beat their chests and went away. 49But those who were known to him and also the women who had followed him from the Galil stood at a distance, watching all this.

The body in linen entombed in rock

50And look, there was a man by the name of Yosef, and though a member of the Sanhedrin,[269] he was a good and a just man 51and had not

---

266. The Greek has the sixth hour (noon) and the ninth hour (three in the afternoon). Yeshua had been on the cross since the third hour, about nine in the morning.

267. In Luke we have a Yeshua who is without protest and with confidence in paradise that very day, for himself and his companions on the cross. His last words bespeak faith in the father to whom he is returning: "Father, into your hands I commend my spirit." In Mark and Matthew, however, Yeshua's last words leave us in doubt and with open interpretation. The human immediacy of those last words "Lord, why have you abandoned me?" makes Yeshua into a supremely solitary soul bespeaking human desperation and reproof at his abandonment by the father who, it appears, has not intervened to alter his pain and momentary death.

268. Innocent from the Greek δίκαιος (dikaios), translated literally as "just" or "righteous," may be read by implication as "innocent." That the military commander of the Roman death squad, who presumably oversaw executions on a routine basis, should at the instant of killing his victim glorify the Jewish God Yahweh and declare Yeshua a righteous or innocent man suggests a miracle of conversion or an invention by author or copyist. This specific apology for Rome, making the executioner pious, jolts human credulity. For more information on the centurion, see note 142 on Luke 7.2, note 174 on Mark 15.39, and note 191 on Matthew 27.54.

269. The council, which was said to have voted to have Yeshua killed.

agreed with the council and their action. He was from Arimathaia,[270] a city of the Jews, and he was waiting for the kingdom of God. 52He came to Pilatus and asked for the body of Yeshua. 53Then he took it down, wrapped it in linen cloth, and placed it in a tomb cut in the rock where no one had yet been laid. 54It was the day of Preparation and Shabbat was dawning.[271]

55The women who had come from Galil with him followed Yosef and saw the tomb and how his body was laid in it. 56Then they returned and prepared spices and myrrh. And on Shabbat they rested according to the commandment.

Chapter 24

The women at the empty tomb

On the first day of the week at early dawn the women came to the tomb, bringing the spices which they had prepared. 2And they found that the stone had been rolled away from the tomb, 3and when they went inside they did not find the body [of the lord Yeshua].[272]

4And it happened that while they were at a loss about this, look, two men stood near them in clothing that gleamed like lightning.

5The women were terrified and bowed their faces to the earth but the men said to them,

Why do you look for the living among the dead?
6He is not here, but has risen.
Remember how he spoke to you when you were in the Galil,
7"The earthly son must be delivered into the hands
Of the wrongdoers

---

270. Arimathea from the Greek Ἀριμαθαία (Arimathaia). Among places the city may be is ancient Ramathaim, also called Ramah, the birthplace of Samuel. It is identified uncertainly with present-day Ramallah, fifteen or twenty miles east of Jaffa.

271. Shabbat (the Sabbath) begins at sunset on Friday evening. The dawning of Shabbat leaves unsaid the time between Friday sunset and Saturday dawn.

272. The words in brackets are omitted in early manuscripts.

And be crucified

And on the third day he shall rise again."

8And they remembered his words.

Women inform messengers

9When they returned from the tomb they reported all this to the eleven and to the others. 10The women were Miryam of Magdala and Yohannah and Miryam of Yaakov and the other women with them. They told the messengers these things, 11and to them their words seemed madness. They did not believe them.

12[But Shimon Kefa got up and ran to the tomb and bending over saw only the linen cloth, and he left, wondering what had happened.][273]

On the road to Emmaous

13And look, on the same day, two of them were traveling to a village about seven miles from Yerushalayim, whose name was Emmaous,[274] 14and they were speaking to each other about all that took place. 15And it happened that during their talk and discussion Yeshua came near and went with them. 16But their eyes were kept from recognizing him.

17He said to them,

What are these words you are exchanging

With each other as you walk along?

And they stood still, downcast. 18One of them whose name was Kleopas answered and said to him, "Are you the only one visiting Yerushalayim who does not know what happened there in these days?"

19He said to them,

What things?

And they said to him, "The things about Yeshua the Natzrati,[275] who was a prophet powerful in act and word, before God and all the

---

273. The words in brackets are omitted in some manuscripts.

274. Emmaous from the Greek Ἐμμαοῦς (Emmaous). The location of the village cannot be stated with certainty.

275. Nazarene. Also translated as "Yeshua of Natzeret."

people, 20and how our high priests and leaders[276] handed him over to the
judgment of death and they crucified him. 21We had hoped that he was
going to redeem Yisrael. But now it is already the third day since these
things occurred. 22And more, some women among us amazed us. They
went at dawn to the tomb, 23and did not find the body and came back
saying they saw a vision of angels who say that he is alive. 24Then some
of us went back to the tomb and found it as the women said, but did not
see him.

    25And he said to them,

> O what fools and slow of heart you are to believe
> All that the prophets spoke!
>   26Did not the mashiah have to suffer this
> And enter into his glory?

    27And starting with Moshe and through all the prophets he explained
to them all the things in the Torah concerning himself.[277]

    28And as they approached the village they were traveling to, he

---

276. Our from the Greek ἡμῶν (hemon) "our," the gen. pl. Here, in the resurrection, in contrast to earlier ethnic and religious detachment from identity with Jewish priests and authorities, the speakers at last say "our," mending their estrangement
from Jewish identity. Prior to this moment, the evil ones, meaning those without
faith in Yeshua as the messiah, have been "they" or "the Jews," implying that "they"
the accusers were not themselves Jews. These shifts in pronouns for purposes of
religious politics reflect later scribal redaction. At the end of Luke, the "their" has
become "our" high priests and authorities, and the Jewish sects are seen under one
emblem, while the "they" that follows is reserved for the Roman crucifiers. These
pronominal changes are of significance, since this recounting of Yeshua's life and
death and resurrection is a didactic interruption in the dramatic narration of Yeshua's companionship with his followers on the road to Emmaous.

277. Verse 27 is another interruption in the drama. After Yeshua's taunting of his followers as fools for their less-than-total faith in him as the messiah, which he has
confirmed through his suffering and death for them, there appear two contrasting
messages: one, the routinely didactic lines from the imagination of later churchmen
reporting the Hebrew Bible, from Moses on, as an unbroken prophesy concerning
the coming of Yeshua; and two, the climactic passage of Yeshua walking through the
village with his students, who entreat him to stay with them. His students feel, yet
do not know, who he is until the instant he vanishes from them, when they recognize
him by his presence and speech and because their hearts have been on fire.

pretended to be going on further. 29They entreated him, "Stay with us. It is almost evening and the day has fallen."

So he went in to stay with them.

30And it happened that as he reclined at the table with them, he took the bread and blessed it and broke it and gave it to them.

31Then their eyes opened and they recognized him. But he vanished from them.278

32They said to each other, "Were our hearts not burning inside us when he talked to us on the road as he revealed the Torah to us?"

Yeshua with the eleven messengers in Yerushalayim

33And they rose up in that very hour and returned to Yerushalayim, and found the eleven and those with them.

34They said, "The lord has truly risen and he appeared to Shimon."

35Then they described the things on the road and how they recognized him in the breaking of the bread.

36While they were saying these things, he stood in their midst [and said to them:

    Peace be with you].279

37They were startled and full of fear and thought they were looking at a ghost.

38And he said to them,

    Why are you shaken and why do doubts rise
    In your hearts?
    39Look at my hands and my feet
    And see I am myself.
    Touch me and see,
    Because a ghost does not have flesh and bones
    Which as you see I have.

40[And when he said this, he showed them his hands and feet.]280

41And when in their joy they still could not believe him and wondered, he said to them,

---

278. Or, "he became unseen to them."

279. The words in brackets are omitted in some texts.

280. Other authorities lack verse 40.

Do you have something to eat?

42They gave him a piece of broiled fish.

43And he took it and in their presence he ate it.

44Then he said to them,

> These are my words which I spoke to you
> While I was still with you:
> All that was written about me in the law of Moshe
> And the prophets and Psalms must be fulfilled.[281]

45Then he opened their minds to an understanding of the Torah, 46and he said to them,

> It is written that the mashiah is to suffer and to rise
> From the dead on the third day,
> 47And in his name you will preach repentance
> And forgiveness of sins to all nations,
> Beginning with Yerushalayim.
> 48You are the witnesses.
> 49And look, I am sending the promise of my father
> To you.
> So stay in the city
> Until you are clothed with power from on high.[282]

---

281. In these words the author of Luke has Yeshua declare his Hebrew Bible inheritance as the foretold messiah.

282. Mark ends abruptly, powerfully, and mysteriously; Matthew and John dramatically and with great pathos. Here the drama is also intense until these last ecclesiastical instructions to prepare witnesses for the missionary duties of the church. The instructions "to stay in the city / until you are clothed with power from on high" serve as a perfect afterword to the road and house scenes, and this last formal message contains hope and a promise of power to be delivered from the father on high to the faithful, who will go out from the city to preach the good news. The dramatic narration of the post-crucifixion gospel ends by verse 44, however, preceding the send-off, with the immensely poignant gloom of the followers at the earthly loss of the messiah, their joy at the recognition on the road and at the breaking of the bread, the plain reality and immediacy of his instructions to look at his mutilations of hand and feet—"Touch me and see"—and his last human act, which is to ask for food and then, in the presence of the intimates, to eat the cooked fish.

In Beit Aniyah Yeshua raises his hands and blesses and is carried into the sky

50And he led them out as far as Beit Aniyah, and raised his hands and blessed them. 51And it happened that while he blessed them, he departed from them [and was carried up into the sky].[283]

52And they [worshiped him and][284] returned to Yerushalayim with great joy, 53and they were constantly in Temple blessing God.

---

283. The words in brackets are omitted in some texts.
284. The words in brackets are omitted in some texts.

Yohanan
(John)

Yohanan[1]
(John)

THE PROLOGUE of the Gospel of John, "In the beginning was the word," imitates the first words of the creation in Genesis, "In the beginning God created the heavens and the earth." The word "prologue" in Greek includes *logos*, and *logos* was a familiar philosophical term, already in Greek currency through its usage by the pre-Socratic philosopher Heraclitus and by the Stoics. John uses logos to convey a specific message. The word is the divine savior, who comes into the world to bring hope and eternal life. The "word became flesh" is Yeshua, God's emissary incarnated in the world. In contrast to the synoptic gospels (Mark, Matthew, and Luke), where Yeshua's divinity is always elusive—here and not there—John states that Yeshua is the messiah, that the messiah is divine, and that he is the son of God.

In the prologue there is also an emphasis on light and darkness, on truth and lies, which seems to be in harmony with dichotomies found in the Dead Sea Scrolls of the Essene community. And finally, in the richest and most eloquent passages of spiritual inquiry, which characterize John, there must be observed a strong Gnostic element. In short, John is a mirror to a time of diverse beliefs and philosophies. Key terms and concepts, from the Neoplatonist Jew Philo of Alexandria to the scrolls of the Essenes and the Gnostics, flash in and out of his text with unusual intensity.

1. John from the Greek Ἰωάννης (Ioannes), from the Hebrew יוֹחָנָן (yohanan). It can also be written as *Yochanan*.

445

The authorship of John is a complex puzzle for which there is no solution. Traditionally, the author is John, son of Zebedee, one of Yeshua's disciples and apostles. For many reasons, including the probable dating of the work, this view is not generally accepted today. We do not know the name of the author. Some scholars suggest that the author of the prologue may not be the author of the rest of the gospel or that it may even be the work of a Johannine community (those who followed John's ideas).

John is distinct from the synoptic gospels in many ways. There is no Sermon on the Mount. Yeshua tells no parables (except of the good shepherd), heals no lepers. Demons are not exorcised, there is no Lord's Prayer or Last Supper, and the notion of religious instruction and moral teachings found in the synoptics is transformed into metaphysical discourse. As in the other gospels, the Book of John does use miracles as "signs" to prove the powers of the messiah and God. However, by contrast, Yeshua is a more abstracted figure; and the presentation of his crucifixion, in contrast to that of the other gospels, is not of an especially suffering man, tortured and dying for human sin, but of a controlled, even aloof, figure, following his own divine purpose without fear. There are similarities to the language of Apocalypse, which is ascribed to John. In both texts Yeshua is the Word and the Lamb of God. But it should be emphasized that the apocalyptic nature of Revelation—the epic vision of heaven and hell, the phantasmagoric images—is wholly apart from anything found in the Gospel of John and alone discredits the traditional notion of common authorship.

There is a special problem with regard to the Jews, who did not accept Christ as the promised messiah. Like Matthew, John is a deeply Jewish gospel, steeped in Old Testament thought and allusion. But more than in Matthew, the reference to Jews as the opponents is fierce and constant, while at the same time the gospel vividly presents Yeshua as a Jew and rabbi. One explanation for John's presentation of this intramural struggle between Jews lies in the politics of his own later time. If, as many scholars believe, John dates from early in the second century, anywhere from 100 to near 150 C.E., then it is probable that he is addressing the increasingly tense struggle in many parts of the diaspora world, especially in Asia Minor, between Christian Jews and non-Christian Jews for their place in the synagogues.

Above all, John is a literary document of the Bible. The prologue is magic for believers or nonbelievers, surely one of the summit moments in world literature. As Mark is the most poignant and dramatic, Matthew perhaps the most poetic, Luke the most literarily accomplished in its telling of the nativity and the parables, John is the most spiritual, philosophical, and independent of the gospels.

Chapter 1

In the beginning was the word
　　In the beginning was the word[2]
　　And the word was with God,
　　And God was the word.
　2The word was in the beginning with God.
　3Through it[3] everything came about
　　And without it not a thing came about.
　　What came to be 4in the word was life
　　And the life was the light of people

---

2. John informs us in "In the beginning was the word," Ἐν ἀρχῇ ἦν ὁ λόγος (En arhe en ho logos) (John 1.1). God created through the word, ὁ λόγος. With that utterance God translates divine sound into matter and being, thereby bringing the cosmos, the earth, and the earth's inhabitants, great and small, into temporal existence. The creation through the word in John parallels the creation in Genesis 1.1 of the Hebrew Bible: "In the beginning when God created the heavens and the earth": בְּרֵאשִׁית בָּרָא אֱלֹהִים אֵת הַשָּׁמַיִם וְאֵת הָאָרֶץ (bereshit bara elohim et hashamayim veet ha-aretz). God in Genesis uses "the word" to speak the world into being through his order, "Let there be light," יְהִי אוֹר (yehi or), while in John "the word" of creation may be spoken or written, but it also is the initial cause of creation. And as in the Hebrew Bible, that word is immediately commingled with light. It has been observed that in John's prologue, the use of the logos offers a link between the divine mind and the human mind, which is rational and apprehends the word through reason, reason being another meaning of *logos*. This beginning is often presumed to be a separate poem added or adapted to the gospel.

John is considered the most Gnostic of the gospels, and especially in its prologue. The logical sequence of this poem also suggests the syllogistic reasoning of the Sophists as well as the Cynics to whom leading theologians sometimes compare Yeshua. See John Dominic Crossan, *The Birth of Christianity* (San Francisco: HarperSanFrancisco, 1998), and Burton L. Mack, *Who Wrote the New Testament? The Making of the Christian Myth* (San Francisco: HarperSanFrancisco, 1995). More broadly, *logos* may be given multiple meanings: the word of God, knowledge, science, the Greek principle of reason ordering the universe, and a Kabbalist principle of the primacy of creating words and, before words, an alphabet of letters, so that God has the means of speaking the universe into being.

3. "Through it" is also translated as "Through him."

5And the light in the darkness shines
And the darkness could not apprehend it.

Yohanan came to proclaim light[4]
6There was a man sent from God.
His name was Yohanan.[5]
7He came as a witness in testimony of the light
So that all might believe through him.
8He was not the light,
But came to testify about the light.[6]
9The light was the true light
Which illuminates every person
Who comes into the world.

Light was in the world
10He was in the world
And through him the world was born,
And the world did not know him.[7]
11He went to his own
And his own did not receive him.[8]

---

4. Yohanan the Dipper (John the Baptist).

5. John from the Greek Ἰωάννης (Ioannes), from the Hebrew יוֹחָנָן (yohanan).

6. Yohanan was not the light, meaning not Yeshua the Mashiah, but the lamp carrying the light, defining the testimony of Yohanan the Dipper (John the Baptist) as prophetic but in a secondary role to Yeshua, who is the messiah, and also suggesting rivalry between early followers of the messiah, some favoring Yohanan, who electrified Judaism with his arrival in ways foretold in Isaiah (Isa. 9.2, 42.6–7, 60.1–3). The majority favor Yeshua, but there is considerable evidence that by the second century of the Common Era the number of those favoring Yohanan over Yeshua as the messiah was increasing alarmingly.

7. Yeshua the Mashiah.

8. The Jews in Isaiah and other prophets spoke of one messiah, whom the majority of Jews did not accept when he came. The Jews who did recognize Yeshua, the early messianics, who late in the first century broke off from mainstream Jewry, were the Christian Jews (meaning "messianics," followers of the messiah). They shared with traditional Jews the Torah as their sole holy scripture, since the New Testament was not to be firmly set and canonized until centuries later.

12To all who received him
   He gave power to become the children of God,
   To those who believed in his name,
13Who were born not from blood
   Or from the will of the flesh
   Or from the will of a man,
   But were born of God.

Word became flesh
   14And the word became flesh
   And lived among us.9
   And we gazed on his glory,
   The glory of the only son born of the father,
   Who is filled with grace and truth.

*Yohanan cries out about him who will come after
and who was before*
   15Yohanan testifies about him and cries out, saying,
      He is the one of whom I said,
      "One who will come after me was before me,
      Because before me he was."
   16From his bounty we have all received grace upon grace,
   17And as the law was given through Moshe,10
      Grace and truth have come through Yeshua the Galilean.
   18No one has ever seen God.
      Only the one born of God,11
      Who is in the heart of his father,
      He has made him known.

---

9. God's word became human flesh in the person of Yeshua.

10. Moses from the Greek Μωϋσῆς (Moyses), from the Hebrew מֹשֶׁה (moshe).

11. Other texts have "only begotten son."

In the desert Yohanan the Dipper denies being the mashiah

19And this is the testimony of Yohanan the Dipper when the Jews[12] sent priests and Levites from Yerushalayim[13] to ask him, "Who are you?"

20And he confessed and made no denial, but confessed, "I am not the mashiah."

21They asked him, "What then? Are you Eliyahu?"[14]

He said, "I am not."

"Are you the prophet?"

He answered, "No."

22"Who are you? Give us an answer for those who sent us here. What do you say about yourself?"

23He said,

> I am the voice of one crying out in the desert:
> "Make straight the way of Adonai,"
> As the prophet Yeshayahu said.[15]

24Now they had been sent by the Prushim. 25They questioned him and said to him, "Why do you dip if you are not the mashiah or Eliyahu or the prophet?"

---

12. The Jews. All the people in these scenes are Jews. The appellation "Jew" here and in most places in John has two functions: to distinguish Jews who do not believe Yeshua to be the son of God from those who do; and to cast hatred on and condemn the unbelievers to immediate and eternal punishment at the day of judgment. Such usage of "Jew" cannot reflect initial texts of John but is an anachronism of later interpolators. The followers of Yeshua were initially few in number among the many sects that made up the Jewish population. All thought themselves Jews—Jews and Christian Jews. Therefore, naming the Jews as a hated community existing alongside Yeshua and his follower Jews is linguistically unlikely. Such usage reflects the later competitive period of nascent Christianity when the Jews had expelled Christian Jews from the synagogues and when the traditional Jews, in turn, became the vilified enemy.

13. Jerusalem from the Greek Ἰερουσαλήμ (Ierousalem), from the Hebrew יְרוּשָׁלַיִם (yerushalayim).

14. Elijah from the Greek Ἠλίας (Elias), from the Hebrew אֵלִיָּהוּ (eliyahu).

15. Isa. 40.3. Isaiah from the Greek Ἠσαΐας (Esaias), from the Hebrew יְשַׁעְיָהוּ (yeshayahu). Pharisees from the Greek Φαρισαῖος (Farisaisos), from the Hebrew פְּרוּשִׁים (prushim). "Pharisee" is *Parush*.

26He answered them,

> I dip in water.
> Among you stands one you do not know,

27One who will come after me,

> Whose sandal strap I am unworthy to loosen.

28All this happened in Beit Aniyah,[16] across the Yarden,[17] where Yohanan was dipping.

The lamb of God

29The next day Yohanan saw Yeshua coming toward him and said,

> Look, the lamb of God who takes away the wrong of the
>> world.
> He is the one of whom I have said,

30"A man is coming after me who was before me,

> Because before me he was."

31And I did not know him,

> But so that he might be known in Yisrael[18]
> Is why I came dipping in water.

Spirit descending like a dove

32And Yohanan testified, saying,

> I saw the spirit descending like a dove from the sky
> And it rested on him 33and I did not know him,
> But the one who sent me to dip in water said,
> "The one on whom you see the spirit descend and rest,
> He is the one dipping in holy spirit."

34And I have seen and I have testified that he is the son of God.

We have found the mashiah, meaning "the anointed"

35The next day Yohanan again was standing with two of his students.

---

16. Bethany from the Greek Βηθανία (Bethania), from the Hebrew בֵּית אָנִיָה (beit aniyah).

17. Jordan from the Greek Ἰορδάνης (Iordanes), from the Hebrew יַרְדֵן (yarden).

18. Israel from the Greek Ἰσραήλ (Israel), from the Hebrew יִשְׂרָאֵל (yisrael).

36When he saw Yeshua walking by, he said,

> Look, the lamb of God.

37His two students heard him speaking and they followed Yeshua. 38And Yeshua turned and saw them following him and said,

> What are you looking for?

"Rabbi," which translated means teacher,[19] "where are you staying?" 39"He told them,

> Come and see.

So they came and saw where he was staying, and stayed with him that day. It was about four in the afternoon.

40One of the two who heard Yohanan and followed him was Andreas,[20] brother of Shimon[21] Kefa.[22] 41First he found his own brother Shimon and told him, "We have found the mashiah" (meaning "the anointed").[23]

42He led Shimon to Yeshua.

Looking at him, Yeshua said,

> You are Shimon, the son of Yohanan.

---

19. After Yeshua is addressed as "Rabbi," the next phrase, ῥαββί, ὃ λέγεται μεθερμηνευόμενον διδάσκαλε (rabbi, ho legetai methermeneuomenon didaskale), "which translated means teacher," is a scribal aside that appears to be a later interpolation whose purpose is to persuade the reader that "rabbi" meant a "teacher" or "scholar" rather than a rabbi of the Jews, whose profession was to lead a congregation and interpret Jewish law. "Rabbi" is a Greek word, reproducing in the Hebrew רַבִּי (rabbi), meaning "rabbi," "master," "great one," or "teacher."

20. Andrew from the Greek Ἀνδρέας (Andreas).

21. Simon from the Greek Σίμων, from the Hebrew שִׁמְעוֹן (shimon).

22. Shimon Kefa is Simon Peter. Peter from the Greek Πέτρος (Petros), translated from the Aramaic כֵּיפָא (kefa), meaning "rock" or "stone." In 1 Corinthians 1.12 and elsewhere, Paul Hellenizes כֵּיפָא (kefa), calling Peter Κηφᾶς (Kefas), traditionally Latinized in English as "Cephas." In Greek, as in French (but not in English), the name and the word for "stone" are related as in "Pierre" (the name) and "pierre" (stone).

23. Anointed is the Christ. Christ is from the Greek Χριστος (Hristos), "the anointed," an attribute of the messiah; in the New Testament, Greek Χριστος is used almost synonymously with Μεσσίας (Messias), a Hellenized transliteration of the Hebrew מָשִׁיחַ (mashiah). The parenthetical scribal aside "meaning 'the anointed'" suggests an earlier text in Aramaic or Hebrew.

You will be called Kefa,
(which is translated Petros).[24]

Rabbi, you are the son of God

43The next day Yeshua wished to go out to the Galil.[25] He found
Filippos[26] and said to him,

Follow me.

44Now Filippos was from Beit Tzaida,[27] the city of Andreas and Shimon
Kefa. 45Filippos found Natanel[28] and said to him, "The one whom Moshe
wrote about in the Torah[29] and whom the prophets describe, we have
found, Yeshua, son of Yosef,[30] from Natzeret.[31]

46And Natanel said to him, "Can anything good come out of
Natzeret?"

"Come and see!" Filippos replied.

47Yeshua saw Natanel coming to him and said of him,

Look, a true Jew,[32] one in whom there is no cunning.

---

24. By calling Peter "Kefa," meaning "stone," Yeshua is here suggesting that Peter
will be the rock of the church. There is an irony in this prediction, since elsewhere
in the gospels Yeshua chooses Peter to ridicule among his students. Yeshua predicts
that Peter will deny him three times, and, after the crucifixion, Peter is beaten by
Yeshua's unnamed but "most beloved" student in their race to find Yeshua in the
empty tomb.

25. Galilee from the Greek Γαλιλαία (Galilaia), from the Hebrew גָּלִיל (galil).
"Galil" is a "circle," "district," or "province." It is often used in the phrase גְּלִיל הַגּוֹיִם
(galil hagoyim), meaning "province of the goyim (gentiles)."

26. Philip from the Greek Φίλιππος (Filippos). Accent is on the first *i*.

27. Bethseda from the Greek Βηθσαϊδά (Bethsaida), from the Hebrew בֵּית עֵידָא
(beit tzaida), which is a place north of Lake Gennesaret.

28. Nathanael from the Greek Ναθαναήλ (Nathanael), from the Hebrew נְתַנְאֵל
(netanel).

29. "The Law" in Hebrew is "Torah." Torah most commonly means the five books of
Moses as well as the entire Hebrew Bible.

30. Joseph from the Greek Ἰωσήφ (Iosef), from the Hebrew/Aramaic יוֹסֵף
(yosef).

31. Nazareth from the Greek Ναζαρέτ (Natzaret), unknown village in Galilee probably spelled "Natzeret."

32. The Greek reads Ἰσραηλίτης (Israelites), from the Hebrew (yisraeli), corresponding to "Israeli." Because translations from the Hebrew Bible translate יִשְׂרְאֵלִי

48"How do you know me?" Natanel said.

Yeshua answered,

> Before Filippos called you,
> You were under the fig tree and I saw you.

49Natanel answered, "Rabbi, you are the son of God! You are the king of Yisrael!"

50Yeshua responded, saying,

> Because I told you I saw you under the fig tree,
> Do you believe?

51You will see even greater things.

And he said to him,

> Amain, amain, I say to you,
> You will see the sky open
> And angels of God ascending and descending
> Upon the earthly son.[33]

Chapter 2

Wine and water at a wedding in Kana

On the third day there was a wedding in Kana[34] in the Galil, and Yeshua's mother was there. 2Yeshua and his students had also been invited to the wedding. 3And when the wine gave out, Yeshua's mother said to him, "They have no wine."

---

as "Israelite" (rather than "Israeli," which is accurate), and the Greek New Testament uses the word "Jews" exclusively for the bad Jews and avoids labeling Yeshua or his followers as Jews, here, where the obvious word in Greek should, in first-century Aramaic and Hebrew, be "Jew," the Greek text resurrects "Israelites" (Ἰσραηλίτης) in shocking consistency with its pattern of depicting good Jews as vaguely non-Jews, like John the Baptist and Mary, and nonfollowers as Jews. In the odd instance of Nathanael, there is no recourse but to reach back to the Hebrew Bible and, ignoring time, safely call him an untainted, true *Israelite*. Had any earlier translation gone directly to the Hebrew for "Israelite" rather than to its Greek version, it would have found Hebrew יִשְׂרְאֵלִי, that is, "Israeli," not "Israelite," and it would be clear to today's reader that a biblical Israeli and Jew are one and the same. "Israelite" is from the Greek nominative case version of "Israeli."

33. See note 31 on Mark 2.10 for "earthly son."

34. Cana. A village, probably Khirbert Qana, some miles north of Nazareth.

4Yeshua said to her,
> What is that to me and you, woman?[35]
> My hour has not yet come.

5His mother said to the servants, "Do what he tells you."

6Now there were six waterpots of stone standing there for the Jewish custom of washing,[36] each holding two or three measures.[37]

7Yeshua said to them,
> Fill the pots with water.

They filled them to the brim.

8And he said to them,
> Now pour some of the water out
> And take it to the master of the feast.

They took it.

9When the master of the feast tasted the water become wine, not knowing where it came from—though the servants knew, those who had drawn the water—he called the bridegroom 10and said to him, "Everybody serves the good wine first, and when the guests are drunk brings out the inferior kind. You have been saving the good wine till now."

11Yeshua did this, the first of his miraculous signs in Kana in the Galil, and he revealed his glory, and his students believed in him.

Days in Kfar Nahum with family and students

12After this he went down to Kfar Nahum[38] with his mother and brothers and students. They stayed there for a few days.

---

35. The gruff use of γύναι (gynai), "woman," rather than κυρία (kyria), "lady," is softened in many translations to "Dear woman" (New International Version), and "Madame" (Lattimore). However, in King James Version and New Revised Standard Version it remains "woman."

36. Washing hands in rite of purification.

37. Twenty or thirty gallons.

38. Capernaum. Latin *Capernaum* from the Greek Καφαρναούμ (Kafarnaoum), from the Hebrew כְּפַר נַחוּם (kfar nahum), meaning "village of Nahum." A prosperous town or city near the north end of the Sea of Galilee that Yeshua made a center for his work.

Pesach in Yerushalayim and driving vendors from the Temple

13It was almost the Pesach[39] of the Jews and Yeshua went up to Yerushalayim. 14In the Temple he found the people selling oxen and sheep and doves, and the coin changers sitting there. 15He made a whip out of ropes and drove out all the animals, the sheep and the oxen. He also scattered the coins of the changers and knocked over their tables. 16To the dove sellers he said,

> Get these things out of here!
> Do not make the house of my father
> A house of business![40]

17His students remembered how the Psalms say:

> Zeal for your house will consume me.[41]

18Then the Jews said to him, "What sign can you show us for doing this?"

19Yeshua answered,

> Destroy this Temple
> And in three days I shall raise it up.

20Then the Jews said, "This Temple was built over forty-six years, and you will raise it up in three days?"

21But he was speaking about the Temple of his body. 22After he was raised from the dead, his students remembered what he said and they believed the scripture and the word which Yeshua said.

Yeshua's wondrous signs in Yerushalayim
and his knowledge of people

23When he was in Yerushalayim during the Pesach suppers, many people believed in his name, seeing the wondrous signs he was doing. 24But Yeshua would not entrust himself to them, because he knew all

---

39. Passover from the Greek πάσχα (pasha), from the Hebrew פֶּסַח (pesach). Festival of the Matzot Bread is the Festival of Unleavened Bread. Pesach, meaning "passed over," refers to the escape from bondage in Egypt, celebrated at the Seder by eating the paschal lamb. See Exodus 12.1–13.16.

40. For location of vendors see note 119 on Mark 11.16.

41. Ps. 69.9.

people 25and because he had no need to have anyone testify about a person and he knew what was in a person.

Chapter 3

With Nakdeimon, speaking of spirit and light

Now there was a Parush named Nakdeimon,[42] a leader of the Jews. 2He came to Yeshua at night and said, "Rabbi, we know that you came as a teacher from God since no one can perform these wondrous signs if God were not with him."

3Yeshua answered,

> Amain,[43] amain, I say to you,
> Unless you are born from above
> You cannot see the kingdom of God.

4"How can one be born when one is old?" he asked. "One cannot enter a mother's womb a second time and be born."

5Yeshua answered,

> Amain, amain, I say to you,
> Unless you are born from water and the wind of God[44]
> You cannot enter the kingdom of God.

> 6What is born from the flesh is flesh,
> What is born from the wind is wind.

---

42. Nicodemus from the Greek Νικόδημος (Nikodemos). Originally a Greek word, *Nikodemos* was Hebraized to נַקְדִּימוֹן (nakdeimon). A Parush is a Pharisee.

43. Amen from the Greek ἀμήν (amen), from the Hebrew אָמֵן (amein). The Hebrew word *amain* (*amein* would work just as well for free-sounding English) was used by Paul in his Greek, as it is used in Hebrew at the end of a passage as a liturgical "in truth" or "so be it." Both the Greek and Hebrew words were probably pronounced with a long ay, as in "main." It is appropriate to pronounce English "amen," as in Greek and Hebrew; hence here it is given as *amain*.

44. From the Greek πνεύματος (pneumatos), "of the wind." The Greek τὸ πνεῦμα (to pneuma) is "the wind," and in the New Testament, by metaphorical abstraction, may also mean "the spirit." Verse 3.8 begins, "The wind [τὸ πνεῦμα] blows," where πνεῦμα clearly retains its classical, particular meaning of "wind."

> Do not wonder that I told you
> 7You must be born again from above.

> 8The wind blows where it wants to and you hear its sound
> But you cannot know where it comes from and where it goes.
> So it is for everyone born from the wind of God.
> 9"How can these things happen?" Nakdeimon asked.
> 10Yeshua said to him,
> You are the teacher of Yisrael and do you not know this?
> 11Amain, amain, I say to you,
> We speak of what we know and we testify to what we have
> seen,
> Yet you do not receive our testimony.
> 12If I tell you of earthly things and you do not believe,
> How if I tell you of heavenly things will you believe?
> 13And no one has gone up into the sky
> Except the one who came down from the sky, the earthly
> son.
> 14And as Moshe raised up the snake in the desert,
> The earthly son must be raised up
> 15So that all who believe in him will have eternal life.

God's only son

> 16God loved the world so much he gave his only son
> So that all who believe in him might not be destroyed but
> have eternal life.
> 17For God did not send his son into the world to judge the
> world
> But so through him the world might be saved.
> 18One who believes in him is not judged
> But one who does not believe is judged already
> For not believing in the name of God's only son.

The light

> 19And this is the judgment:
> Light came into the world
> And people loved the darkness rather than the light,

For their works were cunning.

20For all who do shoddy things[45] hate the light

And do not come toward the light

So that their works will not be exposed.

21But those who do the truth come toward the light

So their works may shine as accomplished through God.[46]

Yeshua dipping in Yehuda

22After this Yeshua and his students came into the land of Yehuda.[47] He stayed there with them and dipped.

Yohanan dipping and speaking of the mashiah

23Yohanan also was dipping in Einayim[48] near Shalem,[49] since there were many waters there, and the people came and were immersed. 24Yohanan had not yet been thrown into prison.

25There was a dispute between Yohanan's students and a Jew[50] about ceremonial washing. 26They came toward Yohanan and said, "Rabbi, the one who was with you across the Yarden, to whom you testified, look, he is dipping all who come to him."

27Yohanan answered,

No one can receive anything unless it comes from heaven.

28You are my witnesses. I said,

"I am not the mashiah but I am sent before him."

29He who has the bride is the groom.

---

45. From the Greek φαῦλα (faula), "slight," "trivial," "rough," or "paltry" rather than normal "evil" or "wicked." "Shoddy" suggests "sloppy work" with a darker implication.

46. Yeshua's distinctions between darkness and light and his emphasis on light as spiritual knowledge and salvation imbue this entire passage with Gnostic tenets.

47. Judea from the Greek Ἰουδαία (Ioudaia), from the Hebrew יְהוּדָה (yehuda). Also is the name Yehuda.

48. Ainon, Aenon from the Greek Αἰνών (Ainon), from the Hebrew עֵינַיִם (einayim), meaning "springs."

49. Salim from the Greek Σαλίμ (Salim), from the Hebrew שָׁלֵם (shalem).

50. In this context the Greek μετὰ Ἰουδαίου (meta Ioudaiou), "with a Jew," has been explained as a man from Judea (Yehuda) as opposed to another region of Israel. More likely it is simply to distinguish Yohanan from the Jews, which is how it comes through in Greek and English. Verse 22 already indicates that Yohanan is in Judea.

The groom's friend who stands near and hears him
  Is filled with joy at the groom's voice.
  So my happiness is completed.
30He must increase and I be diminished.

  31The one who comes from above is above all.
  The one who is of the earth is of the earth
  And speaks from the earth.
  The one who comes from the sky is above all.
32To what he has seen and heard he testifies,
  Yet his testimony no one receives.
33Who receives his testimony proves that God is true.
34Whom God sent speaks the words of God,
  For the wind of spirit he gives out is beyond measure.

35The father loves the son and has given all things into his
    hand.
36Who believes in the son has eternal life,
  But one who disbelieves the son will not see life.
  The wrath of God remains upon him.

Chapter 4

With a Shomron woman needing water
  Now when Yeshua realized that the Pharisees had heard that Yeshua
was converting and immersing more students than Yohanan (2though
it was not Yeshua himself who dipped them but his students), 3he left
Yehuda and went again into the Galil. 4But it was necessary to pass
through Shomron.[51] 5He came to a town in Shomron called Shehem[52]

---

51. Samaria from the Greek Σαμάρεια (Samareia), from the Hebrew שֹׁמְרוֹן (Shomron). Samaritan from the Greek Σαμαρίτης (Samarites), from the Hebrew שֹׁמְרֹנִי
(Shomroni). "Samaritans" (pl.) is *Shomronim*.

52. Sychar. *Sychar* is the Aramaic. The Greek Σψηάρ (Syhar) is probably a corruption
of Συχέμ (Syhem), from the Hebrew שְׁכֶם (shehem). *Sychar*, written *Shechem* in
the KJV can also be written *Shekhem* or *Shehem*. It is identified with nearby Jacob's
Well (Bir Yaakov), and modernly with the city of Nablus.

near the piece of land that Yaakov[53] gave his son Yosef. 6There was a well of Yaakov there. Yeshua was tired from the trip and sat down by the well. It was near noon.[54]

7A Shomron woman came to draw water.

Yeshua said to her, "Give me a drink." 8His students had gone off to the town to buy food.

9The Shomron woman said to him, "How can you a Jew ask to be given a drink by me, a Shomroni? Jews do not mingle with Shomronim.[55]

10Yeshua answered, saying to her,

> If you knew the gift of God and who is saying to you, "Give me a drink,"
> You would have asked and he would have given you living water.

11She said to him, "Sir, you have no bucket and the well is deep. Where

---

53. James (Jacob) from the Greek Ἰάκωβος (Iakobos), from the Hebrew יַעֲקֹב (yaakov).

54. Literally, "the sixth hour."

55. "Jews do not mingle with Samaritans" in other editions is put in brackets, parentheses, or a bottom-of-page note, which in effect acknowledges a later scribal commentary. It could be either way, and here it may be better not to set the phrase off as spurious. This notable identification of Yeshua as a Jew by an "outsider" Samaritan contradicts the prevalent dejudaizing of Yeshua and his circle and the normal use of Jew as Yeshua's deadly opponent. Revealed once again is the disturbed and confused nature of the scriptures, as we have it from multiple hands, which in contingent passages esteems and scourges the Jew. To speak of the Samaritan as not a Jew is problematic, since the Samaritans, from Samaria, were Jews among the main sects of Jews, which included Hasids, Essenes, Sadducees, and Pharisees, among whom, as suggested here with regard to Jerusalem Jews and Samaritan Jews, there was much intense rivalry. Individual branches often claimed to be the true Jews. The later rivalry after Yeshua's death between "traditional" and Christian Jews as to the messiah, laws, and rites was to lead to the main schism in Judaism. As to differences between Samaritans and other Jews, the sacred Samaritan capital was at Shechem, not Jerusalem, and its Temple, then in ruin, on Mount Gerizim. The Samaritans had their own version of the Torah (only the first five books were accepted by them), which was slightly different, and they claimed to be the true Israel, following Mosaic law, and opposing Jews from Jerusalem and its Temple. Here the Samaritan woman speaks of their common ancestor Jacob and common father, meaning "God."

do you have this living water? You are not greater than our father Yaakov
12who gave us the well and who himself drank and whose sons and cattle
drank."

13Yeshua answered her, saying,

> Everyone who drinks this water will be thirsty again.
> 14But whoever drinks the water I give them
> Will not be thirsty again.
> The water I give them will become in them
> A fountain of water springing into eternal life.

15The woman said to him, "Sir, give me this water so I won't be thirsty
or have to come here to draw it up."

16He said to her,

> Go and call your husband and come back here.

17She answered and said to him, "I have no husband."
Yeshua said to her,

> You are right to say, "I have no husband."
> 18You had five husbands and the one
> You have now
> Is not your husband.
> What you spoke is the truth.

19The woman said to him, "Sir, I see that you are a prophet. 20Our
parents[56] worshiped on this mountain and you say Yerushalayim is the
place where we must worship."

21Yeshua said to her,

> Believe me, woman, the hour is coming
> When not on this mountain
> Nor in Yerushalayim will you worship the father.
> 22You worship what you do not know.
> We worship what we know
> Since salvation is from the Jews.

---

56. Our parents from the Greek οἱ πατέρες ἡμῶν (hoi pateres hemon), "our fathers."
As in Greek, in contemporary European languages "our fathers" (as in the Spanish
nuestros padres or the French *nos pères*) is the common word for "parents" and, by
extension, "ancestors" or "forefathers."

23But the hour is coming and it is now
When the true worshipers will worship the father
In spirit and truth,
For the father seeks such people to worship him.
24God is spirit
And those worshiping must worship him
In spirit and truth.

25The woman said to him, "I know a mashiah is coming who is called the anointed. When he comes he will declare all things to us."
26Yeshua said to her,
I am he, talking to you.

Students and Shomronim are amazed by Yeshua

27At this his students came and were amazed that he was talking with a woman,[57] but no one said, "What are you looking for?" or "Why are you talking with her?"
28Then the woman left her waterpot and went back into the town and said to the people, 29"Come see a man who told me everything I ever did. Can he be the mashiah?"
30They went out of the town and came toward him.
31Meanwhile the students were saying, "Rabbi, eat."
32But he said to them,
I have a meat[58] to eat which you do not know.
33Then the students said to each other, "Could someone have brought him something to eat?"
34Yeshua said to them,
My meat is to do the will of him
Who sent me and to complete his work.

Grain for eternal life

35Do you not say,
"Four more months and then comes the harvest?"

---

57. It remains unclear whether the students' amazement is due to Yeshua's talking to a woman, a Samaritan woman, or perhaps to both notions.
58. Meat from the Greek βρῶσις (brosis), also means "food."

Look, I say to you, lift up your eyes
And you will see the fields are white for harvest.
36Already the reaper is taking his wages
And gathering the grain for the eternal life
So sower and reaper alike may be happy.
37The words of the proverb are true:
"One sows and another reaps."
38I sent you to reap what you did not labor.
Others worked and you entered their work.

Shomronim believe

39And many Shomronim from the city believed in him, because of what the woman said when she testified, "He told me everything I ever did." 40So when they came near him, the Shomronim asked him to stay with them.

He stayed there two days.

41And many more believed because of his word, 42and they said to the woman, "It is no longer because of your talk that we believe. We ourselves have heard and we know that he is truly the savior of the world."

Yeshua is received in the Galil

43After two days he went from there to the Galil, 44for Yeshua himself had testified that a prophet has no honor in his own country.[59] 45But when he came to the Galil, the Galileans welcomed him, for they had seen all the things he did in Yerushalayim during the festival days, since they too had gone to the festival.

In Kana, treating a sick prince

46Then he came again to Kana in the Galil, where he had made the water wine. There was a certain prince whose son was sick in Kfar Nahum.[60] 47When he heard that Yeshua had come from Yehuda into the

---

59. "Honor in his own country." See texts and/or notes on Mark 3.35, 6.4; Matthew 13.57; and Luke 4.24, 8.21.
60. Capernaum.

Galil, he went to him and asked him to come down and heal his son, for he was near death.

48Yeshua said to him,

> Unless you see signs and wonders
> You will not believe.

49The prince said to him, "Sir, come down before my child dies." 50Yeshua said to him,

> Go, your son lives.

The man believed the word Yeshua told him and left. 51And as he was going down, his slaves met him and told him that his son was alive.

52So he asked them at what hour[61] he had gotten better.

They told him, "Yesterday at the seventh hour[62] the fever left him."

53Then he realized it was the same hour that Yeshua told him, "Your son lives," and he believed and along with all his household.

54And Yeshua had performed a second sign[63] after coming from Yehuda to the Galil.

Chapter 5

In Yerushalayim at sheep pool called Beit Zaita, Yeshua treats a sick man

After this it was the Pesach of the Jews and Yeshua went up to Yerushalayim. 2In Yerushalayim by the Sheep Gate, there is a pool, whose name in Hebrew is Beit Zaita.[64] It has five porches. 3By the porches lay

---

61. "At what time" or "at what hour." The answer "one in the afternoon" is "the seventh hour."

62. At one in the afternoon.

63. Miracle from the Greek σημεῖον (semeion) "sign." "Sign" in this context should be understood as "miracle."

64. Bethzatha from the Greek Βηθζαθά (Bethzatha), thought to be from the Hebrew בֵּית זַיְתָא (beit zaita), "house of olives." The more common form is "Bethesda" from the Greek Βηθεσδά (Bethesda), from the Aramaic בֵּית חֶסְדָּא (beit hesdda), meaning "house of mercy." Hence use of "Bethesda" as a name for hospitals. The meaning and source of "Bethesda" is debated. It is thought that Bethesda is the pool by Sheep Gate and Bethzatha the location.

a crowd of the sick, blind, lame, and paralyzed [4waiting for the water to move, for an angel of the lord came down into the pool, and whoever was first to go into the water after it was stirred was healed of affliction].[65]

5There was one man there who had been sick for thirty-eight years.

6Seeing him lying there and knowing how long he had been there, Yeshua said to him,

> Do you want to get well?

7The sick man answered, "Sir, I have no one to put me down into the pool when the water is stirred up. And while I am going there, someone else gets there ahead of me."

8Yeshua said to him,

> Stand,
> Take up your bed[66]
> And walk.

9And immediately the man was healthy and he took up his bed and walked around.

Healing on Shabbat

And that day was Shabbat.[67] 10The Jews said to the healed man, "It is Shabbat and it is unlawful for you to carry your bed."

---

65. Verse 4 is omitted or bracketed in most translations. It is probably an explanatory gloss inserted by a later copyist to show the pool's miraculous healing powers.

66. Bed from the Greek κράβαττον (krabatton). Can also be understood as a "mat" or "pallet."

67. Sabbath from the Greek σάββατον (sabbaton), from the Hebrew שַׁבָּת (Shabbat). The Pharisees accuse Yeshua of healing on the Sabbath. But such an issue, especially coming from the Pharisees, who were the most liberal and least legalist of the peoples in Jerusalem, is problematic. The issue is unlikely to have been an issue during Yeshua's lifetime. However, *after* Yeshua's death, Paul, arguing as a Pharisee Jew in letters to the more conservative Peter in Jerusalem and to others, contended that in order to bring Greek gentiles into the synagogue, the three restrictions of diet, circumcision, and Sabbath must be modified. Paul was particularly adamant about suspending the rite of physical circumcision, and for spiritual backing he cites the superior "spiritual circumcision" prescribed in Deuteronomy. Here the words about suspending the Sabbath restriction for the sake of doing good deeds on the Sabbath very likely reflect the views and compositional words of a later churchman rather than an active tenet of Yeshua.

11But the man answered them, "The one who made me healthy told me to take up my bed and walk."

12"Which man told you to take up your bed and walk?" they asked him.

13The healed man didn't know who he was, for Yeshua had disappeared into the crowd that was there.

14Afterward Yeshua found him in the Temple and said to him,

> Look, you have become healthy.
>
> Sin no more
>
> Or something worse may happen to you.

15The man went off and told the Jews it was Yeshua who cured him. 16And for this the Jews began to persecute Yeshua, because he healed on Shabbat.

17But Yeshua responded to them,

> My father is still doing his work
>
> And I am doing mine.

18For this the Jews sought all the more to find him and kill him, since he was not only breaking Shabbat but he even called God his own father, making himself equal to God.

19Yeshua answered and said to them,

> Amain, I say to you,
>
> The son can do nothing by himself unless he sees
>
> The father doing the same,
>
> For what he does the son does likewise.

20The father loves the son and shows him everything
> That he is doing,
>
> And he will show him greater works than these
>
> So you will marvel.

21Just as the father wakes the dead and gives them life,
> So the son gives life to whom he will.

22The father judges no one,
> For he has given all judgment to his son

23So all will honor the son as they honor the father.
> One who does not honor the son
>
> Does not honor the father who sent him.

Eternal life

24Amain, amain, I say to you,
> One who hears my word and believes him

Who sent me
Has eternal life and does not come to judgment,
But passes out of death to life.

25Amain, amain, I say to you,
    A time is coming and it is now
    When the dead will hear the voice of the son of God
    And those who hear will live.
26Just as the father has life in himself,
    So he has given the son life to have in himself.
27And he has given him authority to judge
    Because he is the earthly son.
28Do not wonder at this,
    For the hour is coming when all who are in their graves
    Will hear his voice 29and will come out:
    Those who have done good will go to a resurrection of life,
    But those who have done evil will go to a resurrection
    Of judgment.
30I can do nothing from myself.
    As I hear I judge,
    And my judgment is just,
    Since I do not seek my will but the will of him
    Who sent me.

Yeshua's testimony and Moshe's words in the Tanak

31If I testify about myself, my testimony is not true.
32There is another who testifies about me.
33You have sent to Yohanan[68] and he has testified to the truth.
34But from no living man do I take my testimony
    And I say this so you may be saved,
35Yet that man was a lamp that burns and shines
    And you wished to exult for an hour in his light.

36Yet I have a testimony greater than Yohanan's,

---

68. John the Baptist.

For the works that my father gave me to fulfill,
These my own works, testify that the father has sent me.
37And the father who has sent me has testified for me.
His voice you have never heard,
And his shape you have never seen,
38And his word does not live inside you
Since you do not believe the one whom he sent you.
39You search the writings of the Tanak[69]
Because you think in them is eternal life
And it is they that testify about me
40But you do not want to come to me
So that you may have life.
41I do not accept glory from living people,
42But I know you and that you do not have the love
Of God in you.
43I have come in the name of my father
And you do not accept me.
If someone else comes in his own name,
That one you will accept.
44How can you believe when you take glory from each other
And do not seek the glory from the only God?

45Do not suppose I will accuse you before the father.
Your accuser is Moshe in whom you have hoped.
46But if you believed in Moshe you would believe in me,
For he wrote about me.
47But if you do not believe his writings in the Tanak,
How will you believe my words?

Chapter 6

Bread for five thousand on the grass
After this Yeshua left for the other side of the Sea of the Galil, also called Lake Tiberius.

---

69. The Hebrew Bible. Also written "Tanakh" or "Tanach."

2And a big crowd followed him, because they saw the miraculous signs he performed on the sick.

3Yeshua went up the mountain and there he sat down with his students. 4Pesach was near, the holiday of the Jews. 5Yeshua raised his eyes and seeing a big crowd coming toward him, said to Filippos,

Where can we buy some bread so they can eat?

6But he said this to test him, for he already knew what he would do.

7Filippos answered him, "Two hundred denarii worth of bread are not enough for everyone to have a bite."

8One of his students, Andreas, the brother of Shimon Kefa, said to him, 9"There is a young boy here who has five barley loaves and two fish. But what is that for all these people?"

10Yeshua said,

Have the people sit down.

Now there was a lot of grass in this place. So the men lay back on the ground, five thousand of them.[70]

11Then Yeshua took the loaves, and gave thanks and passed out the bread to the people who were reclining there. So also the fishes, as much as they wanted. 12And when they were filled, Yeshua said to his students,

Pick up the leftover pieces so nothing is lost.

13So they picked up and filled twelve baskets with pieces from the five barley loaves that were left over by those who had eaten.

14And when the people saw the miraculous signs he did, they said, "Certainly he is the prophet, the one who is coming into the world."

Yeshua alone on the mountain

15Yeshua, knowing they were about to come and seize him to make him king, went off again to the mountain to be alone.

Walking on the sea

16When evening came the students went down to the sea, 17and got into a boat to cross over the sea to Kfar Nahum. By now it was dark and

---

70. It is unlikely that such a crowd would consist only of men, and though some translations say "they" or "people," the Greek says "men."

Yeshua had not come to them. 18Since there was a strong wind the sea was rough. 19When they had rowed three or four miles, they saw Yeshua walking on the sea and coming close to the boat, and they were afraid.

20But he said to them,

> It is I.
>
> Do not be afraid.

21Then they wanted to take him up into the boat, and at once the boat reached the land where they were going.

Looking for Rabbi Yeshua who preaches to them in the synagogue at Kfar Nahum

22Next day the crowd that had stayed on the other side of the sea saw that there had been only one boat there. They also saw that Yeshua had not gone aboard the ship with his students, but the students had set out alone. 23Then some boats from Lake Tiberius came near the place where they had eaten the bread.[71] 24When the crowd saw that neither Yeshua nor his students were there, they got into the boats and went to Kfar Nahum, looking for Yeshua.

25When they found him on the other side of the sea, they said to him, "Rabbi, when did you come here?"

26Yeshua answered them, saying,

> Amain, amain, I say to you,
>
> You look for me not because you saw signs
>
> But because you ate the loaves and were filled.

27Do not work for the food that spoils

> But for the food that lasts for eternal life,
>
> Which the earthly son will give you,
>
> Since on him God who is father set the seal.

28Then they said to him, "What can we do to do the work of God?"

29Yeshua answered and said to them,

> The work of God is to believe the one he sent.

30So they said to him, "Why don't you do a sign so we may see and

---

71. Some manuscripts continue the sentence, "after the Lord gave thanks." The phrase referring to Yeshua as "Lord" is probably a scribal addition and is omitted in recent translations.

believe in you and in what you do? 31Our parents ate manna in the desert, and as Moshe wrote in Exodus, 'He gave them bread from the sky to eat.'"

32Then Yeshua said to them,

> Amain, amain, I say to you,
> It was not Moshe who gave you bread from the sky,
> But my father gives you bread from the sky,
> The true bread,
> 33For the bread of God comes out of the heaven
> And gives life to the world.

34Then they said to him,

> Sir, always give us this bread.

35Yeshua said to them,

> I am the bread of life.
> Who comes to me will not be hungry,
> And who believes in me will not be thirsty again.
> 36Yet I said to you,
> You have seen me and do not believe.
> 37All that my father gives me will come to me
> And anyone who comes to me I will not turn away,
> 38Since I have come down from the sky
> Not to do my own will but the will of him who sent me.

> 39And this is the will of him who sent me,
> That I should lose nothing of all he gave me
> But raise it up on the last day.
> 40This is the will of my father,
> That all who see the son and believe in him
> May have eternal life,
> And I will raise them up on the last day.

The Jews murmur about Yeshua, who responds to his coreligionists

41Then the Jews murmured about him because he said, "I am the bread that came down from the sky." 42"Isn't he Yeshua, Yosef's son, whose father and mother we know? How can he now say he has come down from the sky?"

43Yeshua said to them,

>Do not murmur gossip among yourselves.

44No one can come to me

>Unless drawn in by the father who sent me,

>And I will raise that person up on the last day.

45It was written by the prophet Yeshayahu,[72]

>"They will all be taught by God."

>Everyone who has heard from the father and learned

>Comes to me.

46Not that anyone has seen the father

>Except one who is from God.

>This one has seen the father.

47Amain, amain, I say to you,

>One who believes has eternal life.

48I am the bread of life.

49Your parents[73] ate the manna in the desert and died.

50This is the bread that comes from the heavenly sky,

>So anyone may eat it and not die.

51I am the living bread

>Who came down from the sky.

>Whoever eats this bread will live forever,

>And the bread is my flesh,

>Which I will give for the life of the world.

*The Jews argue with each other and Yeshua speaks
to them in the synagogue*

52The Jews were arguing with each other, saying, "How can this man give us his own flesh to eat?"

53So Yeshua said,

>Amain, amain, I tell you,

>Unless you eat the flesh of the earthly son

>And drink his blood,

---

72. Isa. 54.13. See also Jeremiah 31.34.

73. Can also be translated as "ancestors." See note 56 on John 4.20.

You have no life within you.

54The one who eats my flesh and drinks my blood
  Has eternal life
  And I will raise that person up on the last day,
55For my flesh is the true meat and my blood
  Is the true drink.

56The one who eats my flesh and drinks my blood
  Lives in me and I in them.[74]
57As the living father sent me and I live
  Because of the father,
  So the one who eats me will live because of me.
58This is the bread that came down from the sky,
  Not like what our parents ate and died.
  Who eats this bread will live forever.

59These things Yeshua said in a synagogue while teaching in Kfar Nahum.

Yeshua's students also murmur about him,
revealing disbelief

60Many of his students heard these things, and said, "His teaching is abrasive. Who can bear to hear it?"

61But Yeshua knew inside himself that his students were complaining about his words, and he said to them,

    Does this shock you?
62What if you see the earthly son ascend to where he was
        before?
63The breath[75] keeps us alive.
  The flesh is of no help.
  The words I spoke to you are the breath of spirit
  And are life.
64But some among you do not believe.

---

74. "Them" is literally "him."

75. Breath from the Greek πνεῦμα (pneuma), meaning "breath" and by extension "spirit."

Yeshua knew from the beginning who among them didn't believe and who would betray him. 65And he said,

> I have told you that no one can come to me
> Unless it be granted by the father.

66Because of this many of his students withdrew to their own place and would no longer walk about with him.

67Then Yeshua said to the twelve,

> You too, do you not want to leave?

68Shimon Kefa answered,

> Lord, whom can we go to? You have the words
> Of eternal life,
> 69And we have believed and known that you are
> The holy one of God.

70Yeshua responded,

> Did I not choose you the twelve?
> Yet one of you is a devil.

71He was speaking of Yehuda son of Shimon of Keriot,[76] for he, among the twelve, was about to betray him.

Chapter 7

Yeshua in danger

And after that Yeshua went about in the Galil. He did not want to go about in Yehuda because the Jews were trying to kill him.

Yeshua's brothers, who do not believe in him, urge him to go into Yehuda and up to the Sukkoth festival in Yerushalayim

2Now the Jewish harvest feast of Sukkoth[77] was near, 3and his broth-

---

76. Iscariot from the Greek Ἰσκαριώθ (Iskarioth), from the Hebrew אִישׁ קְרִיּוֹת (ish keriot), meaning "man of Keriot." In English, "Keriot" is also written "Kerioth." For more on the origin of the betrayer tale of Judas in scripture and post-biblical portrayals in history and the arts, see note 30 on p. 33, in "Mark, the Vernacular Story Teller." For a more complete account of Judas from the Bible to modern times, see Susan Gubar's *Judas: A Biography* (New York: W. W. Norton, 2009).

77. Tabernacle from the Greek σκηνή (skene), "tent," from the Hebrew סֻכָּה (sukkah), "shelter," "tent." The three tents are associated with the Jewish Sukkoth, the

ers[78] said to him, "Leave here and go into Yehuda so your students will see the works you do. 4No one acts in secret who wants to be widely known. Since you do these things, show them to the world."

5Even his own brothers did not believe in him.

6Then Yeshua said to them,

My time has not come, but your time is always here.

7The world cannot hate you, but it hates me,

For I testify concerning it that its works are evil.

8You go up to the festival [I will not go],[79]

Because my time has not yet been completed.

9And saying these things, he stayed in the Galil.

Yeshua goes to Yerushalayim, teaches in the Temple, and debates with the people

10When his brothers went up to the festival, he also went up, not openly but in secret. 11So then the Jews were looking for him in the festival and saying, "Where is that man?" 12And the crowds were murmuring about him, some saying, "He is a good man," yet others saying, "No, he is fooling the crowd." 13But no one spoke openly about him for fear of the Jews.[80]

14About the middle of the festival, Yeshua went up into the Temple and taught.

15The Jews were astonished and said, "How can this man have learning when he has not instructed?"

Festival of the Tabernacles or Booths, חַג הַסֻּכּוֹת (hag hasukkot), an eight-day celebration for autumnal harvest, beginning on the eve of the 15th of Tishri. The sukkah is a small lean-to-like tent in the fields. The festival commemorates the forty years that Moses and the Jews spent in the desert after escaping from Egypt and before entering Canaan.

78. Yeshua had four brothers, James, Joseph, Judas, and Simon (Yaakov, Yosef, Yehuda, and Shimon), mentioned in Mark 6.3 and Matthew 13.54–56. His sisters are also mentioned in these passages, but not by name.

79. Not in early manuscripts.

80. In these passages the word "Jew" cannot mean "Jew" with respect to the people of Jerusalem, since the people in the crowd are Jews, including Yeshua. But here "Jew" refers to any presumed opponent of Yeshua, thereby demarking enemies as Jews, and rabbi Yeshua who is there to teach in the Temple as some undefined other.

Yeshua answered them,

16My teaching is not mine but is his who sent me.

17Whoever wants to do the will of God

Will know whether the teaching is from God

Or whether I speak on my own.

18The person who speaks only from inside

Seeks a personal glory,

But the person who seeks the glory of God who sent us

Is true and has nothing false inside.

19Did Moshe not give you the law?

Yet none of you keeps the law.

Why are you trying to kill me?

20The crowd responded, "You have a demon inside you. Who is trying to kill you?"

21Yeshua answered,

I performed one work and you are amazed.

22So Moshe gave you circumcision—

Not that it comes from Moshe but from the patriarchs—

And on Shabbat you circumcise a man.

23If a man receives circumcision on Shabbat

In order not to break the law of Moshe,

Are you angry with me for making

A man's whole body healthy on Shabbat?

24Do not judge by appearance

But with the judgment of justice.

Gossip in Yerushalayim about Yeshua as mashiah

25Now some were saying in Yerushalayim, "Isn't this the man they are trying to kill? 26And look, here he is, speaking openly, and they say nothing to him. Perhaps the rulers know that this man is the mashiah. 27But we know where this man comes from. When the mashiah comes, no one will know where he comes from."

Yeshua preaches in the Temple

28Then Yeshua cried out in the Temple while teaching, and said,

You know me and know where I am from,

And I have not come on my own,

But he is true, the one who sent me,

And you do not know him.

29I know him because from him I am

And he sent me.

30Then they sought to seize[81] him and no one had laid a hand on him, because his hour had not yet come. 31Many in the crowd believed in him, however, and said, "When the mashiah comes, will he do more signs than this man did?"

Look for me, but I am going where you cannot come

32The Prushim heard the crowd murmuring these things about him, and the high priests and Prushim sent servants[82] to seize him.

33And Yeshua said,

For a little more time I am still with you

And then I go away to the one who sent me.

34You will search me out and not find me,

And where I am you will not be able to come.

35Then the Jews said to each other, "Where is this man about to go where we cannot find him? Is he about to go to the diaspora among the Greeks and teach them?[83] 36What is the meaning of the words he said,

---

81. From the Greek πιάσαι (piasai), "to seize" or "to grab." Often the verb is translated as "arrest," but while the notion of "arrest" may be implied as a later consequence of seizing, here it means only "to seize." "Arrest" initially meant "to stop" or "to seize."

82. Servants from the Greek ὑπηρέτας (hyperetas) means "servants" and also has been translated as "officers" or "policemen."

83. "Is he [Yeshua] about to go to the diaspora among the Greeks" seems like a prophecy of Yeshua's students who indeed later went to preach in the synagogues of the Greek Jews in Greek lands to announce the good news of Yeshua as the messiah. Although the "diaspora" is a common word for the dispersion of the Jews abroad, this phrase has puzzlingly been interpreted to mean ethnic Greeks, not Greek-speaking Jews in Greek lands. The largest center of diaspora Jews was probably in Alexandria, for whom the Septuagint Bible was translated from Hebrew into Greek (second century B.C.E.). At this time, the Jews were dispersed in great numbers from Alexandria and Antioch to Thessaloniki and Rome; most were Greek-speaking, in contrast to the figures in the New Testament who spoke Aramaic, with Hebrew the language of the synagogue.

You will search me out and not find me,
And where I am you will not be able to come?"

Last day of Sukkoth Yeshua cries out in the Temple
to the crowd of the promise of living water

37On the last and greatest day of Sukkoth, Yeshua stood up and cried out,

Let anyone who is thirsty come to me and drink!
38For one who believes in me, as it says in the scriptures,
"Rivers out of his belly will flow with living water.[84]

39He said this about the spirit, which the believers in him were to receive. But the spirit was not yet because Yeshua was not yet glorified.

More crowd discussion of Yeshua as mashiah

40Some of the crowd hearing these words said, "This man is truly the prophet."

41Others were saying, "He is the mashiah."

But some were saying, "Surely, the mashiah cannot come from the Galil? 42Didn't Micah say in scripture that the mashiah will come from the sperm of David and from the village of Beit Lehem[85] where David lived?"

43So there was a split in the crowd over him, 44some wanting to seize him, but no one laid a hand on him.

Nakdeimon, a Parush, defends Yeshua before the council

45Then the servants went back to the high priests and Prushim, who said to them, "Why didn't you bring him?"

46"No one ever spoke like this man," the servants answered.

47The Prushim retorted, "Have you too been taken in? 48Surely none

---

84. The scripture intended is uncertain. It may be Isaiah 44.2–3 or Zechariah 14.8. Zechariah is read at Sukkoh.

85. Bethlehem from the Greek Βηθλέεμ (Bethleem), from the Hebrew בֵּית לֶחֶם (beit lehem), meaning "house of bread."

of the rulers believed in him. 49But the crowd[86] that does not know the law is cursed."

50Nakdeimon,[87] who had gone to Yeshua before, and was one of the council, said to them, 51"Surely our law doesn't judge a person unless it first hears and knows what that person is doing?"

52They replied, saying to him, "You are not also from the Galil, are you? Search and you will find no prophet is to rise from the Galil."

53[Then each went to his own home, but Yeshua went to the Mountain of Olives.[88]

Chapter 8

Woman taken in adultery

2At dawn he went into the Temple and all the people came to him and he sat down and taught them. 3The scholars and Prushim led a woman in who had been caught in adultery, and they stood her before them 4and said to him, "Rabbi, this woman was caught in the act of adultery. 5In the

---

86. The crowd, from the Greek ὄχλος (ohlos). Until this moment, *ohlos* has been translated as "crowd," carrying no pejorative undertones. In this context, where the crowd has been cursed for not knowing the law, the translation remains accurately "crowd" in the NRSV. However, in other versions, it is rendered as "mob" or "rabble," thereby effectively heightening anger against Jewish authorities and Pharisees for having used the unfriendly term "mob" or "rabble" with respect to a crowd in the Temple favorable to Yeshua as the messiah. So the word for "crowd" astonishingly becomes "mob" in the NIV and "rabble" in the Jerusalem, Lattimore, Funk, Hoover (Jesus Seminar), and other earlier versions. The KJV, however, moves in another direction. It renders ὄχλος with precise and wondrous majesty: "But this people who knoweth not the law are cursed." However, turning "this crowd" into "this people" cannot but have the ominous and familiar tone of a curse not only on the crowd but also on the people.

87. Nicodemus.

88. Normally the last half of verse 7.53 is printed as 8.1, after the chapter break. It makes more sense to leave it as a last complete sentence in chapter 7. Adding to the confusion, scholars agree that the movingly adroit story of the adulterous woman was not originally part of the gospel but an emendation based on oral tradition. Lines 7.53 through 8.11 are bracketed.

law, Moshe charged us to stone such women. Now, what do you say?"
6They said this to test him so they could have a charge against him.
But Yeshua stooped down and with his finger wrote on the ground.
7When they kept questioning him, he stood up and said to them,

> The one among you without sin[89]
> Let him first cast a stone at her.

8And again he stooped down, writing on the ground, 9and those who
heard him went away, one by one, beginning with the older ones. And
he was left alone with the woman standing before him.
10Yeshua stood up and said to her,

> Woman, where are they?
> Has no one condemned you?

11And she said, "No one, sir."
And Yeshua said,

> Neither do I condemn you.
> Go, and from now on sin no more.][90]

Yeshua, light of the world

12Then Yeshua spoke to them again,

> I am the light of the world.
> Whoever follows me will not walk in darkness
> But will have the light of life.

Telling the Prushim who is his father

13Then the Prushim said to him, "You are testifying about yourself.
Your testimony isn't true."
14Yeshua answered and said to them,

> Even if I testify about my self, my testimony is true.
> I know where I came from and where I am going.
> And you do not know where I came from

---

89. The Greek is sparse and needs no fleshing out, saying word for word, "The blameless you [gen.] first at her throw stone." The Greek ἀναμάρτητος (anamartetos)
means "one without fault, failing, or wrong" or "one who misses the mark," which in
biblical Greek came to mean primarily "sin."

90. 7.53–8.11 is not in early manuscripts and is thought to be an addition. Although
an interruption in the flow of Yeshua's debate in the Temple and whether authentic
or spurious, it still adds to the narrative complexity.

Or where I am going.

15You judge according to the flesh.

I judge no one.

16And if I do judge, my judgment is true

Because I am not alone,

But I and the father who sent me.

17And in your law[91] it is written in Deuteronomy

That the testimony of two people is true.

18I am he who testifies about myself,

And testifying about me is the one who sent me,

My father.

19They said to him, "Where is your father?"

Yeshua answered,

You know neither me nor my father.

If you knew me,

You would also know my father.

20These words he spoke in the treasury while teaching in the Temple.

And no one seized him, because his hour had not yet come.

Yeshua not of this world

21Then he said to them again,

I am going and you will look for me

And you will die in your sins.[92]

Where I am going you cannot come.

---

91. Deut. 17.6. The Greek reads *"your* law," thus separating Yeshua from his adversaries. While Yeshua was questioning the law, it was still his law, as is clear from the immediately preceding passages citing Mosaic law. Insofar as the story is set in a historical period, "your" rings like a later redaction when the Hebrew Bible was diminished in authority, and was the "old" rather than the "new" covenant.

92. Sins. In the classical Greek ἁμαρτία (hamartia) means "missing the mark," "failure," "wrong," and sometimes "sin." In biblical Koine it has been translated as "sin," though some object. In *Three Gospels* (New York: Scribners, 1996), Reynolds Price translates ἁμαρτία as "wrong" or "error," explaining that the word "appears to have fewer connotations of the fleshpot than the English word *sin,* so long ago hijacked by the puritan and hypocrite" (18). I have translated ἁμαρτία as "sin" when the intention is harsh, and "wrong" or "error" when the intention is more sympathetic to the wrongdoer.

22Then the Jews said to one another, "He won't kill himself, will he, when he says, 'Where I am going you cannot come'?"

23And he said to them,

> You are of things below.
> I am of things above.
> You are of this world,
> I am not of this world.

24So I have told you

> You will die in your sins.
> If you do not believe that I am,93
> You will die in your sins.

25Then they were saying to him, "Who are you?"

Yeshua said to them,

> I am what from the beginning I told you.

26I have much to say about you and much to judge,

> But the one who sent me is true
> And what I heard from him I speak in the world.

27They did not know he was speaking to them about the father.

28Then Yeshua said,

> When you raise up the earthly son,
> Then you will know that I am94
> And from myself I do nothing,
> But I speak as my father taught me.

29And the one who sent me is with me.

> He did not leave me alone,
> For what I do pleases him always.

30When he was saying this, many believed in him.

---

93. This phrase is normally translated "I am he," but the Greek says ἐγώ εἰμι (ego eimi), "I am." "I am he" may be implied, or "I am myself," or the solitary mystery of "I am." It is richer to give only what the Greek gives, "I am," and then, not bound by interpretation in translation, read the verse creatively. As for Yeshua's take on the phrase, in the next line he is asked the essential enigma, "Who are you?" His answer is a riddle, which should be respected.

94. See note 93 above.

The truth will set you free

31Then Yeshua said to the Jews who believed in him,

> If you remain with my word,
>
> Then you are truly my students,
>
> 32And you will know the truth
>
> And the truth will set you free.[95]

Children of Avraham

33They answered him, "We are of the sperm of Avraham[96] and have never been enslaved. How can you say that we will be set free?"

34Yeshua said,

> Amain, amain, I say to you,
>
> Everyone who sins is a slave to sin
>
> 35But the slave does not stay in the house forever.
>
> The son remains forever.
>
> 36If the son frees you, then you will be really free.
>
> 37I know you are the sperm of Avraham
>
> But you are trying to kill me
>
> Because my word has no place in you.
>
> 38I tell what I have seen with the father.
>
> So, what you have heard from the father, do.

39They responded and said to him, "Our father is Avraham." Yeshua said to them,

> If you are the children of Avraham,
>
> Then do what Avraham did,
>
> 40Yet now you are seeking to kill me,

---

95. The passages "You are of things below. / I am of things above," "I am the light of the world," and "the truth will set you free" reflect the distancing from the world on earth in favor of a spiritual world of light elsewhere. In Gnosticism the soul is trapped in darkness on earth and yearns for return to the light principle. As such, these cited passages display the essence of Gnostic beliefs and are used to support a common contention of the essential Gnostic nature of John with regard to the spirit as light.

96. Abraham from the Greek Ἀβραάμ (Abraam), from the Hebrew אַבְרָהָם (avraham).

A man who has told you the truth
Which I heard from God.
That is not what Avraham did.
41You are doing your father's work.⁹⁷
They told him, "We were not born of prostitution.⁹⁸ We have one father, God."

Jews, the children of the devil
    42Yeshua said to them,
        If God were your father you would love me,
        For I came out from God and I am here.
        I have not come from myself but from the one
        Who sent me.
    43Why do you not know my voice?
        Because you cannot hear my word.
    44You are from your father the devil⁹⁹

---

97. The "your father" makes no sense until the next verses, when Yeshua declares that the Jews' purported father of the Hebrew Bible is not God, but another father, the devil, as immediately seen in verse 44.

98. Of prostitution. From the Greek ἐκ πορνείας (ek porneias). Also translated as "filth," "prostitution," and more freely as "illegitimate" (NRSV).

99. In this angry demonization of the Jews as children of the devil, who is their murderous father, Yeshua appears to speak not as a contemporary Jew to a Jew but through the voice of a later writer whose hatred for the Jew is undisguised. However, it is wrong to soften the attack in the gospels by disguising the target of the attack in translating Jews as "the people," "opponents," or "rulers," which is done with good intent in the *New Testament and Psalms* (New York: Oxford University Press, 1995) and in other versions. Here the Jews are portrayed both as unrelated to their Jewish Bible God, yet also related to Abraham, whom Yeshua states that he preceded. This violent attack on his coreligionists also reaches Abrahamic Judaism and the inferiority of the Hebrew Bible compared to the New Testament, though here the polemic is not as specific as elsewhere in the gospels, where the Jews are the murderers of their own prophets as they will be the murderers of their foreseen messiah, Yeshua. However, in these passages the Jews of the New Testament are irrevocably separated from the Jews of the Hebrew Bible, who are called "the Israelites" (Greek for "Israelis"), which safely eases the passage into fiction to readers unfamiliar with the sundry names for Jews.

Before the chapter's last delimiting of Abrahamic Judaism and self-proclamation,

And you want to do the desires of your father.
From the beginning he was a murderer
And he does not stand in the truth,
Because there is no truth in him.
When he lies he speaks from himself,
Since he is a liar and the father of lies.
45And because I speak the truth you do not believe me.
46Who among you proves me in sin?
If I tell the truth, why do you not believe me?
47Whoever is from God hears the words of God.
But you do not hear, for you are not from God.

Yeshua glorified by his father

48The Jews answered him, "Are we not right to say that you are a Shomroni and have a demon?"

49Yeshua answered,

I have no demon, but I honor my father
And you dishonor me.
50And I do not seek my glory.
There is one who seeks it and he is the judge.
51Amain, amain, I say to you,
Whoever honors my word
Will not look on eternal death.

52The Jews said to him, "Now we know that you have a demon. Avraham died, as did the prophets, and you say, 'Whoever honors my word will not look on eternal death.' 53Can you be greater than our father Avraham who died? And the prophets who died? Who do you think you are?"

54Yeshua answered,

"Before Avraham was born I am," Yeshua states that Abraham himself would have seen and exulted at Yeshua's coming. It is not likely that this pride, unpleasant anger, and retribution have much to do with a historic Yeshua and his messianic center in the formation of later Christianity. Rather, we are reading late, redacted documents in Greek, a foreign language to the participants, reflecting a nascent church and its torrid rejection of the parent creed and its member Jews, excluding rabbi Yeshua and followers, who escape all retribution for their birth and observed religion.

If I glorify myself my glory is nothing.
My father glorifies me,
Of whom you say, "He is our God,"
55Though you do not know him.
But I know him.
And if I say that I do not know him
I will be like you, a liar,
But I know him and I keep his word.
56Your father Avraham was glad
That he could see my day.
He saw it and exulted.

57Then the Jews said to him, "You are not yet fifty and you have seen Avraham?"

58Yeshua said,
Amain, amain, I say to you,
Before Avraham was born I am.

59Then they took up stones to throw at him, but Yeshua hid and went out of the Temple.

Chapter 9

Rabbi Yeshua and a blindman

Going on he saw a man blind from birth.

2His students asked him, saying, "Rabbi, who sinned, this man or his parents that he was born blind?"

3Yeshua answered,
Neither he nor his parents did wrong.
He was born blind so the work of God
Might be revealed in him.
4We must do the work of him who sent us
While it is day.
Night is coming when no one can work.
5While I am in the world,
I am the light of the world.

6After saying that, he spat on the ground and made mud with the spit and smeared mud on the man's eyes, 7and said to him,

Go wash in the pool of Shiloah.[100]

Then he went and washed and came back seeing.

8The neighbors and those who had seen him as a beggar said, "Isn't he the one who sat and begged?"

9Some said, "That's him."

Others said, "No, but it looks like him."

The man said, "It's me."

10So they kept asking him, "How were your eyes opened?"

11He answered, "The man called Yeshua made mud and smeared[101] it on my eyes and said to me, 'Go wash in the pool of Shiloah.' So I went and after washing I saw."

12And they asked him, "Where is he?"

"I don't know," he said.

Prushim question and revile the former blindman

13They took the former blindman to the Prushim. 14Now it was a Shabbat day when Yeshua made the mud and opened his eyes. 15Then the Prushim in turn asked him how he regained his sight.

And he told them, "He put mud on my eyes and I washed and now I see."

16Some of the Prushim said, "This man is not from God, for he doesn't observe the Shabbat." But others said, "How can a man be a sinner who does such signs?" And there was division among them.

17They said to the blindman again, "What do you have to say about him because he opened your eyes?"

"He is a prophet," he said.

---

100. Siloam from the Greek Σιλωάμ (Siloam), from Hebrew שִׁלֹחַ (shiloah). "Siloam" is followed by an interpolation: "which translated means the one who has been sent." *Shiloah* is found also in Isaiah 8.6.

101. "Smeared" from the Greek ἐπέχρισεν (epehrisen) here also means "anointed," from the same root as the noun "anointed," χριστος (hristos), as in Yeshua the Anointed, but here the verb means simply "smear" or "spread." The KJV, shifting to third person and upgrading the verb to convey the power of the messiah (the anointed), translates this phrase freely and beautifully: "And he anointed the eyes of the blind man."

18The Jews did not believe he was blind and then regained his sight until they called on the parents of the one who saw again. 19And they said to them, "This is your son who you say was born blind? How is it that he can see now?"

20His parents answered, saying, "We know that this man is our son and that he was born blind. 21But we don't know how it is that now he sees, nor know who opened his eyes. Ask him, he is of age. He will speak for himself."

22His parents said these things because they were afraid of the Jews, for the Jews had already agreed that anyone who confessed that Yeshua was the mashiah would be barred from the synagogue. 23That is why his parents said, "Ask him, he is of age."

24So for a second time they called the man who was blind and said to him, "Glory to God. We know that this man is a sinner."

25This man answered, "If he is a sinner I do not know. One thing I do know. I was blind and now I see."

26"What did he do to you? How did he open your eyes?" they said to him.

27"I told you already and you don't listen," he said to them. "Why do you want to hear it again? Could it be that you too want to be his students?"

28And they reviled him and said, "You are his student, but we are Moshe's students.[102] 29We know that God spoke to Moshe, but we don't know where this man is from."

30The man answered, saying, "Here is what is astonishing, that you don't know where he is from, yet he opened my eyes. 31We know that God does not listen to sinners, but if one is devout and does his will, he hears. 32From the beginning of time we have not heard of one who opened the eyes of a blindman. 33If this man were not from God, he could not have done anything."

34They answered and said to him, "You were born wholly in sins, and you are teaching us?"

And they threw him out.

---

102. A reference to the superiority of Yeshua's teaching over that of Moses and, by extension, of the New Testament over the Jewish Bible.

Yeshua gives a blindman light

35Yeshua heard that they threw the blindman out and he found him and said,

> Do you believe in the earthly son?

36The man replied to him, "And who is he, sir, that I may believe in him?"

37Yeshua said to him,

> You have seen him
> And he is the one talking with you.

38And he said, "I believe, lord."

And he worshiped him.

39And Yeshua said,

> I came into this world for judgment
> So those who cannot see may see
> And those who see may go blind.

Yeshua and the sighted Prushim

40Some of the Prushim who were near him heard this and said to him, "Surely, we are not blind?"

41Yeshua said to them,

> If you were blind you would have no sin.
> Since you say, "We see," your sin remains.

Chapter 10

Good shepherd at the gate, who lays down his life for the sheep

Again Yeshua said,

> Amain, amain, I tell you,
> I am the gate of the sheepfold
> Whoever enters the sheepfold not through the gate
> But climbs up and goes in another way
> Is a thief and a robber,
> 2But whoever enters through the gate
> Is the shepherd of the sheep.
> 3The gatekeeper opens to him

And the sheep hear his voice
And he calls his own sheep by name
And he leads them out.
4When he has put all his own outside,
He goes in ahead of them and the sheep follow
Because they know his voice.
5They will not follow a stranger, but flee from him.
They do not know the voice of strangers.
6Yeshua told them this parable, but they failed to understand what he was saying to them.
7So again Yeshua said,
Amain, amain, I say to you,
I am the gate of the sheepfold.
8All who came before me are thieves and robbers.
The sheep did not listen to them.
9I am the gate.
Whoever enters through me will be saved
And will go in and go out and find pasture.
10The thief comes only to steal and kill and destroy.
I came that they may have life, and have abundance.

11I am the good shepherd.
The good shepherd lays down his life[103] for the sheep.
12The hired man who is not a shepherd
And is not the owner of the sheep
Sees the wolf coming and leaves the sheep and runs,
And the wolf ravages and scatters them
13Since he is a hired man
And cares nothing about the sheep.

14I am the good shepherd
And I know my own and my own know me
15As the father knows me and I know the father.

---

103. Literally "spirit" but figuratively "life."

And I lay down my life for the sheep.
16And I have other sheep which are not from this fold.
And I must also bring them in
And they will hear my voice
And there will be one flock and one shepherd.

17Therefore my father loves me
Because I lay down my life to receive it again.
18No one takes it from me.
But I lay it down of my own accord.
I have the right to lay it down
And I have the power to receive it again.
This command I have received from my father.

19At these words there was again division among the Jews. 20Many
were saying, "He has a demon and he's mad. Why listen to him?" 21Others
said, "These words are not the words of one with a demon. Can a demon
open the eyes of the blind?"

Hanukkah in Yerushalayim, Yeshua announces he is the son of God

22Then came Hanukkah in Yerushalayim, the Festival of Lights. It
was winter, 23and Yeshua was walking around in the Temple, on the
colonnade of Shlomoh.[104] 24The Jews surrounded him and said to him,
"How long will you hold our soul suspended? If you are the mashiah tell
us plainly."
25Yeshua answered them,
I told you and you do not believe.
The works I do in my father's name
Are my witness. They speak for me,
26But you do not believe because you are not of my sheep.
27My sheep hear my voice
And I know them and they follow me.

---

104. Shlomoh from the Greek Σολομών (Solomon), from the Hebrew שְׁלֹמֹה
(shlomoh).

28I give them eternal life

And they will not perish forever

And no one will pluck them out of my hand.

29What my father gave me is greater than all,

And no one can pluck it out of the father's hand.

30I and the father are one.

31Then the Jews picked up stones again to stone him.

32Yeshua answered them,

I have shown you many good works from the father.

For which of these works will you stone me?

33The Jews answered him, "For good work we do not stone you, but for blasphemy, and because you are a man and make yourself God."

34Yeshua replied to them,

Is it not written in your[105] law,

"I have said that you are gods"?[106]

35If God called gods those to whom the word of God came,

And scripture cannot be set aside,

36Can you say that I whom the father sanctified

And sent into the world am blaspheming

Because I said, "I am the son of God"?

37If I do not do the works of my father,

Do not believe me.

38But if I do them, even if you do not believe me,

Believe the works

So you may know and see that the father is in me

And I am in the father.

---

105. Again a question of distancing through the choice of possessive pronouns. "Your" in "your law" appears to be implausible, since Yeshua is a Jew and the law is also *his* law, which means the Bible (Torah). Only "the law" or "our law" is sensible if Yeshua is speaking in his own time. To prove his argument in the following phrase Yeshua cites the law in Psalms 82.6: "you are gods." Then, confirming their mutual possession of biblical law, he adds, "and scripture cannot be set aside." Yeshua argues as if he were not a Jew and the law were not *his* law; yet, as a Jew, he uses the Jews' common law to prove his point.

106. Ps. 82.6.

39They tried to seize him again, and he slipped out of their hands.

Yeshua withdraws to other side of Yarden

40And he went away again across the Yarden to the place where Yohanan was earlier dipping and he stayed there.[107] 41Many came to him and said that Yohanan had not performed a miraculous act, but everything that Yohanan said about Yeshua was true. 42And many believed in him there.

Chapter 11

With Elazar who is dead

There was a man who was sick, Elazar[108] from Beit Aniyah,[109] from the village of Miryam[110] and Marta,[111] her sister. 2It was Miryam who anointed the rabbi with oil of myrrh and wiped his feet with her hair. Her brother Elazar was sick. 3So the sisters sent word to him, saying, "Rabbi, look, one whom you care for is sick."

4When Yeshua heard this, he said,

> This sickness is not close to death
> But to the glory of God that through it
> The son of God may be glorified.

5Now Yeshua loved Marta and her sister and Elazar. 6Therefore when he heard that he was sick, he remained in the place he was for two days. 7After this he said to his students,

> Let us go to Yehuda again.

---

107. Bethany, where John the Baptist dipped his followers, lies beyond the Jordan, and its location is unknown. In some manuscripts it is written "Bethabara." This appears not to be the Bethany on the slope of the Mountain of Olives some two miles east of Jerusalem, where Yeshua visited his friends Mary and Martha and where tradition says Lazarus is buried.

108. Lazarus from the Greek Λάζαρος (Lazaros), from the Hebrew אֶלְעָזָר (elazar).

109. Bethany.

110. Mary from the Greek Μαρία (Maria), from the Hebrew מִרְיָם (miryam).

111. Martha from the Greek Μάρθα (Martha), from the Aramaic מַרְתָא (marta).

8His students said to him, "Rabbi, the Jews were just now trying to stone you[112] and are you going there again?"

9Yeshua replied,

> Are there not twelve hours in the day?
> Whoever walks around in the day doesn't stumble
> Since one sees the light of this world.
> 10Whoever walks around in the night stumbles
> Since the light is not in that person.

11These things he said, and then he told them,

> Our friend Elazar has fallen asleep,
> But I am going there to awaken him.

12So the students said, "Sir, if he has fallen asleep, he will be cured.[113]

13Yeshua had spoken about his death, but they thought he was talking about restful sleep.

14Then Yeshua told them plainly,

> Elazar died, 15and I am happy for you
> That I was not there so that you may believe.
> But now let us go to him.

16Toma,[114] who was called the Twin, said to his fellow students, "Let us also go so that we may die with him."

---

112. The conjunction of "rabbi" and "the Jews" here is an anomaly whose contradiction in identity befuddles the purpose of making the Jews appear abhorrent. In like passages in Matthew and Luke, "rabbi" has been changed to "master," "teacher," or "Lord," and so the anomaly is less apparent.

113. From the Greek σωθήσεται (sothesetai), meaning primarily "he will be saved or preserved" and by extension "he will be cured." So both cure and salvation are implicit. The students have not understood "falling asleep" as a euphemism for death and understand *sothesetai* to mean "he will cure the (sleeping) body" and by extension "he will save the soul" of the dead man, save it for his body, which he will bring back to life.

114. Thomas from the Greek Θωμᾶς (Thomas), from the Aramaic תָּאוֹמָא (toma), from the Hebrew תְּאוֹם (teom).

Because תְּאוֹם means "twin," Thomas has frequently been identified as Yeshua's twin brother, but his name is not one of the four names listed in the gospels as Yeshua's brothers.

I am the resurrection

17When Yeshua arrived, he found that Elazar had already been four days in the tomb. 18Now Beit Aniyah was near Yerushalayim, about two miles away, 19and many of the Jews had come to console Marta and Miryam for their brother. 20When Marta heard that Yeshua was coming, she went out to meet him, but Miryam sat in her house. 21Then Marta said to Yeshua, "Sir, if you had been here, my brother would not have died. 22Even now I know that whatever you ask God, God gives you."

23Yeshua said to her,

> Your brother will rise again.

24Marta said to him, "I know he will rise in the resurrection on the last day."

25Yeshua said to her,

> I am the resurrection [and the life].[115]
> Those who believe in me even if they die
> Will live.
> 26And everyone who lives and believes in me
> Will not die into eternity.

He asked her, "Do you believe this?"

27She said to him, "Yes, lord. I believe that you are the mashiah, the son of God, who is coming into this world."

Raising Elazar

28After she said this, she left and called her sister Miryam, telling her secretly, "The teacher is here and calls for you."

29When that woman heard she got up quickly and came to him.

30Now Yeshua had not yet come into the village, and he was still at the place where Marta had met him.

31The Jews who were with her in the house, consoling her, saw Miryam quickly get up and go out, and they followed her, thinking that she was going to the tomb to weep there.

32Miryam came to where Yeshua was, and seeing him she fell at his feet, saying to him, "Sir, if you had been here my brother would not have died."

---

115. Not in early text.

33When Yeshua saw her weeping and the Jews who had come with her were weeping, he raged at his own spirit, harrowed himself, 34and said,

> Where have you laid him?

They said to him, "Sir, come and see."

35Yeshua wept.

36Then the Jews were saying, "See how he loved him."

37But some of them said, "Couldn't he who opened the eyes of the blindman have done something so this man wouldn't die?"

38Yeshua again raged inwardly and went to the tomb.

It was a cave, and a stone was lying against it.

39Yeshua said,

> Lift the stone.

The sister of the one who died, Marta, said to Yeshua, "Sir, he already stinks.[116] It's the fourth day."

40Yeshua said to her,

> Did I not tell you that if you believed
> You would see the glory of God?

41So they lifted the stone.

Yeshua lifted his eyes up and said,

> Father, I thank you for hearing me,
>   42And I know that you hear me always
>   But because of the crowd standing here
>   I spoke so they would believe you sent me.

43After saying this, in a great voice he cried out,

> Elazar, come out!

44The one who had died came out, bound feet and hands in graveclothes and his face wrapped around in a cloth.

Yeshua said to them,

> Unbind him and let him go.

The Jews plotting to kill Yeshua

45Then many of the Jews who had come to Miryam and seen what he did believed in him. 46But some of them went away to the Prushim and told them what Yeshua had done.

---

116. Stinks from the Greek ὄζει (otsei), meaning "stink." Many translations tone it down, but the KJV renders it "he stinketh."

47So the high priests and the Prushim called a meeting of the Sanhedrin,[117] 48and said, "What can we do about this man who is performing so many miraculous signs? If we leave him like this, everyone will believe in him, and the Romans will come and take away our holy place and nation."

49But one of them, Kayfa,[118] who was high priest for that year, said to them, "You know nothing. 50You haven't understood that it is better for one man to die for the sake of the people and not have the whole nation perish."

51This he did not say on his own, but as high priest for that year he prophesied that Yeshua would die for the sake of the nation, 52and not only for the nation but so that he might bring together the scattered children of God.

53From that day on they planned to kill him.[119]

54So Yeshua no longer walked openly among the Jews but went away from there to the country near the desert, to a city called Efrayim,[120] and he stayed there with the students.

As Pesach draws near, will Yeshua return to Yerushalayim?

55Now the Pesach of the Jews was near, and many went up from the country to Yerushalayim before Pesach to purify themselves. 56They were looking for Yeshua and said to one another as they stood in the Temple, "What do you think? That he won't come to the festival?"

57But the high priests and the Prushim had given orders that if anyone knew where he was, he should report it so they might seize him.

---

117. Council.

118. Caiaphas from the Greek Καϊάφας (Kaiafas), from the Hebrew כֵּיפָא (kayfa).

119. The conversations and substance of a conspiracy to kill Yeshua, like all conversations and events in the New Testament, have no recorded or otherwise historical evidence to corroborate their authenticity outside the gospels themselves. It is reasonable and probable to assume that such material was conceived and shaped by the authors of the gospels, based on unconfirmed story, testimony, or their own emendation.

120. Ephraim from the Greek Ἐφραίμ (Efraim), from the Hebrew אֶפְרַיִם (efrayim).

Chapter 12

*Miryam anointing Yeshua's feet and wiping them
with her hair*

Six days before Pesach, Yeshua came to Beit Aniyah where Elazar
was, whom he had raised from the dead. 2So they prepared a supper for
him, and Marta served, and Elazar was one of those reclining at the table
with him. 3Then Miryam took a pound of spikenard ointment, pure and
precious, anointed the feet of Yeshua, and wiped his feet with her hair.
And the house was full of the fragrance of the unguent.

4Yehuda of Keriot,[121] one of his students, who was about to betray him,
said, 5"Why was this ointment not sold for three hundred denarii[122] and
given to the poor?" 6But he said this not because he cared about the poor,
but because he was a thief and he was the keeper of the money box and
was removing what was dropped into it.

7So Yeshua said,

> Let her be, so she may keep it for the day
> Of my burial.
> 8The poor you always have with you,
> But me you do not always have.[123]

---

121. Judas Iscariot. Judas the Iscariot. Judas from the Greek Ἰούδας (Ioudas),
from the Hebrew יְהוּדָה (yehuda). The name for the messenger (apostle) Judas in
Hebrew, *Yehuda*, was surely invented because it suggests the Hebrew word for "Jew,"
which is יְהוּדִי (yehudi), thereby the betrayer of Yeshua among his followers was a
Jew, as opposed to the others who escape that identity.

122. Three hundred denarii could be a year's wages.

123. Similar stories about anointing Yeshua's body appear in Mark and Luke. In
Mark, the earliest of the gospels and main source of the synoptic gospels Matthew
and Luke as well as John, this occurs in the house of Shimon the Leper, not Elazar
(Lazarus). The grumbling about the money wasted on anointing Yeshua that might
have gone to the poor is voiced by unnamed diners, not Yehuda (Judas), who was
surely added to the supper table in order to further darken his portrait. In Luke, the
scene is more erotic; there is also a Shimon, the speech about the poor is almost the
same, and Yehuda is not mentioned.

The high priests plot to kill Elazar

9Then a great crowd of Jews learned that he was there, and they came, not only because of Yeshua but to see Elazar, whom he had raised from the dead. 10But the high priests planned also to kill Elazar 11since because of him many of the Jews were going away and believing in Yeshua.

Yeshua, king of Yisrael, enters Yerushalayim

12On the next day the great crowd that came to the festival heard that Yeshua was coming to Yerushalayim. 13They took palm branches and went out to meet him and, as in Psalms, they cried,

> Hosanna!
> Blessed is he who comes in the name of the lord,
> The king of Yisrael.[124]

14And Yeshua found a young donkey and was seated on it just as it is written in Zeharyahu.[125]

> 15Do not fear, daughter of Zion.
> Look, your king is coming,
> Sitting on a foal of a donkey.[126]

16His students did not understand these things at first, but when Yeshua was glorified, then they remembered that these things had been written about him and these things had been done for him.

17The crowd that was with him when he raised Elazar from the tomb bore witness to it all. 18That was why the crowd went to meet him, for they heard that he had performed the miraculous sign.

19So the Prushim said to one another, "You see, you can do nothing. Look, the world has gone over to him."

Yeshua foretells death and glorification

20Now there were some Greek Jews[127] among those who went up to

---

124. Ps. 118.25–26.

125. Zechariah or Zacharias from the Greek Ζαχαρίας (Zaharias), from the Hebrew זְכַרְיָהוּ (zeharyahu).

126. Zech. 9.9.

127. Ethnic Greeks who had converted to Judaism.

worship at the festival. 21They came to Filippos from Beit Tzaida of the Galil and asked him, saying, "Sir, we wish to see Yeshua."

22Filippos came and told Andreas. Andreas and Filippos came and told Yeshua.

23And Yeshua answered them, saying,

> The hour has come when the earthly son is glorified.[128]

24Amain, amain, I say to you,

> Unless a grain of wheat falling into the earth dies,
> It remains alone.
> But if it dies it brings forth a great harvest.[129]

> 25Whoever loves life will lose it,
> And whoever hates life in this world
> Will keep it for life everlasting.

> 26Let anyone who serves me, follow me,
> And where I am, there also will be my servant.
> Whoever serves me, the father will honor.

Yeshua speaks of his death and tells others to be children of light

> 27Now my soul is shaken
> And what shall I say?
> Father, save me from this hour?
> But I came for this hour.
> 28Father, glorify your name.

A voice came out of the sky,

> I have glorified it, and I shall glorify it again.

29Then the crowd standing there heard it. They said,

> It has thundered.

---

128. Glorification is the hour of his death, resurrection, and ascension.

129. Fruit from the Greek καρπός (karpos). καρπός is often translated as "harvest" or "crop," since here it refers specifically to the fruit of a wheat grain, which would be a harvest or crop.

Others said,

> An angel has spoken to him.

30Yeshua answered and said,

> Not because of me has this voice come
> But because of you.
> 31Now is the judgment of the world,
> Now the ruler of this world will be cast out.
> 32And if I am raised above the earth
> I shall draw all people to me.

33This he said, signifying what kind of death he was to die.

34The crowd answered him, "We heard from the law that the mashiah remains forever. How can you say the earthly son must be raised? Who is this earthly son?"

35Yeshua said to them,

> For a little time longer the light is with you.
> Walk about while you still have the light
> So that the darkness may not overtake you.
> And someone walking in the darkness
> Does not know where she is going.
> 36While you have light, believe in the light
> So you may be the children of light.

Of the unbelievers

Yeshua said this and went away and went into hiding from them. 37Though he had performed so many miraculous signs before them, they did not believe in him 38so that the word spoken by the prophet Yeshayahu[130] will be fulfilled,

> Lord, who has believed in our message?
> And to whom was the arm of the lord revealed?[131]

39This is why they could not believe, because since Yeshayahu said elsewhere,

> 40He has blinded their eyes and hardened their heart
> So that they might not see with their eyes

---

130. Isaiah.

131. Isa. 53.1. See also Romans 10.16.

And understand with their hearts and turn their ways around
So that I might heal them.[132]

41Yeshayahu said these things because he saw his glory and he spoke about him. 42Still even among the rulers many believed in him, but because of the Prushim they did not admit it so that they would not be put out of the synagogue. 43They loved human glory more than the glory of God.

44But Yeshua cried out and said,

Who believes in me does not believe in me
But in the one who sent me.
45Who looks at me also looks at him who sent me.
46As light into the world I have come
So that who believes in me will not reside in darkness.
47And who hears my words and does not keep them
I do not judge
For I have not come to judge the world
But to save the world.

48Who rejects me and will not receive my words
Has a judge waiting.
The word I spoke will judge him on the last day.
49Because I did not speak from myself
But the one who sent me,
The father has given me his commandment,
What I should say and how I should speak.
50And I know his commandment is life everlasting.
So what I say, as the father told me, I say it.

Chapter 13

Washing his students' feet

Before the feast of the Pesach, Yeshua knew that his hour had come to pass from this world to the father. In this world he had loved his own

---

132. Isa. 6.10. See also Matthew 13.15; Mark 4.12.

people and he loved them to the end. 2And when supper was served, the devil had already put in the heart of Yehuda,[133] son of Shimon of Keriot, that he should betray him. 3Yeshua, knowing that the father had placed everything in his hands and that he had come from God and was going to God, 4rose from the supper table, took off his garment, took a towel and girded his waist. 5And he poured water into the basin and began to wash the feet of his students and to wipe them with the towel he had tied around himself. 6Then he went to Shimon Kefa.[134]

Kefa said to him, "Lord, are you washing my feet?"

7Yeshua said to him,

    What I do for you, you do not know now,

    But these things later you will understand.

Kefa told him, "You will not wash my feet forever."

Yeshua answered him,

    Unless I wash you, you have no part of me.

9Kefa said to him, "Lord, not just my feet but also my hands and head."

10Yeshua told him,

    One who has bathed need wash nothing

    Except his feet

    And he is wholly clean, and you are clean

    But not all of you.

11He knew his betrayer. That is why he said,

    Not all of you are clean.

12So when he washed their feet and put his garments back on and took his place again reclining at the supper table, he said,

    Do you know what I have done for you?

    13You call me the rabbi and lord,[135]

---

133. Judas.

134. Simon Peter.

135. Lord or Adonai from the Greek κύριος (kyrios). When referring to the divine lord, the Greek κύριος (kyrios) may be translated "lord" or "Adonai" (אֲדֹנָי) as here in the Hebrew text cited from Isaiah; when referring to Jesus, *kyrios* may be translated as "sir," "master," "teacher," or "rabbi," when the implicit Hebrew source is רַבִּי (rabbi).

And what you say is right, for so I am.
14So if I your lord and rabbi washed your feet,
    You also ought to wash each other's feet.
15For I have given you an example
    For you to do as I have done to you.

    Amain, amain, I say to you,
    A slave is not greater than his master,
    Nor is the sent one greater than he
    Who sent her.
17If you know these things
    You are blessed if you do them.

18I am not speaking of all of you—
    I know whom I chose—
    But to fulfill the scripture:
    The one who ate my bread[136]
    Lifted his heel against me.
19I tell you now before it happens
    So that when it happens
    You will believe that I am I.

20Amain, amain, I say to you,
    The one who accepts one I send
    Also accepts me,
    And whoever accepts me
    Accepts him who sent me.
21After he said this, Yeshua was troubled in his soul, and bore witness,
and said,
    Amain, amain, I say to you,
    One of you will betray me.
22The students looked at each other, wondering whom he was speaking

---

136. Ps. 41.9.

about. 23One of the students was leaning back on Yeshua's chest, one whom Yeshua loved.[137]

24So Shimon Kefa nodded to him to ask who it was he was talking about. 25The man who was leaning on Yeshua's chest said to him, "Sir, who is it?"

26Yeshua answered,

> It is the one for whom I will dip the matzot
> And give it to him.

So he took the matzot and gave it to Yehuda, the man of Keriot. 27And after he received the matzot, Satan entered into him.

So Yeshua said to him,

> Do what you will do quickly.

28But no one of those lying back at the table knew why he said this to him. 29Some thought that since Yehuda had the money box, Yeshua was telling him,

> Buy what we need for the supper
> Or something to give to the poor.

30But he took the crust of bread and went out at once. Now it was night.

In a short while goodbye. Now love.

31When Yehuda left, Yeshua said,

> Now the earthly son has been glorified
> And God has been glorified in him.
> 32If God has been glorified in him
> God will glorify him in himself
> And will glorify him at once.

> 33Children, I am with you a short while.
> You will look for me,
> And I tell you now as I said to the Jews,
> "Where I go you cannot also come."

---

137. "The beloved student." The mysterious, unnamed student whom Yeshua loves will appear in the last lines of John as the one Yeshua loves most, who outruns Shimon Kefa to his empty tomb, and who will not die until Yeshua comes again.

34I give you a new commandment
  To love each other.
  As I loved you, you also must love each other.
35By this everyone will know
  You are my students
  If you love each other.

Yeshua tells Kefa what he will do
  36Shimon Kefa said to him, "Lord, where are you going?"
Yeshua answered him,
    Where I go
    You cannot follow me now,
    But you will follow later.
  37Kefa said to him, "Lord, why can I not follow you now? I will lay
down my life for you."
  38Yeshua answered him,
    You will lay down your life for me?
    Amain, amain, I say to you
    That the cock will not crow
    Before you have disowned me three times.

Chapter 14

I am the way
    Do not let your hearts be shaken.
    Believe in God and believe in me.
  2In my father's house there are many rooms.
    If there were not, would I have said to you
    That I go to prepare a place for you?
  3And if I go to prepare a place for you,
    I will come again and take you to me
    So that where I am you may also be.
  4And where I go you know the way.
  5Toma said to him, "Lord, we do not know where you are going. How
can we know the way?"
  6Yeshua said to him,

I am the way and the truth and the life.
No one comes to the father but through me.
7If you had known me, you would have also known my father,
And now you know him and have seen him.
8Filippos said to him, "Lord, show us the father, and that is enough for us."
9Yeshua said to him,

All this time I have been with you
And do you not know me, Filippos?
Who has seen me has seen the father.
How can you say, "Show us the father"?
10Do you not believe that I am in the father
And the father in me?
The words I speak to you I do not speak from myself
But the father who lives in me does his works.
11Believe that I am in the father
And the father is in me.
But if not, believe because of the works themselves.

12Amain, amain, I say to you,
Who believes in me will also do the works I do
And you will do ones greater than these,
Because I am going to the father.
13And whatever you ask in my name I will do
So that the father may be glorified in the son.
14If you ask for anything in my name,
That I will do.

15If you love me, keep my commandments,
16And I will ask the father for another comforter[138]
To be with you forever,
17The spirit of truth that the world cannot accept
Because it cannot see or know it.

---

138. The Paraclete (meaning in Greek and Hebrew the "comforter") has been identified with the Advocate, who will work on behalf of the "sinning believer."

You know it because it dwells with you
And in you will be.

18I will not leave you orphans.
I am coming to you.
19A little time and the world will not see me,
But you will see me.
Because I live, you also live.

20On that day you will know I am in my father,
And you are in me and I am in you.
21Who has my commands and keeps them loves me.
You who love me will be loved by my father,
And I will love you and reveal myself to you.

I leave you peace

22Yehuda said to him (not the man of Keriot), "Sir, what has happened
that you are to show yourself to us and not to the world?"
23Yeshua answered him and said,

Anyone who loves me will keep my word,
And my father will love you
And we will come to you and make our home with you.
24Anyone who does not love me
Does not keep the word that you hear,
And what I say is not mine
But from the father who sent me.

25This I have told you while I remain with you
26But the comforter, the holy spirit,
Whom the father will send in my name,
Will teach you all things and recall all things
That I have said to you.

27I leave you peace. My peace I give to you.
Not as the world gives, I give to you.
Do not be shaken in your heart or frightened.
28You heard what I told you.

"I am going away and I am coming to you."
If you loved me you would be happy
That I am going to the father
Since the father is greater than I.

29And now I have told you before it occurs
    So when it happens you may believe.
30I will no longer talk much with you,
    For the ruler of the world is coming,
    And he owns no part in me.
31But so the world knows I love the father,
    What the father has commanded me I do.

Rise up. Let us go from here.

Chapter 15

I am the true vine and my father is the gardener
    I am the true vine and my father is the gardener.
    2Each branch in me bearing no fruit he cuts off,
    And each branch bearing fruit he also prunes clean
    That it may bear even more fruit.
    3You are already clean because of the word
    I have spoken to you.

    4Abide in me as I in you.
    As the branch cannot bear fruit by itself
    Unless it stays on the vine,
    You too cannot unless you dwell in me.
    5I am the vine, you the branches.
    You who dwell in me as I in you
    Bear much fruit,
    But without me you can do nothing.

    6Anyone who does not remain in me
    Is cast away like a branch and dries up,

And these are gathered and thrown into the fire and burned.
7If you dwell in me and my words dwell in you,
Ask whatever you wish and it will be given you.

8So my father is glorified that you may bear much fruit
And be my students.
9As the father has loved me I have loved you.
Dwell in my love.
10If you keep my commandments
You will stay in my love,
Just as I have kept the father's commandments
And dwell in his love.
11These things I have told you so my joy may be in you
And your joy be full.

Love each other as I have loved you
12This is my command,
That you love each other as I have loved you.
13No one has greater love than this,
Than to lay down one's life for one's friends.
14You are my friends if you do what I command you.
15No longer will I call you slaves
Because the slave does not know what the master does.
But you I have called friends
Because all things I heard from my father
I have made known to you.

16You did not choose me
But I chose you and appointed you to go and bear fruit
And your fruit will last
And so whatever you ask for in my name he may give you
17These things I command you
So you may love one another.

A world hating us without cause
18If the world hates you,
Know that before you it hated me.
19If you were from the world

The world would love you as its own.
But I have chosen you out of this world
And because you are not of this world
The world hates you.

20Remember the word I said to you:
No slave is greater than his lord.
If they persecuted me, they will persecute you also.
If they kept my word, they will also keep yours.
21But all this they will do to you
Because of my name,
Because they do not know the one who sent me.

22If I had not come and spoken to them,
They would have no sin,
But now they have no cloak[139] to wrap around their sin.[140]
23Who hates me also hates my father.
24If I had not done among them things
That no one else has done,
They would have no sin.
But now they have seen and hated both me and my father.
25And to fulfill the word written in the law,[141]
"They hated me openly and without cause."[142]

When the comforter comes
26When the comforter comes,
Whom I will send you from my father,
The breath of truth who comes from the father,
He will testify about me.
27You also will be my witness
Since from the beginning you are with me.

---

139. Cloak, in that there is no possible concealment and therefore no excuse.
140. Or, "guilt."
141. "Law" as Torah (Hebrew Bible), which in this case is the Psalms.
142. Pss. 35.19 and 69.4.

Chapter 16

I will go away so the comforter will come
    This I have told you so you will not go astray.
  2They will expel you from the synagogue
   And the hour is coming when those who kill you
   Will suppose they are serving God.
  3And they will do this because they know
   Neither the father nor me.
  4But this I have told you so when the hour comes
   You will recall that I told you.
   I did not tell you at the beginning, since I was with you.
  5But now I am going to the one who sent me,
   And not one of you asks me, "Where are you going?"
  6But because I have said these things to you,
   Sorrow has filled your heart.

  7I tell you the truth: It is better for you that I go away.
  If I do not go, the comforter will not come to you.
  But if I go away, I will send him to you.
  8And when he comes he will expose the world
   Concerning wrongdoing and justice and judgment:
  9Wrongdoing, since they do not believe in me;
  10Justice because I am going to the father
   And you will no more see me.
  11Judgment because the ruler of this world has been judged.

  12I still have many things to tell you
  But you cannot bear to hear them now.
  13When the spirit[143] of truth comes

---

143. Or, "breath." The words in both the Hebrew and the Greek mean "wind" and by extension "spirit." There is usually a crossover in meaning which no one word in English has.

He will be your guide to the whole truth.
For he will not speak from himself but what he hears
And will report to you what is to come.
14He will glorify me
    Since he will take what is mine and report it to you.
15All that the father has is mine,
    So I said he will take what is mine and report it to you.
16In a little while you will no longer see me
    And again in a little while you will see me.

I will go, but when I return grief will turn into joy
17Now some of his students said to each other, "What does he mean
by 'In a little while you will no longer see me and again in a little while
you will see me,' and 'because I am going to the father'? 18What is this
'in a little while'? We don't know what he is saying."
19Yeshua knew they wanted to question him and said to them,

    Are you asking each other what I meant by,
    "In a little while you will no longer see me
    And again in a little while you will see me"?
20Amain, amain, I say to you,
    You will weep and mourn but the world will be joyful.
    You will be grieved but your grief will turn to joy.

21When a woman gives birth she grieves
    Because her hour has come,
    But when she has borne her child
    She no longer remembers her pain
    Because of the joy that a child was born into the world.
22So now you are in sorrow, but I will see you again
    And your heart will be happy
    And your gladness no one will take from you.
23And on that day you will ask me nothing.

    Amain, amain, I say to you,
    Whatever you ask the father in my name,
    He will give you.
24Till now you ask nothing in my name.

Ask and you will receive so your joy may be complete.

25These things I have told you in riddles,
But the hour is coming when no longer in riddles
Will I speak to you, but plainly I will declare
Concerning the father.
26On that day you will ask in my name.
And I do not say to you I will ask the father on your behalf.
27The father loves you because you have loved me
And believed that I have come from God.
28I came from the father and have come into the world.
I leave the world again and go to the father.

Through me, have peace. I have conquered the world
29His students said, "See, now you are speaking plainly and no longer in riddles. 30Now we know that you know all things and we have no need to question you. By this we know that you came from God."
31Yeshua answered them,
Now do you believe?
32Look, the hour is coming and it has come
When you will be scattered each on his own
And you will leave me alone.
But I am not alone, because the father is with me.

33These things I have said to you
So through me you may have peace.
In the world you have pain. Courage.
I have conquered the world.

Chapter 17

Yeshua raises his eyes, converses with the father,
and prays for his students
Yeshua said this, then raised his eyes to the sky and said,
Father, the hour has come.
Glorify your son so that your son may glorify you

2As you gave him authority over all flesh[144]
So he may give life everlasting to all you have given him.

3And this is the life everlasting
So that they may know you, the only true God,
And he whom you sent, Yeshua the Anointed.[145]
4I glorified you on earth
By completing the work you gave me to do.
5And now glorify me, father, with yourself,
With the glory I had with you before the world was.

6I made your name known to the people
Whom you gave me from the world.
They were yours and you gave them to me
And they have kept your word.
7Now they know that all you gave me comes from you.
8Because the words you gave me I gave them.
And they accepted them,
And they knew the truth that I came from you
And believed that you sent me.
9I ask for their sake.
I am not asking for the sake of the world
But for the ones whom you gave me
Because they are yours.
10And all that is mine is yours and yours is mine
And I am glorified in them.

I am not in this world
11And I am no longer in the world
But they are in the world,

---

144. All flesh from the Greek πάσης σαρκός (pases sarkos), which in a larger sense means "all people."

145. The Greek Ἰησοῦς ὁ χριστὸς (Iesous o hristos) can be translated as "Yeshua the Anointed" or "Yeshua the Mashiah."

And I am coming to you.
Holy father, [keep them in your name,
Which you gave me,]¹⁴⁶
So they may be one as we are one.

12When I was with them,
Through your name I kept those whom you gave me.
I guarded them and not one of them was lost
Except the son of perdition
So that the scripture be fulfilled.

I am coming to you

13Now I am coming to you
And these things I say in the world
So my elation be fulfilled in them.
14I gave them your word and the world hated them
Since they are not of the world
As I am not of the world.

Sanctify them in the truth

15I do not ask you to take them from the world
But to keep them from the cunning one.¹⁴⁷
16They are not of this world as I am not of this world.
17Sanctify them in the truth.
Your word is truth.
18As you sent me into the world so I sent them
into the world.
19And for them I sanctify myself
So they may also be sanctified in truth.

I ask for all believers

20I do not ask for them alone,
But for those believing in me through their word

---

146. This phrase is included in this text but not in other ancient texts.

147. From the Greek ἐκ τοῦ πονηροῦ (ek tou ponerou), translated as "from the evil one" or "from the devil."

21That we may all be one
　　As you, father, are in me and I in you;
　　That the world may believe that you sent me.
22The glory you gave me I gave them
　　So they may be one as we are one.
23I in them and you in me
　　So they may be made perfect as one,
　　So the world may know that you sent me
　　And loved them just as you loved me.

24Father, wherever I am I want the ones you gave me
　　Also to be with me and see my glory,
　　Which you gave me since you loved me
　　Before the foundation of the world.
25Just father, the world did not know who you were,
　　But I knew you
　　And these ones knew that you had sent me.
26I made your name known to them
　　And I shall make it known
　　So the love you have had for me
　　May be in them and I in them.

Chapter 18

Yehuda brings soldiers to arrest Yeshua

After saying these words, Yeshua went out with his students across the ravine[148] where there was a garden which he and his students entered.

2Now Yehuda, who betrayed him, also knew the place, since Yeshua often met there with his students. 3Then Yehuda[149] got a band of soldiers

---

148. Cedron from the Greek Κεδρών (Kedron), from the Hebrew קִדְרוֹן (kidron). The valley (or ravine) lies east of Jerusalem, on the way to the Mountain of Olives.

149. For more on the origin of the betrayer tale of Judas in scripture and post-biblical portrayals in history and the arts, see note 30 on p. 33, in "Mark, the Vernacular Story Teller." For a more complete account of Judas from the Bible to modern times, see Susan Gubar's *Judas: A Biography* (New York: W. W. Norton, 2009).

and serving men of the high priests and Prushim, and went there with lamps and torches and weapons.

4Yeshua, who knew everything that was to happen to him, went out and said to them,

> Who are you looking for?

5They answered him, "Yeshua the Natzrati."[150]

6He said to them,

> I am he.

And they stepped backward and fell to the ground.

7So he asked them again,

> Who are you looking for?

And they said, "Yeshua the Natzrati."

8Yeshua replied,

> I told you that I am he.
>
> If you are looking for me, let these men go.

9All this happened to fulfill the word he said,

> "I have not lost one of those you gave me."

Kefa cuts off the slave's ear

10Then Shimon Kefa had a knife and took it out and struck the slave of the high priest and cut off his right ear. The slave's name was Meleh.[151]

11But Yeshua said to Kefa,

> Put your knife back in its sheath.
>
> Shall I not drink the cup the father gave me?

Yeshua bound and taken to Hannan[152] and Kayfa[153]

12Then the guard and the commander and servants of the Jews took Yeshua and bound him. 13And first they led him to Hannan, who was the

---

150. Nazarene from the Greek Ναζαρηνός (Nazarenos), from Natzeret, that is, a Natzrati.

151. Malchus from the Greek Μάλχος (Malhos), probably from the Hebrew מֶלֶךְ (meleh), meaning "king."

152. Annas. *Hannan* or *Anan* means "high priest" in Hebrew, from the Greek Ἅννας (Annas), from the Hebrew חָנַן (hannan), "priest" or "gracious one."

153. Caiaphas.

father-in-law of Kayfa, the high priest for that year. 14Now it was Kayfa who advised the Jews that it is better for one man to die for the people.

Kefa disowns Yeshua in the high priest's court

15Shimon Kefa and another student followed Yeshua. And that student, who was known to the high priest, went with Yeshua into the high priest's court. 16But Kefa stayed outside the door. So the other student, an acquaintance of the high priest, spoke to the doorkeeper and brought Shimon Kefa inside.

17Then the girl who was at the door said to Shimon Kefa, "Aren't you one of that man's students?"

He said, "I am not."

Yeshua answers the high priest, and a servant beats him

18Now the slaves and assistants stood around a charcoal fire they had made, since it was cold and they were warming themselves. Kefa also was standing there with them, keeping warm.

19Then the high priest questioned Yeshua about his students and about his teaching.

20Yeshua replied to him,

> I have spoken openly to the world.
> I always taught in a synagogue and in the Temple
> Where all the Jews gather. And in secret
> I spoke nothing. 21Why question me?
> Ask those who heard what I said to them.
> Look, they know what I said.

22When he said this, one of the serving men slapped Yeshua, "Is that how you answer the high priest?"

23Yeshua answered him,

> If I spoke wrong, testify to the wrong.
> But if I spoke right, why do you beat me?

24Then Hannan sent him bound to Kayfa the high priest.

Kefa disowns Yeshua a second and third time

25Shimon Kefa was standing and warming himself. So they said to him, "Aren't you also one of his students?"

He denied it and said, "I am not."

26One of the high priest's slaves, a relative of the one whose ear Kefa cut off, said, "Didn't I see you in the garden with him?"

27Again Kefa denied it and at once the cock crowed.

Yeshua before Pilatus. Pilatus asks, Are you
the king of the Jews?

28They led Yeshua from Kayfa to the praetorium.[154] It was early morning. They didn't enter the praetorium, so as to avoid defilement that might prevent them from eating the Pesach meals. 29So Pilatus emerged and said to them, "What charge do you bring against this man?"

30They answered him and said, "Unless he was doing wrong, we would not have turned him over to you."

31Pilatus said to them, "Take him and judge him according to your law."

Then the Jews said to him, "It is not lawful for us to put anyone to death."

32This happened to fulfill Yeshua's word when he foretold what kind of death he was to die.[155]

33Then Pilatus again went into the praetorium and called Yeshua and said to him, "Are you the king of the Jews?"

34Yeshua answered,

> Are you speaking for yourself
> Or did others tell you about me?

35"Am I a Jew?" Pilatus answered. "Your people and the high priest handed you over to me. What did you do?[156]

---

154. Governor's house.

155. Verse 32, a commentary and interpretation interrupting the narration, may be a scribal interpolation and is usually placed in parentheses or brackets.

156. Pilate's essential question, "What did you do?" would suggest that Pilate is unaware of wrongdoing. Among historians there is a consensus that Rome executed Yeshua as a seditionist, as one opposed to Roman occupation. Pilate's question to Yeshua, however, as preserved in scripture, means that Yeshua had committed no grievance against Rome, but Pilate would carry out a punishment for the Jews, to crucify a rabbi, because of disagreement with coreligionists on vital issues. Without historical evidence, Pilate's question is not plausible. Its consequence is to accuse coreligionists of initiating Yeshua's execution and to emphasize Rome's unwilling and marginal involvement in it.

₃₆Yeshua responded,

> My kingdom is not of this world.
> If my kingdom were of this world
> My servants would have fought to keep me
> From being delivered to the Jews.[157]
> But now my kingdom is not here.

₃₇Then Pilatus said to him, "Then you are a king?"
Yeshua answered,

> You say I am a king.
> For this I was born
> And for this I came into the world
> That I might testify to the truth.
> Everyone born of truth hears my voice.

₃₈Pilatus said to him, "What is truth?"

Pilatus before the Jews, who shout for Bar Abba

And after he said this, again he went out to the Jews and told them, "I find no fault in him. ₃₉But you have this custom that I should release someone to you at Pesach. So do you want me to release the king of the Jews?"

₄₀They shouted back saying, "Not this man but Bar Abba!"[158]

Now Bar Abba was a robber.

Chapter 19

Crucify!

Then Pilatus took Yeshua and flogged him. ₂And the soldiers wove a wreath out of thorns and put it on his head and threw a purple robe

---

157. Here the "we and them" reference to Jews signifies that the speaker and his supporters are not to be identified as Jews. A Jew has not been crucified, although Yeshua's teaching in the Temple has been to persuade Jews that he represents true Judaism. Near death, the rabbi might disagree with other Jews but not himself deny that he is a Jew, that symbolically he is king of the Jews. The placement of the denial is odd, since it follows immediately upon Pilate's own identification of Yeshua as a Jew in his statements "Are you the king of the Jews?" and "your people."

158. Barabbas from the Greek Βαραββᾶς, from the Aramaic בַּר אַבָּא (bar abba), meaning "son of abba" (father).

around him. ₃And they went up to him and said, "Hello, king of the Jews!"

And they struck him in the face.

₄And Pilatus again went outside and said to them, "Look, I am bringing him out to you so you may know I find no fault in him."

₅Then Yeshua came out, wearing the wreath of thorns and the purple robe.

And Pilatus said to them, "Look at the man."

₆When the high priests and the serving men saw him, they shouted,

Crucify, crucify!

Pilatus said to them, "You take him and crucify him. I find no fault in him."

₇The Jews answered him, "We have a law and according to that law he should die, because he made himself son of God."

Pilatus, afraid, yields to the Jews and orders crucifixion

₈When Pilatus heard this word, he was more frightened. ₉Again he went back into the praetorium and said to Yeshua, "Where are you from?"

But Yeshua didn't answer him.

₁₀Then Pilatus told him, "You don't speak to me? Don't you know that I have the authority to free you and I have the authority to crucify you?"

₁₁Yeshua answered him,

You would have no authority over me at all
Were it not given to you from above.
Therefore the one who handed me over to you
Has the greater sin.[159]

₁₂Thereupon Pilatus sought to release him, but the Jews cried out, saying, "If you free this man, you are not a friend of Caesar! Everyone who makes himself a king defies Caesar."

---

159. Yeshua fully exonerates Pilate, who is acting not through his authority or free will but by the authority given to him from the father. The Jews, however, have acted freely and therefore their sin is greater. It's not clear why God has authority over Pilate, that is, controls him, and not Jesus's coreligionist Jews.

13When Pilatus heard these words, he led Yeshua outside and sat on the judgment seat called Stone Pavement, but in Hebrew Gabta.[160]

14Now it was Friday, the Preparation Day for the Pesach, the sixth hour which is noon. He said to the Jews, "Look, here is your king."

15Then they shouted, "Take him away, take him away and crucify him!"

Pilatus said to them, "Shall I crucify your king?"

The high priest answered, "We have no king but Caesar."

16So he gave him to them to be crucified.[161]

Carrying his cross to the Place of the Skull, Gulgulta, where they crucify him

They took Yeshua. 17Carrying the cross himself, he went to what was called the Place of the Skull, which in Hebrew is Gulgulta,[162] 18where

---

160. Gabbatha from the Greek Γαββαθά (Gabbatha), from an unknown Aramaic word that would be transliterated as *gabta*.

161. With reference to the "them" in 19.16, the commentary in the Jesus Seminar translation in *The Five Gospels* reads, "The resulting implication that all the Jews/Judeans, or perhaps only some Jewish officials, crucified Jesus—as Pilate had suggested—is wholly inaccurate. In historical fact, whatever Pilate's view of Jesus' guilt, it was certainly he who saw to the execution; crucifixion was never practiced by Jews. The monstrous unreality of this half-verse, if it reads as intended, must be entirely a function of theological or political polemic" (Robert W. Funk and Ray W. Hoover, eds. *The Five Gospels*, New York: Macmillan, 1993).

In the introduction to John in Robert J. Miller's *The Complete Gospels: Annotated Scholars Version* (Sonoma, CA: Polebridge Press, 1992–1994), under "A Jewish Christian gospel," there is a full discussion of references to "the Jews." "The ideological milieu of this gospel is thoroughly Jewish: even the abstract and dualistic symbolism (such as light/darkness) comes from a world that has very little to do with Gentile culture. Nevertheless, this document is ardently anti-Jewish. Only here are the Jewish people spoken of monolithically and from the outside; in the other gospels Pilate alone uses the phrase 'the Jews.' The explanation appears to be that this group of Christian Jews has recently been expelled from the synagogue (9.22, 34; 12.42; 16.2) and therefore has a highly ambivalent, and frequently hostile, attitude to Ioudaioi. . . . This gospel has given rise, still more than Matthew, to savage Christian anti-Semitism down the subsequent centuries."

162. Golgotha from the Greek Γολγοθά (Golgotha), from the Aramaic גֻּלְגָּלְתָּא (gulgulta), meaning "skull."

they crucified him, and with him two others, one on either side with Yeshua in the middle.

19Pilatus wrote a placard and put it on the cross. It read,

Yeshua the Natzrati the King of the Jews.

20Many Jews read the placard because the place where Yeshua was crucified was near the city. And it was written in Hebrew, Latin, and Greek. 21So the high priests of the Jews said to Pilatus, "Do not write, 'The King of the Jews,' but write what he said: 'I am king of the Jews.'"

22Pilatus answered, "What I've written I've written."

The soldiers cast lots for Yeshua's clothes

23When the soldiers crucified Yeshua, they took his clothes and divided them in four parts, one part for each soldier. And they took his tunic too. Now his tunic shirt was seamless, woven in one piece from the top straight down. 24So they said to each other, "Let's not tear it, but cast lots for it to see whose it will be. This was to fulfill the words written in the Psalms saying,

> They divided my clothes among them
> And for my clothes they cast lots.[163]

That is what the soldiers did.

Woman, here is your son

25But near the cross of Yeshua stood his mother and his mother's sister Miryam of Klofa[164] and Miryam of Magdala.[165]

---

163. Ps. 22.18.

164. Clopas from the Greek Κλωπᾶς (Klopas), from the Aramaic קְלוֹפָא (klofa). The name cannot be explained with certainty, but it is said to refer to a person who is the husband of the Mary near the cross, or is the father of James, and others identify him with Cleopas to whom the risen Yeshua appeared on the road to Emmaus (Luke 24.18). Cleopas is a Greek name from Κλεοπᾶς (Kleopas). See note 176 on Mark 15.40.

165. Magdalene from the Greek Μαγδαληνή (Magdalene), meaning "from Magdala," from the Greek Μαγαδάν (Magadan), from the Aramaic *Magdala*. A village of uncertain location near Lake Gennesaret.

26Then Yeshua, seeing his mother and the student he loved standing near, said to his mother,

> Woman, here is your son.[166]

27Then he said to the student,

> Here is your mother.

And from that hour the student took her into his home.[167]

I am thirsty. It is ended.

28After this Yeshua, knowing that all had been done to fulfill the words of the Psalms, said,

> I am thirsty.

29A jar filled with cheap wine[168] was lying there. So they put a sponge soaked with the vinegar on a branch of hyssop and held it to his mouth.

30Then when Yeshua had taken the wine, he said,

> It is ended.

And bowing his head he gave up his spirit.[169]

A spear in Yeshua's side

31Since it was Friday the Preparation Day, the Jews asked Pilatus that their legs be broken and they be taken away so that the bodies would not remain on the cross on Shabbat. 32The soldiers came and broke the bones of the first man and then of the other one crucified with him. 33But when they came to Yeshua and saw that he was already dead, they

---

166. Literally, "Woman, look, your son," which is followed by "Look, your mother." In the synoptic gospels, Mary, Yeshua's mother, does not appear. Here she appears briefly, but her name goes unmentioned. The other Marys appear by name.

167. Although "home" or "care" may be the implied translation, it says no more than "He took her into his own," probably meaning "her own place."

168. Vinegar from the Greek ὄξος (oksos), "cheap wine," "sour wine," or "vinegar."

169. Breath or spirit from the Greek πνεῦμα (peneuma), meaning "spirit" or "wind/breath." Here again the word πνεῦμα, with its double meaning of particular "breath" and more general "spirit," retains in the Greek its double message, that is, he stopped breathing and surrendered his spirit. The phrase παρέδωκεν τὸ πνεῦμα (paredoken to pneuma) in KJV is rendered movingly as "gave up the ghost."

did not break his legs. ₃₄But one of the soldiers stabbed his side with his spear, and at once blood and water came out.

₃₅And the one who saw this has testified to it, and the testimony is true, and he knows he is speaking the truth so that you may also believe.[170]

₃₆These things happened to fulfill the scripture: "No bone of his will be broken."[171] ₃₇And in Zeharyahu it says, "They will look at him whom they stabbed."[172]

₃₈After these things Yosef of Arimathaia,[173] being a student of Yeshua, but a secret one for fear of the Jews,[174] asked Pilatus if he could take away Yeshua's body.

Pilatus allowed it.

Then he came and took the body.

₃₉Nakdeimon came too, the one who first came to him during the night, and he brought a mixture of myrrh and aloes, about a hundred pounds. ₄₀So they took the body of Yeshua and wrapped it in aromatic spices in linen cloths, as is the burial custom of the Jews.[175]

---

170. Much of the New Testament centers around questions of belief, particularly in Yeshua's miracles and divinity. Belief is a moral signal of good or evil. In this unusual insertion into the narration, the narrator notes the specific event of blood and water issuing from Yeshua's side and concludes that the event has been witnessed, the testimony is true, and "you may believe." What is apparently miraculous is that water as well as blood has issued from the wound. Raymond E. Brown renders a standard interpretation: "The scene of the piercing of the dead Jesus' side is peculiarly Johannine, fulfilling both 7.37–39 that from Jesus would flow living water symbolic of the Spirit, and (since the bones of the paschal lamb were not to be broken) 1.29 that he was the Lamb of God" (*An Introduction to the New Testament*, New York: Doubleday, 1997, 358).

171. Ps. 34.20; Exodus 12.46; Num. 9.12.

172. Zech. 12.10.

173. Arimathea from the Greek Αριμαθαία (Arimathaia), and identified with either Ramathaim or Rentis, fifteen to twenty miles east of Jaffa.

174. Though a Pharisee and member of the Sanhedrin, by being presented as one in fear of the Jews, Yosef of Arimathaia is at once delivered from his religious identity and wears no stain of Jewish villainy.

175. As is the Jewish custom. Please see commentary to this passage in the Afterword.

41Now in the region where he was crucified there was a garden, and in the garden a new tomb in which no one had been placed. 42So because it was Friday, the Preparation Day of the Jews, and the tomb was near, in it they placed Yeshua.

Chapter 20

Miryam of Magdala discovers the empty tomb

On Sunday the first day of the week, Miryam of Magdala came to the tomb early while it was still dark and saw that the stone had been removed from the tomb. 2So she ran and came to Shimon Kefa and to the other student whom Yeshua loved and said to them, "They took the lord from the tomb and we don't know where they put him."

3Then Shimon Kefa and the other student came out and went to the tomb. 4The two ran together, but the student ran faster than Kefa and reached the tomb first. 5And he stooped down and saw the linen cloths lying there, but didn't go in. 6Then Shimon Kefa came, following him, and he went into the tomb, and saw the linen cloths lying there, 7but the kerchief which had been on his head was not lying next to the cloths but apart and folded up in its own place. 8And then the other student, who had come first to the tomb, saw and believed. 9They didn't yet know the scripture[176] that he must rise from the dead.

Miryam of Magdala cries Rabboni!

10The students went off to their own places.

11But Miryam stood by the tomb, weeping. Then as she was weeping, she stooped and looked into the tomb 12and saw two angels in white sitting there, one at the head and one at the feet where the body of Yeshua had lain.

---

176. There is a resurrection of the dead in Isaiah 26.19 and Daniel 12.2. The notion of resurrection of the dead and immortality of the soul is derived from Jewish apocalyptic literature and probably the influence of Plato, Neoplatonism, and contemporary pagan notions.

13And they said to her,

> Woman, why are you weeping?

She said to them, "They have taken my lord away and I don't know where they put him."

14Saying this she turned around and saw Yeshua standing there and didn't know it was Yeshua.

15Yeshua said to her,

> Woman, why are you weeping?
>
> Whom are you looking for?

Thinking he was the gardener, she said to him, "Sir, if you took him away, tell me where you put him and I will take him."

16Yeshua said to her,

> Miryam!

She turned and said to him in Hebrew, "Rabboni!" (which means my great teacher).[177]

17Yeshua said to her,

> Do not hold on to me,
> Since I have not yet gone up to the father.
> But go to my brothers and tell them:
> "I am ascending to my father and your father
> And my God and your God."

18Miryam of Magdala went and announced to the students, "I have seen the lord." And she told them that he had said these things to her.

Yeshua appears in the locked house of the students

19So when it was early evening of that first day of the week and the doors of the house where the students met were locked for fear of the Jews, Yeshua came and stood in their midst and said to them,

> Peace to you.

20And saying this he showed his hands and his side to them.

---

177. Mary would have been speaking Aramaic, and in "She turned and said to him in Hebrew, 'Rabboni!'" *rabboni* is Aramaic, not Hebrew. *Rabboni* is an augmentative form of the word "rabbi," whose primary meaning is "rabbi," not "teacher." The scribal intrusion, "which means teacher," fails to silence the idea that to Mary, in her moment of dramatic recognition, Yeshua is truly a rabbi.

The students were overjoyed when they saw the lord.

21So Yeshua said to them again,

> Peace to you.
> As the father sent me, so I send you.

22And saying this he breathed over them and said to them,

> Receive the holy spirit.
> 23For any whose sins you forgive,
> Their sins are forgiven.
> For any whose sins you do not release,
> They are not released.

Yeshua tells doubting Toma to touch his wounded side

24But Toma, who was one of the twelve, called the Twin, was not with them when Yeshua came.

25So the other students were saying to him, "We have seen the lord."

But he said to them, "Unless I see the mark of the nails in his hands and I put my finger into the place of the nails and I put my hand into his side, I shall not believe."

26After eight days the students were again in the house and Toma with them. Though the doors were shut, Yeshua stood in their midst and said,

> Peace to you.

27Then he said to Toma,

> Bring your fingers here and see my hands,
> And bring your hand and put it in my side,
> And do not be without faith but of faith.

28Toma answered saying to him, "My lord and my God."

29Yeshua said to him,

> Do you believe because you have seen me?
> Blessed are they who have not seen and believe.

30Yeshua performed many other signs before his students, which have not been written in this book. But these things were written that you may believe that Yeshua is the mashiah, the son of God, and that in believing you may have life in his name.

Chapter 21
(A Supplement)[178]

Yeshua causes fish in Lake Tiberius to be plentiful near the students' boat

After this, Yeshua again showed himself to the students at Lake Tiberius. And this is how he showed himself. 2Gathered together were Shimon Kefa and Toma called the Twin and Natanel from Kana in the Galil and the sons of Zavdai[179] and two other students.

3Shimon Kefa said, "I'm going fishing."

They told him, "We're coming with you."

They went out and got into the boat, and all that night caught nothing.

4At daybreak Yeshua was standing on the beach. But the students didn't realize that it was Yeshua.

5Yeshua said to them,

Children, have you any fish?

"No," they answered him.

6And he said to them,

Cast the net in the waters to the right side
Of the ship and you will find some.

So they cast, and they weren't strong enough to haul it back in because of the swarm of fish.

Yeshua attends a breakfast fishbake

7Then that student[180] whom Yeshua loved said to Kefa, "It is the lord."

---

178. Or, "orphan ending."

179. Zebedee from the Greek Ζεβεδαῖος (Zebedaios), from the Hebrew זַבְדִּי (zavdai).

180. Apparently the unknown student, who ran faster to the empty tomb than Peter, believed what he saw (20.5, 20.8). When fishing, the beloved student, not Peter, recognized Yeshua on the shore (21.4, 21.7). In the same supplement, however, Peter appears to be elevated to leadership (21.18) by virtue of his foretold crucifixion in service of the church. In the missions of the Jerusalem church, Peter, as the "rock" on which the church was founded, was conventionally entrusted with the circumcised and Paul with the uncircumcised (Gal. 2.7).

When Shimon Kefa heard it was the lord, he put on his outer garment, for he had stripped naked and jumped into the sea.

8But the other students came in a small boat—they were not far from the land, about a hundred yards away—dragging the net full of fish.

9When they came out on the shore, they saw a charcoal fire and a small fish placed on it, and bread.

10Yeshua said to them,

Now bring some of the fish you caught.

11So Kefa went on board and dragged the net onto the land, filled with big fish, a hundred fifty-three of them, yet with so many the net didn't tear.

12Yeshua said to them,

Come have breakfast.

None of the students dared ask, "Who are you?" They knew that it was the lord.

13Yeshua came and took the bread and gave it to them, and also the fish.

14This was already the third time that Yeshua appeared to the students after he was raised from the dead.

Yeshua questions Shimon Kefa's love

15So when they had breakfasted, Yeshua said to Shimon Kefa,

Shimon son of Yohanan, do you love me
More than they do?

Shimon said to him, "Yes, lord, you know that I love you."
Yeshua said to him,

Feed my lambs.

16He asked Shimon a second time,

Shimon son of Yohanan, do you love me?

Shimon said, "Yes, lord, you know that I love you."

17He said to Shimon son of Yohanan for the third time,

Do you love me?

Kefa was hurt that he had asked him for the third time, "Do you love me?" And he said to him, "Lord, you know all things, you know that I love you.¹⁸¹

---

181. Peter's threefold profession of love parallels his earlier threefold denial.

Yeshua replied,
> Graze my sheep.

Yeshua foretells Shimon Kefa's death
And he said to him,
> 18Amain, amain, I say to you,
> When you were younger,
> You fastened your own belt
> And walked about where you wished.
> But when you grow old
> You will stretch out your hands
> And another will fasten your belt
> And take you where you do not wish to go.[182]

19This he said, signifying by what death he would glorify God.
After he said this, he told him,
> Follow me.

The unknown, most-loved student who is writing
this passage
20Kefa turned and saw the student whom Yeshua loved following them, the one who also lay next to his chest at the supper and who had said, "Who is betraying you?"

21When Shimon Kefa saw him, he said to Yeshua, "Lord, what about him?"

22Yeshua said to Kefa,
> If I want him to stay until I come, what is that to you?
> Follow me.[183]

23So word went out to the brothers that the student would not die. But Yeshua did not tell Shimon Kefa that the student would not die, but rather, "If I want him to stay until I come, what is that to you?"

---

182. This passage suggests Peter's later crucifixion, which is uncertain.

183. This testy exchange, in which Yeshua tells Peter to follow him and not to question him further about the unnamed other student whom Yeshua loves most, is mystifying. The student will be there when Yeshua comes again, will not die, and declares himself to be the one testifying to and writing the final lines in colophon 21.24–25.

24This is the student who testifies to these things and who has written these things, and we know that his testimony is true.

The world not big enough to hold books
describing Yeshua's doings

25And there are many other things that Yeshua did. If they were written down one by one, I think the world itself would not have room to hold the books that would be written.

Gnostic Gospels

Translated and with introductions
by Willis Barnstone and Marvin Meyer

Toma
(Thomas)

Toma (Thomas)

⌒

In 1946 the Dead Sea Scrolls were discovered in caves at Qumran on the northwest shore of the Dead Sea, yielding copies in Hebrew, Aramaic, and Greek of biblical documents as well as key scriptures of the Essenes who lived on that arid plain. The Dead Sea Scrolls shook the religious world. A year earlier in 1945, the Nag Hammadi Library was discovered in a sealed jar buried in a farm in upper Egypt near the town of Nag Hammadi, yielding twelve leather-bound papyrus codices containing copies in Coptic of fifty-two mostly Gnostic tractates. These are the Gnostic gospels, of which the most famous is the Gospel of Thomas.

A version of this gospel may have been composed, most likely in Greek, as early as the middle of the first century, and may have been written in Syria, possibly at Edessa (modern Urga), where a memory of Thomas was revered and where his bones were venerated. The gospel today exists in translation from Greek into Coptic (late Egyptian), but at Oxyrhynchus were found fragments in Greek dating from about 200 C.E. The year 340 has been a suggested date for the Coptic version buried at Nag Hammadi for safekeeping from the Christian Orthodox church that in those centuries burned whatever Gnostic scriptures it came upon.

Thomas begins with the hidden sayings that the living Jesus spoke and Judas Thomas the twin recorded. Thomas's original Aramaic name, Toma, means twin, as it also does in Syriac and Hebrew. The Gospel of Thomas is a collection of 114 wisdom sayings in the voice of Yeshua. It is appropriate to begin with number 1, which sets the tone, but the larger order seems to be arbitrary. It contains no gospel story of Jesus's life but rather a discourse between himself and his students. The speech has the dialectical flavor of the ancient world.

Wisdom sayings are Yeshua's way. There is a multitude of wisdom sayings from the widely circulating wisdom literature of the Near East and Mediterranean cultures, dating back to the second and third millennia B.C.E. The Jewish Bible is a treasure of verse sayings, from Proverbs and Ecclesiastes to the apocryphal Wisdom of Solomon. Among the cagiest pieces of wisdom logic are the Cynic sayings from Greco-Roman times, collected in textbooks called *progymnasmata*. In many ways the wayfarer Cynic, as Burton Mack suggests, comes closest to the free-speaking dissenter Jesus in Thomas, who is disinterested in end time, in the eschaton, in fact in any time other than time independent of sun time that exists only now in the spirit. And finally there are the two discrete books in the gospels: the life, death, and resurrection of Jesus, fiercely bound to time of day and night; and the wisdom speech of the charismatic rabbi teacher Yeshua whose rhetorical vehicle is the aphorism and parable.

There is a coincidence of wisdom sayings in Thomas and the gospels that immediately spikes critical query: are the gospels the source or the recipient of these wisdom utterances in Thomas?[1] If the gospels are the source of Thomas, then the dating of the platonic dialogue is after 85 C.E. The post-gospels or "late camp" scholars favor a dating in the second or even third century, which is the traditionalist view. One argument for a late dating is that Gnosticism is a later development than earliest Christianity. Yet one need only read Paul, who composed all his letters before the gospels were written and before Christianity had scripture and decisive separation from its Jewish origin and Jewish congregations, to note that the competing theological enemy is not the Greco-Roman pantheon, not Yahweh, not even the weak in belief in

---

1. The third possibility is that the Gospel of Thomas came both before and after the gospels. Thomas, with its Gnostic wisdom of light, contradiction, and immediate salvation, has an eloquent precursor in the nowness of time, in the here-and-now earthly salvation found in the Hebrew Bible from Ecclesiastes to Daniel. If we posit that Thomas precedes and deeply influences the gospels, Thomas's final form may have been affected by the gospels by the time there are copies of copies and translations of translations. I am persuaded that Thomas precedes the canonical gospels, yet aware that New Testament gospels influence each other in parallel passages from Mark to Luke. Likewise, some form and flavor of the gospels may have entered the minds and hands of Gnostic scribes and translators conserving the sayings of Thomas. Having said this, the Yeshua revealed in recordings by Judas Thomas the twin is an amazing figure of light, however he got to us.

his own synagogues and churches. Those formidable intellectual and persuasive enemies are the nefarious teachers who seduce the mind with false knowledge, with faithless *gnosis*. They are the Gnostics. The same perceived threat from the Gnostics pervades most of the letters and even very late Revelation.

For the "early camp" view, that Thomas precedes the gospels, Harold Bloom asserts that one of the effects of the Gospel of Thomas is to "undo the Jesus of the New Testament and return us to an earlier Jesus."[2] Elaine Pagels in turn asserts in her *Beyond Belief: The Secret Gospel of Thomas* that the Thomas community embraced spiritual resurrection in contrast to the doubting Thomas notion in the gospels of spiritual as well as bodily resurrection. In the gospels Thomas Didymos touches the skin of the risen Jesus to ascertain that he has real flesh, wanting assurances that Jesus has risen physically as well as spiritually. Pagels states that the Thomas community, which pointed only to a spiritual salvation, preceded the Gospel of John, and hence the pre-gospel date for *The Secret Gospel of Thomas*.

Given that there are no clear or even vaguely existing sources for the Jesus story in the canonical gospels, the existence of Thomas's wisdom sayings, which appear in like form in the gospels, seems a likely source for wisdom sayings in the gospels. Indeed, the 114 sayings in the Gospel of Matthew could have been key to the combinatory messianic figure of Jesus that the evangelists fleshed out in their own mythic tale of wonder, proselytizing, miraculous healing, crucifixion, and resurrection. Unlike the New Testament gospels, however, the Gospel of Thomas is free of narrative. It contends no virgin birth, and Yeshua performs no physical miracles, reveals no fulfillment of prophecy, announces no apocalyptic kingdom about to disrupt the world order. He is not acclaimed as master or lord or the incarnate and unique son of God. More, Jesus dies for no one's sins and does not rise from the dead on Easter Sunday.

The gospel path to salvation is alien to the Thomas sayings, though Thomas does not exclude later salvation. The secret words of Yeshua propose immediate internal salvation now, independent of world and time. Harold Bloom in his "reading" of Thomas in Marvin Meyer's *The Gospel of Thomas: The Hidden Sayings of Jesus,* tells us dynamically:

2. From Harold Bloom, "A Reading," in Marvin Meyer, *The Gospel of Thomas*, p. 131.

"Unlike the canonical gospels, that of Judas Thomas the Twin spares us the crucifixion, makes the resurrection unnecessary, and does not present us with a God named Jesus. No dogmas could be founded upon this sequence (if it is a sequence) of apothegms. If you turn to the Gospel of Thomas, you encounter a Jesus who is unsponsored and free. No one could be burned or even scorned in the name of this Jesus."[3]

Jesus in Thomas lives on in his secret sayings with hidden meanings: "Whoever discovers what these sayings mean / Will not taste death" (1). That is to say, one who uncovers the interpretive keys to these sayings finds true wisdom and knowledge. "There is nothing hidden that will not be revealed" (5). Yet in its typical is-and-is-not pattern, revelation is and is not revealed. Like Emerson and Whitman, Yeshua finds grace in self-contradiction. Walt tells us:

> Do I contradict myself?
> Very well then I contradict myself,
> (I am large, I contain multitudes.)
>
> —*Leaves of Grass*, 51

With its constancy of focus on a knowledge or awareness of the unsayable hidden wisdom that forever swings back and forth in a balance of equal opposites, the Gospel of Thomas shares the Gnostic centering on the pursuit and absorption of relative knowledge. And Yeshua makes it easy and doesn't make it too easy. He keeps the attainment of knowledge not finite—there are no finalities in this Yeshua—but a process of attainment, a movement. It is never stasis (standing there) but *exstasis*, moving on, ecstasy. Hence we read in saying 2:

> Seek and do not stop seeking until you find.
> When you find, you will be troubled.
> When you are troubled,
> You will marvel and rule over all.

There are two realms in Thomas, the physical and the spiritual. As to personal resurrection, in Thomas's dualistic belief system, the spirit

---

3. From Bloom, "A Reading," in Meyer, *The Gospel of Thomas*, p. 125.

alone, not the body, is saved. And we attain the spiritual through finding the light. Crucially, Elaine Pagels in *Beyond Belief* sees in Thomas the Gnostic notion of Jesus as teacher, who is not the light of the world but one who proclaims a divinity of light within us.

> There is light within a person of light
> And it shines on the whole world.
>
> SAYING 24

But once we hear that Jesus is not the light, wait, or listen again to his Whitmanian declaration:

> I am the light over all things.
> I am all.
> From me all things have come
> And all things have reached me.
> Split a piece of wood.
> I am there.
> Lift up the stone
> And you will find me there.
>
> SAYING 77

Saying 77 is so much like the ending of Walt Whitman's "Song of Myself," one must ask, did Thomas crib from Whitman or Whitman rob Thomas? It is not coincidence, but both poets have come upon universal truths, which are not absolute and in their energy live on debate, dialectic, and contradiction. Look to the earth, they both say. Thomas says to look under a piece of wood or a stone. Whitman says look under his boot-sole on the grass. Whitman's memorable ending is,

> I bequeath myself to the dirt to grow from the grass I love,
> If you want me again look for me under your boot-soles . . .
>
> Failing to fetch me at first keep encouraged,
> Missing me one place search another,
> I stop somewhere waiting for you.
>
> —*Leaves of Grass*, 52

I see Thomas, like the letters, as an early direct or indirect source for the gospels, coming perhaps a decade or two decades before the canonical gospels. Along with Laozi's *Daodejing*, biblical Ecclesiastes and Song of Songs, and Plato's *Phaedrus*, the Gospel of Thomas reaches the summit of wisdom and metaphysical and poetic literature. Bloom says it in appropriate metaphors: "Like William Blake, like Jakob Böhme, this Jesus is looking for a face he had before the world was made."[4] It seems to me incredulous that so many would take this wondrous Jesus figure and deposit him as the scribbles and musings of a misguided monk in a Syrian or Alexandrian monastery.[5] This unreformed Yeshua is a drink of fresh water from a brook on a summer meadow or hill in Judea. His students look on, wondering before his promises and challenge. Dare they drink too? He is the speaker in a vital, sophisticated original work who survives worldly measures and distractions. The knowledge of his vision of peace and light offers all a living breath now.

4. From Bloom, "A Reading," in Meyer, *The Gospel of Thomas,* p. 136.

5. Harold Bloom in a worldly way links the Thomas Jesus to the great mystical poets, while showing his exasperation with writing him off as a late afterthought by an early church father's ditherings: "Whatever surges beneath the surface of the Gospel of Thomas, it is not a Syrian Christian wisdom teaching of the second century." From "A Reading," in Meyer, *The Gospel of Thomas*, p. 136.

The Gospel of Toma[6]

These are the hidden sayings that the living Yeshua spoke and Yehuda Toma the twin recorded.[7]

1Yeshua[8]
Whoever discovers what these sayings mean[9]
Will not taste death.

2Seek and do not stop seeking until you find.
When you find, you will be troubled.
When you are troubled,
You will marvel and rule over all.[10]

3If your leaders tell you, "Look, the kingdom is in heaven,"
Then the birds of heaven will precede you.
If they tell you, "It is in the sea,"[11]
Then fish will precede you.

---

6. The Gospel of Thomas: Nag Hammadi Library, Codex II, 2, pp. 32,10 to 51,28; Greek fragments, Oxyrhynchus Papyri 1, 654, and 655. There are many parallels in the New Testament gospels to the sayings of Jesus in the Gospel of Thomas. The New Testament parallels are not listed in the notes, for reasons of economy of space, but the serious seeker will easily find them.

7. Instead of "hidden sayings," we may translate as "secret sayings" or "obscure sayings" (Coptic *enšaje ethep*, Greek Papyrus Oxyrhynchus 654 *hoi logoi hoi [apokruphoi]*). The Book of Thomas has a similar opening, and the Secret Book of James also calls itself a "secret book." Yeshua is Jesus (here and throughout), and Yehuda Toma is Judas Thomas. The "living Yeshua" is almost certainly not a reference to the resurrected Jesus as traditionally understood, but rather to Jesus who lives through his sayings.

8. The speaker is probably Jesus, otherwise Judas Thomas with an editorial remark. Throughout the Gospel of Thomas the quotation formulae ("Yeshua says," "He says") are given in the present tense, as in the Greek fragments. It is also possible to translate in the past tense ("Yeshua said," "He said").

9. Or, "the interpretation [Coptic *hermeneia*, from Greek] of these sayings."

10. Greek Papyrus Oxyrhynchus 654 adds, "and having ruled, you will rest" (partially restored).

11. Greek Papyrus Oxyrhynchus 654 reads, "it is under the earth."

But the kingdom is in you and outside you.
When you know yourselves,[12] you will be known
And will understand that you are children of the living father.
But if you do not know yourselves,
You dwell in poverty and you are poverty.

4You who are old in days will not hesitate
To ask a child seven days old[13] about
The place of life, and you will live.[14]
Many who are first will be last and be solitary.

5Know what is in front of your face
And what is hidden from you will be disclosed.
There is nothing hidden that will not be revealed.[15]

6STUDENTS
Do you want us to fast?
How should we pray?
Should we give to charity?
What diet should we observe.[16]

YESHUA
Don't lie and don't do what you hate.[17]
All things are disclosed before heaven.

---

12. "Know yourself" (Greek *gnothi sauton*) was a famous maxim from the oracular center dedicated to Apollo at Delphi, Greece.

13. This probably indicates an uncircumcised boy (a Jewish boy was to be circumcised on the eighth day), or else a child of the Sabbath of the first week of creation.

14. Hippolytus of Rome cites a version of this saying from the Gospel of Thomas used among the Naassenes, in his *Refutation of All Heresies*, 5.7.20: "One who seeks will find me in children from seven years, for there, hidden in the fourteenth age, I am revealed."

15. Greek Papyrus Oxyrhynchus 654 adds, "and nothing buried that will not be raised" (partially restored).

16. These questions seem to be answered in saying 14.

17. This is the negative formulation of the golden rule.

There is nothing hidden that will not be revealed,
Nothing covered that will remain undisclosed.

7Blessings on the lion if a man eats it,
  Making the lion human.
  Foul is the human if a lion eats it,
  Making the lion human.[18]

8A person is like a wise fisherman who cast his net into the sea
  And drew it up from the sea full of little fish.
  Among the fish he found a fine large fish.
  He threw all the little fish back into the sea
  And easily chose the large fish.
  Whoever has ears to hear should hear.

9Look, the sower went out, took a handful of seeds,
  And scattered them.
  Some fell on the road
  And birds came and pecked them up.
  Others fell on rock
  And they did not take root in the soil
  And did not produce heads of grain.
  Others fell on thorns
  And they choked the seeds
  And worms devoured them.
  And others fell on good soil
  And it brought forth a good crop,
  Yielding sixty per bushel and one hundred twenty
  Per bushel.

---

18. This obscure saying seems to appeal to the lion as a symbol of all that is passionate and bestial: the passions may either be consumed by a person or consume a person. The Secret Book of John portrays Yaldabaoth, the ruler of this world, as lionlike in appearance. On the saying in general, see Howard M. Jackson, *The Lion Becomes Man: The Gnostic Leontomorphic Creator and the Platonic Tradition* (Atlanta: Scholars Press, 1985).

10I have thrown fire on the world,
  And look, I am watching till it blazes.

11This firmament will pass away
  And the one above it will pass away.
  The dead are not alive
  And the living will not die.
  On days when you ate what is dead
  You made the dead live.
  What will you do when you are in the light?
  On the day when you were one you became two.
  When you become two, what will you do?[19]

12STUDENTS
  We know you will leave us.
  Who will be our leader?

  YESHUA
  Wherever you are, seek out Yaakov the just.[20]
  For him the sky and earth came into being.

13Compare me to something
  And tell me what I am like.

  SHIMON KEFA[21]
  You are like a just messenger.

---

19. This saying consists of four riddles about life in this world and beyond. A different phrasing of the third riddle appears in the Naassene Sermon, in Hippolytus of Rome's *Refutation of All Heresies*, 5.8.32: "If you ate dead things and made them living, what will you do if you eat living things?"

20. Yaakov the just (or the righteous) is James the just, the brother of Jesus and the leader of the church in Jerusalem until his death in 62 C.E. He was given his nickname because of his reputation for piety and Torah observance.

21. Simon Peter.

MATTAI[22]
You are like a wise philosopher.

TOMA[23]
Rabbi,[24] my mouth is utterly unable to say
Who you are like.

YESHUA
I am not your rabbi.
Since you drank you are intoxicated
From the bubbling spring I tended.[25]
And he takes him and withdraws, and speaks three sayings[26] to him.

When Toma comes back to his friends, they ask him,
        What did Yeshua say to you?

TOMA
If I tell you one of the sayings he spoke to me,
You will pick up rocks and stone me[27]
And fire will come out of the rocks and consume you.

14 YESHUA
If you fast you will bring sin on yourselves,
And if you pray you will be condemned,
And if you give to charity you will harm your spirits.[28]

---

22. Matthew.

23. Thomas.

24. Or, "Teacher" (Coptic *sah*).

25. Jesus is the enlightened bartender who serves up wisdom. In general this saying resembles saying 108.

26. Or, "three words" (Coptic *ᵉnšomt ᵉnšaje*). These three sayings or three words are not reported; the reader must discover the interpretation.

27. Within Judaism, stoning was the punishment for blasphemy.

28. These statements seem to be answers to the questions in saying 6.

When you go into any region and walk through the
    countryside,
And people receive you, eat what they serve you
And heal the sick among them.
What goes into your mouth will not defile you,
But what comes out of your mouth defiles.

15When you see one not born of woman,
    Fall on your faces and worship.
    He is your father.

16People may think I have come to impose peace
    On the world.
    They do not know I have come to impose conflicts
    On the earth: fire, sword, war.
    There will be five in a house.
    There will be three against two and two against three,
    Father against son and son against father,
    And they will stand alone.

17I shall give you what no eye has seen,
    What no ear has heard,
    What no hand has touched,
    What has not arisen in the human heart.[29]

18STUDENTS
    Tell us how our end will be.

YESHUA
Have you discovered the beginning and now seek
The end?
Where the beginning is the end will be.
Blessings on you who stand at the beginning.
You will know the end and not taste death.

---

29. Paul may cite this saying in 1 Corinthians 2.9. as a wisdom saying in use among
enthusiasts in Corinth.

19Blessings on you who came into being
  Before coming into being.
  If you become my students and hear my sayings,
  These stones will serve you.
  There are five trees in paradise for you.
  Summer or winter they do not change
  And their leaves do not fall.
  Whoever knows them will not taste death.[30]

20STUDENTS
  Tell us what the kingdom of heaven is like.

  YESHUA
  It is like a mustard seed, tiniest of seeds[31]
  But when it falls on prepared soil
  It produces a great plant
  And becomes a shelter for the birds of heaven.

21MIRYAM[32]
  What are your students like?

  YESHUA
  They are like children living in a field not theirs.
  When the owners of the field come, they will say,
  "Give our field back to us."
  The children take off their clothes in front of them
  To give it back, to return the field to them.

  So I say, if the owner of a house knows that a thief is coming,
  He will be on guard before the thief arrives
  And will not let the thief break into the house

---

30. The five trees of paradise are also discussed in Manichaean texts and in the Islamic Mother of Books.

31. Or, "a mustard seed. It is the tiniest of seeds."

32. Mary.

Of his estate and steal his possessions.
As for you, be on guard against the world.
Arm yourselves with great strength,
Or the robbers will find a way to reach you.
The trouble you expect will come.
Let someone among you understand.
When the crop ripened,
The reaper came quickly with sickle in hand
And harvested it.
Whoever has ears to hear should hear.

22*Yeshua sees babies nursing.* YESHUA
These nursing babies
Are like those who enter the kingdom.

STUDENTS
Then shall we enter the kingdom as babies?

YESHUA
When you make the two into one,
And when you make the inner like the outer
And the outer like the inner
And the upper like the lower,
And when you make male and female into a single being,
So that male will not be male nor female be female,
When you make eyes in place of an eye,
A hand in place of a hand,
A foot in place of a foot,
An image in place of an image,
Then you will enter the kingdom.[33]

23I shall choose you as one from a thousand
And as two from ten thousand
And you will stand as a single one.

---

33. This is a statement of human transformation. The transformation of genders also
is treated in saying 114 but in different terms.

24STUDENTS
Show us the place where you are.
We must seek it.

YESHUA
Whoever has ears should hear.
There is light within a person of light
And it shines on the whole world.
If it does not shine it is darkness.[34]

25Love your brother like your soul.
Protect that person like the pupil of your eye.

26You see the speck in your brother's eye
But not the beam in your own eye.
When you take the beam out of your eye,
You will see clearly to take the speck
Out of your brother's eye.

27If you do not fast from the world
You will not find the kingdom.
If you do not observe the Shabbat as Shabbat,[35]
You will not see the father.

28I took my stand in the midst of the world,
And I appeared to them in flesh.
I found them all drunk
Yet none of them thirsty.
My soul ached for the human children
Because they are blind in their hearts
And do not see.
They came into the world empty
And seek to depart from the world empty.

---

34. Instead of "it" in these clauses, we may also read "he."
35. Sabbath.

But now they are drunk.
When they shake off their wine, they will repent.

29If the flesh came into being because of spirit
   It is a marvel,
   But if spirit came into being because of body
   It is a marvel of marvels.
   Yet I marvel at how this great wealth has come to dwell
   In utter poverty.

30Where there are three deities,
   They are divine.
   Where there are two or one,
   I am with that one.[36]

31A prophet is not accepted in his hometown.
   A doctor cannot heal those who know the doctor.

32A city built on a high hill and fortified can't fall
   Nor can it be hidden.

33What you will hear in your ear in the other ear[37]
   Proclaim from your rooftops.

   No one lights a lamp and puts it under a basket,
   Nor in a hidden place.
   You put it on a stand
   So that all who come and go will see its light.

---

36. Greek Papyrus Oxyrhynchus 1 has been reconstructed to read, "Where there are three, they are without god [or "they are gods"], and where there is only one, I say, I am with that one." The Greek text then goes on to present part of saying 77.

37. "In the other ear" (Coptic *hᵉm pkemaaje*) may be an instance of dittography (i.e., inadvertently writing something twice), or the phrase may refer to another person's ear or perhaps even one's own "inner" ear.

34If a blind person leads a blind person,
Both will fall in a hole.

35You cannot enter the house of the strong
And take it by force without binding the owner's hands.
Then you can loot the house.

36From morning to evening and from evening to morning,
Do not worry about what you will wear.[38]

37STUDENTS
When will you appear to us
And when shall we see you?

YESHUA
When you strip naked without being ashamed
And take your clothes and put them under your feet
Like small children and trample them,
Then you will see the child of the living one
And you will not be afraid.

38Often you wanted to hear these sayings
That I tell you
And you have no one else from whom to hear them.
There will be days when you will seek me
And you will not find me.

39The Prushim[39] and scholars have taken the keys
Of knowledge and have hidden them.

---

38. Greek Papyrus Oxyrhynchus 655 reads, "Do not worry, from morning to evening nor from evening to morning, either about your food, what you will eat, or about your clothing, what you will wear. You are much better than the lilies, which do not card or spin. And since you have one change of clothing, . . . you . . . ? [or "And since you have no garment, what will you put on?"] Who might add to your stature? That is the one who will give you your garment."

39. Pharisees.

They have not entered,
Nor have they allowed those who want to enter
To go inside.

You should be shrewd as snakes
And innocent as doves.

40A grapevine has been planted far from the father.
  Since it is not strong
  It will be pulled up by the root and perish.

41Whoever has something in hand will be given more
  And whoever has nothing will be deprived
  Of the paltry things possessed.

42Be wanderers.⁴⁰

43STUDENTS
  Who are you to say these things to us?

YESHUA
From what I tell you, you do not know
Who I am, but you are like the Jews.
They love the tree but hate its fruit
Or love the fruit but hate the tree.

44Whoever blasphemes against the father
  Will be forgiven,
  Whoever blasphemes against the son
  Will be forgiven,
  But whoever blasphemes against the holy spirit

---

40. Or, "Be passersby" or, much less likely, "Come into being as you pass away" (Coptic *šope etetᵉnᵉrparage*). A parallel to this saying appears in an inscription from a mosque at Fatehpur Sikri, India: "Jesus said, 'This world is a bridge. Pass over it, but do not build your dwelling there.'"

Will not be forgiven,
Either on earth or in heaven.

45Grapes are not harvested from thorn trees
Nor figs gathered from thistles.
They yield no fruit.
A good person brings good
Out of the storehouse.
A bad person brings evil things
Out of the corrupt storehouse in his heart
And spouts evil things.
From the abundance of the heart
Such a person brings out evil.

46From Adam to the baptizer Yohanan,[41]
Among those born of women,
No one of you is so much greater than Yohanan
That your eyes should not be averted.
But I have said that whoever among you becomes a child
Will know the kingdom
And become greater than Yohanan.

47One person cannot mount two horses
Or bend two bows,

And a servant cannot serve two masters,
Or the servant will honor one and offend the other.

No one who drinks old wine
Suddenly wants to drink new wine.

New wine is not poured into old wineskins
Or they may break,
And old wine is not poured into a new wineskin

---

41. John the baptizer.

Or it may spoil.

An old patch is not sewn onto a new garment
Or it may tear.

48If two make peace with each other in one house
They will tell the mountain: "Move,"
And the mountain will move.

49You are lucky who are alone and chosen,
For you will find the kingdom.
You have come from it and will return there again.

50If they say to you, "Where have you come from?"
Say, "We have come from the light,
From the place where the light came into being by itself,
Established itself, and appeared in their image."
If they say to you, "Is it you?"
Say, "We are its children and the chosen of the living father."
If they ask you, "What evidence is there of your father in you?"
Say to them, "It is motion and rest."[42]

51STUDENTS
When will the dead rest?
When will the new world come?

YESHUA
What you look for has come
But you do not know it.

52STUDENTS
Twenty-four prophets have spoken in Israel
And they all spoke of you.[43]

---

42. This saying recalls the accounts of the career of the soul or of the person in the Secret Book of John, the Song of the Pearl, and the Exegesis on the Soul.

43. Twenty-four is sometimes given as the number of books in the Hebrew Bible.

YESHUA
You have disregarded the living one among you
And have spoken of the dead.

53STUDENTS
Is circumcision useful or not?

YESHUA
If it were useful, fathers would produce their children
Already circumcised from their mothers.
But the true circumcision in spirit[44]
Is fully valuable.

54You the poor are lucky
For yours is the kingdom of heaven.

55Those who do not hate their father and mother
Cannot be my students,
And those who do not hate their brothers and sisters
And bear the cross[45] as I do
Will not be worthy of me.

56Whoever has come to know the world
Was discovered a carcass,
And of whoever has discovered a carcass
The world is not worthy.

57The father's kingdom is like someone with good seed.
His enemy comes at night and sows weeds among the good
seed.
He does not let them pull up the weeds
But says to them,
"No, or you might go to pull up the weeds

---

44. Paul also refers to spiritual circumcision in Romans 2.25–29 and elsewhere.
45. This is a common figure of speech for bearing up under burdens or difficulties.

And pull up the wheat along with them."
On harvest day the weeds will be conspicuous
And will be pulled up and burned.

58Who is lucky?
Who has worked hard and found life.[46]

59Look to the living one as long as you live
Or you may die and try to see the living one
And you won't be able to see.

60*He sees a Shomroni*[47] *carrying a lamb*
As he is going to the land of Yehuda.[48]

YESHUA (*to his students*)
He is carrying the lamb around.[49]

STUDENTS
Then he may kill it and eat it.

YESHUA
He will not eat it while it is alive
But only after he has killed it
And it has become a carcass.

STUDENTS
Otherwise he cannot do it.

---

46. Or, "Blessings on the person who has suffered and found life."

47. Samaritan.

48. This saying is partially restored. Instead of "He sees" or "He saw" (Coptic *afnau*), it is also possible to restore to read as "They see" or "They saw" (Coptic *aunau*). The "land of Yehuda" is Judea.

49. Or, "that person . . . around the lamb," "That person is around the lamb," or perhaps, "Why does that person carry around the lamb?" It may be possible to understand that the Samaritan was "trying to catch a lamb," and Jesus says, "That person is after the lamb."

YESHUA
So it is with you. Find a place of rest
Or you may become a carcass and be eaten.

61 Two will rest on a couch.
One will die, one will live.

SALOME
Who are you? You have climbed on my couch
And eaten from my table as if you are from someone.[50]

YESHUA
I am the one who comes from what is whole.
I was given from the things of my father.

SALOME
I am your student.

YESHUA
I say, if you are whole,[51] you will be filled with light,
But if divided, you will be filled with darkness.

62 I disclose my mysteries to those who are worthy
Of my mysteries.[52]
Do not let your left hand know
What your right hand is doing.

63 There is a rich person enormously wealthy.
He says, "I shall invest my money so I may sow, reap, plant,
And fill my storehouses with produce.
Then I shall lack nothing."

---

50. The word translated "couch" (Coptic *cloc*) may also be translated "bed," but the saying probably refers to a couch used for dining. The clause "as if you are from someone" may derive from the phrase "as a stranger."

51. The Coptic text is emended slightly here.

52. Partially restored.

Those were his thoughts in his heart
But that very night he died.
Whoever has ears should hear.

64A man preparing dinner for guests
Sends his servant to invite them.

The servant goes to the first and says,
"My master invites you."

The reply comes, "Some merchants owe me money.
They are coming tonight.

I must go to give them instructions.
Please excuse me from dinner."

The servant goes to another and says,
"My master invites you."

The reply comes, "I have bought a house
And I've been called away for a day. I have no time."

The servant goes to another and says,
"My master invites you."

The reply comes, "My friend is to be married
And I am to arrange the banquet.

I can't come. Please excuse me from dinner."
The servant goes to another and says,

"My master invites you."
He says to the servant,

"I have bought an estate and I am going
To collect rent. I can't come. Please excuse me."

The servant returns and said to his master,

"Those you invited to dinner have asked to be excused."

The master says to his servant,
"Go out into the streets and invite

Whomever you find for the dinner.
Buyers and merchants will not enter the places of
My father."

65A usurer[53] owned a vineyard and rented it
   To farmers to labor in it.
   From them he would collect its grapes.
   He sent his servant for the farmers to give him
   The fruit of the vineyard. They seized, beat,
   And almost killed his servant, who returned
   And told his master. His master said,
   "Perhaps he did not know them." He sent
   Another servant, but they also beat him.
   Then the master sent his son and said,
   "Perhaps they will respect my son."
   Since the farmers knew the son was heir
   Of the vineyard, they seized and killed him.
   Whoever has ears should hear.

66Show me the stone the builders rejected.
   That is the cornerstone.

67One who knows all but has nothing within
   Has nothing at all.

68Blessings on you when you are hated and persecuted,

---

53. The word "usurer" is partially restored. This word may be restored to read as "good person" (Coptic *ourome* *ᵉnchre[sto]s*) or as "usurer," "creditor" (Coptic *ourome* *ᵉnchre[ste]s*), with very different implications. In the first instance, a good person may be interpreted as the victim of violent tenant farmers; in the second instance, (adopted here), an abusive creditor may be understood as opposed by the victimized poor.

And no place will be found,
Wherever you are persecuted.[54]

69You who have been persecuted in your heart are lucky.
Only you truly know the father.
You who are hungry are lucky
When some other hungry stomach might be filled.

70If you reveal what is in you, what you have will save you.
If you have nothing in you
What you don't have in you will kill you.

71I shall destroy this house
And no one will be able to rebuild.[55]

72A MAN
Tell my brothers to share my father's possessions with me.

YESHUA (*to the man*)
Who made me a divider?

YESHUA (*to his students*)
I'm not a divider, am I?

73The harvest is large but the workers few.
Implore the master to send workers to the harvest.

74A STUDENT[56]
Master, there are many around the drinking trough

---

54. This saying may be understood to mean "you will find a place where you will not be persecuted," perhaps alluding to the flight of early Christians from Jerusalem to Pella in Transjordan at the time of the first-century revolt against the Romans.

55. Or, "build it again" (partially restored). It is also possible to restore this passage to read as "build it except me."

56. Or, "Someone says" (Coptic *pejaf*). Sayings 73–75 most likely should be read as a short dialogue.

But nothing in the well.[57]

75 YESHUA
There are many standing at the door
But those who are alone will enter the wedding chamber.

76 The father's kingdom is like a merchant
Who owns a supply of merchandise and finds a pearl.
The merchant is prudent.
He sells his goods and buys the single pearl
For himself. So with you.
Seek treasure that is unfailing and enduring,
Where no moth comes to devour and no worm destroys.

77 I am the light over all things.
I am all.
From me all things have come
And all things have reached me.
Split a piece of wood.
I am there.
Lift up the stone
And you will find me there.[58]

78 Why have you come out to the countryside?
To see a reed shaken by the wind?
Or see someone dressed in soft clothes
Like your rulers and your men of power?
They are dressed in soft clothes
And cannot understand truth.

79 A WOMAN IN THE CROWD
Blessings on the womb that bore you
And the breasts that fed you.

---

57. The word "well" is emended slightly. Instead of "nothing" it is also possible to read as "no one" (Coptic *mᵉn laau*).

58. Greek Papyrus Oxyrhynchus 1 adds a version of this part of the saying after saying 30.

YESHUA (*to the woman*)
Blessings on those who have heard the father's word
And have truly kept it.
A day will come when you will say,
"Blessings on the womb that has not conceived
And the breasts that have not given milk."

80 YESHUA
Whoever has come to know the world
Has discovered the body
And of whoever has discovered the body
The world is not worthy.

81 Let a rich man rule,
And a powerful man renounce.

82 Whoever is near me is near fire,
Whoever is far from me is far from the kingdom.[59]

83 You see images,
But the light in them is hidden in the image
Of the father's light.
He will be disclosed
But his image is hidden by his light.

84 When you see your likeness you are happy,
But when you see your images that came into being before
you
And that neither die nor become visible,
How you will suffer!

---

59. A version of this saying was recently discovered in a Coptic text (Berlin 22220), now referred to as the Gospel of the Savior: "If someone is near me, he will burn. I am the fire that blazes. Whoever is near me is near fire; whoever is far from me is far from life." See Charles W. Hedrick and Paul A. Mirecki, eds., *Gospel of the Savior: A New Ancient Gospel* (Santa Rosa, CA: Polebridge Press, 1999), 40–41.

85Adam came from great power and great wealth
  But was not worthy of you
  Had he been worthy, he would not have tasted death.

86Foxes have dens[60] and birds nests
  But the human child[61] has no place to lay his head
  And rest.

87How miserable is the body that depends on a body
  And how miserable the soul that depends on both.

88The messengers and the prophets will come to you
  And give you what is yours.
  You give them what you have and wonder,
  "When will they come and take what is theirs?"

89Why do you wash the outside of the cup?
  Don't you know that he who made the inside
  Also made the outside?

90Come to me.
  My yoke is easy and my mastery gentle
  And you will find rest.

91STUDENTS
  Tell us who you are so we may believe in you.
  YESHUA
  You examine the face of heaven and earth
  But you have not come to know the one before you,
  Nor know how to see the now.

---

60. Partially restored.

61. This common phrase (here in Coptic *šere* ᵉ*mprome*, from the Greek *huios tou anthropou*) often is translated "son of man" in other translations of Jewish and Christian texts. Sometimes it can mean a person, or it can be a way of referring to oneself, "I." Such seems to be the meaning here. At other times (as in the Book of Daniel and other similar texts) it may have a more apocalyptic meaning.

92Seek and you will find.
  In the past I did not tell you what you asked.
  Now I am willing to tell
  But you do not seek.

93Do not give what is holy to dogs.
  They might throw them on manure.
  Do not throw pearls to swine.
  They might turn it into mud.[62]

94Seek and you will find.
  Knock and the door will open.

95If you have money, do not lend it at interest,
  But give to someone
  From whom you will not get it back.[63]

96The father's kingdom is like a woman
  Who takes a little yeast, hides it in dough,
  And makes large loaves of bread.
  Whoever has ears should hear.

97The father's kingdom is like a woman
  Who is carrying a jar full of meal.
  While she walks along a distant road
  The handle of the jar breaks
  And the meal spills behind her along the road.
  She doesn't know it.
  She notices no problem.
  When she reaches her house she puts the jar down
  And finds it empty.

---

62. The end of this saying is partially restored. Bentley Layton, editor of *Nag Hammadi Codex II, 2–7* (Leiden, MA: E. J. Brill, 1989, 1:87), notes that in addition to the restoration adopted here, the passage may also be restored to read, "They might grind it to bits" or "They might bring it to naught."

63. Restored.

98The father's kingdom is like a man
  Who wants to put someone powerful to death.
  At home he draws his sword
  And thrusts it into the wall
  To find out whether his hand goes in.
  Then he kills the powerful man.

99STUDENTS
  Your brothers and your mother are standing outside.
  YESHUA
  Those here who do the will of my father
  Are my brothers and my mother.
  They will enter my father's kingdom.

100STUDENTS (*showing Yeshua a small coin*)
  Caesar's people demand taxes from us.
  YESHUA
  Give Caesar the things that are Caesar's,
  Give God the things that are God's,
  And give me what is mine.

101Whoever does not hate his father and mother
  As I do
  Cannot be my student.
  Whoever does not love his father and mother
  As I do
  Cannot be my student.
  My mother gives me lies,
  My true mother gives me life.[64]

102Shame on the Prushim.
  They are like a dog sleeping in the cattle manger.

---

64. This saying is partially restored. On the clause "My mother gives me lies or false-hood" (Coptic *tamaau gar ᵉntas[ti naei ᵉmpc]ol*), see Layton, *Nag Hammadi Codex II, 2–7*, 1:89. Another possibility for restoration: "For my mother brought me forth."

It does not eat or let the cattle eat.

103You are lucky if you know where the robbers will enter
So you can wake up, rouse your estate,
And arm yourself before they break in.

104STUDENTS
Come let us pray today and fast.

YESHUA
What sin have I committed
Or how have I been undone?

When the bridegroom leaves the wedding chamber,
Then let the people fast and pray.

105Whoever knows the father and mother
Will be called the child of a whore.

106When you make two into one,
You will become human children.
When you say, "Mountain, move,"
The mountain will move.

107The kingdom is like a shepherd
Who has a hundred sheep.
One of them, the largest, goes astray.
He leaves the ninety-nine and looks for the one until he
    finds it.
After so much trouble he says to the sheep,
"I love you more than the ninety-nine."

108Whoever drinks from my mouth will become like me.
I myself shall become him
And the hidden will be revealed.65

---

65. This saying recalls saying 13.

109The kingdom is like a man who has a treasure hidden in his
   field.
   He doesn't know it,
   And when he dies he leaves it to his son.
   The son doesn't know.
   He takes over the field and sells it.
   The buyer is plowing and finds the treasure,
   And begins to lend money at interest to whomever he wishes.

110You who have found the world
   And become rich,
   Renounce the world.

111The heavens and earth will roll up before you.
   And you who live from the living one will not see death.
   Doesn't Yeshua say,
   The world is not worthy of whoever has found himself?

112Shame on flesh that depends on soul.
   Shame on soul that depends on flesh.

113STUDENTS
   When will the kingdom come?

   YESHUA
   It will not come because you are looking for it.
   No one will announce, "Look, it's here,"
   Or "Look, it's there."
   The father's kingdom is spread out over the earth
   And people do not see it.

114SHIMON KEFA
   Miryam should leave us.
   Females are not worthy of life.

   YESHUA
   Look, I shall guide her to make her male,
   So she too may become a living spirit resembling you.

Every female who becomes male
Will enter the kingdom of heaven.[66]

---

66. A different statement of gender transformation is given at saying 22. Saying 22 goes beyond gender differences. Saying 114 reflects the traditional view that the female symbolizes what is earthly and mortal, as in the earth mother, and the male what is heavenly and divine, as in the sky father.

Miryam of Magdala
(Mary of Magdala)

Miryam of Magdala
(Mary of Magdala)

⸻

THE GOSPEL OF MARY is a wisdom gospel dialogue between Jesus and his follower Mary Magdalene, Mary's vision of the soul's ascent, and a final debate between Mary and the apostles. This rare, brief, mutilated gospel—ten pages are missing—records the most extended conversation between Jesus and a woman that has survived from ancient biblical scriptures. Its leaves disclose the drama of Yeshua in his metaphysical cloak, Miryam's visionary spiritual trip through the universe, and the envy of the male apostles who listen to her grand recital with distress and anger. The battle pits assertive and courageous Miryam against the cynical and derisive students Shimon Kefa and Andreas. The gospel is a loud clear bell celebrating an early woman in that dangerous mix of early Christian and Gnostic camps.

As scriptures take on Gnostic qualities, the role of women rises. Eve is a hero who asserts not obedience and faith but her right to knowledge. She is not a sinner before God who passes her morose condition along to her descendants but a socially active apostolic figure. In this gospel Miryam is not the prostitute or later saint, not the sensual Miryam whom Yeshua loved. She is closer to the Miryam waiting in Yeshua's empty tomb in Mark 16.1–8. But she is less victim and more active as she scraps for her place. As an educated woman she rebuts Shimon Kefa's belittling jibes. Kefa expresses similar insult in the Gospel of Thomas, saying, "Miryam should leave us. / Females are not worthy of life" (114). Kefa is jealous of women and fellow disciples in the canonical gospels. He remains the jealous taunter in this Gnostic tractate. He and Andreas are disturbed that Yeshua loves Miryam more than he loves his other disciples and wonder whether she can be taken seriously as a female teacher of revelatory wisdom. This dispute between Miryam and the male followers of Yeshua reflects the argument between Gnostics and representatives of the emerging orthodox church about whether women can teach in church and whether private revelatory teachings can have the same authority as the official teachings of the priests and bishops.

In the gospel, Miryam takes her place as Yeshua's student in what seems to be the inner circle of students. There is no inner circle of strictly twelve people specified as young men around Yeshua. Rather, Miryam of Magdala, and perhaps other women, form a group of undefined students. According to the text, when Yeshua leaves, other students—which may include women and young men—are weeping, and it is Miryam who with enlightened compassion comforts them. She stands up, greets them, and says to them,

> "Don't cry or break into despair or doubt.
> His grace will go with you and protect you,
> And let us praise the greatness of his work
> For he prepared us, made us truly human."

Yeshua will be with us, Miryam proclaims, for he has humanized us by making us truly human within. As in the Gospel of Thomas, the message of salvation in the Gospel of Mary is one of a mystical realization of true inward being.

Shimon Kefa asks Miryam to say more about the master, and Miryam recalls a conversation with Yeshua about a vision she once had. When she asks the master about the way in which a person sees a vision, she relates that he told her that a person has a vision not through the soul, as an emotional experience, nor through the spirit, as a spiritual experience, but rather through the mind, as an intellectual experience. In other words, a person thinks a vision. After four missing pages, Miryam is in the middle of the account of her vision of the soul's ascent beyond the cosmic powers. Her account is reminiscent of stories of the ascent of the soul from this world of mortality to the realms above, but in this case the story has an ethical quality. The soul in its ascent is liberated from the powers of darkness, desire, ignorance, and wrath, so that the soul can exclaim,

"What binds me is slain and what surrounds me
Destroyed. My desire is gone. Ignorance is dead.
In a world I am freed through another world.
In an image I am freed through a heavenly image.
The fetter of oblivion is temporary.
From now on I'll rest through the time of this age in silence."

Kefa likes none of this. And again he plays the gender card. He admits that Yeshua loved Miryam more than any other woman, but after Miryam recounts her vision of the ascent of the soul, Shimon Kefa questions whether a woman, Miryam, can be taken seriously as an authority on Yeshua and his message. Kefa protests,

"Did he actually speak with a woman in private,
Without our knowledge? Should we all now turn
And listen to her? Did he prefer her to us?"

Shimon Kefa has his doubts on the basis of Miryam's gender, but Miryam does not respond with the same gender preoccupation, and Levi points out that Kefa is just a hothead. "Certainly the savior / Knows her well," Levi continues. "That is why he's loved her more / Than we are loved."

Mary Magdalene is the beloved student in the Gospel of Mary. She is the one closest to Jesus among the students, and she is the one who understands the mind and the message of Jesus. In her *The Gospel of Mary of Magdala,* Karen King tells us that the gospel "presents a radical interpretation of Jesus' teachings as a path to inner spiritual knowledge."[1] Yeshua shares his teachings on a basis of equality with his woman partner whom he trusts and loves, Miryam. The essence of the dialogue centers in eight amazing lines when Miryam and Yeshua analyze the treasure of the mind, which captures vision in something other than mind or spirit. What is it? How do you contemplate a vision? Of course neither Yeshua nor Miryam will reduce the horizon of the secret by telling us,

---

1. Karen King, *The Gospel of Mary of Magdala: Jesus and the First Woman Apostle* (Santa Rosa, CA: Polebridge Press, 2003), 3.

but they do take us through the journey of vision and permit us entry at the daybreak of mystery:

"'Master, today I saw you in a vision.'
He answers, telling me, 'Blessings on you
Since you in no way trembled when you saw me.
Where mind is is the treasure.' I ask him,
'Master, how does one contemplate a vision?
With soul or spirit?' He answers me, saying,
'One sees neither with soul nor with the spirit.
The mind, which is between the two, sees vision.'"

The gospel survives in Coptic translations from the Greek in a fifth-century papyrus discovered at Oxyrhynchus in Egypt in 1896, which contains Mary as well as three other apocryphal scriptures.[2] The Gospel of Mary is identified as the Berlin Gnostic Codex. Two fragments were later found in Greek.[3] Mary was probably composed in Greek in the second century.

2. The Gnostic Sophia of Jesus Christ, the Apocryphon of John, and a summary of the apocryphal Act of Peter.
3. The Gospel of Mary: Berlin Gnostic Codex 8502,1, pp. 7,1 to 19,5; Greek fragments, Oxyrhynchus Papyrus 3525 and Rhylands Papyrus 463.

Gospel of Miryam

STUDENTS (*speaking with the Mashiah*)
Shall matter be destroyed or not?[4]

THE MASHIAH
Each nature and shaped thing and every creature
Lives in and with each other, and will dissolve
Into distinctive roots, but the nature of matter
Will dissolve into the root of nature.
Whoever has ears to hear should hear.

SHIMON KEFA[5]
You have revealed all things to us.
Tell us more.
Tell us what is sin in the world?

THE MASHIAH
There is no sin, but you create sin
When as in adultery you mingle,
Which is called sin, and which is why the good
Came to be with you, to enter every nature
And restore each nature down to its root.
Sin is why you fall into sickness and die.

---

4. The first six pages are missing from the Coptic manuscript, and the extant text begins in the middle of a dialogue between Jesus and his students on the nature of matter. This dialogue includes reflections on Stoic themes.

5. Peter. In the gospels and letters, the same Peter has numerous names: Peter, Simon, and Simeon. And in John 20.6 he is "Simon Peter" from the Greek Σίμων Πέτρος (Simon Petros). In 2 Peter he is "Simeon Peter," from the Greek Συμεὼν Πέτρος (Simeon Petros). And in John 1.42 he is "Simon, the son of John," from the Greek Σίμων ὁ υἱὸς Ἰωάννου (Simon ho huios Ioannou). "Peter" means "rock" or "stone" from the Greek πέτρος, from the Aramaic כֵּיפָא (kefa), from the Hebrew כֵּף (kef), all meaning "rock" or "stone." In his letters Paul calls Peter "Cephas," from the Greek Κηφᾶς (Kefas), based on the Greek transliteration of his Aramaic name *Kefa*.

You love something and what you love tricks you.[6]
Whoever has a mind should understand.

Matter gave birth to passion without form
Because it comes from what opposes nature
And so confusion rose throughout your body.
That's why I told you then to be courageous.[7]
If you despair, stand up and gaze ahead
Before nature's diversity of forms.[8]
Whoever has ears to hear should hear.

After telling his tale, the blessed one
Welcomes all of them and says,
Peace be with you, receive my peace.[9] Take care
That no one sends you lost into the wrong,
Saying, "Look over here," or "Look over there."
The human child[10] exists in you. Follow
The child. And if you look you'll find the child.
Go out and preach the message of good news
About the kingdom. Don't seek any rules
Other than what I give you. Establish
No law as lawgivers have done, or by
Those laws each one of you will end up bound.

After saying these words he goes away.[11]

---

6. Partially restored.

7. Compare with Luke 24.38 and John 14.27.

8. Or, "images of nature." On truth being present in symbols and images, see Gospel of Philip 67.

9. Compare with John 14.27, 20.19, 20.21 and 20.26.

10. Son of man.

11. The departure of Jesus could be either his crucifixion or his resurrection and ascension.

Miryam consoles the students

The students break into despair and cry
Profoundly, saying,
"How can we go out to the gentiles, preach
The message of good news about the kingdom
Of the human child?[12] If even they did not
Spare him, how possibly can we be spared?"

Miryam[13] stands up and greets each of them,[14]
Responding to her brothers,
"Don't cry or break into despair or doubt.
His grace will go with you and protect you,
And let us praise the greatness of his work
For he prepared us, made us truly human."
When Miryam says this, she turns hearts to goodness,
So they begin to inspect the savior's words.

Shimon Kefa challenges Miryam

Then Shimon Kefa says to Miryam,
"Sister, we know the savior loved you more
Than any other woman.[15] Tell us what
The savior said to you, his words as you
Remember them. And you alone know them
And we cannot because we never heard them."

Miryam answers,
"What is hidden from you I shall reveal to you."

She begins to tell his words, saying,

---

12. Son of man.

13. Most likely Mary of Magdala, throughout the text, since this portrayal of Mary resembles Mary of Magdala as presented elsewhere.

14. In Papyrus Oxyrhynchus 3525 it is added that Mary also kissed them tenderly.

15. On the special love of Jesus for Mary of Magdala, see Gospel of Mary, as well as Gospel of Philip 59, 63–64; also Pistis Sophia 17, 19.

"I saw the master in a vision. I said,
'Master, today I saw you in a vision.'[16]
He answers, telling me, 'Blessings on you
Since you in no way trembled when you saw me.
Where mind is is the treasure.'[17] I ask him,
'Master, how does one contemplate a vision?
With soul or spirit?' He answers me, saying,
'One sees neither with soul nor with the spirit.
The mind, which is between the two, sees vision.'"

Miryam recounts her vision of the soul's ascent
Desire says,[18]
"I didn't see you coming down, but now
I see you rising. Tell me why you're lying,
Since you belong to me."

The soul responds,
"I saw you but you didn't see me or know me,
And for you I am nothing more than

---

16. Here Karen King, in *The Gospel of Mary of Magdala: Jesus and the First Woman Apostle* (Santa Rosa, CA: Polebridge Press, 2003, 196) suggests that the Greek of Papyrus Oxyrhynchus 3525 may imply that Jesus appeared more than once ("*Once when the Lord appeared to me in a vision*").

17. Compare with Matthew 6.21.

18. Pages 11–14 are missing from the Coptic manuscript. The text resumes here as Mary is recounting her vision of the ascent of the soul beyond the cosmic powers. The vision apparently described four stages of ascent, and these stages may have depicted the liberation of the soul from the four elements of this world, here described as expressions of cosmic evil and wickedness. The name of the first power is missing from the text, but it may have been "darkness," according to the list of the forms of the fourth power. The names of the other powers are "desire," "ignorance," and, apparently, "wrath," a deadly composite power. As in other texts relating to the career of the soul, the soul ascends through the realms of the powers and is interrogated by them. The soul is successful in her ascent from this world of matter and body, and she is set free at last. Also compare with Gospel of Thomas 50.

A garment.[19] You cannot know who I am."
After the soul says this, she leaves, intensely happy.
The soul approaches the third power, called ignorance.
The power questions the soul, saying,
"Where are you going? You are bound by evil,
You are bound so do not judge."

The soul says,
"Why do you judge me? I haven't judged you.
I was roped up, but I have not bound ropes
On others. Though I wasn't recognized,
I've understood that all will be dissolved,
Both what is earthly and what is heavenly."

When the soul overcomes the third power,
She rises and sees the fourth power. It takes seven forms:
    The first form is darkness,
    The second, desire,
    The third, ignorance,
    The fourth, death wish,
    The fifth, fleshly kingdom,
    The sixth, foolish fleshly wisdom,
    The seventh, wisdom of the angry.

These are the seven powers of wrath.[20]
The powers ask the soul,
"Where are you coming from, you who murder mortals,
And where are you going, you who destroy realms?"

---

19. This garment, which clothes the soul, is made up of all of the features that characterize bodily existence in this world. The soul puts on this garment upon entering the world and removes it when leaving the world.

20. Compare with the seven heavenly spheres (often for the sun, moon, and five known planets—Mercury, Venus, Mars, Jupiter, and Saturn) described by ancient astronomers and astrologers.

The soul answers, saying,
"What binds me is slain and what surrounds me
Destroyed. My desire is gone. Ignorance is dead.
In a world I am freed through[21] another world.
In an image I was freed through a heavenly image.
The fetter of oblivion is temporary.
From now on I'll rest through the time of this age in silence."

Shimon Kefa and Andreas doubt Miryam's word

After Miryam says this she grows silent
For the savior has told her all these things.
Andreas[22] answers, saying to the brothers,
"Say what you will about what she said.
I still don't think the savior said all this.
These teachings are very strange ideas."

Shimon Kefa expresses similar concerns.
He asks the others about the savior:
"Did he actually speak with a woman in private,
Without our knowledge? Should we all now turn
And listen to her? Did he prefer her to us?"[23]

Levi speaks on behalf of Miryam

Then Miryam cries and says to Shimon Kefa,
"My brother, Shimon, tell me what you think.
Do you think that I made all this up myself
Or that I am telling lies about the savior?"

Levi[24] answers and says to Shimon Kefa,

---

21. Or "from," here and later in the next sentence.

22. Andrew.

23. On the hostility of Peter toward Mary of Magdala, compare with the Gospel of Thomas 114; Pistis Sophia 36, 72, 146.

24. Levi was a disciple of Jesus, named Levi son of Alphaeus in the Gospel of Mark and said to be a tax collector from Capernaum. Sometimes Levi is identified with the disciple Matthew, but the historical reliability of the identification is uncertain.

"Kefa, you are always angry. Now I see you
Arguing against this woman like an enemy.
If the savior made her worthy, who are you
To turn her away? Certainly the savior
Knows her well. That is why he's loved her more
Than we are loved.[25] We should be all ashamed
And become the perfect person and assume it.[26]

As he commanded us, preach the good news,
And never invent a rule or law other
Than what the savior has spelled out for us."

When Levi says this, they[27] begin to leave
And they go out to teach and preach.

---

25. On the love of Jesus for Mary, see note 13 above, Gospel of Mary as well as Gospel of Philip 59, 63–64; also Pistis Sophia 17, 19.
26. Or "nurture it."
27. In Papyrus Rylands 463, only Levi is said to leave in order to preach.

Yehuda
(Judas)

Yehuda (Judas)

~

THE GOSPEL OF JUDAS (*Yehuda Iskariot* in Hebrew) was discovered in Egypt in the 1970s, in Coptic translation from a Greek gospel probably composed between 130 and 180 C.E. By 180 the heresiologist Irenaeus of Lyon had already condemned Gnostic scripture as demonic. The vagabond history of its discovery entailed theft and intrigue after it was carried out of Egypt; and its severe decomposition was a result of appalling storage conditions during some years when it was being unsuccessfully peddled at rocket prices. Finally in good expert hands, its more than many fragments were restored into what may be three-quarters of the original Coptic papyrus. Then came editing, translation, and a well-orchestrated world event in all media when this extraordinary document was published by *National Geographic* in 2006. Judas was a document that, like the Dead Sea Scrolls, would thereafter radically challenge and change our understanding of the New Testament tale of Judas's betrayal and the essential theology of spiritual virtue and salvation.

In the Gnostic Gospel of Judas, the apostle Judas is the human hero, and he is Jesus's one enduring confidant among the twelve angry and bumptiously suspicious disciples. Jesus laughs at their jealousy and ignorance. But to Judas he tells his own future and that of Judas. Judas will undertake the infamous task of turning the mortal body of Jesus over to the authorities for crucifixion, after which the real Jesus, the spiritual Jesus, will return to the light of the divine above.

The Gospel of Judas, like the gospels of Thomas and Mary, is a series of conversations between Jesus and others. Here Jesus speaks to all his students, but the focus soon burns in a bright light around Judas. It takes place "in one week three days before" the celebration of the Pesach (Passover). In early Christian literature, Judas Iscariot is vilified and demonized as the quintessential traitor who turns his master over for thirty pieces of silver. In this revolutionary Gnostic gospel, Judas singularly understands who Jesus is, and he learns where he came from and his destiny. Through Jesus he is the recipient of a cosmological revelation about the mysteries of the universe.

The Gospel of Judas represents what may well be described as an early form of Sethian gnosis. In the central portion of the scripture, Jesus invites Judas to attend a brilliant revelation that "no person has ever seen," and the result is a glorious Sethian vision of the world of light and the creation of the universe. Behind the original creation is, Jesus reveals, the great invisible spirit,

> Which no eye of an angel has ever seen,
> No thought of heart has ever comprehended,
> And it was never called by any name.

Like other Christian Sethian texts, the Gospel of Judas incorporates Jewish and Greek themes in the context of Christian Gnostic proclamation, including a theogony and a creation tale of deities leading to Nebro, or Sakla (the creator God), who places humanity on this globe. Judas himself seems to play a role that reflects aspects of Sophia (wisdom) in the text. He is the immediate doer, the changer of a world balance. Judas has been set apart from the realms above, and he is to undergo persecution and suffering here below, until all is resolved. Like the wisdom of any Gnostic figure in the cosmos, Judas is trapped for a time in this mortal world. But through his intimacy with the messenger Jesus, he strives and sacrifices Jesus's mortal self, and his own, in order to attain light and life high, high somewhere in the divinized sky.

In considering the amazing new version of Judas as spiritual brother and martyr for both Jesus and emerging Christianity, one should note a few rarely recognized facts. The biblical version that makes Judas an implacable villain is contradictory in each canonical version, but so too are many key parables and tales. As Bishop John Shelby Spong has stressed in several volumes, the "betrayal" story is a universal stereotype in all cultures, invented to find a good enemy to unify local powers. Since all the major actors of family, disciple, follower, and early saints were Jews, Christianity needed, as did Islam, some powerful way to reject the

Semitic source of its Abrahamic religion and thereby assert its primal worth and originality. It accomplished this obscuration by disguising the Jewishness of the cast. It changed names and invented ugly stories of the villainous Jews while exempting the circumcised rabbi Jesus (*Yeshua ben Yosef*) and his mother and brothers from the Jewish stain, the rejection and the hatred. Hence, as Spong elaborates, the one Jewish figure among the disciples is Judas, which in English comes from a Latinized version of Greek *Ioudas*, from the Hebrew *Yehuda* or *Yehudi*, which means "the Jew." The invented name invites revenge.

In the earliest depictions of the Passion, Judas is recognized as the dark hypocrite with a big Semitic nose and mean, greedy face. A visitor to any fine museum in the world with a medieval and renaissance collection of religious paintings will spot Judas immediately among the other soon-to-be saints. In the twentieth century, Judas made a comeback, especially in the profoundly important world musical *Jesus Christ Superstar* (1976), in which Judas is portrayed with rare admiration and compassion for his tragic and complicated role as one who wishes to save the group, possibly as part of a larger divine plan. Now the ancient Gospel of Judas reflects these outrageous murmurings in *Jesus Christ Superstar*, and indeed Judas is part of Jesus's divine plan. It is predicted that he will hand over the man Jesus, to become popularly demonized by his actions yet be assured that he will find a holy reward. While the Gospel of Judas does not take us away from messianic Christianity, which has found the messiah foretold in Isaiah, it has removed from Judas, and hence from Judaism, the inherited stain, constantly iterated in beautiful, poetic Matthew and philosophical John, that has made Judas the nefarious personage who will justify two millennia of persecution and executions of the descendants of Jesus and Judas.

The linchpin of enduring anti-Semitism in the New Testament is Judas. He is the traitor. He is guilty of causing the crucifixion of Jesus the man and the deicide of Jesus the godhead. The word "Judas" is a curse, and Jews have been regularly demonized as the "Christ-killers." In the Gospel of Judas, Judas is a hero and Jesus does not die.

In the canonical gospels, the fact that Jesus can suffer as a human being on the cross, crying out in his abandonment, fully humanizes him. Christian orthodoxy permits the double role of man and God's son. The fact that Jesus can and does suffer humanly makes his crucifixion the crime of the world. The Gnostics go elsewhere, stating that the man on the cross is a phantom who appears to be a human but is actually a phantom of God, a laughing Jesus, Jesus of the trinity, or a divine angel, depending on the Gnostic sect and scripture. So there can be no question of deicide because God is not on the cross. But can God be killed? In both Orthodox Christian and Gnostic teachings God cannot be killed. What then happens to "deicide," the most famous crime of the world, committed by Romans or Jews or both? There is no deicide.

The nearly complete scripture possesses a Shakespearean fantasy. In its world beyond time, Jesus is King Lear, the wisdom Lear, who instructs Judas, the diffident, conflicted prince Hamlet. In the Gospel of Judas, Jesus is already more of a god figure than in the canonical gospels. As such he—not the Romans—is master, and Judas a truly tragic figure who must obey the master and "betray" him in order for himself to find salvation and for Jesus's earthly mission to be realized. He reluctantly obeys the king's commandment. From their stormy mountain of dialogue and surrender, Judas descends to the streets of Jerusalem and performs his scapegoat mission. As Jesus reveals to Judas, his mortal body, not the true spiritual body, will be handed over. At the time of crucifixion, the spirit of Jesus will already have ascended to the cloud above.

Modernized by its fragmentary presence, the Gospel of Judas is being restored and deciphered to fill in the missing eighth moon of scripture. In theological history the gospel of Judas presents an innocent salvific figure in a major work of art. Its presence, already in more than twenty tongues, is changing the centerpiece of a world religion.

THE COPTIC TEXT of the Gospel of Judas in Codex Tchacos dates to around the beginning of the fourth century, but the Greek original must have been composed no later than around the middle of the second century, before Irenaeus of Lyon denounced it in about 180.

The Gospel of Yehuda[1]

Secret revelation
> Here is the secret revelation Yeshua[2]
> Had with Yehuda Iskariot[3] in one week[4]
> Three days before the Pesach[5] celebration.

Yeshua tells of mysteries beyond this world
> When Yeshua came to live upon the earth
> He did dynamic miracles and wonders
> For the salvation of the peopled world.
> While some traveled along the way of justice,
> Others ambled about in their transgressions,
> And so he called for twelve students to help.
> He spoke to them about the mysteries
> Beyond the world and what would happen when
> The end came upon them. And frequently
> He wouldn't come himself before his students.
> Mingled among them they would find a child.[6]

Yeshua astonishes his students
> One day in Yehuda[7] he went to his students.
> He found them all sitting together as

---

1. The Gospel of Judas: Codex Tchacos 3, pp. 33,1 to 58,29. The English translation presented here remains somewhat provisional, and we anticipate that further restorations and reconstructions of this challenging text will be offered, and more fragments of the papyrus document will be located and identified, in the years to come. The translation is arranged on the pages in such a way as to account for the missing fragments of text.

2. Jesus.

3. Judas Iscariot.

4. Literally, "during eight days."

5. Passover. Or read, "before his Passion."

6. Or, "an apparition."

7. The land of Yehuda, Judea.

They all were practicing group piety.
When he came near, they were giving a prayer
Of thanks[8] over the bread. He laughed.

The students said, "Rabbi, why do you laugh
At us for giving thanks?[9] Are we in error?"
He answered, saying to them, "I don't laugh
At you. You are acting not of your own will
But so that through these things your God will know
Your offerings of praise." They said, "Rabbi,
You⠀⠀⠀are the son of our own God."[10]
⠀⠀⠀⠀⠀⠀⠀⠀⠀⠀⠀⠀⠀⠀⠀⠀⠀⠀⠀⠀And Yeshua
Told them, "How do you know me? Amain[11] I say
To you, no generation of the people
Who walk among you will know who I am."

Angry students

When the students listened to all of this,
They broke into anger and fury. They
Began to execrate him in their hearts.
When Yeshua noticed their deep ignorance
And interior weakness, he asked them,
"Why has your agitation made you furious?
The God who operates inside you[12] spurs
The anger in your souls. Let anyone of you
Endowed with strength among the beings on earth
Produce the perfect human, and stand near

---

8. Or, "they were giving thanks," perhaps even, "they were celebrating the eucharist" (Coptic *eu^e reucharisti*).

9. Or, "offering our prayer of thanksgiving," "celebrating our eucharist."

10. The students confess that Jesus is the son of their own God, the creator of this world, but they are mistaken.

11. Or, "Truly," here and below.

12. Or, "The God within you and his powers," or "The God within you and his servants" (partially restored).

So I can gaze upon him face to face."
They all replied to him, "We have that strength."
Here their beings of spirit didn't dare to stand
Before him, except for Yehuda Iskariot.
He was able to stand before the figure
But couldn't look him in the eye and turned
His face down and away.[13] Yehuda said,
"I know who you are and where you come from.
You are from the deathless realm of the aeon
Of Barbelo,[14] the holy source of all,
And my mouth is unworthy to utter
The ineffable name of him who sent you."

Yeshua speaks to Yehuda privately of his fate
When Yeshua saw Yehuda brooding on the rest
Of what is exalted, he motioned to him,
"Come here and I shall tell you mysteries
Of the kingdom, not that you will go there,
But you will journey through extended grief,
For someone will replace you to complete
The circle of the twelve before their God."
Yehuda said to him, "When will you give
Me these secrets? And when will the great day
Of light spread dawn upon the generation?"
But by the time he spoke, Yeshua was gone.

Yeshua tells his students of earthly and eternal generations
Early in the morning Yeshua came again
Before his students, and they said to him,
"Rabbi, after you left us you disappeared.
Where did you travel to, what did you do?"

---

13. On standing before someone and averting the eyes, see Gospel of Thomas 48.

14. The name "Barbelo" may well derive from the Hebrew for "God in four," that is, God as known in the tetragrammaton, the ineffable four-letter name of God, "YHWH."

Yeshua told them, "I went to a holy and great
Dominion of another generation."
His students asked, "What is the great generation
That lies above us, holier than we are,
And one that doesn't glitter in our world?"

On hearing them, Yeshua laughed and said,
"Why are you mumbling in your hearts
About the strong and holy generation?
Amain I tell you, no one born in this aeon
Will be able to glimpse that generation,[15]
And no army of angels from the stars
Will have dominion over that generation,
And no person of mortal birth can join it,
Because that generation is not from
    what has come to be
The ones that make up the people among you
Are from here, from the human generation
Power   powers   through which you rule."

When his students heard this, each of them sank,
Spirit in turmoil, couldn't say a word.
And on another day Yeshua came up
To be among them. And they said to him,
"Rabbi, we've seen you in a night vision,
In great dreams last night." He answered,
"Why have you fled into hiding?"[16]

The students envision the temple
They said, "We've seen a giant house. It has
A great altar inside. They are the twelve men.

---

15. The phrase "that generation" indicates the generation of Seth, that is, the generation of the Gnostics, the people of gnosis. Because of the connections with Seth as the prototype of true humanity, texts like the Gospel of Judas are frequently described as reflecting Sethian Gnostic themes.

16. Partially restored.

We think that they are priests. There is a name,
And crowds of people are waiting at the altar
Until the priests present the offerings.
We were there too."
Yeshua said, "And what are these priests like?"

They answered, "Some fast[17] for two weeks,
Some sacrifice their children, others wives,
All under ruses of humility
Or praise. Some sleep with men, and others murder.
And some perform a multitude of sins
And lawless acts. And yet these men before
The altar constantly invoke your name,
And in their own practice of sacrifice[18]
They fill the altar with their offerings."
After their speech they were silent and troubled.

Yeshua speaks about the temple and sacrifices at the altar
Yeshua said to them, "Why are you troubled?
Amain I say to you, all the priests standing
Before the altar proclaim my name. Again
I say to you, my name has been set down
In writing   in the generations of
The stars through the human generations.
They operate, planting trees that bear no fruit,
Shamefully, and do so in my name." He went on,
"Those whom you've seen presenting offerings
Before the altar, they are the ones you are.
That is the God you serve, and you are those
Twelve men you also saw. Cattle you saw
Brought in for sacrifice mirror the many
People you lead astray before that same

---

17. Or, "abstain" (restored).
18. Or, "deficiency" (Coptic *šoot*).

Altar. The ruler of the world[19] will stand,
Using my name like that, and generations
Of those with faith and piety stand loyal
By him. Yet after him another man
Will stand before you from the fornicators,
Another from the children slayers, and
Still another from those who sleep with men,
From those who keep the fast,[20] and from all
The others, from the people of pollution,
Lawlessness, and error. Some say, *We are like*
angels. They are stars bringing an end to all.
And to this generation's human beings
It is announced, 'Look, now God has received
Your sacrifice from a priest's hands,' meaning
A minister of error. But it is the lord
Of the universe who commands and speaks.
On the last day they will be shamed and punished."

Stop sacrificing

Yeshua said to them, "Stop sacrificing
What you have   on the altar,
Since they command over your stars, over
Your angels, and already have reached
Their conclusion there. Let them be
    in front of you   and let them go

    generations
A baker cannot feed all of creation
Under heaven." When the students heard this,
They said to him, "Master, help us, save us."
              Yeshua told them,

---

19. Restored. The reference here, with polemics directed against leaders in the emerging orthodox church, may rather be to an overseer (or bishop) or a minister (or deacon).

20. Or, "abstain."

"Stop struggling with me. Each of you has
A star assigned to you and everyone[21]
    that has not come
      a spring of water for the tree
      of this aeon   after a time
      but this[22] has come to water
God's paradise and the enduring generation,
Because it won't defile the walk through life
Of that generation, forever and forever."

Yehuda asks Yeshua to explain

Yehuda asked him, "Rabbi, what kind of fruit
Does this generation yield?"
                Yeshua replied,
"The souls of each human generation will die.
However, when these people end the time
Within the kingdom and the spirit leaves them,
Their bodies die but their souls will stay alive,
And they will be risen above."
                Yehuda asked,
"And what will all the other human generations
Do?"
    Yeshua said, "It is impossible
To sow seed upon rock and harvest fruit.[23]
That is the action   of the defiled peoples
    and of wisdom[24] that is corrupted
    the hand creating mortal people,
So their souls rise up to eternal realms
Above. Amain I say to you,

---

21. This teaching on stars assigned to people recalls the discussion in Plato, *Timaeus*, 41d–42b.

22. Or, "he," "it." The antecedent of the pronoun is uncertain.

23. Compare the parable of the sower in Matthew 13.1–23; Mark 4.1–20; Luke 8.4–15; and Gospel of Thomas 9.

24. Or, "Wisdom," "Sophia"—personified wisdom.

No authority or angel or power
Can see the realms that this great holy generation
Can see."[25]

And after Yeshua spoke these words he left.

Yehuda's vision
Yehuda said, "Rabbi, as you have heard
All the others, hear me. I've had a vision."

When Yeshua heard this, he broke into laughter
And said to him, "You who are the thirteenth
Daimon,[26] why do you try so hard? But speak
To me, and I shall be here to hear you."

Yehuda told him, "In the vision I saw
Myself and the twelve students stoning me
And persecuting me most grievously.
I also came to the place where   you were.
I saw a house   of such
Cosmic dimension that my eyes
Could not perceive the scope. Great people
Surrounded it, and that house had a single

---

25. Partially restored.

26. Or, "spirit," "demon." Judas is described as the thirteenth, which may refer to the fact that he is said, in the New Testament Acts of the Apostles (chapter 1), to have been excluded from the circle of the twelve students and replaced by another student, Matthias. In certain Sethian Gnostic texts (e.g., the Holy Book of the Great Invisible Spirit and Zostrianos), the number thirteen may have a special significance in the context of the aeons, and the thirteen aeons may be understood to describe the world below, with the ruler of the world holding court, it may be, in the thirteenth aeon. Like Judas, Sophia is connected to the thirteenth aeon in the Pistis Sophia, and in this text she refers to herself as a daimon, a spirit, or a demon in this mortal world. The possibility that Judas may be understood to be a demon (i.e., an evil demon) in the Gospel of Judas has caused some interpreters to conclude that Judas could be a negative figure in this gospel.

Room[27] and in the middle of the house
There was a crowd

       I was saying, Rabbi,
Take me in along with all these people."

Yeshua answered, saying,
"Yehuda, your star led you astray. Further,
No person of mortal birth is worthy
To go into the house that you have seen.
It's for the holy,[28] solely for them. Neither sun
Nor moon will have dominion there, nor day,
And yet the holy will live there forever
In the eternal realm with holy angels.
Look, I have revealed to you the mysteries
Of the kingdom and I have taught you
About the error of the stars, and   send
    to the twelve aeons."

Yehuda asks what will happen to him
    Yehuda asked him, "Rabbi, could my seed,
My heritage, fall under the control of
The archons, who are rulers of this world?"

Yeshua answered, telling him, "Come here
That I may

But you know deepest sorrow when you see
The kingdom and all of its generation."

When he heard this, Yehuda said to him,
"What good to me is what I have received?

---

27. Or, "a thatched roof."
28. Or, "saints," here and below.

For you have kept me separated
From[29] that generation."
　　　　　Yeshua answered him,
Saying, "You will become the thirteenth, and
You will be cursed by other generations.
In the end you will rule over them.
In the last days they will oppose you,
So you'll not rise up to the holy generation."[30]

Cosmology of the spirit
Yeshua said, "Come here so I can teach you
　　what no person has ever seen,
For there exists a great and boundless realm
Whose horizons not even a generation
Of angels has looked upon. And therein
Is the great invisible spirit,[31]
Which no eye of an angel has ever seen,
No thought of heart has ever comprehended,
And it was never called by any name.[32]

Then a luminous cloud of light appeared.
The spirit said, "Let an angel come into
Being and he will become my attendant."
A great angel, the enlightened divine
Self-generated, emerged from the cloud.
Because of him four other angels came
Into existence from another cloud,
And they became attendants for the angel,
The self-generated angel, who said,

---

29. Or, possibly, "for." Most likely Judas is thought to be set apart from the other disciples or the heavenly members of "that generation" while he remains in this world.

30. The restoration and interpretation of this passage remains difficult.

31. In Sethian Gnostic texts the highest manifestation of the divine is commonly referred to as "the great invisible spirit."

32. Compare 1 Corinthians 2.9, where Paul cites Isaiah 64.4; Gospel of Thomas 17.

"Let Adamas[33] come into being," and Adamas
Emerged into being. And he created
The first luminary for him to reign over.
He told them, "Let angels come into being
To serve him," and myriads suddenly came
Into being. He said, "Let an enlightened
Aeon come into being," and he came into
Being. Then he created the second luminary
To reign over him, together with myriads
Beyond number to serve and offer worship.
This is how he created other enlightened
Aeons. He made them to reign over them,
And he created for them myriads of angels
Beyond number to serve and offer worship.

Adamas and luminaries

Adamas was in the first luminous cloud
That no angel has ever seen among all
Those who are called "God." He was
    after the image
      and after the likeness of the angel.
He made the incorruptible generation
Of Seth[34] appear to the twelve luminaries,
Twenty-four of them.
He made seventy-two luminaries appear
In the incorruptible generation
In accordance with the spirit's will.
Then the seventy-two luminaries
Made three hundred sixty luminaries
Appear in the incorruptible generation,
In accordance with the spirit's will
That their number might be five for each.
The twelve aeons of the twelve luminaries

---

33. Heavenly Adam.
34. Seth is the son of Adam and Eve, after Cain and Abel.

Constitute their father, with six heavens
For each aeon, so there are seventy-two
Heavens for the seventy-two luminaries,
And for each of them five firmaments.
This comes to three hundred sixty
Firmaments. They were given dominion
And a great army of angels beyond number,
For glory and adoration, and also
Virgin spirits for glory and adoration
Of all aeons, heavens, and their firmaments.[35]

Cosmos, chaos, and underworld

The worldly multitude of those immortals
Is called the cosmos—corruption, inviting
Decay—called by the father and the seventy-two
Luminaries who are with the self-generated
And his seventy-two aeons. In the cosmos
Appeared the first human
With his incorruptible powers. And the
Aeon who appeared with his generation,
The aeon in whom are the cloud of knowledge
And the angel, is called El[36]   an aeon
And later   it was said, "Let twelve
Angels come into being to govern chaos and
The underworld." And look, from the cloud came
An angel. His face flashed with fire, his countenance
Was defiled with blood,[37] and his name was Nebro,
Meaning *rebel*; others call him Yaldabaoth.

---

35. The previous lines (partially restored) are paralleled in Eugnostos the Blessed and the Wisdom of Jesus Christ.

36. The name *El*, which means "God" in Hebrew, may be compared with *Eleleth* in other similar texts.

37. This description of the appearance of the demiurge brings to mind passages in the Secret Book of John and the Holy Book of the Great Invisible Spirit.

Another angel, Sakla, also came from the cloud.[38]
So Nebro made six angels, with Sakla,
To be his assistants, and each of these
Produced twelve angels in the heavens,
Each one possessing a section of the sky.[39]

Rulers and angels of the underworld
> The twelve rulers spoke with the twelve angels,
> "Let each of you   and let them   a generation
>> five angels:
>> The first is Seth, who is called the Christ.
>> The second is Harmathoth, who is   [40]
>> The third is Galila.
>> The fourth is Yobel.
>> The fifth is Adonaios.[41]
> These are the five ruling the underworld,
> And first of all they are over chaos.[42]

Creation of people on the earth
> Then Sakla said to his angels, "Let us make
> A human being after the likeness and after
> The image."[43] They fashioned Adam and his wife
> Eve, who in the cloud is known as Zoe,
> Which means *life*. And by this name all generations

---

38. The names *Yaldabaoth* and *Sakla* are well known in other Sethian Gnostic texts; on *Nebro*, compare *Nebruel* in the Holy Book of the Great Invisible Spirit and Manichaean texts, as well as *Nimrod* in the Hebrew Scriptures (in the Greek of the Septuagint, *Nebrod*).

39. Probably the signs of the zodiac.

40. Perhaps restore to read "who is the evil eye" or "who is the eye of fire."

41. Similar lists of angels are found in the Secret Book of John and the Holy Book of the Great Invisible Spirit. The correlation of Seth and Christ is unusual in this context, and Harmathoth seems to be a composite name (*Harmas + Athoth*).

42. Or, "And the first ones are over chaos."

43. Gen. 1.26.

Seek the man, and each of them calls the woman
By their own names. Now, Sakla didn't command
    except   the generations
           The ruler said
To Adam, "You shall live for a time with your children."

Yehuda asks about Adam's destiny
    Yehuda said to Yeshua, "What is the value
    Of human life?"
                Yeshua said,
    "Why do you ponder these things? Adam
    And his generation have lived their span
    Of life where he received his kingdom, and
    With the longevity in keeping with his ruler."

    Yehuda said to Yeshua, "Does the human spirit
    Die?"
        Yeshua said, "This is why God told Mihael[44]
    To give the people spirits only on loan
    So that they might offer service, but the great one
    Ordered Gavriel[45] to grant spirits to the great
    Generation with no ruler commanding it[46]
    But their spirit and their soul. Therefore,
    The other souls

Yeshua speaks of the destruction of the wicked
    "   light
       chaos
       around
       spirit living in you,
    Which you made to live

---

44. Michael.
45. Gabriel.
46. Or, "the great kingless generation"—a reference to the generation of Seth.

In flesh among the generations of
The angels. But God had knowledge given
To Adam and those with him so that the kings
Of chaos and the underworld might not
Impose dominion over them."
                    Yehuda
Said to Yeshua, "So what will those generations
Do?"
        Yeshua said, "Amain I say to you,
For all of them the stars bring events
To their consummation. When Sakla completes
The span of life assigned him, their first star
Will sparkle with generations, and they
Will finish what it is said they'd do.
They will fornicate in my name, will slay
Their children, and they will

In my name. And your star will rule over
The thirteenth aeon."
                    At this Yeshua laughed.

Yehuda said, "Rabbi, why are you laughing
At us?"[47]
        Yeshua answered, saying, "I don't laugh
At you but at the error of the stars,
Because these six stars are wandering about
With these five combatants,[48] and they
Will all be destroyed with their creatures."
Yehuda said to Yeshua, "Those
Who have been bathed in your name,
What will they do?"
                    Yeshua said, "Amain I say

---

47. Restored.

48. Here the wandering stars are probably understood to be the five known planets
(Mercury, Venus, Mars, Jupiter, and Saturn) plus the Moon.

To you, this bathing   in my name

To me. Amain I say to you, Yehuda,
Those who offer sacrifices to Sakla

              everything evil.

But you will surpass all of them, for you
Will sacrifice the man who bears me.[49]

    Already your horn is raised,
    your anger is on fire,
    your star has passed by,
    and your heart has grown strong.[50]

Amain I say to you, your last days   become

Grieve
       the ruler,
Since he will be destroyed. And then the image
Of the great generation of Adam
Will be exalted. Before there was heaven,
Earth, and angels, that generation coming
From the eternal realms existed. And look,
You have been told everything that is.
Raise your eyes and look at the cloud
And at the light within it and the stars
Surrounding it. The star that leads the way
Is your star."
         Yehuda raised his eyes and
Saw the luminous cloud. And he entered

---

49. The man who bears Jesus is thought to be the fleshly, mortal body that carries around the inner, spiritual person of Jesus for a period of time.

50. These lines resemble passages from the Psalms in the Hebrew Scriptures.

Into it.[51] Those standing on the ground heard
A voice coming from the cloud, saying,
> great generation
> image

Yehuda hands Yeshua over
> Their high priests murmured because he[52]
> Had gone into the guest room to pray. Yet
> Some of the scribes were there, watching sharply
> And carefully in order to arrest him
> While at prayer. They were afraid of the Jews,
> Who esteemed him as a prophet. They came
> Near Yehuda and said to him, "What are
> You doing here? You are Yeshua's student."

> He answered them just as they wished.
> Yehuda received some money
> And then he handed Yeshua over to them.[53]

---

51. The text reads *affok* (for *afbok*) *ehoun eros*. The antecedent of the pronoun (*f*) is most likely Jesus, but it could conceivably be Judas. In this passage it appears that Jesus experiences a transfiguration or ascension.

52. Or, "they" (restored).

53. The conclusion of the Gospel of Judas is understated, and while it resembles accounts of Judas handing Jesus over to the authorities in the New Testament gospels (with the same verb of Greek origin, *paradidonai*, being employed), here the meaning of the account is different, because the true Jesus, the spiritual Jesus, apparently has already left, and so he will not die on the cross.

Shaul/Saul/Paul

Introduction to Paul

Paul's Many Names

PAUL HAS MANY NAMES in the New Testament and their changes have theological and political significance. The names occur in English, Latin, Greek, and Hebrew. "Paul" is his English name. It comes from the Greek Παῦλος (Paulos), which he assumed after he had an epiphany of Jesus. *Paulos* entered Greek as a loan word from the Latin *Paulus*. His birth name was "Saul," from the Greek Σαῦλος (Saulos), from the Hebrew שָׁאוּל (shaul). He was originally called "Saul of Tarsos." After he became a Messianic, that is, a follower of the Christ, he called himself and was called "Paulos," which not only reflects his Greek background as a Greek- and Aramaic-speaking Jew from Tarsos in Cilicia (in present-day Turkey), but also suggests an affinity with the Roman Empire. He effectively changed his name after his missionary trip to Cyprus, thinking he could reach the Greek pagans better with a Greco-Roman appellation. Acts of the Apostles has Paul asserting that he was a Roman citizen as was his father. As recounted in Acts, he used his Roman citizenship to get out of scrapes, and he made major decisions based on not only Jewish but also Roman law, including the legality of taxes and owning slaves (Philemon). These ideas about Paul are largely based on Acts, whose hero is Paul, and this first Christian history book is the longest book in the New Testament.

Who Is Paul?

Is Paul of Acts the same figure as Paul of the letters? No. While Acts is a major book of imagination in tracing an early history of the formation of early Christian missions, from Jerusalem to Rome, the Paul it idealizes has little to do with Paul's self-presentation in his own authentic letters. Acts anoints Paul with Roman citizenship; he deals with Roman officials as a distinguished equal, despite their theological divide. He is indomitable. Through helpful miracles, he possesses powers to heal the afflicted and to raise the dead as Jesus raised Lazarus.

By contrast, the life-size Paul in the letters portrays a struggling man of poor appearance and unfriendly health who possesses neither magical powers nor state distinctions. Rather, he is heroic for being a human being unaided by miraculous advantage, one who suffered nobly like so many early outsider Christians. He lived at the bottom of the social scale as an artisan, pursuing his lifelong mission of formulating his ethical and eschatological beliefs and spreading his Messianic faith to others. He struggled as one dissenting from Rome, from traditional Judaism, and above all from its first apostolic bishops in the Jerusalem church, Peter, James, and John, who insisted that pagan converts abide strictly by Jewish law with respect to diet, circumcision, and Sabbath. The church leaders in Jerusalem opposed Paul's missions.

To perhaps a majority of leading scholars today, Paul was unlikely to have been the Roman citizen that Acts makes him out to be in his adventures and in his dealing with official adversaries of the Roman Empire. Rather, he was a wandering Jew with few credentials. But he possessed obsessive missionary powers after the "Son" was revealed to him on the road to Damascus. He was an instant convert. Thereafter he spent his life proselytizing. He established missions and new synagogues (*synagogue* is Greek for "assembly") or churches, and brought pagans and Jews into his new fold of Jewish Messianics. Again and again he said he was born a Jew and remained a Jew, a Jew who had found the messiah the Jews awaited, and his Christ (Greek word for "messiah") was the true one. That simple message of discovery and redemption and hope for a life after death propelled him and his many followers. He wrote his letters—we probably have only a fraction of them—to the new congregations, ordering the members to behave in the church and in their homes, and to cast their faith in God for salvation through worship of the divine messiah. He elaborated this simple message in the most beautifully elegant epistolary form, developing his motifs as a composer creating a thematic melody. No one has matched his supreme, internally logical but constantly changing message to fit each occasion. He was a philosopher who rambled poetry as he rambled the roads. Has anyone equaled his discourse on love in 1 Corinthians 13? He was Roman only in the sense that he was a Jew subject to Roman law in the vast territories, including his native Tarsos and Israel, possessed by Rome.

Paul's Early Life

In giving a very brief history of Paul here, I mix information from the letters and Acts, as most scholars do, but note much of the time when a reference comes from Acts rather than the letters in order that the reader may distinguish between Paul's voice and a "reported" voice according to later scriptural biographers.

Paul was probably born in the cosmopolitan city of Tarsos (Acts 22.3), in approximately 5–10 C.E., where his first language was Greek, as it was for most of the Jews of Alexandrian North Africa, Rome, Greece, and Anatolia. A Jew, circumcised on the eighth day, he describes himself as belonging to the tribe of Benjamin (Rom. 11.1) and a Pharisee (Phil. 3.5; Acts 26.5). We suppose that he was schooled in Hebrew at a local synagogue school. Also in Tarsos he was surely first trained in Greek grammar, Stoicism, and basic works of other Greek philosophical schools. Wherever he obtained his main instruction, in Hellenistic Tarsos, in Jerusalem, or elsewhere, Paul was highly trained in rhetoric, Jewish law, and Greek philosophy, which in one form or another pervaded the thinking of most religious sects in the Greco-Roman territories. He might have[1] gone to Jerusalem early for guidance under the liberal Rabbi Gamaliel (Acts 26.4), said to be the grandson of the Pharisee reformer Hillel. In Jerusalem Paul states, "I am verily a man *which am* a Jew, born in Tarsus, *a city* in Cilicia, yet brought up in this city at the feet of Gamaliel" (Acts 22.3, KJV). However, we know about his important

[1]. I prefer not to qualify statements, using auxiliary verbs or adverbs like "might have" or "probably." However, since so many aspects of Paul's life and thoughts are by traditional understanding mixed up with information both from Paul's reliable letters and from unreliable Acts and the forged Pauline letters, and since it would be impossibly tedious if each statement were qualified by the echo of a doubting Thomas, the best one can do is make timidly plausible choices and leave it at that.

Pharisee education with Rabbi Gamaliel in Jerusalem only from Acts 5.33–35, and some scholars raise red flags because there is no reference to Gamaliel in the letters.

With respect to the Pharisees (the Prushim), they defended the new Christians from abuse by the traditional Sadducees (Acts 5.34).[2] Among the many contending sects in Jerusalem, the Pharisees were the most liberal and spiritual of contemporary Jewish sects, demotic, oral, promoting the lot of the poor and the notion of an afterlife, a notion that, after Paul's conversion, was to fill the heart of his Messianic convictions. The great Pharisee reformer had been the legendary Hillel. Despite the vilification of the Pharisees in the gospels, they were the one group from which Paul's step into developing Christianity made most sense. Both groups pushed for a more flexible reading of the Torah (meaning the "law") and indeed bent the laws for beneficent purposes, and both groups believed in a life after death. In addition to Greek philosophy, Paul was also thoroughly familiar with popular Hellenistic spiritualism along with his own base in Jewish monotheism and Jewish exegetical methods for developing an argument. There is one statement one can make with no quiver of equivocation: Saint Paul, as spiritual philosopher and reforming activist, was the major founder, missionary, and epistolary historian of the Messianic Jewish sect we now call Christianity.

Supporting himself as a poorish tentmaker or leatherworker artisan, he set out to bring the gentiles (pagan Greeks and Romans) into the synagogue of the new Messianics. He began his sectarian career as a sometime violent pursuer of the Messianics. The most significant event in Paul's life, his epiphany or vision on the road to Damascus, is related in two versions: in Acts and in his letter to the Galatians. The famous highly dramatic one is in Acts. He converts to salvific Messianism on the road to Damascus around the year 36. In Acts 22.6–11, Saul, who became Paul after the vision, heard a voice calling to him:

2. Because of rabbi Gamaliel's New Testament reputation of protecting Christians, a legend developed about Gamaliel. The erudite ninth-century philosopher and historian Photius of Constantinople wrote that John and Peter had baptized Gamaliel and he was killed defending the early Christians. As a result he became a Christian martyr and saint. It was only in 1956 that for lack of baptismal evidence his name was removed from the book of Roman martyrology and he was no longer a Catholic saint.

And while I was traveling and coming near
Damesek at about the noon, it happened
That suddenly out of the skies a great light
Shone around me, and I fell to the ground
And I heard a voice saying to me, "Shaul, Shaul,
Why are you persecuting me?" And I answered,
Saying, "Who are you, sir?" And he said to me,
"I am Yeshua the Natzrati, whom you persecute."
And the ones with me saw the light but didn't hear
The voice speaking to me. Then I said, "What
Can I do, lord?" And the lord said to me,
"Stand up and go to Damesek and there
You will be told about all things that you
Were chosen to do." And because the glory
Of that light prevented me from seeing,
I came to Damesek with my companions
Leading me by the hand.

In the letter Galatians, Paul's personal recollection of his conversion is, by contrast and common wisdom, "understated," although it is the most significant event in his life. In his spiritual anagnorisis he finds "the son of God," who will be called the Messiah or the Christ. This wordless event of revelation changes the course of his lifework and later the religious world. Can we speak of an epiphanic vision? Yes, but in its letter form there is no drama, inflation of rhetoric, or cataclysmic apparition. Rather, he simply mentions his sudden understanding, which he tells no one, then goes off in solitude to "Araby" to evaluate and plan. There is strong reason to suppose that Paul's personal account in Galatians of his revelation is the accurate one. Indeed, a few verses later, in Galatians 1.20, Paul asserts, "Look, in what I write to you, before God I say: I am not lying!" Paul's first-person account in verses 1.14–17 should be believed:

I was an extreme zealot in support
Of ancestral traditions. But when God,
Who took me from my mother's uterus,
And through his grace called on me to reveal
His son in me so I might preach among

The gentiles, I did not turn suddenly
To any flesh and blood, nor did I go
Up to Yerushalayim to find those
Who were the messengers before me, but
I went away into Arabia
And once again came back to Damesek.

These verses in Galatians were surely the source, whether direct or through later rehash, of the third-person stories inscribed in Acts. The collapse, paroxysm, and blind vision in Acts have been celebrated in writings, musical composition, and countless other works of art, such as "The Conversion of St. Paul" in 1600 by the Italian painter Caravaggio. In the liturgical year, January 25 retells the story in Acts in "The Feast of the Conversion of Saint Paul." Like Noah and the flood, the tower of Babel, and Abraham's covenant with God, Paul's conversion has passed into history and legend.

In the new faith he was establishing, Paul made a pivotal addition to monotheistic Judaism. God was sharing powers with his spokesperson, son Jesus, who was at the same time the divine rather than the merely earth-bound messiah of the Torah. Paul's messiah was God's son, or one of a trinity of Father, Son, and Holy Breath, who joined in one divine entity—all theological variations that were in flux in Paul. Despite a Christological history of fierce splits and warring contentions, the faith that Paul—more than anyone on earth—created remains subsumed into the leading world religion, with all its subtitles, which we call Christianity.

It is also imperative to recall, with sorrow and horror, that the sectarian splits that Paul first witnessed in his lifetime within Judaism and later in the formation of the Jesus movement with respect to the "true Christianity" are not over. Internecine war, alas, has characterized the search for religious truth, be it recent fighting in Northern Ireland between Catholics and Protestants; between Orthodox Constantinople and Catholic Rome; the early-second-century to fifteenth-century suppression and execution of Gnostics from Alexandria to Italy and Cathar France; the hundred-year war; reformations and counter-reformations; the 1572 Saint Bartholomew's Day Massacre of the Protestant Huguenots in Paris; the Protestant ax in the Tower of London over a Catholic neck—endless events when Christians in Europe slaughtered each other.

In his writings and his life, Paul, the prime inventor of an earth and heaven faith, was into salvation, not sectarian power murder.

Scripture

In Paul's life, the book of the new Messianics was only one: the Jewish Torah (Old Testament). Three centuries later at Nicea, the book of the Messianic Jews would be set, though not yet canonized in Rome, giving us the future two-volume Christian Bible. Paul died before his greatest hopes could be known to him or realized. Indeed, for at least twenty-five years after his death, his personal mission seemed to have failed or had been discredited by the church in Jerusalem. Yet in Thessaloniki's central square, in the old below-ground-level synagogue with its Roman temple marble columns, Paul once spoke to the faithful Thessalonikians. Three decades later, Acts of the Apostles, splendidly unreliable, re-created Paul and elevated him to a world status he has never lost. And he is a world.

As for the dating of Paul's death, before 62 B.C.E. is a best, poorly informed guess. The place and cause are unknown. As with other saints, his tomb is regularly found—most recently in Rome under Saint Peter's—and then forgotten until there emerges another claimant for the glory. The most astonishing account of his death appears in the second-century intertestamental Acts of Paul, another apocryphal book of miracles and a gem. As in the canonical Acts, Paul is arrested and taken in chains to Rome for trial. In Acts of Paul, however, he has an audience in the palace with the emperor Nero, who orders him beheaded. Fierce Paul warns the Emperor, "Caesar . . . if you behead me, this will I do: I will arise and appear to you in proof that I am not dead, but alive in my Lord Christ Jesus, who is coming to judge the world." In the Gospel of John, the Roman centurion of the crucifixion squad, which has just killed Jesus, is converted on the spot after Jesus gives up the ghost, and becomes the first true Christian to proclaim that Christ has risen. Similarly, in Acts of Paul, when Paul dies, again Nero's soldier executioner converts on the spot and becomes the first official in Rome to glorify God and report the miraculous happening to the troubled emperor.[3]

Or perhaps Saint Paul simply disappeared and died during one of his missions about which no recollection in letter or other contemporary format has survived to inform us. Saint Peter's Cathedral in the Vatican was built over the spot where Paul was said to have been martyred.

Paul the Epistler and Theologian

Paul, to whom are unevenly attributed thirteen or fourteen of the twenty-seven books of the New Testament, was born, lived, and died a Jew. At the same time, he is the singular fully historic personage of the Jewish and Christian bibles. His true names we know, and his existence is verified by diverse sources beyond the scriptural reference. Paul is the philosophical foundation of Christian intellectual history, and while his personal history is seen through diverse glass, he existed historically. And vigorously. Whether Jonah sailed truly or only allegorically in a whale's abdomen, according to the dictated letters Paul did sail into three missionary ventures, five if Acts had other reliable sources to support its story. His name—all his names—are his, not anonymous or invented ones, as with Isaiah 1, Isaiah 2, and Isaiah 3, or John of the gospels, letters, and Apocalypse, who would have had to be thriving at his peak for more than a century and a few decades to play out all his roles.

---

3. In Acts of Paul, see Willis Barnstone, ed., *The Other Bible* (San Francisco: Harper and Row, 1984), where we read that Paul's martyrdom takes place in Rome, which has become the most generally believed story. "His witnesses are the Roman prefect Longus and the centurion Cestus" (446). Later, "Paul stood with his face to the east, and lifting up his hand to Heaven prayed at length; and after communing in prayer in Hebrew with the fathers, he stretched out his neck without speaking further. But when the executioner struck off his head, milk spurted upon the soldier's clothing. And when they saw it the soldier and all who stood by were amazed, and glorified God who had given Paul such glory. And they went off and reported to Caesar what had happened" (457). Then a few hours later, Paul comes into the palace and stands before Nero, saying, "Caesar, here I am—Paul, God's soldier. I am not dead, but alive in my God. But for you, unhappy man, there shall be many evils and great punishment, because you unjustly shed the blood of the righteous (457)."

In contrast to the verifiable Saint Paul, we cannot know much of a historic Moses, whose books were set down a millennium after his death, or of Jesus, whose life story depends entirely on gospel scriptures composed four to six decades after his death, with till now no external source for the narrations. Of those narrations, Paul lacked all knowledge, though he was born less than a decade after Jesus's 4 B.C.E. birth date, which the gospels coincide with the year of Herod the Great's death. Curiously, Paul of the letters knew nothing about the man Jesus other than that he was the messiah foretold in Isaiah; that he had come and was crucified; and as Paul fervently believed, that he would very soon come back to the earth to judge the world and select and redeem the faithful. His belief carried all the qualities of mystical immersion, as in the Eucharist in which one is "in Christ Jesus" (the messiah Jesus), in his body and total godliness.

As for when the crucifixion occurred, Paul doesn't say or perhaps know. While Paul may have been in Jerusalem when Jesus was crucified, he did not meet him "in the flesh." He was later accused by his opponents of this omission, of not knowing Jesus "in the flesh." In Paul's letters there appear three brief references to Jesus's life, for instance, as in 1 Corinthians 11.23, when he refers to the last supper. Since Paul's letters are pieced together from distinct letter fragments, it is unknown whether the references were Paul's or later scribal insertions. What we do know is that in Paul of the letters, no living voice of Jesus the Christ is heard. Paul utters no word about a virgin birth, or of the evangelists' four-times-told story of Jesus's wanderings in Galilee and Judea to heal, perform miracles, and collect followers of a new group that the Romans will ultimately attempt to destroy, as was their practice when confronting a dissenting political entity. For a greater understanding of the birth of Christianity and its messiah Jesus, who was Paul's forever companion in thought, one should look back to the crucifixion, the one event Paul does indeed always cite. He knew neither circumstance nor how the crucifixion took place and surely not the relevant poster initials carved on the cross. All that information was to appear in the later gospels. With respect to Jesus's death for reasons of sedition, the Jesus movement's proclamation of a new Kingdom of God and a negative suasion of loyalty, gave Rome plenty of reason to annihilate the revolution's assumed leader. Jesus was crucified on a cross on which were inscribed the letters,

"INBI": "Jesus of Nazareth King of the Jews" ('Ιησοῦς ὁ Ναζωραῖος ὁ βασιλεὺς τῶν Ἰουδαίων) (John 19.19).

BY CONTRAST with other biblical figures, we know part of the life of the living Paul in vivid detail. And whether the educated Simon Peter to whom Paul wrote letters had anything to do with the probably illiterate, non-Greek-speaking fisherman companion of Jesus is irrelevant. There was someone called Simon Peter of the letters, whom Paul wrote to and with whom he quarreled. We have none of Peter's actual responses except as Peter's words reflect in Paul's own letters. The letters Peter did address to Paul, now in the canon, were composed long after Paul's death. Raymond E. Brown, the Catholic historian, in his *Introduction to the New Testament*, which carries the *Nihil obstat* of the censor deputatus of the Archdiocese of New York, dates Peter's letters as "likely 70–90," and not by Peter but possibly by some later "disciple carrying on the heritage of Peter at Rome."[4]

Paul and Peter wrote each other in Koine, a demotic Greek, the fresh popular language from which Byzantine and modern Greek derived. There was no limit to the stylist flourishes in the work of Paul and the epistler John. Their writing was genial. But Paul did not write in the formally elegant classical Greek of the aristocrats as did his near contemporary, the Jewish neo-Platonist Philo of Alexandria. Part of the dazzling poetic fluency of the letters may result from their being dictated. He could have written them himself, but only in big letters, as he notes in Galatians 6.11, not in the small, neat letters of the professional scribe. Using small letters made them practical for sending them long distances. These anonymous letters carrying Peter's annoyances do reflect the bitter feuds in Antioch and elsewhere over how far it would be permissive to stray from Jewish practices and still be a Messianist. One imagines that Peter's actual letters, now lost, must have contained even more vitriol to have so inflamed and inspired Paul's rumbling responses. That was a true human disputation, giving historical substance to creedal and credential issues in the developing Messianic movement. Both missionaries,

4. Raymond E. Brown, *An Introduction to the New Testament* (New York: Doubleday, 1997), 706.

whoever Peter Simon was, became later saints. They personally dictated their missives to and at each other.

As for the authenticity of Paul's preserved letters, here we are in great luck. Seven of his letters are indisputably dictated by him to his amanuensis Tertius, while six are forgeries, the pseudonymous Pauline letters.

Paul Floating Four Letters out of One Houdini Hat

Linus comes home from church school and meets Charlie Brown.
"Where have you been?" Charlie Brown asks.
"Church school! We've been studying the letters of the Apostle Paul,"
Linus answers.
"That should be interesting."
"It is—although I must admit it makes me feel a little guilty."
"Why?"
"I always feel like I am reading someone else's mail!"[5]

But is Linus really snooping into Paul's private letters? Not at all. The epistles are edited sermons that the author prefaces and concludes with standard greetings and farewells. The addressee is not a private person, an intimate friend, but a crowd who will hear the letters read aloud in a place of worship. So go the ways of ancient publication. When the letter is copied over and sent out for broadcast in many synagogues and churches, its authorial purpose is realized.

In his bright *Paul's Letter Collection*, David Trobisch[6] contends with abundant example that Paul prepared Romans, 1 Corinthians, 2 Corinthians, and Galatians into one document to send out to his congregation in Ephesos. Whether or not the textual scholar's recreation of a Pauline single epistle proves right in every detail is of little import before his major intuition. Clearly these four very long letters do function as

---

5. Jeffrey H. Loria, *What's It All About, Charlie Brown? Peanuts Kids Look at America Today* (Greenwich, CT, Fawcett Publications, 1968) in David Trobisch, *Paul's Letter Collection: Tracing the Origins* (Bolivar, MO: Quiet Waters Publications, 2001), p. 48.

6. Trobisch, *Paul's Letter Collection*.

chapters in one book, and it is illuminating to read them thus. In the familiar mess of manuscript survival, "of the 779 manuscripts of the letters of Paul . . . only eight manuscripts and the Authorized Byzantine Version form the essential base for the reconstruction of the original text" (Trobisch, 26).[7] Yes, the imperfect manuscripts are in the form of letters, but they are literary, not private letters, even though addressed to one friend or a grouping of church "saints." The farewell greetings to friends are a guise to cover the literary art of a universal sermon. Paul composed his letters for a broad audience. Likewise, Cicero's letters to a friend, as in *De senectute*, were carefully composed works meant to be spoken in the Roman senate and absorbed by influential friends. Paul's beautifully crafted letters—like Saint Augustine's writings three centuries later— were modeled on Cicero's logically reasoned literary gems.

What is the evidence for Paul's strategy of commingling his main letters into one authorial recension? Trobisch finds clues in the greetings and farewells to Prisca, Aquila, and Crispus, in Paul's announced travel plans to Corinth, Jerusalem, and Rome, and above all in the development of his fluid theology. In 1 Corinthians 13 he speaks unforgettably about love. Elsewhere he speaks of salvation through faith in God, the pit of disbelief, sexual depravity, and plans for raising funds for the poor in Jerusalem. But one theme consumes the author: his elaborately argued exemptions for gentiles from diet, Sabbath, and—as the painful obstacle to conversion—circumcision. Here he takes aim at enemies of his doctrine in Jerusalem, the new bishops James, John, and Peter, who hold to Mosaic law. From Paul's letters one infers that the bishops discredit him as vociferously as he them. The invective centers on what the "Judaizing" bishops essay and what he, Paul, opposes. Throughout these letters also lurk other crucial questions: who will control the expanding Jesus movement, and what will be the nature of emerging Christianity?

Galatians, last of the main letters, is often dubbed the Magna Carta of Christian thought. It frees gentile converts from the fear of adult circumcision. It contains no customary greeting, and bluntly attacks

7. David Trobisch observes that among the copies of Paul's surviving letters, "no two copies are completely identical." The variants in the letters are due to editorial changes. The result is that "there probably is not a single verse of the letters of Paul that has the same wording in all surviving manuscripts" (Trobisch, 4).

the Jerusalem adversaries. Paul relates how at Antioch he confronts the "self-condemned" Peter face-to-face over the issue (Gal. 2.11). In the same letter Paul also rages against the unnamed Gnostics who drop by to infect his parishioners with insidious ideas of knowledge. These false teachers bring false knowledge.

As a meticulous detective unraveling old scrolls, Trobisch sees the communality of philosophy in Romans, the two Corinthians, and Galatians. Paul has invented one super scroll that he sends to his listeners in Ephesos. The apostle's recension of these very long letters into one grand book sermon provides a new way for the world to receive his meditation. And the rhetorical format is an ideal way to personalize his message. Plato's attractive ploy is his dialogues where we seem to overhear private conversations of debating philosophers. By such graceful presentation Plato and Paul reach the many. So along with Augustine, Descartes, and Bergson, Paul sends a literary missile to declaim and whisper his message.

THE PSEUDO-PAULINE DOCUMENTS, written decades later but attributed to the apostle, reflect the religious politics of a later day. For example, the three Pastoral Letters emphasize antifeminist elements in Paul. In this they are in keeping with the tenets of a by-then more established church, with robed bishops, all men, which excluded women from any significant church position. We can't get Paul off the hook and simply blame the Pastorals. Immediately following his magical discourse on love, which comprises a whole chapter, 1 Corinthians 13, in 1 Corinthians 14.34–35 he states (King James Version cited for proper authority), "Let your women keep silence in the churches: for it is not permitted unto them to speak; but they are commanded to be under obedience, as also saith the law. And if they will learn any thing, let them ask their husbands at home: for it is a shame for women to speak in the church."

In fairness to Paul it must be said that this specific horrific call for female repression, in church and home, is increasingly seen as a later scribal interpolation. More, it stands out oddly as a petulant twitch, contradicting, in the same letter, Paul's gratitude to women friends who are collaborating in the common cause. Biblical scriptures are riddled with interpolations, which one notes even when comparing the standard Greek texts of the Lord's Prayer.

The Role of Silent Women

Paul, like Walt Whitman, loved to contradict himself. In the same book of 1 Corinthians, he permits women to give sermons and prophesy in the church, provided they wear a veil. More telling, Paul speaks frequently of many women as his founding companions in the churches, his most trusted collaborators; he appoints women to keep new missions in order; and in Romans he notes that he has asked Phoebe (Rom. 16.1), a deacon (an ordained minister) in the church located in Cenchrea, an eastern port of Corinth, to carry his letter to the Romans to Rome. Deacon Priscilla (Rom. 16.3) is associated with the same church, and he promotes one of his colleagues to his own missionary status, saying about Junia, later Saint Junia, that she and her companion Andronikos are "outstanding among the messengers [apostles]":

Greet Andronikos and Iounias,
Who were in prison with me. Outstanding
Among the messengers, even before me
They were working furiously for the Mashiah.

ROM. 16.7

From Paul's time, and in large part because of Paul, women were ordained to preach and hold high administrative offices.[8] Those were his actions nearly two thousand years before anything like them was beginning to be permitted in Protestant churches, and more frequently in Jewish synagogues. But insofar as Paul contributed to silencing and separating women, he was following the practice of not only earlier Jewish temple customs but also Hindu, Bhuddist, and later Muslim hierarchies.

---

8. The tradition continued through most of the Byzantine period, though with increasing restrictions between the eleventh and thirteenth centuries. There was also an appearance of female deacons in the Western church in the first centuries before the great schism, but the male hierarchy in Rome did not accept the role of female church officers, and that sickly restriction, a human rights issue, has not yet gone into remission.

Elaine Pagels, the eminent professor of religion at Princeton, emphasized Paul's radically pro-women passages in her *Gnostic Paul*.[9] She finds the Pastorals and all work like them a reaction to the Gnostics, who were distinctly pro-women, not anti-women. Eve was a hero to the Gnostics for choosing gnosis, knowledge, in the Garden. She had the courage of freedom; she was not the traditional fallen and disobedient villain of Genesis. In supporting the Gnostic tendency to favor women, in her exegesis of Valentine scriptures, Pagels elaborates how women were essential creators, not the poor creatures of the pseudo-Pauline letters. Whatever the ultimate messages are from the many-sided apostle angel of the new sect, Paul's own voice is unmistakable. For those who love him, as this translator does, he is the author of Milton's *Paradise Regained*. For those who hear sick bombast, well, Paul is too human to be all the time in tune. The big horns like Milton, Beethoven, Melville do break the rafters on occasion with their volume, but what incomparable beauty they possess. Paul's authentic letters speak with authorial veracity and sing with verbal majesty.

As noted earlier, when we devise a picture of Saint Paul as depicted in Acts of the Apostles (Activities of the Messengers), the question of historicity versus story is paramount. In a few words, Paul of Acts is another Paul. There we enter adventure, miracles, and other superhuman qualities, as well as missions to far places, wonderful escapes, successful debates with Roman authorities whom he effectively brings over to his ethical and spiritual side. These achievements are not found in Paul's words but in third-person descriptions by an unknown author who (in an implausible prefatory sentence to Acts) claims to be the gospeler Luke. Paul of Acts is a fascinating figure, one of the world's courageous adventurers, but as with the gospels, Acts is a story composed decades after Paul's death by an author or authors whose later church politics of evolving dogma were guiding the pen.

While Acts gave us a Paul for its own purposes and circumstance, Paul gave himself in the first person, in all his troubles, contentions, and spiritual flights. In his own words he composed the sonorous, cranky, soaring letters, dictated mainly to his scribe Tertius as missives to be sent out to

9. Elaine Pagels, *The Gnostic Paul: Gnostic Exegesis of the Pauline Letters* (Philadelphia: Trinity Press International, 1992).

his wavering congregations. These spoken letters were later elevated to become the earliest canonical scripture in the New Testament.

Eternity

In the Hebrew Bible, one was born, lived, and died, with no after-death reward or punishment. Whatever notions of eternity are contained in Torah are vague, and with the exception of Isaiah (even in Isaiah eternity is more metaphor of praise than assertion of fact) death is the last stop. But by Paul's time, long after the Hebrew Bible was set in its canonical frame, ideas of an afterlife seized the imagination and were rampant everywhere there were schools of thought. Plato was the popular and revered agent of afterlife of the soul in the Judaism of Paul's days. And the concept of an afterlife of both body and soul was to star in most later Christian sects, including the Gnostic heresies. The biblical life-confined-to-earth of traditional Judaism found kinship in Greek Stoicism, Epicureanism, Aristotelean science, and ultimately in the Roman philosopher and poet Lucretius (ca. 99 B.C.E.–ca. 55), who in *De rerum natura* (On the Nature of Things) spoke for a peaceful but ultimate death, without danger of whimsical gods disturbing one's sleep. None of this earthly confinement influenced Paul. When Paul invented Christianity, he turned the earthly messiahs of the Jewish Bible into the single divine messiah foretold in Isaiah, but one who would die, return soon, and save us.

Christianity was the surviving and successful sect of the day that proposed a reward of afterlife and a punishment of eternal hell. These notions of heaven and hell, so alien to the Hebrew Bible, were, however, commonplace among other ancient major religious movements from Sumeria, Persia, and Babylonia to Egypt, and mystery religions in Rome.

Paul's way to a belief in eternity came apparently after much anger at fellow Jews who believed in the divinity of the crucified Jesus. But on his way to Damascus in Syria something may have happened. Let us pause before the leap. As noted, this essential story of the vision may have been largely Paul's, or one assigned to him by later epistlers and the author or authors of Acts. We go on. Paul was in hot pursuit of Christian Jews who were harboring there when his world-changing vision came to him. In contrast to the subdued reference to his spiritual "turn" in his letters, in Acts he went temporarily blind, speechless, totally overcome. A new Paul was born. Thereafter he was committed to the good news. He realized his belief in missionary work through Greece and Greek-speaking cities and towns in Asia Minor. As for Paul's late voyage to Rome, it is described only in Acts. The great advantage of Acts is that while the letters tell us his piecemeal adventures and, above all, his beliefs, Acts puts it all together in a coherent story, which makes it surely the top page-turner in the Bible. While many cannot see and believe the Paul of the letters transformed into a miracle charismatic, we all must accept that most of Paul's life remains a mystery. I am convinced that the adventure of his actual life, that creative nonfiction, must be more astonishing than anything in Acts of the Apostles, the later Acts of Paul, and even the letters inscribed onto papyrus or later parchment.

PAUL'S MISSIONS AND VISITS to Jerusalem are compared and seem to contradict each other, at least by omission, in our two main sources. Figuring out how many trips Paul did make to Jerusalem (five in Acts, three in his letters) is an exercise some of the readers may wish to explore. For the manuscript scholar there is an enormous ever-developing history of new interpretations based on the best surviving manuscripts. There are even infra-ray scopes to see words under words. This scientific magic promises to dig up a huge find of Greek and Latin texts from palimpsestic Psalters and prayerbooks in old monasteries, where it was the practice to white out with some kind of gesso earlier texts, often classical Greek texts, such as the Archimedes notebook that was completely restored recently. Paul awaits high-tech missionaries to bring more of his light into the light.

There is so much we do not and for now cannot know. Paul's statement near the end of Romans is that he will soon go to Rome on his way to Spain. Did he ever reach Rome? Spain? The first letter is to the Roman Messianic groups in anticipation of a stop there to bring his own gospel, meaning the good news of the Christ—not the canonical gospels, which were a few decades away from composition. There were thousands of Jews already living in Rome who would be obvious targets for his word. Which leads us to ask, how did Acts of Paul flesh out mention of a trip to Rome in the Letter to the Romans into a dramatic death, which was followed by his risen ghost which returned to the palace to haunt Nero? What were the sources for the author or authors of Acts? Paul may have spent years in Rome and not in prison. But despite so much commentary, we still must return to original documents, and the earlier the better, for they are less tampered with. If we search through the abundant fantastic intertestamental pseudepigrapha, a thousand Pauls are born. But most significant is that there was a real Paul who spoke through his letters as a disorganized but astute theologizer and as an avid missionary. That Paul, the tentmaker Jew from Tarsos, laid the first stone of every church and cathedral thereafter that embraces the creed and faith of Christianity.

Letters of
Shaul/Saul/Paul

Romans

Romans

The letter's Greek title is "To Romans," because it addresses the Romans. We assume here, as with all titles of books in the New Testa-ment, that the title was a later addition. This particular letter escapes from the genre of letter or epistle. Yes, it was written as if it were to be sent to others; however, more than any letter, it is an overheard meditation directed to a congregation. But we speak of it as a letter or an epistle. An epistle may be perceived in English to be a more public and elevated form of "letter." The Greek makes no such distinction. Here, as is now general practice, "letter" rather than "epistle" is used when referring to any covenantal letters. And surely to Paul's surprise wherever he is, his letter or meditation has become a canonical book, sacred scripture for the New Testament, of which during his lifetime he had not a page.

The letters were dictated, not written, by the author, which in no way reflects on Paul's literacy in Greek and Hebrew. He dictated Romans to his regular scribe, Tertius. Tertius is responsible for the third-person salutation, formal and formulaic in a tone that scarcely suggests Paul's intelligent intimacy and makes his letters humane and distinctively of his own person and reflection, and the giveaway last chapter of political goodbyes to helpers and friends. As in Acts, ancient letters usually begin with the name of the sender and the recipient, unlike modern formal letters, in which the sender is named in the letterhead and the recipient's name is given below on the left.

Romans is the longest of Paul's letters and unsurpassed in all ways: style, message, and literary peaks. It is the philosophical masterpiece of the New Testament, and most subsequent theology, and a lot more, in the Eastern and Western sects of Europe springs from its declarations, meditations, metaphysics, parables, paradoxes, and contradictions.

Because of its importance and perhaps its length, it is traditionally placed first among Paul's letters, although among the authentic letters it may be the last one that found its way into the canon. It was composed between 54/55 and 58/59 C.E. Since we have probably only a small part of Paul's letters and no responses to them, we can assume that Paul continued writing after this grand epistle. But given its length and significance, it may well be the last major letter he composed. One should also remember that the traditional dating of the letters is tentative.

The immediate background is that after going from town to town in the Aegean region, collecting funds to help the Christian-Jewish church in Jerusalem, Paul was planning first to go to Jerusalem to deliver the moneys and then leave for Rome. He also hoped to keep part of the funds to support a future mission in virgin Spain. He may have had the document sent to Rome ahead of time by Phoebe, the deacon of the church in Cenchrea, a port of Corinth.

In Romans as elsewhere, Paul must defend his work among gentiles, who were among his main new converts and who were a source of funds passed on to other churches. The validity of this work was questioned by the church in Jerusalem because Paul permitted the new converts not to observe some Jewish laws. At the same time, to the gentiles he had to insist on the centrality of Israel in God's plan for redemption.

Here Paul is harsh on himself, speaking of a thorn in his side, with implications of physical as well as spiritual pain. Yet none would accuse him of modesty or humility. The closest to modesty in his character is self-deprecation, as he proudly and impetuously puts himself down as one of the unworthy. Paul's flaws, physical and spiritual, his wild mood changes, make him all the more human and never boring. He is a grand towering force, worthy of Aeschylus or Shakespeare. The "slave of Jesus Christ" formula may be a customary apologia but it is in no way the assertive Paul of the missions. The first passages, as Tertius handles them and undoubtedly stamps them with his traditional scribal piety, formality, and rallying call to faith, are not the best introduction to one of the world's great missives, but soon the scribal tone disappears and is forgotten and Paul speaks to us from heart, head, and soul.

The pervasive theological theme of Romans is justification and salvation through faith, for Jew and gentile, and Paul shows God's plan of salvation and redemption from Adam to the Christ.

Chapter 1

Hello from the scribe
  Shaul,[1] a slave of Yeshua the Mashiah,[2]
  Called on to be a special messenger

---

1. Paul from the Greek Παῦλος (Paulos), from Saul in the Greek Σαῦλος (Saulos), from the Hebrew שָׁאוּל (Shaul). Paul was born in Tarsos as *Shaul*. Paul, a slave of Jesus the Messiah or Jesus the Christ.

2. Christ Jesus. Jesus is from the Greek Ἰησοῦς (Iesous), from the Aramaic יֵשׁוּעַ (Yeshua), a later form of the Hebrew יְהוֹשֻׁעַ (Yehoshua). "Christ" is from the Greek Χριστος (Hristos), and Greek *Hristos* or *Christos* is a translation from the Greek Μεσσίας (Messias), from the Hebrew מָשִׁיחַ (mashiah). "Christ" in Greek also means "the anointed," and "Messiah" in both Greek and Hebrew contains the meaning of "the anointed."

Paul writes Jesus's epithet "Christ" in "Jesus Christ," making "Christ" Jesus's last name. So in his letters we find "Jesus Christ" or "Christ Jesus," but never "Christ the Messiah," a phrase that runs through the gospels. "Christ the Messiah" is a tautology, meaning "Christ the Christ" or the "Messiah the Messiah." Paul, master of Greek, Aramaic, Hebrew, and Latin, knew that "Christ" and "Messiah" have one and the same meaning.

The authors of the New Testament went to the Septuagint Greek translation of the Hebrew Bible, which *translates* mashiah as *hristos*, meaning "the anointed," an attribute of the messiah, rather than as *messias*, the more obvious Greek *transliteration* of Hebrew *mashiah*. Had the Greek used *messias* then rather than "Christ," "Christian," and "Christianity," we would have "Messiah," "Messianist," and "Messianism," and the emerging religion known as "Christianity" would at last speak its central message of messianism through its philological name "Messianism."

By going to the Hebrew, for "Jesus Christ" we would also have "Yeshua the Mashiah." If we cared to Anglicize the name, as happens in normal Bible translation of other Greek, Aramaic, and Hebrew names, then for "Yeshua the Mashiah" we would have "Joshua the Messiah," a natural name, evoking religious and ethnic origin. But standard English translation has settled on "Jesus Christ," which affords no clue that "Jesus" is a Latin-Greek version of a Hebrew name elsewhere in the Hebrew Bible transliterated as "Joshua," and no clue that "Christ" is a translation of "Messiah."

For the good news[3] of God 2that was proclaimed
First through the prophets in the holy Torah[4]
3About his son who came as flesh from seed
Of David, 4who has been declared the son
Of God with power according to the spirit
Of holiness by his resurrection from
The dead, Yeshua the Mashiah our lord,
5Through whom we have been granted grace and rank
Of messenger to make the faith obeyed
Among all nations honoring his name.
6Among them you are also called by Yeshua
Mashiah, 7and to all God's loves in Rome,
Who now are called on as his holy saints.
Grace be to you and peace from God our father
And from the lord Yeshua the Mashiah.

Shaul longs to visit Rome and share the fruit of spirit
8First I thank God through Yeshua Mashiah
Concerning all of you, because your faith
Reverberates throughout the world. 9And God,
Whom I serve in my spirit of good news
Of his son, is my witness how unceasingly
10In my prayers I remember you and ask
If somehow, through God's will, at last I find
My way to come to you. 11I long to see you
And to impart to you spiritual gifts

---

3. Good news or gospel from the Greek εὐαγγέλιον (evangelion). Here the meaning is clearly *evangelion*, in the sense of sacred good news or good report. Since Paul died at least a decade, or more probably two, before the first canonical gospels were composed, the reference cannot be to the canonical gospels. Nor can "good news" refer to other works called the noncanonical gospels, nor specifically to the Gospel of Thomas, which, even if dated as having been composed before the canonical gospels, as many scholars believe, was not likely to have been known by Paul, since it bares no qualities found in Paul's letters.

4. Tanak or Old Testament, or specifically the law in the five books of Moses (Pentateuch).

For your empowerment; 12may you find comfort
Together in our joined faith, yours and mine.
13 And I wish you to know, brothers,[5] how often
I planned to come to you—but I was blocked
Till now—so I might share some fruit[6] with you
As I have when dining with other nations.[7]
14I am indebted to the Greeks, barbarians,
To wise and stupid. 15I'm eager to bring
All the good news also to you in Rome.

Salvation by faith[8]

16I'm not ashamed of my word of good news.[9]
The good news is God's powers for everyone
With faith, first for the Jews, and also for
The Greeks.[10] 17Through his powers, the justice of God
From faith to faith reveals itself. As it is written
In Habakkuk: "The just man will live by faith."[11]

---

5. The Greek plural of brothers, ἀδελφοί (adelfoi), may in principle include the notion of sisters. However, the Greek does have the gender preference of using the masculine form to represent the masculine and feminine. Some translate as "brothers and sisters," which is a generous and inclusive amendment to the Greek word for "brothers." While it would be much preferable in English to say "brothers and sisters," the Greek, with the possibility of saying "brothers and sisters" or "man and woman," does not support that equality of gender, and therefore, it is unfaithful to the intention of the text to improve the translation, which the New Revised Standard Versions and other translations, with good purpose, do.

6. The King James Version translates "fruit," as it reads in Greek. Most versions change the metaphor to "harvest," but the original "fruit" remains more striking.

7. The gentiles.

8. The theme of the letter.

9. The Majority Text adds "of Christ."

10. Paul looked to the Jews in the synagogues, as written here and in Acts, as his first target for preaching and conversion to the notion that the foretold messiah had really come. See note 333 in Acts 20.17 for distinctions between synagogue and church.

11. Hab. 2.4. Habakkuk, a contemporary of Jeremiah, was popular in the intertestamental years. In some ways, on this minor prophet of few lines Paul principled much of his faith and message.

God's anger against the ungodliness of gentiles
    18Out of heaven God's anger is revealed[12]
      Against ungodliness and wickedness
      Of men who in their unjust ways hide truth.
    19What is known about God is plain to them
      And because God then made it plain to them.
    20From the creation of the world they knew
      God's invisible presence, everlasting

---

12. In scripture it is common to personify God with human traits. Here Paul speaks of God's anger against the unrighteous. He does so in the tradition of earthly leaders who have personal knowledge and insight into the emotions, thoughts, and ways of God. In the practice of charting God's ways, we have, on the one hand, Jack Miles, author of *God: A Biography*, who writes significant biographies of God and Jesus Christ, which he bases largely on scripture itself—say, a passage in Genesis or a Psalm where the text is assumed to be a report of God's voice. On the other, there is the broad tradition of religious authors and leaders who speak God's word and feelings derived from their presumed intimacy with God. How they come upon their knowledge of God's emotions and speak for and through them evokes a question: How can a mortal know what God thinks, feels, wishes, and does?

    Those who assume powers by virtue of conversations with the deity and become God's spokespersons may serve great purpose or disaster. It may be a Byzantine monarch saving his empire or the child leaders Stephen and Nicholas of the French and German children's crusades, who in the early thirteenth century led thousands of children into havoc and slavery in the East. Indeed, the chronicle of religious wars against heretic and infidel is peopled with leaders who claim authority directly from God. There being diverse sects, there are diverse notions as to on whom God's anger should fall. In the instance of Paul, we learn in legendary Acts that on the way to Damascus, Paul encounters God—or God finds him—and, through Jesus's voice, God gazes on him, temporarily blinding him, and personally convinces him to believe in the messiah's arrival. It would be significant to know how at other moments Paul acquires his knowledge of God's own voice and emotions—and not only of anger but also of all things from felicity to disappointment with the human condition. Perhaps the key enigma concerning God and religion lies precisely in clarifying how humans divine the godhead's personal qualities, which, of course, can be described only in human speech. Historically, the religious mystics, whose message is the ineffable union with the divine, come closest to giving us clues to the mystery of the nature of God.

Power, and divinity. They've no excuse.
21They knew God, yet they failed to glorify
　Or thank him as our God. And they grew cunning,
　In reasoning and so their mindless heart
　Fell deep into the fathoms of all darkness.
22They thought that they were wise yet they were fools
23And they exchanged God's imperishable glory
　For likenesses of perishable persons,
　And birds and quadrupeds and reptiles.
24So God delivered them in their desires[13]
　To filth and degradation of their bodies
　Among themselves. 25They had exchanged God's truth
　For falsehood in their worship, served the creature
　Rather than the creator blessed forever.
　　　　　　　　　　Amain.[14]

Polluted passions
26So God delivered them to shameful passions.
　Even the women with them changed their ways,
　Making natural relations[15] betray nature[16]
27Similarly, men abandoned natural bond
　With women and their blood burned craving men.
　Men plunged with men into indecent acts

---

13. The Greek ἐπιθυμία (epithymia) is dominantly defined as "desire, longing, craving." To translate it as "lust" makes desire itself sinful, which may seem to be a fair religious interpretation of the general message. The actual meaning of the single word *epithymia* is "desire" or "craving," and that translation, in context, carries enough weight and need not be changed. By heightening the source word ἐπιθυμία to read "lust," the message is not more powerful but weakened. By contrast, the understated metaphor of a *"desire of the heart" that leads to catastrophe* is a formidable warning.

14. Amen from the Greek ἀμήν (amen), from the Hebrew אָמֵן (amein).

15. Intercourse.

16. Homosexuality.

And got due recompense for their mistake.[17]
28Since they did not care for knowledge of God,
   God spun them into their reprobate minds
29Filled with each wrong,[18] cunning greed and evil.
   Bloated with envy, murder, deceit, discord,
   They were whispering backbiters, 30God-haters,
   Arrogant braggarts, inventors of destruction,
   Defiant to parents 31mindless unworshiping,
   Heartless merciless. 32They knew God's decrees

---

17. Death. See note 41 for 1 Corinthians 5.5., and note 45 for 1 Corinthians 6.9. In Paul's army of the observant, there was no save-face "Don't ask, don't tell" motto. Indeed, in the Abrahamic religions, Judaism, Christianity, and Islam, in full discord with classical Greco-Roman culture, the body was the enemy or, at best, a necessary vehicle for the eternal soul. The ethos comprised more than death for homosexuals or for the long list of body crimes for which death was the payment. The modern Greek poet Constantine Cavafy (1863–1933), a Greek Orthodox by birth, who re-created antiquity in unparalleled poetry, addresses this discord between cultures and the temptations of both sides, in his poem written in 1919, "Of the Jews 50 C.E."

> Painter and poet, runner and discus thrower,
> beautiful as Endymion, Ianthis, son of Anthony,
> was from a family friendly to the synagogue.
>
> My most honest days
> are when I leave behind the aesthetic search,
> when I leave behind beautiful and hard Hellenism,
> with its paramount focus
> on perfectly made and moral white limbs.
> And I become the person I wish
> always to remain—of the Jews, the holy Jews, the son.
> His eager declaration: "Always
> to remain of the Jews, the holy Jews—"
>
> But he did not remain that way at all.
> The Hedonism and Art of Alexandria
> held him, a devoted son.

From Aliki Barnstone, trans., *The Collected Poems of C. P. Cavafy: A New Translation* (New York: W. W. Norton, 2006), 120.

18. The Majority Text adds "whoring."

And that the practice of these things was death.
Yet those in error not only thrived in error
But bloated with joy when others did the same.

Chapter 2

God's judgment
    You, whoever you are, have no excuse
Or defense, since when you condemn the others,
You damn yourself, for you who are the judge
Do equal things. 2But we know that God's judgment
Is really against those who do such things.
3Do you imagine that you, being a person
And judge of others doing what you practice,
Will escape God's judgment? 4Or do you scorn
His plenitude of kindness and forbearance
And his long suffering. Do you not realize
That God's kindness will lead you to repentance?

5Through your hardness, your unrepentant heart,
You are storing up anger for yourself
On the day of the anger and the revelation
Of God's judgment. 6Both Psalms[19] and Proverbs[20] say:
    God will repay each according to deeds.
7And those who patiently do their good work,
Seek glory, honor, and an incorruptibility[21]
He will bequeath you an eternal life.
8For selfish ones who don't obey the truth
But what is wrong, there will be wrath and fury,
9Affliction and despair for every soul

---

19. Ps. 62.12.
20. Prov. 24.12.
21. Others interpret the metaphor as "immortality."

Doing evil, Jew first and also Greek,

10Yet glory and honor and peace to all

Doing good, Jew first and also Greek.

11God shows no favoritism. 12All who sin[22]

Outside the law, perish outside the law,

And all who sin within the law are judged

By the same law. 13It's not hearers of law

Who are in God's sight just. It is the doers

Of the same law who will be justified.

14When gentiles who do not possess the Torah

Practice it naturally, these without Torah

Are themselves Torah. 15They show that the work

Of Torah is, as Yirmiyahu[23] writes:

Written in their hearts.[24]

And their own conscience also bears it witness.[25]

Just as their thoughts accuse or else defend

Each other, 16on that day God will judge

The secrets of these men concordant with

My good news through Yeshua the Mashiah.

---

22. Literally, "miss the mark or target."

23. Jeremiah.

24. Jer. 31.33. Jeremiah writes more fully, "[Yahweh speaking]: Within them I shall plant my law, writing it on their hearts." We will see that Paul will take the "law of the heart" to prevail over all written law, since, as here stated in Jeremiah, it is written in the heart by God: Moreover, Jeremiah continues, the least and the great will know him, and he will forgive them and never more call sin to their mind.

25. According to "their own conscience" is key to Paul's thinking. Paul was trained by the highest Pharisee priests, the most liberal sect of Jews, who were given to oral instruction and which was superior to the written law in Torah or the whole Tanak. Here, in Pharisee tradition, Paul suggests that gentiles can practice a law written in their hearts, which will be seen as not only equal to but also above the written Torah. In such way Paul was able to use his Pharisidic training to change and reform Jewish law for Jews like himself as well as for the Greek gentiles in ways to accommodate their entry into the new Judaism. Such reform was accomplished through his innovations with respect to circumcision (the *pact*) as well as many other tenets of Torah.

Jews and Torah

17But if you call yourself a Jew, and rely
On Torah law[26] and glory in your God

---

26. The word "Torah," meaning "law" or "instruction" or "teaching," refers to the entire Hebrew Bible, which is also called "Tanak" (an acronym of T, N, and K, from the first letter of the three parts of the Bible: Torah, Prophets, and Writings). The Greek word for the Torah as the five books of Moses is "Pentateuch," meaning "five scroll cases."

In any legal context, "Torah" simply means "law." Depending on context, "Torah" is used synonymously for each of these designations: the whole Jewish Bible, the five books of Moses, and the law. As Paul uses the Greek word νόμος (nomos) for law, he never speaks of civil law but religious law, and he is referring to Jewish law. It should be remembered that in Paul's day the only religious law for Paul was that of the Jewish Bible, in Hebrew, which he followed and which was called and is still called "Torah." While Paul speaks of law as Torah, in some instances he goes beyond Torah to speak of "God's law," or "God's law given us through his son Jesus the Christ" (Yeshua the Mashiah). God's unwritten law can prevail over the written Torah, though once Paul pronounces God's law, it becomes God's law established in written form by Paul. The gospels, Acts, and Revelation were not yet written, nor were the letters compiled, including Paul's authentic as well as his disputed letters, all of which were to comprise the full New Testament (New Covenant). Though Torah and the New Testament, including Paul's letters, will eventually shape church law, the New Testament's books are not in themselves composed as law. They are not a self-consciously composed constitution. They contain no Ten Commandments in form or statement. Yet Paul's own letters come closest formally among New Testament books to having the shape of law.

In a word, the Hebrew Bible and the sayings and actions of Jesus remain the spiritual core on which later church law will be developed, but Paul is judge, lawmaker, and philosophical patron of the new movement. As we speak of "Moses the Jewish lawmaker," Paul, too, writing as a Messianic Jew, we may speak of and think of Paul as the Christian lawmaker. While we distinguish between Moses's and Paul's contribution to later Christianity, it must always be kept in mind that insofar as Christianity accepts the Jewish Bible as its own, it also accepts Jewish law, including the Ten Commandments, however its interpretation of Jewish law may differ. The difference lies in the Christian faith that the foretold messiah has come in the person of rabbi Yeshua ben Yosef, and in the additional New Testament scriptures composed by the early Christian Jews who established Christianity.

18And know his will and choose the excellent
   Because you are instructed in the Torah,
19Then you are confident to become guide
   To help the blind, bring light to those in darkness
20And be a teacher for the fools and children,
   Since you have the embodiment of truth
   And knowledge of the Torah. 21You who teach
   Others, will you not be teacher of yourself?
   In Exodus[27] and Deuteronomy[28]
   You preach not to steal, but do you steal?
22In Exodus[29] and Deuteronomy[30]
   You forbid adultery, but are you adulterous?
   You loathe idols, but do you steal from temples?
23Do you who glory in Torah not dishonor God
   By breaking the law? 24So it has been written
   In both Yeshayahu[31] and Ezekiel.[32]
      God's name is profaned among nations.

Philosophy of spiritual circumcision
   25Obey Torah and circumcision helps,
   But if you break the law your circumcision
   Becomes uncircumcision. 26Others who
   Are the uncircumcised yet keep the law,
   Will their uncircumcision not be seen
   As circumcision? 27And if that is so,
   The physically uncircumcised who keep

---

27. Exod. 20.15.

28. Deut. 5.19.

29. Exod. 20.17.

30. Deut. 5.21.

31. Isaiah from the Greek Ἠσαΐας (Esaias), from the Hebrew יְשַׁעְיָהוּ (yeshayahu). The passage appears in Isaiah 52.5.

32. Ezek. 36.20.

Torah will judge you of the written code
And circumcision yet transgress the law.
28Someone is not a Jew by what is seen.
Rather, one is a Jew by what is hidden.
29Circumcision is of the heart, the spirit,33

---

33. See Afterword section "Old Circumcision and New Circumcision in Greek and Hebrew Leading to Old Testament and New Testament" for general commentary on the wider implications of circumcision. For the first Christian Jews who had been gentiles, circumcision was a dire issue in the days when the new sect of Messianics was establishing itself. Paul leaves the door wide open for new Christian Jews not to be circumcised. With eloquence and Talmudic logic, he argues in favor of a lofty meaning of the circumcision, the pact with God, the conventional price for becoming a Jew and upholding the law (the commandments of Torah). Paul writes that it is worse to be circumcised and break the law than not to be circumcised yet obey the law.

We observe that in the years that Paul is writing about a mitigated and higher form of circumcision, such ideas are very much in the air. In the wisdom Gospel of Thomas, we find an extraordinary parallel that is more severe in its ridicule of physical circumcision. Yeshua is derisive, saying that the physical must yield to the spiritual. In saying 53, he is asked about circumcision. His followers said to him,

Is circumcision useful or not?

YESHUA
If it were useful, fathers would produce their children
Already circumcised from their mothers.
But the true circumcision in spirit
Is fully valuable.

The advantage of "true circumcision in spirit" for the gentile who would join the developing sect of Christian Jews was enormous. It meant that without going through an adult mutilation of their genital organ, they could enjoy equality of acceptance before the Messianics who were born as Jews and who represented the greater body of the followers of Yeshua, including Peter and Paul, who had had their circumcision on the eighth day after their birth, hence avoiding the adult trauma of the rite.

Not from the literal law. So one finds praise
Not from the ranks of men. It comes from God.[34]

Chapter 3

What good is it to be a Jew and circumcised?
     What then is the advantage to the Jew,
     What is the value of the circumcision?
     2Great in all ways. In the first place, the words

---

34. Here Paul defines the truly spiritual Jew—not by external signs or by old laws but by a spiritual renewal. Within the realm of Judaism, Paul was working the synagogues, temples, and independent communities during his travels and in letters to convince fellow Jews of the good news as he was welcoming gentiles to become true Jews. He lived and died decades before the split between Jews and Christian Jews carried the distinguishing labels of Judaism and Christianity (Messianism). While there is a confrontational tenor to coreligionists with whom he feuds, it is not cataclysmic, like that between the Essene Jews of the desert and the Jews of Jerusalem. In the Dead Sea Scrolls we read that the "children of light" swear conquest and death to the "children of darkness" in Jerusalem.

In Paul's letters each community claims itself as the true Jews, far different from the constancy of the concealed Jewish identity of Messianics found in the later gospels in which those who do not share belief in the foretold messiah will be, as proved by their after-the-fact prophecy of the Jewish Wars and destruction of the Temple (70 C.E.), utterly destroyed, with no place to hide, in neither city, in field, nor on mountainside. In the deepest sense, Christianity, like Islam, as another child of Judaism, retains virtually the same pillars of belief. Indeed, the three Abrahamic sects share belief in the good, in spirit, in love, in one invisible God, and in a messiah. In the intertestamental period, Judaism and Christianity were exposed to Greek philosophy, absorbing key neoplatonic notions of eternity, of the immortal soul and its residence in a heavenly thereafter, ideas later to be central to Christianity, Islam, and postbiblical Judaism.

Another characteristic of Paul's Messianism and of many sects of Judaism was the openness to gentiles, to the *ethnoi* (the nations), who were mainly Greeks. This openness is manifest in the first and second centuries, which saw the greatest period of conversion to Judaism in the Roman world, similar to the powerful expansion of Christianity and Gnosticism. Ironically, a major cause for this expansion of converts was the destruction of the Temple and of Jerusalem in 70, and the subsequent diaspora of Jewish and Christian Jewish communities to many nations.

Of God were entrusted to them. ₃What then?
What if some of them did not find belief
In words of God? If some did not believe,
It did not void belief in God. ₄Never!
Let God alone be true, though everyone
Become a liar. As written in the Psalms:
    So you may be justified in your words
    And triumph when you are judged.³⁵
₅But our injustice confirms our God's justice.
What are we to say? Can God be unfair
In meting out his wrath on us? ₆(I speak
As a human.)³⁶ Never! How then could God
Be judge on earth? ₇If through my lies God's truth
Resounds his glory, why am I still judged
A sinner? ₈Am I not what some opponents
Slander and charge us with, who claim I say,
Let us do evil so that good may come?
Their condemnation we fully deserve.

No one is good

₉What then? Are we Jews better? Not at all.
We have already charged both Jews and Greeks
To be sinful. ₁₀As written in the Psalms:
    There is no good person. Not a one.
    ₁₁There is no one who understands.
    There is no one who seeks God.
    ₁₂They have all turned away and become useless.
    There is no one turning good, not a one.³⁷
    ₁₃Their throats are open graves,
    Their tongues are working trickery.
    The asp's venom is on their lips.³⁸

---

35. Ps. 51.4 (Septuagint).
36. "I speak as a man" is added in Majority Text.
37. Ps. 14.1–3.
38. Ps. 140.3.

14Their mouths are bloated with curses and bitterness.[39]
15Their feet are quick to shed blood.[40]
16Ruin and misery stand on their path
17And they don't know the way of peace.[41]
18They have no fear of God before their eyes.[42]

Faith and God's judgment

19Now we know that whatever Torah says,
It speaks to those who are within the Torah
So that every single mouth will be silenced
And the whole world accountable to God.
20As it is written in the Psalms:
No mortal being will be justified in his sight
By deeds prescribed by Torah, since in Torah
There is a complete recognition of sin.[43]

21But now God's justice, and distinct from Torah,
Is known and attested to by Torah law
And the prophets: 22a justice of God through faith
In Yeshua the Mashiah to all who believe.
23All have sinned and come short of God's glory,
24Yet now are justified by gift of grace
Through the redemption of Yeshua the Mashiah.
25God presented him as a propitiation
Through faith in his blood. He accomplished this
To demonstrate his justice. In forbearance
He has forgiven earlier committed sins.

---

39. Ps. 10.7.

40. Isa. 59.7.

41. Isa. 59.1–8

42. Ps. 36.1. This New Testament compilation of lines from Psalms achieves an example of the thrilling poetic powers with a vast range of imagery to instruct and inspire.

43. Ps. 143.2.

26More, he did this to show his present justice,
  That he is just, justifies one with faith.44

Faith and Torah
  27Where is boasting45 then? By what Torah law
  Was it excluded? And by what works? No.
  Only through a Torah of faith. 28We hold
  That now one can be justified by faith
  Without the work demanded by the Torah.
  29Is God the God only of Jews? Is he
  Not also for the gentiles? Yes for gentiles.
  30Since God is one and he will justify
  The circumcision by faith
  And uncircumcision by faith.46
  31Then are we making Torah void through faith?
  Never. We are only confirming Torah.

Chapter 4

Example of Avraham
  What shall we say that our forefather Avram47
  Discovered by way of the flesh? 2If Avram
  Was justified by his works, he has something
  To boast about, but not before God. 3Genesis

---

44. In these subtle, logical turnings of concepts from myriad angles, we have the beginning of what will later be known as "scholasticism."

45. "Boasting" may also be read more positively, as Richmond Lattimore does, as "exultation."

46. In these references to "circumcision," Paul is returning to the original meaning of circumcision in Hebrew, *brit,* meaning both "circumcision" and what it means metaphorically and conceptually, which is "covenant," indeed a new covenant through faith.

47. Abram from the Greek Ἀβραάμ (Abram), from the Hebrew אַבְרָם (avram). Avram was the patriarch Abraham's original name. After his circumcision, "Abram" became "Abraham," from the Hebrew אַבְרָהָם (avraham).

Says Avram believed God. For his belief
He was accounted with justice.[48]
4For one who works, his payment isn't measured
As gift but as his due. 5But to the man
Who without work trusts God, who justifies
The ungodly, his faith is seen as goodness.
6David also extols the blessedness
Of one whom God considers good apart
From actions and his work. In Psalms he tells us:
7Blessed are those whose lawlessness is forgiven
And sins are covered.
8Blessed is the man whose sin God does not reckon.[49]

9Is blessedness won by the circumcised
As well as the uncircumcised? We say
That Avram's faith was clarified to him
As goodness. 10Yet how was it told to him?
In circumcised or uncircumcised state?
11He received the sign of the circumcision
As a seal of the goodness of this faith
While he was uncircumcised. 12He's also
The father of circumcision to those
Who are not only circumcised but walk
In his footsteps through faith that Avraham
Our father had while he was uncircumcised.

God's promise realized through faith
13The promise of inheriting the world
Did not reach Avraham or his descendants
Through Torah but through the justice of faith.
14If those who live by law are the inheritors,
The faith is canceled and the promise gone.

---

48. Gen. 15.6.
49. Ps. 32.1–2.

15The law brings anger but where no law is,
   No Torah, there can be no lawbreaking.
16It is because of faith, and therefore grace,
   That the promise holds good for all the seed,
   And not only to adherents of Torah
   But to the seed of the faith of Avraham,
   Who is father of us all. 17As in Genesis:
      I have made you the father of nations![50]
   In the sight of God in whom he believed,
   Who gives life to the dead, and calls the things
   That are not in being into being. 18Beyond hope,
   In hope he believed that he could become
   The father of many nations. As in Genesis.[51]
      So your descendants will be numerous.
19And Avraham did not weaken in his faith
   When he considered his own body, a dead man's,
   Who was then about a hundred years old,
   And also the deadness of Sarah's womb.
20He didn't flag in his belief in God's promise.
   Indeed, he was strengthened in his belief,
   Giving glory to God, 21fully persuaded
   That what God promised he could fulfill.
22So his faith counted as goodness in him.
23Now the words, "it counted for his goodness"
   Were not written for him alone,[52] 24but also us,
   Counted for us who have belief in him
   Who raised Yeshua our lord from the dead,
25Who was handed over to death by our
   Trespasses, and raised for our justification.

---

50. Gen. 17.5.
51. Gen. 15.5.
52. Gen. 15.6.

Chapter 5

Faith and joy

Therefore, since we are justified by faith,
We've peace with God through our lord Yeshua
The Mashiah. 2Through him we have by faith
Our access to this grace in which we stand.
We exult in the hope and glory of our God.
3We exult also in our afflictions, knowing
Afflictions carry us to enduring patience,
4And patience to a quality of character,
And quality to hope. 5Hope does not fail
Because God's love has poured into our hearts
Through the holy spirit we have been given.

6When we were powerless, Mashiah died
For us who were ungodly.[53] 7One dies rarely
For a just man, though perhaps one might dare
To die for a good man.[54] 8God shows his love
For us. While we were sinners, Mashiah died
For us. 9And since we have been justified
By his blood we are more sure to be saved
Through him and from God's wrath. 10When enemies,
We were reconciled to God through the death
Of his son, now reconciled how much more
Will we be saved through his life! 11Even more,
We exult in God through our lord Yeshua
The Mashiah through whom we are reconciled!

---

53. Meaning "those of us lacking belief in God."

54. "Good man" may be thought of as a good cause. Otherwise, it is uncertain what distinctions Paul wishes to make between a just and a good man.

Adam's fall

12Therefore, just as sin came into the world
Because of one man,[55] so death came through sin
And death spread to all men, since all men sinned.
14Death held dominion from Adam to Moshe,[56]
And even over those whose sins were not
Similar to the transgression of Adam,
Who was a model of one who was to come.[57]

Gift of grace

15But the gift of grace[58] is not of the nature
Of the transgression. If by the transgression
Of one, many died, far greater the abundance
For the many of God's grace and the gift
That came by the grace of one man, Yeshua
The Mashiah. 16The gift is not as when a man

---

55. Adam. It is curious that Paul ignores Eve, who is usually assigned the cause of our first condemnation. One can only speculate that either Eve was considered not important enough in God's or Paul's eyes to bring in death, or Eve as woman might not have been thought capable of altering the fate of all humanity. Women would later be so disesteemed among some Church fathers as to be described as without a soul. In any case, it cannot be assumed that she was eliminated from the equation of disobedience, sin, and death as a gesture of generosity. The omission is a slight to women, revealing that even "Eve's first transgression" was ignored in favor of her presumed master, Adam, who was more worthy of committing this evil deed of disobedience for purposes of acquiring knowledge.

In mainstream Gnosticism, however, Eve is seen as the Promethean hero precisely for bringing the fire of knowledge to humans as a weapon against the dominion of the creator God. Likewise, the serpent, as in Egyptian and Mesopotamian religions, is a good omen, and in Gnosticism the serpent is described as the first illumination of the foretold Jesus. In these ways Gnosticism is in great part born of this divergent interpretation of Eve's first deed.

56. Moses from the Greek Μωϋσῆς (Moses), from the Hebrew מֹשֶׁה (moshe).

57. The Greek says "type" of who was to come, implying "later sinners."

58. The Greek word χάρισμα (harisma) means "gift," and in this context, it has the frequent meaning of a divine gift or a "gift of grace." The word for "grace" alone is χάρις (haris).

Has sinned, since the judgment from one stumble
Leads to reprimand, but the gift of grace
After many transgressions leads to justification.
17For if because of one man's trespass, death
Held dominion, far greater the abundance
Of God's grace and gift of receiving justice,
Holding dominion in life through the one man,
Yeshua the Mashiah. 18As one man's blunder
Meant condemnation for all people, through
One just act all of us are justified for life.
19Just as from one man's disobedience,
The many became sinners, by one man's
Obedience the many will be justified.
20Torah law came in, trespasses multiplied.
But where sin multiplied, grace increased too,
21So as sin held dominion in death, grace
Will reign through justice leading to eternal
Life through Yeshua the Mashiah our lord.

Chapter 6

Dead in sin, alive in Mashiah
What then are we to say? Shall we persist
In sin so grace be multiplied? 2Never!
Can we who've died in sin keep living in it?[59]
3Do you not know that we who have been dipped[60]

---

59. Here as in 2.1–5 and elsewhere, Paul uses the diatribe style, a Greek device of rhetoric, in which the speaker states an apparent truth and demands an answer.

60. The Greek βαπτίζω (baptizo) means "dip," "immerse," "wash," "bathed," which is normally translated into English as "baptize," which has largely lost its immediate meaning in Greek and Hebrew, coming as it does from the Jewish ritual of dipping, immersing, and thereby being washed clean and purified.

In Mashiah Yeshua[61] were washed in his death?
4So we were buried with him by our being dipped
In him in death so that just as Mashiah
Was raised from the dead by our father's glory,
We too might walk in a new life. 5And if
We were joined together with him in a death
Like his, we will also be joined with him
In a resurrection like his. 6We also know
That our old self was crucified with him
So the body of our sin be destroyed
And we no longer will be slaves of sin.
7Whoever has died is absolved from sin.
8And if we also died with the Mashiah,
We believe we will also live with him,
9Knowing that Mashiah, raised from the dead,
Dies no more. Death no longer has dominion
Over him. 10When he died, he died for sin
One time. But when he lives, he lives for God.

11You must also count yourselves dead for sin,
But living in God through the mashiah Yeshua.
12Don't make sin king in your mortal body,
Surrender to its passions. 13Do not give
Your limbs to sin as weapons of wrongdoing,
But give yourselves to God as the living
Who have been dead, and give your limbs to God
As weapons of goodness. 14Then sin won't wield
Dominion over you. You will be subject
Not under Torah law but under grace.
15What then? Are we to sin because we're not
Under Torah but under grace? Never!
16Do you not know that if you try to pass
As obedient slaves of the one whom you obey,

---

61. The messiah Jesus.

You are the slaves of the one whom you obey,
Whether it be concerning sin or death
Or obedience that brings goodness.[62] 17By grace
Of God,[63] although you were a slave of sin,
You obeyed from the heart that form of teaching
To which you were committed. 18Freed from sin
You were enslaved to goodness. 19I tell you
In human terms because of the weakness
Of flesh. 20Just as you once surrendered limbs
To lawlessness, debauchery that led
To more debauchery, now give your limbs
As slaves to goodness and sanctification
For goodness. 21What fruit did you then possess
For which you now feel shame? Death is the end
Of those things. 22But you are set free from sin,
Enslaved to God, and have your fruit that brings
Sanctification and eternal life.
23Sin's stipend is our death, but grace of God
Is life eternal in Mashiah Yeshua our lord.

Chapter 7

Analogy of marriage

Do you not know, my brothers—and I speak
To those who understand Torah[64]—that Torah

---

62. The Greek δικαιοσύνη (dikaiosyne) means "justice," "goodness," and "righteousness." The context determines the translation. Normally, "righteousness" is avoided because of its implication of "better than thou" piety or of belonging to a selected and morally upright group. The classical Socratic meaning is "justice."

63. Or more colloquially, "thank God" or "through God's help" or "by the grace of God." The Greek χάρις (haris) means "grace," "favor," "help," and is an essential Pauline word.

64. Here it is clear that Paul is speaking to the Jews who know Torah (the law), since he wishes to change the nature of their obedience from that to only the holy Torah to an obedience to God and his law beyond all written law. His theological

Is binding only during one's lifetime?
2A married woman's bound by Torah law
To her husband as long as he is alive.
But if the husband dies, she is set free
From husband law. 3While he is still alive
She will be called adulterous if she joins
With another man. But if her husband dies,
She's free from the Mosaic law. If she weds
Another man she isn't an adulterer.
4So brothers, you have also died to Torah
Through the Mashiah's body and to join
Another, join him who has been raised
From death that we might bring forth fruit to God.

5When we were in the flesh, the passions of
Our sins, aroused by Torah law, were working
Through our bodies to bear the fruit of death.
6But now by dying to what has captured us,
We are released from that law to be slaves,
And not in the old way of scriptural words
But in a new way opening the spirit.

Spiritual Torah sin and mortal sin

7What then are we to say? Is Torah sin? Never!
Yet I would not have known sin if not for

---

method is in part determined by classical rhetoric, Hellenistic cosmology, and Pharisaic Judaism. As a Pharisee, Paul shares the views of contemporary Pharisees, who modify holy Torah from a body of frozen law to a new, oral interpretation of it, and who, like Paul, in spiritual interpretation of Torah, embrace the key notions of resurrection of the soul and eternal life for the good and just, which had entered Judaism by then as it had religious movements all over the Middle East and in Greece and Rome. The Middle Eastern religions, from Egypt and Mesopotamia—along with India, in contrast to traditional Judaism for whom God alone was eternal—by the time of Pharisaic Judaism were imbued with notions of the eternal soul that pervaded the cauldron of earlier civilizations in the Levant.

Torah law. Nor would I have known desire
Were it not for Torah that says, "You must not
Desire what is not yours."[65] 8But I found sin
Through the commandment and it caused in me
Diverse desire.[66] So without Torah law
Sin is dead. 9Once I lived without Torah.
When the commandment came, then sin came too
Into my life. 10I died and I discovered
That my commandment for life was for death.
11Then sin, through the commandment, seized this chance,
Fooled me, and through it killed me. 12So Torah
Is holy, its commandment holy, just, and good.[67]

My inner struggle

13Then did the good turn into death to me?[68]
No! But sin revealed death in me through good
To show that sin, through the commandment, might
Be utterly sinful. 14We know that Torah
Law is spiritual, but I am carnal, sold
Into sin. 15I do not know what I do.

---

65. This passage is normally translated not as "desire" but as "covet" or "lust for something." The Greek verb ἐπιθυμέω (epithymio) classically means "desire," as it continues to mean "desire" in modern Greek, but essentially without a notion of sin, unless it be a religious context. However, to "covet" is also a possible meaning here, and so the significance is ambiguous.

66. Again, "desire" or "desire for what belongs to others," that is, "covetousness."

67. In this complex back-and-forth reasoning as Paul now explains, the problem is not the law in 7.7–12., it is not Torah but Torah's inability to curb sin. In itself Torah is holy and good, but its commandments may be misused to deceive one into sin and death. When Paul states that he died or that sin killed him, he is using the form of the diatribe to make a dramatic point: "Sin brings the gloom of death, the good brings the spirit of life."

Paul's voice is paradox, and while his contradictions and scholastic wordplay may at times startle, their power lies precisely in their poetry and logic to awaken thought and convince.

68. Or, "bring me death."

I don't do what I want, but what I hate.

16Now if I do what I don't care to do,
   I must agree that Torah law is good.
17No longer is it I who do it now
   But sin that lives in me. 18And yet I know
   That good does not live in me, that is, not
   Within my flesh. There is a will in me,
   But not for doing good. 19I do not do
   The good I want to, but the bad I hate.
20Yet if I do what I don't care to do,
   It's not I doing it, but sin living in me.

I see another law
   21I find this law: when I want to do good,
   The bad things live in me. 22While I delight
   In the law of God, regarding inner man,
   23I find another law in my own body
   In combat with the law fixing my mind.
   I'm in captivity to laws of sin
   Bloating my limbs. 24I am a wretched being!
   Who will save me from this body of death?[69]
   25I thank God through our lord Yeshua Mashiah.
   In my mind I'm a slave to laws of God
   But in my flesh I'm slave to laws of sin.

---

69. What began as a didactic first-person diatribe to prove a spiritual principle has
become in these last verses a wholly personal and pained Paul, who in all his pathos
sees the light of God that might rescue him from the trap of flesh, yet finds himself,
at least for now, lacking and condemned, presumably like so many of us, to the law
of carnal temptation. What here is an irreconcilable battle between soul and body
will become a tradition of soul/body conflict pervading not only Christianity as religion but also multiple sectors of our culture, as exemplified in startling force and
beauty in the great seventeenth-century metaphysical poets George Herbert and
John Donne and on to the grandeur of despair in Gerard Manley Hopkins and the
tortured self-deprecations of T. S. Eliot. Here Paul's endlessly elegant tropes combine in a great passage of religious literature.

Chapter 8

Life in spirit

    Therefore there is no condemnation for
    Those in Mashiah Yeshua. 2The Torah
    Of the spirit of life in Mashiah Yeshua
    Has freed you from the law of sin and death.
    3God did what Bible law could never do
    Since in it it was weakened by the flesh.
    He sent down his own son in the likeness
    Of sinful flesh,[70] and he found sin in the flesh
    Guilty of sin. 4The requirements of Torah
    May be fulfilled in us who walk not in
    The way of flesh but in the way of spirit.
    5Those who are in flesh think about the things
    Of flesh, but those who are in the spirit
    Think things of spirit. 6Thinking of the flesh
    Is death, but thinking of the spirit is life
    And peace. 7The mind that fixes on the flesh
    Is hostile to God; it does not obey
    God's Torah. It cannot do so. 8And those
    Who are in the flesh cannot please God.

    9You are not in the flesh but in the spirit,
    Since the spirit of God is living in you.

---

70. The statement of Jesus coming "in the likeness of sinful flesh" introduces what will become among the later Christian and Gnostic sects a central issue: the nature of Jesus. Is he a man or God in the appearance of a man? This Christological question essentially pits the Monophysites, who believed that in the person of Jesus there was a single, divine nature, a view held by Copts, Syrians, and many other sects, including most of the Gnostics who saw Jesus as more than an angel, against those who would triumph as the orthodox Christians, who saw Jesus as both human and divine. At the other extreme were the Arians—and Constantine himself called in an Arian bishop to baptize him on his deathbed—who believed that Jesus did not share God's divine substance but was the true earthly messiah and the highest of created beings.

But one who does not possess the spirit
Of the Mashiah, that one is not of him.
10Yet if the Mashiah is in you, although
Your body may be dead because of sin,
Your spirit is alive because of goodness.
11If the spirit of him who raised Yeshua
Lives in you, the one who raised the Mashiah
From the dead will also make your doomed bodies
Live through his spirit that inhabits you.

12So my brothers, we have an obligation
But not to flesh and living by the flesh
13For by living by the flesh you will die.
But if you kill the practices of body,
You will live. 14All who are led by spirit
To God are the sons of God. 15And you received
Spirit of slavery not to be in fear
Again, you received the spirit of being
Adopted as sons. When we cry, "Abba!71
My father!" 16this very spirit bears witness
to our spirit that we are children of God.
17And if we are children, we are also heirs,
Heirs of God and co-heirs of the Mashiah.
Suffering with him, we may be glorified.

18I reason that the present sufferings
Are not comparable to the coming glory,
Which very soon will be revealed to us.
19The created world waits longing eagerly
For the children of God to be revealed.72
20The created world is subjected to vanity,

---

71. My father or "dad" from the Greek ἀββά (abba), from a familiar usage of the
Hebrew word for father, אָב (ab or av).

72. Or, "unveiled" or "disclosed," from the root word "apocalypse," in the Greek
ἀποκάλυψις (apokalypsis).

Not willingly but by reason of him
Who has subjected it; 21did so in hope
Creation will be freed from slavery
To corruption and obtain the freedom
Of the glory of the children of God.

Pain before invisible spirit

22We know that all creation groans. Till now
It suffers labor pains, 23and not only creation
Aches but we too, the first fruits of the spirit,[73]
Groan and in eagerness wait for adoption
And for the redemption of our bodies.
24In hope we were saved. But hope that is seen
Is not hope. Why hope for the seen?[74] 25Yet if
We hope for what we do not see, we wait
For it with patience. 26Similarly the spirit
Helps our weaknesses and we do not know
What we should rightly pray for, but the spirit
Intercedes with groans[75] that cannot be uttered,
27And he searching our hearts perceives the mind
Of the spirit, since as God commands
The spirit intercedes to help the saints.

Everything, even death, pales before God's love

28And we know that for those who love God,
All things work together for the good,
And for what may be called his preference.[76]
29For those whom he foresaw, God predestined
To share the image of his son as the firstborn

---

73. A foretaste of what is to come.

74. The unseen may suggest the invisible spirit, which also has no words to describe it. Such is the mystical and ineffable direction of Paul's message.

75. Again the phrase "unsaid groans or sighs" suggests a deeper, mystical consciousness below words, which mere mind can only guess.

76. Or, "purpose."

Among his many brothers. 30He also called
Those he predestined and also justified them,
And those he called he also justified,
And those he justified he glorified.
31What then are we to say about those things?
If God is for us who can be against us?
32He did not spare his son, but gave him up
For all of us. Will he not, with his help,
Give us all things? 33Who will speak against God's
Chosen ones? It is God who justifies.
34Who will condemn us? The Mashiah died,
But he has been raised and is at the right hand
Of God. He intercedes for us. 35And who
Will separate us from the Mashiah's love?
Will it be tribulation or distress
Or persecution or starvation, nakedness
Or the danger of the sword? 36As written
In the Psalms:
> For your sake we are killed all day long.
> We are counted like sheep for slaughter.[77]
37But in all of this we are more than victors
Through him who loves us 38and I am persuaded
That neither death nor life nor angels, rulers,
Things now or things to come, nor powers 39nor height
Nor depth nor anything in all creation
Is capable of severing us from the love
Of God in the Mashiah Yeshua our lord.

Chapter 9

God's promise to Yisrael and the seed of Yitzhak
I am speaking the truth in the Mashiah.
I am not lying. My conscience confirms it

---

77. Ps. 44.22.

Through the holy spirit. 2There is a great
And unceasing pain in my heart. 3I could
Have wished myself as an anathema,[78]
Cast far from the Mashiah for my kinsmen
According to the flesh, 4who are Yisraelis,[79]
To whom belong adoption as the sons
And glory and the covenants, receivers
Of the law and the worship in the temples
And the promises. 5And from them have come
The patriarchs[80] and from them have descended
Mashiah in the flesh. He came and is
Over all. May he who is God be blessed
Into all the ages.[81] And let us say, amain.

---

78. A curse.

79. Israeli, or, in its Greek form, Israelite, from the Greek Ἰσραηλίτης (Israelites), from the Hebrew יִשְׂרְאֵלִי (yisraeli), meaning "Israeli" or "Jew." The bizarre neologism "Israelite" comes from the Greek inflected transcription of the original Hebrew word. Its usage firms up the unfriendly notion that Jews of the Hebrew Bible, Israelites, are distinct from Israelis in modern Israel.

80. Abraham, Isaac, and Jacob.

81. This passage is often cited in the New Testament as the clearest statement of Jesus's descent from the Jewish patriarchs, of the God-selected nature of Israel in all essential qualities, and of their messiah being both Jesus and God. It has also been interpreted as Israel's rejection of the messiah. However, the text at this point does not speak of rejection by Jews of the messiah, but rather that knowledge of the messiah and of his acceptance may be more inclusive, and be not only by those of the biological seed of Isaac, like himself, but also by gentiles who believe that the true messiah has come. This later interpretation corresponds to both the text and the times. Paul lived in the years before the stronger division of Jew and gentile of the later first and early second centuries: This division is painted anachronistically and fiercely in the gospels about an even earlier period, that of Jesus. Paul speaks as a true Jew, with the pedigree of blood and Pharisee education, hoping to persuade fellow Jews and gentile converts to his splinter movement, which believes that the messiah had indeed arrived. As such he is speaking forcefully for the diaspora and more open-minded Jew, in contrast to James and the church of Jerusalem, which was demanding of the gentiles and obliging strict observance of Jewish law.

6It is not as though the word of God failed,
   For not all from Yisrael[82] are of Yisrael.[83]
7It's not because we are of Avraham's seed
   That we're his children, but as in Genesis,[84]
     Through Yitzhak[85] your seed will be reckoned.
8This means it is not the children of the flesh,
   Who are the children of God, but the children
   Of the promise who are counted the true seed.[86]
9This is what the promise says: "I shall come
   And at this time Sarah will have a son."
10Not only that, but there was Rivkah[87]
   Whose children were conceived by one man
   Our father Yitzhak.[88] 11Yet before her children
   Were born or did anything good or bad,
   So God's purpose in his election might hold—
12And not because of their works but of him

---

82. Israel from Greek Ἰσραήλ (Israel) from Hebrew יִשְׂרָאֵל (yisrael).

83. Reference is not necessarily to Israel's biological children but to the children of Israel's faith, to faith in and recognition and promise of Jesus the messiah. On the immediate level in Genesis, the promise is God's promise to or covenant with Abraham with regard to circumcision, a child by Sarah, descendants, and leader of nations, who by later Christian (Messianic) recognition will be the messiah.

84. Or, "descendants."

85. Isaac from the Greek Ἰσαάκ (Isaak), from the Hebrew יִצְחָק (yitzhak). *Yitzhak* means laughter as in "he will laugh."

86. Again, "descendants" or "offspring." "Descendants" and "offspring" are the usual translations of Greek σπέρμα (sperma), meaning "seed" or "sperm," yet there is no reason not to permit Greek "seed" to function as a metaphor for "offspring" rather than to interpret the image into conceptual diction, and thereby lose the poetic imagination and openness of the striking phrase.

87. Rebecca from the Greek Ῥεβέκκα (Rebekka), from the Hebrew רִבְקָה (rivkah). Rebecca is the wife of Isaac, the mother of Esau and Jacob, who were twins, Esau being the first born. In Genesis 26.6–11, Isaac claims that Rebecca is his sister, which may give her a special marital status.

88. "Father" as "forefather" or "ancestor."

Who called them—Rivkah was told, "The elder
Will be the slave of the young."[89] 13As in Malachi:
    I loved Yaakov but Esav[90] I hated.[91]

God's mercy and pity
    14What can we say? Can God be unjust? Never!
    15He says to Moshe in Exodus:
        I will have mercy on whom I have mercy
        And I will pity whom I pity.[92]
    16But it is not a matter of wanting or racing
    To an end but of God's mercy. 17In Exodus
    The Pharaoh is told:
        For this very thing I have raised you up,
        To demonstrate my power through you
        So that my name may be proclaimed
        In every corner of the earth.[93]

---

89. "The elder" is Esau, the one who will be slave to "the young" Jacob. This refers to Rebecca's hatred for her older, hairy son, and also to her giving the younger Jacob a goatskin to cover his arms and neck so that he might impersonate the firstborn Esau and obtain Isaac's blessing and promises to him (Gen. 25.20–27.16). The plan worked, and consequently Jacob, rather than angry Esau, became the father of nations, and his twelve sons carried the names of the later twelve tribes of Israel. The notion of the twelve-tribal-son confederacy determined by a covenant between Abraham and God became a model for the early Christian Jewish twelve apostles (messengers or missionaries) determined by a new covenant between the apostles and Jesus son of God.

90. Esau from the Greek Ἠσαῦ (Esau or Esav), from the Hebrew עֵשָׂו (esav).

91. The speaker here is not Rebecca, as one might assume from the context, but God speaking to Israel through an oracle. The hatred for Esau seems extreme. God is asked how he loves Esau and Jacob. He answers, contrasting the brothers, "Yet I have loved Jacob, but Esau I have hated, and I have turned his mountains into a wasteland and left his inheritance to the desert jackals" (Mal. 1.2–3).

92. Exod. 33.19.

93. Exod. 9.16 (Septuagint).

18He pities the one whom he cares to pity
And hardens into stone the one he wants to.94

God's anger

19Will you ask me, "Why does God still blame us?
But who has ever stood against his will?"
20Who are you, a mortal being, to dispute God?
Will the image made say to the image maker,
"Why have you made me like this?" 21Has the potter
No right with his clay to fashion one piece
To be esteemed and another to be despised?
22But if God desiring to show his anger
And make his power known, has endured
With great patience the vessels of his anger
That were made for destruction, 23is it not
So that he can make known the abundance
Of his glory to the vessels of mercy,
Which he prepared beforehand for glory?
24And it is for us whom he has called,
And not only from among the Jews
But also from among the gentiles?
So he says in Hoshea.95

I will call those who were not my people my people
And her who was not beloved my beloved,96
26And in the place where it was said to them:
"You are not my people,"

---

94. Literally, "hardens," and usually translated as "hardens the heart" or "hardens," but these renderings suggest a change in the person's posture toward God or a change in the person's feelings. The meaning is probably more dire, meaning that the person will harden into death.

95. Hosea from the Greek Ὡσηέ (Hosee), from the Hebrew הוֹשֵׁעַ (hoshea).

96. Hos. 2.23.

There they will be called sons of the living God.[97]

27And as Yeshayahu[98] cries for Yisrael:

Though the number of the sons of Yisrael is like

The sands of the sea, only a segment will be saved.

28 The lord will execute and complete his sentence on the
earth.[99]

29And as Yeshayahu said earlier:

If the lord of Sabaoth[100] had not left us seed,

We would have become like Sedom and appeared like
Amorah.[101]

---

97. Paul, versed in the Bible, finds passages referring to the restoration of Israel as proof of God's openness to gentiles, thereby permitting a Christianization of the Jewish Bible. For later church fathers and scribes, the Christianization of the Bible will often be line for line. In translations of the Hebrew Bible into other languages, there will also be a process of separating the Bible from the Jews, specifically by using select names for the Jews, who will not be called Jews but Israelites or Hebrews, with the curious exception of the Book of Esther. By contrast, in the New Testament, the word "Jews" enters as a common word for the Jews who are not of Jesus's family or the Jesus movement. Their designation as Jews most often indicates opponents, conspirators, villains, those who are demonized as descendants of the devil, as in John 8.44, where the rabbi Jesus is made to say of his coreligionists, "You are from your father the devil / and you want to do the desires of your father. / From the beginning he was a murderer," and a people and their descendants are forever cursed, or as in Matthew 27.25, where the Jews stand in the street and shout, "Let his blood be upon us and upon our children!" In Paul, who wrote before the gospels were written and argued and reasoned his belief as a Torah scholar, there is none of this angry and harmful rhetoric against the Jews. Again and again Paul declares himself a Jew.

98. Isaiah.

99. Isa. 10.22–23 (Septuagint).

100. Of great armies.

101. Sodom from the Greek Σόδομα (Sodoma), from the Hebrew סְדֹם (sedom), and Gomorrah from the Greek Γόμορρα (Gomorra), from the Hebrew עֲמֹרָה (amorah).

The stone of faith

    30What are we to say? That the gentiles, pursuing
      Justice, found justice a justice of faith?
    31But that Yisrael, who pursued the Torah law
      Of justice, did not attain it. 32And why?
      Because they did not pursue by way of faith
      But by way of works. They stumbled against
      The stone of stumbling.[102] 33As written in Yeshayahu:
        Look, I place in Tziyun[103] a stone of stumbling
        And a rock, which is a trap,[104]
        But those who believe in him
        Will not be put to shame.

Chapter 10

Prayer

      Brothers, my heart's desire and prayer to God
      Are for Yisraelis and for their salvation.[105]
    2I testify that they have a zeal for God,
      But not through knowledge. 3Being ignorant
      Of God's justice and trying to establish
      Their own justice, they did not yield to God's
      Justice. 4The Mashiah is the fulfillment

---

102. It is not certain what Paul means by "stone," but it is generally interpreted to mean that Israel, that is, traditional Jews, sought to fulfill the law of Torah not by good works, but by the stone of the messiah one attained through faith and belief. Over that stone Israel stumbles.

103. Zion from the Greek Σιών (Sión), from the Hebrew צִיּוֹן (tziyon).

104. Isa. 8.14, 28.16 (Septuagint).

105. Paul seems to be offering the prayer for those who may be saved, and particularly the Jews who can do so by finding new faith in the messiah. Others suggest that the prayer is for the survival of the new churches.

Of Torah law, which signifies that justice
Is there for everyone who has belief.

Salvation for all
    5Moshe writes about the justice that comes
    From Torah, as said in Leviticus:
        The person who does these things
        Will live by them.[106]
    6But justice that comes from faith, as written
    In Deuteronomy, states:
        Do not say in your heart,
        "Who will rise to heaven?"[107]
    This is to bring the Mashiah down. 7Or,
        Who will descend into the abyss?[108]
    This is to raise the Mashiah from the dead.
    8But what does it say in Deuteronomy?
        The word is close to you,
        In your mouth and in your heart,[109]
    Which is the word of faith that we declaim.
    9If you confess in your mouth that Yeshua
    Is lord and believe it in your heart that God
    Raised him out of the dead, you will be saved.
    10While with the heart one believes in justice,
    With the mouth one confesses and is saved.
    11The scriptures of Yeshayahu say:
        Everyone who believes in him will not be shamed.[110]
    12For there is no difference between Jew and Greek.
    The same lord of all is bounteous to all

---

106. Lev. 18.5.
107. Deut. 30.12.
108. Deut. 30.13.
109. Deut. 30.14.
110. Isa. 28.16 (Septuagint).

Who call on him.[111]13And as Yoel[112] says,
  All who call on the lord's name will be saved.[113]

14Yet how are they to call on one in whom
  They did not believe? How can they believe
  In one of whom they have not heard? And how
  Are they to hear if no one proclaims him?
15And how are they to preach if they are not
  Sent out to preach? As it is written in Yeshayahu:
    How beautiful are the feet of those bringing
    Good news, the good things![114]
16But not everyone heeded the good news.
  And Yeshayahu says:
    Lord, who has believed our message?[115]
17Then faith comes from what is heard,
  And what they hear is through the word.[116]
18But I ask, "Didn't they hear?" Yes, they did.
  As it is sung in the Psalms:

---

111. In the verse, "For there is no difference between Jew and Greek, for the same lord of all is bounteous to all who call on him," we hear the essential Pauline statement of conscience and belief, an all-embracing Paul speaking at once with hope, joy, and welcome to Jew and Greek, indeed to all people and peoples who in heart and spirit recognize the messiah. Here is the diasporic Christian Jew enticing entry to the Jesus movement, with no demands but a faith that triumphs over distinctions of rule, sect, and person. This is a formative, virgin period of growth, a period of wonder and wander, occurring years before the canonical gospels and an established selection of New Testament scripture were composed. In the decades after Paul's mission, there will arise rigorous rules and demands; harsh and unpleasant distinctions between Jew, gentile, Christian, Roman, Greek, pagan, Gnostic, and heathen; and severe condemnation of those who fall outside each sectarian fold.

112. Joel from the Greek Ἰωήλ (Ioel), from the Hebrew יוֹאֵל (yoel).

113. Joel 2.32.

114. Isa. 52.7.

115. Isa. 53.1 (Septuagint).

116. The Majority Text adds "of Christ."

Their voice went out all over the earth, their words

Went to the ends of the inhabited world.[117]

19But I say, "Did Yisrael not understand?"

First Moshe says:

I will make you jealous of who are not a nation.

I will make you angry at an ignorant nation.[118]

20Yet Yeshayahu is forthright and says:

I was found by those who didn't seek me.

I showed myself to those who didn't care to know me.[119]

21And to Yisrael he says:

All day I stretched out my hands to a people

Who would not obey and argued with me.[120]

Chapter 11

I am an Yisraeli

Then I ask, "Did God reject his own people?"[121]

Never! I am also an Yisraeli,[122] from the seed

Of Avraham and of the tribe of Binyamin.[123]

2God did not reject his people, not those

Whom he has chosen before. Do you not know

---

117. Ps. 19.4 (Septuagint).

118. Deut. 32.21.

119. Isa. 65.1 (Septuagint).

120. Isa. 65.2 (Septuagint).

121. "Pushed aside" is literal Greek meaning of ἀπώσατο (aposato), from ἀπωθέω (apotheo), which conceptually (figuratively) means "I reject" (reject is Latin *rejicere* for "throw aside"). The reference is to Leviticus 26.44, in which God says he will not reject the Jews and thereby break his covenants with Abraham, with Isaac, and with Jacob.

122. Israelite or Jew.

123. Benjamin, from the Greek Βενιαμίν (Beniamin), from the Hebrew בִּנְיָמִין (binyamin).

What Eliyahu[124] says in his writing, how he pleads
With God against Yisrael? As written in Kings:
  3Lord, they killed the prophets,[125] torn down your altars,
And I alone am left and they are after my life.[126]
4But what is the holy reply to him? Eliyahu wrote:
  I have kept for myself seven thousand men
  Who did not bend their knee to Baal.
5So even now there is a remnant through
  Election by grace.[127] 6But if it's by grace,
  It's not by deeds, or grace would not be grace.[128]
7What then? Yisrael did not find what it sought.

---

124. Elijah or Elias from Greek Ἠλίας (Elias), from Hebrew אֵלִיָּה (eliyah) or אֵלִיָּהוּ (eliyahu).

125. 1 Kings 19.1, 10, 14. Prophet from the Greek προφήτης (profetes), from the Hebrew נָבִיא (navi), meaning "one who calls." A prophet in Greek is one who serves to communicate between human and divine worlds, as in "divine messengers." There are several words for prophet in Hebrew, meaning diversely "messenger," "seer," "visionary," sometimes in a positive sense, sometimes as a condemnation, and especially so when referring to prophets of Baal or other competing sects. In the phrase "to kill your prophets," the word "prophet" may mean a holy man or simply one of your sect. All these usages are not to be confused with "prophets" meaning the great and minor prophets after whom the books of the Bible are named. There are accusations in the Hebrew Bible of killing the prophets, notably the confusing ones in 1 Kings 19 in which these prophets may be false ones of Baal, but whoever they are supposed to be, none is identified by name. Indeed, there exists no word or verse in the books of the prophets themselves or in commentaries on their writings and lives that any prophet, minor or major, was killed. Were a prophet killed and identified by name, he would have been a martyr, whose name, like that of Socrates and Jesus, would be known by all. This isolated accusation in Paul, and frequent one in Matthew and, except for Mark, in the other gospels, has been uniformly repudiated by biblical scholars.

126. 1 Kings 19.10, 14.

127. 1 Kings 19.18. As there was apostasy in the past, in Elijah's days, so there is today, but there are also those who remain faithful to the notion of the messiah.

128. The Majority Text has another version: "But if it is by works, it is no longer grace; otherwise work would no longer be work."

The elect found it but others became hardened.[129]

8As written in Deuteronomy and Yeshayahu:

> God gave them a spirit of stupor,[130]
> Eyes that would not see and ears
> That would not hear
> And down to this present day.[131]

9And David says in his Psalms:

> Let their table turn into a snare and a trap
> And a stumbling block and a retribution for them.
>   10Let their eyes be darkened so they cannot see
> And their backs be forever bent over.[132]

11I ask, "Did they stumble into transgression
So they might fall?" Never! But through their stumbling,
Salvation came to gentiles to make Jews
Wish to emulate them.[133] 12Now if stumbling
Means fortune for the world and their defeat
Will signify a fortune for the gentiles,
Then how much greater will their fullness be.[134]

I, a messenger to the gentiles, speak of the olive tree root

13To you the gentiles I speak, and in speaking
I become a messenger to the gentiles,
And I praise my ministry 14so my flesh
And blood I can make jealous and save them
Or some of them. 15And if their own rejection
Means reconciliation of the world,
What will their acceptance mean? Surely life

---

129. Paul is speaking for himself and for the elect among the Jews who found faith, meaning the messiah.

130. Deep sleep.

131. Deut. 29.4, Isa. 29.10.

132. Ps. 69.22–23 (Septuagint).

133. The Jews of Israel.

134. Fulfillment from the Greek πλήρωμα (pleroma), which is coincidentally the term the Gnostics use not only for fullness but also for the Gnostic divinity. In other contexts, as in verse 11.25, it means "full number."

From the dead. 16If the first fruit is holy
So are the branches. 17But if some branches
Have been broken off and you graft a wild
Olive shoot in them, which shares the root
Of the olive tree in fatness, 18do not glory
Over those branches. Though you boast,
Know it is not you who supports the root
But is the olive root that supports you.[135]

19Then you will say, "Branches were broken off
So that I could be grafted on." 20Very well.
They were broken off for lack of faith,
But by faith you stood. Do not stand too high
But in fear. 21If God did not spare the branches
That were by nature his, he won't spare you.
22See goodness and severity of God:
Severity to those who are the fallen,
For you his justice if you have good ways
Or else you will be severed from the tree.

23As for the others, if they do not stick
To lacking faith, they will be grafted on.

---

135. Paul explains to the gentiles that they have or are the new branches of a tree
because they have been grafted onto the original parent root, which is Judaism, its
patriarchs, and their old covenants with God. The whole olive tree represents the
people of God. Some branches, of those who do not have faith, have been broken
off from the tree. These are the Jews who do not recognize the new covenants being
made. It may also be remembered that from the point of view of the Jews who hold
to the Bible and are still waiting for the messiah to come, Paul and other Jews are
those who have broken off as apostates into a new Jewish movement. Paul lives in
a moment of maximum contention between many branches or sects of Judaism.
Given the turmoil and contention, it is extraordinary that the authorial Paul of the
letters (though not the Paul as depicted much later by others in Acts) is so graciously
welcoming to gentile and Jew, wishing concordance rather than rivalry and punishment for the other. This extended metaphor of the olive tree assumes the parabolic
device used extensively in the gospels, revealing the parable as a universal means
of wisdom instruction.

God has the power to graft them on again.
24If you were cut away from a wild olive tree
And then were grafted against your nature
Onto the good olive tree, how much sooner
Will they also be grafted back onto
The olive tree so naturally their own!

Salvation for Yisrael

25Brothers, so you will not see yourselves wise,
I want you not to be ignorant of mystery:
A hardness has come over part of Yisrael
Until the full number of gentiles join.
26Then all of Yisrael will find salvation.
As written in Yeshayahu:
The deliverer[136] will come out of Tziun.
And he will turn godlessness away from Yaakov.
27And this is my covenant with them[137]
When I take their sins away.[138]

God's favor of mercy

28As for the good news, they are your enemies
For your sake, and to be among the chosen
They are beloved for the sake of their fathers.[139]
29God's gifts and call are irrevocable.
30And just as you once disbelieved in God,
Your mercy comes from their disobedience.
31They have disbelieved so that by the mercy
Given you they may also receive mercy.
32God has imprisoned everyone in disbelief
So that he may be merciful to all.

---

136. Messiah.
137. Isa. 59.20–21 (Septuagint).
138. Isa. 27.9 (Septuagint).
139. Ancestors or patriarchs.

Knowing God

33O depths of riches, wisdom, and the knowledge
Of God! How inscrutable his judgments,
How untraceable his ways! 34In the words
Of Yeshayahu and Yov:[140]
Who knows the mind of the lord?
Or who became his counselor?[141]
35Or who has given him a gift
To receive a gift in return?[142]
36From him and through him and to him
Are all things. To him glory forever. Amain.[143]

Chapter 12

Renewing the mind

So I urge you, brothers, by God's mercy,
To offer your own bodies as a living
And holy sacrifice pleasing to God,
Which is your reasonable temple worship.
2Do not conform to this age, but be changed,
Transformed through a renewal of the mind
For you to prove what is the will of God,
The good, the pleasing, and the perfect.

3Through the grace given me I say to all
Among you not to think of yourself more
Highly than you ought to. Be of sober
Judgment according to the faith God gave
Each one of you. 4For as in one body we

---

140. Job 41.11. Job from the Greek Ἰώβ (Yob), from the Hebrew אִיּוֹב (yov).

141. Isa. 40.13 (Septuagint).

142. Job 41.11.

143. Amen.

Have many parts, and all parts do not perform
In the same way, 5so we who are many
Are one in the Mashiah, and individually
Parts of each other. 6We have gifts that differ
According to the grace granted to us.
If it is prophecy, base it on faith.
7If it is serving, then serve. Or if teaching,
Teach. 8If one is the comforter, comfort.
The contributor should be generous,
The leader capable, the mercy cheerful.

Ways of love and companion virtues
9Let love be candid and abhor the crafty,
Hold to the good. 10Love each other as brothers,
Honor each other more than your own self.[144]
11Do not be lazy in your eagerness
But burn in spirit serving the lord. 12Be happy
In hope, patient in grief, constant in prayer.
13Contribute to the needs of the holy.[145]
14Bless your persecutors. Bless, do not curse them.
15Be happy with the happy, weep with those
Who are weeping. 16Consider every person
Equally, not with hauteur, and be pleased
To be with the poor in station. Don't see
Yourself as wise. 17Do not repay the bad
With bad, before all do the good. 18If possible,
Be for your part in peace with everyone.

---

144. These extraordinary humane verses may be heard as the Pauline Sermon on the Mountain or a list of affectionate commandments. In contrast to many of Paul's ingenious and intricate homilies regarding faith, grace, God, and salvation, here he essentially addresses human behavior, of one to another, rather than ultimate salvific tests of one's aloneness with the divinity.

145. Normally translated "saints," which in this context appears anachronistic and inflated. Paul is not speaking of canonized saints but holy persons, whose qualities suggest a connection with the divine. "Holy" captures the fine suggestions of ἅγιος (hagios).

19Don't seek revenge, dear ones, and leave some room
    For God's anger. It is written in Deuteronomy:
        I am the avenger. I will repay.
    Those are the lord's words. 20No, if the enemy
    Is hungry, feed him, and if he is thirsty,
    Give him something to drink. In doing this
    You will heap burning coals upon his head.[146]
21And do not be defeated by the bad
    But overcome the bad with the good.

Chapter 13

Living in God's estate
    Let every soul be subject to the higher
    Powers.[147] There is no power but of God
    And those existing ones have been appointed
    By God. 2Therefore anyone who contends
    Against the powers, rebels against what God
    Ordains. The rebels will bring judgment on
    Themselves. 3The Romans[148] are no terror to those

---

146. Prov. 25.21–22 (Septuagint).

147. From personal love, there is a shift to civil duties designed by God, and the moral and legal rewards and punishments for keeping or rejecting a complex social contract. In the divine hierarchy and its lower minions come God as governor, and then the everyday ministers and tax collectors, and enforcers of civic law, who carry authority's sword, meaning death.

148. The authorities or powers are the Romans. Paul is a paradoxical mixture of revolutionary original thinker and organizer and at the same time one who demands obedience of the congregation, of women, and even, as we note, of slaves to their masters. Yet with courageous daring he is central to beginning a new religious order, altering, rebelling against earlier beliefs and practices as he sees he must. Here, though the ruler is the tyrannically mad Nero, Paul offers no worldly plaint. Rather, he calls for submission to the ruling powers. More than anything else, one may attribute these passages to necessary pragmatism in light of the mortal consequences of rejection of Roman rule.

Who do good work but to those who do wrong.
Do you wish not to be fearful of the powers?
Do good, and you will find applause from them.
4They are God's servant to you for the good.
But if you do wrong, then you should be in fear.
The ruler wreaks a sword for his good reason.
5And so submit to the ruler. He is
God's power and revenger to execute
Anger against one who does bad. Submit
Not only because of the real anger. Submit
Because your conscience tells you to obey.
6For these reasons you also pay your taxes.
Collectors are also servants of God,
Engaged in duties. 7Give to everyone
What you owe them, and to the tax man pay
The taxes, to the toll man pay the toll.[149]
To one who makes you fearful be in fear
And to the one whom you should honor honor.

Beyond the dark, love is near
    8Owe no one anything except to love
    One another. For in loving the other,
    Torah is fulfilled.[150] 9And the commandments[151]
        You shall not commit adultery.

---

149. Revenue. The same theme of civil obedience appears especially in Matthew, who himself in the Gospel of Matthew has Jesus order the Galileans to pay Rome what is Rome's and he himself is identified as a tax collector. There is an irony here, an understandable one, given the history of rebellious Galilee, especially since the Galileans were notable for their popular opposition to paying taxes to Rome, a position that led to catastrophic retribution.

150. Leviticus 19.18 gives us the Mosaic law from Torah, "Love your neighbor (a stranger) as yourself," which Jesus cites in Mark 12.31, Matthew 22.39, and Luke 10.27.

151. The list of the commandments is found in Exodus 20.13–17 and Deuteronomy 5.17–21.

You shall not murder.
You shall not steal.
You shall not covet.[152]
And any other commandment there may be
Is comprehended in this one statement:
Love your neighbor as yourself.[153]
10Love does not work harm on your neighbor.
Love is the fulfillment of Torah law.

Night is far gone
11And do this, knowing what time is, how now
Is the hour for you to wake from sleep.[154]
12Night is advancing and the day draws near.
So let us put away the works of darkness
And let us put on the armor of light.
13As in the day let us stroll decently,
Without wild lovemaking or drunkenness,
Nor in debauchery or licentiousness,
Nor in contention and no jealousy.
14Rather, dress in the lord Yeshua Mashiah,
And of desire and flesh, give them no thought.[155]

---

152. Ex. 20.13–15; Deut. 5.17–19, 21.

153. Lev. 19.18.

154. Here, as so often, Paul ends his sermon chapter with a summation in insuperably beautiful poetry, of moving from sleep and darkness to the "armor of light." The "armor" or, more specifically, "weapon" is a military metaphor, lending strength, whose omission would not, however, weaken the spiritual equation of "wakening to light."

155. The rejection of body, flesh, sexuality as a dark temptation and as the enemy of spiritual light and union has many counterparts in the Hebrew Bible, which Paul draws on and which will be a central theme of Christianity. This rejection of the physical is less pronounced in the gospels, which with all their summits of spiritual transformation and mystery, also reveal Jesus as a man whom the uncertain Marys are attached to and whom he cares for and respects. In Paul there is no scent of male-and-female attraction, or none exemplified or spoken of except as a collapse of will and virtue, as a sin to be averted.

Chapter 14

Welcome the weak in faith

Welcome those who are weak in faith, and don't
Cast critical or dubious eyes on them.
2One man believes he can eat anything
While the weak consume only vegetables.
3One who eats should not despise the abstainer,
One who abstains should not despise the eater
Since God has welcomed all of them as his.
4And who are you to judge another's servants?
Before their master they must stand or fall.
They'll be upheld, for the lord makes them stand.

Days and food for the lord

5One man prizes one day more than another.
Another man delights in every day.
Let everyone be persuaded in his own mind.
6Who favors a day favors it for the lord,
The eater eats for the lord and thanks God.
And one who is not eating for the lord
Does not eat but he also thanks his God.

Living and dying for the lord

7No one of us lives for himself
And no one of us dies for himself.
8If we live we live for the lord.
If we die we die for the lord.
Then whether we live or we die,
We are in the hands of the lord.

9To this end the Mashiah died and lived
To be lord over the dead and the living.
10Why do you stand in judgment of your brother,
Why do you treat your brother as a fool?
We all shall stand before God's judgment seat

11Since, as written in Yeshayahu
　　　　　　　The lord says:
　　I live that every knee bend before me,[156]
　　And every tongue will confess to God.[157]
12Everyone of us will account to God.

13So let us stop judging each other,
　　But rather agree to this judgment:
　　　　Place no stumbling block or trap
　　　　Before any brother. 14I know,
　　　　And am persuaded through the lord
　　　　Yeshua, that nothing is itself
　　　　Unclean. It is only unclean
　　　　If one thinks it unclean. 15Your brother
　　　　If he is grieved by your meat,[158]
　　　　You're no longer walking in love.
　　　　Do not let your meat become
　　　　The cause and ruin of one
　　　　For whom the Mashiah died.

Using food for goodness
　　16Don't let your good be seen as blasphemy.
　　17God's kingdom isn't built of meat and wine
　　　　But justice, peace and cheer in the holy spirit
　　18And one who in these ways serves the Mashiah
　　　　Is joy to God and is approved by men.
　　19Let us then pursue the byways of peace
　　　　And those things that will edify another.
　　20Do not destroy God's work for plates of food.
　　　　All things have purity but it is bad
　　　　When you are eating to make someone fall.

---

156. Isa. 45.23 (Septuagint).
157. Isa. 45.23 (Septuagint), vaguely.
158. By what you have to eat.

21It is good not to eat meat or drink wine
  Nor do anything to make your brother fall.
22The faith you have, you have solely with God.
  Happy is he who need not judge himself
  By what's approved, 23and he who doubts and eats
  Is damned because he doesn't eat from faith.
  Everything not rising from faith is sin.

Chapter 15

The Mashiah of the Jews can also be accessible to the gentiles
  We who are strong should feel obliged to bear
  Infirmities of the weak; and not to please
  Only ourselves. 2Let every man attempt
  To please his neighbor for the good purpose
  Of building him up. 3Even the Mashiah
  Did not please himself, but, as written
  In the Psalms:
    The insults of those insulting you have fallen on me.[159]
  4All that was once written for our instruction
  Was written so with patience and the comfort[160]

---

159. Ps. 69.9.

160. Also "encouragement." The Greek word παράκλησις (paraklesis), meaning the "comforter," "consoler," or "encourager," is the same root word as for "Paraclete," which the evangelist John mysteriously uses as a synonym for the messiah in John 15.26, and 16.7. The "comforter" was a common word that Jews, and in particular the Essenes, used for the messiah, who in the case of the Essenes, as in the Messianics (Christians), had already come. See diverse references to the Hebrew word for "comforter," מְנַחֵם (menahem), as in Ecclesiastes 4.1 and Lamentations 1.16. The Essene messiah, Menahem (menahem), was crucified in Jerusalem in 4 B.C.E. by Augustus's soldiers during a major revolt following the death of Herod the Great. His body, which was forbidden to be buried, disappeared after the third day and his disciples believed that the suffering servant was resurrected and rose to heaven. Whatever happened to the body, the historical event of the slain messiah

Of the scriptures[161] we might have hope. 5May God
Of patience and of comfort spread concord
Among you according to Mashiah Yeshua
6So that with one voice you may glorify
God, father of Yeshua the Mashiah.

7Welcome one another as the Mashiah
Has welcomed you for the glory of God.
8I say that the Mashiah was born to be
The servant of the circumcised and truth
Of God in order to confirm the promises
Made to the patriarchs, 9and for the gentiles,
And for his mercy to glorify God. As in 2 Shlomoh:
  So I will recognize you among the gentiles
  And sing praises to your name.[162]
10And again he says in Deuteronomy:
  Be happy, gentiles, along with his people.[163]
11And again in Psalms:
  Let all nations praise the lord,
  And let all people praise him.[164]

---

of forgiveness and redemption was a precursor model to the Jesus story. The Dead
Sea Scrolls describe this event of the crucifixion in two hymns. See Israel Knohl,
The Messiah before Jesus: The Suffering Servant of the Dead Sea Scrolls (Berkeley:
University of California Press, 2002).

161. Commentators agree that the references to the Psalms, as the scriptures, or to
other Old Testament books, are intended to confirm the teachings and thought of
Jesus, since later Christianity assumed the Jewish Bible (the Old Testament) as the
great resource for depicting the messiah and his meaning to humanity on earth. However, when Paul as a Jew refers as he does here to the Jewish scriptures, commentators normally cite Matthew 20.28 and Mark 10.45, which speak of suffering and
even death, carrying the burden of Jesus further. It should be clear that Paul was not
referring to the later composed gospels, but to the standard Hebrew Bible.

162. 2 Sam. 22.50; Ps. 18.49.

163. Deut. 32.43.

164. Ps. 117.1.

12And once more in Yeshayahu:[165]
> There will come a scion of Yishai[166]
> And he will rise and rule over the gentiles[167]
> And in him the same gentiles will have hope.

To Yerushalayim with funds for the poor among the saints
> 13May God of hope fill you with joy and peace
> And through belief may you abound in hope
> And know the power of the holy spirit.

> 14Concerning you, my brothers, I'm persuaded
> That you are filled with goodness and this knowledge
> Which you are capable of sharing with
> 15Each other. I write boldly to remind you,
> Because of grace that God has given me
> 16To be a servant of Mashiah Yeshua
> To gentiles in the holy governance
> Of all good news of God so that this offering
> To gentiles be acceptable to him
> And sanctified by the holy spirit.
> 17Through the Mashiah Yeshua I am able
> To boast of things of God. 18I will not dare
> To speak of anything but what Mashiah
> Accomplished through me to make sure the gentiles
> In word and work obey 19the power of signs

---

165. Isaiah.

166. Jesse from the Greek Ἰεσσαί (Iessai), from the Hebrew יִשַׁי (yishai). Reference is often said to be the messiah. This idea may be reinforced by the table in Luke showing Jesus descended directly from David who is ultimately the son of Adam, who is son of God (Luke 3.23–38). However, such reference depends on a genealogical table unavailable to Paul in his time, and so it is sufficient to limit reference to Jesse, father of David.

167. The foreign nations.

And wonders through the powers of the spirit.[168]
So from Yerushalayim[169] and as far
As Illyricum,[170] I have gone on preaching
The good news of Mashiah. 20My ambition
Has been to bring the good news not to where
Mashiah got his name so as not to build
On another man's foundation,[171] 21but as
Yeshayahu has written:
> They who have not been told of him will see,
> And they who have not heard will understand.[172]
22And so I have been hindered from coming
To you. 23But with no other place for me
To stay, I have desired for many years
To come to know you. Whenever I go
To Spain, 24I hope to see you on my journey
And, after I've enjoyed your company
A while, for you to send me on my way.
25Now I am going to Yerushalayim
And labor in the service of the saints.[173]

---

168. The word "spirit" appears in some but not all versions, giving us "spirit"; in other texts "holy spirit" appears; and in others, "spirit of God." Phrase is uncertain.

169. Jerusalem from Greek Ἰερουσαλήμ (Ierousalem), from Hebrew יְרוּשָׁלַיִם (Yerushalayim).

170. A Latin word appearing in Greek transliteration, Ἰλλυρικόν (Illyrikon). Illyricum is an area across the Adriatic Sea from Italy, which corresponds to Dalmatia (Upper Illyris) and Pannonia (Lower Illyris), an otherwise unmentioned place where Paul carried out his missions. It is speculated that he would have entered Illyricum from Macedonia.

171. Here is as clear as any statement by Paul of his desire to bring his missions not to Israel, where the messiah was born as forecast in the biblical texts, but to where he was unknown in presence and conception.

172. Isa. 52.15 (Septuagint).

173. The "saints" were the holy Messianics (early Christian Jews) living in Jerusalem. See note 148 above.

26Makedonia and Ahaia[174] with kindness
   Have offered their funds to help the poor saints
   In Yerushalayim. 27They agreed to do this,
   And feel themselves indebted to these saints,
   For since the gentiles share in spiritual matters,
   They also are obliged to share with them[175]
   Materially. 28When I have done all this
   And sent them the fruit[176] of my work, I'll go
   For Spain, stopping on route to visit you.
29I know that when I come to be with you,
   I'll come with the Mashiah's full blessing.

Help me in my struggle with the faithless
   30I urge you, brothers, by our lord Yeshua
   The Mashiah and by the love of the spirit,
   To help me in my struggle through your prayers
   For me 31that I may be safe from the faithless
   In Yehudah,[177] and that my ministry
   In Yerushalayim be acceptable
   To the saints, 32and so that I may come to you
   With happiness, coming to you through will
   Of God, and take my rest in you. 33And may
   The God of peace be with you. Amain.

---

174. Achaia or Latinized Achaea, from the Greek Ἀχαΐα (Ahaia). Acts and Paul's letters follow the Roman designations of Macedonia as northern Greece and Achaia as southern Greece. Paul specifically uses "Achaia" to refer to Corinth and its surrounding areas. See note 305 Acts 18.12 for more on the historical designations of Achaia.

175. Literally, "carnal" ways.

176. Fruit" as in "reward." Richmond Lattimore translates καρπόν (karpon), literally, "fruit," as "bounty," implying a monetary fee or payback for entry into the spiritual realm, which underscores the materialistic aspect of the contribution.

177. Reference is to the Jews of Judea who have not recognized Yeshua as the messiah of the Christian (Messianic) Jews, whom Paul represents in his mission of convincing both Jew and gentile to his faith.

Chapter 16

Greetings to Phoebe

Now I commend our sister Phoebe[178] to you,
Who is the shammash[179] of the synagogue[180]
Of Keghreai.[181] 2Receive her in the lord's name,
As befits saints. Help her in anything she needs.
She has attended many, including me.

Greetings to Priska and Akylas and fellow workers

3Greet Priska[182] and Akylas,[183] my fellow workers
In the Mashiah Yeshua. 4They risked

---

178. Phoebe, from the Greek Φοίβη (Foibe), had the function of *shammash*, a rabbinical function of women in the synagogue in Cenchreae.

179. Phoebe of the Christian (Messianic) Jews. This period is many decades before any thought that Paul's recognition of the messiah is not that of a Jew, as Paul himself constantly affirms. Hence, when we use later Christian titles and epithets for these early Christian Jews, such as a deacon or a deaconess of the church instead of *shammash*, it should be understood that these words are intentionally anachronistic in order to minimize, to later Messianics (Christians), both the Jewish period of Christianity and the significant nature of Paul's revolutionary years as a reformer of and within Judaism. We simply don't know who most of these people were outside of what the letters inform.

180. We know from 1 Corinthians that Sosenthes, Paul's spiritual brother in Corinth, is a leader of the synagogue, which has recognized Yeshua as the messiah. It is probable that Prisfa was also a leader in a similar synagogue, which was the main target for conversion in all places where there were existing Jewish communities. Prisfa and Aquila, close friends of Paul, worked like Paul in the trade of tentmaking.

181. Cenchreae from the Greek Κεγχρεαί (Kenghreai), the seaport of Corinth on the eastern side of the Isthmus.

182. Prisca from the Greek Πρίσκα (Priska). The diminutive Priscilla is from the Greek Πρίσκιλλα (Priskilla).

183. Aquila from the Greek Ἀκύλας (Akylas). Aquila of Pontus, a tentmaker, is not to be confused with Aquila of Pontus, a convert to Judaism who in about 130 C.E. translated the Hebrew Bible into Greek in a literalist manner, even reproducing Hebrew syntax in the Greek.

Their own necks for my life,[184] and I thank them

As well as all the churches of the gentiles.

5And greet the church that is in their own house.

And now, greet my love Epainetos,[185]

Who is first fruit[186] in Asia for the Mashiah.

6Greet Miryam,[187] who works very hard for you.

7Greet Andronikos[188] and Iounias,[189]

Who were in prison with me. Outstanding

Among the messengers, even before me

They were working furiously for the Mashiah.

8Greet Ampliatos,[190] my love in the Mashiah.

9Greet Ourbanos,[191] who is our fellow worker

In the Mashiah, and also my love Stahys.[192]

10Greet Apelles,[193] honored in the Mashiah.

Greetings to the household of Aristoboulos.[194]

11Greet Herodion[195] my countryman. Greetings

---

184. It was apparently well known that Prisca and Aquila risked their lives for Paul, but it can only be guessed how they might have saved him since there is no other reference in the New Testament to such an event.

185. Epaenetus from the Greek Ἐπαίνετος (Epainetos).

186. The first convert to Messianism.

187. Mary from the Greek Μαρία (Maria), from Hebrew מִרְיָם (miryam), often Anglicized in English as "Miriam." There are six Marys mentioned in the New Testament and nothing is known of this Mary except this reference to her.

188. Andronicus from the Greek Ἀνδρόνικος (Andronikos).

189. Junias from the Greek Ἰουνιᾶς (Iounias). Junias may be Junia or Julia, and the pair a couple. It is said that Junias was a Christian Jew and Andronikos a gentile, and both were imprisoned for their faith.

190. Ampliatus from the Greek Ἀμπλιᾶτος (Ampliatos), as well as Urbanus, Stachys, and Apelles are all common slave names found in an imperial household.

191. Urbanus from the Latin Urbanus, in Greek Οὐρβανός (Ourbanos).

192. Stachys from the Greek Στάχυς (Stahys).

193. Apelles from the Greek Ἀπελλῆς (Apelles), a common Jewish name.

194. Aristobulus from the Greek Ἀριστόβουλος (Aristoboulos).

195. Herodion from the Greek Ἡρῳδίων (Herodion), a Christian Jew.

To the household of Narkissos,[196] who are
In the lord. 12Greet Tryfaina[197] and Tryfosa,[198]
Who have worked diligently in the lord.
Greet my love Persis,[199] who has worked very hard
In the lord. 13Greet Roufos,[200] chosen in the lord,
And greet his mother—a mother to me too.
14Greet Asynkritos,[201] Flegon,[202] Ermes,[203]
Patrobas,[204] Ermas,[205] and all the brothers
Who are with them. 15Greet Filologos[206] and
Ioulia,[207] and Nereïs[208] and his sister,
And Olympas,[209] and all the saints with them.
16Greet one another with the sacred kiss.
All the churches of the Mashiah greet you.

---

196. Narcissus from the Greek Νάρκισσος (Narkissos), a common name of slaves and freedmen.

197. Tryphaena from the Greek Τρύφαινα (Tryfaina).

198. Tryphosa from the Greek Τρυφῶσα (Tryfosa).

199. Persis from the Greek Περσίς (Persis).

200. Rufus from the Latin *Rufus*, in Greek Ῥοῦφος (Roufos). *Rufus* is a common Latin name that entered Greek as a common name.

201. Asyncritus from the Greek Ἀσύγκριτος (Asynkritos).

202. Phlegon from the Greek Φλέγων (Flegon), common name of a slave or freedman.

203. Hermes from the Greek Ἑρμῆς (Hermes), receiver of greetings from Paul and the ancient god of messengers, mystery, cunning, and commerce.

204. Patrobas from the Greek Πατροβᾶς (Patrobas). A shortened form of Πατρόβιος (Patrobios).

205. Hermas from the Greek Ἑρμᾶς (Hermas).

206. Philologus from the Greek Φιλόλογος (Filologos).

207. Julia from the Greek Ἰουλία (Ioulia).

208. Nereus from the Greek Νηρεύς (Nereus). The name is also the name of Nereus, a sea god, son of Oceanus and Gaea, and father of the Nereids.

209. Olympas from the Greek Ὀλυμπᾶς (Olympas).

Be good not deceived by the belly of evil

17I urge you, my brothers, to keep an eye
On those who cause dissension and misconduct,
Which goes counter to what you all have learned,
And turn away from them. 18Such people are
Not slaves, not servants of the Mashiah
But their own bellies, and by golden words
And flattery deceive hearts of the simple.
19Your obedience is known to everyone.
So I am happy in you, and I wish you
To be wise and good and pure before evil.
20Soon the God of peace will trample Satan
Under your feet.²¹⁰ [And may the grace of our lord
Yeshua the Mashiah be with you.]²¹¹

Tertius, the letter writer, also sends greetings

21Timotheos,²¹² my fellow worker greets you,
As do Loukios²¹³ and Iason²¹⁴ and Sosipatros,²¹⁵

---

210. The "militant God of peace" seems to be an elementary contradiction, not only inherent in the Abrahamic religions but also in all religions. Commentators suggest that this entire warning, lines 17–20, is a later scribal emendation, reflecting not Paul but later thoughts. It comes here as a surprising intrusion in the middle of Paul's farewell list of greetings. The ending of line 20 (see next note) is more clearly an addition.

211. This line does not follow and appears to be a later scribal emendation, perhaps to affirm with a blessing, perhaps to soften, the notion of the militant God of peace. It is not in the earliest Greek texts; the Nestle-Aland 26th Greek New Testament (the source of this translation) brackets the line as suspect.

212. Timothy from the Greek Τιμόθεος (Timotheos), a companion of Paul and said to be the later cowriter of six letters attributed to Paul.

213. Lucius from the Greek Λούκιος (Loukios).

214. Jason from the Greek Ἰάσων (Iason). See note 288 on Acts 17.5.

215. Sosipater from the Greek Σωσίπατρος (Sosipatros).

My fellow countryman.[216] 22And I Tertios,[217]
Who wrote down this letter, send you greetings
In the lord. 23Gaios,[218] who is host[219] to me
And to the entire church, sends his greetings.
Erastos[220] the city treasurer greets you
As does his brother Kouartos.[221]

25Now to the one[222]
Who has the power to establish you
By my good news,[223] by preaching of Yeshua
The Mashiah, and by the revelation
Of a mystery that was silenced through the ages
26But which is glowing through prophetic writings
To all nations by order of our everlasting God
Making them obedient to faith, and to
The only wise God, 27may his glory be given,
Through Yeshua the Mashiah, forever. Amain.[224]

---

216. The Greek συγγενής (syngenes) also has the immediate familiarity of "relatives" or "kinsmen."

217. Tertius from the Greek Τέρτιος (Tertios). Tertios is the scribe who takes down Paul's letters.

218. Gaius from the Greek Γάϊος (Gaios). Paul lived with Gaius when the missionary wrote Romans. He also baptized Gaius (1 Corinthians 1.14). In Acts Gaius was a companion to Paul in Macedonia (Acts 20.4).

219. Paul is living in his house.

220. Erastus from the Greek Ἔραστος (Erastos), the city treasurer, and Paul's companion in Acts 19.22 and in 2 Timothy 4.20.

221. Quartus is Κούαρτος (Kouartos) in Greek. *Quartus* is the original Latin name.

222. God.

223. Here Paul significantly uses the word "gospel" or "good news," εὐαγγέλιον (evangelion), to designate his own letter, which he wrote before the canonical gospels were composed. His letter is "my gospel" (evangel).

224. Verse 24 is not in the early manuscripts. It reads as follows in the KJV: "The grace of our Lord Jesus [be] with you." Verses 25–27 are called the doxology, the praise, and in some manuscripts appear earlier in the letter.

Korinthians alpha
(1 Corinthians)

Korinthians alpha[1]
(1 Corinthians)

⸺

I N OTHER PROLOGUES, notably in Luke and Acts, we see the hand or hands of scribes other than those who first wrote down the main text. The prologue to 1 Corinthians being a necessary salutation to significant brothers and sisters and to Yeshua and God, it may have been written by Paul alone, or in collaboration with his letter writer, Tertios, or by Tertios alone. In any case the real letter begins after chapter 1 verse 10, when Paul urges members of the Yeshua movement to unite and leave aside egotistical differences. The extended beginnings of most of Paul's letters reflect formal theological statements of faith, obedience, and authority to the emerging sect and to God and Yeshua the Mashiah. All these flourishes were standard fare in ancient letters that were to be read aloud, and here may be from the dominant scribe's hand or the scribe's hand with Paul's approval. They do not reveal the great thinker, rhetorician, and metaphysical poet of extended skills that cumulate into an inimitable power of persuasion and even flowery passion. Paul wears his heart and spirit very close to his spoken voice. He does not hide his knowledge and dexterity in Greek reasoning any more than his commanding, pleading, even thundering voice, which he directs to a specific audience that is to hear him and be persuaded.

Beyond his call to behave, both in the congregation and in one's personal life, especially with respect to sexual deviance, which maddens the future saint into death threats and eternal fellowship with the devil,

---

1. Corinthians from the Greek Κορίνθιος (Korinthios). The Greek title is followed by ἄλφα (alpha) representing the letter "a" as well as the number "1."

there is the Paul of love and deliverance. He is many-sided, learned, and unstoppable. His letters are sermons—instructive, moral, spiritual, and frequently ecstatic. The words are at once a rod to behave and a paean on love, and, along with Matthew's lamps of light poems, "Luke's Parable of the Lost Son," and the epic poem of Revelation, are the poetry chef d'oeuvres of the New Testament.

Chapter 13 is the most cited lyrical flight in the Bible, that is, other than Isaiah's words on peace, of which we can never have too much. In Paul's brief chapter, presenting an ultimate yet atypical apostle, we hear the poet Paul who is Shakespeare, or the poet Shakespeare who is Paul. His poem on love begins:

> If I speak in the tongue of men and angels
> But have no love, I am but sounding brass
> Or a clanging cymbal. If I have prophecy
> And understand all mysteries and all knowledge
> And if I have all faith to remove mountains
> But love I do not have, then I am nothing.
> If I give all my goods to feed the poor
> And give my body to be burned, and love
> I do not have, in all I have gained nothing.

While there are words in Paul's verses that may be read for specific theological meanings, here the means are metaphor and poetry. God and the messiah, the synagogue and clergy, go unnamed. This deeply moving meditation on love, directed largely to human love of other human beings, remains a miracle of the spirit.

Agape as Love or Charity

By intent or ignorance, theologians, translators, and dictionaries have done strange things in order to clean up Paul's word *agape,* "love," which resonates through chapter 13. For theological, as opposed to classical, dictionaries, agape is love of Christ for humanity, or it is *spiritual* as opposed to *erotic* and sexual love. But Paul was using a lexicon that he and his congregations understood, and it was *love* with no qualifying allegories to make it pious and respectable. In other chapters of 1 Corinthians, Paul speaks against sexuality and favors abstention. But not here. It is said that if Paul meant love between men and women, he would have used the word *eros*, as in the fanciful god Eros, son of the love goddess Aphrodite. In Greek, *agape* is like *eros* an elemental word for love. From classical Greek, to the demotic Koine that Paul spoke and wrote in, through Byzantine and modern Greek, *agape* means love in all its meanings. And Paul means love in the most expansive and joyous senses. He holds up mountains with his love. Surely he had in mind the exalting love in Song of Songs, where the common Hebrew word for love is אָהַב (ahav) or אַהֲבָה (ahavah) which in the Hebrew Bible means both affective and sexual love between man and woman.

The official culprit in later distortions of *agape* is the Vulgata (or Vulgate), the authorized translation of the Greek and Hebrew Bible by Saint Jerome at the end of the fourth century. The Vulgata renders Greek *agape* as Latin *caritas*, "charity," a true abuse of Paul's words. Until the Revised Version in English, most translations adhered to Vulgata's mistranslation, turning *caritas* into "charity." Paul's love/charity has often been used as a Pauline pastoral argument for proper comportment and church tithing. However, the always demotic and enlightened 1526 translation from William Tyndale gives, "Though I spake with the tonges of men and angels and yet had no love I were even as soundinge brasse: or as a tynklynge Cymball." Tyndale translated directly from the Greek and was the first in the English language to do so (for which he was burned at the stake by the then-still-Catholic Henry VIII), but the King James Version still went back to Jerome's Vulgata and its *caritas* became "charity." Hence, the Authorized King James Version begins, "Though I speak with the tongues of men and of angels, and have not charity, or a tinkling cymbal," and ends, "And now abideth faith, hope, charity, these three; but the greatest of these *is* charity." "Charity" overcomes "love" eleven times in the King James tax-exempt version.

The word and notion of charity in religious thought has a sanctified aroma in English, intensified by its being the infelicitous leitmotif in both Latin and Authorized Paul. Paul, often in terrible health and emotional turmoil, railed against many kinds of bad love and sexuality. In Corinthians, Paul says it is best to be celibate but better to marry than to sin. When he speaks that it is best not to marry, he is not hoping we will all disappear from the earth. As scholars comment, Paul expects salvific Christ to return soon, perhaps within the decade, and so it matters little whether one bears children or not. Enough people will be here to be saved when the Day of Judgment cometh. Paul also condemns sexuality outside marriage and especially unnatural sex. But none of that chiding Paul pertains to chapter 13, and we should let him have it as he says it.

After these shots at the wondrous King James, it must be said that its memorable phrase "For now we see through a glass, darkly" (1 Cor. 13.12) should be a coup de grâce against any detractor. It is beautiful, making tepid the New Revised "For now we see in a mirror, dimly." However, the King James "glass" must be understood as "mirror," since there were no mirrors then of glass. Paul's word ἔσοπτρον (esoptron, mirror) means just that, an ancient polished bronze mirror. Were it glass, his word would be ὕαλος (valos) as in "clear as glass" (Rev. 21.18). Moreover, Paul meant "mirror," not "glass." One can argue that glass also signifies "looking glass." But the King James Version has "see *through* a glass, darkly." So this is a glass one looks through, not at. The Authorized has splendidly improved on Paul. The notion of a transparent glass pane, emphasized by "darkly," though wrong, is here even more mysterious than Alice's looking glass.

There is a second translation quandary. The Greek αἴνιγμα (ainigma) means an "enigma" or "riddle," written here as ἐν αἰνίγματι (en ainigmati, in enigma). The words ἐσόπτρου ἐν αἰνίγματι signify "enigmatic mirror." There is no "darkly" modifying the act of seeing. Again the King James Version errs on the side of beauty.

Chapter 1

Greetings

Shaul[2] was called to be a messenger
Of the Mashiah Yeshua[3] by God's will
As was our brother Sosthenes,[4] 2also
Called to God's temple[5] in the city of
Korinthos,[6] he consecrated in Yeshua
Mashiah called to be deemed saint along
With all who here and every place, in theirs
And ours, are calling out the name of lord
Yeshua the Mashiah. 3Let there be grace,
Let there be peace from God who is our father
And from the lord Yeshua the Mashiah.

---

2. Paul from the Greek Παῦλος (Paulos), from Saul in the Greek Σαῦλος (Saulos), from the Hebrew שָׁאוּל (shaul). Paul was born in Tarsos as *Shaul*.

3. "Christ" in English derives from the Jewish Septuagint translation of Old Testament Hebrew מָשִׁיחַ (mashiah), meaning "messiah" as Χριστος (Hristos), from which we have "Christ," meaning the "anointed," an attribute of the messiah. The more expected version into Greek and thereafter into all tongues from the Greek would be a direct transliteration of *mashiah* as "messiah" rather than "Christ," an attribute of the messiah. As a result of this misleading translation from Hebrew *mashiah* to Greek *Hristos*, even in Greek we have "Christ the Messiah," which should be "Messiah the Christ," meaning "the anointed Messiah." The phrase "Christ the Anointed" is a redundancy meaning "Anointed the Anointed," but by now it is common speech.

4. Sosthenes from the Greek Σωσθένης (Sosthenes), a synagogue leader in Corinth at the time of the missionary work there of Paul. Sosthenes also appears in Acts 18.12–17, where he is beaten, for undisclosed reasons, before the Roman proconsul.

5. Or synagogue. See Acts 20.17, note 340, for distinctions between synagogue and church.

6. Corinth from the Greek Κορίνθος (Korinthos).

4I thank my God at all times for the grace
Given to you in the Mashiah Yeshua.[7]

---

7. Paul and his congregation do not receive grace directly from God but through his son Yeshua the Mashiah with whom God shares powers. As Christianity emerges in identification and doctrine from Judaism, Yeshua becomes the popular focal point of the laity as a result of his sacrifice, his suffering in the hideous crucifixion, his pathos and last cry of despaired abandonment. In ordinary life he is there, personified as a human in churches and prayer; he is eternally available, and his help is sought in moral and practical matters. It may be noted that the cross, the ultimate sign of Christianity, signifies specifically the Christ (the Mashiah), not God. It is the drama of Christ on the cross, and to Christ one crosses oneself, not to God. So too the name "Christianity" signifies Christ directly in a religion founded on the life and teachings of Jesus. In the Hebrew Bible each reference to the "lord" is to God, and since God's true name is unsayable and unknowable, one writes the tetragrammaton "YHWH" from the four Hebrew letters that are phonetically as *yahweh* or descriptively as *adonai*, meaning "lord." By contrast, in Paul and elsewhere in the New Testament each reference to the "lord" or "master" in Greek is to *kyrie*, from the Greek κύριος (kyrios). But *kyrie* refers not to God but to Yeshua.

Hence, while the God in the Torah of the Hebrew and Christian Bibles speaks frequently in his all-powerful voice, in the New Testament God is not only invisible but essentially remotely silent. God is referred to for ultimate authority while designating advice, deeds, and cures, miracles to Yeshua. The son Yeshua is his immediate speaker and doer.

When one says that one is a Christian, "Christian" signifies, above all, that one accepts Christ the Messiah. God may be implied, assumed, spiritually near, but reference in all these instances is to Christ. In this, Christianity has moved decisively from its reputed source in the foretold Jewish messiah as represented in Isaiah and elsewhere in the Torah, where the messiah is an earthly leader with no divine powers. His biblical epithets "son of man" and "son of God" proclaim him and all people on earth children of God. In the preserved Hebrew Bible there is no passage concerning the awaited messiah as a divinity in a holy trinity of shared powers. But from its inception, with the personification of God through his son, Christianity has had a triple godhead with distinct faces: the invisible one of God whose face cannot be seen or depicted, the familiar and universally portrayed Jesus, and the less distinct holy ghost.

Paul's letters, the earliest canonized scriptures in the New Testament, primordially fashioned Christianity from the Jewish Bible, his Hellenistic Greek background (with Platonism as a principle source of eternity, immortality, resurrection, and afterlife), and the word he heard of the crucifixion and resurrection of Jesus the

₅In every way you have become rich in
  His being, in every word and in all knowledge,
₆And the Mashiah's testimony has
  Become confirmed in you. ₇Therefore you lack
  No spiritual gift as you await the revelation
  Of our lord Yeshua the Mashiah.
₈He will confirm your strength until the end
  So that you may be blameless on the day
  Of our lord who is Yeshua the Mashiah.
₉God is faithful. And by him you were called
  To enter into fellowship with his son
  Yeshua the Mashiah who is our lord.

Let good news Jews of Korinthos be united
  ₁₀Now I beseech you, brothers,[8] in the name
  Of our lord Yeshua who is Mashiah
  That you all speak the same with no divisions[9]
  Among you so that you will be conjoined
  In the same mind and one in the same thought.
  ₁₁My brothers, Chloe and her people told me
  Of you and the contentious rife among you.
  ₁₂I ask you this: Can each one of you say,
  "I am with Shaul or am with Apollos,

Messiah. With his devoted emphasis on the meaning of Jesus's death (he did not know Jesus in the flesh in Jerusalem when both were there, nor does he address the life of Jesus in his letters), Paul gives us, in all its depth and complication, the divine Messianic Jesus. Having been a missionary of a Messianic movement, he also fashioned Yeshua the Mashiah as the beloved and pathetic figure at its center, and demanded faith in Yeshua's reality. It is not surprising that despite the Protestant reformation, which somewhat diminished the powers of the Christ the Messiah, Christ developed from the symbolic son of God, in a trinity of spirit, to be at the center of Christianity itself.

8. See note 5 on gender preference in Romans 1.13.

9. Schisms.

I am with Kefa[10] or with the Mashiah?"

13Can the Mashiah be partitioned? No.

And was our Shaul crucified for you?

Or in the name of Shaul were you bathed?[11]

14I am thankful[12] that I dipped[13] none of you

In water except for Krispos and for Gaios[14]

15So no one can affirm that you were dipped

In my name. 16I also dipped the household

Of Stefanas[15]—I don't know if I immersed

Anyone else. 17The Mashiah did not send me

To dip but to preach the good news, and not

With words of wisdom but so that the cross

Of the Mashiah will not lose its meaning.

---

10. Peter. In the gospels and letters, the same Peter has numerous names: Peter, Simon, and Simeon. And in John 20.6 he is "Simon Peter" from the Greek Σίμων Πέτρος (Simon Petros). In 2 Peter he is "Simeon Peter," from the Greek Συμεὼν Πέτρος (Simeon Petros). And in John 1.42 he is "Simon, the son of John," from the Greek Σίμων ὁ υἱὸς Ἰωάννου (Simon ho huios Ioannou). "Peter" means "rock" or "stone" in Greek from πέτρος, from the Aramaic כֵּיפָא (kefa), from the Hebrew כֵּף (kef), all meaning "rock" or "stone." In his letters Paul calls Peter "Cephas," from the Greek Κηφᾶς (Kefas), based on the Greek transliteration of his Aramaic name *Kefa*.

11. Baptized, ἐβαπτίσθητε (ebaptisthete), here meaning "bathed" or "ceremonially dipped in water," is second person, plural, aorist, passive, indicative form of the verb βαπτίζομαι (baptizomai), meaning "to wash," "dip," "bathe," or "immerse in water." The English word "baptize" transliterates the Greek word but does not convey the specific image of dipping in water.

12. The text has "God" in brackets as in "I thank God," which the King James Version keeps, but which seems to be a later emendation.

13. Baptized.

14. Crispus from the Greek Κρίσπος (Krispos) and Gaius from the Greek Γάϊος (Gaios). In Paul, *Krispos* and *Gaios* are loan words from the Latin *Crispus* and *Gaius*. Krispos in Acts 18.8 was president of the synagogue in Corinth before he was baptized into Paul's Messianism. About Gaius less is known. He is mentioned at the end of Romans, 16.23, as being his host at the church in Corinth and was perhaps similarly baptized by Paul.

15. Stephanas from the Greek Στέφανᾶς (Stefanas).

Nonsense and true wisdom

18The word about the cross is folly to
 Those racing toward perdition, but to us
 Who saved that word it is the power of God.
19In Yeshayahu[16] the prophet's word tells us:
 I will destroy the wisdom of the wise
 And void discernment of those discerning.[17]

Where is the sage?

20Where is the sage? I ask. Where is the scholar?[18]
 Where is the great debater of this age?
 Did God not turn the wisdom of the world
 To folly? 21So in deeper wisdom of God
 The world through its wisdom did not know God,
 And God was pleased to save the believers
 Despite the folly that was preached to them.

22Jews[19] ask for signs and Greeks[20] ask for wisdom,
23But we preach the Mashiah crucified.
 For Jews this is a stumbling block, and nonsense
 To the gentiles, 24but to us who are chosen,
 We Jews and Greeks alike, proclaim Mashiah
 The power of God and also God's wisdom.
25And the folly of God is wiser than men,
 And the weakness of God is stronger than men.

---

16. Isaiah from the Greek Ἠσαΐας (Esaias), from the Hebrew יְשַׁעְיָהוּ (yeshayahu).

17. Isa. 29.14 (Septuagint).

18. From the Greek *grammateus* (γραμματεύς), traditionally translated as "scribe" and in recent translations rendered as "scholar" or "expert." In the Hebrew סוֹפֵר (sofer).

19. The Jews who have not recognized Yeshua's messiahship.

20. Greek pagans or gentiles who have not been converted to belief in the Yeshua's messiahship.

Consider your calling

26Look at your calling, brothers. Few of you
  Have become wise in habits of the flesh,
  Few of you are strong, and few are well born,
27But God selected the fools of the world
  To shame the wise. And then God chose the weak
  Of the world 28to shame the strong, and God chose
  The low-born and the despised of the world.
  He chose what is not—to abolish what is,
29So that no flesh might glory[21] before God.
30You are from him in the Mashiah Yeshua,
  Who became our wisdom drawn from God,
  Our justice and holiness and redemption,
  So that as it is written in Yirmiyahu[22]
  Let him who boasts boast in the lord.[23]

Chapter 2

Coming in weakness, fear, and trembling

  When I came to you, my brothers, I came
  Not with eloquence or superior wisdom
  When I announced to you God's mystery.[24]
2I determined to know nothing among you
  But Yeshua the Mashiah, the crucified.[25]
3I came to you in weakness and deep fear

---

21. "Glory" in the sense of "boast" or be "prideful."

22. Jeremiah from the Greek Ἰερεμίας (Ieremias), from the Hebrew יִרְמְיָהוּ (yirmiyahu).

23. Jer. 9.24.

24. Other texts have "testimony of God."

25. Paul's statement here pinpoints his focus, which is not on the course of Yeshua's life, unknown to him, or Yeshua's wisdom sayings, but on his crucifixion and its mysterious meaning.

And trembling. 4Yet my speech and ministry
Lay not in the persuasion of my words
Of wisdom[26] but in revealing the spirit
And power 5so that your faith may not rest
On men's wisdom but on the power of God.

Wisdom from the mystery of spirit
    6While we still speak wisdom among the mature,
    The wisdom is not of this age or of doomed
    Rulers, 7but we speak the wisdom of God
    In a secret mystery that God decreed
    Before the ages for our glory. 8No one
    Among the leaders of this age[27] caught on.
    If they had, they would not have crucified
    The lord of glory. 9But as Yeshayahu[28] wrote:
        What the eye did not see or the ear did not hear
        And did not enter the heart of man,
        These things God has prepared for those who love him.

    10Through spirit God revealed these things to us
    Since spirit searches everything, even
    The depths of God. 11Who knows the things in man
    Except the spirit of man which is in him?
    So things that are of God no person knows
    Except God's spirit. 12Now we have received
    Not spirit of the world but the one spirit
    That is from God so we may understand
    A grace that has been freely given us.
    13We speak of these things in those words not taught

---

26. Paul, who often uses the reasoned diatribe (debate) of the Stoics (of whom the most famous was Socrates), here disclaims the stoic or sophist approach to persuasion. Rather, as throughout Paul, he wishes to reveal the power and spirit of God upon which faith resides.

27. Roman leaders.

28. Isaiah.

By human wisdom but in words that are
The teaching of the spirit that combines
Spiritual with spiritual. 14The sensual man
Does not accept the things that are of spirit;
They're nonsense to him and he cannot know
Their meaning since they only are discerned
Spiritually. 15Now the spiritual man
Discerns all things while he ends up discerned
By no one. 16As Yeshayahu has said:
    Who has known the mind of the lord
       Who will instruct him?[29]
But we possess the mind of the Mashiah.

Chapter 3

Jealousy in the synagogue and God's architecture
    And I, my brothers, could not speak to you
    As spiritual people but as carnal men:
    Infants in the Mashiah. 2I gave you milk
    To drink, not meat,[30] for you were not yet strong
    Enough to eat. Nor are you even now,
  3Since you are men of flesh and blood. And when
    Among you there is jealousy and strife,
    Are you not carnal men and don't you walk
    As mere men do? 4And when one of you says,
    "I am for Shaul," and another says, "I am
    For Apollos,"[31] are you not human beings?

---

29. Isa. 40.13 (Septuagint).

30. Literally, "meat," which the KJV and older versions render. Modern versions say "solid food."

31. Apollos from the Greek Ἀπολλῶς (Apollos). For more on Apollos, see Acts 18.24–28, where he is described: "a certain Jew named Apollos, an Alexandrian by birth, came to Efesos. He was eloquent and learned in scripture." In Acts 18.24–28 Apollos worked in the established new congregations, preaching to those whom Paul had already converted.

5But what then is Apollos? What is Shaul?
You are servants through whom you found belief,
As the lord gave to everyone. 6I planted
And Apollos watered, but only God
Made the field grow. 7The planter and waterer
Have a common purpose, 8and each receives
Reward according to his work. 9We are
Fellow workers of God. You are the field
Of God, you are the architecture of God.[32]

Testing the foundation with fire

10In keeping with God's grace given to me
I laid a foundation like a wise architect,
But someone else builds on it. Each man
Must look to how he builds. 11No one can lay
A foundation but the one who laid it down,
And that one is Yeshua the Mashiah.
12But if one then constructs on the foundation
With gold, silver, and precious stones, with wood,
Hay, straw, 13the work of each one will be seen
The day of its disclosure, and be bright
Since revelation comes with fire, and fire
Will test the kind of work. 14If any part
Of what was built on the foundation lasts,
The builder will receive a good reward.
15If it is burned up, he will suffer loss
But saved only as having passed through fire.

You are the temple

16Do you know that you are the temple of God
And the spirit of God resonates in you?
17If anyone tries to destroy the temple,
God will destroy him, since the temple of God
Is holy and the temple is what you are.

---

32. Normally, οἰκοδομή (oikodomé) is translated as "construction" or "building" but
I have taken Richmond Lattimore's universal word "architecture."

The wisdom of folly

18Let no one deceive himself. If anyone
   Thinks himself wise among you in this age,
   Let him become a fool to become wise.

19The wisdom of this world is foolishness
   With God. It is written in Job:
      He catches the wise
      In their shiftiness.[33]
20And in the Psalms:
      The lord knows that the reasoning of the wise
      Is futile.[34]

No pride in leaders

21Let no one boast among men. All is yours.
22Whether Shaul or Apollos or Kefa,[35]
   Or the world or life or death, or the present
   Or coming things. And all these things are yours.
23You are of Mashiah. Mashiah is of God.

Chapter 4

Messengers of the mystery

   So let a man reason us to be servants
   Of the Mashiah and managers of God's
   Mysteries. 2More, a manager must be
   Reliable. 3I have little concern
   That I be judged by you or any earthly
   Day of judgment.[36] I do not judge myself

---

33. Job 5.13.

34. Ps. 94.11.

35. Peter.

36. In "day of judgment" the Greek does not include "judgment," but in context the idea is intended.

4Since I am unaware of any guilt
But I am not therefore acquitted since
It is the lord who judges me. 5Do not
Judge then until the lord has come. He will
Bring light to things hidden in the darkness
And bring a light to yearnings of the hearts
And then to each of us will come God's praise.

Foolishness of would-be kings

6Now, my brothers, I have fashioned these words
To Apollos and to myself for you
To learn the meaning of: "You must not go
Beyond the written words" so none of you
Will become lordly, favoring one against
Another. 7Who has given you distinction?
What do you have that wasn't given you?
Why do you boast as if it were not a gift?
8Now you are gloating and you have turned rich.
Without our help you have turned into kings.
I wish you had become the kings so we
Might all parade together as we were kings.[37]

The true outcast messengers

9I believe that God has displayed us last
In a procession—messengers like men
Condemned to death—and to the world we are
A spectacle to men and angels. 10We
Are fools for the Mashiah, but you are wise
In the Mashiah. We are weak, you are strong.
You are respectable, we are despised.
11Until this day we are hungry and thirsty,

---

37. Paul speaks with extreme sarcasm and irony about the pretensions of the Corinthian leaders, hoping to shame them into moderate behavior. He compares their frivolity to the true apostolic messengers who, like Paul, are attacked, tortured, and die for the message.

And naked, beaten and homeless everywhere.
12We are worn out working with our own hands.
Reviled, we bless. Persecuted, we endure.
13Slandered, we respond kindly. As the filth
Of the world, we're its garbage till this day.

Shall I come with a rod or love?
14I am not writing this to shame but warn you
As my loved children. 15Though you have ten thousand
Tutors in the Mashiah, not many fathers,
But in Mashiah Yeshua I became your father
Through the good news. 16Imitate me, I beg you.
17So I sent you Timotheos,[38] who is my child,
Loved and faithful in the Mashiah. He will
Remind you of my ways in the Mashiah[39]
As I teach them in every synagogue.

18Some of you thinking that I will not come
Grew arrogant. 19But I'll be coming soon
To be with you, lord willing, and find out
Not only how the arrogant are speaking
But what their powers are, 20since the kingdom
Of God is not in talk but power. 21Tell me,
What do you want? Shall I come to you holding
A rod or come in spirit of our gentleness?

Chapter 5

Fornication
Word comes of fornication rife among you.
Not even among gentiles is there news

---

38. Timothy from the Greek Τιμόθεος (Timotheos).
39. Some editions follow "Christ" with "Jesus."

Of such fornication: a man takes his father's
Wife[40] 2and you look on it with arrogant
Pleasure! Shouldn't you mourn that in your midst
One of you performed these acts? 3I was absent
In body but was there in spirit. Now,
As if I had been present, I have judged
The man who did this act. 4So in the name
Of lord Yeshua, assembled here with you
And with my spirit, with the power of lord
Yeshua, 5I hand this man over to Satan
For the destruction of his flesh so that
His spirit may be saved on the lord's day.[41]
6Your arrogance is bad. Do you not know
A small amount of yeast leavens all dough?
7Purge the old yeast so you may be a new

---

40. The usual gloss of the phrase "his father's wife" is "stepmother," which commentators are guessing or reasoning that were the woman his mother, Paul would have said "mother."

41. In contrast to Acts, where the figure who represents Paul operates with the miraculous powers of the lord Yeshua, here for the first time Paul of the letters assumes the power and authority of Yeshua, not to perform miracles, however, but to judge and sentence to death. The order to destroy the flesh is perfectly clear in Greek and its English translation. To interpret the order as a mere metaphor, suggesting that it really means to expel the guilty man from the new congregation, is wishfully to deny the authority of Paul's plain words, which are to have the man destroyed in the flesh. This destruction, moreover, may make possible his salvation, not on earth but on Judgment Day. In Romans 1.27 Paul lists the polluted moral acts, particularly male and female homosexuality, for which the punishment is death. Also see note 43, 1 Corinthians 6.2. Severe punishment, or capital punishment, for uncondoned sexual acts is common in both ancient religions and secular governances, even today.

Paul's order to destroy the fornicator is followed by the denunciation of his arrogant enemies in the emerging Jesus movement who apparently resent his presence, powers, and the nature of his preaching. Here he recalls the Passover need to cleanse the old bad yeast (a metaphor for evil) when baking the unleavened bread at Passover, as well as the need for the sacrificial lamb. Much can be read into this congruence of parallel examples of impurity and necessary purgation as embodied in the fornicator, the bad yeast, and the Jewish sacrificial lamb who is Jesus.

Baking of dough, and be truly unleavened,[42]
And indeed our paschal lamb, the Mashiah,
Was sacrificed. 8So let us feast, not with
Old yeast nor with the yeast of bad and cunning
But matzoh bread of truth and purity.

9I wrote you in my letter not to mix
  With anyone who is a fornicator,
10But not to break with every fornicator,
  Idolater, or glutton in this world,
  Since you would have to get out of the world.
11But now again I write you not to mix
  With any brother called a fornicator,
  Idolater, or glutton in this world
  Or drunkard or a swindler. With this kind
  You shouldn't eat. 12Yet what have I to do
  With judging those outside? 13God judges them.
  So rid yourself of evil men among you.

Chapter 6

Lawsuits among believers
  Will anyone among you with a case
  Against another dare to have it judged
  Before the unjust rather than the saints?
  2Do you not know the saints will judge the world?[43]

---

42. As in the gospels this is a reference to matzoh, the unleavened bread used at the Passover Seder, normally called the Last Supper. By the time many of the Jewish holidays observed in the New Testament reach English translation, they seem, by means of the chosen lexicon, to be Christian innovations rather than Jewish rituals.

43. Paul infers that the saints (the members of the Jesus movement), not Roman courts, should determine legal disputes. This gives religious law priority over secular courts. There is revealed here not only a struggle of dominion between religious and secular law but also, probably, an antipathy for Roman power, which in all ways is then persecuting Christian Jews. In Acts 22.25, however, Paul draws on his Roman citizenship to save himself from being flogged. See note 366, Acts 22.27.

And if the world is to be judged by you,
Are you not fit to judge trivial lawsuits?
3Do you not know that we are to judge angels,
And certainly this ordinary life?44
4And if you have an ordinary case,
Can you seat one to judge of slight esteem
Within the synagogue? 5I speak to shame you.
Is there among you not just one wise man
Able to judge in cases between brothers?
6And can a brother go against a brother
In court and then be tried by unbelievers?

7It is already a complete defeat
For you to be engaged at all in lawsuits
Against each other. So why not be wronged?
Why not be cheated? 8But you are unjust
And cheat, and you are brothers! 9Or do you
Not know that the unjust will not inherit
The kingdom of God? Don't fool yourselves. None
Of the fornicators or idolaters or adulterers
Or effeminates45 or pederasts46 10or thieves

---

44. In Isaiah 24.21–22, in speaking of God's devastation of the earth, Isaiah writes, "In that day the lord will punish the powers in the heavens above / and the kings on the earth below," the "powers above" being angels. These verses in Isaiah are echoed later in 2 Peter 2.4, 2.9, and Jude 6, but the judge remains God. In no other place in the Bible are human agents called upon to judge angels, which is an extraordinary delegation of power to members of the emerging Messianics.

45. Homosexuals. One of the Greek words for homosexual, μαλακός (malakós), means "soft" or "effeminate," and can refer to the passive adult homosexual or boy who lets himself be used homosexually. The word has multiple meanings. Other modern translations have "male prostitutes," which is probably an anachronistic interpretation. These terms are significant in modern times when questions of clergy or even membership in a congregation are tied up in interpreting biblical interdictions and condemnations. Paul is a principle textual source in these debates. See also note 17, Romans 1.27.

46. From the Greek ἀρσενοκοίτης (arsenokoites), which can mean male homosexual, pederast, or sodomite. Paul may be referring in these two condemnations to active and passive homosexuality, but from our uncertain knowledge of his usage, none of these categories is precisely clear.

SCRIPTURES · LETTERS OF SHAUL/SAUL/PAUL

> Or the greedy or drunks or the abusive
> Will ever inherit the kingdom of God.
> 11And you have been some of these things
> But were washed clean, and you were sanctified
> And justified in the name of lord Yeshua
> The Mashiah and in the spirit of our God.

The price of fornication

> 12All things for me are lawful, but not all things
> Are beneficial. All things are for me
> But I will not be mastered by anything.
> 13Meats are for the stomach and the stomach
> For meats[47] but God will destroy both of them.
> Body is not for fornication but for the lord[48]
> And the lord for the body. 14God raised
> The lord and will also raise us through his power.
> 15Do you not know that bodies are the limbs
> Of the Mashiah? Should I take the limbs
> Of a whore? No, never! 16Do you not know
> That clinging to a whore makes you one body?
> For as it says in Genesis:
>> The two will be one flesh.[49]
> 17But one clinging to the lord is one spirit.

---

47. Food.

48. Here as elsewhere "lord" or "Lord" refers to Jesus rather than to God, which is not possible to read in the Hebrew Bible. If the Hebrew Bible said, "God raised the Lord," it would signify that God raised himself. The more common statement in the New Testament is "God raised his son."

49. Gen. 2.24. The passage reads (KJV), "Therefore shall a man leave his father and his mother, and shall cleave unto his wife: and they shall be one flesh. 25And they were both naked, the man and his wife, and were not ashamed." Here, Paul connects the moral dangers of fornication by a brother in Corinth to Adam and Eve in their first seconds in Eden. To compare a man sleeping with a whore to Adam saying, "A man shall cleave unto his wife" is a forced or ungenerous observation. Adam and Eve, freshly created on their first day of life on earth, know total innocence. The parallel is gauche and reflects qualities of Paul with respect to human physicality. In chapter 7, Paul raises the question of whether sexual intimacy is compatible with life in Christ.

18Flee from fornication! Any sin you do
   Occurs outside the body, but the one
   Who fornicates sins against his own body.[50]
19Or don't you not know that body is a temple
   Of holy spirit deep in you. From God
   She comes, and you are not your own?
20You were bought for a price.[51] And so I say:
   Glorify God who glistens in your body.

Chapter 7

Fire or marriage
   Concerning those things about which you wrote,[52]
   It's best when a man doesn't touch a woman,[53]
2But because of filthy sex[54] let each man have
   His own wife and each woman her own husband.

---

50. In many of the letters, Paul rages against fornication and "Satanic" urges of the body. Bishop John Shelby Spong in his *The Letters of Paul* (New York: Riverhead 1998) suggests that Paul's fury against fornication, and sexuality in general, is his defensive posture against his own desires as one who was probably gay—gay before a time when homosexuality might be accepted as perfectly normal. He was "horrified by the realization that he was experiencing desire for something he had been taught to regard as so totally evil. . . . He would, therefore, do battle against this evil impulse with every resource his religion offered to him" (Preface, xxviii).

51. That price is, scholars comment, probably Jesus's death atoning for human sin. Here, if indeed the reference is to Jesus's death, the financial metaphor is inflated as was the prior reference to Eve and Adam. If Jesus's death reflects the messiah's atonement for human sin, that human sin for which he gave his life must hold greater significance than the sin of fornication.

52. Questions of celibacy and marriage from the congregation in Corinth.

53. In order of virtue, Paul poses celibacy first, which he states is "not to touch a woman," and presents himself as the model celibate; then, if one cannot resist the temptation to fornicate, marriage.

54. The Greek πορνεία (porneia) is "prostitution" and "filth" as in "morally filthy." English "pornographic" means sexually immoral written material. πόρνη (porne) is "prostitute." The KJV "fornication" is a flamboyant word for illicit sex, which can be adultery, sex with a whore, or any number of overlapping sexual and social meanings.

₃Let the husband pay his debt[55] to his wife
  And let the wife render hers to her husband.
₄The wife does not possess authority
  Over her own body. That is her husband's.
  The husband does not have authority
  Over his body. That belongs to his wife.
₅You mustn't spurn each other's needs except
  Through an agreement for a time so as
  To give yourselves to prayer. But then come back
  Again together out of fear that Satan
  Seduce you both into incontinence.
₆To the unmarried men and widows I say
  To you as a concession—not a command—
₇I wish all men to be like me. Yet each man
  Has his own gift from God, his special thing.
₈I say to the unmarried men and widows,
  It's best for them to be contained like me,
₉But if they can't control themselves, go marry.
  Better to marry than to live on fire.

Commands on divorce

₁₀And to those married, I command—not I
  But the lord[56]—a wife should not separate

---

55. A financial metaphor for "conjugal duty."

56. And to those married, I command—not I / but the lord." Normally, when Paul wishes to argue a key change in Jewish practice, notably that of circumcision, dietary law, or keeping the Sabbath, he argues elegantly by citing passages from the Hebrew Bible—especially from the Pentateuch, Isaiah, and Psalms—to prove a point. He writes so persuasively that his interpretation of Hebrew Bible law opens the door to gentile conversion. Here, in giving his commands on marriage and divorce, he does not support his renovations by writing "as it is written" or "as it says in scripture" or "as Isaiah says," which is his practice elsewhere. Rather, he says that the lord, not he Paul, commands, and then goes on to delineate the laws of marriage and divorce between believers. One may say that Jesus or God is speaking *through* Paul, yet he does not cite personal revelation, which is his practice elsewhere. Moreover, Paul confirms his claim that the lord alone commands is intentional and not a rhetorical trope or slip of the tongue by fully reversing his position two verses later when dealing with a mixed marriage. Now,

From her husband 11but if she separates,
Then stay single or reconcile with her spouse,
And a husband should not divorce his wife.

Commands in marriage about non-believers[57]
   12And to the rest I say—I, not the lord—
   If any brother has a wife who is

Paul asserts that he himself, *not* the lord, is the legal arbiter. Turning the phrase around in order to contrast it with his former assertion, he writes, "And to the rest I say—I, not the lord" (7.12).

In many religious traditions Paul's name alone is sufficient to make a statement law. Paul's name is traditionally assigned to the earliest holy scripture in the New Testament, to fourteen of its twenty-seven books (seven attributions are certain), and as an apostolic author his commands have been accepted as apostolic law. In effect, Paul's words have almost universally been taken as his own words—as Paul writes—in which he becomes his own authority to set up his complex legal system for celibacy, marriage, and divorce. In doing so he is consciously creating laws to counter the prevailing secular Roman law. Yet a quandary of authority remains. While the reader may wish to receive Paul's own commands as religious duty based solely on his apostolic stature, he claims and immediately disclaims apostolic and personal authority by writing, "I command," followed by his denial of command: "not I but the lord." And then, as stated two verses later, reclaims the authority for himself. What is one to think?

Can Paul possibly be implying that *both* he and the lord command, thereby sharing control? Not so. In the course of three verses Paul makes three distinct assertions: I Paul command, the lord commands, I Paul command. Perhaps because of these confusing signals of authority, the Pauline decrees on marriage and divorce, so contested among the diverse Christian faiths, continue to be championed, questioned, modified, or rejected.

It can be seen that commentators normally regard Paul's assertion in 7.12 that "the lord commands" as a reference to a command by Jesus found in Matthew 5.32 or elsewhere in the gospels. *The NIV Study Bible* notes, "Paul is citing a command from the Lord Jesus in his earthly ministry that married couples must stay together (Mt 5:32; Mk 10:12; Lk 16:18)." Aware that the gospels were written decades after Paul's death, the editors implausibly conclude, "Paul probably heard such commands from other disciples (cf. Gal 1:18–19) or from Jesus himself by a special revelation" (NIV 1 Cor. 7.10). See *The NIV Study Bible*, gen. ed. Kenneth Barker (Grand Rapids, MI: Zondervan Publishing House, 1995), 1744.

57. One who is not a Christian Jew.

An unbeliever[58] and she will consent
To live with him, let him not divorce her.
13And if a wife has a husband who is
An unbeliever, and he will consent
To live with her, let her not divorce him.
14The unbelieving husband is hallowed
Through his wife. And an unbelieving wife
Is hallowed by the brother. Otherwise,
Your children will be unclean, but this way
They are hallowed.[59] 15But if the unbeliever
Separates, let him go. The brother or sister
In these things isn't bound. God has called us
To live in peace. 16Yet wife, how can you know?
Maybe you'll save your husband, or husband,
How can you know? Maybe you'll save your wife.

Don't worry about circumcision

17Unless the lord has called him, let each one
Walk about on his own, and so are my orders
About the temple. 18If a man was circumcised
When he was called, let him not conceal it.
If a man was uncircumcised when called,
Let him not be circumcised. 19A circumcision
Is nothing and uncircumcision is nothing,
But keeping God's commands is everything.
20Let each remain in the condition of
When he was called. 21Were you a slave when you
Were called? Don't worry. If you can be free,
Be free. 22That way a slave called to by the lord
Is the lord's freedman, a slave of the Mashiah.

---

58. A gentile or a Jew who has not accepted Yeshua as the messiah.

59. The reference to children from parents of two different faiths—children of a mixed marriage—remains the basis for diverse sects' demand that children be brought up according to a certain faith, whether this faith be between a Christian couple or between a Christian and a non-Christian couple.

23You too were purchased for a price. Don't be
  A slave of men. 24So in whatever state
  You were, my brothers, may you be with God.

Care for little in this world, the time is short
  25Concerning virgins, I have no commandment
    From the Mashiah, and I judge as one
    Who through the mercy of the lord you trust.
  26I think, because of the impending crisis,
    It's better for a man to stay as is.

  27If anchored to a wife, don't look for freedom.
    If you are still unmoored, don't seek a wife,
  28But even if you marry, do not sin.
    And if a virgin marries, do not sin.
    Though men and women feel the torment of
    The flesh, my purpose is to spare you pain.

  29Brothers, I tell you this: the time is short.
    From now on, let those who have wives be
    As if they had no wives. 30And the weepers,[60]
    Let them be as if they were not weeping.
    And the happy ones as if they weren't happy.
    And the buyers as if they kept nothing. 31And those
    Who use the world, as if they had no world
    To use. The form[61] of this world is passing away.

Pleasing the lord or enjoying things of the world
  32I want you free from care. An unmarried man
    Cares for things of the lord, 33the married man
    Cares for things of this world, how he can please
    His wife. 34He's of two minds. The unmarried man
    And virgin care for the things of the lord

---

60. Mourners.
61. Or, "fashion."

That they may be holy in body and spirit.
The married woman cares for things of this world
And how to please her husband. 35I say this
For your own profit. I say this not to throw
A noose around your neck[62] but to promote
Good order and firm devotion to the lord.

Virginity and wedlock
    36If a man acts shamefully to his virgin[63]
    And she is beyond her spring days, so be it,
    Let him follow his passions. Let him marry,
    It is no sin. 37If a man stands firm in his heart,
    Mastering his desire and unled by fire,
    And decides in his own heart to keep her
    A virgin, he does well. 38So the man who marries
    Does well. The man who doesn't marry better.

The widow's choice
    39The wife is bound as long as her spouse lives.
    But if the husband sleeps,[64] then she is free
    To marry whom she wants, only in Mashiah.
    40If she stays chaste, I think of her as blessed
    And think myself to have the spirit of God.

Chapter 8

Puffed-up knowledge and idol meat offerings
    Concerning idol offerings, we know
    That all of us have knowledge. Yet knowledge

---

62. Meaning "to restrain."

63. May be translated "girlfriend," but the Greek word is "virgin" from παρθένος (parthenos), meaning "virgin" or "pure."

64. Dies.

Inflates[65] while love builds up.[66] 2If someone thinks
He knows something, he doesn't know it yet
As he should know it. 3Someone who loves God
Is known by God. 4Concerning then the eating
Of idol offerings, we know an idol
Is nothing in the world, and there is no god
But the one God. 5And even if there are
The so-called gods either in heaven or earth
Just as there are many gods and many lords,
6Yet for us there is but one God the father,
From whom all things are and in whom we are,
And our one lord Yeshua the Mashiah

---

65. Or, "constructs." Knowledge "inflates" or, using Old English, "puffs up," from the
Greek φυσιόω (fusiöo), to blow up, puff up, inflate, and by extension, cause arrogance or pride. All these negative connotations of one with knowledge counter Platonism and Gnosticism, which were in the philosophical air of the Greek-speaking
Hellenistic world.

Knowledge from the Greek γνῶσις (gnosis). Even in Paul's day there was more
than a glimmering of Gnostic speculation, which was threatening to and abhorred by
early Christianity (see the articulate denunciations in *Against the Gnostics* by the early
Christian father Iranaeus). Paul, influenced by Greek philosophers, would not have
been attracted by any aspect of this major heresy. Knowledge (gnosis) among the Gnostics was the gift Eve gave the world, but in the Judeo-Christian tradition Eve's defiant
gift of knowledge led to human downfall, the expulsion from Eden, and God's edict of
death. The Gnostics pitted knowledge against faith, faith being, in their mind, a surrender of reason and self-knowledge to the clerical powers. Already in the first century
there were the beginnings of Gnosticism among the Jews (see the "Book of Baruch"
in Willis Barnstone and Marvin Meyer, eds., *The Gnostic Bible*, Boston: Shambhala
Books, 2004), and among the early Christian Jews in the Hellenic and Roman diaspora
(see Simon Magos excoriated in Acts 8.9–24, and later Marcion [died ca. 160]), who
attempted to discard the Hebrew Bible and retain only John among the gospels, John
being the gospel venerated by many Gnostic sects. For an elaborate study of Paul and
the Gnostics, see Elaine Pagels, *Gnostic Paul: Gnostic Exegesis of the Pauline Letters*
(Philadelphia: Trinity Press International, 1994).

66. The KJV captures the beauty of this phrase, saying, "Knowledge puffeth up, but
charity edifieth."

Through whom all things have being, through whom we are.[67]

---

67. In this distinction between father and son, Paul establishes God as the maker in whom we are *and* Jesus as the lord through whom our existence unfolds. In short, God is the creator and his realm of persons and things are governed and determined by his son with whom we have an intimate communication. In verse 6 Paul cites the most sacred line in the Bible, the *shema*: "Hear O Israel, the Lord our God, the Lord is one." In the *shema* God and Lord are one and the same figure, "Lord" being an attribute of God's power just as in the New Testament the Christian messiah and Christ are one, "Christ" being an attribute (the anointed) of the messiah.

The *shema* is the monotheistic cornerstone of the Hebrew Bible, which is Paul's only bible, his letters having not yet been made canonical and the gospels decades away. However, in 1 Corinthians 8.6 Paul speaks of a dual god or two gods, the *father god* "from who all things are for whom we are" and the *son god*, whom he calls *kyrios* (lord), "through whom all things have being" and "through whom we are." While in the *shema* God and the Lord are one divine being, in 1 Corinthians Paul evokes God and the Lord Yeshua as two divine beings. In word and practice these gods have distinct functions in the holy family of God the father and Jesus the son. How is this apparent dualism explained? The monotheistic notion of the emerging movement of Christianity rests on verbal descriptions—notably the trinitarian formula promoted by the Council of Nicene in 325 that Son and Father are equal and of same substance (*homoousios*) but not identical—to justify the notion of a singular godhead in three parts. But the elevation of Yeshua as a discrete figure in God's family has in word and practice given us a deutero-theistic or polytheistic theogony. The new theogony, for all to read and see, contains two divinities, with separate seats in heaven, separate duties, each presumably with human physiognomies since Adam and Eve were created in the image of God. God's face, like his true name, is unknowable and invisible, while the son deity has a name and a face that will be commonly depicted in statue and on walls. One can claim that Christianity remains monotheistic because God is Christ (the messiah) or Christ is God, yet in all verbal and semiotic signs of communication God is not Christ the Messiah, and they are in the New Testament presented in human speech, actions, and reception as two distinct divinities. We have in 1 Corinthians 8.6 three simultaneous assertions: Paul first cites the *shema* to proclaim traditional Jewish monotheism; he then defines the position and functions of the father and son, distinguishing them coherently; and finally he denounces other religions with their visible idols and multiple gods.

Abraham's and Isaiah's predicted messiah will come for the Jews as an anointed *mortal* leader of nations and the salvation of Israel. The same foretold Hebrew Bible messiah is the source and model for the Christian messiah, who has been transfigured into the Christ (meaning "the anointed"), and who is an *immortal* divinity and a powerful filial activist in God's threshold. Shaul, who is originally a Pharisee scholar,

Knowledge, idols, and meat

> 7But there is not this knowledge in all men
> And until now some are used to the idol
> As idol offerings,[68] and so their conscience,
> Being weak, is soiled. 8Food will not bring us to God.
> And if we do not eat, we have not less,
> Yet if again we eat, we have not more.

> 9But see that your freedom does not become
> A stumbling block to the weak. 10If one
> Sees you—one who has knowledge—eating in
> A temple of idols, will not the man
> Of weak conscience be encouraged to eat
> Offerings to the idol? 11So by your knowledge
> The weak believers, for whom the Mashiah
> Died, are destroyed. 12In sinning against brothers
> And in wounding their conscience, which is weak,
> You sin against the Mashiah. 13So if food
> Makes my brother stumble, then I will never
> Eat meat, not to cause a brother to stumble.[69]

---

becomes as Paul the epistler and apostle the father of Christianity. Paul expands the confines of the traditional Torah, giving the European West and later the entire world a new theology based on the Platonic notion of an immortal soul (not in Torah) and a divine leadership under God and his son the messiah. In the letters Paul also gives us moral law, hope, and a profound and fully developed vision of God and the Christ.

68. From the Greek εἰδωλόθυτον (eidolothyton), meaning "offering or sacrifice to an idol," from εἴδωλον (eidolon), idol, and θυτον (thiton), which derives from θύειν (thyein), to sacrifice.

69. Apparently in the market, much of the meat sold came from sacrifices in the temples. Some had "knowledge" of this and did not mind. Paul rebukes those with this arrogant knowledge and even states that he personally will nevermore eat meat in order to prevent his weaker brothers and sisters from its temptation when the source is the temple of idols. Here is an unperceived discourse for promoting vegetarianism.

Chapter 9

Privileges of a messenger

Am I not free? Am I not a messenger?[70]
Have I not seen Yeshua our Mashiah?
Are you not my handiwork in the lord?
2Even though I am not a messenger
To others, at least I am a voice to you.
You are the seal of my message in the lord.

Having a wife and other gains in life

3My defense to those who examine me
Is this: 4Have I no right to eat and drink?[71]
5Do we not have the right to take with us
A sister, a wife like other messengers
And brothers of the lord, and Kefa too?[72]
6Do only Bar Nabba[73] and I have no right
Not to be merely laborers? 7Who serves
Time in the army at his own expense?
Who plants a vineyard and can't eat the fruit?

---

70. Apostle from the Greek ἀπόστολος (apóstolos), means "one who is sent" as in delegate, emissary, missionary, angel, or envoy. English "apostle" has often assumed a reverential and pompous garment, losing its original barefoot humility of one who undertakes a possibly painful and dangerous mission. In modern Greek, an *apostolaki* (a little apostle) retains the original demotic tone of the ancient word, now meaning an errand boy sent out for coffee or the like.

71. Commentators suggest that Paul demands that Barnabas and he, doing God's work, should at least have their meals given to them free in exchange for their ministry.

72. Paul refers to other apostles, including Peter (Kefa), who have wives to accompany them. While Paul is personally given to chastity and self-denial, here he asserts his right to have a wife. If Paul is seen as a model for the clergy not to wed, these lines contradict the obligation of celibacy.

73. Barnabas from the Greek Βαρναβᾶς (Barnabas), from the Aramaic בַּר נְבָא (bar nabba). Barnabas was Joseph, a Levi from Cyprus.

Who herds a flock and cannot eat its milk?[74]
8Do I speak as a man or does the law
Also say this? 9In the law of Moshe[75]
It is written:
    You must not muzzle an ox threshing grain.[76]
Is God concerned only about the oxen
10Or is he not speaking for all of us?
For us it once was written, whoever plows
Must plow in hope. Whoever threshes hopes
To share the crop. 11But if we sow the things
Of spirit, is it too much to hope to reap
A carnal[77] crop from you? 12If others have
This right from you, should we not even more?

My rewards

We have not used our rights, yet suffered all
With the one thought of spreading the good news
Of the Mashiah. 13Don't those who perform
The temple services eat temple foods,
Or who attend the altar eat altar shares?
14The lord instructs those preaching the good news[78]
To live from the good news. 15I have not used
Any of these privileges. I did not write
These things for my own gain. I'd rather die
Than let someone assume my pride as gone.
I have my obligations. 16When I preach
The good news I have good grounds to boast,

---

74. The Greek uses "eat" rather than "drink."

75. Moses from the Greek Μωϋσῆς (Moses), from the Hebrew מֹשֶׁה (moshe).

76. Deut. 25.4.

77. Material.

78. Often translated "gospel," rather than "good news." εὐαγγέλιον (evangelion) means both "good news" and, by extension, "gospel." It is not used to mean a canonical gospel, since the canonicals were composed after Paul's death.

And what misery if I do not preach!
17So when I do it willingly, I know reward,
But if I cannot do it with good will—
And I have been entrusted with this duty—
18What's my reward? I preach the good news free
In order not to flaunt my gospel rights.

Freedom in slavery
19From all men I am free and made myself
A slave to all, and so gain more from them.
20To Jews I've been a Jew that I may win
The Jews. To those who are under the law
(Though I am not under the law myself)
I'm like one under the law that I may gain them.
21For those outside the law79 I am like one
Outside the law, yet not outside the law
Of God but with the law of the Mashiah
That I may gain the ones outside the law.
22To the weak I was the weak to win the weak.80
To all men I became all things to save
A few of them. 23I do it for the good news
And so that I might also share its blessing.

Winning the true race
24Do you not know that of those who compete
As runners in the stadium81 they all run
But only one wins the prize. Run to win.
25All who compete train hard so they might win
A perishable wreath, but we are after

---

79. Gentiles under Roman law. Paul distinguishes between Torah law of the Jews, which he uses as his source and then modifies for purposes of his good news mission, and Roman law, which the gentiles follow.

80. The new Messianists whose conscience might be weak.

81. Corinth was the site of the Isthmian games, which were second in importance only to the Olympic games. In ancient times the prize was a wreath, a perishable token.

The imperishable. 26And I do not race
Without a goal. I box[82] but not as one
Beating the air. 27I batter my own body,
To make a slave of it so when I preach
To others I will not be called unfit.

Chapter 10

Moshe below a cloud and in the sea
    I do not wish for you, brothers, not to know
    That our fathers all went below the cloud
2And all passed through the sea, and all were dipped
    Into Moshe in the cloud and in the sea,[83]
3And all ate the same spiritual food, and drank,
4Drinking from the same spiritual rock that went
    Beside them, and the rock was the Mashiah.

---

82. The reader may be surprised to discover that Paul, ferocious in his beliefs, was also a boxer in his efforts to be physically fit. Boxing was an early Olympian Greek sport. His discourse on stadium racing and boxing is a rare moment that takes us away in metaphor from the beautiful but grim majesty of his usual letter. Paul was not alone as a sportsman among the great philosophical thinkers. As a young man, Plato was a wrestler and gained the name *Plato*, meaning "broad," because he was a broad-shouldered wrestler. Not only athletics were popular during Greek antiquity, but also the games, played each year at a different site including Olympia and Corinth, served as a unifying force for peace. Sports continued until the early Roman Christian emperor Flavius Theodosius (379–395) banned the Olympics in 391 as bodily indulgence. In his campaign to destroy classical Pagan Greco-Roman civilization, Theodosius decreed the destruction of Greek and Roman temples and cultural centers in 392, including the massive Serapeum museum complex in Alexandria, which contained the great Alexandrian library.

83. The cloud and sea of the lord in Exodus 13.21: "And the LORD went before them by day in a pillar of a cloud, to lead them the way" (KJV). And from the passage through the Red (Reed) Sea in Exodus 14.22: "And the children of Israel went into the midst of the sea upon the dry *ground*: and the waters *were* a wall unto them on their right hand, and on their left." Also in Exodus 16.4–35, 17.6, and Numbers 20.7–11.

5But God was not happy with most of them,
And they died scattered in the wilderness.
6These things took place, an example for us:
Not to long for the bad as they longed for
The bad. 7You should not be idolaters[84]

---

84. Exod. 32.1–9. Reference is to the golden calf, probably representing the Egyptian bullgod Apis. Moses's brother Aaron had the wives, sons, and daughters remove their gold earrings to have them melted and with wood to build a golden calf. The next morning the people made food offerings and indulged in sexual revelry and orgies, bringing God's wrath upon them for breaking the second commandment. But in return for obedience to his commandment, God transferred the covenant, originally given to Abraham, to Moses, and promised to make his people into a great nation. It may be observed that sons, too, wore gold earrings in biblical times.

The revelry of these Jews in the desert is described with moral censure. It is relevant to see a similar celebration through approving eyes in the competing classical Greek culture. In an ecstatic religious poem to Aphrodite, Sappho (seventh to sixth century B.C.E.) conveys the beauty of young women dancing before their god in Minoan Crete:

Afroditi of the Flowers at Knossos

Leave Kriti and come here to this holy
temple with your graceful grove
of apple trees and altars smoking
    with frankincense.

Icy water babbles through apple branches
and roses leave shadow on the ground
and bright shaking leaves pour down
    profound sleep.

Here is a meadow where horses graze
amid wild blossoms of the spring and soft winds
    blow aroma

of honey. Afroditi, take the nectar
and delicately pour it into gold
wine cups and mingle joy with
    our celebration.

The Complete Poems of Sappho, trans. Willis Barnstone (Boston: Shambhala Books, 2009), 5.

Like some of them. As written in Exodus:
The people sat down to eat and drink
And they stood up to play in sexual revelry.[85]
8Let us not fornicate as some of them
Fornicated and twenty-three thousand fell.[86]
9Let us not test the Mashiah as some did
And be destroyed by snakes. 10And do not grumble
As some did and be destroyed by the destroyer.[87]

Temptations and eating at the lord's table
11Now things took place as lessons for the others
But they were written down to instruct us
For whom the ending of the age has come.
12You who are standing, watch out, you may fall.
13It's just human temptation seizing you.
God is faithful and will not let you be tempted
Beyond your powers, but with the trial you'll have
A way out through your fervor to endure.

14So my loves, flee idolatry.[88] 15I speak

---

85. Exod. 32.4, 32.6, 32.19.

86. See note 86 below.

87. Others translate "destroyer" as "the angel of death" or "the destroying angel," based on other texts. Paul joins the three incidents of grumbling against Moses and Aaron in Numbers 16.41, the angel of death in Exodus 12.23, and the plague in which 24,000 died (Num. 25.9) as punishment for Israel's joining with the Baal of Peor, worshiping its god and engaging in sexual depravity with "prostitute virgins" who worshiped the God. Paul sets the number at 23,000.

88. There is an allegorical parallel between the temptations of Baal in the desert, but Paul's remarks are especially addressed to gentiles and their Greek and Roman gods, and all practices of pagan worship, including food offerings to statues, that might linger in their memory. There should be no suppers comparable to the lord's Passover supper, and the symbolism and rites of that supper, the wine for the blood of the Messiah, the bread for participation in the body of the Messiah, must not be confused with empty sacrifices to demons. One cannot be both Messianist and pagan is the message.

To thoughtful men. Judge what I say. 16The cup
Of blessing that we bless, is it not communion
In the blood of the Mashiah. The bread
We break, is it not communion in the body
Of the Mashiah? 17Because there is one bread,
We many are one body, and we all
Partake of the one bread. 18Look at Yisrael[89]
And of the flesh. Are those who eat a food
Of sacrifice not partners at the altar?[90]
19What am I saying? That what's sacrificed
To idols means something? That the idol
Means something? 20No. What gentiles sacrifice,
They sacrifice to demons but not to God.
I would not have you partners with the demons.
21You cannot drink from the cup of the lord
And from the cup of demons. You can't eat
At the lord's table and the demons' table.
22Can we provoke the lord to jealousy?
In no way are we more powerful than he.

Do good

23All things are lawful, but not all things are
Beneficial. And all things may be lawful
But do not edify.[91] 24Do not look for
Your own welfare but seek another's good.

Do not offend but freely work for the good

25Eat anything sold in a low meat market
And do not discriminate out of conscience.
26The earth and its fullness is of the lord.
27If an unbeliever asks you to a meal
And you care to go, eat everything set

---

89. Israel from the Greek Ἰσραήλ (Israel), from the Hebrew יִשְׂרָאֵל (yisrael).
90. Reference is to Jews at the altar (Lev. 7.6, 7.15).
91. Literally, "build up."

Before you, and do not discriminate
Out of conscience. 28Yet if someone tells you:
This is sacrificial meat, do not eat
Out of consideration for the man
Who told you and for your conscience. 29Not yours,
I say to you, but for the other's conscience.
Why should my freedom yield to judgment of
Another's conscience? 30If I eat in grace,
Why should I be blasphemed for what I do
With thankfulness? 31Whether you eat or drink,
Or whatever you do, do it for the glory
Of God. 32Do not offend the Jews or Greeks[92]
Or synagogue of God. 33Just as I seek
To please all people in all ways, I don't
Look out for me but just to save the many.

Chapter 11

Imitate me

Imitate me since I'm of the Mashiah.[93]

Women and head coverings

2Now I praise you since you remember me
In all things and you conserve the traditions
As I delivered them to you. 3I want
You now to know the head of every man
Is the Mashiah, and the head of a woman
Is her husband.[94] The head of the Mashiah

---

92. "Jews" refers to the other Jews who do not accept Jesus as their messiah; "Greeks" refers to gentiles.

93. Here Paul clearly establishes his place in the holy hierarchy of command among the Messianists. After the messiah, Paul, who is *of* the messiah, is to be imitated and followed.

94. In this significant phrase Paul defines the relation of husband to wife: the man is the head. He will here and elsewhere elaborate.

Is God.[95] 4Any who pray or prophesy
With his head covered disgraces his head,[96]
5But any woman who prays or prophesies
With her head uncovered[97] brings shame to her head.
It is as bad as if her head were shaved.
6If a woman's uncovered, let her be shorn!
But if it is hideous, disgraceful, for a woman
To be shorn and shaved, let her remain covered.

7Indeed, a man should not cover his head,
Since he is the semblance and glory of God,
But the woman is man's glory. 8Man comes
Not from woman, but a woman from man.
9Man was not created for the sake of woman,

---

95. In parallel speech, as believers submit to Paul as their head, Paul submits to the messiah as the head, and the messiah submits to God as the head.

96. Paul reverses the biblical command, followed by Jews and Muslims. After the fifth century the clerical hierarchy of the Catholic Church wore the Jewish skull-cap, that is, the kippah, from the Hebrew כִּפָּה (kippah). In later Yiddish (medieval Alsatian German) the kippah is called the yarmulke. Today the Pope wears a white kippah.

97. The Greek ἀκατακάλυπτος (akatakályptos), meaning "uncovered" or "without head covering," which the KJV gives, is rendered in many versions as "unveiled." The older meaning of "veiled" suggests a cloth worn over a woman's head, face, and shoulders, but the common meaning today of veil is a cloth or netting to shield only the face, which could not have been Paul's intended meaning. He is contrasting the woman whose head must be covered, with the man whose head must *not* be covered (11.4). The more general meaning of the head covering is to give freedom to the man and to confine the woman to modest subservience. It is said that a woman exposing her hair in public reveals loose general morals and promiscuity.

In the next lines Paul develops the intense differences in station between man and woman, husband and wife, by the exposure or revelation of hair. He tells us that a man needs no cover since he is "the semblance . . . of God," but a woman needs cover because she is the semblance of man. Paul pushes the parallel metaphor too far, since if the woman is indeed the semblance of man (even as a small reflection), she is a semblance of an *uncovered* man and so she too should necessarily be uncovered.

But woman for the sake of man.[98] 10So woman
Should have a sign of authority on her head
Because of the angels.[99] 11Yet in the lord
A woman is not without man, nor man
Without woman.[100] 12Yet just as a woman
Is of the man, the man is through the woman,[101]
And all things are of God. 13Judge for yourselves.
Is it proper for a woman to pray
To God if her head remains uncovered?

Propriety of long hair and short hair
14But does nature herself not inform you:
If a man has long hair, it's a disgrace,
15But if a woman wears long hair, to her
It is her glory? To a woman, her long hair
Is given her for her own covering.[102]
16But if anyone cares to be contentious,
We and God's churches have no such custom.

---

98. The basis for Paul's assertion is that man was created before woman in both creation stories, in Genesis 1.27 and 2.7. The notion that woman was created "for the sake of man" has been a sore point emphasizing Paul's less-than-amenable position concerning the position of women, which is always subservient to men.

99. Many explanations are proposed for why the woman should have a covering "because of the angels": whether the angels are messengers of a divine order in which the woman's covering reveals respect (or its absence disrespect), or whether the angels represent a cosmic demonic power against whom her covering serves as a protection. These speculations are not convincing and the meaning of "angels" remains a mystery.

100. "without" may suggest "independent from."

101. A woman gives birth to a man.

102. Paul now acknowledges that women have a natural covering, which should imply that they need no head covering. Then, catching the trap into which his metaphors have led him, he states succinctly that if anyone wishes to take up a "contentious" line of reasoning, neither he and his group nor the synagogues of God have the custom of permitting women to go bare-headed.

Behavior in the temple at the Lord's supper

17In these instructions I cannot praise you.
When you have meetings, it is not for better
But for the worse. 18I hear there are dissensions
Among you when you meet, and this in part
I do believe. 19There must be factions. Else
How will one of you prove to be the true one?
20Yet when you meet it's not to eat the Lord's
Supper, 21but each one grabs his supper first,
And one man is hungry and another drunk.
22Don't you have your homes to eat and drink in?
Or do you hate the synagogue of God?
Or do you want to put the poor to shame?
What can I say to you? Praise you? I can't.

23I received from the lord what I pass on
To you. The lord Yeshua on the night
He was betrayed took bread.[103] 24When he gave thanks
And broke the bread, he said:
This is my body, which is for you.
Do this in remembrance of me.
25In the same way after the supper he took
The cup, saying:
This cup is the new covenant in my blood.[104]

---

103. In this rare reference to the life of Yeshua, Paul writes about the last seder of Yeshua with his students (disciples). He mentions a betrayal, but no name, and no mention that it came from within the ranks of his own followers. The assignment to Judas does not appear until the gospels, and increases in ferocity and disgust as the story works its way, a decade at a time, through the gospels from Mark to John. It remains strange to find this crucial passage on Yeshua's life and imminent death inserted, with no follow-up here or later, between comments on women's attire and hair length and eating and drinking habits at the table. The seder passage has the usual characteristics of emendations, its meaning out of place, with little connection to what precedes and follows it.

104. The new covenant of the blood recalls the older Mosaic covenant of the blood, (Exod. 24.8).

> As often as you drink
>   Do this in remembrance of me.
> 26As often as you eat this bread and drink
>   The cup of the lord, you proclaim the death
>   Of the lord till the day of his return.

Examine yourself before eating
> 27Whoever eats the bread or drinks the cup
>   Of the lord unworthily will be guilty
>   Of the body and the blood of the lord.
> 28Let a man examine himself. Only then
>   Let him eat from the bread, drink from the cup.
> 29Whoever eats and drinks without discerning
>   The body, eats and drinks his own damnation.
> 30Because of this many of you are weak
>   And a good many have fallen asleep.[105]
> 31If we judged ourselves we would not be judged;
> 32But judged by the lord, we are disciplined
>   So as not to be condemned in the world.
> 33My brothers, when you assemble to eat,
>   Wait for each other. 34And if you are hungry,
>   Eat in your home so you will not be damned.

> Of other things I'll right them when I come.

Chapter 12

Power of the holy spirit
> Concerning matters of the spirit, brothers,
> I do not want you ignorant. 2You know

---

105. Died.

When you were gentiles[106] you were led away
By dumb idols. 3I make it known to you
That no one speaking in the spirit of God
Says: "Yeshua is anathema!"[107] and no one
Can say lord Yeshua except the holy spirit.

Spiritual gifts

4There are diversities of gifts but one
Same spirit. 5And there are
Diversities
Of services[108] and one same lord. 6There are
Diversities of activities—and the same God
Activating all things in everyone.
7But the manifestation of the spirit
Is given to each one so as to gain
From it the good. 8And through the spirit one
Is given a word of wisdom, 9to another
A word of knowledge through the same spirit,
And to another faith by the same spirit,
10And to another workings of the miracles,
And to another prophecy and power
To discern spirits, to another speaking
In diverse tongues, to another interpret
The tongues. 11All these are driven by one

---

106. Instead of "gentiles," most other versions give "pagans" or "heathens," depending on what level of depreciation is desired for the nonbelievers. The KJV has "Gentiles," which is a neutral word for nonbelievers. "Gentile" will eventually move from its original meaning of "non-Jew" in Paul and the gospels to signify "Christian" in English and other languages.

"Gentile" (usually lowercase) comes from the Greek ἐθνικός (ethnikos), meaning a "national" or "ethnic," and sometimes, as here, from ἔθνος (ethnos), meaning "a nation." In this instance Paul does have a measure of scorn for the gentiles, who were beguiled into worshiping dumb idols, but he does not express the scorn in the epithet *ethnos* but rather in idol worship that these nonbelievers indulged in.

107. Others say "curse." The religious imprecation is conveyed more fully in "anathema," which also lets the Greek ἀνάθεμα (anathema) cry out in English, which in more than two millennia has not changed spelling, pronunciation, or meaning.

108. Or, "ministries."

And the same spirit, giving them separately,
One by one, and to each one as he wills.

Many parts of one body
12Just as the body is one with many parts,
All members of the body, although many,
Are one body. Likewise is the Mashiah.
13So in one spirit all of us were dipped[109]
Into one body, whether we're Jews or Greeks,
Whether slave or free, and we were all given
One spirit to drink. 14For one body is not
One member but many. 15If the foot says:
"Since I am not a hand, I am not part
Of the body," the hand would not be less
Of the body for that. 16If the ear says:
"Since I am not an eye, I am not part
Of the body," the ear would not be less
Of the body for that. 17If all the body
Were just one eye, then where would hearing be?
If all were hearing, where would smelling be?
18Now God has set the parts, each of them in
The body as he willed it. 19If all were
One member, then where would the body be?
20Now there are many members and one body.
21The eye can't tell the hand, "I don't need you."
The head can't tell the feet, "I don't need you."
22Rather, parts of the body seeming feeble
Are its most necessary members. 23Parts
Of the body we esteem of little honor
We dress with great regard. Our shameful parts
Have the most prominence. 24Our lovely parts
Need nothing from us. God arranged the members
Of the body, giving the inferior parts honor,
25So there be no dissensions in the body
And one part care for every other part.

---

109. Baptized.

26And if one member suffers, all suffer
   With it. And if one member comes on honor,
   All members join as one in happiness.

You are the Mashiah's body in your diverse appointments
   27Now you are the body of the Mashiah
   And its members individually.
   28God has appointed first the messengers,[110]
   Second the prophets, third the teachers, then
   Those with miraculous powers, gifts of healing,
   Then helpers, leaders, and varieties
   Of tongues. 29Can all of us be messengers?
   Surely not. Can all be prophets? All be teachers?
   Are all workers of miracles? 30Not all
   Have gifts of healing. Can they speak in tongues?
   Surely not everyone is an interpreter?
   31But you long earnestly for greater gifts.
   Hence I will show you a more sterling way.

Chapter 13

Of love
   If I speak in the tongue of men and angels
   But have no love, I am but sounding brass
   Or a clanging cymbal. 2If I have prophecy
   And understand all mysteries and all knowledge
   And if I have all faith to remove mountains
   But love I do not have, then I am nothing.
   3If I give all my goods to feed the poor
   And give my body to be burned, and love
   I do not have, in all I have gained nothing.

   4Love suffers long and love is kind. Love has
   No jealousy and cannot boast and has

---

110. Apostles or missionaries.

No pride. 5Love isn't crude and doesn't seek
Things for itself, is not provoked to anger,
Nor counts up wrongs. 6Not gloating in misdeeds,
Its happiness is truth. 7Love bears all things,
Believes all things; it hopes and it endures.

8Love never falls.¹¹¹ Yet prophecies will cease
And tongues turn dumb and knowledge also vanish.
9We know only in part, we prophesy
Only in part, 10yet when perfection comes,¹¹²
Then what is but a part will disappear.

11When I was a child I spoke like a child,
I thought like a child and reasoned like a child.
When I became a man I put an end
To childish things. 12For now we look into
An enigmatic mirror.¹¹³ One day we will gaze
Face to face.¹¹⁴ Now I know in part, but then
I will know in full even as I am fully
Known. 13Now faith, hope, and love remain,
These three. Of these the greatest one is love.

Chapter 14

Prophecies and speaking in tongues
Pursue love and aspire to things spiritual,
And especially so you may prophesy.
2For one who speaks in tongues, speaks not to men

---

111. Or more freely, "fails."

112. "Perfection" may signify the completion of the circle of life, salvation, or any ultimate transcendence. The meaning is deciphered diversely and remains uncertain, which is one of its strengths.

113. See the introduction to 1 Corinthians for comment on "glass, darkly."

114. Presumably looking at the face of God.

But God, since no one hears him.[115] And he speaks

---

115. No one understands. Speaking in tongues is from the Greek γλῶσσα (glossa), meaning "tongue."

There are diverse views as to what Paul means when referring to those who speak in tongues, and what speaking in tongues signifies in religious experience.

Paul has, at best, qualified sympathy for the mystery of the tongues. In his diatribe (argument), he first suggests with irony that these broken utterances may be heavenly speech that only God comprehends (14.2). Then he withdraws this divine excuse to contrast one who prophesies and edifies others with one who speaks in tongues and edifies only himself (14.4). Subsequently, Paul ruminates on more general notions of language, including which tongues one should use for enlightening gentiles in the temple.

A more universal notion of the phenomenon of speaking in tongues is its relation to religious ecstasy, that is, to the experience of being outside of or apart from oneself. In this sense "tongues" is parallel to the loss of intelligible speech and babbling that in many religions is embodied in instants of ecstasy. Then, ordinary speech, as ordinary time, body, and mind, is lost and left behind. During these manifestations of otherness, one speaks nonsense as a sign of saying the ineffable, of what cannot be uttered in human speech but which a divine power may understand.

So in the sixteenth century, the Spanish mystic Saint John of the Cross (1542–1591), in his main poem "The Spiritual Canticle" based on the biblical Song of Songs, is left knowing nothing, stuttering and babbling: *balbuciendo*. Similarly, in other religions of ecstasy and detachment from earthly mind, body, and time, the old Quakers quaked, the Shakers shook, Dirvishes whirled, and some Holy Rollers still roll and speak in tongues.

Another view is that Paul is referring to the conflict between high learned speech and vernacular. In many houses of worship, then and now, there is a schism between the language of the holy books and the clerical caste that reads and interprets them. In Islam the Qur'an cannot be translated. Therefore in Afghanistan, Iran, Pakistan, Indonesia, and most parts of Muslim Africa, the ordinary and educated people cannot understand the Qur'an unless they are fluent in classical Arabic. In Greece the Koine biblical Greek is understood with moderate difficulty by parishioners. In most Catholic countries until recently, the Latin service was opaque, and in most synagogues the Hebrew Bible is read, but few, except among the orthodox sects, understand.

In Paul's day there was only one source of holy scripture among the Christian Jews, and that was the Hebrew Bible. After the sixth-century B.C.E. Babylonian captivity, Aramaic, rather than Hebrew, was the language spoken by the Jews who returned to Israel; Hebrew was the language only of the temple, that is, of prayer and the reading of Torah. Paul, as one who knew the Hebrew Bible intimately (though many of his references were, as we have them, to the Septuagint Greek translation

Mysteries. 3But one who prophesies to people
Speaks edification and exhortation
And consolation. 4One who speaks in tongues
Edifies himself; one who prophesies
Edifies the synagogue. 5Now I wish
All of you to speak in tongues, but still more
For you to prophesy. Greater is one
Who prophesies than one who speaks in tongues
Unless he translates to edify the temple.

6Now, brothers, if I come speaking to you
In tongues, what possible good am I to you
If I don't speak in revelation, prophecy,
Teaching, or understanding? 7In like ways

---

of the Hebrew Bible), would have had no difficulty in understanding readings from Torah in the Messianist synagogues. But to the many gentile converts, Hebrew would have been an unheard, unknown language—as someone speaking in tongues. Paul may have been principally opposed to ecstatic utterance of speech only to oneself. However, what language to use in the church—Hebrew, Aramaic, Greek, Latin, or some other gentile speech—was a question in Paul's time, as it was for centuries among the early Christians, where the church language was not understood by the laity. Constantine the Great, though he was the first Christian Roman emperor in Greek-speaking Byzantium, could not speak Greek or read the Greek holy scriptures. The speaking and reading out loud in not-understood tongues later fueled the Protestant Reformation, which consequently replaced the Latin Vulgate with new translations and interpretations in national vernaculars.

It is not known whether the references in Acts and 1 Corinthians are to the tongues of foreigners or to the oral tongue of holy scripture, meaning Hebrew. In the mixed synagogues of Messianic Jews and Messianic gentiles, the question was intense, and conversion depended on communication, on not alienating outsiders with insider tongues. The tension was between demotic Greek and classical Greek (for some written texts), demotic Greek or Aramaic in speech, and readings from Hebrew texts or its translations into Greek and Latin.

Whatever the signification of "in tongues," whether it be the utterance of a real foreign tongue, an ecstatic utterance when worldly speech is lost, or an ecstatic utterance when a heavenly speech is found (between speaker and God), Babel, with its diverse interpreters and dictionaries, still commands the condition of world speech.

Even lifeless things have sounds, whether a flute
Or harp. If they don't have a distinct note,
How will you know what is played on the flute
Or on the harp? 8Or if a ram's horn[116] blasts
An unclear call, who will prepare for battle?

9So too with you, if you speak in a tongue
Which is not intelligible, how can one
Comprehend what is said? You will be talking
To the air. 10Yes there are so many tongues
In the world. Not a one is without sound.
11If I don't know the meaning of a voice,
I will be a barbarian to the speaker,
And the speaker a barbarian to me.
12Thus if you are also zealots of the spirit,
Be zealous and edify the synagogue.

Translate for the spirit

13Let him speaking in tongues pray to translate.[117]
14If I pray in tongues, my spirit prays, my mind
Is nothing. 15What then? I will pray with spirit
But I will also pray with my own mind.
I will sing[118] with my spirit but also sing
With my mind. 16If you praise only in spirit,
How can an uninitiate add amain[119]

---

116. Ram's horn or shofar from Greek σάλπιγξ (salpinks), usually translated "trumpet," but is the ceremonial shofar from the Hebrew שׁוֹפָר (shofar). The shofar is actually a ram's horn from the Hebrew קֶרֶן הַיּוֹבֵל (keren hayovel), referring to the ancient battle of Joshua at Jericho when the rams' horns were blown (Joshua 6.4, 6.9). The gentile Greeks would hear an equivalent battle signal in Homer (*Iliad* 18.219).

117. Or, "interpret." The meaning of "translation" or "interpreting" is not an interpretive explanation but a direct translation of intended meaning.

118. Or, "sing psalms."

119. Amen from the Greek ἀμήν (amen), from the Hebrew אָמֵן (amein).

To your thanksgiving when he cannot know
What you are saying? 17You may give good thanks,
But the other man is not edified.
18I thank God that I speak in tongues—and more
Than all of you,[120] 19but in the synagogue
I would rather say five words with my mind
To teach you than ten thousand words in tongues.

Power of prophecy

20Brothers, don't be like children in your minds,
But to the bad be childlike and in thought
Grown up. 21In Torah Yeshayahu writes:
In other tongues and the lips of others
I will speak to this people
Yet even then they will not listen to me,[121]
Says Adonai.[122]
22So the tongues[123] are a sign
Not for believers but for unbelievers
While prophecy is not for unbelievers
But for believers. 23So if the whole temple
Comes together and you are speaking in tongues

---

120. A reference not only to Paul's spiritual tongues but also to his actual knowledge of probably at least Greek, Latin, Aramaic, and Hebrew.

121. Isa. 28.11–12.

122. The lord in Hebrew. Lord or Adonai from Greek κύριος (kyrios). When referring to the divine lord, Greek *kyrios* may be translated "lord" or "Adonai" from the Hebrew אֲדֹנָי (adonai) as here in the Hebrew text cited from Isaiah; when referring to Jesus, *kyrios* may be translated as "rabbi," "sir," "master," or "teacher," when the implicit Hebrew source is רַבִּי (rabbi). Frequently, the Greek gives ῥαββί (rabbi) as in Mark 11.21: "And Peter says to him, Rabbi, look! The fig tree you cursed has dried up" (ὁ Πέτρος λέγει αὐτῷ· ῥαββί, ἴδε ἡ συκῆ ἣν κατηράσω ἐξήρανται). Greek *Rabbi* is normally translated in older versions of the New Testament English as "Lord" or "Master" to conceal the fact that Peter is addressing Jesus as his rabbi. The KJV renders this passage, "Master, behold, the fig tree which thou cursedst is withered away."

123. Speaking in tongues.

And the unlearned[124] or unbelievers enter,
Will they not say that all of you are mad?

24But if all prophecy floats in the air
And an unbeliever or an unlearned
Comes in, he is examined and he is judged
By everyone. 25Hidden things of the heart
Are laid open. And he flings himself
Down on his face and he will worship God,
Declaring: "Yes, God is now among you!"

After songs, prophecy, and revelation, silence
26What then, my brothers? When you meet, you each
Have a psalm of praise, lesson, a revelation,
And tongues and a translation. Let all be
Edification. 27If anyone speaks
In tongues, let there be two, or three at most,
And taking turns with someone to translate.
28But if there is none to translate, be silent
In the synagogue, and speak to yourself
And to God. 29And let two or three speak
As prophets while the rest sit and pass judgment.
30If a revelation comes to someone else
Sitting there, let the first speaker be silent.
31You can all prophesy, one by one, so
That all may learn, with everyone encouraged.
32The spirits of the prophets are controlled
By prophets. 33God is not confusion but peace.[125]

---

124. Unlearned from the Greek ἰδιώτης (idiótes). The notion of uninstructed, private, and unskilled remains, but "idiots" is too strong. The word *idiótes* comes from the Greek ἴδιος (idios), meaning "one's own," as in English "idiolect," one's own language.

125. In other ancient texts, the second part of verse 33 begins verse 34.

Women must be silent at meetings

    As in the other synagogues of saints,

34Women must be silent in the synagogues.

    They do not have the right to speak. Let them

    Submit as Torah law dictates.[126] 35And should

    They wish to learn something, then let them ask

    Their own husbands at home. It is disgraceful

    For a woman to talk in the synagogue.

To prophecy hear my commandments from the lord

    36Did the word of God originate in you?

    Or did it come from you alone? 37If someone

    Claims that he is prophet or a charismatic,[127]

    Let him perceive that things I write to you

    Are a commandment of the lord. 38Anyone

    Who disregards it will be disregarded.

39And so, brothers, eagerly prophesy

    And be not opposed to speaking in tongues

40But do it all properly and in order.

Chapter 15

Good news of the Mashiah

    Brothers, I remind you of the good news,

    Which I have preached to you and you received

    In which you stand, 2and by which you are saved

---

126. For other restrictions on women, see note 96 on 11.5–6. Paul evokes the law, meaning Torah law of the Hebrew Bible rather than Roman law. It is not clear whether he has a specific verse in mind or whether there is one for his purpose. Normally, when Paul wants to alter a habitual practice or interpretation of law, such as the laws on circumcision, Sabbath, marriage, and divorce, he refers to Deuteronomy or Exodus in Torah. Here he does not do so. Most commonly, without reference to Torah, he proposes his own moral code for the emerging Jesus movement with respect to marriage, homosexuality, and deportment in the temple.

127. Or, "spiritual man."

If you hold fast, unless your belief was flawed
With frivolity. 3To you I handed on,
Of supreme range, the news that I received:
The Mashiah died for our sins, as it's said
In Yeshayahu,[128] 4ānd he was buried and rose

---

128. Isa. 53.5. Paul says in 15.3–4 that the Mashiah died for our sins "in accordance with the scripture." As elsewhere, the scriptural reference, where possible, is identified and included in the verse, rather than only in marginalia or footnotes, so the reader may understand the source text that Paul had in mind. Here instead of the common "as it is written," he says more fully, "according to the scripture." The scripture, from the Greek γραφή (grafe), which he refers to, is the Hebrew Bible, not the gospels, since the gospels were not composed during his lifetime.

The Pauline portrait of the messiah and the gospel's messiah differ. In the gospels, Christ as Messiah appears most often identified as a descendent from the royal house of King David who, in the eschatological tradition of early Torah, will in the last days of the rule of Israel, or the last days of the world, arise and save Israel and the world. By contrast, in the undisputed letters, Paul focuses on the messiah as prophet, on his humiliation, suffering, and death for our sins, and on hope revealed through his resurrection. Paul sees confirmation of the messiah in Isaiah's verses on the "servant of God," who in Paul and in writings by later Christian theologians is received as Isaiah's prophecy of the messiah. Isaiah has four "servant" songs—42.1–9, 49.1–6, 50.4–11, 52.13–15—and the magnificent 53.1–12. Isaiah's description of the servant remarkably mirrors Paul's suffering messiah who dies for human transgressions. The humiliation, imprisonment, the metaphor of the innocent lamb, his death, all seem to be a passionate model for the gospel drama:

Surely he hath borne our griefs, and carried our sorrows: yet we did esteem him stricken, smitten of God, and afflicted. But he *was* wounded for our transgressions, *he was* bruised for our iniquities: the chastisement of our peace *was* upon him; and with his stripes we are healed.

All we like sheep have gone astray; we have turned every one to his own way; and the LORD hath laid on him the iniquity of us all. He was oppressed, and he was afflicted, yet he opened not his mouth: he is brought as a lamb to the slaughter, and as a sheep before her shearers is dumb, so he openeth not his mouth. He was taken from prison and from judgment: and who shall declare his generation? for he was cut off out of the land of the living: for the transgression of my people was he stricken. And he made his grave with the wicked, and with the rich in his death; because he had done no violence, neither *was any* deceit in his mouth. (Isa. 53.4–9, KJV)

And in verse 53.12, Isaiah sums up the Passion scene: "He poured out his life onto death."

On the third day, as said in Yeshayahu,[129]
5And seen by Kefa,[130] and then by the twelve.[131]

Witnessing the Mashiah
6Later he was seen by more than five hundred
Brothers at once,[132] of whom most of them

---

129. In verse 15.4, Paul again cites biblical scripture to prove the messiah's resurrection, saying "he was buried and rose on the third day, as said in Yeshayahu." The reference in Isaiah most often given is splendid verse 53.11: "After the sufferings of the soul he will see light." "To see light" can mean many things. There is nothing inherent in the phrase to confirm or deny resurrection and immortality. Other references in Psalms, of less persuasion, are also cited. Psalm 16.10 has "For thou wilt not leave my soul in hell; neither wilt thou suffer thine Holy One to see corruption" (KJV). In the psalm the "Holy One" is David, and by modeling Jesus the Messiah after King David, he also will not see corruption and hence be immortal. It is known that holy men, and particularly saints in the Christian tradition, do not decay after death. When the body of Saint John of the Cross was dug up many months after his burial, there was no smell of decay, only a sweet perfume, which was deemed one of the proofs of his sainthood. The absence of decay may prove Christian saints and biblical kings; however, in a line concerning David's death, the absence of decay proves neither that there was nor that there was not a resurrection. This verse concerning decay is not compelling biblical evidence for the resurrection of the soul.

With respect to "on the third day," there is no apparent source in Isaiah or other Hebrew Bible texts for resurrection on the third day. Jesus predicts his death and rise to life on the third day in Matthew 16.21 and elsewhere in the gospels, but Matthew, Luke, and John, where the third day references appear, were not available to Paul. As for other scriptures or written texts that Paul might have seen, none related to the gospel stories have survived in Hebrew, Aramaic, or Greek. To fill this gap of textual sources, some speak of possible Aramaic or Greek oral witness accounts from which the crucifixion and resurrection narration might have reached Paul. The Gnostic Gospel of Thomas, containing 114 wisdom sayings by Jesus, may have been contemporary with Paul, but Thomas has no narration. It survives in later Coptic translation from the Greek. See in Afterword "The Gospels' Unknown Sources" in "On Authorship and Absence of Sources."

130. Peter.

131. The twelve messengers (apostles), or eleven, if Judas is considered gone and not replaced.

132. Most commentators say Paul came up with this larger number to help bolster the faith by the Corinthians in the resurrection of the Messiah.

Are still alive, but some have gone to sleep.[133]
7And then he was seen by Yaakov[134] and all
The messengers. 8And last of all he was seen
By me who was an aborted child.[135] 9I am
The least of messengers, and am unfit
To be acclaimed a messenger[136] because
I persecuted the temple of God.

10By the grace of God I am what I am.
His gift of grace to me was not in vain.
I worked harder than all of them together,
No, not I, but the grace of God with me.
11And whether it was I or other ones
We preached our messages and you believed.

Bodies raised from the dead

12Now if it is preached that the Mashiah
Has been raised from the dead, how can someone
Among you say there is no resurrection
Of the dead? 13And if the dead are not raised,
There is no resurrection of Mashiah.
14And if Mashiah was not raised, your preaching
Is empty and your faith is empty too.
15We are found out as hollow witnesses
Of God because we testified of God

---

133. Have died.

134. The reference to James (Yaakov) is made after that to the twelve and so it seems not to be to James of the twelve apostles, but to James, Jesus's brother, who was said not to believe in him before the resurrection.

135. Also a miscarriage or untimely birth from the Greek ἔκτρωμα (éktroma), meaning, usually in a pejorative sense, "an abortion."

136. Paul is here defensively modest about declaring himself one of the apostles, since he was not of the original twelve, nor did he know Jesus in the flesh during his years in Jerusalem.

That he raised the Mashiah whom he did
Not raise if it is true the dead are not raised up.
16But if the dead are not raised up, Mashiah
Has not been raised. 17If he wasn't raised,
Your faith is futile, you are still in sin.
18Then those who fell asleep[137] in the Mashiah
Have perished. 19And if only for this life
We hoped in the Mashiah, we are then
Among all people the most pitiful.

20But in fact the Mashiah has been raised
From the dead: he's the first fruit of the sleepers
Who have been raised. 21And since death came
Through man, the resurrection of the dead
Came through man too. 22Since all in Adam die,
All in Mashiah will come back alive.
23Each one in his own order: first of the fruits
Is the Mashiah, and at his coming those
Of the Mashiah. 24And when the end comes,
He hands his kingdom over to his God
And father. After he destroys all rule,
Dominion, and authority, 25he must
Be king until, as it is sung in Psalms:
    He puts all enemies under his feet.[138]
26And the last enemy abolished is death.
27He has brought all things beneath his feet.
Clearly, when he has told us all these things,
It does not include one who subjected all
To him. 28But when all is subject to him,
The son too will be made a subject to
The one who put everything under him,
And only then God will be all in all.

---

137. Died.
138. Ps. 8.6.

Let us eat and drink, for tomorrow we die

29Otherwise, what will they do who are dipped
  In water for the sake of their dead bodies?
  If the dead are not raised at all, why dip them
  In water for the dead? 30Why do we go
  Into danger each hour? 31Each day I die.
  I swear it by my pride in you, just as
  I glory in you through Yeshua Mashiah
  Our lord. 32If as a man I fought with beasts
  In Efesos,[139] What good was it for me?
  If the dead do not rise, as Yeshayahu said:
     Let us eat and drink,
     For tomorrow we die.[140]
33Do not be fooled: "Bad company corrupts good character."[141]
34Awake to good and do not sin. Some lack
  Knowledge of God. I say this to your shame.

Nature of the resurrected body

35Some will ask, "In what form are the dead raised?
  In what kind of body will they appear?"
36Idiot! What you sow does not germinate
  Until it dies.[142] 37And when you sow, you sow

---

139. Ephesus (Latinized version) from the Greek Ἔφεσος (Efesos), an elaborate Greek and later Roman city south of Smyrna on the western coast of present-day Turkey, and one of the Seven Wonders of the World. Artemis (Diana by her Roman name) was worshiped there. Paul is said to have founded a synagogue there. It is unknown whether he had bestial enemies with whom he fought in Ephesus, or whether he is speaking metaphorically of strong opposition to his beliefs and projects.

140. Isa. 22.13.

141. Paul is citing an aphorism from the comedy *Thais* by the Greek playwright Menandros (Menander) (342–292 B.C.E.).

142. Paul uses the metaphors of agriculture as a principle source for his wisdom speech, though verses 40–41 speak figuratively of celestial bodies. It should be understood that Paul's early audience for emerging Christianity was the common people, the modest peasant and village workers. By contrast, the Gnostic philosophers in

Not the body to come but a naked seed,
Perhaps of wheat or other grains. 38But God
Gives it a body according to his wish,
And to each seed its proper body. 39Not
All flesh is the same flesh, but there is one
Alone for people, and another flesh
For beasts, and one for birds and one for fish.
40There are celestial bodies and earthly bodies,
And glory of the celestial is different
From glory of the earthly. 41There is glory
Of the sun and another glory of the moon,
And there is another glory of the stars,
But the stars' glory differs from star to star.

The body is sown in corruption

42Such is the resurrection of the dead.
The body is sown in corruption and raised
In incorruption. 43It is sown in dishonor
And raised in glory. It is sown in weakness
And raised in power. 44It is sown a natural[143] body
And raised a spiritual body. If there is
A natural body, there is also
A spiritual one. 45So in Genesis
It is written:
The first man Adam became a living soul.[144]

Alexandria, especially Valentinos, who gave the early Church fathers their earliest model for a hermeneutic examination of biblical texts, appear to have directed their "heretical" scriptures to a more educated audience. Paul's intellectual background derives from his Pharisee education as well as his absorption of Greek thought, such as Socrates' "doctrine of the soul" elaborated in Plato. His elegant mastery of rhetorical tropes was enriched by Greek principles of dialectical speech. Only in Paul would be found a reference to words of a classical Greek (and pagan) playwright. His authentic letters comprise the core of intellectual, metaphysical, and theological speculation in the New Testament.

143. Or, "physical."

144. Gen. 2.7.

The last man Adam became a giving soul.
46But the spiritual is not first. The natural
Is first. Then afterward the spiritual.

Made of earth, made of sky
47The first man came from earth, from dust.
The second man came from sky. 48So from dust
Are also those who are of dust. So from sky
Are also those who are of sky. 49We wore
The image of the man of dust just as
We'll wear the image of the man of sky.[145]

Where, death, is your sting?
50Now, brothers, I say this, that flesh and blood
Cannot inherit the kingdom of God,
Nor will corruption inherit incorruption.
51Look, I am telling you a mystery:
Not all of us will sleep,[146] but we will all
Be changed. 52In an instant, in the twinkling
Of an eye, suddenly the last ram's horn,[147]
The ram's horn will blow and the dead will wake
Uncorrupted, and we shall all be changed.
53Then the perishable body will put on
Imperishability, and the mortal
Immortality. 54When the perishable
Puts on immortality, then the word

---

145. In these six lines, beginning, "The first man came from earth, from dust," we see Paul's rhetorical genius in turning message into a spare, lyrical wisdom poem.

146. Die.

147. As noted earlier, "trumpet" is incorrect as a biblical metaphor, which in Isaiah and elsewhere in the Bible is a ram's horn, and not the anachronistic trumpet of the occupying Romans. The trumpets are particularly out of place in later Revelation, which, while an allegory against contemporary Roman terror against the Christian Jews, takes place in ancient Babylonia of the sixth century B.C.E. Essentially, the biblical ram's horn is a biblical sound of triumph and salvation, while the blasting trumpet means the victory of Roman troops.

Will be fulfilled as written in Yeshayahu
And Hoshea:[148]
   Death is swallowed up in victory.[149]
  55Where, death, is your victory?
  Where, death, is your sting?[150]

The sting of death is sin
    56The sting of death is sin,[151] and the power
    Of sin is the law.[152] 57Now thanks be to God,
    Who gives us victory through our lord Yeshua
    The Mashiah. 58Therefore, beloved brothers,
    Be steadfast, immovable, excelling always
    In the work of the lord, knowing your work
    Is not in vain by reason of the lord.

Chapter 16

Money for the poor
    Concerning the collection for the saints,[153] proceed
    To do it as I have done in synagogues
    Of Galatia.[154] 2On every Sabbath,

---

148. Isaiah and Hosea.

149. Isa. 25.8.

150. Hosea 13.14 (Septuagint).

151. The "sin of death" refers to Adam's sin that brought death into the world. These concluding verses firmly state hope through obedience, but are, dramatically, a descent from the peak. Paul is abruptly speaking as a cautionary theologian, not as the supreme rhetorician and soaring literary visionary telling how the soul will put on imperishability and gain victory over death.

152. God's law.

153. A euphemism for the poor in the congregation or at times for anyone, including outstanding figures, among the believers.

154. Galatia from the Greek Γαλατία (Galatía). A district between Roman provinces of Asia (western Turkey) and Cappadocia, Galatia is sometimes called Galatia of the East to avoid confusion with where the Gauls and Celts live in Europe.

Each one of you is to put funds aside
In keeping with your gains so when I come
There will be no collections. 3When I arrive
I will send any whom you recommend
With letters to carry your charities
To Yerushalayim.¹⁵⁵ 4And if important
That I go too, they will go on with me.

Shaul's journey map

5I will come to you after passing through
Makedonia.¹⁵⁶ I will be going there
To Makedonia, 6and maybe I will spend
The winter so you can send me on my way
Wherever I may go. 7I do not want
To see you only in passing, for I hope
To spend some time with you, if God permits.
8Yet I will stay in Efesos¹⁵⁷ till Shavuot.¹⁵⁸
9A great and vibrant door opened for me,
And there I have my many enemies.¹⁵⁹

Word about some brothers

10But if Timotheos¹⁶⁰ comes, see that he

---

155. Jerusalem from the Greek Ἰερουσαλήμ (Ierousalem), from the Hebrew יְרוּשָׁלַיִם (Yerushalayim).

156. Macedonia from the Greek Μακεδονία (Makedonia).

157. Ephesus.

158. Pentecost is a purely Jewish festival, which has been given a Greek name. Jews and Christian Jews celebrated it equally as they did the other Jewish festivals. "Pentecost" is from the Greek πεντηκοστή (pentekoste), meaning "fiftieth," from the Hebrew חַג שָׁבֻעוֹת (hag shavuot), meaning "feast of weeks." The Shavuot, one of the four major Jewish holidays, is a harvest festival, celebrated seven weeks (fifty days) after the Passover, commemorating God's giving of the Ten Commandments to Moses on Mount Sinai.

159. Who are the enemies? Ephesus was a large sophisticated city, still beautiful today for its extant Hellenistic marble architecture. The enemies, commentators have conjectured, were Gnostics and Hellenistic Jews.

160. Timothy.

Be unafraid with you. He does the work
Of the lord as I do. 11Let none despise him.
Send him on his way in peace and to come
To me. With the brothers I wait for him.
12Now concerning our brother Apollos,
I urged him to come to you the brothers,
But he was not willing to come just now
But will come whenever he has the time.

Do everything with love

13Be on your guard, stand firm in faith, be men,
Be powerful. 14Do everything with love.[161]

Goodbye, friends

15I urge you, brothers. You know the household
Of Stefanas,[162] that they were the first fruit[163]
In Achaia.[164] They gave themselves to serve

---

161. After a few charges appealing to masculinity comes the amazing brief and gentle sentence: "Do everything with love." This phrase may slip through unnoticed, but it should be seen as a great ideal, a summation, for the emerging sect, found in its totality in resplendent chapter 13. It foretells Martin Luther King's dream of standing firm in faith and power through love.

162. Stephanas from the Greek Στεφανᾶς (Stefanas).

163. Converts.

164. Achaia or Latinized Achaea, from the Greek Ἀχαΐα (Ahaia). The Roman province of Achaia, created in 146 B.C.E., included the main parts of Greece, Attica, Boeotia (perhaps including Epiros), and the Peloponnesos. In the *Iliad*, "Achaians" is Homer's word for those who attacked Troy. The Achaian League refers to the city-states, led by Corinth, that formed a military alliance to fight the Roman invaders. When the Romans defeated the Greeks and destroyed Corinth, Achaia moved north and became a Roman province attached to but distinct from Macedonia. However, in 27 B.C.E. Augustus designated all of the Peloponnesos and the mainland south of the Eubian Gulf to be Achaia, with Corinth again as its capital, and Macedonia became a separate province. For the Romans, reflecting a Homeric memory, all of Greece was popularly called Achaia.

Acts and Paul's letters follow the Roman designations of Macedonia as northern Greece and Achaia as southern Greece. Paul specifically uses "Achaia" to refer to Corinth and its surrounding areas.

The saints. 16I urge you to submit to them
And everyone who joins and toils with them.

17I am happy at the coming of Stefanas
And Fortounatos[165] and Ahaïkos,[166]
Because they made up for your absence, 18they
Refreshed my spirit as they did your own.
So give recognition to men like these.
19The temples of Asia greet you. Akylas[167]
And Priska[168] greet you warmly in the lord
And so the temple meeting in their house.
20And all the brothers here send you their greetings.
Greet one another with a holy kiss.

21This greeting is in my own hand, the hand
Of Shaul. 22If anyone does not love the lord,
A curse be on him. 23The grace of the lord
Yeshua be with you. 24My love be with you
And with all of you in Mashiah Yeshua.

---

165. Fortunatus from the Greek Φορτουνᾶτος (Fortounatos). *Fortunatus* is a Latin name that entered Greek. The person is an unknown early Christian and friend of Stephanas in Corinth.

166. Achaicus from the Greek Ἀχαϊκός (Ahaïkós), another friend of Stephanas in Corinth.

167. Aquila from the Greek Ἀκύλας (Akylas). See note 297 in Acts 18.1.

168. Priscilla (dim.) or Prisca from the Greek Πρίσκα (Priska). See note 299 in Acts 18.1.

Korinthians beta
(2 Corinthians)

Korinthians beta[1]
(2 Corinthians)

THE LETTER OR LETTERS under the title "2 Corinthians" are authentic, deeply Paul, with the exception of 6.14–7.1, which is probably an interpolation by an unknown follower. Scholars are divided on how many separate letters have been combined to yield 2 Corinthians. The jury judges between two and five self-contained letters. All the parts comprise a good editorial match of distinct moods in a troubling time. Among scholars espousing the two-to-three-letter reconstruction theories, the consensus is that Paul's "severe letter" came from Ephesus (10.1–13.10), and a second letter of reconciliation was composed in Macedonia when his messenger Titus informed him that the earlier 1 Corinthians had been well received in Corinth. The second half of 2 Corinthians contains many voices, ranging from reconciliation to anger, in three disparate parts joined only by the names of Paul and Corinth, the city whose Messianic assembly Paul had founded. The problem is that the severe answers to his challengers come late in the second half of the letter while the more positive sections come earlier—just the opposite of what one might expect—and so this enormously moving but disjointed letter in no way follows the emotional chronology of his encounters with Corinth.

The dating is middle to late 57, perhaps in the summer and autumn. Paul made the last of his three visits to Corinth—spending there the winter months of 57–58, when he wrote his letter to the Romans—before he made his fateful funds-carrying trip to Jerusalem, and in anticipation

---

1. 2 Corinthians from the Greek Κορίνθιος (Korinthios). The title is followed by βετα (beta) representing the letter "b" and the number "2."

of setting sail for a missionary trip to Rome and Spain. It is there in Jerusalem where we lose track of what happened to him. Acts speaks of huge adventures when he became a prisoner in Ephesus and then in Rome, and the imaginative but pseudo Pastoral Letters, especially 2 Timothy, give lots of details, as fine fiction should. Something happened. Destination Rome is dubious. He could have been a prisoner or an undocumented alien in Asia Minor; he could have been sent to Rome. He may have simply settled someplace, disappointed, and written nothing more that has been preserved. We certainly have no extant personal letters to corroborate the Roman work and travails and possible execution. To speculate more is to err.

In the Corinthians Paul deals with local troubles: squabbling between factions; Gnostic intruders bringing false knowledge; the territorial intrusion of Simon Peter and his original circle in Jerusalem, whose presence and ideas undermine Paul's own authority; and above all their unwillingness to listen to their founder. In 1 Corinthians he threatened to come with a whip (1 Cor. 4.21). In this grand oratorio of the all too human, Paul postpones a physical visit to Corinth because of the pain and failure of his last "painful" appearance in the city. He notes in 2 Corinthians 2.1 that he sends instead this letter with "endless tears" (2.3–4) with Titus, at the same time admonishing against more rebellious confrontations. Above all, he hopes to prevail by emphasizing his love for all community listeners to his epistle. Ultimately, that later strategy will quiet the crises, and so he will return to Corinth to write his masterly letter to the Romans. But his postponement now is because matters are worse since his last turbulent visit.

Paul answers accusations. He is accused of everything under the sun, including vacillation, intimidation, manipulation, maybe embezzlement of funds collected for the Jerusalem church. (Chapters 8 and 9 speak most fully about funds for Jerusalem.) In turn Paul attacks his accusers more clearly here than in any missive. He fires back at his presumed enemies, noting their theological heresies and unacceptable behavior. Only in Galatia is there as mighty a blowup, and that is confined to a few topics, the main one being his deep and ongoing contention with Simon Peter, who is leader of the Jerusalem forces, the so-called Judaizing teachers who insist on circumcision and obedience to other laws of entry for the gentiles. Ultimately, Paul wins the battle in that he, and later

Christianity, supported by the authority of Acts and the gospels, permit and even praise the gentile Greeks or the founding Messianic Jews for rejecting restrictive aspects of Judaism. In their victory they establish a great opening to pagans, an expansion of the church body, and a greater distinction from traditional Hellenistic Judaism, which also leads to a desired and convenient cover-up of Christianity's origin as a Jewish persuasion.

There are four major theories and a fifth minor one about the chronology of Paul's movements and vacillation in his plans, the authenticity of individual parts, and the sequence of the several letters embedded in 2 Corinthians. Much of the letter is in response to earlier letters to him, which we lack. It may be noted here that more known and lost letters, seven in all, are sent to Corinth, the booming sin city of sexuality on the water and the entry to the Peloponnesos.

What can we say about this fascinating major document? It is uneven in subject, not atypical of Paul but here even more so. It is Sunday sermons varying by the week. At the same time it is always Paul at his rhetorical best, angry or joyous and moving about in theology, where he dwells much less than in his letter to the Romans, his great theological meditation. Here we have a complete and complex man, an unraveling politician plotting his next moves, a thoroughly believable superfigure who can never be monochromatic. On the contrary, lovers of Paul want to read each serial on this road after Damascus to see how, community by community, Christianity was formed and spread. One is also invited to a great document of confessions, confessions that reveal perhaps more than they may have intended to. In so doing, the letter impresses most for his struggle to live through misery, to find peace, to find and dwell in faith to justify existence before God. Then—in part because of the inept ordering of the parts—once new resolutions are made, and problems solved, new episodes bring them all back again and the offending forces return to batter his equanimity. Perhaps the disorder of the parts is a greater truth reflecting his life, and many lives. A straight and narrow trip to the top is not Paul's way. So the tearful or powerful Paul goes on as a complete, complex person in the ancient world—flawed, his accusers say, and endowed, his friends proclaim, with endless purposeful energy. There is no dull or dulling feature in his spectacular character. His physical ailments add to the pathos of his lifestyle. He carries no pocketful of tranquilizers. Paul, whose life is a relentless drive to self-discovery and the acquisition of knowledge of an ideal person on earth, on his or her way to salvation, walks difficult roads as he pursues his missionary steps, all recorded magnificently in these surviving letters. How important the word was in ancient times that a founder of a small and strange dissenting faith should have been read in so many major documents that record how the leader founds, keeps in touch with, tangles with, and guides old and new communities to a nascent faith celebrated in the utmost modest dwellings. Paul could not have dreamt that these modesties would in time be replaced on earth by city-dominating cathedrals in stone.

This grand letter is steeped in the reality of the time, meaning they are steeped in heights and caverns of emotion, intellect, and theological assertions. As a New Testament work of art, the verses are fashioned in unfailing rhetoric and shine in an astonishing flow of poetry.

Chapter 1

Hello

Shaul,[2] a messenger of the Mashiah
Yeshua[3] by the will of God and Timotheos[4]
Our brother, to the temple of God
In Korinthos,[5] and all the saints in the whole
Of Ahaia,[6] 2grace to you and peace from God
Our father and lord Yeshua Mashiah.

Thank you

3Let us praise God and father of our lord
Yeshua the Mashiah, father of mercies
And all compassion, 4who comforts us in our
Affliction so that we are able to console
Those in affliction through the consolation
That we ourselves in need received from God.

5For as the sufferings of the Mashiah flow
Into us, so also through the Mashiah

---

2. Paul from the Greek Παῦλος (Paulos), from Saul in the Greek Σαῦλος (Saulos), from the Hebrew שָׁאוּל (Shaul). Paul was born in Tarsos as *Shaul*.

3. Christ Jesus. "Jesus" is from the Greek Ἰησοῦς (Iesous), from the Aramaic יֵשׁוּעַ (Yeshua), a later form of the Hebrew יְהוֹשֻׁעַ (Yehoshua). "Christ" is from the Greek Χριστος (Hristos), and Greek *Hristos* or *Christos* is a translation from the Greek Μεσσίας (Messias), from the Hebrew מָשִׁיחַ (mashiah). "Christ" in Greek also means "the anointed," and "Messiah" in both Greek and Hebrew contains the meaning of "the anointed."

4. Timothy from the Greek Τιμόθεος (Timotheos).

5. Corinth from the Greek Κόρινθος (Korinthos).

6. Achaia or Achaea, from the Greek Ἀχαΐα (Ahaia). The Roman province of Achaia, created in 146 B.C.E., included the main parts of Greece, Attica, Boeotia (perhaps including Epiros), and the Peloponnesos.

Our consolation overflows. 6If we
Are afflicted, it is for your comfort
And your salvation. If we are comforted
It is for your comfort, inciting patience
In you before the same sufferings that we
Also undergo. 7Our hope for you is firm.
We know that as you share our suffering,
So you also share in our consolation.

Tribulation in Asia

8We do not want you to be unaware,
Brothers, of the affliction that befell us
In Asia, how we were utterly burdened
Beyond our powers, and we despaired even
About whether to live. 9We were so lost
We felt we had the sentence of death in us,
And that our trust could not be in ourselves
But solely God, who raises up the dead.
10He who from the great death delivered us
Will keep delivering us. It is in him
We set our hope that he'll deliver us
Again. 11You also help by joining us
In prayers for us and that thanks may be given
By many for that grace we got from many.

Shaul says he behaved well in this world

12Here is our boast: by testimony of our
Consciousness, we have behaved in this world
With holiness and the sincerity
Of God,7 and done so not with fleshly wisdom

---

7. The collective "we" here, and often elsewhere, may be taken as a polite form of saying "I."

But in the grace of God, and especially
Toward you. 13We write you nothing but what you
Can read and understand. I hope, as in the past
14You understand in part, and in the end[8]
You'll come to understand us in total
And you will boast of us just as we boast
Of you in the day of our lord Yeshua.

He was not fickle in changing plans
15With confidence I changed my earlier plan
To come to see you so you might enjoy
A double grace from me. 16So on my way
To Makedonia[9] I'd come to you,
And on my return from Makedonia
I'd come again so you could send me on
To Yehuda.[10] 17When I wished to change plans,
Was I fickle? Those were my wishes then.
Did I do it, falling into the flesh?
So I might say at once *Yes, yes* or *No, no?*[11]
18As God is faith our word to you was not
Yes and *no.* 19And the son of God, Yeshua
Mashiah, who was preached among you through

---

8. End Day or Day of Judgment.

9. Macedonia from the Greek Μακεδονία (Makedonia).

10. Judea from the Greek Ἰουδαία (Ioudaia), from the Hebrew יְהוּדָה (yehuda).

11. In this most troubled and fluent of Paul's letters, patched together of letter segments, throbbing with spirit and fulminations, the rhetorician of high speech becomes unusually intimate and demotic, as if his lines were imbedded in the highly demotic Gospel of Mark. At some moments, except for noun and verb endings, his sentences seem taken from a modern Greek narrative. These passages represent, again, the many-voiced Paul, dictating his letters to his world.

Myself and Silouanos[12] and Timotheos,[13]
Was never yes and no but *yes* in him.[14]
20And all the promises of God through him[15]
Are yes, and so through him we say amain[16]
21He who confirms us with you in Mashiah
Is God. He has anointed us 22and set
His seal on us. He has deposited
The first payment of spirit in our hearts[17]

It was to spare you
23I call God as the witness of my soul:
It was to spare you that I gave up coming
To Korinthos.[18] 24We do not shape your faith,
But work with you for deepening your joy,
Since in your faith you have been standing firm.

---

12. Silvanus from the Greek Σιλουανός (Silouanos), probably from the Hebrew
סִילְוָנִי (sylvany). Silvanus seems to be the same Silas, a prophet and leader in the
Jerusalem synagogue, who was said to accompany Paul in his second missionary
journey (Acts 15.22, 15.32).

13. Timothy.

14. The "yes and no" means "vacillation"; it is Paul's turn of phrase for defending himself against ambiguity. He wishes to convince the congregation that he is straightforward, one who utters only "yes," which is equivalent to a yes affirmation in Jesus
and a resounding yes for God's promises.

15. Jesus.

16. Amen from the Greek ἀμήν (amen), from the Hebrew אָמֵן (amein).

17. Paul infrequently uses financial metaphors to show obligations and relationships with God, in contrast to the gospels, where this rhetorical device is common.
Here, following the series of yes-and-no tropes, the "payment of the spirit in our
hearts" enters effectively and with great beauty. The apologies and self-exculpation
and defense of his decisiveness that might appear otherwise reflect the most intimately personal and reflective documents we have of Paul, revealing, at least in such
moments, an anguished but candid voice, speaking from the heart.

18. Corinth. The "you" refers to the congregation in Corinth.

Chapter 2

I told myself I must not come again
To you in grieving circumstance. 2If I
Hurt you, then who is there to make me happy
But those I hurt? 3I wrote precisely this,
Fearing that if I come to visit you,
I will be hurt by those who ought to bring
Me joy. I have a confidence in all
Of you, and my joy enters everyone.
4I wrote to you with somber tribulation,
With anguish in my heart and endless tears,
Not to afflict you, but so you may know
The abundance of the love I have for you.

Forgive the troublemaker

5If someone has caused trouble, he has not
Hurt me—maybe a little, yet let me
Not exaggerate—but pained all of you.
6For such a type the punishment by the
Majority has been enough. 7So now,
Instead, you should revise your thought, forgive
And comfort him that he not be swallowed up
By too much sorrow.¹⁹ 8Therefore, I implore you,

---

19. In this remarkable reversal, where Paul surges from punishment to love in treatment of a "sinner," as others call the dissenter, the text gives us a strong, perfect metaphor in the Greek verb καταπίνω (katapino), from "down" plus "drink," meaning "swallow up." This is the image Paul uses and wants, but modern translations uniformly give the explanatory conceptual meaning of "overwhelm" (itself once a metaphor—over-whelm—but now lost to its general sense). The King James Version, alone among available versions, sticks to Paul and his powerful speech rhetoric, giving us the insuperable "lest perhaps such a one should be swallowed up with overmuch sorrow."

Declare your love for him. 9For these concerns
I wrote to learn how serious you are.
Are you obedient in everything?
10Whoever you forgive, I too forgive.
And what I have forgiven—was there something?—
I did for you before the face of the
Mashiah 11so Satan will not outwit us.
We are not ignorant of his designs.

Worried in Troas

12Then I came to Troas,[20] to speak the good news,[21]
And when a door was opened by the lord
For me,[22] 13my spirit couldn't find relief.
I failed to find my brother Titos,[23] so
I said my farewells to the people there
And wandered on into Makedonia.

We are the fragrance of the Mashiah

14But through the grace of God who constantly
Leads us triumphantly in the Mashiah,
The aroma of his knowledge is revealed
Through us in every place. 15We are the fragrance

---

20. Troas or Troy from the Greek Τρῳάς (Troas), a city and district in northwest Turkey, site of the ancient city of Troy's walls, from many earlier periods, which are still extant as extensive ruins.

21. Or gospel. The Greek for gospel, εὐαγγέλιον (euangelion), means "good news." "Gospel," from Old English "godspel," consisting of god, "good," plus spel, "news," "Godspel" is a translation of Greek euangelion.

22. An opportunity to evangelize.

23. Titus from the Greek Τίτος (Titos). Titus accompanied Paul to Jerusalem, and despite the pressure of the "Judaizers," that is, James, Peter, and John, to have him circumcised, Paul did not yield to them.

Of the Mashiah for God in those being saved
And in those perishing. 16To the perishing,
Fragrance of death to death, but to the saved
Fragrance of life to life. Who is up to this?
17We do not go around, as many do,
Peddling the word of God.24 We are speaking
From purity, from God; and in the presence
Of God, we speak only through the Mashiah.

Chapter 3

Written in the heart

Are we beginning to commend ourselves
Again? Or maybe we don't need letters
Of commendation—as the others do—
To you or from you? 2You are our true letter
Written in our hearts, known and read by all.
3Clearly you are the letter from the Mashiah,
Fashioned by us and not composed with ink
But with the spirit of the living God,

---

24. The disparaging reference to roaming peddler is presumably to rival false prophets, who have accused him of being a false prophet. As in all the letters, "false prophets" refers to the struggle against the Gnostics to define the true "orthodoxy," and
much more forcefully than his opposing views with Peter and James, or traditional
Jews who have not accepted Yeshua as the messiah they still await. In many of the
epistles, those who come with knowledge, with *false* knowledge, meaning the Gnostics, provoked the greatest wrath, depreciation, and presumed danger to the orthodox
faith. Here the anger against the intruders is seen in the phrase "peddling the word
of God." Paul triumphs against all competitors by speaking "through the Mashiah,"
that is, with Christ's authority.

And not on tablets but on hearts of flesh.[25]

25. Paul's metaphor of ink and spirit refers to the written and the oral law. He was brought up in Jerusalem "at the feet of Gamaliel" (Acts 22.3), who was pupil of the great Pharisee thinker Hillel. Gamaliel was noted for his spirit of tolerance (Acts 5.34–39). Paul was, as a Pharisee, probably a member of the Sanhedrin, the council, of which many members were Pharisees (Prushim). The Pharisees were seen as liberal, erudite, and spiritual, and their notion of resurrection was a bridge to Christian Judaism. In contrast to the Sadducees, who were on friendly terms with the Hasmonean monarchy, the Pharisees were fierce opponents of Roman occupation and stood for oral rather than solely written law, which was presumably Jesus's position, and such opposition, it can be said, led to his crucifixion. So, as opposed to popular assumption concerning the Pharisees that completely reverses their historic position, we have Paul's Pharisaic affirmation and preference for flexible oral law as opposed to Mosaic law written "on stone tablets." So too he preferred circumcision "of the heart" (of the spirit) (Rom. 2.29 and Deut. 10.16), not of the flesh. The flexibility of the oral law also corresponds precisely as well to his openness to change, namely, in matters of circumcision, dietary law, and the Sabbath, which opened the door to large gentile conversion to Messianic Judaism, that is, what would later, long after Paul, be called Christianity.

All these preferences pitted Paul against the Jerusalem faction of the Jesus movement, headed by James and Peter, who, though sharing his belief in the messiah, held strictly to Mosaic law and were reluctant to alter that law to permit entry to gentiles. Paul's deepest struggle during his lifetime, as revealed in the letters, was not against Romans, though they posed a constant danger to his life, nor to rabbinical Jews, but to his fellow Christian Jews who opposed him and to the Gnostics, whom he mentions repeatedly, not by name, but by their views, as purveyors of false knowledge.

While Acts, like the gospels, paints a much later third-person narrative of Paul's pleasant accommodation with powerful Romans and near-fatal struggles with nasty Jews in the Temple, who conspired against him (as they were alleged to have conspired against Jesus), modern scholarship suggests quite the opposite. Paul's problems were not primarily with Romans or traditional Jews but with the makeup of his congregations in Corinth and elsewhere. The autobiographical letters of Paul, who is the most historically clear figure of the Old and the New Testament, reveal such extreme opposition among the new Christian Jews that he altered travel plans because of troublemakers and rebellion. The letters also show him raging and blessing, threatening and loving, punishing and forgiving, all to bring order, obedience, and growth to his missionary venture. James Carroll summarizes Paul's quandary in Corinth, showing that "the Jews who would have felt most passionately about Paul, the Jews most likely to have erupted at the sight of him, were in fact Jewish followers of Jesus—Christians—who disagreed with him about the observance of the Law." See James Carroll, *Constantine's Sword: The Church and the Jews: A History* (Boston: Houghton Mifflin, 2001), 142–143.

Ministers of the new covenant
    4Such is our confidence we have in God
    Through the Mashiah. 5Not that we are skilled
    Enough to think of things whose origin
    Is ours. Our skill and competence derive
    From God, 6who also gave us competence
    As ministers of a new covenant,
    Not of the letter but of the spirit since
    The letter kills whereas the spirit gives life.

Not the ministry of death but glory
    7Now if the ministry of death, in letters
    Chiseled[26] on stone, appeared in such glory
    That sons of Yisrael[27] could not look at
    The face of Moshe,[28] though it was fading,[29]
    8How much more will the ministry of spirit
    Come into glory? 9If the ministry
    Of condemnation is glory, much greater

---

26. Or engraved.

27. Israel from the Greek Ἰσραήλ (Israel), from the Hebrew יִשְׂרָאֵל (yisrael).

28. Moses from the Greek Μωϋσῆς (Moyses), from the Hebrew מֹשֶׁה (moshe).

29. In speaking of the New Covenant, as opposed to the Old Covenant of Noah, Abraham, and Moses, the desire to compare the Jewish Bible negatively to the revolutionary tenets of the new Messianism is as irresistible as it is understandable. These two factions are competing for dominance and prestige for the hearts of Jews and would-be gentile converts. The new understanding and covenant is in the minds of believers, in part revealed in letters, which are not perceived or accepted, however, as scripture. The New Testament, including Paul and the other epistlers' letters, which have not yet been collected for a new canon of scripture, does not yet exist. The gathering and rough establishment of order and text may have happened as early as around 150 C.E., as David Trobisch asserts in *The First Edition of the New Testament* (New York: Oxford University Press, 2000), though struggles over inclusion and order will not, for the most part, cease until the ecumenical council convened by Constantine I in 325 C.E. And even then the controversies over the Apocrypha continued for a millennium.

Is the ministry of kindness. 10What once
Was glorified no longer walks in glory,
Because of greater glory. 11If what was
A glory fades, enduring glory glows.
12With all this hope, we act with courage,
13Not like our Moshe who put a veil over
 His face so that the sons of Yisrael not see
 The end of something perishing.30 14Their minds
 Were impenetrable. Until this day
 When they read the Old Covenant31 the veil
 Lingers, because only with the Mashiah
 Will it be set aside. 15Indeed, till now
 When the books of Moshe are read, a veil
 Lies on the heart, 16and for one who turns
 To the Mashiah the dark veil is dropped.
17The lord is spirit, and where spirit of
 The lord is, freedom resides. 18Now all
 Of us, with unveiled faces, seeing the glory
 Of the lord as reflected in a mirror, are
 Transformed into the same image, from one
 Degree of glory to another, as from
 The perfect spirit of the true Mashiah.

---

30. Paul speaks with pride of his heritage in biblical figures, and cites the books of
the law (Torah) regularly to justify his arguments. Yet Moses is associated with the
old law, and so the patriarch must be presented as a once-glorious has-been who
even in his day was fading. But he is not disdained or demonized. By contrast, in
his glorious statue of Moses, Michelangelo cannot resist placing half-concealed
devil's horns discreetly under his hero's abundant hair, revealing the Christian
dilemma of how to accept the Hebrew Bible: are the prophets and patriarchs pre-
Christian or incarnations of the devil? Michaelangelo chose to make Moses glorious Lucifer.

31. The Hebrew Bible or Torah.

Chapter 4

Light of knowledge in the glory of God

We have this ministry through God's mercy
And don't lose heart. 2We have dropped the shame
Of hidden things, and do not walk around
With cunning, nor falsify the word of God.
By making plain the truth we can commend
Ourselves to every conscience in the sight
Of God. 3But if the good news is concealed,
It has been hidden to the perishing.
4For them the god of this age blinded them—
The minds of unbelievers—so the radiance
Of good news of the glory of the Mashiah,
The true image of God, can't shine on them.
5We don't proclaim ourselves but vow the lord
Yeshua Mashiah and ourselves as your slaves
For Yeshua's sake. 6Because the God who said,
"Out of the darkness light will shine," made light
Shine in our hearts in order to give us
A radiance of the knowledge of the glory
Of God through Yeshua Mashiah's face.

Fragility of clay vessels, our bodies

7We keep our treasure in these jars of clay[32]
So the supremacy of power be God's,
Not ours. 8We are afflicted in all ways
But we do not lose faith.[33] Bewildered, yes

---

32. Clay jars refers to the weakness of the body (Gen. 2.7), its limitations, and the
true treasures it contains, being the spirit and knowledge of God through Christ.

33. Ps. 116.10 (Septuagint). Verse 8 is close to the Psalms verse. The notion of belief
as a form of faith is also in verse 13.

But not hopeless; 9and we are persecuted
But not forsaken. Cast down but not destroyed,
10And always carrying the death of Yeshua
In our bodies so that his life glows clear.
11Constantly, we the living are delivered
To death for Yeshua's sake so that the life
Of Yeshua glows clear in mortal flesh.
12Hence death works in us but in you it's life.

We do not lose heart
13Just as we have the same spirit of faith,
And as it is written in Psalms:
I believed, therefore I spoke,34
We also believe and so we speak, 14knowing
That he who raised lord Yeshua will raise
Us up with Yeshua and bring us to him
Along with you. 15Yes, everything's for you
So that grace, reaching more and more people,
May increase thanksgiving to the glory of God.

16So we don't faint away. Though even if
Our outer man is crushed, our inward man
Is renewed day by day. 17Our momentary
Light affliction is preparing in us
A greater and ever greater weight of glory.
18We do not gaze at what is visible
But the unseen; for the things that are seen
Are temporal.35 The unseen is eternal.

---

34. See note 33 on 2 Cor. 4.8.
35. Or momentary.

Chapter 5

In the earthly tentfonts

We know that if our house, this earthly tent,[36]
Collapses, we still have a house from God,
Which is a building not made by frail hands
But an eternal structure in the sky.
2While we live in our tent we groan, longing
To be clothed in its cloth,[37] 3so when we drop
Our earthly robes we won't be found naked.
4We still live in this tent and groan, and we
Are weighed down, wanting not to go unclothed
But clothed so death may be drunk down by life.[38]
5God is the one who formed us for all this
And gave the holy spirit as our guarantee.

---

36. Tent or tabernacle. "Tent" is from Greek σκηνή (skene), meaning "tent." "Tabernacle" is here a misleading translation of σκηνή, suggesting primarily a sacred box in which Jews in the desert carried the Ark of the Covenant, or in churches a case or box kept on the altar in which the consecrated host and wine of the Eucharist is kept. The word means "tent," an apt metaphor for Paul, said to be the son of a tentmaker or himself a tentmaker, for a temporary earthly dwelling place. "Tent" is elsewhere misleadingly translated as "tabernacle" in the Feast of the Tabernacles or Feast of the Booths, which is actually the Jewish Feast of the Sukkoth, a harvest feast in which a farmer's shelter was built in the fields and kept there for eight or nine days to commemorate the forty years of living in temporary shelter, in nomadic "tents," in the desert after the flight from Egypt.

37. Presumably with the holy tent cloth. Here again the metaphor, if it is to work, demands "tent cloth" rather than "a wooden structure" if one asks to be clothed in the heavenly σκηνή .

38. This translation of the Greek καταπίνω (katapino) is usually "swallow up," which is strong and not incorrect, but the exact meaning of the verb is "down" + "drink," that is, "drink down," which here is a more striking rendition. So life drinks "death" down as a "poison" one must drink in order for life to overcome death. One immediately thinks of "poison" in the Greek φάρμακον (farmakon), which has the same dual threat and cure, meaning both "poison" and "medicinal cure."

Known to God

6So always confident, we are informed
 That while we are at home in the body,
 We live in absence from the lord. 7We walk
 By faith and not by sight. 8We're confident
 And pleased to leave our house, to leave
 Our body and be present with the lord.39
9Whether at home or away, we aspire
 To please him. 10We must all appear before
 The judgment seat of the Mashiah so
 That each one may receive his payment for
 Those acts that we have practiced, good or bad,
 Through the body. 11Therefore knowing the terror
 Of the lord we attempt to persuade men,
 But what we are is plain to God. I hope
 We're also plain to your own consciences.

We speak to persuade you toward God

12We don't commend ourselves again to you,
 But offer you a chance to boast of us
 And answer those who boast externally
 And not in heart. 13Whether we were beside
 Ourselves, it was for God; or if we were
 In our right mind, it was for you. 14The love
 Of the Mashiah drives us, since we know
 That he alone died for us all. Really,
 All died. 15He died for all so that the living
 Might live no longer for themselves, but for
 The one who died for them and has been raised.

Reconciliation

16From now on we know no one in the flesh.
 And even if we did know the Mashiah
 In the flesh, now no longer do we know
 Him so. 17And if one is in the Mashiah,

---

39. Or, "be at home with."

He is a new creation. The old is gone,
And everything is new. 18All is of God,
And he has reconciled us with himself
Through the Mashiah, and he gave to us
The ministry of reconciliation,
19And when God reconciled the world to himself
Through the Mashiah, he didn't calculate
Their trespasses, and placed in us the word
Of reconciliation. 20Now we are
Ambassadors for the Mashiah. It is
As if God summoned you through us. We ask
For the Mashiah that you be reconciled
To God. 21He made the one who knew no sin
Into the sin, and only for our sake,
That we might be the righteousness of God.

Chapter 6

We commend ourselves in endurance
Working with him, we implore you not to take
The grace of God in vain. 2Yeshayahu[40] says:
In a time of my favor I heard you
And in the day of salvation I helped you.[41]
Look, now in a favorable time, look now

---

40. Isaiah from the Greek Ἠσαΐας (Esaias), from the Hebrew יְשַׁעְיָהוּ (yeshayahu).
41. Isa. 49.8. Normally, the Greek has "as it is written" or "in the scriptures," which informs the reader that a passage from the Jewish Bible is being directly cited. The uncertain assumption is that the reader will be so familiar with the text that to cite the source is unnecessary. In annotated editions, to compensate for incomplete information, footnotes or marginalia provide the sources. Here, however, Paul writes, "he says." Without annotation, it is improbable that the reader will know that "he" refers to Isaiah. The only significant difference in the Isaian text between the Greek and Hebrew versions is that in Isaiah God's words are placed in the future as a prophecy, and in Paul the text uses past tenses, permitting him to transfer God's message from a promise of help given to the Jews in their flight from Egypt to an affirmation that Christ has come and now is "the day of salvation."

Is the day of salvation! ₃We put no cause
For stumbling in the way of anyone,
So that our ministry will not be blamed.⁴²
₄But we have shown ourselves to be servants
Of God in stern endurance, in afflictions,
In duress, in misery, ₅through beatings,
Through imprisonments, in riots, in labors,
Through sleeplessness, in starvation,
₆In purity, in knowledge, in long suffering,
In kindness, in the holy spirit, in love
That is not hypocritical, ₇in the word
Of truth, in the power of God, through weapons
Of justice of the right hand and the left,
₈By honor and dishonor, by disgrace⁴³
And good report, by imposters and the true,
₉As the unknown and known, as dying, and look,
We live, as punished and not put to death,
₁₀In grief but always in a state of joy,

---

42. When Paul raises his voice against detractors and commends his own ministry, which in mild modesty he shares with others by writing in the first-person plural, his detractors are the others in the Jesus movement who call him at once a false apostle and one given to ecstatic writings. He in turn will depict his accusers of being not servants of God but servants of Satan. The struggle with fellow Christian Jews (not traditional Jews or Romans) was intense, and had Acts, which uniformly praised and glamourized his missionary adventures, not been written a decade, or more likely two decades, after his death, the letters might have been left unread and certainly not become the earliest canonized scripture in the New Testament. In these pages detailing his hardships, Paul is appealing to the congregation, not to other leaders, to hear and obey his words and his version of the new movement. After citing Isaiah, who cites the lord, who has heard and helped his people, Paul tells not only how he has helped the people but also how he and his people have endured. It is one of the greatest rhetorical litanies of protest, passion, and pathos that has ever been uttered in religious scriptures. It is hot with conviction and desperation. To use one of Paul's often-pleasured Greco-Roman sports' analogies, this time his runner has raced at top speed from start to finish.

43. Or, "slander."

As poor yet making many rich, as having
Nothing and yet possessing everything.

I speak to you as my children
11Our mouths are open to you,[44] the Korinthians,[45]
Our hearts are large. 12You're not restrained by us,
But you are held in tight in inner passions.
13Now in a fair exchange, I speak to you
As to my children. Open up your hearts.

Sanctuary for the living[46]
14Do not be badly yoked with unbelievers.
What partnership is there with the injustice
Or fellowship between the light and darkness?
15What harmony is there between Mashiah
And Beliyal?[47] Or what does a believer
Share with an unbeliever? 16How does agreement
Hold between a temple of God and idols?
We are the temple of the living God,
As God said in Leviticus, Ezekiel,
Yeshayahu, and Shmuel:[48]
I will live among them and walk among them[49]

---

44. We are speaking candidly.

45. Corinthians.

46. Verses 6.14–7.1 comprise an extraordinary and beautiful interruption to Paul's entreaties to his unruly congregation in Corinth to open their hearts to his love. Verse 7.2 picks up again where 6.13 ends. It is suggested that this parenthetical passage is a fragment from an earlier letter, possibly 1 Corinthians.

47. Belial or Beliar, a name for the devil, from the Greek Βελιάρ (Beliar) or Βελιάλ (Belial), from the Hebrew בְּלִיַּעַל (beliyal), as in Deuteronomy 13.13 and 15.9, where Belial is a troublemaker, scoundrel, and Satan. He is also a significant wicked creature in intertestamental literature. In this visionary fragment, Paul quotes Hebrew Bible passages, urging separation from pagans: Leviticus 26.12, Samuel 7.14.

48. Samuel.

49. Lev. 26.12.

And I will be their God and they will be my people.[50]
17Therefore come out from among them[51]
And be apart from them, says the lord,
And touch nothing unclean
And I will welcome you in,[52]
18And I will be your father
And you will be my sons and daughters[53]
Says the lord of the mountains.[54]

Chapter 7[55]

Let us purify
My love, since we have made these promises,
Let us clean filth from body and the spirit,
Perfecting holiness in fear of God.

---

50. Ezek. 37.12.

51. Rev. 18.4. In numerous study Bibles Paul's impeccable verse "We are the temple of the living God" has its source in or was influenced by Revelation 18.4. Revelation was composed three to six decades after Paul's death. If Revelation is the source of line 6.16 in 2 Corinthians, then the line is a late interpolation. Conversely, it is unlikely that Revelation took the verse from Paul. How could Revelation's author know the line? And if known, why would the author of the finest body of verse in the New Testament turn its magic into pedestrian Revelation 18.4? Allusion to or borrowing from other scripture occurs on most pages in the New Testament. Examples are so plentiful that biblical exegetes go overboard in finding intertextuality. Indeed, some translations annotate each line of the Hebrew Bible as either wrong or as correctly prefiguring and confirming events and theological ideas in the New Testament.

52. Isa. 52.11.

53. Exod. 4.12

54. Sam. 7.8. As indicated earlier, among the possible meanings of "Almighty," which the Greek Septuagint used here, is the metaphoric "God of the Mountains." Here the Greek is Pantokrator, from the Septuagint Greek Παντοκράτωρ (Pantokrator), from the Hebrew צְבָאוֹת (tsvaot).

55. 2 Corinthians 7.1 ends fragment 6.14–18. Verse 7.2 takes up from 6.13.

Shaul causing grief for joy

2Make room for us. We have done wrong to no one,
We have corrupted no one, nor defrauded
Any. 3I do not say this to condemn you.
I've said before that you are in our hearts:
To die with you, to live with you. 4I trust you,
And brag about you. Filled with eagerness,
I overflow with joy amid our grief.

5And even when we reached Makedonia,
Our flesh got no relief. We were consumed
By outer battles and our inner dreads.
6But God who comforts low and downcast
Comforted us by the arrival here
Of Titos,[56] 7and not only by his presence,
But in the encouragement he gave to you.
He told us of your longing, of your sorrows,
Your zeal for me, which made me happiest.
8I grieved you by my letter. I've no regret.
If I regretted it, I see that if
My letter hurt you for an hour, 9I'm pleased—
Not that you hurt but that you sorrowed into
Repentance, and your sorrow found you God,
So in the end you weren't harmed by us
In any way. 10A sorrow through God's will
Causes repentance leading to salvation,
And not to be regretted. The world's sorrow
Generates death. 11Look, you suffered Godly
Wretchedness. See how now you're fortified.
Now what defense, what indignation, what
Alarm, what longing and what zeal! And now
What vengeance! In all things you've done you're pure.

---

56. Titus.

Defending his harsh letter that gave joyful redemption
> 12Then if I wrote you, it was not for some wrong
> One did, or for one who was wronged, but for
> You to see before God your innocence.
> 13For all of this we now are comforted.

Happy for Titos and you
> Beside our own encouragement, we joy
> Greatly before the happiness of Titos.
> His spirit is at ease because of you.
> 14If I have boasted about you to him,
> I'm not ashamed, but as we spoke with truth
> To you about all things, so too our boasting
> To Titos has been truth. 15And so his heart
> Goes out to you even more as he remembers
> Your full obedience, and how with fear
> And trembling you received him as your own.
> 16I am jubilant with confidence in you.[57]

Chapter 8

Deep poverty, rich generosity
> Brothers, we have you recognize God's grace
> Bequeathed to temples in Makedonia,[58]

---

57. Chapter 7 ends on one of the highest notes in this Corinthians. Paul is jubilant that with Titus's appearance and reception, good relations appear to have been restored in Corinth. In the drama of Paul's confession of rage, love, and sympathy, as well as transcendent obedience to the divine, this letter, which many have called a mess, a mishap of joined epistles, becomes a mediation between a dramatic monologue of early Aeschylus and a long soliloquy of Milton. Between those literary and moral inventors lie two more, Shakespeare, who invented the world, and Paul, who invented the letter as a great art form, his worldly and cosmic drama to the world. To this we might add Søren Kierkegaard's *Fear and Trembling*, but though Kierkegaard got the title of his book from Paul, who gave him the theme of his masterpiece, it is usually said to be from Philippians 2.12, not from 2 Corinthians 7.15.

58. These were the synagogues in Philippi and especially Thessaloniki.

2And how amid a dread ordeal of sorrows
  Their boundless joy and extreme poverty
  Have mingled into their abundant wealth
  Of generosity. 3According to
  Their means, I witness how beyond their means
  And of their own free will 4they begged and begged
  Us to allow them favor[59] and to share
  The ministry for the impoverished saints,[60]
  5And not as we expected, since at first
  They gave themselves to the Mashiah,[61] .
  And through the will of God to us. 6We asked
  Titos, since he began this gift of grace
  Among you, if he might complete it now.
  7As you abound in everything—in faith,
  In speech, in knowledge, will, and in our love
  For you, be lavish in this work of grace.

For you he became poor
  8I am not speaking with commands, yet test
  The nature of your love against the eager
  Example of the others. 9You know the gift
  Of lord Yeshua Mashiah, that for you
  He became poor so by his poverty
  You would be rich. 10I tell you my opinion

---

59. To accept the gift of their liberality.

60. Paul asks the congregation of Corinth to recognize the exemplum of the generosity of poorer synagogues in the north, which, with all their needs, implored their leaders for the gift of being permitted to help the impoverished "saints," that is, the Christian Jews, in Jerusalem. Their acts should serve as a precedent for the apparently wealthier congregation in Corinth to contribute money. Paul knew that if the movement was to spread among Jew and Greek, it needed funds to support its missions, and he expressed this need by coupling generosity with faith in and obedience to the messiah and to God.

61. It is not certain if "giving themselves first to the lord" means reaffirming belief in Christ, giving moneys to the temple, or both.

About this. It could help you. Not only
For what you've done but also for the will
To work, which you began last year. 11Complete
Your work so that your eagerness be matched
By finishing what you have now. 12If will
Is there, that gift becomes acceptable
By what you have—not by what you have not.
13I do not mean that others find relief
   And you in need. There should be a fair balance.
14For now your surplus should be matched against
   Their need, and their abundance also be
   For what you lack so that equality
   Exist. 15As written in Exodus:
      He who gathered much had not too much,
      And he who gathered little did not go short.[62]

Titos off to Korinthos with blessings and a letter
     16Our thanks to God for putting in the heart
      Of Titos the same fire I have for you,
     17And he accepted our appeal, and filled
      With zeal, he's going to you on his own.
     18With him we send a brother who is famous
      In all our synagogues for how he broadcasts
      The good news. 19More, he was handpicked by temples
      As our companion in our journey on
      This mission of grace that we did for him,
      For the lord's glory and to satisfy
      Our eagerness to help, 20and to avoid
      Our being blamed for the abundance of
      The contributions we arrange. 21We look
      For the good, not only before the lord,
      But also before men. 22We sent the brother
      Whom we've approved of in a hundred ways,
      A hundred times, who's even more thrilled now

---

62. Exod. 16.18.

Because of his great confidence in you.
23And as for Titos he is my partner
And for you our fellow worker; as for
The brothers they are temple messengers
For the glory of the Mashiah. 24Prove
Your love for them, and openly in temples,
And prove us right in boasting about you.

Chapter 9

More contributions for the saints in Yerushalayim[63]
　　It is superfluous for me to write to you
　　About the contributions for the saints.[64]

---

63. Jerusalem from the Greek Ἰερουσαλήμ (Ierousalem), from the Hebrew יְרוּשָׁלַיִם
(Yerushalayim).

64. The collections for the relief of the poor (the saints) in the Jerusalem temple,
which have appeared in Romans 15.25–27 and 1 Corinthians 16.1–4, are present in
2 Corinthians 8.1–9.15, and will be a theme again in Galatians 2.1–10. They reflect
Paul's needs to raise funds to keep the movement alive and expanding. Because of
the abruptness of their appearance, the difference in tone from spiritual to everyday financial operations of the churches, and the emphasis on practical envoys
who work on behalf of fund-raising, these passages and chapters are sometimes
taken to be separate "stewardship appeal" or "administrative" letters. There is no
question that while imbued with Paul's rhetorical grandeur, these necessary fund-
raising speeches for charity speak to a different topic—not to spiritual or theological meditation but to financial pragmatism. As such, whether these passages were
originally from other fragments and lost letters inserted in the undisputed seven
epistles, or were, as is less likely, all written at one time in each of the titled letters, be it Romans, the two Corinthians, or Galatians, is of scant consequence.
The knowledge of origin pertains to manuscript history. However, it is helpful for
the reader to recognize these disjunctions in the letters and leave it at that. And
what is paramount is what we have. These extant, exultant letters are not tidy
short missives in a few pages but long discursive documents, a new art genre, in
a profoundly personal voice. The voice we hear is that of Paul, a historic man,
not an impersonal third-person narrator or anonymous visionary. He is of many
minds, spirits, and levels, and he will attempt to persuade us on all these levels in
his quest as messenger, as apostle, and, to use the most elevated of these word-
carrying epithets, as angel of the crucial good news.

2I know your eagerness[65] and boast of it
To Makedonians, saying that Ahaia[66]
Has been a year prepared, and your own zeal
Has stirred up many. 3Now I send the brothers
To prove that when we boast of you, it's not
Empty chatter about our cause, but that
You will prepare to help with funds,[67] and I
Have said you will. 4If some Makedonians
Should come with me and find you unprepared,
We'd feel humiliated. Now think how
You'd feel for having been so confident.

5So we thought it a true necessity
To urge the brothers to go off to you
Before we do, to arrange for the blessing
From you (already put in place and promised)
And to confirm the gift, which is a blessing
From you that should not seem like an extortion.[68]

---

65. Good will, willingness, readiness from the Greek προθυμία (prothymia). Paul uses this word not as a passive willingness but in its more affirmative meaning of "eagerness" and "enthusiasm."

66. Acts and Paul's letters follow the Roman designations of Macedonia as northern Greece and Achaia as southern Greece. Paul specifically uses "Achaia" to refer to Corinth and its surrounding areas. See note 163, 1 Corinthians 16.15, for more on the historical designations of Achaia.

67. Ready to contribute funds.

68. In these financial dealings, Paul is anxious to appear upright yet firm. It is good to look at a few key words used in raising charity funds. The beautiful word χάρις (haris), with many meanings, here means "grace" and "gift." Another euphemism is εὐλογία (eulogia), meaning "blessing" or "gift." For gaining collections from the congregation for worthy causes, Paul speaks of "grace" and "blessing" to describe what the gift truly represents. Such praise and persuasion cannot easily be rejected. Yet Paul's anxiety about these moral pressures is apparent when in the last phrase of this part he self-consciously defends his actions, warning that a "blessing" should not be interpreted as πλεονεξία (pleonexia), a negative word meaning variously "extortion" and "exaction" or "greed" and "avarice." The KJV translates πλεονεξία as "covetousness."

792

God loves a cheerful giver

6Consider this. He who sows sparingly
Will reap sparingly. He who
Sows bountifully his bounty will also reap
A blessing.⁶⁹ 7Each of you must give as you
Decided in your heart—not out of pain,
Not forcibly. God loves a cheerful giver.
8God has the power to make all grace abound
For you,⁷⁰ and by always having enough,
You share abundantly in all good work.
9As it is written in the Psalms:
    He scattered everywhere. He gave to the poor.
    His justice endures forever.⁷¹
10He who supplies seed to the sower and bread⁷²
    For food will grow and multiply your seed
And will increase the harvest of your justice.
11You will be rich enough for every kind
Of generosity to generate
A thanksgiving to God through us, 12because
The ministry of this service not only
Provides for the saints' needs, but also flows
Rich and deep into thanksgivings to God.
13And through the testing of this ministry
You're glorifying God by your obedience
To the good news of the Mashiah and
Through generosity of all you share
With them and everyone. 14They pray for you,
Love you for the surpassing grace of God
In you. 15Thank god for his ineffable gift.⁷³

---

69. Here "blessing" also means a "gift" or a "bounty."

70. Grace or gift from the Greek (χάρις). Here, another example of the crucial binary meaning of χάρις.

71. Ps. 112.9.

72. Line 9.10 goes back directly to a line in Isaiah 55.10.

73. Or, "indescribable" gift. The important notion is that God's face, name, and many attributes are unknowable, and therefore indescribable or ineffable as they are great.

Chapter 10[74]

In a taste of the "painful letter" Shaul defends
his ministry against charges of cowardice and
weakness, and demands obedience[75]

Now I Shaul appeal to you by the
Meekness and gentleness of the Mashiah.
I am timid and lowly face to face
With you, but bold when I am far away
From you. 2I ask that I need not be bold
When I am with you, not with that courage
Of confidence, which I think lets me face
Others with daring, who have charged us[76]
As if we walked according to the flesh.[77]

---

74. It is thought that the last chapters, 10–13, of 2 Corinthians, in which the embattled Paul attempts to vindicate his authority, contain such an abrupt change in tone and message that they were a separate letter from chapters 1–9, and may represent the "painful" letter, which we seem to have snippets of or references to in verses 2.3–9 and 7.8–12. However, again, whatever the documentary history of the letters, the last chapters of 2 Corinthians reveal Paul at his most powerful, strident, and eloquent. In mortifying speeches, his anger and pain at the opponents are as real as are his opponents, who engage him at every level of his ministries. In combating their appeal and powers, Paul reaches a grandeur of Lear shouting against his enemies, of Job crying out against the firmament, yet the messenger of God does not raise his voice in indignation and sorrow against bastard princes or heaven, but against those who do not have confidence in the messiah and would undercut his mission. And unlike abused Lear and Job, his roar—his overboasting, he calls it—is mingled with demands for obedience to his authority and an acknowledgment of his weak body in appearance and fact. These currents of grandeur and self-deprecation give a reality and sometimes unbearable pathos to his person and his message. He holds the future of the world's soul, he believes, in his hands. He will not let it go.

75. Literally, "according to my face."

76. From here on, in contrast to preceding chapters, Paul refutes those who charge him with many defects.

77. A number of translations render the beautiful phrase ὡς κατὰ σάρκα περιπατοῦντας, "as if we walked according to the flesh," in speech remote from

₃Though we walk in the flesh, we do not war
According to the flesh. ₄For the weapons
Of our warfare are not of flesh but powers
Of God to overthrow strongholds. We crush
Dissension, ₅anything exalted against
Knowledge of God; we make each thought a captive
To the obedience to the Mashiah.
₆We are prepared to punish every act
Of disobedience, when your obedience
Is complete. ₇Look at what's before your eyes.

He boasts and with good cause
If anyone is confident of living
With the Mashiah, think again. As he
In his own heart belongs to the Mashiah,
We also do. ₈Now even if I boast
Too much of our authority, which God
Gave us to build you up, not tear you down,
I will not feel ashamed. ₉I do not care
To frighten you with letters. ₁₀Yes, they say
His letters come as fat and powerful
But the appearance of his body's weak,
His speech contemptible! ₁₁Let such people
Know that whatever we are, far away
In letters, so shall we be in their presence.

Paul's words, for example, "we live by the standards of this world" (New International Version), and "we are acting according to human standards" (New Revised Standard Version). These and most contemporary versions interpret an important metaphor by eliminating it only to replace it with a weak and pedestrian one that lacks the intrinsic reverberating mystery of the Greek Bible. The KJV and the New King James Version let Paul's phrase stand. Theirs are faithful to Paul's word and his intended use of the word. While many think the King James old-fashioned, with some mistakes and some prejudices that may slant a passage to a prescribed theology, in almost every way it remains (along with the even older Tyndale version) the most faithful to the plain Greek text. It also serves as a vital and constant dictionary of meaning and understanding for any translation into modern English.

Let him boast, who boasts in the lord!
> 12We do not dare to rate or to compare
> Ourselves with those heaping praise on themselves.
> But when they measure themselves and compare
> Themselves to one another, they don't have
> A clue about what they are doing. 13We
> Don't lose all measure when we boast. We keep
> Within the canon measure granted us
> By God, reaching as far away as you.
> 14Yet we don't reach to you, stretching beyond
> Our limits when we got to you. We came
> With the good news of the Mashiah. 15We
> Do not scatter endless claiming of the work
> Of others, but as your faith grows our hope
> Is that our sphere of mission also grows
> Into its plenitude. 16Then we can preach
> The good news in far regions without claiming
> Authority already in the hands of others.
> 17But one who boasts, let him boast in the lord.
> 18Not the man who commends himself wins praise,
> But he who gives his praise to the Mashiah.

Chapter 11

My folly compared to the false Mashiahs[78]
> I wish you could put up with a bit of
> My foolishness. Do bear with me. 2I feel
> A jealousy for you, a jealousy
> Of God.[79] I promised you, virgin and pure,

---

78. Often the subtitles in study Bibles give "false prophets," which is correct in that Paul is furious against the false prophets, his rivals and antagonists, but the first reference in the text implies but does not yet clarify the "someone" as a false prophet but does state that "someone" has proclaimed another Yeshua as the messiah.

79. Or, "godly jealousy" or "as God might have." The version about is literal and open to interpretation, as is the Greek.

In marriage to a bridegroom, the mashiah,
3Yet fear that as the serpent through its cunning
Beguiled Havah,[80] your minds may be corrupted
From the simplicity and purity
In the Mashiah. 4But if someone comes
And preaches another Yeshua[81] whom
We do not preach, or you receive a spirit
Which you have not received before, other
Good news, which you have not accepted, welcomes
The man with cheer. 5But I am in no way
Inferior to these super messengers.[82]
6I may be rude in speech,[83] but not in knowledge,
Which I have shown to you in every way.

Shaul robbed other temples to serve you
7Was it a sin for me to lower myself
So you might be exalted while I preached
Good news of God as a free gift to you?
8I even robbed other synagogues, taking
Stipends so I could serve you at no charge.[84]
9When I was with you and had needs, I never
Burdened any of you, since the brothers
Who came down from Makedonia took care
Of them. I always kept from loading you

---

80. Eve from the Greek Εὖα (Eva), from the Hebrew חַוָּה (havah).

81. See note 78 on first subtitle in this chapter.

82. Or, "super-apostles," Paul writes, sarcastically.

83. Or, "an amateur in oratory." Paul, the master rhetorician, in a flight of false modesty, speaks of himself as rude or unskilled in his *logos*. The word he uses, ἰδιώτης (idiotes), from which "idiot" derives in English, is less pejorative in Greek, related to ἰδίως (idios), meaning "in one's own special or personal way," as found in the English word "idiolect," a personally invented language that may be applied to Emily Dickinson, another idiosyncratic master of rhetoric.

84. Paul feels beleaguered. If he does not charge, his free gifts are proof that his ministry is worth nothing. If he charges, he is unworthy for expecting payment for his work. In turn Paul strikes back, colorfully boasting of robbing others to care for his own, accusing enemies of grasping, greedy ways, and keeping for themselves.

With my encumbrances, and will not now.
10And as for the truth that the Mashiah
Lives in me, I will not silence this boasting
Through all of Ahaia. 11Why should I?
Because I don't love you? God knows I do!

Pseudo prophets as Satans of light

12What I am doing I will keep on doing
To cut the chance of those who want the chance
To boast that they are seen to be our equals.
13These are the pseudo prophets, phony workers,
Disguised as messengers of the Mashiah.
14No wonder! Even Satan is disguised
As an angel of light.[85] 15So it's not strange
That Satan's ministers are robed as ministers
Of justice, but their end will match their deeds!

---

85. In the Hebrew Bible, Satan remains within the ranks of the heavenly court: an adversary, a legal prosecutor, often as agent provocateur who coaxes people into their worst moral tendencies. Only in intertestamental literature is Satan associated with the devil as the serpent in the Garden of Eden. Drawing from intertestamental example, Paul is the first in the New Testament and in Christianity to assail his rival teachers in the Messianic movement with the infamous titles of Satan and satanic. In the later gospels the satanic theme is a well-established curse and weapon for demonizing Jews and Judaism. It should be noted that for the smooth development of later Christianity, the fact that Jesus and his entourage were Jews escapes popular perception, and in the gospels the New Testament fumes against the diabolical and satanic Jew (John 8.44). There are fine studies about the history of Satan, from his earliest appearance in Numbers, 1 Kings, and the Psalms to his many disguises and names, including heroic roles as Mephistopheles in Goethe's *Faust* and Milton's *Paradise Lost*. The finest recent book on Satan is Elaine Pagels's *Origin of Satan*. She writes, concerning these verses in Paul, "The apostle Paul himself, confronted two generations earlier by rival teachers, tried to prevent them from speaking, calling them Satan's servants, 'false apostles, deceptive workers, disguising themselves as apostles of Christ. And no wonder! Even Satan himself disguises himself as an angel of light. So it is not strange if his servants disguise themselves as servants of righteousness' (2 Cor. 11:13–15). 'But,' Paul adds ominously, 'in the end they will get what they deserve.'" See Elaine Pagels, *The Origin of Satan* (New York: Vintage, 1995), 150.

Shaul boasting as the fool of god

16Again I say, let no one take me for
A fool, but if you do, then as a fool
Accept me so I too can boast a little.
17What I say now has nothing sanctioned by
The lord, but in my foolishness I speak
In this confidence of boasting. 18Many boast
Of matters of the flesh. 19I also boast,
And you're cheerful with fools since you are smart.
20You put up with anyone who makes you slaves,[86]
Who eats you live, who robs you and exults
If someone slaps you in the face. 21I say
In shame, we are too weak! Yet when someone
Dares boast, I also boast, the daring fool!

Sufferings

22Are they Jews? So am I. Are they Yisraelis?[87]
So am I. Are they from the seed of Avraham?[88]

---

86. Suddenly, after self-mockery and humbly playing the satiric jester, Paul shifts to mocking the Corinthians who put up with the imposters who are actively abusing them. If ever there is a politician at work (politician, from the Greek *politikos*, of the city, citizen), here Paul uses the political instrument of the long letter, which he has invented, as the new media power of his day. With it he reaches the Corinthians in the Messianic synagogues who have been disobedient to his authority. By turning an ear to rival teachers, the congregation is out of control. As he responds to challenge, his compelling descriptive speech renders this portrait of a man rarely in tranquility. Rather, he is an articulate, tormented fighter for the cause, for his version of what will, in triumph of scripture and movement, be the foundation of Christianity.

87. *Yisraeli* (Israeli) meaning "one from Israel." Israeli, or, in its Greek form, Israelite, from the Greek Ἰσραηλίτης (Israelites), from the Hebrew יִשְׂרְאֵלִי (yisraeli), meaning "Israeli" or "Jew." The initial "y" (yod in Hebrew) is, in both transcriptions, changed to English "i." "Israelite" in English comes not from the Hebrew but directly from its Greek transcription of the Hebrew original. Going from Greek to English, the Greek masculine singular nominative case "es" becomes English "e." See note 79 on Romans 9.4.

88. Abraham.

So am I. 23Are they ministers of the Mashiah?[89]
As a madman I speak: I'm a better one,
With more labors and more often in jail,
With far more floggings, in many near-deaths.
24Five times I have received the forty lashes
Less one.[90] 25Three times I was beaten with rods,

---

89. For Paul, the enemies, whom he refers to in letter after letter, are not rabbinical Jews but fellow Christian Jews (see note 25 on 2 Cor. 3.3). These are the adversaries in Jerusalem or their emissaries abroad who compete with him for direction of the Messianic movement. Once again, when Paul calls himself a Jew, he is speaking as an ethnic Jew, as opposed to a gentile (a Greek convert), who has recognized that the rabbi called Yeshua ben Yosef was the messiah prophesied in Isaiah, in the Psalms, and elsewhere in the Hebrew Bible. In claiming his Jewish ancestry, he wishes to declare that he is as integrally part of the good news as Christian Jews in Jerusalem. The apostles who knew Jesus in the flesh have been in ministerial and theological combat with Paul, whom they accuse of falsifying the good news by compromises with the gentiles. Paul, in turn, accuses them of Judaizing, meaning raising Mosaic law over the messiah's law and imposing Jewish practices and observances, which Paul had freed the gentile converts from following. Indeed both sides accuse each other, with different meanings, of being pseudo prophets, super-apostles, and Judaizing. Name-calling and theology aside, the battle is personal and territorial. By his successful missions to synagogues in Greece and Asia Minor, Paul has outflanked the Jerusalem core of Messianic Jews. His de facto control of much of new Christendom outside of Israel deeply challenges those with memories of Jesus. Their presumed knowledge of Yeshua in the flesh endows the Jerusalem apostles with enormous prestige. The battle between these major parties will persist through Paul's life. Even his alleged execution, whose place and year are unknown, is also clouded by the uncertainty of who, Roman or Christian Jew, was behind it.

90. Thirty-nine lashes were given so as not to exceed by miscount the forty prescribed in Deuteronomy 25.3. Presumably, as with his other bad encounters, this flogging was the work of his enemies, the Christian Jews. The Messianic movement grew, but until after the 70 Diaspora it represented such a small segment of the Jewish population that there is scarce mention, outside the later New Covenant, of its development. The large problems were with Rome, with which they were to culminate in the Jewish War of 66/67–70; in disputes between Essenes, the children of light, who, as the Dead Sea Scrolls record, wished to destroy the Jerusalem children of darkness; or between anti-Roman Pharisees and pro-Roman Sadducees who favored the Hasmonean monarchy. Once again Paul rises to great estate in his Shakespearean speech on his miseries and persistence. Inevitably, his catalogue of abuse anticipates the cry of another outsider Jew concerning persecution, that is, the compelling passage of Shylock in *The Merchant of Venice*.

And one time stoned. Three times I was shipwrecked,
And passed a night and day down in the deep.
26On frequent journeys I lived through the danger
Of rivers, danger of robbers, danger
From my own countrymen, danger
From gentiles, danger in the city, danger
In the wilderness, danger in the sea,
And danger among the false brothers. 27With toil
And hardship, I passed endless, sleepless nights,
In hunger, thirsting, often without food.
I went naked and cold, 28and day on day
I felt the weight of caring for the temples.

His weakness

29Who is weak when I'm not weak? Who stumbles
In a morass when I don't burn inside?
30If I must boast, I'll boast of what reveals
My weakness. 31God, father of lord Yeshua,
Blessed into ages, knows that I'm not lying.

Fabulous escape

32In Damesek[91] King Aretas[92] compelled
His governor to set a garrison
Of guards around the city with one goal:
To capture me. 33But I hid in a basket
And was lowered from a window down
The wall, and slipped out through his hands.[93]

---

91. Damascus from the Greek Δαμασκός (Damaskos), from the Hebrew דַּמֶּשֶׂק (damesek).

92. Aretas IV was king of Nabataea, southeast of Roman Palestine, which at this time included Damascus.

93. This adventurous gem, more typical of Acts than the letters, is lovely but startlingly illogical as an ending for the chapter. Its appropriate place would seem to be after verse 28, the catalogue of calamity and suffering. Yet following the confessional plaint of physical blows and emotional turmoil, this vivid picture of a picaresque escape works as a fresh, almost mythical diversion in which the "weak" man reveals his powers of survival.

Chapter 12

Shaul's vision

I have to boast. No good can come of it
Yet I'll know visions and apocalypses[94]
About the lord. 2I know about a man
Who fourteen years ago knew the Mashiah.
Was it in body? I don't know. Was it
Outside the body? I don't know. God knows,
3But he was caught up into the third heaven.[95]
And I know such a man. Was it in body?
Outside the body? I don't know. God knows,
4But he was caught up into paradise
And heard ineffable words that no man
Can be allowed to speak. 5For such a man
I'll boast, but for myself I will not boast
Except in weaknesses. 6But if I care
To boast, I shall not play the role of fool
Since I speak truth. I stop. I will refrain,
Not wanting anyone to credit me
With something more than he can see and hear,
7Above all with my flood of revelations.

Thorn in his flesh

7Therefore, to keep from being too elated,
A thorn was stuck into my flesh, an angel
Of Satan who had come to batter me,
To keep me from being too elated. 8Three times
I called upon the lord to yank it from
My body, 9and he said to me, "My grace
Is quite enough for you. Know that your power

---

94. Or revelations.
95. The highest ecstasy.

In weakness finds perfection."[96] So I'll boast
More happily about my weaknesses
That the power of the Mashiah lives
In me. 10And I enjoy weakness, outrage,
The persecutions and calamities
For the Mashiah. When I am weak I'm strong.

A *fool and nothing*

11I've been a fool. You forced me into it
When you should have commended me. I'm not
At all inferior to the super messengers,
Though I am nothing. 12You have seen performed
Among you signs of the true messenger:
My utmost patience, all in portents, wonders,
And major works. 13Have you been any less
Than other temples? I was not a burden,
Was I?[97] Can you forgive me for this wrong?[98]

He *didn't cheat but loved you*

14Look, here I am prepared to see you for
A third time, and I will not be a burden.
I do not want your money. I want you.
Children should not store up their treasures for
The parents, but the parents for the children.
15I will happily spend and become spent

---

96. There are multiple interpretations of the intended symbolism of the thorn, a common one being that in weakness humans have an opportunity to rely on God's strength. It may be Paul's cross, his anger, some deformity in his physical body he is alluding to, or even a cyst or unnatural growth. Paul doesn't say. And were he to say, that too would be a speculation. As a writer he knows that if one reveals too much in speech, the door is closed to richness of meaning and possibility. Closure is to be avoided. His symbol remains open.

97. He did not demand funds or excessive funds from the synagogue.

98. In asking to be forgiven for his wrong, that is, of not burdening his people with financial cares, Paul snaps back to an ironic voice.

All for your souls. And if I love you more,
Am I to be loved less? 16Let us agree.
I didn't burden you. But being crafty,
You say, I got you by my guile. 17Did I
Exploit you through any of those I sent?
18I asked Titos to go and sent a brother
With him. Did Titos exploit you? Like them,
In that same spirit, were we not walking?
Did we not follow in their very steps?

Worried about slander and fornication
19I wonder if all along you think of us
As making a defense before you? No,
We're speaking before God through the Mashiah.
Dear loves, it's all for your edification.
20I am fearful that maybe when I come
I will find you not as I want, and you
Find me not as you want. There may be strife,
Jealousy, rages, factions, slander, gossip,
Conceit, and chaos. 21I am fearful God
Will humble me before you, and I'll mourn
The many who have sinned before and not
Repented for their filth and fornication
And the debauchery of their indulgence.

Chapter 13

Last warnings
This is the third time I am coming to you,
And every uttered word must be confirmed
By the mouths of two or three witnesses.
2I warned the sinners and the rest before
When I was with you on my second visit,
And tell you from my absence, if I come
Again I will not spare them. 3Now you seek
A proof that the mashiah speaks in me.

He isn't weak but powerful in you.
4He was crucified in weakness, but he lives
  By the power of God. We too are weak
  In him, but we will be alive in him
  Bolstered by the power of God toward you.
5Test yourselves. See if you are still in faith.
  Assess yourselves. Do you not realize
  That Yeshua the Mashiah is in you?
  Unless you're unapproved.99 6I hope you know
  That we're not unapproved. 7We pray to God
  That you do nothing wrong, not so that we
  Appear approved, but so that you may do
  The good and we may be the unapproved.
8We can do nothing against truth, but for
  The truth. 9And we are happy when we're weak
  And you are strong. We also pray for this,
  For your perfection. 10I write this away
  From you, so when I come I may not need
  To treat you with severity, but use
  The authority the lord has given me
  For your edification—not destruction.

Goodbye

11So my brothers, goodbye and be restored
  And be encouraged with each other, think
  The same, and be at peace. The God of peace
  And love be with you. 12Greet each other with
  A holy kiss. And all the saints send greetings.
13May the grace of lord Yeshua the Mashiah
  And the love of God and the fellowship
  Of the holy spirit be with you all.

---

99. The KJV translated this as "reprobates," a powerful version implying moral rejection and damnation, which can be read into it, but the extended metaphor of testing and failing is closer to the Greek ἀδόκιμος (adokimos), meaning "not standing the test" or "worthless."

Galatians

Galatians

GALATIANS HAS BEEN CALLED the Magna Carta of Christian Liberty.[1] The comparison of Galatians to the Magna Carta, 1215 C.E., the declaration of civil liberties in England, signifies that in Galatians Paul has given religious liberty to gentile Greeks, making them equal to Christian Jews. He tells the gentile converts that they need not hold to the laws of circumcision, diet, and Sabbath, and that as gentiles they can be as Jewish as he Paul is, though without his birthright Jewish "blood." In establishing this freedom, Paul strikes out against James and John (traditionally Jesus's brothers by Mary) and the Jerusalem apostles, leaders of the Council of Jerusalem, who insist that gentile converts must observe Jewish practices. Paul further castigates the Jerusalem group and the serpentine emissaries to gentile temples who undermine him. With prophetic fervor and peak passion, he derides them as "Judaizers" for holding strictly to Mosaic law and their insistence on circumcision for converts. In the eyes of the Council of Jerusalem, led by Peter, Paul has the derisive credentials of being the "Apostle to the Uncircumcision."

1. Magna Carta, Latin for "Great Letter" or "Charter," or Magna Carta Liberatum (Great Letter of Freedoms), represented in multiple rewritings and interpretations as a restraint on powers of the ruling king in favor of the barons, and ultimately the shift of power from the monarchy and House of Lords to the House of Commons. After the Reformation it was used against the papal Counter-Reformation. The Magna Carta sanctified habeus corpus and influenced the American Constitution and the Bill of Rights. Oliver Cromwell overthrew the monarchy, his followers evoking the Magna Carta, though Cromwell called it the "Magna Farta." It was all things. It targeted Jews for increased restrictions while it promoted personal liberty and human rights. The Great Letter is uniquely appropriate to Paul's singular letters of liberation and especially to the letter to Galatians, which foments freedom of choice for gentiles and a brake on the reigning Council of Jerusalem.

This definitely authentic letter is dated to 54–55, and it is likely to
have originated in Ephesus rather than in Macedonia, its traditionally
sited home. Paul is infuriated about the Galatian churches, which consist largely of Jews converted to Messianism, that is, Christian Jews as
opposed to gentile pagans, and side with the Council of Jerusalem in
upholding Mosaic code. Paul contends that Christians live and are justified by faith, not adherence to law. More than elsewhere, the debate is
about *not* requiring gentiles to be circumcised. He turns to Deuteronomy,
which says, "Circumcise the foreskin of your heart" (10.16), asserting that
an invisible spiritual vow is a true covenant with God and as binding
as a mere external physical body mark. God promised Abraham that
if he were circumcised, he would be the leader of all nations and they
would be blessed. But law (Torah) is not fixed, Paul says. Indeed, law is a
temporal command modified with Christ's coming. And the works of the
flesh are secondary to the works of the spirit. Therefore, not the external
pact of circumcision but the faith pact with God extends justification to
Jews and gentiles.[2] In the end, it makes no difference whether one is
circumcised or not. One is saved through a spiritual agreement through
faith. Through faith alone.

When Paul first spoke to the Galatians, he was sick and they called
him the "angel of God," meaning the "messenger" of God (Gal. 4.13–14.)
But after he left them, other missionaries came, the opponents, who
demanded circumcision. They are not defined but it is clear that they
are the Jerusalem Council's instigators. Each side modifies Abraham
to justify its position. Paul's harshest words are for those who justify
themselves through the law and separate themselves from Christ (5.4).
The Council accuses him of making a direct break with Jewish heritage
and biblical scripture. But he defends himself. During his life he has
no holy scripture other than the Jewish Bible, but he disagrees with
traditionally selective commands in the huge book and comes up with
other biblical verses to legitimize his views, such as the Deuteronomy
interpretation of true circumcision. Paul a Pharisee claims he is fully a
Jew in altering adherence to laws. The Pharisees gave oral word priority
over scriptural letter, and circumstance required change. Paul accords

2. Here Paul's prophetic views come full circle. As early as the late nineteenth century, Reformist Jews rejected circumcision as a bloody and unnecessary ritual.

with God's promise to Abraham by reading his words as an allegory of spiritual commitment. He says that all who are baptized into Christ are descendants of Abraham (3.29).

Paul's expansion of meaning of circumcision is clear if one knows Hebrew and Greek as Paul did. In Torah the word for circumcision and covenant is *berit/brit* (בְּרִית): "circumcision," from "cut," and "covenant" from the ritual of circumcision that symbolized a covenant. Hence Paul speaks not only of a new covenant but also of a "New Circumcision." He contends that the Abrahamic edict to circumcise all males in the household down to servants and slaves no longer holds, and certainly not for gentiles. It is strange that the book of Christianity is called the "New Testament," two words that in Paul's Greek and Hebrew signify, in their double meanings, a new acceptable condition of the adult penis for gentile members.

This debate over foreskin occupied a group of Messianic Jews in the first century. How in religious and intellectual history could an emblem on the body be dominatingly at the conflictive center of epistolary writing? Whatever the practice of *berit* was—a hygienic precaution become law or, like traditional tattoo, an unremovable sign in a shamanistic right of passage—the fights over circumcision split the Jesus movement. Entry into new Messianism and its justification by faith for newcomers depended on what lay physically hidden under a robe. Paul won the debate but, as revealed in Acts, only decades after his death.

Paul provided choice on how to treat the male organ that for Jews got a new look on the eighth day after birth: freedom to cut or not to cut. His decision was the first schism in the emerging sect. For Paul the churches he had planted were in danger of being lost because of their turn to the gentlemen in Jerusalem. He exhorted them at the highest register of fever and word not to abandon his gospel. He saw the members as hypnotized, evil, foolish. He demanded change and warned of afterlife punishment for dissenters. More comforting, he saw change as liberation, a liberty from older scriptural interpretations in order to live in the spirit of Christ, and to pass their day on earth with faith and love.

The crisis in Galatia mirrors larger Christendom. After his death, Paul's views on all these essential differences were to become the general practice of Christians, both Jewish converts and gentiles and their descendants. He opened the new Judaism to the world. There would be other sectarian heresies, but the condition of the penis excited no further arguments within Christianity itself. Debate over the male organ should long ago have disappeared like a bad dream, but the story has lived on between Jews, Christians, and Muslims. In Shakespeare's *Othello*, the traitor Iago, by lies and tricks, dupes the noble Moor Othello, general of the Venetian army, into believing his wife's infidelity. Othello kills Desdemona. When he hears the truth, in despair and self-loathing he kills himself, uttering his ultimate self-degrading anatomical epithet:

> I took by the throat the circumcised dog,
> And smote him thus. [*Stabs himself.*]

The twentieth century gave us the Austro-German Nazi period with another version of that ill debate, horrendously and anachronistically in full swing. The Abrahamic mark on the flesh signified death for the Jew. In a time warp, a 1940s Gestapo officer rounding up the "vermin Semites" would hear Paul's explanation of "freedom to choose" as a lie confirmed by counterfeit identity papers, those self-incriminating epistles, an alibi to conceal who he was. Depending on place, the loud-mouth activist would have been shot on the spot (if it were Ukraine) or shoved into a gas chamber on arrival at the nearest extermination camp.

Galatians is quintessential Paul. No masks, no politeness. You see his face, his rage, his hope, his endless defense of what he knows is the right. Paul was not only a great mind and philosopher of the spirit but a practical and steaming organizer and activist who opened the world to the new Messianism. He fought to rid the emerging sect, based on a human and divine Christ (in Hebrew *mashiah*), of impediments to growth and survival. He rid it of negative commandments, the foremost being the ritual of the circumcision, which would kill his dream of increase. So, free at last, Christianity became a world religion of tested endurance and, as Abraham predicted, in all nations.

Chapter 1

Hello

I Shaul[3] a messenger sent not by men,
Nor by a human being but by Yeshua
Mashiah[4] and by God who is our father,
Who raised him from the dead; 2and all
The brothers who are with me, to the temples
Of Galatia,[5] 3grace to you and peace
From God our father and from our lord Yeshua
Mashiah, 4who gave himself for our sins,
To free us from this present evil age
According to the will of God our father,
5Whose glory goes from aeon to aeon.[6] Amain.[7]

---

3. Paul from the Greek Παῦλος (Paulos), from Saul in the Greek Σαῦλος (Saulos), from the Hebrew שָׁאוּל (Shaul). Paul was born in Tarsos as *Shaul*.

4. Christ Jesus. "Jesus" is from the Greek Ἰησοῦς (Iesous), from the Aramaic יֵשׁוּעַ (Yeshua), a later form of the Hebrew יְהוֹשֻׁעַ (Yehoshua). "Christ" is from the Greek Χριστος (Hristos), and Greek *Hristos* or *Christos* is a translation from the Greek Μεσσίας (Messias), from the Hebrew מָשִׁיחַ (mashiah). "Christ" in Greek also means "the anointed," and "Messiah" in both Greek and Hebrew contains the meaning of "the anointed."

5. Galatia from the Greek Γαλατία (Galatia). A district between the Roman provinces of Asia (western Turkey) and Cappadocia, Galatia is sometimes called Galatia of the East to avoid confusion with where the Gauls and Celts live in Europe. There remains uncertainty among scholars, however, exactly where in Asia and Cappadocia, north or south, the Galatians were.

6. "From aeon to aeon" is from the Greek εἰς τοὺς αἰῶνας τῶν αἰώνων, ἀμήν (eis tous aionas ton aionon, amain), from the Hebrew for "aeon," which is עוֹלָם (olam), meaning "forever" or "long time." The Greek *eis tous aionas ton aionon, amain*, "from aeon to aeon, amain," or literally "to aeons of aeons," is hauntingly alliterative in chant or prayer (as is the Hebrew in liturgy), and is carried over into a close equivalence in English through the three words that derive from the Greek and Hebrew: from aeon to aeon, amain. In offering the Greek and Hebrew words that survive in English rather than "forever and ever, amen," I do not intend to diminish the powerful Anglo-Saxon resonance of words like "forever" and "evermore."

7. "Amen" from the Greek ἀμήν (amen), from the Hebrew אָמֵן (amain). The Hebrew

Only one gospel of faith[8]

    6I am amazed that you have so soon turned,
      Forsaking him who called you by the grace
      Of the Mashiah for another gospel.
    7There is no other, but a few confuse
      You and pervert the gospel of Mashiah.
    8But if we or an angel out of heaven
      Should preach a gospel to you contrary
      To one we preach, let an anathema
      Consume him. 9And again I say, if someone
      Should preach a gospel contrary to one
      We preach, let an anathema consume him.[9]

---

word *amain* was used by Paul in his Greek, as it is used in Hebrew at the end of a passage as a liturgical "in truth" or "so be it." Both the Greek and Hebrew words were probably pronounced with a long ay as in "main." It is appropriate to pronounce the English "amen" as in Greek and Hebrew; hence here it is given as *amain*.

8. "Gospel" here retains its literal meaning in the Greek εὐαγγέλιον (euangelion) of "good news." In this translation, as in most translations, the gospel of faith revealed in his letters precedes in date of composition the four canonical gospels. Paul himself died before the gospels were composed. The canonical gospels tell the life and death of Jesus. Paul's gospel of faith speaks of virtually no moment in the life of Jesus other than the crucifixion. His gospel of faith concerns the revelation of Jesus as the messiah and son of God.

    When Paul speaks of one gospel of faith, he is referring to the revelation of Christ the messiah and the law implicit in his divinity as opposed to the Mosaic law of the Torah. However, Paul rejects the latter in only three significant areas: circumcision, dietary laws, and the Sabbath. By not enforcing these three laws, he makes way for gentile converts to the sect of Messianic Judaism. He rejects no other essential Torah law, and will always cite the Torah to authenticate his ministry. Indeed, he states that the foundation of Christ's law is "Love your neighbor as yourself," a Torah commandment found in Leviticus 19.18.

9. Or let him be cursed or damned. By his repetition of the curse, Paul very early reveals his wrath against competing faiths and beliefs. The anathema gospel would be that of the competitive Gnostics or the gospel of strict observance to Mosaic law championed by the opposing "Judaizing" emissaries from the apostles in charge of the Jerusalem community, who threatened Paul's position favoring openness and eventually Paul's life.

    A staple of religious societies is factional conflict in which each sector demands faith and obedience to its cohesive doctrine, and rejection, by word or war, of

Called by men or God?

10Do I seek approval from men or God?
    Or trying to please men? If I pleased men,
    I wouldn't be the slave of Yeshua Mashiah.
11My brothers, I want you to know the gospel
    I preach is not from men. 12I got it not from men
    Nor was I taught it, since it came to me
    Through revelation of Yeshua Mashiah.

My old ways

13You heard about the manner of my life
    In Judaism, how I persecuted

---

factional dissent. Here we see the beginnings in Christianity of later splits, in which the victor assumes the title of orthodoxy and the loser the edict of heresy. The battle between orthodox core-doctrine leaders and heresiarchs, between faithful and infidel, is universal. We see it in the first century in the Essene "Children of Light" of the desert against the "Children of Darkness" in Jerusalem, in the Umayyad and Abbasid wars in Islamic Spain, in the Albigensian Crusade against Gnostic heresy in Languedoc France.

The battle for doctrinal control in Christendom began with the declarations of Saint Paul against the Jerusalem faction. Though the Jerusalem apostolic leader was James, brother of Jesus, rank did not diminish the bitterness of conflict, as Paul's letters document. Paul's letters of philosophy, love, faith, messiahship are also a detailed history of ceaseless battle for dominion of doctrine and missionary authority. Such battle will continue. Soon after the establishment of Christianity as the official religion of the Roman Empire, Emperor Constantine convoked the Council of Nicaea in 325 to address the threat of Arianism, which it condemned as heresy. A few years later, as he lay dying, Constantine chose an Arian bishop to baptize him into Christianity. On a personal scale we have the burning of Giordano Bruno in the Piazza Campo di Fiori in 1600 in Rome for his metaphysical digressions and acceptance of the Copernican cosmology, and the execution in Brussels by order of Henry VIII of William Tyndale in 1536 for his translation of the New Testament into demotic English, which became the basis for the later King James Version. The larger consequence of sectarian conflict is a history of religious wars. The personal implication is the attack on the individual and condemnation to damnation and an eternity of punishment. What begins with Paul's anathema against the Jerusalem cabal stands out because Christianity has been the dominant religion of the West, but the process began earlier everywhere and will continue everywhere unless a miracle of peace seizes the world.

The synagogue of God[10] and ravaged it,
14And I went further in my Judaism
Than many of my age among my people.
I was an extreme zealot in support
Of ancestral traditions. 15But when God,
Who took me from my mother's uterus,
And through his grace called on me 16to reveal
His son in me so I might preach among
The gentiles, I did not turn suddenly
To any flesh and blood,[11] 17nor did I go
Up to Yerushalayim[12] to find those
Who were the messengers before me, but
I went away into Arabia
And once again came back to Damesek.[13]

18In three years I went to Yerushalayim
To get to know Kefa[14] and I stayed on

---

10. The church of God. The word usually translated from the Greek into English as "church" is ἐκκλησία (ekklesia), from the Hebrew קָהָל (kahal). Using the word "church" is an anachronism. The purpose of its usage is to separate members of the Jesus movement, which met in Jewish temples or synagogues in Jerusalem, from other Jews, thereby suggesting a markedly different period, after the first century, when there was indeed a full break between Jews and Christians. Jesus and Paul spent their lives addressing Jews in temples or synagogues and sometimes, as in Galatia, in temples or synagogues of Greek converts to Messianic Judaism. Ironically, the word "synagogue" is not Hebrew or Aramaic, but an ancient Greek word from the Greek συναγωγή (synagoge), "a meeting place," while the word for English church is a Hebrew word, from the Greek ἐκκλησία (ekklesia), from the Hebrew קָהָל (kahal). From the Greek *ekklesia* comes English "ecclesia" and "ecclesiastical." Going through the Greek back to *ekklesia*'s Hebrew root we have קֹהֶלֶת (kohelet), the book of Ecclesiastes, the "Preacher," referring to the speaker of the synagogue.

11. He did not confer with another human being.

12. Jerusalem from Greek Ἰερουσαλήμ (Ierousalem), from Hebrew יְרוּשָׁלַיִם (Yerushalayim).

13. Δαμασκός (Damascus), from the Hebrew דַּמֶּשֶׂק (damesek). On the road to Damascus, Paul saw an image of Jesus and heard his voice and converted to Messianism, and changed his name from Hebrew *Shaul* to Greek *Paulos*, originally from the Latin name *Paulus*.

14. Cephas or Peter or Simon Peter. Paul's word for "Peter" is the Aramaic "Kefa,"

For fifteen days. 19I saw no other messenger
Except for Yaakov,[15] brother of the lord.[16]
20Look, in what I write to you, before God
I say: I am not lying! 21Then I went
Up to the lands of Syria and Kilikia.[17]
22But I was personally unknown among
The synagogues of Yehuda[18] that are
In the Mashiah, 23and they only heard:
"The man who once assailed us speaks the faith
He ravaged," and they extolled God in me.

Chapter 2

Meeting the leaders in Yerushalayim
Then after fourteen years I went again
Up to Yerushalayim[19] with Bar Nabba,[20]
Along with Titios.[21] 2I went there responding
To an apocalypse, and I revealed
To them the gospel I preach to the gentiles.

---

meaning "rock," which he gives in its Greek transliteration, adding ς (s) to put Kefa in the nominative singular case, giving Κηφᾶς (Kefas). In English we use "Cephas," romanizing Paul's Greek form of "Kefa." Jesus gave his student and presumably later apostle the nickname "Kefa." His given name was Simon from the Greek Σίμων (Simon), from the Hebrew שִׁמְעוֹן (shimon). In English שִׁמְעוֹן is "Shimon," "Simon," and "Simeon." We may call him "Kefa" or "Shimon Kefa."

15. James from the Greek Ἰάκωβος (Iakobos), from the Hebrew יַעֲקֹב (yaakov).

16. According to the gospels, in addition to Jesus, Mary had four sons, who are named, and two unnamed daughters. One of the sons was James (Yaakov).

17. Cilicia from the Greek Κιλικία (Kilikia). Cilicia is the southeast province of Asia (Anatolia) in which Tarsos was and remains a major city.

18. Judea from the Greek Ἰουδαία (Ioudaia), from the Hebrew יְהוּדָה (yehuda). Also is the name *Yehuda*.

19. Paul is probably counting fourteen years from his conversion.

20. Barnabas from the Greek Βαρναβᾶς (Barnabas), from the Aramaic בַּר נְבָא (bar nabba). Barnabas was Joseph, a Levi from Cyprus.

21. Titus, a common Latin name found in the Greek as Τίτος (Titos).

I did it privately—to those who seemed
To be the leaders—overcome with fear
That I was running, or should run, yet all
Would fail. 3But even Titos who was Greek
Was not compelled to become circumcised.

4Yet secretly they brought in pseudo brothers,
Who smuggled in to meddle with the freedom
That we have in Mashiah Yeshua,
And they stole in secret to enslave us.
5But we never surrendered to their guile,
Not even for an hour, so that the truth
Of the good news might always live in you.

Who are these leaders?

6For those who seemed to be important—well,
They made no difference to me. God cares
Nothing at all for mere appearances.
For me they came to nothing. 7Immediately
They saw that I was one entrusted with
The gospel for the uncircumcised as Kefa
Was for the circumcised, 8and he who worked
In Kefa as the apostle of circumcision
Worked in me for my mission to the gentiles,
9And when Yaakov,22 Kefa, and Yohanan,23
The renowned pillars, recognized the grace
Given to me, they offered their right hand
Of fellowship to Bar Nabba and me,
That we should take our mission to the gentiles,
They to the circumcised. 10But one proviso:
That we should keep remembering the poor,
Which for me too was my impassioned task.

---

22. James.

23. John from the Greek Ἰωάννης (Ioannes), from the Hebrew יוֹחָנָן (yohanan).

Shaul accuses Shimon Kefa of hypocrisy[24]

11When Kefa came to Antioheia,[25] I stood
Against him face to face. He stood in clear
Self-condemnation. 12Before certain men
Came from Yaakov, Kefa ate with the gentiles.
But when they came, he drew back, separating
From them, fearing the circumcision faction,
13And the other Jews[26] joined him in his hypocrisy,
So that even Bar Nabba was carried away
By their hypocrisy. 14And when I saw
That they were not walking upright before
The truth of the good news, I said to Kefa,
Before them all, "If you a Jew are living

---

24. In the struggle for control and doctrine between Paul and Jerusalem, although Peter shares James's strict views on observing Jewish law, he is thought to waver in tolerating Paul's opening to the gentiles. The fact of his coming to Antioch to encounter Paul is a sign of mediation. But soon Paul is aware that Peter is there not to accommodate but to contend with him and to convince Paul's own companions to come over to the side of Peter and James. Paul brims with invectives when "certain men," Paul's words for James's emissaries, arrive to promote their mission. As for Peter, he changes, becomes afraid, and will no longer eat with the gentiles. More, Peter's actions bring others around to his hypocrisy, including Paul's most trusted traveling companion, Barnabas, who temporarily is "carried away by their hypocrisy." When Paul sees that "they were not walking upright before the truth of the good news," that is, that they were lying hypocrites, Paul accuses Peter, before everyone, of his missteps. He assails him of both not eating and eating with the gentiles. The talk is one-sided since Paul, as author, reports the incident with only his words to Peter but not Peter's words to him. Given the stakes and temper of the discourse, we assume Peter's retorts to be equally inflammatory. Though Peter's words are unheard, Paul vividly describes his opponent's actions and body movements at the meal and in the room. In this encounter there is an uncanny parallel of the contention between Paul and Peter to the recurrent riffs between Jesus and Peter, culminating in Jesus's proven prophecy that before the cock crows Peter will betray him three times.

25. Antioch from the Greek Ἀντιόχεια (Antioheia).

26. "Jews" here refers to Jews by birth who became Christian Jews like Peter. They are being contrasted with the suddenly untouchable gentile converts to Messianic Judaism at the table.

Like a gentile and not as a Jew lives,
How can you force gentiles to live like Jews?[27]

Jews and gentiles saved by faith
    15We, who are Jews by birth and are not gentile
    Sinners, 16know that a man is not found just
    By Torah law[28] but through faith in Yeshua
    Mashiah, and we have believed in Mashiah
    Yeshua that we might be justified
    By faith in the Mashiah, and not by books
    Of law, since no flesh can be justified
    By Torah law. 17But if we want to be
    Justified in Mashiah and we are sinners,
    Then is the Mashiah a deacon of sin?
    Never! 18If I rebuild what I tore down,
    I prove that I break Torah. 19Through its books
    I died to Torah law to live in God.
    And I was crucified with the Mashiah.
    20It is not I who live but the Mashiah

---

27. These early skirmishings over first-class and second-class Messianic Jews, over Jews by birth and gentile converts to Messianic Judaism, reveal early intrafamily conflict in the Jesus movement. Both sides assert to being Jews, with no hint of the fuzzy dissemblance of Jewishness intrinsic in the gospels. Paul, who has taken the gentiles as his cause, stands against James, Peter, and John, who give priority to born Jews and make excessive demands on the gentile converts. For Paul these Jerusalem apostles and their emissaries are his target, his danger, his grief.

As for traditional Jews, they are not feared opponents and their role is minor. However, they remain the main source for converts to Messianism: hence Paul's missions to distant synagogues.

It is hard to keep members of the cast straight, but critical to do so.

Since the apostles are Jews, without exception, without denial, without reservation, to confuse the Christian Jews of Jerusalem, the Judaizers, with traditional Jews is, alas, inevitable, but wrong casting. This mistake in identity has an obvious parallel, of terrible consequence, with the intentionally blurred identity of Jews in the later gospels and Acts. Once again, all major actors in the cast are Jews, but the implausible acceptance of Jesus and followers without Jewish identity has permitted a history of extreme anti-Judaism.

28. Or books of law. The books of law are Torah.

Lives in me. Now the life I live in flesh
I live by faith in our God's son, who loved me
And gave himself to me. 21I don't reject
The grace of God, yet if I'm justified
Through Torah, then Mashiah died for nothing.

Chapter 3

Torah law or faith

O foolish Galatians! Who bewitched you?
Before your eyes Yeshua the Mashiah
Was publicly displayed upon the cross!
2I want to learn one thing from you. Did you
Take in the spirit from the books of Torah
Or from listening to faith? 3Where is your mind?
Did you begin in spirit to end up
In flesh? 4Did you suffer through all of this
For nothing? 5Just for nothing? He who gave
You spirit and worked wonders before you,
Was it through Torah law or hearing faith?

Avraham's faith rewards all peoples

6As Avraham[29] had faith in God, and he
Was singled out for justice,[30] 7you must know
That those of faith are sons of Avraham.
8Scripture foresaw that God would justify
The nations by their faith. God told the gospel

---

29. Abraham from the Greek Ἀβραάμ (Abraam), from the Hebrew אַבְרָהָם (avraham). "Abraham" means "father of many."

30. Gen. 15.6. "Sons" in the next verse can be interpreted as children or descendants of Abraham. According to Paul, because the gentiles accept Judaism, they also are true descendants of Abraham, and need not be Jews by birth and circumcision to be considered fully Jews, and with all privileges of other Jews like Paul and Peter (see Gal. 2.14).

At first to Avraham, saying, "All nations
Will be blessed in you."³¹ ₉So those with faith
Are blessed like Avraham, one who had faith.

A curse hanging from a tree
 ₁₀All under Torah books of law are under
A curse. It is written in Deuteronomy:
    A curse on anyone who does not obey
      All things written in Torah
      And fails to do them.³²

---

31. Gen. 12.2, 18.18, 22.18, 26.4, 28.14. Nation, people, gentile, heathen (depending on context and intention) from the Greek ἔθνος (ethnos), from the Hebrew גּוֹי (goy), and plural גּוֹיִם (goyim).

Genesis 18.18 reads, "Abraham will surely become a great and powerful nation, and all nations on earth will be blessed through him." The word "nations" can mean "gentiles" in the general sense of non-Jews, but not one nation, people, or religious sect. This is significant because by Hellenistic times, the Greek *ethnos* has evolved into multiple meanings, one of which in biblical Koine signifies gentiles who were converts to Messianic Judaism. But God's speech in the Hebrew scripture of Genesis 18.18 does not destine the *goyim* to be Paul's converts or be Christians in general. In Abraham's mythical day, there were no Pauline converts nor later Christians about, but hosts of other peoples and religions in the world for Abraham to understand as targets for God's promise of blessings.

In Galatians 3.6 Paul paraphrases Genesis correctly in Greek, rendering *ethnos* as "nation" or "people." But in almost all old and new English translations of Galatians, *ethnos* becomes "gentiles." The widespread and judicious New Revised Standard Version yields, "And the scripture, foreseeing that God would justify the Gentiles by faith, declared the gospel beforehand to Abraham, saying, 'All the Gentiles shall be blessed in you'" (Gal. 3.8.). A thousand years after Genesis, the polyvalent Greek *ethnos* could mean "Gentiles," but not here. Paul respects the Abrahamic covenant. By not selecting any one nation, people, or sect to gain dominion, his Greek passage retains the majesty of the inclusive Hebrew scripture. True to his classical and biblical erudition, Paul sticks close to Genesis 16.6 and 18.18. Most English versions of the promise to Abraham have changed God's prophecy of a broad sweep of nations to a wishful designation of a saint's gentile converts. Such parochial renderings underscore the frequent difficulties in Bible translation when anachronistic exegesis is applied to early scripture and historical event.

32. Deut. 27.26.

11No one is justified with God, who lives
  By law, since clearly the just live by faith.[33]
12But law is not from faith. Rather, one says:
  "Whoever does the things of law will live
  By them."[34] 13Mashiah ransomed us from
  The curse of law by becoming a curse
  For us. It is written in Deuteronomy:
      Cursed is anyone hanging from a tree.[35]
14Through the Mashiah Yeshua, let the blessing
  Of Avraham come to the nations[36] so that we
  Receive the promised spirit through our faith.

Promise to Avraham

15Brothers, I speak for man.[37] No one can add
  Or nullify a confirmed covenant.

---

33. Hab. 2.4.

34. Lev. 18.5.

35. Deut. 21.23. A most moving symbolic reference. Paul, as always, has a trained and imaginative eye for scouring the Hebrew Bible for his authority and poetry.

36. "Gentiles," rather than "nations," again appears elsewhere as the singular target for Abraham's blessing.

37. Although both "brothers" and "for man" are sexist, to substitute "brothers and sisters" or "humanity" or "human beings" for these two words, as other versions do, would make the text sound proper to men and women alike, which would be admirable if that propriety were also true in the Greek. But the Greek usage is sexist in content and grammatical forms, and as with questions of anti-Judaism in the gospels, if we wish a translation to reveal original text, it is best not to sweeten it.

More, it is historically important and interesting to understand the societal realities in first-century regions where Paul took his mission. Yet one sees little about everyday life in the letters. In this regard the gospels, serializing the life and death of Jesus in a described environment, are vivid and colorful while Paul's settings are bare or invisible. His fullness appears in his spirit and incessant struggles: abysses of despair and heavenly metaphysics; by ways of faith, law, and salvation; passionate encounters with missionaries and congregations; bedlam of friends and tormenters. With scant description of thing and place, the missionary Paul triumphs in a perhaps unwitting autobiography that remains unique in the world. In epistolary episodes, through a deceptive harmony of rhetorical phrasing, he confesses a sorrowing, cranky, raging, loving, and ecstatic mind.

16The promises were made to Avraham
And to his seed.[38] It doesn't say to seeds,
As to the many but to one, your seed
Who is Mashiah. 17And this is what I say.
Torah that came four hundred thirty years
Later[39] does not annul a covenant
Confirmed by God and nullify the promise.
18If the inheritance comes by the Torah,
It would no longer come from promise 18but
A promise made to Avraham by God.

Message of angels

19Why speak of Torah?[40] Law was added for
Transgressions, till the seed would come to whom
The promise had been made, ordained by angels
But through the mediator's hand. But now 20a mediator has
        propriety
Over many, not one. "But God is one."[41]

---

38. Descendants.

39. According to some manuscripts of the Septuagint Greek translation of the
Hebrew Bible, in Exodus 12.40 there was a sojourn of 430 years in Egypt and Canaan,
while in the original Hebrew Bible, Exodus 12.40 destines the 430 years solely to
the sojourn in Egypt.

40. The argument is legalistic in the best Greek traditions of logic and sophistry
and later Jewish traditions of Talmudic reasoning.

41. Galatians 3.20 is elliptical, and this beautiful among beautiful verses remains
not clarified, being brief yet replete with word-next-to-word allusions. Standard
commentaries suggest that while God through Moses, and later through Abraham,
made covenants, resulting in the written law and God's promise, now Christ has
come to replace all parties of mediators through his angels. Therefore, since the
coming of the messiah, Christ has direct access to the promise of God. This also
means that being in, or having faith in Christ, supersedes all earlier mediation.

As proof of God as the source of mediation, Paul's sentence ends with the last two
key words of the Shema. "God [is] one." These words end the Shema from Deuteronomy 6.4–9 and Numbers 15.37–41 שְׁמַע יִשְׂרָאֵל יהוה אֱלֹהֵינוּ יהוה אֶחָד (shema yisrael yhwh elohanu yhwh ehad), "Hear O Israel, yhwh our God, yhwh [is] one." יהוה
(yhwh) called by its Greek description the "tetragrammaton," is often sounded out by

Schoolmaster law yielding to faith

21Does Torah law refute the promises
Of God? Never! If given law gave life,
Then justice would have come through law. 22But scripture
Declares that everything is locked in sin
So that a promise born of faith in Yeshua
Mashiah be delivered to believers.
23Before faith came we felt the custody
Of Torah law until the instant when faith

---

adding vowels under the consonants, yielding יְהֹוָה (yahweh or yahveh). In popular older renditions יהוה is pronounced by its euphemism *adonai*, meaning "my lord."

In going back to the debates over written law versus law through faith in Christ, and matters of promise and mediators, Paul cites the Shema. In the face of early polytheistic temptations the Shema became the foundation of Jewish, Christian, and Islamic monotheistic faith in an eternal God, who is one as opposed to many. In Christianity this monotheism is expressed through three manifestations of God: God, the son, and holy ghost. As always, Paul returns to the Bible for confirmation of his belief. Jesus identifies the later part or continuation of the Shema in Deuteronomy 6.5, "Love God with all your heart and all your soul and all your strength," which he calls the greatest of the commandments (Mark 12.29–30; Matt. 22.34–40).

There is a fascinating importance, or appears to be, in the almost non sequitur but strikingly brief ending to verse 3.20: ὁ δὲ θεὸς εἷς ἐστιν (ho de theos heis estin), "but God is one." Paul alternates in referring to the Jewish Bible and the as-yet-unwritten story of the messiah and his meaning to the faithful. When he reinterprets the messianic purpose, he adamantly presents the law of faith in messiah as superior to the written Mosaic convening. The former is to be selected over the latter when the two diverge. After arguing persuasively about Christ's authority, as our immediate godhead who deals with "man," in a gesture of respect and remembrance he omits the messiah's immediate intervention and restates the great credo that God is one, which becomes thereby the core belief of the old and emerging covenants. Some might suggest that because the Galatians are mainly Greek gentiles who have come from a polytheistic background, this affirmation of monotheism is a reminder and a warning. In his missionary role of bringing good news of Jesus to Jews and gentiles, Paul must recall to all and to himself Judaism's revolutionary doctrine of the oneness of God, of God as the supreme father and creator of the divine and earthly worlds. Without the foundation of belief in an omniscient, just and loving God, there is no Judaism, nor its Abrahamic offspring of merging Christianity and a future Islam.

Would be revealed. 24Torah was our schoolmaster[42]
Bringing us to Mashiah so through faith
We might be justified. 25After faith came,
No longer under schoolmaster, we're free.

In Mashiah the seed of Avraham

26All of you now are sons of God through faith
In the Mashiah Yeshua. 27As many of you
Who have been dipped[43] are dressed in the Mashiah.

---

42. Schoolmaster, teacher, guardian, tutor, slave teacher from the Greek παιδαγωγός (paidagogos), from which we have English "pedagogue." The KJV gives "schoolmaster," which better reflects the intended relationship of Torah law to law through faith, which Paul wishes to convey in his metaphor.

The polemic between Paul and the Galatians is over liberalizing attempts to free gentile converts from the strictures that Christian Jews have followed and that the Jerusalem apostles Peter, James, and John demand. Paul's wrath will reach its peak in chapter 5, for which these denunciations are a preparation. Raymond E. Brown, the esteemed Catholic theologian at Princeton, comments, "We can only guess what happened when this letter was read in the churches of Galatia. Some would have been offended by the intemperate language that called them fools (3:1). Was it proper for a Christian apostle to indulge in gutter crudity by wishing that in the circumcision advocated by the preachers the knife might slip and lop off the male organ (5:12)? . . . Was that polemic not a sign of the weakness of his position?" Paul's polemic is against the "so-called pillars of the Jerusalem church," especially "against Peter who was not on the right path about the truth of the gospel (2.14)" and "the Jerusalem Christian authorities sympathetic to the Jewish heritage," that burdensome heritage of the laws of circumcision, diet, and Sabbath. See Raymond E. Brown, *An Introduction to the New Testament* (New York: Doubleday, 1997), 473–474.

It is well to remember that while during his life Paul battled against his fellow apostles on the issue of truly opening Christianity to the gentiles, the *goyim*, and while he seemed in tangible ways to have failed in convincing his equals in the mission of his way, in the end after his death his way prevailed. Christianity, through the missions and writings of Paul, its most educated and philosophically keen Jewish proselytizer, accepted the gentiles. By the middle of the second century the gentiles became the dominant faction. Paul won and his Jewish Bible and the later gospels, also Jewish documents in person and authorship, prevailed. However, Paul, ever proud of being an enlightened Jew from the tribe of Benjamin, could not have approved the later unnecessary amnesia that disguised Jewish personage and authorship of scripture, and through emendation and interpretation, demonized the source.

43. Baptized, meaning "dipped, immersed, washed."

28There is no Jew or Greek,[44] there is no slave
Nor free, no male or female.[45] You are all one
In the Mashiah Yeshua. 29If you are of
Mashiah, you are the seed of Avraham
And are the heirs by covenantal promise.

Chapter 4

Child slave under law
But I say, as long as an heir is a child,
Even if a landlord, he's no better than
A slave. 2He's under guardians and caretakers
Until the time set by the father. 3So
We too when we were children were the slaves
Of the globe's earthly elements. 4Then came
The pleroma[46] of time, which God sent to

---

44. The word "Greek," Ἕλλην (Hellen), from which in English we have "Hellene," refers to Greeks who have become the gentile converts to Christ, who will become the larger gentile Christian population. The Greek input was dominant in culture, philosophy, and rhetoric, as clearly revealed in the person of Paul, who was not a Greek gentile converted to Judaism but a natively Greek-speaking Jew, as were most Jews in the world during those centuries in greater Greece, including Hellenistic North Africa. Hence, we have the New Testament, composed in Greek, by the Greek-speaking Messianic Jews. The Greek-speaking Jew, as opposed to the Greek gentile convert, is a Ἑλληνιστής (Hellenistes). Paul was a Ἑλληνιστής, a Greek-speaking Jew, as were the evangelists, whose names remain unknown to us, who composed the gospels.

45. Although Paul has been often used to justify the subjugation of women into inferior status in church and family—a woman should remain silent in the congregation (1 Cor. 14.34)—these key words at a crucial moment of revelation can be used equally well to speak to the promise of women's freedom in all areas of religious and personal life. The words are important because they include not only woman and man but also Greek and Jew, slave and free; in other words, they reach to all group distinctions of national ethnicity, religion, and social status, and say that difference is irrelevant, that we are all one and the same, and equally the seed of Abraham, with privileges of God's promise.

46. Fullness, a favorite Greek word of the Gnostics.

His son, born of a woman, under Torah,
5To ransom those under the law so we
Might then receive adoption. 6Since you are
The sons, God sent the spirit of his son
Into our hearts, crying, "Abba,47 father!"
7Now you are no longer a slave but a son
and as a son, an heir because of God.

Will you be a slave again?

8Now at that time when you did not know God
You were enslaved to beings who in their nature
Were not true gods.48 9Now when you do know God,
Or rather you are known by God, how can
You turn back to those weak and beggarly
Elements? Do you want to be their slave
Again? 10You observe special days, months, seasons,
And years. 11I fear I've worked for you in vain.49

12Brothers, I plead with you, be as I am
For I too have become like you. 13You did
No injury to me. 13You know that I
Was sick in body when I first brought you
The gospel.50 14When because of my poor state
Of flesh I was a trial to you, you paused,
You never loathed or despised me, but took
Me in as if I were the angel of God,
As the Mashiah Yeshua. 15What's become

---

47. Aramaic word for "father," from the Greek ἀββά (abba), from the Aramaic אַבָּא (abba).

48. A reference to the Galatian gentile population's pagan deities.

49. The opponents in the following verses are not now the pagan temptation, but the doctrines and persons of the opposing apostolic faction in Jerusalem, which is still under bondage to the Mosaic law that Moses received on Mount Sinai: the Ten Commandments.

50. An allusion to personal sickness, probably of his eyes.

Of your good will? I testify that then
You would have torn your eyes out to give them
To me, 16but now I am an enemy
For telling you the truth. 17The others want
To win you over, not for your own good.
They want to keep you in seclusion, so you
Will want their favor. 18It is good for them
To be so zealous always, not only when
I am with you. 19My little children whom
I suffer birth pains for till the Mashiah
Is formed in you. 20I wanted now to come
And be with you right now, to change my tone,
For about you I'm utterly perplexed.

Allegory of Hagar and Sarah

21Tell me, you who wish to be under Torah,
 Will you not hear the law?[51] 22In Genesis
 It records that Avraham had two sons,[52]
 One by his slave girl,[53] one by his free woman.
23The son by the slave girl was engendered
 By flesh, but the free woman's through the promise.
24These tales are allegories,[54] the women are

---

51. As ever, Paul is ambivalent about Torah law, by which he here seems to refer more generally to Genesis scripture. He repeatedly makes the case for the greater importance of law through faith in Christ, yet will not reject the Torah—meaning "law" as well as those first five books of the Bible where the law is laid out. However, because of his stern opposition to the Jerusalem faction, which he believes is undermining his mission, he associates Torah above all with them, the symbol and fact of their presence, since they oppose him precisely because of their stricter respect for and interpretation and observance of Torah.

52. Gen. 16.15. The sons were Ishmael born to his Egyptian slave girl Hagar, and Isaac (Gen. 21.1–5) to the free woman Sarah.

53. A child or girl slave from the Greek παιδίσκη (paidiski), a diminutive of παῖς (pais), "girl," from the Hebrew יַלְדָּה (yalda).

54. Paul's allegorical reading of Genesis reverses the story. According to Genesis, Isaac symbolizes Israel, and Ishamel the gentiles (21.4).

Two covenants[55] [25]the girl is Hagar[56] from
Mount Sinai in Arabia, born to slavery,
And corresponds to Yerushalayim here.[57]
She and her children live in slavery.
[26]The other woman is Yerushalayim
Above and she is free.[58] She is our mother.
[27]In Genesis it is written:

> Be happy, barren one, who bore no child,
> break into song and shout,
> you who have had no labor pains,
> Since many are the children of the one
> Who has a husband.[59]

Children of the free

[28]Now you, my brothers, like Yitzhak[60] are children
Of the promise,[61] [29]but just as then the child
Born of the flesh tormented the child born
From spirit,[62] so too now. [30]What does the scripture

---

55. The two covenants are not the conventional Old and New Testaments, but the covenant of law and the covenant of promise.

56. Hagar or Agar from the Greek Ἁγάρ (Hagar), from the Hebrew הָגָר (hagar). The association of Hagar with Mount Sinai is unrelated to the Genesis story, but is a way of associating Torah law with slavery.

57. Of the opposing faction in Jerusalem.

58. The Jerusalem "above" corresponds to the archetype of a Jerusalem in heaven, which in the Messianic period will descend to earth (Rev. 21.2). The story is also found in rabbinical teaching.

59. Isa. 54.1. Paul relates this passage in Isaiah of hope to exiled Jerusalem to a promise of restoration though belief in the gospel. Isaiah's song suggests a parallel to slavery and freedom, and the two covenants of law and promise. The usual explanation of Isaiah 54.1 (and earlier 51.2, concerning Abraham and Sarah, and 49.19–20, concerning children born during desolation) is that the desolate times of exile and slavery in Babylon, as earlier in Egypt, will end and the people in freedom will return to a restored Israel and Jerusalem, where there will be many new children.

60. Isaac from the Greek Ἰσαάκ (Isaak), from the Hebrew יִצְחָק (Yitzhak). *Yitzhak* means "he will laugh."

61. Gen. 17.19–20. God's covenantal promise to Abraham of a son with descendants.

62. Gen. 21.9. The notion that Ishmael persecuted Isaac is found in rabbinic Mid-

Report? Cast out the slave girl and her son.
The son of a slave girl will never share
Inheritance with the son of a free woman.[63]
31So, brothers, we are not the children of
The slave girl but the woman who is free.

Chapter 5

Freedom in the Mashiah

For freedom the Mashiah has set us free.
Therefore, stand firm, and don't be caught again
Under the ponderous yoke of slavery.

Freedom not in circumcising but faith

2Look, I Shaul tell you that if you are
Circumcised, it won't win you benefit
With the Mashiah. 3Once more I testify,
To everyone who becomes circumcised,
That you become a debtor to perform
The entire law. 4Whoever is justified
By law becomes estranged from the Mashiah,[64]

---

rash (Jewish commentaries on the Bible from 400 to 1200 C.E.) and goes back to Genesis 21.9, though in Genesis, Ishmael, Hagar's son by Abraham, merely mocked Isaac, as Sarah complained about the child of rival Hagar. When mother and child were sent into the desert and the boy was near death, God rescued the boy, giving him water, and promised to make him a great nation.

63. These are Sarah's words in Genesis 21.10.

64. Here Paul seems to say that obedience to all laws of the Hebrew Bible's Pentateuch includes circumcision. Elsewhere, Paul argues effectively that a spiritual circumcision of the heart or spirit is more important than that of mere flesh, and to prove his point he goes back to passages in Deuteronomy 10.16, Jeremiah 9.26, and Ezekiel 44.9. So in effect Paul argues against injudicious acceptance of popularly understood points of Torah, but not against the entire Hebrew Bible. At times in making a point, he rejects, or seems to reject, more than may be intended, as when in chapter 4 he associates Moses's law received at Mount Sinai (Ten Commandments) with all that he despises in blind obeisance to old law.

And falls from grace. 5Yet through spirit and faith,
We wait in hunger for the coming of
Justification. 6In Mashiah Yeshua
Not circumcision nor uncircumcision
Has force, but only faith working through love.[65]

Enemies

7You were running well, yet who broke your stride
And stopped you from persuasion by the truth?
8Persuasion was not from him who called you.[66]
9A little yeast raises a lump of dough.
10And I am confident that through the lord
You will have no other thought. Yet those
Who trouble you, whoever they may be,
Will bear the blame. 11I still preach circumcision.
Why am I downtrodden? That blunder at
The cross is void.[67] 12I wish those bothering you
Would simply chop off their own testicles![68]

---

65. In "not circumcision nor uncircumcision / has force, but only faith working through love," Paul says precisely and fully his dominant vision of openness and his faith in faith through love. Elsewhere it is faith in the messiah or God.

66. Meaning not from the "Judaizers," that is, the apostles James and Peter, who, Paul argues, want to take the Messianic movement back to unpleasantly enforced laws in the Bible.

67. The blunder or stumbling block at the cross was failure of some Jews not to recognize the rabbi Yeshua ben Yosef as the awaited messiah. However, those Jews who saw Jesus, not as a Galilean whom the Romans executed as a seditionist but as indeed the messiah, became the core of the Jesus movement, which at this time was experiencing expansion and conflict. The nature of that collision of beliefs, between Paul and his apostolic brothers in Jerusalem, is a principle drama of these letters.

68. The KJV avoids the meaning. Modern versions give "castrate themselves," which is correct, though lacking the graphic sense of the exhorting command in the Greek ἀποκόπτω (apokopto), which means "to chop off from oneself." Since the subject concerns circumcision, it makes a bit more sense to assume that Paul is asking the listener to lop off the penis rather than the testicles. Either way Paul is not happy with those, presumably the apostles, who have given the Galatians bad information. Being a true person of conflicting feelings, after this outburst of hatred for those who

By spirit not by flesh

    13You have been called to freedom. A freedom,
      My brothers, not for the impulse of flesh,
      But be the slaves of love to one another.
    14The entire law is summed up in one saying:
      Love your neighbor as yourself.[69]
    15But if you bite and swallow one another,
      See by one another you're not consumed.

Walk in spirit

    16I tell you, walk in spirit and don't yield
      To longing of the flesh. 17Flesh has its desires
      Against the spirit, spirit against flesh.
      These two oppose each other to keep you
      From doing what you wish to do. 18If led
      By spirit, you're not under law. 19The works
      Of flesh are manifest. They're fornication,
      Filth and debauchery, 20idol worship
      And witchcraft, discord, hate and jealousy,

---

are undoing his missions, in the next lines he returns to the Torah to cite Leviticus's dictum on love, and at the same time adds a cautionary note about the dangers of fighting with each other and getting consumed in the process, followed by a longer passage on the evils of sinful behavior of the flesh. See next note on love.

69. Leviticus 19.18 reads, "Love your neighbor as yourself. I am the lord." In verse 4, Paul writes, "Whoever is justified by law becomes estranged from the Mashiah." A few verses later he turns to law to find, in Leviticus 19.18, this passage on loving one's neighbor as the key commandment to live by. In Romans 13.8–10 he also informs us that the commandments are summed up in "Love your neighbor as yourself." In this instance he justifies love through Torah, ending verse 10 with "Love is the fulfillment of the law."

    Paul may give the impression of contradicting his words against the Bible law. However, when temperate, he distinguishes between law crucial to the spirit and law that, for the sake of the gentiles, he must reinterpret or reject. When he speaks about circumcision, he is passionately unsettled in assailing the Jerusalem apostles, and then logical and erudite in finding those passages in Jewish law that reveal that circumcision of the heart (spirit) is better than of the flesh just as love of spirit is better than lust for flesh.

Fits of rage, selfishness, dissension, sects,
21Envy, nights of drunkenness and orgies,
And things like that. I warn you now and warned
You in the past: Practice this kind of thing
And you will not enter the kingdom of God.

22But the fruit of the spirit is love, joy,
Peace and long-suffering, kindness, the good,
Faith, 23gentleness, and self-control. Against
Such things there is no law. 24But those who stand
With the Mashiah Yeshua have crucified
The flesh with passions and desires. 25If we
Live by the spirit, let us walk in spirit.
26Let us not be conceited, challenging
Each other, envious of another's good.

Chapter 6

Be gentle and work for good

Brothers, if a man is found out in a sin,
You who are spiritual should turn him back
To a spirit of gentleness, on guard
In fear that you might succumb to temptation.
2Take up each other's burdens and fulfill
The law of the Mashiah. 3If a man thinks
He is something and is nothing at all,
He fools himself. 4Each man must prove his work,
And then boast of it in himself and not
Compare it to a neighbor's work. 5Each man
Must carry his own burdens. 6Let those taught
The word share all good things, share with the teacher.
7Don't fool yourself. God isn't mocked by you,
For what you sow you reap. 8If you are sowing
To your own flesh, you reap corruption from
The flesh, but one who sows to spirit reaps
Eternal life. 9You're doing well. Let us not weaken

In doing what is good. In time we'll reap.
Don't faint. 10So when we have a chance, let us
Do good to all, and work especially
For those who make a family of faith.

Writing big

11See what tall letters I have drawn for you,
In writing all this down in my own hand![70]

Goodbye, no circumcision, peace

12Those who wish to look good in the flesh try
To compel you to circumcision, if only
So they won't be molested for the cross
Of the Mashiah.[71] 13Even the circumcised
Do not obey the law, yet ask for you
To undergo the circumcision so
That they can boast about your flesh. 14May I
Not boast of anything unless it be
The cross of our lord Yeshua Mashiah
Through whom the world is crucified to me,
And I to the world. 15Neither circumcision
Nor uncircumcision means anything.
Only a new creation signifies
The world! 16Peace be to those who keep the rule,
And mercy also to Yisrael[72] of God.[73]
17From now, let no one give me trouble. On

---

70. Paul apparently had poor vision. He dictated his letters, but here he tells us that he is finishing this one by himself.

71. The notion here is that the apostolic Judaizers (the Messianics who stick to all Jewish law) would like to present a good appearance to the Jews who do not accept Jesus as the messiah, and by urging circumcision they can suggest that they too hold to Jewish law, are Jews, and should be treated as one of the many diverse Jewish sects. For Paul this presentation is false, which is clear from his fiercely reprimanding tone.

72. Israel from the Greek Ἰσραήλ, from the Hebrew יִשְׂרָאֵל (yisrael).

73. In this context, Paul's words suggest Israel of Christ.

My body I wear stigmata of Yeshua.[74]

18Brothers, may the grace of our lord Yeshua
Mashiah be with your spirit. Amain.[75]

---

74. The stigmata are scars, which correspond to Jesus's wounds on the cross. Here the scars or marks on Paul's body are marks of a slave and are meant to reflect sufferings of his missionary work for Christ.

75. Amen.

Thessalonikians alpha
(1 Thessalonians)

Thessalonikians alpha[1]
(1 Thessalonians)

In Thessaloniki, a northern Greek city on the sea, Paul founded an early synagogue church in the central square. Its still-extant half-standing Roman temple, with words in Hebrew clearly inscribed on the marble columns, stands below street level in a large excavation site where Paul once preached. Each year as sand, muck, and brick-hard rubble are hauled out, its restoration restores Paul and his good news in the letter 1 Thessalonians. A few months after he spoke in Thessaloniki, Paul sent back this letter from Corinth. The document is the earliest extant letter that Paul composed, in early 50 or 51, and is the oldest writing of the New Testament and of Christianity.

Paul's followers in this great city of mixed peoples were half Jews and pagan Greeks, now converted to and practicing the new messianism. Even today, there is a tangible tie with the most vibrant source of early Christianity. A few hours away by ferry from Thessaloniki, almost in salt air–smelling distance from the port, stands Mount Athos. Six thousand feet above sea level on a peninsula plain is the center of Greek Orthodoxy, called in Greek the Holy Mountain (Ἅγιον Ὄρος). Each of its medieval monasteries from Orthodox Eastern Europe and Greece has its monks, libraries, mosaic walls and ceilings, icons and icon painters, and small wooden boards that are tapped in a special rhythm for waking the "good old men" for midnight prayer. They are trying to live out the religion that Paul designed for them.

---

1. Thessalonians from the Greek Θεσσαλονικεύς (Thessalonikeus). The Greek title is followed by ἄλφα (alpha) representing the letter "a" as well as the number "1."

Thessaloniki is the capital of Macedonia in northern Greece. There in the large port King Philip of Macedonia and his young son Alexander the Great plotted the future of vast territories far into Asia and North Africa, which the son would eventually conquer and colonize. So the title, at least in English not in Greek, misinforms. Salonika and Thessaly have a stirring historical connection. Thessaloniki means "Victory of the Thessalians," taking us south, referring to the brave horsemen from Thessaly who helped Philip II of Macedon to defeat the Phocians. To commemorate his victory, Philip named his newborn daughter "Thessaloniki." When Cassander, king of Macedon, who founded the port city, married Philip's daughter, he honored the present metropolis by titling it with his wife's name.

Paul writes with affection for the congregation, encouraging them to persevere as he warns against threatening community opposition and their own loose sexuality. He defends himself against an array of slanderous accusations about his character and motives. But these negative words and notions do not dominate. Paul writes a happy and encouraging letter. He preaches to be fearless of death, since the Parousia (from Greek παρουσία), the second coming of the Christ, is imminent. Paul and his congregation believe that the Christ will return soon. So too the end is near. Yet members of the new faith fear that the recent dead may not be eligible for salvation. Paul tells them that they are passing through a previously unequaled Satanic opposition to God, but Christ will return, punish the wicked, and save the living as well as those who have gone to sleep. All believers will be with the lord (4.13–18). The people must hold firm (2.1–17). Paul's response is often apocalyptic (5.1–11), with the fiery imagination of the still-to-be-written Revelation. Paul never lacks ascending eloquence in his letter sermons.

The text is debated, as it is in most of the letters, about whether it consists of one or several joined letters. It is one constancy of breath. With one brief exception. Between verses of gratitude and lyrical passages of Paul's yearning love for faraway faces in the port city appear lines 2.14–16, a terrifying anti-Judaic interpolation. These lines foretell a dark cloud in the later gospels:

And so, my brothers, you were imitators,
Of synagogues of God in the Mashiah

Yeshua in Yehuda, for you suffered
The same things from your own compatriots
As they have suffered from the Jews, who killed
Lord Yeshua and the prophets, and who drove
Us out. They displease God and are against
All men, preventing us from speaking to
The gentiles so they might be saved. Their sins
Abound beyond all measure, always,
Until God's wrath will come on them at last.

This same accusation appears in the gospels of Matthew and John. Here it is punched in "brazenly," as some critics say, as a stain unjustly penned into a superb document. Amid good cheer, fellowship, and upbeat aspirations comes the hateful charge that the Jews of the Old Testament killed their prophets. Its presence mocks Paul's missions to the Jews in the synagogues, be they in Corinth or Thessaloniki, which has been to persuade Jews to accept Jesus as the messiah and so advance his ministry of good news. Paul's target for conversion in the big cities *is* the large Jewish communities, whom he approaches as a Jewish reformer for a new Judaism within the synagogue soon to be called "church." In a mission promising brotherly love and salvation, he would not alienate the Jews by demonizing accusations supported by no biblical text. Christian theologians have long asserted that these vilifications are a blight in the history of the Christian conscience and should be exposed as such.

How can these lines jive with Paul, who in the letters asserts that he was and is a Jew? In Philippians he describes himself as "circumcised on the eight day, of the tribe of Benyamin, a Jew and born of Jews, in law a Pharisee" (Phil. 3.5). Paul is expanding his faith by declaring Judaism's fulfillment in Jesus. However, the insertion of the anti-Pauline verses 2.14–16 cannot diminish 1 Thessalonians. Paul could no more control his posthumous imitators who gave us six pseudo-Pauline epistles than he could erase interpolations of later eager clerical scriveners. The interpolation, which suspiciously appears as a non sequitur intrusion in Paul and also in the gospels, suggests a post-gospel scribe since the evangelists were unfamiliar with Thessalonikians. If these textual emendations are accepted as genuine, or excused as insignificant, the interpolation adds the cruelest face of anti-Judaism as a specter within his mission, which is an injustice to Paul. Paul's mission was to universalize contemporary Judaism, not to create demons of his biblical ancestors.

As Paul's probably earliest extant letter—surely not the first piece of lyrical-philosophical writing by the master artist from Tarsos—its themes are not yet the justification through faith. Rather they are simply love, faith, and happiness, watch how you live and behave in the holy room. He does assuage fears about death, which is a strength of all religions. One wonders if biological death were not part of the miracle of consciousness, if the end, the unknown were not a constant in human awareness, what place religion might hold. But in this first essay, Paul addresses the end through the resurrection and its meaning for the people, for the people with faith in the messiah who does not die forever.

Chapter 1

Hello

 Shaul[2] and Silouanos[3] and Timotheos[4]
 To the temple of the Thessalonikians[5]
 In God the father and in the lord Yeshua
 The Mashiah.[6] Grace to you all and peace.

Thank you

 2We thank God at all times for all of you,
 And in our prayers endlessly mention you,
 3Remembering your work of faith and labor
 Of love and patience and hope in our lord
 Yeshua the Mashiah before our God
 And father, 4and we know my brothers who
 Are loved by God because he's chosen you.
 5Because our good news came to you not solely
 By way of word but also filled with power
 And holy spirit and immense assurance,
 You know what kind of men we were with you.

---

2. Paul from the Greek Παῦλος (Paulos), from Saul in the Greek Σαῦλος (Saulos), from the Hebrew שָׁאוּל (Shaul). Paul was born in Tarsos as *Shaul*.

3. Silvanus from the Greek Σιλουανός (Silouanos), probably from the Hebrew סִילְוָנִי (Sylvany). Silvanus seems to be the same person as Silas, a prophet and leader in the Jerusalem synagogue who was said to accompany Paul in his second missionary journey (Acts 15.22, 15.32).

4. Timothy from the Greek Τιμόθεος (Timotheos).

5. Thessalonikian from the Greek Θεσσαλονικεύς (Thessalonikeus), an inhabitant of Thessaloniki, the ancient port capital of Macedonia in northern Greece.

6. Christ Jesus. "Jesus" is from the Greek Ἰησοῦς (Iesous), from the Aramaic יֵשׁוּעַ (Yeshua), a later form of the Hebrew יְהוֹשֻׁעַ (Yehoshua). "Christ" is from the Greek Χριστος (Hristos), and Greek *Hristos* or *Christos* is a translation from the Greek Μεσσίας (Messias), from the Hebrew מָשִׁיחַ (mashiah). "Christ" in Greek also means "the anointed," and "Messiah" in both Greek and Hebrew contains the meaning of "the anointed."

6You were like us and like the lord. The word
Reached you with suffering and joy. Joy came
From holy spirit 7making you a model
To all believers in Makedonia7
And Ahaia.8 8For from you the lord's word_
Is heard not only in Makedonia
But resonates in every place your faith
In God is known. Therefore we have no need
To speak of anything 9and they report
What kind of welcome we received from you
And how you turned to God, rejected idols,9
To serve a true and living God, 10await
His son from heaven, whom he raised up from
The dead, Yeshua. It is he who will
Deliver us from anger which is coming.10

Chapter 2

Paul's way of life in Thessaloniki
    You know, brothers, how my visit to you
    Was not in vain, 2but though we suffered once,

---

7. Macedonia from the Greek Μακεδονία (Makedonia).

8. Achaia or Achaea, from the Greek Ἀχαΐα (Ahaia). The Roman province of Achaia, created in 146 B.C.E., included the main parts of Greece, Attica, Boeotia (perhaps including Epiros), and the Peloponnesos.

9. "Idols" of Greek gods and goddesses. The agon between Christianity and Greco-Roman civilization was resolved only in the early fourth century when the Caesar Constantine became the first Christian emperor of the Roman Empire. For Paul and other writers of the intertestamental period, this conflict between two cultures is contrasted, and not in flattering terms for the Greco-Romans, in the words "idol" and "God." Here, as in virtually all religions, the emerging Jesus movement, though eclectic in origin, is monolithically chauvinist in the politics of survival. In future divisions in Christianity, as in all faiths, each side sees itself as orthodoxy (uprightness) and the rival "other" as heresy or witchcraft.

10. The anger or wrath, also called "justice," on the second coming of Christ was considered imminent, and much of the philosophy of life, death, and resurrection was affected by belief in the impending coming.

Were miserably mistreated in Filippoi,[11]
As you know, we were bold in God to speak
To you God's good news amid agony
Of conflict. 3Our appeal to you is free
Of trickery, impurity, and guile,
4But just as we have been approved by God
  To be entrusted with the gospel, so
We speak not to please men but to please God.
He is the one examining our hearts.

5We uttered not a word of flattery,
  As you know, nor with any hankering
  Of greed—God is my witness—nor did we
  Seek praise from men, neither from you nor others.
7As messengers of the Mashiah we may
  Have made demands, but we were innocent
  With you the nurse ever tending her children,
8So we desire to share with you not only
  Good news of God but also our own souls
  Because to us you have become so dear.

9My brothers, you remember the harsh toil,
  How night and day we worked not to become
  A burden on any of you. We preached
  Good news of God. 10You are the witnesses,
  And also God, how piously and justly
  And blamelessly we were with you believers.
11Likewise you know how we have dealt with each
  Of you as would a father to his children,
12Exhorting and encouraging and pleading
  For you to walk in ways honoring God,
  Who calls you to his own kingdom and glory.

---

11. Philippi from the Greek Φίλιπποι (Filippoi), a city in Macedonia founded by
Philip of Macedonia, in Paul's time under Roman rule. Paul founded the first church
in Europe in Philippi.

13Therefore we also endlessly thank God
That when you heard the word of God from us
You accepted it not as the word of men
But as it truly is, the word of God
That also works in you who do believe.

Of Jews who killed the lord and prophets
14And so, my brothers, you were imitators,
Of synagogues of God in the Mashiah
Yeshua in Yehuda,[12] for you suffered
The same things from your own compatriots
As they have suffered from the Jews, who killed
15Lord Yeshua and the prophets, and who drove
Us out. They displease God and are against
All men, 16preventing us from speaking to
The gentiles so they might be saved. Their sins
Abound beyond all measure, always,
Until God's wrath will come on them at last.[13]

Paul's longing to see the Thessalonikians
17My brothers, we have been apart from you
For a short time, in person, not in heart,
We have even greater desire to see
Your face again. 18So we wanted to come
To you, I Shaul, over and again,
But Satan cut us off. 19What is our hope
Or joy or wreath of boasting, if not you,
Before our lord Yeshua at his coming?
You are our glory and our happiness!

---

12. Judea from the Greek Ἰουδαία (Ioudaia), from the Hebrew יְהוּדָה (yehuda). The Hebrew word is also the name *Yehuda.*

13. See introduction to Thessalonians, pages 840–41. Verses 14–16 are not by Paul. They are routine interpolations by later church scribes and a major source of anti-Semitism in the New Testament. See note 165 on Matthew 23.37.

Chapter 3

Please God by abstaining from lechery
>So when we couldn't bear it any longer,
>We made a choice to stay back in Athenai,[14]
>Alone. 2We sent Timotheos[15] our brother
>[And coworker of God][16] in the good news
>Of the Mashiah to bring strength and heart
>To keep you in your faith 3so none be shaken
>By these afflictions. But such is our fate,
>Which you have known. 4And even when we were
>With you, as we had said before to you,
>We were about to suffer persecution,
>No other word for it, and you have known it.
>5So when I couldn't bear it any longer,
>I sent Timotheos to test your faith
>Fearing that a magician might dupe you
>Into temptation, with all our labors lost.

Timotheos
>6But now Timotheos has come to us
>From you with good news of your faith and love
>And told us how we are in your good memory
>And how you always long to be with us
>As we with you. 7So we are animated
>About you, brothers, during our distress
>And suffering because of your good faith.
>8If you are steadfast in the lord, we are now
>Alive. 9What thanks can we return to God
>For all the joy we have in you before
>Our God, 10while night and day most urgently

---

14. Athens from the Greek Ἀθῆναι (Athenai)
15. Timothy.
16. Uncertain in ancient texts.

We pray to see you face to face and mend
Any and all shortcomings in your faith?
11May God our father and our lord Yeshua
Direct our way to you. 12You and the lord
May multiply and overflow with love
For one another and for all, as we
Love you. 13Strengthen your hearts so they
Are blameless and are holy before God
Our father at the coming of our lord
Yeshua and with all his saints. Amain.[17]

Chapter 4

For God do not fornicate

Finally, brothers, we ask you and we urge
You in the lord these things: As you have learned
From us how you must walk and please our God,
Which you are doing now, improve and keep
On walking and do more. 2You know what orders
We gave you through the lord Yeshua. 3Here is
God's will: sanctification of your body.
You must abstain from fornication. 4Know
Each one of you how to control your penis[18]
In sanctity and honor, 5not in lust and passion
Like the gentiles who don't know God, 6and do
Not wrong your brother, taking advantage
Of him in prurient ways, because the lord
Is the avenger concerning all these things,
As we have said to you before, and warned
You solemnly. 7God did not call us to

---

17. Amen from the Greek ἀμήν (amen), from the Hebrew אָמֵן (amein).

18. Or vessel or body, from the Greek σκεῦος (skeuos). Here, in this warning against fornication, to control one's vessel, the word σκεῦος functions as a euphemism for the male genital organ.

Unchastity but holiness. 8He who
Rejects this rejects not a man[19] but God,
Who also offers you his holy spirit.

Brotherly love

9As for brotherly love I need not write
To you. You yourselves have been taught by God
To love each other. 10And you practice this
With all brothers in all Makedonia,
But we encourage you, brothers, to go
Even further. Abound in love. 11Aspire
To live in quiet peace, mind your own work
And labor with your hands, as we have charged
You to. 12Then walk respectably before
An outsider, needing nothing from anyone.

Returning from sleep

13We do not want you to be ignorant,
Brothers, concerning those of you who've slept[20]
So that you do not sorrow like the others
Who have no hope. 14If we believe Yeshua
Died and arose, so God will also bring
The sleepers[21] back along with him to life.

Coming of the lord

15For this we say to you by the lord's word
That we the living, the survivors left
Until the coming of the lord, will not
In any way precede those who have slept,

---

19. Human authority.

20. Here "slept" is a euphemism for "died."

21. These words have been suggested to mean that the parishioners of the synagogue in Thessaloniki have misunderstood that the messianists will not have to sleep (die) until the coming of the messiah. In these verses "sleeper" carries the verb "sleep" from euphemism to an extended metaphor for "dying."

16For at the signal, the archangel's cry,
And with the blast of God's ram's horn[22] the lord
Himself will come down from the sky, and then
The dead in the Mashiah will rise first. 17Then we
The living, the survivors, joining them
Will be caught up in clouds to meet the lord
Resting in air, and so be with the lord
Forever. 18Courage to all with these words.

Chapter 5

Day of the lord will come like a thief in the night
Concerning times and seasons, there's no need
To write to you, my brothers. 2You yourselves
Know accurately that the day of the lord
Will come like a thief in the night. 3They say,
"Peace and security." Then doom arrives
Like birth pangs in the belly of a woman,
And they cannot escape. 4But you, my brothers,
Are not in darkness for that day to catch
You like a thief. 5You all are sons of light
And sons of day. We are not of the night
Or dark. 6Therefore, let us not sleep like others
But be awake and sober. 7They the sleeping
Sleep through the night. The drunks get drunk again
At night. 8But we belong to day, are sober,
And wear a breastplate of our faith and love,
Wearing a helmet of our hope of salvation,
9But God did not choose us for anger but
To gain salvation through our lord Yeshua
Mashiah, 10who died for us. So if awake

---

22. The Greek reads "trumpet" from the Greek σάλπιγξ (salpinks). The Bible reference is to Isaiah 27.13, and it is not a Roman trumpet that blasts, however, but a Jewish ram's horn, which in Hebrew is the shofar, from the Hebrew שׁוֹפָר (shofar).

Or sleeping, we shall live with him. 11Comfort
Each other and give strength as you do now.

Final instructions and goodbye
12We ask you, brothers, to know those who work
With you, who look out for you through the lord,
And counsel you. 13Consider them with love
Because of what they do. But be at peace
Among you. 14We urge you, brothers, to warn
The lazy ones, comfort the faint of heart,
Protect the weak, be patient toward all.
15See that no one gives evil back to evil,
But always follow good for everyone.

16Always be happy and pray endlessly.
17Give thanks for everything. 18This is the will
Of God in the Mashiah Yeshua for you.
19Don't quench the spirit, 20nor spurn prophecies.
21Examine everything. Hold onto good.
22Abstain from every form of wickedness.

23May the true God of peace sanctify you
Completely, and may all your soul and spirit
And body be blameless for the Parousia[23]
Of our lord Yeshua Mashiah. 24Faithful
Is he who calls you, and he will do so.
25And now I ask you, brothers, pray for us.
26Greet all our brothers with a holy kiss.
27I charge you by the lord to read this letter
To all the brethren. 28May the grace of lord
Yeshua the Mashiah be with you.

---

23. The Second Coming.

Filemon
(Philemon)

Filemon[1]
(Philemon)

THE LETTER TO PHILEMON is generally assigned to Paul, though not always. It is one of the most dramatic letters traditionally assigned to him, wild in spirit like the Book of Acts and the imaginary Paul created by the unknown author or authors of Acts. Unlike the Paul of Acts, however, the Paul here has no powers to walk through prison walls to find liberation. But like that later reincarnation of Paul in Acts, Paul of Philemon assiduously follows legalist Roman law, here with respect to slavery, a notion obnoxious to developing Christianity. Such support of Roman slave laws makes this letter to Philemon suspect as a true document by Paul. At the same time, it is superior, almost supreme in pathos and eloquence, and of much greater interest than the docile letters questionably attributed to Paul. We are in the dark with respect to its full Pauline authorship.

Philemon is a slave owner. His slave Onesimus has escaped from him. Fleeing is a capital offense, and if caught, the slave can be severely punished or put to death by his master under Roman law. Paul meets Onesimus in prison and converts him. Onesimus then works diligently with Paul in his mission. Both Onesimus and Philemon become Messianic Jews. Paul asks Onesimus to return to his master and to deliver Paul's letter to him, which asks Philemon to accept Onesimus back as his slave, in the context of *agapi*, love, without severe punishment but as a brother like himself, Paul. Paul also implores Philemon to permit Onesimus to return to work for Paul in his mission once his slave

---

1. Philemon from the Greek Φιλήμων (Filemon).

has paid him back in full for losses accrued because of his escape. It is uncertain whether the home town of Philemon is Colossae or nearby Laodicea, and the place of Onesimus's confinement is also unknown, though it was probably Ephesus. It is unknown what the results of the letter were, though in Ignatius, *Eph.* 1.3, there is an unconfirmed claim that the slave Onesimus later became bishop of Ephesus.

Apparently Paul is himself in prison when he writes this letter, which he does so again through the good office of Timothy.

As for the reprehensible practice of slavery, in all continents slave labor, by one name or form or another, has been the norm, and continues in huge numbers today.

Slavery was accepted by the church. When the Roman Empire became Christian, under Constantine, slavery continued, flourishing in the Byzantine Empire as well as in the West. It came to the New World in the sixteenth century under the Spaniards, a century before the English and French brought in slaves from Africa. Bartolomé de Las Casas (1474–1566), a Spanish missionary and historian called "the Apostle of the Indies," heroically devoted his life to obtain, though without success, the complete abolition of slavery (the *encomienda*) among the native populations in the New World. In order to save the souls of the Indians for Christian conversion, he proposed to import black slaves from Cuba, who had no souls, he claimed, to work in the mines. In Mexico, slavery was normal even in monasteries and convents. When Sor Juana Inés de la Cruz (1648/51–95), the major poet of the colonial period, entered the cloistered Hieronymite convent of Santa Paula in Mexico City, she brought with her to her luxurious apartment two slaves, one Indian, one black, one of whom she later sold to her sister Josefa for 250 gold pesos. Although Sor Juana's biography, *Response to Sister Filotea* (1691), was the first and truly most significant literary book concerning a woman's right to intellectual and artistic freedom prior to the publication in 1929 of Virginia Woolf's emancipatory *Room of One's Own*, Sor Juana was unconcerned with the slavery that prevailed in the working class in Mexico during her lifetime.

Anciently, slavery was present in Israel and Christianity, in the Hebrew Bible and the Greek scriptures. There were rules concerning slavery in both the authentic and the disputed letters of Paul. He asked for kindness to slaves and commanded that in the spiritual realm they be treated as brothers in Christ. With respect to the slave's obligations in the material world, in the letters in which he discusses slavery, he commands that a slave, under threat of punishment, obey his master and not escape. Until powerful Protestant rumblings in the early nineteenth century, when slavery was condemned as a rupture of the covenant between humans and God, there were effectively no moral prescriptions against slavery in the world churches.

The biblical words for slave, in Hebrew עֶבֶד (eved) and Greek δοῦλος (doulos), had a wide range of meaning, from forced labor to table servant. In both the Hebrew Bible and in the New Testament, *eved* and *doulos* were also used metaphorically to express the relationship of humans to God. So Moses in Deuteronomy 34.5 and David in Psalm 18.1 speak of themselves as "slaves of God," and Paul in Roman 1.1 speaks of himself as "a slave of Christ Jesus."

Hello

I Shaul[2] prisoner of the Mashiah
Yeshua[3] and Timotheos[4] the brother,
I send this to Filemon[5] our beloved
Fellow worker, and to Afia[6] our sister,
2To Arhippos[7] who is our fellow soldier,
To you who are the temple in your house,
3And grace to you and peace from God our father
And from the lord Yeshua the Mashiah.

Shaul's love for Filemon

4I thank my God and always mention you
In my prayers, 5hearing of your love and faith
Which you have for the lord Yeshua and all
The saints. 6I pray that sharing of your faith
May work in recognizing all the good
We have in the Mashiah. 7I was happy
And comforted by your strong love, and you
Refreshed the inner hearts[8] of saints, my brothers.

---

2. Paul from the Greek Παῦλος (Paulos), from Saul in the Greek Σαῦλος (Saulos), from the Hebrew שָׁאוּל (Shaul). Paul was born in Tarsos as *Shaul*.

3. Christ Jesus. "Jesus" is from the Greek Ἰησοῦς (Iesous), from the Aramaic יֵשׁוּעַ (Yeshua), a later form of the Hebrew יְהוֹשֻׁעַ (Yehoshua). "Christ" is from the Greek Χριστος (Hristos), and Greek *Hristos* or *Christos* is a translation from the Greek Μεσσίας (Messias), from the Hebrew מָשִׁיחַ (mashiah). "Christ" in Greek also means "the anointed," and "Messiah" in both Greek and Hebrew contains the meaning of "the anointed."

4. Timothy.

5. Philemon.

6. Apphia from the Greek Ἀπφία (Apfia).

7. Archippus from the Greek Ἄρχιππος (Arhippos).

8. The metaphor of deep heart or inner parts is expressed through the intestines, σπλάγχνον (splanghnon), which the King James Version regularly renders as "bowels," and here, "the bowels of the saints are refreshed by thee, brother."

He pleas for Onesimos

8So though I have the full authority
In the Mashiah to do what must be done,
9But because of our love now I prefer
To appeal to you, and I Shaul do this
As an old man⁹ and now a prisoner¹⁰
Of the Mashiah Yeshua, 10I beg you
About my child Onesimos,¹¹ whom I
Gave birth to in my chains.¹² 11He was at first
Useless to you, but now to both of us
He is useful.¹³ 12I sent him back to you,
He is my heart.¹⁴ 13I wanted to keep him

---

9. The primary meaning in this context of πρεσβύτης (presbytes) is "old man" or "aged," but it also can mean "ambassador" or "elder" with ecclesiastic authority. A touch of both meanings comes through. Lattimore gives "ambassador." However, since in context, Paul is speaking of himself with self-pity, referring to himself in the next phrase as a prisoner, not pulling rank on Philemon, it makes more sense to interpret *presbytes* as "old man."

10. Prisoner of Christ can mean indebted to Christ and an actual prisoner for professing Messianic Judaism.

11. Onesimus from the Greek Ὀνήσιμος (Onesimos). He is a companion of Paul and slave of Philemon for whom Paul writes this brief letter. For more on Onesimus as Philemon's slave, see the introduction to Philemon.

12. Paul converted him when they were in prison.

13. Paul is playing with the meaning of Onesimus, which means "useful," as in a useful helper, as opposed to "useless," his former self before he converted.

14. The letter to Philemon, more than a letter, is a heartbreak monologue, beginning with "I sent him back to you, he is my heart." These words epitomize Paul's (or a later author's) quandary. Paul, like the later church, needed to support Roman law or risk immediate reprisal; but he also wished the benefits of the law, including that of legal slavery. Yet, concerning Onesimus there is a human element. Paul needs the slave for his personal help and his mission and at the same time wishes to improve the lot of the slave, whom he has converted. What lacks in the equation is a critical rejection of (or at least a reference to) the law and practice of slavery. That is taboo and will remain so. It would be dangerous to question slavery, since

slave labor serves the economic welfare of the wealthy, the less wealthy, as well as the church. While the author writing in Paul's name evokes sympathy, the legal practice of slavery is not addressed as an ethical issue. Indeed, he denounces Onesimus's illegal escape. There is no moral rage, as against false prophets or debauchery. Yet Paul does offer a spiritual solution, one that does not entail making Onesimus a freeman. He asks Philemon not to dissolve the bondage but to let Onesimus attend to him, Paul, for a while, and not as a mere slave but in a higher state of brotherly love. Then he will return Onesimus to be with Philemon forever. Paul is also quick to point out that Philemon the slave owner owes his own deliverance to Paul, so *he* has a moral debt to pay off.

Christians in the next centuries, along with teachers, workers, and farmers, will be slaves. No state or religion opposes the system. In the slave-versus-freeman question, a rare exception in the ancient world was that of Solon (638?–559? B.C.E.), the Athenian poet and ruler (archon) of Athens who ended serfdom in Attica Greece. Yet as Philemon reveals six centuries later, Solon's reforms did not endure. His slavery poem decries slavery and abolishes it at least for citizens who for reasons of debt had fallen into slavery:

Apologia of His Rule

Where did I fail? When did I give up goals
for which I gathered my born people together?
When the judgment of time descends on me,
call on my prime witness, Black Earth, supreme
excellent mother of the Olympian gods,
whose expanse was once pocked with mortgage stones,
which I dug out to free a soil in bondage.

Into our home, Athens, founded by the gods,
I brought back many sold unlawfully as slaves,
and throngs of debtors harried into exile,
drifting about so long in foreign lands
they could no longer use our Attic tongue;
here at home men who wore the shameful brand
of slavery and suffered the hideous moods
of brutal masters—all these I freed. Fusing
justice and power into an iron weapon,
I forced through every measure I had pledged.
I wrote the laws for good and bad alike,
and gave an upright posture to our courts.

From Willis Barnstone, *Sappho and the Greek Lyric Poets* (New York: Schocken Books, 1988), 98.

With me, to serve me on behalf of you
While I remain in chains for the good news.
14But without your consent I would do nothing
Forced as a need but through your generous will.
15Perhaps that's why he was taken from you
A while so he might be with you forever,
16Not as a mere slave, more than a slave,
A brother loved by me and even more
By you, both in the flesh and in the lord.

Promise of repayment for losses

17If then you think of me a partner, welcome
Him back. 18But if he wronged you, owes you money,
Charge it to me. 19I Shaul write in my hand
I will pay. Not to mention that you also
Owe me your very self.15 20Yes, brother, let
Me have good word from you of being in
The lord. Refresh my heart in the Mashiah.

Now obey

21Confident in your obedience, I
Wrote you, knowing that you'll do even more.
22At the same time, prepare a room for me.
I hope that through your prayers, it won't be long
Before I am set free and restored to you.

Greetings

23Epafras,16 who is my fellow prisoner
In the Mashiah Yeshua, sends his greetings.

---

15. An allusion that he Paul has converted Philemon.

16. Epaphras from the Greek Ἐπαφρᾶς (Epafras), probably a gentile convert and founder of the church in Colossae.

24So do Markos,[17] Aristarhos,[18] Demas,[19] Lukas,[20]
Fellow workers. 25May the grace of the lord
Yeshua the Mashiah be with your spirit.

---

17. Mark.

18. Aristarchos from the Greek Ἀρίσταρχος (Aristarhos), a companion on his journeys.

19. Demas is a shortened form of Demetrios.

20. Luke.

Filippians
(Philippians)

Filippians[1]
(Philippians)

WHERE PAUL WROTE Philippians cannot be confidently stated. Older scholars give Rome, because Paul is writing from prison, and his letter is referred to as one of the "captivity epistles." But that assertion is based on Acts, and we have no information on whether Paul ever succeeded in reaching Rome, as he intended to, after going to Jerusalem in 60–61 to prepare for his trip to Rome. While in Corinth he had written his letter to the Romans and sent it ahead to Rome to prepare the community for his visit. Apart from Acts, which is historically unreliable, we simply do not know where Paul was when he wrote Philippians. The other three cities where a good case can be made are Corinth, Ephesus, and Caesarea. The site must contain a Roman praetorium (1.12–13), that is, it must be a grand city with important royal headquarters and officials, which makes Rome and Caesarea better candidates. The letter is perhaps two letters or even three pieced together, but the authorship has never been doubted, nor are there any significant interpolations, unless one considers the exquisite Christian hymn (2.6–11), which may be from another time, perhaps earlier and refashioned by Paul, with all its Christological implications.

But the vagueness of place and integrity of letter or letters is of little importance. What signifies is the great quality of the writing, the feeling of love for the new community, gratitude for its contributions though it is poor, and his ongoing struggle with the community to behave and hear his words. No letter is free of ethical remonstrance. Paul himself

---

1. Philippians. *Filippians* is from the Greek Φιλιππήσιος (Filippesios), a Philippian.

must feel poor, indeed. He has been stripped naked, thrashed, placed in chains, probably for being a bothersome Jew stirring up the local people. In Acts 16.16–40 he has driven bad spirits out of a slave girl, and so the local magistrates haul him and his friend Silas into jail. When the prison doors pop open after an earthquake and they refuse to escape, showing loyalty to the Roman Empire, the jailer converts on the spot, a conversion reminiscent of other implausible conversions, notably of the Roman centurion executioner at the cross just after Jesus dies. These many events happen in this once-prosperous city of Philippi, now merely ruins, where a century earlier Antony and the emperor Octavian (Augustus) defeated the armies of Brutus and Cassius, the assassins of Julius Caesar. Octavian made the city a Roman colony, giving local Greeks from Macedon the rights and privileges of a Roman citizen. More, the city was on the Via Egnatia, a main road going from the port of Brundisium (Brindisi) in Italy across the Adriatic Sea to Macedonia and on to Byzantium.

But more fascinating than the adventures and miracles found in Acts is the absolute beauty, simplicity, and depth of these disjointed letters, which still work so well together. Paul thinks of his own death in a morose self-revelation, of Christ and the philosophy of emptiness he attributes to Christ as revealed in the hymn, where Christ empties himself to take on the role of the slave. The act of emptiness is not different, except in lexicon, from the universal emptiness we find in many mystical figures, ranging from John of the Cross to Wang Wei to the Buddha in Nepal. Paul specifically seems to be recalling, most personally, his own self-emptying as he formally left his Pharisee past to join the new messianism, which gave him Christ as the risen incarnation of the divine. So the apostle ventured into the perils of his proselytizing missions.

These high ideas are also accompanied by the customary rage against the intrusive disbelievers, especially the Gnostics and so-called Judaizers, meaning Peter and his fellow apostles in Jerusalem, and against circumcision and other laws that Paul opposes if they are applied compulsorily.

This letter is short and bumpy as Paul moves from one point to another, perhaps because of the joining of the parts. He truly loves the church, and his thanksgiving and gratitude section exceeds that in any of the other authentic letters. The people of his church are with him in their suffering and their common mission.

Chapter 1

Hello

Shaul[2] and Timotheos,[3] the slaves of Yeshua[4]
Mashiah, to all the saints in the Mashiah
Yeshua who are in Filippo[5] with the bishops
And deacons. 2Grace to you and peace from God
Our father and lord Yeshua Mashiah.

From my chains I send love

3I thank my God for all of you whenever
I mention you in prayers. 4I always pray
With joy for you 5because you've shared the gospel
From the first day till now. 6And confident
That he who began the good work in you
Will carry it to completion till the day
Of the Mashiah Yeshua. 7And it is right
For me to feel this, since you all keep me
Embedded in your heart. Whether in chains

Or in defense and confirmation of
The gospel, you all partake in my grace.

---

2. Paul from the Greek Παῦλος (Paulos), from Saul in the Greek Σαῦλος (Saulos), from the Hebrew שָׁאוּל (Shaul). Paul was born in Tarsos as *Shaul*.

3. Timothy from the Greek Τιμόθεος (Timotheos). Timothy is a companion of Paul, and some say the later cowriter of six letters attributed to Paul.

4. Christ Jesus. "Jesus" is from the Greek Ἰησοῦς (Iesous), from the Aramaic יֵשׁוּעַ (Yeshua), a later form of the Hebrew יְהוֹשֻׁעַ (Yehoshua). "Christ" is from the Greek Χριστος (Hristos), and Greek *Hristos* or *Christos* is a translation from the Greek Μεσσίας (Messias), from the Hebrew מָשִׁיחַ (mashiah). "Christ" in Greek also means "the anointed," and "Messiah" in both Greek and Hebrew contains the meaning of "the anointed."

5. Philippi from the Greek Φίλιπποι (Filippoi), a city in Macedonia founded by Philip of Macedonia, in Paul's time under Roman rule. Paul founded the first church in Europe in Philippi.

8God is my witness how I yearn for you
With the compassion of Yeshua Mashiah.

9Here is my prayer. I pray that your love grows
Greater and greater in its deeper knowledge
And full perception 10so that you can tell
What is superior and you may be pure
And blameless till the day of the Mashiah,
11When you are satiated with the fruit
Of goodness coming through Yeshua Mashiah
To sing the glory and the praise of God!

12I want you, brothers, now to know that what
I've suffered only has increased diffusion
Of the good news, 13and my imprisonment
For the Mashiah has illuminated
The whole praetorian camp and everywhere.
14Most of the brothers, trusting in the lord,
Because of my imprisonment began
To preach the word of God more fearlessly.

Motives for speaking the word

15Some preach Mashiah out of rivalry
And strife, and others in good will. 16They know
I lie in jail defending the good news.
They preach with love. 17As for those who preach
Mashiah out of spite and selfishness,
They do it not purely but to augment
My sufferings where I live in these chains.
18But what of this? In every way, falsely
Or through the truth, Mashiah's preached. For this
I'm happy and will go on being happy.

19I know this will be my salvation through
Your prayers and the supporting spirit of
Yeshua the Mashiah. 20I hope and eagerly
Expect nothing to stumble me in shame,

And now as always the Mashiah, with
Extraordinary courage, now and always,
Will be exalted in my body, whether
Through life or death. 21Living is the Mashiah
For me. Dying is gain. 22But living in flesh
For me is labor's fruit. What should I choose?
I don't know what to do. 23I'm caught between
A passion to depart and be embraced
In the Mashiah. That would be much better,
24Yet to stay on in flesh is paramount
For you, 25and so persuaded I'll stay on,[6]
Go on with all of you in your progression
And joy of faith. 26Then I'll participate
In your abounding pride in Yeshua Mashiah
When I come back to be with you again.

Be firm, with or without me
27Be solely as a citizen of life
Worthy as it befits the good news of
Mashiah so that if I come to see you,
Or absent hear about you, that you stand
Straight in one spirit, with one soul contending
In faith for the good news, 28fearful of nothing
From those opponents. They are single proof
Of their destruction and of your salvation,

---

6. Here Paul presents a basic ethical dilemma, which is how, for a man of faith, can one go on living on earth when salvation and paradise are promised in the afterlife. Paul's argument here is that he agrees to live in order to spread the word of the messiah. So altruistically he resists his preference, which would be to depart immediately to his reward, in order to save other souls. Insofar as others may have the same mission of communal devotion, to live is therefore an imperative. However, by the same reasoning, for those whose life, say, a carpenter or mason, or a young man or woman, has no responsibilities to others, in effect a large part of the population, what reason would there be not to end their life immediately in order to enter heaven? This primordially important question may be answered elsewhere but not here.

And this from God. 29Because of the Mashiah
Grace came to you not only to believe
In him, but suffer too for him. The contest
That now is yours, you saw in me. 30It is
The same one. Hear me now. I have it still.

Chapter 2

Consolation of love
> If there be consolation in the Mashiah,
> If there be the comfort of love, if there
> Be fellowship of spirit and compassion,

> If there be mercy, 2then complete my joy
> So you will think the same, with the same love
> As in joined souls,7 one thinking being in full

> Concord. 3Do nothing found in rivalry,
> Do nothing out of vacuous conceit,
> But in humility, in lowliness

> Of mind. 4Consider others better than
> You are, not brooding only on yourself,
> And feel compassion for another's cares.

Paul's song
> 5Let the same purpose be foremost
> In you that also was in the Mashiah:

---

7. John Donne (1572–1631), the English metaphysical poet, was dean of St. Paul's
Cathedral and learned his divinity and metaphysics from St. Paul's magic tinker-
ing with "joined souls" in the "comfort of love," as in his poem "The Ecstasy." This
developing passage by Paul, like his discourse on love in 1 Corinthians 13, comes
through as a passionate ethical plea for generosity of spirit. Like 1 Corinthians 13, it
is a major poetic utterance.

6He shared the form of God, but had
No thought of robbery, of being
Equal to God. 7He came empty,[8]

Assuming the form of a slave
Born in the likeness of a man.
Appearing like a man 8he lowered

Himself and was obedient
Until his death—but it was death
Upon a cross. 9Therefore our God

Exalted him, gave him a name,
Gracing him with a name above
All names, 10and every knee should bend

Before that name of Yeshua:
Those who live in heaven, on earth,
And underground. 11Let every tongue

---

8. Or "poured out." The notion of being empty, of being nothing, is an example not only of Paul's view of the humility and humiliation of Jesus in assuming a human form but also of a world concept of emptiness and nothingness. In the West a culmination of the tradition of emptiness, of denigrating loss of self, is articulated in Saint John of the Cross's *nada* (nothingness) in "The Dark Night of the Soul." Here the Spanish poet-saint traces a spiritual ladder from the dark night of oblivion, which is a detachment from the senses, to ecstatic illumination, total union with the divinity, and an aftermath of oblivion. The experience is ineffable and must, John writes, be expressed in simile (the poem). Across the globe, in Buddhism there is a similar scheme of emptiness, the loss of mind and self, the ascension to satori (enlightenment), and the ultimate rest, wisdom, and transformation, which is Nirvana. The programmed lexicon of self-transformation changes, be it shamans in Africa or Asia, Hindus in India, Zoroastrians and Manichaeans in Mesopotamia, but there are universal constants that connect the validity and actuality of the experience everywhere. So here, in Paul's hymn, we have another version, the early Christian-Jewish form of Messianic emptiness, loss of identity, denigration of senses, and ascension in felicity and light in the return to the father God.

Confess that he is Yeshua,
Who is the Mashiah, who is
In glory of the father God.[9]

Shining like stars

12Therefore, my love, you always obeyed me,
Not only in my presence but so much more
Now in my absence. Hence, in fear and trembling[10]
Work out your own salvation. 13God's at work
In you, impelling you with will and skills
To work for his good favor. 14Do what you do
Without the grumblings and the arguments,
15So without blame, you are in innocence
Children of God, unblemished in the midst
Of a crooked and perverse generation
In which you glitter in the world like stars.

16Through your harboring in the word of life,
I can be happy, boasting of the day
Of the Mashiah, that I did not run this course
In vain,[11] nor do my work in vain.
17Yet if I'm poured out[12] as a sacrifice

---

9. There is speculation, and no agreement, on the source of this song, usually set off as a song, within the larger verse of Paul's letter. It is thought to be an early Christian hymn adapted by Paul. Whatever the degree to which these words are Paul's, his form in Greek is not different from the grand poetic flow of words in all the letters dictated in his own balanced and resonant voice.

10. The Danish religious philosopher Søren Kierkegaard (1813–1855), took the title of his famous and influential book, *Fear and Trembling* (1843), from the Philippians 2.12. In searching for religious truth, he seized on the Pauline "leap of faith;" which he opposed to Protestant rationalist theology.

11. Here again is another favored reference to racing, which Paul, as a Greek-speaking Jew, surely absorbed in the Greek environment in which the athletic contest was not only a sport and office for regional reconciliation but also a spiritual event in which force of mind led the body to a culminating expenditure of energy.

12. Or, "emptied" or "offered up."

In priestly[13] service of the faith, I joy
And joy together with you all. 18Likewise,
You too are glad and share our joy together.

Timotheos the good angel

19I hope in the lord Yeshua to send
Timotheos to you that I may soon
Learn your news and be cheered. 20I have no one
Of equal spirit here, deeply concerned
For you. 21Others care only for themselves,
But not of the Mashiah Yeshua. 22You
Know how he's proven who he is: a son
To father he has been for me, and served
Me in the gospel. 23So I hope to send him
As soon as I see how things go with me.
24I trust the lord that soon I too will come.

Epafroditos on his way

25I need to send to you Epafroditos,[14]
Brother and helper and my fellow soldier,
Your messenger to minister my needs.
26He longs to be with you and was distressed
Because you heard that he was sick. 27He was,
So sick he came near death. But God took pity,
And not only on him but also me
So I should not build sorrow upon sorrow.
28I send him now more eagerly. I've been
With him. Now you again may joy, and I
Put off my sorrow. 29Take him in the lord
With extreme happiness and honor him
30For all his work in the Mashiah. He came

---

13. The Greek λειτουργία (leitourgia), from which English "liturgy" derives, means a "service," and here a ceremonial or priestly service.

14. Epaphroditus from the Greek Ἐπαφρόδιτος (Epafroditos), a companion of Paul.

Near death, risking his life to fill the need
Of services you felt I had to have.[15]

Chapter 3

Finally, be glad, my brothers, in the lord.
It isn't troublesome for me to write you
Things I have said—for you a reassurance.[16]

Paul tells his life
2Watch out for dogs. Watch out for harmful workers.
Watch out for those who mutilate the flesh.
3We are the circumcised. It's we [who worship
God in the spirit],[17] and who boast about
Mashiah Yeshua but have no confidence
In flesh, 4though I have confidence in flesh.
If someone else has reason to confide
In flesh, I still have more: 5circumcised on

---

15. The end of chapter 1 and first half of chapter 2 present stunning song of Paul at his strongest. Then suddenly the rhetoric plunges to cheerful comradely business reports, in letter form, on recent church organization events. As biblical scripture they do not contain the literary magic of Isaiah or Revelation. For their stylistic differences alone, scholars ruminate that segments of distinct letters have been pieced together under one book title.

If we knew the letters' manuscript history and could hence separate luminous parts from pedestrian church business, the lesser verses might be placed in a volume of church history and the New Testament would be a bit leaner and stronger. But no worry. Not only the letters but even the great book of Isaiah is segmented, consisting of three parts composed by three authors. Since one can possess no more than a hypothesis about their survival, there will be no wars over epistolary canon. In reading the letters one sees lyrical and philosophical voyages, from Paul to John, all amazing for their essential human questions, the "fear and trembling," and the spiritual elevation, paradoxes found elsewhere perhaps only in unique Ecclesiastes.

16. Chapter 2 effectively ends with 3.1.

17. Uncertain text that is not in all editions.

The eighth day,[18] of the tribe of Benyamin,[19]
A Jew and born of Jews, in law a Pharisee,
6And zealous in his persecution of
The temples of the Messianic Jews,[20]
Of justice by the law and without flaw.

7But what I then counted as gains, because
Of the Mashiah are now a loss. 8More so,
Since *all* of that I count a loss because
Of the surpassing knowledge of Mashiah
Yeshua my lord. For him I suffered loss
Yet all those things I count as garbage now
So I may gain Mashiah 9and be found
In him. I have no justice now that comes
From Torah,[21] but from faith in the Mashiah,
And righteousness from God that's based on faith.
10I want to know him and the power of
His resurrection and the fellowship
Of sharing in his sufferings. I do it,
Becoming like him in my death, 11so I
Might share his resurrection from the dead.

---

18. Paul as a Jew was circumcised on the eighth day, which is the traditional day for circumcision of a newborn male child. Paul's strong affirmation of being a Jew and a Pharisee belies virulently anti-Judaic interpolations found in 1 Thessalonians 3.14–16, Matthew 23.37, and elsewhere.

19. Benjamin from the Greek Βενιαμίν (Beniamin), from the Hebrew בִּנְיָמִין (benyamin).

20. Here it is clear that Paul is speaking only of Jews, in Jerusalem, who had become Messianic (Christian) Jews, as opposed to the gentile converts. Their congregations were always in the synagogues or temples. The Messianics whom Paul was persecuting were, without exception, Jews who thought themselves as being of the true Jewish movement, which had encountered the true messiah. "Messiah" in Greek is "Christ" and "Messianic" in Greek translation is "Christian."

21. The law. Torah, meaning "law," is the Pentateuch, in which the Mosaic law is prescribed. In a more general sense, Torah also means the Hebrew Bible.

Moving to perfection

12Not that I have already reached or am
　　Perfection, but I try to capture it
　　As the Mashiah Yeshua captured me.
13Brothers, I do not count myself as one
　　Who's captured it. One thing I do. I leave
　　Behind those early days, forgetting them,
　　And strain, pushing ahead, 14to reach the prize
　　I seek, which is to be summoned aloft
　　By God through the Mashiah Yeshua.
15For you who would be perfect you should think
　　Like this, and if you've other thoughts, that too
　　God will reveal to you. 16But let's be firm
　　And hold onto the place we have attained.

17Imitate me, my brothers. Look at how
　　The ones are walking who pursue the model
　　I gave to you. 18As often I described them,
　　Many who walk are weeping now. They are
　　Enemies of the cross of the Mashiah.
19Their end is pure destruction, and their God
　　Their belly, and their glory in their shame,
　　Their minds contrived by earthly things. 20For us
　　Our city is in heaven, and from there
　　We avidly await a savior, the lord
　　Yeshua Mashiah. 21He'll transform
　　The body of our lowliness to be
　　Reformed into the body of his glory,
　　And through the workings of his power subject
　　All living things on earth to be his own.

Chapter 4

Therefore, my brothers, whom I love and long for,
My joy and wreath,[22] be steadfast in the lord.

Paul asks companions to spread the joy
2I beseech Euodia[23] and beseech Syntyche[24]
That they be of the same mind in the lord.
3Yes. I ask you, my true companions, help
These women who have struggled for the gospel
Alongside me and Klemens[25] and the rest
Of my coworkers. Their names are in the book
Of life. 4Always be happy in the lord.
I say again, rejoice. 5Let everyone
Know of your gentleness. The lord is near.
6Never be anxious but in every prayer
And each entreaty, add your thanks to God,
7And so the peace of God and his supreme
And understanding mind will guard your hearts
And keep your thoughts in the Mashiah Yeshua.

---

22. Elsewhere translated "crown," from the Greek στέφανος (stefanos), whose literal meaning is a "wreath," which on athletes—and Paul adored athletic metaphors—represented victory. One can say in English that one is crowned with a wreath. However, by itself, "crown" signifies a metal circlet, often set with jewels, for regal events, unless the word is modified as "crown of thorns," a reference to Jesus's forced headdress, which Paul very likely had in mind. But here, too, the English version "crown of thorns" is an unnecessary inflation of "wreath of thorns," a more accurate translation from Koine Greek of the gospels, and a humble and more appropriate symbol for Jesus at the cross. In Greek a "wreath" needs no inflation, since, whether for athletes or grooms and brides, the wreath carries a precious and ancient authority.
23. Euodia from the Greek Εὐοδία (Euodia).
24. Syntyche from the Greek Συντύχη (Syntyche).
25. Clement from the Greek Κλήμης (Klemes).

8Lastly, my loves, whatever may be true,
  Whatever may be honorable, just
  And pure or something lovely to be praised,
  If there is any virtue, think of them,
  9Of what you got and heard and saw in me,
  And then the God of peace will be with you.

My up and down ways
  10I am in ecstasy about the lord
  Now that at last your concern over me
  Is blossoming again! You were concerned
  Before but had no chance to be of help.
  11I do not say this because I'm in need.
  I've learned to be content with what I have.
  12I know the lows, I know abundance in
  All kinds of matters. I know secrets of
  Eating good food and passing through starvation,
  Of having plenty and of lacking all.
  13I'm quiet for all through him who strengthens me,
  14But you were kind to share my miseries.

Being with you bounteous Filippeans
  15You my Filippeans also know how in
  Early days of the good news, when I
  Left from Makedonia,²⁶ there was none,
  No other temple that would share with me
  My gains and losses except you alone.
  16Even when I was in Thessaloniki,²⁷
  You sent me help one time and then again
  When I was suffering want. 17Not that I seek

---

26. Macedonia from the Greek Μακεδονία (Makedonia).

27. Thessalonica, now regularly called Thessalonika, Thessaloniki, Salonika, or Salonica, from the Greek Θεσσαλονίκη (Thessalonike), a great ancient port city in Macedonia, where Paul also founded an early synagogue of Christian Jews.

A gift. I seek the fruit[28] increasing in
Your own account. 18I am paid full and more,
Am filled with what I got from Epafroditos
And gifts I got from you, a fragrant offering,
A proper sacrifice, pleasing to God.
19My God will fill each need you have by way
Of his great wealth in glory of Mashiah
Yeshua.
20To God our father glory
from aeon into aeon.[29] Amain.[30]

Goodbye

21Greet every saint in the Mashiah Yeshua.
The brothers who are with me greet you too
22And all the saints greet you, especially
The ones in Caesar's household[31] 23May the grace
Of lord Yeshua Mashiah be with your spirit.

---

28. For profit.

29. "Aeon to aeon" repeats the Greek in English, meaning "from age to age" or traditionally, forever and ever, which is beautiful but less specific. In the Greek "aeon to aeon" gives us the spread of time as opposed to "forever and ever," which gives eternity. These two lines are Paul's doxology (praise of God) to end the letter before the final salutation.

30. Amen from the Greek ἀμήν (amen), from the Hebrew אָמֵן (amein).

31. The reference to Caesar is a reminder of the Roman Empire's dominion in Greece, and how, at least in the letters, despite the Roman crucifixion of Jesus and the later Passion drama related in the gospels but virtually unknown to the epistlers, Paul pays homage to Rome.

LETTERS
ATTRIBUTED TO
SHAUL/SAUL/PAUL

Efesians
(Ephesians)

Efesians[1]
(Ephesians)

⁓

THIS POWERFUL AND POETIC LETTER is attributed to Paul, but most historians believe it was written not by Paul but by a follower of the missionary who had access to Paul's letters. It celebrates the history of the early church with respect to the gentiles and interprets Paul's life and his ideas to a later church. This letter has strong parallels with the one to the Colossians, also an anonymous, forged Pauline letter. The title "Ephesians" does not appear in early manuscripts. The letter contains some extremely long sentences, not characteristic of Paul's purist style, and a lexicon distinct from the authentic letters. It is called a "circular letter" composed for distribution to the new gentile churches in Asia Minor. In form it slips between traditional genres of the letter and may be more appropriately esteemed a sermon or a collection of wisdom speeches, congratulatory homilies, and theological essays. These qualities also appear in the authentic letters, but missing here is the monumental spirit and personality of Paul, in combat and in love with his own virtues and failings and those of his immediate world. Beyond person, doctrine, and transcending spirit of his faith, there are the subtlety and power of unfailing rhetoric, which it imitates.

In justice to the unknown author or authors of Ephesians, however, whose sources are also unknown, many passages read as if directly from

---

1. Ephesians from the Greek Ἐφέσιος (Efesios). An Ephesian is one from Ephesos, a Greek city then under Roman rule where most of the people, including Jews, spoke Greek. Paul was a Greek-speaking Jew, that is, a Ἑλληνιστής (Hellenistes), from the city of Tarsos, northwest of Ephesos. Both cities are in present-day Turkey.

the pen of Paul, as when a bold Paul is, figuratively or actually, on his knees, beseeching, through God, his remote congregation to come into enlightenment and the mystery. Paul's spirit and rhetoric clearly pervade the letters by his imitators. They were excellent inspired forgers whose forgeries until recent times have passed.

To preserve Paul's unique poetry, the authentic letters are lineated into blank verse. The anonymous ones ascribed to Paul, despite long passages of great beauty and felicitous speech, are rendered into prose, except where song or chant is apparent, especially in the lyrical prayers in the opening chapters of the letter.

Chapter 1

Hello

Shaul[2] a messenger of the Mashiah Yeshua[3] by the will of God, to saints[4] who are in Efesos[5] and the believers in the Mashiah Yeshua, 2grace to you and peace from God our father our lord Yeshua the Mashiah.

Blessings in the Mashiah

    3Blessed be God and father of our lord
    Yeshua the Mashiah, who blessed us
    With every spiritual blessing in heaven,
    As he chose us in the Mashiah, 4before
    The foundation of the world, to be holy
    And blameless in love in his presence.[6]
    5He destined us adopted as his children
    Through Yeshua Mashiah according to
    The pleasure of his will, 6and for the praise
    Of glory of his grace that he bestowed
    On us through his beloved son. 7In him
    We have redemption through his blood, forgiveness
    Of sins through the abundance of his grace
    8That he lavished on us. With all his wisdom

---

2. Paul from the Greek Παῦλος (Paulos), from Saul in the Greek Σαῦλος (Saulos), from the Hebrew שָׁאוּל (Shaul). Paul was born in Tarsos as *Shaul*.

3. Christ Jesus. "Jesus" is from the Greek Ἰησοῦς (Iesous), from the Aramaic יֵשׁוּעַ (Yeshua), a later form of the Hebrew יְהוֹשֻׁעַ (Yehoshua). "Christ" is from the Greek Χριστος (Hristos), and Greek *Hristos* or *Christos* is a translation from the Greek Μεσσίας (Messias), from the Hebrew מָשִׁחַ (mashiah). "Christ" in Greek also means "the anointed," and "Messiah" in both Greek and Hebrew contains the meaning of "the anointed."

4. The saints are impoverished Christian Jews in the synagogues.

5. Ephesus from the Greek Ἔφεσος (Efesos). The phrase "in Efesos" is not in early manuscripts of Paul's letters. It does appear in the King James Version, the American Standard Version, and other recent translations.

6. This first section, verses 3–14, of praise, a doxology, is one sentence in the Greek. In all old and modern translations, it is broken up into smaller sentences.

And insight 9he revealed to us the mystery
Of will by his good pleasure deep in him.
10For his plan for the fulfillment of time
So that all things in heaven and on earth
Be summed up in Mashiah, 11and from him
We also received our inheritance
Destined according to his purpose, from him
Accomplishing all things as he decides
And wills it so that we, 12who were the first
To hope in the Mashiah, might praise his glory.
13In him whom you also trusted when you heard
The word of truth, gospel of your salvation,
You too believed and you were sealed with that
Holy spirit of promise, 14which is a pledge
Of our inheritance until redemption
Of our possession of praise for his glory.

Paul's prayer for the Efesians

15I've also heard of your faith in the lord
Yeshua and love you have for all the saints,
And 16so I never cease to give you thanks.
In my prayers I remember you. 17I pray
That the God of our lord Yeshua Mashiah,
Father of glory, may give you a spirit
Of wisdom and revelation in a fuller
Knowledge of him 18in order that the eyes
Of your heart shine illuminating you
To know what hope he's calling you to take,
What wealth of glory in the inheritance
He offers you among the saints, 19and what
Is the surpassing greatness of his power
For us believers before the supremacy
Of strength 20that he infused in the Mashiah.
He did all this when he raised him from death
And seated him by his right hand in heavenly
Domains 21and far above authority
And rule and power and dominion, far
Above each name that's named, not only

In this age but in the ages to come.
22And he has placed all things under his feet,
And made him leader of the entire church,[7]
23Which is his body and the pleroma,[8]
Which is of him who fills all things in all.

Chapter 2

We are his poem[9]
You died through trespasses and sins 2in which
You walked, following the world's course, following
The ruler of the dominion of the air,[10]
The spirit that is now at work among
The sons of disobedience. 3Among
You we once also lived in the desires
Of flesh, surrendering to passions of
The flesh and thoughts, and we were nature's children
Angry like all the rest. 4But God was rich
In mercy through the great love he held out
For us 5even when we were dead from sins.
He made us live again with the Mashiah—
You have been saved by grace—6and then he raised us
With him and seated us along with him

---

7. Here "church" or "synagogue" or "gathering place" is possible, but since this late letter is addressed principally to gentile converts to Christian Judaism, the word "church" may be appropriate. But there is not yet a decisive split, in name or understanding, between Christians and Jews, which will characterize second-century separations. Even then, the Hebrew Bible will be the same and only Bible for Christians and Jews, there being nothing close to a New Testament text until after about 150 C.E. Here, the same questions of circumcision or uncircumcision, of how close or far one is to keep to doctrines of the apostolic fathers Peter, James, and John (one of the many Johns) in Jerusalem (who preserve Messianic Judaism according to the Hebrew Bible), pertain in the letter.

8. Fulfillment or fullness.

9. See note 11 below.

10. The ruler is Satan.

In heaven in Mashiah Yeshua
7To show to coming ages an unending
Abundance of his grace of kindness. We
Received it through Mashiah Yeshua.
8By grace you have been saved through faith, but not
From you. Salvation is God's gift, 9and not
From earthly works. I say, Let no one boast.
10We are his poem,[11] created in Mashiah
For all the good works that our mighty God
Prepared us for so in them we might walk.

Gentiles near in the Mashiah

11Remember that once you were gentiles in the flesh,[12] who were called "the foreskins"[13] by ones called "the circumcision," done in the flesh by hand. 12Remember that at that time you were without Mashiah, separated from citizenship[14] in Yisrael[15] and strangers to the covenants of promise, without hope and godless in the world. 13But now in Mashiah

---

11. Or, usually, "creation," "handiwork," "masterpiece," from the Greek ποίημα (poiema), meaning "poem," or abstractly as "creation." In Greek a poet is "one who makes" or "a maker," ποιητής (poietes). In this apparitional phrase, however, ποίημα is not translated elsewhere as "poem."

The author of this work in Greek, by the nature of the text's classical ring, knew the direct meaning of ποίημα as "poem" (from which English "poem" derives), and while "creation," "handicraft," and "masterpiece" are defendable as puffed-up versions, the elegant plainness of "poem," from ποιέω (to make), is too rich and important not to be intended as primary meaning. Whatever the authorial intention, the common philological history of the word offers the dominion of "poem"; and the beautiful Greek phrase, αὐτοῦ ἐσμεν ποίημα, "we are his poem," should never be forgotten.

12. By birth.

13. The usual translation is "the uncircumcision." However, ἀκροβυστία (akrobystia) is the proper word for "foreskin" as in ἀπερίτμητος ἀκροβυστίαν (aperitmetos akrobystian), meaning "uncircumcised in foreskin." The Greek for "foreskin" comes through as a strong insult, while the euphemism "uncircumcision" is often a positive word, as Paul uses it, to praise the fleshly state of the gentiles.

14. Or "state" or "commonwealth" from the Greek πολιτεία (politeia). *Politeia* carries both meanings equally, depending on context, of "citizenship" or "the body politic." Here either or both meanings can work.

15. Israel from the Greek Ἰσραήλ, from the Hebrew יִשְׂרָאֵל (yisrael).

Yeshua you, who once were far, have been drawn near by the blood of the Mashiah.

Gentiles no longer strangers and aliens

14He is our peace.[16] He made the two one, breaking down the middle wall of partition, the hatred, by his own flesh. 15He has abolished the law of the commandments and its dogmas. He did this in order to create in himself one new man to make peace, 16and in one body he could reconcile both groups[17] to God through the cross, and thereby kill the hatred.

17He came to preach peace to you who were far off, and peace to you who were near. 18Through him we both have access in one spirit to the father. 19No longer are you strangers and aliens but fellow citizens of the saints and members of the household of God, 20built on the foundation of the messengers[18] and prophets, whose capstone is the Mashiah Yeshua himself. 21In him the whole structure is joined together, and grows into a holy temple in the lord. 22In him you also are joined together into a residence for God in the spirit.

Chapter 3

Paul the minister to gentiles

Because of this, I Paul, the prisoner of the Mashiah Yeshua for you the gentiles, say this to you. 2You must know of the commission of God's grace that was given to me to bring to you. 3Through revelation a mystery was made known to me, as I wrote above briefly. 4And reading this you will understand my insight in the mystery of the Mashiah. 5In other generations this was not made known to the sons of men as now it has been revealed to his holy messengers and prophets in spirit.

6This mystery is that the gentiles are now heirs and members and partners in the promise of the Mashiah Yeshua through the good news.[19]

---

16. The succinct and epigraphic "He is our peace" follows the "We are his poem" of a few verses earlier (2.10).

17. Gentiles and Christian Jews.

18. Apostles.

19. Or gospel.

7Of this I became a minister by the gift of God's grace that was given me through the working of his power. 8I am the least of all the saints, yet this grace was given me to preach the good news to the gentiles of the incalculable bounty of the Mashiah, 9and to bring light to the nature of the scheme of mystery. It had been hidden away for ages in God who created all things. 10But now through the church God's manifold wisdom may be made known to the rulers and authorities in the heavenly places. 11All this is done in concordance with the plan of the ages, which God made in the Mashiah Yeshua our lord, 12in whom we have confidence and access to through our faith in him.

13Therefore I ask you not to despair because of my suffering for you. This is your glory.

Prayer for readers
 14Because of this I bend my knees to God,
 15From whom each family in the heavens and
  On earth is named, 16pray that from the abundance
  Of glory and through spirit he may grant
  Your strength to be confirmed in the inner man,
 17And that Mashiah live through your heart's faith,
  Since you are rooted and grounded in love.
 18I pray that you have powers to understand
  The breadth and length and height and depth
  That his love spans, 19surpassing knowledge so
  That you be filled in the fullness of God.

 20To him who has the powers to create
  Enormously more than we ask or think
  Of through the powers at work in us,
 21To him glory in the church and in
  Yeshua Mashiah for all generations
  And from aeons to aeons more. Amain.[20]

---

20. Amen from the Greek ἀμήν (amen), from the Hebrew אָמֵן (amein).

Chapter 4

From the prisoner in the lord

So I the prisoner in the lord encourage you to walk worthy of the calling by which you were called. ₂Be with all humility and meekness, with long suffering, and patient with each other in love. ₃Be eager to preserve your singleness of spirit in the bond of peace. ₄There is one body and one spirit, just as you were called in one hope of your calling. ₅One lord, one faith, one dipping,²¹ ₆one God and father of all, the one over all and through all and in all.

₇To each one of us was given grace in accordance with the measure of the Mashiah's gift. ₈As it sings in the Psalms:

When he climbed to the high summits

He led captives in his train

And brought gifts to his people.²²

₉What it reads, "he climbed to the high summits," what can it signify other than that he also went down into the lower parts of the earth?²³

---

21. Baptism or immersion.

22. Ps. 68.18.

23. The psalm here refers to God's ascension to his throne in the Temple of Jerusalem, that is, God's residence in heaven. The writer of Ephesians, following the manner of Christian Jews and later Christians, interprets, in Christological exegesis, the biblical Hebrew psalm, replacing "God" with "Christ." Jews reading the text in Hebrew would keep "God," rather than his descended son. In Paul's authentic letters the main biblical allusions to the messiah in the Jewish Bible are to his preferred Isaiah, where the figure is indeed the foretold description of the messiah, whom Christians determine lived in the human figure of Jesus son of Joseph (Yeshua ben Yosef).

Christianizing the Bible was a practice and necessity for the Jewish Bible's acceptance in the emerging Jesus movement, where, after the fifth century when the books of the Greek New Testament were fully set and canonized in Rome (405), the two volumes were combined as the one Christian Bible, with variations depending on the rejection or degree of acceptance of the Apocrypha. Many of the passages in the next verses, particularly the listing of duties of those in "the work of ministry," suggest a later dating than what is usually given to this letter commonly attributed to Paul. Since some parts of the letter are truly outstanding, it is always possible that, as with many of the letters, this one has fragments of writings by Paul later filled out in full letter form by the pious forgers.

10He who went down is the same one who climbed far above all the skies that he might fulfill all things.²⁴ 11The gifts he gave were that some would be messengers, some prophets, some evangelists, some shepherds and teachers. 12For training the saints for the work of ministry, for the building of the body of the Mashiah, 13until we all attain a singleness of faith and knowledge of the son of God, to attain manhood and the measure of the full maturity of the Mashiah.

14So we must no longer live as children, tossed by waves and blown about in every wind of doctrine, contrived in the cunning of men, in their craftiness leading to means of deception. 15Keeping to the truth of love, let us grow up into him in all things, who is the head, Mashiah. 16From him the whole body, joined perfectly as one and knit together by every connective sinew and supplied with all parts working in measured activity, leads the body to build itself into love.

Leave the dark

17So I say, and charge you by the lord, you must no longer walk as the gentiles walk in their futility of sense.²⁵ 18They are darkened in what they understand, alienated from the life of God, since ignorance is in them and their hearts are hard. 19In their insensibility, they are given into debauchery and every form of license, filth, and greed. 20This is not how you learned from the Mashiah! 21If you ever heard of him and were taught in him how truth is in Yeshua! 22You must throw off your former life, corrupted by desire for pleasure, 23and be renewed in the spirit of your mind. 24Put on the new person, the one created in justice and the sanctity of truth.

Commandments for the new man

25So put aside the lies, and then let each of you speak truth to your neighbor. We are members of each other. 26Be angry but do not sin.

---

24. The fulfillment of the risen Christ.

25. Here the author refers to the lost gentiles who have not yet converted to Jesus. Although the word in Greek remains the same, *ethnos*, to distinguish between gentiles who have become Christian Jews and those who remain senseless, *ethnos* is translated as the "heathen."

27Don't make room for the devil. 28Let the thief give up stealing. Rather, let him work hard with his own hands to do something good and have something to share with the poor. 29Let no corrupt word come out of your mouth, but only what will be helpful to those in need and to extend grace to those who hear you. 30Do not upset the holy spirit of God by whom you were sealed for the day of redemption. 31Let all bitterness and rage and wrath and clamor and slander be gone from you. And also every kind of evil. 32Become kind to one another and compassionate, forgiving each other as God through the Mashiah forgave you.

Chapter 5

Walk in love

> Imitate God as loving children.
> 2Walk in love as the Mashiah
> Who loved us and who gave himself
> For us as a fragrant offering
> And as a sacrifice to God.

Be children of light

3But fornication and all filth or greed, let all that not be mentioned among you, which is proper for saints. 4Avoid indecency and silly talk or dirty jokes. All that is unbecoming. You should be giving thanks. 5For you know well that any fornicator or filthy person or rapacious person (that is, an idolater) will have no inheritance in the kingdom of the Mashiah and God.

6Let no one deceive you with empty talk. Through these things come God's anger against the sons of disobedience. 7Spend no time with them.

> 8Once you were darkness, now you are light
> Through the lord. Walk as children of light.
> 9The fruit of light lies in goodness, justice,
> And truth. 10Discover what pleases the lord,
> 11And don't participate in works of
> Unfruitful darkness. Rather, expose them.
> 12The secret things done by those people
> Are shameful, even to speak about them,

13But everything exposed by the light
Is illuminated. 14Everything
Contains the totality of light.
So as it is said in scriptures:
    Awake, sleeping one![26]
    Rise from the dead.[27]
    The mashiah will shine on you.[28]

15Be very careful how you walk, like the wise, not the fools, 16making the most of time, because these are evil days. 17So do not be a fool but learn what is the will of God. 18Don't get drunk on wine, which is dissipation, but fill yourself with spirit. 19Speak to each other in psalms and hymns and spiritual songs, singing and making melody in your hearts to the lord, 20always giving thanks for all things to God the father in the name of our lord Yeshua the Mashiah.

21Be submissive to each other in awe and fear of the Mashiah.

Husbands, wives, and rules of the household
22Wives, submit to your husbands as to the lord.[29]

---

26. Rom. 13.11.

27. John 5.25. With respect to these words, which the speaker says are from scripture, it is reasonable to assume that, as commentators assign them, they are from the Gospel of John. The author of the Ephesians presumably had access to Johannine writings, or perhaps to an early Christian hymn containing the words from John. But if the author had access to the Gospel of John, that fact alone would expose the letter as pseudepigraphic, that is, a falsely ascribed imitation trying to pass as an original, since Paul was dead before John's gospel was composed. The other possibility is that the phrase καὶ ἀνάστα ἐκ τῶν νεκρῶν, "rise from the dead," was itself a common religious phrase said or sung by early Christians and not confined to John's gospel. In that case, the ascription by commentators to John is wrong and its inclusion here in no way reflects on the dating of the letter.

28. See Isaiah 26.19.

29. Few passages have aroused more controversy and ire, on both sides, than these instructions about wives and husbands. As an apology for the commanding position of the husband, it is argued that there is a reciprocal agreement of responsibility that affects both husband and wife, especially with regard to love and loyalty. However, in the end the wife must obey her husband, and given his CEO position (financial images, from wages to redemption, are favorite metaphors in New Testament persuasion), there is no question where ultimate authority lies: "Wives,

23The husband is the head of the wife as the Mashiah is the head of the church, of which he is savior of the body.[30]

24Just as the church is submissive to the Mashiah, so the wives should be submissive to their husbands in everything.

25Husbands, love your wives just as the Mashiah loved the church and gave himself up for her sake, 26to make her holy by washing her clean with water in the word, 27so as to present a glorious church to himself with no spot or wrinkle or any such thing, yes, for her to be holy and without flaw. 28So also the husbands should love their wives as their own bodies. He who loves his wife loves himself.

29No one ever hates his own flesh. He nourishes and cares tenderly for it as the Mashiah does for the church. 30We are members of his body.

31For this reason a man will leave father and mother and be joined to his wife, and the two of them will be in one flesh.

32This is a great mystery.

I speak of the Mashiah and the church, 33but each one of you should also love his wife as himself, and a wife should be in awe and fear of her husband.

---

submit to your husbands as to the lord." However, one should not place the mantle of authority, with its benevolent-or-onerous commanding officer stars, on Paul's shoulders, since the letter is not by Paul but an imitator. Paul, being dead, could not approve or disapprove of the nature and depth of these rules. Before it was accepted by informed scholars that half of the letters carrying Paul's name are pseudepigraphal, the church—its officers and parishioners—turned to "Paul" for direction. Now that authorship is unknown with respect to many of those questions for which Paul has been traditionally praised or reproached, one must, in all fairness, dissociate the missionary saint from the debate. However, Paul makes enough degrading statements about women's inferiority not to depend on Ephesians to reveal his positions. The happy rule with regard to these famous pronouncements on family roles is simply, "Do not credit Paul" or "Do not blame Paul."

Between the initial and end verses that prescribe a wife's position in the household, it should be seen that there is also a core of idealized love between man and woman, with emphasis on the mystery of caring for person and flesh. After the diatribe against ill use of the body, an idealized love appears immediately in verses 31–32, ending with "This is a great mystery." However, the author immediately catches himself and warns inconsolably in verse 33, "and a wife should be in awe and fear of her husband."

30. In the Greek body-and-head metaphor for the family and church, "head" is to be taken as real and not only figuratively. "Head" is from the Greek κεφαλή (kefale), as in "cephalic," meaning anatomically the "head."

Chapter 6

Children and parents

Children, obey your parents [in the lord,][31] for this is right. 2Honor your father and your mother, which is the first commandment, with the promise: 3That it may be well with you and you may be a long time on earth.

4Fathers, do not provoke your children to wrath,[32] but nurture them in training and admonition of the lord.

Slaves and masters

5Slaves, obey your fleshly masters with fear and trembling in simplicity of the heart, as you obey the Mashiah, 6not by catching the eye and pleasing people, but as slaves of the Mashiah. Do the will of God from your soul, 7doing slave work with enthusiasm as to the lord and not for men. 8Know that every man, whatever good thing he does, he will receive good from the lord, whether slave or free. 9Masters, do likewise to them, sparing your threats, knowing that you and they have the same lord in the skies, and with him there are no distinctions of person.

God's armor

10Lastly, be strong in the lord and in the strength of his power. 11Put on the whole armor of God[33] so you can stand against the schemes of the devil. 12We wrestle[34] not against blood and flesh but against the rulers, against the authorities, against the world powers of darkness, against the spiritual forces of evil in heavenly places. 13Therefore take up the whole

---

31. "In the lord" is not found in the earliest manuscripts.

32. Or exasperate or provoke.

33. Isa. 11.5 and 59.17. The Greek word πανοπλία (panoplia) exists also in English as "panoply," from *pan,* "full," + *hopla,* "armor"; but it has lost its etymological meaning of full armor to signify a ceremonial attire or a striking display as in "a panoply of flags."

34. Or struggle. The literal gripping meaning of the Homeric word πάλη (pale) is "wrestle," which gives a more lively image than the indefinite "struggle."

armor of God that you will be able to withstand them on the day of evil, and having done everything 14stand belted to the waist with truth, and put on the breastplate of justice. 15Shod your feet with the firmness of the good news of peace. 16With all this take up the shield of faith by which you will be able to put out all the burning arrows of the cunning one.[35] 17Seize the helmet of salvation and the sword of spirit, which is the word of God.

Pray for me ambassador in chains

18And do this with prayer and entreaty, praying in the spirit on every occasion. To this end, be alert and with perseverance, praying for all the saints. 19And pray for me, so that when I open my mouth utterance will come and I will boldly make known the mystery of the good news. 20I am its ambassador in chains. Pray that I may speak with courage, since I must speak.

Goodbye

21Now that you know how I am and what I am doing, Tyhikos[36] will tell you everything. He is my loved brother and faithful minister in the lord, 22whom I send to you so that you may learn about us and he may comfort your hearts.

23Peace to the brothers, and love with faith, from God the father and lord Yeshua Mashiah. 24Grace be with all who love our lord Yeshua the Mashiah in his immortality.

---

35. The devil.

36. Tychicus from the Greek Τυχικός (Tyhikos), a man from the province of Asia who accompanied Paul on a journey to Jerusalem.

Kolossians
(Colossians)

Kolossians[1]
(Colossians)

THE LETTER TO THE COLOSSIANS does not figure among the authentic letters, which does not mean that it lacks passages of extraordinary importance and beauty. However, in significant ways it differs in rhetorical style, syntax, and theology from other letters, except for Ephesians, which draws closely on Colossians and which is similarly said by most scholars to be pseudepigraphal. Probably written by a follower of Paul a decade or two after the missionary's death—some suggest as late as the second century because of references to a more flourishing Gnosticism—the forged Colossian letter was to be read in the Colossian and Laodicean churches. As in Ephesians, many of the sentences are long and the tone often formal. It lacks the personal debates, passions, and transcendence of Paul's letters.

An interesting point about the abundant pseudepigrapha of the Hebrew Bible and New Testament, usually assigned to the intertestamental period, is their inevitable goal, which is to be taken as authentic, to be received in faith, to have been written by a prestigious author whose very name might lead to acceptance into the canon. In Colossians the speaker narrates in the first person, as Paul in his letter to companions and church parishioners—in other words, the forger makes it look genuine.

1. Colossians. Colossae from the Greek Κολοσσαί (Kolossai), a city in the highlands of Asia Minor in Phrygia, close to larger Laodicea and Hieropolis. The Messianic community in Roman Colossae was probably founded by Paul's companion Epaphras. There were many competing religions and mystery cults in the city, including early Gnosticism, which appears to be one of the speaker's targeted enemies.

In the Pauline compositions, the question of ascription is of cardinal significance. Matters of authorship have widely occupied (and divided) scholars since the later part of the nineteenth century. Seven of Paul's fourteen letters are seen by virtually all serious scholars as indisputably historical (although some have emendations or parts of other letters pieced in, such as 2 Corinthians). As for the other books of the Bible, from Genesis to the gospels, names and ascriptions are uncertain and the authors are anonymous. We have no idea who composed the four canonical gospels. As for their sources, they remain an enigma. We speak of three authors of Job: of the preface, main body, and afterword. Historical scholarship accepts that Psalms and Song of Songs were composed some five centuries after the death of David and Solomon. And there is no more external evidence beyond the scriptures for the existence of David and Solomon than there is for Moses or John of Ephesos or Patmos, who is said to be the single author of Revelation, the letters of John, and the Gospel of John, and John the Apostle of the early Jerusalem church. The names of the evangelists appear to have been assigned to the gospels in the second century. None of these uncertainties reflects, or should reflect, on the intrinsic value of a text. Scholarship tells us simply that ascribed names are in doubt. A common name for the inauthentic letters is the "Deutero-Pauline Writing." Although nearly half of the letters traditionally attributed to Paul were composed anciently as forgeries, they are ancient, informative despite their unknown authorship. Each letter assumes a unique place in the world's religious literature. Colossians is also a seminal document in intellectual history. It shares the words of other letters and the later Church fathers to beware of the heresy of the "deceitful teachers" who threaten their faith. These intruders are the sinful Gnostics offering false and corrupting knowledge.

Chapter 1

Hello

Shaul[2] messenger of the Mashiah Yeshua[3] by the will of God, and Timotheos[4] our brother; 2to the saints in Kolossai and faithful brothers in the Mashiah. Grace to you and peace from God our father.

Thanksgiving

3In our prayers to God the father of our lord Yeshua Mashiah, we give thanks for you. 4We have heard of your faith in the Mashiah Yeshua, and the love you have for all the saints.[5] 5Faith and love spring from hope stored in heaven and that you know about in the word of truth of the good news. 6The good news comes to you, bearing fruit and growing in the whole world. It has grown for you from the day you heard it and you truly understood the grace of God. 7You learned from our beloved fellow slave Epafras.[6] He is for you a faithful minister for the Mashiah, 8who also revealed to us your love in the spirit.

9Therefore, we too, from the day we heard about you, we have not paused in our prayers for you, asking that you be filled with the knowledge

---

2. Paul from the Greek Παῦλος (Paulos), from Saul in the Greek Σαῦλος (Saulos), from the Hebrew שָׁאוּל (Shaul). Paul was born in Tarsos as *Shaul*.

3. Christ Jesus. "Jesus" is from the Greek Ἰησοῦς (Iesous), from the Aramaic יֵשׁוּעַ (Yeshua), a later form of the Hebrew יְהוֹשֻׁעַ (Yehoshua). "Christ" is from the Greek Χριστος (Hristos), and Greek *Hristos* or *Christos* is a translation from the Greek Μεσσίας (Messias), from the Hebrew מָשִׁיחַ (mashiah). "Christ" in Greek also means "the anointed," and "Messiah" in both Greek and Hebrew contains the meaning of "the anointed."

4. Timothy from the Greek Τιμόθεος (Timotheos), a companion of Paul and, according to some, the later cowriter of seven letters attributed to Paul.

5. In Colossians and Ephesians the saints are of the new Messianic community who are particularly destined for the ministry. In other letters, Paul speaks of them with compassion as the poor who need help and will help others, and who are at the heart of the congregations, in Jerusalem and elsewhere.

6. Epaphras from the Greek Ἐπαφρᾶς (Epafras), probably a gentile convert and founder of the church in Colossae.

of God's will, in full wisdom and spiritual understanding, 10so that you may walk worthy of the lord, in every good work bearing fruit and growing in the knowledge of God.[7] 11Strengthened greatly with power from might that comes from the supremacy of his power, may you be prepared to endure and suffer everything with patience, 12and you joyfully thank the father, who has made you fit to share in the inheritance of the saints, in the light. 13He has truly rescued us from the authority of darkness and transferred us into the kingdom of his beloved son 14in whom we find our redemption and remission of sins.

Hymn of the supreme Mashiah

> 15He is the image of the unseen God,
>> Firstborn of all creation. 16And in him
>> Were made all things in heaven and on earth,
>> Visible things and the invisible,
>> Whether the thrones or lordships or the rulers
>> Or powers, all things through and for him were made.
> 17He is before all things and all things are
>> Possessed commingled in him.[8] 18He is head,
>> Head of the body of the church. He is
>> Beginning, firstborn from the dead, so he
>> Might hold first place in everything that is.
> 19The pleroma[9] was pleased to live in him,
> 20And through him reconcile all things to him,
>> Whether the things on earth or in the skies.

---

7. While Paul is at times formulaic in brief salutations and farewells, these series of long sentences are alien to his speech and reasoning. In the Greek edition, the editors have broken up long sentences into shorter units, and in English the sentences are shortened more.

8. Held together.

9. Fullness or fulfillment. "Pleroma" in Gnosticism is the full transcendence of God. Here Paul means the full nature of God is now in Jesus's abundance. Such an assertion of paternal rank is not needed for clarity or Christology, since in verse 15 the lines of authority are clearly drawn: Jesus the Christ is the image of invisible God.

The Mashiah saved you from flesh

21You were once alienated and hostile in your mind by works of cunning, 22but now Yeshua has reconciled his fleshly body through his death so as to present you as holy and blameless and beyond reproach before him, 23provided that you keep the faith, steadfast, without straying from the hope of the good news which you have heard, which has been proclaimed in all creation under heaven, and of which I Shaul have been made the minister.

Shaul laboring for the Kolossians

24I am happy in my suffering for you, and in my flesh I am filling up what is still lacking in the Mashiah's afflictions of the body, which is the church. 25I have been made a minister through God's commission that was given me for you, to present you the word of God in all its fullness, 26which is the mystery hidden away for ages and generations. Now the mystery has been revealed to his saints. 27God wanted to make known, among the gentiles, the full glory of the mystery: the Mashiah is in you, and is your hope of glory. 28We proclaim him, warning everyone and teaching everyone in all wisdom in such way as to present every man complete and perfected in the Mashiah. 29For this I labor, struggling with all his working powers in me.

Chapter 2

I want you to know how great is my struggle for you and those in Laodikeia[10] and many I have not seen in the flesh.[11] 2I do it to comfort their hearts so that they may come together in love and in the wealth and full resources of understanding in the knowledge of God's mystery, [who is the Mashiah,][12] in him are all the treasures of wisdom and hidden

---

10. Laodicea from the Greek Λαοδίκεια (Laodikeia), a city in Phrygia, near Colossae, where there was a large colony of Jews from whom converts started a synagogue of Christian Jews.

11. Face to face or in person.

12. Not found in all early texts.

knowledge. 4I say this so no one can trick you with candied argument. 5If I am absent in the flesh, in spirit I am with you, joyful to see the discipline and firmness of your faith in the Mashiah.

Walk in him

6As you have received the Mashiah Yeshua the lord, now walk in him,[13] 7rooted, built in him, and established by the faith you were taught with such abounding gratitude. 8See that no one takes you captive through philosophy and empty deceit by ways of human tradition and according to the fundamentals of the world and not according to the Mashiah.[14]

---

13. The literal meaning of the verb περιπατέω (peripateo) is "to walk," or "about" + "walk," giving us "walk about." The verb in this context in several letters is almost always rendered as "live in" or "dwell" and sometimes "go," which is closer. The literal meaning is surreal by our terminology yet is exactly the symbolic image the speaker has in mind, and it is best to let the author have his way.

14. Here (and in 16–23) in this late letter, perhaps more vehemently and clearly than elsewhere, is a statement of the threat of competing religions, interpretations of religion, and humanist philosophy. The other religions and interpretations included orthodox Judaism and Jerusalem Christianity, which was more strictly based in observance of Jewish law and ceremonial practice. The humanist philosophy was based on Greek reason and the traditional classical philosophers, which include not only Plato but also in Pauline learning, the pre-Socratics whose writings formed Platonism. The other religion and philosophy was the nascent and rapidly growing Gnosticism, which eventually dwarfed other heresies by its wide-ranging appeal geographically and its persistence, under many names, well into the early fifteenth century, and thereafter in literary esoteric writings.

The reference to those who come and capture minds with their deceitful philosophy of *knowledge* is clearly targeted on the Gnostics who prized *gnosis*, meaning "knowledge," over faith as the means of meditative transport to the spiritual world. It shared with Christianity many fundamentals, including the notion of transcending flesh, but the Gnostic philosophers taught that through gnosis one could find spiritual salvation now, not necessarily after death. Understanding—rather than faith, error, darkness, false senses—was the engine of their ascent into the pleroma (the fullness) and return to the divine mind. Hence Eve, who gave us gnosis, was prized rather than vilified as the first fallen woman. Apart from Colossians, Revelation (Apocalypse) is, especially in its opening chapters, most replete with rage against heretical churches that have been identified or accused of being Gnostic-

9In him the full pleroma of deity lives in the body, 10and you have come to fullness in him. He is the head of every ruler and authority. 11In him you were circumcised with a circumcision not made by hands in cutting flesh from body, but in the circumcision of the Mashiah.¹⁵ 12You were buried with him in the immersion.¹⁶ And with him you were also raised together through your faith in the power of God, raised him from the dead. 13When you were dead because of your trespasses and the foreskin¹⁷ on your flesh, he made you alive with him, forgiving all our trespasses, 14erasing the handwritten code, its dogmas,¹⁸ that were against us. He

---

inspired. This fact is particularly significant in that the most mythological and spiritually transcendent book of the New Testament, perhaps of the Bible, is Revelation, the history of apocalyptical thought and ascension to a detailed heaven of salvation. Though faith-versus-knowledge seems to sum up the agon between Christianity and other religions, in all essential stylistic and thematic means, the mystery and mystical ascension in Christian meditation has deep commonality with the myths, spiritual ascension, and deliverance described in Gnostic scriptures. Colossians and Revelation in these ways suggest that despite different nominal sectarian affiliations, some experiences, however they are classified, remain universal in the human and spiritual condition.

15. As in other letters, the reference here is to the superiority of a spiritual, rather than a physical, circumcision. Paul's arguments, or arguments by the unknown author who repeats them, are elegant and based on Torah law. The fact that a circumcision remains a central question, of replacing the disconcerting adult circumcision for would-be converts, with a painless spiritual rite, points to the ever-enduring symbolism of circumcision, the *brit* in Hebrew, which means both "circumcision" and "covenant." Hence, by way of spiritual "circumcision of the heart"—Paul's words derived from Deuteronomy—a signal notion of the covenant persists. A new covenant signifies on the immediate level a new (spiritual) circumcision; on the symbolic level, a new agreement. We move from physical rite to spiritual rite, from old circumcision to new circumcision, from old Bible to new Bible.

16. Baptism or dipping. Baptism, signifying a dipping or immersion, is the ritual Jewish bathing, which John the Dipper or Immerser is first seen performing in the early pages of Mark. The emphasis on baptism suggests an author who may be as late as the evangelists, or emendations that brought in a knowledge of the authors of the gospels.

17. Elsewhere euphemistically translated as "uncircumcision," a word invented to avoid using the ordinary anatomical word "foreskin." See note 13 on Ephesians 2.11.

18. Or ordinances or regulations.

took it from our midst, nailing it on the cross.[19] He disarmed the rulers and authorities in public show, triumphing over them.[20]

Beware of false teachers

16So do permit anyone to judge you in questions of food or drink or a new moon or festivals or Sabbath days.[21] 17These are the shadows of things to come. The reality is in the Mashiah. 18Do not let anyone deprive you of your reward by demanding excessive lowliness and adoration of angels, dwelling on his visions. Such a one is deftly puffed up, using the mind of the flesh. 19He does not hold onto the head, from which the whole body, nourished and held together by ligaments and sinews, grows in a growth that is from God.

20If with Mashiah you died to the fundamentals of the world, why do you still live in the world as one subject to its dogmas? 21*Do not handle, do not taste, do not touch.* All these pertain to human commands and teachings that perish. 23They have the show of reason[22] in a self-willed

---

19. The cross is a violent and defining moment of change. By nailing it to the cross, the Christ is publicly saying, the past is gone and discarded.

20. This metaphor of a Roman triumphant march may refer to one or many circumstances: a triumph over past law, over the devil and his cohorts. It could not, however, with any degree of safety, have signaled a triumph over the Roman authorities and rulers of the occupation of these lands. These were especially dangerous and fearful years for Jews and emerging Christians with respect to Roman rulers. Any overt protest, subversion, or rebellion would have been punished immediately. During the Jewish War (67–70), which coincides with this time frame, according to Josephus, Roman Titus was executing up to five hundred Jews and Christian Jews a day as his army moved to capture Jerusalem.

21. Reference is to Jewish dietary laws and ceremonies, which the author informs the gentile converts are under a shadow since the coming of the Mashiah, and multiple demands of observance will no longer be enforced.

22. Literally, they have the *logos,* the "word." In the Greek tradition the word, λόγος (logos), is invested in reason, philosophy; and in Judeo-Christian theology the word may contain supernatural creation powers, as in Genesis 1.3 when God speaks creation into existence, or in parallel John 1.1, when, as in Kabbalah, God creates the divine verb of the mind: "In the beginning was the word."

religion and lowliness and severe treatment of the body, but they are of no value against the indulgence of the flesh.[23]

Chapter 3

You once walked on earth

If then you were raised[24] with the Mashiah, look for what is above where the Mashiah is, seated by the right hand of God. 2Think about things above, not what is on the earth, 3for you died, and your life has been hidden away with the Mashiah in God. 4When the Mashiah appears, your life, and you also will be revealed with him in glory.

5Mortify your members[25] that are of the earth: fornication, filth, passion, wicked desire, and greed which is idolatry. 6From them comes the wrath of God [on the sons of disobedience].[26] 7Once you also walked among them, when you were living amid those things. 8Put them down. Be away from anger, rage, malice, blasphemy, foul language from your mouth. 9Do not lie to one another. Strip away the old man with his practices, 10and dress in the new man, renewed in knowledge after the

---

23. It is impossible to know what heresy the speaker is targeting. However, the attack lists qualities praised by the Gnostics, that is, reason and knowledge, a self-centered meditation, and the notion, in common with Paul's letters, that the illusory body is an erroneous, dark manifestation of ignorance that can be transcended only through bodily detachment and spiritual ascension. The absence of specifically Jewish observances or Greco-Roman idols (statues) strengthens the case for early Gnosticism as the enemy sect.

24. Or wakened.

25. Mortify from the Greek νεκρόω (nekroo), which can mean "put to death," and commonly "deaden" or "make impotent," which connotes a sexual meaning, particularly if related to a body part. Here "member[s]" is from the Greek μέλος (melos). It occurs as the first key word in the condemnation of unclean sexual practices. *Melos* probably signifies "penis" rather than a general notion of limbs or body. *Melos* functions in Greek as "member" in English, not as a symbol but a strong synonym of penis.

26. Not found in some early texts.

icon[27] of the one who created the new man. 11 In that renewal there is no Greek and Jew, circumcision and foreskin, barbarian, Scythian, slave, free man. There the Mashiah is all and in all.

Love, bond of perfection

12So as the chosen of God, holy and loved, clothe yourselves in compassion, kindness, lowliness, gentleness, 13patience with each other, and forgiving one another if someone has a complaint. As the lord forgave you, so should you. 14To all these things add love, which is a bond of perfection. 15And let the peace of the Mashiah rule in your hearts, to which you were called in one body. Be thankful. 16Let the word of the Mashiah live within you abundantly, in all his wisdom, teaching and admonishing one another with psalms, hymns, spiritual songs to God. 17And do all you do in word or in work, all things in the name of the lord Yeshua, giving thanks through him to God the father.

Rules of the household[28]

18Wives, be submissive to your husbands as is proper in the lord.

19Husbands, love your wives and do not be bitter against them.

20Children, obey your parents in all things, for this is pleasing to the lord.

21Fathers, do not provoke your children, for they may lose heart.

22Slaves, obey your earthly masters in everything, not merely as eye-catchers to please people when being watched, but in simplicity of heart, fearing the lord. 23Whatever you do, work from the soul as for the lord and not for men, 24knowing that from the lord you will receive your inheritance as a reward. You were a slave to the lord Mashiah. 25The wrongdoer will be repaid for wrong and there is no partiality.[29]

---

27. Image or likeness.

28. For similar rules of the household, see Ephesians 5.22–32. These rules, including the ones concerning the submission of the wife, appear as doctrine in many quarters, and while the most famous incarnation appears in two disputed letters, Ephesians and Colossians, their origin cannot be assigned or unassigned to Paul.

29. No favorites.

Chapter 4

Justice for slaves

Masters, be just and fair with your slaves.[30] Give, and know that you also have a master in the sky.

A few more rules

2Be constant in prayer, alert and with thanksgiving. 3And at the same time pray for us that God may open a door of the word to us, to speak the mystery of the Mashiah, for which I am in chains,[31] 4so that I may speak and reveal it. 5Walk in wisdom toward those outside, making the best of your time. 6May your speech always be gracious, seasoned with salt so you may know how to answer everyone.

News through his messengers Tyhikos and Onesimos

7I will tell you all my news. He is Tyhikos,[32] my loved brother and faithful minister and fellow slave in the lord. 8I sent him to you for this purpose, that you know how we are and he may guide your hearts. 9With Onesimos,[33] my faithful and loved brother, who is one of you, will inform you about all things here.

Greetings and goodbye

10Aristarhos,[34] my fellow prisoner, and Markos, cousin of Bar Nabba[35]

---

30. The letter offers no criticism of slavery itself but how slaves should be treated by Christian slave owners.

31. In prison. It is not known what imprisonment means here—actual or symbolic, and if actual, where.

32. Tychicus from the Greek Τυχικός (Tyhikos), a man from the province of Asia who accompanied Paul on a journey to Jerusalem.

33. Onesimus from the Greek Ὀνήσιμος (Onesimos), a companion of Paul and slave of Philemon for whom Paul wrote a brief letter. Onesimos in Greek means "useful," as in a useful helper.

34. Aristarchos from the Greek Ἀρίσταρχος (Aristarhos). Aristarhos of Thessaloniki accompanied Paul on his journeys.

35. Barnabas from the Greek Βαρναβᾶς (Barnabas), from the Aramaic בַּר נְבָא (bar nabba). Barnabas was Joseph, a Levi from Cyprus.

from whom you have received instructions from me, if he comes to you, receive him, and 11Yeshua[36] who is called Ioustos,[37] greets you. These of the circumcision[38] are my only coworkers in the kingdom of God, and they have been a comfort to me. 12Epafras sends you greetings. He is one of you,[39] a slave of the Mashiah Yeshua, always struggling for you in his prayers that you might stand perfected and fulfilled in every way God wishes. 13I testify for him that he works hard for you and as do those in

---

36. Jesus.

37. Justus from the Greek Ἰοῦστος (Ioustos), a Latin name.

38. These labels are Paul's way of saying that Barnabas and Jesus are Jews, rather than gentiles who have become Messianics. Paul has developed a new theory of signs for quick identification of the groups in the confusing complexity of merging ethnicities and sects, where a name and the changing of a name might signify good or evil, and even life or death by execution, particularly in Paul's background, which comprehended Roman citizenship, Greek and Aramaic speech, and Christian and Jewish faith. It is a sign of the day, and an ominous one that has not gone away in light of the twentieth-century Nazis' systematic searches in Europe for the "circumcised," that circumcision should have been made so central a theme by Paul and other primitive Christians. Throughout the letters, Paul extensively discusses the nature of circumcision, "of the body" and "of the heart." Here and elsewhere he identifies his followers in the Greek as "foreskins" (gentiles) or "circumcisions" (Jews converted to Messianism). Like many religions, the Jesus movement elevates spirit over body, identifying spirit as eternal, good, and pure, and body as temporal, sinful, and unclean (*akarthatos*). It is unusual that it should nametag its followers by the condition of their penis, distinguishing the faithful as the "foreskins" and the "circumcisions."

In this centering on the male genital organ as a showpiece of membership in early Messianism, women are omitted, failing to have neither presence nor a sign of their physicality in the gender-favored nomenclature. The neglect and degradation of women are particularly apparent, since this greetings-and-farewell section is preceded by the passages on "rules of the household" (3.18–22). While rules require a husband to love his wife as his wife her husband, they command wives to "be submissive to your husbands as is proper in the lord," and order obedience of children to parents and of slaves to masters.

With regard to women, Colossians, composed after Paul's death, may be seen, along with Ephesians of a similar late date and with a more detailed discussion of women, children, and slaves (5.22–6.9), as reflecting views, perhaps more than Paul's, of later church leaders in the diaspora communities.

39. Implying, not a circumcision but a foreskin, not a Jew but a gentile.

Laodikeia and those in Hieropolis. ₁₄I greet you, Loukas⁴⁰ the beloved physician, and Demas⁴¹ greets you. ₁₅Give greetings to the brothers in Laodikeia and to Nymfa⁴² and the church in her house.

₁₆When this letter is read before you, have it read also in the church of the Laodikeans, and also the letter sent from Laodikeia to you, which you should also read.⁴³ ₁₇And tell Arhippos,⁴⁴ "See that you complete the task that received in the lord."

₁₈This greeting is written in my hand, Shaul.⁴⁵ Remember my chains. Grace be with you.

---

40. Luke. This reference to Luke the physician, as well as those in 2 Timothy 4.11 and Philemon 24, is used to support the notion of a Luke-Acts and Luke-gospel axis of authorship. To most scholars the authors of Acts as well as of the Gospel of Luke and the other gospels are anonymous. Were Luke, or another single person, the author of the Luke gospel and Acts, he would have composed twenty-eight percent of the New Testament, many more pages than are contained in Paul's authentic letters. For more discussion, see "The Authorship of Luke-Acts Reconsidered," in Joseph A. Fitzmyer's *Luke the Theologian* (New York: Paulist Press, 1989), 1–26.

41. Demas from the Greek Δημᾶς (Demas), probably shortened from Δημήτριος (Demetrios). Demas was a companion of Paul.

42. Nympha from the Greek Νύμφα (Nymfa), a female name, or from Νυμφᾶς (Nymfas), a male name. In the Greek text we have this single reference in the letters in its accusative form, Νύμφαν (Nymfan), which is the same form for masculine and feminine spellings of the name. Hence, we do not know whether the name is of a man or a woman. If it is a woman, which is likely, it shows, as in Acts 16.15 and 16.40 and Romans 16.3–6, a woman leader whose church is in her household. If this is so, it gives a strongly alternate infusion of information about the roles of women in primitive Christianity, which in other aspects are minor and subservient. Here, the scriptural evidence asserts that a woman in the formative days of Christianity might be a clerical leader, which stands in contrast to contemporary circumstance, at least in traditional Catholicism, which forbids women in the clergy.

43. Reference is apparently to a letter sent by Paul, or by the anonymous author of Colossians, from Paul to the Laodiceans. Nothing is known of this letter.

44. Archippus from the Greek Ἄρχιππος (Arhippos).

45. Paul's habit was to dictate his letters and write the farewell greetings in his own hand. It is unknown how, when in chains in prison, he was able to dictate his long letters and arrange for their delivery. Whatever means he had, he speaks of being in chains, in both the authentic and the disputed letters.

Thessalonikians beta
(2 Thessalonians)

Thessalonikians beta[1]
(2 Thessalonians)

THE SECOND LETTER to the Thessalonikians is late, perhaps written about the time of Revelation, at the end of the first or beginning of the second century. It is an impersonal work of no distinction, with no specific references to Paul's actual dilemmas. One wonders why it was included in the original compilation of the New Testament in the mid-second century, and how it survived the final selection at Nicea (325 C.E.). It does have an ever increasing missionary anger against the deceptive false teachers, meaning the Gnostics, who in major Greek cities were doing very well. That jealous hatred reveals contemporary politic but in no way reflects Paul's activities and philosophy.

As early as the beginning of the eighteenth century, 2 Thessalonians' validity was questioned. The debate has gone back and forth but there is little support today for not placing the book among the pseudo-Pauline letters. Its better place would be among the huge collection of pseudepigrapha from this period, of which many figure in the history and mythology of early Christianity. From the pseudepigrapha we have the main stories of Jesus's immediate extended family.

The author's main theological issue is how to cope with God's promise of the return of the Christ. He has not yet come, and apocalyptic struggles with evil are offered as reasons for the delay. It repeats the promise in 1 Thessalonians that at the Parousia, the coming of the Christ, the dead

---

1. Thessalonians from the Greek Θεσσαλονικεύς (Thessalonikeus), inhabitants of Thessaloniki, the ancient port capital of Macedonia in northern Greece. The Greek title is followed by βῆτα (beta) representing the letter "b" as well as the number "2."

will be awakened from their sleep. Therefore, the author admonishes to keep on working, live in this world, obey church law, and believe in the gospel. Those who fail to obey the gospel of Jesus will suffer the punishment of eternal destruction by "Yeshua's mighty angels of flame" (1.9).

The letter imitates as far as it can Paul's style and phrases, such as "in Christ," and begins, as in the earlier letter, asserting how Paul loves his brothers and sisters, and that his love for them increases each day. But it is more a sermon of generalities, its freshness fading before the dry platitudes. The letter might pertain for church readings at any period, since, apart from mentioning Paul's name and notions of the end, it doesn't add to the writings of Paul, the grand philosopher with the quick inventive mind. Sadly, it is hard to find a consensus of praise for the brief epistle.

Chapter 1

Hello

> Shaul[2] and Silouanos[3] and Timotheos[4]
> To the temple of the Thessalonikians
> In God the father and in the lord Yeshua
> The Mashiah.[5] 2Grace to you all and peace.[6]

Thank you

3We must thank you at all times concerning you, brothers, and it is fitting because our faith in you is growing abundantly and increases the

---

2. Paul from the Greek Παῦλος (Paulos), from Saul in the Greek Σαῦλος (Saulos), from the Hebrew שָׁאוּל (Shaul). Paul was born in Tarsos as *Shaul*.

3. Silvanus from the Greek Σιλουανός (Silouanos), probably from the Hebrew סִילְוָנִי (Sylvany). Silvanus seems to be the same person as Silas, a prophet and leader in the Jerusalem synagogue who was said to accompany Paul in his second missionary journey (Acts 15.22, 15.32).

4. Timothy from the Greek Τιμόθεος (Timotheos).

5. Christ Jesus. "Jesus" is from the Greek 'Ιησοῦς (Iesous), from the Aramaic יֵשׁוּעַ (Yeshua), a later form of the Hebrew יְהוֹשֻׁעַ (Yehoshua). "Christ" is from the Greek Χριστος (Hristos), and Greek *Hristos* or *Christos* is a translation from the Greek Μεσσίας (Messias), from the Hebrew מָשִׁיחַ (mashiah). "Christ" in Greek also means "the anointed," and "Messiah" in both Greek and Hebrew contains the meaning of "the anointed."

6. Thessalonians 1.1–2 is identical to 2 Thessalonians 1.1–2, and many later passages are also almost identical, helping the author of the Deutero-Pauline letter make it pass as Paul's voice (Paul dictated his letters). Of course, the purpose of a forgery is to make it pass, and in this instance the author almost outdoes himself by wonderful Daniel-like rhetoric and Revelation apocalypse, which prompts Raymond E. Brown to suggest a date of composition near the end of the first century. There is more similarity in word and form in these two letters than in any others in the canon. There remains much dispute concerning the certainty "of the uncertain," as Brown skillfully phrases it, though the majority view is for pseudonymity. See Raymond E. Brown, "Second Letter to the Thessalonians," in *An Introduction to the New Testament* (New York: Doubleday, 1997), 596.

love of each one of you for one another. 4So we ourselves boast of you in the temples of God for your endurance and faith during all your persecutions and the afflictions you are suffering. 5This is a demonstration of God's correction judgment, and for you to be counted worthy of the kingdom of God, for whose sake you are in pain.

6It is indeed just for God to repay with affliction those who afflict you, 7and give relief to the afflicted and to us when the lord Yeshua is revealed from the skies with angels of power, in blazing fire, 8and punishes those who don't know God and those who don't obey the gospel of lord Yeshua. 9They will pay a penalty of everlasting destruction, and be far from the presence of the lord and from the glory of his strength 10when he comes to be glorified by his saints and to be admired among believers on that great day, because our testimony to you was believed.

We Pray for You

11Till then we pray, always for you, that our God may consider you worthy of his call, and by his power fulfill every desire for goodness and work of faith 12so that the name of our lord Yeshua be glorified in you, and you in him by grace of God and lord Yeshua Mashiah.

Chapter 2

Day of the lord

Now we ask you, brothers, in the matter of the Parousia,7 of the coming of our lord Yeshua the Mashiah, and our meeting with him, 2not to be easily shaken from your mind or terrified by any spirit or word or letter, as if the letter were from us and the day of the lord already here.

The lawless man who claims to be God

3Let no one deceive you in any way. For that day of the coming will not be here until first come the apostasy, the rebellion and revelation [of the

---

7. Parousia or coming as in "the coming of the lord," from the Greek παρουσία (parousia).

lawless man],[8] of the son of destruction, 4who opposes and exalts himself above anything that is called God or worshiped so that he can sit in the temple of God, declaring himself to be God. 5Do you not remember that I told you this when I was with you? 6And you know now what restrains him so that he will be revealed when his time comes. 7The mystery of lawlessness is already at work, but the one who is restraining him will go on doing so until he is gone. 8Then the lawless one will be exposed, and the lord [Yeshua] will consume him with a breath from his mouth and annihilate him by the manifestation of his own day of coming.[9] 9The coming of the lawless one is apparent in the workings of Satan with all his power and signs and wonders of falseness, 10and with every wicked deception for those who are perishing because they did not accept the love of truth for their salvation. 11Therefore God sends them a powerful delusion for them to believe the lie 12so that all who did not believe the truth but enjoyed injustice may be judged.

We thank God for salvation

13But we owe constant thanks to God about you, brothers, loved by the lord because from the beginning he chose you as the [first fruits][10] of salvation through sanctification of the spirit and belief in the truth. 14He called you to this through our good news that you might share in the glory of our lord Yeshua the Mashiah. 15So then, brothers, stand firm and hold to the traditions you were taught by us, either in word or by letter from us.

---

8. Not in all ancient texts. "The lawless man" has also been translated as "a man of iniquity." The Greek ἀνομία (anomia) means "lawlessness," equivalent to English "anomie" or "anomy," from *a* (without) + *nomos* (law).

Who this apocalyptic lawless man is remains a mystery: a false prophet or god, Satan, a Roman emperor—all are candidates. God himself may have sent the lawless man down as a delusion to test the true believers. To darken the lawless man's person, he is described with language found in Daniel or Revelation that is reserved for depicting the anti-God or anti-Christ.

9. The manifestation or appearance of his coming refers to the coming of the lord, not that of the lawless man.

10. Not found in all ancient texts.

16May our lord Yeshua the Mashiah, and God our father, who loved us and through grace gave us everlasting comfort and splendid hope, 17may he animate your hearts and strengthen you in every work and each good word.

Chapter 3

Pray

For the rest, pray for us, brothers, so that the word of the lord may race about and be glorified everywhere, just as it is among you, 2and that we may be safe from wicked and crafty men. Not everyone has faith. 3But the lord is faithful. He will strengthen and guard you from the cunning one.¹¹ 4We have confidence in the lord about you that you will do the things that we tell you to do. 5May the lord direct your hearts to the love of God and the endurance to await the Mashiah.

6Now we charge you, brothers, in the name of our lord Yeshua Mashiah to keep away from any brothers walking idly and not in accordance with the tradition you received from us. 7You know how you should imitate us, since we were not lazy when we were among you. 8We did not

---

11. Or "wicked one" or "devil" from the Greek πονηρός (poneros). The word has multiple meanings, from its classical and modern Greek meaning of smart, nimble-minded (as in the epithet for Odysseus) to evil and crafty, which is its New Testament usage. When it signifies "wicked," it carries the notion of cunning and evil intelligence. In its biblical usage, there is frequently a fundamental agon between faith and knowledge, pitting the Judeo-Christian demand for faith and obedience (hence, disobedient Eve and our human downfall) against the heretical Gnostic demand for knowledge, *gnosis*, where Eve is praised for her dissent and disobedience in the Garden. The struggle between Christianity and Gnosticism is seen in brief references in Paul, more fully in pseudonymous Paul (Timothy), and Revelation, but will not have major consequences until after the first century. The temptations and denunciations of Gnosticism as a rival meditation are epitomized by Saint Augustine (354–430), who in *Confessions* (397) speaks of his early nine years (377–86) as an active Gnostic missionary in North Africa and Italy. His own denunciations of Manicheanism and Donatism have been a major source on Gnostic theology, especially before the 1945 discovery of the Nag Hammadi Gnostic scriptures.

eat bread as a gift from anyone, but in labor and hardship by night and day, working so as not to be a burden to you. ₉This was not because we do not have the right, but in order not to give you an example to imitate. ₁₀Even when we were with you, we taught you that anyone who does not work does not eat. ₁₁We hear that some of you are walking about idle, not working but are busybodies. ₁₂And these we ask and exhort them in the lord Yeshua Mashiah to go to their work in quiet and work so they may eat. ₁₃Brothers, do not lose heart in doing good, ₁₄and if anyone does not obey our word in this letter, have nothing to do with him that he may be put to shame. ₁₅But do not think him an enemy but admonish him as a brother.

₁₆May the lord of peace bring you peace of every kind always. The lord be with you.

Goodbye

₁₇This greeting is Paul's, by my hand, which is my signature to every letter. This is my writing. ₁₈The grace of our lord Yeshua Mashiah be with you all.

THREE LATE PASTORAL LETTERS ATTRIBUTED TO SHAUL/SAUL/PAUL

Timotheos alpha
(1 Timothy)

Timotheos alpha[1]
(1 Timothy)

⁓

Timothy was born in Lystra, today Turkey, of a Greek father and a Christian-Jewish mother (Acts 16.1). When Paul invited Timothy to be part of his mission, he had him circumcised so that he would not be a liability when proselytizing Jews to the good news (Acts 16.3). This action points to how central it was for Paul, a circumcised Jew, to be able to reach traditional Jews as a principle group for conversion. Timothy was part of Paul's evangelization in Macedonia and Achaia and a frequent traveler with him on other missions, especially in Ephesos. Six of Paul's letters name Timothy as a co-sender, which reveals how close he was to Paul in life and in their common ministry.

The two letters to Timothy and the letter to Titus, often called the Pastorals because they deal with church officers and their "flocks," are judged to be forgeries by most scholars. This first letter to Timothy is cast in a more directly personal style to its recipient, and would seem to have more claim for authorship by Paul or by one of his students. In this regard, however, it is regarded as a letter from a veteran missionary to a younger colleague. Stylistic and theological differences, along with anachronisms, militate against Pauline authorship. The style, however,

1. The First Letter of Paul to Timothy. Timothy from the Greek Τιμόθεος (Timotheos). The title of these three epistles, "Pastoral Letters," may connote the country life of the shepherd and lyrical meadows as in Bach's *Pastocella* and Beethoven's Pastoral Symphony, but such is not the intended meaning. The title of these anonymous letters came as an afterthought, not in earliest documents.

is fluent and often pleasing. Its singular purport seems to be, again in contrast to Paul's polythematic letters, uniformly didactic. It articulates standards for accepting church officers (including rules on celibacy, women, and slaves) and the usual warning against false prophets and rival messages.

Chapter 1

Hello

Shaul[2] a messenger of the Mashiah Yeshua[3] by order of God our savior and the Mashiah Yeshua our hope, 2to Timotheos,[4] my own true child in faith, grace, mercy, peace from God the father and the Mashiah Yeshua our lord.

Aim of my instruction is love

3I urge you, as I did on my way to Makedonia,[5] to stay on in Efesos[6] so you could instruct people not to teach heretical doctrines[7] 4nor to pay attention to myths and endless genealogies, which lead to speculations rather than the plan of God in faith. 5But the aim of my instruction is love from a clean heart and a good conscience and unhypocritical faith. 6Some miss the mark on these qualities and drift into vain chatter. 7They wish to be teachers of the law, without understanding either what to say or what they want seriously to assert.

---

2. Paul from the Greek Παῦλος (Paulos), from Saul in the Greek Σαῦλος (Saulos), from the Hebrew שָׁאוּל (Shaul). Paul was born in Tarsos as *Shaul*.

3. Christ Jesus. "Jesus" is from the Greek Ἰησοῦς (Iesous), from the Aramaic יֵשׁוּעַ (Yeshua), a later form of the Hebrew יְהוֹשֻׁעַ (Yehoshua). "Christ" is from the Greek Χριστος (Hristos), and Greek *Hristos* or *Christos* is a translation from the Greek Μεσσίας (Messias), from the Hebrew מָשִׁיחַ (mashiah). "Christ" in Greek also means "the anointed," and "Messiah" in both Greek and Hebrew contains the meaning of "the anointed."

4. Timothy.

5. Macedonia from the Greek Μακεδονία (Makedonia).

6. Ephesos or Ephesus (Latinized version) from the Greek Ἔφεσος (Efesos), an elaborate Greek and later Roman city south of Smyrna on the western coast of present-day Turkey, which was one of the Seven Wonders of the World.

7. Probably referring to Gnosticism here, as in later verses. The references to false teachings insofar as the letter is dated to after 70 C.E. would be to Greco-Roman mystery religions or more likely to Gnosticizing Judaism, whereas if, as some contend, the Pastoral Letters are from the second century, then the references would be to Gnosticizing Christianity.

8We know that the law is good, if one uses it lawfully. 9This means that law is not for the just and innocent,[8] but for the lawless and disobedient, the ungodly and sinners, the unholy and profane, for the patricides and matricides, murderers, 10fornicators, sodomites,[9] slave traders, liars, perjurers, and whatever else is contrary to healthy teaching 11according to the gospel of the glory of blessed God in whom I believe.

I was a blasphemer

12I am grateful to him who gave me power, to the Mashiah Yeshua our lord, because he considered me trustworthy and appointed me to his service, 13though earlier I was a blasphemer and persecutor and a violent man. But I was given mercy because I had acted ignorantly in unbelief 14and God's grace overflowed for me with faith and love, which is in the Mashiah Yeshua. 15The word is to be believed and worthy of full acceptance: that the Mashiah Yeshua came into the world to save the fallen of whom I am the foremost. 16For that reason I received mercy and so that in me, foremost of all, Yeshua Mashiah might display his utmost patience, making me an example to those who would come to believe in him for eternal life.

17Now to the king of ages, incorruptible, invisible, the only God, be honor and glory into the aeons of aeons. Amain.

Timotheos, my child

18Timotheos, my child, I give you these instructions according to prophecies you pointed to before so that you might fight the good campaign, 19keeping faith and with a good conscience. Some have lost that faith. Some have shipwrecked in their faith. 20Among these are Ymenaios[10] and Alexandros,[11] whom I have turned over to Satan so they may be taught not to blaspheme.

---

8. Here the notion of law does not pertain to the innocent but to naming and condemning the guilty.

9. The word ἀρσενοκοίτης (arsenokoites), "male-loving," is a general word for homosexuality, but it can also be translated as "sodomite" and "pederast."

10. Hymenaeus, from the Greek Ὑμέναιος (Hymenaios). Hymenaeus and Alexander were excluded from the temple by Paul for disciplinary reasons.

11. Alexander from the Greek Ἀλέξανδρος (Alexandros).

Chapter 2

Praying

First of all I ask you to make your entreaties, prayers, intercessions, and thanksgivings for everyone, 2for kings and all of high estate, so that we may lead a peaceful and quiet life in all piety and reverence. 3This is good and acceptable before God our savior, 4who wants all people to be saved and to come to a knowledge of the truth:

5There is one God.[12]

There is one mediator between God and person,

Mashiah Yeshua a man,

6Who gave himself as ransom for everyone,

a testimonial to his days.[13]

Commandments for men to pray and women in silence to submit

7I was appointed herald and messenger, I speak truth, I do not lie, a teacher of the gentiles in faith and truth:

8I wish then that in every place the men to raise holy hands without anger or dispute.

9So too I wish women to dress in decorous style with modesty and propriety,[14] and to adorn themselves not in hairstyles and gold or pearls or expensive fabrics, 10but as becomes a proper woman professing godly reverence by way of good works.

11Let a woman learn in silence and in full submission.

12I do not allow women to teach, nor to usurp authority over the man.[15]

She must be in silence.

13Adam was formed first. Then Eve.

---

12. The core of Jewish belief expressed in the Shema.

13. This passage, with reason, has been set apart in other translations, as a prayer psalm, worthy of any.

14. The King James Version gives a striking version of the Greek: "with shamefacedness and sobriety."

15. The word "man" in Greek can also mean secondarily "husband." However, by not choosing a specific word for husband, the Greek leaves the command open to all states of womanhood with respect to men.

14Adam was not deceived, but the woman was deceived and became a transgressor.

15She will be saved through childbearing, if she remains in faith and love and holiness and good behavior.[16]

Chapter 3

To be a bishop

The word is believed.

If someone aspires to be a bishop,[17] he desires a good work.

2Now the bishop must be irreproachable, a man of one wife, sober, sensible, worldly, hospitable, and teacherly, 3not a wine drunk, no brawler, but forbearing, not quarrelsome, not a lover of money. 4He must manage his own household well, keeping his children submissive, and respectable. 5If one does not know how to manage one's own household, how can he care for a church of God?[18] 6He must not be a new plant, a new

---

16. The extreme degradation of women in these famous verses, while often explained away, remains a fierce source of contemporary debate and protest. The kindest thing one can say in Paul's defense is that they were in all likelihood composed by church authorities between two and five decades after his death. However, the forgers using Paul's name were attempting to reproduce Paul's presumed thinking.

17. A bishop from the Greek ἐπίσκοπος (episkopos), meaning literally "overseer," from *epi* (over) + *skopos* (seer).

18. If this letter is not from Paul's hand but from a later period when gentile or Greek Jews and Christian Jews did not meet primarily in a synagogue (a Greek, not a Hebrew, word), then "church" is appropriate. However, if it is pretended that it is from Paul's time, then "synagogue" remains the probably right word. The claim of contemporaneity with Paul is particularly weakened by the later idea of office for a respectable bishop as opposed to an overseer, which is the original meaning of "bishop" in classical Greek. As the church developed, many ordinary words, which in English would be "student," "messenger," "overseer," and "waiter," took on, in Greek usage, high office, pomp, and respectability. In an anachronistic translation into English, high-sounding words were chosen to turn what at the time was a plain-garbed, impoverished survival reality into the later-church power and rich-robed respectability. Hence, a student became a "disciple," a messenger an "apostle," an overseer a "bishop," and a servant and table waiter a "deacon."

convert,[19] who might become conceited and fall into the devil. 7And he must be well thought of by outsiders so as not to fall into disgrace and the devil's trap.

To be a deacon

8So deacons[20] also must be dignified, not two-tongued, not lost in heavy drinking, not fond of obscene gain. 9They must keep the mystery of faith with a clean conscience. 10And let them first be tested, then serve as deacons,[21] irreproachable. 11Women deacons[22] must similarly be respectable, not gossips, sober, faithful in all things. 12Let deacon husbands be of one wife, manage their children well, and also their household. 13Those who serve well as deacons gain for themselves a good standing and much confidence in faith in the Mashiah Yeshua.

14I write these things to you, hoping to come to you quickly. 15But if I am slow in coming, you may know how to conduct yourself in the house of God, which is the temple of a living God, pillar and foundation of the truth. 16And clearly great is the mystery of godliness:

> He appeared in flesh
> made good by spirit
> seen by angels
> Preached among nations
> believed in the world
> risen in glory.[23]

---

19. The word in Timothy is νεόφυτος (neofytos), from which we get "neophyte," and which in New Testament translation becomes ultimately "new convert," but "neophyte" in Greek carries its strong etymological meaning of "new plant" from *neo* (new) + *fytos* (plant).

20. Deacon from the Greek διάκονος (diakonos), a servant, a table waiter, or helper.

21. The Greek ironically plays on the double meaning of "deacon" in saying "serve" with "deacon" imbedded in the verb διακονέω (diakoneo), "to serve," and διάκονος (diakonos), which is "deacon" and "minister," as well as its root meaning of "servant."

22. Deaconesses.

23. Or taken up into the skies.

Chapter 4

Demonic Gnostic ascetics

The spirit expressly says that in later times some will forsake the faith, heeding deceitful spirits and teachings of demons in hypocrisy, 2liars whose consciences have been seared with a hot iron.[24] 3Opposing marriage they abstain from foods that God created to be eaten with thanksgiving by those who are believers and know the truth. 4Because every creature of God is good and nothing is to be thrown away that is received with thanksgiving, 5for it is hallowed by the word of God and prayer.

Be trained in godliness

6If you instruct these things to the brothers, you will be a good servant of the Mashiah Yeshua, nourished on words of faith and the good teachings that you have followed. 7Reject profane old wives' tales, and train yourselves in godliness. 8While training the body is of some value, godliness is valuable, containing promise for this life and the coming one. 9My sayings are to be believed and worthy of full acceptance. 10To this end we labor and [struggle],[25] because we put our hope in the living God, who is the savior of all people, and especially of the believers.

Believe, behave, and teach

11Teach and promote these beliefs. 12Let no one scorn your youth, but make yourself a model of the faithful in speech, in behavior, in love, in

---

24. The Gnostics, whose main seat was Alexandria, were heavily Platonized philosophers, as was Paul, who in the later Valentinian school gave us the first exegesis of the Bible, which was to establish an imitated example for the main early Christian exegetes, especially the Platonist Origen (185?–254?), whose work was to set a high standard for early Christian text hermeneutic analysis and allegorical interpretation. As philosophers the Gnostics preferred knowledge to faith, and offered salvation now, independent of death, through meditation where through ascetic detachment one became one with the eternal pneuma (spirit) as opposed to the hylic (earthly and temporal) psyche or soul. See note on Eve and knowledge and Satan in note 31 on 1 Timothy 5.15.

25. Not in all ancient texts.

faith, in purity. 13Until I come, attend to public reading of scripture,[26] to exhortations,[27] to teaching.[28] 14Do not ignore the gift in you, given to you

---

26. Reading of what scripture? one must ask. If the letter is by Paul, the only scripture during his time was the Torah, that is, the Hebrew Bible (Old Testament). There was no New Testament, of which the earliest sections would have been Paul's letters, but these letters were in Paul's times circular epistles to be read at the synagogues and new gentile synagogues, but not as scripture. If by "scripture," the writer means the gospels or Revelation, and by the middle of the second century there was an official but nearly finished version of the twenty-seven books of the New Testament, then we must place the date for 1 Timothy well into the middle of the second century, which is at least a few decades too late. What is clear is that whether 1 Timothy was composed in Paul's day, or two or four decades later, there were not yet New Testament texts available to be read. Hence, these public sermons in the synagogues and nascent churches were Greek translations from the Hebrew Bible, the Septuagint or variations of it (the Hebrew Bible in Greek), or letters from other missionaries like Paul, his colleagues, or, in other meeting places, his opponent apostles, who in his lifetime outnumbered him in person and power.

27. Exhortations were speeches to animate, encourage, and advise. In this they were calls to faith by spiritual cheerleaders.

28. The liturgical practice of public reading of scripture, exhortation, and teaching was intrinsic to the traditional Jewish synagogue, and taken over in exact practice and purpose by the Christian Jews. The concept of the synagogue was itself a revolutionary development in Judaism, whose earliest examples are still impossible to date. It meant that isolated priests did not perform ceremonies alone for those outside in courtyards, streets, or elsewhere in a village or city, but carried on in public view of participants. It shifted worship from sacrifices on altars or in shrines, by the few, to worship in communal institutions to whom the leaders depended for help and on whom they depended for acceptance.

The sequence of these ceremonial happenings was prayer and study (silent or publicly read aloud), exhortations, and teaching. In synagogues and meeting houses where early Messianists met up, to and including later churches, the Jewish liturgical practice was continued in order and content. To the books read, chanted, instructed were added, when available, passages from the New Testament. In rebellious Protestantism the role of the priest was diminished and the congregation enhanced. By the time of George Fox (1624–1691), founder of the Society of Friends, or Quakers, the clergy all but disappeared and was replaced by a communal audience; the scriptures that had been read aloud were replaced by silent meditation, and the exhortation was gone. Without a clergy, the word was turned over to those in the communal audience who stood up in the meeting house in order to speak a personal encounter with "the inner light." So individual public revelation became, among the Quakers, their significant instrument of instruction.

by prophesy, which is the laying on of hands on you by the presbytery.[29]
15Practice and meditate on these things, and devote yourself to them so
that your progress may be visible to all. 16Attend to your teaching, persevere in such things, for by doing that you will save both yourself and
those who hear you.

Chapter 5

Instruction about old people, widows, and slaves

Do not rebuke an old man, but entreat him as a father, younger men as
brothers, 2old women as mothers, younger women as sisters in complete
chastity.

3Honor widows who are really widows. 4But if any widow has children
or grandchildren, let them first respect their own household and show
piety to and recompense their parents, which is acceptable in the sight
of God. 5She who is really a widow and lives alone has placed her hope
in God and is constant in her entreaties and prayers night and day. 6But
the widow who lives in pleasure has died even while she is alive.

7Charge people with these concepts that they be beyond reproach.
8And if one of the members of the household does not take care of his
own people, and especially his own family, he has denied his faith and
is worse than an infidel.

9No widow can be put on the list of widows unless she is not less
than sixty years old, the wife of one man, 10is well known for her good
deeds, has brought up her children, been hospitable, washed the saints'
feet, given assistance to the afflicted, and been devoted to all good
work.

11As for younger widows, do not put them on the list. For when

---

29. The council of elders. In Judaism the presbytery was the highest Jewish council in Jerusalem. The laying of hands was a practice in many parts of Israel, by the
Essenes and by wise men and miracle-doers in Jesus's Galilee. In Torah, "laying
hands" is the Hebrew word סָמַךְ (samah). In the ceremony of laying hands on an
object, סָמַךְ signifies transferring identity from person to object, that is, transferring healing powers of the miracle-maker to the flesh of the sick person.

their sexual desires are in disregard of the Mashiah, they want to marry. 12They have committed a crime by violating their first pledge. 13At the same time they learn to be shiftless, going from house to house. And not merely shiftless but they are also gossips and weird busybodies, saying what they should not say.[30] 14So I wish the younger widows to marry, to have children, to rule the house, and give an adversary no occasion to slander us. 15Already some have turned to Satan.[31]

16If any believer woman has widows in her family, let her take care of them, and so that the church is not burdened and can assist those who are really widowed.

---

30. This rage against young widows is part of a pattern of discriminating cruelly against women in the household, in the street, and in the church. There is no equivalent rage against young widowers for any of these presumed moral failures. Their being rushed into marriage is not presented as a means of attaining higher virtue—which for them would be to be well behaved like good widows over sixty, an apparent impossibility for younger widows, who are necessarily lustful—but a reluctant necessity for keeping them out of further wickedness and laziness.

31. The facile association of women with their sexuality and weakness, and the need to control them for fear of woman as the initiator of temptation, begins in the Garden where God created "the garden [with] the tree of the knowledge of good and evil," וְעֵץ הַדַּעַת טוֹב וָרָע (v'atz ha-daat tov vara) (Gen. 2.9). The fruit of the tree of the knowledge of good and evil is the source of evil, for it will make her wise (Gen. 3.6). "Knowledge" in this Genesis passage means "understanding," "wisdom." Eve, seeing that the fruit is beautiful, desires its knowledge, takes the first step and the blame. God asks Adam if he ate the fruit. Adam informs God that Eve gave him the fruit and he ate it. By shifting the first transgression to Eve for giving the fruit to him, Adam is partially cleared (though both are punished with mortality) while Eve assumes an everlasting deeper guilt. She has committed the first disobedience in the Garden. In the unchanging hierarchy of blame, Eve is beguiled by the serpent and eats. Adam is given the fruit by the serpent/devil-beguiled Eve. Hence, woman is the serpent devil and man is the seduced victim of that devil woman. The logic of guilt, making Eve the first temptation and sinner, is thereafter inexorably applied to women under many circumstances on most days of their lives.

In praise of old churchmen

17The presbyters, the elders, who direct the church well deserve double honor, especially those who labor in preaching and teaching. 18It says in Deuteronomy:

You shall not muzzle an ox treading grain.[32]

And in Loukas:

The laborer deserves his wages.[33]

19Do not accept a charge against an elder until there are two or three witnesses, 20but convict those who do sin before everyone so others will be afraid. 21I order you before God and the Mashiah Yeshua and the chosen angels to keep these commandments with no reservations, doing nothing in partiality. 22Do not lay hands hastily on anyone, or join in sins of others. Keep yourself pure. 23Do not go on drinking water, but take a little wine because of your stomach and your frequent sicknesses.

24The sins of some people are obvious and lead the way to their judgment, while the sins of others remain obscure. 25Likewise, the good works of the elders are obvious, and those that are not evident cannot remain concealed.

---

32. Deut. 25.4.

33. Luke 10.7. 1 Timothy 5.18 cites Luke, the latest of the gospels, which, in the minefield of dating, was probably composed about three decades after Paul's death; it is unknown how long after its composition it took before Luke was dispersed and considered holy script. By including Luke in 1 Timothy it would seem that the ascription to Paul was not to be taken seriously, but until well into the twentieth century, opinion was divided. Today, even the colloquial, well-respected, and conservative New International Version, in the introduction to 1 Timothy still states, "[E]vidence is still convincingly supportive of Paul's authorship." (See NIV: *The NIV Study Bible: New International Version*, gen. ed. Kenneth Barker, Grand Rapids, MI: Zondervan Publishing House, 1995.) In effect, Paul's citing of Luke simply means that Paul dictated his letter to Timothy decades after his death from his unknown grave.

Chapter 6

Of slaves

All who are slaves under the yoke should consider their masters worthy of full honor so that the name and teaching of God not be scorned.[34] 2Those of you who have masters who are believers, do not disrespect them. They are brothers, and therefore slave for them even harder because they who benefit from your work are believers and beloved.

Of love of money

Teach and encourage these principles. 3If any teaches another doctrine and does not adhere to the healthy words of our lord Yeshua the Mashiah, and to the godliness of his teaching, 4that person is conceited and has understood nothing. He is sick over controversies and word wars out of which come envy, strife, blasphemy, base suspicions, 5wrangling of men corrupted in mind and bereft of truth, who think that godliness is gain. 6Gain combined with godliness and happiness is great, 7yet we came into the world with nothing so that we can carry nothing out of it. 8Yet if we have food and clothing, these things are enough. 9Those who wish to be rich fall into temptation and are trapped by senseless and and harmful desires that plunge people into ruin and destruction. 10The root of all evil is the love of money. Some have craved it and strayed from faith and pierced themselves with many sorrows.

---

34. For whatever reasons—and over the centuries many justifications for accepting slavery have been advanced—early Christian Jews and emerging Christians not only accepted the cast of slavery in society and church but also commanded, in the name and teachings of God, as said above, and in Ephesians and elsewhere, that obedience to and honoring of the master be wholehearted and absolute, and that failure to do so is sin and blasphemy. It may be remembered that excuses for the realpolitik of slavery are proposed by mortals even when God is cited as favoring the practice: "Such regulations did not encourage or condone such situations but were divinely-given practical ways of dealing with the realities of the day." See note on "Slaves," Ephesians 6.15, in NIV, p. 1801.

Orders to Timotheos

11You, man of God, flee from these things. Seek justice, godliness, faith, patient love, gentleness. 12Fight the good campaign of faith, seize eternal life to which you were called and confessed the good before many witnesses. 13I command you before God, who gave life to all things, and before the Mashiah Yeshua, who before Pontius Pilatus[35] testified to the good confession, 14keep the commandments stainless and irreproachable until the appearance of our lord Yeshua the Mashiah, 15which in his own time the blessed and sole sovereign will display. He is the king of kings and lord of lords, 16the sole immortal living in unapproachable light, whom no human has seen or can see. To him honor and eternal dominion. Amain.[36]

Of the rich

17Command those who are rich in our present age not to be haughty nor to set their hope on the uncertainty of riches, but on God, who richly provides us with everything, with happiness. 18They are to do good, be rich in good words, generous, glad to share, 19and to lay up a treasure for themselves so that will be a good foundation for the future so all may share in the real life.

---

35. Pontius Pilate. Paul knew nothing of Pontius Pilate, not being privy to the gospels composed after his death. Until 1961 Pontius Pilate had been largely dismissed as an invented figure, though there were ancient writers who mentioned him, including Philo and principally the Jewish historian Josephus. In his *Antiquities of the Jews*, (18.63–64), Josephus notes that "Pilate ordered the crucifixion of a man called Jesus, who was Christ [Messiah] after whom the Christian tribes were named." These words are an interpolation, that is, a much later emendation which scholars have dated to three or four centuries after Pilate's rule. Popularly, the legends were that Pilate's huge number of crucifixions caused him as prefect (governor) of Judea to be transferred elsewhere after two years. In 1961 the first physical evidence of his existence was found with the discovery of a block of limestone in the Roman theater at Caesarea Maritima in Judea. Though the block is damaged, its readable letters say Pilate a Tiberieum [. . .]ECTVS IUDA[. . .], read as *praefectus iudaeae* (prefect or governor of Judea). The black stone block, dated 26–37, is in the Israel Museum in Jerusalem.

36. Amen from the Greek ἀμήν (amen), from the Hebrew אָמֵן (amein).

Timotheos, goodbye

20O Timotheos, guard what has been entrusted to you. Turn away from profane babbling and antitheses of what is falsely named gnosis,[37] 21which some profess, having failed in their faith.

---

37. *Gnosis*, the word used in the Greek text and which also exists in English, means "knowledge." Jewish Gnosticism or other forms of Gnosticism held knowledge, *gnosis*, above faith. A recurring theme in 1 Timothy is the powerful rejection of Gnostic heresy, which even ends the book. Such preoccupation with Gnosticism is itself a strong marker of the probable late dating for 1 Timothy, since Gnosticism began to flourish in Syria and North Africa, and in cities of Italy and Greece, in the first and beginning of the second centuries, when the threat was more real and troubling than during Paul's lifetime. At the same time, Paul's education was deeply in Greek. Most of early Gnosticism has survived in Greek and Coptic (the language of the non-Greek native Egyptians), with only references in Aramaic. It is certain that just as Paul was deeply Platonized with respect to concepts of a transcendent soul and immortality, so too he was in all likelihood more familiar with Gnostic thoughts and their presence than were his apostolic opponents in Jerusalem. In Acts 8.9–24, Simon Magus (Simon the Magician), who is called the "father of heresy" and is a symbol of greed and "simony," which is the buying of ecclesiastical pardons and offices, was a Gnostic. There is much conflict between him and Saint Peter in later noncanonical scriptures, where the powers of Christianity are pitted against the false powers of the Gnostic magus.

The use of the word "gnosis" here to identify Gnosticism is one of the earliest instances of such usage of what will later become its general title. Gnosticism includes many sects over fifteen centuries, including Valentinian speculation, Sethianism, Manichaenism, Mandaeanism, and Catharism. See Willis Barnstone and Marvin Meyer, eds., *The Gnostic Bible* (Boston: Shambhala Books, 2004).

Timotheos beta
(2 Timothy)

Timotheos beta[1]
(2 Timothy)

WHILE, LIKE 1 TIMOTHY, 2 Timothy clearly is a late pseudonymous letter, it is not largely restricted to cataloguing harsh homilies about the wicked, orders for obedient women, and praise for the deacons and high bishops of the emerging church. The author of 2 Timothy, along with paraphrases of Pauline admonitions, gives us a more spiritual Paul, which in parts finds expression in true poetic passages. Then, like 1 Timothy, the letter attacks the Gnostic deceivers with huge sectarian wrath.

If the letter is by Paul, the "sacred scriptures" are from the Hebrew Bible, since during Paul's lifetime no accepted sacred scriptures existed other than those in the Torah. The gospels were written more than a decade after Paul's death and available for public reading an unknown number of years after their composition. Since 2 Timothy is presented as a letter by Paul to Timothy in which he urges his Timothy to stay with the sacred scriptures learned since childhood, the sacred scriptures cannot be from books of the New Testament. If Paul's exhortation is meant to include New Testament scriptures, it is an anachronism subverting Pauline authorship and establishing the letter as apocryphal from a later period. As such the epistle may be read allegorically like Revelation, which changes its time frame to avoid Roman retribution, disguising a harsh criticism of Rome by clamoring against Babylonian lords of six centuries earlier. This second letter to Timothy, along with six other remarkable letters of uncertain authorship, lives among the "disputed

---

1. The Second Letter of Paul to Timothy. Timothy from the Greek Τιμόθεος (Timotheos).

letters." The letter was probably composed by later Church fathers, at least a generation, and perhaps more, after Paul's death, writing from the perspective of their period, when church and church doctrines were relatively stable, when a clearer separation of Jew and Christian prevailed, and when the troubling and stronger enemy was the heretical Gnostic who perverted the faith of the believer.

Here, since the text itself appears in Paul's voice, out of respect for the extant document, one must keep to the intended time frame set in the text and convey that "sacred scriptures" are indeed Torah scriptures, that is, from the Hebrew Bible (Old Testament). Torah scriptures would have been read by Timothy, who was born of a Greek father and a Jewish mother, in their Septuagint Greek translation. As for finding in Jewish biblical scripture instruction for salvation through faith in Christ Jesus, the references in Paul are to diverse messianic passages in the Hebrew Bible, and especially to Isaiah and Psalms and their prophecies and descriptions of the coming of the messiah of the nations.

The clarification of "sacred scriptures" as Torah, rather than New Testament, eliminates the possibility of unintended, or intended, misreading of 2 Timothy. Should "sacred scriptures" conjure up writings from the New Testament, then, as said, it invalidates Paul's authorship and message.

Although the main features of 2 Timothy, including the absence of leading theological themes such as the union of the believer with Christ, militate against Pauline authorship, there are Pauline patches. Some have suggested that fragments of earlier letters may have survived and been inserted into the pseudepigraphal letter. On a personal level some of Paul's pleasures and angers concerning his companions of the word ring of experience, such as his stinging anger against Alexander the bronzemaker (4.14), which seems too passionate and minor to have been invented as mere goodbye decoration. While the cause of this annoyance is unspecified, his response is in keeping with his fury against his Jerusalem rival, the apostle Peter, and his conviction that in due time the doctrinal opponent will receive proper retribution. What is lacking in these special pastoral letters is Paul's great transcendent vision and spirit, which give his letters to the Romans and Corinthians their special voice in world religion and literature.

Chapter 1

Hello

Shaul[2] a messenger of the Mashiah Yeshua[3] by the will of God through the promise of life in the Mashiah Yeshua, 2to Timotheos,[4] my loved child, grace, mercy, peace from God the father and the Mashiah Yeshua our lord.

Remembering your tears

3I thank God whom I serve with a clean conscience, which is from my ancestors, when I remember you constantly in my prayers. 4Night and day, remembering your tears, I long to see you that I may be filled with happiness. 5I recall your genuine faith that lived first in your grandmother Lois,[5] and in your mother Evnik,[6] and also in you. 6Because of this I remind you to re-light the gift of God in you through the laying on of my hands. 7God did not give us the spirit of cowardice but of power and love and self-discipline.

Prisoner of the lord of light

8Do not be ashamed of the testimony of our lord or of me his prisoner, but share with me in suffering for the gospel, with strength from

---

2. Paul from the Greek Παῦλος (Paulos), from Saul in the Greek Σαῦλος (Saulos), from the Hebrew שָׁאוּל (Shaul). Paul was born in Tarsos as *Shaul*.

3.Christ Jesus. "Jesus" is from the Greek Ἰησοῦς (Iesous), from the Aramaic יֵשׁוּעַ (Yeshua), a later form of the Hebrew יְהוֹשֻׁעַ (Yehoshua). "Christ" is from the Greek Χριστός (Hristos), and Greek *Hristos* or *Christos* is a translation from the Greek Μεσσίας (Messias), from the Hebrew מָשִׁיחַ (mashiah). "Christ" in Greek also means "the anointed," and "Messiah" in both Greek and Hebrew contains the meaning of "the anointed."

4. Timothy.

5. Lois from the Greek Λωΐς (Lois).

6. Eunice from the Greek Εὐνίκη (Eunike).

the lord, 9who called us with a holy calling, not for our works but through our purpose and grace, grace given to us in Mashiah Yeshua, before eternal time began, 10which is now revealed by the appearance before us of savior Mashiah Yeshua, who abolished death and brought life and imperishability into light through the gospel. 11For this gospel I was a herald, messenger and teacher, 12for which I also suffer, but I am not ashamed. I know in whom I believed and placed my trust, and I'm persuaded that he can guard my trust until the day.[7] 13Follow the pattern of healthy words[8] that you heard in faith and love in Mashiah Yeshua. 14Guard the good entrusted in you through the holy spirit living in us.

Desertions and loyalties

15You know this, that all those in Asia[9] turned away from me, and among them Fygelos[10] and Ermogenes.[11] 16But may the lord grant mercy to the house of Onesiforos,[12] because many times he refreshed me, and he was not ashamed of my chains. 17When he got to Rome, he eagerly sought and found me. 18May the lord grant that he find mercy from the lord on that day! You know so well how many ways he helped me in Efesos.[13]

---

7. The day of judgment.

8. Sound teaching.

9. Roman province, which is in western Turkey today.

10. Phygelus from the Greek Φύγελος (Fygelos). Nothing is known of Phygelus and Hermogenes other than they were among those in the diaspora who deserted Paul.

11. Hermogenes from the Greek Ἑρμογένης (Hermogenes).

12. Onesiphorus from the Greek Ὀνησίφορος (Onesiforos), a loyal believer, who was probably from Ephesos.

13. Ephesos from the Greek Ἔφεσος (Efesos). A seaport in Asia Minor (present-day Turkey), famed as a prosperous Greco-Roman city and for its sanctuary for Artemis, Ephesos also served as an important base for Paul in his missions.

Chapter 2

Be strong, Timotheos

You my child be strong in the grace which is in the Mashiah Yeshua. 2What you have heard from me through many witnesses, pass on to faithful people who will be able to teach others. 3Take your share of suffering like a soldier of the Mashiah Yeshua. 4No one serving as a soldier gets involved in civilian life, if he is to please the officers. 5And if an athlete, he is not wreathed with victory unless he keeps to the rules. 6The working farmer should be the first to share the fruit of the harvest. 7Think about what I say, for the lord will give you understanding in all things.[14]

Maxims for a godly life

8Remember Yeshua Mashiah, of the seed of David, raised from the dead, which is my good news 9for which I suffer even to the point of being chained as a criminal. But the word of God is not in chains. 10And for this I endure all things for the elect[15] that they may obtain salvation in Mashiah Yeshua with eternal glory.

11Faithful is the word:

If we die with him, we will live with him.

12If we suffer with him, we will be kings with him.

If we deny him, he will deny us.

13If we are faithless, he will remain faithful.

He cannot deny himself.

14Remind people of this, and warn them before God not to squabble over words, which is of no use other than to destroy those who are listening.

15Strive to present yourself before God as one who is without shame, drawing a straight line of words for the truth.

16Avoid profane and empty chatter, since it will lead people into more

---

14. The apparent lesson concerning the soldier, athlete, and farmer is work hard and honorably and the fruit of your work is yours.

15. Or chosen ones.

ungodliness,[16] [17]and their word will spread like gangrene. Among them are Ymenaios[17] and Filetos,[18] [18]who stray from the truth and say that resurrection has already happened, and they are overthrowing the faith of some.[19] [19]But the foundation of God stands firm, with this seal upon it from Numbers:

> Yahweh knows those who are his.

and

> Let everyone who names the name of Yahweh
> abstain from wrongdoing.

Allegory of the house

> [20]In a great house there are not only vessels
> Of gold and silver but of wood and clay.[20]
> Some are of honor. Others of dishonor.[21]
> [21]If someone cleans himself of all these things
> I mention, he will be a special vessel
> Of honor, hallowed, useful to his master,
> And be prepared for every good work.
> [22]Scorn youthful passions and pursue the good
> And faith and love and peace, and call the lord
> From a clean heart. [23]Put aside ignorant
> And foolish speculations.[22] They breed fights.
> [24]And the lord's slave should not be quarreling

---

16. Or impiety.

17. Hymenaeus from the Greek Ὑμέναιος (Hymenaios).

18. Philetus from the Greek Φίλητος (Filetos).

19. More references to the wordy thoughts of the Gnostics. Hymenaeus and Philetus seem to have strayed into Gnosticism, claiming that resurrection has already taken place. This accords with the Gnostic notion that physical or bodily resurrection is merely allegorical. The real resurrection or salvation is spiritual and need not wait for a day of judgment or after-death salvation.

20. The allegory can be, in part, reduced to a distinction between good ministers and the false teachers.

21. Some to be prized, some to be despised.

22. Do not be tempted by the Gnostic speculation.

But gentle to everyone, a skillful teacher,
Patient, 25enlightening his opponents mildly
So perhaps God may grant them to repent
And come to know the truth, 26come to their senses,
Free of the devil's trap, though they were held
Captured by him, ready to do his will.

Chapter 3

False teachers

Know this, that in the last days harsh times will come. 2Men will be lovers of themselves, lovers of money, pretentious, blasphemous, disobedient to their parents, ungrateful, impious, 3unloving and implacable troublemakers, slanderers, out of control, savage, not lovers of God, 4treacherous, reckless brutes, swollen with conceit, lovers of pleasure rather than God, 5holding to the form of piety but denying its power.

6Among them are those who creep into homes and captivate women filled with sin and swayed by sundry desires. 7They are always learning but never can recognize the truth.

8In this way Iannes[23] and Iambres[24] opposed Moshe,[25] so these men will also stand up against the truth, their minds corrupted and failures with respect to faith. 9But they will not progress further. Their madness is, as was the madness of the two Egyptians, plain for everyone to see.

Timotheos, hear my teaching

10Now you who have followed my teaching, my way of life, my faith, my patience, my love, 11my persecutions, my sufferings, what happened

---

23. Jannes from the Greek Ἰάννης (Iannes).

24. Jambres from the Greek Ἰαμβρῆς (Iambres). Jannes and Jambres do not appear in the Hebrew Bible, but in Jewish tradition. These sorcerers with mellifluously like names were opponents of Moses. They do appear in the Dead Sea Scrolls, Damascus Document, 5.18–19.

25. Moses from the Greek Μωϋσῆς (Moses), from the Hebrew מֹשֶׁה (moshe).

to me in Antioheia,[26] in Ikonion,[27] and Lystra. What persecutions I have borne! But the lord rescued me from all of them.

12And everyone who wishes to live a godly life in the Mashiah Yeshua will be persecuted. 13But cunning men and mind swindlers[28] will advance, for the worst, deceiving and being self-deceived. 14But for you, stay with what you have learned and came to believe, knowing from whom you learned it, 15and that from childhood you knew the sacred scriptures of Torah that can make you wise in salvation through faith in the Mashiah Yeshua. 16All scripture is God-inspired and useful for teaching, for argument, for correction, for education in the good 17so that the man of God may be proficient and prepared for every good work.

---

26. Antioch from the Greek Ἀντιόχεια (Antioheia), the capital of the Seleucid Empire, on the Orontes River in Syria. Many Jews lived there, which meant that Paul could find abundant converts to Messianism. Acts comes many years after Paul's life, contemporary with the gospels, containing fable, miracles, and stunning adventure. As a source for Paul, it lacks the reliability of Paul's authentic letters. There is in Acts an intended mixture of person between the "Judaizing" apostles of Jerusalem, the traditional Jews, and despised Gnostics. In his authentic letters there is no rage against traditional Jews, but rather against the James-Peter-John faction in Jerusalem, who, for its part, is equally opposed to Paul. There are also fierce denunciations, especially in the disputed letters, of the Gnostics. Given these facts during Paul's lifetime, it is not possible to ascertain or even guess the sectarian identity of Paul's real opponents in Acts as, for example, in Acts 13–14, where Paul is harmed. Whatever the shortcomings of Acts as history, it should also be remembered that these missionary adventure stories rescued Paul from possible oblivion, since in a severe conflict for dominion, Acts chose Paul rather than the Jerusalem Christian Jews as the mainstream hero of later Christianity, whose thought and revolution would survive in the letters as New Testament scripture.

27. Iconium from the Greek Ἰκόνιον (Ikonion).

28. Or cheats, sorcerers. The colorful Greek γόης (goes) has a classical meaning of swindler. In New Testament usage, the meaning shifts "swindling" or "deception" in religious concepts. The King James Version sexualizes its version, making it neither financial nor theological, rendering "seducers." Lattimore, whose renderings are both classical and fresh, and frequently entail a return to insights found in the KJV, gives "wizard."

Chapter 4

Timotheos's charge

I charge you before God and Mashiah Yeshua, who will judge the living and the dead: 2preach the word, be persistent, be ready in season and out, convince, rebuke, encourage with complete patience and instruction. 3There will come a time when people will no longer accept healthy instruction but, with itching ears, will find masses of teachers to speak to their personal desires. 4They will turn their ear away from truth and wander into myths. 5But as for you, be in sober control, suffer hardship, work to evangelize, and fulfill your ministry.

6I am already being poured out as an offering and the time of departure has come. 7I have caught the good fight, I have finished the race, I have kept faith. 8For the rest, waiting for me is a wreath of righteousness, which the lord, the good judge, has reserved to give me on that day. And it is not only to be given me but to all who have loved his appearing.

Come soon

9Try to come to me soon. 10Demas[29] deserted me, loving the present age, and has gone to Thessaloniki. Kreskes[30] went to Galatia, Titos[31] to Dalmatia.[32] 11Loukas[33] alone is with me. Find Markos[34] and bring him with you, for he is useful in the ministry. 12I sent Tyhikos[35] to Efesos.[36]

---

29. Demas is short for Demetrios, a companion of Paul.

30. Crescens from the Latin *Crescens*, from the Greek Κρήσκης (Kreskes), a companion of Paul who may be Κρίσπος (Krispus), a leader of the synagogue in Corinth, whom Paul baptized.

31. Titus.

32. Dalmatia from the Greek Δαλματία (Dalmatia), in Illyricum in Latin, which remains today Dalmatia.

33. Luke from the Greek Λουκᾶς (Lukas).

34. Mark from the Greek Μᾶρκος (Markos).

35. Tychicus from the Greek Τυχικός (Tyhikos), a companion of Paul who went with him to Jerusalem.

36. Ephesos.

13When you come, bring the cloak I left behind with Karpos[37] in Troas,[38] and when you come bring the scrolls,[39] and especially the parchments.

Some deserted but God stood with me

14Alexandros[40] the bronzesmith did terrible things to me and the lord will repay him according to his acts. 15You also should be aware, for he strongly opposed our message.

16At my first defense, no one came to stand with me. Everyone abandoned me. May it not be counted against them. 17The lord stood with me and gave me strength that through me the message might be fully made and all gentiles might hear it, and I was rescued from the lion's mouth.[41] 18The lord will rescue me from every bad act and bring me safely into the kingdom of the skies. To him glory into aeons and aeons. Amain.[42]

Greetings and Goodbye

19Greet Priska[43] and Akylas[44] and the household of Onesiforos.

---

37. Carpus from the Greek Κάρπος (Karpos).

38. Troy from the Greek Τρῳάς (Troas).

39. Books.

40. Alexander from the Greek Ἀλέξανδρος (Alexandros), a Jew from Ephesos with whom Paul had a falling out.

41. Here the plea for gentiles to hear is convincing. In fact, it is one of the most moving utterances in the New Testament, ending with "and I was rescued from the lion's mouth." Yet something is missing. While Paul distinguished himself from the Jerusalem faction by facilitating entry of the gentiles into messianic Judaism, he certainly wished to address with equal ardor the Jews in the synagogues where he preached to bring the message to them. The first generation of messianics was all Jews, and Paul was one of that generation. Hence the absence of asking "all Jews" to also hear the message suggests a plea and prayer made by an eloquent missionary in a later generation, after the Jewish War diaspora of 70 C.E., after changes and events that occurred after Paul's death.

42. Amen from the Greek ἀμήν (amen), from the Hebrew אָמֵן (amein).

43. Priscilla (dim.) or Prisca from the Greek Πρίσκα (Priska). See note 298 on Acts 18.2.

44. Aquila from the Greek Ἀκύλας (Akylas). See note 296 on Acts 18.2.

20Irastos[45] stayed on in Korinthos.[46] I left Trofimos[47] in Miletos.[48] 21Hurry, before winter comes. Greetings to you Eyvoulos[49] and Poedes[50] and Linos and Klaudia[51] and all the brothers. 22The lord be with your spirit.

---

45. Erastus from the Greek Ἔραστος (Erastos), a city treasurer in Corinth and Paul's companion.

46. Corinth.

47. Trophimus from the Greek Τρόφιμος (Trofimos), a companion on Paul's last trip to Jerusalem whose home was in Ephesos.

48. Miletus from the Greek Μίλητος (Miletos), a seaport on the west coast of Asia Minor, with a large Jewish population, and an earlier center of pre-Socratic philosophy.

49. Eubulus from the Greek Εὔβουλος (Euboulos).

50. Pudens, a Latin name, found in Greek as Πούδης (Poudes).

51. Claudia from the Greek Κλαυδία (Klaudia).

Titos
(Titus)

Titos[1]
(Titus)

THE PERVASIVE CONCERN in the Pastoral Letters with the structure of families and the conduct of church officials has been taken as a signal of their post-apostolic authorship. The letters are fascinating with respect to these questions of family and clerical behavior. They are nominally addressed to a missionary friend but are actually constructed as general teachings on righteous comportment to be read aloud in the churches. Since they do not paint the passions and spirit infusing the person of Paul as revealed in the authentic letters, they contrast with the brief letter to Philemon, which follows them in the standard ordering of the books of the New Testament. There, Paul in prison, using all his powers of persuasion, flattery, love, and orders to obey, hopes to get the slave owner Philemon to return to him Onesimus, a slave whom Paul had earlier converted in his cell, and whom he now wants fervently to have again at his side as his missionary helper and companion. The letter to Titus is generally perceived as an embarrassment and the least worthy short book to have somehow slipped into the unparalleled achievement of the New Testament.

1. Titus from the Greek Τίτος (Titos). Titus accompanied Paul to Jerusalem, and despite the pressure of the "Judaizers," that is, James, Peter, and John, to have him circumcised, as were all gentiles whom the Jerusalem apostles permitted to enter the Jesus movement, Paul resisted their demands.

Chapter 1

Hello

Shaul[2] a slave of God and a messenger of Yeshua the Mashiah[3] in the faith of those of God's elect and the recognition of the truth which comes with godliness 2and in the hope of eternal life that God, who is not a liar, promised aeons of time ago, 3but in his own time revealed in the annunciation with which I was entrusted by command of God our savior. 4To Titos, my true child,[4] through faith we share, grace and peace from God our father and the Mashiah Yeshua our savior.

Leaving you Titos in Crete with the bishops

5For this reason I left you in Crete[5] so that you could straighten out and appoint an elder in every city that lacks elders,[6] as I have instructed you to do. 6Such a person must be blameless, a man who has had one wife, with children who are believers, and not charged with debauchery or disobedience. 7The bishop,[7] as God's housemaster, must be blameless, not arrogant, not quick-tempered, not a wine drunk, not a brawler, nor fond of dishonest gain, 8but hospitable a lover of the good wise just holy self-controlled,[8] 9with a firm grip on the word, according to doctrine, so

---

2. Paul from the Greek Παῦλος (Paulos), from Saul in the Greek Σαῦλος (Saulos), from the Hebrew שָׁאוּל (Shaul). Paul was born in Tarsos as *Shaul*.

3. Christ Jesus. "Jesus" is from the Greek Ἰησοῦς (Iesous), from the Aramaic ישׁוּע (Yeshua), a later form of the Hebrew יְהוֹשֻׁעַ (Yehoshua). "Christ" is from the Greek Χριστος (Hristos), and Greek *Hristos* or *Christos* is a translation from the Greek Μεσσίας (Messias), from the Hebrew מָשִׁיח (mashiah). "Christ" in Greek also means "the anointed," and "Messiah" in both Greek and Hebrew contains the meaning of "the anointed."

4. By "true," Paul seems to mean one whom he has personally converted.

5. A confirmation that Paul and Titos were in Crete together.

6. Presbyters. The reference, as we will see in a few verses, is to bishops, who may come from the council of the elders.

7. Originally an overseer and, during Paul's time, not a richly robed figure of great ecclesiastical circumstance.

8. The unpunctuated flow of the Greek is repeated here.

that he can have the power to encourage by his healthy teaching and to expose those who contradict it.

False teachers

10There are many who are disobedient, vain talkers and deceivers, especially those of the circumcision.9 11One must stop up their mouths,10 those who subvert whole family households, who teach for sordid gain what is not right to teach. 12One of their own prophets said:

Cretans are always liars, horrible beasts, lazy gluttons.11

13That testimony is true. For this reason, reprove them severely so they may grow healthy in faith, 14not paying attention to Jewish myths and commandments of men turning away from the truth.12 15To the pure all things are pure; but to the corrupt and unbelieving nothing is pure. Their mind and conscience are defiled. 16They claim to know God, but in their actions they deny him, since these are abominable and disobedient, and unfit for any good work.

---

9. Those of the circumcision does not refer to orthodox or traditional Jews but to the Christian Jews of Jerusalem, the apostolic leaders James, Peter, and John who hold to the Jewish ritual of circumcision as an obligation for gentiles wishing to join the Jesus movement.

10. Reads rude and direct in the Greek.

11. The statement is attributed to the Cretan poet Epimenides (ca. 600 B.C.E.). Later the Sophists picked up the idea that all Cretans were liars and, with Aristotelean logic, came up with impossible syllogisms such as "All Cretans are liars. I am a Cretan. I am a liar." Can the Cretan be telling the truth when he claims to be a liar? These traditional slurs against Cretans (whose Minoan civilization preceded by a millennium that of the mainland) were still current in Paul's time. Later "Cretan," or "Cretin," with a somewhat dubious etymology but certain intention, was a Greco-Roman insult of the competing Christians, meaning an idiot or fool.

12. "Jewish myths" may refer to genealogies to prove descent. However, here as elsewhere, the Jerusalem apostles are given code names of "Judaizers" and "Jews," both of which do not reflect Paul of the authentic letters, who was furious with his apostolic opponents in Jerusalem but not with the Jews. By the times of Acts, however, where a distinctive Paul of miraculous powers is presented, the confusion between Judaizer and Jew is cruelly pervasive.

Chapter 2

Rules of behavior for teachers

You must speak what is correct in healthy[13] teaching.

Old men

2Old men need to be sober, dignified, discreet, healthy in faith, in love, and in patience.[14]

Old women

3Old women in their behavior similarly must be reverent, not slanderers, not slaves to excessive wine drinking, and teachers of the good.

Young women

4Old women should encourage young women to be husband lovers, children lovers, 5discreet pure[15] home workers good,[16] and submissive to their own husbands so that the word of God is not blasphemed.

Young men

6You must similarly exhort younger men to behave. 7Above all you must show yourselves as models of good works, and in your teaching show incorruption, gravity, 8unblemished healthy speech so that those who oppose you find no shame in what you say, there being in it nothing bad about us.

---

13. The normal and universal translation is "sound." However, the primary Greek is a sharply defining metaphor, meaning "healthy" or "good health," from ὑγιαίνω (hygiaino), a verb signifying being in good health or healthy, from which English "hygiene" is derived. "Healthy" suggests both physical and moral health and carries a moral bite. "Sound" is close, yet it primarily means "balanced," "levelheaded," "proper," or "valid," all less persuasive interpretations of *hygiaino*.

14. Or, "in endurance."

15. The word is "pure" and implies "chaste" or "faithful" in a sexual sense.

16. The unpunctuated flow of the Greek is repeated here.

Slaves

9Slaves must be obedient to their masters and please them in every way, not talk back, 10not pilfer, but demonstrate complete good faith so that the teaching of our savior God may be an ornament in all things.[17]

Salvation to everyone

11The grace of God has appeared, bringing salvation to everyone, 12instructing us to renounce ungodliness[18] and worldly desires, and in the present age to live sensibly and justly and godly, 13looking forward to blessed hope and the appearing of the glory of our great God, and of our savior Yeshua the Mashiah, 14who gave himself for us, to redeem us from all lawlessness and purify for himself a people of his own, making them zealous for good works.

15Speak these things and encourage and rebuke with every command. Let no man despise you.

Chapter 3

Do what is good

Remind them to be submissive and obedient to rulers and authorities,[19] ready for every good work, 2to blaspheme[20] no one, not to be a brawler, to be gentle, displaying all modest courtesy to everyone. 3Once we too were foolish, disobedient, led astray, slaves to desires and sundry pleasures, with malice and envy, spending our lives in hatred, hating each other. 4But when kindness and people loving of our savior God were revealed, 5not because of good works we had done but through his mercy he saved us: through the washing of regeneration and the renewing by the holy spirit. 6This spirit he poured abundantly on us

---

17. In his articulation of church prescriptions on obedient slavery, the author, clearly not Paul, is extreme in declaring slavery an ornament of God.

18. Or impiety.

19. The authorities are earthly, whether of synagogue (assuming Paul), of church (assuming a later author), or of Rome.

20. Or slander.

through Yeshua the Mashiah, our savior, 7so that justified by grace we might become heirs with hope of life eternal.

8This word is to be believed.

And I want you to insist on these principles so that those who believe in God may be involved with good works. These are good and profitable for people.

9But avoid stupid controversies and genealogies and quarrels and fights over Torah law, for they are unprofitable and futile. 10Banish a heretic after he ignores one and the second warning. 11You know that such a man is perverted and sinful and has condemned himself.

Last words

12When I send Artemas[21] to you or Tyhikos,[22] come here quickly to me in Nikopolis,[23] for I have decided to spend the winter there. 13Send Zenas the lawyer and Apollos[24] on their way, and see that they lack nothing. 14Let our people learn to devote themselves to good works in order to take care of urgent needs. They must not be unfruitful.

Greetings

15All who are with me send greetings to you. And greet those who love us in the faith.

Grace be with you all.

---

21. Artemas from the Greek Ἀρτεμᾶς (Artemas), a friend of Paul.

22. Tychicus from the Greek Τυχικός (Tyhikos), a friend from the province of Asia who went with Paul to Jerusalem, whom he sent to Ephesos and whom he plans to send to Crete.

23. Nicopolis from the Greek Νικόπολις (Nikopolis). Of three cities with this name, it is thought that one in northern Epirus is likely the city Paul means.

24. Apollos from the Greek Ἀπολλῶς (Apollos), a companion of Paul who worked in Corinth and Ephesos. He was probably a Christian Jew born in Alexandria, though some scholars identify him as a gentile convert. Martin Luther first suggested Apollos as the author of the letter to the Jews, but there is no solid evidence to identify anyone as the author of that exhortation.

General Letters

Yaakov
(James)

Yaakov[1]
(James)

THE CANONICITY OF THE LETTER of James came gradually, and
not without dispute: by the church in Alexandria in the third century of
the Common Era, by churches in the West in the fourth century, and by
the Syrian church in the fifth. Jerome has James as the son of Alphaeus
(Mark 3.18). The usual attribution has been to "James, brother of the
Lord," Yeshua's younger brother, also identified as the head of Christian
Jews in Jerusalem. Today the work is thought to be anonymous, of late-
first- or early-second-century composition. Paul was in deep conflict with
James and Peter over circumcision, kosher dietary laws, and the Sabbath,
yet these subjects do not figure in this letter of James. But in other matters, James gives importance to strict Jewish law. In contrast to Paul's
letters, where the crucifixion and resurrection are central, there is curiously no reference to cross, resurrection, or salvation in this missive. All
parabolic exempla of moral comportment are to the Hebrew scriptures.
Here the word is spoken to God. And the lord, as in the Hebrew Bible,
is *Adonai*, meaning "lord." It returns to the familiar usage in Hebrew
scriptures of "lord": the Lord is God. Jesus is mentioned twice and based
on both placements—the first verse of the first two chapters—they may
be insertions. In other books the salutations are the least credible verses
with respect to attribution, as in the anonymous Luke and Acts, where in
the opening paragraphs, in lengthy, formal Greek, not found elsewhere
in the gospel or in Acts, Luke is declared to be the author.

1. James or Jacob from the Greek Ἰάκωβος (Iakobos), from the Hebrew יַעֲקֹב (yaakov). Yaakov, meaning "Jacob."

Among the surviving documents of this intertestamental period of religions in ferment, there is no clear demarcation between inspired Jewish and Christian pseudepigrapha and the scriptures later determined to be canonical. The first letter of James and the letter of Jude fall into this indeterminate category. As Christianity, growing out of the earth of Judaism, developed, many Gnostic and pseudepigraphal texts began as Jewish wisdom texts and in their preservation were lightly Gnosticized or Christianized to fit the frame of normative sects. Justin's Book of Baruch, the earliest surviving Gnostic text, is, as found in Hippolytus's *Refutation of All Heresies*, a transitional Jewish document. The door is open to the letter of James, which may be seen as a document of the period composed by a Christian Jew or a highly Hellenized Jew whose message is wisdom and goodness. The letter, in sophisticated high Greek, which would not have been known by a Galilean rabbi and younger son of Mary, coincides with Jewish and Christian wisdom literature and other pseudepigrapha of the time.

James is an insight into faith and works (or acts), and the necessity of the latter to justify the former, and into the purpose of works, which is alleviation of the suffering of the poor. It finds its argument from a wealth of biblical parables, from faithful Abraham, whose deeds justified him, to Rahab the good prostitute, who endangered her life for Jericho. There is throughout a dextrous harmony of wisdom proverbs intricate in the verse.

James is a letter in external forms, but it is not correspondence. Rather, it is a sermon essay speaking in high poetic discourse to the poor. During a period when Christian (Messianic) Judaism was increasingly attempting to distance itself from its Jewish foundation, like most new Jewish sects during a period of tremendous ferment, except for the slight Christianizing salutations at the beginning of chapters 1 and 2, typical scribal forgeries performed in piety, this marvel of wisdom, philosophy, theology, and poetry should be taken as a superior example of Jewish pseudepigrapha composed during the intertestamental period.

This intertestamental period of the emerging Christian movement had no testament of its own other than the Hebrew Bible, which it interpreted as a prophetic book in which the messiah was realized in Jesus Christ. The New Testament was scarcely an idea, with confusion, contention, and cries of heresy as each side vied for supremacy. Figures like

Marcion of Sinope (ca. 85–160) were among the early, if not the earliest, to propose a new covenant; Marcion was also the first famous heretic in the early church. As the first Christians went to the Jewish Bible as the mainstay of their religious documents, they took from the multitude of contemporary pseudepigrapha (Jewish works written between 200 B.C.E. and 200 C.E.) some key works, such as the sermons of James and John, that were lightly Christianized to make them acceptable in an emerging canon.

James's sophisticated letter also provides translucent scriptural evidence, however, that the closeness between traditional Judaism and Messianic Judaism persisted for decades after the death of Paul, who insisted that he was a Jew and a Pharisee from the tribe of Benjamin. We see the closeness to the entirety of Judaism in Jews (Hebrews), an extraordinary apocalyptic sermon from an unknown, sophisticated intellectual from Philo's Alexandria. The stunning letters of James and John are major philosophical and literary documents, a fact usually overlooked because of the higher profile given to the gospels, Acts, Paul's Romans and Corinthians, and mysterious Revelation. It is good that the general letters begin with James's literary gem, whose emotive wisdom poetry finds expression in primal nature metaphor.

Chapter 1

Sun rises with burning heat and the flower of grass shrivels
    Yaakov[2] slave of God and of the lord
    Yeshua the Mashiah,[3] to the twelves tribes
    In their diaspora,[4] I send you greetings.

    2My brothers, think of it as happiness
    Whenever you face falling into trials,
    3And know that testing of your faith creates
    Endurance. 4Let endurance be perfected.
    Complete it through your work, and you will lack
    In nothing. 5But if anyone is short
    In wisdom, let him ask for it from God,
    Who gives to all and generously without
    Reproach, and it will be accorded him.
    6But ask in faith and never doubt. The one
    Who doubts is like a sea wave tossed about
    By blowing winds. 7And let the doubter know
    8That one who vacillates is no way sound,
    And wavering gets nothing from the lord.

    9Let the lowdown boast of being raised up
    10And let the rich man fall in lowliness

---

2. James or Jacob.

3. Christ Jesus. "Jesus" is from the Greek Ἰησοῦς (Iesous), from the Aramaic יֵשׁוּעַ (Yeshua), a later form of the Hebrew יְהוֹשֻׁעַ (Yehoshua). "Christ" is from the Greek Χριστος (Hristos), and Greek *Hristos* or *Christos* is a translation from the Greek Μεσσίας (Messias), from the Hebrew מָשִׁיחַ (mashiah). "Christ" in Greek also means "the anointed," and "Messiah" in both Greek and Hebrew contains the meaning of "the anointed."

4. The letter is formally dedicated to the twelve tribes of his coreligionist Jews of Israel, in their diaspora outside Jerusalem and Israel.

And pass away like a flower of the field.
11The sun rises with burning heat and shrivels[5]
The grass. Its flower falls and the beauty
Of its appearance perishes. The rich
Amid their busywork will also fade.

The wreath of life

12Blessed is any man who endures trials.
He is approved and will receive the wreath[6]
Of life he promised to the ones who love him.

Sin when fully grown is death

13Let no man who is tempted say, "I'm tempted
By God." God can't be tempted by the bad,
And he himself tempts none. 14By one's desire
Each one is tempted, lured away, seduced.
15Then the desire that one feels gives birth
To sin, and sin when fully grown is death.

16Do not be taken in, brothers, my loves.
17Every generous act and perfect gift
Is from above and descends from the father
Of lights, with whom there is no variation
Or turning shadow. 18Issuing the word
Of truth, he gave us birth for us to be,
And we became the first fruit of his creatures.
19Know this, brothers, my loves. Let everyone
Be quick to hear and slow to speak, and slow

---

5. Or dries. For "the sun rises" there are precedents in Catullus and followers in John Donne and Ernest Hemingway. Hemingway's *The Sun Also Rises* is taken from Ecclesiastes 1.5. As for the flower of the field burning in a day, there is Matthew's lily (6.26–30); for the perishing beauty there are a thousand poets of the Renaissance.
6. "Wreath" rather than "crown" is the primary meaning of Greek στέφανος (stefanos), the classical award given to excellence. Here its modesty is appropriate.

To anger. 20Anger doesn't gain the good
Of God. 21So put away all filthiness
And remnants of the base and sordid. Welcome
With meekness the implanted word, and so
The power will prevail to save your souls.

22Become the doer of the word, not a
  Mere listener who lets himself be fooled.
23A hearer of the word who cannot do
  Is a man looking in the mirror at
  His natural face, 24who suddenly goes off,
  Forgetting what he's like. 25But he who looks
  Into the perfect law, inside the Torah7
  Of freedom, and holds on, he's not the hearer
  Who has forgotten but a doer of work,
  And in his doing he will then be blessed.
26If someone thinks himself religious, yet
  Can't keep his tongue flat in his mouth, he tricks
  His heart and his religion is worth nothing.
27Religion that is undefiled and clean
  Before our God the father comes to this:
  Visit the orphans and the widows when
  They are distressed. Be unstained by the world.

---

7. Law, the books of law comprising the Pentateuch, or Bible.

Chapter 2

In shabby clothes in the synagogue
>   My brothers, do your favoritizing acts
>   Go with your faith in Yeshua Mashiah,
>   Who is our glorious lord? 2If a man comes
>   Into your synagogue[8] with rings of gold
>   Around his fingers and in splendid robes,
>   And then a poor man comes in filthy rags,
>   3You look at him in all his splendid robes
>   And say, "Sit here in a good place," and to
>   The shabby man you say, "Stand there, or sit
>   Under my footstool." 4Do you make distinctions
>   Among yourselves and judge your crafty thoughts?

Torah of love and mercy
>   5Listen, brothers, my loves, has God not chosen
>   The poor ones of the world to be the rich
>   In faith and make them heirs to the kingdom
>   Which he has promised to the souls who love him?
>   6But you dishonored the poor man. Are you
>   Not by the rich oppressed? And don't they drag

---

8. The text gives "synagogue" from the Greek συναγωγή (synagoge), meaning a synagogue or gathering place. The word "synagogue" is not a Hebrew but a Greek word like "pedagogue" a leader or gatherer of children. Whether James is speaking to Christian Jews or Jews is not clear. If the prefatory verse 2.1, which speaks to Jesus the Messiah, is original text, then he is speaking to Christian Jews. If the letter is an earlier text that has been very slightly Christianized by the addition of the two references to Jesus, then James was originally speaking wisdom literature to first-century or early-second-century unconverted Jews. Amid the plethora of pseudepigrapha from this period, there is no way of establishing firm probability. However, the text is as we have it, and it is well to accept it as it is, in transition, as was Christianity itself, from the Hebrew Bible to a Hebrew and Greek Bible of scriptures, which for countless reasons remain eternally commingled.

You into law courts? 7And don't they insult
The noble name which has been given you?
8If you perform the regal9 law, but keep
To Torah, you will love your neighbor as
Yourself,10 and you do well. 9But if you show
Partiality, you sin, and be convicted
By law as a transgressor. 10Anyone
Who keeps the law but stumbles before one
Of them is guilty of stumbling in all.11
11Now one of the Ten Commandments tells us:
    You shall not murder.
And:
    You shall not commit adultery.
If you have not engaged in adultery
But you have murdered, then you too transgress
Our Torah law.12 12So speak and act as if
You will be judged by Torah law of freedom.
13Judgment is merciless to one who shows
No mercy. Mercy triumphs over judgment.13

Faith and works

14What good is it, my brothers, if you say
That you have faith but have no works?14

---

9. Roman.

10. Lev. 19.18.

11. There follows some of the Ten Commandments, Exod. 20.13–14; Deut. 5.17–18.

12. As opposed to Roman law, which also forbade murder.

13. No line of biblical scripture is more compassionate, humane, and central to the human condition than James's line 2.13: κατακαυχᾶται ἔλεος κρίσεως, "Mercy triumphs over judgment." In this unusual instant, the King James Version, "mercy rejoiceth against judgments," fails in a literal and connotative sense to convey the power and lawless marvel of James's phrase. The verb does not mock joy against judgment and criticism, but rather "powers down" common judgment with understanding and sympathy.

14. In the much-discussed difference between Paul and James with respect to

Can faith save you? 15If a brother or sister
Is naked, short of daily food, 16and one
Of you says, "Go in peace. Keep warm and eat,"
But you give nothing for the body's needs,
What good is it? 17So even faith, if by
Itself and not backed up by works, is dead.
18Someone will say, "You have the faith, and I
   Have works." Show me your faith apart from works
   And I will show you from my works my faith.
19You do believe that God is one,15 and you
   Do well. As it reads in Deuteronomy:
      Even demons believe and shudder.16
20O hollow man, are you prepared to know
   That faith alone, without the works, is barren?

---

faith, while there is much coincidence, Paul always deems faith primary. When works require gentile converts to obey the Jewish rites of circumcision, dietary practice, and Sabbath, Paul is not for works, or at least, such works. The author of James, as the James whom Paul met in Jerusalem, countered what they angrily termed "false slogans," which was Paul's willingness to free gentiles from holding to Jewish law, to Torah. James the author of the exquisite "letter," or more correctly "treatise," is not the Jerusalem apostle, and does not enter into the dispute between factions over what laws of Judaism to hold or reject (there is no evidence that the author had a clue of any of that) but rather emphasize the necessity for works to be fully concordant with faith. Specifically, works must be principally devoted to a compassionate and pragmatic concern for the poor, the widowed, the orphan, and the outsider who is suffering. James's faith, he writes with ardor, is with societal good deeds. He states it all in "Show me your faith apart from works / and I will show you from my works my faith" (2.18). Here he repeats commands of the prophets and others to favor, through tithing and deeds, the poor and those in great need. In this he is like the Quakers, who return to the Hebrew Bible, to perform deeds on this earth as their religion. As for an enforcing hierarchy, there is none at all. Playing on Hamlet's last words, one can say, "The meeting house is silence." So too James is silent.

15. The statement echoes the fundamental Jewish Shema, "God is one."

16. Deut. 6.4. Demons know about God but are not saved.

21Avraham,[17] father of us all, was he
  Not justified when, as in Genesis:
    He offered his son Yitzhak[18] on the altar?
22You see that faith was working with his works
  And from his works his faith was made complete.
23And so the scripture was fulfilled that said:
    And Avraham believed God and he was counted
    Among the good.[19]
  And he was called a friend of God. 24You see,
  A man is justified by works and not
  By faith alone. 25Likewise Rahav[20] the whore
  When she took in the messengers and sent
  Them on an undetected road she too,
  Was she not justified? 26Just as the body
  Without spirit is dead, so also faith,
  If not accompanied by works, is dead.

---

17. Abraham from Greek Ἀβραάμ (Abraam), from the Hebrew אַבְרָהָם (avraham).

18. Isaac from the Greek Ἰσαάκ (Isaak), from the Hebrew יִצְחָק (yitzhak).

19. Gen. 22.1–14.

20. Rahab from the Greek Ῥαάβ (Raab), from the Hebrew רָחָב (rahav). Josh. 2.1 and 6.17. The spies are Jews sent as scouts "to view the land" for Joshua's later siege of the city, and Rahab protects them, unwilling to reveal them to the local king.

  In Hebrew the men Rahab hides are called spies, while here they are called messengers, for which the word "angels" is used, who are normally celestial messengers, as opposed to "apostles" who are earthly messengers.

Chapter 3

The tongue is a fire
    Brothers, not many of you become teachers,
    Knowing you will come under greater judgment.
    2All of us stumble.[21] And if anyone
    Does not stumble in speech, that man is perfect
    And able to control all of his body.
    3Since we put bits into the mouths of horses
    To make them obey us, so we guide
    Their whole body. 4Look also at the ships,

---

21. Or fall. The word "fall" or "stumble," from the Greek πταίω (ptaio) is often used as a word for moral error, and usually translated as "sin," depriving the original Greek metaphor from working in English. Here KJV and Tyndale avoid "sin," but abstract the beautiful demotic Greek into the implausible "offend." Standard translations of the verse also kill the metaphor by *interpretation*, the capital sin of translation, giving "make a mistake," a weak generalization. The crime is compounded in the next verse where "to stumble in speech," a metaphor for controlling the body, becomes unintelligible. The need for physical metaphors becomes clear in the next verses, which compare body parts to horses, ships, and fire. James's splendor of language offers a triple paratactic trope (three side-by-side comparisons to make the argument). Whether the well-educated author knew it or not, the most famous classical use of this rhetorical device in his day was in Sappho's poem fragment 16 of the seventh century B.C.E. beginning:

> ο]ἰ μὲν ἰππήων στρότον οἰ δὲ πέσδων
> οἰ δὲ νάων φαῖσ᾽ ἐπ[ὶ] γᾶν μέλαι[ν]αν
> ἔ]μμεναι κάλλιστον, ἔγω δὲ κῆν᾽ ὄτ-
>   τω τις ἔραται·

> Some say cavalry and others claim
> Infantry or a fleet of long oars
> Is the supreme sight on the black earth.
>   I say it is the one you love.

The Complete Poems of Sappho, trans. Willis Barnstone (Boston: Shambhala Books, 2009), 46.

Great as they are and driven by fierce winds,
They are guided by a tiny rudder
And shift to where the governor impels
His craft. 5So too the tongue is a small part
And yet it boasts, clamoring about great feats.

Look how a small fire burns down a forest.
6The tongue is fire. Among the members of
Our body, the tongue is a world of wrong
Staining the entire body, setting ablaze
The wheel of the creation, itself
Delivered into fire by Gei Hinnom.[22]
7Every species of beasts and birds, reptiles
And sea creatures is tamed and has been tamed
By human beings. 8But the tongue no one
Can tame. It is an uncontrollable evil
Full of deadly poison. 9We bless the lord
Our father, and with the same tongue we curse
The people made in the image of our God.
10Out of the same mouth comes blessing and curse.
My brothers, these things should not be like this.
11Surely from the same opening, a spring
Does not pour out the sweet and bitter waters?

---

22. Gehenna, for "hell," from the Greek γέεννα (Gehenna), from Hebrew גֵּיא הִנֹּם (gei hinnom), meaning "Valley of Hinnom." *Gehenna* superseded the older term, *Sheol*, for the underworld. Gei Hinnom is a special pit of darkness of the Hebrew Bible. *Gei Hinnom* and *Sheol* are normally translated into English as "hell." In other New Testament books, the author goes back to Greek mythology and puts in Greek ἅδης (Hades) for English "hell" or "underworld." James goes back to biblical hell, the Valley of Gehenna, in the Hebrew Bible, originally a garbage pit just south of Jerusalem where the dead were placed, but which later took on in Isaiah (30.33) and in Jewish apocalypticism (Esdras 7.36) an eschatological notion of eternal punishment. The English "hell" is an Old English and Germanic word going back to the Old Norse mythological realm of the dead, presided over by the giant goddess Hel.

12Surely, my brothers, a fig tree won't yield
  Olives, nor can a grapevine create figs?
  No more than can salt water give us fresh.

13Who among you is wise and understanding?
  Let him show it by good conduct and works
  He does with gentleness that comes of wisdom.
14But if a bitter envy takes hold of you
  And you have thick ambition in your heart,
  Do not boast, do not lie against the truth.
15Such wisdom doesn't descend from above
  But is of earth and natural and demonic.
16Where there is jealousy and selfishness,
  There is disorder and everything that's bad.
17But wisdom from above—first it is pure,
  Peaceable, loving, thoughtful, and is full
  Of mercy and good fruits, with no favoring
  Or hypocrisy. 18It is fruit of goodness,
  Is sown in peace by those makers of peace.

Chapter 4

God not for the proud but the lowly
  Where do those wars and quarrels among you
  Come from? Are they not from the pleasures warring
  Inside your bodies? 2You desire and don't
  Possess. You envy, murder, and yet you still
  Do not possess it. You fight and make war.
  You do not have because you fail to ask.
  3You ask and don't receive because you ask
  Wrongly so you can spend it on your pleasures.
  4Adulterers, do you not know that friendship
  With things of the world makes you enemy
  Of God? 5And do you think it meaningless
  When it says in Genesis:

The spirit he sent to live in us is jealous cravings.[23]
6But grace he gives is stronger as in Proverbs:
God opposes the proud
And graces the lowdown.[24]

Go close to God

7Submit to God. Oppose the devil and he
Will flee from you. 8Draw close to God and God
Will draw close to you. Wash your hands, you sinners,
And sanctify your hearts, you of two minds.
9Lament and mourn and weep. Your laughter will
Be turned to sorrow and your joy to gloom.
10Be low before the lord. He will exalt you.

Don't judge

11Do not speak nastily about each other.
The brother who rages against his brother
Or judges him also speaks against Torah.
Now if you judge Torah you are not a doer
Of Torah law but are a judge. 12A lawmaker
And judge is one who can save and destroy,
But who are you who dares to judge his neighbor?

A mist appears and disappears

13Come you who say, "Today or tomorrow
That we shall go a year to another city
And we shall buy and sell, and in such work
We'll earn a life and make a profit there."
14Yet you have no clue what tomorrow brings.
What is your life? You are a little while
A mist. It appears and then it disappears.
15Instead you ought to say, "If the lord wishes
And we are alive, then we'll do this or that."

---

23. Gen. 2.7.
24. Prov. 3.34

16But now with all your pretensions and boasting,
All that boasting is bad. 17If one knows good
And fails to do the good, sin is in him.[25]

Chapter 5

The rich have cheated and killed the laboring poor
    Come now, you rich men. Weep, wail, howl
    Over the miseries coming to you. 2Your wealth
    Is rotted, fled, your clothes eaten by moths,
    3Your gold and silver rusted and their rust
    Will testify against you, feed on your flesh
    Like fire. You've stored your treasures for the last
    And final days. 4Listen! The workmen's pay
    For mowing fields which you held back by fraud
    Cries out. The cries of harvesters have reached
    The ears of Yahweh Tzvaot.[26] 5You lived
    On earth in luxury and self-indulgence,

---

25. Verses 13–16 read like a source or early version of Constantine Cavafy's well-known poem, "The City," beginning, "I will go to another city."

26. Yahweh Sabaoth or Lord of Hosts. Sabaoth, meaning armies from the Greek Σαβαώθ (Sabaoth), from the Hebrew יהוה צְבָאוֹת (YHWH/YHVH tzvaot), meaning "God of the armies." The armies may refer to heavenly or earthly armies but they are of Yahweh. Yahweh is the most common name for God in the Hebrew Bible, occurring 279 times. In the New Testament it occurs once in James and once in Paul's Romans (9.29). It is of great interest that James goes back to the primordial yet most common title of the lord in the Hebrew, Yahweh Sabaoth, to invoke the lord (kyrie) as God who will have the power to punish the corrupt rich. It confirms, as most of his usages do, that in James, in contrast to other books in the New Testament, "lord" normally refers only to the Hebrew Bible *Yahweh* or *Adonai*.

Yahweh is the tetragrammaton, the four letters in "YHWH," which are the meaningless letters of Hebrew יהוה, whose true name is unknown and must remain unknown and unsaid. *Yahweh*, or *Adonai*, meaning "my lord," are the two common pronunciations of יהוה (YHWH). *Adonis*, the Greek god, also means "lord." Both Semitic *Adonai* and Greek *Adonis* share the earlier Phoenician common root word *adon*, also meaning "lord."

And nourished your hearts on the day of slaughter.
6You have condemned and murdered the just man.
He who is left cannot resist your force.

Suffer in patience

7Be patient, brothers, till the coming of
The lord. And look, the farmer's waiting for
The precious fruit out of the earth.[27] Be patient
Until it drinks the first and later rains.
8Be patient. Gather strength, make your hearts firm.
Drawing near is the coming of the lord.[28]
9And brothers, do not groan[29] against each other
For fear you may be judged. And look, the judge
Is standing at the doors! 10As an example
Of suffering and patience, brothers, see
The prophets who spoke in the name of God.
11Look, we call blessed those who have endured.
You have heard of the endurance[30] of Job,
And you have seen the purpose of the lord,
How the lord is generous and takes pity.

Don't swear

12Before all things, my brothers, do not swear,
Neither by skies nor earth, nor by an oath

---

27. "Fruit" here means "harvest." The same fruit of the tree is used as a rich symbol for many agricultural and other precious rewards.

28. It can be waiting for God, that is, for Yahweh, Yahweh Tzvaot, the lord Adonai, or waiting for the Jewish messiah (mashiah), who in Christianity is called Christ (*mashiah* in Greek is "Christ") and also the son of God. The foretold messiah is described in multiple passages through the Hebrew Bible, and, especially for Christians, in Psalms and in Isaiah, which is sometimes called the "Fifth Gospel." Some of the more important and familiar references in Isaiah, revealing diverse aspects of the anointed, the suffering servant, son of God, and redeemer, are found in 2.2–4, 9.2–7, 11.2, 11.6–9, and 42.2–3.

29. Also can mean "complain" or "gossip."

30. Or patience. The Greek ὑπομονή (hypomone) can also mean "fortitude, steadfastness, perseverance."

From anywhere. And let your *yes* be *yes*,
Your *no* be *no*—so you will not be judged.

And pray
13Is anyone among you suffering?
Then pray. If anyone is glad, sing psalms.
14Is anyone among you sick? Then call
The elders of the temple. Let them pray
Over them, anoint them with olive oil
In the name of the lord. 15A prayer of faith
Will save the sick and the lord will raise him.
If he has sinned, he'll be forgiven. 16Confess
Your sins to one another and then pray
For one another so that you'll be cured.
The prayer of a good man at work has strength.
17Eliyahu[31] was a human man like us,
And prayed a prayer for there to be no rain.
It didn't rain on earth the next three years
And six months more. 18Again he prayed. The skies
Gave rain and the earth blossomed with its fruit.

Don't lie and save a wandering soul
19My brothers, if anyone among you
Wanders from truth and someone turns him back,
20Let him know: He who turned the sinner back
From ways of wandering will save the soul
From death and cloak a multitude of sins.[32]

---

31. Elijah from the Greek Ἠλίας, from the Hebrew אֵלִיָּהוּ (eliyahu).

32. In rendering this last passage, with its indeterminate references, Richmond Lattimore shows the author's mischievous humor in his free version: "be sure that the man who brought back the sinner from the error of his ways will save his own soul from death, and cover up a multitude of sins" (5.20).

After the magnificent tirade against the rich (5.1–6), this brief ending breathes the air of church rules that conclude the Pastoral Letters, making it a suspect ending. It remains unclear whether James or a follower wished to express a pious warning or impious fun. For that reason, and because of other quick shifts in tone, some scholars say that parts of this letter of James contain parts from other letters.

The Shimonian Letters

Shimon Kefa alpha (1 Simon Peter)

Shimon Kefa beta (2 Simon Peter)

～

Shimon Kefa alpha
(1 Simon Peter)

Shimon Kefa alpha[1]
(Shimon Kef)
(1 Simon Peter)

⁓

PETER IS THE PSEUDEPIGRAPHIC NAME of the author or authors of two letters composed decades after Paul's death to pass as contemporary letters. The author of these letters is neither Jesus's fisherman disciple nor the historic later apostle of the emerging church. The fact that Paul wrote letters to a missionary named Peter in Jerusalem indicates that the apostle Peter was alive during Paul's lifetime. There is no external evidence of a gospel Peter outside the gospels themselves, and neither the apostle Paul, nor Peter to whom Paul writes, knew anything about the gospel fisherman Peter. So we have at least three levels of famous Peter: the legendary Peter in the gospels, the historic apostle Peter with whom Paul quarrels in his letters, and the late Peter who assumes the early apostle's identity, and whose name is on two books of the Bible, 1 Peter and 2 Peter.

1. Peter. In the gospels and letters the same Peter has numerous names: Peter, Simon, and Simeon. And in John 20.6 he is "Simon Peter" from the Greek Σίμων Πέτρος (Simon Petros); in 2 Peter he is "Simeon Peter," from the Greek Συμεὼν Πέτρος (Simeon Petros); and in John 1.42 he is "Simon, the son of John," from the Greek Σίμων ὁ υἱὸς Ἰωάννου (Simon ho huios Ioannou).

"Peter" means "rock" or "stone" in Greek from πέτρος, from the Aramaic כֵּיפָא (kefa), from the Hebrew כֵּף (kef), all meaning "rock" or "stone." In his letters Paul calls Peter "Cephas," from the Greek Κηφᾶς (kefas), based on the Greek transliteration of his Aramaic name, *Kefa*. Here I have gone back to *Shimon Kefa*, Peter's full Aramaic name.

Alpha is the letter "a" in Greek and the number "1."

Babylon as the place of authorship is, as in Revelation, a code word for Rome, where the author, in educated Greek, writes to constituents. There is no way of knowing where the letter was composed. There is also no consensus about dating, but it is reasonable to assume it was written after 80 C.E. and before 120, when reference to the epistle appears in other early works. Nominally a letter, with a greeting at the beginning and an exhortation and farewell at the end, it is principally a sermon to far communities, and precisely for this reason is alive as scripture. It does not have the personally passionate or transcendental nature of the authentic Pauline letters. One major consolation is the hope this letter extends to the new Christians, the hope of the prophets, of rebirth and redemption when the messiah returns, which, it reveals, will be soon. The thought of Jesus's imminent return was universal among early communities. This later forgery in the good intertestamental tradition of pseudepigraha also informs about general Christian behavior in a harsh and terrifyingly hostile environment, and specific duties of free citizens, slaves, wives, and husbands. Throughout, the sociological sermon tells of the historic persecutions and sufferings of the new sect and how they mirror Jesus's own pains, which he underwent for the salvation of his believers.

Chapter 1

Hello

Shimon Kef[2] a messenger[3] of Yeshua the Mashiah,[4] to the chosen exiles of the diaspora[5] in Pontos,[6] Asia,[7] Galatia,[8] Kappadokia,[9] and Bithynia,[10] 2according to the foreknowledge of God the father, and sanctified by the spirit to be obedient to Yeshua the Mashiah and to be sprinkled with his blood.

Grace and peace be multiplied in you.

---

2. Peter.

3. Apostle.

4. Christ Jesus. "Jesus" is from the Greek Ἰησοῦς (Iesous), from the Aramaic יֵשׁוּעַ (Yeshua), a later form of the Hebrew יְהוֹשֻׁעַ (Yehoshua). "Christ" is from the Greek Χριστός (Hristos), and Greek *Hristos* or *Christos* is a translation from the Greek Μεσσίας (Messias), from the Hebrew מָשִׁיחַ (mashiah). "Christ" in Greek also means "the anointed," and "Messiah" in both Greek and Hebrew contains the meaning of "the anointed."

5. A reference to the Jewish experience of exile in the diaspora. In 5.13 Peter picks up the theme, specifically referring to Babylon, from which he sends his greetings, signifying that he is speaking from a synagogue of the Jews of the diaspora in the Babylonian city where Jeremiah once prophesied.

6. Pontos from the Greek word πόντος (pontos). Greek *pontos* means "sea" and is also associated with the Black Sea or Euxine Sea, to the north of Turkey's northern coast. In Peter's day, capitalized "Pontos" was a large Roman province south of the Black Sea.

7. Asia, a large Roman coastal province in Asia Minor, on Turkey's western coast. To the east is Galatia, and further east is Cappadocia.

8. Galatia from the Greek Γαλατία (Galatia). A district between the Roman provinces of Asia (western Turkey) and Cappadocia, Galatia is sometimes called Galatia of the East to avoid confusion with where the Gauls and Celts live in Europe.

9. Cappadocia from the Greek Καππαδοκία (Kappadokia), a mountainous Roman province in the interior of Asia Minor. There remain today extensive caves and chapels within the caves where early Christians hid and lived during Roman times.

10. Bithynia from the Greek Βιθυνία (Bithynia), a Roman province in northern Asia Minor, located on the Black Sea, to the west of and adjacent to Pontos.

Safe in the skies for you

3Blessed be God and father of our lord Yeshua the Mashiah! Through his great mercy he has granted us to be born again into living hope of the resurrection of Yeshua the Mashiah from the dead, 4to an inheritance imperishable and stainless and unfading, which has been kept safe in the skies for you 5by the power of God and through your faith in the salvation which is ready to be revealed in the final time. 6Be happy about this, even if for a little while you must suffer all kinds of trials. 7The quality of your faith—far more valuable than gold, which, though perishable, is tested by fire—results in the praise and glory and honor in the revelation of Yeshua the Mashiah. 8Although you didn't see him, you love him, and though you don't see him now, you believe in him, are glad, with inexpressible and glorious joy, 9since you win the end of your faith, the salvation of your souls.

Grace promised by the prophets

10This salvation was the concern of the prophets. They prophesied about the grace that was to come to you, studied diligently, 11trying to determine the time when the spirit of the Mashiah in them foretold the Mashiah's suffering and the glory that would follow. 12It was revealed to them that they were serving not themselves but you in these matters, which have now been announced to you through those who brought you the good news by the holy spirit sent from the sky, and into things where angels long to look.

Like a lamb unblemished and unspotted

13So gird up the loins of your mind, sober, and set your perfect hope on the grace brought to you in the revelation of Yeshua the Mashiah. 14As children of obedience, do not slip back into the former ignorance of your passions. 15Rather, as he who called you is holy, in all be holy in your behavior. 16It is written in Leviticus:

You will be holy because I am holy.[11]

---

11. Lev. 19.2.

17If you invoke as father the one who judges impartially according to what each has done, live in reverend fear during this time of exile.[12] 18You know that it is not with perishable things like silver or gold that you were ransomed from your futile ways inherited from your fathers,[13] 19but with the blood of the Mashiah, who was like a lamb unblemished and unspotted. 20He was foreknown before the foundation of the world, but he was revealed at end of the ages for you. 21Through him you have come to believe in God who raised him from the dead and gave him glory so that your faith and hope would be in God.

All flesh is like grass

22Now that you have purified your souls by obedience to the truth, leading you to unfeigned brotherly love, love each other from the heart, deeply. 23You have been born not from a perishable seed but one that is imperishable through the living and enduring word of God. 24As in Yeshayahu.[14]

All flesh is like grass and all its glory is like the flower of grass.
The grass dries and the flower falls,

---

12. Exile in 1 Peter will concern two communities: the Jesus communities, some of whose peoples and leaders are being hounded into caves and prisons, or executed, and the parallel community of the ancestral Jews in Babylonia, who were the subject of the prophets and the Psalms. The reason for a supposedly Roman author (the unknown writer of 1 Peter) to speak as if from and about Babylon is exactly the same one which prompts the unknown author of Revelation (Apocalypse) to mask his furious and apocalyptic struggle against Rome as a war against a corrupt and tyrannical Babylon. (There is no connection of influence between these works that shared the same code word, "exile.") Had either author spoken overtly of Rome rather than of a fabled Babylon, that word would have caused instant and violent punishment. For similar reasons of escaping Roman wrath, the gospels accommodate Rome. There is nothing like this in 1 Peter or in Revelation, whose opposition to Roman persecutions is constant, though by necessity concealed by the semi-mythical metaphor of Babylonia. In reality Babylon was a true and terrible trial—by the rivers of Babylon we sat down and wept (Ps. 137)—as was the emerging Christian suffering in Asia Minor, where the book of 1 Peter is set.

13. Ancestors.

14. Isaiah from the Greek Ἡσαΐας (Esaias), from the Hebrew יְשַׁעְיָהוּ (yeshayahu).

25But the word of the lord remains into the aeons.[15]
That word is the good news proclaimed to you.

Chapter 2

Crave the guileless milk of reason

Let us place aside all badness and all treachery and hypocrisy and
envy and all calumny. 2Like newborn babies, crave the guileless milk of
reason so that by it you may grow into salvation—3if you have tasted and
know that the lord is good.

A stone alive

4Come to him, a living stone,[16] rejected by people but selected by God
for honor. 5And let yourselves, like living stones, be built into a spiritual
house for a holy priesthood to offer spiritual sacrifices pleasing to God
through Yeshua the Mashiah.[17] 6It stands in the book of Yeshayahu.[18]

Look, I place a stone in Tziyun,[19] a precious cornerstone
And who believes in him will never know shame.[20]

7So to you who believe, he is precious, but to the unbelievers, it says in
Psalms:

---

15. Isa. 40.6–8.

16. Or a stone alive. The reference is to Christ, "a living stone," as written later in the
Gospel of John's "living water" (John 4.10, 7.38) and "living bread" (John 6.51). There
is inevitably a remembrance, too, of Peter himself, *petros* in Greek, meaning "stone,"
and *kefa* in Aramaic, meaning "stone," which is Peter's name to Paul, which he gives
as a Greek noun, *kefas*, normally transcribed in English as "Cephas," all names and
ways of saying "stone." In other languages "Peter" is still the word for both the person and stone as in French *Pierre* and *pierre*.

17. In this verse is the cornerstone of the later church and cathedral, just as the biblical stone, as heard in Isaiah and Psalms, is the cornerstone for temple or synagogue
and spiritual sacrifices performed therein.

18. Isaiah.

19. Zion from the Greek Σιών (Sión), from the Hebrew צִיּוֹן (Tziyun).

20. Isa. 28.16 (Septuagint).

> A stone rejected by the builders
> Became the very head of the corner.[21]

8And further in Yeshayahu:

> A stone for stumbling on
> And a rock to make one fall.[22]

Those who stumble are disbelieving of the word, as they were destined to be.

Out of darkness into his wonderful light

9You are a chosen race, a kingly priesthood, a sacred nation, a people to be preserved, so that you may proclaim the virtues of who called you as Yeshayahu says:

> Out of darkness into his wonderful light,[23]

10And as Hoshea[24] says:

> You who were not a people, now are a people of God.[25]
> You who did not receive mercy, now have mercy.[26]

My loves, fight the flesh

11My loves, I encourage you as strangers and exiles[27] to refrain from desires of the flesh, which war with the soul. 12Conduct yourselves with the gentiles[28] so that they do not speak of you as doers of wrong so that they may see your good work and glorify God in his day of visitation.

---

21. Ps. 118.22.

22. Isa. 8.14–15.

23. Isa. 43.16.

24. Hosea from the Greek Ὡσηέ (Hosee), from the Hebrew הוֹשֵׁעַ (hoshea).

25. Hos. 2.23.

26. Exod. 19.6.

27. As in transitory sojourners.

28. "Gentiles" is ambiguous here. If we follow the grand parable that the author is speaking from Babylon, then the gentiles are non-Jews in Babylonia. If it is his own time, he cannot mean the gentile converts to messianic (Christian) Judaism, who would be a large part of the Jesus movement converts in Asia Minor, but pagan gentiles who have not yet found Yahweh and his messiah.

Obey governor and emperor

13Submit to every human authority[29] for the sake of the lord, whether it be to a king as supreme, 14or governors sent by him to punish wrongdoers and to praise those who do good. 15It is God's will that by doing right you should silence the ignorance of senseless people, 16As slaves of God, live as free men, but do not to cover up baseness. 17Honor all people in the fellowship of love. Fear God. Honor the king.[30]

Slaves, obey and endure pain

18Slaves of the house, submit in full fear to your masters, not only to the good and gentle ones but also to the harsh ones.[31] 19It is a grace when, through consciousness of God, one endures pain while suffering unjustly. 20What credit is there if you endure a beating when you have done wrong? But if you have done good and endure suffering, this is grace with God. 21To this you were called, because the Mashiah also suffered for you, leaving you his example so that you might follow in his footsteps. As Yeshayahu said:

> 22He did no wrong
>   and no treachery was found in his mouth.[32]

23He was reviled and did not return insult. He suffered and did not threaten, but handed himself over to him who judges justly. 24He carried up our sins with him in his body on the tree[33] so that, dying for sins,

---

29. Or institution or authority.

30. Here Peter warns people to respect Roman authority as Paul does in Romans 13.1–7, where he tells his people to pay taxes and respect Roman governance, then under the emperor Nero. Depending on the dating, the passage may come directly from Romans. See note 147 on Romans 13.1 and Matthew 22.21, "Then give the things of Caesar to Caesar." See note 127 on Mark 12.14.

31. The demanded behavior of slaves in 1 Peter, while stupefying, is not as offensive to contemporary understanding as its fuller articulation in the Pastoral Letters and in Paul's letter to Philemon. However, here as there, there is no hint of moral dilemma with respect to the institution. Indeed, the author of the sermon, as in the Pastorals, associates God's grace with obedience of slaves to masters.

32. Isa. 53.9.

33. The cross.

we might live for the good. By his wounds you were healed. 25You were like sheep led astray, but you came back now to your shepherd and the guardian of your souls.

Chapter 3

Wives, submit to husbands

Likewise, you wives be submissive to your husbands so that even if some of the men do not believe in the word,[34] they may, even without the word, be won over by the wives' behavior, 2as they observe how in fear they live in chastity.[35] 3Your adornment should not be outward braiding of hair and putting on gold ornaments or wearing fine clothing. 4Your beauty should be the being hidden in the heart, and the incorruptibility of a lowly and peaceful spirit, which before God is of great worth. 5Long ago this was the way that holy women, those hoping in God, adorned themselves, submitting to their own husbands. 6So Sarah was submissive to Avraham,[36] and called him lord. You have become her daughters, as long as you do what is good and fear no threat.

Husbands, honor the weaker vessel

7Likewise, you husbands, live with them with the knowledge of them as a weaker female vessel, and honor them as heirs of the grace of life, so that your prayers not be blocked.

Love one another

8Finally, all of you be as one in your thoughts, have sympathy, love like brothers, compassionate, lowly, 9not returning hurt or insult for insult but, on the contrary, bless. You were called for this, to inherit a blessing.

---

34. Word of God.

35. Most of verses 3.2–7 repeat, in this order, phrases and lines from the pseudo-Pauline Ephesians 5.22–24; Colossians 3.18; 1 Timothy 2.9–15; Ephesians 5.25–33; and Colossians 3.19.

36. Abraham from Greek Ἀβραάμ (Abraam), from the Hebrew אַבְרָהָם (avraham).

10The Psalm[37] sings:

> Whoever wants to love life
> > and see good days
> Let him stop his tongue from speaking evil
> > and his lips from uttering cunning,
> 11And let him turn away from evil and let him do good,
> > let him seek out peace and chase it
> 12Because the eyes of the lord are on the just
> > and his ears are open to their prayers
> But the face of the lord is against those doing harm.

Have no fear

13And who will harm you if you are zealous to do the good? 14But if you suffer because of doing the right thing, you are blessed. And do not fear what they fear or be shaken, 15but in your hearts hallow the Mashiah as lord. Always be ready to answer anyone who demands a word about the hope in you. 16But do so with gentleness and awe, with good conscience so that those who attack your good life in the Mashiah may be ashamed. 17It is better to suffer for doing good, if God wills it, than for doing wrong. 18Even the Mashiah once suffered for sins, a just man on behalf of unjust men, that he might bring you to God. He was put to death in the flesh and brought to life in the spirit.

He went into the prisons

19He even went to the spirits in prison and preached to them.[38]

20They had been disobedient long ago, once when the long patient God was waiting for them. Then in those days Noah prepared the ark in which a few, that is, eight souls, were saved through the waters. 21This

---

37. Psalm 34 is very much what "psalm" means in Hebrew, "song of praise," which in this psalm signifies, "Do not speak evil but speak the good." "Psalm" is from the Greek ψαλμός (psalmos), from the Hebrew תְּהִלָּה (tehilah), "song of praise."

38. This passage has been interpreted by some as Christ's descent into hell to judge the condemned or, less dreadfully, into the realm of the dead to redeem those who remain in the prison of death. Or, on the most modest level, and more compassionate, the lines may be taken as a direct allusion to his own days of imprisonment and his desire to alleviate the suffering of those in captivity.

flood as immersion in a pool[39] now saves you. And its fulfillment is not
a riddance of the body's filth but a plea to God for good conscience,
through the resurrection of Yeshua the Mashiah, 22who has gone into
the sky and is at the right hand of God with angels and authorities and
powers subjected to him.

Chapter 4

Drunks and fornicators, a day will come

Since the Mashiah suffered in the flesh, arm yourself with the same
understanding, since one who has suffered in the flesh is relieved from
sin 2to live the rest of his earthly life no longer driven by human passions
but by the will of God. 3You have already spent enough time in the past
doing what the gentiles like to do, living in fornications, desire, drunkenness, orgies, drinking parties, and lawless idolatry. 4They find it strange
that you no longer race with them into the same flood of dissipation,
and so they slander you. 5Yet they will have to answer him who stands
ready to judge the living and the dead. 6This is why the good news was
preached to the dead that they might be judged as men in the flesh, as
everyone is judged, and that they might live in the spirit as God does.

The end is near

7The end of all things is near. Be sober in mind and controlled in
prayers. 8Above all, be constant in loving each other fervently, since
love covers a multitude of sins. 9Be hospitable to each other without
grumbling. 10As each of you has been given the gift of grace, take care of
each other like good stewards of the complex grace of God. 11If anyone
speaks, let it be as if he were citing the sayings of God. If he serves, let
him serve with the strength that God assigns. Then God in all things

---

39. Baptism. The great flood, in which Noah and his family were saved, becomes
a great parable for the baptism in water, the Jewish ritual of dipping practiced by
John, which now saves you, as once it destroyed but saved the virtuous Noah. Being
saved in water, however, is not the removal of external dirt but reaching into the
body and purifying the spirit.

will be glorified through Yeshua the Mashiah, to whom is the glory and the dominion into the aeons and the aeons. Amain.⁴⁰

Let none of you suffer as murderer or thief

12My loves, don't be surprised at the trial by fire that will come to you as a strange thing that happened to you, 13but since you share in the sufferings of the Mashiah, be happy so that in the revelation of his glory you may rejoice and be glad. 14If you are blamed in the name of the Mashiah, you are blessed, because the spirit of glory and the spirit of God is resting on you. 15Let none of you suffer as murderer or thief or wrongdoer or meddler. 16But as a Christian,⁴¹ let him have no shame, but let him glorify God in his name.

17It is time to begin the judgment with the household of God. If it begins first with us, what will be the end for those who refuse to hear the good news of God? It tells us in Proverbs:

18If it is hard for the good to be saved,

Where will the ungodly and sinner appear?⁴²

19So even those who suffer by the will of God should, by doing good, entrust their souls to their faithful creator.

Chapter 5

Be a shepherd to God's flock

To the elders among you, including me, I, a fellow elder and witness of the sufferings of the Mashiah and sharer of the glory soon to be revealed, send you this appeal: 2Be a shepherd to God's flock among you [and an overseer].⁴³ Be so not under compulsion but willingly [according to

---

40. Amen from the Greek ἀμήν (amen), from the Hebrew אָמֵן (amein).

41. Christian. The epithet "Christian," heretofore unheard except in later Acts, which suggests a late date for 1 Peter, began as a word of abuse by outsiders who referred to those who followed the Messiah (which in Greek is "Christ").

42. Prov. 11.31 (Septuagint).

43. Not in all ancient manuscripts.

God],[44] not in sordid greed but freely, 3not as overlords of your charges but as exempla of the flock. 4When the chief shepherd appears, you will win the unfading wreath of glory.

Be lowly

5Likewise, young men, be submissive to the elders and to everyone and clothe yourselves in lowliness toward one another. As Proverbs say:

> God opposes the proud
> But to the lowly he gives grace.[45]

6Be lowly under the mighty hand of God so that in time he may exalt you. 7Cast all your worries on him, because he cares for you.

The devil, a prowling lion

8Be sober. Guard against your adversary the devil, a roaring lion prowling around, seeking someone to devour. 9Resist him, stand firm in faith. You know that your brothers in the world are undergoing the same suffering. 10After you have suffered a while, the God of all grace, who called you to his eternal glory in the Mashiah [Yeshua],[46] will himself restore, confirm, and strengthen, and make you whole again.

11To him the dominion into the aeons. Amain.

Greetings, goodbye

12Through Shilas[47] whom I consider my faithful brother, I have written this short letter to encourage you, testifying that this is the true

---

44. Not in all ancient manuscripts.

45. Prov. 3.34 (Septuagint).

46. Not in all ancient manuscripts.

47. Silvanus from the Greek Σιλουανός (Silouanos). "Silvanus" is a Latinized form of the Greek Σίλας (Silas), which is in Hebrew שָׁאוּל (shaul). *Saul* is the same name that Paul had before he took the road to Damascus. Here, his ordinary Aramaic name *Shilas* is given, the name he would have had during his lifetime in Jerusalem. Silvanus, prominent in Acts, was a companion of Paul and was with him on his second missionary journey.

Here Silvanus is introduced to claim fellowship with a close friend of Paul and to give the anonymous author the authority of the name Peter for his letter, which is preserved as 1 Peter.

grace of God. Stand fast in it. 13She, your chosen sister synagogue in Babylon,[48] greets you, as does my son Markos.[49] 14Greet each other with the kiss of love.

Peace to all of you who are in the Mashiah.

---

48. The letter is written as if the events occurred during the Babylonian Captivity in the sixth century B.C.E. The Greek says "she" greets you, and it is presumed that Peter means his meeting place in Babylon, which, six centuries before Jesus, was a synagogue or temple rather than a church. The later Greek word for church, ἐκκλησία (ekklesia), originally meant "meeting place." ἐκκλησία first appears in the second-century B.C.E. Septuagint translation of the Hebrew Bible, where it means "synagogue." The word "synagogue" is Greek, also meaning "meeting place," and is not found in the Hebrew scriptures. Richmond Lattimore solves the problem of synagogue, temple, and church by not guessing what the Greek pronoun "she" means. He gives, "My fellows among the chosen in Babylon." The King James Version, which here is probably responsible for the conjecture, gives, "The *church that is* at Babylon," but safely puts "*church that is*" in italics, indicating not in original text.

49. Mark from the Greek Μᾶρκος (Markos).

Shimon Kefa beta
(2 Simon Peter)

Shimon Kefa beta[1]
(2 Simon Peter)

THE PSEUDEPIGRAPHAL LETTER 2 Peter speaks in the name of Peter of the synoptic gospels who witnessed the transfiguration of Jesus (Matt. 17.1–5). It is presented as a last will and testament of the apostle Peter in a farewell speech revealing how he wished to be remembered after his death. This intertestamental work is probably by a Greek-educated Jew in Rome, of strong Hellenistic and Jewish backgrounds, who has accepted the messiah. The letter begins with the quirks of Jewish and Christian first-century epistles but quickly moves into Jewish apocalyptic imagery and ideas, as seen in 3.3–13. In his polemical voice of apocalyptic eschatology, he opposes the false teachings of pagan Hellenism as well as the insidious Gnostics, though by veiled references. For a Jewish convert to messianism, imbued with Hellenistic Judaism, living in the post-apostolic period of great religious upheaval and threats from diverse sources, Peter picks his opponents, but it is not perfectly clear who they

---

1. 2 Peter. In the gospels and letters, the same Peter has numerous names: Peter, Simon, and Simeon. And in John 20.6 he is "Simon Peter" from the Greek Σίμων Πέτρος (Simon Petros). In 2 Peter he is "Simeon Peter," from the Greek Συμεὼν Πέτρος (Simeon Petros). And in John 1.42 he is "Simon, the son of John," from the Greek Σίμων ὁ υἱὸς Ἰωάννου (Simon ho huios Ioannou).

"Peter" means "rock" or "stone" from the Greek πέτρος, from the Aramaic כֵּיפָא (kefa), from the Hebrew כֵּף (kef), all meaning "rock" or "stone." In his letters Paul calls Peter "Cephas," from the Greek Κηφᾶς (Kefas), based on the Greek transliteration of his Aramaic name *Kefa*. Here I have gone back to *Shimon Kefa*, Peter's full Aramaic name.

Beta is the letter "b" in Greek and also the number "2."

are, who the heretics are, to what extent the Gnostics are truly Gnostics (a perennial debate), and who the pagans are. To the extent that Peter is aware of the Johannine tradition, the heterodox teachers among them, though not their leaders, are heretics within the broader Jesus movement. These dissenting teachers rejected key traditional Christian ideas of Jesus's suffering as sacrifice to wash away sin, the salvific powers of his death, and even the very reality of Jesus, son of God, as a fully human body on the cross, all docetist notions later developed by Gnostics. For all these reasons, some Johannine figures and their followers may be included among the false teachers. What is paramount about the opponents is that to him they all share an eschatological skepticism that he abhors. As for classical pagans who assail Christians for their moral restraints, he hurls back a swift spear of denunciation of their moral libertinism.

In this letter, as well as in other letters, there is both the promise of the Parousia (the Second Coming of the Christ), which Peter bases on his witnessing of the transfiguration, and the troubling delay in its arrival. The writing is highly polished Greek (not of an Aramaic-speaking Peter), with poetic consistency and narrative flair in retelling the Hebrew Bible story for his sermon. The dating is insecure, being estimated after 80 C.E. and as late as the first or second decade of the second century. Its apparent references to Acts and gospels rule out an earlier dating. There is also a back-and-forth borrowing or lending of verses between 2 Peter and Jude, but independent of insecure dating, Jude appears more likely to be the source than the borrower. There is no significant connection between 1 Peter and 2 Peter in terms of authorship or message.

Chapter 1

Hello

Shimon Kefa[2] slave and messenger[3] of Yeshua the Mashiah,[4] to those who have received faith as precious as ours through the goodness of our God and savior Yeshua the Mashiah, 2may grace and peace be multiplied for you in the knowledge of God and of Yeshua our lord.[5]

Not blind or myopic but in him

3His divine power has given all things to us for life and godliness, through the knowledge of the one who called us to his [own][6] glory and virtues. 4By this precious and great promise that he has given you, you may become sharers in the divine natures and through them escape from the desires and corruption of this world. 5For this same reason you must make every effort to support your faith with virtue, and virtue with knowledge, and 6knowledge with continence, and continence with endurance, and endurance with godliness, 7and godliness with brotherly love, and brotherly love with love.

8All these qualities are yours and abound in you, they will keep you from being useless and unfruitful in your knowledge of our lord Yeshua the Mashiah. 9Anyone who lacks these qualities is blind, myopic, forgetful of how he has been purified from past sins. 10So brothers, be diligent

---

2. Peter.

3. Apostle.

4. Christ Jesus. "Jesus" is from the Greek Ἰησοῦς (Iesous), from the Aramaic יֵשׁוּעַ (Yeshua), a later form of the Hebrew יְהוֹשֻׁעַ (Yehoshua). "Christ" is from the Greek Χριστος (Hristos), and Greek *Hristos* or *Christos* is a translation from the Greek Μεσσίας (Messias), from the Hebrew מָשִׁיחַ (mashiah). "Christ" in Greek also means "the anointed," and "Messiah" in both Greek and Hebrew contains the meaning of "the anointed.

5. In contrast to 1 Peter, where the lord is God, in the introduction to 2 Peter the lord is Jesus. Some verses later, however, the emphasis will not be on virtuous living today but a retelling of a Bible story from Noah on as a background to an ultimate apocalypse of return and salvation in the day of the lord.

6. Not in all ancient manuscripts.

and certain of your calling and election. If you do things you will never stumble, 11and so you will be provided with the wealth of entry into the eternal kingdom of our lord and savior, Yeshua the Mashiah.

My death will come soon

12So I shall constantly remind you of these matters, even though you know them and are firm in the truth that is in you. 13I think it right as long as I am in this tent of flesh to waken you to remember, 14knowing that soon I will lay aside this tent of mine as even our lord Yeshua the Mashiah has made clear to me. 15And it is essential to me always to be certain that you keep these things in your memory after my departure.

On the holy mountain a voice from the sky

16It is not by following artfully devised myths that we made known to you the power and the coming of our lord Yeshua the Mashiah, but we have been eyewitnesses of his majesty.[7] 17When he received from God the father honor and glory, a voice like this came to him from the magnificent glory, saying in Matthew:

> This is my son whom I love,
> In whom I am happy.[8]

18We heard this voice out of the sky, while we were with him on the holy mountain.

19So we have verified the prophetic word. You will do well to watch it as a lamp shining in a dark place until the day dawns and the light-carrying morning star rises in your hearts. 20Know this first so that no prophecy of scripture is one's personal interpretation 21for no prophecy

---

7. This important verse, speaking of "artfully devised myths," is an attack on undisclosed heretics or opponents. Among rivals, one sect's true history is another sect's myth. The rejection is elegantly severe and beautiful in speech and passion but the reference so vague that it remains a general ethical dictum rather than a historical observation.

8. Matt. 17.5. This quotation from Matthew, the first specific line in the letters cited from a gospel, dates 2 Peter as composed not only after Matthew but, more significantly, after its dispersion as known scripture. Up to this time all quotation of scripture was from the Hebrew Bible, frequently through the Greek Septuagint.

ever came from the will of man, but men, carried along by the holy spirit, have spoken from God.[9]

Chapter 2

False prophets

There were also pseudo prophets among the people, as among you there will also be pseudo teachers, who will secretly bring in destructive heresies.[10] They will even deny the master, thereby bringing swift destruction on themselves. 2And many will follow their vicious ways because they will blaspheme the way of truth, 3and in their greed they will exploit you with their fictive words. The judgment against them, pronounced long ago, has not been idle and their destruction has not slumbered.

God did not spare the angels

4If God did not spare the angels when they sinned, but cast them into Gehenna[11] and consigned them to [chains of][12] deepest darkness to be

---

9. Other texts have a variation: "holy men of God spoke."

10. Heresy from the Greek αἵρεσις (hairesis), originally meaning "sect," "party," or "school" as in "school of philosophy," and later in the Greek Philo texts "opinion" or "dogma," and ultimately "heretical sect" or "heresy." Here, the meaning is negative, but the notion of "opinion" or "dissenting opinion" still lingers. A candidate for these heretics may be another Christian sect, such as the Johannine community—there will be so many in the next century—or more probably the Christian Gnostics of Alexandria and Syria, and not the classical pagans, since pagans would not be thought to have an opinion on the master.

11. Gehenna, for "hell," from the Greek γέεννα (geenna), from Hebrew גֵּיא הִנֹּם (gei hinnom), meaning "Valley of Hinnom." *Gehenna* superseded the older term, *Sheol*, for the underworld. Gei Hinnom is a special pit of darkness of the Hebrew Bible. *Gei Hinnom* and *Sheol* are normally translated into English as "hell." See note 22 on James 3.6. The Greek gives ταρταρόω (tartaroo), derived from Tartarus, which in Greek mythology was a region below Hades where the Titans were confined, and the word was used in Jewish apocalyptic, including in Philo, Exs., 152, but since the period in question is early in the creation, Hebrew *Gehenna* or *Sheol*, rather than Greek *Tartarus*, is appropriate to designate the underworld where God hurled the angels.

12. Not in all ancient manuscripts.

kept for judgment, and the ancient world did not spare but the eight.[13] 5Noah a herald of goodness he saved when he loosed a flood on a world of the ungodly. 6And he reduced the cities of Sedom and Amorah[14] to ashes,[15] making them an example of the judgment coming to the ungodly. 7And he rescued Lot the good, tormented by the lawless in their vicious behavior. 8The good man saw and heard them, living among their lawless behavior, and day after day their unprincipled works tormented his good soul. 9The lord knows how to rescue the godly ones from their trial, and to keep the wrongdoers under punishment until the day of judgment; 10especially those who are into desire for the flesh in all depravity, and despise the governing authority.

Unreasoning beasts and children of the curse

Daring, headstrong, they do not tremble at insulting the glorious, 11whereas angels, greater in strength and power than they are, do not bring against them an insulting judgment from the lord. 12But these men are unreasoning beasts, bred as creatures of nature for capture and slaughter. They slander what they do not understand, and when those creatures are slaughtered they will be slaughtered. 13And they are damaged for the damage they have done. They think of happiness as daytime luxurious pleasures.[16] They are blots and blemishes partying in their drunken deceits while they feast with you. 14Their eyes are full of adultery, insatiable in sinning, and they seduce unstable souls. Their hearts are trained in greed. Children of the curse, 15they left the straight road and went astray, following the road of Bilam son of Bor,[17] who longed for the wages of going

---

13. Noah and seven others in his family.

14. Sodom from the Greek Σόδομα (Sodoma), from the Hebrew סְדֹם (Sedom), and Gomorrah from the Greek Γόμορρα (Gomorra), from the Hebrew עֲמֹרָה (Amorah).

15. Other ancient texts add "by a catastrophe."

16. Or indulgences. The word classically was positive and became, in usage, an abuse of happiness.

17. Balaam, Bilam, or Bosor from the Greek Βαλαάμ (Balaam), from the Hebrew בִּלְעָם (bilam); and Bosor from the Greek Βοσόρ, from the Hebrew בְּעוֹר (beor). Considered a sorcerer, Balaam was a Midianite prophet who led Israel astray in sexual sin and idol worship.

wrong 16but was reproved for his transgression. A speechless donkey spoke in a human voice and halted the madness of the prophet.[18]

A dog returns to his vomit

17These men are waterless springs and clouds carried by a tempest, for whom the deepest dark gloom awaits. 18They speak in swollen words of vanity, and with depraved bodily desires seduce others who are barely escaping from living in error. 19They promise them freedom, but they themselves live in corruption. You are a slave to anyone who defeats you. 20If after they have escaped the defilements of this world by a knowledge of our lord, and savior Yeshua the Mashiah, they are again entangled therein and again defeated, the last state is worse than the first. 21It would have been better for them not to have known the way of goodness, then, after knowing it, to turn from the holy commandment handed down to them. 22What happened to them in the true proverb in Proverbs:

> A dog returns to his own vomit,[19]

and,

> A washed sow goes back to roll in mud.

Chapter 3

One day is like a thousand

This, my love, is the second letter I write you. In them I try to quicken your wholesome thinking 2to remember the words spoken earlier by the holy prophets and the commandment of the lord and savior spoken to you through your messengers.[20]

3But first understand. In the last days the scoffers will come, scoffing and following the way of their desires. 4They will go about saying, "What

---

18. Not a traditional prophet, but a false one.

19. Prov. 26.11.

20. Apostles.

happened to the promise of his coming?[21] Since our fathers fell asleep,[22] all things go on as from the beginning of creation!" 5But they purposefully forget that by God's word[23] the skies existed from long ago and the earth was formed from water, and the water came from the word of God, 6and in waters the world was flooded and perished. 7Now, by the same word the present skies and earth have been reserved for fire, kept for the day of judgment and destruction of ungodly people.

The day of the lord will come like a thief

8Do not ignore this, my love, that for the lord one day is like a thousand years and a thousand years are like one day. 9The lord is not slow about his promise, as some think of slowness, but is patient with you, not wishing any to perish, but all to come into repentance. 10But the day of the lord will come like a thief in the night[24] and then in a roaring blast the skies will pass away, and the elements burn and be destroyed, and the earth and everything done on it [will be found out.][25]

New skies and new earth

11With the world dissolving like this, what kind of person must you be in leading lives of holiness and godliness, 12while waiting for and urging the coming of the day of God when the skies will blaze and fall apart

---

21. Meaning, Where is the soon-expected coming of the lord, the Parousia? It is usually said the scoffers are the Gnostics, but here there is no evidence on which to ascertain the reference other than that they are opponents.

22. Our ancestors died.

23. Gen. 1.3. Through speech God spoke the cosmos into creation—"And let there be light," יְהִי אוֹר (yehi or)—and thereafter the word has been central in Abrahamic religions. In mystical Kabbalism the letter is created first to make the word. But both word and letter (and letters also signify numbers) take on major importance as in the famed Book of Formation (Sepher Yetzirah), where, it is claimed, by examining combinations of ten divine numbers and twenty-two letters the cosmological secrets of the universe may be revealed.

24. A Hebrew Bible expression found in Isaiah 34.4, and also in Matthew 24.43–44, 1 Thessalonians 5.2, Mark 13.25, and Revelation 6.13–14.

25. Not found in all ancient manuscripts.

and the element of earth dissolve and melt in fire. 13Then, according to the promise, there will be new skies and new earth, where goodness is at home.

Be spotless, waiting for heaven

14So, my loves, in this expectation, be eager to be spotless and unblemished and at peace with him, 15and believe in the great patience of our lord as salvation. Our brother Shaul,[26] by the wisdom given him, 16speaks of these matters in all his letters. There are things of them hard to fathom, which the ignorant and unstable distort to shape their own destruction as they do other scriptures. 17So you, my loves, being forewarned, guard against being carried away into lawless error and thereby lose your centering. 18Grow in grace and knowledge of our lord and savior Yeshua the Mashiah. To him be the glory now and to the day of eternity.

---

26. Paul from the Greek Παῦλος (Paulos), from Saul in the Greek Σαῦλος (Saulos), from the Hebrew שָׁאוּל (Shaul).

The
Johannine
Letters

YOHANAN ALPHA
(1 JOHN)

YOHANAN BETA
(2 JOHN)

YOHANAN GAMMA
(3 JOHN)

Yohanan alpha
(1 John)

Yohanan alpha[1]
(1 John)

~

TRADITIONALLY, THE THREE LETTERS OF JOHN are said to have been written by the same John, son of Zebedee, who wrote the Gospel of John and the Book of Revelation. Modern critics reject common authorship of the three so-called Johannine letters. As for authorship of each letter, the name or names are also unknown. Certain is that the author or authors of the letters were older authority figures in the Johannine sect of early Christian Jews. Dating is less problematic in that since there is frequent reference to and citing from the John gospel, the letters were written no earlier than in the last decade of the first century and possibly, as some think, well into the second (110 C.E.). Their central concern about Gnostic tendencies among teachers and the laity heightens the probability of a later date, when Gnosticism had become a full-blown speculation in the larger centers of the Greco-Roman world.

John's three letters are relatively brief, but are among the greatest ever written. They are keenly cognizant of the Gnostics, who by then were the foremost sectarian threat to orthodoxy. The letters warn that these urbane pseudo-scholars and preachers come to the temples and churches with notions of ascetic meditation and false knowledge, and attack the very basis of early Christianity, which is the family.

The Gnostics were so important as a competing sect of Christianity that Valentinos of Alexandria, leader and major Gnostic author, narrowly

---

1. John from Greek ʼΙωάννης (Ioannes), from the Hebrew יוֹחָנָן (yohanan). Alpha is the Greek letter for "a" and also for number "1."

missed being elected bishop of Rome, that is, the pope, in the mid-second century. Like the Arians, the Samaritans, and a host of other competing Christian movements, the Gnostics lost in achieving dominion. So too their own scriptures, or their variations of canonical scripture, lost out in finding a place during the centuries of canon definition. The Gospel of John is unique in that it was a centerpiece of Christian Orthodoxy as it was of Gnosticism, each claiming it as its own. It is a pity that the Gospel of Thomas did not find a place in the canon, since despite naysayers, it is as close to being an amazing early discourse attributed to Jesus as is likely to be discovered.

The first of the letters ascribed to John is a sermon, without epistolary salutation or conclusion. It is addressed to a troubled and disintegrating Johannine congregation with secessionist teachers who preach docetic ideas that cast doubt on the human nature of Jesus on the cross (is this a man or a divine facsimile?), on his suffering, and on whether or not such uncertain suffering has cleansed his followers from sin. The author condemns the antichrists, deceivers, and false prophets who doubt that Jesus came in the flesh, by recalling the gospel's "the word became flesh" (John 1.14). The danger was real (1 John 2.19). Dissident groups were already established, circulating false teaching and being behind the secessionist movement. They contended that some could be without sin (1.8, 1.10). Their general rejection of worldliness made them close to what would indeed be central to Gnosticism, which is that this material world is a mistake, a darkness, an illusion. A succinct summary of the problems and the conflicting elements besetting the Johannine community is contained in an essay by Stephen S. Smalley, dean of Chester Cathedral, England, on the letters of John:

> By the time the Johannine letters were written (some ten years after the gospel), friction between the two heterodox groups had developed, and a polarization had begun to emerge. Those with a low view of Jesus had moved further toward the Jewish position and denied that Jesus was the Christ (2.22). Those who espoused a high Christology had become more clearly Gnostic and docetic by inclination and refused to acknowledge that the Christ was Jesus (4.2). On both sides, problems of behavior accompanied those of doctrine (2.7–8, the Law is wrongly regarded as indispensable; right conduct is falsely

deemed unimportant). As a result secession from the community began to take place (2.18–19).[2]

After the greater part of 1 John, which assails the threatening oppo-nents and consequences of their false teaching, chapters 4 and 5 center on God of the Hebrew Bible, of Psalms and Isaiah, rather than on the human nature of Jesus the savior. These last chapters speak of the truth of God, of God in us, and say, "God is love."

The literary virtues of 1 John, in clear and esteemed imitation of the opening passages of the Fourth Gospel, have resulted in one of the most illuminated and sustained lyrical documents among the letters.

2. See Bruce M. Metzger and Michael D. Coogan, eds., *The Oxford Companion to the Bible* (New York: Oxford University Press, 1993), 378.

Chapter 1

What was from the beginning

What was from the beginning[3] what we heard,
What we saw with our eyes, what we looked on
And touched with our own hands, it was the word
Of life, 2a life that shone and we have seen
And testified and clamored it to you
Eternal life! It lives within the father
And was revealed to us. 3What we have seen
And heard, we also call to you that you
May share a fellowship with us, and yes,
Our fellowship is with the father, with
His son Yeshua the Mashiah.[4] 4We
Pen this so that your joy may be complete.

---

3. The first line of the Letter of John imitates the first line of the Gospel of John, which imitates Genesis 1.1. Such an observation is supportable only if the author, who is unknown, had access to the Fourth Gospel. If the dating of this book is around or after 90 C.E., it is more than possible. If there is doubt about accessibility to a finished Gospel of John, then one must conclude that this Johannine community shared ideas enunciated in the gospel, whatever the connection, and this link is confirmed immediately in the first verses of John, which say that God is the word, the word is life, and life is the light (John 1.1–4), which comes to "God is light." "God is light" in 1 John appears in verse 5. It should also be understood that "God is light" was central to the Gnostics, which is why for many sects from North Africa and Asia Minor into Mesopotamia, and in later sects, especially the Mandaeans, the Gospel of John was primary scripture and Johannine ideas the guide. The first substantive exegesis, Christian or Gnostic, on the Gospel of John was accomplished by the Gnostic Herakleon (Heracleon), a student of Valentinos, in Alexandria at the end of the second century, who gave a verse-by-verse analysis of the Fourth Gospel. See Willis Barnstone and Marvin Meyer, eds., *The Gnostic Bible* (Boston: Shambhala Books, 2004), 307–325.

4. Christ Jesus. "Jesus" is from the Greek Ἰησοῦς (Iesous), from the Aramaic יֵשׁוּעַ (Yeshua), a later form of the Hebrew יְהוֹשֻׁעַ (Yehoshua). "Christ" is from the Greek Χριστος (Hristos), and Greek *Hristos* or *Christos* is a translation from the Greek Μεσσίας (Messias), from the Hebrew מָשִׁיחַ (mashiah). "Christ" in Greek also means "the anointed," and "Messiah" in both Greek and Hebrew contains the meaning of "the anointed.

God is light

    5This is the message we have heard from him
    That we announce to you, that God is light,
    In him no darkness lives in any way.
    6If we say we share fellowship with him
    While we are walking in the dark, we lie
    And do not practice truth. 7But if we walk
    In light as he is in the light, we share
    A fellowship with one another. Then
    The blood of Yeshua his son cleans us
    From every sin. 8Yet if we say we have
    No sin, we fool ourselves and truth is not
    In us.[5] 9If we confess our sins, he who
    Is good and faithful will forgive our sins
    And cleanse us of all wickedness. 10If we
    Say we are free of sin we transform him
    Into a liar. His word is not in us.

Chapter 2

Little children, don't sin

    My little children,[6] I pen this to you
    So you won't sin. And even if you sin,
    We have a Paraclete[7] serving the good

---

5. John is speaking to the secessionist false teachers in the Johannine community, who in their docetist tendencies deny the suffering of Jesus on the cross for human sin.

6. "Children" refers in complimentary fashion to the whole congregation and is not directed to young children. The sins referred to are adult practices.

7. Advocate, mediator, or comforter from the Greek παράκλητος (parakletos), the Paraclete, a translation of the Hebrew מְנַחֵם (menahem), meaning "the comforter," which is also the name of the Essene messiah killed by the Romans in Jerusalem in 7 B.C.E., eulogized in two hymns in the Qumran scrolls. The mysterious Para clete appears in John 14.16, 14.26, 12.26, and 16.7 and here in 1 John. He is an advocate or mediator for the Father. The Paraclete, like the Beloved Disciple in John, is an extremely significant figure in the gospels, making brief but crucial appearances under his distinctive title. Here in 1 John the Paraclete is Jesus the Messiah. Among the Essenes, the comforter (paraclete) Menahem is the messiah.

Father, and he is Yeshua Mashiah,
2And his atoning sacrifice wipes out
Our sins and sins of the entire world.

Walk the good way or you are a liar
3By this we know that we have known him—if
We keep to his commandments. 4If one says,
"I too have known him," but his own commandments
He has ignored, he is a liar. In him
There is no truth. 5Whoever keeps his word,
In him his love of God has reached perfection.
By this we know that we are deep in him.
6Whoever says that he abides with him
Must also walk in ways that he has walked.

Whoever loves a sister or brother stands in light
7My loves, I am not writing you a new
Commandment but an old one,[8] which you know
From the beginning is the word you heard.
8I write a new commandment that is true
In him and you because the darkness passes
And light is true and is already shining.
9Whoever says, "I am in light" and hates
His brother, he is in the darkness now.
10Whoever loves his brother stands in light.
In him there is no cause for him to stumble,
11But he who hates his brother is in darkness
And in the darkness walks and doesn't know
Where he is going. Darkness blinds his eyes.

Why he writes to you
12I am writing to you, little children,
Because your sins have been forgiven in his name.

---

8. The commandment of love in Torah, "Love your neighbor like yourself" (Lev. 19.18).

₁₃I am writing to you, fathers,
 Because you have known him from the beginning.
I am writing to you, young men,
 Because you had victory over the cunning one.
₁₄I am writing to you, young children,
 Because you have known the father.
I wrote to you, fathers,
 Because you have known him from the beginning.
I am writing to you, young men,
 Because you are strong,
The word abides in you,
 And you have had victory over the cunning one.

Do not love the world

₁₅Do not love the world,⁹ nor things of the world.
If someone loves the world, love of the father
Is not in him. ₁₆All that is in the world,
The craving of the flesh, the craving of
The eyes, an arrogance about this life,
Does not come from the father but the world.
₁₇The world and craving it will pass away,
And yet whoever does the will of God
Will persevere into eternity.

Comes the antichrist

₁₈Children, it is the final hour! And as
You heard, the antichrist¹⁰ is coming now,
And many antichrists have come. From this

---

9. While this command is found throughout the letters, here, because of the Gnostic emphasis on seeing the world as a material illusion, the command not to love the world takes on the contextual importance of clarifying John's vision of the world.

10. The word "antichrist" appears but a few times in the New Testament, in 1 John 2.18, 2.22, 4.3, and 2 John 7, yet over the centuries the name of Christ, as formulated here negatively for accusatory purpose, became a much used and abused epithet for damning heretics to extreme punishment.

We know it is the final hour.[11] 19They issued
From us but they were not of us, for if
They were they would have stuck it out and stayed,
But they have made it clear that none of them
Belongs to us. 20But you have been anointed
By the holy one [as all of you know].[12]
21I write to you not because you don't know
The truth, but because you know it, because
You know that no lie comes out of the truth.

Who is the antichrist?

22Who is the liar but he who has denied
That Yeshua is the Mashiah? He is
The antichrist, the one denying the father
And son. 23Anyone who denies the son
Has not the father. But as John has said,
"Who knows the son must know the father too."[13]
24Let what you heard in the beginning last.
If what you heard in the beginning lasts
In you, you will rest in the son and father.
25This he has promised us: eternal life.

Remain in him

26I wrote these things to you concerning those
Who try to fool you. 27As for you the anointing
Which you received from him remains in you,
And so you have no need for anyone
To teach you. Yet the anointing teaches you

---

11. The coming of the Christ is imminent.

12. Not in all ancient manuscripts. Usually, as here, the words amended appear to be of an exhortatory nature to confirm belief and certainty in a statement.

13. John 14.7. 1 John cites an important verse in the Fourth Gospel, but in the gospel Jesus is speaking and there is a difference in statement: "If you had known me, you would have also known my father."

About all things and is the truth, no lie.
Since he himself taught you, remain in him.

Children of God
28And now, little children, remain in him
So when he is revealed we're confident
And do not feel shame before him at his coming.
29And if you know that he is good, you know
That all who perform good are born from him.

Chapter 3

The father gave us love
See what is love the father gave to us,
That we are called children of God. We are.
The world does not know us because it didn't
Know him. 2My loves, we are children of God.
What we will be has not yet been revealed.
We know that when he is revealed we'll be
Like him, for we shall see him as he is.
3And everyone who has this hope in him
Makes himself pure as also God is pure.

Sin is from the devil
4Each one who sins is violating Torah[14]
And sin is violating Torah law.
5You know that he was manifested to
Remove our sins. There is no sin in him.
6All who abide in him commit no sin,
While all who sin have not seen or known him.
7My little children, let no one fool you.

---

14. "Torah" means law, as in Moses's Ten Commandments. "Torah" also means the Pentateuch and, in the broader sense, the whole Hebrew Bible. At the time of John there was only one religious law, which was found in Torah.

Who has performed the good is good just as
The lord is good. 8The one who commits sin
Is of the devil, since from the beginning
The devil sins. The son of God was shone
For this, that he destroy the devil's works.
9Those who are born of God are not with sin
Because the seed endures in him, and he
Cannot know sin because he sprang from God.
10Children of god and children of the devil
In these ways are revealed. Those who do not
Do good are not of God, nor love their brothers.

Love one another

11This is the message we heard from the start,
That we love one another, 12not like Kayin[15]
Who came out of the evil one, who murdered
His brother and why did he murder him?
His actions had been bad, his brother's good.

Who doesn't love remains in death

13Do not wonder, my brothers, that the world
Hates you. 14We know that we have passed
Out of death into life because we love
Each other. He who doesn't love remains
In death. 15But all who hate each other are
Clear murderers. And every murderer,
You know, has no eternal life in him.

He lay down his life for us

16We have known love by this, that he lay down
His life for us. We should lay down our lives
For our brothers. 17Now anyone who has
His world possessions and comes on a brother
In need and closes all his heart to him,
How can the love of God be in that man?

---

15. Cain from the Greek Κάϊν (Kain), from the Hebrew קַיִן (kayin).

18My little children, let's not love in word
Or tongue but in our deeds and in our truth.

Commandment of love
19By this we'll know that we are from the truth,
And before him we will persuade our hearts
20That if our hearts condemn us for being cold,
That God is greater than our hearts. He knows
All things. 21My loves, and if our hearts do not
Condemn us, we have confidence with God,
22And what we ask from him, we will receive,
Because we keep to his commands and do
What pleases him. 23And this is his command
That we believe the name of his son Yeshua
The Mashiah, and we love one another
As he commanded us to do. 24All who
Keep his commands reside in him and he
In them. And so we know that he resides
In us, and through the spirit he gave us.

Chapter 4

Spirit of truth and spirit of error
My loves, do not believe each spirit.[16] Test

---

16. Lines 1–7 of chapter 4 are crucial in 1 John for distinguishing between the author's assertion that Jesus came incarnate, that is, in the flesh, and the docetic assertion, shared by most Gnostic sects, that denies that the word, the *logos*, could become a fully human Jesus, and describes Jesus as a phantom, an illusion on the cross, the "laughing God," who laughs at mortals who believe they can make God suffer and die. In speaking of these teachers (mainly of Alexandria) as "spirits of error," John uses a terminology most often used by the Gnostics themselves—error, darkness, hylic (material)—to describe the traditionally "misled" Christians. Hence each group, on the question of the Christological nature of Jesus, uses similarly charged words to denounce the falsity of the opponent. The verse in question, about which the main dissension centers, is John 1.14: "And the word became flesh and tented (lived) among us" (Καὶ ὁ λόγος σὰρξ ἐγένετο καὶ ἐσκήνωσεν ἐν ἡμῖν, Kai ho logos sarks egeneto kai eskenosen en hemin).

The spirits to see if they are from God,
Because many false prophets have gone out
Into the world. 2By this you know the spirit
Of God: each spirit that acknowledges[17]
Yeshua Mashiah has come in flesh,
It is from God; 3and each spirit that fails
To recognize *Yeshua,* it's not from God.
This is the spirit of the antichrist,
And you have heard that he was coming. He
Has come, he is already in the world.[18]

We are of God

4You are of God, my little children, and
You have overcome these pseudo prophets,
Since he who is in you is greater than
He who is in the world. 5They're of the world,
And so they speak as of the world, and so
The world hears them. 6We are of God. Those who
Know God hear us. Those who are not of God
Do not hear us. From this we know the spirit
Of truth, and know the spirit of their error.

God's love in us

7My loves, let us love one another since
Love is from God, and everyone who loves
Is sprung from God, and he knows God.[19] 8But he
Not loving can't know God, since God is love.

---

17. Or confesses or recognizes.

18. The antichrist has come.

19. At this point in 1 John, there is a shift from concern with false prophets to God's love of the believer. There follows through the chapter a major articulation of love in the New Testament. Not the mystical erotic love of Song of Songs, it is the societal love in the Torah commandment "Love your neighbor like yourself" (Lev. 19.18.) and the personal love between God and his people, heard as song through the Psalms.

9In this way God's love was revealed in us,
  And he sent his only engendered son
  Into the world that we might live through him.
10Love is in this, not in that we've loved God
  But he loved us and gave his son to be
  As a propitiation for our sins.
11My loves, since God loved us, then we should love
  Each other. 12No one ever has seen God,
  But if we love each other, God resides
  In us, and in us his love is made perfect.

See Yeshua as son of God

  13By this we know that we remain in him
  And he in us, because he's given us
  His spirit. 14We have seen and testify
  That the father sent his son as savior of
  The world. 15Whoever confesses that Yeshua
  Is the son of God, God lives in him and he
  In God. 16We know, believe God's love for us.

God is love

  Since God is love, he who resides in love
  Resides in God and God resides in him.
  17By this, love has been made perfect in us
  So on the day of judgment we may have
  Full confidence, because as he is in
  The world, so we are too. 18Fear has no place
  In love, since perfect love casts out the fear,
  Because fear has to do with punishment
  And one who is afraid has not been made
  Perfect in love. 19We love because he first
  Loved us. 20If anyone says, "I love God,"
  And hates his brother, then he is a liar.
  He who cannot love his own brother whom
  He's seen, cannot love God whom he's not seen.
  21The commandment we have from God is this:
  He who loves God must love his brother too.

Chapter 5

Faith overcomes the world

All who believe Yeshua is the Mashiah,
And was fathered by God, all those who love
The one who fathered should love him who was
Engendered. 2So by this we love the children
Of God when we love God and carry out
His commandments. 3This is the love of God,
That we keep his commandments and that they
Are not a burden. 4Whatever is born
Of God will overcome the world, and so
Our faith is victory that overcomes
The world. 5And who can overcome the world
But he who believes Yeshua is God's son?

Of him who came through water and blood

6This is the one who came by water and blood,
Yeshua Mashiah, and not by water
Alone but in water and blood. 7The spirit
Testifies, because spirit is the truth.
8There are three who testify, the spirit,
And the water, and the blood, and the three
Are one. 9If we receive the testimony
Of men, then testimony coming from God
Is greater, for this is God's testimony
Where he is testifying about his son.
10And he who believes in the son of God
Contains the testimony in his heart.
And those who don't believe in God have made
Of him a liar, since they don't believe
In testimony that God gave himself
Concerning his own son. 11I tell you then
His testimony: God has given us
Eternal life. This life is in the son.

12Whoever has the son also has life,
 Who does not have the son does not have life.

Farewell
 13I write these things to you so you may know
 That you will have an everlasting life,
 You who believe in the name of God's son.

Two Supplements to 1 John[20]

Prayer for Sinners

14And this is the confidence we have in him, that if we ask him anything in accordance with his will, he hears us. 15And if we know that he hears us, whatever we ask for we know we are given what we ask from him.

16If anyone sees his brother committing a sin, which is not a deadly sin, he will ask and God will give him life. There is sin that leads to death. I do not say that you or he should pray for that kind. 17All wrongdoing is sin, but there is sin which is not deadly.

Summary of the Book

18We know that those who are born of God do not sin, and one who is born of God obeys him, and the evil one doesn't touch him. 19We know that we are of God and the world lies under the power of the evil one. 20We know that the son of God has come and has given us understanding so we may know who the true one is, and we are in him who is true, in his son, Yeshua the Mashiah. He is the true God and eternal life.

21My little children, keep yourselves from idols.

---

20. 1 John effectively concludes with 5.13. The provenance of verses 14–21 is uncertain; they may be a later pious emendation. Following John's tremendous ending, it certainly seems like scribal scribble.

Yohanan beta
(2 John)

Yohanan beta[1]
(2 John)

⌁

THE LETTERS DESIGNATED 2 John and 3 John are the shortest ones in the New Testament, each about the same length, and containing only one chapter. Indeed, they are compact enough to have been written on a single page of papyrus. In contrast to 1 John, they are presented as real private letters, though 2 John seems to be addressed to a community while 3 John is addressed to Gaius, a personal acquaintance. The place and dating of the letters are unknown, but like 1 John, they probably were composed after 90 C.E. and at some place in Asia Minor where the Johannine communities developed, later, as in the warning of these letters, as Gnostic communities. Especially in the John letters, in part because of their late date, when Gnosticism was beginning to peak, the Gnostics, with their false intellectual pretensions, overly esteemed view of Eve and women, and their anticreator God message, are the diabolical threat and enemy.

This second letter of John deals precisely with the commandment of love and the dangers of false teachers. It adds a warning not to be hospitable to such false teachers and the danger of lurking docetic views. The letter is addressed to an unnamed lady and her children. Although there is no basis for identification, it has been suggested that the "lady" and her children may be a sister congregation of gentile women converts or of

---

1. John from Greek Ἰωάννης (Ioannes), from the Hebrew יוֹחָנָן (yohanan). Beta is the Greek letter for "b" and also for number "2."

Christian Jews, or a woman elder in another Johannine community. The main dedication to a woman and her children is unique among the New Testament books, and the actual reference of a haphazard encounter, perhaps in the street, adds a touch of ordinary reality to dedications, which are normally lofty and formulaic.

To the chosen lady

The elder[2] to the chosen lady and to her children, whom I love in truth, and not only I but also all who have known the truth, 2and through the truth residing in us and which will be with us into the aeons. 3Grace, mercy, peace from God the father and from Yeshua the Mashiah,[3] the son of the father, in truth and love.

Walking in truth and love

4I was overjoyed that I found some of your children walking the truth, just as in the commandment received from the father. 5Now I ask you, madame, not as one who writes you a new commandment, but thinking of one from the beginning,[4] that we should love one another. 6And this is love, that we should walk according to his commandments. This is the commandment as you heard it from the beginning, to walk in love.

Beware of deceivers

7Many tricksters have gone out into the world, those who do not acknowledge the coming of Yeshua the Mashiah in the flesh.[5] One is a trickster and the other an antichrist.[6] 8Look into yourselves so you do

---

2. The author, who may or may not be the author of 1 John. If he is the author of 1 John, this letter is still separate and not a fragment of 1 John.

3. Christ Jesus. "Jesus" is from the Greek Ἰησοῦς (Iesous), from the Aramaic יֵשׁוּעַ (Yeshua), a later form of the Hebrew יְהוֹשֻׁעַ (Yehoshua). "Christ" is from the Greek Χριστος (Hristos), and Greek *Hristos* or *Christos* is a translation from the Greek Μεσσίας (Messias), from the Hebrew מָשִׁיחַ (mashiah). "Christ" in Greek also means "the anointed," and "Messiah" in both Greek and Hebrew contains the meaning of "the anointed."

4. The commandment of love in Torah, "Love your neighbor like yourself" (Lev. 19.18).

5. A clear reference to the docetic Gnostics, who did not see Jesus as a God fully incarnated as mortal capable of death. See introduction to 1 John.

6. It remains unclear who the antichrists were among the opponents: Gnostics, Jews, pagans, or other dissenters. The Johannines were themselves a dissenting faction that was saved from unpleasant titles by disappearing as an entity, except insofar as their descendants may have indeed slipped into the Gnostic speculation, with the Fourth Gospel as the base.

not lose [what we worked for][7] but gain the full reward you may receive. 9Whoever goes ahead and does not abide by the teaching of the Mashiah does not have God. Those who keep to the teaching have both the father and the son.

Give no house welcome to false teachers

10If anyone comes to you and does not bring you this doctrine, do not welcome him into your house and do not greet him. 11Anyone who greets him shares in his cunning works.

Goodbye

12Though I have many things to write you, I would rather not do it with paper and ink but I hope to be with you and to speak mouth to mouth[8] so that our joy may be complete. 13The children of your chosen sister send you greetings.[9]

---

7. Not in all ancient manuscripts.

8. Face to face, intimately and in person.

9. This final greeting may be taken as from a real woman, rather than an uncertain John, or be a pleasant heteronymic title for a letter from an elder in a kindred church.

Yohanan gamma
(3 John)

Yohanan gamma[1]
(3 John)

THE LETTER 3 JOHN closely follows the conventions of the ancient letter format. It recommends a new Christian, Demetrios, probably a gentile convert, to the messianic (Christian) Jewish sect. The normal earlier internal conflicts in New Testament books were between the Jerusalem apostles and Paul, with respect to how close (the Jerusalem view) and how far (Paul's view) one was permitted to be in observing Jewish law (Torah) on diet, circumcision, and the Sabbath, especially concerning new gentile converts for whom these questions of openness were a problem. Now, in this post-apostolic generation, the conflict deals with the Gnostics, who pose a new threat to the stability of the larger Jesus movement, one that will, in the case of the Johannine community, lead to its ultimate disappearance, at least as nominal Christians. They will survive transformed into the despised heresy, as they do even today among the Mandaean Gnostics in Iraq and Iran, and in some American cities, especially Detroit, Chicago, and Cambridge. So, in 3 John, as in the earlier John letters, the question of the false teachers overrides other issues. Diotrephes has refused to render hospitality to bearers of suspect letters. In this administrative controversy—and the contents of the actual letters remain vague—the elder author threatens to intervene in the mess to force Diotrephes to receive and be hospitable to the traveling missionaries he had refused. Since the letter comes from an elder of a new Christian church, the refusal to receive his letter implies that this

---

1. John from Greek Ἰωάννης (Ioannes), from the Hebrew יוֹחָנָן (yohanan). Gamma is the Greek letter for English "g" or "c" and also for number "3."

bitter controversy has already seen the Johannine congregation yield to the false teachings of the Gnostics or antichrists (who may be Gnostics, Jews, or some other heresy). Hence, the purpose of 3 John is to fight the apostates among them, centering on Diotrephes.

As with 1 John and 2 John, dating and place are uncertain, but 3 John was most likely composed late, certainly after 90 C.E., and someplace in Asia Minor. The author is unknown.

Hello

The elder to the beloved Gaios,[2] whom I truly love.

2My love, concerning all things I wish you to do well and be in good health and that your soul also do well.

3I was exceedingly happy after the visit of the brothers, who testified that truth is in you and you walk in truth. 4I have no greater joy than to hear that my children are walking in the truth.

Be kind to foreigners

5My love, you are being faithful when you work for the brothers, even when they are foreigners. 6They have testified about your love before the congregation, and you have done well to send them on their way in a manner worthy of God. 7They began their journey for the sake of his name, and they take no support from the gentiles.[3] 8So we should receive cordially such men so that they may become coworkers in the truth.

Of the troublemaker Diotrefes

9I wrote something to the congregation. But the one who loves to be first among them, Diotrefes,[4] does not receive us.[5] 10Therefore, when I come I will remember his works, which he does with malicious words, talking nonsense about us. And not being satisfied with these actions, he refuses to welcome brothers, and those who would like to welcome us he prevents from doing so and expels from the congregation.

---

2. Gaius, a common Latin name here found in Greek as Γάϊος(Gaios).

3. Here, "gentiles" is still used in its original meaning, of non-Jews, nonbelievers, that is, Greeks, whom in another context might be called pagans. It does not mean "gentile" in the Christian context, which is new converts from Greek paganism to Christian Judaism. The word in Greek for the Latin word "gentile," from Latin *gentilis*, is derived from Greek ἔθνος (ethnos), from the Hebrew גּוֹי (goy), and plural גּוֹיִם (goyim). An *ethnikos* is an ethnic.

4. Diotrephes from the Greek Διοτρέφης (Diotrefes).

5. The charge against Diotrefes goes from personal to doctrinal, from calling attention to his big ego—he loves to make himself first—to his refusal to accept letters from his denomination. This comes through not only as an unwillingness to recognize the authority of the elders but also as apostasy.

Demetrios the good

11My loves do not imitate the bad but the good. Who does good is from God. Who does bad has not seen God. 12By contrast, Demetrios[6] has favorable testimonials from all and from the truth itself. We also testify for him, and you know that our testimony is true.

Speaking mouth to mouth

13I had many things to write to you but I do not write them to you with ink and pen. 14I am hoping to see you immediately and mouth to mouth we will talk.[7]

Goodbye

15Peace to you. Our friends send you greetings. Greet our friends in person by name.

---

6. Demetrios, a Greek name that becomes Latin *Demetrius* in English, from the Greek Δημήτριος (Demetrios). This Demetrios should not be confused with the earlier silversmith Demetrios in Ephesos, who led a rebellion against Paul (Acts 19.24–38).

7. Face to face, intimately and in person.

An
Apocalyptic
Letter

An
Apocalyptic
Letter

Yehuda or Judas
(Jude)

Yehuda or Judas[1]
(Jude)

⁓

THE LETTER OF JUDE is a perfect song before the extended allegory
of the Apocalypse, the great epic of the New Testament. "Apocalypse"
means "revelation" or "uncovering" in Greek, and only secondarily its
cognate "apocalypse." Yet the Apocalypse that ends the Bible recovers
the cosmic, destructive, and salvific vision of true apocalypse, with
angels, pale horses, a Babylonian whore in the sky, prophetic beasts,
and a heavenly city whose walls are glass and sapphire. The brief letter of
Jude is also a Dantesque visionary work. It begins and ends in epistolary
tropes, but they yield to a powerful retelling of biblical event, which
he knows with Midrashic eyes. He is steeped in contemporary Jewish
and Christian-Jewish apocrypha, pseudepigrapha, and apocalypses.
His citing from a no-longer-extant version of Enoch, quoted in verses
14 and 15 and echoed in other verses, reveals his interest in multiple
genres of intertestamental writings; Enoch, which still exists in Greek
and Ethiopic, suggests the range of his sources. With a firm hand, Jude
gathers image and word to produce an intellectual dream and spiritual
wandering unique in religious literature.

The author directs his passions against enemies of the messiah and
the father God. These are charismatic intruders, demons, false teachers,
pseudo prophets, and ungodly sensualists, all of whom are not made
topical with names or other identifications. Scholars have observed that
whoever these enemies are, they are decisively antinomians (the lawless),

---

1. Jude. Judas from the Greek Ἰούδας (Ioudas), from the Hebrew יְהוּדָה
(yehuda).

going their own way, outside of doctrine and authority, toward grace and salvation. Like Plotinos who denounced the Valentinian Gnostics, with whom he actually shared many metaphysical ideas, it is not unlikely that this teacher, warning us so imaginatively against enemies whom he describes with extracanonical inspiration, was affected by the imagination of the renegade antinomians and their ways to his own personal transcendence.

The degree to which the list of enemies contained the names of lapsing Jews (if an early work) or of rising Gnostics (if a late work) can only be guessed by considering the period of composition, but its date is unknown. Scholars have argued that the letter was written as early as the 50s and well into the second century. Something closer to the later date is more probable. Ephesos is again suggested, almost by habit, as a possible place of composition.

As for who Jude was, the name attached to the letter is suggestive. In 1.1 the author identifies him as a slave of Jesus and brother of James. Scholars agree that "Jude" came into English naming in order to dissociate Judas of this letter from Judas Iscariot, the betrayer of Jesus. In concordance with the struggle of early Christian communities to establish their identity independent of the Judaism from which they emerged, the gospels blurred the identity of their main personages, of Jesus and God. Yahweh is no longer "Yahweh" ("the name") but *Kyrie*, and debts to antecedents are diminished. The change from "Judas" to "Jude," however, occurs only in English translations, not in Greek scripture, yet it upholds the practice of the Greek scriptures and patristic writings to alter names for church purposes. Hence the unparalleled King James Version translates a common name found in Hebrew and its Greek version 813 times as "Judah," and 33 times as "Judas," reserved for the Iscariot. In 813 occasions, its version precludes association of other biblical Judases with Judas the betrayer. Hence, today we have the Letter of Jude rather than the Letter of Judas.

Hello

Yehuda a slave of Yeshua the Mashiah[2]
And brother of Yaakov,[3] to those of you
Chosen ones who are loved in God the father
And kept safe in Yeshua the Mashiah.
2May mercy, peace, and love abound in you.

Doom of the godless among you

3My loves, I'm writing hastily to you
Concerning our salvation that we share.
I am in need of writing you to plead
With you to contend for the faith that was,
Once and for all, handed down to the saints.
4Some men have secreted in among you,
Men who were long ago marked down in writings
For condemnation, who were judged the ungodly,
Who twist the grace of God into depravity,
And who deny the being our one master
And lord who is Yeshua the Mashiah.

Debauched angels lie now in fire

5I want you to remember, though you know
All of these things, that once the lord rescued
His people out of Egypt. Later he
Destroyed all those who lacked belief. 6And angels
Failing to obey in their dominion, leaving
Their proper residence, he locked them in
Eternal chains under a deepest darkness

---

2. Christ Jesus. "Jesus" is from the Greek Ἰησοῦς (Iesous), from the Aramaic יֵשׁוּעַ (Yeshua), a later form of the Hebrew יְהוֹשֻׁעַ (Yehoshua). "Christ" is from the Greek Χριστος (Hristos), and Greek *Hristos* or *Christos* is a translation from the Greek Μεσσίας (Messias), from the Hebrew מָשִׁיחַ (mashiah). "Christ" in Greek also means "the anointed," and "Messiah" in both Greek and Hebrew contains the meaning of "the anointed."

3. James from the Greek Ἰάκωβος (Iakobos), from the Hebrew יַעֲקֹב (yaakov).

To wait for judgment on the giant day.[4]
7Just like Sedom and Amorah[5] and the cities
Around them, like the fornicating angels
Who fell into unnatural sex, they all
Serve as examples as they undergo
The punishment of everlasting fire.

Archangel Michael and the devil
8Likewise those dreamers who defile the flesh
Deny authority and they blaspheme
The glorious beings,[6] 9and yet the archangel
Mihael,[7] when he was matched against the devil,
Contending over the body of Moshe,[8]
He lacked the audacity to retort
With a slandering insult, but he said,
    May the lord punish you!
10These people slander what they do not know,
And like the unreasoning beasts they know
Things naturally and in them are corrupted.

---

4. Judgment Day.

5. Sodom from the Greek Σόδομα (Sodoma), from the Hebrew סְדֹם (sedom), and Gomorrah from the Greek Γόμορρα (Gomorra), from the Hebrew עֲמֹרָה (Amorah).

6. Celestial beings or angels.

7. Michael from the Greek Μιχαήλ (Michael), from the Hebrew מִיכָאֵל (mihael), the archangel and protector of the Jewish nation. Michael is a major figure in Jewish apocalyptic, which pervades this work as it does the earlier Jews (the book), James, and 1 John, and here serves as a prelude for Revelation, the ultimate Apocalypse.

8. Moses from the Greek Μωϋσῆς (Moses), from the Hebrew מֹשֶׁה (moshe). In an apocryphal story Michael and the devil contend over the body of Moses. The devil said that Moses was a murderer, going back to Moses's killing of an Egyptian who was abusing Jews (Exod. 2.11–12), and therefore unworthy of burial. Michael knows this is slander, but rather than retort in kind, condemning the slandering devil, he refers the matter to God. Hence, Michael comes through as one not guilty of easy judgment or leading others into sin, and shines when he suggests a higher judgment.

11A plague on them! They go the way of Kayin[9]
  And lose themselves in the error of Bilam,[10]
  Driven by gold, and die rebelling like Korah.[11]

They are rainless clouds
  12They are reefs and stains[12] in your love feasts.
  They come into your banquets shamelessly,
  Caring only for themselves, rainless clouds
  Driven by gales that uproot autumn trees
  And leave them fruitless and twice dead; 13wild waves
  Of the sea foaming their own shame, and stars
  Wandering to blackest aeons saved for them.

Enoch warns of ten thousand holy ones
  14Hanor,[13] seventh from Adam,[14] prophesied,
  Saying, "Look, the lord comes amid his myriads
  Of holy ones 15to pass judgment on all
  And to convict each soul of the ungodly,
  For each harsh thing ungodly sinners spoke

---

9. Cain from the Greek Κάϊν (Kain), from the Hebrew קַיִן (kayin).

10. Balaam, Bilam, or Bosor from the Greek Βαλαάμ (Balaam), from the Hebrew בִּלְעָם (Bilam). Considered a sorcerer, Balaam was a Midianite prophet who led Israel astray in sexual sin and idol worship.

11. Korah or Core, from the Greek Κόρε (Kore), from the Hebrew קֹרַח (kerah). Korah led a rebellion against Moses in the desert. He was punished by God, who had him swallowed up by the earth (Num. 26.9; Deut. 11.6; Ps. 106.17).

12. The Greek σπιλάς (spilas) has a twofold but connected meaning, signifying a rock or reef in the sea for wrecking a ship, or a stain or spot; both are lurking hidden dangers to destroy.

13. Enoch from the Greek Ἐνώχ (Enoch), from the Hebrew חֲנוֹךְ (hanoh). Enoch first appears in Genesis 5.18–24. The vision of the wild beasts and the lord amid myriads of holy ones is found in Daniel. The prophecy of Enoch is found in an equivalent passage in 1 Enoch 1.9 in the Jewish pseudepigrapha. For Enoch's dream vision journeys through heaven and hell, see epigrapha under Enoch in Willis Barnstone, ed., *The Other Bible* (San Francisco: Harper and Row, 1984), 485–497.

14. Seven generations from Adam.

Against him." 16They are grumblers and complainers,
Walking around in search of flesh, their mouths
Talking loud, flattering to gain a victory.

My loves, scoffers walk around
    17My loves, remember the words of prophecy
    Said earlier by messengers of our lord
    Yeshua the Mashiah. 18They told you,
    "In final days there will be scoffers walking
    Around, ungodly ones in search of flesh."
    19They cause divisions, these sensual men,
    And in them there is no spirit at all.

Be strong, there is the mercy of the lord
    20My loves, be strong. Build on the holy faith
    And pray in holy spirit. 21Keep to love
    Of God. Keep looking forward to the mercy
    Of our lord Yeshua the Mashiah, who leads
    Us to eternal life. 22Pity some who waver.
    23Save them by snatching them from the fire,
    And pity others who are afraid, but hate
    Even their garment which is stained by flesh.

Song of praise[15]
    24To him who has the power of guarding you,
    To keep you from a fall, to set you blameless,
    Exulting in the presence of his glory,
    25To the only God our savior through Yeshua
    The Mashiah, our lord, glory and majesty,
    Dominion and authority before
    All aeons, now and into all the aeons.
                                    Amain.[16]

---

15. The doxology.

16. Amen from the Greek ἀμήν (amen), from the Hebrew אָמֵן (amein).

ANONYMOUS

Yehudim or Jews
(Hebrews)

Yehudim or Jews
(Hebrews)

⁓

JEWS[1] DOES NOT BEGIN with the traditional salutation of the Pauline letters. It has been traditionally called an epistle or letter, but it follows no known ancient genre of the letter. Rather, it is a sermon or exhortation, by a grand master of hermeneutics, anticipating Origen, who introduces "the interpretive tyranny of a Plato or Paul"[2] more fully to the Hebrew

1. "Jews" refers to Christian or Messianic Jews of a congregation, not to unconverted traditional Jews. The presumed audience is unknown. Some argue that both Christian Jews and Jews are the intended readers; others argue gentiles. The traditional title of this document is "Letter to the Hebrews" or, as in the Greek text of the United Bible Societies fourth corrected edition, used here, "Hebrews." The word "Hebrew" is from the Greek Ἑβραῖος (Hebraios), the word for a Jew in Hellenistic Greek. In Genesis the word for Jew is עִבְרִי (Ivree). The word "Hebrew" in modern English, however, refers only to language, not to person or people. While its use in English biblical translations is customary, this usage follows the pattern of finding alternate words or euphemisms to distinguish between Messianic Jews, who were the first followers of Jesus, and other Jews. Paul in modern English was a Jew, not a Hebrew. Today the word "Hebrew" for a Jew is derogatory, what dictionaries label "offensive." To use "Hebrews" as the title for the nineteenth book of the New Testament is not to be intentionally derogatory, but rather to employ words that free the author and reader of the discomfort of using the "J word" to identify Jews as the first Christians, the "J word" being reserved for all the Jews who are demonized in the gospels.

The proper title in English for the book is not "Letter to the Hebrews" or "Hebrews" but "Letter to the Jews" or "Jews." With respect to the traditional Greek title, it is, like most biblical titles, unknown and based on inferences and the pen of a later scribe.

2. Gabriel Josipovici, "The Epistle to the Hebrews and the Catholic Epistles," in Robert Alter and Frank Kermode, eds., *The Literary Guide to the Bible* (Cambridge, MA: Harvard University Press, 1987), 521.

scriptures. The language used is a high Hellenistic Greek, no longer the beautiful flowing demotic of the narrative gospels or the spell of Paul's flourishing letters. It has the rhetorical elegance and breadth of lexicon of a classical grammarian from Alexandria.[3]

The elegant exegesis of the Old versus the New Testament has in Jews a different tone of Alexandrian reason and identification with the author's presumed Jewish fathers, which stands in contrast to the diatribe in the disputed Pauline letters and many passages in the gospels. The latter are of later composition, in which the Jews, depicted as alien enemies plotting against a Jew-free Jesus movement, are demonized as killers of their prophets and savior. The argument against the Jews is carried on by citing passages, Christianized through interpretation, of the Torah.

Completely different, Paul's authentic letters follow the philosophical Greco-Roman tradition of letters—essays in epistolary form—of his contemporary Seneca and of Pliny and Cicero, whose logical arguments are part of his extended essays, carried out in the familiar first person. But that first-person passion of Paul or presumption of an epistle is scarcely present in the work of the Alexandrian apologist. His is a didactic essay or sermon in which he asserts a way to make the Hebrew Bible, seen through the Alexandrian Septuagint version, truly one with a messianic vision of a savior, better than angels, more divine than the divinely supported Moses.

Composed before the gospels presented a picture of Jesus's actual life prior to the crucifixion (although the dating is up in the air), Jews, like the Pauline letters, concentrates on the suffering savior, who is from the Jews and now the hero of Messianic Jews like himself who labor for a way to faith and salvation. In all these letters of persuasion, there is an intellectual and spiritual struggle for control of the sundry Jewish movements. As Gabriel Josipovici notes, these conflicts led each of the diverse Jewish sects to attempt "to gain control of the interpretation of Scripture. Pharisees, Sadducees, Essenes and Christians were all firmly convinced and bent on convincing others of their views."[4] The author's long elegant essay-poem attempts to make his Jews, and his word to them, prevail.

3. For a reading "superior to the angels" of Jews, see Josipovici, "Epistle to the Hebrews and the Catholic Epistles."

4. Josipovici, "Epistle to the Hebrews and the Catholic Epistles," 510.

All books in the New Testament, except the cosmic Revelation and learned Jews, regularly cite the Hebrew Bible, usually Isaiah and Psalms, to validate Christ as the foretold messiah. At the same time they demean the Old Testament's "inferior" message. By contrast, the author of Jews generously returns to Genesis and the Psalms with clear adoration. And God, rather than Jesus, is the main divine actor on the stage, almost completely through more than the first half of the sermon, which is unique in the books of the New Testament. Where Jesus is prominent, he is not a divinity in heaven but the high messianic and immortal priest on earth, selected by Aaron, which is again a revolutionary change in emphasis. As Jews progresses, Jesus's leading role is to show how the new covenant with God (New Testament) supersedes the old covenant and Jesus is the mediator to bring this truth into being. It is not that the anonymous gentleman from Alexandria has embraced the pagan freedom of C. P. Cavafy or the earlier detachment from the world of Neoplatonic Philo the Jew, who set the steps of ascension for later Plotinos and the European mystics to spiritual oneness with sun or divinity found within themselves. His New Testament messiah does embrace the desolation and blazing punishment for sin as a weapon for not selecting the stimulation of love for good deeds. Here his otherwise individualistic messianism coincides, not with Paul, but with the gospels' evocation of Sodom and Gomorrah and endless grinding of teeth for the faithless and the wicked. In keeping with the other epistlers, however, the anonymous author has no inkling of the gospel life of Jesus, though his writing may have coincided with that of the gospels. However, if he composed his letter as early as 70 C.E., which is the early speculative date of composition, then Mark's writings could not have been known to him. But apparently there were no contemporary extant intertestamental scriptures from Alexandria that convey the astonishing narratives of the gospels from which he might have drawn another view of the messiah.

As a Christian Jew, steeped like Paul in Platonist notions of eternity, this first Messianic exegete of the Hebrew Bible prepares the way for the study of one full Bible, which will contain both covenants with equality rather than selective praise and scorn. A century later, such study will truly be possible—and inequalities will prevail—when the second covenant is fully composed and assembled in the first edition of the New Testament, around 150 C.E. "First edition" means only that no new scriptures are being considered after that date, but fierce squabbling over the proper canon and even over whether strange books like Revelation have a place will continue until the late fourth century, and the entire New Testament will not become official until the first five years of the sixth century.

The author of Jews is also a fervid apologist for the emerging Jesus movement. He takes a lovely mythical moment in the tale of Abram (before God made him Abraham), and incredulously turns the obscure and undeveloped figure of Melchizedek into a full-blown prefiguration of Jesus Christ. In this way the anonymous erudite grammarian once again follows the needlessly justificatory practice of looking hard and wishfully at Hebrew Bible scripture, through Septuagint translation, to prove the presence of the messiah. In the instance of Jews the focus is on a few verses in Genesis and a verse in Psalms.

Jews was composed in Alexandria, where in response to the Gnostic philosophers' biblical exegesis there appears the next Christian exegete, the Alexandrian Origen (185?–254?), whose threefold interpretation of scripture (literal, ethical, and allegorical) gained him the reputation as the first and most significant Christian textual critic. His *Hexapla* is a critical edition of six Hebrew and two Greek versions of the Bible. But in the history of textual criticism, all later Christian scholarly interpretation of the Bible, including that of Origen and Augustine, finds its origin in anonymous Jews. In Jews the division between literary creation and its commentary breaks down, for the work is both. We must wait till Kafka (1883–1924) and Borges (1899–1986) to find equally brilliant genre-breakers whose story is commentary and commentary, story.

Note that Jews has no typical Pauline salutation to a specific person or audience and ends as a written exhortation. But somehow Jews, which was said to be by Paul, found itself among the accepted epistles. Had Jews not carried its earlier Pauline attribution, it would not have made it into the canon. Therefore, we should be grateful for an earlier misattribution of authorship. But once it lost Paul's powerful name, Jews became homeless. It sank to the "anonymous," a hurtful epithet for finding its place as a signal book in the covenant. How can there be groupies around Saint Anonymous? At the same time, "anonymous" is an accurate and perfect name for this learned poetic sermon. While all the other books claim personal authorship, the one certain name is that of Paul for seven letters, if Philemon is included. The remaining books in the New Testament are pseudepigraphical—that is, the books possess authorial names added later to gain prestige and a more likely place in the canon.

We know the telling place of the composition of Jews: for most of the other books, the place of composition is a guess. We also know the approximate period of its composition and the prevailing winds that shape its philosophy. Indeed, we seem to have more factual information about Jews and its place in the history of religious and intellectual thought than we do for other volumes in the canon. It may be good to remember that even the sacred names of Homer and Isaiah are at once vital and uncertain. We have their work. Why ask for more?[5] And names aside, nameless Jews is a unique, undeclared, and secret achievement of the New Testament.

5. William Shakespeare, pioneer of language theory, rescues us again. Juliet says, "What's in a name? That which we call a rose / By any other name would smell as sweet." *Romeo and Juliet,* II, ii, 1–2.

Chapter 1

The son is superior to angels[6]

Long ago and in many ways God spoke
To our fathers[7] by the prophets, but now
2In these last days he spoke to us by his son
Whom he appointed heir of everything,
By whom he also made the worlds. 3The son
As brightness of his glory and the exact
Impression of his person upholds all
By word of power. When he had made us pure
From sins, he sat down at the right hand of
The majesty on high. 4He is superior
To angels since the name that he inherited
Is further excellent than theirs. 5To which
One of his angels did God say in Psalms?[8]

You are my son.
Today have I become your father?[9]

---

6. The "son" in Hebrew is taken as "Christ," who, the author says, is superior to the angels, who only serve. The author correctly goes back to the original meaning of "angel," which was to carry the word of God, and not, like the son, to carry the majesty of office.

The Greek word "angel" is ἄγγελος (angelos), meaning a "celestial messenger," while the word "apostle" ἀπόστολος (apostolos) means an "earthly messenger," or in Paul's time a modest "missionary." In the later church, *apostolos* took on robes and pomp, and the iconic title "apostle" signified the highest office of spiritual and patriarchal authority and no longer the lowly place of messenger. It is hard to remember that once angels and apostles were God's service messengers of sky and earth.

7. Or ancestors. From the first sentence, the author identifies himself as a descendant of the Jews.

8. The author's source is often the Greek Septuagint translation of the Hebrew Bible, as in the following notes.

9. Ps. 2.7.

or again,

> I will be his father
> And he will be a son to me?[10]

6And once more, when he brings his first-born to the world, he says in Deuteronomy:

> And let all of God's angels worship him.[11]

7Of the angels he says in Psalms:

> He makes his angels into winds
> And his servants into flame of fire.[12]

8And to the son he says in Psalms:

> Your throne, O God, is from aeon to aeon,

and:

> And the scepter of goodness is the scepter
> Of the kingdom.
> 9You loved the good and hated lawlessness
> And so God, your God, anointed you
> With the oil of happiness, beyond your companions.[13]

10And:

> In the beginning, lord, you laid the foundation
> And the skies are the work of your hands.
> 11They will perish, but you remain,
> And they will all like a garment grow old,[14]
> 12And like a robe you will roll them up,
> And like a garment they will be changed
> But you will remain the same,
> And your years will not come to an end.[15]

13But to which of the angels has he ever said:

---

10. 2 Sam. 7.14.

11. Deut. 32.43 (Septuagint).

12. Ps. 104.4 (Septuagint).

13. Ps. 45.6–7.

14. Wear out.

15. Ps. 102.25–27 (Septuagint).

Sit at my right hand
Until I make your enemies into a footstool
For your feet?[16]

14Are all angels not ministering spirits sent out for divine service for those who are about to inherit salvation?

Chapter 2

Hear the word

Because of this, we must pay more attention to what we have heard, lest we slip away from it. 2So if the word spoken by the angel was certain,[17] then every transgression and disobedience got its just punishment. 3How can we escape if we neglect so great a salvation? This began when it was received through God, and those who heard confirmed it. 4God adds his testimony with signs and wonders and various miracles and by gifts of the holy spirit, distributed according to his will.

Yeshua made like his brothers

5God did not subject the coming world, of which we speak, to angels.[18]
6To this someone has testified, saying in Psalms:
What is a person that you remember him,
or the son of a man that you care about him?
7You have made him for a short time lower than angels,
placing a wreath of glory and honor on him,
and put everything under his feet.[19]
8Now in subjecting everything under his feet, God left nothing beyond human control. As it is now, we do not see everything in subjugation to

---

16. Ps. 110.1.

17. The Mosaic law.

18. The angels fly high, and Jesus is low on earth when taking care of people, but he, not the angels, offers the key to redemption.

19. Ps. 8.4–6 (Septuagint).

him, but we do see Yeshua,[20] 9who for a short time was made lower than angels, and because of the suffering of death he wears the wreath of glory and honor so that by the grace of God he should taste death for all of us.[21]

10It was right for him, through whom and for whom all things are, to bring many children to glory, and make the author of their salvation perfect through his sufferings. 11The one who sanctified and the one who is sanctified all have one father. So Yeshua is not ashamed to call them brothers, 12as it says in Psalms:

> I will proclaim your name to my brothers
> And in the midst of the congregation I will sing hymns to you.[22]

13And again in Yeshayahu:[23]

> I will put my confidence in him,

and again,

> Look, here I am again with my children,
> Whom God gave me.[24]

14Since children have shared Yeshua's blood and flesh, so he likewise shares theirs so that through death he might destroy the one having dominion over death, who is the devil, 15and free all those who are held

---

20. "Jesus" is from the Greek Ἰησοῦς (Iesous), a later form of the Hebrew יְהוֹשֻׁעַ (yehoshua).

21. The notion "and because of the suffering of death he wears the wreath of glory and honor so that by the grace of God he should taste death for all of us" may not seem common, yet making Jesus's death one directed by the grace of God for all of us seems clearly to justify and redeem Judas, who consciously, if unhappily, follows Jesus's orders to denounce him for the greater good as stated in Ireneaus of Lyons's *Against the Heresies* and in the newly published *Gospel of Judas*, edited by Rodolphe Kasser et al. (Washington, DC: National Geographic, 2008). What follows further confirms this view of Jesus's earthly death as helpful to the seed of Abraham, meaning specifically the Jews, since all the early Christians deemed themselves the enlightened Jews, and in a larger sense, we can project, all of later Abrahamic religions.

22. Ps. 22.22.

23. Isaiah from the Greek Ἡσαΐας (Esaias), from the Hebrew יְשַׁעְיָהוּ (yeshayahu).

24. Isa. 8.17–18.

in slavery by the fear of death.²⁵ ₁₆Clearly, he did not come to help the angels, but to help the seed²⁶ of Avraham.²⁷ ₁₇So he had to be made like his brothers in every way so that he might become the faithful high priest for all that concerns God, and to expiate the sins of the people. ₁₈Because he himself suffered through trial, he is able to help those who undergo trial.

Chapter 3

Moshe built the house, God built all

Therefore, holy brothers, partners in a heavenly calling, consider that Yeshua, the messenger²⁸ and high priest of our confession, ₂was faithful to the one who made him just as Moshe²⁹ was faithful [to all of God's house].³⁰ ₃Yet Yeshua is worthy of greater glory than Moshe just as the builder of the house has more honor than the house.

₄Each house is built by someone, but he who
Built everything is God. ₅Moshe was faithful
Throughout his house, a servant to testify

---

25. The author speaks about those who are condemned to the slavery of fearing death and God or Yeshua who sets them free. The metaphor of slavery of fear is meant to evoke the worst of human conditions, demonstrating, one should think, that slavery itself is a wicked human fate. Yet Paul and the author of this letter to the Hebrews and the later church exhort, in the word and name of the savior, the slave to obey and please the master and, should a slave escape the lawful master, to return and make up for the losses borne by the master during the slave's absence. It is baffling why the church, as a guardian of morality, did not condemn slavery, without reservation, and act vigorously upon that judgment. Yet there was no crossover from the horror of slavery as a metaphorical figure in the mind to its actual daily presence.

26. Descendants.

27. Abraham from the Greek Ἀβραάμ (Abraam), from the Hebrew אַבְרָהָם (avraham).

28. Or apostle.

29. Moses from the Greek Μωϋσῆς (Moyses), from the Hebrew מֹשֶׁה (moshe).

30. Not in earliest manuscripts.

To things that would be spoken about later,
6But Mashiah[31] was the faithful son over
His house. We are his house, if we conserve
Our courage and the pride that is of hope.
7So as the holy spirit says in Psalms:
Today if you hear his voice, 8do not harden your hearts
As you did in the time of rebellion
As in the day of the trial in the desert
9When your fathers[32] put me to the test
Though they saw my works for forty years.
10So I was angry with this generation,
And I said, "They always go astray in their hearts
And they do not understand my ways."
11And in my anger I swore:
"They will not come into my rest."[33]

12See, brothers, that none of you has a cunning heart of disbelief that turns away from the living God. 13Encourage each other every day while it is still called today so that none of you may be hardened by the beguilement of sin. 14We have become partners in the Mashiah, if we only can keep our original conviction until the end. 15As it is said in Psalms:

Today if you hear his voice, do not harden your hearts
As you did in the time of rebellion.[34]

16Who heard and rebelled? Was it not all those who went out of Egypt led by Moshe? 17And with whom he[35] was angry for forty years? Was it

---

31. "Christ" is from the Greek Χριστος (Hristos), and Greek *Hristos* or *Christos* is a translation from the Greek Μεσσίας (Messias), from the Hebrew מָשִׁיחַ (mashiah).

32. Ancestors.

33. Ps. 95.7–11 (Septuagint). In the psalm the speaker is God. "Rest" may be thought of as the place in Canaan, and ultimately in God's heaven where on the seventh day God rests.

34. Ps. 95.7–8 (Septuagint).

35. God.

not those who sinned, whose "dead bodies fell in the desert"?[36] 18And against whom did he swear that they would never come into his rest, if not the disbelievers? 19And we see that they never came into peace because of their disbelief.

Chapter 4

Rest and the seventh day

We should be afraid that while the promise to come into his rest is still open, any of you may be judged to have fallen short of it. 2We also received the good news as the others did, but the word they heard did them no good, since they were not united in faith with those who heard. 3We who believe come into rest. As said in Psalms,

> And in my anger I swore:
> "They will not come into my rest."[37]

Yet his works had been done since the beginning of the world. 4And it said somewhere[38] concerning the seventh day:

> And on the seventh day God rested from all his labors.

5And in this place again, "They will not come into my rest." 6Since it remains open for someone to come into it, and those of an earlier time who received the good news failed to enter because of disobedience, 7again he sets a certain day, and saying again in David's Psalm what was said before:

> Today if you hear his voice, do not harden your hearts.[39]

---

36. Num. 14.29.

37. Ps. 95.11 (Septuagint).

38. Gen. 2.2. The vagueness of "somewhere" is inexplicable, perhaps ironic, since the line in Genesis is perhaps the most familiar passage in Torah, which is the first creation story.

39. Ps. 95.7–9 (Septuagint).

Yeshua after the battle of Yeriho[40]

8While Yeshua[41] gave them a place to rest, he would not have spoken of another day after that.[42] 9But there remains a Shabbat[43] for the people of God. 10One who enters God's rest also ceases from one's own labors as God did from his own. 11So let us make every effort to come into that rest so that we do not tumble into that same example of disobedience.

---

40. Jericho from Greek Ἰεριχώ (Ieriho), from Hebrew יְרִיחוֹ (yeriho).

41. Joshua. The name for Joshua of Jericho and Jesus of Nazareth is one and the same in Hebrew (Yeshua) and in Greek (Iesous). In English the two Yeshuas should also carry the same name, whether it is Yeshua (Hebrew), Jesus (Latin through the Greek), or Joshua (Elizabethan). Elsewhere, we have the Jacob-versus-James controversy, of how one Hebrew Yaakov leaps into English as both the patriarch Jacob and the saint James. Composers of the Greek scriptures and translators from the Greek into the world's tongues give two names to these figures, "Joshua" for the Jewish Bible and "Jesus" for the Christian scriptures, to make Jesus unique and as one who has never appeared in the Old Testament even by name, yet always by code interpretation, as the foretold messiah. No one from the Jewish Bible carries the name "Jesus." The purge was carried out initially by authors, clerics, and scribes intent on demonizing Jews as an alien people, erasing all trace of them as the founders of Christianity (Messianism) in the source Old and New Testaments, while at the same time appropriating the aliens' Tanak, the Jewish Bible, as the Christian Bible. The writers, translators, and textual commentators have been linguistically erroneous and ethically shaky, but they achieved an enduring worldwide media success.

Harold Bloom elaborates in his pioneer *Anxiety of Influence* (New York: Oxford University Press, 1973) how major poets and artists have similarly practiced denial of the past. There is no end to the religious and authoritarian political entities that repeat the Roman model, erasing precursors by name or other revealing tags. Even the biblical Noah's Flood tale (Gen. 7–10) derives from Sumerian and Akkadian cuneiform versions of the flood story in *Gilgamesh*, including details of the raven-and-dove sighting as the craft nears land.

42. After Joshua's victory at Jericho, near the northwest shore of the Dead Sea, the Jews had an earthly resting place after their wanderings, their Sabbath, which the author will compare with the resting place in heaven for the believers.

43. Sabbath from the Greek σάββατον (sabbaton), from the Hebrew שַׁבָּת (shabbat).

God's word like a sword in mind and bone
> 12The word of God is active, lively, sharper
>> Than any two-edged sword. It cuts through till
>> Dividing soul and spirit, joints and bone
>> Marrow, and can discern the thoughts and purposes
>> Of the heart. 13There is no creature hidden
>> Before him. All are naked and exposed
>> To his eyes to whom we render our account.

Yeshua the great high priest
> 14And so we have a great high priest,44 the son
>> Of God. Let us hold fast to our conviction.
> 15We have a priest able to sympathize
>> With our frailties,45 who was in all ways tested
>> As we are without slipping into sin.
> 16Let us approach the throne of grace and go
>> With confidence so we may receive mercy
>> And come upon his grace in time of need.

Chapter 5

Work of the high priest46

Every high priest is chosen by people and appointed, for people, to do the things of God that he may offer both gifts and sacrifices for sin. 2He can deal moderately with the ignorant and gone astray, since he is

---

44. In the gospels the high priest or archpriest, ἀρχιερεύς (arhiereus), from the Hebrew כֹּהֵן גָּדוֹל (kohen gadol), signifying a great priest (a cohen), is the code for a high-placed plotting head of the despised Sanhedrin authority. However, in Hebrews the authority is Jesus himself, the high priest king of the Jews.

45. The Greek expresses this positive statement through a double negative.

46. Here the high priest described is one appointed by the people, just as was Aaron (Aaron from the Greek Ἀαρών, from the Hebrew אַהֲרֹן, *Aaron*, meaning "bringer of light"). It is astonishing that Jesus was chosen by Aaron, as opposed to being chosen by God, for the messianic position of high priest.

surrounded by weakness, 3and because of this he must offer sacrifice for his own sins and those of his people. 4And the priest does not assume this honor by himself but from being called by God just as was Aaron.[47]

Parable of the encounter of Abram with Malki-Tzedek, king of justice
5So also the Mashiah did not glorify himself in becoming a high priest, but was appointed to the one who said to him, in Psalms:
> You are my son.
> Today have I become your father.[48]

6As in another place he says, in Psalms:
> You are a priest for the ages
> By the order of Malki-Tzedek.[49]

7In the days of his flesh[50] Yeshua addressed prayers and entreaties, with loud cries and tears, to the one who could save him from death. And he was heard because of his reverent submission. 8Though he was the son he learned obedience from all that he suffered, 9and made perfect, he became to all who obey him the source of eternal salvation. 10He was designated by God as high priest according to the order of Malki-Tzedek of Shalem.

---

47. Exod. 28; Lev. 9.7.

48. Ps. 2.7.

49. Ps. 110.4. Melchizedek from the Greek Μελχισέδεκ (Melhisedek), from the Hebrew מַלְכִּי־צֶדֶק (malki-tzedek), meaning "my king is righteous or just." Melchizedek was actually the king of Salem and priest of the Most High God; also Genesis 14.18. "Salem" is from שָׁלֵם (shalem), meaning "righteous," which the author of Jews erroneously relates to שָׁלוֹם (shalom), meaning "peace." The author's etymology is close but erroneous, since the Hebrew words *shalem* and *sholem* (Salem and shalom) are *faux cousins*.

The city of Salem situated in Massachusetts was appropriately called *Shalom*, for "city of peace," at the beginning, the settlers also believing that King Melchizedek meant "King of Peace." "Salem" in Isaiah refers to ancient Jerusalem, which means "the city of peace." The *sedek* in King Melchizedek's name is Zedek, the name of the main deity worshiped in Salem who will merge with YHWH. See note 57 on 7.3.

50. While Jesus was in human form.

Milk for infants, meat for the wise

    11About him we have much to say to you
      Yet it's hard to tell you since you've become hard
      Of hearing.[51] 12While you should be teachers now,
      You still need someone to instruct you in
      The basic oracles of God. You need
      To drink milk, not eat strong meat.[52] 13Everyone
      Who lives on milk is still unacquainted with
      The word of goodness. You are an infant still
      Among us. 14Strong meat is for the mature,
      Whose wits are trained to make out good from evil.

Chapter 6

Moving toward perfection

  So let us leave the elementary things of the Mashiah and move toward perfection, and not again be laying down the foundations: repentance for dead works, faith toward God, 2the teaching of washings and the laying on of hands, the resurrection of the dead and eternal judgment. 3And this we shall do, if God permits.

Earth drinking rain and sprouting or falling into thorns

    4For men who once have known enlightenment,
      Who once have tasted the heavenly gift,
      Who once were partners with the holy spirit,
      5Who once have tasted the good word of God
      And known the powers of the coming age
      6But have collapsed, it is impossible
      For them to come into a new repentance,
      Since they are crucifying the son of God
      And making him a public spectacle.

---

51. Failing to understand.
52. Or food.

7And when the earth has drunk the coming rain
Constantly falling across it, and sprouted
A lovely plant for those who made it grow,
These men receive God's blessing. 8But if it
Sprouts thorns and thistles, then it drops to nothing,
Is nearly cursed, and waits an end in fire.

God will not forget your work

9Dear friends, we are confident of better things for you and things that belong to salvation, and we speak, 10not for an unjust God who will forget your work and the love you have shown toward his name, how you served the saints and still are tending them, 11and we desire each one of you to show the same enthusiasm toward the realization of hope until the end 12so that you do not turn dull and lazy, but to imitate those who, with faith and patience, inherit the promises.

13When God made his promise to Avraham, since he had no one greater to swear by, he swore by himself, 14saying,

I will surely bless you and in my multiplying
Multiply you.[53]

15And so Avraham, after waiting patiently, gained the promise. 16People swear by the greater person, and an oath given as confirmation puts an end to every dispute. 17In the same way, God, wishing to show even more clearly to the heirs of his promise how unchangeable was his will, guaranteed it with an oath. 18So by these two acts, the promise and the oath, there are two unchangeable things about which it is impossible for God to lie. So we who have fled into refuge may be encouraged strongly enough to seize the hope that lies before us. 19We have that hope as an anchor of the soul, sure and reliable, a hope that penetrates a curtain 20where the forerunner has raced before us. By order of Malki-Tzedek, Yeshua has become the high priest forever.

---

53. Gen. 22.16–17.

Chapter 7

Malki-Tzedek, God's appointed priest

This Malki-Tzedek, King of Shalem,[54] priest of the most lofty God, who met Avraham as he returned from the slaughter of the kings, and blessed him, 2and Avraham apportioned the king one tenth of his spoils. His name means "King of the Righteousness,"[55] and then "King of Shalem,"[56] which means "King of Peace." 3Fatherless, motherless, without genealogy, with neither a beginning nor an end of life, but made like the son of God, he remains a king eternally.[57]

Avraham the blessed inferior to Malki-Tzedek the blesser

4Consider how great this man was, to whom Avraham gave a tenth of his spoils.[58] 5And those sons of Levi[59] who assume the priestly office have a commandment in the law to collect tithes according to the law from the people, their brothers, even though they are of the loins of

---

54. Salem. See note 49 on 5.6.

55. The name Malki-Tzedek does not here have a double meaning of "King of Righteousness" and "King of Peace." It has only the first meaning, "King of Righteousness." It does not mean "King of Peace."

56. Salem. See note 49 on 5.6 on Salem and the king.

57. The king blesses Abraham ("the less is blessed by the better," 7.7, KJV), and therefore the king is greater than Abraham. Melchizedek, who is said to be a Canaanite priest king, is related perhaps to a Canaanite deity called Uru-Salim, who in later times merged with Yahweh.

The mysterious king is depicted virtually on the level of the son, without death, and even more strangely without genealogy. This follows the Bible verses, which give no information on Melchizedek's birth, death, or parenthood. Precisely because there are but two brief references to Melchizedek, in Genesis 14 and Psalm 110, the author of Hebrews determines that the King of Peace (should be "Righteousness") is, like Christ, divine. More, the king is depicted as an earlier incarnation or icon of the messiah manifested to Abraham during their encounter after the battle. Other legends have Melchizedek as an early king of Jerusalem before the arrival of the Jews.

58. Spoils or booty of war.

59. Descendants of Levi.

Avraham. 6But this man, who does not have ancestry from them,[60] yet has received tithes from Avraham, and he blessed him who has the promises.[61] 7Beyond all argument the inferior is blessed by the superior.[62] 8In one case the tenth[63] part, the tithes, is received by men who die; in the other it goes to one of whom it is testified that he lives.[64] 9One might even say that even Levi, who received the tenths, also paid his tenths through Avraham, 10since he was still in the loins of his ancestor when Malki-Tzedek met him.

Yeshua like Malki-Tzedek

11If perfection were attainable through the Levitical priesthood,[65] through which people received the Torah,[66] what good would there be in having another priest rise according to the order of Malki-Tzedek rather than being called the order of Aaron? 12When there is a change in priesthood, there is necessarily a change in law. 13Now the one about whom we speak belongs to another tribe from which no member has ever approached the altar. 14It is clear that our lord has descended from Yehuda,[67] and in connection with that tribe Moshe said nothing about

---

60. Again, we have the "argument from absence," which is that because there is no mention of his ancestry, Melchizedek cannot have the seed of Abraham or anyone in him and is therefore immortal. It may be noted that almost all biblical figures are cited without reference to ancestry, which should, by this reasoning, confer immortality on them all.

61. The promises are God's covenantal promises.

62. Now we are informed that the king is better than Abraham for three reasons: he is of no seed and immortal; he is a reflection or image of the son of God, that is, of Jesus; and he is greater than Abraham because he, Melchizedek, blesses Abraham.

63. The tithe.

64. There is no mention of the king's death, which signifies that he is alive and that he is immortal.

65. Equated with the order of Aaron.

66. The law.

67. Judah or Judas from Greek Ἰούδας (Ioudas), from the Hebrew יְהוּדָה (yehuda). Only in the instance of Judas of Keriot is Greek Ἰούδας (Ioudas) translated as "Judas" rather than "Juda," "Judah," or "Jude," in order to make Judas, Jesus's heroic savior for the Gnostics, a unique villain by both act and name.

priests.[68] 15And it is even clearer when another priest rises in the likeness of Malki-Tzedek, 16who not by the law of the flesh[69] has become a priest but through the power of imperishable life.[70] 17For it is testified of him in Psalms:

> You are priest forever
> According to the order of Malki-Tzedek.[71]

18The former commandment is canceled because of its weakness and uselessness. 19Nothing is perfected in Torah. There is, however, a better hope by which we can draw near to God. 20And this was done with an oath. Other priests took their offices without an oath, 21but he became a priest with an oath on hearing the one who said to him:

> The lord has sworn
>   and he will not change his mind:
> "You are a priest forever."[72]

22And so Yeshua has also become the guarantee of a better covenant.

The son, the perfect, forever

23The priests became many because they were prevented by death from continuing in office. 24But because he endures into the aeons,[73] he has an unchangeable priesthood. 25He can save for all time those who come through him to God, since he lives always to intercede for them.

---

68. The suggestion in these genealogies is that Levi is not perfect because he comes down from the tribe of Aaron, brother of Moses, while the lord comes from Judah, whose person and tribe are perfect like the immortal Melchizedek, who has no earlier seed. This extended exercise in pure and impure seed is fascinating but fantastical. If Levi is impure because he is already present in the seed in Abraham's loins, does Judah not also share the same seed as Levi, since he too is there in Abraham's loins? Judah was Abraham's great-grandson in the descent from Abraham, Isaac, and Jacob, whose fourth son was Judah. These errors are frequently noted by scholars, compared to the genealogies put forth in Matthew and Luke, but in the end the imperfect descent chart serves the greater purpose of identifying the priest king with the high priest Jesus, who at the chapter's dramatic end is revealed.

69. Not by earthly law.

70. Or indestructible life.

71. Ps. 110.4.

72. Ps. 110.4.

73. Forever.

26For us it was fitting that we had a high priest, holy, blameless, separated from sinners, and higher than the skies. 27Unlike the other high priests, he has no everyday need to make sacrifices for his own sins, and then to offer sacrifices for the sins of the people. He did this once when he offered himself. 28Torah appoints as priests men who have weakness, but the word of sworn oath, which came after Torah, appoints the son perfect into the aeons.

Chapter 8

The Mashiah in a higher ministry

The main point of what we are saying is this: We have a high priest who sat down at the right hand of the majesty in the skies, 2a minister in the true tent[74] pitched by God, not by a person. 3Now every high priest

---

74. "Tent" is the literal and beautiful translation of Greek σκηνή (skene), meaning "tent." In virtually all translations of *skein*, there is an inflation of a modest object, a tent, into a sanctuary, which conveys a large structure and not at all the plain tent worthy of a desert God for a desert people. The KJV compromises, always with beauty, by saying "pitch a sanctuary or tabernacle." The word "pitch" acknowledges that *skene* refers to some kind of tent, since one cannot pitch a sanctuary or a tabernacle. The tabernacle is the wood box or case to carry the Ark of the Covenant (the Ten Commandments on stone carried by the Jews in the desert during the exodus from Egypt), and the tabernacle goes within the tent. A sanctuary may be used, uncommonly, as a case for carrying a holy object, but its evocation in modern languages is a church, temple, or mosque. The notion of setting up a church, temple, or mosque in the sky or in heaven is unfair to humble words in the Greek and its reference to a history of wandering desert Jews. The wood case or tabernacle dwells in the sukkah in commemoration of God's protection of Israel when it was wandering in the desert after escaping from Egypt. The history is that of the celebration among Christians as the Festival of the Tabernacles, coming from the Jewish holiday of Sukkot, or of the Sukkah (the object itself). Sukkah is from the Hebrew סֻכָּה (sukkah), "tent" or "shelter." Sukkot (סֻכּוֹת) or Festival of the Tabernacles (or Booths), as in חַג הַסֻּכּוֹת (hag ha-sukkot), is an eight-day celebration for the autumnal harvest, beginning on the eve of the 15th of Tishri. The sukkah is a small lean-to-like shelter in the fields. Hence in Jewish and Christian celebrations there is combined a memory of the desert trek and carrying the precious Ten Commandments on the journey, and commemoration of that journey in the autumnal harvest holiday, appropriately observed by pitching a temporary tent or lean-to in the countryside. Such ancient relics do not fit well with grandiose aspirations for a cathedral in the sky.

is appointed to offer gifts and sacrifices. It is necessary for him too to have gifts to offer. 4If he were on earth, he would not even be a priest at all, since there are priests who offer gifts in harmony with Torah. 5They serve a copy and shadow of the heavenly, as Moshe directed when he was about to pitch the tent. He warned in Exodus:

> See that you make it on the model
> of what you were shown on the mountain.75

6But Yeshua has been given a higher ministry in that he is the mediator of a better covenant, which has come about through better promises.

7If the first covenant had been without fault, there would be no place for a second one. 8It says in Yirmiyahu:76

> Look, the days are coming, the lord says,
> when I will make a new covenant with the house of Yisrael77
> and with the house of Yehuda,78
> 9Not like the covenant I made with their fathers
> on the day I took them by the hand
> to lead them out of the land of Egypt,
> Because they did not keep to my covenant
> and I put them out of mind, says the lord.
> 10This is the covenant I will make with the house of Yisrael
> after those days, says the lord,
> Putting my Torah in their mind,
> and I will write it on their hearts
> And I will be their God,
> and they will be my people,
> 11And they must not teach each neighbor79
> and each brother, saying "Know the lord,"
> Because all will know me

---

75. Exod. 25.40.

76. Jeremiah from the Greek Ἰερεμίας (Ieremias), from the Hebrew יִרְמְיָהוּ (yirmiyahu).

77. Israel from the Greek Ἰσραήλ, from the Hebrew יִשְׂרָאֵל (yisrael).

78. Judah.

79. The Greek is "citizen," too urban for a desert people.

from the small child to the greatest of them,
12For I will be merciful with the wrongdoers
and toward their sins
And I will remember their sins no longer.[80]
13When he says new, he has made the first one antiquated, and antiquated and growing old, it is close to disappearing.[81]

Chapter 9

Worship in the earthly tent
> The first covenant had rules for service in the earthly holy
> place.[82]

---

80. Jer. 31.31–34.

81. This passage is not a jeremiad, expressing doom and lamentation. It says what it says, which is that God will give a new covenant. It says nothing about how little or much of the old in that new covenant God will retain. To reason that the passage supports the notion that the first covenant (the Torah) is obsolete is, as with the immortality of the priest king Melchizedek, to surrender to "argument by absence" of information. It is crucial that here and elsewhere the author of Hebrews, in his persuasion about the new being superior to the old covenant, has been, in contrast to New Testament tenor, less defensive and belligerent, and more generously persuasive in reaching Jews to come over and Christian Jews to stick to the new movement. Especially in Alexandria, where there was enormous intellectual activity, this was a quiet period in the formative years of the Messianic movement.

In the next centuries, when Christianity has triumphed, there will be complete destruction of Gnostic and pagan (classical Greco-Roman) books, objects, and art, including the great libraries of Alexandria, for which Islam is regularly and erroneously faulted. The obliteration of classical antiquity as well as the Gnostic speculation—surfacing in large part in 1945 with the discovery at Nag Hammadi of the extensive Gnostic scriptures in Coptic translation from Greek, including the Gospel of Thomas—is, like anti-Judaism, one of the burdens of conscience that Christianity, and all religions, must bear with respect to rival faiths. Among the early Jews the "romantic" Essenes of the Dead Sea Scrolls desired nothing more than for their "children of light" to annihilate the "children of darkness" inhabitants of Jerusalem. Religious wars, from the Crusades before and after, are always ignoble.

82. Here "holy place" (literal meaning) or "sanctuary" is appropriate.

₂A tent[83] was pitched and graced with a menorah,[84]
   A table and a setting out of bread,
   And named a holy place or sanctuary.
₃Behind a second curtain was the tent,
   And named the holy of the holy places[85]
₄Behind the second curtain stood a gold
   Incense altar and ark of the covenant
   Entirely overlaid with gold. It held
   A golden jar with manna and the rod
   Of Aaron that had blossomed. And also
   The tablets of the covenant. ₅Above
   It were the keruvim[86] of glory, shading
   The seat of mercy. About all these things
   It is impossible to name each piece.

₆With these arrangements the priests always enter the first tent and perform the ceremonies. ₇But only a high priest enters once a year and not without blood offering, which he offers for his own errors and that of his people. ₈This is what the holy spirit makes clear: the way into the sanctuary has not yet been disclosed as long as the first tent[87] is still standing, ₉this is a parable of the present time, during which gifts and sacrifices are offered that cannot make the worshiper conscious of

---

83. Or sukkoh.

84. A seven-branched candelabrum symbolizing the seven days of the creation. Normally translated "lampstand" from the Greek λυχνία (lyhnia), from the Hebrew מְנוֹרָה (menorah).

85. Here the word *skene* for "tent" is not clear, since the area seems to be an inner sanctuary. Perhaps the original intention was to call the holy place within the holy place the tent within the tent, meaning a further curtained-off place where the ark would be protected in its gilded box.

86. Cherubim from the Greek Χερούβ (Heroub), from the Hebrew כְּרוּב (keruv), in plural form כְּרוּבִים (keruvim).

87. Or sanctuary.

perfection. 10It concerns only matters of meat and drink and various washings, regulations for the flesh until the days of the new order.

Blood of the Mashiah sealing the covenant
          11Now Mashiah has come as the high priest[88]
          By way of a greater and perfect tent

          Not made by hands, not hands of this creation,[89]
          12And not by blood of goats and bulls but through

          His unique blood. He entered once into
          The holy place to gain for us eternal

          Redemption. 13But if blood of goats and bulls
          And sprinkled ashes of a heifer hallow

          Those who have been defiled so that their flesh
          Is purified, 14how greater is the blood

          Of the Mashiah. Through eternal spirit
          He gave himself blameless to God to purify

          Our conscience far away from mere dead works
          That serve us when we worship living God.

15For this reason he is the mediator of a new covenant so that those who are called may receive the promised eternal inheritance, because by means of his death he redeemed the transgressions committed under the first covenant.

---

88. "Of good things to come," not in all ancient texts.
89. Or world.

Covenant and will and testament

16So where there is a will,[90] the death of the one who made the will must be established. 17A will and testament is in force only when someone dies. 18That is why even the first covenant was not in force without blood.[91] 19Therefore when Moshe told the people every commandment in accordance with Torah, he took the blood of bulls and goats, with water and red wool and hyssop, and sprinkled the scroll and all the people, 20saying in Exodus:

> This is the blood of the covenant that God
>   has commanded you to keep.[92]

21And in the same way he sprinkled blood on the tent and all the vessels used in eating and worship. 22So under the law everything was purified. But without shedding of blood there is no remission of sins.

> 23While patterns of our earthly things
> Are purified in the heavens by these means,
>   The heavenly things in the skies
> Are purified with greater sacrifices.
>   24And the Mashiah did not enter
> The sanctuary of holy tents that human hands
>   Once raised by human hands, for they're
> Mere copies of true things, but he entered
>   Into the heavens to appear
> Before the face of God for us, 25and not
>   To offer himself once again

---

90. The Greek word διαθήκη (diatheke) had two meanings: "covenant" and "last will and testament," or simply "will." In the New Covenant the normal meaning of *diatheke* is "covenant," going back to Hebrew *b'rit*, meaning "covenant" or "pact" or "agreement," as between God and Abraham. In some moments, as in 9.16, the author chooses to use *diatheke* to signify "will," and he plays with the double meaning, going back and forth in his elegant style. It is this dual meaning, however, that led Jerome to translate *diatheke* into Latin uniquely as *testamentum*, erroneously, since the dominant meaning is that of an agreement, a pact, or covenant.

91. Here, the author has switched back to the covenantal meaning of *diatheke*.

92. Exod. 24.8. The larger context and the language of these lines appear in the first verses of Exodus. This line also will appear later in Psalms 50.5 and in almost the exact words in Matthew 26.28, which, like the passage in Hebrews, come from Exodus.

As the high priest enters the holy place
    Year after year with blood belonging
To another. 26Then he would have had to suffer
    Over and over and once again
Since the foundation of the world. Now at
    The ending of an age he's come
Appearing through his sacrifice to free it
    Of errors. 27He's been appointed
To die for mortals once, and after that
    Will come the judgment. 28Offered once
To bear away the sins of many, in
    His second coming no longer
Will the Mashiah cope with sin through blood
    But simply save the souls of those
Who wait for him eager for their salvation.

Chapter 10

The Mashiah speaks in David's voice[93]

Since Torah law possesses only the shadow of good things to come, not the actual image, even after the constantly offered year after year sacrifices it can never offer perfection to those who come to it. 2Otherwise, would the people not cease being offered perfection, since were they truly cleansed once and for all, would these worshipers still be aware of sin? 3Rather, in these sacrifices persists the yearly remembrance of sin. 4It is impossible for the blood of bulls and goats to wash away sins.

    5So coming into this world the Mashiah says, citing the psalm:
    You did not want sacrifice and offering
        But a body you prepared for me.
    6Whole burnt offerings even for sin you did not enjoy.
        7Then I said,
    "Look, I have come to do your will, O God!"

---

93. In Psalm 40, David speaks to God.

In a book scroll this is written of me.[94]

8And while he said above that you did not want nor enjoy sacrifices and offerings and whole burnt offerings even for sin, offered according to Torah, 9then he said, "Look, I come to do your will." He abolishes the first so that the second may stand. 10And by his will we are made holy through the offering of the body of Yeshua the Mashiah, once and for all.

11Every priest stands day by day at his service and often offering sacrifices, which are never able to remove sins. 12But when the Mashiah offered for all time a single sacrifice of sin, he sat down at the right hand of God, 13waiting until his enemies are made a footstool for his feet.[95] 14With one offering he made the holy perfected forever.

15And the holy spirit also testifies to us, saying in Yirmiyahu:[96]

16After those days this is the covenant I will make with them,
Says the lord:
I will put Torah laws in their hearts,
And write them in their minds,

17and adds:

And their sins and lawlessness I will remember no longer.[97]

18Where these things are forgiven, there is no longer an offering for sin.

Beware of punishment for trampling down the son's word

19So my brothers, since we feel confident about entrance into the sanctuary by the blood of Yeshua, 20by a new and living way opened for us through the curtain, that is, his flesh, 21since we have a great priest over the house of God, 22let us approach with a true heart and full confidence of faith, and with our hearts purged of cunning conscience and our bodies washed with pure water. 23Let us hold fast to the confession of our hope, without wavering, for he who gave his promise is trustworthy.

---

94. Ps. 40.6–8. In this typically extraordinary segment of a psalm attributed to David, through Christian interpretation the messiah sings through David's voice.

95. Allusion to Psalm 110.1.

96. Jeremiah.

97. Jer. 31.33–34. It is the lord himself, rather than the holy spirit, in Jeremiah who makes this declaration.

24And let us study each other to stimulate love and good works, 25not neglecting to meet together, as some do, but encouraging one another all the more as you see that the day is drawing nearer.

26When we willingly sin after we have received the full knowledge of truth, there is no longer a sacrifice for sins, 27but a terrible expectation of judgment and a blazing fire about to consume the opponents. 28Anyone who has violated the law of Moshe's Torah, on the basis of two or three witnesses, dies. 29How much worse do you think the cost of the punishment will be for those who have trampled down the son of God, called unclean the blood of the covenant by which he was made holy, and outraged the spirit of grace? 30We know the one[98] who said in Deuteronomy:

> Vengeance is mine and I will repay.[99]

and again:

> The lord will judge his people.[100]

31It is a dreadful thing to fall into the hands of the living God.

Remember when you knew the light

32Remember the earlier days, when you the enlightened, how you endured a hard struggle with suffering. 33Sometimes you were publicly exposed to revilement and persecutions, and sometimes you were partners of those who were so maltreated. 34You sympathized with the prisoners and you cheerfully accepted the seizing of your possessions, knowing that you had a better possession and more lasting. 35Do not throw away, then, your confidence, which has great reward. 36You need patience so that when you have the will of God, you may receive the promise. For it is written in Habakkuk:

> 37In a short short while
> the one coming will come and not delay.
> 38My good ones will live by faith,
> but if one draws back, my soul is not pleased.

---

98. Moses in "The Song of Moses."
99. Deut. 32.35.
100. Deut. 32.36.

39But we are not among those who falter and flounder into destruction, but with those of faith who save the soul.

Chapter 11

History of faith

Now faith is the substance of things hoped for,
The evidence of things unseen. 2Through this
The elders have obtained a good report.
3By faith we understand the world was framed
By word of God so what is seen is made
From the invisible. 4By faith Abel
Offered God greater sacrifice than Kayin.[101]
Through this he was proved good, and God bore witness
To Abel's gifts. He died yet speaks. 5By faith
Hanoh[102] was translated high up so not
To see his death. He wasn't found since God
Translated him, a proof that he pleased God.

6And without faith it is impossible
To please him. One who goes to God believes
That he exists and he awards the seeker.
7By faith Noah was warned about events
Unseen, received the warning, built the ark
To save his household. He condemned the world
By such an act, inherited the good
That comes through faith. 8By faith Avraham
Obeyed when he was called to voyage into
A place where he'd obtain some promised land.
He traveled to that region, was unknowing
Where he journeyed to. 9By faith he sojourned

---

101. Cain from the Greek Κάϊν (Kain), from the Hebrew קַיִן (kayin).
102. Enoch from the Greek Ἐνώχ (Henoh), from the Hebrew חֲנוֹךְ (hanoh).

In the land of promise, a stranger in
A foreign country, lived in tents with Yitzhak[103]
And Yaakov,[104] who were heirs of that same promise.
10He looked for a city that had foundations
Whose architect and builder was his God.
11By faith Sarah, a barren woman, found
Strength to give birth, though past her time in life
Since she believed the one who promised her.
12So from one man,[105] and he long dead, came his
Descendants numerous as the celestial stars
In multitudes, and as innumerable sands
Along the edge of the sea.[106] 13All these died
In faith without winning the promises,
But seeing them far off they were persuaded
To embrace them,[107] and confessed that they were strangers
And exiles[108] on the earth. 14And they who say
These things declare with clarity they seek
A country. 15If they had recalled the land
From which they came, they'd have had time

---

103. Isaac from the Greek Ἰσαάκ (Isaak), from the Hebrew יִצְחָק (yitzhak), meaning "he will laugh."

104. James from the Greek Ἰάκωβ (Iakob), from the Hebrew יַעֲקֹב (yaakov).

105. There is a grace reserved for this letter to the Hebrews in its original presenta-
tions. While it describes Abraham as the father of countless generations, albeit dying
without the promise, the text does, in keeping with its primary celebration of faith,
praise Sarah for faith by which she overcame natural age. No other book of the New
Testament so celebrates the scope, primal beauty, and passions of generations in legendary Genesis and moreover cites the Hebrew Bible for poignant examples of celebrated faith. Most New Testament citations from the Hebrew Bible, which appear on
virtually every page, include a line or two from Deuteronomy, Psalms, or the prophets
to justify a messianic truth or a moral pitfall. Hebrews re-creates a mythical period,
land, and its parabolic figures who are the foundation of the Bible.

106. See Genesis 22.17 for these images of stars and sea.

107. "Them" seems to refer to the heavenly realities of the promises.

108. Or visitors.

For a return. 16But they longed for better
Country, for a heavenly land where God
Is not ashamed at being called their God,
And for them he has made ready a city.

17By faith Avraham when tested offered
Yitzhak, and he had even received promises
Offered his only son. 18Of him he said:
In Yitzhak will your seed be named.[109] 19He thought
That God might even raise the dead, and he
Symbolically took Yitzhak home from death.
20By faith Yitzhak blessed future Yaakov and
Esav,[110] 21and by faith dying Yaakov blessed
Each of his sons, and prayed for them leaning
Upon the top of his staff. 22By faith Yosef,[111]
When he was dying, mentioned the departing
Children of Yisrael, giving his commandments
Concerning his bones.[112] 23By faith when Moshe
Was born his parents hid him for three months
Because they saw the beautiful child and were not
Afraid of the king's edict.[113] 24By faith Moshe
Refused to be called the son of Pharaoh's daughter.
25Rather, he chose to be maltreated with
His people than to enjoy pleasures of sin
For a season,[114] 26and esteemed Mashiah's

---

109. Gen. 21.12. "Named" in the sense that through his name "Isaac" his descendants will be named and known.

110. Esau from the Greek Ἠσαῦ (Esau), from the Hebrew עֵשָׂו (esav). Esau was Jacob's brother.

111. Joseph from the Greek Ἰωσήφ (Iosef), from the Hebrew יוֹסֵף (yosef).

112. His burial.

113. To kill all Jewish male infants at birth by throwing them into the Nile, a task to be done by the midwives. See Exodus 2.1–10.

114. These good thoughts are not recorded in Exodus 2.11–15, the references usually given as the source for this passage in Hebrews. Rather, Moses kills an Egyptian who is beating a Jew, and when the Pharaoh is informed, he tries to kill Moses, who

Reproach greater than the rich treasures of Egypt,
And he thought also of his own reward.[115]
27By faith he left Egypt, not fearing anger
Of the king, 28and he endured as though he saw
The invisible. By faith he observed Pesach[116]
And sprinkling of blood[117] so the destroyer could
Not touch Yisrael's first-born. 29By faith they went
Through the Red Sea[118] as across a dry land,
And when the Egyptians tried to do so they
Were drowned.[119] 30By faith the walls of Yeriho[120]
Fell after they had been encircled seven
Days.[121] 31By faith the harlot Rahav[122] did not
Perish with those who disobeyed. She welcomed
The spies with peace.[123] 32And what more should I say?
My time would fail me to tell you of Gideon,[124]

---

flees to Midian. Later Moses returns with God-given powers of the magician to bring plagues on Egypt unless the Pharaoh agrees to let the Jews leave the country.

115. The idea that Moses chooses to renounce Egyptian treasures because he fears Christ's reproach, and looks for his reward from the messiah (an earthly leader as later conceived by Jews in Isaiah and Psalms, or the son of God as later understood by Christians), is not supported in words found in Exodus.

116. *Pesach* is Passover from Greek πάσχα (pasha), from the Hebrew פֶּסַח (pesach), to pass over, referring to the escape from bondage in Egypt. Pesach is celebrated at the Seder by eating the paschal lamb. See Exodus 12.1–13.16.

117. On the lintels and the doorposts.

118. The Reed Sea or Sea of Marshes.

119. Exod. 14.

120. Jericho.

121. Josh. 6.

122. Rahab from the Greek Ῥαάβ (Raab), from the Hebrew רָחָב (rahav).

123. Josh. 2.1, 6.17. The spies are Jews sent as scouts "to view the land" for Joshua's later siege of the city, and Rahab protects them, unwilling to reveal them to the local king. In Matthew 1.5 she is counted as one of Jesus's ancestors, praised for her living faith.

124. Gideon from the Greek Γεδεών (Gedeon), from the Hebrew גִּדְעוֹן (gidon or gideon).

Of Barak, of Shimshon,[125] of Yiftah,[126] and
Both David and Shmuel,[127] and prophets, 33who
By faith conquered the kingdoms and performed
The good, got promises, shut lions' mouths
34And quenched the power of fire, escaped the edge
Of swords,[128] were strengthened out of weakness, were
Fearful in war, routed the enemy
And all their armies. 35Women found their dead
Resurrected. Others were tortured to death,
Refusing to accept deliverance
So they would find a better resurrection.
36Others went through the test of mockery
And scourging, and still others were in bonds
And prison. 37They were stoned to death,[129] died by
The sword. They walked around in sheepskins, walked
In goatskins, destitute, oppressed, tormented.
38And the world wasn't worthy of them. They
Wandered in deserts, in the mountains, caves,
Holes in the ground. 39And all of them, though they
Were given good report through faith, did not
Receive the promise. 40God foresaw something
Better: Those who are far from us be perfect.[130]

---

125. Samson from the Greek Σαμψών (Sampson), from the Hebrew שִׁמְשׁוֹן (shimshon).

126. Jephthah from the Greek Ἰεφθάε (Iefthae), from the Hebrew יִפְתָּח (yiftah).

127. Samuel from the Greek Σαμουήλ (Samouel), from the Hebrew שְׁמוּאֵל (shmuel).

128. Others give "edges," but the Greek gives "mouth" as in being devoured by a beast, and so the Greek metaphor stands.

129. "Sawn in two," but not in all ancient manuscripts.

130. The early figures were faithful to the promises of God. Now fulfillment or perfection will come through something more complete, which is redemption through Jesus Christ.

Here, unlike elsewhere in the New Testament, Jesus Christ has not become the single figure of divinity in terms of action, presence, relationship with humanity,

Chapter 12

Yeshua enduring in the world

Therefore, surrounded by a cloud of witnesses, let us also put aside every obstacle and the sin that easily ensnares, and with endurance let us run the race that lies before us. 2Let us fix our look at the founder and perfect Yeshua, who instead of joy that was set before him endured the cross, and despised shame, and who has taken his seat at the right hand of the throne of God.[131] 3Think of him who endured such great rebellion by sinners against himself so that you may not falter and weaken in your spirit.

Disciplining sons for them not to be bastards

4In your struggle against sinfulness, you have not resorted to shedding blood, 5and have forgotten the appeals that speak to you as children:

My son, do not look lightly on the lord's discipline,
 and do not lose heart when you are punished by him.
6Whom the God loves he disciplines,
 and he whips every son he receives.

---

fulfillment, and redemption or salvation. God is the highest figure. Until this point God has remained the main actor. In the remaining portion, Jesus gains his place, at least in part, found totally in the other books of the New Testament. God is God but works through his son, who in terms of attention and use of given powers, though not rank, predominates. God does not endure the cross. That is the suffering labor of his son, who does it in the street, not in the sky. The singular distinction between later Judaism and Christianity centers on the role of the Jewish messiah, who is common to both religions. In Judaism the messiah has not yet appeared, and when he comes he will free and lead nations, as a human. In Christianity the Jewish rabbi messiah (who will soon change ethnicity and sect) is the divine son of God and in God.

131. Though Christ is determined to be in God and to emanate from God, by his presence as a separate figure on earth on the cross, and in heaven at the right hand of God, whatever the symbolism or theological and Christological understanding that makes these two figures one God, their presences preside in people and in literatures as two figures from a common source. While the son has a thousand faces, God the father has by definition no knowable or known face.

7Put up with discipline. Where is there a son whom a parent does not discipline? 8If you go on with no discipline that all are born to share, you are bastards, not sons. 9Also, we had parents of the flesh to discipline us, and we respected them. Should we not be willing to submit further to the father of spirits and live? 10The others disciplined us for a few days according to what seemed right to them, but he does it for our good so we can participate in his holiness. 11All discipline for now does not seem pleasant but painful, but later, to those who have endured it, it brings the fruit of peace.

Hear and see: our God is a consuming fire

    12So, restore your weak hands and feeble knees,
    13Make straight paths for your feet so that your lameness
      Does not dissuade but makes you heal it. 14Seek
      To be at peace with everyone and choose
      The holy. Without it no one sees the lord.
    15See that no one falls from the grace of God,
      That no earth root of bitterness springs up
      And troubles and defiles 16as did lewd Esav[132]
      Profane, who sold his birthright for a meal.
    17You know that later, when he wanted to
      Inherit blessing, he inherited
      Rejection, found no course left for repentance,
      Even though with tears he sought the blessing.

    18You haven't come to a mountain-high place
      That can be touched, a blazing fire, the dark
      Of gloom, a storm, 19the groan of a ram's horn,
      And sound of words that makes a hearer beg
      Not to hear words again. 20And they could not
      Endure the orders that were given them:
          If even an animal touches the mountain
          it will be stoned to death.[133]

---

132. Esau.
133. Exod. 19.12–20.

21And there appeared such a fearful thing that Moshe said:

I am terrified and tremble.[134]

22But you have come to Mount Tziyun,[135] the city

Of the living God, to the heavenly Yerushalayim,[136]

To myriads of angels, to a festival, 23and to the temple

Where the first-born have been registered in the heavens

And before the God of all and the spirits of the good made perfect,

24And to Yeshua the mediator of the New Covenant,

And to the blood sprinkled which speaks louder than the blood of Abel.

25See to it that you do not ask not to hear the one speaking.

If those who asked not to hear him did not escape him

Who warned him on earth, how much less will we escape

If we do not hear him who warns us from heaven!

26At that instant his voice shook the earth. Now he has given a promise, saying once again:

Once again I will shake not only the earth but also heaven.[137]

27The phrase "Once again" means the abolition of what cannot be shaken so that what cannot be shaken, the creation of things, remains. 28Then, taking over an unshaken kingdom, and let us have grace, through which we may please God, and do so with modesty and fear.

29Our God is a consuming fire.

---

134. Deut. 9.19.

135. Zion from the Greek Σιών (Sión), from the Hebrew צִיּוֹן (Tziyun).

136. Jerusalem from Greek Ἰερουσαλήμ (Ierousalem), from Hebrew יְרוּשָׁלַיִם (Yerushalayim).

137. Hag. 2.6 (Septuagint).

Chapter 13

Be good and love

Let love among us go on. 2Do not forget your hospitality, and take care, for without knowing it some have entertained angels.[138] 3Remember the prisoners as if you were in prison with them, the abused, as if you with there in your own body. 4Let marriage be honored and undefiled, for God condemns the fornicators and adulterers. 5Keep your life free of greed, be happy with what you have, 6for the lord said in Deuteronomy:

> I will never abandon you.
>
> I will never forsake you.[139]

and in the Psalms:

> The lord is my helper and I will not fear.
>
> What can anyone do to me?[140]

7Remember your leaders, who spoke to you the word of God, and like you consider the end of their life, imitate their faith. 8Yeshua the Mashiah yesterday and today the same and into the ages. 9Do not be carried away by strange and complex teachings.[141] It is good for the heart to be strengthened by grace not by food regulations,[142] which have not been those who walk in the street. 10We have an altar from which those who officiate in the tent must not eat. 11Concerning those animal bodies

---

138. The notion of not knowing when one is with an otherworldly being and to take care occurs in many literatures: as Odysseus in Book 1 of the *Odyssey* when he first encounters Athena disguised as a beggar; or in Genesis 18.1, when the three shadowy strangers come to Abraham with advice, and they are angels; or later in Mark 16.5–8, when the two women, Mary Magdalene and Mary mother of James, are in the empty cave where Jesus is not to be found, and a young man dressed in a white garment, an angel, informs them that he has been raised, and the women hear and rush out afraid, seized with trembling and ecstasy.

139. Deut. 31.6, 31.8.

140. Ps. 118.6 (Septuagint).

141. Reference is to Gnostics, and in Alexandria the philosophers and teachers of *gnosis*, knowledge. The Gnostics were centered in Alexandria for centuries, and hence the danger of their teachings was of utmost concern.

142. Reference is to Jewish dietary laws.

brought into the holy sanctuary by the high priest as a sacrifice for sin, the carcasses are burnt outside the camp.

Looking for the other city

12So Yeshua too, so that he might with his own blood sanctify the people, suffered outside the gate. 13So let us go out to him outside the camp and bear the abuse that he bore. 14Here the city our city will not endure but we are looking for a city that is to come. 15Through him let us offer a sacrifice of praise to God, constantly. Let it be the fruit of lips confessing his name. 16But do not forget to do good and share what you have, for such sacrifices please God.

An Orphan Ending[143]

Obey your leaders

17Obey your leaders and give way to them, for they watch over your souls and will give you an accounting. Let them do it with joy and not with groaning, for that would be unprofitable for you. 18Pray for us, for we are persuaded that we have a good conscience, and wish to act honorably in all things. 19I urge you all the more to do so that I may be restored to you soon.

Blessing

20May the God of peace, who brought back from the dead the great shepherd of sheep through the blood of the everlasting covenant, our lord Yeshua, 21make you complete with every good thing so that we may do his will and be pleasing in his sight through Yeshua the Mashiah to whom there be glory into the aeons and [aeons].[144] Amain.[145]

---

143. The last pages, beginning with verse 13.16, are the only words in this document suggesting that it may be a letter, and the epistolary conclusion is strange in the text. It is almost certainly a scribal addition to make the essay seem a personal letter of Paul's, which it fails completely in doing. It is a pity that the marvelous, impeccably styled and balanced essay or sermon is not allowed to finish after the plain call to goodness of verse 16: "But do not forget to do good and share what you have, for such sacrifices please God."

The "few words" in verse 22 is typical of the classical apologia of modesty to the reader in a letter. If taken as a letter, this work is one of the longest in the New Testament. Whatever it is called, it is a high point of thoughtful eloquence, bringing the reader and listener close to early scripture and to hope in a coming city.

144. Not in all ancient manuscripts.

145. Amen from the Greek ἀμήν (amen), from the Hebrew אָמֵן (amein).

Greetings and goodbye

22I urge you, brothers, be patient with my word of exhortation, for I have written to you in only a few words. 23Know that our brother Timotheos[146] has been released, and if he comes quickly I will see you. 24Greet all your leaders and all saints. Those from Italy send you greetings. May grace be with you all.

---

146. Timothy from the Greek Τιμόθεος (Timotheos). The reference to Timothy is suspect. Stylistically, the familiar letter ending of "it won't be long before I am set free and restored to you" from Philemon 22, in verse 19 (Paul from prison) and repeated in verse 23 (Timothy released), is improbable in the work of one who is an unflawed Alexandrian grammarian or the equivalent from Rome or an urbane setting. Unlike other letters, where Paul's intimate and trusted companion Timothy is mentioned at beginning and end, here Timothy's sudden appearance, along with the well-known news of his release, is out of place. These inserted verses in the essay-sermon are meant to establish both an epistolary form and Pauline authorship. The anticlimax should not blur the fresh splendor of the unknown author of Hebrews.

ACTS

Activities
of the
Messengers
(Acts of the Apostles)

Activities of the Messengers
(Acts of the Apostles)

LIKE THE FOUR GOSPELS, Acts is an anonymous book. It is the fifth book, sometimes called the "fifth gospel," of the New Testament in the common arrangement, and covers the first three decades of church events from after the death of Yeshua to Paul's appearance in Rome. In dynamic Rome of conflicting sects and peoples, the narrative suddenly stops, as if this well-composed book were a first large fragment of a larger story. This fifth gospel has profoundly determined succeeding attempts at reconstructing the story of Christianity, beginning with Irenaeus's *Adversus haereses I,* or *Against Heresies I* (ca. 180), and Eusebius's *Ecclesiastical History* (third to fourth century).

The actual title in Greek of this theological narrative, Πράξεις Ἀποστόλων (Praxeis apostolon), containing the word "apostle" in English translation, is misleading in that few of the apostles are prominent in Acts. The word "apostle" is also misleading in that the root meaning and usage in Greek remain simply a "messenger," an "envoy," and when the messenger carries a religious message, a "missionary." However, English "apostle" by now inevitably carries an undeniable import of richly robed ambassador, as king, patriarch, pope, rather than the modesty "slave of God," sometimes jailed, with scant funds, surviving on the borders of society. "Apostle" conveys no early Christian humility. Similarly, the English word "acts" vaguely implies either an edict or an epical act. Neither is right. Greek *praxeis* signifies "activities" or "doings." Here, reflecting the Greek, the English title is "Activities of the Messengers."

Some have suggested that the title "The Acts of the Holy Spirit" would be equally appropriate since the book shows in detail the help and guidance of the Holy Spirit in early days of the developing church. Indeed, the cast of guides to Paul is the trinity of God, Jesus, and the Holy Spirit, the latter more immediate than in any book of the New Testament. And unlike the gospels, God in his earthly presence is more significant than Yeshua. The radical difference between this fifth gospel and the earlier four is that the historical account is not about Yeshua but about a Pharisee, Shaul the tentmaker, who had not seen Jesus in the flesh, and who would be celebrated by his cognomen "Paul," and with the triumph of the church, Saint Paul.

Acts was composed after 80 C.E., and the place of composition is unknown. More significant than where it was written is its vast geography, which also tells the spread of early Christendom. It goes from Jerusalem to Samaria (8.5); someplace on the Asian seacoast (8.40); Damascus (9.10); Antioch, where the disciples meet (11.26); Asia Minor (13.13); Europe (16.11); and then Rome, where we lose track of Paul as he, relatively free and well treated, awaits trial. Acts is correctly called "colorful" and "vivid" in its narrations, from the dramatic punishment of death to Ananias and Sapphira (5.1–11), who lied about their wealth when giving the tithe, to tales of martyrdom, arrests, miraculous escape, and missionary ships on the dangerously stormy Mediterranean. It is a page turner.

By church tradition Acts is attributed to a gentile physician named Luke, who is also the author of the Gospel of Luke, and the same Luke attributes both books to Theophilus, presumably, by Hellenistic literary convention, a distinguished patron. The prologues to Theophilus are specious.[1] Acts was composed in elegant demotic Greek, with no artificial rhetorical complication of the Lukan prefaces. It is unlikely that anonymous Luke and anonymous Acts have a single authorship. The most one can say is that the author Luke was a Christian Jew and the author of Acts, a later book, is unknowable.

Luke and Acts are radically different. Luke is the life, death, and resurrection of Yeshua. Acts is about the holy trinity and Paul. Luke contains the unsurpassed poetry of the nativity scene and the parable of the prodigal son. Acts is swift activist narrative, intended as spell-binding

---

1. Luke 1–4, Acts 1.1–3.

documentary propaganda. Its earthly hero Paul becomes, at least unofficially, the thirteenth apostle.

The portrait of Paul in Acts, a third-person description, is profoundly different from the first-person Paul of the epistles. Seven of the fourteen letters attributed to Paul are genuine. They reveal the historic Paul. We have no other figure in the Bible whose person, philosophy, and events we can examine with the same authority. To know Paul of Acts and Paul of the letters provides a double perspective of Paul.

In his memoir epistles, Paul reveals all: himself, his thought, his congregation, the external competitors, and an intimate picture of the first-century Jesus movement. In the letters Paul is a systematic philosopher whose work will shape later Christian metaphysics and theology, as well as prescribed modes of social behavior. For the latter, Paul gets a bad rap. The sections where the missionary slams women, silences them at church services, orders strict obedience to husbands or absence from church administration are interpolations. They are presumably the mischief of a later Church father or scribe. More, the famous antifemale putdowns contradict passage after passage in which Paul praises his closest women friends who support him in his hardships and whom he makes deacons and apostles to "grow" the movement.

Sometimes cranky with respect to opponents, Paul's meditations and fervent pronouncements define Christ's followers, their new law as Christian Jews, and Yeshua the Mashiah's death and resurrection. The letters define the mystical body of Christ, and Paul's words on higher law and grace characterize Christian faith. Though Letters traditionally follow Acts, they precede Acts in composition by at least three decades.

In his incarnation in Acts, Paul is no longer a confessing memoirist but the main character in the first Christian novel. He is the creation of unknown authors who send him off legendarily as an implacably heroic saint figure, moving from city to city, from sea trip to shipwreck, miraculously surviving and thriving. The tale is related in thrilling, novelistic suspense.

In both Acts and Paul's letters, the missionary's end is to enlarge the community of Christian (Messianic) Jews to include gentiles (Greeks) in the new movement that has found its messiah Yeshua, through whom God acts on earth. In keeping with the widespread Platonism and Egyptian hermeticism of the time, Paul preaches the immortality of the soul, and perhaps by implication the body, which is destined to reside in heaven or hell. But while on earth, the missionary Paul is an epic and episodic hero like Odysseus. Acts is the lively story of Shaul, a Pharisee Jew, who at Damascus becomes Messianic Paul, who sets out on his holy mission of return to Rome and God in the great Odyssey of Christendom.

Chapter 1

Prologue: Yeshua risen and revealed

In the first account,[2] O Theofilos,[3] I wrote about everything that Yeshua[4] began to do and teach 2up to the day when, after instructing his chosen messengers through the holy spirit, he rose.[5] 3To them he showed himself as living after he had died, and did so with many proofs. For forty days he appeared to them and spoke to them about the kingdom of God.

In the holy spirit

4And while Yeshua stayed with them, he ordered them not to leave Yerushalayim,[6] but said,

> Wait for the father's promise that you heard
> From me. 5Whereas Yohanan[7] immersed in water,
> In a few days you will be bathed in the holy spirit.[8]

6So when they came together they asked him, saying, "Lord, is this the hour of your restoring the kingdom of Yisrael?"[9]

---

2. Word, account, narration, speech from Greek λόγος (logos), traditionally translated "book."

3. Theophilus from the Greek Θεόφιλος (Theofilos), meaning "friend of God."

4. "Jesus" is from the Greek Ἰησοῦς (Iesous), from the Aramaic יֵשׁוּעַ (Yeshua), a later form of the Hebrew יְהוֹשֻׁעַ (Yehoshua). "Christ" is from the Greek Χριστος (Hristos), and Greek Hristos or Christos is a translation from the Greek Μεσσίας (Messias), from the Hebrew מָשִׁיחַ (mashiah). "Christ" in Greek also means "the anointed," and "Messiah" in both Greek and Hebrew contains the meaning of "the anointed."

5. He ascended (to heaven).

6. Jerusalem from Greek Ἰερουσαλήμ (Ierousalem), from Hebrew יְרוּשָׁלַיִם (Yerushalayim).

7. John from Greek Ἰωάννης (Ioannes), from the Hebrew יוֹחָנָן (yohanan).

8. Breath or spirit from the Greek πνεῦμα (pneuma), meaning "breath" or "spirit," from the Hebrew רוּחַ (ruah), which also means "breath" or "spirit." The holy spirit (the Holy Ghost) is from the Greek πνεύματος ἁγίου (pneumatos hagiou), and a forced origin in the Hebrew רוּחַ הַקֹּדֶשׁ (ruah hakodesh).

9. Israel from the Greek Ἰσραήλ, from the Hebrew יִשְׂרָאֵל (yisrael).

7He said to them,

> It's not for you to know the times or seasons
> The father set through his authority,
> 8But when the holy spirit moves in you
> You will receive the power, and you will be
> My witnesses in Yerushalayim and in all Yehuda[10]
> And Shomron[11] and to the far ends of the earth.

Yeshua rises

9When he said this and as they looked, he was raised high and a cloud took him from their eyes. 10And as they stared into the sky where he went, look, two men in white clothing stood beside them.[12] 11They said, men of the Galil,[13]

> Why do you stand there gazing into the sky?
> This same Yeshua who has been taken from you
> Into the sky will come back in the same way
> That you saw him disappear beyond the clouds.

In a room upstairs in Yerushalayim

12Then they returned to Yerushalayim from the place called the Mountain of Olives, which is near Yerushalayim, a Shabbat day's walk away. 13When they were indoors they climbed to the upstairs room where they were staying. They were Shimon Kefa[14] and Yohanan, and

---

10. Judea from the Greek Ἰουδαία (Ioudaia), from the Hebrew יְהוּדָה (yehuda).

11. Samaria from the Greek Σαμάρεια (Samaria), from the Hebrew שֹׁמְרוֹן (shomron).

12. The two figures in white are apparently informing angels. See last lines of Mark.

13. Galilee from the Greek Γαλιλαία (Galilaia), from the Hebrew גָּלִיל (galil).

14. Peter. In the gospels and letters the same Peter has numerous names: Peter, Simon, and Simeon. And in John 20.6 he is "Simon Peter" from the Greek Σίμων Πέτρος (Simon Petros). In 2 Peter he is "Simeon Peter," from the Greek Συμεὼν Πέτρος (Simeon Petros). And in John 1.42 he is "Simon, the son of John," from the Greek Σίμων ὁ υἱὸς Ἰωάννου (Simon ho huios Ioannou). "Peter" means "rock" or "stone" from the Greek πέτρος, from the Aramaic כֵּיפָא (kefa), from the Hebrew כֵּף (kef), all meaning "rock" or "stone." In his letters Paul calls Peter "Cephas," from the Greek Κηφᾶς (Kefas), based on the Greek transliteration of his Aramaic name Kefa. Here I have gone back to Shimon Kefa, Peter's full Aramaic name.

Yaakov,[15] and Andreas[16] and Filippos[17] and Toma,[18] Bar Talmai[19] and Mattityahu,[20] Yaakov son of Halfai and Shimon the Zealot,[21] and Yehuda son of Yaakov. 14All were devoting themselves single-mindedly to prayer[22] along with Miryam[23] and Yeshua's brothers.[24]

Field of blood and replacing Yehuda

15And on one of those days Shimon Kefa stood up among the brothers.[25]

---

15. James from the Greek Ἰάκωβος (Iakobos), from the Hebrew יַעֲקֹב (yaakov).

16. Andrew from the Greek Ἀνδρέας (Andreas). "Andreas," like "Filippos," "Markos," and "Lukas," are Greek names used by Jews in Israel.

17. Philip from the Greek Φίλιππος (Filippos).

18. Thomas from the Greek Θωμᾶς (Thomas), from the Aramaic תְּאוֹמָא (toma), from the Hebrew תְּאוֹם, meaning "twin." In Aramaic, *Toma* means "twin," which is concordant with the notion that Thomas was a twin, perhaps Jesus's twin brother, as often asserted and often denied.

19. Bartholomew from the Greek Βαρθολομαῖος (Bartholomaios), from the Aramaic בַּר תַּלְמַי (bar talmai).

20. Matthew from the Greek Μαθθαῖοσ (Maththaios), from the Hebrew מַתִּתְיָהוּ (Mattityahu), or from the Aramaic *Mattai.*

21. Shimon Kefa. See note 14 on 1.13.

22. The Majority Text adds "and supplication."

23. Mary from the Greek Μαρία (Maria), from the Hebrew מִרְיָם (miryam).

24. Here, for the first time and in contrast to the gospels, Mary and Jesus's brothers, James, Joses (Joseph), Judas, and Simon (Yaakov, Yosef, Yehuda, and Shimon), are brought into the immediate life of the adult earthly Jesus as intimate participants. In the gospels while Mary is glorified in the Magnificat (Luke 1.39–55) as the mother of the infant child, Jesus expresses resentment at his family's lack of faith in his powers, stating that his true mother and brothers are those out in the fields (Mark 3.33–35) and that a prophet is without honor in his own house and in his own family (Mark 6.4). Jesus's one sentence addressed to his mother occurs in John, after it is noted that while on the cross, he spots his mother standing next to "the student he loved." It reads cryptically, "Then Yeshua seeing his mother and the student he loved standing near said to his mother, 'Woman, your son.'" After Jesus's death, Acts brings Mary and Jesus's brothers firmly into the fold. The later Mariolatry that developed around Mary was not based on Jesus's words to and concerning his mother in the gospels.

25. The King James Version has "disciples," modern translations give "believers," the Greek reads "brothers."

There was a crowd of about one hundred twenty names in the same place.
Shimon Kefa said:

> 16Men and brothers, the scripture was destined
>   To be fulfilled which the holy spirit foretold
>   Long ago through David's mouth about Yehuda,[26]
>   Who acted as a guide for those who seized Yeshua.
> 17He was numbered among us and had his share
>   In this ministry. 18He bought a field with the reward
>   Of his crime,[27] and fell headlong, burst in the middle
>   And all his entrails poured out of him.
> 19This was known to all who live in Yerushalayim,[28]
>   And that field is called in their own[29] language
>   Hakel Dema,[30] that is, the Field of Blood.
> 20For it is written in the Book of Psalms:

> > Let his home be desolate
> > And no one live in it[31]

and

> > Let someone else
> > Take over his office.[32]

---

26. Judea.

27. Or iniquity.

28. Jerusalem.

29. The use of *"their* own" is the first instance in Acts of distancing the residents of Jerusalem and wicked Judas from the messengers, by suggesting that Peter and the brothers now are speaking a language different from the Aramaic of the Jews, which is wrong, since this speech by Peter as a first-century Jew of Jerusalem is not gentile Greek but biblical Aramaic, as is the place name. The correct possessive pronoun should be "in *our* language." For more on the origin of the betrayer tale of Judas in scripture and post-biblical portrayals in history and the arts, see note 30 on p. 33, in "Mark, the Vernacular Story Teller." For a more complete account of Judas from the Bible to modern times, see Susan Gubar's *Judas: A Biography* (New York: W. W. Norton, 2009).

30. Hakeldama (or Akeldama) from the Greek Ἀκελδαμάχ (Hakeldamah), from the Aramaic חֲקֵל דְּמָא (hakal dema), meaning "the field of blood."

31. Ps. 69.25.

32. Ps. 109.8. The Greek ἐπισκοπή (episkope) means "charge" or "visitation" but also suggests the office of apostle or bishop from the Greek ἐπίσκοπος (episkopos).

21So from among those men who were with us
In all that time when rabbi Yeshua came
And went among us, 22beginning with Yohanan
And his immersions until the day
He was taken up from us, let one of them
Join us as a witness to his resurrection.

23And they put forward two men, Yosef[33] called Bar Shavva,[34] who was also known as Justus,[35] and Mattityahu.[36] 24And they prayed and said, "Lord, you who know the hearts of all, reveal whom you chose of these two 25to take the place in this ministry and mission, which Yehuda turned away from in order to go to his own place. 26And they cast lots and the lot fell to Mattityahu, and he was added to the eleven messengers.[37]

---

33. Joseph from the Greek Ἰωσήφ (Iosef), from the Hebrew/Aramaic יוֹסֵף (yosef).

34. Barsabbas from the Greek Βαρσαββᾶς (Barsabbas), from the Hebrew בַּרשַׁבָּא (bar shavva). The name may be from בַּרשַׁבָּת (bar shabbat), meaning "son of the Sabbath." In Aramaic it may have been *Bar Sheba*.

35. Justus from the Greek Ἰοῦστος (Ioustos), a Latin name.

36. Matthew's name in English comes from the Greek Μαθθαῖος (Maththaios), from the Hebrew מַתִּתְיָהוּ (Mattityahu) or מַתִּתְיָה (Mattityah), meaning "gift of Yahweh." Another candidate for Matthew's name is the Hebrew *Mattai* or the Aramaic *Matai*.

37. Here and in the later appended preface, in contrast to the gospels, which tell some of these events in other words, Jesus's disciples (students) before his death have already been promoted to apostles (messengers or envoys). In going from student to apostle, Acts represents a transition from the gospels, where the disciples are most frequently corrected and reprimanded, and the disciples became apostles, thereby showing the movement from a peasant tale of the poor and hungry to a more lordly hierarchy of significantly titled members of the church. As such this later phase of the movement similarly militates for a distinctly later period of composition of Acts, unlike the letters, which were certainly begun within a decade or so of the crucifixion.

Chapter 2

Tongues of fire at Shavuot

Now when the feast day of Shavuot[38] came, they were all together in one place. 2Suddenly there came a sound in the sky like the blowing of a great wind, and it filled the whole house where they were sitting. 3There appeared to them divided tongues of fire and a separate flame settled on each side of them, 4and they were filled with the holy spirit and began to speak in other tongues as the spirit gave them utterance.

5Now there were devout Jews living in Yerushalayim from all nations under the skies, 6and at the sound of these voices, the crowd came together, and they were confused because each one heard them speaking in his or her own language. 7They were amazed and marveled, saying, "Look, are all these non-Galilean speakers? 8And how is it that we hear each speaking in the language to which we were born? 9Parthians and Medes and Elamites, and inhabitants of Mesopotamia, Yehuda and Cappadocia, Pontos and Asia, 10both Frygia[39] and Pamfylia,[40] Egypt and the parts of Libya by Cyrene, and visitors from Rome, 11both Jews and proselytes, Cretans and Jews from Arabia, we hear them all speaking in other languages of the greatness of God."[41] 12They were all astonished and perplexed, saying to one another, "What can this mean?" 13But others scoffed and said, "They are drunk on new sweet wine."

---

38. Pentecost from the Greek πεντηκοστή (pentekoste), meaning "fiftieth," from the Hebrew חַג שָׁבֻעוֹת (hag shavuot), meaning "feast of weeks." The Shavuot, one of the four major Jewish holidays, is a harvest festival, celebrated seven weeks after the Passover, commemorating God's giving of the Ten Commandments to Moses on Mount Sinai.

39. Phrygia from the Greek Φρυγία (Frygia), a large district in Asia Minor during Roman times consisting of the eastern portion of the Roman province of Asia. In Greek times King Midas established the Phrygian Empire (ca. 725–675 B.C.E.), whose capital was at Gordion.

40. Pamphylia from the Greek Παμφυλία (Pamfylia), a Roman province in southern Asia Minor on the Mediterranean, which Paul visited several times.

41. Jerusalem was an international and cosmopolitan city of Jews from Greece, Rome, North Africa, the Arabian peninsula, and vast areas of Mesopotamia.

Shimon Kefa addresses the Shavuot crowds

14But Shimon Kefa, standing up with the eleven, raised his voice and said to them, "Jews and all who live in Yerushalayim, let this be known to you and hear my words. 15These men are not drunk as you suppose. It is only the third hour of the day,[42] 16but the prophet Yoel[43] said,

17On the last days, God said, it will happen

That I shall pour my spirit on all flesh,

And your sons and your daughters will prophesy

And your young men see visions, your old men dream dreams,

18And in those days I will pour my spirit on my male and my
female slaves

19And I shall show wonders in the sky above and signs on the
earth below,

All of blood and fire and smoky mist.

20The sun will be turned into darkness and the moon into
blood

Before the coming of the great and glorious day of the lord.

21And all who call on the name of the lord will be saved.[44]

22"Yisraeli men,[45] listen to these words. There was a Yeshua the Natzrati,[46]

---

42. Nine in the morning.

43. Joel from the Greek Ἰωήλ (Ioel), from the Hebrew יוֹאֵל (yoel).

44. This passage is commonly said to signify the coming of the Messianic age, meaning the coming of the Christ (the Messiah), and to all nations. In Joel, however, it is the coming of God to the Jews rather than of the messiah to all nations. The messiah for the Jews is an earthly leader of salvation, not, as for the early Christian Jews, which is to say, the *Messianic* Jews, a divine figure who is one of the three parts in the tripartite God. In the first years when Christianity was developing in Jerusalem, all the Messianics were Christian Jews, but in subsequent decades there were Christian pagans as conversions multiplied. The first center of pagan Christians, that is, of the gentiles, was in Antioch, which Luke identified as his city.

45. Israelite from the Greek Ἰσραηλίτης (Israelite), from the Hebrew יִשְׂרְאֵלִי (yisraeli), meaning "Israeli." Other translations of the awkward phrase are "Men of Israel" (KJV, New King James Version, and New Revised Standard Version) or simply, "Jews," which is the common epithet throughout the gospels.

46. Nazarene from Greek Ναζαρηνός (Nazarenos), from Natzeret, that is, a Natzrati.

a man attested to you by God with deeds of powers,[47] wonders, and signs that God performed through him while he was among you, as you yourselves know. 23This man was, according to God's purpose and fore-knowledge, handed over to you by lawless men, spiked on to the cross, and you killed him,[48] 24but God loosened the pains of death, since it was not possible for him to be held by it. 25David said of him,[49]

---

47. Often translated as "miracles."

48. As in the infamous and fully incredulous passage in Matthew 27.23, where on the second night of the Seder the Jews are purportedly not in their houses celebrating the holy day but in the streets shouting, "Crucify him!" and, two verses later (Matt. 27.25), proclaim their own guilt and curse. The curse is against an ethnic people who must be forever punished for the unpardonable crime of being Jews. One would suppose that a reasonable reader of goodwill would immediately note something grave and ill-intentioned. However, until recently good readers of scripture have been blind to the obvious impossibility of the scene.

In contrast to the gospel story, now the "reluctant" Roman execution of a presumed seditionist is, for the moment, left out. Rome is no longer in the picture, and Peter need not bother to exonerate Rome for Jesus's death. Rome's exoneration is complete. However, Rome was the law, and to identify its execution squad as "lawless Jews" is a shift of identity of person surely unacceptable to Israel's Roman occupiers. In Acts 3.13 Rome returns but only to exonerate itself again and to speak once more of the Jewish deicide of rabbi Jesus. This shifting, disguising, or blurring of a people's identity follows the same pattern as in the forgetting of the Jewish identify of Jesus, his family, and his first-century followers. See note 185 on Matthew 27.25.

49. Peter quotes the Psalms of David to make David speak prophetically of "him," that is, of Jesus citing David in order to authenticate Jesus's divinity. This Christianization of the Psalms (a psalter of many minds composed over many centuries) has the presumed historical David, a millennium before Jesus, write of Jesus. This Christianization of the Hebrew Bible is essential for the very early Christian Jews, the Jewish Bible being their sole scripture. Here Peter's allegorical reading of the psalm has David identify Jesus as the messiah. However, in these two psalms David speaks only of God, Yahweh, YHWH, or Adonai (lord), not of the foretold messiah whom Christians will identify with God or God's son or one of a trinity including God. So this citation in Acts remains enigmatic. This instance of changing identity for a good purpose, God the creator for Jesus the messiah, immediately follows Acts 2.23. I have translated the psalm from the Greek, based on the Septuagint Greek, which differs from the Hebrew Bible in some small but significant ways. "Hell" (a Germanic word) is pagan *Hades* in the Greek, but *Sheol*, the pit of hell, in the Hebrew, is similar to

I keep the lord always before my face,
For he is at my right hand that I may not be shaken.
26My heart was glad and my tongue exulted,
And my body will live in hope.
27Because you will not abandon my soul to Sheol[50]
Or let your holy one[51] look upon corruption.
28You made me know the ways of life
With your presence you will fill me with joy.

David and Yeshua

29Men and brothers, let me speak confidently to you about the patriarch David, that he died and was buried, and his tomb is with us to this day. 30Since he was a prophet, he knew that God swore an oath to him that one who was the fruit of his loins would sit upon his throne.[52] 31Foreseeing this, he spoke about the resurrection of the Mashiah,[53] saying in the Psalm,

He was not abandoned to Gei Ben Hinnom[54]
and his flesh not seen corruption.[55]

32God raised this Yeshua, and of this we are all witnesses. 33He exalted him at his right hand, and having received the promise of the holy spirit from his father, he inspired what you see and hear. 34David did not ascend into the skies, but he himself said,

---

Gehenna, another Hebrew word for "hell" translated into Greek. Surprisingly, from the KJV to modern versions such as the NRSV, *Hades* rather than *Sheol* is still used. However, in the Old Testament section of each of these Bibles, the same psalms in their English translations, we find *Sheol* and the "Pit," but no *Hades*.

50. Hell.

51. The Hebrew psalm writes that your faithful one will not see the Pit or the grave. Again Peter allegorically interprets the psalm to mean that David is foreseeing the resurrection of the messiah. As there is no reference to the messiah in Psalm 16, there is no reference to his resurrection.

52. Ps. 132.11

53. Messiah from Greek Μεσσίας (Messias), from the Hebrew מָשִׁיחַ (mashiah).

54. Destruction, Hades, hell, Gehenna, Valley of Gehenna. Gei Ben Hinnom from the Hebrew גֵּיא בֶּן־הִנֹּם (gei ben hinom).

55. Ps. 16.10.

The lord said to my lord:

"Sit on my right so 35that I may make your enemies

your footstool."56

36Yisrael knows with certainty that God has made this Yeshua both lord and Mashiah, whom you crucified.57

Conversion of the Jews

37When they heard this they were pierced to the heart and said to Shimon Kefa and the other messengers, "Men and brothers, what should we do?"

38Shimon Kefa told them,

Repent and let each of you be dipped58 in the name

Of Yeshua the Mashiah for remission of your sins

And you will receive the gift of the holy spirit.

39The promise is for you and your children

And for all of you who are far away

And whom the lord our God calls to him.

40And he testified with many other words and exhorted them, saying,

Save yourselves from this crooked generation.

41So those who welcomed his word were dipped in the waters, and

---

56. Ps. 110.1.

57. Early Christians saw Jesus as the messiah on earth as well as in heaven, hence the resurrection. Peter the fisherman, who in Acts 4.13 is depicted as illiterate (ἀγράμματος), is here cast as an early theologian determining doctrine in a sermon to a Jewish crowd, whom he again castigates, saying that the entire house of Israel (presumably Jesus, family, and disciples) must know that it has crucified Jesus. More, if its children are to be forgiven from all that will befall this corrupt generation of Jews, they must be baptized, that is, converted. If anti-Judaism begins in the gospels, the chant of deicide seems to dominate early in Acts. On the other hand, the figure carrying the name "Peter" in the letters and his Messianic church in Jerusalem are normally characterized as being strictly Jewish, observing circumcision, dietary law, and its close interpretation of Torah (the law) in contrast to Paul, who wrote as a Jew liberated from these structures. Peter's converts to Messianic Judaism were the Jews of Jerusalem, while Paul addressed Jews and gentiles of a large diaspora.

58. Baptized or dipped. "Baptize" is from the Greek βαπτίζειν (baptizein), meaning to dip, wash, or immerse, as in Jewish ritual washings.

on that day about three thousand souls were added. 42And they devoted themselves to the messengers' teaching and fellowship, to the breaking of the bread[59] and to prayers.

43And there was fear[60] in every soul, and many wonders and miraculous signs were performed by the messengers. 44All who believed were in the same place and held many things in common, 45and they sold their properties and their possessions and shared things as each one had need. 46Day after day they attended the temple,[61] and broke bread in their houses, and shared food with cheerfulness and simplicity of heart, 47praising God and in favor with all the people. And every day the lord added to the number of those who were saved.

Chapter 3

Healing the crippled

Shimon Kefa and Yohanan went up to the Temple[62] at the hour of prayer, at the ninth hour,[63] 2and a man crippled from his mother's womb was being carried in. They would lay him by the Temple gate, the one called the Beautiful[64] so that he could beg alms from those entering the Temple. 3When he saw Shimon Kefa and Yohanan about to go into the Temple, he was begging for alms.

4Shimon Kefa looked intensely at him, as did Yohanan, and said,
　　Look at us.

---

59. The breaking of the bread derives from the eucharist ceremony at the Last Seder in which Jesus presents the matzah (unleavened bread) as his body and the wine as his blood in the cup, which holds a new covenant. See Luke 22.19.

60. Or "awe."

61. The word in Greek is ἱερόν (hieron), meaning "temple," the same word as in the great Temple. These events take place in a temple (church) of the early Messianic Jews.

62. The great Temple of Jerusalem.

63. Three o'clock in the afternoon.

64. Others give "Beautiful Gate," but the Greek says only "the Beautiful," which is characteristic of the Greek and in English has its own beauty.

5And he fixed his gaze on them, expecting to get something from them. 6Shimon Kefa said,

> I have no silver or gold, but what I have
> I give to you. In the name of Yeshua the Messiah,
> The Natzrati, *stand up and walk*.[65]

7And he took him by the right hand and lifted him. Immediately his feet and ankles became strong. 8And jumping up, he stood and walked around and went inside the Temple with them, walking and leaping and praising God. 9Everyone saw him walking and praising God 10and they recognized that he was the one who sat and begged for alms at the Beautiful Gate of the Temple, and they were filled with wonder and ecstasy at what had happened to him.

11As he clung to Shimon Kefa and Yohanan, all the people ran up to them on the Porch of Shlomoh,[66] utterly astonished. 12When Shimon Kefa saw this, he answered the people,

> Yisraeli men, why do you wonder at this or at us?
> Why do you stare at us as if by our own power
> Or godliness we have made him walk?
> 13The God of Avraham[67] and of Yitzhak[68]
> And of Yaakov,[69] the God of our fathers,
> Glorified his own child[70] Yeshua,
> Whom you handed over and denied before Pilatus[71]
> When he had decided to release him
> 14But you rejected the holy and just one
> And asked to have a murderer delivered to you.

---

65. The Majority Text has "rise up and walk." Peter and John assumed Jesus's miraculous powers to heal.

66. Solomon from the Greek Σολομών (Solomon), from the Hebrew שְׁלֹמֹה (shlomoh). The Porch of Solomon was probably on the east side of the Temple.

67. Abraham from the Greek Ἀβραάμ (Abraam), from the Hebrew אַבְרָהָם (avraham).

68. Isaac from the Greek Ἰσαάκ (Isaak), from the Hebrew יִצְחָק (yitzhak).

69. James or Jacob from the Greek Ἰάκωβος (Iakobos), from the Hebrew יַעֲקֹב (yaakov).

70. Elsewhere translated "servant" or "suffering servant of the Lord."

71. Pilate.

15And you killed the author of life,[72]
Whom God then raised from the dead.
To this we are witnesses. 16And by faith
In his name, his name made him
Whom you see and know strong.
And faith, through Yeshua, has given him
This wholeness before all of you.
17Now, brother, I know that you acted
In ignorance as did your authorities.
18But God fulfilled the sufferings of the Mashiah,
Which he had foretold through the mouth
Of all the prophets.[73] 19Repent, then, and turn[74]
To remove your sins 20so a time of refreshment
Will come from the face of the lord
And he may send you the pre-appointed one,

---

72. The Greek ἀρχηγός (arhegos), meaning literally "arch" or "head ruler" or "leader," also carries the meaning of "originator" or "founder." In this latter sense "author" has been used in this and other versions.

73. In verse 3.17 the shift in the possessive pronoun from the intimate "our" authorities to the distancing "your" authorities blurs the circumstance that Peter is a Jew, a Messianic (Christian) Jew, in the great Temple, speaking to brother Jews, whom he calls his brothers, to convince them that they should see that *our* foretold messiah is here in the figure of Jesus, whose arrival and suffering he substantiates in verse 3.18 through the Jewish prophets, whose authority he shares with his brothers. He could say that *our* authorities are ignorant or wicked or murderous, but to speak to his brothers in the Temple both as contemporary brother and as a later outsider is an anachronism. Two voices are heard: a reprimanding voice of many decades later, when Christianity has already split from Judaism, and a heartening voice speaking shortly after Jesus's crucifixion, when the Messianics are in emerging sect of Jews attempting to convince and convert fellow Jews that *our* messiah has arrived.

74. The Greek verb is ἐπιστρέφω (epistrefo), meaning "turn around," "turn back," "return," and in a metaphorical sense to turn one's beliefs around, that is, to convert. In "Ash Wednesday" (1930), T. S. Eliot uses this same multivalent verb in his refrain "Because I do not hope to turn again," exactly echoing the medieval Italian poet Cavalcanti's "Perqu'io non spero di tornar jiammai." Other translations do not give the specific metaphorical "turn" and translate it piously and unnecessarily conceptually, as in the KJV's "and be converted," or explain it by adding "to God" as in the NRSV "and turn to God." The one word "turn" (as Cavalcanti and Eliot knew) is more beautiful and powerful without improvements.

Yeshua the Mashiah, 21who must remain in the sky
Until the time of the restoration of all things,
Which God spoke through the eternal mouth
Of his holy prophets. 22Indeed Moshe[75] said,
"The lord Yahweh will raise up a prophet like me
From among our own people. You will listen to all things
He tells you.[76] 23Every soul who does not hear that prophet[77]
Shall be utterly destroyed from among the people.[78]
24And all the prophets who have spoken, from Shmuel[79]
And his successors, have also predicted these days.
25You are sons of the prophets and the covenant[80]
That God gave to your ancestors, saying to Avraham:
"In your seed all the families of the earth will be blessed."
26When God first raised his child, he sent him first to you
To bless you by turning each of you away from cunning.

---

75. Moses from the Greek Μωϋσῆς (Moses), from the Hebrew מֹשֶׁה (moshe).

76. Deut. 18.15–16.

77. Deut. 18.19.

78. Lev. 23.29. The citations from the Torah are through the Greek intermediary of the Septuagint. In this instance they are three sentences or parts of sentences patched together from two places in Deuteronomy and one in Leviticus, and transformed freely for instructive purpose. The King James version of these passages, as translated not from the Greek and later New Testament but from its Old Testament, reads as follows, "The LORD thy God will raise up unto thee a Prophet from the midst of thee, of thy brethren, like unto me; unto him ye shall hearken" (Deut. 18.15–16). "And it shall come to pass, that whosoever will not hearken unto my words" (Deut. 18.19). "For whatsoever soul it be that shall not be afflicted in that same day, he shall be cut off from among his people" (Lev. 23.29). It can be easily seen that words are taken from three places, seriously altered in syntax and word meaning, and joined to make a new coherent prophecy corroborating the assertion that Moses foresees the coming of Jesus. The majority of quotations directly from the Hebrew Bible, which appear throughout, are loosely quoted and shaped for New Covenant persuasions.

79. Samuel from the Greek Σαμουήλ (Samouel), from the Hebrew שמואל (shmuel).

80. "Covenant" from the Greek διαθήκη (diatheke), is the word used by Greeks and most Orthodox Christians for the New Covenant.

Chapter 4

Conversions in the Temple and confinement

As they were speaking to the people, the priests and the captain[81] of the Temple and the Tzadokim[82] came up to them, 2disturbed because they were teaching the people and announcing that in Yeshua there is the resurrection of the dead. 3And they laid hands on them and put them in prison until the next day. It was already evening. 4But many who had heard the word believed and the number of men came to five thousand.

5And it happened that on the next day, the leaders and the elders and the scholars assembled in Yerushalayim, 6and also Hannan[83] the priest and Kayfa[84] and Yohanan[85] and Alexandros[86] and all who were of the high priest's family. 7And they stood the captives in their midst and questioned them, saying "By what power and in whose name have you done this?"

8Then Shimon Kefa, filled with the holy spirit, said to them,

> Leaders of the people and elders, 9if today
> Because of a kindness rendered to a weakened man,
> We are judged as to how he has been healed,
> 10Let all of you and all the people of Yisrael[87] know
> In the name of Yeshua Mashiah the Natzati,[88]
> Whom you crucified,[89] whom God raised from the dead,

---

81. Also "general."

82. Sadducee from the Greek Σαδώκ (Sadok), from the Hebrew צָדוֹק (tzadok), meaning "Tzadok" and "Sadducee." Plural is *Tzadokim*.

83. Annas, Hannan, or Anan, meaning "high priest" in Hebrew, from the Greek Ἄννας (Hannas), from the Hebrew חָנָן (hannan), "priest" or "gracious one."

84. Caiaphas from the Greek Καϊάφας (Kaiafas), from the Hebrew כֵּיפָא (kayfa).

85. This Yohanan has been identified as Annas's son or Jonathan ben Zacci, who was later president of the great Temple, but all this is speculation.

86. Alexander from the Greek Ἀλέξανδρος (Alexandros).

87. Israel.

88. Jesus Christ the Nazarene.

89. In this new confrontation, the chant of later anti-Judaic charges continues in the pronouncement of guilt. As in earlier condemnations, there is no mention, not even exculpatingly, of the Roman military crucifiers. Rome is by now omitted from the equation. Given that there are no documents, no recorders, old or modern, to preserve

It is through him that his man who stands before you
Is in good health. 11As said in the Psalms,
    He is the stone rejected by you, the builders,
    Which has become the cornerstone.[90]
  12And there is salvation in no one else,
    For there is no other name under the sky
    By which we are to be saved.

13Now when they saw the plain courage of Shimon Kefa and
Yohanan[91] and understood them to be illiterate and untrained, they
marveled, and they knew that they had been with Yeshua. 14And on
seeing the man standing with them, healed, they had nothing to say
against them. 15So they ordered them out of the council[92] while they
conferred with each other, 16saying, "What will we do with these men?
They have performed an extraordinary sign,[93] which is clear to everyone living in Yerushalayim and we cannot deny it. 17But to keep it from
spreading further among the people, let us warn them not to speak and
not to teach in this name." 18They they called them back in and ordered
them not to speak or teach at all in the name of Yeshua.[94]

19But Shimon Kefa and Yohanan answered, saying to them, "You decided
whether it is right before God to listen to you rather than to God, 20but we
cannot keep from speaking about what we have seen and heard."

21After threatening them again, they let them go, finding no way
to punish them, because of the people, who were all glorifying God

---

Peter's accusatory words, their welcome or regrettable ascription to Peter is unverifiable. However, the one fact of Jesus's life, largely uncontested by secular or religious
scholars, is that Jesus "King of the Jews" was crucified by Israel's Roman occupiers.

90. Ps. 118.22; "cornerstone" is literally "head of the corner."

91. In Acts Peter has developed far from the person of the gospels, whom Jesus derides
as one who doubts him and will and does deny him three times before the cock crows.
Now he has powers to heal and in moments of danger is frank and courageous.

92. Sanhedrin.

93. Miracle.

94. Here, as in the gospel reports of secret conversations by conspirators against
Jesus in the Sanhedrin quarters, the author uses skillful dramatic means to heighten
a key moment of intrigue. Though again it is unknown what means were available
to record secretive off-stage speech, the narration, as in the best creative nonfiction, is consummately effective.

for what had happened. 22The man on whom this sign of healing had been performed was over forty years old.

23After they were released they went to their friends and reported what the priests and elders said. 24When they heard it, they raised their voices in harmony to God and said,

> Master, you who made the sky and the earth
> And the sea and all things in them,
> 25And by the holy spirit and through the mouth of David,
> Our father and by your child, as you said in the Psalm:
> Why did the nations[95] rage and the people plot vanities?
> 26The kings of the earth took their stand
> And the rulers assembled against the lord and his Mashiah.[96]

---

95. "Nations," (ethnics) or *gentiles* or *goyim* are Greek, Latin, and Hebrew words for non-Jews and all these words are appropriate.

96. Ps. 21–12. In the Hebrew, the *mashiah* is the anointed one, on having had sacred oil poured ceremonially on one's head and given leadership authority as a prince or special priest, being the choice of God (Dan. 9.25, 9.26). So in Hebrew *mashiah* means both "messiah" and "anointed." The English "messiah" is a transliteration of Hebrew מָשִׁיחַ (mashiah) while "Christ" is a transliteration of the Greek Χριστος (Hristos) meaning "anointed," which is itself a translation of Hebrew *mashiah*. Hence, there are at least four ways of rendering Greek into English: 1) "mashiah," 2) "messiah," 3) "anointed," and 4) "Christ." "Mashiah" transcribes both the Hebrew consonants and vowels. "Messiah" transcribes the consonants but Englishes the vowels. "Anointed" translates the Hebrew into English. "Christ" transliterates into English the Greek translation of the Hebrew *mashiah*.

"Christ" survives in English mainly as a name rather than as a title or epithet, and in usage does not evoke its primary Greek and Hebrew meanings. In adjectival form, few are aware that "Christian" means "Messianic." The original meaning of "anointed" does survive in the Greek scriptures, since *hristos* is also the classical Greek word for "rubbed on with salve." But the loss in the transformation of "mashiah" into "Christ" in Psalm 2 is not inadvertent. Rather, it conforms to the ecclesiastical intention of turning each mention of the Jews' awaited earthly messiah and anointed leader into the divine Christ, thereby confirming that in the Hebrew Bible the Christ has been foretold in Exodus, 1 Kings, Isaiah, Daniel, and so on. However, the transformation of *mashiah* into "Christ" does not occur in renderings of the Hebrew Bible into English (as distinct from citations of the Hebrew Bible in the New Testament). Then *mashiah* is not "Christ" but "messiah" or the "anointed." For example, here in Psalm 2.2 cited in the New Testament, the KJV has "Against the Lord and against His Christ," but for the exact same line in its Old Testament source, the same KJV has "against the LORD, and against his anointed." In translations of

27Herod, Pontius Pilatus, gentiles, and the people of Yisrael
    Gathered in this city against your holy child, Yeshua.
    You anointed him 28to do what your hand and will
        had predestined to occur.
29Now, lord, look at their threats and grant you slaves
    That with all courage they may speak your word
30While you stretch out your hand to heal and perform signs
    And wonders through the name of your holy child, Yeshua.

31And when they prayed, the place where they were meeting shook, and they were all filled with the holy spirit and spoke the word of God with courage.

Selling possessions and sharing with the poor

32Now there was one heart and spirit in the whole body of the believers, and no one said his possessions were his own, but everything was held in common. 33And with great force the messengers gave their testimony to the resurrection of rabbi Yeshua, and great grace was upon them all. 34Nor was anyone among them in need, for those among them who owned lands or houses sold them and they brought the proceeds of what was sold 35and laid them at the feet of the messengers, and they distributed to each one according to need.

36And there was Yosef, whom the messengers named Bar Nabba,[97] which translated means "son of encouragement,"[98] a Levite[99] and a Cypriote by birth. 37He sold a field that belonged to him, and brought the money and laid it before the feet of the messengers.

---

the Hebrew Bible, the transformation of the messiah into the Christ in the KJV is found only in annotation, note, and commentary.

97. Barnabas from the Greek Βαρναβᾶς (Barnabas), from the Aramaic בַּר נְבָא (bar nabba). Barnabas was Joseph, a Levi from Cyprus.

98. The Greek παράκλησις (paraklesis) means "encouragement" or "consolation" but is not a correct translation from the Hebrew נְבָא (nabba), the meaning of which is unknown. It is not "son of the prophet." See previous note.

99. Levite from the Greek Λευίτης (Leuites), from the Hebrew לֵוִי (levi), meaning "one from the tribe of Levi" or a "Levite."

Chapter 5

Calamity of Hananyah and Shappira

But a man by the name of Hananyah[100] with Shappira[101] his wife sold property 2yet held back some of the profits, with his wife's knowledge, and brought only a part and laid it at the feet of the messengers. 3Shimon Kefa said, "Hananyah, why has Satan filled your heart so that you lie to the holy spirit and hold back some of the profit. 4While unsold was it not yours? And once sold, was the profit not still under your authority? Why did you place this deed in your heart? You lied not to people but to God." 5When Hananyah heard these words, he fell down and died, and great fear came upon all who heard. 6The young men rose and wrapped him and after carrying him out buried him.

7There was an interval of about three hours and his wife came in, not knowing what had happened. 8Shimon Kefa answered her, and said, "Tell me how much you sold the land for?"

"Yes, for that much," she said.

9And Shimon Kefa to her, "Why did you agree to test the spirit of the lord? Look, the feet of those who buried your husband are at the door and they will carry you out."

10And at once she fell at his feet and died, and the young men came in and found her dead and carried her out and buried her beside her husband.

11And great fear came upon the whole congregation and upon all who heard of these things.[102]

---

100. Ananias from the Greek Ἀνανίας (Hananias), from the Hebrew חֲנַנְיָה (hananyah). In the Hebrew Bible the name appears frequently as in Daniel 1.6, where Hananyah is Daniel's friend.

101. Sapphira from the Greek Σάπφιρα (Sapfira), from the Aramaic שַׁפִּירָא (shappira).

102. This communal living and sharing of goods was also a contemporary practice of the Essenes. In intertestamental scriptures there are many mortal punishments, but no episode in the New Testament is as drastic as the brief report on the husband and wife who are accused of having Satan in their hearts for not turning the full profit of a property sale over to church authorities and are therefore immediately struck dead and buried.

The messengers perform miraculous healings in the Temple

12Now through the hands of the messengers, many signs and wonders were performed among the people. And they all were coming together in the Porch of Shlomoh. 13None of the rest dared join them yet the people glorified them, 14and a multitude of believers, both men and women, came over to the rabbi. 15So they carried their sick out into the streets and put them on cots and mats so that when Shimon Kefa came by at least his shadow might fall on some of them. 16And also a multitude from the cities around Yerushalayim gathered, bringing their sick and those tormented by unclean spirits, and they were all healed.[103]

The messengers and the angel

17Then the high priest and all those with him, the sect of Tzadokim[104] rose up, filled with jealousy, 18and laid their hands on them and put them in the public prison. 19But during the night an angel of the lord opened the doors and led them out, saying,

20Go stand in the Temple
  And tell the people all the words of this life.
21When they heard this they went into the Temple at daybreak and were teaching.

When the high priest came he called together the council[105] and the whole body of elders of the sons of Yisrael, and he sent word to the prison to have them brought back, 22but when the servingmen got there they did not find them in the jail. They came back and reported,

---

103. In the gospels only Jesus can heal and perform miracles. In Acts, Simon Peter (along with John and Paul) has been give the powers of Jesus to heal many who lie waiting for him in the streets. The gospel portrait of Peter is different from that in Acts. In the gospels Peter is close to Jesus but is also a fumbling disciple who asks to sit next to Jesus and God in heaven, which Jesus reproaches him for. In the famous footrace to Jesus's tomb, Peter, we are told, loses the race to the unnamed disciple, whom Jesus loves most, and who at the Last Seder had sat next to Jesus and reclined on his chest. In a word, in Acts Saint Peter is elevated to a power with great resources.

104. Sadducees.

105. Sanhedrin.

saying, 23"We found the prison securely locked and the guards standing at the doors, but when we opened it there was no one inside." 24When the captain of the Temple and the high priest heard these words, they were puzzled about them. What could it mean? 25Then someone came and informed them, saying, "Look, the men you put in jail are standing in the Temple and teaching the people." 26Then the captain and his servingmen took them away, but not forcibly for they feared that they might be stoned by the people.

The messengers at the Sanhedrin and Gamliel's counsel

27And taken away, they stood in the Sanhedrin and the high priest questioned them, 28saying, "We formally commanded you not to teach in this name, and look, you have filled Yerushalayim with your teaching and are determined to bring this man's blood upon us."

29And Shimon Kefa and the messengers said, "We must obey God rather than people. 30The God of our fathers raised up Yeshua whom you killed, hanging him on a tree.[106] 31God raised him, at his right hand, as prince and savior that he might give repentance to Yisrael. 32And we are witnesses to these things, we and the holy spirit which God gave to those who obey him."

33When they heard this, they were enraged and wanted to kill them. 34But a Parush[107] in the council, Gamliel,[108] a teacher of the law, esteemed

---

106. Peter refers to hanging Jesus from a tree, and he will use similar words in a great poetic passage in 10.39, where the author of Acts has Peter repeat the horrific condemnation of the Jews. This general condemnation as the *Christ-killers* will be against all Jews forever more. We hear Peter say, "We are all witnesses / to all that he did in the country of the Jews / and in Yerushalayim. They put him to death / by hanging him for a tree." By condemning "the other" when Peter the accuser *is* himself the other, he successfully conceals to readers that he and his brethren are observant Jews. They are the people of the book who in rabbi Jesus have found their Jewish messiah foretold in Isaiah and elsewhere.

107. Pharisee from the Greek Φαρισαῖος (Farisaios), from the Hebrew פְּרוּשִׁים (prushim or perushim), "Pharisees." Singular is *Parush*.

108. Gamaliel from the Greek Γαμαλιήλ (Gamaliel), from the Hebrew גַּמְלִיאֵל (Gamliel). Gamaliel was the most famous Jewish teacher of his day. He may have been the son of Hillel, and Paul (Shaul) was one of his students.

by all the people, stood up and ordered these men to be taken outside for a little while, 35and said to the men, "Men, Yisraelis, be careful what you are about to do with these men. 36Some time ago Theudas[109] rose in rebellion, saying he was someone and had about four hundred men with him, yet he was killed and all who obeyed him were scattered and came to nothing. 37After him Yehuda the Galilean[110] arose in the days of the census and misled people into following him. He also was killed and all who obeyed him were scattered. 38So now I tell you, keep away from these men and release them. If this matter and work come from men, it will fail; 39but if it comes from God, then you cannot overthrow them, lest you be found fighting against God."

40They were persuaded by him, and they called the messengers back in and beat them. Then they warned them not to speak in the name of Yeshua, and released them. 41And they left the council, joyful that they had been found worthy to suffer shame for his name, 42and every day in the Temple and in each house they did not stop teaching Mashiah Yeshua.

Chapter 6

Choosing the seven ministers[111]

Now in those days, as the number of students multiplied, there was a complaint by the Greek-speaking Jews against the native Jews, because the Greek widows were being neglected in the daily distribution of food.

---

109. Theudas from the Greek Θευδᾶς (Theudas). This Greek name may or may not be a shortened form of Θεόδωρος (Theodoros), Theodore, meaning "gift of God." There are several Theudas's mentioned, before and after this moment in the Temple, including a later Jewish insurrectionist who was killed by the Romans in 44 C.E. according to Josephus (*Antiquities*, 20.97–98).

110. This Galilean was a revolutionary leader and charismatic who opposed new taxes after the census of Quirinius in 6–7 C.E. his revolt was crushed. He may have been a Zealot. Galilee was known for its rebellions.

111. Or "servants" or "deacons."

₂Then the twelve called together the multitude of students,[112] saying, "It is not right to neglect the word of God in bringing food to the tables. ₃So, brothers, select seven[113] among you who are well recommended, filled with spirit and wisdom, whom we will put in charge of this matter. ₄We will devote ourselves to prayer and the ministry of the word." ₅And the whole group liked their word and they chose Stefanos,[114] a man filled with faith and the holy spirit, and Filippos[115] and Prohoros[116] and Nikanor[117] and Timon[118] and Parmenas[119] and Nikolaos,[120] a proselyte from Antioch. ₆They set them before the messengers, who said a prayer and laid their hands upon them.

---

112. Disciples. "Pupil" or "student" is the common meaning of μαθητής (mathetes), which in Latin is *discipulus*. By usage "disciple" has come to mean an adherent to a sect of philosophy or its leader, and in Christianity the twelve messengers (apostoles). Greek *mathetes* is the ordinary word for "student," including the disciples. In this instance the multitude had become students, and would have been called in Hebrew *talmidin* (singular is *talmid*) from *lamad*, to learn, and in classical Arabic *taleban* (singular is *taliban*).

113. These seven are sometimes called the seven deacons of Jerusalem.

114. Stephen from the Greek Στέφανος (Stefanos). Stephen was from Antioch and a proselyte, that is, a pagan convert to Judaism before becoming a Christian Jew. Yet Stephen also claims Jewish heritage from his ancestor Abraham, so we are left in doubt. See note 16 above, on Andreas (1.13). In Acts, in contrast to the other books of the New Testament, the power of miracle—healing, resurrection, walking through walls, being in two places at once—has now come into the possession of many members of the new movement, including the apostles and many outstanding figures designated for sainthood because of their skills in the miraculous. The acts or activities (*praxeis*) of the apostles might be called "The Book of Miracles." Here, as with the ancient Egyptian performers of magical spells, we have the activities of the wonder-makers.

115. Philip.

116. Prochorus from the Greek Πρόχορος (Prohoros).

117. Nicanor from the Greek Νικάνωρ (Nikánor), from Rabbinical literature נִיקָנוֹר (nikanor).

118. Timon from the Greek Τίμων (Timon).

119. Parmenas from the Greek Παρμενᾶς (Parmenas), a shortened form of Παρμενίδης (Parmenides).

120. Nicolaus from the Greek Νικόλαος (Nikolaos), meaning "victory of the people."

7And the word of God spread and the number of students in Yerushalayim grew greatly, and a great number of priests obeyed the faith.

Stefanos with the face of an angel

8Stefanos, filled with grace and power, performed wonders and great signs among the people. 9Then some from the synagogue of the Freedmen,[121] as it was called, and Cyrenians and Alexandrians and others from Cilicia and Asia stood up and debated Stefanos. 10And they were to withstand the wisdom and spirit with which he spoke. 11Then they stirred up men to say, "We have heard him saying blasphemous words against Moshe[122] and God." 12And they aroused the people and the elders and the scholars and they came after him and seized him and took him to the council 13and they set up false witnesses who said, "This man never stops speaking words against this holy place and Torah.[123] 14We heard him saying that Yeshua the Natzrati[124] will destroy this place and change the ethics[125] handed down to us from Moshe."

15Yet everyone sitting in the Sanhedrin stared at him and saw his face like the face of an angel.

Chapter 7

Stefanos remembers Avraham, Yitzhak, Yaakov, and Yosef down in Egypt

The high priest said, "Is this so?"

2And Stefanos said, "Men, my brothers and fathers, listen. The God

---

121. The Freedmen were men freed from slavery. The Greek word Λιβερτῖνος (Libertinos) is a Latin loan word in Greek.

122. Moses.

123. The law.

124. Nazarene.

125. Or customs.

of glory appeared to our father[126] Avraham in Mesopotamia before he lived in Haran ₃and he said to him,

> Go out of your country and your relatives,
> And come to the land I will show you.[127]

₄Then he left the land of the Chaldeans[128] and settled in Haran. And after his father died, God moved him to this land in which you now live, ₅and gave him no inheritance, not a foot's length of it, but he promised to give him and his seed after him possession of the land.[129] But he had no child. ₆And God spoke to him in this way, saying:

> Your descendants will be aliens in another's land
> And held as slaves and afflicted for four hundred years,[130]

₇And God said:

> And I will judge the nation they serve
> And they will come out and serve me here.

₈Then he gave him the covenant of circumcision.[131] So Avraham became the father of Yitzhak[132] and circumcised him on the eighth day, and Yitzhak became the father of Yaakov and Yaakov of the twelve patriarchs.[133]

---

126. In contrast to chapters 1 and 2, where the apostles refer to contemporary villainous Jews as *they*, as if they the apostles are unaffiliated aliens in a city of Jews, throughout Stephen's speech recalling Abraham, Joseph, and Moses from the Hebrew Bible, it is *our* ancestors as Stephen proudly claims his Jewish ancestry in arguing with the rabbis and members of the council. Here there is no denial or blurring of people or religion but a debate about recognition of the biblically announced messiah in which Stephen claims, as Paul will also assert, that his Judaism is the true branch, for he has seen the prophesied light.

127. Gen. 12.1.

128. Southern Babylonia.

129. Gen. 17.8, 48.4.

130. Gen. 15.13–14. In Egypt as slaves for 400 years (Gen. 15.13) or 430 years (Exod. 12.40).

131. Gen. 17.10–11.

132. Isaac.

133. Jacob had thirteen children, twelve sons and one daughter, by his wife Leah, her maidservant Zilpah, his second wife Rachel, and her maidservant Bilhah. The

9The patriarchs were jealous of Yosef and sold him into Egypt. But God was with him, 10and rescued him from all his afflictions and gave him grace and wisdom in the presence of Pharaoh, King of Egypt; and Pharaoh appointed him ruler over Egypt and his entire household. 11Now a famine came over all of Egypt and Canaan, and bringing great affliction, and our ancestors could find no food. 12But when Yosef heard that there was wheat in Egypt, he sent our ancestors there on their first visit. 13On their second visit, Yosef made himself known to his brothers, and Yosef's family became known to Pharaoh. 14Then Yosef sent for and called his father Yaakov and all his relatives to him, some seventy-five souls,[134] 15and Yaakov went down into Egypt. And he died and so did our ancestors. 16They were all brought back to Shehem[135] and were placed in the tomb that Avraham bought for a sum of silver from the sons of Hamor in Shehem.[136]

---

twelve sons were the patriarchs. From Leah came his daughter Dinah and six sons: Reuben, Simeon, Issachar, Zebulun, and Levi, who did not found a tribe but was the ancestor of the Levites, and Judah, from whom the Davidic monarchy was descended. From Zilpah came Gad and Asher. From Bilhah came Dan and Naphtali. From Rachel came Benjamin and their youngest child, Joseph, who did not found a tribe but whose sons founded the tribes of Manasseh and Ephraim. Through Jacob's sons and grandsons came the twelve tribes of Israel. Jacob was given the name "Israel" by a mysterious divine stranger, perhaps an angel, with whom he had wrestled all night until daybreak (Gen. 32.24–32). Jacob's new name also became an epithet for Jews in the Hebrew Bible, as in the "sons of Israel," meaning the "sons of Jacob," or as in "Israelites," the Greek word for the Hebrew *Yisraeli*, which in English is "Israeli." The names of Jacob's descendant twelve tribes were Asher, Benjamin, Dan, Ephraim, Gad, Issachar, Judah, Manasseh, Reuben, Simeon, Levi, and Zebulun.

134. In Genesis 42.27 the number is 70. The Hebrew Bible reads "seventy." The Septuagint translation of the Hebrew Bible into Greek, which is the source of this phrase, incorrectly reads "seventy-five."

135. Shehem from the Greek Συχέμ (Syhem) or Sychar, from the Hebrew שְׁכֶם. Shehem is a city in Samaria, near present-day Nablus, from the Greek *Neapolis*, meaning "New City."

136. Stephen combines the accounts of land purchases by Abraham and Jacob. Jacob bought land at Shehem (Gen. 33.19), where his son Joseph was buried (Josh. 24.32).

Moshe born in Egypt, beautiful before God

17When the time drew near for the promise that God had made with Avraham, our people in Egypt increased and multiplied 18until another king loomed in Egypt, one who had not known Yosef. 19This one contrived against our people and oppressed our ancestors, forcing them to leave our babies exposed outside so that they would die.

20At this time Moshe was born and he was beautiful before God, and was nurtured for three months in the house of his father. 21And when he was set outside, Pharaoh's daughter took him and raised him as her own son. 22And Moshe was instructed in all the wisdom of the Egyptians, and he was powerful in his words and actions.

23When he was fully forty years old, it came into his heart to visit his brothers, the sons of Yisrael.[137] 24When he saw one of them being wrongly abused, he brought justice to the oppressed man by striking down the Egyptian. 25He thought that his brothers would understand that through him the hand of God was saving them, but they did not understand. 26The next day Moshe appeared to them as they were fighting with each other and he tried to make peace, saying, "Men, you are brothers. Why are you hurting each other?" 27But the one who was injuring his neighbor shoved Moshe and said, "Who made you a ruler and judge over us? 28Do you want to kill me as yesterday you killed the Egyptian?"

29And Moshe fled and became a stranger in the land of Midyan,[138] and had two sons.

30And when forty years had passed, an angel appeared to him in the desert near the Mountain of Sinai, in the flame of a thornbush on fire.[139] 31When Moshe saw this, he wondered about the vision. As he came near it to look, and the voice of the lord came near.

32I am the God of your fathers,
    The God of Avraham and Yitzhak and Yaakov.
Moshe trembled and didn't dare look.

33The lord said to him,

---

137. In Exodus 7.7 he is 80.

138. Midian from the Greek Μαδιάμ (Madiam), from the Hebrew מִדְיָן (midyan), a desert area in northwest Arabia.

139. The burning bush (Exod. 3.2).

Untie your sandals, for the place
Where you stand is holy ground.
₃₄I looked and saw the evil done
To my people in Egypt and I heard their groaning
And I came down to bring them out.
Come now. I will send you back to Egypt.

₃₅This was the Moshe whom they denied, saying, "Who appointed you ruler and judge?" But he was sent by God as ruler deliverer through the hand of the angel who appeared to him in the thornbush.¹⁴⁰ ₃₆He led them out, having done wonders and signs in the land of Egypt and in the Red Sea and in the desert for forty years. ₃₇This is the Moshe who said to the sons of Yisrael,

God will raise up a prophet for you,
Like me, from among your brothers.

₃₈He is the one who was in the congregation in the desert with the angel who spoke to him on the Mountain of Sinai, and with our ancestors. He received the living words¹⁴¹ to give us. ₃₉But our fathers would not obey him. They thrust him aside, and in their hearts turned back to Egypt. ₄₀They told Aharon,¹⁴² "Make us gods who will go before us. As for Moshe, who led us out of Egypt, we don't know what became of him."

The golden calf and the sukkah

₄₁And they made a calf in those days and made offerings to the idols and were happy with the work of their hands.¹⁴³ ₄₂But God turned them around and sent them to serve in the army¹⁴⁴ of heaven as it is written in the book of the prophet Amos:¹⁴⁵

Did you bring me sacrifices and offerings

---

140. Exod. 3.2.

141. Elsewhere translated "oracles," an interpretation of "words."

142. Aaron from the Greek Ἀαρών, from the Hebrew אַהֲרוֹן (aharon).

143. Exod. 32.1.

144. The common word for "army" is elsewhere translated as "host."

145. Amos 5.25–27 (Septuagint).

For forty years in the desert?

43No, you took along the sukkah[146] of Moloch

and the star of your god Keinun.[147]

44Our fathers had the sukkah of testimony in the desert as he who spoke to Moshe commanded him to build it according to the image he had seen. Our ancestors inherited it 45and brought it in with Yeshua when he took possession of the land from the gentiles, whom God drove out of the sight of our father.[148] And the sukkah remained in the land until the days of David; 46and David found favor before God and he asked to make a sukkuh [for the house of Yaakov].[149] 47And Shlomoh built a house, but the highest one does not live in a house built by human hands. 48As the prophet Yeshayahu[150] said:

49The sky is my throne

And the earth is my footstool.

What kind of place will you build for me? says the lord,

50Didn't I make all these things with my hand?

Or what is my place of rest?

51"Stiff-necked and uncircumcised in your heart and ears, you always resist the holy spirit as your fathers did. 52Who among the prophets did

---

146. Tabernacle from the Greek σκηνή (skene), "tent," from the Hebrew סֻכָּה (sukkah), "shelter," "tent." The Festival of the Tabernacle or Booths is in the Greek σκηνοπηγία (skenopegia), which represents the usually three tents of the Jewish Sukkah, also called the Sukkoth, or in the Hebrew חַג הַסֻּכּוֹת (hag hasukkot), meaning Festival of the Weeks, an eight-day celebration for autumnal harvest, beginning on the eve of the 15th of Tishri. The sukkah is a small lean-to-like shelter in the fields. The festival commemorates the forty years that Moses and the Jews spent in the desert after escaping from Egypt and before entering Canaan.

147. Rephan from the Greek Ραιφάν (Raifan). In Amos 5:26 it is the Hebrew כִּיּוּן (kiyun), referring to the Babylonian star god Saturn (now called a planet), whom the Jews worshiped in the desert.

148. Literally, "from the face of our father."

149. Not found in the United Bible Societies fourth corrected edition of the *Greek New Testament* but is in the Majority edition and other editions of the Greek New Testament.

150. Isaiah from the Greek Ἠσαΐας (Esaias), from the Hebrew יְשַׁעְיָהוּ (yeshayahu).

your fathers not drive out? And they killed those who foretold the coming of the just one,[151] of whom you are now his betrayers and murderers. 53You received the law ordered by the angels and did not keep it."

Stefanos falls into sleep

54When they heard this they were furious in their hearts and gnashed their teeth at him. 55But filled with the holy spirit, he gazed into the sky and saw the glory of God and Yeshua standing on the right hand of God.[152] 56And he said,

> Look, I see the skies open and the earthly son[153]
> Standing on the right hand of God.

57They cried out in a great voice and covered their ears, and all rushed together against him. 58They dragged him outside the city and began to stone him. And the witnesses laid their garments at the feet of a young man called Shaul.[154] 59While they were stoning him, Stefanos called upon God and said,

---

151. The notion that the Jews killed their prophets is not found in the Hebrew Bible. It is an invention found in the gospels. See note 165 on Matthew 23.37.

152. The frequent citing of God, the Holy Spirit, and Jesus, with Jesus in heaven standing to the right of God, reveals three separate entities that are interpreted allegorically as one, the trinity, the tripartite god, by the early church, which prevailed against other sects of Christianity (Messianic Judaism) who disagreed, lost out, and survived in church history as heresies.

153. "Son of Man" or "son of man" is the usual translation of the Greek ὁ υἱὸς τοῦ ἀνθρώπου (ho huios tou anthropou), which literally means "son of a person" or "son of people." Greek anthropos is not "man." It lacks gender as "person" does. In the Hebrew Bible "son of people" was an idiomatic way of saying "human being." In the gospels it may also suggest the son on earth rather than the "son in heaven," the "earthly son" rather than the "heavenly son." Hence, "earthly son," rather than "son of man," "son of people," or "human being," may work better poetically and theologically. "Son of man" is normally interpreted in theology to mean allegorically "son of God," that is, Jesus the Christ.

154. Paul from the Greek Παῦλος (Paulos), from Saul in the Greek Σαῦλος (Saulos), from the Hebrew שָׁאוּל (Shaul). Paul was born in Tarsos as *Shaul*. In the Greek and in English translation he is still called "Saul," and will be until on the road to Damascus he has a vision of Jesus, whom he never knew in person in Jerusalem, and thereafter he was called "Paul," which is *Shaul* in Greek.

> Lord Yeshua, receive my spirit.
> 60Then he fell on his knees and cried out in a great voice,
>> Lord, do not hold this sin against them.
> And on saying this, he fell asleep.[155]

Chapter 8

Shaul ravaging the church

Shaul approved of their killing Stefanos.

And that day began a great persecution against the church in Yerushalayim, and everyone except the messengers was scattered throughout the countryside of Yehuda and Shomron. 2A few devout men buried Stefanos and made a great lamentation over him. 3But Shaul went on outraging the church, house by house, entering them, dragging both men and women off and putting them in jail.

4Those who were dispersed went about preaching the word of God.

Filippos in Shomron

5Filippos went to a city in Shomron and preached the mashiah to the people. 6The crowds listened eagerly to what Filippos said and were of one mind when they heard him and saw the signs[156] he was performing. 7Many who had unclean spirits cried out in a great voice and were relieved, and many paralyzed and lame were healed. 8And there was great joy in that city.

Shimon the Gnostic magician

9Now there was a certain man named Shimon,[157] who had been in

---

155. The Greek says, "he slept." Others write, "he died," which is implied. In saying, "Do not hold this sin against them," Stephen acknowledges sin in his murder, but his purported killers are accorded a conciliatory dispensation against the execution, since Shaul, the later Paul, appears to be the leader complicit in the death.

156. "Signs" is interpreted as miracles.

157. Shimon is Simon Magus (Simon the Magician), a major early Gnostic who is held by the early church to be an arch heretic. Gnosticism was in reality a more

the city before Filippos, practicing magic[158] and amazing the people of Shomron, saying that he was a great man, 10and everyone, from lowly to the great, followed him, saying, "This is the power of God, which is called Mighty." 11And they followed him because for some time he had captured them with his magic. 12But when they believed Filippos as he preached about the kingdom of God and the name of Yeshua the Mashiah,[159] they were dipped[160] in water, both men and women. 13And even Shimon himself believed. And when he was baptized, he followed Filippos everywhere, and when he saw the signs and the great powers,[161] he was astonished.

Shimon Kefa and Yohanan in Shomron

14When the messengers in Yerushalayim heard that Shomron had accepted the word of God, they sent Shimon Kefa and Yohanan to its

---

dangerous heretical enemy to the early Messianics and later Christians than the traditional Jews, since the majority of the classical Gnostics in Alexandria held themselves to be the true Christians, as was characteristic of each contending sect within the church. Augustine was a proselytizing Gnostic as a young man until his conversion to traditional Christianity. With their main early intellectual centers in Alexandria, Syria, and Rome, the classical Gnostics in Europe and North Africa were ultimately destroyed, meaning that Gnostic scriptures of diverse Gnostic sects were burned or hidden and the sects themselves killed or silenced. Nevertheless, Gnosticism continued in central Asia as Manichaeans and Mandaeans, and was the national religion of northwestern China (Xinjiang) from the eleventh through the thirteenth centuries, which roughly coincided with its dominance in southern France, in the Languedoc area, as the Neo-Manichaen Cathars. The Cathars were wiped out as a result of the thirteenth-century papal Albigensian Crusade and the establishment of the Inquisition in France, carried out by the Dominicans. It was not until the discovery in 1945 in Egypt of the great Nag Hammadi Library that at last we had fifty-one scrolls with major Gnostic scriptures, which have since been translated from Coptic (itself a translation from the Greek) into the world's languages. See Marvin Meyer, ed., *The Nag Hammadi Library* (San Francisco: HarperOne, 2007), and Willis Barnstone and Marvin Meyer, eds., *The Gnostic Bible* (Boston: Shambhala Books, 2004).

158. The feats of one's own sect are signs and miracles; those of an opposing sect are magic and sorcery. Similarly, one's own scripture is history; a rival's scripture is myth.

159. Jesus.

160. Baptized.

161. Usually translated "miracles." The Greek δύναμις (dynamis) means "power," "force, "energy." An English derivative is "dynamism."

people. 15They went down there and prayed that the Shomronim might receive the holy spirit, 16since though they had been dipped in water in the name of rabbi Yeshua, none had yet received the holy spirit. 17Then they laid their hands on them and they received the holy spirit.

Shimon the Magician offers silver for the gift of God

18When Shimon the Magician saw that the holy spirit was given by the messengers' laying on of the hands, he brought them money, 19saying, "Give me too this authority so that anyone I lay my hands on will receive the holy spirit."

20But Shimon Kefa said to him,

> May the silver in your hand perish. You thought
> You could buy the gift of God with money.
> 21You have no part or rightful share in this,
> Since your heart is not upright before God.
> 22So repent of evil and pray to the lord
> For the intention of your heart to be
> Forgiven. 23I see that you stand in the gall
> Of bitterness and the bonds of injustice.

24Shimon responded, "Pray for me to the lord that nothing you have said will come upon me."

25Then, after testifying and speaking the word of the lord, Shimon Kefa and Filippos returned to Yerushalayim, but not before speaking the good news in many villages of the Shomronim.[162]

An angel, Filippos, and an Ethiopian eunuch

26An angel of the lord spoke to Filippos saying,

> Rise and go to the south to the road
> Going down from Yerushalayim to Gaza,
> Where it is desert.

27And he rose and went and look: an Ethiopian eunuch, an important court official of the Queen Candace[163] who was in charge of all her

---

162. Samaritans.

163. Candace from the Greek Κανδάκη (Kandake), a title for the queen or queen mother of the Ethiopians. Ethiopian at this time meant Nubian, from southern Egypt or the northern Sudan.

treasury. He had come to Yerushalayim to worship, 28and was on his way home, sitting in his chariot and reading the prophet Yeshayahu.[164] 29Then the spirit said to Filippos, "Go to that chariot and join it."

30Then Filippos ran up to the chariot and heard him reading the prophet Yeshayahu and he said, "Do you understand what you are reading?"

31And the eunuch replied, "How can I, if I have no one to guide me?" And he invited Filippos to come up and sit by him. 32And this was the passage he was reading:

> As a sheep is led to slaughter
> And as a lamb before the shearer is silent,
> So he does not open his mouth.
> 33In humiliation he is deprived of justice.
> Who can speak of his descendants
> Since his life has been taken away from the earth?[165]

34The eunuch answered, saying to Filippos, "I ask you, about whom does the prophet say this? About himself or someone else?"

35Filippos opened his mouth and, beginning with this passage of scripture, gave him the good news of Yeshua.

36As they were going along the road, they came to some water and the eunuch said, "Look, water. What is preventing me from being dipped in it?"[166] 38And he ordered the chariot to stop and both of them, Filippos and the eunuch, went into the water and Filippos immersed him. 39But when they came out of the water, the spirit of the lord took Filippos away. The eunuch did not see him any longer, but he went on his way in joy.

40But Filippos found himself in Ashdod,[167] and he went through the region, preaching the good news to all the cities until he came to Caesarea.[168]

---

164. Isaiah.

165. Isa. 53.7 (Septuagint).

166. Verse 37, probably a later emendation, appears in other earlier texts. "Then Filippos said, 'If you believe with all your heart, you may.' And he answered, saying, 'I believe that Yeshua the Mashiah is the son of God.'"

167. Azotus from the Greek Ἄζωτος (Azotos), from the Hebrew אַשְׁדּוֹד (ashdod). About twenty miles north of Gaza, Ashdod is one of five principal Philistine cities.

168. Caesarea (Caesarea Maritima) was a major Roman harbor and settlement named for Caesar Augustus. It was rebuilt by Herod. It served as headquarters of

Chapter 9

Shaul on the road to light

But Shaul, still breathing threats and slaughter against the students of the lord, went to the high priest,[169] 2and asked him for letters to the synagogues of Damesek[170] so that if he found anyone, men or women, who were students of the way,[171] he could bring them back to Yerushalayim bound in-ropes. 3On his journey as he came near Damesek, suddenly a light from the sky shone around him, 4and he fell to the ground and heard a voice saying to him,

> Shaul, Shaul, why do you persecute me?

5And he said,

> Who are you, sir?

And he said,

> I am Yeshua whom you persecute.
> 6But rise and go into the city
> And you will be told what you must do.

7And the men who were traveling with Shaul stood there speechless. They heard the voice but saw no one. 8Shaul got up from the ground, and when he opened his eyes, he saw nothing. So they led him by the hand into Damesek. 9And he was three days blind, and didn't eat or drink.

10There a student in Damesek by the name of Hananyah,[172] and the rabbi said to him:

> Hananyah.

---

the Roman procurators, including that of Pontius Pilate. It was also an urban center of Christian Jews.

169. "Priest" is "kohen" or "cohen." "High" or "big priest" is from the Hebrew כֹּהֵן גָּדוֹל (kohen gadol), as in 2 Kings 12.10.

170. Damascus from the Greek Δαμασκός (Damaskos), from the Hebrew דְּמֶשֶׂק (damesek or dammesek).

171. "Way" from the Greek ὁδός (hodos) means "way" or "road." In the universal sense, in the West or East, "the way," whether of Saint John of the Cross's *via oscura* (dark way) or the *dao* of the *Daodejing*, marks a spiritual path and revelation. Here "students of the way" refers to the Messianics (Christian Jews) in the synagogues.

172. Ananias. See note 100 above for Greek and Hebrew philology.

And he said,

> Look, I am here, rabbi.

11The rabbi said to him:

> Get up and go to the street called Straight
> And look in Yehuda's house for a man from Tarsos.[173]
> Look, he is praying
> 12And in a vision[174] he saw a man named Hananyah
> Coming in and laying his hands upon him
> So he can see again.

13Hananyah answered,

> Lord, I heard from many about this man,
> Of how much wrong he did to your saints
> In Yerushalayim. 14And here he has the right
> From the chief priests to put into bonds all
> Who are calling out to you in your name.

15But the lord said to him:

> Go, for this man is my chosen vessel
> To carry my name before the gentiles[175] and kings[176]
> And the sons of Yisrael. 16I will show him
> How much for my name's sake he must suffer.

---

173. Tarsos from the Greek Ταρσός (Tarsos). Tarsos was a Greek city of commerce and learning and the capital of Cilicia in southwest Asia Minor; later as "Tarsus" (in Latin), it was the Roman Greek-speaking city where Paul was born. Tarsos is on the southern coast of Turkey, close to Syria and directly south of Cappadocia.

174. "In a vision" is not in some other texts.

175. Gentile from the late Latin *gens*, meaning "pagan," from the Greek ἔθνος (ethnos), meaning a "nation" or a "people." *Ethnikos* in the plural means "gentiles, non-Jews, Christian Jews, Christians, pagans," or "heathens," from the Hebrew גּוֹי (goy), plural גּוֹיִם (goyim), meaning "a people, nation, non-Jew." The diverse meanings given in usage and especially in translation of the Greek depend on the context. Normally, in the gospels and Acts a gentile is a non-Jew, usually a Greek, who may be converted to Jewish Messianism or, as in later church koine, a "Christian Jew who is a convert from paganism," as in parts of Acts and the letters; and if the word is used disparagingly to mean both a non-Jew and non-Christian, it refers to a pagan. In its fully wicked sense, "gentile" means a "heathen." In modern English the commonest meaning of "gentile" has come to be a Christian as opposed to a Jew.

176. Probably Agrippa in Israel and Nero in Rome.

17Hananyah left and entered the house, and placed his hands on him and said, "Brother Shaul, Yeshua, who appeared to you on the road you came on, the lord has sent me so that you may see again and be filled with the holy spirit."

18And suddenly something like scales fell from his eyes, and he saw again, and got up and was dipped in water. 19When he took food, he regained his strength.

Shaul in Damesek and a plot

Shaul was with students in Damesek for some days, 20and immediately began to proclaim in the synagogues that Yeshua is the son of God. 21All were amazed who heard him and said, "Isn't he the same one who in Yerushalayim attacked those who evoked this name?[177] And didn't he come here to take those people away in bonds back to the high priests?"

22But Shaul became even stronger and confounded the Jews living in Damesek by demonstrating that he was the Mashiah.[178]

23After many days passed, the Jews conspired to kill him,[179] 24but Shaul learned of their plot. They were watching the gates day and night, to kill him. 25However, the students took him through an opening in the wall and lowered him out in a basket.

Shaul in Yerushalayim and conspiracies

26Arriving in Yerushalayim, Shaul tried to attach himself to the students, yet all were afraid of him, not believing he was a disciple.[180] 27But

---

177. That of Yeshua or Jesus.

178. Messiah or the Christ (in Greek translation of *mashiah*).

179. The use of the word "Jew" to represent the "other," and in this instance a *killer* of Christians, is anachronistic in that Paul declared himself a Jew before and after his vision of Jesus as the Jewish messiah. Hence, if this ugly, provocative event has a historical source, the designation of the Jews as wicked killers makes no sense. Similarly, we must find Paul and Jesus typed as hateful and murderous for being Jews? The passage reflects not Paul's period but decades after Paul's death when the gospels and Acts were composed and when a division between Christian and Jew was a reality and hatred of the Jew in scriptures normal.

180. In Galatians 1.15–20 Paul suggests that he came first to Jerusalem three years after his conversion.

Bar Nabba[181] took him to the messengers and told them how on the road Shaul saw the rabbi and the rabbi talked to him, and how in Damesek he spoke out in the name of Yeshua. 28So he was with them, going in and out of Yerushalayim, speaking out in the name of the rabbi. 29He spoke to and debated with the Hellenized Jews,[182] and they were trying to kill him. 30But when his brothers learned of this, they secreted him down to Caesarea and sent him to Tarsos.

Peace

31Meanwhile the Messianic church throughout all Yehuda and the Galil and Shomron had peace, was building up, lived in the fear of the lord and in the comfort of the holy spirit as its numbers increased.

Shimon Kefa in Lod with Aineas a paralytic

32It happened that while Shimon Kefa was passing through many areas, he came to the saints who lived in Lod.[183] 33And there he found a man named Aineas,[184] who had been lying on a floor bed for eight years. He was paralyzed. 34Shimon Kefa said to him, "Yeshua the Mashiah heals you. Get up and make your bed." And immediately he got up.

---

181. Barnabas.

182. Hellenists. Here in Acts a Hellenist (Ἑλληνιστής, Hellenistes) is a Greek-speaking Jew as opposed to an Aramaic-speaking Jew. Paul, of Tarsos, was a Hellenist, that is, a Greek-speaking Jew, as were most of the Jews who lived in the cities of the diaspora except for those living in Persia, Babylonia, and regions of the Mesopotamia and the Arabian Peninsula where, as in Israel, they spoke Aramaic, the language of Babylonia. The Jews of the Captivity adopted Aramaic, reserving Hebrew for the temple and for scripture.

183. Lydda from the Greek Λύδδα (Lydda), from the Hebrew לֹד (lod), a city southeast of Jaffa on the road to Jerusalem. The city's inhabitants suffered under Pompey and Cassius, who sold the people as slaves. Mark Antony freed them, but Cestius Gallus burned the city in 66 C.E. while its inhabitants were celebrating the Sukkoth. It was a rabbinic center of learning and an early Christian-Jewish center. The Crusaders named it Saint George for George's martyrdom there.

184. Aeneas from the Greek Αἰνέας (Aineas). Aeneas, as in the *Aeneid*, is a Latin version of the Greek name. Because of his Greek name, Aeneas may have been a gentile convert, although many Greek names had entered Aramaic and had been adopted by Jews, including the gospel names Markos, Lukas, Filippos, and Andreas—Mark, Luke, Philip, and Andrew.

35And all those who lived in Lod and Sharon[185] saw him and turned to the lord.[186]

Shimon Kefa in Yafo with Tavita a corpse

36In Yafo[187] there was a student named Tavita,[188] who in Greek translation is Dorkas,[189] a gazelle. She was filled with the good works and alms to the poor. 37And it happened that in those days she fell sick and died. After washing her, they laid her out in an upper room. 38Lod is close to Yafo, and the students, hearing that Shimon Kefa was there, sent two men to him, urging him, "Please come to us at once."

---

185. Sharon from the Greek Σαρών (Saron), from the Hebrew שָׁרוֹן (sharon). Sharon is fertile coastal plain from Jaffa down to Mount Carmel, and anciently a caravan route connecting Asia Minor with Egypt and Mesopotamia.

186. Peter (Simon) has a distinguished role as healer, miracle maker, missionary, and saint in Acts and the letters.

After his hard going in the gospels, he (or a figure named Peter) rises in stature from a humble fisherman to the illustrious and learned founder, along with James, of the Jerusalem church, a missionary and saint. He is in conflict with Paul, who rebukes him (Gal. 2.11–14), and especially since Peter and James represent a home church in Jerusalem where the main converts to Jesus as the messiah are Jews, while Paul represents a world diaspora and more flexibility in moving away from onerous elements of Jewish law in order to welcome gentiles into Messianic Judaism. Peter is a mediator, or attempts to be, between Paul and James (who is traditionally but improbably held to be Jesus's brother), who is by contrast hostile to opening this splinter movement of Jews to uncircumised gentiles. The feud between Paul and James was, like all feuds in both emerging and established religions, elemental and at times fierce. Paul worked in the diaspora, converting Jews and gentiles to the good news of Jesus, while James replaced Peter as titular head of the more conservatively Christian Jews in Jerusalem.

187. Jaffa, Joppa, from the Greek Ἰόππη (Ioppe), from the Hebrew יָפוֹ (yafo). Jaffa or Joppa, a major ancient port of Israel on a promontory near Tel Aviv, was originally allotted to the tribe of Dan. In fifth century B.C.E. the Persians gave it to the Syrians, and after Alexander the Great it was populated by Greeks and Syrians. The Hasmoneans reconquered it around 140 B.C.E. In the early Christian period it was a seat of a bishop.

188. Tabitha from the Greek Ταβιθά (Tabitha), from the Aramaic טְבִיתָא (tavita).

189. Dorcas from the Greek Δορκάς (Dorkas), a "gazelle."

₃₉Shimon Kefa got up and went with them, and when he arrived they took him to the upper room, and all the widows stood near him, crying and displaying all the tunics and mantles that Dorkas had made when she was with them. ₄₀Then Shimon Kefa put everyone outside, fell on his knees and prayed, and turned to the body he said, "Tavita, stand up." Then she opened her eyes, and when she saw Shimon Kefa she sat up. ₄₁He gave his hand to her and raised her up, and called out to the saints and widows and presented her alive. ₄₂This became known throughout Yafo and and many believed in the Yeshua.

Shimon Kefa and the tanner
₄₃And it happened that he stayed on in Yafo with Shimon a tanner.¹⁹⁰

Chapter 10

Cornelius the Italian centurion and the angel
There was a man in Caesarea named Cornelius, a centurion from

---

190. Peter's staying with a tanner may have an intended significance in that a tanner worked with animal hides and was therefore virtually an outcast, ritually unclean. While the Jewish laws of cleanliness had a health basis, like all laws in a theocratic society they also took on a sacred ritual meaning. To stay with a tanner has been widely interpreted as a sign that Peter wished to disregard Jewish practices. If so, there is a certain irony in the gesture, since Peter, at least Peter of the letters as opposed to Peter of Acts, remained closer to Jewish law and ritual than did any other important figure and found himself in conflict with Paul and others for that very reason.

There is anecdotal evidence about Peter's life, death, and travels, and extensive accounts on Peter in the noncanonical apocrypha, including a contest in which both Peter and Simon Magus fly over the city of Rome. Simon flies higher but Peter causes Simon to fall and be killed, so in this tale Peter is triumphant. Most of these pseudepigraphical stories date from mid-second-century scriptures composed a century after the gospel events, by which time Christianity was distinct in identity, if not origin, from its parent religion. For more on Peter in the intertestamental scriptures, see Willis Barnstone, *The Other Bible* (San Francisco: HarperSanFrancisco, 2005).

the cohort called the Italian division,[191] 2who was pious and feared God, along with all his household. He gave alms generously to the poor and constantly prayed to God. 3In a vision about the ninth hour of the day,[192] the Roman saw an angel of God coming to him and saying to him:

> Cornelius.

4He gazed at him and in terror said to him,

> Lord, what is it?

The angel said to him:

> Your prayers and all your charities,
> As portions of grain burnt on the altar,
> Are a memorial offering before God.[193]
> 5Now send men to Yafo for Shimon,
> Whose surname is Shimon Kefa. 6He is staying
> With Shimon the tanner who lives
> In a house you will find by the sea.[194]

7And when the angel left, he called in two of his household servants and a pious soldier from among his attendants, 8and after informing them about everything sent them to Yafo.

---

191. Probably the Italian Cohort from the Cohors II of the Italica Civium Romanorum. Peter is credited with converting the first gentile to messianic Judaism, but there were other conversions of gentiles in the gospels, including that of the Samaritan, though the Samaritans were, like the Essenes and the Messianics, one of many Jewish sects. This event is recounted in Mark, Matthew, and Luke. By the time Acts was composed, the Roman executioner is visited by an angel who praises him for his charities and tells the officer to send men to the house of Shimon the tanner. In John, however, there is no conversion and the sole action after the execution has a Roman soldier pierce Jesus's stomach with his spear. In Acts, following the pattern of the gospels of exculpating Rome and its military from the onus of having executed the messiah, a Roman officer gives alms and prays like a pious Jew and becomes the first gentile Christian, and first among all to recognize Jesus's divinity.

192. Three in the afternoon. As others have noted, the centurion follows Jewish religious practices. The ninth hour of the day corresponds to the Jewish hour of prayer. See verse 3.1.

193. "portions of grain burnt on the altar," not in the Greek, explains "a memorial offering."

194. Later manuscripts add, "He will tell you what to do" (20.6).

Shimon Kefa in ecstasy

9On the next day as the travelers drew near to the city, Shimon Kefa went up to the roof about the sixth hour to pray.[195] 10And he got hungry and wanted to eat. As the meal was being prepared for him, he came into ecstasy. 11And he saw the heavens opened, and descending was an object like a great linen sheet being lowered by its four corners down to the earth. 12In it were all the four-footed beasts and reptiles of the earth and birds of heaven. 13And a voice came to him:

> Stand up, kill and eat.

14But Shimon Kefa said,

> Surely not, lord, since I have never eaten
> Anything common and unclean.[196]

15And a second time the voice came down to him:

> What God made clean, don't make unclean.[197]

16This happened three times and the object was suddenly raised into the sky.

17While Shimon Kefa pondered the meaning of the vision he had seen, look, the three men sent by Cornelius were looking for Shimon's house. 18And after asking for Shimon, they stood before his gate.

19Shimon Kefa was still pondering the meaning of the vision, when the spirit said to him, "Look, the men are looking for you. 20Stand up, go downstairs, and go off with them. Don't hesitate, since I sent them."

21Shimon Kefa came down and said to the men, "Look, I am the one you are looking for. Why are you here?"

22And they said, "Cornelius, a centurion, a just God-fearing man, well-spoken of by the whole Jewish nation, was summoned by a holy angel to send for you to come to his house and hear your words."

23So Shimon Kefa invited them in as his guests.

---

195. At noon.

196. Peter protests breaking the dietary laws of what is proper to eat, which as a Jew he has followed.

197. God has made all things clean. See Matthew 15.11. By a subversion of the dietary laws, along with those on circumcision, the way was open to make Messianic Judaism more welcome to a large gentile conversion and eventually to distinguish Judaism from emerging Christianity.

The next day he awoke and went out with them and some of the brothers from Yafo accompanied him. 24And the following day he entered
Caesarea. Cornelius was expecting them and had called together his
relatives and close friends.

Cornelius and the angel

25When Shimon Kefa met him, Cornelius fell at his feet and worshiped him. 26But Shimon Kefa raised him and said, "Stand up. I am also
a man."[198] 27And he talked with him and went inside and found many
gathered there, 28and said to them, "You know that it is unlawful for one
who is a Jew to approach or mingle with a foreigner.[199] God has shown
me that I must not call anyone common or unclean. 29Therefore when
I was summoned I came without any objections. So I ask why have you
invited me here?"

30And Cornelius said, "Four days ago I was praying in my house at the
ninth hour,[200] and look, a man stood before me in shining clothes 31and
he said:

> Cornelius, God has heard your prayer
> And remembers your alms to the poor.
> 32So send to Yafo and summon Shimon
> Who is surnamed Shimon Kefa, living in the house
> Of Shimon the tanner by the sea.
> 33So I immediately sent for you
> And you have had the goodness to come.

---

198. Or, "person." Peter is saying he is human, not a god.

199. The Bible and its commentaries abound in mingling between Jews and foreigners. Philo of Alexandria was a major Neo-Platonist and at the same time a prolific
Jewish scholar, the most esteemed Jew in Egypt just as the Jewish historian Josephus lived out his life in Rome under the personal patronage of the emperor. Especially in this period of major Jewish proselytizing in many nations, these words are
inexplicable except to convey the notion that only the Messianic Jews (Christian
Jews) could mix with and welcome outsiders on a personal, commercial, political,
and religious level. However, with regard to conversion, there is no question that
by abolishing the dietary laws, a significant obstacle to Messianism (Christianity)
was removed.

200. Three in the afternoon.

So now we are all here in God's presence
To hear all the lord ordered you to say."

34Shimon Kefa opened his mouth and said,
I understand the truth: God shows no partiality.
35In every nation he accepts one who fears him
And does what is right. 36He sent the word
To the sons and daughters of Yisrael, speaking
The good news of peace through Yeshua the Mashiah,
Who is lord of all. 37And you know the things
That have happened through all of Yehuda,
Beginning in the Galil after the dipping in water
Which Yohanan preached, 38and how God anointed
Yeshua from Natzeret with the holy spirit
And with power, how he went about doing good
And healing all who were under the power of the devil,
For God was with him. 39We are all witnesses
To all that he did in the country of the Jews
And in Yerushalayim. They put him to death
By hanging him from a tree. 40God raised him
On the third day and granted him to be visible
41Not to everyone but to those witnesses
Whom God earlier selected, who ate and drank together
With him after he rose from the dead.
42And he commanded us to preach to the people
And to testify that he was chosen by God
To be judge of all the living and the dead.
43All prophets testify that all who believe in him
Receive forgiveness for sins through his name.

The holy breath falling on Jew and gentile
44While Shimon Kefa was still speaking these words, the holy spirit
fell on everyone hearing his word. 45And the circumcised faithful who
accompanied Shimon Kefa were amazed that the gift of the holy breath[201]

---

201. Spirit. The Greek has the double meaning of "breath" and, by extension, "spirit."

also was poured down on the gentiles.²⁰² ₄₆They heard them speaking in tongues²⁰³ and magnifying God.

₄₇Then Shimon Kefa asked, "Can anyone prevent these people from being dipped in the water, who have, like us, received the holy spirit?" ₄₈And he commanded them to be dipped in the name of Yeshua the Mashiah.

Then they asked him to stay a few days.

Chapter 11

Shimon Kefa defends embracing the uncircumcised

The messengers and the brothers who were in Yehuda heard that the gentiles also had received the word of God. ₂When Shimon Kefa went up to Yerushalayim, the circumcised²⁰⁴ criticized him ₃and said, "You ate in the house of the uncircumcised and ate with them."

₄Then Shimon Kefa explained everything to them in order and from the beginning:

₅I was in the city of Yafo, praying,
And in the ecstacy of a vision I saw
Coming down an object, like a big linen sheet,
Being let down by the corners from the sky,
And it came close to me. ₆As I looked at it closely
I saw four-footed beasts of the earth
And reptiles and birds of the sky.
₇And I heard a voice saying to me,
"Stand up, Shimon Kefa. Kill and eat." ₈But I said,
"Surely not, lord, since I have never let anything
Common and unclean enter my stomach."
₉The voice answered a second time from the sky:
"What God made clean, don't make unclean."

---

202. "Gentiles" here signifies "proselytes to Judaism."
203. In languages other than Aramaic.
204. Christian Jews.

10This happened three times and then everything
    Was drawn up again into the sky. 11And look,
    Suddenly three men stood before me in my house,
    Sent to me from Caesarea. 12And the spirit told me,
    "Go with them, without worrying about distinctions
    Between us." These six brothers also came
    And we entered the man's house, 13and he reported
    How he saw an angel standing in his house,
    And it said, "Send to Yafo and summon Shimon
    Whose surname is Shimon Kefa. 14He will give you words
    To save all of you and save your household."
15And as I began to speak, the holy spirit
    Fell on them as it had on us in the beginning.
16And I remembered the word of our rabbi,
    How he had said, "Yohanan dipped with water,
    But you will be dipped in the holy spirit."
17If God gave them the same gift he gave us
    When we believed in rabbi Yeshua the Mashiah,
    Who was I to block the ways of God?

18When they heard this, they were silent. Then they glorified God, saying, "So God has given even the gentiles repentance to lead them into life."

Bar Nabba in Antioch and early Messianics

19Those who were dispersed because of the persecution after the events of Stefanos, traveled as far as Phoenicia and Cyprus and Antioch, and they spoke the word to no one but the Jews.[205] 20But some of them were from Cyrene, and when they came to Antioch they also spoke to the Greek Jews,[206] preaching word of rabbi Yeshua. 21And the hand of the lord was with them, and a great number believed and turned to the rabbi. 22Word of this came to the ears of the church in Yerushalayim, and they sent Bar Nabba to Antioch. 23When he arrived and saw the grace of God, he was joyful and he animated them all to devote their hearts to the rabbi, 24since he was a good man and filled with the holy spirit and

---

205. Reference is probably to Greek-speaking Jews.
206. The "Hellenized," meaning Greek Jews or Greek-speaking Jews.

faith. And many people were brought to the rabbi. 25Then Bar Nabba left for Tarsos to look for Shaul, 26and when he found him he brought him to Antioch. So for a whole year they met with him in the church and taught a great many people, and it was in Antioch that the students were first called Messianics.[207]

Prophets and famine in Yehuda

27In these days prophets came down from Yerushalayim to Antioch, 28and one of them by the name of Agav[208] stood up and predicted that there would be a great famine over all the inhabited world. This took place during the reign of Claudius.[209] 29The students, each according to their means, each decided to send help to the brothers living in Yehuda. 30This they did by sending gifts to the elders through Bar Nabba and Shaul.

Chapter 12

Herod's tyranny and Shimon Kefa and the angel

About this time King Herod[210] used his own hands to harm those

---

207. Christians. Even today the questions of ethnic, religious, and political identity possess and sometimes ravage the world, when any polarity assumes the need to clean the world of the unwashed enemies.

208. Agabus or Hagabus from the Greek Ἄγαβος (Hagabos), from the Hebrew עָגָב (agav).

209. Later texts give Claudius Caesar. The emperor Claudius ruled from 41 to 54. The famine may have occurred in 46. Since Acts was written many decades after 46, the question of correct or false prophecy is problematic, since the prophetic knowledge is already a fact or a fiction. In the instance of sybils and other traditional and mythical prophetic figures, the actually written "witness" account of the prophecy usually postdates the prophesied event by decades or centuries.

210. Herod (Agrippa I by his Roman name) was made king of Judea by Claudius in 41. He also had the title of Tetrarch of Galilee and Paraea. Born Marcus Julius Agrippa, son of Aristobolus IV, in the New Testament alone Agrippa I is King Herod (41–44). During his reign Peter was arrested and James executed. His grandfather was Herod the Great (37–4 B.C.E.), the builder of the second Temple, and his uncle was Herod Antipas (4 B.C.E.–39 C.E.), who was said to have had John the Baptist beheaded and, according to the gospels, was hostilely present during Jesus's trial. His son, Agrippa II, ruled during the Jewish War (66–70) and the great diaspora of 70.

of the church. 2He killed Yaakov,[211] brother of Yohanan, with a sword. 3Seeing that this pleased the Jews,[212] he then went on to arrest Shimon Kefa. These events took place during the Days of the Matzot Bread.[213] 4And having seized Shimon Kefa, he put him in jail, and handed him over to four squads of soldiers to guard him, intending to bring him before the people after the Pesach. 5While Shimon Kefa was in prison, the church prayed fervently to God for him.

6When Herod was about to bring him out, that night Shimon Kefa was sleeping between two soldiers and bound with two chains. Guards in front of the door were watching the prison. 7And look, an angel of the lord came near and shone in the room. He hit Shimon Kefa on the side, raised him, and said:

Rise quickly.

And the chains fell off his wrists.

8Then the angel said to him:

Fasten your belt and tie your sandals.

And he did so. Then the angel said to him:

Wrap your cloak around you and follow me.

9And he followed him out, and he didn't know that what was happening through the angel's help was real. He thought he had a vision.

10They passed through the first guard and the second and came to the iron gate leading to the city. The gate opened of its own accord, they went out, walked along the street and suddenly the angel left him. 11And Shimon Kefa came to himself and said, "Now I truly know that the lord has sent his angel and that he has delivered me from the hand of Herod and from all the expectations of the Jews." 12And when he

---

211. James (Yaakov) was one of the sons of Zebedee.

212. The Jew-hating accusation that the Romans killed James, a Jew, because "it would please the Jews" has no historical basis. The Jews revolted against Rome many times, and Rome's response was to massacre the Jews, usually by ostentatious crucifixion, as when Titus crucified Jews along a long section of the walls of Jerusalem during the 66–70 Jewish War. To suggest that the Romans, the occupying power, took any major step to please the Jews, their rebellious subjects, is nonsense.

213. Literally, "days of the unleavened bread." The feasts or suppers of the Pesach or Passover. See note 142 on Mark 14.1.

realized this, he came to the house of Miryam, the mother of Yohanan, also called Markos, where many were gathered and praying. 13When he knocked on the courtyard door, a young servant named Roda[214] came to answer. 14When she recognized Shimon Kefa's voice, she was so happy she didn't open the door but ran inside and announced that Shimon Kefa was standing at the gate.

15Those near her said, "You are crazy!"

But she insisted he was there.

"It is his angel," they said.

16Meanwhile Shimon Kefa kept knocking, and when they opened the gate they were amazed. 17Shimon Kefa motioned with his hand to be quiet, and explained to them how the lord had led him out of the prison, and said, "Report this to Yaakov[215] and his brothers."

Then he went to another place.

18When day came, there was no small commotion among the soldiers over what had become of Shimon Kefa. 19Herod searched for him and couldn't find him. Then he interrogated the guards and ordered them to be taken away and executed. Then he went down from Yehuda to Caesarea and stayed there.

Herod and the angel of death

20Herod was furious with the people of Tzor[216] and Tzidon.[217] They came to him in a group and, after winning over Blastus, the king's personal chamberlain,[218] asked for peace, since their country depended on the king's country for food. 21And on an appointed day, Herod put on his

---

214. Rhoda from the Greek Ῥόδη (Rode), meaning "rose" or "rose tree" or "rose-bush." The name can also be translated simply as "Rose."

215. James. Not James, one of the sons of Zebedee (as in verse 12.2), but James, Jesus's brother, next in age, and titular head of the Jerusalem church.

216. Tyre from the Greek Τύρος (Tyros), from the Hebrew צוֹר (tzor), צֹר (tzor), or טוּר (tur), meaning "hard quartz" or "a flint knife," from the Aramaic טוּר (tur), meaning "a rock."

217. Sidon from the Greek Σιδών (Sidon), from the Hebrew צִידוֹן (tzidon).

218. Officer head of Herod's household and his treasurer. To win him over probably signified having access to Herod.

royal clothing and sat down on the platform throne[219] and made a speech to the populace. 22The crowd was screaming, "The voice of God, not of a person!" 23Suddenly an angel of the lord struck him down because he had not glorified God, and he was eaten by worms and died.

24And the word of God grew and increased.

25And after fulfilling their mission, Bar Nabba and Shaul returned to Yerushalayim.[220] They brought with them Yohanan, whose other name was Markos.[221]

Chapter 13

Bar Nabba and Shaul journey to Cyprus

In the church in Antioch there were prophets and teachers: Bar Nabba, and Shimon who was called Dark,[222] and Loukios[223] the Cyrenian, and Menahem[224] who grew up with Herod the Tetrarch, and Shaul. And while worshiping the lord and fasting, the holy spirit said:

2Set apart for me Bar Abba and Shaul

To do the work for which I've called them.

3Then after fasting and praying, the others laid hands on them and sent them off.

4So these men went down to Seleukeia[225] and from there sailed

---

219. May also be translated "judicial bench."

220. "Returned to Jerusalem" is not in all texts.

221. It is uncertain who this John Mark is. Some say it is the young man who fled the night Jesus was arrested (Mark 14.51–52).

222. Niger, a Latin loan name and word meaning "dark" or "black."

223. Lucius from the Greek Λούκιος (Loukios).

224. Manaen from the Greek Μαναήν (Manaen), from the Hebrew מְנַחֵם (menahem). "Menahem" means the "comforter," as does "Paraclete" (comforter), meaning the holy spirit or the messiah (uncertain) in John 14.16. Menahem is also the Essene messiah in the Dead Sea Scroll "Thanksgiving Hymn 2."

225. Seleucia from the Greek Σελεύκεια (Seleukeia), about sixteen miles west of Antioch, serving as its seaport. It was also called Seleucia Pieria.

to Cyprus, 5and in Salamis[226] they preached the word of God in the synagogues of the Jews. And they had Yohanan[227] with them as a helper.

Shaul blinds a false Jewish prophet

6When they had gone through the whole island as far as Pafos,[228]
they found a certain man, a false Jewish prophet, whose name was Bar
Yeshua[229] 7who was with the proconsul Sergius Paulus, an intelligent
man. The proconsul invited Bar Nabba and Shaul in and wanted to hear
the word of God, 8but the magician Elymas (for this is how his name is
translated)[230] opposed them and tried to turn the proconsul away from
his faith. 9But Shaul, who is also Paul,[231] was filled with the holy spirit,
glared at him and said, 10"You are full of all trickery and all fraud, you son
of the devil, enemy of justice, and will you not stop making the straight
path of the lord crooked? 11And look, now the hand of the lord is against
you and you will be blind and not see the sun for a while."

Suddenly mist and darkness fell on him and he went about groping
for someone to lead him by the hand.

12When the proconsul saw what had happened, astounded by the
teaching of the rabbi, he believed.[232]

---

226. A city on the northeast coast of Cyprus.

227. The first John or John Mark mentioned in 12.25.

228. Paphos from the Greek Πάφος (Pafos). Paphos was the ancient capital of
Cyprus and also the legendary birthplace of Aphrodite.

229. Bar Jesus or Barjesus from the Greek Βαριησοῦς (Bariesous), meaning in Aramaic and Hebrew (where *ben* is usually "son"), "son of Jesus," from the Aramaic
בַּר יֵשׁוּעַ (bar yeshua). *Bar* in Aramaic is "son."

230. "Elymas" does not mean *Barjesus*, which means "son of Jesus." "Elymas" is a
Semitic name meaning "magician" or "sorcerer."

231. From now on Shaul (Saul) is called by his Greek name *Paulos* or *Pavlos*, but
Shaul here is restoring the Hebrew name. His Latin name was *Saulus*, by which he
was probably known to the Romans, which Latinizes *Shaul*.

232. As in the gospels, it is significant that although Paul has gone to Cyprus to convince Jews in the synagogues that the foretold savior has arrived in the person of
Jesus, on his first mission and upon assuming the Roman name of Saulus (Shaul),
his first conversion should be a Roman official and gentile, which parallels, at the
crucifixion, the on-the-spot conversion to Jewish Messianism by the Roman centurion Cornelius, who has just directed the execution of Jesus.

In Pisidian Antioch and of death without decay

13Sailing from Pafos, Shaul and his party came to Perga in Pamfylia,[233] but Yohanan left them and went back to Yerushalayim. 14And journeying from Perga, they went up to Antioch in Pisidia,[234] and entered the synagogue on Shabbat[235] and sat down. 15After the reading from Torah[236] and Prophets, the heads of the synagogue sent them a message saying, "Brothers, if you have a word of encouragement for the people, say it."

16Shaul got up and gesturing with his hands said, "Yisraelis[237] and those fearing God, listen. 17The god[238] of this people, Israel, chose our ancestors[239] and exalted the people during their stay in Egypt, and with his raised arm led them out. 18For about forty years he nurtured them[240]

---

233. Pamphylia. Perga was the capital of Pamphylia, a coastal province of present-day Turkey, some two hundred miles west of Tarsos, where Paul was born.

234. Pisidia is a mountainous region in central Asia Minor that Paul traversed, well west of the Taurus mountains, to reach Antioch. Pisidian Antioch is not to be confused with the major city of Antioch in Syria, far to the southeast.

235. Day of the Sabbath.

236. Torah, meaning "the law," refers to the first five books of the Hebrew Bible (Pentateuch or five books of Moses), but also means the entire Hebrew Bible. Here the reference is to the Pentateuch.

237. Israeli, or, in its Greek form, Israelite. See note 32 on John 1.47, and for a fuller account note 79 on Romans 9.4.

238. "God" is not capitalized in Greek or Hebrew. Here it is uncapitalized because God is not being addressed by his name but is distinguished as the god of Israel as compared, presumably, to less significant gods.

239. Here, in the synagogue, Paul is speaking as one of his time, not anachronistically from a later period when Messianic Jews were Christians. Hence, in contrast to earlier moments in Acts, when there is Paul and then the Jews, Paul speaks in first person plural of "our ancestors" (literally, "fathers") and identifies with the members of the congregation at the same time that he attempts to persuade them that "our" messiah has arrived in the person of Jesus the Messiah. In the next passages, giving the history of God and the Jews, he speaks no longer of "us" but of "them," thereby distancing himself from Hebrew Bible Jews. However, when announcing the good news in the synagogue, Paul returns to "our ancestors." The shifting of identity from Jew "us" to Jew "them" reflects the extended complexity of recognition and denial that was huge in the late first and the second century, and has continued in related forms until now.

240. Other ancient texts have "put up with" them in the desert. These significant

in the desert. 19After he destroyed seven nations in the land of Canaan, 20he gave them the land as an inheritance for about four hundred fifty years.241 Then he gave them judges until the prophet Shmuel. 21And when they asked for a king, God gave them Shaul son of Kish, from the tribe of Benyamin,242 for forty years. 22After setting him aside, he raised up David as their king, to whom he bore witness, saying:

> I found David, son of Yishai,243
>
> After my own heart. He is a man
>
> Who will carry out all my wishes.

23From this man's seed, according to his promise God brought Yisrael its savior, Yeshua. 24Before his Yeshua's coming, Yohanan had proclaimed repentance for all the people of Yisrael. 25And as Yohanan was completing his road, he would say:

> What do you suppose I am? I am not he.244
>
> But look, there is one coming after me
>
> And I am not worthy to untie the sandals of his feet.

26Men and brothers, children of the family Avraham and you who fear God, the word of this salvation has been sent to us. 27Those in Yerushalayim and their leaders have not recognized him nor the voices of the prophets read on every Shabbat. Those words were fulfilled by their judgment245 of them. 28And without finding any reason for his death, they asked Pilatus to have him killed. 29And when they had completed all that was written about him, they took him down from the wood, and put him in a tomb. 30But God raised him from the dead. 31And he was seen for some days by those who had come up from the Galil to Yerushalayim, who are witnesses of him before the people.

---

antithetical verbs, one of nurturing and caring, the other of disapproving toleration, indicate that one copyist wished to show God's protective care of the Jews in this period while another chose a verb to reveal God's annoyance.

241. The rabbinic calculation covers the period from the entrance into Canaan to the building of the first Temple.

242. Benjamin, from the Greek Βενιαμίν (Beniamin), from the Hebrew בְּאנְיָמִין (benyamin).

243. Jesse from the Greek Ἰεσσαί (Iessai), from the Hebrew יִשַׁי (yishai).

244. "He" is omitted but implied in the Greek.

245. Implying a rejection.

32We bring you the good news of the promise made to our ancestors and 33which God has fulfilled for us, his children. He has raised Yeshua. As it is written in psalm two:

> You are my son.
> Today I have engendered you.[246]

34As for raising him from the dead and no more to return to corruption, he has spoken in the way of Yeshayahu:

> I give you the holy promises of David,
> In which you may put your trust.[247]

35And in another psalm he says:

> You will not let your sacred one
> Know corruption.[248]

36David, who in his own generation had served the will of God, fell asleep[249] and was laid among his ancestors and experienced decay, 37but he whom God raised experienced no decay. 38Let it be known then, men and brothers, that through him, Yeshua, the remission of your sins is proclaimed, and of all things which the Torah of Moshe could not justify. 39By this all believers are justified and set free. 40And see that what the prophets said could happen does not happen to you:

> 41Look, you who doubt and scoff,
> Be in wonder and become nothing,
> Since in your days I am performing
> A deed which you will not believe
> Even if someone tells you."[250]

42When Shaul and Bar Nabba went out, the people asked them to speak about these words at the next Shabbat. 43And when the meeting broke up, many of the Jews and devout converts to Judaism followed Shaul and Bar Nabba, who spoke to them, urging them to remain in the grace of God.

---

246. Ps. 2.7.
247. Isa. 55.3 (Septuagint).
248. Ps. 16.10 (Septuagint).
249. Meaning "died."
250. Hab. 1.5 (Septuagint).

44On the next Shabbat almost the whole city gathered to hear the word of the lord. 45But when the Jews[251] saw the crowds they were filled with envy and attacked the words spoken by Shaul as blasphemy. 46But Shaul and Bar Nabba spoke out boldly, saying, "It was imperative that the word of God be spoken first to you. Since you reject it and consider yourselves unworthy of eternal life, look, we are turning to the gentiles.[252] 47For so the lord commanded us in Yeshayahu:

> I have appointed you to be the light to the gentiles
> So you can bring salvation to the ends of the earth."[253]

48When the gentiles heard this they were happy and glorified [the word of God][254] and all those who were destined for eternal life believed. 49And the word of God was spreading through the entire land.

50But the Jews incited the prominent women who were worshipers and the leading men of the city and initiated a persecution of Shaul and Bar Nabba and drove them out of their region. 51So they shook the dust off their feet against them, and went to Ikonion,[255] 52and their students were filled with happiness and the holy spirit.

---

251. The key word "Jew" has shifting, conflicting meanings. Immediately after the text speaks favorably of the Jew in the synagogue whom the messengers Paul and Barnabas have come to Cyprus to enlighten and lead to Jesus, now the word "Jew" is used as an ugly stereotype, implicating a people, evoking a jealous, murderous figure, although the crowd of new believers presumably consists of Jews who have heard the words of God. The lesson is that those who listen to Paul and Barnabas may be initially identified as Jews without denigration, while those who do not hear, like the false prophet blinded by Paul, are Jewish villains.

252. Turning exclusively to the gentiles contradicts the statement of the first converts who were the Jews in the synagogue, revealed a few lines earlier: "And when the meeting broke up, many of the Jews and devout converts to Judaism followed Shaul and Bar Nabba" (13.43).

253. Isa. 49.6.

254. Bracketed words are not in all ancient texts.

255. Iconium from the Greek Ἰκόνιον (Ikonion). Iconium is today's Konya in Turkey, now venerated for the Persian poet Rūmī (Jalāl al-Din Rūmī), the Persian Sufi and mystical poet who died in Konya in 1273. He is called Rūmī because he came from the Rum; Persian for "Rome," meaning the Byzantine Empire. So Greek, Latin, Persian, and Turkish are among the main languages that have been spoken in this part of Asia Minor where Shaul proselytized.

Chapter 14

In Ikonion, preaching and fleeing stones

In Ikonion as before, Shaul and Bar Nabba entered the synagogue of the Jews and spoke so that a great multitude of Jews and Greeks became believers. 2But the Jews who were unwilling to believe stirred up the gentiles and poisoned their spirits against the brothers. 3So Shaul and Bar Nabba spent much time speaking fearlessly for the lord, who testified to the word of his grace by granting signs and wonders that happened through their hands. 4The multitude in the city was divided, and some were with the Jews but others with the messengers. 5But when there was a movement by gentiles and Jews, with their leaders, to hound and stone them, 6the messengers learned of it and fled to Lystra and Derbe, cities of Lykaonia,²⁵⁶ and the surrounding countryside.

7There they were speaking the good news.

In Lystra with a cripple and a priest of Zeus

8Now there was a certain feeble man in Lystra, who was sitting on his feet, lame from his mother's womb, who had never walked. 9He heard Shaul speaking. Shaul gazed at him, and seeing that he had faith to be healed, 10said in a loud voice, stand up straight on your feet. And he sprang up and walked. 11When the crowds saw what Shaul had done, they cried out in their own Lykaonian speech, saying, "The gods have become like people and come down to us." 12And they called Bar Nabba Zeus and Hermes, since he was the main speaker.

13The priest of the Zeus temple, whose temple was outside the city, brought bulls and garlands in through the gates. He and the crowds wanted a sacrifice. 14When the messengers Bar Nabba and Shaul heard of this, they tore their robes and rushed into the crowd screaming, 15"Men, why are you doing this? We are also people of the same nature, who feel like you, and we bring you good news, which is to turn from these worthless things to the living God, who made the sky and the earth and the sea, and all the things in them. 16Who in past generations

---

256. Lycaonia from the Greek Λυκαονία (Lykaonia), a province in the interior of Asia Minor that included the cities of Lystra and Derbe.

allowed the nations to go their own ways? 17Yet he has not let himself lack proof of his goodness—bringing you rains from the sky and seasons bringing fruit, filling your hearts with food and with joy."

18With these words they managed to stop the crowds from sacrificing to them.

19But Jews came from Antioch and Ikonion and won over the crowds. They stoned Shaul and dragged him outside the city, thinking him dead. 20But when his students made a circle around him, he got up and went into the city. The next day he left with Bar Nabba for Derbe.

Through cities on their way back to Antioch in Syria

21After they had spoken the good news in this city and had converted many students, they returned to Lystra and to Ikonion and to Antioch,[257] 22strengthening the souls of the students, encouraging them to persist in the faith, and telling them that only through suffering can we enter the kingdom of God. 23And Shaul and Bar Nabba selected the elders in every church, and with prayers and fasting they committed them to the lord in whom they believed.

24Then they went through Pisidia and came to Pamfylia. 25When they spoke the word in Perga, they went down to Attaleia.[258] 26And from there they sailed back to Antioch[259] where they were committed to the grace of God in the work they had now completed. 27When they got there and convened the church, they related all that God did with them and how he had opened a door of faith for the gentiles. 28And they spent much time there with the students.

Chapter 15

Conflict over circumcision and the gentiles

Some people came down from Yehuda and were teaching the brothers,

---

257. Pisidian, not Syrian, Antioch.

258. Attalia from the Greek Ἀττάλεια (Attaleia), the port for Perga, in Pamphylia, lying in the southwest corner of Asia Minor. It is modern Antalya.

259. The great Greek and later Roman city in Syria, named after Antiochos, King of Syria, after the death of Alexander the Great. It had a large Jewish population.

"If you are not circumcised according to the custom of Moshe, you cannot be saved." 2And after many arguments and debates between Shaul and Bar Nabba and these men, Shaul and Bar Nabba and some of the others were appointed to go up to Yerushalayim to discuss this matter with the messengers and elders. 3So those sent by the church passed through Phoenicia and Shomron,[260] telling of the conversion of the gentiles, and they brought the brothers great happiness. 4When they reached Yerushalayim, they were received by the church and the messengers and the elders, and they reported all that God had done through them.

5But some believers who were from the sect of the Prushim[261] stood up and said, "They must be circumcised and keep the law of Moshe."

6The messengers and the elders met to see about the matter. 7After much discussion, Shimon Kefa got up and said to them,

> Men and brothers, you know that in early days
> God chose among you that through my mouth
> The gentiles should hear the good news and believe.
> 8And God, knower-of-hearts, testified to them
> By giving them the holy spirit as he did to us.
> 9And he did not distinguish between them
> And us while purifying their hearts through faith.
> 10Why now are you testing God by placing a yoke
> On the necks of students that neither our fathers
> Nor we might bear? 11But by the grace of rabbi Yeshua,
> We believe we are saved in the same way as they.

12Then the whole congregation was silent and listened to Bar Nabba and Shaul describe the signs and wonders that God had worked through them among the gentiles. 13When they were silent, Yaakov answered, saying, "Men and brothers, hear me. 14Shimon Kefa has related how God first concerned himself with the gentiles to accept a people in his name. 15This agrees with the words of the prophets as it is written in Amos:

> 16After this I will return
> And rebuild the fallen sukkoth[262] of David

---

260. Samaria.

261. Pharisees.

262. "Tent," which is the Greek word for "sukkoth" or "tabernacle."

And from its ruins I will rebuild it
  and restore it
17So that others might seek the lord,
  And all the gentiles to whom my name
    has been spoken.
18So the lord has done these things
  known since eternity.²⁶³

19So I have decided that we should not trouble those gentiles who turn to God 20but instruct them to keep away from food polluted by idols and by prostitution and from the meat of strangled animals and from blood. 21In every city for generations, there are those who preach Moshe and every Shabbat his work is read in the synagogue."

Letter to the gentiles

22Then the messengers and the elders and the entire church selected some men to send to Antioch with Shaul and Bar Nabba. They sent Yehuda, called Bar Shabbat²⁶⁴ and Shila,²⁶⁵ leaders among the brothers. 23And they wrote a letter by hand for them: "From the brothers, both messengers and elders, to our gentile brothers in Antioch and Syria and Cilicia.

Greetings.

24We have heard that some have gone out to you from us without our instruction, and have disturbed your souls with their words. 25Of one mind we have chosen men to send you, our beloved Bar Abba and Shaul, 26those who have risked their lives for the name of our rabbi Yeshua the Mashiah. 27Therefore we have sent Yehuda and Shila, who will give you the same message by word of mouth. 28It seemed best to the holy spirit and to us not to impose any further burden on you except what is essential. 29Abstain from meat sacrificed to idols and blood and strangled animals and prostitution. If you keep yourselves from these things, you will do well. Farewell."

---

263. Amos 9.11–12.
264. Barsabbas.
265. Shilas from the Greek Σίλας (Silas), from the Aramaic שִׁילָא (shila).

New mission to Antioch

30So they were sent on their way and they went down to Antioch, and after gathering the congregation together they delivered the letter. 31When they read it, they were happy for its advice. 32Yehuda and Shila were also prophets and spoke many words with them and comforted the brothers and strengthened them. 33After being there a while they were sent back in peace from these brothers to those who had sent them.[266] 35And Shaul and Bar Nabba stayed on in Antioch and, along with many others, taught and brought the good news of the word of the lord.

Bitterness over Yohanan

36After some days Shaul said to Bar Nabba, "Let us return and visit the brothers in each city where we have proclaimed the word of the lord to see how they are."

37Bar Nabba wanted to take along Yohanan, who is called Markos, 38but Shaul insisted that it would be wrong to take with them the man who had deserted them in Pamfylia and not gone along with their work. 39And there was a bitter disagreement and they separated from each other. Bar Nabba sailed to Cyprus, taking Markos with him.

40Shaul chose Shila and left, commended by the grace of the lord to the brothers, 41and they journeyed through Syria and Cicilia, strengthening the churches.

Chapter 16

Timothy joins the mission and is circumcised

Shaul went to Derbe and to Lystra, and look, there was a student named Timotheos,[267] son of a Jewish woman who was a believer and a Greek father. 2He was well spoken of by the brothers in Lystra and

---

266. Verse 34 reads, "It seemed good to Shila to remain there." This verse is not in the United Bible Societies fourth corrected edition but does appear in the KJV and other texts. It accounts for Shila's presence when Paul and Barnabas separate.

267. Timothy from the Greek Τιμόθεος (Timotheos), a companion of Paul and said to be the later cowriter of the Timothy letters attributed to Paul.

Ikonion. 3Shaul wanted Timotheos to accompany him and took him and circumcised him because of the Jews who were in those places, since they all knew that his father was a Greek.[268]

4As they traveled through the cities, they told the people to keep the commandments decided on by the messengers and elders in Yerushalayim. 5So the churches grew in faith and increased in number day by day.

6They journeyed through Frygia and Galatia,[269] being forbidden by the holy spirit from preaching the word in Asia.[270] 7When they reached Mysia, they were trying to go on to Bithyia,[271] but the spirit of Yeshua would not let them. 8So passing through Mysia, they came down to Troas.[272] 9And during the night a vision appeared to Shaul. A Makedonian stood there pleading with him, saying, "Cross over into Makedonia[273] and help us." 10When he had seen the vision, we immediately sought to go to Makedonia,[274] concluding that God has called us to preach the good news to them.

Lydia a seller of purple cloth

11We sailed from Troas and went directly to Samothraki[275] and the next day to Neapolis,[276] 12and from there to Filippoi,[277] which is the first

---

268. Here meaning that his father was a pagan or a Greek gentile, not a Greek-speaking Jew, like Paul.

269. A district between Roman provinces of Asia (western Turkey) and Cappadocia.

270. Asia was a Roman province in western Asia Minor, which included western Phrygia.

271. A province in northern Asia Minor.

272. Troas or the Troad, a peninsula in northwestern Anatolia in Asia Minor that contains the ancient site of the ancient city of Troy.

273. Macedonia from the Greek Μακεδονία (Makedonia).

274. At this point the narrative voice changes to the first-person plural "we," suggesting to some that the author has joined the party (16.11–40).

275. Samothrace from the Greek Σαμοθράκη (Samothrake), an island in the northeast Aegean Sea.

276. Neapolis is the seaport of Philippi.

277. Philippi, a city in Macedonia named after Philip II, father of Alexander the Great.

city in the district of Makedonia and a Roman colony. We stayed some days in this city. 13And on Shabbat we went outside the gate by the river where we thought there was a place for prayer, and we talked with women gathered there. 14A woman named Lydia, a seller of purple cloth in the city of Thyatira[278] and one who worshiped God, was listening to us. The lord opened her heart to pay attention to what Shaul said. 15And when she and her household were dipped in holy water,[279] she invited us, saying, "If you have judged me close to the lord, come into my house and stay."[280]

She made us do it.

The screaming slave girl diviner

16And it happened that as we were on our way to the place of prayer, we met a slave girl with a spirit of prophecy, and she made a lot of money for her masters by her fortune-telling. 17While following Shaul and us she screamed out, saying, "These people are slaves of the highest God, who are proclaiming to you the way of salvation." 18She screamed like this for many days. But Shaul was annoyed and said to the spirit, "I command you in the name of Yeshua Mashiah to come out of her."

And the spirit came out of her in that same hour.

19But when her masters saw that their hope of profit was lost, they seized Shaul and Shila and dragged them into the market place before the authorities.

20When they brought them to the chief magistrates, they said, "These men are disturbing our city. They are Jews 21and are proclaiming practices that we as Romans cannot accept."

Shaul and Shila beaten, in jail, and an earthquake

22The crowd joined in the attack on Shaul and Shila, and the magistrates had their clothing torn off them and ordered them to be beaten. 23After flogging them repeatedly, they threw them in jail and ordered

---

278. Thyatira from the Greek Θυάτειρα (Thyateira), a city in the Asia Minor province of Lydia, about twenty miles south of Pergamon.
279. Baptized.
280. A synagogue.

the jailer to guard them securely. 24And on receiving these orders, the jailer put them in the innermost room and fastened their feet in the stocks.

25About midnight Shaul and Shila were praying, singing hymns to God, and the prisoners were listening to them. 26Suddenly there was an earthquake so great that it shook the foundations of the prison, and all the doors came open and everyone's chains came loose. 27The jailer woke and seeing all the doors open, he drew his sword and was about to kill himself, thinking that all the prisoners had escaped. 28But Shaul shouted in a great voice, saying, "Don't harm yourself! We are all here!"

29The jailer called out for lights and rushed in and fell trembling before Shaul and Shila. 30Then he led them outside and said, "Sirs, what must I do to be saved?"

31"Believe in rabbi Yeshua," they said, "and you and your household will be saved."

32And they spoke the word of the lord to him and everyone in his house.

33At that hour of the night the warden washed their wounds and he, and all who were with him, were dipped in holy water, right on the spot. 34Then he took them into his house, set a table before them, and he and all those who were in house believed in God.[281]

Shaul rejects secrecy

35When day came, the magistrates sent the policemen, saying, "Release those men." 36And the jailer reported these words to Shaul, saying, "The magistrates sent word that you be released. Now go in peace."

37But Shaul said to them, "After flogging us in public, without trial, who are Romans, thrown us in jail, and now secretly they are slipping us out of the city? No. Let them come themselves and lead us out."

38The policemen reported all this to the magistrates and they were afraid when they heard they were Romans. 39So the officials came and apologized and conducted them out and asked them to leave the city.

---

281. This miracle story of prison, earthquake, escape, and resolution is a perfect, masterly literary chronicle, revealing the power of tale and belief.

40When they left the prison, they went to Lydia, and when they saw and had animated the brothers[282] they departed.

Chapter 17

In Thessaloniki lecturing on the scriptures

Making their way through Amfipolis[283] and Apollonia,[284] they came to Thessaloniki[285] where there was a synagogue of the Jews. 2And as was his custom Shaul visited them and on three Shabbats he lectured to them on the scriptures, 3explaining and demonstrating, and saying, "The Mashiah had to suffer and rise again from the dead, and he was Yeshua the Mashiah whom I proclaim to you." 4And some were persuaded and joined Shaul and Shila, a great many Greeks, and not a few prominent women.[286]

Iason under seige

5But the Jews became jealous, and with the help of some cunning men from the market place, they formed a mob and set the whole city in an uproar. They besieged the house of Iason,[287] looking for Shaul and Shila

---

282. The Greek speech and gender are sexist, using the masculine. It can be argued that women were included but as shades, not persons. Nevertheless, some translations render this last "brothers" as "brothers and sisters." It is a good gesture of correction but scarcely reflects the word and intention of the text. Women may have been there, but they were not represented as there.

283. Amphipolis from the Greek Ἀμφίπολις (Amfipolis), the capital of southeast Macedonia. The Strymon River flows around the city, hence its name meaning "both sides of city."

284. Apollonia from the Greek Ἀπολλωνία (Apollonia), a city in Macedonia that Shaul passed through.

285. Thessalonica or Salonica from the Greek Θεσσαλονίκη (Thessalonike), meaning "victory of Thessaly."

286. Shila and Paul are apparently back on good terms and are proselytizing together.

287. Jason from the Greek Ἰάσων (Iason). It was common for Greek Jewish Messianists to take the name *Iason* which resembled *Iesous*, from the Greek Ἰησοῦς (Iesous), from which Latin *Iesus* and English "Jesus" come. Greek *Iesous* is from

in order to bring them out to the crowd. 6Not finding them, they dragged Iason and some of his brothers to the city authorities, screaming, "These men who have been turning the world upside down have come here. 7Iason has taken them in, all of them acting against Caesar's decrees, saying there is another king named Yeshua."

8And they stirred up the crowd and the city authorities, 9but after taking bond money from Iason and the others, they let them go.

In Beroia at a more welcoming synagogue

10The brothers immediately sent Shaul and Shila off during the night to Beroia.[288] When they got there, they went to the synagogue of the Jews. 11These people were more noble than those in Thessaloniki, for they welcomed word with eagerness, and studied the scriptures every day to see if this was really so. 12And many of them believed, including not a few prominent women and men. 13But when the Jews of Thessaloniki learned that even in Beroia the word of God was proclaimed by Shaul, they also came there to stir up the masses. 14Then the brothers immediately sent Shaul off as far as the sea, and Shila and Timotheos stayed there. 15Those who were escorting Shaul took him as far as Athens. Then, after receiving instructions to have Shila and Timotheos join him in Athens, they went off on their own.

Shaul and the Athens philosophers

16While Shaul waited for them in Athens, he was upset in his spirit by observing the city filled with idols.[289] 17Then he went into the synagogue

---

the Aramaic *Yeshua* (Joshua) and the Hebrew *Yehosha* (Jehoshua). Jason may have been Paul's cousin.

288. Beroea from the Greek Βέροια (Beroia), an old city in Macedonia at the foot of Mount Bermius, fifty miles southwest of Thessaloniki by the Astraeus River, which is now modern Veria, by Mount Vermion.

289. Paul's anger about idols is a harbinger of the later deep conflict between classical civilization and Judaism, Christianity, and Islam, which, in iconoclastic periods, saw the demolition of classical temples and the destruction of statues and classical libraries and museums. At the same time, classical authors, especially Plato and first-century Neoplatonists, were to infuse Judaism and Christianity, and especially Paul, with notions of heaven, hell, and the immortality of the soul, which were undeveloped in the Hebrew Bible.

and conversed with the Jews and with the worshipers and every day in the market place with anyone he happened to meet. 18Some Epicurean and Stoic philosophers[290] conversed with him, and some said of him, "What is this seed-picking babbler saying?" Others said, "He seems to be proclaiming foreign deities." This was because he was bringing the good news of Yeshua and the resurrection.

Shaul on the Areiopagos

19So they took him to the Areiopagos,[291] saying, "Can we know what this new teaching of yours is? 20You bring something strange to our ears. We want to know what it means."

21All the Athenians and visitors from abroad would spend their time on nothing but looking for and talking about the latest idea.

22Then Shaul standing in the middle of the Areiopagos said,

> Athenians, I see how you are superstitious.[292]
> 23As I went through your city and examined
> Your sanctuaries, I even found an altar
> With the inscription TO THE UNKNOWN GOD.
> While not knowing what your worship is,
> This is what I announce to you. 24The God
> Who made the world and all the things in it,
> Who is the lord of sky and of the earth,
> Does not live in temples built by human hands,
> 25Nor is he served by men's hands as if he were
> In need, since he has given life and breath

---

290. Here is an early meeting of what will be the tragic struggle between emerging Christianity and classical Greco-Roman civilization, which was defeated legally and definitively with the conversion of the Roman emperor Constantine and baptism on his Byzantine deathbed to Christianity, albeit it to an Arian denomination that was to yield to Greek Orthodoxy.

291. Areopagus from the Greek Ἀρειοπάγος (Areiopagos), the hill of Ares (Latin Mars), Greek god of thunder and war, on a rocky hill west of the Acropolis and south of Agora, where open talk and formal discussions of the governing Council of the Areopagus, as well as judgments of capital crimes, took place.

292. The Greek δεισιδαιμονεστέρους (deisidaimonesterous) means "religious" or "superstitious," containing in it *daimon*, meaning a Greek god or demon, which by the time of the gospels had a purely negative connotation.

And all things to everything. 26And out of one
He made all nations of people to live
On the face of the earth. He chose the shape
Of seasons and the borders of their dwellings;
27And he made them seek God and maybe grope
For him and find him not far from every one
Of us. 28In him we live and move and are.[293]

And as some of your own poets have said:
"We are also the offspring of God"[294]
29So we should not think that the deity
Is gold or silver or of stone, an image
Devised and fashioned by a human being.
30While God has winked at times of ignorance
Now he commands all people of the world
Wherever they may be: they must repent
31Because he has fixed a day for having
The world be judged as it adheres to justice
And through a man whom he one day appointed.
To everyone he gave assurance of
His coming since he raised him from the dead.

32When they heard about the resurrection of the dead, some derided him but others said, "We will hear you again about this matter."

33So Shaul left them, 34and some joined him and became believers among whom was Dionysios the Areiopagite[295] and a woman named Damaris and others with them.

---

293. Attributed to the Cretan poet Epimenides (ca. 600 B.C.E.) in his *Kretika*.

294. The Cilician poet Aratos (ca. 315–240) in his *Fainomena* and also Kleanthes (331–233) in his *Hymn to Zeus*.

295. Nothing is known of this Dionysios other than that he was a court judge and legendarily became a bishop. He is often confused with another figure, the writer Dionysios the Areiopagite or now called the Pseudo-Dionysios, who was apparently a fifth-century Syrian monk and author of *The Celestial Hierarchy*, *The Ecclesiastical Hierarchy*, *Divine Names*, and *Mystical Theology*. The Pseudo-Dionysios wrote about the ecstatic steps of mysticism, ending with the ray of darkness.

Chapter 18

Shaul in Corinth with Akylas of Pontos

After that Shaul left Athens and went to Corinth 2and found a Jew named Akylas,[296] a native from Pontos,[297] who had recently come from Italy, with his wife Priskilla,[298] because Claudius[299] had ordered all Jews to leave Rome. Shaul went to see them 3and because he was of the same trade he stayed with and was working with him, for they were both tentmakers by trade. 4Every Shabbat he debated in the synagogue and he was winning over both Jews and Greeks.

Shaul's vision

5When Shila and Timotheos arrived from Makedonia,[300] Shaul was eagerly proclaiming the word to the Jews that Yeshua was the Mashiah. 6And when they opposed him and abused him, he shook out his clothing and said to them,

> Your blood on your heads! I am clean.
> From now on I will go to the gentiles.

7And leaving this place, he went to the house of a man named Titios Justos,[301] who worshiped God. His house was near the synagogue. 8Krispos,[302] the synagogue leader, and all his household believed in the

---

296. Aquila from the Greek Ἀκύλας (Akylas). Aquila of Pontus, a tentmaker, is not to be confused with Aquila of Pontus, a convert to Judaism who in about 130 C.E. translated the Hebrew Bible into Greek in a literalist manner, even reproducing Hebrew syntax in the Greek.

297. A Roman province in northeastern Asia Minor bordering on the south shore of the Black Sea.

298. Priscilla from the Greek Πρίσκιλλα (Priskilla), a diminutive of Πρίσκα (Priska), the form in which it appears in Shaul's letters.

299. The Roman emperor.

300. Macedonia.

301. Titus from the Greek Τίτιος (Titios). Titus and Titus Justus were common Latin names used in Greek.

302. Crispus from the Greek Κρίσπος (Krispos).

rabbi,[303] and many of the Corinthians who heard Shaul believed and were dipped in the water. 9And in a vision one night the lord said to Shaul:

> Do not fear but speak and do not be silent.
> 10Because I am with you, no one will attack you
> To do you harm,
> For I have many people in this city.

Gallio the judge

11And he stayed for a year and six months among them teaching the word of God.

12When Gallio[304] was proconsul of Ahaia,[305] the Jews made a concordant attack against Shaul and brought him before the tribunal, 13saying, "In unlawful ways this man is persuading people to worship God."

14But as Shaul was about to open his mouth to speak, Gallio said to

---

303. As in the gospels, in Acts there is a merging of the notion of God and Jesus. If the reference is indeed to Jesus and he is called rabbi in the Greek text, he is called rabbi in English, a practice normally followed only in the recent NKJV. When a synoptic passage in Mark or Matthew uses "rabbi" in the Greek but Luke, in the identical passage, has changed Greek "rabbi" to *kyrie* in order to distance Jesus from his rabbinical position, faith, and people, "rabbi" is retained as the English epithet. Here, while there is no gospel precedent for the incident and it is uncertain whether the *kyrie* in the Greek text is addressed to Jesus or to God, the personification of the divinity suggests the antecedent is Jesus, and hence, as in Luke, "rabbi" is restored. Elsewhere, when *kyrie* appears to refer to God, the English title, then "lord" or "God," is given.

304. Gallio was the brother of Seneca, the Roman philosopher and playwright. Both were from Cordoba (Roman Corduba) in Spain. Gallio, reputed for his fairness and calm, was originally "Lucius Annaeus Novatus." His name as Gallio is inscribed at Delphi in 52 C.E. The information that he was proconsul in Greece from 51 to 52 helps us date Paul's visit to Corinth on his second journey as well as his letters to the Thessalonikians. Cordoba was the city of Seneca, and later the Jewish philosopher Maimonides and the Arabic philosopher Averroes. The caliphate of Muslim Spain was also in this renowned city from soon after 755 until the early eleventh century.

305. Achaia or Achaea from the Greek Ἀχαΐα (Ahaia). The Roman province of Achaia, created in 146 B.C.E. included the main parts of Greece, Attica, Boetia (perhaps including Epiros), and the Peloponnesos.

the Jews, "If it were wrong or a bad crime, O Jews, I might reasonably go along with you, 15but since it is a matter of a word or names and your law, I do not wish to be a judge of those things." 16And he drove them from the tribunal. 17Then the other Greeks all seized Sosthenes, the head of the synagogue, and beat him outside the tribunal, but none of this concerned Gallio.

Shaul sails to Syria

18Shaul stayed on for many days and then said goodbye to the brothers and sailed to Syria, and Priskilla and Akylas went with him. In Kengreai[306] he had his head shaved in accordance with a vow he had taken. 19They put in at Efesos[307] and he left the others there and went into the synagogue and conversed with the Jews. 20When they asked him to stay for a longer time, he refused. 21But when he said goodbye, he said, I will come back to you again, God willing, and he sailed from Efesos. 22He went ashore in Caesarea and went up to Yerushalayim and greeted the church, and went down to Antioch. 23And after spending some time there, he left. He went from place to place through the region of Galatia[308] and Frygia, strengthening all the students.

Learned Apollos and the way

24A certain Jew named Apollos, an Alexandrian by birth, came to Efesos. He was eloquent and learned in scripture. 25He had been instructed in the ways of the lord, and burning with spirit he spoke and taught the exact facts about Yeshua, though he knew him only through his dipping of Yohanan in the water. 26He began to speak freely in the synagogue, and when Priskilla and Akylas heard him they took him aside and more accurately explained the way to him. 27When he wished to

---

306. Cenchreae from the Greek Κεγχρεαί (Kenghreai), the seaport on the eastern side of the isthmus of Corinth.

307. Ephesos or Ephesus from the Greek Ἔφεσος (Efesos).

308. Galatia from the Greek Γαλατία (Galatia), a district in Roman Asia Minor but also the name of Celtic Gaul. The meaning of "Galatians" is much disputed and commented on, and held by now to be the same name, if not the same people, of all the Celtic peoples in northern France, northern Spain, and England and Ireland.

go to Ahaia, the brothers encouraged him and wrote to the students to welcome him. And when he got there, he greatly helped those who had become believers. 28He was refuting the Jews in public, showing through the Hebrew scriptures that Yeshua was the Mashiah.[309]

Chapter 19

In Efesos with students and bathing in a name

While Apollos was in Corinth, Shaul was traveling through the north and came down to Efesos, and there he found some students 2and said to them, "When you believed did you receive the holy spirit?"

They said to him, "We have not even heard that there is a holy spirit."

3He said, "In what were you bathed?"[310]

---

309. Here, as throughout the New Testament, the use of the word "Jew" is anachronistic, reflecting not the period of the personages but a later period when Christianity had broken or appeared to have broken with Judaism. In this early moment in the formation of later Christianity, we note that while Apollos is introduced to us as "Apollos the Jew," by the end of the paragraph he is found refuting "the Jews," implying that he has converted from Judaism and is free of it, a feat of alienation achieved by claiming that Jesus is the proclaimed messiah of the Jews. Then, adding more paradox, in order to prove his case and convert his coreligionists to Messianism, he cites Jewish scripture. There was not yet any "Christian" scripture to quote because none had yet been composed, much less selected and canonized. All these characters are Jews—those who accept and those who do not accept Jesus as the messiah. To make the scene more plausible and reasonable, one could say, in the English conversion, that Apollos was debating with *traditional Jews* or with *Jews who failed to recognize Jesus as messiah*. But to add these distinctions to the text would also subvert its integrity. Alas, it is better to let contradictions hang out clearly with the hope that people of goodwill—Jews, Christians, believers, and skeptics—will bring a historic eye to a scene inevitably construed and determined by religious imperatives of later church figures long and far removed from the time and spirit of the episode.

310. Dipped, bathed, immersed, washed, from the Greek βαπτίζω (baptizo). Normally translated "baptized," this rendering lacks the immediate significance of being dipped or immersed in water. By contrast, the word for breath in Greek, πνεῦμα (pneuma), is rendered into English as "breath" and only metaphorically as "spirit"

And they said, "Into Yohanan's immersion."

4Shaul said, "Yohanan dipped with the waters of repentance, telling the people to believe in the one who was coming after him, that is, in Yeshua."

5When they heard this, they were bathed in the name of lord Yeshua.

6When Shaul placed his hands on them, the holy spirit came over them. They spoke in tongues and were prophesying. 7In all there were about twelve men.

Preaching in the synagogue and in the school of Tyrannos

8Then he went into the synagogue and spoke for three months, arguing and persuading concerning the kingdom of God. 9But when some were hardening into disbelief and spoke poorly about the way to the crowd, he withdrew from them, taking his students with him, and argued daily in the school of Tyrannos.³¹¹ 10This went on for two years so that all who were living in Asia,³¹² both Jews and Greeks, could hear the word of the lord.

Jewish exorcists and evil spirits

11God performed extraordinary powers through the hands of Shaul 12so that even if a handkerchief or towel touched the skin of the sick,

---

or "soul." While in Greek *baptizo* and *pneuma* function multivalently, in English *baptizo*'s original sense of "ceremonially dipping or immersing" is either lost or secondary to its conceptual significance of "religiously initiating and converting." In the name "John the Baptist," "Baptist" serves as a pious title. In an attempt to restore the original meaning, other translators have begun to call John "John the Baptizer." In this instance to ask in English, "In what were you baptized?" carries a shock of incongruity, since the metaphor of being physically immersed in something, be it water or spirit, has been truncated.

311. Tyrannos from the Greek Τύραννος (Tyrannos), an Ephesian in whose hall Shaul preached for two years after he found opposition in the synagogue.

312. Here "Asia" refers to the Roman province including Ephesos, a Greek city then under the Romans where most of the people spoke Greek, including Jews like Shaul, who was a Greek-speaking Jew from the city of Tarsos, northwest of Ephesos. Both cities are in present-day Turkey.

their disease was taken away and evil spirits would leave them. 13Then some itinerant Jewish exorcists tried pronouncing the name of the lord over those possessed with evil spirits, saying, "In the name of Yeshua, to whom Shaul preaches, I command you to come out."

14There were seven sons of Skevas,[313] a Jewish high priest who were doing this. 15But the evil spirit said to them, "Yeshua I know and I know about Shaul, but who are you?" 16Then the man with the evil spirits leapt on all these men, overpowered them so that they fled naked and wounded out of the house. 17This became known to all the Jews and Greeks living in Efesos and fear fell on them and the name of lord Yeshua was held in high honor.

Book burning by the new believers

18And many who became believers were disclosing and confessing what they had done, and they gathered their books together and burned them before everyone. 19A number of them who had strange practices[314] calculated the value of the books burned and found them to be worth fifty thousand pieces of silver.[315] 20So the power of the word of the lord grew and gathered strength.

21When these things were fulfilled, Shaul resolved in his spirit to travel through Makedonia and Ahaia[316] on his way to Yerushalayim. He said, "After I have gone there I must see Rome." 22So he sent two of his assistants, Timotheos and Erastos,[317] to Makedonia while he stayed for some time in Asia.

---

313. Sceva from the Greek Σκευᾶς (Skeuas).

314. This phrase has also been translated as "magical practices."

315. The silver coins are probably drachmas. Books at the time were rolled up as scrolls. The practice of burning presumably Greek religious and philosophical texts foretells the oncoming iconoclastic period of struggle between the developing religion and classical antiquity, for which there would be largely no tolerance of its pagan books, statues, and temples. The suggestion here is that the Greek mystery religions represent sorcery and despicable magic.

316. Achaia.

317. Erastus from the Greek Ἔραστος (Erastos), Shaul's companion.

Silversmith of the goddess

23About this time there was a considerable disturbance about the meaning of the way. 24A man named Demetrios,[318] a silversmith who built shrines of Artemis,[319] gave much work to the artisans. 25He assembled them with others of the same trade and said, "You know that our prosperity comes from this work. 26You also see and hear that not only in Efesos but throughout almost all of Asia, this Shaul has convinced and turned away crowds of people, saying that gods made by hands are not gods. 27There is a danger not only that our art may fall into disrepute but also that the temple of the great goddess Artemis will be despised and, her magnificence destroyed—she whom all Asia and the world worship."[320]

A city of confusion and anger

28When they heard this they were filled with rage and screamed, "Great is Artemis of the Efesians!"

29The city was filled with confusion, and they rushed with one impulse into the theater, seizing and taking with them Gaius[321] and Aristarhos,[322] Shaul's traveling companions from Makedonia. 30Shaul wanted to go in among the people, but his students would not let him. 31And some of the Asian officials[323] who were friendly to him sent him a message and urged him not to venture into the theater.

---

318. Demetrius from the Greek Δημήτριος (Demetrios).

319. Artemis, the sister of Apollo, is the virgin goddess of the moon and the hunt. In Latin she is *Diana*.

320. Here are among the first words in scripture that prophesy the coming destruction of classical temples. In this period, while Christianity was neither a dominant nor an official religion, the notion of destroying Greek temples is not a realizable dream, but its mention here does reflect a later period when destruction of pagan antiquity and its icons of worship is an urgent and a commanding concern and endeavor.

321. Gaius from the Greek Γάϊος (Gaios), a common Latin name.

322. Aristarchos from the Greek Ἀρίσταρχος (Aristarhos). Aristarhos of Thessaloniki accompanied Shaul on his journeys.

323. In Greek the men are called "Asiarchs," that is, wealthy and influential elected leaders in the province of Asia who comprised a council that promoted the worship of the emperor. Shaul was friendly with this group.

32Now some were shouting one thing and some another. The crowd was in turmoil and most of them did not know why they had come together. 33Some in the crowd told Alexandros what to say. The Jews had pushed him forward, and he motioned to them with his hand, wanting to speak in defense before the people. 34But when they recognized that he was a Jew, in a single voice and for about two hours everyone screamed, "Artemis of the Ephesians is great!"

35When the secretary of the city quieted the crowd, he said, "Men of Efesos, who is there among the living who does not know the city of Efesos as the temple keeper of the great Artemis and the statue that fell from heaven? 36Since these things are undeniable, you must be calm and do nothing reckless. 37You have brought these men here, who are neither temple robbers nor blasphemers of our goddess. 38So if Demetrios and the artisans with him have any complaint against anyone, the courts are open and the proconsuls are there. Let them bring their charges. 39And if you seek anything else, it will be settled in the lawful assembly. 40But we are in danger of being charged with rioting today, and have no excuse for this commotion."

When he said these things, he dismissed the assembly.

Chapter 20

Sailing the islands and coastal cities

After the uproar quieted, Shaul summoned his students and encouraged them and said his farewells and left for his trip to Makedonia. 2When he had gone through those regions and animated the people with many words, he came to Greece. 3He spent three months there when there was a plot against him by the Jews just as he was to sail for Syria. 4He decided to return through Makedonia with Sopatros,324 the son of Pyrros,325 from Beroia, Aristarhos and Secundus from Thessaloniki, Gaius of Derbe326

---

324. Sopater from the Greek Σώπατρος (Sopatros), a Greek convert.
325. Pyrrus from the Greek Πύρρος (Pyrros).
326. A city in Lycaonia in the Roman province of Galatia.

and Timotheos, and the Asians Tyhikos[327] and Trofimos.[328] 5And they were waiting for us[329] in the Troas.[330] 6And we sailed away from Filippoi after the days of the Feast of the Matzot Bread,[331] and we came to them in the Troas, and for five days we stayed there.

Shaul performs a miracle

7On the first day of the week when we came together to break bread, Shaul was lecturing them. Since he planned to leave the next day, he continued speaking until midnight. 8There were a number of lamps in the room upstairs where we had assembled. 9A young man named Eutyhos[332] was sitting in the window when he was overcome by a deep sleep while Shaul was speaking at length. He fell down from the third story and they found him dead. 10Shaul went down and fell on him and hugged him, saying:

> Don't be troubled, for his life is in him.

11Then Shaul went upstairs and after he broke bread and ate it, he went on speaking for a long time until daybreak. Then he departed. 12Meanwhile they led the boy away, alive, and they greatly comforted him.

13We went ahead to the ship and sailed for Assos,[333] intending to take Shaul on board there. He had arranged it, intending to go himself by land.

---

327. Tychicus from the Greek Τυχικός (Tyhikos).

328. Trophimus from the Greek Τρόφιμος (Trofimos), an uncircumcised gentile from Ephesos.

329. In this and other lines the author changes grammar and voice, as if in unconscious enthusiasm, from normal third-person narration to a first-person plural memoir accounting of the venture.

330. Troas or Troad.

331. Feast of the Matzot Bread is the Feast of Unleavened Bread. Matzo bread from the Greek ἄζυμος (azymos), "unleavened bread." The matzo is eaten during the Passover, the *Pesach*, from the Greek πάσχα (pasha), from the Hebrew פֶסַח (pesach), to pass over, referring to the escape from bondage in Egypt, celebrated for the first two nights at the Seder by eating the paschal lamb. See Exodus 12.1–13.16.

332. Eutychus from the Greek Εὔτυχος (Eutyhos).

333. A city on the coast of Asia Minor, near Pergamum. Aristotle lived in Assos and founded his academy there.

14When he met us in Assos, we took him aboard, and went to Mitylene.³³⁴ 15From there we sailed the next day opposite Hios,³³⁵ and then we crossed over to Samos,³³⁶ and the following day we came to Miletos.³³⁷ 16Shaul decided to bypass Efesos so as not to lose time in Asia. He was hurrying as quickly as possible to be in Yerushalayim on the day of Shavuot.³³⁸

Sermon in the synagogue

17From Miletos he sent word to Efesos, summoning the congregation³³⁹ elders. 18When they came to Shaul he told them,

---

334. Mitylene was the capital city of the island of Lesbos (now called Mitylene), the birthplace of the ancient Greek poet Sappho, perhaps the greatest poet in antiquity. Sappho was a Lesbian in the geopolitical and sexual sense. The astonishing poet wrote love poems to women as well as to men and to her daughter Atthis.

335. Chios from the Greek Χίος (Hios), a Greek island in the eastern Aegean, off the coast of Ephesos, and one of the main claimants for Homer's birthplace.

336. Greek island off the coast of Asia Minor, and reputed birthplace of the fabulist Aesop.

337. Miletus from the Greek Μίλητος (Miletos), on the coast south of Ephesos, and home of the pre-Socratic Greek philosopher Thales of Miletus. Miletus is today Balat.

338. The Festival of the Pentecost. This major Jewish holiday was associated with the covenant at Sinai and the giving of the law. For the later Christians, Shavuot came to mean the celebration of the first Christian communities as a parallel to the first Jewish communities at Sinai. See note 38 for philology and more information.

339. The Greek word ἐκκλησία (ekklesia) is "church" when referring to this institution as it would exist in a later period. Paul lived before the gospels were written and before Judaism and Messianic Judaism had separated to become Judaism and Christianity. So here, ἐκκλησία (a gathering place) should be translated as "congregation" or "synagogue." Paul's Messianism is largely directed to Jews who attend the synagogue (or temple) or to the Greek converts to Messianic Judaism, who similarly attend the synagogue. "Synagogue" is from the Greek συναγωγή (synagoge), meaning, as does ἐκκλησία, an "assembly" or "gathering place." Using "church" rather than "synagogue" reflects the general practice of clerical writers to predate a later condition and to diminish the parent religion, as in altering names of Jews and their institutions, ceremonies, and holidays. When Shavuot, the Feast of Weeks, becomes the Pentecost, the new Greek term, in Greek and English, it retains none of its Jewish resonance.

The gospels were composed decades after the life and Passion of Jesus described

You know from the first day I walked in Asia,
How I was all the time with you, serving
19The lord with humility, tears and hardship
That came to me from intrigues of the Jews.
20I never shrank from doing all I could
For you, revealing the good news and teaching
Publicly and going from house to house.
21I've testified to both the Jews and Greeks
About repentence before God and faith
In our lord Yeshua the Mashiah.
22And now, low, in bondage to the spirit,
I am on my way to Yerushalayim,
Not knowing what will happen to me there
23Save that the holy spirit in each city
Informs me, saying chains and tribulations
Are waiting for me. 24But none of these things
Move me, nor do I count my life of any
Value if I can just complete my road
And ministry received from our lord Yeshua
Which is to testify to the good news
Of God's grace. 25And look, now I know
That none of you among whom I have gone
To preach the kingdom will ever again
Look on my face. 26I tell you to record

---

in them, and Acts was written after the gospels, and it covers the period of Paul's missions some decades before the canonical gospels were written. Yet the figures in Acts breathe a gospel spirit and a detailed knowledge of acts and conversations recounted in the gospels, which they cite and discuss, although such acts and conversations had not yet been recorded as far as we know. One could say that Paul in Acts and his comrades knew what the later gospels said because they shared with the evangelists a common source of oral gospeling or witnessing. Such conjecture seems fully implausible since the letters of Paul breathe a different air. And elsewhere in Acts he states, "I am a Jew born in Tarsos" (22.2) and "I am a Parush, the son of Prushim" (23.6). Paul was unequivocal about being a true Jew, and his own letters contain neither miraculous healings nor relentlessly fearful caricatures of Jews. What is clear is that Acts, in its confusion of ethnic and religious identities, was shaped for a later period in Christianity's trajectory when its Jewish past will be concealed.

On this day I am clean of blood of all
Of you. 27I never shun revealing God's
Purpose to you. 28Take good care of yourselves
And over the whole flock. The holy spirit
Made you the guardian of the church of God,
Which he bought with blood of his own son.
29I know once I leave savage wolves will come
Among you, not sparing the flock 30and some
Among you will rebel and speak perversely
To draw the students into their following.
31Be alert, recall how for these three years,
Night and day, I never ceased to weep
As I admonished every one of you.
32Now I commend you to God and his word
Of grace, which has the power to give you
Inheritance among the sanctified.
33I never longed for gold, silver, or clothing.
34You know that with my hands I have provided
For my needs and for those of my companions.
35In all this I have shown you to work hard
To help the weak and to recall the words
Of lord Yeshua Mashiah, those he said,
"More blessed is to give than to receive."

36And when he said this, he bent his knees and prayed with them.
37There was much sobbing and they fell over Shaul's neck and kissed
him. 38What pained them most was when he said that they would never
see his face again. And they walked with him to the ship.

Chapter 21

On to Yerushalayim and Shavuot

When it happened that we were about to set sail and had to break
from them, we took a straight course to Kos[340] and the next day to Rhodes

---

340. A large island in the Aegean, near the coast of Asia Minor.

and from there to Patara.[341] 2When we found a ship crossing over to Phoenicia, we went on board and set sail.

3After sighting Cyprus and leaving it behind on the left, we sailed to Syria and we arrived in Tzor[342] and unloaded the cargo. 4We found the students and stayed there for seven days, and they warned Shaul, as the spirit had told them, not to go up to Yerushalayim. 5When our days were over, we left and started on our way; everyone, with their wives and children, accompanied us outside the city, and we all kneeled on the beach and prayed. 6We said goodbye to one another and climbed into the ship. The others turned back to their homes.

Shaul is warned in Caesarea about dangers

7When our voyage from Tzor was over, we came to Ptolemais,[343] greeted the brothers, and spent a day with them.

8The next day we left and came to Caesarea and went on to the house of Filippos the evangelist, one of the seven,[344] and we stayed with him. 9He had four virgin daughters who prophesied. 10After many days a prophet of the Jews[345] came down, named Agav,[346] 11and coming to us he took Shaul's belt, bound his own legs and hands, and said, "This is what the holy spirit says":

> This is how the Jews in Yerushalayim
> Will bind the man who owns this belt
> And hand him over to the hands of gentiles.

12And when we heard these things, we and the others there all begged him not to go up to Yerushalayim. 13Then Shaul answered,

---

341. Patara from the Greek Πάταρα (Patara), a city in Lycia on the southwest coast of Asia Minor.

342. Tyre.

343. Ptolemais from the Greek Πτολεμαΐς (Ptolemais), an important city on the coast named for the Hellenistic Egyptian monarch Ptolemy II Philadelphus, near modern Haifa.

344. "One of the seven" evangelists establishes a parallel with the seven prophets.

345. The spelling is ambiguous in Greek. The KJV has "Jews," other versions give "Judea."

346. Agabus.

What are you doing, crying and breaking my heart?

I am ready not only to be bound but to die

In Yerushalayim for the name of rabbi Yeshua.

14Not able to persuade him, we held our peace, saying, "The lord's will be done."

15After these days we made preparations for going up to Yerushalayim, 16and some students from Caesarea came along and took us where we could lodge with an early student, Mnason of Cyprus.

Tremors of Yerushalayim

17When we reached Yerushalayim, the brothers welcomed us gladly. 18The next day Shaul went with us to Yaakov, and all the elders were there. 19He greeted them and related, one by one, those things that God had done among the gentiles through his ministry. 20When they heard, they glorified God. But they said to Shaul, "You see how many myriads among Jews have come to be believers and they are all zealots for the law. 21They have been told about you that you teach all the Jews who live among the gentiles an apostasy: to turn away from Moshe, not to circumcise their children, nor to observe customs. 22What can be done? They will certainly learn that you have come.[347] 23So do what we tell you. We have four men who have taken a vow. 24Join them and be purified with them, and pay for them to have their heads shaved. All will realize that there is nothing in what they have said about you, and that you yourself keep and guard the law.[348] 25As for the gentiles[349] who have become believers, we have written that they should avoid meat offered to idols, and blood, and strangled beasts, and fornication."

26Then Shaul purified himself and on the next day took the men with him into the Temple and gave public notice of the expiration of the days

---

347. The Majority Text includes at the beginning of the sentence, "An assembly will come together."

348. There is always ambiguity as to whether it is good or wicked to be a Jew. Here, for reasons of safety and strategy, Paul is urged to prove that he has acted like a good Jew before the law, observing the essential principles of his people.

349. In most instances, "the gentiles" refers to non-Jewish Greeks, in contrast to Paul, who was a Greeking-speaking Jew, from Tarsos, in Greece (modern-day Turkey), which was then under Roman domination.

of purification when a sacrifice would be made for each of them.

27When they were about to complete the seven days,[350] Jews from Asia,[351] who had seen him in the Temple, stirred up the whole crowd and they laid hands on him, 28shouting, "Yisraeli men, help us! This is the man who is teaching everywhere against the people, the law, and this place. He has brought Greeks into the Temple and profaned this holy place."[352]

Mobs and anarchy in the Temple

29They had earlier seen Trofimos the Efesian[353] with him in the city, and supposed that Shaul had brought him into the Temple. 30The whole city was aroused and the people rushed in and seized Shaul and dragged him out of the Temple, and immediately the doors were shut. 31While they were trying to kill him, a word reached the commanding tribune[354] of the Roman cohort that all Yerushalayim was in chaos. 32Immediately he took soldiers and centurions and ran to the scene. When the tribune saw them, they stopped beating Shaul. 33Then the tribune arrested him and ordered him to be bound in two chains, and he asked who he was and what he had done.[355]

---

350. The seven days required for purification according to Jewish ritual.

351. The Roman province of Asia.

352. Bringing Greeks into the Temple was held to be a capital crime.

353. See Acts 20.4.

354. In the Roman army, a tribune commanded a cohort, a cohort a centurion. Here the tribune is Claudius Lysius, who commanded a regiment of perhaps a thousand soldiers.

355. As in the gospels, the Roman presence is ambiguous. In the gospels, the Romans execute Jesus, but that execution is blamed on crowds of unruly Jews, who are accused of initiating charges against Jesus that the reluctant Romans pursued. Paul, who heals and performs parallel miracles in imitation of Jesus and other itinerant wise men, is accused by the Jews of blasphemy. When he is in danger, he is rescued from death by soldiers of the Roman authority occupying Israel, who represent order and just law. Ultimately, many years later, like Jesus, Paul will be executed, it is said, by the Romans under legendary circumstances, though we have no certain knowledge of his death in terms of date or circumstance. In each instance, the Jews are portrayed as malignant inciters, and their victims, though also Jews, are dissociated from being Jews and bear no blame. The Romans come through without guilt, free of all historic memory of enduring condemnation for their apparent execution of later Christendom's two major figures.

Romans take Shaul to barracks for scourging[356]

34Some in the crowd shouted one thing, some another. Since the commander cannot know exactly what has happened, he ordered him to be taken to the barracks.

35When he reached the steps, he had to be carried by the soldiers 36because of the violence of the mob, which followed him and shouted, "Kill him!"[357]

37Then as he was about to be taken into the barracks, Shaul said to the tribune, "May I say something to you?"

He said, "Do you know Greek? 38Then are you not the Egyptian who some days ago started a riot and led four thousand assassins into the desert?"

39Shaul said,

> I am a Jew from Tarsos in Kilikia,[358]
>
> A citizen of not an insignificant ordinary city,[359]
>
> And I ask your permission to speak to the people.

40When he was given permission, Shaul stood on the steps and motioned with his hands to the people, and there came a great silence, and he addressed them in the Hebrew language,[360] saying:

---

356. The barracks is a euphemism for the room of scourging where cruel instruments are used to extract information from ordinary prisoners. Once Paul identifies himself as a Roman citizen, he escapes this torture. Here the barracks refers to the Fortress of Antonia, connected to the northern end of the Temple.

357. Usually translated "Kill him." The literal metaphor is "Away with him." Here the parallel with the gospel death of Jesus is exact: the mob of Jews shouting, "kill," and the Romans representing order arresting the dissenting Jew. As in the instance of the gospels, there is no evidence outside texts to prove, disprove, or describe these events.

358. Cilicia from the Greek Κιλικία (Kilikia). Cilicia is the southeast province of Asia (Anatolia) in which Tarsos was and remains a major city.

359. The phrase "not from an insignificant city" is probably an allusion to Euripides's phrase to describe Athens.

360. Hebrew, but Paul spoke to Jews in Aramaic. After the sixth-century B.C.E. Babylonian Captivity, Hebrew became the language of the temple and of prayers, but the spoken language was Aramaic of the Babylonians, the lingua franca of the region of Mesopotamia and along the coast from Caanan to Syria. In this situation, Paul would have addressed the crowd in Aramaic and saved Hebrew for his prayers. There were no prayers he could utter other than Jewish prayers because no Christian scripture, including the "lord's prayer," had yet been composed.

Chapter 22

Shaul speaks his life

Brothers and fathers, hear the defense
I make before you.

2When they heard him addressing them in Hebrew, they became even
more quiet. He said,

3I am a Jew born in Tarsos of Kikilia,
Brought up in the city at the feet of Gamliel,[361]
Instructed in the strictness of our ancestral law,
And I was zealous for God as you are today.[362]
4I persecuted the followers of this new way
Even to the death, binding and putting in jail
Both men and women, 5as the high priest
And entire council of elders can testify to.

---

361. Gamaliel from the Greek Γαμαλιήλ (Gamaliel), from the Hebrew נַמְלִיאֵל
(gamliel). Paul was trained at the feet of Gamaliel, a famous Pharisee figure, which
added distinction to Paul's education and background. Grandson of the great Hillel, Gamaliel was held to be the most revered rabbi in Judaism. As a leader of a liberal, pragmatic form of Judaism emphasizing oral tradition as opposed to legalistic
argument, Gamaliel reflected Paul's background as a Pharisee. The Pharisees were
the group most opposed to Roman occupation, and this anti-Romanizing sentiment
was also true in the Sanhedrin, of which Gamaliel was the president, though the
same Sanhedrin came to be presented in gospel and Christian tradition as an odi-
ous assembly, a nest of murderous conspirators. In his writings Gamaliel emphasized
ways of promoting peace, goodness, and the improvement of the role of women,
whom he championed. Gamaliel also reached out to Jews of the diaspora, to gentiles for whom he asked generosity, and to the Greek language, which he loved. After
the Jewish War (66–70), he helped consolidate Judaism.

362. Although Paul was proud of having been instructed by Gamaliel, and mentions
this point as his first credential of solidarity with the crowd, Gamaliel was not at all a
Zealot who wished to persecute Christian Jews, but rather a reformer and opponent
of strictness, as were the Pharisees, who spoke for changing oral tradition. For these
flexible qualities Gamaliel was known. The implication here is that Paul should be
seen not as a strict but a liberated interpreter of Judaism, and indeed he was so. However, his own liberation was not in rebellion from a zealous teacher. On the contrary,
one may fairly speculate that from his apprenticeship with Gamaliel, Paul learned to
question and form his own ideas, which he practiced in his own ministry.

From them I also received letters sent
To the brothers in Damesek. And I went there
To bind and lead them away and bring them back
Bound to have them punished in Yerushalayim.

A brilliance from above
    6And while I was traveling and coming near
    Damesek at about the noon, it happened
    That suddenly out of the skies a great light
    Shone around me, 7and I fell to the ground
    And I heard a voice saying to me, "Shaul, Shaul,
    Why are you persecuting me?" 8And I answered,
    Saying, "Who are you, sir?"363 And he said to me,
    "I am Yeshua the Natzrati, whom you persecute."
    9And the ones with me saw the light but didn't hear
    The voice speaking to me. 10Then I said, "What
    Can I do, lord?"364 And the lord said to me,
    "Stand up and go to Damesek and there
    You will be told about all things that you
    Were chosen to do." 11And because the glory
    Of that light prevented me from seeing,
    I came to Damesek with my companions
    Leading me by the hand.

    12Then Hananyah,
    Who was a devout man about the law

---

363. *Kyrie* is translated as "Lord" in other editions. *Kyrie* can be translated as "rabbi," "sir," "master," "lord," or "Lord," depending on context and approach. Since at this moment Paul does not know who has spoken to him, he could not have intended his question to be addressed to Jesus or to God. Had he known whom the speaker was, why ask? The question would have been unnecessary and unthinkable. We should trust that Paul was truly asking for the speaker's identity. In the end, this particular translation of *kyrie* as "Lord" imposes a later translator's conviction and knowledge of what follows in the text on Paul, and deprives him of the innocence and plausibility of his question.

364. With "the lord" identified as Jesus, a translation of *kyrie* as "rabbi" or "lord" makes sense.

And well esteemed by all the Jews there,
13Came to me and stood near. "Brother Shaul,"
    He said, "Recover your sight!" At that moment
    I recovered my sight and saw him. 14He said,
    "God of our ancestors has appointed you
    To know his will and to see the just one
    And to hear the voice from his mouth,
15Because you will be a witness before
    All people about what you have seen and heard.
16And now, why delay? Stand up, be dipped
    And wash away your sins, calling his name."

Ecstasy in Yerushalayim and Stefanos

17When I returned to Yerushalayim,
    It happened that as I was praying in
    The Temple, I fell into an ecstasy,
18And saw him telling me, "Hurry and go
    From Yerushalayim. They will not accept
    Your testimony about me." 19And I said,
    "Lord, they know that in every synagogue
    I jailed and flogged those who believed in you.
20While the blood of your martyr Stefanos
    Poured out, I stood near him and approved
    And protected the garment of his killer."
21He said to me, "Go, for I am sending you
    Out to the gentiles who are far away."

Shaul the Roman

22They listened to him up to this moment and then they raised their voices, saying, "Take this fellow away from the earth. He has no right to live!" 23And as they screamed and threw their coats down and kicked dust into the air, 24the tribune ordered him to be brought into the barracks. He ordered him to be examined with lashes to find out the reason for this outcry against him.

25But when they stretched him out for the flogging, Shaul said to the centurion standing near him, "Is it legal for you to flog an uncondemned Roman citizen?"

26When the centurion heard this, he went up to the tribune and reported, saying, "What are you about to do? This man is a Roman."

27The tribune went to Shaul and said to him, "Are you a Roman?"

He said, "Yes."365

28The tribune responded, "I paid a huge sum of money to become a Roman citizen."366

Shaul answered, "I was born one."367

29Immediately, those who were about to examine him through the lash drew away from him; and the tribune was frightened after learning that Shaul was a Roman and that he had put him in chains.

30The next day, wanting to find out precisely why he was accused by the Jews, the tribune released him and ordered the high priests and the whole Sanhedrin to meet. Then he brought Shaul in and set him before them.

Chapter 23

Confrontation with the Sanhedrin

Glaring intensely at the Sanhedrin, Shaul said,

Men and brothers, in full good conscience
I have lived as God's citizen down to this day.

2Then the high priest Hananyah ordered the men who stood beside him to strike him on the mouth.

---

365. Paul's "Yes" is a signal moment in the strategic history of Christianity. While the new Messianic movement will suffer severe persecutions by Rome, Paul's declaration of himself as a Roman citizen portends a triumphant union of Christendom and Rome. Three centuries will pass of outsider Christian growth among pagans. But in the early fourth century Roman emperor Constantine will see a cross in the sky and alter the Western world by moving his seat of power from Rome to Constantinople and declaring Christianity the Roman Empire's official religion.

366. Literally, "to acquire this citizenship."

367. The confession by the high Roman officer that he had to buy his citizenship (an implausible confession), followed by Paul's statement of his birthright citizenship, permits Paul not only to outmaneuver the officer but also to foretell a day in the fourth century when a Christian will possess the true Roman birthright.

3At this Shaul said to him,

> God will strike you, you whitewashed wall!
> Do you sit judging me according to the law
> When violating the law you order me struck?

4Those standing beside him said, "Are you reviling the high priest of God?"

5And Shaul said,

> Brothers, I didn't know he was the high priest.
> In Exodus it is written:
>> You will not speak evil of a ruler of the people.[368]

6When Shaul noticed that some of them were Tzadokim[369] and some others were Prushim,[370] he cried out to the council:

> Men and brothers, I am a Parush,[371]
> The son of Prushim, and I am on trial
> For hope of resurrection of the dead.

7When he said this, there was a discord between the Prushim and the Tzadokim that divided the assembly. 8The Tzadokim say there is no resurrection, nor angel, nor spirit, but the Prushim believe in all these. 9Then there was a great uproar and some of the Parush scholars stood up and dissented, saying, "We find no evil in this man. What if a spirit or angel spoke to him?"

10The dissension increased and the tribune, fearing that Shaul might be torn to pieces, ordered the soldiers to go down, take him away amidst them, and take him into the barracks.

The lord urges courage

11The following night the lord said,

> Be of courage. As you have testified
> About this to me in Yerushalayim
> So you must also testify in Rome.

---

368. Exod. 22–28.

369. Sadducees.

370. Pharisees.

371. Pharisee. Here, in contrast to other sinister depictions of the Sanhedrin, some Pharisee scholars are said to believe in resurrection and find no evil in Paul.

The Jews conspire

12When day came the Jews joined in a plot, binding themselves by an oath not to eat nor to drink until they had killed Shaul. 13There were more than forty who were in the conspiracy. 14They went to the high priests and the elders and said, "We are bound by oath not to taste food nor drink until we kill Shaul. 15Now you must inform the tribune and the council to bring him down to you as if you are intending to determine more accurate things about him. And we are ready to kill him."

16Now the son of Shaul's sister heard about the ambush, and he went to the barracks, got in and told Shaul.

17Shaul called one of the centurions and said, "Take this young man to the tribune, since he has something to report to him."

18So the centurion took him to the tribune and he said, "The prisoner Shaul called me over and asked me to bring this young man to you, since he has something to report to you."

19The tribune took him by the hand, drew him aside privately, and asked him, "What is it you have to tell me?"

20And he said, "The Jews have decided to ask you to bring Shaul down to the Sanhedrin tomorrow as if for the purpose of obtaining more accurate information from him. 21You must not be persuaded to do so, for more than forty of them are waiting in ambush, men who have bound themselves by oath not to eat nor to drink until they have killed him, and now they are ready and waiting for your word from you."

22The tribune dismissed the young man, ordering him, "Tell no one about what you have revealed to me."

Troops canter away with Shaul

23Then he summoned two of the centurions and said, "Prepare two hundred foot soldiers and seventy horsemen and two hundred spearmen so they can leave for Caesarea at the third hour of the night.[372] 24Have horses for Shaul to ride so he can get safely to Felix the governor."[373]

---

372. At nine in the evening.

373. At this dramatic moment, with a flourish of infantry and cavalry, the tribune decides to rescue Paul from the Jews and deliver him to the justice of the governor. From here to the end of Acts, Roman authorities will support Paul, permitting him to survive, to present his case against the conspiring Jews, and once in Rome to carry

25And he wrote a letter in the following manner:

26Claudius Lysias to the most excellent governor Felix,[374]
Greetings.

27This man was arrested by the Jews and was about to be killed by
them, when I went with my soldiers and rescued him on learning that
he was a Roman citizen. 28I wanted to know the reason behind their
accusations. I brought him down to the Sanhedrin. 29I found that he
was accused because of questions of their law, but was charged with
nothing that warranted death or imprisonment. 30After I was informed
that there would be a plot against the man, I sent him to you at once.
I also gave orders for his accusers to charge him in your presence.

---

out his ministry. None of the Roman military authorities or judges who hear Paul
find him guilty of any charge. The book reveals the triumphant progress of spreading the good news in the Roman provinces, and proving once again that the new
Messianism is not a dangerous anti-Roman element in the empire. Anonymous Acts
is skillful in composing and shaping speeches in the mouths of prominent historical figures to show both Roman goodwill to its colonies and the favored position of
the early Christians. During Paul's time and for the next centuries the plight of the
new Christians was worse than that of the Jews, who, fewer in number, did not represent a grave threat to Roman religion and rule. During Paul's life until his death,
whose time and place remain unknown, the lives of Jews and Christian Jews were
horrendous. Caesar Augustus had some four thousand Jews crucified alone in 4
B.C.E. during the chaotic moment after King Herod's death; during the Jewish War,
66–70, the daily crucifixions did not end, and sometimes, according to Josephus,
the number reached five hundred a day. The caves in which the Christians of Anatolia hid and worshiped and the Book of Revelation (a thunderous condemnation of
a demonic Rome) reflect another historical view in contradiction to the praise and
apologia for Roman hegemony that color the gospels and Acts. Twenty-five awkward
years after Paul's death, during which his contributions and direction can at best be
described as minor, Acts re-creates Paul, endowing him with superhuman qualities
as the major figure in early Christianity.

374. Antonius Felix, a favorite of Roman emperor Claudius, was governor (procurator) of Palestine from 52/53 until his removal in 60. Although in Acts he is a model of
patience and benevolent justice, he was not perceived kindly elsewhere. In Rome we
hear from Tacitus about the infamous character of his administration who helped to
lay the ground for the revolt of 66–70: "He reveled in cruelty and lust, and wielded
the power of a king with the mind of a slave" (*Historiae*, 5, 9).

31So the soldiers according to their orders took Shaul with them through the night to Antipatris,[375] 32and the next day, letting the horseman go on with him, they returned to the barracks. 33When they came to Caesarea and delivered the letter to the governor, they also brought Shaul before him. 34When he read it and asked what province he was from and he learned he was from Kilikia, 35he said, "I will hear you when your accusers arrive." And he ordered him held in Herod's residence.

Chapter 24

On trial before the governor

Five days later the high priest Hananyah came down with some elders[376] and a certain orator[377] Tertullus. 2When Shaul was summoned, Tertullus began to accuse him, saying, "We have enjoyed long peace because of you and your foresight, most excellent Felix, and with gratitude we acknowledge 3your reforms that have come to our nation in every way and from everywhere. 4But so as not to detain you further, I beg you in your graciousness to hear us briefly. 5We have found this man a plague, who incites riots among all the Jews throughout the world and is a leader of the sect of Natzrati. 6He was even trying to desecrate the Temple when we caught him.[378] 8You yourself will be able to learn by questioning him about all these things we accuse him of." 9And the Jews also assented, saying that these things are true.[379]

---

375. Antipatris from the Greek Ἀντιπατρίς (Antipatris), a city in Judaea on the way to Caesarea. The city was founded by Herod the Great and named for his father.

376. There were seventy-one elders in the Sanhedrin.

377. A lawyer or advocate for the case, skilled in oratory and the law.

378. In the NRSV verses 6b–8a are not included. They are included in the KJV and other Majority Text versions: "and we would have judged him according to our law when the tribune Lysias came and violently took him out of our hands, commanding his accusers to come before you."

379. It is not possible to know from his name Tertullus who the orator is or represents—he may be a Roman gentile, or Tertullos a Greek gentile, or a Jew with a gentile name. Verse 9, reading, "And the Jews also assented," seems to separate him from the Jews as he unattractively represents them, making his literal identity even more murky. However, in the parallel allegory of vile Judas and Jesus, Judas is now

Shaul tells his mission

10Shaul responded when the governor nodded him to speak:

Knowing you for many years to have been judge
Over this nation, I make a heartfelt defense
Against these charges now brought against me.
11It is more than twelve days since I went up
To worship in Yerushalayim, 12and no one
Found me arguing with anyone, or causing trouble
In the Temple, in other synagogues,
Or anywhere in the city, 13nor can they prove
Any of those things they accuse me of.
14But I confess this to you: the way I serve
The God of our fathers, they call a heresy,
Yet I believe all things written in the law
And prophets, 15and have hope—a hope
They share—that there will be a resurrection
Of the just and the unjust. 16In all this
I always try to have a blameless conscience
Before God and people. 17Now after some years
I came to bring alms to my nation and offer
Sacrifices. 18While doing this they found me
In the Temple after doing the ceremony
Of purification, not with any crowd
Or causing an uproar. 19But some Jews
From Asia, they should be here today
To accuse me before you if they possess

---

vile Tertullus and the Sanhedrin denouncing Paul, who continues the work of the spiritual Jesus on earth.

These intratribal wars of influence in the first century, as here seen between Christian Jews and Jewish villains of Jerusalem, were commonplace. The Essenes of Qumran on the northwest bank of the Dead Sea called themselves "the children of light" and aspired to conquer Jerusalem and its "children of darkness," where liberal city reformists abounded, as seen in rabbis Hillel and Gamaliel and other Pharisees in the Sanhedrin.

Something to say against me. 20Or let them state
What crime I committed when I stood
Before the Sanhedrin, 21other than my one
Declaration which I cried out among those
With whom I stood. I am before you on trial
Today over the resurrection of the dead.

Shaul lingers in Felix's hands

22After learning specifically about the nature of the way, Felix said,
"When Lysias comes down, I will decide your case." 23He ordered the
centurion to keep him under guard but give him some freedom and not
to prevent any of his friends from taking care of him.

24Some days later Felix arrived with his own wife, Drusilla, a Jew. He
sent for Shaul and listened to him speak of faith in Yeshua the Mashiah.
25Now as he reasoned about justice and continence and the coming judgment, Felix was afraid and answered him, "Go away for now, and when I
have a proper moment, I will send for you." 26Also, he hoped that Shaul
would give him money. Therefore, he sent for him and talked with him
ever more frequently.

27After two years went by, Felix was succeeded by Porcius Festus.[380]
Wanting to do the Jews a favor, he left Shaul bound in prison.

Chapter 25

Plotting and a trial before Festus

Three days after Festus set foot in the province, he went up to
Yerushalayim from Caesarea, 2and the high priests and leaders of the
Jews made a report against Shaul and appealed to him, and 3as a favor to
them urged that he transfer Shaul to Yerushalayim. They were concoct-
ing a plot to kill him on the way there.[381]

---

380. Felix Porcius Festus followed Felix as governor. Eventually, Festus permitted
Paul to go to Rome to plead his destiny.

381. With regard to the historicity of charges by both sides in Acts, the witnessing
evidence resides entirely within Acts itself. The author (or authors) is unknown, the

4But Festus answered that Shaul should be held in Caesarea, and he himself planned soon to go there. 5So, he said, let those of you who have authority among you come down with me and, if there is anything wrong with this man, bring charges against him.

6Then, after spending no more than eight days there, he came down to Caesarea, and on the next day he sat on the judgment seat and ordered Shaul to be brought in.

7When he arrived, the Jews who had come down from Yerushalayim surrounded him and made many grave charges against him, which they couldn't prove. 8Shaul defended himself, saying:

> I have not sinned against the law of the Jews,
> Nor against the Temple, nor against Caesar.

9But Festus, wishing to store up favor with the Jews, answered Shaul, "Do you want to go up to Yerushalayim and there be tried about these matters before me?"

10And Shaul said,

> Before Caesar's judgment bench I have stood
> Where I should be tried. 11Now if I have done wrong
> And something that deserves death,
> I do not refuse to die. But if there is nothing

---

date uncertain. As to the charge that Paul incited riots in synagogues, it would seem an unlikely way of persuasion. With regard to the charge that Paul was attempting to convert Jews and gentiles to Messianic Judaism, it is clear that Paul's mission in spreading the good news was successful, which is confirmed, with or without turning to Acts, by the rapid historical spread of the emerging faith throughout the Roman Empire. So the charge against Paul of proselytizing is true and may be thought of as benevolent. As to specific charges that Jews plotted to kill Paul, there is no evidence outside Acts to confirm or deny these events, and no way of knowing how a record of such events and conversations reached the author of Acts. Whatever the veracity of these events, the depiction of Jews in this conflict within Judaism repeats the diction and logic found in the gospels' demonization of the Jew; over the centuries these severe caricatures have had cataclysmic effects on the life and death of Jews. As for the demonization of a parent faith or of other sects and faiths, scripture from major religions (with rare exceptions) reveals unremitting hostility to "the infidel other" unless that infidelity is healed by the redemption of conversion.

> To their charges against me, no one can turn me
> Over to them. So I appeal to Caesar.[382]

12Then Festus, after conferring with the council, answered, "You have appealed to Caesar and to Caesar you will go."

With King Agrippa and his sister

13After a few days went by, King Agrippa[383] and Bernike[384] arrived in Caesarea to greet Festus. 14Since they were staying a few days there, Festus referred Shaul's case to the king, saying, "There is a certain man whom Felix left behind in prison. 15When I was in Yerushalayim, the high priests and elders of the Jews informed me about him and request his condemnation. 16I told them that it is not the Roman way to hand over anyone being accused before the accused met the accusers face to face and to have the opportunity of a defense against the charge. 17So when they assembled here I made no delay, and the next day I sat down on the judgment seat and ordered the man to be brought before me. 18When the accusers stood up, they did not charge him with any of the evil crimes that I had expected. 19Instead they disagreed about areas in their own religion and about a certain Yeshua who died, whom Shaul said lived. 20Not knowing how to examine these matters, I asked him if he would

---

382. Nero had just become Caesar (54–68), if indeed Paul's imprisonment was in 54. It has been suggested that were Paul to have won his case in Caesar's court, it would have been not only a personal victory but one that recognized a distinction between Judaism and emerging Christianity.

383. Herod Agrippa II was seventeen when his father Herod Agrippa I died, in 44. At first replaced by Roman procurators, later he became an influential king whose territorial reign and powers greatly increased during his lifetime. He died around 100 C.E.

384. Bernice from the Greek Βερνίκη (Bernike). Bernice was King Agrippa's sister and had an important and colorful life. She had several marriages and several marital relationships, including an extended one with her brother the king. During the Jewish wars, at first she and Agrippa sided strongly with the Jews, who were being slaughtered by Titus. Eventually, both supported the Romans. Bernice became the mistress of Titus, and they went to Rome together. But Titus, son of the emperor Vespasian, broke away from Bernice when he himself was about to become emperor.

be willing to go to Yerushalayim and there be tried. 21But when Shaul appealed to be held for the judgment of the emperor,[385] I ordered him to be kept until I could send him to Caesar."

22Agrippa said to Festus, "I would like to hear the man myself."

"Tomorrow," he says, "you will hear him."[386]

---

385. The emperor was the newly inaugurated Nero. The Greek reads "emperor," but the grand KJV says, "Augustus": "Paul appealed to be reserved for the decision of Augustus" (25.21). This elegant error may have occurred in order to put Paul before a more worthy judge, but Augustus reigned from 27 B.C.E. to 14 C.E., making Jesus fourteen years old and Paul nine in the last year of his rule. It can be said that "Augustus" suggests a more general title of respect, as in "Imperial Majesty," but the context here does not warrant that interpretation.

386. The historical frame presented in the gospels and Acts is that of a benevolent and just Rome of decent law, perverted by Jewish ambition. While Jews are the enemy of Christianity, Rome is the great patient power, wanting accommodation with the new sect. In Acts we encounter the listening powers of Governor Festus and King Agrippa, each curious and eager to hear Paul speak, to hear his good news, and to comprehend his spiritual way. Entering the scene with imperial pomp and followed by his military retinue, the king comes to pay homage to the prisoner, whose ideas have prompted the visit. In this beautiful imaginary scene a king visits an unknown man accused, as was Jesus, of social insurrection, in order that he may be informed and perhaps prepared for future conversion. In such a way one day in the fourth century, a Constantine emerges from terrible internecine warfare and is worthy of leading Christianity in all dominions of what was, until that hour, the pagan Roman Empire.

Paul is on talking terms with the great figures of his time, with Festus, the governor of Roman Palestine (Israel); with King Agrippa, the Hasmonean ruler of Israel; and eventually, Paul hopes, with Caesar, from whom he hopes for full pardon and understanding, which is a metaphor for Rome's understanding and eventual espousal of Christianity, and a parallel to the passion scene in which Jesus actually goes before Pilate, Jesus's "good but reluctant crucifier," and they have a conversation in some common language. When Acts ends, Paul, freed in Rome to pursue his ministry, awaits his audience with the emperor. As Paul stands before the understanding King Agrippa, he experiences the king's ultimate goodwill.

The much earlier letters, composed by contemporaries of Jesus, should be the logical place for confirmation of the gospel life and death of Jesus, but in the Pauline and pseudo-Pauline Pastoral Letters, there is no Pilate, no Herod, no centurions, nor any of the earlier figures in the life of Jesus, including his mother and precursor in John the Baptist.

In Acts the rise of Paul as the spiritual and political leader of the emerging

23On the next day Agrippa and Bernike came with great fantastic pageantry and entered the audience room, with both tribunes and prominent men of the city. Then Festus gave the order and Shaul was brought in. 24And Festus said, "King Agrippa and all here present with you, you are looking at this man about whom a multitude of Jews has petitioned me, both in Yerushalayim and here, crying out that he should not live any longer. 25Yet I found that he had done nothing to make him deserve death. And when he wished to appeal to the emperor, I decided to send him. 26But I have nothing definite to write to our master, and so I have brought him before all of you and above all before you, King Agrippa, so that after examining him I will have something to say. 27For it seems unreasonable to send a prisoner without any charges to report against him."

Chapter 26

Shaul about himself

Agrippa said to Shaul, "You have permission to speak for yourself."
Then Shaul extended his hand and began his defense:
    2For all I have been accused of by the Jews,
      King Agrippa, I think myself fortunate
      That I am to defend myself before you,
    3Who are an expert in the customs and concerns

Christians is a key historical reconstruction in early Christianity that majorly parallels the biblical legend of Moses and the Pharaoh in the formation of a Jewish coherent entity. In each instance the titular founder of the new religion operates at the highest level of governance, talking to monarchs, with appropriate honors and punishments bestowed on that risky role. When crisis arises for the second millennium Jews, Moses rejects the privilege of palace familiarity and leaves to take his people into exile and freedom, leaving Egypt behind. When crisis comes to Paul, though Paul like Jesus is imprisoned by the Romans and like Jesus, according to scripture, will die by Roman sword, Paul does not reject the privilege of Roman familiarity, indeed, he works toward more understanding and embraces the possibility that Rome itself will find redemption. This posture of reconciliation conforms to early aspirations that reveal Rome not as the enemy but as the church's eventual eternal home.

Of the Jews.[387] I beg you to hear me patiently.
4All Jews know my way of life from my youth
Spent from the beginning in my own country
In Yerushalayim. 5They know me from then,
If they are willing to testify. I was a member
Of the strictest sect of our religion,
A Parush.[388] 6And now I stand on trial
For my hope in that promise made by God
To us, 7a promise our twelve tribes pray for
Fervently night and day to attain. My king,
For this hope, king, I am accused by the Jews.
8Can it be unbelievable to any of you
Who are here that God raises the dead?[389]

---

387. King Agrippa, a Hasmonean Jew descended from the original Maccabean family of patriots who successfully fought the invading Greeks (sent there by Rome) in
the second and first centuries B.C.E. would be familiar with the customs of the Jews,
and perhaps surprised or offended to hear Paul accuse them of being his would-be
killers. The Paul in these verses, written after his death, in which Paul speaks of the
Jews in the harshest speech, as if by his conversion he no longer thinks or identifies
himself as a Messianic Jew, is not related to the Paul of his own letters. While Acts
is a glorious and exciting book of fervent mission and adventure through the geographies of the Near East and part of Europe, it would be deeply unfair to confuse the
speculations of an unknown later author with the spirit and speech of the historical
Paul, who has recorded his wisdom and his soul in his own meditative letters.

388. A Pharisee. Of the two major political sects of the Second Temple period (the
second commonwealth), the Pharisees were the least strict in terms of oral and written law. They were the sect of the people, as opposed to the aristocratic Sadducees
of the priestly cast. In their politics they were against Hellenization and opposed to
Roman rule. The intellectual and spiritual leaders, Hillel, Gamaliel, Paul, and perhaps Jesus, came from their sect, though more recently Jesus has also been identified with the Galilean Hasid ascetic healers. Prushim (Pharisees) means "separatists"
or "deviants," an epithet given them because of their own liberal interpretation of
religious concerns, such as eternal life and resurrection.

389. It is unlikely that Paul would have accused the Jews, and especially his own
Pharisees, of being against him because he believed in God's resurrection of the
dead, since the Pharisee tenet of resurrection was the source of Paul's own spiritual formation. It is equally unlikely that Paul would have expected sympathy from

Paul remembers

9Now I thought that I should strongly oppose
The name of Yeshua the Natzrati,
And with authority from the high priests390
I not only locked up many of the saints
In jail but cast my vote for death. 10I went
Into all the synagogues 11and often
I punished them, forcing them to blaspheme
And in my fury and rage against them
I even pursued them in foreign cities.

On the road

12On the road to Damesek I traveled
With the authority of the high priests.
13At noon along the way, O king, I saw
A light from the sky brighter than the sun,
Shining around me and those companions
With me.391 14When all of us fell to the ground
I heard a voice saying to me in Hebrew,392
"Shaul, Shaul, why do you persecute me?
It is hard for you to kick against the goads."393

Roman Festus and especially from Hasmonean Agrippa on the question of resurrection, since they both allied themselves with the Sadducees, who rejected the notion of resurrection, and Agrippa himself appointed the Sadducee high priests. It is also unexpected that Paul would have directed his anger at the Pharisees, who supported his position, and spared the Sadducees, who were his real opponents. This anomaly does not reflect the historic Paul, but the more general survival doctrine of the later church, which was accommodation with Roman authority.

390. Since Paul was a Pharisee, and the Pharisees and Sadducees bitterly opposed each other, it is not apparent why the Sadducee high priests would have accorded Paul authority to lock up the "saints" unless, indeed, he had changed his allegiance to the Sadducees.

391. Paul gives two earlier accounts of his conversion in 9.1–19 and 22.4–21.

392. Probably in Aramaic. See note 360 on 21.40.

393. The meaning of the Greek proverb is that it is futile to resist. A "goad" is a sharp pointed stick used to prod a donkey or an ox.

15And I said, "Who are you, sir?" "I am Yeshua,
   Whom you persecute. 16But get up and stand
   On your feet. This is why I have appeared
   To you, to appoint you as servant and witness
   Both to things in which you have seen me
   And in those times when I will appear to you,
17Delivering you from the people[394] and the gentiles
   To whom I send you 18to open their eyes
   And to turn them from the darkness to light
   And from the power of Satan to God
   And for them to receive remission of sin
   And a share among those who until now
   Are sanctified by their belief in me."

19So then, King Agrippa, I have not disobeyed
   The vision in the sky, 20and I have preached
   First in Damesek and then in Yerushalayim
   And all the lands of Yehuda[395] and the gentiles,
   Asking them to repent and to turn to God
   And to do works that merit their repentance.

21Because of these things the Jews seized me
   In the Temple and tried to kill me.
22I have got help from God and till this day
   I stand here and testify to both great and small,
   Saying nothing but what the prophets and Moshe
   Said would happen:[396] 23that Yeshua must suffer
   And by being the first to rise from the dead light,
   He would proclaim it to the people and the gentiles.

Agrippa counters Shaul's appeal

24While he was making his defense, Festus said in a loud voice, "You are mad, Shaul, and too much learning is driving you mad."

---

394. The Jews.
395. Judea.
396. Exod. 2.10–11, 2.14–15.

25But Shaul said,

> I am not mad, most excellent Festus,
> But I am speaking true and wisdom words.

26The king to whom I speak to openly

> Knows about these matters and I think
> That nothing has escaped his eye. All this
> Was not accomplished in a corner. 27King
> Agrippa, do you believe in the prophets?
> I know that you believe.

28And Agrippa said to Shaul,

> In a little while
> You will persuade me to become a Christian.[397]

29And Shaul said,

> I pray to God that sooner or later all
> Who listen to me now will one day be
> As I am now—except for all these chains.

30Then the king and the governor and Bernike got up and also those who had been seated with them, 31and as they were leaving they spoke to one another, saying, "This man has done nothing to deserve chains or death."

32Agrippa said to Festus, "This man could have gone free, if he had not appealed to Caesar."

Chapter 27

Shaul sails for Italy

When it was decided to sail for Italy, we handed Shaul and some other prisoners over to a centurion named Julius.[398] 2After boarding a ship of Adramyttium[399] about to sail to ports along the coast in Asia, we set sail. Aristarhos, a Makedonian[400] of Thessaloniki, was with us. 3On the

---

397. In a final parallel to gospel, King Herod the Roman, who appointed Hasmonean King Agrippa, also declares Paul innocent and good, thereby making Rome the wise and understanding master in the play of dominance.

398. For some lines the speaker is again using the first-person plural "we."

399. An important seaport in Mysia on the west coast of Asia, southeast of Troas.

400. Macedonian.

next day we docked at Tzidon.[401] Julius treated Shaul with kindness and allowed him to go to friends and receive their care. 4Then putting out from there, we sailed under the lee of Cyprus because the winds were against us. 5After we sailed the open sea off Kilikia and Pamfylia, we came to Myra[402] of Lykia.[403] 6There the centurion found an Alexandrian ship bound for Italy and we boarded it. 7Then for a number of days we sailed slowly on harsh waters until we reached Knidos,[404] and since the wind held us up we sailed under the lee of Krete[405] across from Salmone,[406] 8and barely managed to move past it till we finally came to a place called Beautiful Harbors[407] near Lasaia.[408]

The seawind strikes

9Since much time had passed and sailing was already risky, because even Yom Kippur[409] had come and gone, 10Shaul said to them,[410]

---

401. Sidon, a major port in Phoenicia, modern Lebanon.

402. A city on the south coast of Lycia in Asia Minor.

403. Lycia from the Greek Λυκία (Lykia), a wooded, mountainous area on the southwest coast of Asia Minor and a major trading center with Alexandria. The Lycians are mentioned in the *Iliad* as a brave people who sided with the Trojans. Lycia was also famous for the worship of Apollo, who spent his winters there.

404. Knidos from the Greek Κνίδος (Knidos), a peninsula and city on the coast of Caria in Asia Minor.

405. Crete from the Greek Κρήτη (Krete), the largest of the Greek islands, far south of the mainland.

406. Salmone from the Greek Σαλμώνη (Salmone), a promontory on the northeast corner of Crete.

407. Beautiful Harbors from the Greek Καλοὶ Λιμένες (Kaloi Limenes), meaning "beautiful harbors," and normally translated "Fair Havens." It is a port on the southern coast of Crete, a few miles from the city of Lasea.

408. Lasea from the Greek Λασαία (Lasaia), a city on the southern coast of Crete.

409. The Fast or Day of Atonement from the Greek νηστεία (nesteia), meaning "fasting," from the Hebrew יוֹם כִּפּוּר (yom kipur), meaning "day of covering or atoning." Yom Kippur or the Day of Atonement, in early September, is a day of fasting to atone for sins. There is no way that Paul, a Christian Jew, will ignore the holiest of Jewish holidays.

410. The text reverts back to a third-person account and then back and forth between third person and first person.

> Gentlemen, I perceive our voyage to be
> Dangerous, with great loss not only of cargo
> And ship but of the lives of us on the trip.

11But the centurion was persuaded rather by the helmsman and ship-owner than by the concerns that Shaul stated. 12Since this harbor was unsuitable for spending the winter, most were in favor of sailing so that if they could somehow reach Phoenix, there they could spend the winter. It was Kretan harbor facing southwest and northwest.

13With a south wind blowing gently, they thought they had what they needed, and raised anchor and sailed near the shore of Krete. 14But soon a violent wind, called the northeaster, battered us from the island. 15The ship was caught and could not be turned to face the gale. We gave in and let our craft be swept along. 16By running below a near sheltering small island named Kauda,[411] they were barely able to keep control of the life-boat, 17which they hoisted up aboard. Then they used cables to undergird the ship. Fearing we might run aground on the shoals of the Syrtis gulf, they let down the sea anchor and we were so driven along. 18But the storm battered us, and on the next day they threw the cargo overboard. 19On the third day with their own hands they threw the tackle overboard. 20But when neither sun nor stars appeared for a number of days, and huge winter storms were raging, we lost all hope of being saved.

The angel of courage

21After a long time with no one having any appetite to eat, Shaul stood up in the midst of them and said,

> Gentlemen, you should have obeyed me
> And not have sailed from Krete and spared yourselves
> From battering and loss. 22Now I urge courage.
> There will be no loss of life among you,
> But only the ship. 23All through this last night
> An angel of God stood by me, whom I serve,
> 24Saying, "Have no fear, Shaul. You must stand
> Before Caesar, and look, God has granted safety

---

411. Cauda from the Greek Καῦδα (Kauda), found in other manuscripts as Κλαῦδα (Klauda), a small island south of Crete.

To you and all who are sailing with you."
25So courage, gentlemen. I believe in God
  And it will be exactly as he's told me.
26But we must run aground on some island.

Battling the sea and crew
  27Now on the fourteenth day of being tossed
  And drifting in the Adriatic Sea,
  The night was coming and around midnight
  The sailors thought we might be nearing land,
28And they took soundings. Twenty fathoms deep.
  Sailing a little further, they took soundings.
  Fifteen fathoms. 29Fearing we might be driven
  Onto rocky shores we let down four anchors
  From the stern and prayed for day to come.
30Now the sailors were trying to flee from
  The ship, and had lowered the lifeboat down
  Into the sea, pretending they were dropping
  The anchors from the bow. 31But Shaul said
  To the centurion and to the soldiers,
  "Unless these men remain here in the ship
  You cannot be saved." 32Then the soldiers cut
  The lifeboat's ropes and let it fall away.

Shipwreck
  33When day was coming on us, Shaul urged
  Everyone to eat our rations. "Today
  Is our fourteenth day of waiting, worried,
  Tasting nothing. 34Now I ask you to eat
  What's left. It will help you survive, and none
  Of you will lose a hair from your heads."
35On saying this he took bread and thanked God
  Before everyone. He broke it and ate.
36Then all were animated and took food.
37We were two hundred seventy-six souls
  In all. 38After eating their fill, they lightened
  The ship by throwing grain into the sea.

39When day came they didn't recognize land,
But they saw a bay and a beach, and there
They hoped to ground the ship. 40So they let go
The anchors, leaving them in the sea,
And at the same time loosened the ropes
On the rudders and hoisted the mainsail
Into the wind, and steered for the beach.
41But they struck a shoal concealed in the waters
And ran the ship aground. The bow was stuck
And unmovable while the stern was breaking up
By crashing waves. 42The soldiers had a plan
To kill the prisoners so none might flee
By swimming off. 43But the centurion, wanting
To save Shaul, ordered those who could swim
To jump overboard first and make for land.
44The rest to follow, some on floating boards,
Others on pieces torn from the ship. And so
It happened that all got safely to the land.

Chapter 28

Waking in Melite

Once safely on shore, we learned that the island was called Melite.[412]
2And the islanders[413] showed us unusual kindness. They lit a fire and
welcomed us all around it, since it was raining and cold. 3Shaul gathered
a load of brushwood and placed it on the fire 4when a viper emerged from
the heat and fastened onto his hand. When the natives saw the creature
angling from his hand, they said to one another, "This man must be a
murderer. Though he made it safely out of the sea, justice will not let
him." 5Then he shook the creature into the fire and suffered no harm.

---

412. Malta from the Greek Μελίτη (Melite), a large island south of Sicily.
413. The word in Greek is βάρβαρος (barbaros), meaning "foreigner." Our word
"barbarian" derives from the Greek, but here the word means simply a "foreigner,"
"native," or contextually an "islander," with no negative inference.

6They expected him to swell up or suddenly collapse dead. For a long time they waited and observed nothing unusual happening to him. So they changed their minds and were saying he was a god.

7Now in the neighborhood of that place were estates belonging to the leading man on the island, whose name was Publius. He greeted us and for three days entertained us with fine hospitality. 8It happened that Publius's father was lying sick with high fever and dysentery. Shaul went in to him and prayed, laying his hands on him and healed him. 9When that happened the rest of the people on the island who were sick came to him and were healed. 10They honored him with many honors, and when we sailed away they supplied us with all our needs.

Voyage to Rome

11After three months we set sail in a ship that had wintered on the island, on an Alexandrian ship marked with Dioskouroi[414] as its figure-head. 12We docked at Syrakousai[415] where we stayed three days; 13then we weighed anchor and arrived at Region.[416] A day later a south wind sprang up and on the second day we reached Potiola.[417] 14There we found believers who invited us to stay seven days, and so we came to Rome. 15When the believers from there heard of us, they came as far as the Forum and the Three Taverns to meet us. On seeing them, Paul blessed God and took courage.

Witnessing to the Roman Jews

16When we entered Rome, Shaul was allowed to stay by himself, with the soldier who was guarding him.

---

414. Castor and Pollux from the Greek Διόσκουροι (Dioskouroi), meaning "Twin Brother" and in Latin "Gemini." Castor and Pollux were the twin sons of Zeus and Leda, after whom the constellation is also named.

415. Syracuse from the Greek Συράκουσαι (Syrakousai), a city on the east coast of Sicily.

416. Rhegium from the Greek Ῥήγιον (Region), a city and promontory at the toe of Italy in Bruttium, opposite Messina in Sicily.

417. Puteoli from the Greek Ποτίολοι (Potioloi), a city whose modern name is Pozzuoli. It is on the Phlegrean peninsula in the province of Naples.

17Now it happened that three days later he called together the prominent Jews. When they assembled, he said to them,

> Men and brothers, though I have done nothing
> Against our people or our ancestral customs,
> I was arrested in Yerushalayim and handed over
> To the Romans, 18who examined me, and they
> Wanted to let me go, since they found in me
> No cause for death, 19but when the Jews objected,
> I was forced to appeal to Caesar, though
> I have no charge to bring against my nation,
> 20And so I've summoned you to speak with you.
> Because of Israel's hopes I wear these chains.

21They told him, "We have received no letters about you from Yehuda, nor has any brother arrived and reported anything evil about you. 22But we would like to hear from you what you think about our sect, since we know that everywhere one speaks against it."

23Then they agreed on a day, and large numbers came to his lodgings, and from morning to evening he lectured them, testifying to the kingdom of God and persuading them about Yeshua both from the Torah of Moshe and from the prophets. 24Some were persuaded by his words and others would not believe, 25and they broke up at odds with each other.[418]

Shaul had one further word,

> The holy spirit, who spoke through the prophet
> Yeshayahu, was right to say to your ancestors:
>> 26Go to this people and say,
> Hearing you will hear but not understand,
>> Seeing you will see but not perceive,
> 27For this people's heart has grown dull
> And they hear with heaviness, and they close their eyes
>> So they will not see with their eyes

---

418. The dispute among the Roman Jews surely centered on whether or not they accepted Jesus as the foretold messiah, which ultimately became the distinguishing point thereafter between Jews, who were waiting for the messiah, and Christians, who believed that he had arrived.

And hear with their ears
And understand with their heart
And turn and I would heal them.[419]

28So let it be known to you that this salvation of God was sent to the gentiles and they will listen.[420]

30And Shaul stayed two whole years in his own rented house and he welcomed all who came to him, 31preaching the kingdom of God and teaching about rabbi Yeshua the Mashiah, with open boldness and with no one hindering him.[421]

---

419. Isa. 6.9–10. Quotations from the Hebrew Bible usually come by way of the Greek Septuagint; in this citation the Acts text is close to the wording in the Hebrew Bible.

420. A last commendation to the gentiles and an implicit rebuke to those Jews who do not listen to the salvific word implicit in the words of the prophet Isaiah. The rebuke is more apparent in verse 29, not included in the United Bible Societies fourth corrected edition, but included in the Majority edition: "And having said these things, the Jews left, arguing vigorously among themselves."

421. Clearly Paul's house arrest does not hinder his ministry, and gives a fine conclusion to his third missionary voyage. It is uncertain whether or not he goes on to Spain at some later time. The book stops abruptly, without climax, without resolution, which is appropriate for a good dramatic novel. It does not truly end but leaves the main personage in a state of deep expectancy and the reader curious to know, with hope and fear, what next will befall the hero of the story. In this scene we must wonder how the mainspring of imminent Christianity will survive and fare.

Apocalypse

Apocalypse or Revelation
by Yohanan of Patmos
or Efesos

(Apocalypse or Revelation
by John of Patmos
or Ephesos)

Apocalypse or
Revelation

⁓

Apocalypse is the alternate title of Revelation, and in verse 1.1
appears the word "Apocalypse" from the greek Ἀποκάλυψις (apokalypsis), meaning "revelation," "disclosure," and literally an "uncovering."[1]
The title conveys the visionary and apocalyptic nature of the book.

Visionary writing is a habit of the Hebrew Bible, found in Isaiah,
Ezekiel, and Jeremiah, and in the Book of Daniel, which contains four
formal apocalypses. The apocalyptic form is found in virtually all religions
of the world, be it as murals in a Tibetan monastery or in the Egyptian
Book of the Dead. These allegorical works, usually prompted by some
historical conflict, have enormous spatial dimensions. In Apocalypse,
characters float between earth, heaven, and hell, and, and with Christ's
help, the good, on defeating the wicked, enter the fulfillment of a New
Age. God declares himself the Alpha and the Omega, and he appears
with the mystery of the seven stars in his hand. The four Horsemen
of the Apocalypse ride by. A woman gives birth in midair. The angel
Michael fights the dragons. Christ and his army throw the beasts of evil
into a lake of fire, whereupon a heavenly Jerusalem descends to replace
the early city, and the millennium arrives.

In the second century Bishop Irenaeus ascribed the Book of Apocalypse
to the evangelist John son of Zebedee, one of the twelve apostles, who
is also credited with writing the Gospel of John and the three Letters of
John. Modern scholars, however, find the style, language, thought, and

---

1. Revelatory writing, as in Isaiah and Daniel, is conveyed in the Hebrew גָּלָה (galah),
"he revealed" or "uncovered."

historic circumstance of Apocalypse so different from the Gospel of John as to obviate the notion of single authorship. John does identify himself as "John" in 1.9, "I Yohanan your brother," and there is good reason to suppose that the author was a Christian Jew named Yohanan, which is Anglicized as John. On the basis of the Greek style, which has elements of Hebrew syntax and vision, it is speculated that the author was a native of Israel who emigrated to Asia Minor, perhaps in the diaspora after the Jewish revolt against Rome (66–70 C.E.) when many had to flee from Jerusalem. One may wonder why one should have falsely ascribed Apocalypse to the evangelist John. It should be remembered that books of the Hebrew Bible and of the New Testament as well as scripture of the Intercovenant period were regularly ascribed to great figures so that such scripture might be taken into the canon. So we have works attributed to Enoch and Moses well into the first and second centuries C.E. in order to give those religious texts major significance. Seven of the thirteen letters traditionally ascribed to Paul are thought not to be by Paul. Similarly, the attachment of the evangelist's name John to Apocalypse gave great authority to the book and surely helped it find its way into the canon.

There is a crypt in a monastery on Patmos, the Greek island to which John was exiled for two years, and in a small cave at the edge of this crypt John is said to have composed Apocalypse. Since the speaker in the book says that the risen Christ appeared to him on the island of Patmos, then part of a Roman province, and ordered him to write the book, there is good reason to suppose that Apocalypse might have been written there. Ephesos is given as an alternative place of composition. The date is uncertain. Because of the scarcely disguised anger against the Romans who were persecuting Jews and Christians, some suggest that the book was composed during the rule of the Roman emperor Nero (54–68), who massacred both Christian Jews and Christian gentiles, or during the rule of Domitian (81–96 C.E.).

During the Intercovenant period when Revelation was written, the apocalypse form was a common, indeed a popular, form, and there are significant extant examples, such as the Book of Enoch (Jewish), the Apocalypse of Peter (Christian), and the Apocalypse of Thomas (Christian). To the apocalyptic mind, a visionary experience yields a revelation of the future, of a holy city of redemption, or a terrible hell of punishment. Apocalypse is peopled by angels, monsters, four-headed beasts, who may represent Satan or a Roman emperor, a woman clothed with the sun, representing the faithful people of God, or the great whore of Babylon, representing nefarious Rome. God in his glorious city of gold and precious stones remains the blessing in wait for the pious reader. Though bestial and chaotic creatures of evil battle against heavenly forces, the heavens will triumph through the intervention of Christ as the Christian message will triumph over the hostility of Rome. In sharp contrast to the gospels, God, rather than Yeshua, has at peak moments a dominant role and roaring voice. It seems to be as if we were reading sublime passages in Daniel. And Yeshua as a force is not the itinerant rabbi wandering the villages of Galilee or Judea but a cosmic God, interchangeable with YHWH, with eyes of fire and a two-edged sword.

Clearly, between the writing of the gospels and their papal canonization in 405 C.E., many hands shaped the words and theology. Apocalypse, which was probably composed in early draft at the end of the first century and the first decades of the second, was one of many apocalypses and, obscure and uncertain in doctrine as it is, barely made it into the final canon, which is perhaps why it may have been less tampered with. Not only is this visionary book of the future and of heaven and hell anti-Roman, but also the Roman soldiers are symbolized as demon monsters of hell, Rome is Babylon, and the beast, whose code name is 666 (13.18), is not the Babylonian Captivity of Israel in the sixth century B.C.E. but primarily a wicked Caesar Augustus, who became the first emperor of Rome. Under Nero and Domitian, Christians and Jews were slaughtered, and there was every reason to feel unfriendly toward Rome the oppressor. When Rome became the seat of Christianity, the politics in the Bible's texts was reshaped and reinterpreted, but little of that apparently in Revelation.[2]

---

2. Rome is ever the enemy of the Jews in Apocalypse, not the benevolent friend as in the gospels. In *The Messiah before Jesus: The Suffering Servant of the Dead Sea Scrolls* (Berkeley: University of California Press, 2000), Israel Knohl shows how in two Dead Sea Scroll hymns the goat-horned beast was the emperor Augustus. He was the Capricorn (goat horn on his coin), "the false prophet" masquerading as Apollo, the "beast rising from the earth" with "two horns like a lamb" but "who spoke like a dragon" (Rev. 13.11). Augustus was the cruel beast who fooled worshipers and killed them.

Another enemy was Publius Quinctilius Varus, who, after the death of Herod the

As a genre of revelatory and visionary works, Apocalypse is narrated by a prophet in the first person and contains great disasters and heavenly salvation. The main source is Daniel. The beasts and surreal dream atmosphere of this late mythical book historically reflect two periods of oppression: the Babylonian Captivity of the Jews, and its mirror, the Roman occupation and oppression that color John's Apocalypse. As a single poem, Apocalypse is the great epic work of the New Testament, with epic length, high conflict, and elevated speech. It was not the custom to lineate either the Hebrew Bible or the New Testament Greek in verse. After the nineteenth-century Revised Edition, large sections of the Hebrew Bible—the Psalms, Proverbs, Song of Songs, Job, and long passages in Isaiah and the other prophets—were uniformly rendered in verse. But not until the mid-twentieth-century French *La Bible de Jérusalem* were even Hebrew Bible verse passages quoted in the New Testament rendered into verse. Apocalypse, like the Book of Job, is an extended poem, as densely poetic as Blake's *Jerusalem*, Whitman's *Leaves of Grass*, or Gerard Manley Hopkins's *Wreck of the Deutschland*. Here it is rendered in loose blank verse. The language is richly symbolic, obscure, allusive; the work is highly structured, yet like the Song of Songs, it is a collage of recapitulations. Apocalypse is a prophecy of doom and salvation, ending with a description of the walls and streets burning in the bejeweled city of heaven.

As an epic poem, Apocalypse takes its place with *Gilgamesh* (Babylonian ca. 2000 B.C.E.), *Beowulf* (eighth century), and John Milton's *Paradise Lost* (1667) as one of the world's critical visionary poems. As a single, unified work, Apocalypse may be seen as the literary masterpiece of the New Testament. The symbolism is complex and obscure, a vision blindingly fearful and beautiful. Although an intensely luminous book,

---

Great in Jericho, in 4 B.C.E., crucified about two thousand Jews who had used the vacuum of power to rebel against the occupying power. For the Apocalypse reader the most recent Roman imprint was the Jewish War (66–70). Nero sent his commander Titus Flavius Vespasianus to win the Judean campaign. Titus razed the city, destroyed the Temple, and drove out its remaining inhabitants. One cannot know the true number of deaths, but a substantial part of the population died in battle or was crucified. The survivors, Jews and Christians, fled the city. To commemorate Titus's victory in the Jewish War, the Roman emperor Domitian erected the Arch of Triumph on the Via Sacra leading to the Forum.

it suggests more mysteries than it discloses. For that reason, the book is unfinished, as great books are, and its open ending permits the reader endless meditation. There is a circular phenomenon in the fact that the Apocalypse, composed perhaps on a pagan Greek island, stands as the last work in the Asian New Testament, which returns, as no other volume in Christian scriptures, to the speech, vision, and hopes of salvation of the Jewish Bible visionaries.

Chapter 1

Prologue

The Apocalypse[3] of Yeshua the Mashiah,[4] which God gave him to show his slaves what must soon happen. And he signified it by sending it through his angel to his slave Yohanan,[5] 2who bore witness to the word of God and the testimony of Yeshua the Mashiah of everything he saw. 3Blessed is the one who reads and blessed are they who hear the words of this prophecy and who keep what is written in it. For the time is near.

Alpha and Omega

4Yohanan said to the seven churches in Asia,
>   Grace be with you and peace from one who is,
>   And one who was, and one who is to come,
>   And from the seven spirits before his throne,
>   5And from Yeshua the Mashiah, faithful
>   Witness who is the firstborn of the dead
>   And is the ruler of the kings of the earth.
>   To him who loves us and freed us from our sins
>   By his own blood, 6and who made us a kingdom,
>   And made priests labor for the God and father,
>   To him glory and dominion forevermore.
>   Amain.[6]

---

3. Apocalypse from the Greek ἀποκάλυψις (apokalypsis), "revelation" or "disclosure of secrets" (literal meaning) or "a vision of heaven, hell, and the end of the world" (in the referential sense).

4. Jesus Christ. "Jesus" is from the Greek Ἰησοῦς (Iesous), from the Hebrew יֵשׁוּעַ (yeshua), traditionally translated "Joshua," a later form of Yehoshua יְהוֹשֻׁעַ. "Christ" is from the Greek Χριστος (Hristos), "the anointed," an attribute of the messiah. In the New Covenant Greek, Χριστος, is used almost synonymously with Μεσσίας, (messiah), a Hellenized transliteration of the Hebrew מָשִׁיחַ (mashiah).

5. John from Greek Ἰωάννης (Ioannes), from the Hebrew יוֹחָנָן (yohanan).

6. Amen is from the Greek ἀμήν (amen), from the Hebrew אָמֵן (amein), meaning "it is so," or "it is true." In English "amain" restores the Hebrew pronunciation of this Old Testament word.

7Look, he is coming with the clouds, and every eye
Will see him, and even they who stabbed him,
And all the tribes of the earth will mourn him.[7]
Amain.
8"I am the Alpha and the Omega," says the lord,
"Who is and who was and who is coming,
And who is the ruler of all, the pantokrator.[8]

Yohanan's vision

9I Yohanan your brother, who through Yeshua
Share with you suffering and kingdom and endurance,
Was on the island called Patmos for the word
Of God and testimony of Yeshua.
10I was fixed in the spirit on the lord's day
And I heard behind me a great voice like a ram's horn[9]
11Saying: "What you have seen, write in a book
And send it off to the seven churches.
To Efesos,[10] Smyrna, Pergamos,[11] and Thyatira,
To Sardis and Philadelphia and Laodikeia."[12]

---

7. Dan. 7.13; Zech. 12.10, 12.14.

8. Pantokrator from the Greek Παντοκράτωρ (pantokrator), from the Hebrew צְבָאוֹת (tzvaot), meaning "the Almighty," "all powerful," or "ruler of all," "of hosts." In the Greek Orthodox church "pantokrator," meaning "all powerful," from pan (all) and kratos (power), is regularly used in the Greek liturgy to signify "Almighty." Here it is chosen to reflect the Greek usage. However, since these first two verses come from Isaiah 6.3, "Almighty" better reflects the tradition of translation from the Hebrew Bible. In Isaiah 6.5, we find the origin of "pantokrator" (or "pantocrator" Romanized) in the set phrase הַמֶּלֶךְ יְהוָה צְבָאוֹת (hamelech yahweh tzvaot), "the king," "lord all powerful" (all powerful, almighty of hosts, etc.).

9. The trumpet (meaning "horn") in Apocalypse is not the modern brass instrument but the shofar, a "ram's horn," sounded as a battle signal.

10. Ephesos or Ephesus (Latinized) from the Greek Ἔφεσος (Efesos).

11. Pergamum from the Greek Πέργαμος (Pergamos).

12. Laodicea from the Greek Λαοδίκεια (Laodikeia).

Yeshua amid seven gold lamps

12And I turned to see the voice speaking to me,
And when I turned I saw seven gold lamps,
13And in the midst of the lamps was one like
The earthly son[13] clothed in a robe down to his feet,
And girt around his breasts[14] with a gold belt.
14His head and his hair were white like white wool
Like snow and his eyes like a flame of fire,
15His feet like fine bronze as if fired in a furnace
And his voice like the sound of many waters.
16And in his right hand he held seven stars
And from his mouth came a sharp two-edged sword
And his face was like the sun shining in its power.
17When I saw him I fell at his feet like a dead man
And he placed his right hand on me and said,
"Don't be afraid. 18I am the first and last
And the living one, and I have been dead,
And look, I am alive forevermore
And I have the keys to death and of hell.
19So write what you have seen and what you see
And after this what is about to happen.
20The mystery of the seven stars you saw
In my right hand, and seven golden lamps.
Seven stars are angels for the seven churches
And seven golden lamps are the seven churches."

---

13. "Son of Man" or "son of man" is the usual translation from the Greek ὁ υἱὸς τοῦ ἀνθρώπου (ho huios tou anthropou), which literally means "son of a person" or "son of people." The Greek ἀνθρώπου is not "man" but without gender, like "person." In the Hebrew Bible, "son of people" was an idiomatic way of saying "human being." In the gospels it may also suggest "the son on earth" as opposed to "the son in heaven," the "earthly son" rather than the "heavenly son." Hence, "earthly son," rather than "son of man," "son of people," or "human being," may work better poetically and theologically.

14. Although the Greek *mastois* means "breasts," it is commonly translated as "chest" or "waist" or sometimes the singular form "breast."

Chapter 2

Efesos

"To the angel of the church in Efesos[15] write:
'So speaks one holding seven stars in his right hand,
One walking amid the seven gold lamps:
2"I know your work and labor and endurance
And that you cannot tolerate bad men.
You have tried those who say they are apostles
And yet are not, and you have found them false.
3You have patience and for the sake of my name
You have persevered and not grown weary.
4But I blame you for abandoning your first love.
5Remember the height from which you have fallen
And repent and return to your first works.
If not, I'll come to you and take your lamp
From its place unless you repent. 6But you
Have this in your favor: You hate the deeds
Of the church of Nikolaos,[16] which I also hate.
7Who has an ear, hear the spirit speaking to
The churches. To the victor I will give food
To eat which comes from the tree of life
And which stands in the paradise of God.'

Smyrna

8"To the angel of the church in Smyrna[17] write:

---

15. Efesos (Ephesos), an important early Christian center and the largest city of the Roman province of Asia. These next parts, commonly called "letters," are messages or edicts to the seven churches of Asia.

16. The heretical Nicolaitians were antimonian sects associated with Ephesos and Pergamos, accused of compromising with pagan idolatry and of being libertine Gnostics. Most scholars now doubt these specific references, and think Nicolaos, from the Greek Νικόλαος (conqueror of people), is a wordplay parallel to Balaam (Rev. 2.14–15), from the Hebrew בִּלְעָם (bilam), meaning "he destroyed people."

17. A harbor city north of Ephesos.

'So speaks he who is the first and the last,
Who was dead and came back into life:
9"I know your suffering and your poverty,
But you are rich, and I know the blasphemy
Of those who say they are Jews and are not
But come out of a synagogue of Satan.[18]
10Do not fear what you are about to suffer.
Look, the devil will throw some of you in prison
To test you and you will suffer for ten days,
And I will give to you the crown of life.
11Who has ears, hear the spirit speaking to
The churches. And the victor won't be harmed
By the second death.'

Pergamos

12"To the angel of the church in Pergamos[19] write:
'So speaks one who has the sharp two-edged sword:
13"I know where you live, where Satan's throne is,
And you keep my name, even in the days of Antipas[20]
My witness, my faithful one, who was killed
Among you in the place where Satan lives.
14But I have a few things I hold against you,
For there you keep the teachings of Bilam[21]
Who taught Balak[22] to snare the sons of Yisrael,

---

18. Satan from the Greek σατάν (satan) or σατανᾶς (satanas), from the Hebrew שָׂטָן (satan). The demonization of the Jews in the gospels persists in Apocalypse.

19. An important Roman city with an imperial cult and major Hellenistic culture.

20. Antipas was, according to tradition, roasted to death in a bronze kettle by those worshiping the Roman emperor at the Asian capital city of Pergamos ("Pergamum" in Latin). Pergamos, meaning "citadel," also held one of the great libraries of antiquity, before Alexandria, and our word "parchment" derives from the Greek *pergamenos*. Parchment was first achieved in Pergamos.

21. Balaam from the Greek Βαλαάμ (Balaam), from the Hebrew בִּלְעָם (bilam).

22. Balak, from the Greek Βαλάκ (Balak), from the Hebrew בָּלָק (balak), was king of Moab, fearful after the Jews defeated the Amorites, Balak summoned Balaam to

To eat food sacrificed to idols and go with whores.[23]
15So you also hold to the teachings of Nikolaos.
16Repent then or soon I will come to you
And battle them with the sword of my mouth.
17Who has ears, hear the spirit speaking to
The churches. To the victor I'll give hidden manna
And I will give a white stone, and on the stone
Will be written a new name no one knows
Except for the one who will receive it.'

Thyatira

18"To the angel of the church in Thyatira[24] write:
'These are the words of the son of God
Whose eyes are like the flame of fire
And whose feet are like burnished bronze.
19"I know your works—your love, faith, your service
And endurance—last longer than the first.
20But I blame you that you forgive Izevel,[25]
Who calls herself prophet and teaches and tricks
My slaves to go with whores and consume food
Sacrificed to idols. 21And I gave her time
In which to repent, but she would not repent
Her harlotry. 22See, I will cast her on a bed
And will hurl those who copulate with her
Into great suffering if they don't repent

---

curse them (Num. 22–24, 21.16). Balaam, in turn, urged Balak to persuade Israel to idolatry with the help of the women of Moab (Num. 25.1–3).

23. "To go with whores" from the Greek πορνεύω (porneuo), "to practice prostitution." The colorful "commit fornication" used in earlier translations does not refer specifically to prostitutes.

24. Inland, between Pergamos and Ephesos.

25. Jezebel from the Greek Ἰεζάβελ (Iezabel), from the Hebrew אִיזֶבֶל (izevel), the Canaanite queen of King Ahab of Israel (1 Kings 18–19; 2 Kings 9) who induced Ahab to worship Canaanite deities. John gave this name to a Christian sect, probably the Nicolaitians, who were leading Christians astray.

Of going with her. 23And I'll kill her children
With death. And all the churches will know
That I am the one who searches their minds
And hearts. And I will give to each of you
According to your works. 24To the rest of you
In Thyatira who do not hold this teaching,
Who have not known the depths of Satan,
I will not lay another weight on you.
25But hold to what you have until I come.
26To one who conquers and keeps my works
    Until the end, and as it says in the Psalms,
        I will extend power over the nations
    27And will shepherd them with a staff of iron
        As pottery is broken.[26]
28And as I have received from my father
    I will give away the morning star. 29Who has an ear,
    Hear the spirit speaking to the churches.'

Chapter 3

Sardis

"To the angel of the church in Sardis[27] write:
'These words are from one holding seven spirits
Of God and seven stars: "'I know your works,
In name you are alive yet you are dead.
2Come and awake and strengthen what is left
And which is soon to die, for I have found
Your works were not enacted before God.
3Remember then the things you have received
And heard, and hold on to it and repent.

---

26. Ps. 2.8–9.

27. Ancient capital of Lydia, then a Seleucid kingdom. It had a temple to Artemis, and, along with Laodicea, received harsh criticism in Apocalypse for its spiritual "soiled clothes."

If you don't wake I'll come in as a thief
And you won't know what hour I'll come to you.
4But you have the names of a few in Sardis
And they have not defiled their garments.
They will walk with me in white because
They're worthy. 5The victorious like them
Will be clothed in white clothing. I will never
Obliterate your name from the book of life,
And I will confess your name before my father
And before his angels. 6Who has an ear,
Hear what the spirit is saying to the churches.'

Philadelphia

7"To the angel of the church in Philadelphia[28] write:
'These are the words of the saint, the true one,
And as Yeshayahu[29] says,
    Who holds the key of David,
    Who opens and none will close,
    Who closes and none will open.[30]
8"'I know your works, look, I have set before you
An open door and no one can shut it,
Since you have little strength and kept my word
And you did not deny my name. 9Look, I give you
Those who are from the synagogue of Satan,
Who say they are Jews and are not. They lie.
Look, I will make them come and worship
Before your feet and know I gave you my love.
10Since you have kept my word of my patience,
I too will keep you from the hour of trial
About to come upon the entire world

---

28. Near Sardis, Philadelphia appears in Apocalypse as a place of rivalry between Christianity and the Jewish community (Rev. 3.9).

29. Isaiah from the Greek Ἠσαΐας (Esaias), from the Hebrew יְשַׁעְיָהוּ (yeshayahu).

30. Isa. 22.22.

To test the inhabitants of the earth.
11I'm coming soon. Hold fast to what you have
So none can take your crown away from you.
12If you conquer I'll make you a pillar in the temple
Of my God and you will never leave it,
And on you I will write the name of my God
And the name of the city of my God,
The new Yerushalayim descending from
The sky, and will record my own new name.
13Who has an ear, hear what the spirit
Is saying to the churches.'

Laodikeia

14"To the angel of the church in Laodikeia[31] write:
'These are the words of the Amen,[32] the faithful
And true witness, the origin of God's creation:
15"I know your works, that you are neither cold
Nor hot, 16and since you are lukewarm, not hot
Nor cold, I will spit you out of my mouth.
17Because you say I am rich and prospered
And need nothing, and you do not know
That you are the wretched and the pitiful
And the poor and the blind and the naked,
18I counsel you to buy from me a gold
Made pure in fire so that you may be rich,
And have white clothes to wear on your body
So the shame of your nakedness not appear,
And salve to rub on your eyes so you can see.
19And those I love I rebuke and discipline.
So strive relentlessly and then repent.
20Look, I am standing at the door, and knock.

---

31. A commercial center one hundred miles east of Ephesos. During Paul's Ephesian ministry, its church was led by a woman named Nympha (Col. 4.15).

32. Not "Amen" of liturgical response, but a transliteration from the Hebrew of "master workman," here signifying Yeshua. The term is also found in Proverbs 8.30, "then I was beside him like a master worker."

If you can hear my voice, open the door,
And I'll come in to you and eat with you
And you with me. 21The victor I will ask
To sit with me on my throne as I too
Was victorious and sat with my father
On his throne. 22Who has an ear, hear
What the spirit is saying to the churches.'"

Chapter 4

An emerald rainbow around a throne in heaven
After this I looked, and there a door opened
In the sky, and the voice of the first I heard
Was a ram's horn speaking with me saying,
"Come up here and I will show you what
Must happen after this." 2At once I was enveloped
In the spirit and saw a throne standing in the sky
And one seated on the throne. 3The one seated
Looked like stone of jasper and carnelian,
And around the throne was a rainbow like an emerald.
4And around the throne were twenty-four thrones
And seated on the thrones were twenty-four elders
Clothed in white garments, and on their heads
Were gold crowns. 5From the throne poured out
Lightning flashes and voices and booming thunder,
And before the throne were seven lamps of fire
Burning, which are the seven spirits of God,
6And before the throne a sea of glass like crystal.

And in the middle and around the throne
Were four live animals teeming with eyes
In front and in back.[33] 7The first was like a lion

---

33. The description of the four animals or "living creatures" is derived from Ezekiel 1.5–10. Since Irenaeus, these four animals were used iconographically as symbols for the four evangelists.

And the second animal was like a calf[34]
And the third animal had a human face,
8the fourth creature was like a flying eagle.
And each of the live animals had six wings
And were full of eyes around them and inside,
And day and night they never ceased saying,
    Holy, holy, holy, lord God the pantokrator,
    The one who was and is and is to come.[35]
9And when the animals gave glory and honor
And thanks to the one seated on the throne
And to the one who lives forevermore,
10The twenty-four elders cast their crowns
Before the throne, and said,
    Our lord and God,
You are worthy to receive this glory, honor, and power,
For you made all things,
And by your will they were and were created.

Chapter 5

The scroll and the lamb
    And I saw in the right hand of him sitting
    On the throne a scroll written on the inside
    And on the back, and sealed with seven seals.
    2And I saw a strong angel who cried out
    In a great voice, "Who is worthy to open
    The book scroll and break its seven seals?"
    3And no one in the sky or on the earth
    Or under the earth could open the book
    Or look at it, 4and I wept much since no one
    Was found worthy to open the book
    Or look at it. 5And one of the elders said to me,

---

34. "Calf" in earlier translations rendered as "ox."
35. Isa. 6.2–3.

"Don't weep, see, the lion from the tribe
Of Yehuda, the scion of David, has conquered
And will open the book and its seven seals."

6I saw, between the throne and the four animals
And elders, a lamb standing as if slaughtered,
With seven horns and seven eyes which are
The seven spirits of God sent all over the earth.
7And he came and took it from the right hand
Of the one seated on the throne. 8And when he took
The book the four animals and twenty-four elders
Fell before the lamb, each holding a harp and gold bowls
Filled with incense, which are the prayers of saints.
9And they sang a new song, saying,[36]
> You are worthy to take up the book scroll
> And to open the seals upon it
> Since you were slaughtered and by your blood
> You bought[37] people for God
> From every tribe and language and nation,
> 10And for our God
> You made them be a kingdom and priests
> And they will reign over the earth.

11I looked and heard the voices of many angels
Around the throne and animals and the elders,
And they numbered myriads of myriads
And thousands and thousands, 12saying in a great voice,
> Worthy is the lamb who was slaughtered
> To receive the power and the riches

---

36. "A new song." From Psalms 33.3 and 96.1 and Isaiah 42.10, "Sing to the Lord a new song."

37. Bought from the Greek ἀγοράζω (agorazo), to "buy." "Buy" is the immediate common meaning of *agorazo*, which may in context take on a religious level of "redemption" (also a financial word) but remains an explanation of a metaphor, not the financial metaphor itself.

And wisdom and strength and honor
And glory and blessing.
And every creature which is in the sky,
On the earth and under the earth and on the sea,
And everything in these, 13I heard them saying,
To the one seated on the throne and to the lamb,
Blessings and honor and glory and dominion forevermore.
14And the four animals said, "Amain,"
And the elders fell down and worshiped.

Chapter 6

Seven seals

And I saw the lamb open one of the seals
And I heard one of the four animals saying
In a voice that seemed like thunder, "Come!"
2And I saw, and look, a white horse
And its rider had a bow and was given a crown
And he went out conquering and to conquer.
3And when the lamb opened the second seal,
I heard the second animal saying, "Come!"
4Another horse of fire red came out.
Its rider was ordered to take peace away
From earth so men might kill each other,
And he was given an enormous sword.

5And when the lamb opened the third seal,
I heard the third animal saying, "Come!"
And I saw, and look, a black horse,
And its rider held a pair of scales in his hand.
6And I heard what seemed to be a voice
In the midst of the four animals, saying,
"A measure of wheat for a single denar
And three measures of barley for a single denar,
And do not damage the olive oil with wine."

7And when the lamb opened the fourth seal,
 I heard the voice of the fourth animal saying,
 "Come!" 8and I saw, and look, a pale green horse,
 And the name of his rider was Death, and Hell
 Was following him. Power was given them
 Over a quarter of the globe to kill
 By sword and by hunger and by death
 And by the wild beasts of the earth.

9And when the lamb opened the fifth seal,
 I saw under the altar the souls of those
 Who were slaughtered for the word of God
 And the testimony which they held.
10And they cried out in a great voice saying,
 "How long, O absolute ruler, holy and true,
 Will you wait to judge and avenge our blood
 From those who live upon the earth?"
11They were each given a white robe and told
 To rest a little time until the number was reached
 Of their fellow slaves, brothers and sisters
 Who are to be killed as they were killed.

12When the lamb opened the sixth seal I looked
 And there took place a great earthquake
 And the sun became black like sackcloth of hair
 And the full moon became like blood,
13And the stars of the sky fell to the earth
 As the fig tree drops its unripe fruit
 Shaken by a great wind. 14And the sky
 Vanished like a scroll rolling up
 And every mountain and island of the earth
 Was torn up from its place and moved.
15And the kings of the earth and the great men
 And commanders of thousands and every slave
 And the free hid in caves and mountain rocks,
16And said to the mountains and rocks, "Fall on us

And hide us from the face of him who is sitting
On the throne and from the anger of the lamb
17Because the great day of his anger has come,
And before him who has the force to stand?"

Chapter 7

144,000 sealed from the tribes of Yisrael
After that I saw four angels standing on
The four farthest corners of the earth,
Holding back the four winds of the earth
So that no wind might blow upon the earth
Or upon the sea or upon any tree.
2And I saw another angel going up
The sky from the rising place of the sun,
Carrying the seal of the living God,
And he cried in a great voice to the angels
Granted power to harm the earth and sea,
3"Do not harm the earth or the sea or the trees
Until we have marked the slaves of our God
With a seal on their foreheads." 4And I heard
The number of those who were marked, a hundred
Forty-four thousand were marked from every tribe
    Of the children of Yisrael:[38]
5From the tribe of Yehuda twelve thousand sealed,
From the tribe of Reuven[39] twelve thousand,
From the tribe of Gad twelve thousand,
6From the tribe of Asher twelve thousand,
From the tribe of Naftali[40] twelve thousand,

---

38. Israel.

39. Reuben from the Greek Ῥουβήν (Rouben), from the Hebrew רְאוּבֵן (reuven).

40. Naphtali from the Greek Νεφθαλίμ (Nefthalim), from the Hebrew נַפְתָּלִי (naftali).

From the tribe of Menasheh[41] twelve thousand,

7From the tribe of Shimon twelve thousand,

From the tribe of Levi twelve thousand,

From the tribe of Yisahar[42] twelve thousand,

8From the tribe of Zvulun[43] twelve thousand,

From the tribe of Yosef twelve thousand,

From the tribe of Binyamin[44] twelve thousand

 Marked with the seal.

9After that I looked, and suddenly a multitude

Whose number no one could count, from every

Nation and tribe and people and tongue,

Standing before the throne and before the lamb,

Wearing white robes, holding palms in their hands.

10And they cried out in a great voice, saying,

 Salvation to our God who is sitting

 On the throne and to the lamb.[45]

11And all the angels stood around the throne

And around the elders and the four animals,

Who fell down before the throne on their faces

And they worshiped God, 12with these words:

 Amain, blessing and glory and wisdom

 And thanksgiving and honor and power

 And strength to our God forevermore. Amain.

13Then one of the elders asked me, saying,

 "These people who are clothed in robes of white,

---

41. Manasses or Manasseh from the Greek Μανασσῆς (Manasses), from the Hebrew מְנַשֶׁה (menasheh).

42. Issachar from the Greek Ἰσσαχάρ (Issahar), from the Hebrew יְשָׂשכָר (yisahar).

43. Zebulun from the Greek Ζαβουλών (Zaboulon), from the Hebrew זְבֻלוֹן (zvulun).

44. Benjamin, from the Greek Βενιαμίν (Beniamin), from the Hebrew בִּנְיָמִין (Binyamin).

45. Ps. 8.3.

Do you know who they are, where they are from?"

14And I replied to him, "My lord, you know."

And he said to me, "These people came from

Great suffering and they have washed their robes

And whitened them in the blood of the lamb.

15So they stand before the throne of God,

And serve him day and night in his temple.

Seated on his throne he'll spread his tent over them.[46]

16They'll not be hungry or thirsty anymore,

No sun will fall on them and scorch their skin,[47]

17Because the lamb in the middle of the throne

Will shepherd them and lead them to the springs

Of the waters of life,[48] and from their faces

God will wipe away every tear from their eyes."

Chapter 8

Angel and censer of fire

And when the lamb opened the seventh seal,

There was a half hour of silence in the sky.

2I saw the seven angels standing before God

And they were given seven ram's horns.

3And another angel came and stood by the altar,

With a gold censer, and was given much incense

To offer with the prayers of all the saints

On the gold altar which was before the throne.

And coming with the prayers of the saints,

4Then the smoke of varied incense arose

---

46. See Leviticus 26.11 and Ezekiel 37.27.

47. An allusion to the idyllic conditions described in Isaiah 49.10. See also Revelation 21.4.

48. For the shepherd metaphor for king (and Yeshua), see 2 Samuel 7.7, Isaiah 44.28, and Jeremiah 3.15. For living springs, see Isaiah 49.10.

Out of the hand of the angel before God.
5And the angel took the censer and filled it
With fire from the altar and threw it down to earth,
And there came thunders and voices and lightning
Flashes and earthquake. 6The seven angels
Holding the ram's horns prepared to blow them.

7The first angel blew the ram's horn. There came hail
And fire mingled with blood and it was thrown
To the earth, and a third of the earth burned up,
And a third of the trees burned up, and all green grass caught
    fire.

8And the second angel blew the ram's horn
And something like a great mountain on fire
Was cast into the sea. A third of the sea was blood
9And a third of the creatures in the sea died,
Who had been alive. A third of the ships sank.

10And the third angel blew the ram's horn.
From the sky a great star fell, a blazing torch,
And the star fell on a third of the rivers
And across the springs of the waters,
11And the name of the star is called Wormwood,
And a third of the waters became wormwood
And many people died from the waters
Because they were made bitter.

12And the fourth angel blew the ram's horn
And a third of the sun was struck by it,
And a third of the moon, a third of the stars,
And a third of their light was darkened,
And the day lost a third of its brilliance
And likewise the night.

13And I looked and I heard an eagle flying
In mid-sky, crying out in a great voice,

"Despair despair despair to the inhabitants
Of the earth at the blasts of more ram's horns
That the three angels are about to blow."

Chapter 9

A star fell from the sky
    And the fifth angel blew his ram's horn
    And I saw a star fall out of the sky
    And down to the earth, and the angel was given
    The key to the shaft of the bottomless pit.
  2He opened the shaft of the bottomless pit
    And smoke rose from the shaft like fumes
    From a great furnace. And the sun was darkened
    And the air was darkened from the smoke
    Of the shaft. 3And out of the smoke came locusts
    Upon the earth, and they were given powers
    Like the powers of scorpions of the earth.
  4They were told not to damage the earth's grass,
    Or any green thing, or any tree, but only people
    Who don't wear the seal of God on their foreheads.
  5They were told not to kill them but to torture them
    For five months, and their torture should equal
    The scorpion's torture when it strikes a person.
  6And in such days the people will seek death,
    But not find it, and they will desire to die
    But they won't fall into escape to death.

  7The locusts looked like horses prepared for war.
    On their heads it was like the crowns of gold
    And their faces were like the faces of people,
  8And they had hair like the hair of women,
    And the teeth in their jaws resembled lions.
  9Their breastplates seemed to be made of iron,
    And the noise of their wings was like the noise
    Of many horse chariots galloping into battle.

10And they have tails like scorpions and stings,
  And in their tails the power to harm people.
11They have a king over them who is the angel
  Of the abyss, whose name in Hebrew is Abaddon
  And in Greek he has the name of Apollyon.[49]
12The first despair is over. After the first,
  Look, there are still two more despairs to come.

13And the sixth angel blew his ram's horn,
  And I heard a voice coming from the four horns
  Of the gold altar standing before God,
14Telling the sixth angel who held the ram's horn,
  "Release the four angels who are bound
  At the great river Euphrates." 15The four angels
  Were freed, prepared for the hour and day
  And month and year to kill a third of the people.
16And the number of cavalry of their armies
  Is two hundred million. I heard their number.

17And so I saw the horses in the vision
  And the riders on them were wearing breastplates
  Of fire red and hyacinth blue and yellow sulfur
  And the heads of horses were like heads of lions
  And fire, smoke and sulfur[50] came from their mouths.
18From these three plagues a third of humankind
  Was killed by the fire and smoke and sulfur
  Spewing from their mouths. 19The power of the horses
  Resides in their mouths and in their tails
  Because the tails are like serpents with heads
  And with their terrible heads they harm.

20The rest of the people who had not been killed

---

49. Abaddon is the angel of the realm of the dead, and "Apollyon" means "destroyer,"
an attribute of Apollo.
50. "Sulfur" from the Greek θεῖον (theion) is also translated as "brimstone."

In the plagues did not repent of the work
Of their hands so they might go on worshiping
The demons and the idols of gold and silver
And bronze and stone and wood, which cannot
See or hear or walk. 21And they did not repent
Of their murders or their poison sorceries
Or their dirty copulations or their thefts.

Chapter 10

An angel clothed in cloud
I saw another strong angel coming down from
The sky, clothed in cloud, and the rainbow
Was on his head, and his face was the sun,
And his feet like pillars of fire, 2In his hand
He held a little book open. He planted his right foot
On the sea and his left foot on the land
3And cried out in a great voice like a roaring lion.
When he cried out, the seven thunders spoke
In their own voices. 4When the seven thunders spoke,
I was about to write, but heard a voice in the sky,
Saying, "Seal what the seven thunders have spoken
And do not write them down." 5Then the angel,
Whom I saw standing on the sea and on the earth,
Lifted his right hand to the sky 6and he swore
By him who is alive forevermore,
Who created the sky and what lives in it,
And the sea and what lives in it, and he said
That the time will be no more. 7But in the days
Of the sounding of the seventh angel, when he
Is about to blow his ram's horn, right then
The mystery of God will be fulfilled
As he informed his slaves who were the prophets.

8And the voice I heard from the sky again
Spoke to me, saying, "Go take the open scroll

In the hand of the angel standing on the sea
And on the earth." 9And I went to the angel,
Telling him to give me the little book.
And he said to me, "Take it and eat it
And it will make your stomach bitter,
But in your mouth it will be like sweet honey."
10And I took the book from the angel's hand
And ate it and in my mouth it was as sweet
As honey but it made my stomach bitter.
11Then they said to me, "You must prophesy
Again about many peoples and their tongues,
And about many nations and their kings."

Chapter 11

Two witnesses in sackcloth
The angel gave me a reed like a staff. He said,
"Stand up and measure the temple of God
And the altar and those who worship there.
2But omit the courtyard outside the temple
And do not measure it, since it has been given
To the gentiles. They will trample the holy city
For forty-two months. 3I will give power to
Two of my witnesses and they will prophesy
For a thousand two hundred days, wearing sackcloth."
4These are the two olive trees and the two lamps
That stand before the lord of the earth.
5And if anyone wants to harm them, then fire
Comes out of their mouths and eats their enemies;
And if anyone wants to harm them,
In this way that person must be killed.
6These have the power to close the sky
So no rain will drench their days of prophecy,
And they have a power over the waters
To turn them into blood and strike the earth
With every plague as often as they want.

7And when they finish their testimony,
The beast rising from the bottomless pit
Will make war with them and conquer them
And kill them. 8Their dead bodies will lie
In the square of the great city,51 which is called
Spiritually Sedom, and Egypt where their lord
Was also crucified. 9For three days and a half,
Members of the tribes and tongues and nations
Will stare at their corpses and not let them be placed
In graves. 10And those who dwell on the earth
Will be happy over them and be cheerful
And send each other gifts, since these two prophets
Tormented those who dwell upon the earth.

11But after three days and a half, the breath
Of life from God went into them, and they
Stood on their feet, and great fear fell upon
Those who saw them. 12They heard a great voice out
Of the sky, saying to them, "Come up here."
And they went up into the sky in a cloud.
Their enemies saw them. 13And in that hour
There was a great earthquake and a tenth of
The city fell. And in the earthquake were killed
Seven thousand of the inhabitants,
And the rest were terrified and gave glory
To the God of the sky. 14The second despair
Is over. Look, the third despair comes soon.

The seventh ram's horn

15And the seventh angel blew his ram's horn
And there were great voices in the sky, saying,

> The kingdom of the world is now the kingdom
> Of our lord and his Mashiah,

---

51. The great city in Apocalypse is normally Babylon, but is also identified as Rome, Jerusalem, Egypt, and Sodom (Sedom), all condemned for crimes against prophets, God's messengers, and Yeshua.

And he will reign forevermore.[52]

16And the twenty-four elders, sitting on their thrones
Before God, fell on their faces and worshiped God,
17Saying,

We thank you, lord God the pantokrator,
The one who is and was,
Because you have taken your great power and become
king.
18The gentile nations raged and your anger came
And also the time for judging the dead
And giving wages to your slaves, the prophets
And your saints, and to all who fear your name,
The small and the great,
And to destroy the destroyers of the earth.

19Then the temple of God in the sky was opened
And the ark of his covenant[53] was seen in his temple
And there came lightning flashes and voices
And thunders and an earthquake and great hail.

Chapter 12

Woman, child, and the dragon
Then there was a great portent in the sky,
A woman clothed in the sun, and the moon
Under her feet, and on her head a crown
Of seven stars. 2In her womb she had a child
And screamed in labor pains, aching to give birth.
3And another portent was seen in the sky,
Look, a great fire-red dragon with seven heads

---

52. Ps. 145.13.

53. "The ark of his covenant" was an acacia wood chest (Deut. 10.1–2), symbolizing the presence of God among his people, kept in the Temple in Jerusalem probably until the Temple's destruction in the early sixth century B.C.E. by the Babylonian king Nebuchadnezzar.

And ten horns, and on his heads seven diadems.
4His tail dragged a third of the stars of heaven
  And hurled them to the earth. The dragon stood
  Before the woman about to give birth
  So when she bore her child he might devour it.
5She bore a son, a male, who will shepherd
  All nations with a rod of iron,
  And her child was snatched away to God
  And to his throne. 6And the woman fled
  Into the desert where she has a place
  Made ready by God that they might nourish
  Her one thousand two hundred sixty days.

7And in the sky were Mihael[54] and his angels
  Battling with the dragon. 8The dragon and his angels
  Fought back, but they were not strong enough.
  No longer was there place for them in the sky.
9The great dragon, the ancient snake, who is called
  Devil and Satan, the deceiver of the whole
  Inhabited world, was flung down to earth
  And his angels were flung down with him.

10And I heard a great voice in the sky, saying,
  "Now has come the salvation and the power
  And the kingdom of our God and the authority
  Of his mashiah, for the accuser of our brothers
  And sisters has been cast down, and the accuser
  Abused them day and night before our God.
11They defeated him through the blood of the lamb
  And by the word to which they testified
  And did not cling to life while facing death.
12Be happy, skies, and those who set their tents

---

54. Michael from the Greek Μιχαήλ (Michael), from the Hebrew מִיכָאֵל (mihael)
in Daniel 12.1, "the great prince, the protector of your people, shall arise." From
Michael as the special protector of Israel came the covenant meaning of "the protecting archangel."

On you. Earth and sky, you will know grief,
Because the devil has come down to you
In great rage, knowing he has little time."

13When the dragon saw that he had been cast
Down on the earth, he pursued the woman
Who had borne the male child. 14And she was given
Two wings of the great eagle that she might fly
Into the desert to her place where she is nourished
For a time, and times, and half a time away
From the face of the snake. 15But from his mouth
The snake cast water, a flood behind the woman,
So he might sweep her away on the river.
16But the earth helped the woman, and the earth
Opened its mouth and swallowed the river
Which the dragon had cast out of his mouth.
17The dragon was enraged at the woman and left
To battle against her remaining seed,
Those who keep the commandments of God
And keep the testimony of Yeshua.

18Then the dragon stood on the sand of the sea.[55]

Chapter 13

Beast from the sea
Then I saw a beast coming up from the sea,[56]
With ten horns and seven heads and on his horns
Ten diadems, and on his heads were the names
Of blasphemy. 2The beast I saw was like a leopard,
His feet like a bear and his mouth like the mouth
Of a lion. And the dragon gave him his power

---

55. Other ancient texts have this line at the beginning of chapter 13.

56. Rome and its emperors are represented as the sea monster Leviathan (Ezek. 29.3; 2 Esd. 6.47–52).

And his throne and fierce power of dominion.
3One of his heads seemed to be stricken to death
But the wound causing his death was healed
And the whole world marveled after the beast.
4They worshiped the dragon since he had given
Dominion to the beast, and they worshiped the beast,
Saying, "Who is like the beast and can battle him?"
5He was given a mouth to speak great things
And blasphemies. And he was given dominion
To act for forty-two months. 6Then he opened
His mouth to utter blasphemies against God,
Blaspheming his name and his tenting place,
And those who have set their tent in the sky.
7He was given powers to battle the saints
And to overcome them, and was given powers
Over every tribe and people and tongue and nation.
8All who dwell on the earth will worship him,
Each one whose name has not been written since
The foundation of the world in the book of life
Of the slaughtered lamb. 9Who has an ear, hear
Yirmiyahu:57
10He who leads into captivity goes into captivity.
He who kills with the sword will be killed by the sword.58
Such is the endurance and faith of the saints.

Beast from the earth
11Then I saw another beast rising from the earth
And he had two horns like a lamb and he spoke
Like a dragon. 12He exercises all the dominion
Of the first beast before him, and makes the earth
And its inhabitants worship the first beast,

---

57. Jeremiah from the Greek Ἰερεμίας (Ieremias), from the Hebrew יִרְמְיָהוּ (yirmiyahu).

58. Jer. 15.2, 43.11.

Whose wound of death was healed. 13He does great portents,
Even making a fire plunge from the sky
Down to the earth in the sight of the people.
14He fools the inhabitants on the earth
By means of the portents he contrives to make
On behalf of the beast, creating an image
To show the beast as wounded by the sword
Yet coming out alive. 15And he had the power
To give breath59 to the image of the beast
And the image of the beast could even speak
And cause all who would not worship the beast
To be killed. 16He causes all, the small and great,
The rich and poor, the free ones and the slaves,
To be marked on the hand and the forehead
17So that no one can buy or sell without the mark,
The name of the beast or number of his name.
18Here is wisdom. Who has a mind, calculate
The number of the beast, which is the number
For a human. And the number is 666.60

Chapter 14

Lamb on Mount Zion
Then I saw, and look, the lamb standing on
Mount Zion and with him one hundred forty-four
Thousand who had his name and the name of
His father written on their foreheads. 2And
I heard a voice out of the sky like the voice
Of many waters, like the voice of great thunder,

---

59. "Breath" from the Greek πνεῦμα (pneuma) is "breath" and by extension "spirit," and sometimes, as in the prologue of John, it means both. Dan. 3.5–6.

60. The number of the beast corresponds in Hebrew to a code, which may be the name of Nero Caesar or Caesar Augustus.

And the voice I heard was like the voice of harpists
Playing on their harps. ₃They sing a new song
Before the throne and before the four animals
And the elders, and no one could learn the song
Except the hundred and forty-four thousand
Who have been bought⁶¹ from the earth. ₄These are
The men who were not defiled by women,
Since they are virgins. They follow the lamb
Wherever he goes. These were bought from men
As a first fruit of God and the lamb. ₅And in
Their mouths no lie was found. They are blameless.

₆Then I saw another angel flying in midair
With an eternal gospel to proclaim
To those inhabiting the earth and each nation,
And tribe and tongue and people, ₇saying
In a great voice,
    Fear God and give him glory.
    The hour of his judgment is come,
    And worship him who made the sky and earth,
    The sea and the springs of water.
₈Another angel, a second, followed, saying,
    Great Babylon is fallen, is fallen.⁶²
    She made all nations drink her wine of passion
    And her filthy copulations.

₉Another angel, a third, followed them, saying
In a great voice, "All those who worship the beast
And his image and receive a mark on the forehead
Or on the hand, ₁₀even those humans will drink
The wine of the wrath of God, which is poured

---

61. See note 37, Revelation 5.9, on "bought" and "redeemed."
62. Isa. 21.9. Babylon may be a code name for Rome.

Undiluted into the cup of the anger
Of their God, and they will be tormented
In fire and in sulfur before the holy angels
And before the lamb. 11The smoke of their torment
Will rise forevermore, and there's no rest
Day and night for any who worship the beast
And his image or wears the mark of his name."
12Such is the endurance of the saints, who keep
The commandments of God and faith in Yeshua.

13And I heard a voice out of the sky, saying,
"Write. Blessed are the dead who from now on
Die in the lord." "Yes," the spirit says to them
"So they may rest from their labors.
Their works will follow after them."

Earthly son on a white cloud and angels with harvest sickles
14Then I looked and there was a white cloud,
And seated on the cloud was one who seemed
To be the earthly son, wearing a gold crown
On his head, and he was carrying in his hand
A sharp sickle. 15Another angel came out
Of the temple, crying in a great voice
To the one sitting on the cloud, "Take out
Your sickle and reap, for the hour to reap
Has come, because the harvest of the earth
Is ripe." 16And the one sitting on the cloud
Swung his sickle on the earth, and reaped the earth.
17Another angel came out of his temple
In the sky, and he carried a sharp sickle.
18Another angel came out of the altar,
Who is in charge of fire, and he called
In a great voice to him with the sharp sickle,
"Thrust in your sharp sickle and gather up
The clusters of the vine upon the earth,
Because her grapes are ripe." 19And the angel
Thrust his sickle into the ground and gathered

The vintage from the earth and threw it into
The great winepress of the anger of God.
20And the winepress was trodden outside the city
And blood came from the press up to the bridles
Of horses for a distance of four hundred furlongs.[63]

Chapter 15

Sea of glass mingled with fire
And I saw another great portent in the sky,
Great and wonderful, seven angels with seven plagues,
The last ones, since the anger of God is fulfilled
In them. 2I saw what seemed a sea of glass
Mingled with fire, and victors over the beast
And his image and the number of his name,
Standing on the sea of glass, holding harps of God.
3They sang the song of Moshe the slave of God
And the song of the lamb:
Great and wonderful are your works,
Lord God the pantokrator.
Just and true are your ways,
O king of nations!
4Who will not fear you, lord,
And glorify your name?
Because you alone are holy,
Because all nations come
And worship before you,
Because your judgments are revealed[64]

---

63. Furlong from the Greek στάδιον (stadion). The Greek says 1,600 stadia. A stade is 606 feet, and 1,600 stadia is about 200 miles. "Stade" is commonly translated as "furlong," 220 feet; hence 400 furlongs.

64. The song of Moses, from Deuteronomy 32.1–47 and Exodus 15.1–18, was sung on Sabbath evenings in the synagogues to celebrate Israel's deliverance from Egypt.

Seven gold bowls with the anger of God
    5After this I looked. The temple of the tent[65]
    Of testimony was opened in the sky,
    6And the seven angels with the seven plagues
    Came out of the temple. They were robed in linen
    Clean and bright, and gold belts girding their breasts.
    7One of the four animals gave the seven angels
    Seven gold bowls filled with the anger of God
    Who lives forevermore. 8The temple was filled
    With smoke from the glory of God and from
    His power, and none could enter the temple until
    The seven plagues of the seven angels were done.

Chapter 16

Angels emptying bowls of God's wrath on the earth
    Then I heard a great voice out of the temple,
    Saying to the seven angels, "Go and pour out
    The seven bowls of the anger of God
    Onto the earth." 2So the first went, and poured
    The bowl out onto the earth, and a sore
    And painful wound came on those with the mark
    Of the beast and those worshiping his image.

    3Then the second poured his bowl on the sea
    And it turned into blood like a dead man's,
    And every living soul died in the sea.
    4And the third poured his bowl on the rivers
    And springs of waters, and it turned into blood.
    5I heard the angel of the waters saying,
        You are just, the one who was, the holy one,
        For you have judged these things.

---

65. Tent from the Greek σκηνή (skene), "tent," from the Hebrew סֻכָּה (sukkah), "shelter," or "tent."

6Because they shed the blood of saints and prophets,
  You gave them blood to drink as they deserve.
7And I heard the altar respond,
  Yes, lord God, the pantokrator,
  Your judgments are true and right.

8And the fourth poured his bowl onto the sun
  And he was able to burn people with great fire.
9And the people were burned in a great blaze
  And they blasphemed the name of his God,
  Who holds dominion over these plagues,
  And they failed to repent and give him glory.

10And the fifth poured out his bowl on the throne
  Of the beast, and his kingdom turned dark,
  And they chewed their tongues from pain.
11They blasphemed the God in the sky because
  Of their pains and their sores and did not repent
  From their works.

            12And the sixth poured out his bowl
  On the great Euphrates river. Its water dried up
  So as to make ready the way for the kings
  From the rising sun. 13I saw coming out
  Of the mouth of the dragon, from the mouth
  Of the beast, from the mouth of the false prophet
  Three unclean breaths like frogs. 14For these are breaths
  Of demons performing portents that go out
  To the kings of the whole inhabited world,
  To poise them for the battle of the great day
  Of God the pantokrator. 15("Look, I'm coming
  Like a thief! Blessed is the one who watches
  And cares for his clothes so he doesn't walk
  About naked and his shame become seen.")[66]

---

66. This unforeseen parenthetical voice, "I'm coming like a thief!" gives the common

16And they brought them together in a place.
  Which is called in Hebrew Har Megiddo.[67]

17The seventh poured out his bowl upon the air,
  And a great voice came out of the temple
  From the throne, saying, "It happened!" 18There were
  The lightning flashes, voices, and the thunders
  There was an earthquake greater than any since
  People inhabited the earth, it was so violent.
19The city was sundered into three parts
  And the cities of the nations fell. Then Babylon
  The great was remembered before God,
  Who gave her the wine cup of the fury of his wrath.
20Every island fled and mountains were not found.
21Huge hail, heavy as talents, fell from the sky
  Upon the people, and they blasphemed God
  For bringing a plague with this enormous hail,
  Because the plague was exceedingly great.

Chapter 17

The great whore on a scarlet beast
      Then came one of the seven angels who held
      The seven bowls and he spoke with me, saying,
      "Come, I'll show you the judgment on the great whore
      Sitting on the many waters, 2with whom the kings
      Of the earth have copulated, and with the wine
      Of her copulations the dwellers of the earth

---

metaphor for the unexpected arrival of Yeshua, as in Matthew 24.42–44 and Luke 12.39–40.

67. Armageddon or Har Magedon from the Greek Ἁρμαγεδών (Harmagedon), from the Hebrew הַר מְגִדּוֹ (har megiddo), meaning, "Mountain or Hill of Megiddo," an ancient archeological site and city in central Israel of decisive battles, by Megiddo, a major Canaanite city in Manasseh. The site has taken on a mystical quality about which there is much fuss and uncertainty.

Have got drunk." 3He took me off to a desert
In the spirit. I saw a woman sitting
On a scarlet beast who was filled with the names
Of blasphemy, with seven heads and ten horns.
4The woman was wearing purple and scarlet
And was adorned with gold and precious stones
And pearls. She held a gold cup in her hand,
Full of the abominations of filth
Of her harlotry. 5On her forehead a name
Was written:

MYSTERY

BABYLON THE GREAT

THE MOTHER OF THE WHORES

AND THE ABOMINATIONS OF THE EARTH[68]

6And I saw the woman drunk on the blood of saints
And from the blood of the witnesses of Yeshua.
I was amazed, looking at her with wonder.
7The angel said to me, "Why do you marvel?
I will tell you the mystery of the woman
And the beast with seven heads and ten horns
Who carries her. 8The beast you saw was
And is not and is about to come up out of
The bottomless abyss and go to his perdition.
And the inhabitants of earth will be stunned,
Whose names have not been written in the book
Of life from the foundation of the world,
When they see the beast that is and is not
And is to come. 9Here is the mind with wisdom:
The seven heads are seven mountains where
The woman sits on them. They are seven kings.
10Five have fallen, one is, the other has not
Yet come, and when he comes, short is the time

---

68. The great whore is often a metaphor for "a godless city" as in Isaiah 1.21 and
23.16–17, or Rome of the emperors, or Babylon of the kings.

He must stay. 11The beast who was and is not,
He too is the eighth and comes from the seven
And goes to his perdition. 12The ten horns
You saw are ten kings who did not yet take
A kingdom, but they will have their kingdom
As kings for one hour along with the beast.
13These are of one mind and render the power
And dominion to the claws of the beast.
14They will make war with the lamb and the lamb
Will conquer them, because he is the lord
Of lords and king of kings. Those on his side
Are the called and the chosen and the faithful."

15Then the angel said to me, "The waters you saw
Where the whore sits, there are peoples and crowds
And nations and tongues. 16The ten horns you saw
And the beast, they will all hate the whore
And will make her desolate and naked,
And eat her flesh and will burn her up with fire.
17For God put in their hearts to do his will
And act with one mind to give their kingship
Until the words of God will be fulfilled.
18And the woman you saw is the great city[69]
With dominion over the kings of the earth."

Chapter 18

All nations have drunk the wine of copulation with fallen Babylon

After this I saw another angel coming down
Out of the sky and with great authority
And the earth was lighted with his glory.

---

69. The great city is now named as Babylon but may signify Rome, or hell, or all three.

2And he cried out in a powerful voice, saying,
>   Fallen fallen is Babylon the great.[70]
>   She has become a home for demons
>   And a prison of every foul spirit
>   And a prison of every foul bird
>   And a prison of every foul and
>   Detested beast, 3since all the nations
>   Have drunk the wine of passion
>   Of her copulation, and the kings
>   Of the earth have copulated with her,
>   And the merchants of the earth
>   Have grown rich on her lechery.[71]

Of merchants, captains, and seafarers who mourn and now cry out
>   4Then I heard another voice out of the sky, saying,
>   Come out of her, my people,
>   So you will not join in her sins,
>   So you won't take on her plagues,
>   5Because her sins are piled up and reach the sky.
>   God has remembered her iniquities.
>   6Render to her as she has rendered,

---

70. Again a reference to Isaiah 21.9 and Jeremiah 51.8, foreseeing Babylon's fall and by extension Rome's fall. These many references to Rome as the terrible enemy reflect how Apocalypse remained outside the redaction process that fashioned the gospels so as to favor Rome (despite its crucifixion of Yeshua), to justify her destruction of "sinful" Jerusalem of the Jews, and, by implication, to speak for Rome's later church. Although the gospels are replete with references to the Hebrew Bible, each page of Apocalypse draws deeply from the Jewish scriptures. Written while the division between Jews and Christian Jews was still a blur of rivalry and not a schism, it is, after Daniel, the other apocalypse of which we have several Jewish and Christian-Jewish texts from the intertestamental period. See James H. Charlesworth, ed., *The Old Testament Psuedepigrapha* (Garden City, NY: Doubleday, 1983–1985, two vols.), and Willis Barnstone, *The Other Bible* (San Francisco: Harper and Row, 1984).

71. Lechery or sensuality from the Greek στρῆνος (strenos), which may also be translated as "luxury."

Mix her a double portion
In the cup she has mixed.
7As she gloried in the luxury of the flesh,
Give her equal torment and sorrow.
In her heart she says,
"I sit, a queen.
I am not a widow
And will never know grief."
8But soon the plagues will come to her,
Death and sorrow and famine,
And in fire she will burn,
For powerful is the lord God who has judged her.

9The kings of the earth, who copulated
With her and lived in lechery, will weep
And beat themselves over her when they see
The smoke of her burning. 10Standing far off
Because they fear the torment, they say,
Despair despair is the great city
Babylon, the strong city,
For in an hour your judgment came.

11The merchants of the earth cry out and mourn
Over her, since no one buys their cargo now,
12Cargo of gold and silver and precious stones
And pearls and fine linen and purple cloth
And silk and scarlet and every cedar wood
And every ivory vessel and every vessel
Of precious wood and bronze and iron and marble
13And cinnamon and spice and incense and myrrh
And frankincense and wine and olive oil
And fine flour and wheat and cattle and sheep,
And horses and chariots and bodies and souls.
14And the autumn fruit your soul longed for
Has gone from you,
And all the luxurious and the brilliant
Are lost to you and never will be found.

15The merchants of these things, who became rich
From her, will stand far off because they fear
Her torment, her weeping, and her mourning,
16Which say,
    Despair despair is the great city
    Who was clothed in fine linen
    And purple cloth and scarlet
    And decorated with gold
    And precious stone and pearl.
  17In an hour that wealth was desert.
And all captains and seafarers on the ship
And sailors and all those who work the sea
Stood far off 18and cried out as they saw
The smoke of her conflagration, saying,
    What city was like this great city?
19And they threw dust upon their heads
And they cried out with tears and groans,
    Despair despair is the city,
    Where all who owned ships on the sea
    Grew rich from her prosperity.
    In an hour came only desolation.

20Heaven and saints, celebrate her downfall,
And apostles and prophets, for God has judged
Against her for you. 21Then one strong angel
Picked up a boulder like a great millstone
And hurled it down into the sea, saying,
    With such violence Babylon will be cast down
        And will be found no more.
  22And the voices of harp players and singers,
        The pipers and ram-horn blowers
        Will be heard no more in you,
        And the artisan of any trade
        Will be found no more in you,
        And the sound of the mill
        Will be heard no more in you,
      23And the light of a lamp

Will shine no more in you,
The voice of the groom and bride
Will be heard no more in you.
Your merchants were the great men of the earth
And all nations were fooled by your sorcery.
24In her was the blood of prophets and saints
And all those who were slaughtered on the earth.

Chapter 19

A great voice in the heaven crying Halleluyah![72]
After this I heard a great voice in the sky,
Like a huge crowd shouting, Halleluyah!
Salvation and glory and honor and power to our God,
2True and just are his judgments,
He judged the great whore
Who has corrupted the earth with her harlotry.
He avenged the blood of his own slaves against her hand.
3A second time they said, Halleluyah!
And her smoke ascends forever and ever.
4Then the twenty-four elders and four animals
Fell down and worshiped God, who was seated
On the throne, and said, Amain Halleluyah!
5And a voice came from the throne, saying, Praise our God
And all his slaves and those who fear him, the small and
the great.

6And I heard the voice of a huge crowd
Like the voice of many waters and thunders,
Saying, Hallelluyah!
Because the lord God and pantokrator reigns.
7Let us be happy and exult and give him glory,

---

72. Halleluyah from the Greek ἀλληλουϊά (hallelouia), from the Hebrew הַלְלוּיָהּ
(halleluyah), meaning "praise Yahweh."

For the wedding of the lamb has come,
And his bride got ready
8And she had to clothe herself in fine linen bright and
clean,
A linen of the good acts of the saints.
9The angel said to me, "Write. Blessed are
Those called to the supper of the wedding
Of the lamb." And the angel said, "These words
Are the true words of God." 10I fell before
His feet to worship him. He said to me,
"You must not do that! I am your fellow slave
And of your brothers and sisters who keep
The testimony of Yeshua. Worship God.
To witness Yeshua is the spirit of prophecy."

Rider on a white horse
11I saw the sky open, and look, a white horse
And the rider on him called Faithful and True,
And in the right he judges and makes war.
12His eyes are flames of fire, and on his head
Many diadems, with names written known
Alone by him. 13And he wore a mantle
Dipped in blood and his name is called the word
Of God. 14The armies in the sky followed him
On white horses, clothed in fine linen white
And clean. 15And from his mouth goes a sharp sword
To smite the nations. He will shepherd them
With a rod of iron. He will trample the wine press
Of the fury of the anger of God, the pantokrator.
16He wears on his mantle and on his thigh
A name written:
KING OF KINGS AND LORD OF LORDS

Into the lake of fire
17I saw an angel standing in the sun
And he cried out in a great voice, saying,
"To all the birds flying in the middle air,

Come, gather for the great supper of God
18To eat the flesh of kings and flesh of captains
And flesh of strongmen and flesh of horses
And of their riders and flesh of both the free
And slaves and small and great." 19I saw the beast
And kings of the earth and their armies poised
To make war against the rider on his horse
And against his armies. 20Then the beast
Was captured and with him the false prophet
Who had worked miracles on the beast's behalf
And so deceived those who received the mark
Of the beast and those who worshiped the image
Of the monster. The two of them were cast alive
Into the lake of fire burning with sulfur.
21The rest were killed by the sword of the rider
On the horse, the sword that came from his mouth;
And all the flying birds gorged on their flesh.

Chapter 20

Angel with a great chain in his hand
I saw an angel coming down from the sky.
He was holding a great chain on his hand
And the key of the bottomless pit. 2He seized
The dragon, and ancient snake, who is the devil
And Satan; he bound him for a thousand years
3And cast him into the bottomless pit
And closed it tight and sealed it over him
So he couldn't fool the nations any more
Until the thousand years should be fulfilled.
After that he must be released a short time.
4Then I saw thrones, and those who sat on them
Were given the power to judge. I saw
The souls of those beheaded for their testimony
To Yeshua and for the word of God
And those who had not worshiped the beast

Nor the image of him and did not take
His mark on their forehead and on their hand,
And they came to life and reigned with Yeshua
For a thousand years. 5The rest of the dead
Did not come to life until the thousand years
Were over. This is the first resurrection.

Devil in sulfur and fire forever

6Blessed and holy are they who take part in
The first resurrection: on these the second death
Has no power. They will become priests of God
And of Yeshua and with him they will reign
A thousand years. 7And when the thousand years
Should be fulfilled, Satan will be released
From his prison 8and will come out to fool
The nations in the four corners of the earth,
Gog and Magog,73 to lead them into battle,
Whose number is like the sand of the sea.
9Then they climbed up and over the width
Of the earth and encircled the encampment
Of the saints and their beloved city,
But fire came down from the sky and consumed
The attackers. 10The devil, who had fooled them,
Was cast into the lake of fire and sulfur
Where both the beast and the false prophet are
And will be tormented forevermore.

Of the dead written in the book

11I saw a throne great and white, and sitting
On it was he from whose face fled the earth

---

73. Ezek. 38–39. Gog and the king of Magog, two names that represent the nations in league who will march against Jerusalem. They seem to appear after the first thousand-year reign of the messiah. In Apocalypse, their defeat, meaning that of Satan and of his forces, will herald the triumph of the Lamb in the New Jerusalem. The war of Gog and Magog is commented on in the Babylonian Talmud.

And the sky, and no place was found for them.
12I saw the dead, the great and small. They stood
Before the throne and there the books were opened.
Another book was opened, which is the book
Of life. The dead were judged according to
Their works as they were written in the books.
13The sea gave up the dead in it, and hell
Gave up the dead in it, and they were judged,
Each one according to their works. 14And Death
And Hell were cast into the lake of fire.
This is the second death, the lake of fire.
15And anyone not written in the book
Of life was cast into the lake of fire.

Chapter 21

A new Yerushalayim descends from heaven
And I saw a new sky and a new earth,
For the first sky and the first earth were gone
And the sea was no more. 2I saw the holy
City, the new Yerushalayim, coming down
Out of the sky from God who prepared her
Like a bride adorned for her groom. 3And then
I heard a great voice from the throne, saying,
"Look, now the tent of God is with them. They'll be
His people, and he God will be with them,
4And he will wipe away each tear from their eyes
And death will be no more. And grief and crying
And pain will be no more. The past has perished."

I am the Alpha and the Omega
5And he who sat upon the throne said, "Look,
I made all new." And he said, "Write, because
These words are true and faithful." 6And he said
To me, "It's done. I am the Alpha and the Omega,
The beginning and the end. And to the thirsty

I will give a gift from the spring of the water
Of life. 7The victor will inherit these things
And I will be his God and he will be
A son. 8But to the cowards and unbelieving
And abominable and murderers and copulators
And sorcerers and all who are false, their fate
Will be the lake burning with fire and sulfur,
Which is the second death."

The city clear gold like clear glass
9One of the angels came with the seven bowls
Full of the seven last plagues, and he spoke
With me, saying, "Come, I will show you the bride,
The wife of the lamb." 10And he took me away
In spirit onto a mountain great and high,
And showed me the city of holy Yerushalayim
Coming down out of the sky from God,
11Wearing the glory of God, and her radiance
Like a precious stone, like a jasper stone
And crystal clear. 12She has a great and high wall
With twelve gates and at the gates twelve angels,
Their names inscribed on them: the twelve tribes
Who are the sons and daughters of Yisrael.

13On the east three gates and on the north three gates,
On the south three gates and on the west three gates.
14The walls of the city have twelve foundations,
And on them twelve names, the twelve apostles of the lamb.
15The angel speaking to me had a gold
Measuring rod to gage the city and her gates
And walls. 16The city lies foursquare, its length
And width the same. He gaged the city with
The reed, twelve thousand furlongs in length,[74]

---

74. About 1,500 miles.

Her length and width and height the same. 17He gaged
Her wall a hundred forty-four cubits,[75]
By human measurement like the angel's.

18The wall is built of jasper and the city
Clear gold like clear glass. 19The foundations of
The city are adorned with precious stones,
The first foundation jasper, the second sapphire,
Third of agate, fourth of emerald, 20fifth of onyx,
The sixth carnelian, seventh of chrysolite,
The eighth beryl, ninth of topaz, tenth of chrysoprase,
Eleventh jacinth and the twelfth amethyst.
21The twelve gates are twelve pearls, each gate
A single pearl, and the great square in the city
Is clear gold like diaphanous glass.

City without need of sun or moon
22I saw no temple in her, for the temple
Is lord God the pantokrator and the lamb.
23The city has no need of sun or moon
To shine on her, for the glory of God
Illuminated her and her lamp is the lamb.
24The gentile nations will walk around
Through her light, and the kings of the earth
Bring glory into her. 25Her gates will never
Be shut by day, and night will not be there.
26Her people will bring the glory and honor
Of nations into her. 27But no common thing[76]

---

75. Almost 200 feet.

76. Common from the Greek κοινός (koinos), meaning "common," "of little value,"
or "communal" (in the sense of being shared). Here this word, as with many ordinary words in New Testament lexicons, is given a religious boost by translating it as
"profane," which suggests "in contrast to the sacred." But its sense of "common" or
"plain" contrasts in a lovely way with the luminous magnificence of the city in the
sky, which is lost when "common" has an ecclesiastical ring.

Will enter her, or anyone who stoops
To abominations and lies, but only those
Written in the book of life of the lamb.

Chapter 22

River of the water of life
    The angel showed me a river of the water
    Of life shining like crystal and issuing
    From the throne of God and of the lamb.
    2Between the great plaza and the river
    And on either side stands the tree of life
    With her twelve fruits, yielding a special fruit
    For every month, and the leaves of the tree
    Are for healing the nations. 3All curses
    Will cease to exist. The throne of God
    And of the lamb will be in the city.
    His slaves will serve him; 4they will see his face. His name
    Will be on their foreheads. 5And night will not
    Be there and they'll need no light of a lamp
    Or light of sun, for the lord God will glow
    On them, and they will reign forevermore.

I'm coming quickly!
    6Then he said to me, "These words are faithful
    And true, and the lord God of the spirits of
    The prophets sent his angel to show his slaves
    Those things which soon must take place. 7Look,
    I'm coming quickly! Blessed is the one
    Who keeps the words of this book's prophecy."
    8I Yohanan am the one who heard and saw
    These things. And when I heard and saw I fell
    And worshiped before the feet of the angel
    Showing me these things. 9And he said to me,
    "You must not do that! I am your fellow slave

And of your brothers and prophets and those
Who keep the words of this book. Worship God."
10And he tells me, "Do not seal the words
Of prophecy of this book. The time is near.
11Let the unjust still be unjust, the filthy
Still be filthy, the righteous still do right,
And the holy one be holy still." 12"Look,
I'm coming quickly, and my reward is with me
To give to each according to your work.
13I am the Alpha and the Omega, the first
And the last, the beginning and the end."

To the tree of life
14Blessed are they who are washing their robes
So they will have the right to the tree of life
And can enter the city through the gates.
15Outside will be the dogs and sorcerers
And copulators and murderers and idolators
And everyone who loves to practice lies.

I am the offspring of David the bright morning star
16"I Yeshua sent my angel to you
To testify these things for the churches.
I am the root and the offspring of David,
The bright morning star." 17The spirit and bride
Say, "Come." Let you who hear say, "Come."
"Let you who thirst come, and let you who wish
Take the water of life, which is a gift."

Come, lord Yeshua!
18I give my testimony to all who hear
These words of the prophecy of this book.
If anyone adds to these, then God will add
To them the plagues recorded in this book.
19If anyone takes away from the words
Of this book's prophecy, God will cut off

Their share of the tree of life and the holy
City, those things recorded in this book.[77]
20And he who is the one who testifies
To all this says, "Yes, I am coming quickly!"
Amain. Come, lord Yeshua! 21And may
The grace of lord Yeshua be with you all.

---

77. These last commands and warnings are from Deuteronomy 4.2 and 12.32.

AFTERWORD

AFTERWORD

History of the Translator's Way

A History

John Wyclif

IN THE CONVERSION of holy scripture each word faces the risky test of theology, canon, and history. From the fourteenth to the sixteenth centuries in England and France, translators burned. John Wyclif (also spelled Wycliffe; mid-1320s–1384), Master of Balliol College and called the flower of Oxford scholarship, was a dissenter against the rich princes of the church. He engaged in open war with Rome and the papacy, which reserved the reading of the Bible for its clergy. For Wyclif it was not enough to overhear the priest's Latin language in the church. He held that the emancipation of the individual soul lay in the possibility of reading the Bible in one's native tongue. He was the first translator of the Bible into vernacular English from the Latin Vulgate, for a public that could not read its Latin translation. He also addressed another language rivalry: the political and class conflict between Norman French and English. With Chaucer writing his masterpieces in English and the Wyclif English Bible reaching large numbers of people orally and in manuscript—this was still the manuscript age—English established itself as the language of England, and Wyclif contributed to its early domination. The Wyclif Bible was immensely popular (some one hundred fifty manuscripts of the Wyclif versions have survived, many times the number of extant copies of Chaucer's *Troilus and Criseyde* or the *Canterbury Tales*), and it was also to serve as source and dictionary for the later Tyndale New Testament in 1525 and Coverdale's Bible in 1535.

Wyclif founded the populist Lollard movement, a precursor to the Protestant Reformation, and he was sometimes called the "morning star of the Reformation." There was a price for Wyclif's populist outrages. The official church was not deaf to the sounds of all this theological and related linguistic activity from Oxford lectures and in the churches and streets in England. It would not remain silent. In 1401 Archbishop Arundel denounced Wyclif as heretical. He fumed, "The peal of the Gospel is scattered abroad and trodden underfoot by swine." He further wrote in his report to claimant John XXIII, "This pestilent and wretched John Wyclif, of cursed memory, that son of the old serpent . . . endeavored by every means to attack the very faith and sacred doctrine of Holy Church, devising—to fill up the measure of his malice—the expedient of a new translation into the mother tongue."

The scholar's death, by natural causes, saved him. Some associates and readers of Wyclif were, however, burned alive for the sins of unauthorized vernacular translation. John Purvey, his follower and author of the second widespread revision of his work, was thrown into prison under the 1401 acts against heresy, *De haeretico comburendo*, and under torture abjured his Lollard principles (the vernacular "mutterings" of poor preachers). Wyclif was by then safely in the earth, or so it seemed. In 1424, forty years after his burial, his bones were dug up, burned, and thrown into the River Swift.

Étienne Dolet
In France the pre-Renaissance scholar Étienne Dolet (1509–1546), historian, painter, printer, and translator of the Bible, was tried and convicted of heresy by the French church for his secularized translation of Plato—not for his scripture. He was burned at the stake. He became the first martyr in the cause of secular translation.

William Tyndale
Meanwhile, in England, Dolet's near contemporary William Tyndale (ca. 1494–1536) was establishing the Renaissance English language of the Bible. The larger part of the Authorized New Testament (and that part of the Jewish Bible that Tyndale lived to translate) is Tyndale's phraseology. His prose is clear, modern, minimally Latinized, and with unmatched narrative powers. Everything is fresh, including the use of very common words, unelevated for religious respectability. So

where the Authorized Version has "and the Lord was with Joseph and he was a prosperous man" (Gen. 39.2), Tyndale has "the Lord was with Joseph and he was a luckie felawe." We have been trying and failing for centuries to get back to that speech, which is at once dignified and ordinary, which a Bible from common but inspired people should be. Working from original sources, Tyndale made the English of his day the language of the Bible, and his vision of biblical speech imposed itself on all subsequent versions in English, particularly the Geneva, which carried the cadence and ordinary magnificence of his words under its own rubric to the masters of English literature.

Not only did Tyndale translate the Bible into English to make it readable for the literate and hearable for the unlettered churchgoer, but he did so with the enthusiastic assertion that English was an excellent language to translate into from Hebrew and Greek, and far better than Latin. English is so flexible that one can translate into it word for word, and not paraphrase as one must in Latin. And Tyndale, working hard to stay close in word and syntax to the original, more than any Renaissance translator, avoided paraphrase, equivalents, and explanation. But he did so with his special gift for finding the grace and sweetness of the English language:

> They will say it cannot be translated into our tongue, it is so rude. It is not so rude as they are false liars. For the Greek tongue agreeth more with the English than with the Latin. And the properties of the Hebrew tongue agreeth a thousand times more with the English than with the Latin. The manner of speaking is both one, so that in a thousand places thou needest not but to translate it into the English word for word when thou must seek a compass in the Latin and yet shall have much work to translate it well-favouredly, so that it have the same grace and sweetness, sense and pure understanding with it in the Latin as it hath in the Hebrew. A thousand parts better may it be translated than into the Latin. (*Obedience of a Christian Man* [1528] in Alter and Kermode, 648).[1]

1. The lines from Tyndale are taken from Gerald Hammond's essay "English Translations of the Bible" in Robert Alter and Frank Kernmode, eds., *The Literary Guide to the Bible* (Cambridge, MA: Harvard University Press, 1987). Hammond's essay and his volume *The Making of the English Bible* (New York: Philosophical Library, 1983) contain uniformly sensitive and informed remarks on Bible translation.

But Tyndale's courageous venture in English did not escape the wrath of those who saw heresy in his vernacular, in his translations which he rendered "for the ploughboy in the fields." The bishop of London called them "persiferous and most pernicious poison." As a sign of those noisy times, Sir Thomas More (who was to lose his head to the axe in 1535) devoted a book, *Dialogue Concerning Tyndale* (1529), to blasting Tyndale the man, reviling the language of his revisionist translation, and even transforming its author into a barking hound: "He barketh against the sacraments much more than Luther (1528)."[2] And no one in his day could surpass More in his sonorous alliterations and orchestration of rhythmic denunciations. But he surpassed his own alliterative flair and brutal magnificence in the rhetoric of insult when he called Tyndale "the devilish drunken soul . . . this drowsy drudge hath drunken so deep in the devil's dregs that if he wake and repent himself the sooner he may hap to fall into draff that the hogs of hell shall feed upon."

For his "cunning counterfeit" and a choice of offensive words— "congregation," not "church"; "senior" and "elder," not "priest"; and "love," not "charity," all lacking ecclesiastical correctness—Tyndale was arrested for heresy in Antwerp, then under the rule of Charles V. By this time he had completed the Pentateuch, Jonah, and the Second Book of Chronicles. In 1535, he was imprisoned near Brussels at Vilvorde, where he continued to translate. Even in prison Tyndale was a hero of translation. We read from a letter to the marquis of Bergen, "And I ask to be allowed to have a lamp in the evening; it is indeed wearisome sitting alone in the dark. But most of all I beg and beseech your clemency to be urgent with the commissary, that he will kindly permit me to have the Hebrew bible, Hebrew grammar, and Hebrew dictionary, that I may pass the time in that study." On October 6, 1536, William Tyndale was taken to the stake, strangled by the hangman, and burned. His last words were, "Lord, open the King of England's eyes."

Translation Registers

The grace of Tyndale's word lay in his chosen way, which I place midway

2. William Tyndale, *An Answer unto Sir Thomas More's* Dialogue, ed. Henry Walker (Cambridge, UK: Cambridge University Press, 1850).

in translation registers.[3] On one side of the register is a straightforward transfer of information to the reader, student, and scholar in need of a denotative crib to read scripture in Hebrew or Greek. On the other side is free re-creation or imitation, such as John Dominic Crossan's adroit transformations of Yeshua's sayings into minimalist poems. And the middle ground, which is Tyndale's, is autonomous restatement.

Interlinear Greek Bibles (Greek text with English between lines under each word or phrase) provide accurate word-for-word information, without syntax, with which the instructed reader can decipher the Greek scripture. The interlinear page usually contains a parallel column translation, as with the King James or a standard modern version, to help the reader return to the Greek. It is the Rosetta Stone of translations.

In the mid-range of the spectrum, the translation stands solitary on the page, without the Greek, as an autonomous text to be read in English as scripture. I should say at the outset that the translation should express, not indulge in, "the heresy of explanation," as Robert Alter states in his introduction to *The Five Books of Moses*.[4] Insofar as the translation does explain, it lacks autonomy to be read as an expressive text and returns in essential function to the interlinear level; that is, it becomes a useful aid, for student and teacher, to read and study the original Greek text. A self-contained literary version needs no self-explanation. Explanation and interpretation go into commentary wherever that is placed—on the page, at the back, or in another volume—but not within the translation itself. The Jesus Seminar translation of the gospels, worthy but heavy

3. In *Poetics of Translation: History, Theory, Practice* (New Haven: Yale University Press, 1993), I suggest a division of three registers: interlinear or Benjamin's word-by-word; Horace's and Cicero's sense-by-sense middle ground; and Dryden's imitation. In a derogatory way, the middle ground is often eliminated, and the work is accused of either unenlightened literalism or infidel license. Actually, the middle ground is very wide, as it should be, and includes both "the chaste, close, responsible version, in which the original author is always visible and the source culture is often allowed to retain an imposing flavor in the target language, and, in opposition, a free transference, in which the translator is most visible, where the work seems to be native and at home in the target language, not a naturalized immigrant, but, as the Spanish mystic Fray Luis de León posited, 'as if born and natural in the language'" (28).

4. See Robert Alter, *The Five Books of Moses: A Translation with Commentary* (New York: W. W. Norton, 2004), xix.

in explanation and conceptualization of image and metaphor, uses key words to clarify rather than to express, and operates, unintentionally, very much like an interlinear version, that is, as a bridge back to study and interpretation of the Greek. The frequent *he basileia ton ouranon* (ἡ βασιλεία τῶν οὐρανῶν), "the kingdom of the skies" (or traditionally "kingdom of heaven"), is rendered as "God's imperial rule." The image and metaphor are lost to abstraction and explanation. Neither God, empire, nor rule is in the Greek. That is interpretation.

At the other end of the register are those who freely re-create literary texts, as Robert Lowell cunningly and brilliantly did in his imitations. The imitator enters into an artistic partnership with the earlier writer. Much of our best literature is imitation—from hunks of Chaucer, Crashaw, and Racine to Yeats, Pound, and Lowell. Some declare their imitations openly as Racine, Pound, and Lowell did, and Chaucer, Crashaw, and Yeats did not seem to. Lowell entitled his collected translations *Imitations*, but Richard Crashaw's well-known poem on Saint Teresa de Avila, "A Song," with its key line, "I dy even in desire of death," is actually a rewording of Teresa's best-known poem, "Vivo sin vivir en mi." Similarly, William Yeats's "When you are Old" is an imitation of Pierre de Ronsard's most famous sonnet, "Quand vous serez bien vieille."

So here are two extremes that can be satisfied happily: a gloss for the reader who wants help in reading the source text, and imitation for the writer who wants to collaborate with, adapt, or rewrite a precursor's work as Dryden did with Shakespeare's *Anthony and Cleopatra* or Anouilh with Euripides' *Antigone*. As for the free approach, it is perfectly fine if the reader knows what it is. But, like the informational gloss, a free imitation should not pass for a close literary translation. It has another creative purpose. Recent free translations of *Gilgamesh* by David Ferry and of Dante by Robert Pinsky are magnificent, and there is no subterfuge of method. There is sharing of authorship that has resulted in versions superior to predecessors, close or free, and these works will endure.

There is also a middle ground between gloss and imitation, whose purpose is to hear the source author more clearly than the translator author. To say what this way is, I offer a brief visual parable rather than the wearily abstract terminology in translation studies (of which I am an offending user). When Robert Fitzgerald decided to translate the *Odyssey,* he went to see Ezra Pound at Saint Elizabeth's Hospital, where the poet was incarcerated. He asked Pound how he should do it. Pound replied, "Let Homer say everything he wanted to say."[5] This was not Pound's normal practice. He himself took tremendous freedoms, imitated, and intimately collaborated with or overcame the author in his best translations from Anglo-Saxon and Chinese—and they may be his own best poems. But Pound gave Fitzgerald generously right advice. Fitzgerald followed it and produced—because he was a great poet in the act of translations—the major literary version of his era. Robert Alter, with equal art, did the same in rendering Genesis and David in 1 Kings and 2 Kings.

This is the difficult middle way.

In looking for a right and good voice for the New Testament, I read and thought but did not experiment. After a certain period it was there, and I was grateful it was clear. I wished to let the Greek talk, not me, and behind the Greek voice a restoration of the Semitic biblical names to temper the lexical anti-Semitism where its source seems to be the eager accretions of later redactors. In short, I believe I have found a plain and close voice—as distinct from gloss, interpretation, or a free authorial collaboration. The great discovery for me was the invisible poet hitherto hidden in unlineated Greek prose.

The closeness, the plainness, and the poetic are just what Fitzgerald and Alter have done in making the literal literary. I quickly add that those who hear "literal" and think "literalist thug" or "academic clunk" are usually right. "Literal" is usually a dismissive word and most often describes the laziest, worst, and least imaginative type of mechanical "correct" translation, with minimal reaches of valence and voice. By "literal," I mean a deep respect for all aspects of the source text; and to make a distinction in definition, I say "literal," not "literalist," the one being as different from the other as "sentiment" is from "sentimental." So the literal should be literary (not the literary's antagonist) and be as literary as any version on the way to pure imitation. To be close to the word and its full connotations need imply no lessening of tonality or song or semantic richness.

5. See Edwin Honig, *The Poet's Other Voice: Conversation on Literary Translation* (Amherst: University of Massachusetts Press, 1985), 113.

Gerald Hammond, in his superb essay on "English Translations of the Bible," praises the Authorized over more interpretive modern versions, which by their very interpretations not only lose in accuracy and literature but limit ambiguity by making choices for us. He writes, "The Renaissance translators were still close to a Protestant Reformation which stressed the primacy of the Bible's literal sense, as opposed to the various allegorical readings which the Catholic Church had foisted upon it. Stressing the literal sense very often involves treating the story with as much care as any writer of narrative should do."[6]

The translator in service of the source author becomes more invisible as the art intensifies, permitting the reader to *see* Homer or Dante or the Bible and, as Pound suggested, to hear them have *their* say. By contrast, in the inevitable collaboration between author and translator, as we move from re-creation to imitation, the earlier author tends to disappear, overcome by the voice of the translating author.

It is hard to hold that middle ground, to be both literal and literary. The literal tends to move one toward information transfer, the literary toward imitation. But these difficulties of balance also liberate. With the imperative to preserve fidelity to both raw content and artistic form, the translator is saved from first-glance easy solutions. To overcome the obstacles, one must leap up or track through the mind to come upon many possibilities until the right, or almost right, one surprisingly appears. Is such translation truly possible? Of course not, in an absolute sense, since *a* is not *b*. But the fact of impossibility makes the translation richer and more desirable, and differences in languages are a plus to all sides. It is good to wrestle with the words, as Jacob wrestled with God until daybreak, for the child of that struggle will come up intact, imperfect, and handsome.

Finally, I restate my enthusiasm for the at-last excellent versions of Genesis and Kings that have recently appeared, and my debt to the beloved Richmond Lattimore of the Greek classics, whose last work was the New Testament. To fulfill the required words about translation practice, it should be enough to ignore what has been done and affirm one's own ways and wait—while acknowledging the debt to others. I have saved particular praise for the older versions, done in dangerous

6. See Hammond, "English Translations of the Bible," 664.

times when a life could be lost to the axe or stake. The King James and especially the Tyndale conversion remain the joy of the literal become literary. I would wish, just wish, the speech and song here to be so plain and lucid for Tyndale's "ploughboy in the fields."

King James Version

The model for high and good translation of the New Testament remains the King James Authorized Version of 1611. Strictly speaking, the King James is, as its title states, "a version" rather than a translation, since about eighty percent of its New Testament comes directly, with minimal change in letter of punctuation, from the William Tyndale translation, which appeared between 1525 and 1536. In rendering about half the Hebrew Bible directly from the Hebrew and the complete New Testament from the Greek, Tyndale produced a lucid version, beautiful in its cadences, plain in its lexicon, favoring the Anglo-Saxon over the Latin word. Erasmus saw in Tyndale "the evangelist of the poor." However, the near century that separates Tyndale from the Authorized, a century of rapid change in the language, also distances Tyndale that much more from contemporary spelling. Consequently, without modernization, the Authorized remains the great Bible of the past and the present that can still be read with perfect linguistic ease. Principally for reason of access, the King James is the most attractive version in English. It has, as Gerald Hammond sees, "the kind of transparency which makes it possible for the reader to see the original clearly."[7]

The "forty and seven scholars who devised the Book of the World" knew the art of translation. And it was in their famous preface (omitted, alas, in almost all editions) that Miles Smith said his unforgettable, "Translation it is that openeth the window, to let in the light." The Authorized let in the light with bright focus and minimum distortion. In comparing nineteenth-century and contemporary versions of the New Testament, I've noted how the King James, with all its recognized magnificence of word, is plainer, less convoluted than any contemporary version, closer to the Greek text, and more accurate (despite the

---

7. See Hammond, "English Translations of the Bible," 664.

frequent slamming the KJV takes for deficient Greek texts and errors). Its authors were genial in deciphering complexity in the Greek and rendering straightforward English prose. Its strength and emotional impact lie not only in the by-now-sacred majesty of memorable phrasing but in its clear and comprehensible speech. No serious writer in English can afford to ignore its speech, and since its publication few major writers have not been strongly affected by it.

The downside of the King James is heard often enough. It is true that recent translations have earlier and more reliable texts than did the king-appointed translators of the seventeenth-century Bible. However, since the present, "more reliable" texts are at best questionable, the common criticism should be softened. It is also true that the King James abounds in archaisms and holds some problems of uncertain meaning for the modern reader; the New King James Bible, which appeared in 1979, responded to those attested frailties, and it modernized spelling, corrected mistakes as it saw them, and moderated gender bias. I confess that I prefer the unmodernized version, as I would an unmodernized Shakespeare, for the Authorized is close enough to be perfectly readable. If one wants to read a modern-spelling version of a text that is endlessly beautiful but not perfectly readable in the old spelling because of the extensive spelling changes in the late sixteenth century, then the David Daniell edition of William Tyndale is fully satisfying and still "old" enough in spelling and speech to make it of the earlier age. There is not a stilted or churchy phrase in Tyndale's everyday word, no obtrusive inversions. Tyndale's English is as plain and compelling as Mark's ordinary Greek.

Having said all these good things about Tyndale and the original Authorized, why a new translation? First, I should say that praise for the Authorized, as praise for Chapman's Homer, does not lessen the need, since we are dealing with translation, not an original Shakespearean play, whose difficulties and obscurities we gladly accept rather than modernize. The Greek and Roman classics, despite the Chapman, Dryden, Pope, and Shelley versions, have been given life today through the dignity and beauty of modern English in translations by Richmond Lattimore, Robert Fitzgerald, and Robert Fagles. They have given readership to the classics. By comparison, the Bible has fared poorly. Exceptions are Lattimore's *Four Gospels* and Alter's *Five Books of Moses*—which I am certain mark the beginning of good things.

My reasons for the translation are literary and philosophical. I want to let the Greek speak, that is, to be close and literal, but make the literal literary. I've also reasoned that the poetry of the New Testament, principally of Yeshua and Yohanan of Patmos and Ephesos, should breathe good light. As noted, I have, when possible, restored proper names to their Greek, Hebrew, or Aramaic original forms, which will also help clarify the identity of the people. I favor both the rhetoric of the ordinary and the magic of the simple line, whether in straightforward Mark or in the poetry of soaring Apocalypse, the epic poem of the New Testament.

The Jewish Bible of
the Early Christians

THE BIBLE of the early Christians remained the Jewish Bible, usually in Greek or Latin translation. In the first decades it was their sole scripture. As for the New Covenant in the church, its earliest compositions are the letters of Paul, who was executed by the Romans, probably around 60 C.E. His death is vague with respect to when, where, and how. The gospels were begun no earlier than after 75–80 C.E. The last books were completed around 150. Paul used the term "the old covenant" for the Hebrew Bible (or Old Testament), referring to the writings of the Mosaic covenant (2 Cor. 3.14). The Church father Tertullian in the late second and third centuries already refers to the New Testament, by which he meant the gospels, the Pauline letters, and Revelation (Apocalypse). These stood out among the much larger body of Christian writings out of which a selection and canon would ultimately be determined. By the fourth century it was common in Western Europe to refer to Christian scripture as the New Testament, and, as mentioned, the main selection of twenty-seven books was allegedly made by Athanasios of Alexandria in 387 C.E., and sanctioned in Rome in 405. However, there remained six competing orderings of the books. By the beginning decades of the third century, there were many copies of scriptures that eventually formed the new covenant. It is now virtually certain that a selection of the twenty-seven books of the New Testament was set and published as early as 150. No codices of the earliest edition are extant, but, with changes, it served as a model for the next centuries. The role of Athanasios in determining anything truly new, which is a traditional truism, is unlikely. If his "Easter Letter" did anything, it confirmed what already was established.

As for the authors, Paul is one whose name is certain for probably seven of the fourteen letters ascribed to him. Peter may or may not be the author of 1 Peter. The other uncertain letters have no known authorship. The gospels claim no authorship within their text, but in the second century Papias, ca. 140, suggested the names of "Matthew" and "Mark" for the books attributed to them, and Irenaeus, ca. 180, put forth "Luke" and "John" for their gospels. Acts was also linked with Luke, a friend of Paul. Luke is often called the one gentile among the Jewish evangelists. That idea is also a second-century invention.

Early Christians Without a Christian Bible

In his *Historical Introduction to the New Testament*, Robert M. Grant writes that the church proclaimed Christianity without possessing the New Testament. He agrees with Helmet Koester that "the Apostolic Fathers (the earliest Christian writers outside the New Testament) did not even make use of written gospels. Instead, they relied upon oral traditions of the same sort as those recorded by the evangelists." Grant acknowledges, with unnecessary apology, the absence of a New Testament canon:

> In dealing with the canon of the New Testament we must begin with some rather negative statements. First, the earliest Christian Bible was not, and did not, include the New Testament. Instead, it was the Old Testament, usually read in Greek, and often interpreted in the light of a number of apocalyptic documents which were not generally recognized as canonical.[8]

The gospel story of a rabbi named Yeshua appeared in diverse documents (as noted, in all or part of seventeen gospels concerning Yeshua), but what served as testimony during that long period of Christianity's formation was the disputed miscellany of written document and oral

---

8. Grant is referring to the enormous pseudepigraphic scripture of the time, in particular Enoch, a Jewish apocalypse. See Robert M. Grant, *A Historical Introduction to the New Testament* (New York: Simon and Schuster, 1972), 25, 28.

tradition. Second-century Marcion,[9] marked as a Gnostic heretic by all branches of later Christianity and expelled from the Church in 144, alone among the prominent messianics attempted, and failed, to exclude the Hebrew Bible[10] from Christianity. By the end of the second century, among the multitude of documents floating around, the books which now comprise the gospels already existed, and there were already disputes, particularly instigated by the figure of Marcion, who, steeped in anger, rejected the Old Testament of the despised "creator God" who had trapped our spirits on this earth. Marcion did accept Paul and part of Luke, though he rejected the remaining gospels. For all his forays, Marcion was the first to attempt to formulate a canon. But despite Marcion, one book remained canon and sacred to the early Christian Jews and Christian gentiles, and that was the Torah (the Hebrew Bible), which was increasingly received in its second-century B.C.E. Septuagint Greek translation. By the time of Constantine's conversion in the early fourth century, the Torah was received in Latin translation.

New Covenant, Essenes, and a Unitarian Dual Torah

In their volume *Judaism in the New Testament*, Bruce Chilton and Jacob Neusner declare that the New Testament consists of "writings by Jews

---

9. Being accused of being a Gnostic was more serious than being thought of as a Jew, since as Gnosticism grew, spreading from Portugal through Europe, North Africa, the Near East, and China, it was the largest and most dangerous heresy. Its last flourishing as neo-Manichaean Cathars in the southwest of France prompted the thirteenth-century Albigensian Crusade and the establishment of the Inquisition, carried out by the Dominican order. As for Marcion, though his theistic dualism, positing a good invisible god and the evil creator god of Genesis, coincided with Gnostic dualism, his message is faith, not gnosis, and with himself as the great messenger or messiah. He had little or no influence on classical Alexandrian Gnosticism.

10. Without quibbling about order and number of included books, I use "Old Testament," "Old Covenant," "Jewish Bible," "Hebrew Bible," "Hebrew Scriptures," "Tanak" (Tanakh), and "Torah" interchangeably. However, the Tanak has a different order and number of books. Torah (the Torah) is the scroll of the five books of Moses but is also customarily used to mean the entire Hebrew Bible. The Bible by itself, or the Christian Bible, includes the Hebrew Bible and the New Testament. The New Testament is also called "New Covenant," "Christian scriptures," and "Greek scriptures."

for Jews who formed a very special Israel."[11] In their essential homily they insist on the intense diversity and dissidence among the Judaisms of the period, one of which was Christianity. As we know now from the Dead Sea Scrolls, the communities at Qumran and elsewhere in southern Israel fiercely opposed the powerful Hasmonean Jews (whom Yeshua also surely opposed)[12] and saw themselves as the true "sons of light" and other Judaisms as representatives of the "sons of darkness." The Essenes sought an apocalyptic triumph over Jerusalem, as foretold in their *War Scroll*—the moral and religious life they would impose after conquest is seen in the *Manual of Discipline*—and the correctness alone

11. See Bruce Chilton and Jacob Neusner, *Judaism in the New Testament: Practices and Beliefs* (London/New York: Routledge, 1993), 9.

12. The Hasmonean rulers were descendants of Judas Maccabeus or Yehuda the Maccabee ("the hammer") and his sons, who fought the Seleucid Antiochus Epiphanes, the Greek ruler who introduced pagan rites in the Temple at Jerusalem. With their victory in 141 B.C.E. an independent Jewish kingdom was established under the ruling dynasty of the priestly Hasmonean family, which persisted until Roman Pompey's conquest of Jerusalem in 63 B.C.E. Yeshua, who was given a political execution as an insurrectionist, would have opposed the Hasmonean rulers, who were by then client kings of Rome. The very moment of original Hasmonean victory in 141 B.C.E. corresponded with the foundations of the Dead Sea Scroll Essene community at Qumran, who as "sons of light" angrily rejected the "sons of darkness" Hasmonean rulers in Jerusalem.

Among those who opposed Rome, the Essene opposition coincided with the militant opposition by the Zealots and the intellectual opposition by the Pharisee leaders to both Rome and their Hasmonean Jewish king. During the later major revolt against Rome by Judea and Galilee, 66–68, the Pharisees survived more intact than did other Jewish sects after the Roman sack of Jerusalem and destruction of the Second Temple in 70.

The question of Jewishness of the Hasmonean kings becomes tricky and murky because of their eventual divided loyalty to foreign rulers. Herod the Great was an Idumean (considered a half-Jew) who married a Jew, Mariamne, whom he later executed along with his mother-in-law, Alexandra. His achievements were enormous with respect to new structures and lowering of taxes, and from 20 B.C.E. until his death in 4 C.E. he expanded the Second Temple in a magnificent style. His domestic life was plagued with intrigue, execution, and new alliances to descendants, and problems with Rome, which was his power source and which permitted him to consolidate his rule. When civil war broke out between Octavius and Antony (32 B.C.E.), he initially favored Antony. After Antony's defeat he cultivated Octavius's friendship.

of their Judaism is elaborated in the *Zadokite Document*. Compared to the Essenes of the Dead Sea Scrolls, the Jews who followed Yeshua, revolutionary as they were, were not extreme and not radically distinct from other centrist Jews.

In the Qumranic texts the Essenes have a special relation to Yeshua for the similarity of the titular designations. One is a royal figure named "son of God," but it is uncertain whether he is a Jew or an anti-god figure. To fill out the portrait of Yeshua, it is important to look at the coincidences of both titles and deeds between Essenes and Yeshua the Messiah. In *Jesus the Jew*, Geza Vermes elaborates these similarities, citing a fragmentary Dead Sea Scrolls poem from the Qumran Messianic Apocalypse (4Q521), which deals with charismatic Judaism:

> . . . [the hea]vens and the earth will listen to His Messiah,
> and none therein will stray from the commandments of the holy ones.
> Seekers of the Lord, strengthen yourselves in his service!
> All you hopeful in (your) heart, will you not find the Lord in this?
> For the Lord will consider the pious, and call the righteous by name.
> Over the poor His spirit will hover and will renew the faithful with His
> power.
>
> And He will glorify the pious on the throne of the eternal Kingdom,
> He who liberates the captives, restores sight to the blind, straightens
> the b[ent].
>
> And the Lord will accomplish glorious things which have never been . . .
> For He will heal the wounded, and revive the dead and bring good news
> to the poor . . .

On this fragment, Vermes comments, "These few lines bind together the concepts of the Messiah, the Kingdom of God, healing, resurrection and the proclamation of good news to the poor, representing the same charismatic-eschatological pattern as the Gospel's announcement of victory over devil and disease."[13] And he cites Matthew 11.4–5, which is one of the many New Testament passages depicting similar miracle

13. See Geza Vermes, *Jesus the Jew* (Philadelphia: Fortress Press, 1981), 12–13.

healings and good news of resurrection for the poor. This Matthew passage derives from Isaiah 35.5, bringing us back once more to the Torah:

> The blind will see again and the lame walk,
> The lepers are made clean and the deaf hear,
> The dead are raised and the poor hear the good news.
>
> MATT. 11.5

The passage in Isaiah differs in that the blind and deaf once cured leap and shout ecstatically:

> Then will the eyes of the blind be opened
> and the ears of the deaf unstopped.
> Then will the lame leap like deer
> and the mute tongue shout for joy.
>
> ISA. 35.5

Here, as we enter the impossible search for the historical Yeshua, we see the Essenes with parallel claims of messiahship through their "Teacher of Righteousness," who heals with his hands. There is much to associate Yeshua with in terms of precedents, and especially in recent years commentators have assigned Yeshua to many prominent groups, from Essenes and Zealots to Pharisees, and Cynics to Gnostics and the Hasidim. Once Christianity takes hold, or even before, the same diversity of beliefs within the Christian fold will initiate millennia of sectarian dogma and conflict. We already see the squabbles of origin, faith, and dogma pronounced by James, Peter, and triumphant Paul. Like all Jewish factions, the leaders of the Christian Jews declared their unique authenticity. James, a conservative Jew with considerable power until his death in ?66 C.E., stayed back to decree from Jerusalem; Peter felt at home, wherever he was, but demanded circumcision for all gentile converts; and allegorical Paul found his own in person and through his letters, as the inclusive missionary, for the circumcised and uncircumcised. All three founders proposed a Judaic way of life through distinctive visions and revisions of who the messiah was and what he signified. Throughout the New Testament, the authors' scrupulous reference to verse in the authoritative Hebrew Bible marks their acceptance, however interpreted, of that covenant between God and Moses at Sinai that resulted in the Torah.

In their book *Judaism in the New Testament*, Chilton and Neusner argue for the multiplicity of Judaisms by listing, apart from the Hebrew Bible and New Testament, "Enoch, the writings found at the Dead Sea, Josephus, Philo, the Elephantine Papyri, and the Mishnah." They speak of Christianity as another Judaism of antiquity, and state "the iron datum that the New Testament writers saw themselves as Israelites teaching the meaning of the Torah." They express their Unitarian conviction about the essence of one holy book assumed by Christians—the Hebrew Bible and New Testament—by giving it the title "the dual Torah."[14]

The Creation of the Septuagint

It is not feasible in a general afterword to the gospels and Apocalypse to deal at greater length with the central matter of historicity in the New Testament. I wish to look into the colorful tale of the translation of the Septuagint Bible, which has remained the Bible for Eastern Orthodoxy and is the source of the canonical Apocrypha. In the New Testament, the Greek translation in the Septuagint is usually given when referring to words from the Hebrew Bible.

Apart from the versions of earlier Aramaic Targums, the first translation of the Hebrew Bible into another language is the Septuagint or Hellenistic Bible (ca. 250–175 B.C.E.), created for the Greek-speaking Jews of the diaspora in Alexandria, who by 300 B.C.E. represented a significant segment of the city's inhabitants rivaling in number the Jews of Jerusalem. As mentioned, the name "Septuagint," meaning seventy, refers to the seventy-two scholars who, according to tradition, by order of King Ptolemy II Philadelphus, undertake the translation of the Hebrew Bible into Greek on the island of Pharos in the port of Alexandria. By divine coincidence, the translation is completed in seventy-two days. The story of the Septuagint translation is first contained in the *Letter of Aristeas*.

Aristeas recounts that as a gesture of goodwill, the king sends sumptuous gifts to the Temple in Jerusalem. The scholars are then sent to Alexandria, where there is an endless banquet at which both king and

14. See Chilton and Neusner, *Judaism in the New Testament*, xv, 6, 4.

scholars display their wisdom in explaining Jewish ethics and theology and Greek reason and virtue, all accomplished with excessive politeness and mutual congratulations. Then the scholars are taken to Pharos and paired off into thirty-six cells. At the end of each day the work of each version is compared with the others until all the versions agree with each other, word for word. After exactly seventy-two days, the work by the seventy-two scholars is complete, "as though this coincidence had been intended."[15] The requisite goal of a perfect translation had been achieved.

To understand this necessary miracle of translation in relation to theological and political conditions of this period, we must speak about historical background. As presented in the text, Aristeas, the author-narrator of the *Letter of Aristeas*, was an influential courtier in Ptolemy's circle and a pagan apologist for the Jews to the king himself, a main character in the work. The king is also sternly devoted to bringing forth an immaculate translation of the Jewish Bible, the first foreign religious scripture ever to be commissioned into Greek translation.

The story of the third-century Aristeas and the creation of the Septuagint was to be retold many times, and of particular interest are those retellings by the Jewish historian Josephus (37–95) and by the Neoplatonist Philo Judaeus (50? B.C.E.–50? C.E.). However, with regard to Aristeas and his era, historical study immediately discloses the literary masks of the author, period, and genre. The author is in temporal and national disguise. Aristeas was not a third-century contemporary of the Egyptian king, and the book is not a letter but rather a *diegesis* (*narratio* in Latin) concerning, among other matters, standards and methodology in the translation of religious texts. Even the designation "letter" (*epistolis*) first appears only in a fourteenth-century manuscript, *epistolis Aristeos pros Philokratin ekphrasis*. The ancient designation of the short book was simply *Aristeas to Philocrates*. The text itself is imaginative in its anachronisms, even in the early lines where the elders are described as selected from each of the six tribes; of course, by the third century B.C.E. the legendary twelve tribes as a unit had long ago disappeared from Judea.

---

15. See *Aristeas to Philocrates* [*Letter of Aristeas*], ed. and trans. Moses Hadas (New York: Harper and Brothers, 1951), 307. See also pp. 56 (*epistolis Aristeos pros Philokratin ekphrasis*), 34–40 (in the early lines), 17–27 (abundant internal evidence).

Who was Aristeas? By abundant internal evidence in this popular book, he was an Alexandrian Jew, not of the third but more likely the second century B.C.E., arguing for harmony between Jews and Greeks, to the point of equating Yahweh and Zeus. Aristeas not only displays a Greek's love for Jewish literature, law, and ethics, but, in a political gesture, pleads for the release of Ptolemy's Jewish slaves, and persuades the king to do so as a precondition for the translation of their laws. Aristeas, in fact, was addressing the Jewish community, and his "letter" may be thought of as a piece of internal encouragement.

If the idea of King Ptolemy commissioning the translation of the Bible for the Jews of Alexandria is a fantasy, then the logical alternative is that the Hellenized Jews commissioned the work of translation themselves. By the time of the actual composition of Aristeas, most if not all of the Hebrew Bible had already been rendered into the Greek Bible of the Septuagint. And the act of translation was not accomplished in seventy or seventy-two days but executed and gathered together during the course of approximately seventy-five years, from 250 to 175 B.C.E.

Here we have a famous story, to which the sacred Bible of Eastern Europe, the Septuagint, is in religious debt. Yet we discover that virtually every aspect of the story that Aristeas recounts is fiction. The story of its translation, though a parable for a Jewish cause, was, nevertheless, picked up and retold a century later by those two most famous men of the period, the historian Josephus and the philosopher Philo. In the instance of the composition of the New Testament, the stakes were much higher than the method of translation of the Hebrew Bible for its Alexandrian Greek-speaking Jewish community. The story of its miraculous identical translation in a few days, like five fish feeding three thousand or five thousand of Yeshua's followers in the Galilee, is beautiful, but today it should be read as allegorical truth.

History and Beyond

In these thoughts on historical investigation, I have raised flags of caution when looking at passages that harshly condemn a person or group. Consider the self-serving spin on a report composed half a century after an alleged event. After the questioning of gospel events and dates, it is best to look for the universal, rather than the sectarian, in the teaching. So the Jewish philosopher Martin Buber saw the greater historic and universal faces of Yeshua when he predicted that "[o]ne day Jesus will be granted a prominent place among the teachers of the Jewish faith."[16] When a Greek passage is complex, I reread, which is a great secret of reading; and when passages test credulity, I delight in the fantasy. A history of acceptance and repetition of unproven events has led me to do close reading always with the premise that the gospels are dramatic story, not arid history. And I prefer the fact that the gospels culminate as heartrending story. Yeshua himself prefers the fantastic parable to the chronicler's argument. The historian Josephus reads almost like story, but nothing captures the fervor of the gospels. The gospels and Apocalypse go beyond interpretation of plain fact, which in any case is illusive. Paramount is the adventure of a wanderer among the deprived, healing the body, and liberating the physical and spiritual eye that explores the astronomy of cloud and mind, or drifts through neighborhoods of prodigal sons and Miryams generous with myrrh.

The scriptures tell the sorrow and pathos of the poor and the hurt. They talk to the crippled and to the blind and possessed. They move through a valley of hunger and luminosity. Parables speak the human and spiritual condition, with extraordinary beauty of word. Chapters are books of being. There is a mustard seed that drinks deep water. On each page lives a solitude of spirit. Some religious poets—the Spaniard Saint John of the Cross, who inhabited mountains of spirit and cellars of love, and the English monk Gerard Manley Hopkins, who found the mind had mountains and suffered the fell of dark—left a record of pain and transcendence that is nonsectarian and ecstatic. In like manner, these gospels and Apocalypse question the very limits of despair and interior light. And in some rooms of Jerusalem and Galilee or high in a solitary sanctuary of rocks on the northern hills, and ultimately in the broken body on the awful mound of crucifixion, there exists a night sun stronger than fact.

16. See Martin Buber, *Two Types of Faith* (New York: Harper and Row, 1961), 13.

The Church Agon Between
the Jewish Bible
and the New Testament
and an Almost
Happy Reconciliation

⁓

*Catholics and Protestants Battle over Bible Translation
and the Reemergence of the Hebrew Bible*

THE RIVALRY BETWEEN the developing Christianity and its source in Judaism comes through at every turn in the New Testament. In *Jesus: A Revolutionary Biography*, John Dominic Crossan reviews the parallels in the birth and the circumcision scenes of John the Baptist and Yeshua, in which John reflects the best of limited figures in the Old Testament, and Yeshua the glory and salvation in the New Testament. Crossan also compares Matthew's parallel treatment of Moses and the Pharaonic killing of the infant males to Yeshua and the Herodian killing of the infant males, as well as the worldly covenant of Moses and God at Sinai and the great spiritual covenant of Yeshua and the Father. "But once again," Crossan writes, "Matthew, like Luke, sends a strong and powerful message by his very structure. Jesus is the new and greater Moses."[17]

In the name of Old Testament, "old" does not signify venerable and worthy but outmoded; and the Hebrew Bible is surpassed by the Messianic fulfillment of the New Testament. Hence, it is not surprising that in many countries, especially Spain, Italy, and Greece, the Old

17. See John Dominic Crossan, *Jesus: A Revolutionary Biography* (San Francisco: HarperSanFrancisco, 1994), 15.

Testament was rarely available to the common reader and when available, little read. The Christian Bible was, in effect, the New Testament. With the Reformation, Protestants rediscovered the Old Testament, and the Jewish Bible moved up a few notches in availability and esteem.

About the Bible in the Reformation, the canonized cliché is "the reformers dethroned the Pope and enthroned the Bible." By making the Bible readable in the vulgates of Western Europe, the reformers and translators into German, French, English, Italian, Spanish, Portuguese, Dutch, and Scandinavian permitted laypeople to read and interpret for themselves the holy scripture and by so doing removed the Bible from the exclusively privileged eyes of the clergy, whom Martin Luther called the "the lords of Scripture."

In his "Address to the Nobility of the German Nation," Luther asked bitterly, why not burn our copies of the holy scripture "and content ourselves with those unlearned lords at Rome, who have the Holy Ghost within them, though in truth the Holy Ghost can dwell only in a godly heart?" In his ironic argument against the church's insistence on keeping the Hebrew Bible and Greek scriptures solely in Roman Latin, Luther even cited Abraham and Sarah as models of understanding the word of God. His reference to the Hebrew Bible alone constituted a major shift in emphasis in the difficult family dispute between the Jewish Bible (effectively in the province of the Jews, among whom at least the males could and normally did read it daily) and the New Testament, which was available in Latin but seldom in the vernacular languages, and consequently largely in the domain of the literate Latin-reading clergy rather than the ordinary parishioner.

Prior to the Reformation, among Christians, the Jewish Bible was relegated so completely to the dark that its figures, beyond the primeval Adam and Eve and a few patriarchs cited in the New Testament were scarcely in the knowledge of parishioners at all levels of education. The Latin translation remained canon pure, while the Hebrew and Greek scriptures were deemed "corrupt originals." Yeshua throughout carried not his Aramaic/Hebrew name of *Yeshua*, nor his Greek name of *Iesous*, but his Latin name *Jesus*. With slight language variations, he still is Jesus in all countries of the West, Protestant and Catholic (but of course not in Orthodox Greece, where he remains *Iesous*). In English, Yeshua bears his Latin name *Jesus* from the Saint Jerome fourth-century Vulgata. For the act of straying from the Latin Vulgata, the punishment could be death. Torture, strangulation, the axe, and fire at the stake awaited many of those audacious translators, including John Wyclif,[18] John Purvey, Étienne Dolet, and William Tyndale, who not only translated into the vernacular tongues but in the case of Tyndale did so heretically from the original Hebrew and Greek texts.

With the Protestant Reformation there was a proliferation of translations made directly from the source text. As a result, the Bible entered the households and literatures of Europe and even the Puritan graveyards of New England where the presidents of Harvard and the farmers of the field carried on their grave slabs the common names of Samuel, Elihu, Ezra, and Elijah. The Hebrew Bible became so central in the education of the young that Yale College, originally a school run by the Puritan elders, not only required the study of Hebrew in its curriculum but incorporated a Greek and Hebrew logo into its full name.

Two Views of the Jew Among the Holy Poets

Prior to the Reformation, the New Testament was essentially the holy scripture, and the Jewish Bible an uncomfortable parent best left unvisited. With the audacious and dangerous translation into the vernaculars, the Hebrew Bible came back into the fold, but the deformation of its speech as the historical and religious history of the Jews was even more acute in the new translations. In Eastern Europe until the most recent times, the Hebrew Bible, for all intents and purposes, went unread except by Jews. And in the West, the Jewish Bible was received as a guide and prophecy of the events in the New Testament. Every page of the annotated Jewish Bible in translation carried explanations to make it into a Christian document. So in John 12.40, to explain the disbelief by some in Jesus's miracles, the prophet Isaiah is cited to explain this lapse, and in the next verse, 12.41, it states that Isaiah saw Jesus's "glory and spoke of him." Thus, the Jewish Bible became a preface to the New Testament in which the true God appeared and which served as the main holy script which Christians would know and by which they would live. This was the price of interpretation that the Torah paid for inclusion in the Christian Bible. Yet the Jewish Bible could not, as the angry Gnostic Marcion of Sinope (second century

18. Wyclif died in his bed, but was unearthed four decades later and his bones were burned.

C.E.) wished, be cast out completely. Although in the New Testament the Hebrew Bible is repeatedly and overtly denigrated as spiritually inferior to the message in the Greek scriptures, it remained the law and the unique religious authority for the dissident Jewish sect of Messianics who had developed around Yeshua. Without the Hebrew Bible, the new Christianity lacked a foundation for its God, its foretold savior, and the example of an old covenant which it might surpass with its emerging new covenant.

So these two Jewish books, the Hebrew Bible and the New Testament, were sewn together under one cloth, which is the Christian Bible. Harold Bloom speaks of the Christian appropriation of the Hebrew Bible as "an act of total usurpation," which was epitomized in the debasement of Abraham (and by direct implication Moses) and his covenant with God in Yeshua's reply to the Pharisee in John 8.58: "before Abraham was [born], I am."[19]

Two divergent sixteenth-century views of "usurpation" are revealed in poems by the English metaphysical poets John Donne (1572–1631) and George Herbert (1593–1633). In later life the dean of St. Paul's Cathedral in London, Donne, in his magnificent work, his nineteen "Holy Sonnets," which include "XI," not only depicts "you Jewes" as vile but as killers of "an inglorious Man," Yeshua, who by a miracle of disguise was not to be perceived as a "Jewe." More, he recalls "Jacob" in a way to make him fulfill the stereotype of the tricky, money-minded Semite. But in his penitence, Donne asserts that he, John Donne, is even worse than the Jewes, since he crucifies Yeshua daily:

> Spit in my face you Jewes, and pierce my side,
> Buffet, and scoffe, scoure, and crucifie mee,
> For I have sinn'd, and sinn'd, and only hee,
> Who could do no inquitie, hath dyed:
> But by my death can not be satisfied
> My sinnes, which passe the Jewes impiety:
> They kill'd once an inglorious man, but I
> Crucifie him daily, being now glorified.
> Oh let mee then, his strange love still admire:
> Kings pardon, but he bore our punishment.

19. See Harold Bloom, "Before Moses Was, I Am: The Original and the Belated Testaments," in Harold Bloom, ed., *The Bible* (New York: Chelsea House, 1987), 291.

And Jacob came cloth'd in vile harsh attire
But to supplant, and with gainfull intent:
God cloth'd himselfe in vile mans flesh, that so
Hee might be weake enough to so suffer woe.

John Donne's contemporary, the metaphysical poet George Herbert
(1593–1633), sees the Jews in another light. He speaks not only of the
Jews' suffering, but of their religion "purloin'd" by Christians. Herbert
rebukes his coreligionists for usurping Jewish words as in the baptism (a
Jewish rite practiced by John the Baptizer), while leaving the nation to
"pine and die":

The Jews
Poore nation, whose sweet sap, and juice
Our cyens have purloin'd, and left you drie:
Whose streams we got by the Apostle's sluce,
And use in baptisme, while ye pine and die.

In the same vein as Herbert, Henry Wadsworth Longfellow, in his
"Jewish Cemetery at Newport," describes the Jews in the cemetery
next to the eighteenth-century Spanish-and-Portuguese synagogue in
Newport, Rhode Island:

How strange it seems! These Hebrews in their graves,
      Close by the street of this fair seaport town . . . . .
How came they here? What burst of Christian hate,
      What persecution, merciless and blind
Drove o'er the sea—that desert desolate—
      These Ishmaels and Hagars of mankind?
They lived in narrow streets and lanes obscure,
      Ghetto and Judenstrass, in mirk and mire;
Taught in the school of patience to endure
      The life of anguish and the death of fire.

Huge Benefits for the World and for Jews Due to the Christian
Misprisoning of the Hebrew Bible
These usurpations and distortions would all seem to be travesties.
I think, however, such stern judgment on the "misprisoning" of the

Jewish Bibles, to use Harold Bloom's preferred word, was temporally acceptable, even though that temporary travesty persisted for nearly two thousand years. For the obstruction could not and would not be eternal, and not to understand the extraordinary benefits from the symbiotic capture of the Jewish Bible by the powerful Christian church is to be severely myopic. Of course the Jews suffered defamation and death. But consider the alternative. Had Christianity *not* appropriated the Jewish Bible to accompany the New Testament, it is almost a given that the Torah would, in the course of twenty centuries, have vanished into the confinement of the ghettos and become at best a significant oddity, a book like *Gilgamesh* or *The Tibetan Book of the Dead*, known by title by a few, and read by fewer. But by being preserved openly in the West, and later in the whole world by Christianity, both books penetrated every level of culture, and spirit in the last two millennia. They were ripped out of Asia and presented universally, albeit in different outfits, to the people of the Earth, in translations seldom made by Jews but nevertheless magnificent. As a result of the appropriation of its Hebrew Bible, the Christian Bible presented its tales, poems, and concepts, and invented and defined huge vocabularies in most spoken languages. Joined together, the Jewish covenants became and remain, as no one would dispute, one of the most important books of the world. And this dual Bible gave not only speech and story to other languages but a sphere of thought, mood, and reference that have shaped and continue to shape the languages of the world.

To help understand the benefits of appropriation, I offer a small travesty. Consider the Elgin marbles that reside in the British Museum today rather than on the Acropolis, taken there by Lord Elgin in 1806. They consist of a Parthenon frieze by Phidias, a caryatid, and a column from the Erechtheum. Whatever the motives, their appropriation by the English was an undeniable act of preservation, but one with grave aesthetic consequences to the statues themselves. In the 1920s, for purposes of cleanliness, the Elgin marbles were sandblasted, which removed their old patina as if they, too, like Greek gods and Greek scripture, were Romanized by the alien owners. Had the English not sequestered the Elgin marbles, their survival would have been, on the basis of the survival of their companion pieces, certain. And the sandblasting was more degrading aesthetically than any weather or pollution threat in Athens. But at least the Elgin marbles have been for nearly two centuries the showpiece of classical Greek sculpture to the world, which is no mean accomplishment.

So the Jewish Bible and its companion New Testament have also survived with splendor, and the Jewish Bible has been given a great worldliness by its dramatic marriage to its offspring and rival. In translation—from Latin *translatio*, "a carrying over"—that treasure which is the Bible has been carried over in the extraordinary translations of the Vulgata, of Luther, Tyndale, and the King James—and that is reward enough.

Anti-Judaism in the
New Testament

New Light of the Gospels

In CONSIDERING JEWS as the people of the New Testament—those who received and those who did not receive Yeshua as the messiah—George W. E. Nickelsburg in "Jews and Christians in the First Century: The Struggle over Identity" states categorically,

> That the first "Christians" were Jewish followers of Jesus of Nazareth is indisputable. At the very least, Paul attests this in 1 Cor. 15.5–7. Thus, while it may seem tautological, it is worth emphasizing that Christianity begins among *Jews* who are *distinguished from other Jews* by virtue of their belief in the special status or role(s) of Jesus of Nazareth. Thus, from the beginning certain Jews (i.e., Christian Jews) isolated a particular factor as crucial to their self-identity as Jews.[20]

The aim of this translation of the last book of the Bible should provide open reading for Jews, Christians, and all peoples and faiths or nonfaiths, without exclusion, without worry whether one is of the elect or the eternally damned. Jews should be able to read this book of marvels, of their authorship, about themselves, about some Jews who believe they have found the Jewish messiah, whose offspring become known as Messianics or Christians. It is imperative to remember that it is not the

20. See George W. E. Nickelsburg, "Jews and Christians in the First Century: The Struggle over Identity," *Neotestamentica* 27(2) (1993): 367.

gentiles (non-Jews) but a body of Jews who nourish and first proclaim Yeshua to be their messiah. Near the end of the first century, these Messianic Jews are called "Christians," which is "Messianic" in Greek translation. The Messianic Jews have a different name for themselves in Greek, "Christians"—hence, the popular confusion by way of names of first separating Jew from Christian, of separating Yeshua's family, followers, and ultimately Yeshua himself from his people and his faith. Yeshua was a rabbi of the synagogue, not a priest of the church. This translation—having made Yeshua's Judaism obvious through its restoration of Jewish names and its annotation and afterword—should encourage Jews to read the New Testament without terror, without fear for their very lives and souls. If that degree of enlightenment is accomplished, apart from literary aspirations, this version will be a happy one.

One cannot alter scripture to eliminate angry slurs, nor erase a resultant history of good-news gospels bringing bad news to Jews. The gospels have been the significant factor during dark centuries of dismal exclusion of the Jew from ordinary society. However, once the gospels are absolutely and clearly understood as a book by Jews arguing among themselves about authority and dominion, we have a new book, with new light, and that light invites us to read one of the essential wonders of spirit and art. In this sense, the Jews should be as deeply concerned readers of the Greek Covenant as they are of the Hebrew Bible, for, however it is presented, it is their history, too, of the last Jewish prophet and of their people—not of Europeans, Australians, or Chinese—and it is a history they share with later Christians and the world. Christians in turn should be able to recognize their origin, to read the New Testament as a book about a Jewish messiah, to share the book with Jews and the world, and read it *without* the grave weight of Christian shame and guilt for the gospels' condemnations and polemical exclusions.

In regard to the New Testament as a tract against Jews, Krister Stendahl, a Christian scholar, speaks of Christian complicity in making the New Testament the first instrument of anti-Semitism. He speaks of the burden that Christianity carries for its record of misuse of its developing majority status with regard to the Jewish minority:

But the Christians burdened by the horrendous history of anti-Semitism have urgent reasons to recognize how the rhetoric of a fledgling and beleaguered minority turned into the aiding and abetting of lethal hatred when endowed with the power of being in the majority. Anti-Semitism could be branded the most persistent heresy of Christian theology and practice.[21]

Anti-Semitism begins its decisive and horrendous world history in the New Testament. Yet had anyone attempted to accuse Yeshua or Paul of not being a Jew, he would have been scandalized.[22] And, by extension, Jeremiah, Isaiah, and Amos were no less harsh in their internal denunciations of Jews; yet theirs is not received as anti-Judaism but self-criticism for purposes of higher virtue. How does such criticism differ in the New Testament?

The circumstance that permits a polemic against the Jew in the Covenant is the misrepresentation of the historical period and the identity of the contending parties. Internal squabbles between Jewish sects during the life of Yeshua are presented in the gospels as shivering conflicts between foreign forces, of gentile Christians without Jewish identity against Jews. How did such flagrant distortions enter the gospels? Although the gospels' narrations read as the history of the life and death of Yeshua, they are not historical documents of key days in Jerusalem but late compositions imposing the political interest and theological professions of a later period on an earlier one. They invent actions and conversations. They devise new personages—such as the figure of Judas, meaning the Jew—in a rehashed version of the traditional betrayer tale, and they shape the character of known personages, such

21. See Krister Stendahl, "Anti-Semitism," in *The Oxford Companion to the Bible*, ed. Bruce M. Metzger and Michael D. Coogan (New York: Oxford University Press, 1993), 34.

22. Through the letters, Paul speaks of himself as a Jew certain that the Jewish messiah has come. In Galatians 2.14–15, he rebukes Peter—whom he addresses as "Cephas," Greek for *Kefa*—for not acting like a Jew,

> I said to Kefa,
> Before them all, "If you a Jew are living
> Like a gentile and not as a Jew lives,
> How can you force gentiles to live like Jews?"
> We, who are Jews by birth and not gentile
> Sinners . . .

as the benevolent Pilate and his soldiers, who unwillingly crucify yet also love and believe in the divinity of their victim. The gospel narration, without annotation to contextualize these compositions, cannot be easy reading for a Jew. Who wishes to see oneself portrayed as deeply evil, demonic, and destined for eternal condemnation?

As noted, we possess no fact about the historical Yeshua other than a faith knowledge of his death by Roman crucifixion. But we know that during his lifetime he had proponents, for within a hundred years of his death his descendants developed a new form of Messianic Judaism. During Yeshua's lifetime, he was a local rabbi of Galilee and Judea, with a following. By anachronistic retelling, the events of his life became a black-and-white conflict between divine and demonic forces. And in the letters, which precede the gospels by decades, we know nothing about Yeshua other than that he was the foretold messiah and crucified.

The horrifying denunciations reflect the fury of a new sect denouncing its parent, inflamed by Rome, textual corruption, and patristic exegesis. The holy books seem to justify the bleak history of Christian oppression and the slaying of Jews for being Jews. So it is perfectly understandable why the gospels, though Jewish books, have become a *noli me tangere*— don't-touch-me—terrain for Jewish readers. As a result, even today, apart from scholars who in the last decades have turned importantly to the New Testament, Jews at all levels of education instinctively hold the New Testament at bay as a dread document, not to be read, whose subtext signifies death to the Jews.

The time is long overdue for translations and editions of the New Testament in English that permit the reader to see beyond the demonization of those outside the later Christian fold. The special attack on Jews must be shown to be implausible, since Yeshua and those he attends are Jews. With that knowledge, his love for the hurt, the hopeless, and those harrowed by poverty of body and thought might prevail. The gospels are unequaled works of art and spirit, extraordinary achievements that should not be rejected because of their sectarian blemishes. The itinerant Yeshua, wise in the tradition of mythical Gautama Siddhartha, Laozi, and all of the great oral teachers on the continent of Asia, where Yeshua lived and died, deserves more. Only with joy should the covenant be received, and by everybody. It contains the poetic speech of the last charismatic Jewish prophet. For those who receive him as the messiah, he gave word of life here, of pain here, and of salvation. For those without belief in his messiahship, he remains, like Socrates or the Buddha, an articulate wisdom figure whose word is indispensable to the life of the spirit.

On Authorship and
Absence of Sources

The Gospels' Unknown Sources

THE PUZZLE of the gospels' unknown sources remains the most disturbing enigma of the Greek scriptures. Much imaginative scholarship has gone into supposing oral or graphic records to fill in the nearly half century between Yeshua's death and the earliest gospels. The lonely absence of any record remains.[23] The question of unknown sources also beset the Hebrew Bible with respect to the canonical Apocrypha. By Old Testament criteria, the gospels are the canonical Apocrypha of the New Testament. As in the instance of the canonical Apocrypha of the Hebrew Bible, we also lack an original Hebrew or Aramaic text to support them. Is it not a wonder that the Church fathers were not as concerned with the absence of a source text for the canonical gospels as they were with Hebrew Bible Apocrypha? The decision by Jerome (347–419/420), the great translator of the Hebrew and Greek Bibles into Latin, to give apocryphal status to the Apocrypha (and to name the Apocrypha) was based on the absence of a Hebrew original, a measure he discarded with respect to the gospels. But that secondary status of the Apocrypha was such that the Jews, Catholics, and Greek and Russian Orthodox churches considered them deuterocanonical, and the Reformation Protestants excluded them altogether from the canon. Among those books in the Septuagint[24] accepted as canonical apocryphal writings by the Jews are

23. If the Gospel of Thomas indeed predates the canonical gospels, it would not shed any light on the narrative, since Thomas is wisdom sayings and no story. Q is the main linguistic reconstruction, which is discussed on p. 1326.

24. The Septuagint is commonly dated as a third-century B.C.E. translation, a notion still shared by the editors of the Tanak Bible published in English in 1985 by the

Tobit, Judith, the Wisdom of Solomon, and Ecclesiasticus; and accepted by the Roman Catholics are First and Second Books of Maccabees, Susanna, and extensive portions of the Book of Esther.

The main difference between the apocryphal status of the gospels and the canonical Apocrypha is that while we still have no earlier documents to authenticate or trace the tradition of the gospels, since the discovery of the Dead Sea Scrolls[25] we now have fragments in Hebrew and Aramaic for some of the Greek Septuagint Apocrypha. Such original source texts in Hebrew had been the indispensable measure for inclusion in the Bible as fully canonical scripture. Since the translation from the rest of the Hebrew Bible into the Septuagint Bible is remarkably accurate, it is reasonable to believe that the translation from the lost Hebrew scriptures into what we call the Apocrypha may be similarly accurate. The Dead Sea Scroll fragments in Hebrew of the Apocrypha, including Tobit, confirm the closeness of the translation. Indeed, Robert Alter notes in his translation of Genesis[26] that he

---

Jewish Publication Society, and standard fare in recent Bible dictionaries, but the translation dates from the second century B.C.E. and took many decades to do.

25. The Dead Sea Scrolls or Qumran Literature, containing ten scrolls and thousands of fragments, were found in 1947 in caves near Qumran on the northwest shore of the Dead Sea. The Qumran Scrolls include fragments of the Apocrypha, and we now have resolved the question of a Semitic language origin for Septuagint Apocrypha. There are one Hebrew and four Aramaic manuscripts of the book of Tobit, fragmentary of course. Tobit was officially published in Joseph A. Fitzmyer's *Discoveries in the Judaean Desert*, vol. 19 (Oxford: Clarendon Press, 1995), 1–76. And newer translation is available in the editions of the Scroll translations by Florentino Garcia Martinez, ed., *The Dead Sea Scrolls Translated: The Qumran Texts in English*, 2nd ed. (New Orleans: E. J. Brill/Grand Rapids, MI; W. B. Eerdmans, 1996), and Geza Vermes, *The Complete Dead Sea Scrolls in English* (London: Allen Lane/Penguin, 1997), 559–565. Since we now have evidence of a Hebrew original, it may be time to move Tobit from deuterocanonical to canonical status in the churches where it resides among the Apocrypha and to be admitted into the Protestant Bibles. All this is not crucial—Tobit has not even entered Writings (Kethuvim), the appropriate place in the Hebrew Bible. Yet clearly the Dead Sea Scrolls have again raised the ancient questions of canonicity that once occupied religious councils.

26. See Robert Alter, *Genesis: Translation and Commentary* (New York: W. W. Norton, 1996).

has looked to the Septuagint for alternate meanings of the Hebrew, for the second-century B.C.E. Septuagint translation is in fact older than the Hebrew Bible texts in the form we know them, as established by the Masoretic scholars centuries later into the Common Era.

As for a similar fidelity in transmitting "the lost gospel," that is, the unknown Semitic sources, written or oral, into the gospels, the parallel breaks down. There are no original fragments in Hebrew or Aramaic and little hope that any will be found. While as the Essenes came to life through the Dead Sea Scrolls and the Apocrypha found fragmentary Hebrew and Aramaic originals, no Semitic scriptures have been found as a source for the gospels.

Before the Greek scriptures is the void. Since there is not a written phrase or verse or record of an overheard word, the gospels, as they exist in Greek, are what we have to read and work with. It is unknown how they moved from Semitic sources into Greek, from conversations carried on largely in Aramaic, except for the words of Pilate, who was speaking Latin. It is not likely that Pilate ever addressed Yeshua in Latin, and whether or not Yeshua had Latin to respond to him is unknown. It is similarly unlikely that Pilate and Yeshua spoke to each other in Greek. If they spoke, it was through interpreters. And because of language differences, it is also improbable that they exchanged those austere life-and-death questions and retorts heard dramatically in the gospels. What fidelity of phrase was there when the Latin of Pilate and the Aramaic of Yeshua moved into the Greek of the gospels? No scholar has been able to answer these critical questions.

As they stand today, the subject of the Greek scriptures is the history of early first-century Jews. However, the writings send both early Jewish and later Christian signals, reflecting a perception of a century or two after the events. It is inconceivable that these accounts about Yeshua the Mashiah were not deeply adjusted or invented in the course of their establishment in Greek by the emerging churches, which were not anxious to own up to Rome's execution of a seditious rabbi.[27] As

27. Raymond E. Brown, in *An Introduction to the New Testament* (New York: Doubleday, 1997), notes in his foreword, "Most of the main NT figures and possibly all the writers were Jews, and NT affirmations have had a major role (often devastating) in relations between Jews and Christians" (xi).

for specific additions to the gospels, there are the well-known "orphan endings" appended to Mark. The "longer ending to Mark" adds a true resurrection scene. Its initial absence in Mark raises questions as to what the model was for the resurrection accounts in the later gospels. The resurrection scene, like the entire gospel narration, leads back to its formation during the gap after Yeshua's death around 30 B.C.E. and the penning of the first gospel by Mark at least four decades after the crucifixion.[28] Once the evangelist Mark—or rather the unknown figure who in the second century was designated as Mark—wrote the earliest gospel, there began the amorphous period of the shaping of the gospels, the redactions, the orphan contributions, and the Christianizing of Jewish events into the narrations that exist today. This writing and shaping of the gospels occurred during the later part of the first century and well into the second. By the third century, despite small variations indicated in brackets in the competing texts of today, the gospels found their final form.

As for that strangely silent gap of about forty to fifty years between the crucifixion and the first gospel, were we to come upon in some cave or burial site the equivalent of the Dead Sea Scrolls of the Essenes or the Nag Hammadi Library of the Gnostics (gifts of the mid-1940s), imagine the monumental news of the discovery of an ur-gospel or letters composed in Hebrew or Aramaic, shortly after Yeshua's death, recording the circumstances of Yeshua's life and death and his messianic movement. Such information would have unimaginable consequences in regard to our understanding of the early formation of Christian Judaism, which by the end of the second century, as accounted in Acts and in the letters, had evolved into Christianity. Its resemblance to or departure from the extant gospels would test and perhaps reshape existing Christian doctrine and faith.

---

28. Paul, who like the evangelists, did not personally know Yeshua, wrote and died during the period before the gospels were formulated, but his work was apparently not known, or if known, not accounted for, in the gospels and so in no way serves as a source or bridge to the gospels.

Authorship

The names of the evangelists are, as Robert W. Funk and Roy W. Hoover observe in their introduction to *The Five Gospels*,[29] "guesses or perhaps the result of pious wishes." About a century after Yeshua's death, the names occur in the writing of the later Church father Papias (ca. 130 C.E.), as reported by Eusebius (d. 325), who suggested the names Matthew and Mark. Matthew, who introduces himself in Matthew 9.9 as the tax collector, is identified in Mark 2.14 as Levi. As for Luke, Funk and Hoover say, "Like the other attributions, this one, too, is fanciful." And John (ca. 180 C.E.) "was produced by a 'school' of disciples, probably in Syria."[30] They sum up: "All the gospels originally circulated anonymously. Authoritative names were later assigned to them by unknown figures in the early church." They affirm what Emily Dickinson perceived in the uncertainty of the blurry faces behind the books in her lines: "The Bible is an antique Volume— / Written by Faded Men." The additional cognomens of Matthew the lion, Mark the ox, Luke the man, and John the eagle derive fancifully from the four living creations in Revelation 4.7.

The tradition of false attribution relates to the pseudepigrapha, which includes many intertestamental scriptures or noncanonical apocrypha

---

29. See Robert W. Funk, Roy W. Hoover, and the Jesus Seminar, eds., *The Five Gospels: The Search for the Authentic Words of Jesus: New Translation and Commentary* (New York: Macmillan, 1993), 20.

30. The formation of the Book of John is the most intriguing and, because of its separate sources from the Synoptics, has given rise among scholars to much speculation. Frank Kermode tells us, "Earlier in the present century there were those who strongly believed John to have been related to a particular form of Gnosticism, the *Mandaean*. This belief was abandoned after the discovery of the Dead Sea Scrolls, which were the work of Jewish writers before the time of John, and which anticipated some of his characteristic imagery and habits of thought. John is now seen to derive from a tradition that is fundamentally Jewish, however influenced by Hellenistic ideas. Such considerations and others, such as the accuracy of his Palestinian topography, have induced most scholars to reject the view that John's was a late theological reworking of the material, lacking direct contact with the original tradition. It is now commonly thought that the Fourth has sources as old as, though largely independent of, those available to the Synoptics." See Robert Alter and Frank Kermode, eds., *The Literary Guide to the Bible* (Cambridge, MA: Harvard University Press, 1967), 43.

assembled largely in the centuries between the closing of the Hebrew Bible and the canonization of the New Testament.[31] Most of the traditional names given the books of the Hebrew Bible—the Psalms of David, Solomon's Song of Songs, the three Isaiahs—also fall into the category of the pseudepigraphical.

The earliest and most reliable texts with regard to both author and validity of the Greek are Paul's letters, which were written as letters, not scripture, but whose inclusion in the canon made them scripture. By and large they have fewer problems of sources and later tampering by inventing hands—by Church fathers, scribes, and evangelists—that make the gospels a subject of intense debate. However, Paul's Pastoral Letters to Titus and to Timothy are not authentic, along with the letters to the Ephesians, Colossians, and Thessalonians. It is hard to understand how most of the pseudo-Pauline Letters slipped into the canon, especially the very weak Pastoral Letters. There are so many fascinating and useful apocryphal documents from the treasure of the pseudepigrapha, including the infancy documents attributed to James, Matthew, and Thomas, on which so many church biographies and major religious paintings are based; other fabled acts of Peter, John, and Paul; and apocalypses of Peter, Paul, and Thomas.

As a historical figure, a Jew born in the Hellenistic city of Tarsos, Paul as a person, name, and author is the least controversial of any figure associated with books of the New Testament. And his actuality as a person,

31. The compendium of pseudepigrapha related to the Hebrew Bible (though most of it is in Greek and other languages) is collected in *The Old Testament Pseudepigrapha*, ed. James H. Charlesworth (Garden City, NY: Doubleday, 1983–1985). *The Other Bible*, ed. Willis Barnstone (San Francisco: Harper and Row, 1984), contains pseudepigrapha as well as noncanonical apocrypha of Torah, New Testament Gnostic scriptures, the Dead Sea Scrolls, and other intertestamental writings. There is an overlapping in this terminology, "pseudepigrapha" meaning "works of false attribution and noncanonical apocrypha." I use "intertestamental" when referring to works not necessarily written between the last books of the Hebrew Bible and the conjectured dates of the Greek scriptures, but in the wider sense of the gap of centuries (first B.C.E. to fifth C.E.) between the canonization of the Hebrew Bible and that of the Greek scriptures. During that period many works were written, ascribed to everyone from Moses to the evangelists, hence pseudepigraphical, with aspirations to find their way back into the Hebrew Bible or into the not-yet-canonized New Testament.

in the seven letters categorically attributed to him, bestows a historic liveliness to what he wrote. In the conceptual, not the manuscript, sense, he was the great translator. He transposed biblical law into Christian practice; he seems to have transformed the Jewish hope for the messiah into a Christian accomplishment. In the same way that he converted Shaul into Paul, in the diaspora synagogues of the Mediterranean and the Near East, Paul translated Judaism into what after his life became a strong foundation for Christianity.

There are problems, however, with this traditional interpretation of Paul's role in giving us the earliest scripture. First, it must be said that Paul knew Yeshua only "after the flesh," and so wrote from accounts and faith. However, Burton Mack points out in great detail in *Who Wrote the New Testament? The Making of the Christian Myth* how the letters do not reflect the scene of those early followers of Yeshua:

> There are two problems with this view [that of Paul's perception of Christianity]. Paul's conception of Christianity is not evident among the many texts from the early Jesus movements. The other is that Paul's gospel was not comprehensible and persuasive for most people of his time, including many other Christians, as we shall see. For historians this means that the traditional picture of Christian origins derived from Paul's letters is suspect and needs to be revised. Instead of reading the material from the Jesus movements through the eyes of Paul, we need to read Paul as a remarkable movement in the history of the Jesus movement.[32]

To whatever extent Paul reflects the actual moment or determines the future Yeshua movement (which is more probable), the existence of his letters, despite early controversy about authenticity, is the most historical frame we have in the writings.

As for the authorship of the gospels, the complexity of the problem and absence of documentary evidence make description of their emergence from the shade difficult. However, we do have factual knowledge of their final emergence, selection, and late canonization. In that final form, the

---

32. See Burton L. Mack, *Who Wrote the New Testament? The Making of the Christian Myth* (San Francisco: HarperSanFrancisco, 1995), 99.

scriptures, consisting of the gospels, letters, apostolic writings and rewritings, represent a small number from a mass of texts that were floating around the ancient world—those rejected pseudepigrapha—including many extant apocalypses, gospels, infancy gospels, psalm books, wisdom poetry, and acts. As mentioned above, by the fourth century the ground was established for the Christian selection and canonization of both the New Testament and the "Christian" Hebrew Bible (based on the Septuagint). Between 325 and 330 C.E., Constantine ordered Eusebius to make a selection of writings that he copied and included in a Christian book of holy scriptures. These are listed in his *Ecclesiastical History* 3, 25. Jerome's translations of the scriptures into Latin were done in 382 C.E. These translation and editorial events, along with Augustine's arguments for a more inclusive selection from the Hebrew Bible, made way for the Hebrew Bible and Christian scriptures as we have them today in the Latin West.

Selection and Canonization of Scriptures

With regard to method and purpose, here are some technical thoughts on the gospels, their selection, canonization, and the names of the active cast in them.

In the Western church, the New Testament was formally canonized in Rome at the beginning of the fifth century. Athanasios[33] was the first to use the word "canon" (from the Greek κανών, *kanon*, a measuring rod, and, in second-century koine, rule of truth), and his canon, listing the present books of the Greek scriptures, was first proposed in his "Thirty-ninth Easter Letter," written in 369 C.E. It was probably approved at the Synod of Rome in 382, and confirmed by papal declaration in 405. Yeshua's citing of passages from the Torah might have been directly from the Hebrew Bible, not as we have it in the gospels, where the authors and redactors went to the well-known second-century B.C.E. Septuagint translation of the Jewish Bible into Greek.

---

33. Bishop (later saint) Athanasios (ca. 297–373) was a strong opponent of Arianism, Christianity's most powerful heresy, concerning the nature of Yeshua. It was widespread, diverse, among emperors and clergy, and lasted until around 560 when, under Pope Gregory I, it disappeared in Italy.

Details About the Texts of the Gospels

The New Testament, as we have it, is in Greek, containing among its twenty-seven books four gospels, which, in probable order of their composition, are Mark, Matthew, Luke and John (Markos, Mattityahu, Loukas, and Yohanan). There is an uneven consensus today that Mark precedes Matthew and that Mark used Q, the hypothetical sayings source, whose recent reconstruction by the members of the Jesus Seminar and others was accomplished by collating coincidences of language in Yeshua's sayings. Yet some prominent scholars still give precedence to Matthew and/ or question that there was Q.[34]

Q is from the German word *Quelle*, meaning "source." Our speculations about Q source texts for the New Testament go back at least 150 years. In the twentieth century, Rudolf Bultmann[35] and B. H. Streeter[36] each published major studies on the two-source theory, which posits that Matthew and Luke derived not only from the Markan account of the life of Yeshua, but also from a hypothetical Q text. With the 1945

---

34. In his "The Gospel according to the 'Jesus Seminar'" in *The Emergence of the Christian Religion: Essays on Early Christianity* (Harrisburg, PA: Trinity Press International, 1997), Birger A. Pearson takes on, with meticulous fury, the notions of the Jesus Seminar with respect to their attempts to measure authenticity in the gospels. The Jesus Seminar, a group of hundreds of liberal American theologians, asserts that most of the gospels are spurious and restrict the authentic *historical* (as opposed to the *canonized*) Yeshua to Yeshua's sayings, which they estimate as less than twenty percent of scripture. The notion of voting and ascribing degrees of truth to passages is comparable to searching for historic events in Homer; the allusions to events are there, but the details of those allusions, which contain the great interest, are certainly the least historical. I prefer the approach of Paula Fredriksen in *Jesus of Nazareth, King of the Jews: A Jewish Life and the Emergence of Christianity* (New York: Knopf, 1999), who begins with the premise that the single verifiable fact of Yeshua's life is that he was a Jew crucified around 30 C.E. and then speculates.

35. Rudolf Bultmann, *The History of the Synoptic Tradition*, trans. John Marsh (New York: Harper and Row, 1966). Bultmann sought and ultimately opposed the notion of discovering "a historical Jesus," since it was impossible and theologically illegitimate, and worldly proof took dominion over faith.

36. Burnett Hillman Streeter, *The Four Gospels: A Study of Origins* (London: Macmillan, 1930).

discovery of the Coptic-Gnostic Gospel of Thomas as one of the documents in the Nag Hammadi Library,[37] found buried near the ancient town of Chenoboskion in Upper Egypt, containing Yeshua's sayings, about thirty-five percent of which coincide with those sayings of the Synoptics (Mark, Matthew, Luke), there has been a major new impetus to pursue the Q hypothesis. A major book on Q and its actual reconstruction is John Kloppenborg's *Formation of Q* (1987). Burton L. Mack has carried the reconstruction further in his *Lost Gospel, The Book of Q & Christian Origins* (1993). Following the model of Kloppenborg in his *Q Parallels* (1987), Mack reconstructed an original text in a fresh translation. The Jesus Seminar translation of *The Complete Gospels: Annotated Scholars Version* (1992–1994) provides a two-column reconstruction (based on Luke and Matthew) of Q, which is less easy to read, but which provides helpful annotation. And since the Mack there is finally *The Critical Edition of Q*, under James M. Robinson, a new masterful 600-page work, with a 106-page introduction, including the Coptic for Thomas, and academic translations into English, German, and French.[38]

Since the late eighteenth century, there has been an attempt to apply historical approaches to the oral and script transmission of the gospels and to speculate on order, source, and veracity. These questions will be debated and are not likely be resolved unless there are major finds of earlier versions of the gospels that cast specific light on questions of New Testament source and composition, or unanticipated related documents. In his introduction to the New Testament in *The Literary Guide to the Bible*, Frank Kermode sums up the problems of order of composition and of Q: "Beginning in the 1830s the view gained ground that priority must be accorded to Mark, and it is probably still the majority opinion that Matthew and Luke used Mark, augmenting him from a collection of sayings (Q) and also from sources peculiar to themselves; there are many variants of this view. Recently, however, inconsistencies

---

37. James M. Robinson, ed., *The Nag Hammadi Library* (San Francisco: Harper and Row, 1977).

38. James M. Robinson, Paul Hoffman, and John S. Kloppenborg, eds., *The Critical Edition of Q* (Minneapolis: Fortress Press, 2000).

and improbabilities in the standard explanation have led to a revival by some of the old assumption that Matthew came first. Other scholars retain the Markan priority but dispense with Q."[39]

Whatever the order, these gospels are the only canonical ones that we acknowledge, and surprisingly we have them in Greek outfit rather than Aramaic or late Hebrew. Traditionally there was more interest in restoring a hypothetical source of information, with little regard for its passage as translation from its Semitic roots and Jewish thought. In the last decades, however, there has been a sea change of interest in Yeshua as an Aramaic-speaking observant Jew, whose words have been presented at one remove in Greek and, for those in the West, at two removes, going from Aramaic to Greek and then on to the second language of their translation (and frequently in past at three removes, if they pass from Aramaic to Greek to Jerome's Latin and then into a West European language). In his *Changing Faces of Jesus*, Geza Vermes attempts to restore "the vague contours of the real Jesus, the charismatic Hasid," and he comments on the language of Yeshua and of his Aramaic-speaking followers, on the virtual absence of a record of their speech, and affirms seminally that the Greek New Covenant is a translation of a Jewish ideology acculturated by an alien pagan Graeco-Roman world:

> The language of Jesus and his Galilean disciples was Aramaic, a Semitic language skin to Hebrew, then spoken by most Palestinian Jews. It was in Aramaic that Jesus taught and argued with friends and foes. The linguistically authentic form of his teaching, with the exception of a dozen or so Aramaic words preserved in the Gospels, soon disappeared. If there ever existed a written Aramaic Gospel, it did not survive for long; we certainly no longer have it. At the same time, as a consequence of the success of the primitive church in the Greek-speaking Gentile (i.e., non-Jewish) world, the whole message transmitted by the apostles—the Gospels, the letters, and the rest—was recorded in Greek, which is the earliest form of the New Testament that we possess. But this Greek New Testament is a "translation" of the genuine thoughts and ideas of the Aramaic-

39. See Alter and Kermode, *Literary Guide to the Bible*, 377.

thinking and -speaking Jesus and of his immediate disciples, a transplantation not just into a totally different language, but also a translation of the ideology of the communication and in his familiar Semitic tongue.[40]

The Greek texts we have are mirrors of lost shadows of Jewish wisdom and thought, and of Aramaic speech and possible script. Although original Semitic texts are unlikely to materialize, above ground or below, one purpose of this translation is, through restoration of Semitic names, to reflect more shadows of those disappeared figures and events.

With regard to the preserved Greek gospels and all the books of the covenant, as noted, this bundle of scripture officially entered the canon in Rome in 405 C.E. In Bruce M. Metzger's *Text of the New Testament, It's Transmission, Corruption, and Restoration,*[41] which deals authoritatively on the approximately five thousand manuscripts that contain all or part of the New Testament, there is abundant information about the survival, changes, emendations, and copying tactics, but absolutely no light on the essential mystery by which Yeshua's words and a history of his life and death migrated into this plethora of early Greek texts. In addition to these untraceable canonical gospels, there are seventeen gospels now included in *The Complete Gospels: Annotated Scholars Version,* edited by Robert J. Miller, including the Gospel of Thomas, which exists in Coptic and fragmentarily in Syriac and Greek (the latter in portions that exist in the *Oxyrhynchus Papyri*). But we also do not know how or from what tongues the Gospel of Thomas was transmitted into Greek, though surely there was an Aramaic or Hebrew source, since only in those languages could one witness and record Yeshua's sayings. So what some scholars claim to be the most authentic of the gospels with regard to Yeshua's wisdom utterances, remains, like all the gospels, a mystery with regard to source.

The Gospel of Thomas, itself a discovery of enormous value—the so-called Fifth Gospel—suggests new possibilities as it casts doubt on

---

40. Geza Vermes, *The Changing Faces of Jesus* (New York: Viking Compass, 2001), 286, 2–3.

41. Bruce M. Metzger, *The Text of the New Testament: Its Transmission, Corruption, and Restoration,* 3rd enlarged ed. (New York: Oxford University Press, 1992).

some older systems of the formation of the gospels. Thomas has passages that parallel the synoptic gospels, and whether indeed it was assembled around 50–55 C.E., as has been asserted, or whether it simply represents a different line of preservation of Yeshua's sayings, it reveals an ancient, completely distinct Yeshua, who is also free of the problems of the narration of the canonical gospels, since it has none. It is uncertain which is the partial source of the other, the gospels or Thomas, or whether both draw on hypothetical Q. Yeshua in Thomas, like the Buddha and Laoze, lives by his speech rather than the myths that his person and sayings later incited. With only dialogue and no background events, Thomas reveals a Yeshua of metaphysical aphorisms, who breathes the spirit of the formal Gnostic scriptures of the Nag Hammadi Library and of their dissident solitude.[42] As a Gnostic version of early Christianity, found in Coptic translation from the Greek, these wisdom sayings early went into hiding (they were found buried in Egyptian soil in a leather pouch in Egypt) and did not publicly survive long enough to have gone through the altering of copying, redaction, scribal insertions, and changes which is the history of the canonical gospels. Nor did Thomas have a narration that was exposed to the Christianizing handiwork of later priestly redactors.

Faith and History

One may ask: Why is it necessary to verify the gospels by finding an earlier version, a source, an original, and why, without an apparent parentage, do the gospels stand in limbo as documents accepted on faith rather than confirmed by history? Why should the gospels need their lost historical sources? We do not ask for Homer's sources. We do not look askance because the Genesis flood story has almost identical mirrors in much earlier Mesopotamian writings. But Homer is literature and myth, and no longer a religion requiring "truth" and belief. And early Genesis is primeval myth of religion and stands self-sufficiently alone. For most readers, however, the gospels utter a historical statement. They tell the life of an actual wandering Mediterranean rabbi

42. There are other late sources for a tradition of Yeshua's sayings, especially in Coptic, Syriac, and Arabic, which may be found in Marvin Meyer's *Unknown Sayings of Jesus* (San Francisco: HarperSanFrancisco, 1998).

healer and exorcist in the Eastern Roman empire, who irked its local rulers enough to be condemned to suffer Roman political execution, for reasons that remain unclear. Those four biographies, the good news of a messiah, cannot escape into myth and literature. In a word, faith makes the documents self-validating; but history leaves them undocumented beyond themselves.

The events in the evangels concern Jews in the city of Jerusalem and the districts of Judea and Galilee. They are in Greek, a language native to Jews of the diaspora, especially in Alexandrian Egypt, Greece, and the former Greek empire in Asia Minor, but not native to the Jews of Israel, of Judea, Samaria, and Galilee. Consider John the Baptizer. Yeshua's precursor and model was not baptizing in Greek. Not only is the language of the gospels suspect, but the time of their composition raises questions. Since the gospels were composed probably between 70 and 95, none of their reputed evangelists witnessed Yeshua in his lifetime. The gospels did not rise from nothingness. How, then, did their authors come upon their account? As previously mentioned, we have hypotheses of origin and linguistic markers that go back to Hebrew phrases. The existence of the Secret Gospel of Mark, the Secret Book of John, the Gospel of Philip, and the Gospel of Thomas, among other extant noncanonical gospels, offers information on other ways that the speech of Yeshua has reached us. But no original Semitic document in the languages of Yeshua from under the sand or in a cave has come to light.

Scholars are looking—not archeologically but through existent texts or ones they wish to be existent.[43] Burton L. Mack tells a mystery story of a lost gospel in *The Lost Gospel*, which is based on his composite of Yeshua's sayings from sundry sources. Mack makes the Yeshua community vividly real. He writes, "Jesus was much more like a Cynic-teacher than either a Christ-savior or a messiah with a program

43. The dry sands of Syria, Israel, and Egypt are likely areas for archeological search, since only in virtually waterless areas can papyrus survive, and even later parchment copies, a stronger medium, do not do well in damp climates. Although three major religions (as well as classical Western literature) are based on common interweaving scriptures, there is relatively little exploration. When there are discoveries, enormous political, scholarly, and religious problems materialize to delay or frustrate further exploration. Ancient documents do not carry the economic and political clout of oil and gas.

for the reformation of second-Temple Jewish society and religion.[44] Yet we scarcely know who the historical teacher was, or what tendencies he shared with the Cynics, the Gnostics, the Essenes, the Pharisees, the healing and miracle-making Hasidim (the charismatic holy men), and the messianic tradition of Isaiah. The main documents, the gospels, are examined for clues, as the theogony of Homer is examined to understand Greece, war, and gods of antiquity. And, curiously, the waves of intense yet mutating theory that saturate literature, film, art, history, and anthropological studies are hardly perceptible in biblical studies, which are usually a strange mix of faith, tradition, and academic inquiry. Nevertheless, a common goal among imaginative thinkers is to look for a historical figure called Yeshua and bring him to life.

For reconstructing the life and times of Yeshua, we lack the documentary material of historians, but there is a story of an extraordinary man; there is a new early Jewish sect vying for dominion over other sects. Yeshua's followers were the sect who saw Yeshua as their teacher, leader, and messiah. In all religions, then and now, such conflict between sects is usual. However, one salient aspect of the historical enigma of the gospels is their view of Rome. One may ask how in the New Testament the military leaders from Rome, Pontius Pilate and his centurion who executed Yeshua, are presented with generously phrased understanding of their difficult assignments. Indeed, they are ultimately seen as ruefully carrying out their role of deicide. The benign view of Yeshua's Roman crucifiers is balanced by the virulently condemnatory view of the Pharisees, who were strong opponents of the Roman occupation and their Hasmonean clerics. Since the gospels reflect a Roman and later church take on the crucifixion of Yeshua, the Romans are spared opprobrium, while opponents of Rome are defamed. Where this leaves Yeshua is the enigma. Since crucifixion was reserved strictly for political insurrection, Yeshua could not have been perceived by his executioners with sympathy, as the scriptures convey. At the same time, why exactly did they crucify him? As Paula Fredriksen points out,[45] the level of insurrection

---

44. See Burton L. Mack, *The Lost Gospel: The Book of Q & Christian Origins* (San Francisco: HarperSanFrancisco, 1993), 245.

45. See Paula Fredriksen, *Jesus of Nazareth, King of the Jews: A Jewish Life and Emergence of Christianity* (New York: Knopf, 1999), 8–9.

must have been minor, since only Yeshua and none of his followers were killed. Had there been a seriously subversive revolutionary movement, such as the mass rallies in Galilee against Rome that preceded and followed Yeshua's death, there would have been crucifixions galore to accompany "the messiah's" execution.

For many years I have pondered how the gospels could be relentlessly an apology for Rome when its essence, regardless of presumed later tampering in copying and redacting by its editors, was established between the years 70, of Mark's gospel, and around 150, the final edition, years of growth but of vast public persecution by Rome, from the catacombs of Rome to the cave chapels and communities in Cappadocia in central Anatolia. Since even despite a few second-century fragments (and these now considered wishfully dated), there is no extant copy in Greek of the gospels before the fourth century, and these are at best fragmentary. I had to assume, *faute de mieux*, that the most furious Romanizing of the gospel texts occurred between the early decades of the fourth century when Constantine became the first Christian emperor of the Roman Empire, and Athanasios's canon in 367. I asked Professor David Trobisch, the distinguished German manuscript historian, about the anomaly of Christian loyalty to their persecutors. His response: "Think of the perfect parallel in Josephus." Here was the greatest of Jewish historians, I realized, who details the day-to-day marches of Roman armies and the concerns of their commander, Titus, as he heads to Rome. And Josephus takes the same line as the gospels, defending the action of the Roman armies that in 70 were to level the walls, raze the city, destroy the Temple, crucify many of its inhabitants, and exile Jews and Christian Jews alike in the greatest diaspora since the sixth-century B.C.E. Babylonian Captivity, which resulted in the destruction of the first Temple. "Why did Josephus placate the Romans?" His response: "Because he was a Jew, living in Rome in a fine villa, in pleasant captivity, and were he to have taken any other line opposing the emperor it would have been his end, exile or the sword."

To survive and grow under the Roman Empire that demanded loyalty, Josephus and the evangels' editors had no choice if their public churches and their texts were to survive. I thought of the earlier parallel of the Maccabees, who in the second century B.C.E. had fought the invading armies of the Seleucid ruler Antiochus IV, saving Israel and Judaism from extinction, yet their Hasmonean descendants, kings and rulers, including Herod, were by the time of Yeshua both Hellenized and pro-Roman. More, even the Apocalypse, which among the twenty-seven scriptures of the Testament remains uniquely and relentlessly anti-Roman, which fully demonizes them to an alert reader, does so only allegorically, going back to the "Whore of Babylonia" and 666, a coded word for a Roman emperor Nero or Domitian or Augustus,[46] to show their furious opposition. Even Revelation could not call a Roman a Roman. With these ideas, the riddle of the political orientation in the gospels seemed to find some solution.

While the gospels of the New Testament may not fit the categories of either historical chronicle or literary fable, they join early Genesis to stand at the summit of the transcendent spirit and of world literature. It also must be stated that uncertainties of origin and sectarian bigotries do not subvert their spiritual and aesthetic impact and the grandeur of their straightforward speech. Even the twentieth century's indifferent translations, though winning few friends, have not threatened them. Especially in their older English-language incarnations, distinguished by the Tyndale and the King James Versions, the gospels are beautiful, fearful, and dramatic; they dwell in the profound labyrinths of the soul. Their poetry and vision have haunted the world. They persist as creation, parable, conspiracy, mystery, apocryphal testament, and essential holy scripture. For the majority readership of the faithful, the gospels are a manual of salvation.

46. See note 2 on Emperor Augustus in Revelation. Research at Stanford University using infrared and other technologies to read palimpsests suggests the code 666 may be 616.

How Yeshua ben Yosef Became Yeshua the Mashiah and Jesus the Christ

Hebrew Names in the Jewish Bible

In the primordial beginnings of the Torah, until Adam gave names to all cattle and to the birds of the air and to every animal of the field, their existence was unfulfilled. With a name, even the humblest ant or bleak raven had a sound to distinguish it from all other species. Names also distinguish good from bad, pleasant from foul, and are a clue to essence. After God formed Adam, and Adam completed his task of endowing all with names, we find names for deities, people, and beasts whose mere utterance implies good or evil, kindness or cruelty, tribal friend or foreign enemy.

Adam's name, meaning "earth," connects him to the earth, paralleling God's molding of Adam from the earth. In the first creation tale (Gen. 1.26), God makes one he calls not a man but an Adam, that is, "one from the earth." And again in the second creation tale (2.7), God makes Adam (אָדָם, adam) from earth (אֲדָמָה, adamah). Adam is still a man-woman. Only after Genesis 2.18, when God puts Adam to work in the garden and delivers Eve to him, does God distinguish his genderless creations by their sexes. Then Adam jubilantly cries that "from his flesh and bones / this one will be called woman / and this one man" (Gen. 2.23). And God calls Adam man, *ish* (אִישׁ), and Eve woman, *ishah* (אִשָּׁה).

Each of these early namings—indeed, most names in the Hebrew Bible—is replete with etymological puns and semantic resonances, from earthly Adam to the pleasant garden of Eden (עֵדֶן, eden), whose name means "delight." By noting the enormous importance of names in the opening passages of Genesis, we have a model for the significance of new names designed for the New Testament.

Greek and English Names in the New Testament

In choosing names for the cast of the New Testament, the authors established a semantic code for recognizing Jew, Christian, and gentile. The code, as with all codes, is often muddled, self-contradictory, and inconsistent, but it has worked both in Greek and in translations from Greek to other tongues. Through the naming and renaming of place, people, and movement, the New Testament has changed identity and position for a new cast of actors who pass distinctly as the Messianics (the Christians), and not as another Jewish faction.

How were these linguistic feats accomplished? How was time moved ahead around a hundred years to early in the second century when indeed Christians were beginning to be distinct from Jews? Here, with respect to anachronistic bias, it is important to restate that while the gospels read as contemporary history, Mark, the earliest gospel, was not formulated in Greek until at least forty or fifty years after Yeshua's crucifixion (ca. 30 C.E.) and the others up to seventy years after his lifetime.

The dissociation of the New Testament as a Jewish book begins with the conversion of Semitic names into Greek names. When referring to members of the messianic movement, the New Testament uses largely Greek or seemingly Greek names. But the Greek name is usually only a shadow of the original Hebrew name in sound and connotation. "James" is the name for Yeshua's brother, the son of Miryam, who was later head of the church in Jerusalem. English James scarcely echoes Greek *Iakobos* (Ἰάκωβος) and Hebrew *Yaakov* (יַעֲקֹב). So James is removed from his Semitic self in his new British costume. To leap from "James" back to *Yaakov* is a stretch, maybe a shocking one to the reader, because of the coded tradition of distinguishing Christian from Jew in days when they were all Jews. But once having understood how far one has been led from the Hebrew name, it should be a pleasure to return and redeem the names that Adam and his descendants dreamed up.

I have earlier noted the problems with the title of the Greek scriptures, namely, that "New Testament" is a mistranslation of the Greek title "New Covenant" based on Jerome's intermediate Latin mistranslation,

which he rendered as *Novum Testamentum*.[47] The title "New Covenant"
itself derives from Luke 22.20, Paul in 1 Corinthians 11.25, and Hebrews
8.8–13.[48] The idea of a "new covenant," a new pact with God, we must
remember, comes from Paul, who takes it directly from Jeremiah 31.31: "I
will establish a new covenant with the house of Israel." In Hebrews 8.13,
Paul quotes this famous passage in Jeremiah and writes, "In [Jeremiah's]
speaking of a 'new covenant,' he has made the first one obsolete. And
what is obsolete and growing old will soon disappear."[49] Paul, a Greek-

47. For the initial discussion of the origin of the title New Testament, please see
note 10, p. 1298. Reference to the Vulgata by Jerome should always be tempered by
the fact that we do not know if portions of the Vulgata that have come down to us
were actually done by Jerome.

In the King James Version there is an inconsistency in the translation of *diatheke*
(διαθήκη) into English. For the title *diatheke* is "Testament" as it is in 1 Corinthians
11.25. However, in Hebrews 8.8–13, the KJV translates *diatheke* as "covenant" both
in citing Jeremiah and in Paul's own speech. Hebrews 8.13 reads, "In that he saith,
A new *covenant*, hath made the first old. Now that which decayeth and waxeth old
is ready to vanish away." In defense of the KJV's inconsistency, one must applaud
the translators of the Authorized (the KJV), who avoided the painful consistencies
imposed on the text in many versions, especially in contemporary ones. Absolute consistency of translation suggests that the original word and the context it falls into in
the English text always hold the same meaning. That is not how language works. In
their preface to the Authorized, the translators say, "We have not tied ourselves to an
uniformity of phrasing, or to an identity of words, as some peradventure would wish
we had done, because they observe that some learned men somewhere have been
as exact as they could that way." Another perhaps more accurate translation from
Hebrew *berit* into Greek is the word συνθήκη (syntheke), which specifically means
"covenant" and "contract." So we would have καινὴ συνηθήκη (kaine syntheke).

48. Few today would ascribe Hebrews to Paul, though the assumption of Paul's
authorship got it its place in the canon. Hebrews, like other letters, carries Paul's
name but is of doubtful ascription.

49. There has been a raising and lowering of the place of the Old Testament in Christianity. Before the completion of the gospels, the Christian Jews, including gentile
converts, had only the Torah as their Bible. Before there was a canonized New Testament, the second-century Gnostic heretic Marcion argued for abolishing the Old
Testament. Paul's argument in Hebrews 8.13 that the "new covenant" made the "old
covenant" obsolete and that the old one would eventually disappear has been mis-
interpreted. In the changing status of the Hebrew Bible in Christianity, the effect
of the Protestant Reformation was to raise the Old Testament, doing so especially
through its translation into vernaculars, along with that of the New Testament. This

speaking Jew from Tarsos, who knew the Hebrew texts, used *diatheke* to convey its meaning in Hebrew, *berit* (בְּרִית), which is "covenant" and also a "cut" or "circumcision," as when Paul speaks of a "new circumcision of the heart" (Rom. 2.25–29).[50]

From Yeshua to Jesus

The New Testament's Greek texts were initially addressed largely to Greek-speaking Jews to persuade them that Jesus (*Iesous*—Ἰησοῦς)[51] was not, or not only, a late Jewish prophet, but was their messiah, hence the name "Christian" for their sect, "Christian" meaning "Messianic."[52] At some point in the process of voyage, the transmission from the probable Aramaic script or oral witness accounts to the Greek, the Hebrew biblical names were Hellenized; that is, they were given to us in a Greek translation or transliteration from late Hebrew or Aramaic. So, as we have seen, Yeshua (יֵשׁוּעַ or, more fully, Yehoshua the Mashiah, which comes from יְהוֹשֻׁעַ (yehoshua) and מָשִׁיחַ (mashiah), is rendered into Greek as *Iesous ho Hristos* (Ἰησοῦς ὁ Χριστος). *Iesous* is a transliteration of *Yeshua* and *Hristos* (meaning the "anointed"), being a translation of *mashiah*. Greek *Iesous ho Hristos* is in turn translated into English as "Jesus [the] Christ." Similarly, *Yohahan* (יוֹחָנָן) becomes *Ioannes* (Ἰωάννης) in Greek, *Johannes* in Latin, and "John" in English.[53]

---

was at the heart of bringing "the word of God" directly to the people and not confining it to a Latin translation associated with Rome.

50. For further discussion on new covenant, see Galatians 3.15ff.

51. See note 1 on p. 3.

52. "Messianic" or "Messianist" signifies "one who follows the messiah," which in Greek translation is "Christian." "Christian" derives from "Christ," whose transfer from Hebrew mashiah is given above.

53. In *The Masks of God: Occidental Mythology* (New York: Penguin Arkana, 1991), Joseph Campbell traces John the Baptist's garb and diet back to Elijah as described in 2 Kings 1.8, but both his baptism practices and his name go back to the water god Ea, "God of the House of Water," from the Sumerian temple city of Eridu. He writes, "In the Hellenistic period, Ea was called *Oannes*, which is in Greek *Ioannes*, Latin *Johannes*, Hebrew *Yohanan*, English *John*." Whether any of these ancient ablutions—and he might have mentioned those of the Essenes—is more than a universal wash is uncertain, but Campbell does trace the journey of the English name John back to Hebrew *Yohanan*. *Ea* (also known as Enki) goes back to both Sumerian and to Old Akkadian *hyw*, which Hebrew of Eve also goes back to, so that *Ea*

But we are not Greek-speaking Jews and gentiles, the gospels' original audience. We speak English. Why not biblical Yohanan in English rather than Greek John? Why adopt an English transcription of a Hellenized Greek transcription of Hebrew names from the Hebrew Bible? It is roundabout. Since we transcribe biblical names from the Hebrew Bible directly into English with minimum changes ("Abraham" may be written "Avraham" since the *b* and *v* in Hebrew, as in Spanish and other languages, are usually interchangeable), why not transcribe biblical names from the New Testament directly into English? And without pausing at an intermediary Greek transcription? Hellenizing "Yeshua the Mashiah" son of God, into "Jesus Christ" is comparable to Hellenizing "Yahweh" (YHWH) into "Zeus." Then Genesis would begin, "In the beginning Zeus created the heavens and the earth," and the Hebrew Bible would be consonant with the presently Hellenized New Testament. It is ridiculous and unacceptable, yet the same translators allow the Greek translation of *Sheol* in Hebrew to carry over into English as "Hades," which designates the pagan underworld in Greek religion and mythology.[54]

As for Yeshua's name, his name is key to the Hellenization and Christianization of the last Jewish prophet, who died for some Jews and later Christians as the messiah, and who in his life was known by his Jewish name and titles. For the early Christian world the life, death, and resurrection of Yeshua was the fulfillment of Jewish prophetic expectations. Yeshua was the messiah, the Lord's anointed one. George Nickelsburg elaborates:

> Early Christians oriented their world view around the belief that the crucified Jesus was exalted in heaven. There he ruled as Lord and

---

and *Eve* both have common Semitic root *hyh*, meaning "living" (as in living water), which is a common phrase both in the gospels and especially in Gnostic scriptures that analyze the Gospel of John.

54. Commonly, a dominant religious faith determines whether a creation or supernatural story is assigned to religious history or mythology; and this determination usually ascribes one's own tales to religious history and the outsider religion to mythology. Hence from our perspective, Hades is part of Greek mythology, although it has slipped into the Christian terminology in the Greek scriptures. Hell is another Germanic/Scandinavian equivalent, but *Sheol* and *Gehenna* really deserve a common place in English, and they evoke accurately and spiritually the original meaning of Jewish underworld notions.

Christ and prepared to return as God's appointed judge, who would vindicate and reward the righteous and punish their oppressors (as if they had such) and the rest of the wicked of this world. They also attached positive value to Jesus' death as a means of dealing with human sin. The categories from which these beliefs were drawn are thoroughly Jewish: the suffering and exalted servant of the Lord; the Lord's Anointed One; the one like a son of man enthroned as the executor of God's reign. Thus these Christians related their self-understanding as heirs of the Israelite tradition to their identification of the crucified and risen Jesus with the aforementioned figures of Jewish expectation. Jesus the crucified, risen, and exalted one was the key to their understanding of their tradition and the polar star by which they oriented themselves. In their view, being a Jew required that one recognize Jesus as the fulfillment of these expectations; to believe in the crucified and exalted Christ was to acknowledge the realization of God's promises to judge all flesh and to extend the divine reign throughout the cosmos.[55]

The gospels preserve the life and death of the messiah and lord of emerging Christianity, and they preserved him, without excuse or explanation, in Greek scriptures with a Greek name, which may not seem to be at all unreasonable for Greek-reading Jews and gentiles. Yes, why not translate Hebrew names into Greek for Greek readers? Yet the non-Greek reader of these names should not be required to be a textual detective to understand Yeshua's probable Jewish name and ethnicity. In the end it must be clear why and how the title of Yeshua the Mashiah[56] becomes in

55. George W. E. Nickelsburg, "Revealed Wisdom as a Criterion for Inclusion and Exclusion: From Jewish Sectarianism to Early Christianity," in Jacob Neusner and Ernest S. Frerichs, eds., *To See Ourselves as Others See Us: Christians, Jews, "Others" in Late Antiquity* (Chico, CA: Scholars Press, 1985), 2.2.6.

56. Coming upon Yeshua the Mashiah is not without complication, as we have seen. "Christ" (from Greek *Hristos*) means "anointed" or "messiah." "Jesus" (from Greek *Iesous*) can be *Yeshua* or Joshua as it is in translations from the Hebrew Bible with the exception of Everett Fox's *Five Books of Moses: A New Translation with Introduction, Commentary, and Notes* (New York: Schocken Books, 1995), which restores "Joshua" to *Yehoshua*. "Joshua" is simply an older English way of transliterating *Yeshua*. So we can have *Yeshua the Messiah* or *Joshua the Messiah* or *Yehoshua the Messiah*. We can also return "messiah" to Hebrew *mashiah*, and then have *Yehoshua Mashiah*. The

Greek Ἰησοῦς ὁ Χριστος (Iesous ho Hristos). Here, and now in other translations, the movement directly from Hebrew and Aramaic into the target languages is beginning, will persist, and perhaps will prevail.

The name "Jesus Christ" has no Hebrew resonance or linguistic identity and, as we'll see, has allowed Yeshua to pass as someone other than a Jew, to have been a gentile in his earthly life. At the crucifixion, the Roman soldiers cast lots and offered Yeshua the sour wine and mocked him with the title "the king of the Jews." The soldiers slipped into the truth, and that title, if true in the eyes of the Roman rulers, reinforces the belief that Yeshua was executed by Roman soldiers for sedition, that is, for being a leader and opponent to Roman occupation to Israel. And in the gospels, for the sect of Jews who followed him, Yeshua was certainly the spiritual king of the Jews.

The paramount reason behind the old tradition of *not* using Hebrew biblical names in English in translations of the New Testament was to distance early Christian Jews and later Christians from Judaism. The immediate effect of bestowing Greek names on the circle of figures around Yeshua created a pantheon of Hellenized venerables who would, by way of a gentleman's agreement, be perceived as Christians rather than Jews and thereby be one step farther removed from their Jewish identity.[57]

---

advantage of saying "Joshua the Messiah" would be that it reproduces the traditional English spelling used in the Hebrew Bible and makes Joshua the same name in both books. But it seems better to use the closer form in English, which is *Yeshua*, and hope that in future translations of the Hebrew Bible, old Joshua will give way to *Yeshua*, as "Jupiter" and *Jehovah* have importantly given way to *Yahweh* and *YHWH*. There is common agreement that Jesus was known in his time as *Yeshua*, the shortened Aramaic and Hebrew version of *Yehoshua*, and I have come, not without other possibilities in mind, to *Yeshua the Mashiah*, which is an understandable shift from "Jesus the Christ." "Messiah" translates both meanings of the Hebrew *mashiah*, of "messiah" and "anointed." The terms "Yeshua ben Yosef" and "Yeshua bar Yosef" (fully Aramaic version) are also becoming increasingly common as Yeshua's proper name before he was given the mantle of the messiah.

57. For an investigation of questions of Jewish and Christian identity in the first century, see two seminal articles by George W. E. Nickelsburg: "Jews and Christians in the First Century: The Struggle over Identity" in *Neotestamentica* 27(2) (1993): 365–390/1–4.5, and "The First Century: A Time to Rejoice and a Time to Weep" in *Religion and Theology*, 1(1) (1994): 4–17/1–5. Nickelsburg speaks of the Jewish traditions from which Yeshua comes and the often-noted "parallels between the New Testament and the Qumran documents." Of special importance are his observations on the parallels between the Jewish tradition of "persecution and vindication of the

From the first pages of the Greek gospels, changing names was essential in the process of dejudaizing Yeshua.

A simple and well-known example of an attempt to free Yeshua in the Greek gospels of the Jewish stain occurs when Andrew and Peter first address Yeshua (John 1.38): "'Rabbi,' which translated means teacher, 'where are you staying?'" ('Ραββί, ὃ λέγεται μεθερμηνευόμενον διδάσκαλε, ποῦ μένεις;).[58] This aside, breaking the narrative flow, seems to be a later scribal interpolation to explain away "rabbi" as "teacher" and to blur Yeshua's identity as a rabbi and Jew; and indeed to persuade the reader that "rabbi" meant an independent teacher or scholar and not a Jewish interpreter of the Bible. "Rabbi" is a Greek word from Hebrew *rabbi* (רַבִּי), meaning "my master," "great one," or "teacher of the law." But primarily "rabbi" means rabbi and Jew and one cannot "mean" that away. That the aside in John 1.38 needs to be "translated" into Greek suggests an earlier version of this passage in late Hebrew or Aramaic. This example of the dejudaizing of Yeshua the Mashiah occurs not only in the Greek version, but, as will be shown, in multiple renderings of Greek *rabbi* into English versions of the New Testament.

In speaking of "the dejudaizing of Jesus," Hugh J. Schonfield writes in *The Original New Testament*, "The story of Christian beginnings has commonly been related with little reference to or comprehension of its Jewish aspects . . . it is a deprivation which resulted in a one-sided and very inaccurate viewpoint with horrifying consequences so far as the Jews of Europe were concerned. Jesus was made not only a stranger to

---

righteous one" with Yeshua's death and his resurrection and exaltation in heaven. Placing Yeshua as the figure of Old Testament prophecy, Nickelsburg writes that Yeshua's sacrificial death makes him the true Son of Man, God's judge in heaven and on earth, and fulfills the multiple tradition of "Second Isaiah's Chosen One, the Servant of the Lord." He also relates Yeshua to the dream vision of the apocalyptic beast who was burned to death and then given glory and everlasting dominion over peoples and nations of the earth, which occurs in Daniel's diaspora novel (Dan. 7.13–15). In short, the main Jewish and Christian-Jewish titles come together in the life and the death of Yeshua: "the son of man/chosen One/Anointed One" (Nickelsburg, 2.2.3), and the heavenly figure seated beside God's throne. In these earliest moments of Christianity, Yeshua was a salvific figure who thoroughly fulfilled Isaianic and Danielic scriptural prophesy.

58. Greek ";" is English "?".

his brethren, but their mortal foe seeking their extermination. . . . The dejudaizing of Jesus was appreciably to affect both the Christian Faith, as in the Church Creeds, and the comprehension of the New Testament, since it was responsible for a good deal of mistranslation and misinterpretation of the text."[59]

Hoping that the practice of dejudaizing Yeshua will cease, in this instance I have followed the now current practice of translating Greek *rabbi* into English "rabbi." When the Yeshua's title is teacher as in the Greek διδάσκαλος, I follow the definition in the *Greek-English Lexicon of the New Testament and Other Early Christian Literature* of διδάσκαλος, giving *rabbi* or *rabboni* as the Hebrew word for Yeshua's title: "Used in addressing Jesus (corresp. to the title רַב or רִבִּי, rabbi) Matt 8:19; 12:38; 19:16; 22:16; 24, 36; Mark 4:38; 9:17, 38; 10:17; 20, 35; 12:14, 19, 32; 13:1; Luke 7:40; 9:38 Ῥαββί w. translation John 1:38, also Ῥαββουνί 20:16. W. the art. Mt 9:11; 17:24; 26:18; Mk 5:35; 14:14; Lk 22:11; J 11:28."[60]

In John 1.38, where the scribe comes out of the closet to add an aside in order to exonerate Yeshua of his Jewish identity, the usual religious mutation of "rabbi" into Greek as teacher, master, sir, or lord has not occurred as the story moves from early Mark to late John, but the revelation of rabbi has been explained away. The Romans achieved a similar trompe l'oeil in their Romanization of Greek deities when they created a pantheon of Latin gods by ingloriously making Greek Zeus into Roman Jupiter, Aphrodite into Venus, Artemis into Diana, and Athena into Minerva. As the Jews took the names for God and Beelzebub from earlier Mesopotamian religions, so the Christians appropriated Yeshua as their own, and the Romans appropriated the Greek gods and heroes. Such borrowings and denials are universal and purposeful, and cannot be explained always as linguistic oddities or casualties of translation. It is not easier phonetically to call Yeshua "Jesus" rather than *Yeshua*, or Yaakov "James" rather than *Yaakov* or "Jacob."

59. See Hugh J. Schonfield, *The Original New Testament* (San Francisco: Harper and Row, 1985), xix.

60. See *A Greek-English Lexicon of the New Testament and Other Early Christian Literature*, 3rd ed., rev. and ed. Frederick William Danker (Chicago: University of Chicago Press, 2000).

Migration of Yaakov to James
In this translation of the New Testament I have in most instances
restored the biblical names to their Hebrew equivalents in English.
An example is the aforementioned Jacob. It is important to see in
some linguistic detail how *Yaakov* migrated to England as "James."
Yaakov—in Hebrew יַעֲקֹב—is traditionally transcribed into English
as "Jacob." The biblical figure Yaakov, son of Yitzhak (Isaac— יִצְחָק),
appears in the genealogies of Matthew and Luke as *Iakob*, which is
as close as the Greek can transliterate the name. But the same name
Yaakov, when applied to Yeshua's brother, is slightly Hellenized; that
is, *Iakob* for "Jacob" is an uninflected foreign borrowing, but when it
refers to Yeshua's brother it is given the Greek nominative ending, and
we have *Iakobos* in order to distinguish in Greek, if only grammati-
cally, between the Old and New Testament figures who carry the same
Hebrew Bible name. So in Greek the name of Jacob when applied to
the Old Testament patriarch remains Jewish, but when applied to a
New Testament brother of Yeshua it takes on a Greek form to help him
be more comfortable in a Greek epithet. When these Greek names are
transcribed into English, *Iakob* becomes "Jacob," but *Iakobos* comes out
implausibly as "James." Now the separation and deception is complete.
The original Hebrew name *Yaakov*, which in its two Greek versions
were distinguished only by a declension ending, has generously spawned
two entirely distinct names in English: Jacob and James. In having his
name taken away from him, Yaakov also loses his cultural and religious
identity. As "James" he appears as a fresh New Testament figure in
no danger of being detected as a Jacob or a Yaakov from the Hebrew
Bible. In keeping up the pretense of two already distinct religions in
Jerusalem, no Old Testament patriarch can have the name "James."[61]

Past translators have been guilty of deceiving the Christian readers. By

---

61. The word for Yeshua's brother Yaakov in Greek is the declined noun: Ἰάκωβος,
Ἰακώβου, Ἰακώβῳ, Ἰάκωβον (Iakobos, Iakobou, Iakobo, Iakobon). The word for
the Jewish patriarch is the "indeclinable" Ἰακώβ. In the standard *Greek-English Lexicon of New Testament and Other Early Christian Literature*, there is an explanation.
Under Ἰακώβ, the entry reads, "indecl. This, the un-Grecized form of the Hebrew
Bible, is reserved for formal writing." The dictionary explanation falters, however,
since undeclined Ἰακώβ (Iakob) is not "formal writing."

using non-Jewish names for biblical figures, and worse, by using different Greek and English names for the same Hebrew name to distinguish
between people in the Old and New Testament, translators are putting a
linguistics screen between the two books and creating the impression that
Christianity did not spring from the messianic tradition in Judaism.

In this version, *Iakob* and *Iakobos*, the two Greek translations from
the Hebrew, are restored to one *Yaakov*, and "Jacob" and "James" are two
memories. The question of what specific traditional biblical name of
the time, in late Hebrew of Aramaic, should be restored will always be
uncertain. What is certain is that the presently accepted Greek names for
Christ and John or the strangely Anglicized names from the Greek such
as "James" and "Jude" are false names to accept and will in a decade or
two give way to names that reflect not Greek but biblical Jewish names.
In Homer, for now more than a century "Ulysses" and "Venus" have
given way to "Odysseus" and "Aphrodite," though the Roman names for
the gods still persist in the romance languages, even in translations of
Homer. Already in recent standard translations "messiah" is replacing
"Christ," when the Greek text refers to the messiah as the savior, as in
"the Christ." While the King James gives us "the Christ," most twentieth-
century versions give us "the messiah."

In summary, since most of the names in the Greek scriptures are
translations or transliterations from the Hebrew, it makes more sense to
do in English what the Greeks did: work straight from Hebrew instead
of doing a translation of a translation. The Alexandrian Neoplatonic
philosopher Plotinus informed his friend and biographer Porphyry that
he refused to let a painter paint his picture. His reasoning: "Why paint
an illusion of an illusion?"

In Spain the Fate of the Suspect Original

Curiously, translating a Hebrew name into English through its Greek
version begins to make the Hebrew original seem like a suspect illusion,
and an attempt to foist that original onto English a radical language act. A
"suspect original," or a more general revulsion against the Jewish origins
of Christianity, occurs in the drama of the Spanish poet Fray Luis de
León (1524–1591), an Augustinian monk and professor of Latin, Greek,
and Hebrew at the University of Salamanca, whose student was the mystical poet Saint John of the Cross. Luis de León, of convert (*converso*)

background, translated Job, Song of Songs, and Psalms directly from the Hebrew, with commentary, in what remain the finest versions of the Bible in the Spanish language. For this, he was four and a half years in the inquisitional prison at Valladolid, accused of Judaizing. He had, according to his accusers, translated from "the corrupt original" Hebrew text rather than from the authorized Latin Vulgata. When the esteemed poet was released, his students carried him on their shoulders back in triumph to his university chair at Salamanca.

An aversion and anxiety about drawing from the original texts was unique to Spain, which in the Middle Ages, because of its large multilingual Jewish population, actually had at least two private translations of the Jewish Bible made directly from Hebrew. They were the Alva Bible, 1422–1433, translated by Rabbi Mosse Arragel de Maqueda, uniquely and restrictively for use in the house of the Duque de Alba, and the Osuna Bible for the house of the Marqués de Santillana. Elsewhere in Europe any translation into a demotic tongue was done at the risk of heresy and punishment. As a result of the domination of Jerome's Vulgate, throughout the Western Middle Ages and in the Renaissance, not only the names in the Bible but the Bible itself contained another layer of Latinizations. The Vulgata was the canonized word of God for the Roman Catholic Church, and insofar as the Bible went into European tongues, it was rendered exclusively from the approved Latin, not the Greek, which even learned Dante and Petrarca couldn't read, or the dark original in Hebrew, which only Jews could read. Spain, in the instance of the aristocratic family translations, was the exception. After the 1492 expulsion of Jews from Spain, there soon appeared new versions from the Hebrew Bible into Spanish editions published in Ferrara (with the papal seal of approval), Amsterdam, and Constantinople.

Restoration of Original Breath

After centuries of covering up and condemning the Hebrew language base of the Hebrew Bible and of the Greek scriptures, modern scholarship is moving to correct traditional infelicities. This is an auspicious time for the New Testament, for the restoration in scholarship and translation of its Semitic names, the religious identity of its main characters as Jews, and above all a spirit of universality which, both in the gospels and in their interpretation, has too often been merely divisive. As sectarian differences drop away, a broader bible may come through to include the Hebrew Bible, the Intertestament, and the New Testament. Easy access to deuterocanonical and noncanonical apocrypha will alone prove the welcome news of diversity. Some may shudder and fume, but such a wider bible will bring in a lot of good news.

As for rethinking old historical assumptions, we may note a biblical prehistory of stories flooding in from Mesopotamia, with many names and many gods, and the spellings of place-names and figures in flux as scholars tinker. Knowledge frees and incites the courage of change. Among obvious changes is the practice of seeking source-language foreign spellings and pronunciations, which is now enjoyably common. Hence "Peking" has yielded to *Beijing* (it was always Beijing, if one knew how to pronounce the old Chinese-English code letters that Wade-Giles established). It is not always possible, however, to jar habit, to call Plato *Platon* or Pindar *Pindaros*. So Everett Fox in *The Five Books of Moses* (1995) notes that he has retained English "Jordan" (rather than Hebrew *Yarden*), while relentlessly returning to a phonetically based English equivalent of most Hebrew names in the Torah. But Everett Fox did something of equal importance to his restoration of Hebrew names: He translated the Torah into verse.

Yeshua Back Home

Yeshua's quintessential poetic sayings were of life, light, soul, and death, and of his source in Adonai the Lord. He himself took on, in his followers' eyes, the earthly incarnation of Adonai the Lord, the traditional ever-waited-for messiah of the Jews, who was to appear salvifically on earth. "For to us a son is born. . . . And he shall be called Wonderful, The Counselor, The mighty God, The everlasting Father, The Prince of Peace" (Isa. 9.6, KJV). Through odd concealment of his person, he became universally known as a Greek-speaking figure ostensibly from Galilee (the Galil), but essentially from nowhere. His universality appeared to take away his simple Jewish origin, including his voice, preserved only in Greek or in translations from Greek, and especially into Latin. That same universality, canonized by the Roman State Church, made him so remote from his native language and origin that in his dialogues his own tongue and person were under cover. Imagine if Odysseus spoke only Aramaic and quoted Hebrew verse as he bounced around the

Mediterranean, and that he was universally known not as Odysseus but Moses. That reversal of Greek and Hebrew has for two millennia been the destiny of Yeshua ben Yosef, who preached around the hills and villages of the Galil and Yehuda (Galilee and Judea).

This conversion of the New Testament into English seeks to bring Yeshua back to his Semitic geography and roots. To bring him back home.

Historical or Mythical Jesus, the Passover Plot, and the Rap of Deicide

When I was a child growing up in a evangelical part of the Christian Church in the United States, I was convinced that Jesus must have been a Swede or at least an Englishman. Every picture I saw of him, and there were many, portrayed him with fair skin, blonde hair, and blue eyes.

— JOHN SHELBY SPONG,
Episcopal Bishop of Newark,
Liberating the Gospels

The virgin by the blooming beans is blonde
And her small Jesus is a blond like her
His eyes are blue and pure like the sky or wave
I guess her seeded by the Paraclete.

— GUILLAUME APOLLINAIRE,
"The Virgin by the Bean
Blossoms in Cologne"

Carts were dashing though the narrow streets of the city; more going on than usual for this town; everything that evening seemed too satisfied.

Jesus withdrew his hand: It was a movement of childish and feminine pride. "All of you, if you don't see miracles, you don't believe."

— ARTHUR RIMBAUD,
"Galilee,"
Illuminations

Discovery of an Early Gospel

ESPECIALLY since the discovery of the Gospel of Thomas in 1945 in Egypt among the scrolls of the Nag Hammadi Library, the historicity of narrations in the New Testament has been increasingly studied and questioned. Since the only real source for Yeshua's life had been the gospels, written long after his death, faith rather than historical documents has prevailed to fashion a picture of Yeshua. The Gospel of Thomas has added information. Without narration and relatively free of anti-Jewish bias, it gives what some scholars assert (and others deny) are the earliest words of Yeshua. Through the sayings, it offers some hints about the personality of a historical Yeshua. The dating is significant but ultimately secondary to the greater contribution, which is that it represents a profoundly different presentation of Yeshua's words, and is obviously one of the earliest distinct sources we have.

The Gospel of Thomas is found in Coptic translation from the Greek of a text that may have had an Aramaic origin. There are also fragments of Thomas in Syriac. In the gospel, we hear Yeshua in the format of a Platonic dialogue. It is also significant that the "Fifth Gospel" was found together with classical Gnostic scriptures, and that Yeshua's appearance in Thomas is itself the centerpiece of early Gnosticism. The extraordinary Gospel of Thomas, reflecting a sage's original thought, is focused in 144 concise entries of oral sayings and parables. The tradition of an itinerant sage's oral sayings and parables clearly derives from both the written Bible and extra-biblical literature.

Among the Nag Hammadi scrolls were also the Gnostic Gospel of Truth and Gospel of Philip. These documents cast a new light on the Yeshua of Gnostic speculation, the special gnosis of light, truth, knowledge, and divinity found inside the person rather than in external scripture. Early Jewish and Jewish-Christian Gnosticism, as in the Book of Baruch, linguistically reveals the transition between Judaism and Christianity; but, aside from the closer character and more traditional format, these early Gnostic scriptures pose the same enigmas of origin and transmission of information as the canonical gospels, since in this presentation of a Greek and Coptic speaker in Gnostic scriptures, the

Semitic atmosphere and textual links that should take us back to an
Aramaic-speaking Yeshua are missing.[62]

Sources and Transmission of Texts[63]

The question of historicity pertains to factual information about the
people in the New Testament, their names and identity, what they did
and said, the miracle story, events (and especially the Passion narration),
and the condition of the texts which offer all this information. As for
specific historical references to Yeshua of Nazareth outside the gospels,
they are pitifully few and uncertain. There are brief allusions in Tacitus,
Suetonius, and Pliny the Younger.

The Jewish historian Josephus (ca. 37–100 C.E.) (Joseph ben Matthias)
has a passage of more significance, though its validity is strongly debated.
In *The Changing Faces of Jesus*, Geza Vermes offers a balanced view: "In
certain circles, Josephus was venerated as the fifth evangelist. Hyper-
critical scholars consider the entire passage to be spurious, i.e., a Christian
gloss inserted into the Antiquities to furnish a first-century Jewish proof
of the existence of Jesus who was the Messiah. Admittedly, as it stands,
the text is unlikely to have originated from the pen of Flavius Josephus.
The flat assertions, 'He was the Christ' and that his resurrection on the
third day fulfilled the predictions of the prophets are alien to Josephus
and must have derived from a later Christian editor of the *Antiquities*."[64]

For a spiritual biography of Yeshua we have Paul, who did not know
Yeshua in the flesh and who is unconcerned with Yeshua in history. Paul
is closer to John of the Fourth Gospel, who wrote three generations
after Yeshua's death. Both authors sought and created a messianic and
eschatological Yeshua, who corresponded to the emerging ideological
development of Jewish Christianity. And then we have Josephus and

---

62. The atmosphere in the Gospel of Thomas will soon change. The fine version of
Thomas in English by Marvin Meyer, *The Gospel of Thomas* (San Francisco: Harp-
erSanFrancisco, 1992), has a stunning interpretation by Harold Bloom, who places
Thomas in its Jewish and Gnostic setting. In the Gospel of Thomas for *The Gnostic
Bible*, Professor Meyer and I have, as here in the RNT, restored all names to their
probable Hebrew and Aramaic forms.

63. For details on authorship, the Q source, and Thomas, see pp. 1326–30.

64. See Geza Vermes, *The Changing Faces of Jesus* (New York: Viking Compass,
2000), 276–277.

Philo to give us specific reporting of the Jews during the life of Yeshua. Of great importance is also the history of Yeshua's time found in the later Talmud (rabbinical writing around 200 C.E., including the Mishnah), which is vital for understanding Yeshua's precursors among the charismatic Hasidic healers and miracle-makers. However, since the gospels are all we have as a detailed record of the life of Yeshua, they are what we investigate and evaluate and about which we come up with guesses and broad theories. In short, all the historical events of Yeshua's life take place within the frame of unverifiable religious scripture.

In the last decades there have been a number of new "biographies" of Jesus, which, in a novelistic manner, fill in the colorful scenes, describing village life, landscapes, the farmers, carpenters, and fishermen, the crowds as well as main figures of the day, including Herod Antipas and his mass crucifixions of dissidents and enemies, and the stoning to death of Yeshua's younger brother James(Jacob/Yaakov), who was head of the Jerusalem church. An excellent example of such re-creations is Bruce Chilton's *Rabbi Jesus: An Intimate Biography* (2000). Generally speaking, these biographies reconstruct speech, ideas, and events recorded in the gospels and in Acts. The historical base is scripture (with reservations), Josephus, later rabbinical writings, and factual knowledge of Roman rule. Since these lives of Jesus draw primarily on unverifiable scripture, however skillfully they are handled, there remains the question of what is knowable and what is guided conjecture. In this regard, the outstanding book on the life of Jesus is *The Changing Faces of Jesus* by Vermes. Vermes looks to the gospels for discrete information to shape a picture of Yeshua, and also to the Essenes of the Dead Sea Scrolls (which he edited and translated), and to Yeshua's antecedents and contemporaries among the Hasidic charismatics. Given the multitude of general sources and paucity of specific references to Yeshua outside of the gospels, I think that Vermes may offer us the most persuasive ways of coming to terms with the evasive "historical Jesus."

The gospels concern the late Second Temple period followers of Yeshua (who are sometimes called "the primitive Christians") and, having been written *after* the Roman destruction of the Herodian Temple in 70 C.E., they direly predict the catastrophe and presage the swiftening separation of Jews from Christian Jews that takes place after the diaspora from Jerusalem. It is imperative to remember that these gospels were long to reach their present form, and the editors who copied, emended, and rewrote are all unknown. In speaking about the formation of Mark, John Drury writes, "A welter of oral and fluid tradition about Jesus got fixed into text. Stories which had been the property of Christian preachers, teachers, and prophets were appropriated by a Christian writer. This written gospel is next-door neighbor to thirty or forty years of oral gospeling."[65]

Faith Moves Mountains, and Its Vehicle Is Translation

As for the four gospels, probably the earliest, the more historical Mark, was not recorded as a written document until around 70 or 80 C.E., generations after Yeshua's death. Mark is closest to the Aramaic-speaking Yeshua, and the few Aramaic words found in the gospels are mainly in Mark: *Rabbuni*, "my rabbi" (10.51), *Abba*, "father" (14.36), and finally, *Eloi, Eloi, lama sabachtani*, "My God, my God, why do you abandon me?" (15.34). In at least this one line from the scripture, the last words Yeshua will utter, we hear the human, Aramaic voice of Yeshua; for the same line in Matthew, Hebrew *Eli, Eli* replaces Aramaic *Eloi, Eloi* (27.46). Each of the gospels reveals a different face of Yeshua.

How did we arrive at the four canonized gospel biographies of Yeshua? Beginning with a changing oral text recorded in now lost sources, the course of translation from original events to the first Greek manuscripts was a very long road. Errors and, more significant, interpretation of those events as they were told and retold (oral copying or oral translation), editorial invention, omission, and alteration on their way to the extant fourth-century codices have all determined the nature of the Christian scriptures. In *A Historical Introduction to the New Testament*, Robert M. Grant gives an overview: "The Gospels testify primarily to the faith and the memories of the communities out of which they came, not the historical reliability of their authors. In many respects the Synoptic Gospels (though not John) resemble folk literature more than the creation of individual artists."[66]

---

65. See John Drury, "Mark," in Robert Alter and Frank Kermode, eds., *The Literary Guide to the Bible* (Cambridge, MA: Harvard University Press, 1987), 404.

66. See Robert M. Grant, *A Historical Introduction to the New Testament* (New York: Simon and Schuster, 1972), 108.

The events that happened one day in Jerusalem to a rabbi called Yeshua represent perhaps the major act of literary composition in history. A version of those happenings appeared, and a new religion was born. Christianity arose. For the Romans, this was a day of a routine crucifixion by its army of three Jews in Jerusalem. Descriptive evidence concerning this event, apart from the uncertain sentence of Josephus ("He was the Christ"), lies uniquely in the Greek version of the gospels. Yeshua's teaching was oral, and there is no claim that there were writings by him. Yet scholars continue to debate, arguing as if the true nature of a transcendent God depended in some definitive way on a discovery of further evidence concealed within the translated words in the text. One looks, of course, for the deepest meaning within a text, but always with the awareness that great religious scriptures of the world, in this and apparently all instances, are not tape recordings or photographs, but late transcriptions that have gone through an unknown plethora of transmission activity.

In its journey from event to gospel,[67] the tale was said to have been translated from oral reports of Aramaic- and Latin-speaking witnesses, perhaps from written reports in Hebrew including something by a man later designed as Matthew. Finally, decades later, the story reached the

---

67. Gospel, meaning "good news," has come also by usage to be used as a specific genre, and many intertestamental works are typed as "gospels," thirteen other extant gospels, such as the Gospel of Philip, the Gospel of Mary, and the Gospel of Thomas. Some point out anomalies in calling gospel a genre of writing including David Trobisch who comments, "The term *Gospel* is used to refer to the content of the message as well as to the act of preaching in the New Testament. It is not used to indicate a specific literary genre. And so far no evidence has surfaced in pre-Christian literature, either, that the term can be used to refer to a literary genre" (*The First Edition of the New Testament*, New York: Oxford University Press, 2000, 38). Elsewhere he comments that the books fall into the genre normally called in early Greek βίος (bios), meaning "a life." However, since the publication of the gospels, which Trobisch posits to be around 150, "genre" has persisted as the common term for the life of Yeshua. Prior to the second century, "gospel" had meant something else. For Paul, who died before the gospels were composed or edited, "gospel" refers to the whole Christian message, above all to the eschatological meaning of Yeshua's death, and there could be only one gospel. By the end of the second century, there were many gospels still claiming to be the one true one, but by then, Mark, Matthew, Luke, and John had found their place as the canonical four.

pens of Greek-writing Jewish scribes. Grant comments on the bilingual authors of the gospels. "Even though none of the New Testament books was written in Aramaic, the authors of some of them thought in Aramaic, at least at times. And behind the sayings of Yeshua in their Greek versions lies a chain of transmission which began in a Semitic language. Obviously this chain cannot be reproduced in a translation. But it has to be taken into account."[68]

Much talk, memory, imagination, creation, and interpretation went into that story, climaxing with the last of the miracles, the miracle of the resurrection, and its first recording. We know that whether true or false in actuality, the Mark version of the resurrection is a spurious "orphan" ending (a late appended text), included in the King James Version but omitted from twentieth-century versions such as the widespread New Revised Standard Version. The NRSV is based on the now standard UBS (United Bible Societies) Greek texts edited by Kurt Aland (1979) and a later edition of them in Eberhard and Erwin Nestle's *Novum Testamentum Graece* (1993), all of which exclude the orphan. The process of recording the gospels, to use an appropriate metaphor, is an oral and graphic palimpsest with endless layers of changing information. The later translation of the Greek scriptures themselves into Latin and the world's languages brings in further changes, due to error or intention, along with the trauma of textual alterations at the time of the radical conversion of uncial[69] into modern letters. Each new stage of transmission carries with it all the problems of interlingual rewording.

The scriptures are insistent about the truth of their recorded events, about the truth of belief and faith in miracle and the supernatural powers of the divine, and in the punishments awaiting those who fail to believe in these truths. Yet with respect to the authenticity of actual events, dialogue, or miracles, there is no way of corroborating the truth of the events. Discomfort about this absence lurks in the statements of the early Latin fathers, such as Origen's claim that the Holy Spirit gave each of the evangelists a perfect memory. Even if true with regard to each

---

68. See Grant, *Historical Introduction to the New Testament*, 56.

69. Uncial letters from the fourth to the eighth centuries were characterized by round capital letters in Greek and Latin manuscripts that provided the model for most modern capital letters.

memory, this solves nothing unless we believe, against widely accepted chronological evidence, that the evangelists were witness to Yeshua's life and death and therefore had a personal recollection of the events which they recorded.

The problems of historicity, of verification of even the most minor facts, remain a barrier to affirming the truth or falsity of gospel events. Despite the documentary vacuum outside the gospels, there is within the gospels, as there would be in any literary document, enormous information that may be examined and conclusions drawn, as I have attempted to do with regard to the straightforward facts of the exist-ing names in the gospels. The danger is to forget, especially during a lifetime of research, that so little is known, and that evidence pertain-ing to miracles, exorcism, the source of the parables and wisdom say-ings, the conspiracy, the crucifixion, and the resurrection can never be ascertained from a literal surface reading of the text. Paula Fredriksen, among so many, states the obvious in her cautionary summary of cap-turing these oral texts:

> This is another way of saying that Jesus' audience, like himself, would have been for the most Aramaic-speaking Jews living in Jewish territory, but the language of the evangelists is Greek, their medium written, not oral. No one knows where the Gospels were composed, nor the identi-ties of their authors—the traditional ascriptions ("Matthew," "Mark," "Luke," and "John") evolved only in the course of the second century: The original texts circulated anonymously. Most scholars assign loca-tions of origin to somewhere in the Greek-speaking cities of the empire. Accordingly the question of their communities' relations with Gentiles, with Gentile culture, and with imperial government looms much larger for the evangelists than it could have for Jesus himself.

As for transmission by eyewitness testimony, which is the usual way of filling the gap between an event and the late transcription of an event, Fredriksen further states:

> But eyewitness testimony is never scientific or objective, first of all because the witness is human. In this particular case their conviction that Jesus has been raised from the dead, or that he was God's special

agent working in history for the redemption of Israel and the world, would inevitably have affected the reports that these witnesses gave: Other witnesses, not so convinced, would, and presumably did, speak differently.[70] [cf. Matt. 28.17]

Surely the biggest gap in source and transmission of gospel information pertains to the letter writers Paul, Peter, James, and John, who preceded the evangelists by three to seven decades. The evangelists knew Yeshua's life from birth to death, his words, his deeds, and the passion scene of his crufixion. None of this information reached Paul, Yeshua's near contemporary, who was in Jerusalem for years when Yeshua was preaching in the synagogues. Paul had not heard of Mary or the virgin birth, nor of the centurion who led the execution squad and was the first to declare Yeshua the risen messiah. For Paul Yeshua was the Christ, that is, the messiah Isaiah foretold, who had come and who had given his life through the crucifixion for our salvation and would soon return to make that salvation explicit. There are in Paul's thirteen letters, authentic and pseudepigraphic, only three references to any event in the gospels. But most of Paul's authentic letters consist of parts patched together, and there is deep suspicion that even these three gospel-story references were emendations patched in at a later date. So for Paul the epistler, the best we can say is that because of his virtual complete ignorance of person, word, and deed of the crucified, he adds no information concerning the historical Jesus.

We can only guess at the nature of pre-gospel information. Sometimes, knowledge of the Hebrew or Aramaic source word deflates the magnificence, as in the proverb of it being harder for a rich man to enter heaven than for "a camel to pass through the eye of a needle" (Mark 10.25; Matt. 19.24; Luke 18.25). "Coarse thread" and "camel" turn out to have the same root consonants (vowels are unmarked in Hebrew and Aramaic). Hence the mistake in transmission to the Greek gives us the memorable, beautiful, and surreal image in the maxim. So, apart from external historical and archeological evidence, the main areas of research are in understanding and interpreting material in the gospels themselves and

70. See Paula Fredriksen, *Jesus of Nazareth, King of the Jews: A Jewish Life and Emergence of Christianity* (New York: Knopf, 1999), 19, 20.

in studying and establishing a history of the great number of surviving complete and fragmentary manuscripts of the gospels.

Manuscript History

The earliest fragment of the gospels is a scrap with five verses from John 18, which was recognized by C. H. Roberts in 1934 from shreds of papyri found by Bernard P. Grenfell in 1920 in Egypt. Roberts dated the piece to the first half of the second century, though the date cannot be confirmed. The first substantial manuscripts with portions of the New Testament are the Bodomer papyrus of John and the Chester Beatty papyrus, which contains ten Pauline letters. These papyri are dated some time in the middle of the third century. The earliest extant uncial parchment manuscript, containing the entire New Testament, is the Codex Sinaiticus discovered in 1844 at St. Catherine's monastery in the Sinai, dating from the fourth century. These early manuscripts have all the expected erasures, rewriting, emendations, and comments about earlier scribes on them, which is helpful in tracing their history. In the case of the Hebrew Bible, the earliest copies are much later, while the Septuagint Greek translation of the Bible is earlier than any surviving Hebrew text (with the exception now of fragments in the Dead Sea Scrolls). Indeed, almost all the ancient literature that has come down to us from every society consists of copies of copies.

As mentioned, the composition of the gospels took place in the late first and early second centuries. There is no manuscript fragment of the gospels themselves for at least a century after Yeshua's death—and at least two centuries for anything substantial. Because of the information gap after Yeshua's life, we have only guesses to describe the mysterious chemistry that turned a Jewish movement in Jerusalem into Greek Christian scripture.

Spreading the Word of God in Many Tongues

Before looking and studying within the Greek New Testament, it is important to know how scriptures spread through the world soon after their selection and order were established. Greek scripture moved into new language bodies, and each transformation assumed a distinct means and purpose of translation. As will be clear in later elaboration, the historical content of the scriptures changed not only as events and dialogue reached through silence and mystery to the Greek scripture, but also, and now fully visibly, as they have been moved out of our extant Greek source text into a thousand and another thousand foreign versions.

The first major employment in the West of the translator—of the translating messenger of the Bible—was to spread the word of God. Curiously, in classical Greek and Latin literatures, while there is imitation of Greek in Latin, as when Catullus adapts a poem by Sappho, there is otherwise remarkably little translation per se. Beyond their own literatures, Greeks and Romans had little interest, and decently educated Greeks and Romans read both Greek and Latin. The power of the Greeks and Romans resided in their civilization and the ruling power of the sword. The power of the proselytizing Christians was in the holy word. And Greek was a chosen language for this purpose, since in eastern Europe, much of North Africa, and the Near East, Greek was the lingua franca. But with the growth of Christianity and the necessity for clergy, if not for the largely illiterate laity, to possess canonized scripture, the serious ecclesiastical industry of Bible translation began. Most of the emphasis was on producing vernacular versions of the New Testament rather than of the Hebrew Bible, for part of the overriding need to propagate Christianity was distinguishing it from its Jewish source. Accordingly, there were soon versions of the Greek scriptures in Syriac, Armenian, Georgian, Ethiopic, Arabic, and even Nubian, Persian, Sogdian, and Caucasian Albanian. In the West, that is, west of the Near East, there was primarily Latin, and then Gothic, Old Church Slavonic, and Anglo-Saxon.[71]

History of the Word After Jerome's Latin Domination

In the early Christian centuries, Latin had the double role of being not only a classical language of Rome but also a true European vernacular, spoken by both clergy and laity in Latin countries before the vulgar Romance tongues predominated. Moreover, like Greek Koine, church Latin in biblical translation and patristic writings had thrown off the artificial elegance of complicated classical Latin syntax. For the common

71. For the most thorough description and analysis of early Bible translations, see Bruce M. Metzger's *Early Versions of the New Testament: Their Origin, Transmission, and Limitations* (Oxford: Clarendon Press, 1977).

reader it was an easier tongue to read. As the Romance languages gained ground, displacing Latin as the vulgar tongue, the need for a true universal Vulgar arose, which was in large part the handiwork of the Latin scholar Jerome (347–419/420). Saint Jerome, as was his later title, revised earlier versions of the gospels and ultimately settled in Bethlehem and with the help of Jewish friends translated the Hebrew Bible from what he called the "true text." He was lucky to be working from the original Hebrew text for the Old Testament as opposed to the mysterious apocryphal New Testament gospels, which were one language removed from their Semitic speakers. The New Testament, like the canonical Apocrypha (until the Dead Sea Scrolls findings), had no Semitic version.[72]

The fifth-century Vulgate dominated the West as the true Bible (the title Vulgate or Vulgata came into being only in the sixteenth century), and by the sixteenth century there was sacred sound but the meaning of the words eluded most of the laity. Latin had remained a learned universal language, but its parish readers were limited. So came the need to bring the biblical story directly to the people and not through a translated version in the priest sermon summary. Hearing the truth of the Bible in a language one could not understand may have been advantageous to clerical authority, but it simply added another layer of the ahistorical to stories already suffering from the absence of verifiable originals. The Protestant Reformation, the break from Rome and Latin, the Roman Catholic language, had at its core the mission of bringing the Bible to the laity in a tongue they could understand.[73]

In returning to the vernacular, the Bible moved back to its original koine (common) purpose, which was to speak to the common people in plain, sharp, uplifting speech. The life-and-death drama of those translation efforts in France, Germany, and England also profoundly affected the language and literatures of each people. In England, the sixteenth-century William Tyndale gave the New Testament back to the people, to "the ploughboy in the field." He followed the aims of Erasmus, who gave us the populist image of the ploughboy who could read scripture. In 1529, Tyndale translated *Exhortations to the Diligent Study of Scripture*

---

72. For more on the gospels as the New Testament Apocrypha, see p. 1318.

73. Halfway through the twentieth century, the Latin Vulgate gave way to the vernacular, but in a few places, such as the Catholic Church in China, it did not.

in which Erasmus asks that the Bible be translated into all tongues, for women and for all peoples and faiths. In Tyndale's lovely words we hear, "I wold to God the ploughman wold singe a texte of the scripture at his plo-bene. And that the wever at his lowme with this wold drive away the tediousness of tyme. I would the wayfaringman with this pastyme wold expelle the weriness of his iorney."

With Tyndale, and in the next century with the spoken grandeur of the King James Version (now raised to a higher rhetorical level beyond the ploughboy), the testaments entered the English language popularly as original text, as "the word of the Bible." Such popular confusion about original document and a translation of a translation reveals just how far the lofty beauty of the King James Version can lead one to ascribe absolute authority to its words, though its title modestly calls itself a version. The King James Version is a Protestant translation. The now omitted prefatory "Translation to the Reader" reveals the struggle between Catholic and Protestant, between London and Rome, concerning dominion, doctrine, and moral law. While the leader of the translation group, Dr. Miles Smith, denounces his rival "Catholicks," whom he defines as "Popish *Romanists*," his introduction ends with a spiritual defense of the art of translation with his plea that the translation let in the light.

Looking Within the Gospels for Historical and Imagined Events

Unfortunately, as the New Testament and the Hebrew Bible multiplied in translation throughout Europe, all the tendencies within the Greek scriptures to disenfranchise Yeshua of his religion and ethnicity were not ameliorated but, rather, enhanced. The original history of a Jewish sect recognizing its messiah became more remote from the Galilee and the streets of Jerusalem and the translation of Greek names into local names increasingly distanced the personages from their Semitic stage. To understand the Greek scriptures in their time, it is helpful to gather information from other writings—some that have remained closer to their linguistic and spiritual sources—including the Dead Sea Scrolls, the Nag Hammadi Library, the intertestamental pseudepigrapha overlapping with New Testament apocrypha, and, above all, the writings of Philo and Josephus.

The gospels are documents composed as histories of the beginnings of Christianity. Their religious purpose is to prove, to inspire, and to convert. However, the events, the people, the names, the conversations are story, not chronicle or history. In telling its story, every religious document necessarily claims and demands belief in its unique and absolute historical truth. Often the punishment for disbelief or even skepticism has been death, death to "the infidel" or "heretic," meaning one who is unfaithful or dissident to a prevailing orthodoxy. To take the gospels as historical event, which their didactic form prescribes, requires an act of faith. This same reasonable assumption of faith pertains to all religions.

As long as there are sects, there will be polemics over who has the correct faith. But a deeper faith does not need revealed truth in immutable words in our translated scripture. Nor does faith require proof or disapproval by external historic document. Faith survives as a beautiful tautology, since faith requires faith in faith. Scripture, however, which is often the source of faith, is fallible, since it is neither written nor dictated by God but is a human, imperfect endeavor. Those who say that faith carries them beyond the word may have the clearest mind and spirit, for perhaps they understand that words are sounded script, imprecise signs, and sometimes wondrous. And even the word under the word, that pause of silence, will not yield a perfect epiphany. So pitting faith against history or history against faith should be taken as a common human activity of medium importance. In the end, faith and moveable mountains will keep their own terrains. In the instance of my translations and comments, they represent another tampering with tradition and perhaps doctrinal faith by seeking to make the words closer to their Greek and Semitic sources. In the cause of progress and frailty, I hope I can add something to the necessary inconstancy of text and their mysterious interpretations.

Gospel Yeshua and Historical Yeshua

For more than a century, those who look for historical truths in texts sacred and secular have come up with two versions of Yeshua: the gospel Yeshua and the historical Yeshua. The unfriendly dilemma of looking for the historical Yeshua is our expanding awareness of what cannot be known. We do not know the fundamental facts of the life of

Yeshua—including the nature of his birth, the sect or segment of Jews (Essenes, Galileans, Zealots, Pharisees, Hasidim) whose views reflect his formation, the specific cause of his crucifixion. Lacking resources, we search in the gospels to prove or disprove a gospel event or statement. We look for special elements within the gospel story, and then examine archeological evidence in Israel, just as in corroborating events in Homer we gaze at the ruins of Troy, its walls, the Labyrinth in Crete, its stone bull, and even Hades as an archaic temple in Southern Epirus. As for patristic documents to confirm the story of Yeshua, the commentary leads not to history but back to the gospels through the Church fathers' passionate convictions and interpretations. Whatever rigor of dispassionate reason, honesty, and nonpartisan intelligence is applied to this search, there remains the limiting fact that in investigating miracles, events, and intimate conversations that are said to have taken place in houses, in the Sanhedrin,[74] and between Yeshua and his opponents, there is no external evidence to support or reject these matters. As for gospel references to peoples and events in Yeshua's time, we do have historic information: Romans in the Seleucid Near East; Pompey's conquest of Jerusalem in 63 B.C.E.; the Jews in Israel, Alexandria, and in the wider diaspora; the Jewish uprising against the Romans in 66–70 C.E. And this external information helps us to receive the meaning of gospel statements in some historical context.

Because the gospels arrive before us from unknown origin, we have only some "negative" facts. It is certain that the authors (the evangelists or gospel writers) are unknown by name or person, that no alleged eyewitness accounts survive, that no intermediary texts exist in Hebrew, Aramaic, Greek, Syriac, Coptic, or Latin—the languages used in areas of early Judaism and Christianity. Where did the evangelists, who were not witness to these events, obtain their information? There is no knowledge about this void. What the gospels say is that a rabbi, whose name was probably Yeshua ben Yosef, was crucified by the Romans for the political crime of conspiring against Rome.

---

74. The highest judicial and ecclesiastical council in Jerusalem. Its members were accused of conspiring in the death of Yeshua, and secret conversations in the Sanhedrin are reported in the gospels to prove the conspiracy. Reports of overhead conversations behind the walls of the Sanhedrin lack credibility.

Given this rude circumstance, we do at least have an important option: While we cannot prove the truth of any described event, we can perhaps convincingly assert the untruth or improvability of some events. Such an option may seem meager, but it is not. Demonstrating the improvability of events that are sinister in their implication for the principal participants may in itself be a crucial achievement.

Passover Plot

The single event in the New Testament that provides the historical or mythical basis for blaming the Jews for the death of Yeshua is the trial before the council or Sanhedrin where, the gospels say, the high priests and whole council were looking for testimony against Yeshua to put him to death, but they found none. "For many gave false testimony against him, and their testimony did not agree" (Mark 14.56, NRSV). Similar words occur in Matthew 26.59. How could the evangelists, or anyone outside the Sanhedrin, have known, at least three decades after the words that were supposed to have been exchanged, what deliberations took place behind closed doors in a private residence? How could one know that such a meeting even took place?

Such passages in the gospels were assembled to exonerate the Romans for their crucifixion of Yeshua and to incriminate and place a curse on the Jews for Yeshua's execution. This selective curse incriminating an entire people forever reveals its own folly and senseless cruelty. Why do Yeshua and his family and followers not share the blanket racial and religious guilt laid upon all Jews for all generations? ("Let his blood be upon us and upon our children!" [Matt. 27.25].) And is Yeshua as a Jew not also the devil and a murderer? ("You are from your father the devil / and you want to do the desires of your father. / From the beginning he was a murderer" [John 8.44].) But rabbi Yeshua is exempt from the terrible epithets and curses laid upon his coreligionists.

It should be clear that in the schizoid way in which Yeshua is presented—as rabbi and as denouncer of Jews—there is a deep confusion of conflicting disguises of identity, and diverse voices speaking through his persona. With regard to the curse that Matthew has the Jews call upon themselves and their children, Vermes declares the consequence of demonization: "Matthew laid the foundation of the Christian concept of the universal and permanent Jewish guilt for

deicide which, unhesitatingly embraced by the church, was responsible for the shedding of much innocent blood over the ages." Vermes
points out fascinating paradoxes in Matthew, who at one moment
has his Yeshua speak as leader of fellow Jews, and the next as a later
Church father: "Matthew's 'schizophrenia' shows itself in many ways.
He is more pro-Jewish than Mark, and much more than the Gentile
Luke. He portrayed a Jesus who was concerned only with Jews—'I
was sent to the lost sheep of the house of Israel' (Matt. 15.24)—and
who actually forbade his disciples to take an interest in non-Jews: 'Go
nowhere among the Gentiles, and enter no town of the Samaritans,
but rather to the lost sheep of the house of Israel' (10.6). However, in
a complete volte-face from the chauvinism expressed in the preceding
passages, Matthew laid a heavier emphasis than any other evangelist
on the Christian mission to all the nations, and on the church being
substituted for Israel."[75]

The sundry faces of Yeshua confound, but it must be remembered that
an emerging new sect needs to erase its parent. So it was essential to fabricate a Socrates-like trial by villainous Jews in order to free the Romans
of their historical execution of Yeshua. Yet there is no historical exoneration of the Romans for Yeshua's execution. The single event in the life
and death of Yeshua that most but not all Bible scholars agree is historical
is his execution by the Romans. If there were exonerating circumstances
that "justified" such execution within the arena of Roman law, such as
Yeshua's being an active leader and opponent to Roman rule, a seditionist, a Jewish revolutionary, indeed, the king of the Jews against the Roman
governor, that, too, we cannot know. We have no official information on
why the Romans ordered the execution but, if this execution is historical, we cannot go further than to suppose that some form of opposition
to Roman rule led to Yeshua's death, since such opposition is the usual
cause for the empire's practice of cruel execution for all to see.

Crucifixion was also applied to robbers. However, if there is truth
or significance in the "King of the Jews" placard that the Romans had
Yeshua carry, or in the anti-Jewish version, which again made it the politics of the Sanhedrin to convince Rome of Yeshua's disloyalty to Rome,
all these hints within the gospels suggest political not civil crime, the

75. See Vermes, *Changing Faces of Jesus*, 232, 231.

latter being normally the responsibility of the occupied people. While nothing is foolproof, it is most unlikely that Yeshua died as a thief.

Despite the negative facts—our absolute ignorance of what led to Yeshua's execution—some excellent scholars, even in books published as late as 1999, perpetuate the myth of ultimate Jewish culpability.

E. P. Sanders states as a firm fact that "Jesus was executed by the Romans as a would-be 'king of the Jews'."[76] His argument that the Romans killed Yeshua as an insurrectionist is proved by his title "king of the Jews." Since this view puts potential blame on the Romans (whereas the gospels show unwillingness by the Romans to carry out the crucifixion), one can think that here, at last, is a plausible motive that does not reflect the evangelists' pattern of making the Romans mere puppets of wicked Jewish will. But while the "king of the Jews" incident may suggest Roman anger against Yeshua as a rebel leader, Sanders still accepts the gospels' version that the "Jews," through their plot, convinced the Romans of Yeshua's role as seditionist, which throws the guilt again fundamentally back on the Jews for suggesting Yeshua's opposition to Rome.

One implication is that it would be slanderous and sinister for Yeshua to have opposed the Romans. This view is compatible with the gospels' view of diminished Roman responsibility as an agent of justice falsely determined by the plotting Jews. It also suggests that we do have knowledge of what the Jewish leaders said behind closed doors, gathered by a miraculous ancient recording device, and we are again back to square one in terms of unverifiable speculation of a Jewish plot to murder Yeshua. Such speculation on the basis of the inherent truth of incidents reported in scripture is common and, until recently, universal. Yet all such speculation founders on its disrespect for the three already noted facts regarding the death of Yeshua: 1) Yeshua died by Roman *crucifixion*; 2) crucifixion was the punishment for *sedition* against Rome, as it was for some forms of civil crime, but in this instance all parties have ruled out civil crime; 3) outside the gospels we have *no information* on the specific nature of the

76. See E. P. Sanders, *Jesus and Judaism* (Philadelphia: Fortress Press, 1987), 294. Sanders looks for discussion of his ideas among many historians who deal with the trial and execution, such as A. E. Harvey, *Jesus on Trial: A Study in the Fourth Gospel* (London: SPCK, 1976), and Paul Winter, *On the Trial of Jesus* (Berlin/New York: De Gruyter, 1974).

political crime of sedition—whether it was his actual opposition to Rome or a plot by his Jewish opponents to convince Rome of his opposition—that persuaded the prefect Pilate to make a public example through crucifixion. Scholars who routinely blame the Jews for setting up Yeshua's death founder on fact 3, which is the unverifiable conspiracy scenario.

A regrettable side of the gospels, as they have come down to us, is the apologetic alibi for Roman authorities in their role in the crucifixion (as well as the acceptance of the depravity of opposing Rome for which the fit punishment will be the destruction of the Temple). Evidence in Acts, Apocalypse, and in routine historical documents about the treatment of Christians in the Roman Empire prior to Constantine's conversion shows an unhappy picture that goes beyond the Christian martyr scenes in the Colosseum. All the miseries of the early Christian under the Roman Empire speak out against the revisionary hands that at critical moments cast the gospels' authors as Roman sympathizers during years of terrible persecution when, among the horror of mass crucifixions, in 70 C.E., the earliest Christian Jews, along with the others, were killed or driven by Roman legions from an incinerated Jerusalem.

In the gospels both the Jewish leaders and the Jews in the street are blamed for Yeshua's death. Those scholars who still contend that the Jewish authority put the Romans up to killing Yeshua are in sad concordance with the Second Vatican Council's diplomatic softening of the universal charge of deicide against the Jewish people. After nearly two thousand years, the Roman Catholic Church, in the *Vatican Council II* document *Nostra Aetate*, announced, "Even though the Jewish authorities and those who followed their lead pressed for the death of Christ (cf. John 19.6), neither all Jews indiscriminately at that time, nor all Jews today, can be charged with the crimes committed during his passion." What is the meaning of "neither all Jews indiscriminately at that time, nor all Jews today"? It shifts the blame of "ancient crimes" from all Jews forever to some Jews discriminately in the past and an unspecified number of Jews today. The Vatican offers an improvement that only reinforces the original change by turning to John 19.6 to validate the ancient, inhuman accusation of deicide. While the Vatican in recent years has officially and courageously acknowledged and apologized for its own crimes over the centuries, here their restatement of Jewish authorities' alleged dominant role in the death of the Galilean is not a happy way of resolving ancient persuasions that have caused so much misery and death.

Graham Stanton comments, "In antiquity crucifixion was the most savage and shameful form of capital punishment. It was so barbarous and inhumane that polite Romans did not talk about it. Crucifixion was carried out by Romans especially on slaves, violent criminals and rebellious subject peoples."[77] With respect to Yeshua's death, Graham Stanton, concurring with E. P. Sanders, states that under Roman law, sedition was a crime for which the crucifixion was a due punishment. But while proposing the accusation of sedition as the active cause of Yeshua's death, like Sanders, Stanton too accepts the plot theory and blames the Jewish Temple authorities for misinformation to the Romans. In both examples, where recent scholars advance a radical and more historical explanation for the crucifixion by seeing more possibilities within the gospel presentation, they assume an impossible premise of knowledge of the intentions and words of the Jewish authorities.

To guess the line of causes of the crucifixion keeps scholars busy speculating about the fate of the historical Yeshua. We do not know the truth of the charge of "king of the Jews." We do not know whether Roman soldiers cast dice for Yeshua's garments, whether he was stabbed with a spear or not (the gospels do not concur on the stabbing). We do not know whether the centurion who was head of the execution squad had an immediate vision after killing Yeshua. Nor do we know that while he and his troops were gazing in awe at the dead Yeshua, he, the centurion, converted on the spot to later Christian credo and declared Yeshua innocent, God, and risen and became the first pagan Christian. We cannot know or argue the veracity or falsehood of these scenes other than to say that certain assertions in the gospels seem likely, unlikely, contradictory, or unverifiable. It is unverifiable which of our assertions has dominion.

In fairness to E. P. Sanders, while he does assert the culpability of the Temple authorities, he elaborates the unknowability of these scenes, and observes that not only theologians but also historians have their "'history' and 'exegesis' dictated by theology." He also observes the well-known

---

77. See Graham Stanton, *Gospel Truth? New Light on Jesus and the Gospels* (London: HarperCollins, 1995), 173.

contradictions and implausibilities about the trial: "It is hard to believe
that a formal court actually convened on the first night of Passover, as
Matthew and Mark have it. Luke, we should note, states that Yeshua
was taken to the Sanhedrin only after daybreak (Luke 22.66). John does
not depict a trial before the Sanhedrin at all." Sanders, who speaks of
himself as a "secularized Protestant," continues:

> The Gospels are all influenced by the desire to incriminate the Jews
> and exculpate the Romans. The insistence of the crowd that Jesus
> be killed, despite Pilate's considering him innocent (Matt. 27.15–
> 26/Mark 15.6–15/Luke 23.18–23; cf. John 18.38), shows this clearly
> enough. The elaborate Jewish trial scenes in the Synoptic Gospels
> also tend to shift responsibility to Judaism in an official way and help
> serve the same purpose.[78]

As for why the evangelists should have wanted so much to exculpate the
Romans, Sanders says, "This reflects the fact that the early Church had
to make its way in the Roman Empire, and did not wish its leader to be
thought of as truly guilty in Roman eyes."[79]

About the actual possibility of the trial and what we can know of it he
writes:

> All we need do is to accept the obvious, that we do not have detailed
> knowledge of what happened when the high priest and possibly oth-
> ers questioned Jesus. We cannot know even that "the Sanhedrin"
> met. Further, I doubt that the earliest followers of Jesus knew. They
> were not privy to the membership list; if people hurried into the high
> priest's house at night there was no one to identify them and tick their
> names off. . . . I am not proposing that the evangelists have deliberately
> deceived us. It seems quite clear that they did not know why Jesus
> was executed from the point of view of the Jewish leaders. We shall
> see, in fact, that they were ignorant even about the composition of a

78. See Sanders, *Jesus and Judaism*, 334, 298.

79. See E. P. Sanders, "Jesus Christ," in David Noel Freeman, ed., *Eerdmans Dictionary of the Bible* (Grand Rapids, MI: William B. Eerdmans Publishing Company,
2000), 706.

Jewish court. New Testament scholars all tell themselves, one another and their students that the Gospel writers were not historians in the modern sense, but we do not apply this fact rigorously enough.

Sanders observes diverse reasons "that could have led the Romans to think that Yeshua was a threat to public order" as grounds for his execution. And he insists that on that confused night "the trial scene of Matthew and Mark is not historical," "that not only do we not know whether the Sanhedrin convened, but our ignorance of all aspects is also shared by the evangelists." Finally, he states, "That the *internal motives* of the actors were known by those on whom the evangelists drew seems impossible." He also castigates fellow modern historians for making assertions not based on historical evidence, for not being rigorous enough.

With all his annoyance at historical presumptions, Sanders still writes, shockingly, "I do not doubt that Jesus was arrested on the orders of the high priest and interrogated."[80] With that declaration Sanders subverts his own detailed and vehement argument that the conspiracy plot, trial, and arrest have no basis in historical reference or probability and that the evangelists wrote to exculpate the Romans. All his argument, historical observations, and his debunking of those who mythologize history and come to facile conclusions disappear. The venom, which entered the gospels and was to persist as a death force directed against Yeshua's coreligionists from early Christendom to the present, is issued once again, implausibly, by an earnest historical interpreter of the gospels.

The story of Jews at the Passover, who kidnap Christian children to perform ritual murder on them to use their blood to prepare the matzo, a tale that exists in virtually every language in Europe, is not heard today. Yet the source of the satanization of the Jews, leading to such tales, lies in the New Testament and, as Elaine Pagels has revealed in *The Origin of Satan*,[81] has not faded; and so the venom, of Jew-hating and Jew-killing, has not vanished. The Jew-hating will not disappear for a reader of the New Testament as long as Yeshua and all his cast continue to have their true identities as observant Jews interacting with Jews obscured. Maybe in a few generations in the Christian West, the dark activity of hatred

80. See Sanders, *Jesus and Judaism*, 299, 300.
81. See Elaine Pagels, *The Origin of Satan* (New York: Vintage, 1995).

and killing will vanish. For now, New Testament scholarship must fully face its responsibility by rejecting as factual history the eternally unforgivable Jewish deeds dramatically presented in the Passion story—a tale about which Paul knew nothing. Then this Jewish scripture will be read with measured understanding and enlightened pleasure. The demonized Jew will be no more. And Yeshua, who escapes demonization only insofar as he is not perceived as a Jew, will have his dignified religious passion fully and jubilantly restored. For the Christian faithful, the undisguised Jew, Yeshua, can be received as the unblemished incarnation of Jewish messianic aspiration.

Recent Scholarship on Yeshua, the Jewish Authorities, Judas, and the Charge of Deicide

Today is a good time with respect to questions of the historical Yeshua, immeasurably good compared to yesterday. But today has a memory. It is hard for many scholars, who must draw primarily on the gospels, to move freely from nearly two millennia of theological exegesis to an unprejudiced walk through historical investigation. The holy precincts of Christianity are a powerful tradition and fortress, and judgment contends with almost insuperable temptations of normative belief. To my surprise, however, these approaches, in commentary and translation, have been welcomed with openness and indeed excitement. With respect to translation, the restoration of Semitic names has already been incorporated in other forthcoming translations. There is enthusiasm in the air for change, which is inevitable.

Among the writers who for many years have moved independently and with great scholarly resources are George Nickelsburg, who has given us his excellent study, *Jewish Literature between the Bible and the Mishnah* (1981), as well as many seminal books and studies on the ties between Judaism and early Christianity. He has dealt meticulously with matters of historicity. Jacob Neusner, in *Judaism When Christianity Began* (2002) and *Judaism in the New Testament* (1995), brings in rabbinic traditions and a knowledge of Mishnaic law. Geza Vermes has pivotal volumes on the historicity of the gospels, including *Jesus the Jew* (1981) and his more recent *Changing Faces of Jesus* (2001). A long important road exists between Albert Schweitzer's *Quest of the Historical Jesus* back in 1906 and Rudolf Bultmann's *History of the Synoptic Tradition* (1966),

W. G. Kümmel's works on the New Testament, Howard Clark Kee's *Jesus in History* (1977), and recent work by Wayne A. Meeks, Burton L. Mack, Elaine Pagels, Paula Fredriksen, Marcus J. Borg, and Graham Stanton, to mention but a few of the scholars who have been innovative and also reach a wide audience. Among younger New Testament scholars, Bart D. Ehrman is fascinating and astute in re-examining God's presence in religion, Jesus quoted and misquoted, and scriptural error, emendations, and misinterpretation. He is a bridge between traditional theological reasoning and modern historical method. His recent books are *God's Problem: How the Bible Fails to Answer Our Most Important Question—Why We Suffer* (2008) and *Misquoting Jesus: The Story behind Who Changed the Bible and Why* (2005).

In studies pertaining to a historical Yeshua, the sticking point is what is worth discussing as a source of history. The quest for the historical Jesus owes its impetus to eighteenth-century Enlightenment and the orientalist Hermann Samuel Reimarus (1694–1768). Schweitzer begins his work on the historical Jesus with Reimarus, as indicated in his title, *Von Reimarus zur Wrede* (1906). Schweitzer elaborates the ethical nature of Yeshua's ministry in first-century Judaism, essentially discounting most information on the historical figure and stressing his idea of a "spiritual kingdom." The Jesus Seminar, which represents a sizable group of contemporary theologians and scholars within the university and clergy, questions the authenticity of Yeshua's words and the events of his life. In their new translation of the New Testament, the Jesus Seminar scholars rate the historical probability of each chapter and verse (which must be taken, at best, as a symbolic gesture toward correction).

As for the historical origins of anti-Judaism that are to be found in the New Testament, no one has written more brilliantly and movingly than Elaine Pagels in *The Origin of Satan*. That disease of anti-Semitism, she informs us, begins with the demonization of the Jews in the Greek scriptures. Pagels finds a historical possibility in the scriptures, however, that leads her to accept, with probability, the story of a Jewish conspiracy, perpetrated by "Jewish leaders," that the New Testament tells. She writes,

I agree as a working hypothesis that Jesus' execution was probably imposed by the Romans for activities they considered seditious—

possibly for arousing public demonstration and (so they apparently
believed) for claiming to be "King of the Jews." Among his own people,
however, Jesus appeared as a radical prophetic figure whose public
teaching, although popular with the crowds, angered and alarmed
certain Jewish leaders, especially the Temple authorities, who probably facilitated his capture and arrest.

Later, in discussing the diverse uses of the term "Jew" in the gospels, she
tells us that "John, like the other Gospels, associates the mythological
figure of Satan with specific human opposition, first implicating Judas
Iscariot, then the Jewish authorities, and finally 'the Jews collectively'."
But, after stating that the gospels associate mythological Satan (presumably unfairly and incorrectly) with both Judas and Jewish authorities
in order to blame them for Yeshua's death, she returns to her original
premise: "Let us assume, first, that it is historically likely that certain
Jewish leaders may have collaborated with Roman authorities in Jesus'
arrest and execution." While she absolutely deplores and disdains the
accusations of guilt and demonization of the Jews, and colors those
accusations as gospel mythology, she too believes (at least in these passages) that these accusations are "historically likely" to be true. Like
well-intentioned Sanders and Stanton, Pagels provides the demonizers of
the Jews with their essential opening for pinning guilt collectively and
eternally on the Jews, as Matthew proclaims, for Yeshua's death.

Who can believe that a Jewish mob on the first night of Passover is
in the street shouting to a reluctant prefect, "Crucify him!" followed by
"Let his blood be upon us and upon our children!"? Would anybody
shout a curse upon themselves and their children? The notion is silly
but noxious, and has followed the Jews for two millennia. At the instant
before his death, Yeshua cries out to God his despair of abandonment,
in Aramaic, his own tongue. At this supreme moment of Yeshua's death
as a tortured Jewish man by Roman crucifixion, he may be "King of the
Jews" in Roman mockery, but to the evangelists and future followers
he is seen as the Christian God, not the Jewish *mashiah*. More, by
inventing a scene of mass Jewish guilt that he notably does not share,
Yeshua at once ceases to be perceived as a Jew. He is defrocked. He is
stripped of his robes of faith and tradition as a messianic Jew preaching
redemption.

These hate scenes lack historicity. We know that the church of Rome needed to find the Jews, not the earlier Romans, guilty for Yeshua's death. Pagels explains that those who wrote about Yeshua were "devoted admirers, even as his worshipers," and she writes, further, that the gospels were "wartime literature" (referring to the Jewish-Roman war in 66–70), and composed to persuade other Jews not to agitate against the Romans. These "wartime literature" gospels were, as Pagels interprets them, citing Josephus, Roman-biased documents warning Jews not to resist Rome or else suffer devastation.[82]

In character with recent historical criticism on killing Yeshua the man, William Nicholls, in his book *Christian Anti-Semitism*, writes,

> Did the Jews kill Christ? We shall discover that the stories in the gospels that suggest they did are exceedingly improbable. The Jews did not kill Jesus because they had no reason to do so. He was not guilty of any religious offense. It is in the highest degree improbable that such a trial before the Sanhedrin as we read of in the gospels of Mark and Matthew ever took place. What we read in the gospels about the trial of Jesus is the project of later Christian imagination, and it reflects Christian, not Jewish, views of the nature of the Messiah.[83]

Nicholls, Nickelsburg, and Vermes reflect at least a strong component of contemporary historical criticism. While, as noted, other distinguished figures state that there was a Jewish plot to arrest and kill Yeshua the lord, the current mood and scholarship of religious studies in university and seminary generally has, increasingly, little patience for dreadful conspiracy theory.

Elaine Pagels is our most original and eloquent interpreter of the period for Jewish, Christian, and Gnostic matters, and a champion of women in her books *The Gnostic Gospels* (1979) and *Adam, Eve, and the Serpent* (1988). Yet Pagels, Sanders, Stanton, and a majority of earlier and many contemporary religious historians seem to hold to the premise

---

82. See Pagels, *Origin of Satan*, xxii, 105, 7.

83. See William Nicholls, *Christian Anti-Semitism: A History of Hate* (Northvale, NJ/ London: Jason Aronson, 1995), 17.

that Jewish authorities plotted and achieved Yeshua's death through the instrument of the weak, innocent, but acquiescing Roman prefect of Palestine.[84] At the very least they accept an active Jewish involvement in the events leading to Yeshua's crucifixion. They do so without malice, with good conscience, based on their sound historical wisdom and experience in the fields. Yet we cannot know that the Jewish conspiracy is factual. Nor can we know that there was not a conspiracy of Jews against the rabbi Yeshua. And since no truth can be established with regard to the drama of Yeshua's death, we must stop there, and escape from the traditional assumptions so hard to lay to rest. It might be that angry Jews conspired horribly against other Jews and even in worse ways than the theatrical scenes that the New Testament enacts. The Essenes, the sons of light, certainly declared their intention to wipe out, through war, the Jewish sons of darkness inhabiting Jerusalem. Nothing is surprising in the history of sectarian conflict. Here it is beyond dispute that we have no references to the Jews and the crucifixion outside the frame of the late gospels. The few historical mentions of Yeshua by name say nothing in this regard, including Josephus.

That ultimate condemnation of the Jews will create the terrible history of Jews and Christians. I should also venture that even were there a historical basis for Jewish plot theory, it should no more lead to global and eternal condemnation of selective Jews (since Christian Jews and Yeshua's family have been spared) than the execution of Socrates should lead to an eternal curse on the souls of Greeks.

84. Though Marcus Borg in his *Meeting Jesus Again for the First Time* (San Francisco: HarperSanFrancisco, 1994) refutes "the popular image of Jesus" and blames "parts of the New Testament" for constructing a picture of Jews against Yeshua, he too refers to Yeshua's crucifixion and his Jewish "opponents." With the kind intention of exonerating Jews in general from Yeshua's death, he asserts, as fact, the evil of a few enemy Jews. He writes, "But Jesus' opponents did not represent the Jewish people or nation. Rather, the few Jewish persons involved in the events leading to his execution were a small but powerful elite whose power derived from the Romans. Instead of representing the Jews, they might fairly be described as collaborating in the oppression of the Jewish people" (22).

To assume that a powerful elite of Herodian Jews collaborated with Romans, or worse, according to scripture, that unwilling Romans were urged by Jews in the street and from the Sanhedrin to execute Yeshua, as Marcus Borg writes, returns us to the fearful conspiracy theory of the Greek texts.

We can believe through Christian faith in 1) Yeshua's virgin birth, 2) his miracles, and 3) his resurrection. And though the New Testament is presented not as a tale but a report, many contemporary theologians will shepherd these key notions onto the meadow of faith and demand no historic proof from the gospels. But the alleged conspiracy plot by Jews against Yeshua has nothing to do with Christian faith. We can guess the circumstance of rivalry and self-exoneration that may have induced the early church to fabricate a conspiracy scene. The grave accusation demands historical credibility or dismissal once and for all.

After all this, is there anything we can say about the crucifixion scene without falling into the trap of purposeful invention of evidence? Having spoken about what can *not* be said, what specific, historical assumption *can* we make? There remain pivotal questions that can be reasonably elaborated. We say or deny that there existed a historic Jew named Yeshua of Nazareth, who especially after his death and witnessed resurrection was called the messiah. It is widely doubted that Yeshua himself assumed the title of messiah during his lifetime, but that, too, is speculation. We can also say or deny that the same Yeshua was crucified in the fourth decade of the first century by order of a historical figure, Pontius Pilate, the prefect or governor of Judea. We can say that those sayings attributed to Yeshua in the Gospel of Thomas and repeated and augmented in the gospels, while reflecting a wide oral rabbinic wisdom tradition based on biblical wisdom scripture, may or may not in small or large part be statements originating with Yeshua. Beyond these bare statements, none of them for the moment provable or unprovable, there is historical speculation and faith.

In the search for historicity, we can go a crucial step further than affirming the absence of historical proof. Sometimes there is enough external textual evidence to assert the improbability of certain events, which is a crucial positive step. For example, the figure of Judas lacks historical probability, since this story of the betrayer seems to be lifted intact and anachronistically from Midrashic tale. There is also the convenient parallel in Genesis of the Joseph story, where Judah sells Joseph for twenty pieces of silver. Bishop John Shelby Spong writes eloquently in *Liberating the Gospels* (1996) of the Judas story as a Christian invention. The common folklore motif of the betrayer was trumped up, in all its telling details, to use against the Jews as one of the colorful ways of exonerating Rome, and the Christians who inherited Rome, from Yeshua's death.

The motive for the insertion of the Judas story into the gospels is clear. Judas carries the name "Judas" to make "a Jew" be the betrayer of Yeshua. "Judas" is from the Greek *Ioudas* ('Ιούδας), from the Hebrew name *Yehuda* (יְהוּדָה), which signifies the province of Judea as well as "one who pertains to the tribe of Yehudi (יְהוּדִי—yehudi)," that is, a Jew. The word "Judea" is a Latin version of the Greek *Ioudaia* ('Ιουδαία). So in Greek as well as in Hebrew, "Judas," "Jew," and "Judaism" are synonymous.

Such is the power of names that *Ioudas* ('Ιούδας) in the King James Version is translated in all other cases as "Juda" so that Judas will remain uniquely the caricature of the evil Jew of the New Testament. In modern versions, such as the NRSV, "Juda" has been given its correct translation of "Judas." Gone is the intent of saving Yeshua's own brother Judas from bearing the name of the betrayer. Among the epistles of the New Testament we still have Jude in the "Letter of Jude" in all translations. The names "Juda," "Judah," and "Jude" are all translation masks to separate Christians Jews from Judas, but in the Greek texts they all have one name, *Ioudas* ('Ιούδας). Judas is a key figure in denigrating the image of the Jew, and his name remains a word in all languages for traitor.

In keeping with making Judas the Jew among the primitive Christians, who are Yeshua and his students, there is a pictorial tradition of making Judas look like the somber thief while the other disciples take on the features of the painter's nation. In the national art museum in Prague in a series of paintings of Yeshua and his disciples, all appear as fair Slavs, except for Judas, who is bent over as the dark, crafty Mediterranean.

The Charge of Deicide

Here we depart radically from the discussion of Rome killing Yeshua as "King of the Jews." Did Rome kill God as well? And, more crucial, can the biblical God be killed? The notion of deicide inevitably takes us to the history of Christological speculation on the human and divine in Yeshua. The early centuries of Christianity saw fearful debates about the nature of Christ, especially in the East. The Docetists (from *dokein*, "to seem"), along with overlapping Gnostics, Nestorians, Arians, and Monophysites, were the main contenders for control of doctrines. The

Docetists held that the figure on the cross was a simulacrum of Yeshua, since divine Yeshua could not be killed by mortals. By the end of the seventh century, these docetic "heresies" yielded to the prevailing orthodoxy of the Church: the incarnation of the divine word in the flesh as expounded in the prologue of the Gospel of John: "And the word became flesh" (John 1.14). In the incarnation, the divine word (the *logos*), which precedes the flesh, lives in union with the flesh during Yeshua's life, and after the flesh's death, the word, which is the divinity of God, survives. Yeshua suffers pain as a human and dies, but the word residing in him is eternal. The eternal God of the Abrahamic faiths cannot be killed by Jews, Christians, Greeks, Romans, or anyone. Hence, God cannot be the victim of deicide. But the charge of deicide presumes that God dies, and that after the crucifixion he disappears. God's death surely is not acceptable to those who have accused Jews of killing God. Indeed, those who charge deicide do so while firmly believing that God not only is alive but also will avenge the deicide, that is, his killing and death. Deep confusion presides.

While the notion of deicide is self-contradictory, this self-contradiction has persisted for two millennia. The gospels have none of it. The Roman centurion who executes rabbi Yeshua is the first to tell the crowds that Yeshua is God and arisen. He does not announce that his now recognized God is dead. A man dies, but not God. And paradoxically, three days after his crucifixion, Yeshua returns to earth in human form. At one moment he asks the doubting Thomas to touch his wounds. For the believer, God lives and his everlasting existence has never lapsed. So the notion of deicide is a cruel rhetorical and logical impossibility, and no person or people should be accused of having the desire or the means of committing what is humanly impossible: to kill the biblical God.

As a summary of the three crucial historical questions, *Rome, deicide,* and *Judas,* I take from Spong's *Liberating the Gospels* two powerful and succinct paragraphs from his chapter on Judas, "Judas Iscariot: A Christian Invention?" After twenty pages of detailing incongruities in the betrayal story, and indicating the source of the spurious betrayal story in Midrashic scripture, Spong concludes,

I only want to register now that it is a tragedy of enormous dimensions that, by the time the story of Jesus' arrest and execution came to be written, the Christians made the Jews, rather than the Romans, the villains of their story. I suggest that this was achieved primarily by creating the narrative of a Jewish traitor according to the *Midrashic* tradition out of the bits and pieces of the sacred scriptures and by giving that traitor the name Judas, the very name of the nation of the Jews. As a result, from that day to this, the blame for the death of Jesus has been laid on the backs, not just of Judas, the Jewish proto-type, but of the entire people of the Jews themselves. "His blood be upon us and upon our children." That was a biblical sentence of death to untold numbers of Jews.

I raise this possibility to consciousness in the hope that as you and I are awakened to the realization of what this story of Judas has done to the Jews of history, we Christians might rise up and deal a death blow to the most virulent Christian prejudice that has for 2,000 years placed on the Jewish people the blame for the death of Jesus. If that result could be achieved, then the darkest clouds that have hung over the Christian church in our history might finally begin to lift.[85]

To Bishop Spong's lucid words, I note what should be obvious. Those who were messianics close to Yeshua were still decades away from being referred to in Greek as Christians. Yeshua, his family, and followers were Jews, not strangers from another faith or ethnicity. They had not fallen to earth from another solar system. Since the Passion tales in the four gospels declared all Jews forever guilty of a horrible crime, Yeshua and the early saints, all Jews, must share this ignominy of hate. If only the identity of the actors in these scenes that shaped worlds were commonly known, the scaffolding of anti-Judaism would collapse.

85. See John Shelby Spong, *Liberating the Gospels: Reading the Bible with Jewish Eyes: Freeing Jesus from 2,000 Years of Misunderstanding* (San Francisco: HarperSanFrancisco, 1996), 276. For more on the origin of the betrayer tale of Judas in scripture and post-biblical portrayals in history and the arts, see note 30 on p. 33, in "Mark, the Vernacular Story Teller." For a more complete account of Judas from the Bible to modern times, see Susan Gubar's *Judas: A Biography* (New York: W. W. Norton, 2009).

Old Circumcision and
New Circumcision in Greek
and Hebrew Leading to
Old Testament and
New Testament

~⁓~

Circumcision in the Heart in Paul's Romans

HAD THERE BEEN any holy scripture around when Paul was writing his epistles, he might have called the New Testament (his "new covenant"), that later gathering of gospels, letters, and Apocalypse, "The Spiritual Circumcision." Paul argued compassionately in his letters that the old traditional covenant of his fellow Jews, which was established by the painful ceremony of the circumcision, need not be solely of the body. He advocated a new covenant, one of the spirit, which is more significant than that of the flesh. He said,

> Someone is not a Jew by what is seen.
> Rather, one is a Jew by what is hidden.
> Circumcision is of the heart, the spirit,
> Not from the literal law. So one finds praise
> Not from the ranks of men. It comes from God.
>
> ROM. 2.28–29

Such an interpretation left an opening to gentile converts to become Messianic Jews by adopting the spirit of the rite of circumcision rather than undergoing the old rite itself. Paul's words about circumcision have usually been interpreted as a rejection of the Old Testament for a yet to be conceived or written New Testament, or a rejection of old Judaism for a new Judaism, which later, when there is scripture and a church, will, after the acknowledgment of the messiah, the Christ, be known as Christianity.

Certainly Paul was seeking to change Judaism, and among these changes one was, in disagreement with Peter, to do away with the obligation of circumcision, for those who wished to join the followers of Yeshua the Messiah. His words about circumcision in the heart as well as of the flesh, in which heart and spirit prevail, also appear in Deuteronomy 10.16, Jeremiah 9.26, and Ezekiel 44.9. Paul returned to the authority of Deuteronomy precisely to show that within the Hebrew Bible there was the tribal obligation not only of a physical sign to represent a pact or covenant with God but also of a spiritual sign, centered in the heart.

Paul's main source is probably a famous passage in Deuteronomy. Moses has climbed Mount Sinai a second time, and remains there forty days and forty nights, when God will write again his commandments on two tablets of stone, which earlier had been destroyed. Moses comes down and reports to Israel, his people, what the lord requires of them. Among the instructions are for a circumcision in the spirit: "Circumcise, then, the foreskin of your heart, and do not be stubborn any longer" (Deut. 10.16, New Revised Standard Version). This line is generally interpreted to mean that one must open the mind to direct the will to God. Again in Jeremiah 9.26 (NRSV), we read, more graphically, "Circumcise yourselves to the Lord, remove the foreskin of your heart." And once more in Ezekiel 44.9 (NRSV), we hear an admonishment against being "uncircumcised in heart and flesh." We see here that Paul does *not* reject Torah by contrasting his Messianism to it, but goes directly to the Hebrew scriptures to show that heart and spirit are more than flesh. Indeed, with respect to circumcision, as he affirms spirit over body he also affirms that one is a Jew who in one's heart hears the voice of God.

Paul as a Torah scholar had the deepest understanding of the diverse covenants in the Jewish Bible: Mosaic, Abrahamic, and Davidic, each signifying a compact or commitment entailing promises and obligations with God. The relationship is sealed by a rite, among which are oath, meal, blood (circumcision), and sacrifice or offerings. The Hebrew word *berit* means both specific circumcision and abstractly moral covenant as in the Sinai *berit*. Paul was concerned with physical and spiritual circumcision, the latter meaning not only of the body but more important in inward parts and as written on the heart, which is sufficient. Jeremiah more than anyone in scripture, even more than Paul's cited sources in Deuteronomy, expresses the larger meaning of "new covenant" to which he aspires:

> Behold, the days come, saith the LORD, that I will make a new covenant with the house of Israel, and with the house of Judah: Not according to the covenant that I made with their fathers in the day *that* I took them by the hand to bring them out of the land of Egypt; which my covenant they brake, although I was a husband unto them, saith the LORD: But this *shall be* the covenant that I will make with the house of Israel; After those days, saith the LORD, I will put my law in their inward parts, and write it in their hearts; and will be their God, and they shall be my people.
>
> JER. 31.30–33,
>
> KING JAMES VERSION

Paul is against physical circumcision for newcomers, but he makes it perfectly clear that for a would-be convert to Judaism, the spiritual pact is essential, while the bodily sign of the pact is neither essential nor obligatory. With regard to the law, Paul breaks no law. On the contrary he finds support in the Jewish Bible for the higher place given circumcision of the heart (the spirit) over physical circumcision. But the Hebrew Bible does not take the extra step, which is to say that if the spiritual covenant is there, the physical circumcision—the covenant's external marker— can be dispensed with. Therein lies the great difference, which was to be crucial to the spread of Christianity.

Paul was a Jew, and purportedly after seeing the light on the way to Damascus, a Christian Jew. And Paul was concerned with a new covenant, which later became the name of the Greek scriptures called the New Testament, by contrasting the spiritual circumcision in the heart in Deuteronomy, Jeremiah, and Ezekiel to the bloody rite of physical circumcision in the covenant between God and Abraham (Gen. 17.1–23), which he wanted to go beyond. God offers to reward Abraham by making him the ancestor of a multitude of nations, and many other good things, that is, an earthly messiah. In exchange Abraham must undergo the rite of circumcision, which becomes a tribal sign of loyalty to the lord.

Paul, the missionary and advocate of Yeshua in the diaspora synagogues of the Mediterranean, was convinced that the covenant with Abraham was, compared to the examples in Deuteronomy, Jeremiah, and Ezekiel, limited, brutal, and a bad marketing tool for the new Judaism.

The word for circumcision in late Hebrew is *berit* (בְּרִית) and means not only circumcision. Since the circumcision was the rite confirming the covenant with God, this physical meaning has a metaphorical and abstract meaning in Hebrew of "covenant." So when Paul speaks in Romans of a circumcision of the heart, he could find in the same word its cross-language levels of meaning. Knowing that in Hebrew physical circumcision and conceptual covenant reside in the same word, he can play with the Greek *peritome* (περιτομή) a cutting around, "circumcision," to ask for the dominant sense of the covenant not to be Abrahamic circumcision, the external act and sign, but the inner circumcision. But why Paul used this particular metaphor, "*berit* of the heart," for spiritual loyalty can only be deeply understood if one understands, as any Hellenized (that is, Greek-speaking) Jew would, the Hebrew equation of circumcision and spirit.[86]

86. To understand how circumcision works as a synecdoche, consider the word "baptism." To say that a Jewish child or an adult has been circumcised means that the person circumcised has formally become a Jew and has entered, during the ceremony, into a covenant with God, with all duties and entitlements. Equivalent to the rite of circumcision was the widespread ancient Jewish rite of baptism, as performed by John the Baptizer (Yohanan the Dipper), a Jew who lived and died before Christianity or Christian Jews existed. In 2 Kings 5.14, we read of immersions (baptism) in the river in order to be cured as by the word of God: "So he went down and immersed himself seven times in the Jordan; according to the word of the man of God; his flesh was restored like the flesh of a young boy, and he was clean." That ceremony of the baptism, meaning in Greek "to dip, as in water," later became the ceremony for formally becoming a Christian, with all duties and entitlements. It was not an unpleasant act. In the physical immediacy of being dipped in water and its covenantal symbolism of becoming a Christian, baptism became a Christian version of *berit*, with its specific physical act of the cutting of the flesh and its covenantal symbolism of becoming a Jew. As for would-be Christians who do not get baptized, or Jews and Muslims who do not get circumcised, the outlook has traditionally been grim, for here and eternity. For the Christian, it may mean an eternity in limbo. For the Jew and Muslim, God does not look on the uncircumcised as his own. Remember Genesis 17.14: "Any uncircumcised male who is not circumcised in the flesh of his foreskin shall be cut off from his people; he has broken my covenant." In every religion God is sectarian

There is an interesting linguistic reason why *berit* or *brit* took on its simultaneous meaning of "covenant." Biblical Hebrew had few abstract and conceptual words. Hence, when a conceptual word was needed, its rich denotative words for things were often upgraded to contain a conceptual meaning. Biblical Hebrew is an immediate, bold language, which carries with it a sonorous roughness and vitality. The first pages of Genesis echo with contrapuntal chant. A parallel between the bold "word as thing" in Hebrew and the "word as idea" in Greek is English words of Anglo-Saxon compared to those of Latin derivation. The Anglo-Saxon tend to be briefer, stronger, and based on image, while the Latin tends to be polysyllabic, abstract, and based on concept. In Hebrew the richness of the word *berit* is that it retains the elemental circumcision of a physical rite as well as the spiritual covenant. Both meanings sound with equal force.

The Church fathers, picking up on Paul's notion of a spiritual circumcision as spiritual covenant, saw in Paul's argument not only a good phrase for their new scriptures, the New Testament, but also a clearly implied rejection of the Old Covenant, that is, the Jewish Bible. Thereafter in languages other than Hebrew, "Old Covenant," became the title for the Hebrew Bible. In the Latin languages based, as noted, on Jerome's mistranslation of covenant, where "covenant" turned into "testament," we have the New Testament and the Old Testament. That invention of Old Covenant versus New Covenant has a precedent in several later fathers of the Church. But insofar as the word derived from Paul, the meaning was in no way a rejection of Hebrew Bible scripture but rather a reconfirmation of spiritual rites established by the Old Covenant. For Paul's physical circumcision versus spiritual circumcision is certainly not an "Old Testament Circumcision versus a New Testament circumcision." The choice was not between the authority of Hebrew and Greek scriptures (there were no Greek scriptures when Paul wrote other than his own letters), but between two ways spelled out in the Jewish Bible.

---

and keeps the faithful obedient to the comportment of the sect. As for women, either by neglect or ignorance of female circumcision, women were (with some notorious exceptions) exempt from genital circumcision. For the Christian woman and man, the required rite of baptism was painless and carried none of the terror of adult male circumcision for Jews and Muslims.

Paul chose a spiritual way to know and make a pact with God. His words say that the true Jew is one who follows the inward meaning of circumcision. He rejects neither the Torah nor his Jewishness. His words "old" and "new" are to affirm his preferred example of virtue. As for using old and new as a powerful vehicle for rejecting the worth of the Old Testament, that was the work of later Church fathers.

Spiritual Circumcision that Opens the Way for Painless Conversion

In the first years when Christian Jews were busily proselytizing Jews and gentiles to a belief that the messiah had come to earth, died, and risen in the figure of Yeshua, a major obstacle for outsider conversion to the new sect of the Jews was the painful and dangerous ritual of the circumcision, which involved the cutting away of the foreskin. Let us look with some detail at the Abrahamic example, and how Paul, by advocating spiritual over physical proof of faith, opened the door to a rapidly expanding sect. Abraham cut a deal with God. "You shall circumcise the flesh of your foreskins, and it shall be a sign of the covenant between me and you" (Gen. 17.11).[87] The sign of the covenant inflicted by God was crucial. It sealed their agreement.

Abraham was ninety-nine when he submitted to the cutting, which provoked his unsettling laughter as he worried whether a man could father a child at his age; and he flung himself on his face and he laughed, and spoke out loud to himself, wondering whether this was a reward or a painful joke (Gen. 17.17). As for Sarah, upon learning that she, at ninety, already "withered and dry," was to have a child, her first reaction was also to laugh (18.12–15). A year later, their son Yitzhak (Isaac) was born, and so began a line of progeny that would be the first linear family of the Jews. Appropriately, Abraham's son bore the name *Yitzhak*, meaning "he will laugh," reflecting his laughter of happiness and pain.

This covenant established Abraham as the patriarchal ancestor of the Jews, the progenitor of kings, the father of his nation and of a multitude of

---

87. The covenant begins in chapter 15 when in a dream Abram has a vision in which Adonai tells Abram, "Do not be afraid, Abram, I am your shield; your reward shall be very great." The name "Abraham" is explained for its similarity in Hebrew to "multitude of nations," but the roots of "Abraham" are *ab* "father" + *raham* "exalted."

nations. These were extraordinary rewards and protections for Abraham, a simple nomadic shepherd, owner of herds and a few slaves in his household, from perhaps the Middle Bronze Age (2000–1900 B.C.E.) or as late as the Iron Age (1200–900 B.C.E.), who could have been a historical person, or more likely and eponymous figure representing a people, Israel. In return, God, the generous landlord, demanded recognition of his sovereignty and obedience to his law. That recognition and obedience would be forever etched in the skin by circumcision of his children, the Jews, and even of foreign slaves brought into their houses. The narration of this deal between God and Abraham is fully elaborated in Genesis 17.1–14:

> And Abram was ninety-nine years old and the Lord appeared to Abram and said to him, "I am El Shaddai.[88] Walk with Me and be blameless, and I will grant My covenant between Me and you and I will multiply you very greatly." And Abram flung himself on his face, and God spoke to him, saying, "As for Me, this is My covenant with you: you shall be father to a multitude of nations. And no longer shall your name be called Abram but your name shall be Abraham, for I have made you father to a multitude of nations. And I will make you most abundantly fruitful and turn you into nations, and kings shall come forth from you. And I will establish My covenant between Me and you and your seed after you through their generations as an everlasting covenant to be God to you and to your seed after you. And I will give unto you and your seed after you the land in which you sojourn, the whole land of Canaan, as an everlasting holding, and I will be their God."
>
> And God said to Abram, "As for you, you shall keep My commandment, you and your seed after you through their generations. This is My covenant which you shall keep, between Me and you and your seed after you: every male among you must be circumcised. You shall circumcise the flesh of your foreskin and

88. *El Shaddai* is translated in KJV and even in the modern New Revised Standard Version as "God Almighty." Actually, it is a beautiful name, meaning "God of the Mountains." Robert Alter calls the translator's habit of explaining or interpreting a metaphor rather than giving a literal version "the heresy of explanation." Robert Alter, *The Five Books of Moses: A Translation with Commentary* (New York: W. W. Norton, 2004), xix.

it shall be the sign of the covenant between Me and you. Every
eight-day-old male among you shall be circumcised through your
generations, even slaves born in the household and those purchased with silver must be circumcised, and My covenant in your
flesh shall be an everlasting covenant. And a male with a foreskin,
who has not circumcised the flesh of his foreskin, that person
shall be cut off from his folk. My covenant he has broken."

The rite was performed not only on Abraham but also on his son and
his household:

And Abraham was ninety-nine years old when the flesh of
his foreskin was circumcised. On that very day Abraham was
circumcised, and Ishmael his son, and all the men of his household, those born in the household and those purchased with
silver from the foreigners, were circumcised with him.

GEN.17.23–27

For the first Christian Jews, circumcision was a dire question in those
days when the new sect of messianics was establishing itself. Paul leaves
the door wide open for new Christian Jews not to be circumcised. With
eloquence and Talmudic logic, he argues in favor of a lofty meaning of
the circumcision, the pact with God, the covenantal price for becoming
a Jew and upholding the law (the commandments of Torah). Paul writes
that it is worse to be circumcised and break the law than not to be
circumcised yet obey the law.

In the years that Paul is writing about a mitigated and higher form of
circumcision, we observe that such ideas are very much in the air. In the
contemporary wisdom Gospel of Thomas, we find an extraordinary parallel that is more severe in its ridicule of physical circumcision. Yeshua
is derisive, saying that the physical must yield to the spiritual. In saying
53, he is asked about circumcision:

STUDENTS
Is circumcision useful or not?
YESHUA
If it were useful, fathers would produce their children

Already circumcised from their mothers.
But the true circumcision in spirit
Is fully valuable.

GOSPEL OF THOMAS[89]

The advantage of "true circumcision in spirit" for the gentiles who would join the developing sect of Christian Jews was enormous. It meant that without going through an adult mutilation of their genital organ, they could enjoy equality of acceptance before the Messianics who were born as Jews, who represented the greater body of the followers of Yeshua, including Peter and Paul, who had had their circumcision on the eighth day after their birth, hence avoiding the adult trauma of the rite.

Covenants and Testaments and Their Names of Old and New

I have tried to convey some notion of the related meanings of "circumcision" and "covenant,"[90] and of a sign in the flesh of an everlasting covenant. When the Christian Bible became traditionally separated into two covenants or testaments, they took on the names of "Old Covenant" and "New Covenant," and in Western Europe, "Old Testament" and "New

---

89. In his *Gospel of Thomas* (San Francisco: HarperSanFrancisco, 1992), Marvin W. Meyer comments on saying 53: "This saying critiques the value of physical circumcision and instead recommends spiritual circumcision. Compare Romans 2.25–29, as well as other passages in Paul. According to a Jewish tradition, a governor of Judea once commented to Rabbi Akiba, 'If he (that is, God) takes such pleasure in circumcision, why then does not a child come circumcised from his mother's womb?'"

90. As "covenant" increasingly gains acceptance as the translation of διαθήκη, the persistence of "testament" as the traditional translation of *diatheke* has prompted explanations of covenant as "an alternate translation of the Greek words (*kaine diatheke*)" (*The HarperCollins Bible Dictionary*, ed. Paul J. Achtemeier, San Francisco: HarperSanFrancisco, 1996, 750). To say "alternate" suggests a choice between possible meanings. It would be better to say that "testament" is an error and "covenant" the right transfer of *diatheke* into English. Greek *diatheke* means a covenant, agreement, and can also mean "a last will and testament," but this latter possible meaning does not contain the notion of "covenant" in the Hebrew Bible. "Testament" by itself suggests not a two-way covenant, in which each party does his or her share, but a credo, a statement, or witnessing (etymological meaning) as in testimony, none of which is intended in *diatheke*. It should be noted that the Greek word διαθήκη (diatheke) does not have, like its Hebrew antecedent, בְּרִית (berit), the other meaning of "circumcision," which in Greek is περιτομή (peritome).

Testament." These two temporal signs of old and new were fashioned to distinguish two religions in a single Bible.

"Old Testament" is a Christian Greek name for the Jewish Bible. The Jews did not participate in the renaming of their scripture, the Tanak or Torah or simply Bible, but in the languages they spoke, they, too, in public communication have used the common appellation. In a chronological sense this appellation is accurate, for the New Testament was accepted in its final form in the late fourth century. However, while "the new" is undoubtedly appropriate for the Greek scriptures, for it followed the earlier Hebrew scriptures, the question of the epithet "old" is pragmatic but problematic.

We first encounter the actual Greek words "new covenant" (not "new testament") in Paul:

> Our skill and competence derive
> From God, who also gave us competence
> As ministers of a new covenant,
> Not of the letter but of the spirit since
> The letter kills whereas the spirit gives life.
>
> 2 COR. 3.5–6

In his letter to the Corinthians, he calls for a new covenant, but Paul did not speak of "old covenant" as a metonym to represent the larger Jewish Bible any more than was "new covenant" a metonym for future New Covenant scriptures. In no place in his letters did Paul call for new scriptures to be assembled into a Christian Bible. As a Jew who died before the gospels were composed, who sought to convince coreligionists that Yeshua was the messiah, Paul would scarcely have foreseen a new compendium of holy scripture that might be added to or replace the long-since canonized Hebrew Bible, and certainly not his own letters included in his canon.

It was the Church fathers Tertullian (ca. 160–230) and Origen (ca. 185–254) who were among the first to use the term "Old Covenant" for the Hebrew Bible. The earliest use of "Old Covenant" seems to be by Melito, bishop of Sardis, who, according to Eusebius,[91] made a list of

---

91. *Ecclesiastical History* 4.26.12, in Eusebius Pamphilus, *Eusebius' Ecclesiastical History*, trans. C. F. Cruse (Indianapolis: Hendrickson Publisher, 1998).

writings of the Old Covenant. Eusebius quotes a letter by Melito to a certain Onesimus: "I came to the East and learned the books of the Old Covenant." This letter is dated ca. 170 C.E. We find in the New Covenant the frequent notion of witnessing and testimony or last will and testament, but the notion of witnessing or a testimony between God and his people is definitely not the primary meaning of *diatheke*.

In Western Catholic and Protestant countries, we still have the universal usage of "New Testament" as a synonym for "New Covenant." The meanings of words always change, including within a language, and especially in translation. For Christians of the Catholic and Protestant West, "New Testament" determined the name of the earlier holy scripture, which logically had to balance and also contrast with the old name for holy scripture. Hence the invention of "Old Testament" as the proper Western Christian name for the Jewish or Hebrew Bible[92]—without input from Jews about their Bible's title in its diverse translations. Jews, of course, have gone along, since public language, whatever its history, demands that in order to communicate one follows common usage.

Whether "testament" or "covenant," either word imposes a non-Jewish title on the Jewish Bible preserved in Hebrew and Aramaic.[93] By contrast, the Qur'an or Koran, while pronounced and spelled differently in other languages, remains the Qur'an, and though schisms also exist in the Muslim world, the title of the Qur'an has not been an issue.

Although, as mentioned, Jews have gone along in common speech with using the term "Old Testament," this is the traditional Christian name, not the Jewish name, for their Bible. So *berit*, the source name of the Christian Bible, whether you translate it "circumcision" or "covenant," is not relevant to diverse "right" titles of the Jewish Bible in English, in other tongues, or in Hebrew. First, it must be said that for Jews, as

92. "Jewish Bible" and "Hebrew Bible" are both used for the Old Testament. "Jewish Bible" implies Bible of the Jews, equivalent to "Christian scriptures" for New Covenant, and "Hebrew Bible," referring to language, suggests Bible in Hebrew as opposed to "Greek scriptures" for the New Covenant.

93. Some portions of Daniel and other scriptures survive and were probably written in Aramaic, which took over in later biblical times. Aramaic was the greater language of the Near East, covering much of the western Asian coast and into Mesopotamia. Eventually koine-Greek replaced Aramaic in parts of this same region and elsewhere in the Seleucid (312–364 B.C.E.) and until late Byzantine periods.

for Christians, the common word in English for their holy scriptures is "the Bible." Academics, to distinguish the holy scriptures of the Jews from the combined holy scriptures of Jews and Christians, speak of the Jewish Bible, the Hebrew Bible, the Law, the Scrolls. Hebrew names for the Bible are Torah (meaning "law" or "instruction") or Tanak (an acronym from initial Hebrew letters for Torah, Prophets, and Writings), or the three major divisions of Tanak: Torah (Five Books of Moses), Nev'im (Prophets), and Kethuvim (Writings). Whatever name is given by Jews to the Bible, it is not properly the old, nor the testament, nor the covenant.

The matter of the covenant is, of course, a fundamental and deeply Jewish concept. But this Jewish concept was never used by Jesus for the naming of their sacred book. "Old Testament" is used by Christians who uneasily assumed and interpreted the Jewish Bible as their own, and who found new terms to ensure their original and unique possession of it, while at the same time expressing discomfort about their possession of an imperfect, blemished old book, with alien pre-Christian figures in it. To cite one of many commonplaces, there is "the stern God of anger and vengeance of the Old Testament" as opposed to "the God of love and compassion of the New Testament," which inexorably implies two godheads in the Christian Bible. If God is the same immutable figure in both books, then his "human" character is inferior to and other than the God described in the New Testament. Such interpretation that makes eternal God fickle of personality, changing his ways and authority with the age and book, might seem irreverent, but such views have been perfectly normal. Indeed, Jack Miles, a former Jesuit, in his erudite *God: A Biography*,[94] traces the changing nature of God in the Old Testament with respect to his relationship with man and woman. Miles is right. God's "human" personality changes from book to book. In the Old Testament God speaks to his human creations. God has a minor, third-person silent role in the New Testament compared to his prominence in the Hebrew Bible. In the New Testament, Yeshua is the main figure. It is fair to say that God of the Hebrew Bible and the New Testament appears equally castigating and loving. There is God whom one appeals to in battle and God of the Ten Commandments who tells

94. See Jack Miles, *God: A Biography* (New York: Knopf, 1995).

us not to kill; there is also Christ militant sending sinners and unbelievers to hell for eternity and Yeshua who heals and turns the other cheek.
Miles works from within scripture. What is perhaps most significant is
that the relation of Christians to the Old Testament itself, as a book to
be read, disparaged, discarded, or revered, changes with the century and
Christian sect. The Reformation was in part fueled by new translations
of the "Old Testament" into the vernacular, when the Hebrew Bible
definitely rose for many Christians from damaged goods to a renewed
source for information, names, and law.

Altering Names of Biblical Characters

There is an extraordinary anomaly with respect to names. While the
Jews have been historically thought of, and not always as a compliment,
as the authors of the Old Testament, in the Old Testament there are,
in standard English editions, almost no Jews. Translation has virtually
caused the magical disappearance of the Jew from the Hebrew Bible.

In the Christian Old Testament (and also in Bibles translated by Jews
who accept the received Christian naming), the English term for Jew is
"of the children of Israel," "an Israelite," "a Hebrew," which come to about
three thousand references in *The New Strong's Exhaustive Concordance
of the Bible*. To Jews, there are some ninety references. Of the ninety
Old Testament references to Jews, seventy-one appear in the Book of
Esther. Esther (whose name derives from the Babylonian deity Ishtar,
and whose Hebrew name is Hadassah) is a heroine celebrated in the
holiday of Purim. In a legend that takes place in the Persian period
(400–332 B.C.E.),[95] Esther's courageous actions deliver the Jews from a
pogrom (Esther 8.3–10.3). Apart from Esther, in the entire Hebrew Bible
there are, in standard English translations, less than twenty references
to a Jew, and no one has a name. Queen Esther is the only Jew designated by name in the Christian Old Testament. Although "the children
of Israel," "Israelites," and "Hebrews" abound in the Old Testament, in
the New Testament gospels there is hardly a mention of children of
Israel, Israelites, or Hebrews. But the Jews have reappeared. In the New
Testament there are some two hundred references to them, designated

95. Over the centuries the Book of Esther's place in the canon has been contested
and was denounced by Luther.

by name or Jewish title of rabbi, ranging from John the Baptist and Yeshua to the Pharisees, high priests, and Judas.

The Jews in the Jewish Bible are Jews, whether or not they are called Israelites. But for the traditional English reader, to read "Israelite" for "Jew" provides an unnecessary distancing, suggesting that this ancient people is distinct from New Testament Jews. As with other Hebrew epithets, Israelite comes into English through the Greek Ἰσραηλίτης (Israelites), from the Hebrew יִשְׂרְאֵלִי (yisraeli), corresponding to "Israeli." Were any translation today to use a direct transliteration from Hebrew, giving us "Israeli" rather than "Israelite," it would be clear that the Israelis and Jews are one and the same. Because of this practice of omitting the word "Jew" in the Hebrew Bible, until recently, standard reference books on the Bible speak of Jews as a people who appear in New Testament times. There are, of course, variations in presenting this information of when the Jews appear historically, but it all comes to the same, and bears no reference to history. In effect, the history of the Jews in the Hebrew Bible has been obscured. Such is the great power of names and translations of names. The Jews, whose ancient history is in the Hebrew Bible, which forms the greater part of the Christian Bible, are missing through disenfranchisement. They return as the hypocritical, plotting personalities in the Christian-Jewish gospels. It is through the conscious means of translation that almost total disguisement and disenfranchisement have occurred. A Jew or Christian who reads only the English translations of the Hebrew Bible will know none of these odd illusions. For the Hebrew reader, for whom the word *Yehudim* (Jews) occurs throughout the Bible, the Jews have not lost their history.

It can be argued that the Jews had diverse appellations in the Hebrew Bible, and so no one word is appropriate. However, translation is to convey information, not etymology, and the Jews of the Old and the New Testament are the same people and should not be designated otherwise. It is enough to say that this argument for excluding the Jews from the Jewish Bible is specious. No translation of Homer suggests that Odysseus and his crew were not Greeks, though there were many words for the Greeks in ancient Greek (*Hellene*, not the tribal word *Graikos*, was the common ancient word), but in English translation and commentary there is not the slightest question that the Greeks were Greeks. So, too, the Jews were Jews.

How can it be then that the Jews, by their naming, arrive strangely from nowhere in the New Testament as inimical aliens? In the gospels, as opposed to Paul, the Jews are not clearly the Jews of the Psalms and prophets. They are rather the mortal enemy of Christian Jews. Yeshua ben Yosef and his immediate family, friends, and followers are ultimately spared the stain of being Jews. The Virgin Mary is not seen as a Jew. Mary in translation, church iconography, and common understanding is not seen as a Jew. Therefore somewhere in the passing of information to the Christian reader and worshiper, the truth of Mary failed to get through.

I have noted that there is a linguistic effort in Greek and later translations to conceal the Jewishness of gospel heroes as shown in the earlier-discussed passage "Rabbi, which translated means teacher, where are you staying?" (ῥαββί, ὃ λέγεται μεθερμηνευόμενον διδάσκαλε, ποῦ μένεις;)[96] (John 1.38). Yet the Christianizing of this Semitic book about Jews is not complete. There remains the Greek word "rabbi." In the tabernacle scene, whose telling is virtually identical in the Synoptics, in Mark 9.5, the first gospel, we have *ho Petros legei to Iesou, "Rabbi"* (ὁ Πέτρος λέγει τῷ ᾿Ιησοῦ· ῥαββί), "Peter says to Jesus, 'Rabbi.'" In Matthew 17.4, whose source is in part Mark, we have *ho Petros eipen to Iesou, "Kurie"* (ὁ Πέτρος εἶπεν τῷ ᾿Ιησοῦ· κύριε), "Peter said to Jesus, 'Lord.'" In Luke 9.33, whose source is also Mark and perhaps Matthew, we have *eipen ho Petros pros ton Iesoun, "Epistata"* (εἶπεν ὁ Πέτρος πρὸς τὸν ᾿Ιησοῦν· ᾿Επιστάτα), "Peter said to Jesus, 'Master.'" "Rabbi" of Mark has been changed in the later gospels to *Kyrie*, "Lord," and *Epistata*, "Master." We can think that in other instances when Yeshua is addressed as "Teacher," "Lord," or "Master" in Greek that "Rabbi" has, as in the example of the tabernacles, been changed to suppress Yeshua's Jewish title of rabbi. In the King James Version (1611) of these three passages, "Rabbi," "Lord," and "Master" are *all* rendered into English as "Master."

In the New King James Version (1982), however, the English text has been corrected to follow the Greek, and we have for Mark 9.5, "Peter answered and said to Jesus, 'Rabbi.'" The New King James's rendering of "Rabbi" in their English translation of Mark 9.5 happily shows the new editors' imperative not to conceal Yeshua's title.

96. Greek ";" is English "?".

Along with the Christian name-changing, the Jews have their ways of shaping the Hebrew Bible, which they traditionally take as a book uniquely of their authorship and history. Yet the Bible has its precursors, which turn earlier Mesopotamian figures into Jewish patriarchs and heroes. The Mesopotamian myth of the flood story in *Gilgamesh* appears in the Hebrew Bible as intrinsic to the history and origin of the Jews, though it is a reworked story from the previous millennium, whose Babylonian names have been changed into Noah and other good Hebrew names to make them appear to be the earliest Jewish patriarchs, Jews and Christians still look on mountains of Armenia for their ancestral ark when they would do better to search in the sands of present-day Iraq.

The New Covenant and Its Precursor and a Parable from China

One invents new names for the past so that the present can influence and reform the past. In his masterful essay "Kafka and His Precursors," Jorge Luis Borges understood that the present shapes, influences, and even creates the past. Normally, one thinks that history creates the present and that influence travels only one way: forward. Yet Borges, a child of Kafka, influences how Kafka is seen, because he, Borges, came into being and his own prominence alters our perception of his Czech precursor. So the New Testament influences how the Jewish Bible is seen, because the New Testament, a child of the Jewish Bible, came into being and its own prominence alters our perception of the Jewish Bible. In a hypothetical essay, "The New Covenant and Its Precursors," one would see how later and earlier biblical works and the names they give them mutually and inexorably explore and affect each other.

So a parable on the Bible.

Jews have imagined that they live in the Torah, and have carried their Bible, in many languages, into all continents of their multiple diasporas. They took it from Ethiopia and India to London and Buenos Aires, and even to Beijing in China where in the late sixteenth century the Jesuit missionary Matteo Ricci (1552–1610)[97] was unable to persuade a delegation of the ancient community of Jews in Kaifeng, for centuries cut off

---

97. The parable of the Chinese Jews and Bishop Ricci is taken from Jonathan Spence's *The Memory Palace of Matteo Ricci* (New York: Viking Penguin, 1994).

from their coreligionists, that he, Bishop Ricci, who carried the word of their Bible through Asia, was not, like them, a Jew and indeed a rabbi of the Jews. He had their book. The Kaifeng Jews were by then completely Chinese in appearance and were unconcerned that the missionary had with him some additional Christian scriptures (they themselves may have had nothing after the Babylonian Captivity). Bishop Ricci, for his part, though he could not accept their request to be the rabbi for their synagogue, didn't care to persuade them of sectarian distinctions that had come to separate Jews and Christians, who were both "peoples of the book." The visions of the Chinese Jews and the Italian Catholic bishop and memory master were perfectly in harmony, ecumenical, and joined in vision.

If the reader from any quarter will forgive me, there should be no worry as once in the city of Kaifeng there was no worry about two covenants, an old one and a new one.

Christian Jews or
Jewish Christians

We TURN NOW to other aspects of historicity in the gospels, which is the identities of the participants. To understand this first-century setting, it is crucial to look at key Adamic names that describe the contending factions of Jews in the gospels. Traditionally, those who followed Yeshua have been called Christians or, more recently, "Christian Jews" (as there were Essenic Jews or Jews from any of perhaps seventeen sects seeking authority within Second Temple Judaism). Those who did not follow Yeshua are often called "Orthodox Jews," an essentially useless term of identity in a period of contending sects of first-century Jews, including the entourage around Yeshua.

In the touchy and highly charged game of naming people, sects, and places, which is at the heart of religious politics, the epithet "Jewish Christians" became widely popular in the last century, with some daring, as an acceptable title for those Jews who followed Yeshua. There was indeed no singular name for the first-century Jews who accepted Yeshua as the messiah. They were originally widely called Nazoreans, the general name for Aramaic-speaking Christian Jews and specifically for a sect who lived in Borea, which gave us the late second-century Gospel of the Nazoreans. They were also called Ebionites ("the poor") as in the Gospel of the Ebionites,[98] and Sampsaeans ("servants of God"). Since all who first followed Yeshua, who formed the religion that was

98. For the Gospel of the Ebionites and Gospel of the Hebrews (another Christian-Jewish gospel), see Ron Cameron, *The Other Gospels* (Philadelphia: Westminster Press, 1982), 103–106; and Willis Barnstone, *The Other Bible* (San Francisco: Harper and Row, 1984), 333–338.

to be called Christianity, were Jews, some word must account for them. Yet the term "Jewish Christians" is seriously misleading in its emphasis. I prefer "Christian Jews," or the more accurate "Christianized Jews." "Jewish Christian" suggests that the followers of Yeshua *had* been Jews, and were now apostates who had renounced Judaism and converted to Christianity. This is all wrong, since the early "Christians" certainly thought themselves Jews, and when they addressed Yeshua as rabbi, which happens throughout the gospels, it was not as a rabbi of some religion other than Judaism. The followers of the messiah, the Messianic Jews, were Jews, vying among other sects of Jews for persuasion and dominance.

There are also among the Christian Jews distinctions, and it gets complicated. We will stick to "Christian Jews" as the main appellation, but it should be understood that in the formation of early Christianity, there were both Jewish and gentile coverts to Christianized Judaism. Among the Jews who joined the Christian Jews, Paul represented a break from many of the traditional Jewish rites and practices, while the Jerusalem Christian Jews more strictly observed the laws of the Torah. Among the gentiles, many welcomed the break from some demanding Jewish rites, while others, as exemplified by those whom Paul addressed in his Letter to the Galatians, were against laxity, and required strict observance of the Torah, including circumcision, dietary laws, and the Sabbath. Then there is the ambiguous term of "gentile Christians." Initially it means simply those gentiles (pagans) who converted to the sect of the Christian Jews but later, as Christianity drifts from its center in Judaism—or thinks it does—it will be known simply to mean the gentiles (the non-Jews), or Christians.

Until the destruction of the Second Temple in 70 C.E., more than three decades after Yeshua's death, the overwhelming number of the followers of Yeshua remained Jews. Those who were gentile converts were converts not to Christianity but to a first-century Judaism that accepted Yeshua as the foretold biblical messiah. So, insofar as we speak of Jews, Hasmonean Jews, Diaspora Jews, Second Temple Jews, Hasidic Jews, we call the followers of Yeshua the Mashiah "Christian Jews." We would never say "Jewish Hasmoneans," "Jewish Essenes," or "Jewish Sadducees." For this reason it is awkward and misleading to say "Jewish Christians." Since "Christian" means "Messianic," a Christian Jew is a Messianic Jew who has found the messiah. The Greek word *Hristos* (Χριστος) for "Christ," meaning "the anointed one" and "the messiah" from Hebrew *mashiah* (מָשִׁיחַ), would never have been used or understood by the Jewish peasants who looked to Yeshua. For Jews of the day, a central meaning of "messiah" was, as Graham Stanton summarizes, "the hope that an anointed King of David's line would set up a glorious kingdom by removing Israel's enemies." Whether there was a more transcendental meaning, which we would presume from Isaiah's reference to a spiritual son or whether he was instead the practical guardian that Stanton suggests he was, there is no question that soon "messiah" became synonymous with Yeshua, in effect his name, and hence his followers eventually took on his name. When the Messianic Jews became dominantly Greek-speaking, the sect took on a Greek name and were the Christians. Stanton writes,

> Paul refers to Jesus as "Christ" on every page of his letters—271 times in all in his seven undisputed letters. However, with only clear exception and a handful of marginal cases, "Christ" has become simply a name for Jesus; it no longer refers to the *messiahship* of Jesus. Elsewhere when Paul speaks about the significance of Jesus for Christians, he prefers to use "lord," or "Son"/"Son of God," because these terms made sense to Gentiles. Without explanation, Messiah meant nothing in non-Jewish settings.[99]

Unfortunately, even today the word "Christian" has for almost everyone lost its original meaning of "Messianic," and consequently Christians rarely understand that "Christian" is not only the name of a religious denomination but is primarily a title of Jewish faith in the messiah. To speak now of "Messianics" and "Messianic Jews" restores the essence of the meaning of early Christianity (Messianism). In the history of Christianity, Yeshua is seen as the messiah and his followers Christian Jews. To resort to the older term of "primitive Christians" obscures the fact that the followers belonged to a new branch of first-century Judaism, and demeans these followers as "primitive," suggesting that the

99. See Graham Stanton, *Gospel Truth? New Light on Jesus and the Gospels* (London: HarperCollins, 1995), 178.

Christian Jews were the good but uninformed and uninstructed pioneers of a future-great faith.

Once having observed that for early Christians Yeshua was the Jewish messiah, he was one of many declared messiahs. The title of messiah is at the heart of Jewish biblical scripture and rabbinic tradition. The mythical king David—apart from all his human political accomplishments and swashbuckling passions—assumed for many the anointed role of messiah, and in 1 Samuel 16 he is singled out as the divinely chosen ruler. In Psalm 2.2 he is identified "as God's anointed" whom God addresses as "son." The Jewish Messianic hope is one of a promised, ideal future on earth, of a leader from the seed of David (as defined in Ezra 4) who will restore divine rule to Israel and reign in goodness and truth. Christian messianism, primarily fashioned by Paul, was scarcely interested in the teachings of Yeshua who will restore divine rule to Israel and reign in goodness and truth. Messianism for the Christians was less centered on earthly paradise. The epistler Paul, who fashioned the eschatology of Christian messianism, did not speak of the teachings, words, and acts of Yeshua on earth, and apparently had no knowledge of them. He was interested in Jesus Christ not as a man Jesus but as the Christ meaning messiah. He called him Jesus Christ by name, which became a synonym for the Christ or savior. He knew alone that the messiah foretold had come—he doesn't say when he came or when he died—and had been crucified, dying for our sins and later salvation, and would return, soon, to judge us for an afterlife. The crucified "son of God" would judge and resurrect both body and soul of the saved into eternal, celestial salvation.

Early in Matthew and Luke, the Galilean Yeshua ben Yosef's Davidic seed is established where the evangelists trace his lineage back to King David (Matt. 1.17; Luke 3.23–38). It should be added that these two genealogies are separate in linguistic style and are surely later additions to the gospels. Yeshua's contemporary Essenes had their messianic figures as revealed in the Dead Sea Scrolls, but Yeshua, according to Geza Vermes in his *Changing Faces of Jesus*, appears to come directly out of the strong Hasidic tradition in Galilee, of these holy charismatic men, the healers and miracle workers, who represented not the official religion of the priests in the synagogues, but a popular personal figure, "the man of God" (ish ha-elohim). This tradition goes back to the prophets Elisha and Elijah, who were the most revered popular healers and miracle-makers in the Hebrew Bible.

As we move to Yeshua's time, in the Apocrypha and the Dead Sea Scrolls, the references to healers and miracles are legion, and especially in northern Israel, which was the site of Yeshua's ministry. The later Mishnah and the Talmud note two major healers: Honi (whom Josephus calls Onias) and his grandson Hanina ben Dosa, a contemporary of Yeshua.[100] Honi, called "the Circle Drawer" in the Mishnah and the Talmud, was a rainmaker. These itinerant charismatics were normally ascetic, caring little for food or personal possessions, which they would share with others. Like Yeshua, Honi was eventually put to death for political reasons, not willing to take sides in disputes between ruling factions (Josephus, *Antiquities* 14.22–24). Hanina ben Dosa from the first century, came from Araba or Gabara, near Yeshua's Nazareth, and was the best known of those who through prayer performed miracles. To follow the road of his many healings, of his changing vinegar into oil (as Yeshua changed water into wine), is to trace the path of Yeshua in his many therapeutic visits to the sick and, when called upon, his miracles of changing few provisions into necessary abundance. Vermes observes the Galilean holy men, whose messianic traits are shared by Yeshua: "Jewish, and perhaps in particular Galilean, popular religiosity tended to develop along the path followed by Honi, Hilkiliah, Hanan, Jesus, and Hanina. Compassionate, caring, and loving, they were all celebrated as deliverers of the Jews from famine, sickness, and the dominion of the forces of darkness, and some of them at least as teachers of religion and morality. . . . The Jesus of the New Testament fits into this picture, which in turn confers on his image validity and credibility; for there is no denying that a figure not dissimilar to the Honis and Haninas of Palestine Judaism lurks beneath the Gospels."

In late Kabbalah (a body of mystical teachings of rabbinic origin), there are important messianic leaders, especially after the expulsion from Spain when Lurian mysticism established itself in Amsterdam, Safed in Israel, and Constantinople. The most fascinating later messianic is

---

100. For extensive information on healers and miracle workers in Galilee, see "Beneath the Gospels" in Geza Vermes's *The Changing Faces of Jesus* (New York: Viking Compass, 2001), 246–279. Quote below is on p. 267.

Rabbi Shabbetai Tzevi of Smyrna (1626–1676),[101] who proclaimed himself messiah in 1665. For a century he had thousands of faithful followers among Jews and Muslims, in part because of Nathan of Gaza (ca. 1644–1690), who found a parallel between Gnosticism and Kabbalah and explained Tzevi through the Lurian theory of repair, which entailed the descent of the just into the abyss in order to liberate the captive particles of divine light. The chain of "messiahs" continues to our time, where the Hasidim again have a special interest in discovering and proclaiming the revered, anointed leader.[102]

Moving from Jewish Messianism to Christianity

While the term "Jewish Christian" is widely used today, neither "Jewish Christian" nor "Christian Jewish" is used to describe the gospels. Only writings from non- or extra-canonical scripture, as say those of the Ebionites or the syncretistic Gospel of the Hebrews and Gospel of the Nazoreans, are described as Jewish Christian. How can this be if texts written later than the gospels still carry the epithet "Jewish Christian"?[103] Although the gospels have been traditionally accepted as Christian, they deal with a period before the later followers of Yeshua established a religion now called Christianity. Christian theologians increasingly assert that the gospels are simply Jewish texts. The whole problem of names is crucial here. Historically, a Christian was a Jew who saw Yeshua as the messiah. We are so far from understanding that simple fact, though the word "Christian" (Messianic) tells it all, that we must quibble, like

101. See Gershom Scholem, *Sabbatai Sevi: The Mystical Messiah, 1626–1676* (Princeton: Princeton University Press, 1973).

102. Martin Buber (1876–1965) traces the history and tales of Hasidism in *Die Chassidische Botschaft* (Heidelberg: L. Schneider, 1922), which appeared in English as *Tales of the Hasidim* (New York: Schocken Books, 1975), beginning with the revival of Hasidic speculation in the eighteenth century as exemplified by the clairvoyant charismatic Jacob Isaac (d. 1815) of Lublin in Poland.

103. Among the important noncanonical gospels is the Gospel of the Hebrews, which is preserved in fragments recorded in Cyril of Jerusalem, Jerome, and Clement, and may precede Mark. It contains the second saying in the very early Gnostic Gospel of Thomas. In the Gospel of the Hebrews, James (Jacob/Yaakov), brother of Yeshua, is mentioned as the first to see the resurrected appearance of Yeshua. The fragment confirms the authority assigned to James, who was the leading figure of the conservative Jewish church in Jerusalem that followed Yeshua.

parties making peace with each other, who must learn again how to address each other.

The quibbling over names should, one hopes, bring us back to history and to who these followers of Yeshua were. During his lifetime and for at least four decades after his death, the followers of Yeshua were Jews. This means they thought themselves Jews and were also made up largely of Jews in the ethnic sense, and seldom of gentile (ἐθνικῶς) background until after the diaspora of 70 C.E. The historical establishment of an independent Christian church was not yet the issue during that intra-Jewish struggle for dominance in the recognition of the messiah. Christians did not come to recognize Yeshua when the Jews failed to do so (a falsehood repeated to death as gospel truth). On the contrary, there were originally no outsiders, no gentiles, who recognized Yeshua.[104] Only Jews did, Messianic (Christian) Jews. Precisely from those Christian Jews grew a body of followers and also a quartet of Jewish gospels concerning the life of rabbi Yeshua, which became the centerpiece of an independent religion, and which eventually gained the unhyphenated title of Christianity.

By the end of the first decades of the second century of the Common Era, the Jewishness of the two covenants, the wrangling over biblical imperatives, and the religion and ethnicity of the principal figures in this first-century Israel drama were denied and forgotten. It was necessary for the early Christians to make this final divorce. Forgotten was the Jewish center of Yeshua, of the gospels about him, and of all the other books of the New Testament. Conversions to Christianized Judaism gave way, in the wake of a swiftly expanding and apparently independent Christian church, to conversion to an autonomous Christianity whose amnesia of origin was paramount. The survival of a strong notion of Christianity's Jewish origin threatened the church's illusion

---

104. No gentiles except the centurion at the crucifixion, who first declares Yeshua God and risen. This on-the-spot conversion, after executing Yeshua, poses problems. As for Yeshua himself, his character toward gentiles is presented ambivalently by the unknown hands who composed him: While Yeshua praises one centurion as having more faith than anyone in Israel (Luke 7.9), he also speaks as one concerned solely with Jews—"I was sent only to the lost sheep of the house of Israel" (Matt. 15.24), and he embarrassingly refers to the gentiles (the non-Jews) as dogs and swine (Mark 7.27; Matt. 15.26).

of self-creation. After 70 C.E., with the collapse of Jerusalem as the base of the formative sect, the Christian movement found its converts among Jews and pagans (gentiles). And though both the Hebrew Bible of the Jews and the New Testament, which were written by, about, and for Jews, remained the Bible of the new messianic faith, by the second and third decades of the second century, Jewish messianism had been translated, in all senses, into Christianity.

Gentleman's Agreement
in Gospels that Jews
in Yeshua Movement
Not Be Perceived as Jews

Disappearing the Jews from the Yeshua Movement

THE CENTRAL religio-political quandary of the writers, editors, and copyists of the New Testament was how to make a book about Jews into a Christian Bible. That task was imperative if Christianity was to be independent of its creators. Yet there were mighty obstacles. The characters existed before Christianity had scriptures or temples of its own name. And in the decades after Yeshua's death, circa 30 C.E., Peter and Paul went forth to convert other Jews and gentiles to a belief in a Jewish messiah foretold in the Hebrew Bible. These Christian Jews in the mold of Paul, dependent on the Jewish Bible and the sayings of Yeshua the Mashiah, did not know who they were. They knew they were in conflict with the Jews who had not accepted Yeshua as the Jewish messiah; with Christian Gnostics, who as philosophical exegetes and "heretics" saw the appeared Yeshua as a simulacrum and the creator God of Genesis as the Demiurge; and, above all, with Rome, who remained the great political enemy. The contention with Rome and its religious gods and icons is depicted especially fiercely in intertestamental scriptures of noncanonical Apocrypha and pseudepigrapha.

Pagan rulers, with their figures of high office and their idolatry, had to be buried. Indeed, the removal of Judaism from Christianity was minor compared to the three-century battle to overcome Greco-Roman religion, civilization, and political dominion. The battle was won when

Constantine I shifted his capital to Constantinople and on his deathbed converted to Christianity, probably baptized by the Arian bishop
Eusebius of Nicomidia. The general iconoclastic period (not the specific
eighth- and ninth-century Byzantine debate on worshiping Christian
statues and images) included the demolition of Greek and Roman stat-
utes and temples; the razing by patriarch (later Saint) Theofilus of the
Mouseion Library of Alexandria, with its some 700,000 rolls, in 391
C.E. (falsely attributed to later Muslim conquest); and the closing of the
academies in Alexandria and Athens. These events were symptoms of
a larger fundamental world change as classical civilization gave way to
the cross.

How did these early diaspora Christian Jews define themselves?
Eventually, they were simply Christians. But until they got to be
Christians, they had the burden of accounting for all these events
that had happened to a body of Jews in Jewish Galilee and Jerusalem.
So the gospels' authors had the task of blurring the Jewish identity of
its pre-Christians so that later they might pass as Christians (and of
demonizing those Jews who were not pre-Christians). Strictly speaking, it was impossible to make all these Jews—Yeshua, Miryam, Yosef,
Yohanan the Dipper—fully pass. Yet in practical terms, the passage to
Christian honor was a monumental success. The changing of the masks
was achieved despite the discomfort of hearing, in the same sentence,
Yeshua addressed as rabbi while he is denouncing the Jews as children
of the devil, who are called sinner, liar, fraud, thief, and murderer (John
8.44). The incongruity would seem to sink the message, but the slander
of the Jew is so constant, and the obfuscation of Jewish identity of pre-
Christians so pervasive, that the traditional reader, if not the recent
reader and scholar, has accepted this subversion of identity as truth. If
Yeshua himself denounces the Jews as offspring of the devil, how can he
himself be perceived as a Jew? Indeed, the very denunciation and hatred
of the Jew serve to distance and free the accuser from Jewish identity.
The essayist I. F. Stone, with respect to what he called the two famous
suicides, noted that Jesus did not run away from his predicted crucifixion
and needed the cross to fulfill his mission as similarly Socrates did not
accept an offer to escape and needed his hemlock to fulfill his ethical
mission.[105]

105. See I. F. Stone, *The Trial of Socrates* (New York: Knopf, 2000), 3.

In summary, we witness a remarkably enduring gentleman's agreement to keep all Jews out of Christianity's mythological beginnings by changing the religion and ethnicity of Yeshua, his family, and his disciples. The anachronistic Christianization takes place in the gospels as we have them, and in commentary on them—both as annotation and external texts, in scribal interpolations, in translations of the gospels, and in the resultant general perception by the public about who Yeshua and his circle were.

Some might argue that there is little deception in the text, for a careful reader can find abundant evidence that Yeshua was a Jew. Yes and no. The evidence is there and a careful reader *should* respond to it, but reading theories inform us why this text is received otherwise. Consider the pressures on a reasonable and alert reader to ignore the evidence of Jewish identity. We have gone over in detail the pattern of changing the title of rabbi to teacher, master, or lord going into and out of the Greek scriptures, and of the changing of Semitic names to Greek names and then to foreign names, such as Jesus, Mary, James, Paul, Peter, and John, which have all lost the Hebrew ring. But one might still argue that the ample evidence is there for identifying Yeshua as a Jew. True again, but by formal reader reception theory, or virtually by any sensible notion of reading, a reader-deception practice has in the past, and for the vast majority of contemporary readers today, persuaded the reader that Yeshua, Miryam, Yohanan, and the disciples are not truly Jews but early Christians whose translated names are Jesus, Mary, and John, words that come through as fine English names, with no ring or taint of Near Eastern Semitism. (The same name changes exist in other language translations of the New Testament.) In the case of noncompetitive Greek heroes, Odysseus, Achilles, and Agamemnon are not rebaptized with the fine English royal names of William, Richard, and Edward. There is no need to forget the Greekness of the Greeks. But for the shadowy Jews, the reader is persuaded to suppress or forget that Semitic shade by the virulence of the anti-Jewish speech emanating from the implied narrator as well as from Yeshua and he Jewish members of his circle.

In the subjective process of reading, there is, to begin with, a physical objective text, which comes alive only as it passes into the reader's mind, where the text's subjective transformation occurs. The reader participates in the transformation on the basis of signs inside and outside the text to receive and resolve significance. Traditionally, the extratextual element that encourages a probable reading in which Jewish identity is suppressed has come principally from Christian theology and clerical pronouncements. The most hopeful factor in altering an inevitably biased and myopic reading comes from the same extratextual sources, theologians and clergy, who are moving rapidly to a more balanced reception of the scriptures. Also, the place in the curriculum of courses or parts of courses on the Bible as literature permits an instructed reading in which religious persuasions do not deny the book an objective reception accorded to other major books. In the new school, faith and history are not in conflict. However, the full extent of the inconsistencies in the text and the overwhelming pressures on the reader to forget Yeshua as the rabbi who died on the cross (as Marc Chagall painted him in full-rabbinical attire on thirteen canvases) still remain largely unperceived. The present correction of disguisement is real, but in its initial period.

In this translation, the restoration of biblical for Hellenized personal names is by itself a hugely powerful marker throughout the scriptures that should signal the reader to receive the text with sensibility to the cast's Jewish identity. Christianity is no longer a struggling religion that needs to placate the Roman Empire and to attack its parent religion in order to defend its own identity. By these restorations of the Semitic names, I would like to serve both Christianity and Judaism by highlighting the illogic of anti-Judaism in a Jewish book. I hope these versions begin to free both religions from misinformation that has led to outmoded and unnecessary strife.

The Jesus Movement and the Emergence of a Historical Yeshua[106]

Insofar as the Hebrew Bible and New Testament are assumed to be historical documents, they are scrutinized for their authenticity. Hence, we find the worried who complain, as Thomas Jefferson did in a letter of January 24, 1814, to John Adams, "In the New Testament there is internal evidence that parts of it have proceeded from an extraordinary man; and that other parts are of the fabric of very inferior minds. It is as easy to separate those parts, as to pick out diamonds from dunghills."

---

106. See also earlier section on historicity.

Scripture in the New Testament is for some holy and inviolate, and for others pages to be read with Jeffersonian reservations, but for devout or skeptical alike the book is constantly analyzed and interpreted. Others read the very early letters, constituting half of the New Testament, where Yeshua is the Christ, the messiah, but not a fleshed-out person, and conclude that, like Confucius or the Buddha, Yeshua, of uncertain period, is not a single person but a composite of wisdom sayings, which is the text and message of the Gospel of Thomas, which has only wisdom verse, no figures other than his students and no narrative history at all.

Geza Vermes construes a Yeshua who is an ascetic charismatic. While the Dead Sea Scrolls reveal a messianic figure among the Essenes at Qumran with similar messianic qualities, Vermes writes emphatically that "Jesus did not belong among the Pharisees, Essenes, Zealots or Gnostics, but was one of the holy miracle-workers of Galilee."[107] Two decades later, while still asserting that the essential Yeshua corresponds to earlier and contemporary Hasidic holy men, Vermes now moves on to describe Yeshua as one of the Pharisees, or at the very least, as one portrayed in the traditional costume of the Pharisees. In *The Changing Faces of Jesus*, he writes, "The evangelists implicitly portray Jesus as a Jew profoundly attached to the laws and customs of his people, and some of his most obvious authentic sayings confirm this picture. The gospels attest his presence in Galilean synagogues and in the Temple of Jerusalem. We are told that he had eaten the Passover just before he was arrested. His garment was like that of the Pharisees [Matt. 23.5], with the traditional tassels hanging from its edge (Matt. 9.20; Luke 8.44; Mark 6.56; Matt. 14.36; cf. Num. 15.38;–40; Deut. 22.12)."[108]

But in stressing Yeshua's Galilean nature, Vermes in no way reflects the French historian Ernest Renan's *Life of Jesus* (1862), which treated Yeshua as a non-Semitic, Aryan Galilean from a roaming northerner tribe. We have come a long way from the once revolutionary Renan, whose perversion of Yeshua's origin was taken up by the greater Protestant Church in divinity school and pulpit in Germany during the Nazi period in order to strip the messiah of all taint of Jewishness.

---

107. See Geza Vermes, *Jesus the Jew* (Philadelphia: Fortress Press, 1981), 223.
108. See Geza Vermes, *The Changing Faces of Jesus* (New York: Viking Compass, 2001), 208–209.

In the endless search of the historical Yeshua, in addition to Jesus the Cynic, Mediterranean peasant, Hasidic charismatic, desert Essene, Pharisaic populist, and Galilean Aryan, there have been many speculations in film, theater, poetry, and novel about the real Yeshua, including Norman Mailer's syncretistic re-creation of Yeshua's everyday life and death in *The Gospel According to the Son* (1997).

Since its beginnings, the interest in "the historical Jesus" has presented many Yeshuas at odds with the biblical figure. The gospel portrayal of Yeshua as one who acquiesces to Roman administration and law is unconvincing. Beyond possible credence is his presentation in Luke as a soothsayer apologist for Titus's destruction of Jerusalem, which Luke informs us, through Yeshua's words, is the punishment the Jews deserve because of their lack of belief.

Yeshua and Miryam Speaking Greek That Is a Translation or an Invention

In these preliminary observations, it is not possible to do more than raise questions about the nature of a historical Yeshua and transmission of texts. What is certain is the uncertainty of earlier-held truths. For example, the curious notion of Yeshua with a Latin name "Jesus," speaking Greek to a circle of Greek-speaking followers, raises questions of credulity. Then we have the question of originality of the Greek gospels. I am often asked whether I have translated the gospels from the original Greek texts. My answer is yes. Yet am I being truthful? I translate from the extant Greek texts, our earliest texts, but these "original" scripts are either an edition or a translation or transformation of earlier material, or one new gospel story that has come down to us in four versions. If not new compositions, what are they and what is their source? While there exist no earlier manuscripts or editions of the Greek gospels, no gospel has been traditionally called a "translation" or even a Greek text acknowledged to be derived from unknown sources that once held Yeshua's words in Aramaic. However, the alternative to being a translation of a written oral source is that the gospels are the pure, fabled invention of the evangelists, with no historical basis in text or earlier persons, which is the skeptic's view. There is nothing in between. The gospels are either grounded in history or are dramatic fiction.

"Translation" is a carrying of information from one place to another, inter- or intralingually. For the Greek scriptures to be deemed more than a translation, a carrying of information from an earlier to a later period adds an unfounded authority to the Greeks and deprives the texts of their plausibility as a retelling of possible events in an earlier period. The Greek texts do not contain Yeshua's Aramaic speech, so at some point in the process of transmission there could have been a translation. However, with regard to Miryam's singing the beautiful Magnificat in Luke (1.39–55), I suspect this canticle may not be a translation from Aramaic or Hebrew but an original Greek composition written many decades after young Miryam sang.

Did I translate from the *original* Greek texts? Yes, but only in the sense that they are the earliest texts in which the good news survives. As of now, source texts are hypothetical—from Q, from Aramaic, or from surviving eyewitnesses. It is better to use the word "mystery," "silence," or some noun to suggest that the enigma of source will remain unsolved.

The Exact Word of God in Translation and the Illusion of the Quijote

It is largely accepted by the lay reader that in the Bible resides the exact word of God, the gospel truth, as it is sometimes called, whether this truth be in Greek, Latin, or King James English. Yeshua used the parable as one of his main vehicles for conveying mysterious truths. But to find his exact words we cannot look to the gospels, unless we speak of the exact words in translation, suggesting the $a = a$ perfectability of translation, which no one grants translation. Literary translation is a rich way of moving information, but neither literal nor free ways re-create perfectly. Imperfection is the nature of language, not a defect but a richness that keeps literatures alive as they pass through centuries and between languages. Yeshua himself, master of the parable, told tales and asked his listeners to translate each mysterious image into a living conceptual truth.

As for the truth in translation in the New Testament, a story by Jorge Luis Borges, the modern parabolist, enlightens. Monsieur Pierre Menard, a cultivated French intellectual in the early twentieth century, copied in Spanish two chapters of Miguel de Cervantes's *Don Quijote de la Mancha*. But the difference is amazing. Menard's handwriting and presentation are sophisticated. He bequeaths us the true noble

Knight of the Sad Countenance. The voice in Menard's fragmentary *Quijote* is more subtle than the crude speech composed by the barbaric seventeenth-century Spaniard Miguel de Cervantes, an old, tired ex-soldier. The Cervantes text and the Menard text are identical, but the latter is infinitely richer. Influenced and formed by Stéphane Mallarmé, Paul Valéry, and the philosopher Bertrand Russell, Menard renovated the art of reading. He proved that everything we read we transform to our vision and needs. He imposed his time, civilization, and interpretation on the original. The translators of the New Testament actually translated the text from one tongue to another, but then the Menard principle intervened. Like Menard in his new version of *Quijote*, the translators of the Greek scriptures read the scriptures as they wished, rescuing it whenever they could from its barbaric Jewish origin. As if it were true, they have Yeshua speak late first- and second-century Greek, a more civilized tongue than Yeshua's Aramaic, the spoken language of the Jews. And the forty-seven marvelous King James translators of that Greek covenant have presented us the exact word of God in a civilized and memorable seventeenth-century English, which is far superior to the rudimentary demotic koine of Greek scriptures.

At each new level of translation, the new version diminishes the authority of the source text, if not its aesthetic component.

The failure to acknowledge a source language is not an accident. Were the source language clear, this change alone would make the Jewish ethnicity of all major characters in the New Testament perfectly clear. Harold Bloom addresses precisely this question of the language of speakers and related questions of transmission and historicity in his essay "An Interpretation." Bloom writes,

> Of the veritable text of the sayings of a historical Jesus, we have nothing. Presumably he spoke to his followers and other wayfarers in Aramaic, and except for a few phrases scattered throughout the Gospels, none of his Aramaic sayings have survived. I have wondered for some time how this could be, and wondered even more that Christian scholars have never joined in my wonder. If you believed in the divinity of Jesus, would you not wish to have preserved the actual Aramaic sayings themselves? Were they lost, still to be found in a cave somewhere in Israel? Were they never written down in the first

place, so that the Greek texts were based only upon memory? For
some years now, I have asked these questions whenever I have met
a New Testament scholar, and I have met only blankness. Yet surely
this puzzle matters. Aramaic and Greek are very different languages,
and the nuances of spirituality and of wisdom do not translate readily
from one into the other. Any sayings of Jesus, open or hidden, need
to be regarded in this context, which ought to teach us a certain
suspicion of even the most normative judgments as to authenticity,
whether those judgments rise from faith or from supposedly positive
scholarship.

Bloom wonders about the great absence, about those decades between
the death of Yeshua and the Gospel of Mark: "Between Jesus and any
Christianity, at least a generation of silence intervenes."[109] What happened in the most crucial initial years of Christianity's formation? Why
is there no record, and from where and through whose hands come the
scriptures we do have? How could the identity of a Jew, of one who
will be known as man, the messiah, and God, become so thoroughly
confused and blurred?

As Bloom implies, there is a double vision with regard to Yeshua and
the Jew throughout the New Testament. Here we have, in translations
of translations, texts in which a messianic figure, a God-Man, speaks
to us in Greek about himself and about his followers and condemns his
enemies "the Jews" as the spawn of Satan. The double vision with regard
to the Jew is the overriding paradox of the New Testament.

Satanizing Jews in John and the Other Gospels

We see this double vision—about as clearly as double vision can be
isolated and focused—in the Gospel of John. The anomalies of history
and myth, of spiritual mystery and elemental hate, all assemble most
intensely in John.

Many have written about the disturbing characterization of the Jews
in John, the most Jewish, most poetic, and most philosophical and mysterious of the gospels. I have tried to make sense of it, and like others

---

109. Harold Bloom, "A Reading," in Marvin Meyer, *The Gospel of Thomas* (San Francisco: HarperSanFrancisco, 1992), 113–114, 119.

I have made guesses and have been tempted to come up with a way of rendering *hoi Joudaioi*—"the Jews"—as something else in English, without violating the text. But there is no way of getting around John's epithet "the Jews."

The Satanization of the Jew in John persists. At least its context clarifies the usage, highlights the implausibility of its veracity, and annotation may invent an essential mirror in which those words, "the Jews," will not appear so sinister, and not have such sinister consequences in the religious and social history of Jews and Christians. The magnificent gospel is attributed to John, a Greek name (*Yohanan* is his Jewish name), who has been identified as a Jew writing in a period before Christianity had a separate identity. His treatment of Yeshua as a Jewish prophet,[110] as a rabbi teaching in the synagogue and attending the holiday feasts of Sukkoth and Pesach (Tabernacles and Passover), is enforced by Yeshua's constant citations of earlier Jewish prophets in his sermons, all of which indicate no rupture with the Hebraic tradition. Yet, implausibly, we read in John, "Rabbi, the Jews were just now trying to stone you."

The conjunction of "rabbi" and "the Jews" is an anomaly, with cross signals that befuddle the purpose of making the Jews appear abhorrent. Yet, readers are apparently not shocked to find Yeshua addressed as rabbi, and then utter words as if to suggest that he is not a rabbi of the Jews but an outsider attacking the Jews. And his talmidim,[111] are they not also Jews as is their rabbi? Or have they too suddenly lost their Judaism to be able to speak of "the Jews" as a people whom they and Yeshua are not, and do not represent in any way? To make further sense of this is a stretch, bringing us to the hypothetical. As they are, the gospels reflect a Christianizing of Jewish scriptures that characterizes dozens of extant second- and third-century pseudepigraphica, such as the beautiful "Jewish-Christian" Gnostic scripture, the Book of Baruch.[112] In this

110. George Nickelsburg comments in a letter to the author on Yeshua as a Jewish prophet: "Jesus spoke as a Jewish prophet to the Jews. However, once Christianity separated from Judaism, they took these sayings out of context and as outsiders to Judaism hurled them back to the Jews, who were the others."

111. Hebrew for "students," "disciples."

112. The Book of Baruch, attributed to Justin, is in spirit and probably in fact the earliest extant Gnostic text, though it is preserved only as a paraphrase in Hippolytus of Rome's *Refutation of All Heresies*. Robert M. Grant calls Baruch "an example of a

process of converting early Jewish scripture into Christian documents, the perspective changes. The implied author speaks as a much later Christian about early events in which the Jew is normally, as in the New Testament, depicted either as villainous or disguised, in a time warp, as a later Christian.

What is probable is that in the process of redacting whatever texts were used for John, at some point in their transmission to the present Greek form the changing of identity from Jew to non-Jew was not completed. And hence the paradox in John 11.8 of a rabbi as one who is momentarily, after the utterance of his title, rabbi, not a rabbi but an unidentified non-Jew whom his opponents, the Jews, want to murder. We have two texts and two authors working against each other, and consequently Yeshua changes person. A minimal close look should alert us to foul scribal play. The attack on "the Jews" here, and about seventy times elsewhere, points to a later redaction of a text that is fashioned to appeal exclusively to gentiles as it praises those who have shed their Jewish name tag and Satanizes those it selectively identifies as the Jew.

So we see that the shaping of Yeshua and his circle as later Christians remains always uneven. Not only does Yeshua lead a rabbinical life of teaching in the synagogues and great Temple, but Yeshua as a Jew makes compelling declarations of his kinship with the Jews as the chosen, as in John 4.22, where he declares the Jews are the people of salvation: "You Shomronim worship what you do not know, for salvation is from the Jews." But then come equivocal appearances of Yeshua, where he both affirms himself as a Jew and defames the people "over there" for being Jews.

In the Temple scene (John 2.12–16), Yeshua enters with the rage of the prophets against the impious to expel the animal and coin merchants who are sullying this holiest of Jewish monuments. Is Yeshua to be taken here as an unknown alien enemy among the Jews, overturning their tables and whipping them for their sins? Or is he a devout Jew in his own

---

gnosis almost purely Jewish" in *Gnosticism and Early Christianity* (New York: Columbia University Press, 1959), 19. It should be remembered that Jewish heterodoxy and Gnosticism preceded Christian Gnosticism, though alas, we lack texts other than in Christianized Jewish scripture such as Baruch and the evidence Gershom Scholem elaborates on in his opus magnum *Jewish Gnosticism, Merkabah Mysticism, and Talmudic Tradition* (New York: Schocken Books, 1961).

Temple, admonishing his people, in violent family dispute, to reform, to clean house in order to reclaim their orthodoxy? Yet however vile the Jews are made to appear before a righteous Yeshua militant, Yeshua's reform takes place *inside* the Temple. He doesn't destroy the Temple as an *outsider* with Roman fire, nor does he urge followers to do so.

The notion of a family feud among diverse Jewish sects is essential for understanding how the angry feuds of the day, viewed later through the polemic in the gospels and after almost twenty centuries of enmity, could lead to the tragic divisions between Christians and Jews, and the massacres by Christians of Jews. The change from family feud to massacre was made possible as the historical Yeshua—*a Jew speaking as a Jew to Jews*—is altered in the interpretive gospels to be received as *a non-Jew speaking against Jews*. Concerning the many voices heard in first-century Judaism, George Nickelsburg writes, "First century Judaism was a remarkably diverse phenomenon, which could breed Pharisees, Essenes, children of Enoch, and Christians of various sorts—all of whom claimed to be faithful to their mother religion."[113]

Yeshua's Vilifications of Jews in the Tradition of the Prophets

There is nothing unusual about Jews, perceived as Jews, scourging Jews. Vituperation for sin and wrongdoing is a familiar act of self-criticism scripted in the Hebrew Bible from Genesis through the last prophets. Indeed, the Bible ends with Malachi's polemic against the priesthood, a furious assault in which he execrates the cast of priests as well as its seed. The prophet's oracle does so by assembling the Lord's words of abuse and threats from Exodus 29.14 and Leviticus 8.17 and 16.29. Nothing in the Greek scriptures outdoes the sheer wrath of his attack on corrupt authorities:

> And now, O ye priests, this commandment is for you. If you will not hear, and if ye will not lay it to heart, to give glory unto my name, saith the Lord of Hosts, I will even send a curse upon you, and I will curse your blessings: yea, I have cursed them already,

113. See George W. E. Nickelsburg, "Jews and Christians in the First Century: The Struggle over Identity" in *Neotestamentica* 27(2) (1993): 365–390/1–4.5.

because ye do not lay it to heart. Behold, I will corrupt your seed,
and spread dung upon your faces, even the dung of your solemn
feasts, and one shall take you away with it.

MAL. 2.1–3, KJV

But after the curses and threats, even the wayward priest is shown a
place within God's society, if he will listen, for he is the messenger
(*malak* or angel) of the lord:

> For the priest's lips should keep knowledge, and they should
> seek the law at his mouth: for he is the messenger of the Lord of
> hosts. But ye are departed out of the way; ye have caused many
> to stumble at the law; ye have not kept my ways, but have been
> partial in the law.

2.7–9

Exasperated by the priest who causes others to stumble and to violate
the covenant with God, Malachi asks,

> Have we not all one father? Hath not one God created us? Why
> do we deal treacherously every man against his brother, by pro-
> faning the covenant of our fathers?

2.10

The prophet tells the priests that they should not live by treachery. And
he asks for reconciliation, making clear that he, Malachi the accuser,
and the offending clergy are of one family, created by the same God.

Malachi's attack is fierce. Excrement is slapped on the faces of the
cursed priests, yet no one would or could look to Malachi as a source of
anti-Semitism or Satanization of the Jew. Although the accusations are
as grave as any in John or Luke, the drama of treason occurs *within* the
tribe—as it did even in the messiah drama in the unlikely self-serving
tale of a Roman execution of a Jew instigated by other Jews. Were Yeshua
the Mashiah truly and always perceived as Rex Judeorum and his circle
truly and always perceived as Jews throughout the texts of the messiah
passion, then the Greek scriptures' horrendous and fatal historical impact
on the life and death of the Jew could not have happened. In some other

imaginary tale in which the Yeshua circles at the Sukkoth or Passover were depicted as ordinary Jews, anti-Judaism and the Satanization of the Jew of the historical diaspora could never have sprung from that new covenant with God. And most tellingly, in no century after the crucifixion of "rabbi Yeshua" could the epithet "Jew," during the bloody murder of a Jew for being a Jew, have been reasonably hurled at the victim if the would-be killer knew that his own inherited savior Yeshua was also a Jew. Cossacks, even in moments of killing, don't kill Cossacks simply because they are Cossacks.

The in-house nature of Yeshua's invective is seen by the Christian scholar Krister Stendahl, who accounts for the heavy rhetoric of "brood of vipers" in Matthew and Luke, writing, "When such words are spoken they are spoken by a Jewish prophet for a Jewish people. Jesus identifies with his people." He further elaborates: "The Jesus-movement was a totally Jewish event—the gospels know of few contacts of Jesus with gentiles. Christianity begins as a Jewish reform movement, and the formative conflicts by which the Christian identity is formed are conflicts within Judaism."[114]

The characteristic attack mode against "the Jews" occurs in the episode of the Sukkoth (Festival of Booths), 7.10. Yeshua has gone up to Jerusalem for the Sukkoth feasts and he will enter the great Temple and teach there. Members of the crowd are speaking about Yeshua, for and against him. We read that "no one spoke about him openly for fear of the Jews" (7.13). Yet Jews at a Jewish festival cannot sensibly be made to whisper to each other that they must not speak openly about Yeshua, who is also a Jew, "for fear of the Jews." Although in this crudely redacted sentence the identity of the speaker and the speaker's "fearful" referents are identical—they are all Jews—by the condemnation of the referent, the reader is instructed to disassociate speaker from referent. A Jew condemns a Jew for being Jewish, and consequently the condemner ceases to be seen as a Jew. In another reversal, we have the condemnation of the Jews reinforced by having the referent Jews crying out their own self-condemnation. In the notoriously implausible

114. See Krister Stendahl, "Anti-Semitism," in *The Oxford Companion to the Bible*, ed. Bruce M. Metzger and Michael D. Coogan (New York: Oxford University Press, 1993), 33, 32.

street scene before Pontius Pilate, earlier discussed in the segment
on historicity, the author or authors have miraculously made the Jews
themselves scream out their collective guilt for the immediate moment
and, prophetically, a guilt to be inherited by their children for all time
in the future (Matt. 27.25).

In John and throughout the gospels, the term "the Jews" is an embracing code word for a composite enemy consisting of opponents, authorities,
and unbelievers in rabbi Yeshua. Although the means of stereotyping
are crude and self-contradictory, the effect is unequivocal: The Jew is
Satanized. Elaine Pagels eloquently documents the Devil-making enter-
prise in *The Origin of Satan* (1995). The demonization is explicit and
complete in John 8.44. There Yeshua declares the children of Abraham
to be the children of the devil:

> You are from your father the devil
> And you want to do the desires of your father.
> From the beginning he was a murderer
> And he does not stand in the truth,
> Because there is no truth in him.
> When he lies he speaks from himself,
> Since he is a liar and the father of lies.

It should be said that the vindictive demonization of the Jews in the
Abraham and the Sukkoth scenes has less to do with the historic moment
of an evangelist John or of his subjects but more with the needs of a
second-century retrenchment of Christianity. As the movement became
increasingly gentile, Christianity split from Judaism, the messiah was
converted into the Christ, and the children of the unreconstructed Jews
were converted into the children of Satan. With Yeshua's Jewish identity
all but muted and dead after his crucifixion by the Romans in Jerusalem,
the new Christian fathers of the church in Rome and elsewhere could
breathe independence from a Jewish parentage.

In George Nickelsburg's article, "The First Century: A Time to Rejoice
and a Time to Weep," the weepers were the Jews and the rejoicers were
those who, as Christian Jews and increasingly by the time of the gospels simply as Christians, rejoiced at the destruction of the Temple and
Jerusalem as an act of God's justice. Nickelsburg writes,

Once again revisionist history [the gospels not as chronicles but as "interpretive history"] reflects the standoff between Christians and Jews at the end of the first century and reveals a startling difference in their responses to the events of the year 70. Baruch and Ezra [late noncanonical apocrypha] may attribute the destruction to sin, but their account is explicitly tempered with grief and puzzlement over the extremity of the punishment. For the evangelists, there is no pause. The Jews had it coming to them. Nor does it make any difference in the final analysis. God's redemptive activity will go on without the Temple, and God's covenantal relationship is transferred to the gentiles. There are losers, but there are winners, and the winners hardly pause to think of the losers, except with a certain satisfaction that God's justice has been enacted.[115]

However, the matter of Christianity's origins remained to plague the new sect's equanimity. The religion had its origin in these despised Suasionist Jews. The continued existence of the Jews kept the problem alive, and so there was no end to targeting them for their Satanic ways.

Code Words in the New Covenant
Let us look carefully at the logic of a passage, typical throughout the gospels, which reveals the hand disguising the Jewishness of both Yeshua and the circle he was speaking to. The failure in completely concealing the alterations provides our clues. In John 13.33 we have:

> Children, I am with you a short while.
> You will look for me,
> And I tell you now as I said to the Jews,
> "Where I go you cannot also come."

The author of this passage has Yeshua say, "and I tell you now as I said to the Jews." This verse designates three parties: the I, the you, and the Jews. Now the intimate instruction fails, because Yeshua designates the Jews as other than the I and the you, who are also Jews. If instead of

115. See George W. E. Nickelsburg, "The First Century: A Time to Rejoice and a Time to Weep," in *Religion and Theology* 1(1)(1994): 4–17.

saying "as I said to the Jews," Yeshua had said, "as I said to other Jews or to my Jewish opponents," the phrase would have been that of a credible Jewish leader distinguishing those who were in his movement from those who were not. Then the reader could assume truthfully that Yeshua and his confidants were Jews, but that some of the Jews were antagonists and worthy of punishment. An in-house drama. But the author of the passage clearly leaps ahead to a later time when Christianity existed as a distinct group of largely non-Jewish followers and the people in this scene were gentiles rather than Jews. There, in the historical context of Yeshua's day, the words fail by being too greedy, by making Yeshua a Christian (one following himself?), not a Jew, and by making his students not Jews, and finally by designating himself and his students as belonging to some people other than the Jews. This meddling reveals that the words are not likely to be those of a historic evangelist reigning over a Jewish Passover supper in Jerusalem, but of a gentile scribe from a later time when the separation between Christian and Jew had been realized. In these ways, the authors and redactors of the gospels established a mythical identity for the founders of Christianity.

Pharisees: Who Were They, and Was Yeshua or Paul a Pharisee?

As the Greek scriptures read today, there is an inexplicable shift in implied reference, which occurs when the Jews around Yeshua excoriated the Jewish priesthood, especially the Pharisees.[116] The Pharisees, meaning "separatists," were rivals of the priestly temple cult of the Sadducees. Associated with the small synagogues and the houses of prayer rather than the great Temple, they emphasized faith in the one God, with whom an individual could have, as Yeshua did, a direct relationship, without going through the formalities of the Temple. As noted earlier, Christianity was in deep debt to the Pharisees, despite the vilification of them as "hypocritical actors" and "brood of vipers" in Matthew, for

---

116. For discussion of slander in the Greek scriptures, see Luke T. Johnson, "The New Testament: Anti-Jewish Slander and the Conventions of Ancient Polemic," *Journal of Biblical Literature* 108 (1989): 419–441, and "Matthew's Campaign against the Pharisees: Deploying the Devil," in Elaine Pagels's *Origin of Satan* (New York: Vintage, 1995). For further discussion of Matthew, see Krister Stendahl, *The School of Matthew* (Uppsala: C. W. K. Gleerup, 1954).

the Pharisees believed in the divine revelation of both written and oral law, and in eternal life and resurrection. They centered on the soul's immortality, which was also at the heart of Yeshua's spiritual redemption, a Platonic notion that entered Judaism and consequently Christianity during the two centuries B.C.E. of high Greek influence in Israel, which paralleled the Hasmonean struggle against and accommodation with the Greeks. It is said that the Pharisees were aloof toward quotidian politics, including the revolt against the Romans in 70 C.E., in which few took part, and as a progressive sect the Pharisees held that religious ritual and practice could take place in one's own home as opposed to public synagogues and the Temple. This fact was to be of extreme significance in the survival of the Jewish tradition after the destruction of the Temple, and in the lives of the early Christians, who struggled to survive amidst enemies. They separated the worldly and spiritual spheres, and, like Yeshua, they ceded the former to Caesar in order to pursue the salvation of spiritual eternity. At the same time, other sources say that the Pharisees were not aloof but distinctly with the people in opposing Roman rule. The New Testament is a strange book pitting Yeshua the Jew against the Pharisees, who probably shared his deviant persuasion, but whom the gospels reduce to a parody of legalistic constraints.[117]

Harold Bloom sees the Pharisees as the primary ally of Yeshua with regard to the belief in the resurrection, but he distinguishes between resurrection and the Platonic immortality of the soul, which he contends was the domain of Hellenistic Jews (surely Philo) and Paul and had less to do with Yeshua and the gospels. In *Omens of Millennium*, Bloom writes,

> Saint Paul, like the Hellenistic Jews, seems to have absorbed Platonic notions of immortality, but there seems no Platonic influence upon Jesus himself, with his altogether Pharisaic belief in resurrection: "He is not the God of the dead but of the living." The intertestamental Jewish texts that fuse immortality and resurrection are themselves

117. E. P. Sanders debunks the "authenticity of the charges against the Pharisees in Matt. 23" (*Jesus and Judaism*, Philadelphia: Fortress Press, 1987, 277), and develops this notion fully in *Paul and Palestinian Judaism: A Comparison of Patterns of Religion* (Philadelphia: Fortress Press, 1977) and in *Paul, the Law, and the Jewish People* (Philadelphia: Fortress Press, 1983).

Platonized, but Jesus, despite the New Testament polemic against the
Pharisees falsely argued in his name, seems less Platonized even than
the Pharisees. He is in the tradition of "Yahweh alone," even if his
vision of Yahweh is extraordinarily benign, at least in those passages
of the gospels (and *The Gospel of Thomas*) that have the authentic
aura of his voice.[118]

Burton Mack also describes the coincidences of dissent between the
Jesus movement and the Pharisees. Along with the Essenes, who withdrew
to Qumran near the Dead Sea, the Pharisees were opposed not only to
the secular Hellenization of the Jews but also to the Hasmonean Jewish
leaders. Originally, the Hasmonean family under Judas Maccabeus, who
led the successful rebellion in 167–64 B.C.E. against the Greek monarchy,
represented Jewish resistance to Hellenization and foreign rule; but after
nearly two centuries of accommodation to Greek and Roman rulers,
the Hasmonean descendants, like Herod, became puppets of their earlier adversaries. Mack writes, "The Pharisees were harsh critics of the
Hasmonean establishment and, together with the priests at Qumran,
they wore the Hasmoneans down."[119]

In effect, the existence of the Pharisees was an embarrassment to
later Christian writers, for not only were they separatists like the early
Christian Jews, but from their rank came converts—Paul claimed to
be a Pharisee—to the Jesus movement.[120] Moreover, they were fiercely
opposed to Roman occupation. If there is one historical reason that
most contemporary scholars agree upon, it is that Yeshua was executed
as a seditionist, that is, a Jewish revolutionary who wanted out of the
Roman occupation. But since the gospels picture Yeshua as one who

118. See Harold Bloom, *Omens of Millennium: The Gnosis of Angels, Dreams, and
Resurrection* (New York: Riverhead Books, 1996), 158.

119. See Burton L. Mack, *Who Wrote the New Testament? The Making of the Christian Myth* (San Francisco: HarperSanFrancisco, 1993), 23.

120. In *The Mythmaker: Paul and the Invention of Christianity* (San Francisco: HarperSanFrancisco, 1986), Hyam Maccoby asserts that Paul was not a Pharisee, writing, "The contention of this book is that Jesus, usually represented as anything but a
Pharisee, was one, while Paul, always represented as a Pharisee in his unregenerate
days, never was. In the course of the argument, it will become plain why this strange
reversal of the facts was brought about by the New Testament writers" (33).

accommodates the Romans—"What is of Caesar give to Caesar" (Mark 14.25) and the Roman soldiers who execute Yeshua are made the first to affirm him as innocent, God, and risen—there is also an inescapable conclusion that there is a terrible quandary of how the evangelists should treat these Romans who killed Yeshua, Paul, and all those Christian Jews, which is the concern of Apocalypse (Revelation). The Pharisees' uncomfortably similar views with the historical Yeshua executed by the Romans as a seditionist, together with their failure to accept Yeshua's divinity, could not be tolerated. The solution was to co-opt the essential position of the dissenting Pharisees and turn them from opponents of Rome to instigators and enforcers of the Romans' "unwilling" execution of Yeshua—to make the Pharisees into the establishment by demonizing them as shameless legalists, liars, and killers. In one stroke, the enemy authority was Pharisee, unbeliever, murderer, and devil.

There is also a notion among scholars that not only Yeshua's views coincided with the Pharisees (hence the special need to defame these Jews who were in spiritual harmony with Yeshua) but also Yeshua was a Pharisee.[121] Hyam Maccoby writes, "Jesus speaks and acts as a Pharisee, though the gospel editors have attempted to conceal this by representing him as opposing Pharisaism even when his sayings were most in accordance with Pharisee teaching." Since the Pharisees "were the centre of opposition to the Roman occupation, it was of the utmost importance to the Gospel editors to represent Jesus as having been a rebel against Jewish religion, not against the Roman occupation. The wholesale re-editing of the material in order to give a picture of conflict between Jesus and the Pharisees was thus essential."[122]

Maccoby sees the Pharisees as the center of opposition to Rome which, if Yeshua was executed for anti-Rome activities, would make them allies in the struggle. Others see the Pharisees and Yeshua as disinterested in the struggle against Rome and link them accordingly to similar positions. The evidence about the Pharisees appears in the New Testament, in

121. Geza Vermes in *The Changing Faces of Jesus* remarks that at the Passover meal Yeshua is described as wearing a Pharisee garment, "including the traditional tassels hanging from its edge" (209). Then he notes places in the New Testament and Hebrew Bible that describe the Pharisee attire.

122. See Maccoby, *Mythmaker*, xi, 34.

Josephus, and in rabbinic literature. The accounts are contradictory, and modern descriptions also differ widely as to their position on Rome and revolt. In Josephus and elsewhere, the Pharisees strongly opposed Herod and his successors, which would imply opposition to Rome. In rabbinic literature, the Pharisees are associated with the great philosophical schools of Shammai and Hillel, who were Pharisiac leaders. In the New Testament, the Pharisees are reduced to perfidious clones of evil.

Ultimately, the Pharisees had to be condemned by the authors of the gospels, who surely were writing for the survival of later Christianity amid the widespread Roman Empire. So they condemned Rome's enemies, especially the Pharisees, to appease Rome and to demonstrate their own innocence and loyalty to the empire. But while they fiercely condemned Rome's enemies, it was unthinkable that their wrath might extend to Yeshua himself as an enemy of Rome. So Yeshua was not only fashioned as a loyal subject of Rome and enemy of the Jews but forced ungenerously into the illogical role of the most famous defender of his own executioners. Such a position was hugely unfair to Yeshua, the greatest and best-known world victim of the Roman rulers of occupied Israel.

New Translations Forming a Christian Bible

The formidable shaping of a Christian Bible came in the unknowable beginnings. The contradictions remained, and in reading these texts, one can conjecture about the blank time of rewriting when purposeful redaction was intense, censorial eyes not there. When the evangelists were converting early Jews to Christianity, it was convenient for the evangelists to use the Septuagint Greek Bible of the Jews. Paul used the Septuagint for his apostolate and, as Lowry Nelson observed, "In the early century of proselytizing and establishing the doctrine, Greek was the prime language and Hellenized Jews the prime body of converts."[123] With the later separation of Jews from the new Judaism of the Christian Jews came the need on both sides to separate the Septuagint Greek Bible of the Jews from the one of the Christians: hence, the redaction of the Septuagint for Christian usage by a series

123. See Lowry Nelson Jr., *Poetic Configurations* (University Park: Pennsylvania State University Press, 1992), 118.

of translations, culminating in the third-century Hexapla of Origen, a polyglot version of the Hebrew Bible (named for its six columns: a Hebrew text, a Greek transliteration of it, and four Greek versions—Aquila's, Symmachus's, Theodotion's, and Origen's own corrected version of the Septuagint). The Hexapla was lost with the seventh-century destruction of the library at Caesarea by the Muslims, but we do hear that in the fourth century Jerome consulted it at Caesarea for his own translation of the Vulgate. With the Romanization of the Christian movement, the Latin translation took precedence over Hebrew and Greek scripture, becoming for the Catholic Church, like the Authorized for many Protestants, the word itself.

All these transformations of identities, through scripture, corresponded to requirements for establishing by the beginning of the fifth-century "a Christian epic," as Mack describes the Christian Bible, which would include both the Hebrew Bible and the Greek scriptures. As Christianity became dominant in southern Europe in the fourth century, it was increasingly important for the Greek scriptures to be a single authoritative book, no longer a disputed collection of disparate texts, but the dominant Bible within the "dual" Bible and the definitive guide to keep alive the stories of Yeshua and the apostles and to spread the word of God to the faithful and potential proselytes. The shaping of the New Testament required that the enemies be defined, and so they were. The New Testament also required miracles to match those in the Old Testament. The older Bible had to fit the new one, whatever their relative status, and the exegetes found the Hebrew Bible rich in symbolism that could be seen as a source for Christian virtues and predictions of the messiah. The fitting of the two covenants together, the joining together of the authority of Moses with the apostolic writings, gave a firm and deep legitimacy to the Christian religion.

Yeshua's Changing Self

Throughout the gospels, there remain the inconsistencies and mutations of Yeshua's character during his residence on earth, within or between sentences and paragraphs, whether presented as messiah, Jew, rabbi, savior, gentile, pre-Christian, or simply alien. The schizophrenic presentation of Yeshua's Jewishness and non-Jewishness is nowhere revealed more poignantly than in the passage in John 19.40: "So they took the body of Yeshua and wrapped it in aromatic spices in linen cloths, as is the Jewish custom." John reveals that it is mandated that Yeshua be buried in the Jewish manner. Now Pilate has just washed his hands to show his innocence, his heartfelt reluctance to kill Yeshua. While Pilate appears to have made himself an acceptable gentile by washing his hands, in doing so he performs an ancient Jewish ritual. So even Pilate, in this supposedly sanitized script, is portrayed as resorting to a Jewish symbolic rite of purification. Elaine Pagels points out, "[I]n a most unlikely scene, Pilate performed a ritual that derives from Jewish law, described in the book of Deuteronomy. He washed his hands to indicate his innocence of bloodshed."[124]

After these back-and-forth passages of Yeshua's split presentation in the gospels, as Jew and abused non-Jew, the emphasis on Yeshua's Jewishness in the ritual of handling his body appears again, in John 20.16, when Mary the Magdalene first encounters Yeshua. The text has her say "Rabboni!" (which means "teacher").[125] We note, however, the inevitable and illogical cover-up in the interpolation "which means teacher" that has again been added to the text, in instructive parenthesis, to dissuade the reader from the unwelcome notion that "rabbi" actually means "rabbi," and that Yeshua is a rabbi and therefore a Jew. That a rabbi might also be a teacher does not, as some contend, excuse the intentions of the parenthesis, which is to suggest that he is not a Jewish rabbi but an unattached local teacher.

In practice, the changing of identity was accomplished by persuading the reader that Yeshua was in opposition to Jews (not to "other" Jews), to their purity laws, to their inhumane keeping of the Sabbath, to their brutish, enforcing authorities. The Jews were always *they*, not *we*. By an accumulation of convincing details in a blistering anti-Jewish message, the itinerant charismatic was disenfranchised of his Jewish culture and ethnicity. The reader could thereby hate the Jews without hating Yeshua the Mashiah. Yeshua, rather than being portrayed by the assemblers of the gospels as a God of love, is depicted as a figure who hates his fellow Jews, which can have little to do with a historic Yeshua. At this point, it is right to put this scene in a modern context. It is enough to

124. See Pagels, *Origin of Satan*, 87.
125. It means "my great teacher or master."

say that Yeshua and his circle, whatever masks their writers gave them, would have fared less well in Germany between 1933 and 1945. In those days, the designation of the Jew as "vermin," found famously first in Matthew's "brood of vipers," was fixed, and even the intervention of Pope Pius XII could not have altered that designation of Yeshua's blood and racial identity, and his inevitable way to the chamber. His parents, brothers, sisters, students, and messengers (apostles) would also have been picked up in trucks and sent to the death camps as Jews. In the eyes of the master race, the identity of Yeshua as one of the Jews had no way out.

Sparing Greeks for Execution of Socrates

The Jews are the named enemy in the gospels of the Jews, which is no less insensible than having the Greeks as the named enemy in the other great death in history, the death of Socrates. The Jews at least had Romans to get them off the hook, if a literal reading of scripture is followed. While the story of the crucifixion is uncertain in all its larger facts and smaller details, the tale of the death of Socrates is certain indeed. We may not know whether Plato's reporting of Socrates' last conversations is accurate or invented. We do know that a Greek tribunal ordered the death of perhaps the greatest of the Greek philosophers and theologians. If the same criterion of inherited guilt by association were applied to the Greeks, then even the most generous eyes could not save the Greeks from the damnation of the ages. They had no alibis, neither Romans nor other aliens to save their people from everlasting infamy. At this, let us say there are some good turns in history. One is the surprising, blessed fact that the Greeks for their treatment of Socrates, and the Romans for theirs of Yeshua have not been condemned and vilified through the ages. There is no inheritance of alleged guilt, and there are simply and happily no takers of such profoundly mean-spirited vision.

Abandonment of Yeshua

Those who invented a Yeshua in life who was clean of Jewish stain and whose people were wicked and tainted with everlasting guilt of being a Jew were not kind to Yeshua, nor to his tribal kin, nor to their descendants. To Yeshua's people his angry creators stained their savior with a ghost of fear echoing even in the utterance of his name.

When Yeshua was on the cross as a man, desolate that his God had not saved him, he cried out, "Why have you forsaken me?" He shouted in Aramaic, his language as a Jew (not in later Christian Greek), and reproached God, asking, Why have you let Rome kill a Jew? Over the centuries his cry has not been heard.

Evangelists as
Apologists for Rome

~~~

A Roman Miracle

As we have seen, in order to bring the messiah of the Jews into the church in Rome, Yeshua as Jew was blurred and essentially absolved from his religion, his ethnicity, and from his occupation as an itinerant charismatic rabbi. He was the *other*—and the other is never clarified—to be contrasted with those around him, who were identified specifically and uniformly as vile and wicked Jews. He could not be one of them. But the clergy of the Roman church still had an urgent and fierce dilemma about Rome's role in the execution of this stubbornly independent rabbi.

The clergy in Rome saw themselves as Romans and therefore as direct descendants of Pompey, who conquered Judea in 63 B.C.E. and deported large numbers of Jews as slaves to Rome; of Pontius Pilate, who ordered the centurion and his guard to execute Yeshua; and of Florus and Titus, who crucified thousands of rebelling Jews, including the Christian Jews, and their entire families with extraordinary speed and efficiency. How could a Roman clergy in Rome, where Messianism had taken hold, cope with the past? It did not entirely fall into historic amnesia, which is the most common way of coping with periods and events one would prefer forgotten. Its solution was to shift blame from Romans to Jews for all untoward events and, as noted, make the Roman officials the first to recognize Yeshua's earthly innocence, his God, and his own divinity as the son of God. That Roman invention of history shines as an unworthy miracle of the gospels.

The most benign explanation for the clergy's praise for its persecutors is that Rome reluctantly tolerated the expanding Christian churches, and the clerics feared that any sharp criticism of Rome with respect to the death of the messiah, any accusation of Roman deicide, would certainly lead to lethal repression.

So the gospels were shaped as an apology for Roman occupation of Israel, whose benign officials had been forced involuntarily into unpleasant acts to maintain obedience to Rome and its treasury. The evangelists were unfailing apologists for Rome. Foremost, they exonerated Rome from the death of Yeshua. They have Yeshua proclaim militantly the necessary and absolute punishment of his fellow Jews for challenging the Romans. They have Yeshua, who offers salvation, condemn the Jews for Titus's destruction of the Temple and Jerusalem four decades later. In condemning Jews, Yeshua personally exculpates Rome for the devastation of Jerusalem and its expulsion of the inhabitants, Jews and Christian Jews, into a new diaspora.

Pontius Pilatus

The secular moral hero of the gospels is Pontius Pilate. His ennoblement, which after his death will give him a place among the saints in Ethiopian Orthodoxy, is not merely an apology. He is Rome in Israel and its reasonable, humane emperor. He is certainly not a nondescript Eichmann banally following orders to kill Jews. A weak man, he kills Yeshua with a pained heart, unable to intimidate the high priests or resist the crowds in the street. He is the good bridge to Rome. Unlike Herod or his own soldiers, at no moment does Pilate participate in the maligning or mockery of Yeshua. Rather, he asks some simple questions, whose intent is to give Yeshua a way out, and then declares his distinctively personal judgment that Yeshua is innocent and states that he wants to release him. He yields only after three attempts to win his release, and then only under the insistent pressure of the Jewish high priests and leaders, does he order him scourged and crucified. The event occurs on Friday, the day of preparation for the Passover Sabbath that will begin that evening, which makes the presence of the crowds in the street even more extraordinary. That Pilate accedes to the release of Barabbas, an insurrectionist and murderer, only emphasizes by contrast Yeshua's innocence.

Pilate's contemporaries were not so solicitous about preserving the ruler's good name. The Alexandrian Neoplatonist philosopher Philo (20 B.C.E.–50 C.E.), whose allegorical method of interpreting biblical scripture was to profoundly affect later Christian theology, wrote prolifically about Hellenistic Judaism, though without any awareness of Christian figures or events. Yeshua and his dissident Jewish sect had not, during Philo's lifetime, made a strong resonance in Alexandria, which it was later to do when it became, among other things, the initiator of Christian monasticism. Pilate, however, was known to him. In *Embassy to Gaius* (301–302), Philo "describes Pilate, whom the evangelists present as a helpless pawn, as a man of 'ruthless, stubborn and cruel disposition,' famous for, among other things, ordering 'frequent executions without trial'."[126] As Mary Smallwood notes in *The Jews under Roman Rule from Pompey to Diocletian*, "At a time when the Romans in Israel were crucifying thousands of Jews for trouble making and sedition,"[127] Pilate was renowned for his cruelty, venality with regard to Temple funds and other local moneys, and abundant killings. The Roman prefect of Judea was recalled to Rome in 36 C.E. to answer for the massacre and executions of the Samaritans at Mount Gerizim.

How did Pontius Pilate become the good figure of the gospels? Mark begins the process of converting Pilate into a virtuous Roman governor and Yeshua into a non-Jewish victim of Jews. Elaine Pagels, tracing the changing portraits of Pilate through the gospels, develops in great depth the shifting of blame from Romans to Jews in the crucifixion and its resultant demonization of the Jews:

> Mark's benign portrait of Pilate increases the culpability of Jewish leaders and supports Mark's contention that Jews, not Romans, were the primary force behind Jesus' crucifixion. Throughout the following decades, as bitterness between the Jewish majority and Jesus followers increased, the Gospels came to depict Pilate in an increasingly favorable light. As Paul Winter observes, the stern Pilate grows more mellow from Gospel to Gospel [from Mark to Matthew, from Matthew and Luke to John]. . . . The more removed from history, the more sympathetic a character he becomes.[128]

126. See Elaine Pagels, *The Origin of Satan* (New York: Vintage, 1995), 10.

127. See Mary Smallwood, *The Jews under Roman Rule from Pompey to Diocletian* (Leiden: E. J. Brill, 1981), 164.

128. Pagels, *Origin of Satan*, 33. See also Paul Winter, *On the Trial of Jesus* (Berlin/New York: De Gruyter, 1974), 88.

In the gospels, the evangelists demonstrate Pilate's benevolence and impotence before higher forces. He is embellished as a good man, played with by evil forces. Pilate is mentioned only once more in the gospel. In his last good act he permits Yeshua's body to be taken away (Luke 23.52). The fact that the corpse was not left to rot on the cross for the vultures and dogs to pick apart and the remains thrown into a fire indicates special treatment, since part of the punishment of Roman crucifixion was the dismemberment and public humiliation of the victim. By permitting the body to be removed from the tomb, Pilate sets the stage for the discovery of the resurrection.

Apart from Yeshua and perhaps Peter, the personages in the gospels are fixed. They appear briefly, episodically, as in a travel book, and reveal little personal development. In the parables, there is perhaps more development, as in the figures of the prodigal son story, but they are a story within a story and once removed from the drama of the narration. The clear exception is Pilate. He has a crisis of conscience. He must as a Roman ruler kill in order to maintain a continuity of control, which his position requires. He is caught between loyalties to Rome and to his conscience, and sensitivity to the Jewish hierarchy and street mob. As in good theater, his order to proceed with the crucifixion establishes the tragedy. He may seem weak but not evil. And like his city of Rome, he will after his death float slowly back to the future church and be sanctified.

Rome Seen from the Catacombs Where the Christians Cower
During the period when the gospels were assembled, we assume between 70 and 95 or later, neither Rome nor the Romans were viewed with pleasure. They were, as we see vividly in Revelation, the human incarnation of evil, although for obvious reasons Rome and its emperors are not mentioned by name in this wild allegory. In the Apocalypse, the Whore of Babylon may be the Roman emperor Nero or Domitian or, after the publication of Israel Knohl's *Messiah before Jesus: The Suffering Servant of the Dead Sea Scrolls* (2000), is surely the goat-horned monster emperor Caesar Augustus. The purpose of the apocalypses was to reveal and conceal through allegorical disguise, thus making historical-critical analysis at best tentative.[129]

129. See Bernard McGinn's "Apocalypse," in Robert Alter and Frank Kermode, eds., *The Literary Guide to the Bible* (Cambridge, MA: Harvard University Press, 1987), 523–541.

Revelation surely escaped the Romanizing that characterizes the gospels. Written well after the gospels, its oddity and obscurity set it aside—it was not an early centerpiece of the emerging New Testament—and so this revelation, including its not very veiled attack on Rome, remained intact at the heart of the poem. By the third century, when after much debate this controversial book was included in the canon, it reached us without marked political alteration of its text. It reflects its own period. The fear and fury it expresses toward the Roman Augustus and his forces can hardly be reconciled with the friendliness in the synoptic gospels. The catacombs of Rome, where Christian fugitives lived in terror, would not have recognized the Roman political and military figures depicted in the gospels. Their historical experience clamors against the whitewash of Roman behavior in scripture.

Coins for Rome

We have observed the gentle way made for Pontius Pilate to his later beatification and canonization. The goodness trickles down to his centurion, and even to the tax collectors for Rome, who took payments from farmers, city people, and the Temple. The famous scene of Yeshua and the Roman coin is normally received as a convenient separation of state and religion. It begins with the Jewish authorities who are trying to trap Yeshua by making it seem wrong to cooperate with Rome,

> "Is it right to pay the tax to Caesar or not? Should we give or
>   not give?"
> But he saw their hypocrisy and said to them:
>   Why are you testing me?
>   Bring me a denarius to look at.
> They brought one.
> And he said to them,
>   Whose image is this and whose name?
> They said to him, "Caesar's."
> Yeshua said to them,
>   The things of Caesar give to Caesar
>   And the things of God give to God.
>   MARK 12.14–17

The Pharisees remain embarrassed into silence after Yeshua's response. He has trapped them by his turn of phrase and has proven that it is not a fault to pay Rome what is Rome's.

Historically, this period was a touchy time of contention between Jew and Roman over religious matters—such as Caligula's attempt in 44–45 C.E. to set up a statue of himself in the Temple, and the tax rebellions, which, Josephus reports, were ruthlessly put down. Since the scriptural position held Roman authority to be good and Jewish authority bad, especially as represented by the Pharisees (who, as noted, opposed Hellenization and Roman occupation), it was imperative to prove that tribute to Rome in the form of payment to Caesar did not interfere with tribute to God. So this passage of the coins showing Caesar's head establishes three principles: 1) Yeshua's recognition of the authority of the emperor for things of the emperor; 2) the hypocrisy of Jewish authorities who cast doubt on the authority of the emperor; and 3) that payment to the emperor does not imperil the things that are God's.

In Luke 23.2, Yeshua in captivity is accused falsely of "forbidding taxes to be paid to Caesar." Under Roman law not to pay taxes to Caesar was a crime. The gospel position here is that Yeshua is being falsely accused of opposition to Roman rule, and it affirms his goodness in going along with Roman law.

In summary, the question of paying taxes identifies the position of the parties toward the Roman occupation of Israel. One accused of disobeying Roman law (by way of not paying taxes) is a corrupting force and not a patriot to Rome. The gospels portray Yeshua as one who acquiesces to Caesar, and even have him falsely accused by fellow Jews of being a revolutionary against Rome in order to show how despicable these Jews are in accusing Yeshua of having opposed Rome.

This consistent gospel picture of a Yeshua who states "The things of Caesar give to Caesar" is an unfair portrait of the charismatic rabbi who was received as the messiah. And the prevailing view by contemporary Bible historians holds that Yeshua died because he was perceived by the Romans as a political opponent with large crowds of followers, which the crucifixion of a seditionist underscores. As for the alleged poor relations with other Jews, with Temple or Sanhedrin authorities, these were Jewish matters and, as Paula Fredriksen and others note, Pilate couldn't have cared less about them.

In scripture, the Jewish tax collectors who work specifically for the Romans are fashioned in the parables and other incidents as humble and good, and in contrast to the Jewish authorities, high priests, and their scholars, who are arrogant and wicked. Such is the prevalent coloring of Jew and Roman in the gospels. In Matthew 10.3, the tax collector is Matthew. In Mark 2.13–14 and Luke 5.27–28, the same tax collector is called Levi. That Matthew and Levi are the same person (the traditional view) is unclear, and also unclear is the traditional view that the tax collector Matthew is Matthew the evangelist. While the actual names of the evangelists may be later attributions, it is very clear that the figure of a tax collector called Matthew, traditionally identified with the authorial evangelist of the same name, is portrayed not only as a good man, but also as good enough to be an evangelist.

The Good Centurions

The centurions are Roman officers who appear on two occasions in the gospels. Like the tax collectors, they are modest and virtuous. Their favorable presentation foretells the need of the later church in Rome to prepare for Yeshua's messiahship and to make Rome and Pilate, its representative in Israel, appear beneficent. The first mention of a centurion in the synoptics is the Roman officer who implores Yeshua to heal his son who is near death. He is introduced as one "who loves our people and built our synagogue" (Luke 7.5). After Yeshua has healed the centurion's son, Yeshua praises him, for the centurion has stated that while as a stern commander his soldiers and the slaves under his orders obey his word at once, he, before the powers of Yeshua, is unworthy to ask him to come under his roof. Yeshua is so amazed by this assertion of the centurion's humility that he says to the others, "I tell you, / I have not found such faith in Israel" (Luke 7.9). Effectively, the faith of this Roman soldier of the occupation of Israel exceeds that of any Jew, whether a follower or not of Yeshua. This hyperbole of praise for the Roman *ethnikos* ("national" or "pagan gentile") seems unfathomable and out of place, yet it corresponds accurately with the practice of making servants of Rome exemplary in their benevolence and Christian piety.

The role of the centurion, as noted, takes on a crucially dramatic role at the crucifixion. Although again unnamed, the centurion, who has just overseen the crucifixion of Yeshua by his death squad, experiences, like Paul on the way to Damascus, sudden revelation and conversion. At the instant of Yeshua's death he not only proclaims to the world Yeshua's divinity, with faith in the messiah, but presumably by doing so renounces the gods of the Romans to praise Yahweh, who is still the God of the Jews. With that event, so early in Christian history, Rome recognizes Christianity and the Christian God. In Luke, we read, "When the centurion, commander of the company of soldiers, saw what had happened, he glorified God, saying: 'Surely this was a just man'" (Luke 23.47). In Mark, the earliest gospel and in large part the source of Matthew and Luke, the praiser of Yeshua is the centurion commander of the execution who saw Yeshua breathe his last. He said, "Truly this man was the son of God" (Mark 15.39). As in Luke, at this climactic moment, the evangelist author has made a Roman utter the first spoken word after Yeshua's death, and it is the praise of Christian faith, proving that even then Romans who killed Yeshua shared the later Christian conviction of Yeshua as the son of God. Matthew enlarges the scope, and his converts to Christianity include both the centurion and his troops: "When the centurion and those with him guarding Yeshua saw the earthquake and all that took place, they were terrified, and said, 'Surely he was the son of God!'" (Matt. 27.54). Only after the Romans have had their say does the narrator turn briefly to the women onlookers, who are watching from the distance. The women of Yeshua's faith, who stand there on his behalf, say nothing. Their silence is telling.

In John we find a sharply contrasting scene from that depicted in the synoptic Mark, Matthew, and Luke. There is no mention of any Roman *sur-le-champ* conversion. No centurion or common soldier steps forward to declare his epiphany of faith in the messiah. The soldiers are merely brutal. They come to break Yeshua's legs, but, finding him already dead, "one of the soldiers stabs his side with his spear, and at once blood and water came out" (John 19.34). The omission of the pious Roman soldiers brings John's version in contention with the synoptics. For whatever reason, John was not about to show the Roman miracle of the executioner's conversion.

Titus and the Stones of Jerusalem

Flavius Titus, emperor of Rome in 79–81 C.E., is not mentioned in the gospels. As a young man he directed the siege of Jerusalem that

culminated in the piercing of the city walls and the destruction of the
Temple, the heart of Jewish identity and resistance. For his conquest and
the razing of Jerusalem, the Arch of Titus was built at the entrance to
the Roman Forum, bearing the Latin inscription "The Senate and the
Roman people to the divine Titus, son of the divine Vespasian, and to
Vespasian Augustus." And the Roman biographer Suetonius called Titus
"the darling of the human race." Josephus gives us a close-up of Titus
and his soldiers during the worst days of the siege when the city was
starving: "[They] caught every day five hundred Jews; nay, some days
they caught more." "They were first whipped, and then tormented with
all sorts of tortures, before they died, and were then crucified before the
walls of the city."[130]

The gospels transform Yeshua into a prophet of the city's destruction,
and while he weeps at the thought of its future ruin, he assigns its
demise to two terrible wrongs committed by the Jews. The first offense
takes place four decades after his death, which is that they will not
choose the ways of peace but rebellion against Rome. The second wrong,
as Luke says, is the Jews' failure to recognize Yeshua as their savior when
he visited them. The Gospel of Luke, composed not earlier than 80–85
C.E., fifty years after Yeshua's death, fashioned a Yeshua who would be a
rebel against the Jews of his country and scold them for their opposition
to the Roman empire. Luke writes,

> If you only knew on this day those things
> Creating peace! Yet now they are hidden
> From your eyes. But days will come upon you
> And your enemies will set up ramparts
> Against you and encircle you and hem you in
> From all sides. They will crush you and your children,
> And not leave a stone on a stone intact in you
> Since you did not know the time of your visitation.
>
> 19.41–44

For Luke, the Jews' great sin is "not knowing the time of your visitation,"

130. See Josephus, "The Jewish War," in *The New Complete Works of Josephus*, trans.
William Whiston (Grand Rapids, MI: Kregel, 1999), book 5, chapter 11, 450, 459.

which points to a major thesis of the gospels: The Jews brought eternal calamity upon themselves by failing to accept Yeshua and Rome.

There were clearly Jews who did and Jews who did not accept Yeshua's messiahship, but the destruction of Jerusalem, "stone upon stone," had nothing to do with such matters. It came about because of the rejection by Jews of Roman rule. This was not the first revolt against Roman or Greek rule, nor would it be the last. Centuries earlier the Maccabees had rebelled against Syro-Hellene rule, and under Judas Maccabeus recaptured Jerusalem. Hanukkah (Feast of Dedication or of the Lights) is an annual celebration of the recapturing in 167 B.C.E. of the Temple from the Syrian Antiochus IV, a Hellenizing Seleucid ruler. The rebellion was prompted by Antiochus's decrees: "All Jewish customs and ceremonies were forbidden, including Sabbath and festival observance and circumcision. All Torah scrolls were to be seized and burned. All sacrifices and offering to God at the Jerusalem Temple were abolished."[131] Those who disobeyed the decrees were to be executed. The Temple became a place of worship for the Greek god Zeus Olympus, and its altar was used for sacrificing pigs. Antiochus called for eradication of monotheistic Judaism. Had the Jews not rebelled then against foreign rule, Judaism would surely have disappeared, which was the intention of the rulers, and without Judaism there would not have been its early sect of Christianity.

Now such rebellion by Jews against foreign rule was treason. And the disaster was not unknown to the evangelists. By the time of their writing, the prophecy had occurred. As the prophecy said, children were crushed, no stone unturned. During the reign of terror by Titus, thousands of Christian Jews, including whole families, were crucified.

It is not likely that a Yeshua of love would have wished these indiscriminate devastations upon his people, upon Christian Jews and other Jews. The detailed description of the scenes has not the quality of prophecy but of data reported to the evangelists. Hence, virtually all scholars date Mark after 70 in order to account for the author's knowledge of the Roman razing of Jerusalem. But apart from detective work on chronology,

131. See Leonard J. Greenspoon, "Between Alexandria and Antioch: Jew and Judaism in the Hellenistic Period," in *The Oxford History of the Biblical World*, ed. Michael D. Coogan (New York: Oxford University Press, 1998), 437.

this depiction of a militant Yeshua, siding with Rome, in anger against the people of Jerusalem should be seen as a portrait wrongful to Christians at all levels of faith. It is wrongful to have the Yeshua of love and spirit call for the later Roman slaughter of his people and their condemnation to an afterlife of eternal pain. It may be best to remember that these translated scriptures are the labor of mortals—not chronicles whispered down from heaven—who record as best they can. The literal word in the gospels, especially when disturbing, is often allegorized to remove it from its surface meaning. But it may be more prudent to look for human frailty in composition, for later redaction and interpolation, and to Rome as an ever-present worry. In the gospels, beauty, love, spirit, and salvation may reside one page away from anger, battle, and condemnation to sulfurous Sodom and Gomorrah. The reader can choose which verses to take into the critical mind or soul.

To Soften Blows
by Softening Translation
or to Let It All Hang Out

Christianizing Yeshua

THE WORDS OF A Jewish sage speaking in Aramaic to his followers
were reported to others, and what he said and what happened to him
became an oral memory that ended up in Greek texts by means we
do not know and by authors and editors we cannot guess. The tirades
against the Jews are the gospels' way of Christianizing the rabbi Yeshua.
The needs of a developing religion to put its house in order made this
conversion of the person of Yeshua imperative.

Concerning these questions of textual and credo history, professors of
the Jesus Seminar, under the theme of "the storyteller's license," say,

> We know that the evangelists not infrequently ascribed Christian words
> to Jesus—they made him talk like a Christian, when, in fact, he was
> only the precursor of the movement that was to take him as its cultic
> hero. They also supplied dialogue for him on many narrative occasions
> for which their memories could not recall an appropriate aphorism or
> parable. In a word, they creatively invented speech for Jesus.

With regard to the Christianizing of Yeshua, they write, "Christian
conviction eventually overwhelms Jesus: he is made to confess what
Christians had come to believe." They list how the Christianization
comes about:

• Sayings and parables expressed in "Christian" language are the
  creation of the evangelists or their Christian predecessors.

- Sayings or parables that contrast with the language or viewpoint of the gospel in which they are embedded reflect older tradition (but not necessarily tradition that originated with Jesus).
- The Christian community develops apologetic statements to defend its claims and sometimes attributes such statements to Jesus.[132]

Soften the Blows or Let It All Hang Out?

How does a translator deal with the antipathy to Jews in the New Testament that appears as pervasive slander? The antipathy itself may connect with a Bloomian "anxiety of influence," meaning the authorial denial and Oedipal fear of and hostility to *precursors* and *original sources*. The precursors were the Jews, and all early followers of Yeshua were Messianic Jews. The original sources were Judaism and its Hebrew Bible, which the Christian Jews appropriated as their own with nominal and doctrinal changes. Harsh denial of a heritage that one cares to obliterate is common in emotional and artistic development. But how in a holy text to handle the consequences of self-anger—the donning of masks, the castigation of the original incarnation—is the uneasy problem. Hostility to women, the eternal "gender discrimination," is now routinely mitigated stylistically in most new versions of the Hebrew Bible and Greek scriptures. Can or should one also soften, in the translation, the harm of the Satanization of the Jew, which in subsequent centuries justified the thicket of oppression and slaughter?

In the introduction and afterword, one can explain, if not explain away, the polemic. To deflect scribal interpolations and alterations, I considered making "the Jews" simply "the person" or "some people," when referring to gatherings. But in the end I came back to the need to let the Jews take their seventy hits, and I comment in the introduction and sometimes in the annotation. To tamper with the text would, whatever the aim, carry the free license of translation into deception. In a word, let the extant Greek version say what it says.

As the texts stand now, especially the beautiful and deep book of John, the message is contradictory and untenable. At least the contradictions

132. See Robert W. Funk, Roy W. Hoover, and the Jesus Seminar, eds., *The Five Gospels: The Search for the Authentic Words of Jesus: New Translation and Commentary* (New York: Macmillan, 1993), 29, 24.

are helpful to the observant reader to recognize a highly redacted text. It is obviously untenable that the accuser lose his identity as a Jew when accusing another Jew of being "of the Jews." That kind of denial of one's position is already castigated by Yeshua himself in the instance of his follower Peter, who in the course of one day denies being of those with Yeshua three times before the dawn cock crows. In a great irony of the New Testament, Yeshua severely castigates Peter for denying his identity and does not forget or forgive that transgression. One must ask, Would Yeshua have also castigated his gospel biographers who, exactly like Peter's denial of himself, denied Yeshua's identity? Dostoyevsky in *The Brothers Karamazov* poses the same matter of the identity of Yeshua in the parable of the Grand Inquisitor: Would Jesus have been arrested as an imposter had he appeared in sixteenth-century Sevilla?

The overt racism and intense anti-Judaism must remain in the text as it is. The informed reader can see the bigotry and reject the message of sectarian hatred. The abuse to the historical Yeshua himself—here turned into a man of angry bias to his own people—one can hope will eventually sink from credibility. So, unlike well-intentioned new versions, these translations leave Jews as Jews, with no euphemism, change, omission, or addition.

There is also in traditional editions of the New Testament a problem parallel to the textual disguisement of Yeshua's identity: the scholarly annotations that anachronistically Christianize both the Hebrew Bible and the New Testament. There is no proselytizing commentary in this edition.

Good-Hearted Reforming of the Text

What are the good-hearted reforms?

In recent years, there have been radical changes in both translation and commentary. In *The Five Gospels*, translators Robert W. Funk and Roy W. Hoover change the wicked "Jews" to the wicked "Judeans." This is surely done with the intention of softening the blow, yet it also raises questions. Who are the Judeans? Isn't "Judean" another name for "Jew"? And whoever they are, are not Judeans now the wicked accusers and the wicked accused, just as the Jews were made to be both the accusers and the accused in standard versions? And if the accusers are not Jews, who are they?

Most pitiful is that in their desire not to hurt the Jews, the translators have eliminated them completely, even in the annotations, where we read about "conflicts between Christians and Judeans." We are back to traditional translations of the Old Testament where the Jews also disappeared in favor of the "Israelites" and the "Hebrews." *The Five Gospels* does not resolve the central question of whether the conflict is to be considered an internal dispute between Jews or, as in traditional translations, one between good outsiders who effectively pass as non-Jews and bad rejectionist Jews. To make Jews into Judeans does not eliminate the "good outsider" versus the "bad locals" persuasion. What happens when a name changes and a people disappear is disquieting.

Another solution by the editors of the 1995 *New Testament and Psalms: An Inclusive Version* is singularly noble and, I am afraid, impossible. The editors are clearly appalled by the extant scriptures because of the described disguisements and the intrinsic hatred of the Jews. In their missionary translation they omit the words "the Jews" when those words function as an exclusively accusatory epithet. It distinguishes, on the one hand, between the term "the Jews" as a straightforward, historical way to refer to the ethnic people, of whom Yeshua was one, and, on the other, "the Jews" as "the code-word for religious people . . . who miss the revelation." They call the Jews "opponents" or "the enemies" or "the religious authorities" or "the leaders," which they do "in order to minimize what could be perceived as a warrant for anti-Jewish bias."[133] Yet we soon learn who these opponents are, and they turn out to be "the most despicable" of the Jews.

Felicitations to the Oxford translators for their goodwill. They have changed the New Testament to overcome unpleasantness, but the serious problems remain. As the Jesus Seminar directs us to hate Judeans rather than Jews, so the Oxford translators would have us hate Jewish authorities and Jewish priests and the unidentified "opponents." The changes are fishy. In making the text more friendly to some of the Jews, the editors have violated the unfriendly intention of the scriptures toward the Jews. To bowdlerize the essence of the scripture as we have it may be thought to be a form of benevolent book-burning.

133. See Victor Roland Gold, Thomas L. Hoyt Jr., Sharon H. Ringe, and Susan Brooks Thistlethwaite, eds., *The New Testament and Psalms: An Inclusive Version* (New York: Oxford University Press, 1995), xvii.

The solution is to leave the text alone. When the Jews are demonized, let the Jews be called Jews. Then problems are clear, and through commentary the hatred may be seen in the context of polemical struggles of a certain time—many decades after Yeshua's life and death—and this knowledge alone diminishes the bite. The slurs appear too often but do not hold dominion and must not be allowed to do so. They are finite human blunder. They fade before the huge wonders and sundry messages of the story. And these wonders are beyond measure.

Holding dominion in the New Testament is not the anger of a new dismissive tribalism but the beauty of the word, the compassion for the poor and hungry, the blind and the leprous, the crippled and the possessed. The wisdom narration explores physical and mental suffering and offers earthly and spiritual hope. Preserved in plain Koine Greek, this supreme telling of roaming and parable is intrinsically so powerful that it survives translation with distinction in every tongue. And on each page the reader may enter the interior landscapes of the spiritual and the solitary mystery of love.

APPENDICES

APPENDICES

Names of God

⁓

The names of God are the hardest words to wrestle with in the Bible. Their conversion into other languages raises as many questions as the face of God, which no one and everyone knows. God changes names in the Hebrew Bible. He is the patristic *Elohim* of the first creation and final judgment, and, in the middle of Genesis 2.4, he is the more pervasive Lord God, *Yahweh*, who is characterized as less distant and more merciful. In the New Testament, God is *theos*, a word taken over from classical Greek literature, where beginning with Homer and Hesiod's *Theogony, theos* designates the supreme god Zeus and the lesser gods. It is problematic how and when to replace the Greek *theos* in the New Testament with an English word that reflects the Hebrew Bible, for one cannot choose one Hebrew name without exiling others with equal credentials as God's true epithet. But clearly the English word "God," a name loaned to us from the Germanic and Scandinavian languages, does not, as do *Elohim* and *Yahweh*, evoke the biblical creator in the Hebraic tradition. So the New Testament is a text in search of the name of God.

God's first name we encounter as the third word in the Hebrew Genesis (reading right to left): בְּרֵאשִׁית בָּרָא אֱלֹהִים אֵת הַשָּׁמַיִם וְאֵת הָאָרֶץ (bereyshit bara elohim et ha-shamayim ve-et ha-aretz), which following the Hebrew word order in the English reads: "In the beginning | created | Elohim | the skies | and the earth." *Elohim*, a plural of majesty but with a singular meaning,[1] derives from *Eloah* (found mainly in Job), or from

---

1. *Elohim* has also been taken as a singular noun whose plural form is an augmentative, rendering it something like "mighty God." There is no unanimity in accepting a "plural of majesty" for what seems to be a simple plural. In a note on this manuscript

El, which has an independent life of its own, meaning "God" as in *El Shaddai*, "God of the Mountains," or *El Elyon*, "God Most High"; and from *El* derives Islam's *Allah*.

In the first creation story (Gen. 1–2.4), Elohim creates skies, earth, beasts, and humans, male and female, in six days. In the second creation story (Gen. 2.4), much happens all in one day: "In the day that the lord Elohim made the earth and the skies," בְּיוֹם עֲשׂוֹת יְהוָה אֱלֹהִים אֶרֶץ וְשָׁמָיִם (be-yom asot adonai elohim eretz ve-shamayim), we have not only the godhead called *Elohim* but *Adonai*, meaning "lord," and in that single day that godhead makes not only the skies and the earth but every plant of the field before it was in the earth, and dust of the ground out of which he forms a man, Adam, who has a rib destined to become Eve. Now Genesis has provided two words for God: *Elohim* and *Adonai*. Yet since the deity's secret *name*—or any *word* signifying that name—is ineffable, the true name cannot be known, written, or sounded. However, there is a way to represent God with letters that do not spell or reveal his secret name. This is the tetragrammaton (also tetragram), consisting of the four Hebrew consonants YHWH (*yod, he, waw* or *vav, he*), which is written יהוה, *Jehovah*, but is normally pronounced *Adonai* (the Semitic word for "lord"). Sometimes, however, YHWH is sounded out to become *Yahweh*, and thereby becomes another surrogate name for the nameless one. And then, as in Genesis 2.4, the word for God is combined with "lord," giving the epithet *Adonai Elohim* ("Lord God"). We have now identified seven principal ways in English of evoking the deity: *Elohim, Adonai, Adonai Elohim,* YHWH, YHVH, *Yahweh, Yahveh*; and we can add an eighth, *Jehovah*, the spelling in the King James Version and the Catholic Bible. Other less common names for God are *Baal* ("lord"), *Yah* instead of *Yahweh*, and *Meleh* ("king"), and combinations thereof. If these onomastic vicissitudes appear complicated and elusive, that is proper for the name of a spiritual God, whose reality does not descend to earthly script or voice. Finally, the surrogate name *Yahweh* has an etymological meaning too (adding another dimension for Kabbalist

page, Professor Marvin Meyer in private correspondence to the author comments on Genesis 1.1: "I'm not really convinced by the 'plural of majesty' argument foisted on us by die-hard monotheists who cannot abide the thought of polytheism in the tradition. Hebrew religion and the whole Judeo-Christian-Islamic tradition emerged (but never fully) from polytheistic traditions. I see in Elohim's plural form the shadow of polytheism, still visible in a Yahwist or Elohist or Priestly context."

play), since *yahweh* is a synonym for "creator," carrying the meaning of "he brings into existence," from the Hebrew *hayâ*, "to be."

When Yeshua quotes the Hebrew Bible scripture in the Greek, his biblical citations come from the second-century B.C.E. Septuagint Greek translation of the Bible for the Greek-speaking Jews of Alexandria who could no longer read the Hebrew with ease. In the Septuagint, God is *theos*. As the Hebrew names for God pass from their Semitic source into other languages, it would be appropriate to use those same traditional Hebrew names for God in the English translation from the Greek—*Elohim, Adonai*, and *Yahweh*—and were I more confident and courageous, I would have translated *theos* throughout with a Hebrew rather than a Germanic word. The difficulty is that with the Greek standing as a linguistic screen between the Hebrew and the English, one can make intelligent supposi-tions but not know with certainty which Hebrew name stands behind the Greek. While the Greeks may care to Hellenize the Semitic epithets for God, in English there is no reason (other than the lethargy of tradition) why the Hellenized, Romanized, and Germanized words for God do not yield to *Elohim, Adonai*, and *Yahweh* in the New Testament.

Yahweh, which was "Jehovah" in the King James Version, is now used for God in many translations of the Hebrew Bible (and especially in the headings). Since it is the same God in both the Hebrew Bible and the New Testament, why not *Yahweh* in the New Testament? So the absence of an intermediary text, or oral or transcribed witness accounts, keeps us with *theos* (θεός), and choosing a name, particularly one name, for God in the English is also a guess. I am confident that in future translations, the decisions and the arguments for those decisions will be well made, and God in the New Testament will sound not like a north European or a Greek but a deity bearing a Hebrew name.

The English "God" exists in Old English and is cognate with Dutch *god*, German *Gott*, Icelandic *godh*, and Goth *guth*. The epithet "God" has no more connection with the Greek or the Hebrew than "hell," which is also given to us by Germanic peoples. "Hell" comes from an old Norse saga preserved in Iceland. In the Greek scriptures "hell" is *Hades*, in the Hebrew Bible it is *Sheol* or *Gehenna* (Gei Hinnom). *Sheol* appears sixty-five times in the Hebrew Bible, the Greek word "Hades" ten times in the New Testament and twenty-six times in the Apocrypha. In most recent translations of the Hebrew Bible and the New Testament, *Sheol* or *Gehenna* has replaced "hell" or "Hades." *Sheol* not only restores the Hebrew resonance but suggests the dwelling place of the dead, and *Gehenna* geographically suggests specific dark pits outside Jerusalem where the less-worthy dead dwelled in punishment, just as "Hades" suggests not only a history of references in Greek literature but also the extant archaic temple in Epirus, whose underground stone basement is Hades, lying less than a kilometer from the small river of the dead, the Acheron. As the Greek has its own Greek words for God, hell, and the devil, it would be similarly right for English, which is the most open language in the world to visiting words, to incorporate names of God that reflect the Hebrew Bible. About half our proper names in English, from "Abraham" to Elizabeth's husband "Zecharias," as well as "Sabbath," "amen," and "halleluyah," are loan words that long ago entered the English from the Hebrew.

I do not know how "God" of the New Testament should enter the English language. Each way incites positive and negative reasons for its selection. For the moment "God," the name of a northern pagan divinity, is standard English usage and for the most part is retained in this and most texts, though I suspect that *Elohim, Yahweh*, and *Adonai* will soon be calling. God has upper-case status as a name. But if it is an idea, an entity, simply a divinity, the lower case would be equally appropriate, as it was originally in all the source languages, and God may go the way of the Lord, from piety to friendly companionship. To speak about the wisdom of having the word "God" be the key sound in the Judeo-Christian tradition does not diminish the Viking and Germanic monosyllable's deep resonance when it evoked Thor, the Old Norse god of thunder, who also gave us "Thor's Day," our day of God in the middle of the week, which we keep as "Thursday."

In his translation of the Pentateuch in *The Five Books of Moses* (1995), Everett Fox uses "God" when the name in the Hebrew is *Elohim*, and "YHWH" when it is the corresponding name in the Hebrew. He sometimes uses "God, YHWH" as one entity. It's not very neat, because the variables are obstinately complex. The easy solution is "God," which is a weak watering down in the English of the great sonorous words in the Hebrew. In the Catholic *Jerusalem Bible* (1990), *Yahweh* is used to represent God through most of the Hebrew Bible.

Since God's face is unseeable and his name unknowable, the best any language can offer us is a simulacrum for the visage, and various signs for the name—but not the one name that resides in mystery. Ultimately, the word "God," or whatever name some version comes up with, has minor importance. No name will lessen or increase our knowledge of God, nor inform belief in the deity's being or deny it. It is no wonder that in the Hebrew writings, God had no singular epithet. He was at once nameless, but with a secret sign that was ineffable, and so the deity took on the one name that meant itself, which was *Ha-Shem*, which means "The Name."

A Note on Transcription

For purposes of easy reference to the English and Greek texts, in the introduction, afterword, and annotation, the evangelists are referred to by their traditional English names. *Yeshua* has largely replaced "Jesus" in all parts of the book, except in quotations and bibliography. The probable original proper nouns are here transliterated into English followed by their traditional spelling as they appear in other translations. In the annotation, these nouns are also given in the Greek and, when possible, in the original Aramaic and/or Hebrew.

The question of restoration is not only *what* the probable original name was, clear in most instances (with exceptions like Matthew where there are several to choose from), but what *system* to use for transcription from Aramaic and Hebrew into English. Some words, such as "Tanakh," already exist in English, but it might have been "Tanak." I chose to double the Hebrew *b* in "Shabbat," which is common practice, but to drop the *h* after *k* in "Tanak," since we do not make that consonantal distinction in English. With regard to Hebrew *bet* or *vet*, *b* or *v*, the solutions old and new are vexing. As in transcribing Greek, I prefer not to be held to reflecting source-text spelling but to reflect plain English practice. Such is especially true in transcribing Greek words, where I follow modern translators from classical Greek literature. They drop all the screens of Latin and French (as the Germans also do) when moving a word from Greek into English. So it is not Latinized "Seriphus" but Greek-lettered "Serifos" for the island from which Perseus flew off in pursuit of the Medusa, or it is not Latinized "Alcaeus" but Greek "Alkaios" for the poet from Lesbos.

With respect to complexities of choice, I cite the enlightened *American Heritage Dictionary*, which explains its pauses in transcribing the word

"Kabbalah." It summarizes vowel problems and the doubling of consonants in transcribing Hebrew and Arabic:

> Usage Note: There are no less than two dozen variant spellings of kab-
> balah, the most common of which include kabbalah, kabala, kabalah,
> qabalah, qabala, cabala, cabbala, kaballah, kabbala, quaballah, and
> qabbalah. This sort of confusion is frequently seen with Hebrew and
> Arabic words borrowed into English because there exist several dif-
> ferent systems of transliterating the Hebrew and Arabic alphabets
> into Roman letters. Often a more exact or scholarly transliteration,
> such as Qur'an, will coexist alongside a spelling that has been heavily
> Anglicized (Koran). The fact that the Hebrew and Arabic alphabets
> do not as a rule indicate short vowels or the doubling of consonants
> compounds the difficulties. Spellings of kabbalah with one or two *b*'s
> are equally "correct," insofar as the single *b* accurately reproduces the
> spelling of the Hebrew, while the double *b* represents the fact that it
> was once pronounced with a double *b*.[2]

2. *American Heritage Dictionary of the English Language*, 4th ed. (Boston: Houghton Mifflin, 2000), 952.

Glossary of Greek and Biblical Proper Nouns

Abba. Father.

Adonai. Lord.

Agav. Agabus.

Aharon. Aaron.

Aineas. Aeneas.

Alexandros. Alexander.

Amfipolis. Amphipolis.

Amminadav. Amminadab.

Amorah. Gomorrah.

Amotz. Amos

Anan. Hannas.

Andreas. Andrew.

Arimathaia. Arimathea.

Arpahshad. Arphaxad or Arpachad.

Asa. Asaph.

Ashdod. Azotus.

Attaleia. Attalia.

Avihud. Abiud.

Aviyah. Abijah.

Avraham. Abraham.

Avram. Abram.

Azur. Azor.

Baal Zebub. Beelzebub.

Baal Zebul. Beelzebul.

Bar. Son.

Bar Abba. Barabbas.

Bar Nabba or Barnabba. Barnabas.

Bar Shavva or Bar Shabbat or Bar Sheba (Aramaic). Barsabbas.

Bar Talmai. Bartholomew.

Bar Yohanan. Barjona.

Bat. Daughter.

Beit Aniyah. Bethany.

Beit Hesda. Bethesda.

Beit Lehem. Bethelehem.

Beit Pagey. Bethphage.

Beit Tzaida. Bethsaida. Bethseda.

Beit Zaita. Bethzatha.

Ben. Son.

Benei Regesh. Boanerges.

Berehyahu, Berehyah. Barachiah.

Bilam. Balaam.

Binyamin. Benjamin.

Caesarea Filippi. Caesarea Philippi.

Damesek or Dammesek. Damascus.

Dekapolis. Decapolis.

Efesos. Ephesos or Ephesus.

Efrayim. Ephraim.

Einayim. Ainon or Aenon.

Elazar. Eleazar or Lazarus.

Eli. Heli.

Eli (Aramaic). My God.

Eliakim. Eliakim.

Elisha or Eliseus. Elisha.

Elisheva. Elizabeth.

Eliud. Eliud.

Eliyahu or Eliyah. Elijah or Elias
(from Greek version).

Elohi (Hebrew). My God.

Elohim. Gods or God.

Enosh. Enos.

Esav. Esau.

Ever. Eber.

Evyatar. Abiathar.

Fanuel. Phanuel.

Filippos. Philip.

Galil. Galilee.

Gat Shmanim. Gethsemane.

Gavriel. Gabriel.

Gei Hinnom, Gei Ben Hinnom, Gei
Ben Hinom. Gehenna (hell).

Gulgulta. Golgotha.

Hades. Hell.

Hakel Dema. Hakeldama or
Aceldamach (KJV).

Halfi. Alphaeus.

Hananyah. Hananias or Ananias.

Hannah. Anna.

Hanoh. Enoch.

Har Megiddo. Armageddon.

Havah. Eve.

Hesli. Esli.

Hetzron. Hezron or Esrom.

Hevel. Abel.

Hizikiah. Hezekiah or Ezekias.

Horazim. Chorazin.

Hoshea. Hosea.

Hymenaios. Hymenaeus.

Iairos. Jairus.

Iason. Jason.

Ikonion. Iconium or Konya.

Ioustos. Justus.

Irastos. Erastus.

Izevel. Jezebel.

Kayfa. Caiaphas.

Kayin. Cain.

Kefa or Shimon Kefa. Cephas
(Latinization) or Peter or Simon
Peter or Simeon Peter.

Keinan or Kainan. Cainan.

Keriot. Iscariot.

Kfar Nahum or Kefar Nahum.
Capernaum.

Klofah. Clopas.

Korazim. Chorazin.

Korban. Corban.

Kosam. Cosam.

Kuza. Chuza.

Laodikeia. Laodicea.

Lemeh. Lemech.

Levi. Levi, Matthew.

Lod. Lydda.

Loukas. Luke.

Loukios. Lucius.

Lykaonia. Lycaonia.

Magdala (town on the Sea of
Galilee). Mary the Magdalene
(from Magdala).

Mahalalel. Mahalaleel.

Mahat. Maath.

Makedonia. Macedonia.

Malah. Melea.

Malki. Melchi.

Manah. Menna.

Markos. Mark.

Marta. Martha.

Mashiah. Messiah.

Mathias. Maththias.

Mattan. Matthan.

Mattat. Matthat.

Mattatah. Mattatha.

Mattityah. Mattathias

Mattityahu, Mattai. Matthew.

Meleh. Malchus.

Meleh. King.

Menasheh. Menasses, Menasseh.

Metushelah. Methuselah.

Midyan. Midian.

Mihael. Michael.

Mihaihu or Mihayhu. Micah.

Miryam. Mary.

Moshe or Mosheh. Moses.

Naftali. Naphtali.

Nakdeimon. Nikodemos,
    Nicodemus.

Naon. Nain.

Natan. Nathan.

Natanel. Nathanael.

Natzeret. Nazareth.

Natzrati. Nazarene.

Nikolaos. Nicolaus.

Obev. Obeb.

Pafos. Paphos.

Pamfylia. Pamphylia.

Pantokrator. Pantocrator.

Parush. Pharisee.

Patmos. Patmus.

Paulus. Paul.

Peretz. Perez.

Pergamos. Pergamum.

Pesach, Pesah. Passover.

Pilatus. Pilate.

Pnuel. Panuel. Phanuel.

Priska. Prisca.

Prushim or Perushim. Pharisees.

Rahav. Rahab.

Rahel. Rachel.

Ram. Aram.

Rehavam. Rehoboam, Roboam.

Reisha. Rhesa.

Reuven. Reuben.

Rivkah. Rebecca.

Rodi, Rhoda, Rode. Rose.

Rut. Ruth.

Samothraki. Samothrace.

Sanhedrin. Council.

Sdom, Sedom. Sodom.

Seleukeia. Seleucia.

Shabbat, Shabat. Sabbath.

Shalem. Salim.

Shaltiel. Shealtiel.

Shaul. Saul, Paul.

Shealtial. Shealtiel, Salathiel.

Shehem. Sychar or Syhem.

Shem. Name.

Sheol. Hell.

Shet. Seth.

Shiloah. Siloam.

Shimi. Semein.

Shimon. Simon or Simeon.

Shimon Kefa. Simon Peter.

Shimshon. Samson.

Shlomit. Salome.

Shlomoh. Solomon

Shmuel. Samuel.

Shomron. Samaria.

Shomroni. Samaritan.

Shomronim. Samaritans.

Shoshannah. Susanna.

Silouanos. Silvanus.

Stefanos. Stephen.

Sukkah. Sukkoth or
    Tabernacle.

Taddai. Thaddeus.

Tamar. Tamar, Thamar.

Tavita. Tabitha.

Theofilos. Theophilus.

Thessaloniki. Thessalonica or
    Salonica.

Timotheos. Timothy.

Toma. Thomas.

Torah. The Torah is the
    Pentateuch or used to
    signify the Hebrew Bible.

Tzadok. Zadok.

Tzidon. Sidon.

Tziyun or Tziyon. Zion.

Tzor, Tzur, Tur. Tyre.

Uriyahu, Uriyah. Uriah.

Uziyah, Uziyahu. Uzziah.

Yaakov. Jacob, James.

Yafo. Jaffar, Joppa.

Yahin. Achim.

Yahweh, Yahveh (the sounded
    four Hebrew vowels of the
tetragrammaton for *Adonai*,
    meaning "God" or "Lord").

Jahweh, Jahveh, Jehovah, God,
    Lord.

YHWH, YHVH (the written
    four Hebrew vowels of the
    tetragrammaton for *Adonai*,
    meaning "God" or "Lord").

Jahweh, Jahveh, Jehovah, God,
    Lord.

Yair. Jairus.

Yannai. Jannai.

Yarden. Jordan.

Yehoniah. Jechoniah.

Yehoshafat. Jehoshaphat.

Yehuda. Judas, Juda, Judah, Jude.

Yehuda. Judea.

Yehuda man of Keriot. Judas Iscariot.

Yered. Jared.

Yeriho. Jericho.

Yerushalayim. Jerusalem.

Yeshayahu, Yeshayah. Isaiah.

Yeshua. Joshua, Yehoshua, Jehoshua,
    Jesus.

Yeshua the Mashiah. Jesus the
    Christ.

Yeshua bar Yosef (Aramaic). Jesus
    son of Joseph.

Yeshua ben Yosef (Hebrew). Jesus
    son of Joseph.

Yiftah. Jephthah.

Yirmiyahu, Yirmiyah. Jeremiah.

Yisahar. Issachar.

Yishai. Jesse.

Yisrael. Israel.

Yitzhak. Isaac.

Yodah. Joda.

Yoel. Joel.

Yohanan. John.
Yohannah or Yohanna. Joanna.
Yona. Jona.
Yonah. Jonah.
Yoram. Joram, Jorim.
Yosef. Joseph.
Yoseh. Josech.
Yoshiyahu, Yoshiyah. Josiah,
    Josias.

Yotam. Jotham.
Yov. Job.

Zakai. Zacchaeus.
Zavdai. Zebedee.
Zeharyahu, Zharyahu. Zacharias or
    Zechariah.
Zerubavel. Zerubbabel, Zorobabel.
Zvulun. Zebulun.

Works Cited and
Selected Bibliography

Alter, Robert. *The Art of Biblical Poetry.* New York: Basic Books, 1987.

————. *Genesis: Translation and Commentary.* New York: W. W. Norton, 1996.

————. *The David Story: Translation with Commentary of I and II Samuel.* New York: W. W. Norton, 1999.

————. *The Five Books of Moses: A Translation with Commentary.* New York: W. W. Norton, 2004.

————. *The Book of Psalms: A Translation with Commentary.* New York: W. W. Norton, 2007.

Alter, Robert, and Frank Kermode, eds. *The Literary Guide to the Bible.* Cambridge, MA: Harvard University Press, 1987.

American Heritage Dictionary of the English Language. 4th ed. Boston: Houghton Mifflin, 2000.

Aristeas to Philocrates [*Letter of Aristeas*]. Ed. and trans. Moses Hadas. New York: Harper and Brothers, 1951; New York: Ktav Publishing, 1974.

Armstrong, Karen. *The Bible: A Biography.* New York: Grove Press, 2008.

Barnstone, Aliki, trans. *The Collected Poems of C. P. Cavafy: A New Translation.* New York: W. W. Norton, 2006.

Barnstone, Willis. *The Poems of Saint John of the Cross.* Translation and Introduction. Bloomington: Indiana University Press, 1967; rev. ed. New York: New Directions, 1972.

————. *The Poetics of Translation: History, Theory, Practice.* New Haven: Yale University Press, 1993.

————. *With Borges on an Ordinary Evening in Buenos Aires: Memoir with Poems.* Champaign/Urbana: University of Illinois Press, 1993.

————. *To Touch the Sky: Spiritual, Mystical and Philosophical Poems in Translation.* New York: New Directions, 1999.

————. *The Apocalypse.* New York: New Directions, 2000.

————. *The New Covenant.* New York: Riverhead Books, 2002.

———, ed. *The Other Bible*. San Francisco: Harper and Row, 1984; 2nd rev. ed. San Francisco: HarperSanFrancisco, 2005.

———. *The Complete Poems of Sappho*. Boston: Shambhala Books, 2009.

Barnstone, Willis, and Marvin Meyer, eds. *The Gnostic Bible*. Boston: Shambhala Books, 2004.

Bloom, Harold. *Anxiety of Influence*. New York: Oxford University Press, 1973.

———. "Before Moses Was, I Am: The Original and the Belated Testaments." In *The Bible*, ed. and intro. Harold Bloom. New York: Chelsea House, 1987.

———. "A Reading." In *The Gospel of Thomas. New Translation with Introduction and Notes*, by Marvin Meyer. San Francisco: HarperSanFrancisco, 1992.

———. *Omens of Millennium: The Gnosis of Angels, Dreams, and Resurrection*. New York: Riverhead Books, 1996.

———. "Who Will Praise the Lord?" *New York Review of Books*, November 27, 2007.

Borg, Marcus J. *Meeting Jesus Again for the First Time*. San Francisco: HarperSanFrancisco, 1994.

Borges, Jorges Luis. *Collected Fictions*, trans. Andrew Hurley. New York: Viking, 1998.

Brown, Raymond E. *An Introduction to the New Testament*. New York: Doubleday, 1997.

Buber, Martin. *Die Chassidische Botschaft*. Heidelberg: L. Schneider, 1922.

———. *Two Types of Faith*. New York: Harper and Row, 1961.

———. *Tales of the Hasidim*. New York: Schocken Books, 1975.

Bultmann, Rudolf. *Jesus and the Word*. Trans. Louise Pettibone Smith and Erminie Huntress Lantero. New York: Scribner, 1958.

———. *The History of the Synoptic Tradition*. Trans. John Marsh. New York: Harper and Row, 1966.

Cameron, Ron. *The Other Gospels*. Philadelphia: Westminster Press, 1982.

Campbell, Joseph. *The Masks of God: Occidental Mythology*. New York: Penguin Arkana, 1991.

Carroll, James. *Constantine's Sword: The Church and the Jews: A History*. Boston: Houghton Mifflin, 2001.

Carson, Anne. *If Not, Winter: Fragments of Sappho*. New York: Knopf, 2002.

Charlesworth, James H., ed. *The Old Testament Pseudepigrapha*. 2 vols. Garden City, NY: Doubleday, 1983–1985.

Chilton, Bruce. *Rabbi Jesus: An Intimate Biography*. New York: Doubleday, 2000.

Chilton, Bruce, and Jacob Neusner. *Judaism in the New Testament: Practices and Beliefs*. London/New York: Routledge, 1995.

Cohen, Shaye J. D. *From the Maccabees to the Mishnah*. Philadelphia: Westminster Press, 1989.

Crossan, John Dominic. *The Essential Jesus: Original Sayings and the Earliest Images*. San Francisco: HarperSanFrancisco, 1994.

———. *Jesus: A Revolutionary Biography*. San Francisco: HarperSanFrancisco, 1994.

————. *Who Killed Jesus? Exposing the Roots of Anti-Semitism in the Gospel Story of the Death of Jesus.* San Francisco: HarperSanFrancisco, 1996.

————. *The Birth of Christianity.* San Francisco: HarperSanFrancisco, 1998.

Dickinson, Emily. *The Complete Poems of Emily Dickinson.* Ed. Thomas H. Johnson. Boston: Little, Brown, 1958.

Ehrman, Bart D. *Misquoting Jesus: The Story behind Who Changed the Bible and Why.* San Francisco: HarperSanFrancisco, 2005.

————. *Misquoting the Bible.* San Francisco: HarperOne, 2007.

————. *God's Problem: How the Bible Fails to Answer Our Most Important Question—Why We Suffer.* San Francisco: HarperOne, 2008.

Ferry, David. *Gilgamesh: A New Rendering in English Verse.* New York: Farrar, Straus and Giroux, 1992.

Fideler, David. *Jesus Christ, Son of God: Ancient Cosmology and Early Christian Symbolism.* Wheaton, IL: Quest Books, 1993.

Fitzgerald, Robert, trans. *The Odyssey.* Garden City, NY: Doubleday, 1961.

Fitzmyer, Joseph A. *Luke the Theologian.* New York: Paulist Press, 1989.

————. *Discoveries in the Judaean Desert*, vol. 19. Oxford: Clarendon Press, 1995.

Fox, Everett. *The Five Books of Moses: A New Translation with Introduction, Commentary, and Notes.* New York: Schocken Books, 1995.

Fredriksen, Paula. *From Jesus to Christ: The Origins of the New Testament Images of Jesus.* New Haven: Yale University Press, 1988.

————. *Jesus of Nazareth, King of the Jews: A Jewish Life and the Emergence of Christianity.* New York: Knopf, 1999.

Funk, Robert W., Roy W. Hoover, and the Jesus Seminar, eds. *The Five Gospels: The Search for the Authentic Words of Jesus: New Translation and Commentary.* New York: Macmillan, 1993.

García Martínez, Florentino, ed., Wilfred G. E. Watson, trans. *The Dead Sea Scrolls Translated: The Qumran Texts in English.* 2nd ed. New Orleans: E.J. Brill/Grand Rapids, MI: W.B. Eerdmans, 1996.

Gaster, Theodor H. *The Dead Sea Scrolls in English Translation.* Translation with Introduction and Notes. New York: Doubleday Anchor, 1956.

Gold, Victor Roland, Thomas L. Hoyt Jr., Sharon H. Ringe, and Susan Brooks Thistlethwaite, eds. *The New Testament and Psalms: An Inclusive Version.* New York: Oxford University Press, 1995.

Grant, Robert M. *Gnosticism and Early Christianity.* New York: Columbia University Press, 1959.

————. *A Historical Introduction to the New Testament.* New York: Harper and Row, 1963; New York: Simon and Schuster, 1972.

A Greek-English Lexicon of the New Testament and Other Early Christian Literature, 3rd ed. Rev. and ed. Frederick William Danker. Chicago: University of Chicago Press, 2000.

Greenspoon, Leonard J. "Between Alexandria and Antioch: Jew and Judaism in the Hellenistic Period." In *The Oxford History of the Biblical World*, ed. Michael D. Coogan. New York: Oxford University Press, 1998.

Gubar, Susan. *Judas: A Biography*. New York: W. W. Norton, 2009.

Hammond, Gerald. *The Making of the English Bible*. New York: Philosophical Library, 1983.

The HarperCollins Bible Dictionary. Ed. Paul J. Achtemeier. San Francisco: HarperSanFrancisco, 1993, 1996.

The HarperCollins Study Bible: New Revised Standard Version. Gen. ed. Wayne Meeks. New York: HarperCollins, 1993.

Harvey, A. E. *Jesus on Trial: A Study in the Fourth Gospel*. London: SPCK, 1976.

Hedrick, Charles W., and Paul A. Mirecki, eds. *Gospel of the Savior: A New Ancient Gospel*. Santa Rosa, CA: Polebridge Press, 1999.

Heschel, Susannah. "Transforming Jesus from Jew to Aryan: Protestant Theologies in Nazi Germany." The Albert T. Bilgray Lecture, University of Arizona, April 1995. Alexander Jones, Gen. ed.

Honig, Edwin. *The Poet's Other Voice: Conversation on Literary Translation*. Amherst: University of Massachusetts Press, 1985.

Jackson, Howard M. *The Lion Becomes Man: The Gnostic Leontomorphic Creator and the Platonic Tradition*. Atlanta: Scholars Press, 1985.

Johnson, Luke T. "The New Testament: Anti-Jewish Slander and the Conventions of Ancient Polemic." *Journal of Biblical Literature* 108 (1989): 419–441.

Josephus. *The New Complete Works of Josephus*. Trans. William Whiston. Grand Rapids, MI: Kregel, 1999.

Kasser, Rodolphe, Marvin Meyer, Gregor Wurst, et al., eds. *The Gospel of Judas*. 2nd rev. ed. Washington, DC: National Geographic, 2008.

Kee, Howard Clark. *Jesus in History: An Approach to the Study of the Gospels*. 2nd ed. New York: Harcourt Brace Jovanovich, 1977.

Kermode, Frank. *The Genesis of Secrecy: On the Interpretation of Narrative*. Cambridge, MA: Harvard University Press, 1979.

King, Karen. *The Gospel of Mary of Magdala: Jesus and the First Woman Apostle*. Santa Rosa, CA: Polebridge Press, 2003.

Klein, Charlotte. *Anti-Judaism in Christian Theology*. Trans. Edward Quinn. Philadelphia: Fortress Press, 1978.

Kloppenborg, John. *The Formation of Q: Trajectories in Ancient Wisdom Collections*. Philadelphia: Fortress Press, 1987.

———. *Q Parallels: Synopsis, Critical Notes and Concordance*. Sonoma, CA: Polebridge Press, 1988.

———. *Excavating Q: The History and Setting of the Sayings Gospel*. Minneapolis: Fortress Press, 2000.

Knohl, Israel. *The Messiah before Jesus: The Suffering Servant of the Dead Sea Scrolls*. Berkeley: University of California Press, 2002.

Koester, Helmut. *Ancient Christian Gospels: Their History and Development*. Philadelphia: Trinity Press International, 1990.

———. *Introduction to the New Testament*. Vol. 1., *History, Culture, and Religion of the Hellenistic Age*. Vol. 2., *History and Literature of Early Christianity*. 2nd ed. Philadelphia: Fortress Press, 1994–1996.

Kümmel, Werner Georg. *Introduction to the New Testament*. Rev. ed. Trans. from German by Howard Clark Kee. Nashville: Abingdon Press, 1975.

Lattimore, Richmond. *The Four Gospels and the Revelation: Newly Translated from the Greek*. New York: Farrar, Straus, Giroux, 1979.

―――. *The New Testament*. New York: North Point Press, 1997.

Layton, Bentley, ed. *Nag Hammadi Codex II, 2–7*. New York: E. J. Brill, 1989.

Maccoby, Hyam. *The Mythmaker: Paul and the Invention of Christianity*. San Francisco: HarperSanFrancisco, 1986.

Mack, Burton L. *The Lost Gospel: The Book of Q & Christian Origins*. San Francisco: HarperSanFrancisco, 1993.

―――. *Who Wrote the New Testament? The Making of the Christian Myth*. San Francisco: HarperSanFrancisco, 1995.

Mailer, Norman. *The Gospel according to the Son*. New York: Random House, 1997.

McGrath, Alister E. *In the Beginning: The Story of the King James Bible*. New York: Doubleday, 2001.

Meeks, Wayne. *The First Urban Christians: The Social World of the Apostle Paul*. New Haven: Yale University Press, 1983.

Metzger, Bruce M. *The Early Versions of the New Testament: Their Origin, Transmission, and Limitations*. Oxford: Clarendon Press, 1977.

―――. *The Text of the New Testament: Its Transmission, Corruption, and Restoration*. 3rd. enlarged ed. New York: Oxford University Press, 1992.

Meyer, Marvin. *The Gospel of Thomas: New Translation with Introduction and Notes*. A Reading by Harold Bloom. San Francisco: HarperSanFrancisco, 1992.

―――. *The Unknown Sayings of Jesus*. San Francisco: HarperSanFrancisco, 1998.

―――. "Judas and the Gnostic Connection." In *The Gospel of Judas*, ed. Rodolphe Kasser, Marvin Meyer, and Gregor Wurst. Washington, DC: National Geographic, 2006.

―――, ed. *The Nag Hammadi Library*. San Francisco: HarperOne, 2007.

Miles, Jack. *God: A Biography*. New York: Knopf, 1995.

Miller, Robert J., ed. *The Complete Gospels: Annotated Scholars Version*. Sonoma, CA: Polebridge Press, 1992–1994.

More, Thomas. *The Dialogue Concerning Tyndale*. Ed. W. E. Campbell. Facsimile of the 1557 edition. London: Eyre and Spottiswoode, 1927.

Nelson, Lowry, Jr. *Poetic Configuration*. University Park: Pennsylvania State University Press, 1992.

The New Jerusalem Bible. Garden City, NJ: Doubleday, 1990.

Neusner, Jacob. *Judaism When Christianity Began: A Survey of Belief and Practice*. Louisville, KY: Westminster John Knox Press, 2002.

The New Oxford Annotated Bible, with the Apocryphal/Deuterocanonical Books. New Revised Standard Version. Ed. Bruce M. Metzger and Roland Murphy. New York: Oxford University Press, 1994.

New Testament and Psalms. New York: Oxford University Press, 1995.

Nicholls, William. *Christian Anti-Semitism: A History of Hate*. Northvale, NJ/London: Jason Aronson, 1995.

Nickelsburg, George W. E. "The Genre and Function of the Markan Passion Narrative." *Harvard Theological Review* 73 (1980): 153–184.

———. *Jewish Literature between the Bible and the Mishnah: A Historical and Literary Introduction.* Philadelphia: Fortress Press, 1981.

———. "Revealed Wisdom as a Criterion for Inclusion and Exclusion: From Jewish Sectarianism to Early Christianity." In *To See Ourselves as Others See Us: Christians, Jews, "Others" in Late Antiquity,* ed. Jacob Neusner and Ernest S. Frerichs, Chico, CA: Scholars Press, 1985.

———. "Jews and Christians in the First Century: The Struggle over Identity." *Neotestamentica* 27(2) (1993): 365–390.

———. "The First Century: A Time to Rejoice and a Time to Weep." *Religion and Theology* 1(1) (1994): 4–17.

The NIV Study Bible: New International Version. Gen. ed. Kenneth Barker. Grand Rapids, MI: Zondervan Publishing House, 1986, 1995.

The Oxford Companion to the Bible. Ed. Bruce M. Metzger and Michael D. Coogan. New York: Oxford University Press, 1993.

Pagels, Elaine. *The Gnostic Gospels.* New York: Random House, 1979.

———. *Adam, Eve, and the Serpent.* New York: Vintage, 1988.

———. *Gnostic Paul: Gnostic Exegesis of the Pauline Letters.* Philadelphia: Trinity Press International, 1994.

———. *The Origin of Satan.* New York: Vintage, 1995.

———. *Beyond Belief.* New York: Vintage Books, 2004.

Pagels, Elaine, and Karen L. King. *Reading Judas: The Gospel of Judas and the Shaping of Christianity.* New York: Viking, 2007.

Pamphilus, Eusebius. *Eusebius' Ecclesiastical History.* Trans. C. F. Cruse. Indianapolis: Hendrickson Publisher, 1998.

Pearson, Birger A. "The Gospel according to the 'Jesus Seminar': On Some Recent Trends in Gospel Research." In *The Emergence of the Christian Religion: Essays on Early Christianity.* Harrisburg, PA: Trinity Press International, 1997.

Petersen, Norman R. *The Gospel of John and the Sociology of Light: Language and the Characterization in the Fourth Gospel.* Valley Forge, PA: Trinity Press International, 1993.

Philo. *Embassy to Gaius.* In *Philo.* Loeb edition. Vol. 10. Trans. F. H. Colson. London: Heinemann, 1962.

Pines, Shlomo. *An Arabic Version of the Testimonium Flavianum and Its Implications.* Jerusalem: The Israel Academy of Sciences and Humanities, 1971.

Pinsky, Robert, trans. *The Inferno of Dante.* Foreword by John Freccero. New York: Farrar, Straus and Giroux, 1994.

Price, Reynolds. *Three Gospels.* New York: Scribners, 1996.

Rathmell, J. C. A., ed. *The Psalms of Sir Philip Sidney and the Countess of Pembroke.* Garden City, NY: Doubleday, 1963.

Renan, Ernest. *Life of Jesus,* trans. William J. Hutchison. Whitefish, MT: Kessinger Books, 2003.

Robinson, James M., ed. *The Nag Hammadi Library.* San Francisco: Harper and Row, 1977.

Robinson, James M., Paul Hoffman, and John S. Kloppenborg, eds. *The Critical Edition of Q.* Minneapolis: Fortress Press, 2000.

Sanders, E. P. *Paul and Palestinian Judaism: A Comparison of Patterns of Religion.* Philadelphia: Fortress Press, 1977.

———. *Paul, the Law, and the Jewish People.* Philadelphia: Fortress Press, 1983.

———. *Jesus and Judaism.* Philadelphia: Fortress Press, 1987.

———. "Jesus Christ." In *Eerdman's Dictionary of the Bible,* ed. David Noel Freedman. Grand Rapids, MI/Cambridge, UK: William B. Eerdman's Publishing, 2000.

Scholem, Gershom. *Jewish Gnosticism, Merkabah Mysticism, and Talmudic Tradition.* New York: Schocken Books, 1961.

———. *Sabbatai Sevi: The Mystical Messiah, 1626–1676.* Princeton: Princeton University Press, 1973.

———. *Origins of the Kaballah.* Princeton: Princeton University Press, 1987.

Schonfield, Hugh J. *The Original New Testament.* Trans. and intro. San Francisco: Harper and Row, 1985.

Schweitzer, Albert. *The Quest of the Historical Jesus.* Intro. James M. Robinson, trans. W. Montgomery of *Von Reimarus zur Wrede* (1906). New York: Macmillan, 1968.

Sidney, Sir Philip. *The Psalms of Sir Philip Sidney and the Countess of Pembroke.* Ed. J. C. A. Rathmell. Garden City, NY: Doubleday, 1963.

Smallwood, Mary. *The Jews under Roman Rule from Pompey to Diocletian.* Leiden: E.J. Brill, 1981.

Spence, Jonathan. *Memory Palace of Matteo Ricci.* New York: Viking Penguin, 1994.

Spong, John Shelby. *Liberating the Gospels: Reading the Bible with Jewish Eyes: Freeing Jesus from 2,000 Years of Misunderstanding.* San Francisco: HarperSanFrancisco, 1996.

Stanton, Graham. *Gospel Truth? New Light on Jesus and the Gospels.* London: HarperCollins, 1995.

Stendahl, Krister. *The School of Matthew.* Uppsala: C. W. K. Gleerup, 1954.

———. "Anti-Semitism." In *The Oxford Companion to the Bible,* ed. Bruce M. Metzger and Michael D. Coogan. New York: Oxford University Press, 1993.

Stern, M. "The History of Judea under Roman Rule." In *A History of the Jewish People,* ed. H. H. Ben-Sasson. Cambridge, MA: Harvard University Press, 1976.

Stone, I. F. *The Trial of Socrates.* New York: Knopf, 2000.

Streeter, Burnett Hillman. *The Four Gospels: A Study of Origins.* London: Macmillan, 1930.

Strong, James. *The New Strong's Exhaustive Concordance of the Bible.* Nashville: Thomas Nelson Publishers, 1997.

———. *The New Strong's Exhaustive Concordance of the Bible.* Nashville: Thomas Nelson, 1999.

Trobisch, David. *The First Edition of the New Testament*. New York: Oxford University Press, 2000.

———. *Paul's Letter Collection: Tracing the Origins*. Foreword by Gerd Thiessen. Bolivar, MO: Quiet Waters Publications, 2001.

Tyndale, William. *An Answer unto Sir Thomas More's* Dialogue. Ed. Henry Walker. Cambridge, UK: Cambridge University, Press, 1850.

———. "The Obedience of a Christian Man" (1522). In *The Work of William Tyndale*. ed. and intro. G. E. Duffield. Preface by F. F. Bruce. Philadelphia: Fortress Press, 1965.

———. *Tyndale's New Testament*. Trans. William Tyndale and ed. David Daniell. New Haven: Yale University Press, 1989.

Vermes, Geza. *Jesus the Jew*. Philadelphia: Fortress Press, 1981.

———. *The Complete Dead Sea Scrolls in English*. Trans. and Ed. from the Hebrew and Aramaic. London: Allen Lane/Penguin, 1997.

———. *The Changing Faces of Jesus*. New York: Viking Compass, 2001.

———. *The Resurrection*. New York: Doubleday, 2008.

Wilson, A. N. *Jesus: A Life*. New York: Ballantine Books, 1993.

Wilson, Ian. *The Evidence*. Washington, DC: Regnery Publishing, 2000.

Winter, Paul. *On the Trial of Jesus*. Rev. and ed. T. A. Burkill and Geza Vermes. Berlin/New York: De Gruyter, 1974.

Greek Texts

The Greek New Testament, ed. Kurt Aland and Barbara Aland. 4th ed. Stuttgart, Germany: Deutsche Bibelgesellshaft: United Bible Societies, 1993.

Greek-English New Testament, ed. Eberhard Nestle, Erwin Nestle, Kurt Aland, and Barbara Aland. 7th ed. Under the title *Novum Testamentum Graece*. Includes parallel texts of 2nd ed. of Revised Standard Version. Stuttgart, Germany: Deutsche Bibelgesellshaft, 1993.

Brown, Robert K., and Philip W. Comfort, trans. J. D. Douglas, ed. *The New Interlinear New Testament with the New Revised Standard Version. The Greek New Testament*, United Bible Societies fourth corrected edition (same text as the *Novum Testamentum Graece*, 26th edition), originally ed. Eberhard and Erwin Nestle; reed. Kurt Aland, Matthew Black, Carlo M. Martini, Bruce M. Metzger, and Allen Wilgren. Wheaton, IL: Tyndale House Publications, 1990.

Index